TORAH · PROPHETS · WRITINGS
THE ENGLISH KOREN TANAKH

THE MAGERMAN EDITION

TORAH · PROPHETS · WRITINGS
THE ENGLISH KOREN TANAKH

A NEW ENGLISH TRANSLATION OF THE HEBREW BIBLE

TRANSLATIONS BY
RABBI LORD JONATHAN SACKS,
RABBI TZVI HERSH WEINREB,
AND OTHERS

KOREN PUBLISHERS JERUSALEM

The English Koren Tanakh
The Magerman Edition
First Edition

Koren Publishers Jerusalem Ltd.
POB 4044, Jerusalem 91040, ISRAEL
POB 8531, New Milford, CT 06776-8531, USA

www.korenpub.com

Compact size, Hardcover, ISBN 978-965-7766-37-8
Large size, Hardcover, ISBN 978-965-7766-38-5

Printed in PRC

EOT01

The Torah is eternal.

Humanity is ephemeral and dynamic.

The Torah is the cornerstone of the world, of our People, and it forms the baseline of the Tanakh, the holy writings of God and His prophets. The changing nature of human society demands a fresh Tanakh translation which speaks to each and every one of us while remaining rooted in the eternal essence of the Torah. The Tanakh is a living script, the screenplay of the history of humanity from Creation to the present.

Rabbi Lord Jonathan Sacks זצ"ל was the authentic Torah voice for our generation, simultaneously steeped in Torah tradition and deeply engaged with people of all faiths. He succinctly understood and eloquently conveyed both the particular Jewish identity of our sacred writings as well as their universal relevance.

We pray that this unique, traditional, and painstakingly researched and annotated translation of Tanakh animates and enlivens Torah for *Klal Yisrael*, uniting us in our traditions, exposing us to new ways of thinking, and ultimately bringing us closer to the Redemption.

אֲנִי מַאֲמִין בֶּאֱמוּנָה שְׁלֵמָה
בְּבִיאַת הַמָּשִׁיחַ
וְאַף עַל פִּי שֶׁיִּתְמַהְמֵהַּ עִם כָּל זֶה אֲחַכֶּה לּוֹ
בְּכָל יוֹם שֶׁיָּבוֹא.

I believe with perfect faith
in the coming of the Messiah,
and though he may delay,
I wait daily for his coming.

We are pleased that we were able to contribute to this critically important edition of the Tanakh which will reach so, so many Jews and non-Jews alike.

Debra and David Magerman
Philadelphia, Pennsylvania

RABBI MOSES FEINSTEIN
455 F. D. R. DRIVE
New York 2, N. Y.
—
ORegon 7-1222

משה פיינשטיין
ר"מ תפארת ירושלים
בנוא יארק

בע"ה

נאום משה פיינשטיין

הנה ראיתי את התנ"ך שלם הנדפס עתה מקרוב בירושלים עיה"ק בדקדוק
גדול בחלוק הפרשיות אף בנביאים וכתובים כפי המסורת, וכדאשכחן
בגמ' שגם בנביאים איכא פרשיות פרשיות וגם סימני הסדרים שלא נדפס
כן עד עתה וכן דקדקו בהנקודות והטעמים ויישר הדבר הזה בעיני
גדולי א"י, וגם אני מחזיק זה לענין גדול שיהיה בכל בית תנ"ך
מדוקדק זה בשלימות אף שעיקר הלמוד הוא באלו שנדפסו עם מפרשים
כפירש"י ועוד, אבל הא לתנ"ך הוא בנביאים וכתובים ספר הנכתב
כדין אף שאינו בגלילה, וגם ברוב ספרי תנ"ך איכא שגיאות מטעותי
הדפוס שיש שנשרשו כבר ברוב הדפוסים שאין מדקדקים כל כך וספר
תנ"ך זה הוא טובה ומדוקדק כפי שמעידין עליו ולכן מן הראוי שיהיה
בכל בית תנ"ך כזה וכן בכל ביהכ"נ וביהמ"ד ובפרט שנדפס ע"י פועלים
שומרי תורה. וע"ז באתי על החתום בכ"ו טבת שנת תשכ"ו בנוא יארק
נאום משה פיינשטיין

I have just viewed the full Koren Tanakh printed in Jerusalem. I was impressed by the great meticulousness with which the passages are laid out, even in the Prophets and Writings, according to the Masora. As we know from the Talmud, the books of the Prophets, too, are divided into *parashot* as well as *sedarim*, divisions which have not been conveyed in previous printed editions. In addition, Koren's editors were very scrupulous regarding the placement of vocalization and cantillation marks, and their work in this respect has met with the approval of the greatest rabbis of Israel. I too consider it of great importance that every Jewish home own such a comprehensive Tanakh… Most Tanakhs include mistakes and typographic errors which have become entrenched over time and printing in many successive editions. Yet the Koren Tanakh is accurate and reliable, as testified by its users. Therefore it is advisable that such a Tanakh be found in every household, synagogue, and *beit midrash*, all the more since it was published by a Torah-observant firm.

26th of Tevet, 5726 (1966), New York
Moshe Feinstein

This approbation refers to the first Hebrew edition of this work.

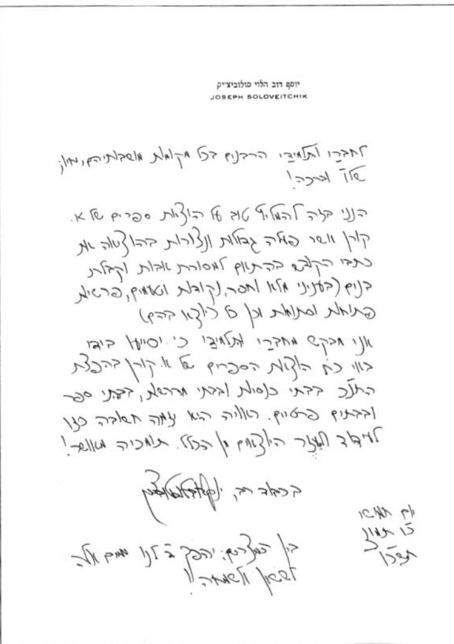

יוסף דוב הלוי סולובייצ'יק
JOSEPH SOLOVEITCHIK

To my rabbinical colleagues and students throughout the world,

I hereby recommend the publications of Eliyahu Koren, who has performed a great service in publishing the Holy Scriptures according to Jewish tradition, with careful regard for accuracy in spelling, vowels and accentuation, paragraph divisions, and the like.

I call upon my friends and students to assist the representatives of Koren Publishers Jerusalem by distributing the Tanakh in synagogues and *batei midrash*, in schools and in private homes. Such an important initiative is worthy of outstanding encouragement and assistance.

"... and joyous are those who hold her fast!"

Respectfully,
Joseph B. Soloveitchik
Thursday, 26 Tammuz, 5726 (1966)
Between the straits:
May God transform these days into ones of joy and happiness!

This approbation refers to the first Hebrew edition of this work.

CONTENTS

TORAH

PROPHETS / NEVI'IM

WEEKLY TORAH PORTIONS

GENESIS

EXODUS

LEVITICUS

NUMBERS

DEUTERONOMY

FOREWORD
RABBI LORD JONATHAN SACKS

"When God began creating heaven and earth, the earth was void and desolate, there was darkness on the face of the deep, and the spirit of God moved over the waters...." Thus unfolds the most revolutionary as well as the most influential account of creation in the history of the human spirit.

Yet what I find so profound and counterintuitive is how the Torah frames creation. It does so not from a vantage point of physics or cosmology, but rather through a phrase we hear repeatedly in the opening verses: "And God said, Let there be... And there was...." What is truly creative, we learn, is not science or technology per se, but rather the word. That is what forms all being.

Judaism treats mere words with a great degree of seriousness: "Life and death are in the power of the tongue," says the book of Proverbs (18:21). Likewise the verses in Psalms (34:13–14), "Whoever of you loves life and desires to see many good days, keep your tongue from evil and your lips from telling lies."

There are ancient cultures who worshipped the gods because they saw them as powers: lightning, thunder, the rain and sun, the sea and ocean that epitomized the forces of chaos, and sometimes wild animals that represented danger and fear. Judaism was not a religion that worshipped power, despite the fact that God is more powerful than any pagan deity. Judaism, like other religions, has holy places, holy people, sacred times, and consecrated rituals. What made Judaism different, however, is that it is supremely *a religion of holy words*.

Creation, revelation, and the moral life begin with the creative word, the idea, the vision, the dream. Language – and with it the ability to remember a distant past and conceptualize a distant future – lies at the heart of our uniqueness as the image of God. Just as God makes the natural world by words, so we make the human world by words. Already at the opening of the Torah, at the very beginning of creation, the Jewish doctrine of revelation is foretold: that God reveals Himself to humanity not in the sun, the stars, the wind, or the storm but in and through words – sacred words that establish eternal covenant between heaven and earth, and thus become co-partners with God in the work of redemption.

This new translation of our foundational texts, this collection of words, has been a true partnership. First, with the outstanding team at Koren Publishers inspirationally led by Matthew Miller, its tireless and visionary driving force. What Koren have achieved in reviving Jewish publishing is remarkable, and particular thanks must be paid to Rabbi Tzvi Hersh Weinreb, Jessica Sacks, Sara Daniel, Rabbi Reuven Ziegler, and Ashirah Yosefah Firszt, together with the other Koren professionals and translators who have contributed so much to this particular project.

Second, with Debra and David Magerman, whose friendship I cherish, and whose support for this project and the Koren Ḥumash is so deeply appreciated. Their generosity will benefit generations of Jews around the world who will make use of these publications for decades to come.

My deepest thanks, as always, are to Elaine and my family, who remain my inspiration and strength, and who have taught me to be open to the Divine Other.

Ultimately, though, all thanks belong to God, whose timeless words continue to provide endless guidance for us today.

Rabbi Lord Jonathan Sacks
London, 5781 (2020)

PUBLISHER'S PREFACE

"One generation will praise Your works to the next..." (Ps. 145:4)

To undertake a new English translation of the Tanakh – the Jewish scriptures comprising the Torah, Nevi'im (Prophets), and Ketuvim (Writings) – requires chutzpah and humility in equal measure, but neither more than *yirat Shamayim* – fear and trembling before God. In translating God's words and those of His prophets, one assumes the precarious position of mediator between Him and the reader, searching for the formulation that will do His work the greatest measure of justice, while simultaneously bringing the reader closer to the text. While there are already numerous English translations of the Bible in the Jewish world, ours aims to stand out through its emphasis on authentically conveying the *hadrat kodesh*, the sacred majesty, of the original Hebrew. More specifically, we have created a translation which

- is readable and stylistically sound to the modern eye and ear, without compromising accuracy or scholarly integrity,
- whispers the tonality of the Hebrew original,
- maintains the beauty and the majestic quality of the poetry and prose of Tanakh,
- is faithful to the classical Jewish interpretive tradition, while cognizant of contemporary scholarship,
- invites the contemporary reader to experience afresh the timeless stories and wisdom contained in the Hebrew scriptures.

This work has been the fruit of a happy collaboration between many people. While this preface cannot list everyone involved, we must acknowledge the contributions of those few without whom the new *Koren Tanakh* simply would not have been produced.

Rabbi Lord Jonathan Sacks, זצ"ל, translated the Torah and much of Psalms. His profound learning, moral depth, and sheer eloquence, expressed in his many published works, made him a leading religious figure not only within contemporary Judaism, but throughout the greater religious world. His untimely passing as the first edition went to press was an irreparable loss to the Jewish people, but we take a measure of consolation in the knowledge that this brilliant translation, to which he devoted his final years, will help carry on his legacy for generations to come. We are honored to have been Rabbi Sacks's publishers, students, and friends.

Rabbi Dr. Tzvi Hersh Weinreb, שליט"א, translated the books of Jeremiah and Proverbs and reviewed many of the other translations. A leading American rabbi and former Chief Executive of the Orthodox Union, Rabbi Weinreb spans the divide between the publishing world in Israel and the needs of American Jewry. We have benefitted greatly from both his scholarship and his sage advice.

Debra and David Magerman, whose unfailing support for this edition as well as the accompanying new *Koren Ḥumash* has demonstrated their faith and friendship – and no small amount of patience – for the invaluable work contained therein. We thank you both, on behalf not only of the many dozens of professionals involved, but of the generations of Jews who will use and cherish this groundbreaking publication.

Translation Team Manager and Senior Translator Jessica Sacks, Sara Daniel, and the other translators, who have invested inestimable time, scholarship, and their prodigious literary talents in this Tanakh.

Rabbi Reuven Ziegler, Ashirah Yosefah Firszt, Rabbi Avishai Magence, and Rabbi Yedidya Naveh, whose management and guidance of scores of translators, scholars, editors, proofreaders, and designers have been superb. Without their skills, no fruit of the above literary talents would have seen the light of publication, and without their expertise, the final product would not have attained the same exacting standards of quality.

Typographer Esther Be'er – who studied under Eliyahu Koren himself – and her colleagues **Rina Ben Gal** and **Tomi Mager** designed the clear, elegant, and functional layout of this Tanakh, which is worthy of our founder's name and of the superb typographical quality of past Koren titles.

In addition to the above, the new *Koren Tanakh* is a testament to the many gifted professionals who had a role in its creation: consulting experts, reviewing scholars, editors, and proofreaders. Their names and contributions are in the Acknowledgments pages which follow.

We are presently developing an extensive range of publications built around this new translation as a core text: the forthcoming **Magerman Edition of the Koren Ḥumash** with extensive commentaries by Rabbi Sacks, the **Rohr Edition of the Koren Mikraot HaDorot**, the **Hertog Edition of the Koren Tanakh of the Land of Israel**, the **Nagel Edition of the Koren Ḥumash Lev Ladaat for Young Adults**, and more. Each of these will fulfill different needs and address specific purposes. What they will share is this intelligent, eloquent translation. It is our hope that the new *Koren Tanakh* will provide its readers with insights beyond and behind the text, and perhaps even a glimpse into their own story.

Matthew Miller, Publisher
Jerusalem, 5781 (2021)

ABOUT THIS EDITION

THE KOREN TANAKH IN HISTORY

Early Printed Hebrew Bibles

Hebrew biblical texts were first printed in Italy in Bologna (1477), with other publications soon following in Soncino, Casale, and Naples. The first complete Hebrew Bible, in folio, was printed in 1488 at Soncino, without any commentary, and was riddled with errors. Further Jewish editions were soon published – one in 1490 in Isola del Liri, with Rashi's commentaries; a very accurate edition of the Ḥumash in Lisbon in 1491; and a second complete edition of the Tanakh in 1494 at Brescia.

But soon thereafter – from 1514 onwards – biblical books in Hebrew began to be printed by Christians, the most notable among them being the Catholic Venetian printer Daniel Bomberg. Bomberg's second edition (1524–25), known as the *Mikraot Gedolot*, was printed in a large format with commentaries and philological notes, and in a smaller format without commentaries. This edition formed the basis of almost every subsequent edition of the Hebrew Bible to this day, including many of those printed by Jews.

Since then, many Hebrew editions of the Tanakh have been brought out by Christian publishers, who dominated the editorial and textual scholarship of Hebrew printing for almost 450 years. Most Jews in the nineteenth century used Bibles published by Christian missionaries (or reprinted from such editions). While this may be difficult to imagine today, for much of modern history the only books available to the Jewish student of Torah were those printed by gentiles intent on converting them.

The Hebrew Koren Tanakh

Along with the establishment of the State of Israel, the spiritual reconstitution of the Jewish people in their ancient homeland was expressed in no way more than by the preparation and printing of the famous *Koren Tanakh*. Mr. Eliyahu Koren understood that the miracle of the nation's return to the land of Israel demanded a clear spiritual response, one which struck to the heart of the question – still debated to this day – of what drives the spirit of the Jewish people. This response would take the shape of a new Tanakh – with text meticulously researched by Torah scholars and free of errors, and with a new typeface that combined classical aesthetic sensibilities with a meticulously modern insistence on clarity and legibility – printed by a Jewish publishing house in Jerusalem, in the modern State of Israel.

Over the course of the 1950s, Eliyahu Koren, along with scholar Meir Medan and a team that included Dr. Daniel Goldschmidt and Avraham Meir Haberman, worked to create an unprecedentedly accurate edition of the Hebrew scriptures. The *Koren Tanakh,* first published in Jerusalem in 1962, was the first fully Jewish bible to be published since the end of the fifteenth century, with Jewish scholars and editors, type designers, printers, and binders. It was remarkable also for being the first publication ever set in the famous Koren Tanakh typeface, which was painstakingly designed especially for it. Since that first printing, the publication of Jewish texts worldwide has made great strides. Koren Publishers too has continually updated and improved its editions, of which this new volume joins a long and worthy tradition.

The Hebrew text of the original *Koren Tanakh* was meticulously researched and reviewed by some of the foremost Masoretic scholars of the generation. The text itself was based for the most part on the earlier work of Rabbi Wolf Heidenheim and *Minḥat Shai,* as well as the Leningrad Codex, the oldest complete surviving manuscript of the Tanakh in Hebrew. The text was met with critical acclaim on its publication and received the approbation of rabbinic luminaries such as Rabbi Joseph B. Soloveitchik and Rabbi Moshe Feinstein.

Another notable feature of the Koren Tanakh in both Hebrew and English is its presentation and organization of the text. In early modern bibles printed by gentiles and used by Jews, the chapter divisions were not based on any Jewish tradition, but on a Christian one. Because this system has by now become an accepted standard of reference even for Jews, it is retained on the inside margin of the page. However, the *Koren Tanakh* is the first to also mark and number the division of the biblical text into the traditional Jewish system of *sedarim.* These appear on the outer margin of the page, as do the divisions for *aliyot* and weekly *parashot.* These distinctions are more than mere intellectual curiosity: they have significant theological import. Many of the disputes between Judaism and Christianity are reflected in the different designation of chapters and sections. The page itself is printed in the style of a *sefer Torah,* including proper graphical representation of the *petuḥa* and *setuma* line breaks according to the Masora, as opposed to the placeholder letters *peh* and *samekh* typically used by older editions to save paper.

The First Koren English Edition

The translation used for the first English *Koren Tanakh* of 1967 was not entirely new. It was, rather, a thoroughly corrected, modernized, and revised version of the Anglo-Jewish bibles that had long been accepted for home and synagogue use throughout the English-speaking world. The Koren translation was based upon *The Jewish Family Bible,* edited by M. Friedlander and published in 1881 with the sanction of the Chief Rabbi of the British Empire, Dr. N. M. Adler. The translation had two important merits: it was faithful to the Masora, while retaining as much of the excellent language and rhythm of the King James "Authorized Version" of 1611 as Jewish sentiment permitted.

That translation was revised for Koren by Professor Harold Fisch, a renowned scholar of English literature and Rector of Bar Ilan University. The language of the older versions was modernized to some extent, and fresh translations and interpretations were included based on comparisons with other Jewish bible translations, *targumim,* and classical and contemporary scholarship. Names of biblical characters, until then invariably rendered in their Hellenized/anglicized versions such as "Eve" and "Jeconiah," were newly presented as they are pronounced in Hebrew, using a transliteration scheme approved by the Academy of the Hebrew Language. Still, more than fifty years later, the language of that translation – especially the retention of the pronouns "thee," "thou," "thy," and "thine" – can feel archaic to the contemporary reader, and the academic, technical style of transliterating names dry and detached.

Now, Koren Publishers has had the great privilege of partnering with Rabbi Lord Jonathan Sacks, who was perhaps the most eloquent spokesman for Judaism in our times, in publishing a completely new and fully Jewish translation of the Tanakh – one which aims to wed the Masoretic authenticity and attention to detail that are the hallmarks of Koren with the literary majesty and elegance that characterize all of Rabbi Sacks's English works. It is the fruit of this great undertaking which you hold in your hands.

NAMES IN THE ENGLISH KOREN TANAKH

The system used by the 1967 Fisch translation for transliterating names possessed the advantage of authenticity and a more Hebrew feel. However, the style was technical and academic, and it sometimes had the opposite of its desired effect by making the characters appear foreign. In this edition, we have opted for a middle path. We transliterate personal names – as well as those of places and tribes – using a simpler, more popular style, eschewing doubled letters and apostrophes except where needed to ensure correct pronunciation. The result is that personal names are spelled much as contemporary Israelis might spell their names in English – e.g., Yaakov (not Ya'aqov) or Rivka (not Rivqa). Whether with respect to august figures such as Moshe – "drawn from the water" – or minor ones such as Ikhavod – "without honor" (contrast to the comic Ichabod of Washington Irving) – we see the rendering of names in contemporary transliteration as imparting a new dimension of the Tanakh that weds cultural authenticity with intimacy.

In certain rare cases where anything but the common anglicized version of a name would feel jarring – e.g., "Israel" or "Pharaoh" – the anglicizations have been preserved, as well as with demonyms (such as "Moabites") whose suffixes indelibly mark them as English words. In addition, the names of many places and geographical features with straightforward meanings that describe them have been translated outright – for example, the Mount of Olives.

As regards names of God, we have followed Rabbi Sacks's direction in maintaining the elegant and accurate distinction between "God," used for *Elohim*, and "LORD" for the tetragrammaton (the ineffable name of God spelled *yod-heh-vav-heh*). This reflects the Almighty's twin roles as Creator of the universe and God of Israel. The appellation "LORD" is set in block capitals to symbolize how the name in Hebrew, while pronounced *Adonai* (which literally means "my Lord"), is in fact written as God's personal name, which may not be uttered. Thus, in those cases where the tetragrammaton is traditionally pronounced *Elohim* rather than *Adonai*, the name is rendered in English as "GOD," in block capitals.

THE PROCESS OF TRANSLATION

The translators who took part in this project, all of whom have deep understanding of the Hebrew texts, were chosen primarily for their uniformly superb literary abilities. After translation, each text was edited and reviewed several times by leading scholars of biblical history, language, and literature to ensure the high level of accuracy and integrity readers should expect from a flagship Koren publication. This process provided our translators with clear parameters in which to creatively render into contemporary English the beauty, drama, and nuances of the original Hebrew texts. With consummate skill and close attention to style, our literary editors helped craft the translations in dialogue with the translators, followed by the attentions of copy editors and consistency editors, as well as multiple rounds of proofreading. Throughout, we have prioritized the experience of the English, with the aim that those holding this volume will forget that they are reading a translation and lose themselves in the drama of the narrative, the elegance of the poetry, the holiness of the law, and the relevance of the wisdom.

Our translation adheres to the Masoretic text of Tanakh. In cases where the Masoretic text distinguishes between the way the word is written (*ketiv*) and the way it is pronounced (*keri*), the translation follows the latter.

Hebrew is a grammatically gendered language, and masculine words and forms are often used to refer to both sexes. In such cases, we have favored the use of gender-neutral forms in English – for example, "people" and "children" rather than "men" and "sons."

To fit the requirements of English style, we occasionally replaced names with pronouns and vice versa, and changed the position of speech markers ("she said") in the sentence, thereby ensuring the clarity and fluidity of the dialogue. In the case of prophecy, introducing modern punctuation to the ancient text is especially difficult. The prophets often shift between the first and third person when conveying God's word, identifying so closely with their message that it is difficult at times to distinguish between God's voice and the prophet's own. The approach we found most organic to the text was to use quotation marks when God appears in direct "dialogue" with the prophet. When, however, the prophet conveys or is asked to convey a message to others, that message is introduced merely by the use of a colon: "The LORD said to Moshe, 'This is what you shall tell the Israelites: You yourselves have seen....'"

Every translation is an interpretation. While we have made use of contemporary approaches to understanding Tanakh, we are also committed to the way the Tanakh, and in particular the Torah, has been received and understood in the Jewish tradition. The acute discernments of Rashi and other commentators, especially those of the school of the *pashtanim*, will be felt in many parts of the translation. In the instances where a rabbinic reading was chosen against the apparent grain of the literal one, we have marked this with a footnote.

This edition of the *English Koren Tanakh* is intentionally sparing in its use of footnotes and explanatory texts. Rather than producing a comprehensive commentary (which would be a titanic undertaking in its own right), we have largely restricted ourselves to pointing out elements of the Hebrew – such as wordplay – that cannot come across in translation, or crucial background information without which the reader might find him- or herself simply unable to understand the text at hand.

To aid the reader further, we have appended to this volume a selection of maps, charts, timelines, genealogies, and illustrations. Drawing upon the extensive collection of high-quality supplementary material developed over the past six decades by Koren Publishers Jerusalem, we have thoroughly updated the material to reflect contemporary graphic sensibilities and to facilitate comprehension.

We sincerely pray that our efforts will "find favor and approval in the eyes of God" (Prov. 3:4) and in the eyes of all to whom the word of God is dear.

ACKNOWLEDGMENTS

THE ENGLISH **KOREN TANAKH** TRANSLATORS

The responsibility of a translator cannot be overstated: for normal books, the best translators are those who transmit words and concepts fluidly from one language to another, from one culture to another, seamlessly, quietly, innocuously. Indeed, it is those translations which jar the reader, which call attention to the text being a translation, that may be considered failures. The success of a translator is his or her very anonymity.

To translate the words of God and His prophets only heightens the responsibilities. Beyond the standard requirements, Bible translators must rephrase these ancient words for the eye and the ear of the contemporary English-speaking reader, conveying the true sense of each word with respect, reverence, love, belief, erudition, elegance, and fluency. Such challenges require translators gifted with extraordinary abilities and sensitivities.

We are truly blessed to have worked with a team of brilliantly literate and highly educated professionals, and are proud to acknowledge their contribution – together with that of our consulting scholars, editors, managers, and staff – to the Jews of the English-speaking world and their *avodat Hashem.*

Rabbi Lord Jonathan Sacks: Genesis, Exodus, Leviticus, Numbers, Deuteronomy, Psalms 1–4, 6, 9, 15, 16, 19, 20, 23, 24, 27, 29, 30, 33, 34, 47, 48, 49, 67, 81, 82, 90–100, 103, 104, 113–118, 120–137, 139, 144–150

Rabbi Dr. Tzvi Hirsch Weinreb: Jeremiah, Proverbs

Jessica Sacks: Isaiah, Jonah, Song of Songs, Ruth, Lamentations, Ecclesiastes, Esther

Sara Daniel: Joshua, Judges, I and II Samuel, I and II Kings, I and II Chronicles, Psalms 5, 7, 8, 10–14, 17, 18, 21, 22, 25, 26, 28, 31, 32, 35–46, 50–66, 68–80, 83–89, 101, 102, 105, 106–112, 119, 138, 140–143

Rachel Ebner: Ezekiel 40–48, Daniel

Lauren Gordon: Ezekiel 1–39

Serylle Horwitz: Ezra 2, Nehemiah

Annie Kantar: Job 3–31, 38–42:6

Tichye Krakowski: Joel, Amos, Obadiah, Haggai, Zechariah, Malachi, Job 1–2, 32–37, 42:7–17

Adina Luber: Ezra 1, 3–10

Dafna Renbaum: Nahum, Habakkuk, Micah, Hosea, Zephaniah

THE ENGLISH **KOREN TANAKH** TRANSLATION SCHOLARS

We extend heartfelt appreciation to the esteemed scholars of Tanakh who invested many hours reviewing draft translations and providing our translators with valuable corrections, translation guidance, and textual and historical insights. The scholars are listed in alphabetical order, followed by the translations they reviewed.

Rabbi Dr. Tzvi Hersh Weinreb: Consultancy scholar for translation queries and final decisions

Dr. Baruch Alster: Haggai

Prof. Joseph L. Angel: I and II Kings, Ezekiel 1–39, Psalms, Daniel

Rabbi Prof. Elie Assis: Joel

Prof. Michael Avioz: Bibliography and resources scholar

Prof. Shawn Zelig Aster: Isaiah, Hosea, Amos, Micah, Haggai

Rabbi Prof. Yitzhak Berger: Genesis, Exodus, Leviticus, Numbers, Deuteronomy, Jeremiah 1–26, Jonah, Malachi

Prof. Emerita Adele Berlin: Jeremiah 27–52, Proverbs, Lamentations

Rabbi Dr. Ezra Frazer: Zechariah, Ezra, Nehemiah

Dr. Tova Ganzel: Ezekiel

Dr. Binyamin Goldstein: I and II Samuel, I and II Chronicles

Rabbi Prof. Isaac B. Gottlieb: I Kings 1–21 , Ecclesiastes

Prof. Emeritus Edward Greenstein: Job

Rabbi Michael Hattin: Joshua, Song of Songs

Prof. Aaron Koller: Judges, Esther

Dr. Yael Landman: Nahum

Dr. Bryna Jocheved Levy: Obadiah, Habakkuk, Zephaniah

Dr. Yael Ziegler: Ruth

THE ENGLISH **KOREN TANAKH** FOOTNOTE SCHOLARS

As noted above, the footnote style chosen for our initial editions of the new *Koren Tanakh* is one of brief clarification. The Tanakh scholars listed below, in alphabetical order, spent many hours researching and composing richly informative footnotes from which we have drawn and adapted the short footnotes appearing in this Tanakh edition.

Prof. Joseph L. Angel: I and II Kings, Ezekiel, Psalms, Daniel

Prof. Shawn Zelig Aster: Joshua, Judges, Isaiah, Jeremiah, Ezekiel, Hosea, Joel, Amos, Obadiah, Micah, Nahum, Habakkuk, Zephaniah, Haggai, Zechariah, Malachi

Rabbi Prof. Yitzhak Berger: Genesis, Exodus, Leviticus, Numbers, Deuteronomy

Prof. Emerita Adele Berlin: Jonah, Proverbs, Job, Song of Songs, Ruth, Lamentations, Ecclesiastes, Esther

Rabbi Dr. Ezra Frazer: Ezra, Nehemiah

Dr. Binyamin Goldstein: I and II Samuel, I and II Chronicles

Rabbi Yedidya Naveh: Selection and editing of footnotes

THE ENGLISH **KOREN TANAKH**
EDITORS, TYPESETTERS, AND GRAPHIC DESIGNERS

EDITOR IN CHIEF
Rabbi Reuven Ziegler

MANAGING EDITORS
Ashirah Yosefah Firszt (Project)
Rabbi Avishai Magence (Production)

LITERARY EDITORS
Prof. Emeritus William L. Lee: Joshua, Judges, I and II Samuel, I and II Kings, Isaiah, Jeremiah, Ezekiel, Hosea, Joel, Amos, Obadiah, Jonah, Micah, Nahum, Habakkuk, Zephaniah, Haggai, Zechariah, Malachi, Psalms, Proverbs, Job, Song of Songs, Ruth, Lamentations, Ecclesiastes, Esther, Daniel, Ezra, Nehemiah, I and II Chronicles
Jessica Sacks: Genesis, Exodus, Leviticus, Numbers, Deuteronomy

COPY EDITORS
Shira Finson
Debbie Ismailoff
Rachel Meghnagi
Ita Olesker

CONSISTENCY EDITORS
Caryn Meltz
Rabbi Yedidya Naveh

PROOFREADERS
Debbie Ismailoff
Caryn Meltz
Ita Olesker
Dvora Rhein

REFERENCE MATERIAL
Editors:
David Arnovitz
Rabbi Alan Haber (Translator)
Caryn Meltz

Content:
Rabbi Dan Beeri
Rabbi Yinon Chen
Efrat Gross
Tamar Hayardeni
Dr. Neriah Klein
Rabbi Menachem Makover
Hanan Moses
Rabbi David Nativ
Eliav Stollman

Graphic Designers:
Tani Bayer
Eliyahu Misgav

Map Designers:
A. D. Riddle
Jay Rosenberg

TYPESETTERS
Rina Ben Gal
Tomi Mager

TORAH READINGS FOR SPECIAL DAYS

Rosh Ḥodesh	Numbers 28:1–15, p. 228
Fast Days	Exodus 32:11–14, p. 123 Continues with Exodus 34:1–10, p. 125
Ninth of Av	Shaḥarit: Deuteronomy 4:25–40, p. 251 Minḥa: See Fast Days, above.
Ḥanukka – Day 1	Ashkenazim: Numbers 7:1–17, p. 194 Sepharadim: Numbers 6:22–7:17, p. 194
Ḥanukka – Days 2–7	Read the offering for the respective day, Numbers 7:18–53, p. 195 On Rosh Ḥodesh, read the Rosh Ḥodesh reading from the first Torah scroll, and the Ḥanukka reading from the second Torah scroll.
Ḥanukka – Day 8	Numbers 7:54–8:4, p. 196
Purim	Exodus 17:8–16, p. 104

TORAH READINGS FOR SPECIAL SHABBATOT

(READ FROM THE SECOND TORAH SCROLL)

Shabbat Rosh Ḥodesh	Numbers 28:9–15, p. 228
Shabbat Ḥanukka	Read the passage for Shabbat Rosh Ḥodesh from the second Torah scroll and for Ḥanukka from the third Torah scroll.
Parashat Shekalim	Exodus 30:11–16, p. 121 If Rosh Ḥodesh falls on Parashat Shekalim, the passage for Rosh Ḥodesh is read from the second Torah scroll and Parashat Shekalim from the third Torah scroll.
Parashat Zakhor	Deuteronomy 25:17–19, p. 278
Parashat Para	Numbers 19:1–22, p. 213
Parashat HaḤodesh	Exodus 12:1–20, p. 95 If Parashat HaḤodesh falls on Rosh Ḥodesh, the passage for Rosh Ḥodesh is read from the second Torah scroll and Parashat HaḤodesh from the third Torah scroll.
Purim on Shabbat (in Walled Cities)	Exodus 17:8–16, p. 104 *Haftara*: Same as Shabbat Zakhor

TORAH READINGS FOR FESTIVALS

Pesaḥ – Day 1	Exodus 12:21–51, p. 96 On Shabbat, Sepharadim read Exodus 12:14–51, p. 95 *Maftir*: Numbers 28:16–25, p. 229
Day 2	Leviticus 22:26–23:44, p. 170 In Israel: *Revi'i* (second Torah scroll): Numbers 28:19–25, p. 229 In the Diaspora: *Maftir*: Same as Day 1
Day 3	Exodus 13:1–16, p. 97 *Revi'i* (second Torah scroll): Numbers 28:19–25, p. 229
Day 4	Exodus 22:24–23:19, p. 110 (If it falls on a Sunday, Sepharadim read the passage for Day 3.) *Revi'i* (second Torah scroll): Numbers 28:19–25, p. 229
Day 5	Exodus 34:1–26, p. 125 (If it falls on a Monday, Sepharadim read the passage for Day 4.) *Revi'i* (second Torah scroll): Numbers 28:19–25, p. 229
Day 6	Numbers 9:1–14, p. 198 *Revi'i* (second Torah scroll): Numbers 28:19–25, p. 229
Shabbat Ḥol HaMoed Pesaḥ	Exodus 33:12–34:26, p. 125 *Maftir*: Numbers 28:19–25, p. 229
Day 7	Exodus 13:17–15:26, p. 98 *Maftir*: Numbers 28:19–25, p. 229
Day 8 (Diaspora)	Deuteronomy 15:19–16:17, p. 267 On Shabbat: Deuteronomy 14:22–16:17, p. 265 *Maftir*: Numbers 28:19–25, p. 229
Shavuot – Day 1	Exodus 19:1–20:23, p. 105 *Maftir*: Numbers 28:26–31, p. 229
Day 2 (Diaspora)	Deuteronomy 15:19–16:17, p. 267 On Shabbat: Deuteronomy 14:22–16:17, p. 265 *Maftir*: Same as Day 1
Rosh HaShana – Day 1	Genesis 21:1–34, p. 29 *Maftir*: Numbers 29:1–6, p. 229
Day 2	Genesis 22:1–24, p. 30 *Maftir*: Same as Day 1
Yom Kippur – Shaḥarit	Leviticus 16:1–34, p. 161 *Maftir*: Numbers 29:7–11, p. 230

Minḥa	Leviticus 18:1–30, p. 163
Sukkot – Day 1	Leviticus 22:26–23:44, p. 170 *Maftir*: Numbers 29:12–16, p. 230
Day 2	Israel: Numbers 29:17–19, p. 230 Diaspora: Same as day 1
Day 3	Israel: Numbers 29:20–22, p. 230 Diaspora: Numbers 29:17–25, p. 230
Day 4	Israel: Numbers 29:23–25, p. 230 Diaspora: Numbers 29:20–28, p. 230
Day 5	Israel: Numbers 29:26–28, p. 231 Diaspora: Numbers 29:23–31, p. 230
Day 6	Israel: Numbers 29:29–31, p. 231 Diaspora: Numbers 29:26–34, p. 231
Hoshana Rabba	Israel: Numbers 29:32–34, p. 231 Diaspora: Numbers 29:26–34, p. 231
Shabbat Ḥol HaMoed Sukkot	Exodus 33:12–34:26, p. 125 *Maftir*: Read the offering for the respective day (in the Diaspora adding the offering for the previous day).
Shemini Atzeret (Diaspora)	Deuteronomy 15:19–16:17, p. 267 On Shabbat: Deuteronomy 14:22–16:17, p. 265 *Maftir*: Numbers 29:35–30:1, p. 231
Simḥat Torah (Israel and Diaspora)	First Torah scroll: Deuteronomy 33:1–34:12, p. 292 Second Torah scroll: Genesis 1:1–2:3, p. 5 Third Torah scroll (*Maftir*): Numbers 29:35–30:1, p. 231

HAFTAROT
(WITH VARIATIONS FOR ASHKENAZIM, SEPHARADIM, YEMENITES, AND MINHAG ANGLIA)

Bereshit	Ashkenazim:	Isaiah 42:5–43:10, p. 641
	Sepharadim:	Isaiah 32:5–21, p. 623
	Yemenites:	Isaiah 32:5–16, p. 623
Noaḥ	Ashkenazim:	Isaiah 54:1–55:5, p. 666
	Sepharadim:	Isaiah 54:1–54:10, p. 666
	Yemenites:	Isaiah 54:1–55:3, p. 666
Lekh Lekha	Ashkenazim & Sepharadim:	Isaiah 40:27–41:16, p. 637
	Yemenites:	Isaiah 40:25–41:16, p. 637
Vayera	Ashkenazim & Yemenites:	II Kings 4:1–37, p. 521
	Sepharadim:	II Kings 4:1–23, p. 521
Ḥayei Sara		I Kings 1:1–31, p. 471
Toledot	Ashkenazim & Sepharadim:	Malachi 1:1–2:7, p. 982
	Yemenites:	Malachi 1:1–3:4, p. 982
Vayetze	Ashkenazim:	Hosea 12:13–14:10, p. 910 (some add Joel 2:26–27, p. 917)
	Sepharadim:	Hosea 11:7–12:12 / –13:5, p. 908
	Yemenites:	Hosea 11:7–12:14, p. 908
Vayishlaḥ		Obadiah 1:1–21, p. 932 (Minhag Anglia: Hosea 11:7–12:12, p. 908)
Vayeshev		Amos 2:6–3:8, p. 921
Miketz		I Kings 3:15–4:1, p. 477
Vayigash		Ezekiel 37:15–28, p. 871
Vayeḥi		I Kings 2:1–12, p. 473
Shemot	Ashkenazim:	Isaiah 27:6–28:13, p. 611, and 29:22–23, p. 617
	Sepharadim:	Jeremiah 1:1–2:3, p. 693
	Yemenites:	Ezekiel 16:1–14, p. 828
Vaera	Ashkenazim & Sepharadim:	Ezekiel 28:25–29:21, p. 855
	Yemenites:	Ezekiel 28:24–29:21, p. 855
Bo	Ashkenazim & Sepharadim:	Jeremiah 46:13–28, p. 779
	Yemenites:	Isaiah 19:1–25, p. 596
Beshalaḥ	Ashkenazim:	Judges 4:4–5:31, p. 345
	Sepharadim:	Judges 5:1–31, p. 346
	Yemenites:	Judges 4:23–5:31, p. 346

Yitro	Ashkenazim:	Isaiah 6:1–7:6, p. 573, and 9:5–6, p. 580
	Sepharadim:	Isaiah 6:1–13, p. 573
	Yemenites:	Isaiah 6:1–13, p. 573, and 9:5–6, p. 580
Mishpatim	Ashkenazim & Sepharadim:	Jeremiah 34:8–22, p. 764, and 33:25–26, p. 763
	Yemenites:	Jeremiah 34:8–35:19, p. 764
Teruma		I Kings 5:26–6:13, p. 480
Tetzaveh		Ezekiel 43:10–27, p. 881
Ki Tisa	Ashkenazim:	I Kings 18:1–39, p. 505
	Sepharadim:	I Kings 18:20–39, p. 506
	Yemenites:	I Kings 18:1–45, p. 505
Vayak'hel	Ashkenazim:	I Kings 7:40–50, p. 484
	Sepharadim:	I Kings 7:13–26, p. 483
	Yemenites:	I Kings 7:13–22, p. 483
Pekudei	Ashkenazim:	I Kings 7:51–8:21, p. 485
	Sepharadim & Yemenites:	I Kings 7:40–50, p. 484
Vayikra	Ashkenazim & Sepharadim:	Isaiah 43:21–44:23, p. 645
	Yemenites:	Isaiah 43:21–44:6, p. 645
Tzav	Ashkenazim & Sepharadim:	Jeremiah 7:21–8:3, p. 711, and 9:22–23, p. 717
	Yemenites:	Jeremiah 7:21–28, p. 711, and 9:22–23, p. 717
Shemini	Ashkenazim:	II Samuel 6:1–7:17, p. 432
	Sepharadim:	II Samuel 6:1–19, p. 432
	Yemenites:	II Samuel 6:1–7:3, p. 432
Tazria		II Kings 4:42–5:19, p. 523
Metzora	Ashkenazim & Sepharadim:	II Kings 7:3–20, p. 528
	Yemenites:	II Kings 7:1–20, p. 527, and 13:23, p. 539
Aḥarei Mot		Ezekiel 22:1–16, p. 841 (Minhag Anglia ends at 22:19)
Kedoshim	Ashkenazim:	Amos 9:7–9:15, p. 931
	Sepharadim:	Ezekiel 20:2–20, p. 836
	Yemenites:	Ezekiel 20:1–15, p. 836
Emor		Ezekiel 44:15–31, p. 883
Behar	Ashkenazim & Sepharadim:	Jeremiah 32:6–27, p. 760
	Yemenites:	Jeremiah 16:19-17:14, p. 731

Beḥukotai	Ashkenazim & Sephardim:	Jeremiah 16:19–17:14, p. 731
	Yemenites:	Ezekiel 34:1–27, p. 865
Bemidbar		Hosea 2:1–22, p. 895
Naso	Ashkenazim & Sephardim:	Judges 13:2–25, p. 361
	Yemenites:	Judges 13:2–24, p. 361
Behaalotekha	Ashkenazim & Sephardim:	Zechariah 2:14–4:7, p. 967
	Yemenites:	Zechariah 2:14–4:9, p. 967
Shelaḥ		Joshua 2:1–24, p. 303
Koraḥ		I Samuel 11:14–12:22, p. 392
Ḥukat	Ashkenazim & Sephardim:	Judges 11:1–33, p. 358
	Yemenites:	Judges 11:1–40, p. 358
Balak		Micah 5:6–6:8, p. 944
Pinḥas (before 17 Tamuz)		I Kings 18:46–19:21, p. 507
Shabbat following 17 Tamuz (Pinḥas or Mattot)		Jeremiah 1:1–2:3, p. 693
Masei	Ashkenazim & Sephardim:	Jeremiah 2:4–28, p. 694, and (for Ashkenazim) 3:4, p. 698, or (for Sephardim) 4:1–2, p. 700 (Minhag Anglia includes both additions.)
	Yemenites:	Isaiah 1:1–20, p. 563
Devarim	Ashkenazim & Sephardim:	Isaiah 1:1–27, p. 563
	Yemenites:	Isaiah 1:21–31, p. 565
Vaetḥanan	Ashkenazim & Sephardim:	Isaiah 40:1–26, p. 635
	Yemenites:	Isaiah 40:1–27, p. 635, and 41:17, p. 639
Ekev		Isaiah 49:14–51:3, p. 657
Re'eh		Isaiah 54:11–55:5, p. 667
Shofetim		Isaiah 51:12–52:12, p. 661
Ki Tetzeh		Isaiah 54:1–10, p. 666
Ki Tavo		Isaiah 60:1–22, p. 676
Nitzavim (or Nitzavim-Vayelekh)	Ashkenazim & Sephardim:	Isaiah 61:10–63:9, p. 679
	Yemenites:	Isaiah 61:9–63:9, p. 679

Shabbat Shuva (Vayelekh or Haazinu)	Ashkenazim:	Hosea 14:2–10, p. 911, and Joel 2:15–27 p. 915 (some begin at 2:11, p. 915). Some also read Micah 7:18–20, p. 948 (Minhag Anglia reads in the order: Hosea, Micah, Joel.)
	Sephardim:	Hosea 14:2–10, p. 911, and Micah 7:18–20, p. 948
	Yemenites:	Hosea 14:2–10, p. 911
Haazinu (after Yom Kippur)	Ashkenazim & Sepharadim:	II Samuel 22:1–51, p. 459
	Yemenites:	Ezekiel 17:22–18:32, p. 833
Special Shabbatot and Holidays		
Shabbat Rosh Ḥodesh		Isaiah 66:1–24, p. 686
Shabbat Erev Rosh Ḥodesh		I Samuel 20:18–42, p. 408
Shabbat Ḥanukka	(1)	Zechariah 2:14–4:7, p. 967 (Yemenites read until 4:9)
	(2)	I Kings 7:40–50, p. 484
Fast Day Minḥa		Isaiah 55:6–56:8, p. 668
Ninth of Av – Shaḥarit	Ashkenazim & Sepharadim:	Jeremiah 8:13–9:23, p. 714
	Yemenites:	Jeremiah 6:16–17, p. 708, and 8:13–9:23, p. 714
Ninth of Av – Minḥa	Ashkenazim:	Isaiah 55:6–56:8, p. 668
	Sepharadim:	Hosea 14:2–10, p. 911
	Yemenites:	Hosea 14:2–10, p. 911, and Micah 7:18–20, p. 948
Parashat Shekalim	Ashkenazim & Yemenites:	II Kings 12:1–17, p. 536 (Minhag Anglia begins at 11:17, p. 536)
	Sepharadim:	II Kings 11:17–12:17, p. 536
Parashat Zakhor	Ashkenazim:	I Samuel 15:2–34, p. 398
	Sepharadim & Minhag Anglia:	I Samuel 15:1–34, p. 398
	Yemenites:	I Samuel 14:52–15:33, p. 398
Parashat Para	Ashkenazim:	Ezekiel 36:16–38, p. 869
	Sepharadim & Yemenites:	Ezekiel 36:16–36, p. 869
Parashat HaḤodesh	Ashkenazim:	Ezekiel 45:16–46:18, p. 885
	Sepharadim:	Ezekiel 45:18–46:15, p. 885
	Yemenites:	Ezekiel 45:9–46:11, p. 885

Shabbat HaGadol		Malachi 3:4–24, p. 986
Pesaḥ Day 1		(Some begin with Joshua 3:5–7, p. 305) Joshua 5:2–6:1, p. 307, and 6:27, p. 309
Pesaḥ Day 2 (Diaspora)	Ashkenazim & Sepharadim:	II Kings 23:1–9, p. 554 and 21–25, p. 556
	Yemenites:	II Kings 22:1–7, p. 553 and 23:21–25, p. 556
Shabbat Ḥol HaMoed Pesaḥ	Ashkenazim & Sepharadim:	Ezekiel 37:1–14, p. 871
	Yemenites:	Ezekiel 36:37–37:14, p. 871
Pesaḥ Day 7		II Samuel 22:1–51, p. 459
Pesaḥ Day 8 (Diaspora)		Isaiah 10:32–12:6, p. 584
Shavuot Day 1	Ashkenazim & Sepharadim:	Ezekiel 1:1–28, p. 807 and 3:12, p. 810
	Yemenites:	Ezekiel 1:1–2:2, p. 807 and 3:12, p. 810
Shavuot Day 2 (Diaspora)		Habakkuk 2:20–3:19, p. 956
Rosh HaShana Day 1		I Samuel 1:1–2:10, p. 379
Rosh HaShana Day 2		Jeremiah 31:1–19, p. 756
Yom Kippur – Shaḥarit		Isaiah 57:14–58:14, p. 671 (Yemenites add 59:20–21, p. 675)
Yom Kippur – Minḥa		The Book of Jonah, p. 934 and Micah 7:18–20, p. 948
Sukkot Day 1	Ashkenazim & Sepharadim:	Zechariah 14:1–21, p. 980
	Yemenites:	Zechariah 13:9–14:21, p. 980
Sukkot Day 2 (Diaspora)	Ashkenazim & Sepharadim:	I Kings 8:2–21, p. 485
	Yemenites:	I Kings 7:51–8:21, p. 485
Shabbat Ḥol HaMoed Sukkot	Ashkenazim & Sepharadim:	Ezekiel 38:18–39:16, p. 873
	Yemenites:	Ezekiel 38:1–23, p. 872
Shemini Atzeret (Diaspora)	Ashkenazim:	I Kings 8:54–9:1, p. 488
	Sepharadim, Yemenites, & Minhag Anglia:	I Kings 8:54–66, p. 488
Simḥat Torah	Ashkenazim:	Joshua 1:1–18, p. 303
	Sepharadim & Yemenites:	Joshua 1:1–9, p. 303 (Yemenites add 6:27, p. 309)

BLESSINGS BEFORE AND AFTER READING THE TORAH

Before the Torah is read, the Oleh says:

Barekhu et Adonai hamevorakh.

Cong: Barukh Adonai hamevorakh le'olam va'ed.

Barukh Adonai hamevorakh le'olam va'ed.

Barukh Ata Adonai, Eloheinu Melekh ha'olam,
asher baḥar banu mikol ha'amim
venatan lanu et Torato.
Barukh ata Adonai, noten haTorah.

After the reading, the Oleh says:

Barukh Ata Adonai, Eloheinu Melekh ha'olam,
asher natan lanu Torat emet,
veḥayei olam nata betokhenu.
Barukh Ata Adonai, noten haTorah.

BLESSINGS BEFORE AND AFTER READING THE HAFTARA

Before reading the Haftara, the person called up for Maftir says:

Barukh Ata Adonai, Eloheinu Melekh ha'olam,
asher baḥar binvi'im tovim
veratza vedivreihem hane'emarim be'emet.
Barukh Ata Adonai, haboḥer baTorah uvMoshe avdo,
uvYisra'el amo, uvinvi'ei ha'emet vatzedek.

After the Haftara, the person called up for Maftir says the following blessings:

(Goalenu Adonai Tzevaot shemo,
Kedosh Yisrael.)

Barukh Ata Adonai, Eloheinu Melekh ha'olam,
Tzur kol ha'olamim, tzadik bekhol hadorot,
haEl hane'eman, ha'omer veoseh, hamedaber umkayem
shekol devarav emet vatzedek.
Ne'eman ata hu Adonai Eloheinu,
vene'emanim devarekha,
vedavar eḥad midevarekha aḥor lo yashuv reikam,

BLESSINGS BEFORE AND AFTER READING THE TORAH

Before the Torah is read, the Oleh says:

Bless the LORD, the blessed One.

Cong: Bless the LORD, the blessed One, for ever and all time.

Bless the LORD, the blessed One, for ever and all time.

Blessed are You, LORD our God, King of the Universe,
who has chosen us from all peoples
and has given us His Torah.
Blessed are You, LORD, Giver of the Torah.

After the reading, the Oleh says:

Blessed are You, LORD our God, King of the Universe,
who has given us (His Torah ,) the Torah of truth,
planting everlasting life in our midst.
Blessed are You, LORD, Giver of the Torah.

BLESSINGS BEFORE AND AFTER READING THE HAFTARA

Before reading the Haftara, the person called up for Maftir says:

Blessed are You, LORD our God, King of the Universe,
who chose good prophets
and was pleased with their words, spoken in truth.
Blessed are You, LORD, who chose the Torah, His servant Moshe,
His people Israel, and the prophets of truth and righteousness.

After the Haftara, the person called up for Maftir says the following blessings:

(As for our redeemer, the LORD of hosts is His name,
the Holy One of Israel.)

Blessed are You, LORD our God, King of the Universe,
Rock of all worlds, righteous for all generations,
the faithful God who says and does, speaks and fulfills,
all of whose words are truth and righteousness.
You are faithful, LORD our God,
and faithful are Your words,
not one of which returns unfulfilled,

ki El melekh ne'eman (veraḥaman) Ata.
Barukh Ata Adonai, haEl hane'eman bekhol devarav.

Raḥem al Tziyon ki hi beit ḥayeinu,
vela'aluvat nefesh toshiya bimhera veyameinu.
Barukh Ata Adonai mesamei'aḥ Tziyon bevanei'a.

Samḥeinu Adonai Eloheinu,
be'Eliyahu hanavi avdekha,
uvmalkhut beit David meshiḥekha –
bimhera yavo veyagel libenu.
Al kis'o lo yeshev zar,
velo yinḥalu od aḥerim et kevodo,
ki veshem kodshekha nishbata lo
shelo yikhbeh nero le'olam va'ed.
Barukh Ata Adonai magen David.

On Shabbat, including Shabbat Ḥol HaMo'ed Pesaḥ, say:

Al haTorah ve'al ha'avoda,
ve'al hanevi'im ve'al yom haShabbat hazeh
shenatata lanu Adonai Eloheinu likdusha ve'limnuḥa,
lekhavod ultifaret. –
Al hakol Adonai Eloheinu, anaḥnu modim lakh umvarekhim otakh
yitbarakh shimkha befi kol ḥai,
tamid le'olam vaed.
Barukh Ata Adonai, mekadesh haShabbat. (Amen.)

On Yom Tov and on Shabbat Ḥol HaMo'ed Sukkot, say
(adding on Shabbat the words in parentheses):

Al haTorah ve'al ha'avoda ve'al hanevi'im,
(ve'al yom haShabbat hazeh) ve'al yom

On Pesaḥ:	Ḥag haMatzot hazeh
On Shavuot:	Ḥag haShavuot hazeh
On Sukkot:	Ḥag haSukkot hazeh
On Shemini Atzeret and Simḥat Torah:	haShemini Ḥag ha'Atzeret hazeh

shenatata lanu, Adonai Eloheinu (likdusha velimnuḥa,) lesason ulsimḥa,
lekhavod ultifaret. Al hakol, Adonai Eloheinu,
anaḥnu modim lakh umvarekhim otakh,
yitbarakh shimkha befi kol ḥai,
tamid le'olam vaed.
Barukh Ata Adonai, mekadesh (haShabbat ve)Yisrael vehazemanim. (Amen.)

for You, God, are a faithful (and compassionate) King.
Blessed are You, Lord, faithful in all His words.

Have compassion on Zion for it is the source of our life,
and save the one grieved in spirit swiftly in our days.
Blessed are You, Lord, who makes Zion rejoice in her children.

Grant us joy, Lord our God,
through Eliyahu the prophet Your servant,
and through the kingdom of the house of David Your anointed –
may he soon come and make our hearts glad.
May no stranger sit on his throne,
and may others not continue to inherit his glory,
for You promised him by Your holy name
that his light would never be extinguished.
Blessed are You, Lord, Shield of David.

On Shabbat, including Shabbat Ḥol HaMo'ed Pesaḥ, say:

For the Torah, for Divine worship,
for the prophets, and for this Sabbath day
which You, Lord our God, have given us for holiness and rest,
honor and glory –
for all these we thank and bless You, Lord our God,
and may Your name be blessed by the mouth of all that lives,
continually, for ever and all time.
Blessed are You, Lord, who sanctifies the Sabbath. (Amen.)

On Yom Tov and on Shabbat Ḥol HaMo'ed Sukkot, say
(adding on Shabbat the words in parentheses):

For the Torah, for Divine worship, for the prophets,
(for this Sabbath day) and for this day of

On Pesaḥ: the Festival of Matzot
On Shavuot: the Festival of Shavuot
On Sukkot: the Festival of Sukkot
On Shemini Atzeret and Simḥat Torah: the Festival of Shemini Atzeret

which You, Lord our God, have given us (for holiness and rest), for joy and gladness,
honor and glory – for all these we thank and bless You, Lord our God,
and may Your name be blessed by the mouth of all that lives,
continually, for ever and all time.
Blessed are You, Lord, who sanctifies (the Sabbath), Israel and the festivals. (Amen.)

TORAH

GENESIS / BERESHIT

EXODUS / SHEMOT

LEVITICUS / VAYIKRA

NUMBERS / BEMIDBAR

DEUTERONOMY / DEVARIM

From Creation	The Patriarchs	Enslavement in Egypt	Wanderings in the Desert	Conquering Canaan	The Judges
2,000 years	Approx. 200 years	210 years	40 years	14 years	Approx. 300 years

Book	Period covered
Genesis	From Creation – The Patriarchs
Exodus	Enslavement in Egypt
Leviticus	Wanderings in the Desert
Numbers	Wanderings in the Desert
Deuteronomy	Wanderings in the Desert
Joshua	Conquering Canaan
Judges	The Judges
Chronicles	From Creation – The Judges

Tabernacle in the Desert	Wanderings in the Desert
Tabernacle in Gilgal	Conquering Canaan
Tabernacle in Shilo	The Judges

GENESIS/BERESHIT

GENESIS	Beginning of humanity – from Adam to Avraham	Avraham	Yitzḥak	Yaakov	Yosef and his brothers – the descent to Egypt
	Chs. 1–11	12:1–25:18	25:19–26:34	27–36	37–50
	2,309 years				

1 1 2 When God began creating heaven and earth, the earth was void and desolate, BERESHIT
there was darkness on the face of the deep, and the spirit of God moved
3 4 over the waters. God said, "Let there be light." And there was light. God
saw the light: it was good; and God separated the light from the darkness.
5 And God called the light "day," and the darkness He called "night." There
was evening, and there was morning – one day.

6 Then God said, "Let an expanse stretch through the water; let it separate
7 water from water." So God made the expanse, and it separated the water
8 beneath the expanse from the water above. And so it was. God called the
expanse "heavens." There was evening, and there was morning – a second
day.

9 Then God said, "Let the water beneath the heavens be gathered to one
10 place, and let dry ground appear." And so it was. God called the dry ground
"earth," and the gathered waters He called "seas." And God saw: it was
good.

11 Then God said, "Let the earth produce vegetation: seed-bearing plants
and trees of all the kinds on earth that grow seed-bearing fruit." And so it
12 was. The earth produced vegetation: plants bearing seeds, each of its kind,
and trees bearing fruit containing seeds, each of its kind. And God saw:
13 it was good. There was evening, and there was morning – a third day.

14 Then God said, "Let there be lights in the heavens' expanse to separate day
15 from night and to serve for signs and seasons, days and years. They shall be
lights in the heavens' expanse, shining upon the earth." And so it was.

16 God made the two great lights – the greater light to rule by day and the
17 lesser light to rule by night – and the stars. God set them in the heavens'
18 expanse to shine upon the earth, to rule by day and by night and to separate
19 light from darkness. And God saw that it was good. There was evening,
and there was morning – a fourth day.

20 Then God said, "Let the water teem with swarms of living creatures, and
21 let birds fly over the earth across the heavens' expanse." So God created the
great sea creatures, and all the kinds of crawling, living things that swarm
in the water, and all the kinds of winged, flying creatures. And God saw
22 that it was good. God blessed them, saying: "Be fertile and multiply and
23 fill the waters of the seas, and let flying creatures multiply on earth." There
was evening, and there was morning – a fifth day.

24 Then God said, "Let the land produce every kind of living thing: all the
different species of cattle, crawling things and wild animals of the earth."
25 And so it was. God made the different kinds of wild animals of the earth,
and cattle, and all the species of creature that creep upon land. And God
saw that it was good.

26 Then God said, "Let us make humankind in our image, our likeness, that
they may rule over the fish of the sea and the flying creatures of the heavens,
the cattle and all the earth, and every living creature that moves upon the
earth."

27 So God created humankind in His image:
in the image of God He created him;
male and female He created them.

28 God blessed them, saying, "Be fertile and multiply. Fill the earth and
subdue it. Rule over the fish of the sea, and the flying creatures of the
heavens, and every living thing that moves upon the earth."

29 Then God said, "I give you all these seed-bearing plants on the face of the
earth and every tree with seed-bearing fruit. They shall be yours to eat.
30 And to all the beasts of the earth and birds of the heavens and everything
that crawls over the earth and has within it living spirit – I give every green
plant for food." And so it was.

31 Then God saw all that He had made: and it was very good.

There was evening, and there was morning – the sixth day.

2 1 2 So the heavens and the earth were finished, and all their vast array. On the
seventh day God finished the work that He had done, and on the seventh
3 day He rested from all the work that He had done. God blessed the seventh
day and sanctified it, because on it He rested from all His work, from all
that God had created and done.

4 This is the story of the heavens and the earth when they were created, on
5 the day the Lord God made earth and heaven. No shrub of the field yet
grew on earth, and no plant had yet sprouted, for the Lord God had not
yet brought rain upon the earth, and there was no one to work the land.
6 A mist would rise up from the earth and water all the face of the land.

7 Then the Lord God formed man from the dust of the land[1] and breathed
8 the breath of life into his nostrils, and the man became a living being. The
Lord God planted a garden in Eden, in the east, and there he put the
9 man He had formed. And from the land, the Lord God caused all kinds
of trees to grow, pleasant to look at and good to eat from, and the Tree
of Life stood in the middle of the garden, and the Tree of Knowledge of
good and evil.

10 A river flows from Eden to water this garden, and from there divides into
11 four headwaters. The name of the first is Pishon. It surrounds the land of
12 Ḥavila, where there is gold. And the gold of that land is good; bdellium
13 and rock crystal are there also. The name of the second river is Giḥon; it
14 is the one that surrounds the land of Kush. The name of the third river

1 | The Hebrew *adam* (man) resonates with *adama* (land).

is the Tigris, and it flows to the east of Assyria. The fourth river is the
Euphrates.

15 The LORD God took the man and placed him in the Garden of Eden to
16 work it and safeguard it. And the LORD God commanded the man: "You
17 are free to eat from any tree in the garden. But the Tree of Knowledge of
good and evil – you may not eat from that, for on the day you eat of it,
you shall die."

18 Then the LORD God said, "It is not good for man to be alone. I will make a
19 fitting partner for him." The LORD God formed all the wild animals, and all the
birds of the heavens, out of the land. He brought them to the man to see what
he would call them, and whatever he called each living thing, that became its
20 name. So the man gave names to all the animals, the birds of the heavens, and
all the wild creatures. But he found no fitting partner for himself.

21 Then the LORD God made the man fall into a deep sleep, and while he
22 was sleeping He took one of his ribs and closed the flesh in its place. And
the LORD God built the rib He had taken from the man into a woman. He
23 brought her to the man. And the man said:

"This, at last
is bone of my bones
and flesh of my flesh.
This shall be called Woman,
for from Man was this one taken."[2]

24 That is why a man leaves his father and mother and cleaves to his wife and
25 they become one flesh. The man and his wife were both naked, but they
were not ashamed.

3 1 The serpent was the slyest of all the wild animals the LORD God had made.
"Did God say," it asked the woman, "that you must not eat from any tree in
the garden?"

2 The woman told the serpent, "We may eat the fruit of the trees in the garden,
3 but God did say, 'You must not eat fruit from the tree in the middle of the
garden, and you must not touch it, or you will die.'"

4 5 But the serpent told the woman, "You will not die; God knows that on
the day you eat from it your eyes will be opened, and you will be like God,
knowing good and evil."

6 The woman saw that the tree was ripe for eating, enticing to the eyes, and
desirable too for granting insight. She took some of its fruit and ate, and she
7 gave some to her husband and he too ate. The eyes of both of them were
opened, and they realized that they were naked. So they sewed fig leaves
together and made coverings for themselves.

---

2 | *Isha* (woman) resonates with *ish* (man).

8 They heard the sound of the LORD God walking in the garden in the cool of
the day, and the man and his wife hid from the LORD God among the trees
9 of the garden. The LORD God called to the man: "Where are you?"

10 He answered, "I heard Your voice in the garden, and I was afraid, because I
was naked. So I hid."

11 "Who told you," God asked, "that you were naked? Have you eaten from the
tree from which I commanded you not to eat?"

12 The man said, "The woman You put here with me – she gave me fruit from
the tree and I ate."

13 Then the LORD God said to the woman, "What is this you have done?"
The woman said, "The serpent beguiled me and I ate."

14 And the LORD God said to the serpent,

"Because you have done this,
    you are accursed
more than all the animals
    and all wild beasts.
You will creep on your belly
    and dust will you eat
        all the days of your life.
15 I will plant hostility
    between you and the woman,
        between your children and hers.
And man will strike your head,
    and you will strike his heel."

16 To the woman He said,

"I will make your pain in pregnancy
    searingly great;
        in sorrow will you bear children.
You will long for your husband,
    but he will rule over you."

17 To Adam[3] He said, "Because you listened to your wife and ate of the tree
from which I commanded you not to eat –
cursed will be the land on your account.
    By painful toil you will eat from it
        all the days of your life.
18 It will sprout thorns and thistles for you,
    and you shall eat plants of the field.

3 | The Hebrew *adam* can be read, depending on usage, as a common noun (man; cf. 2:7) or as a proper name.

19 By the sweat of your brow will you eat bread
until you return to the land,
for from there you were taken.
You are dust, and
you will return to dust."

20 Then the man named his wife Ḥava, for she would become the mother of
21 all life.[4] Then the LORD God made garments of skins for Adam and his
wife and clothed them.

22 The LORD God then said, "Now that man has become like one of us,
knowing good and evil, he must not be allowed to reach out his hand and
23 take also from the Tree of Life, eat, and live forever." So the LORD God
sent him away from the Garden of Eden to work the land from which he
24 had been taken. He drove out the man, and east of the Garden of Eden
He placed the cherubim and the flaming, whirling sword to guard the way
to the Tree of Life.

4 1 The man knew[5] his wife Ḥava, and she conceived and gave birth to Kayin.
2 She said, "With the LORD's help I have made a man."[6] Later, she gave birth
to his brother Hevel.[7] Hevel became a shepherd, while Kayin was a worker
of the land.

3 Time passed, and Kayin brought fruit of the land as an offering to the
4 LORD. Hevel too brought an offering: fat portions from the firstborn of
5 his flock. The LORD looked favorably on Hevel and his offering, but upon
Kayin and his offering He did not look with favor. Kayin became very
angry, and his face downcast.

6 The LORD said to Kayin:

"Why are you angry;
why is your face downcast?
7 If you act well,
will you not be uplifted?
If you fail to act well,
sin is crouching at the door;
it longs to have you,
but you must rule over it."

8 Then Kayin said to his brother Hevel[8] –

and when they were in the field, Kayin rose up against his brother Hevel
and killed him.

---

4 | The name Ḥava resonates with *ḥai* (life).

5 | A euphemism for sexual relations.

6 | The name Kayin resonates with *kaniti* (I have made).

7 | *Hevel* means "breath" and carries connotations of transience.

8 | It is not specified what Kayin told Hevel.

9 The Lord asked Kayin, "Where is your brother, Hevel?"

"I do not know," he said. "Am I my brother's keeper?"

10 He said, "What is it you have done? The voice of your brother's blood
11 cries out to Me from the land! Now you are cursed, more so than the land[9]
that has opened its mouth to receive your brother's blood from your hand.
12 When you work the land, it will no longer grant you its powers. You will
be a fugitive wanderer over the land."

13 14 Kayin said to the Lord, "My sin is more than I can bear. You have banished
me today from the face of the land, and from Your face too I will be
hidden. I will be a fugitive wanderer over the land, and whoever finds me
15 will kill me." The Lord said to him, "Whoever then kills Kayin will suffer
vengeance seven times over." Then the Lord put a mark on Kayin so that
none who found him would kill him.

16 So Kayin departed from the Lord's presence and lived in the land of Nod,[10]
17 east of Eden. Kayin knew his wife, and she conceived and gave birth to
18 Ḥanokh. He built a city, naming it Ḥanokh after his son. Ḥanokh had a
son Irad, and Irad had a son Meḥuyael. Meḥiyael had a son Metushael, and
Metushael had a son Lemekh.

19 20 Lemekh married two women, one named Ada and the other Tzila. Ada
gave birth to Yaval. He was the ancestor of those who live in tents and raise
21 livestock. His brother's name was Yuval. He was the ancestor of all those who
22 play the lyre and the pipe. Tzila, too, had a son, Tuval-Kayin, who forged all
kinds of bronze and iron tools. Tuval-Kayin's sister was Naama.

23 Lemekh said to his wives:

"Ada and Tzila, listen to my voice;
  wives of Lemekh, heed my words.
I killed a man for wounding me,
  killed a boy for bruising me.
24 If Kayin will be avenged seven times,
  then Lemekh, seventy-seven."

25 Adam knew his wife again, and she gave birth to a son and named him Shet,
"because God has granted[11] me another child in place of Hevel," for Kayin
26 had killed him. And Shet too had a son, and named him Enosh. That was
when people began to pray in the name of the Lord.

5 1 This is the book of Adam's descendants:
On the day God created humankind,
  He made them in the likeness of God.
2   Male and female He created them,

---

9 | Cf. 3:17.

10 | "Land of Nod" bears the simultaneous meaning "land of wandering."

11 | The name Shet resonates with *shat* (granted).

and on the day they were created,
He blessed them and called them Humankind.[12]

3 Adam lived one hundred and thirty years and then had a son in his own
4 likeness and image, and named him Shet. After Shet was born, Adam lived
5 eight hundred years and had other sons and daughters. Altogether Adam
lived nine hundred and thirty years, and then he died.

6 7 Shet lived one hundred and five years and then had a son, Enosh. After
Enosh was born, Shet lived eight hundred and seven years and had other
8 sons and daughters. Altogether, Shet lived nine hundred and twelve years,
and then he died.

9 10 Enosh lived ninety years and then had a son, Keinan. After Keinan was
born, Enosh lived eight hundred and fifteen years and had other sons and
11 daughters. Altogether, Enosh lived nine hundred and five years, and then
he died.

12 13 Keinan lived seventy years and had a son, Mahalalel. After Mahalalel was
born, Keinan lived eight hundred and forty years and had other sons and
14 daughters. Altogether, Keinan lived nine hundred and ten years, and then
he died.

15 16 Mahalalel lived sixty-five years and had a son, Yered. After Yered was
born, Mahalalel lived eight hundred and thirty years and had other sons
17 and daughters. Altogether, Mahalalel lived eight hundred and ninety-five
years, and then he died.

18 19 Yered lived one hundred and sixty-two years and had a son, Ḥanokh. After
Ḥanokh was born, Yered lived eight hundred years and had other sons and
20 daughters. Altogether, Yered lived nine hundred and sixty-two years, and
then he died.

21 22 Ḥanokh lived sixty-five years and had a son, Metushelaḥ. Ḥanokh walked
faithfully with God for three hundred years after Metushelaḥ was born,
23 and had other sons and daughters. Altogether, Ḥanokh lived for three
24 hundred and sixty-five years. Ḥanokh walked faithfully with God and then
he was no more, for God took him.

25 Metushelaḥ lived one hundred and eighty-seven years and had a son,
26 Lemekh. After Lemekh was born, Metushelaḥ lived seven hundred and
27 eighty-two years and had other sons and daughters. Altogether, Metushelaḥ
lived nine hundred and sixty-nine years, and then he died.

28 29 Lemekh lived one hundred and eighty-two years and had a son. He named
him Noaḥ, saying, "This one will bring us comfort[13] after all our labor and
30 the sorrow of our hands on the land the Lord has cursed." After Noaḥ

12 | Hebrew *adam*.

13 | *Noaḥ* resonates with *yenaḥamenu* (will bring us comfort).

was born, Lemekh lived five hundred and ninety-five years and had other
31 sons and daughters. Altogether, Lemekh lived seven hundred and seventy-
seven years, and then he died.

32 After Noaḥ was five hundred years old, Noaḥ had three sons: Shem, Ḥam,
6 1 and Yefet. Humans began to multiply on earth, and daughters were born to
2 them. When the sons of God[14] saw that the daughters of man were lovely,
3 they began to take whomever they chose to be wives to them. Then the
Lord said, "My spirit will not forever judge man; he is of flesh. His life
shall be but one hundred and twenty years."

4 In those days the Nefilim[15] were on earth, and later also, for the sons of
God had gone to the daughters of man and had children with them. These
were the heroes of old, men of legends.

5 The Lord saw how great man's wickedness was upon the earth, and that his
6 thoughts constantly inclined toward evil. Then the Lord regretted that He
7 had made man on earth, and His heart was touched with sorrow. The Lord
said, "I will erase My creation, humankind, from the face of the land – man,
even animals and creeping things, even birds of the heavens – for I regret
8 having made them." But Noaḥ found favor in the Lord's sight.

NOAḤ

9 This is the story of Noaḥ. Noaḥ was a righteous man, a person of integrity
10 in his generation; Noaḥ walked with God. And Noaḥ had three sons: Shem,
Ḥam, and Yefet.

11 12 The earth had become corrupt in God's sight, full of violence. And when
God saw how corrupt the earth had become, all flesh corrupting its ways
13 upon the earth, God said to Noaḥ, "The end of all flesh has come before
Me, for the earth is full of violence because of them. I am about to destroy
14 them, along with all the earth. So make yourself an ark of cypress wood.
15 Make it with compartments and coat it in pitch inside and out. This is
how you shall make it: the ark shall be three hundred cubits long, fifty
16 cubits wide, and thirty cubits high. Make a window for the ark, and taper
the latter to within a cubit of the top.[16] Put a door in the side of the ark
17 and make lower, middle, and upper decks. And I – I am about to bring
floodwaters over the earth to destroy all flesh that has within it the breath
18 of life under the heavens. Everything on earth will die. But I will establish
My covenant with you, and you will enter the ark – you, your sons, your
19 wife, and your sons' wives with you. And you shall take two of each living
20 creature, male and female, into the ark to keep alive with you. Of every
21 kind of bird, animal, and wild beast, bring two to keep alive. As for you,
take all the food to be eaten and store it: it will be for food for you and for
22 them." Noaḥ did so: all that God commanded him, he fulfilled.

---

14 | Opinions vary regarding the meaning and proper translation of this phrase.

15 | Apparently giants (see Num. 13:33).

16 | That is, the ark should slant upward, becoming narrower as it approaches the top.

7 1 Then the LORD said to Noaḥ, "Enter the ark, you and all your household,
for I have seen you alone to be righteous before Me in this generation.
2 Take seven and seven of every pure animal, seven pairs, and two of every
3 animal that is not pure, of each kind a pair. Also take seven pairs of each
4 kind of bird, male and female, to keep their kind alive across the earth. For
in seven days' time I will send rain on the earth for forty days and forty
nights, and I will wipe from the face of the earth every living creature I
5 have made." Noaḥ did all that the LORD commanded him.

6 Noaḥ was six hundred years old when the floodwaters came upon the
7 earth. Noaḥ, with his sons, his wife, and his sons' wives, came into the
8 ark to escape the waters of the flood. The pure animals, the animals that
9 were not pure, the birds, and all that walked the earth came two by two
to Noaḥ into the ark, male and female, as God had commanded Noaḥ.
10 11 Thus, after seven days the floodwaters came upon the earth. In the six
hundredth year of Noaḥ's life, in the second month, on the seventeenth
of the month – on that day, all the wellsprings of the great deep burst, and
heavens' floodgates opened.

12 13 The rain fell on the earth for forty days and forty nights. On that very day,
Noaḥ, his sons, Shem, Ḥam, and Yefet, Noaḥ's wife, and his sons' three
14 wives entered the ark. With them came every kind of wild beast, every
kind of animal, every creeping, crawling creature of the land, every kind
15 of flying creature, every bird, and each winged thing. They came to Noaḥ,
16 to the ark, two by two, of all flesh that had within it the breath of life. They
came, male and female of all flesh, as God had commanded him. Then the
LORD shut him in.

17 For forty days the flood came upon the earth. The waters swelled, lifting the
18 ark so that it rose above the land. The waters surged, swelling enormously
19 on the earth, and the ark began to drift on the surface of the water. The
waters surged ever more, until all the high mountains beneath all the
20 heavens were covered. Fifteen cubits above them the waters surged
21 as the mountains were covered. All flesh that moved upon the earth
perished – birds, animals, wild beasts, and all the creatures that swarm
22 on the earth, and all humankind. Everything on dry land that had breath
23 of life in its nostrils died. Every living thing on the face of the earth was
wiped out: from humans to animals, from creeping creatures to winged
birds of the heavens, all were wiped from the earth. Only Noaḥ and those
24 with him in the ark survived. For one hundred fifty days, the waters surged
over the earth.

8 1 Then God remembered Noaḥ and all the wild beasts and animals with
him in the ark. God sent a wind over the earth, and the waters began to
2 subside. The wellsprings of the deep and heavens' floodgates closed, and
3 the heavens' rains were reined in. The water steadily receded from the
4 earth, and by the end of one hundred fifty days, the water had abated. In

the seventh month, on the seventeenth day of the month, the ark came to
5 rest on the mountains of Ararat. The water continued to abate until the
tenth month, and on the first day of the tenth month, the mountaintops
became visible.

6 7 After forty days Noaḥ opened the window he had made in the ark and
sent a raven forth. It flew to and fro until the water on the earth had dried.
8 After that he sent forth a dove to see whether the water had subsided from
9 the face of the land. But the dove found no resting place to plant its foot,
and so it returned to him, to the ark, for water still covered the face of the
earth completely. He reached out his hand and brought the dove back to
him, into the ark.

10 Then he waited another seven days, and again he sent the dove forth from
11 the ark. The dove came back to him in the evening – and in its beak was
a freshly picked olive leaf. Noaḥ knew then that the water had subsided
from the earth.

12 He waited another seven days and again sent forth the dove – and it
returned to him no more.

13 So it was that, by the first day of the first month of Noaḥ's six hundred and
first year, the water on the earth dried up. Noaḥ removed the covering of
14 the ark and saw that the face of the land was dry. By the twenty-seventh
day of the second month, the earth had dried completely.

15 16 Then God said to Noaḥ, "Leave the ark – you, and your wife, your sons,
17 and your sons' wives with you. And every living thing with you – birds,
animals, and all wild beasts that walk the earth – bring them out with you.
Let them swarm again on the earth and be fertile and multiply upon it."
18 19 So Noaḥ came out with his sons, his wife, and his sons' wives. Every beast,
creeping thing, winged creature, everything that creeps across the earth,
emerged from the ark by families.

20 Then Noaḥ built an altar to the Lord and, taking of each of the kinds of
21 pure animals and pure birds, sacrificed burnt offerings on the altar. The
Lord smelled the fragrant aroma and said in His heart, "Never again will I
curse the land because of man;[17] the devisings of the human heart are evil
22 from its youth. And never again will I destroy all life as I have done. As
long as earth and time endure – sowing time and harvest, cold and heat,
summer, winter, day, and night will not cease."

9 1 Then God blessed Noaḥ and his sons, saying to them, "Be fertile, multiply,
2 fill the earth. Fear and dread of you shall fall upon all beasts of the earth,
upon all winged creatures of the heavens, upon all that creeps upon the
3 land and all fish of the sea. Into your hand they are given. Every moving

17 | Cf. 3:17, 5:29.

thing that lives shall be food for you; I allow them all to you, like green
4 plants. But flesh with its lifeblood still in it you may not eat. And for your
5 own lifeblood I will demand account; I will demand it from every wild
beast. For human life I will demand account, of every man toward his
fellow man:

6 "One who sheds the blood of man –
by man shall his blood be shed,
for in God's image
man was made.

7 "As for you, be fertile and multiply, abound on earth and become many
on it."

8 Then God said to Noaḥ and to his sons with him: "I – I am about to
9
10 establish My covenant with you and your descendants after you, and with
every living creature that is with you – the birds, the animals, and all the
wild beasts of earth that are with you, everything that left the ark, every
11 living creature on earth. I will establish My covenant with you, that never
again may all life be destroyed by the waters of a flood; never again will
there be a flood to destroy the earth."

12 God said, "This is the sign of the covenant I am making between Me and
you – and every living creature with you – for all generations to come.
13 I have laid down My bow in the clouds to be the sign of the covenant
14 between Me and the earth. Whenever I bring clouds over the earth and the
15 rainbow appears in the clouds, I will remember My covenant that binds
Me and you and every living creature of all flesh so that never again will
16 the waters become a flood to destroy all life. The rainbow will be there in
the cloud, and I will see it, remembering the eternal covenant between
17 God and every living creature, all flesh upon the earth." So said God to Noaḥ:
"This is the sign of the covenant that I have established between Me and all
flesh that is on earth."

18 Noaḥ's sons who came out from the ark were Shem, Ḥam, and Yefet. Ḥam
19 was the father of Kenaan.[18] These three were Noaḥ's sons; and from them
20 all the world branched out. Noaḥ began to be a man of the land, and he
21 planted a vineyard. He drank some of the wine, became drunk, and lay
22 uncovered in his tent. Ḥam, father of Kenaan, saw his father's nakedness
23 and told his two brothers who were outside. Shem and Yefet then took
a cloak and put it over both their shoulders. They walked backward and
covered their father's nakedness, averting their faces so as not to see the
24 nakedness of their father. Noaḥ woke from his wine and realized what his
25 youngest son had done to him. He said,

18 | The ancestor of the Canaanites, whose land would ultimately be given to Israel, descendants of Shem.

"Cursed be Kenaan!
The lowest of slaves
shall he be to his brothers."

26 Then he said,

"Blessed be the LORD, God of Shem;
Kenaan shall be his slave.
27 May God enlarge Yefet,
and let him dwell in the tents of Shem;
Kenaan shall be his slave."

28 29 After the flood Noaḥ lived three hundred and fifty years. Noaḥ lived a total
of nine hundred and fifty years, and he died.

10 1 These are the descendants of Noaḥ's sons, Shem, Ḥam, and Yefet; after
2 the flood, children were born to them.[19] Yefet's sons were Gomer, Magog,
3 Madai, Yavan, Tuval, Meshekh, and Tiras. Gomer's sons were Ashkenaz,
4 Rifat, and Togarma. Yavan's sons were Elisha, Tarshish, Kitim, and
5 Dodanim. From these the seagoing nations spread out to their territories,
each with its own language, by their clans and their nations.

6 7 Ḥam's sons were Kush, Mitzrayim,[20] Put, and Kenaan. Kush's sons were
Seva, Ḥavila, Savta, Raama, and Savtekha. Raama's sons were Sheva and
8 Dedan. Kush was the father of Nimrod, the first mighty warrior on earth.
9 He was a mighty hunter before the LORD, which is why people still say,
"Like Nimrod, a mighty hunter before the LORD."

10 His kingdom began with Babylon, Erekh, Akad, and Kalneh in the land
11 of Shinar. From that land, Ashur went out and built Nineveh, Reḥovot Ir,
12 13 Kalaḥ, and Resen between Nineveh and Kalaḥ; that is the great city. Mitz-
14 rayim fathered the Ludim, Anamim, Lehavim and Naftuḥim, Patrusim,
Kasluḥim – from whom the Philistines descended – and the Kaftorim.

15, 16 Kenaan fathered Tzidon, his firstborn, and Ḥet, and the Jebusites, Amor-
17, 18 ites, and Girgashites, the Hivites, Arkites, and Sinites, the Arvadites,
Zemarites, and Hamatites. Later, the Canaanite families were dispersed.

19 The Canaanite borders were from Sidon toward Gerar near Aza, and
toward Sedom, Amora, Adma, and Tzevoyim, near Lasha.

20 These were the descendants of Ḥam, by their clans and their languages,
with their lands and their nations.

21 Sons were also born to Shem. The older brother of Yefet, he was the ancestor
22 of all the sons of Ever. Shem's sons were Elam, Ashur, Arpakhshad, Lud,
23 24 and Aram. Aram's sons were Utz, Ḥul, Geter, and Mash. Arpakhshad was

19 | The following are the eponymous ancestors of various nations.

20 | In this translation, Ḥam's son is rendered "Mitzrayim," while the nation is called "Egypt"; see introduction.

25 the father of Shelaḥ, and Shelaḥ was the father of Ever. To Ever, two sons
were born. One was named Peleg, for in his time the earth was divided.[21]
26 His brother was named Yoktan. Yoktan was the father of Almodad, Shelef,
27, 28, 29 Ḥatzarmavet, Yeraḥ, Hadoram, Uzal, Dikla, Oval, Avimael, Sheva, Ofir,
30 Ḥavila, and Yovav; all these were Yoktan's sons. Their settlements extended
31 from Mesha toward Sefar, in the eastern hill country. These were the
descendants of Shem, by their clans and their languages, with their lands
and their nations.

32 These, then, are the clans of the sons of Noaḥ, by their lines, in their
nations. And from these, the nations spread out across the earth after the
flood.

11 1, 2 The whole world spoke the same language, the same words. And as the
people migrated from the east they found a valley in the land of Shinar and
3 settled there. They said to each other, "Come, let us make bricks, let us
4 bake them thoroughly." They used bricks for stone and tar for mortar. And
they said, "Come, let us build ourselves a city and a tower that reaches the
heavens, and make a name for ourselves. Otherwise we will be scattered
across the face of the earth."

5 But the LORD came down to see the city and the tower being built by the
6 children of men. The LORD said, "If, as one people with one language,
they have begun to do this, nothing they plan to do will be impossible
7 for them. Let us go down and confuse their language so that one will
8 not understand the speech of another." From there the LORD scattered
9 them all over the earth, and they abandoned the building of the city. That
is why it was called Bavel, because it was there that the LORD confused[22]
the language of all the earth; and from there the LORD scattered them all
across the face of the earth.

10 These are the descendants of Shem. When Shem was one hundred years old,
11 he had a son, Arpakhshad, two years after the flood. After Arpakhshad was
born, Shem lived five hundred years and had other sons and daughters.

12, 13 When Arpakhshad was thirty-five years old, he had a son, Shelaḥ. After
Shelaḥ was born, Arpakhshad lived four hundred and three years and had
other sons and daughters.

14, 15 When Shelaḥ was thirty years old, he had a son, Ever. After Ever was
born, Shelaḥ lived four hundred and three years and had other sons and
daughters.

16, 17 Ever lived thirty-four years and then had a son, Peleg. After Peleg was
born, Ever lived four hundred and thirty years and had other sons and
daughters.

---

21 | Peleg evokes the Hebrew *niflega* (divided). This is often understood to refer to the dispersion recounted in 11:1–9.

22 | The name Bavel (Babylon) resonates with *balal* (confused).

18 19 Peleg lived thirty years and then had a son, Reu. After Reu was born, Peleg
lived two hundred and nine years and had other sons and daughters.

20 21 Reu lived thirty-two years and then had a son, Serug. After Serug was born,
Reu lived two hundred and seven years and had other sons and daughters.

22 23 Serug lived thirty years and then had a son, Naḥor. After Naḥor was born,
Serug lived two hundred years and had other sons and daughters.

24 25 Naḥor lived twenty-nine years and then had a son, Teraḥ. After Teraḥ was
born, Naḥor lived one hundred and nineteen years and had other sons
and daughters.

26 27 Teraḥ lived seventy years and fathered Avram, Naḥor, and Haran. These
are the descendants of Teraḥ. Teraḥ was the father of Avram, Naḥor, and
28 Haran, and Haran had a son, Lot. While his father Teraḥ was still alive,
29 Haran died in the land of his birth, Ur Kasdim. Avram and Naḥor married;
the name of Avram's wife was Sarai, and the name of Naḥor's wife was
30 Milka. She was the daughter of Haran, father of Milka and Yiska. And Sarai
was barren – she had no child.

31 Teraḥ took his son Avram, and his grandson Lot, son of Haran, and his
daughter-in-law Sarai, his son Avram's wife, and together they set out from
Ur Kasdim to go to the land of Canaan. But when they arrived at Ḥaran,
32 they settled there. Teraḥ lived two hundred and five years, and he died in
Ḥaran.

LEKH LEKHA

12 1 The Lord said to Avram, "Go – from your land, your birthplace, and your
2 father's house – to the land that I will show you. I will make you a great
nation, and I will bless you and make your name great. You will become a
3 blessing. And I will bless those who bless you, and those who curse you I
will curse. And through you, all the families of the earth will be blessed."

4 So Avram went, as the Lord had told him, and with him went Lot. Avram
5 was seventy-five years old when he left Ḥaran. Avram took Sarai his wife,
and Lot his nephew, and all the wealth they had acquired and the people
they had gathered in Ḥaran. They set out to go to the land of Canaan, and
6 they entered the land of Canaan. Avram traveled through the land to the
region of Shekhem, to the Oak of Moreh. The Canaanites were then in
the land.

7 Then the Lord appeared to Avram and said, "To your descendants I will
give this land." There he built an altar to the Lord, who had appeared to
8 him. And from there he moved on to the hills east of Beit El, and pitched
his tent with Beit El to the west and Ai to the east. There he built an altar
9 to the Lord and called on the name of the Lord. Then Avram journeyed
on, traveling toward the Negev.

10 There was a famine in the land. Avram went down to Egypt to stay there
11 for a while because the famine in the land was severe. And as his arrival in

Egypt drew close, he said to Sarai his wife, "I know what a beautiful woman
12 you are. When the Egyptians see you, they will say, 'She is his wife'; they
13 will kill me and keep you alive. Please, say you are my sister. Then I will
be treated well for your sake, and because of you my life will be spared."

14 When Avram came to Egypt, the Egyptians saw the woman, saw that she
15 was very beautiful indeed. And when Pharaoh's officials saw her, they
praised her to Pharaoh, and the woman was taken into Pharaoh's palace.
16 He treated Avram well for her sake: he acquired flocks, herds, donkeys,
17 male and female servants, she-donkeys, and camels. But the Lord struck
Pharaoh and his household with terrible afflictions because of Avram's
wife Sarai.

18 Pharaoh summoned Avram and said, "What have you done to me? Why
19 did you not tell me she was your wife? Why did you say 'She is my sister,'
20 so that I took her as a wife? Now – here is your wife. Take her. Go." Pharaoh
gave orders to his men about him, and they sent him on his way, together
with his wife and all that he had.

13 1 Then Avram went up from Egypt to the Negev with his wife and all he had,
2 and with him went Lot. And Avram had become very wealthy in cattle,
3 silver, and gold. From the Negev he continued on his journey to Beit El,
4 to the site between Beit El and Ai where his tent had previously been, and
where he had first made an altar. There Avram called on the name of the
5 Lord. Lot, who went with Avram, had flocks, herds, and tents as well,
6 and the land could not support them living together; so many were their
7 possessions that they were unable to live side by side. A dispute broke out
between Avram's herdsmen and those of Lot; and the Canaanites and the
8 Perizzites were then too living in the land. Avram said to Lot, "Please, let
there be no friction between me and you, and between my herdsmen and
9 yours, for we are brothers. The whole land lies before you; please separate
yourself from me. If you go to the left, I will go to the right; if you go to
the right, I will go to the left."

10 Lot raised his eyes and saw that the whole plain of the Jordan up to Tzoar
was well watered. It was like the garden of the Lord, like the land of Egypt;
11 this was before the Lord destroyed Sedom and Amora.[23] So Lot chose
for himself the entire plain of the Jordan. He traveled eastward, and the
12 two men separated. Avram settled in the land of Canaan while Lot settled
13 in the cities of the plain, pitching his tent near Sedom. But the people of
Sedom were evil, great sinners against the Lord.

14 After Lot had separated from him, the Lord said to Avram, "Raise your
eyes and look around from where you are to the north, south, east, and
15 west. All the land you see I will give to you and your descendants forever.
16 I will make your descendants like the dust of the earth: if anyone could

23 | See chapter 19.

17 count the dust of the earth, then could your descendants be counted. Get
up and walk through the length and breadth of the land, for to you shall I
18 give it." So Avram took his tent and came to settle by the Oaks of Mamre,
in Ḥevron. There he built an altar to the Lord.

14 1 In the days of Amrafel, king of Shinar, Aryokh, king of Elasar, Kedorlaomer,
2 king of Eilam, and Tidal, king of Goyim, they all waged war against Bera,
king of Sedom, Birsha, king of Amora, Shinav, king of Adma, and Shemever,
3 king of Tzevoyim, and the king of Bela – that is, Tzoar. These had all come
4 together in Siddim Valley – now the Dead Sea; for twelve years they had
5 served Kedorlaomer, but in the thirteenth year they had rebelled. In the
fourteenth year Kedorlaomer and his allied kings came and defeated the
Refaim in Ashterot Karnayim, the Zuzim in Ham, the Eimim in Shaveh
6 Kiryatayim,[24] and the Horites in the hill country of Se'ir as far as Eil Paran
7 by the wilderness. Then they swung back and came to Ein Mishpat – that
is, Kadesh – conquering the whole territory of the Amalekites, as well as
8 the Amorites living in Ḥatzetzon Tamar. Then the kings of Sedom, Amora,
Adma, Tzevoyim, and Bela – that is, Tzoar – marched out and drew up
9 their battle lines in Siddim Valley against Kedorlaomer, king of Eilam,
Tidal, king of Goyim, Amrafel, king of Shinar, and Aryokh, king of Elasar:
four kings battling five.

10 The Siddim Valley was riddled with tar pits, and when the kings of Sedom
and Amora tried to flee, they fell into them. The others fled to the moun-
11 tains. The victors seized all the possessions of Sedom and Amora and all
12 the food, and they left, taking with them – since he had been living in
Sedom – Avram's nephew, Lot, and his possessions.

13 A fugitive came and reported this to Avram the Hebrew, who was then
living near the Oaks of Mamre the Amorite, a kinsman of Avram's allies,
14 Eshkol and Aner. When Avram heard that his own kinsman had been taken
captive, he marshaled the three hundred eighteen trained men born in his
15 household, and went in pursuit as far as Dan. He divided his forces against
the captors at night and defeated them, pursuing them to Ḥova, north of
16 Damascus. He recovered all the plunder, as well as his kinsman Lot and
his possessions, the women, and the other survivors as well.

17 When he returned from defeating Kedorlaomer and the kings with him,
the king of Sedom came out to greet him at Shaveh Valley – that is, the
18 Valley of the King. And Malki Tzedek, king of Shalem, offered bread and
19 wine. He was a priest of God Most High, and he blessed Avram, saying:

"Blessed be Avram by God Most High,
Maker of heaven and earth,
20 and blessed be God Most High
who delivered your foes into your hand."

24 | Concerning these peoples, see Deuteronomy 2:10–11, 20.

21 Then Avram gave him a tenth of everything. And the king of Sedom said
22 to Avram, "Give me the people, and keep the possessions for yourself." But
Avram said to the king of Sedom, "I raise my hand in oath to the LORD,
23 God Most High, Maker of heaven and earth, that I will not accept anything
of yours, not even a thread or a shoe strap, so that you never shall say, 'I
24 made Avram rich.' I will accept nothing but what my young men have eaten
and the share that belongs to the men who went with me – Aner, Eshkol,
and Mamre; let them have their share."

15 1 After these events the word of the LORD came to Avram in a vision, saying:
"Do not be afraid, Avram. I am your shield. Your reward shall be very
great."

2 But Avram said, "My LORD GOD, what will You have given me if I remain
childless, and the one who will take charge of my household is Eliezer of
3 Damascus?"[25] Avram said, "You have given me no children. A man of my
household will be my heir."

4 Then the word of the LORD came to him: "That man will not be your heir;
5 one who comes forth from your own loins will be your heir." He took him
outside and said, "Look at the heavens and count the stars – if indeed you
can count them." He said to him, "That is how your descendants will be."
6 And because Avram put his trust in the LORD, He reckoned it to him as
righteousness.[26]

7 And He told him, "I am the LORD who brought you out from Ur Kasdim
to give you this land to possess it."

8 And he said, "My LORD GOD, how shall I know that I will possess it?"

9 And he said to him, "Take for me a three-year-old heifer, and a three-year-
old goat, and a three-year-old ram, and a turtledove, and a young pigeon."
10 And he took all these and cut them in two and put each half opposite its
11 other half, but the birds he did not cut.[27] Birds of prey descended on the
12 carcasses, but Avram drove them away. And so it was that, as the sun went
down, a deep sleep fell upon Avram and a deep, dark dread came upon
13 him. And God said to Avram, "Know with certainty that your descendants
will be migrants in a land not their own, and there they will be enslaved
14 and oppressed for four hundred years. But I will bring judgment on the
nation they will serve, and afterward they will go free with great wealth.

15 "As for you, you will join your ancestors in peace; you will be buried in
16 ripe old age. And the fourth generation will return here, for the guilt of
the Amorites is not yet resolved."[28]

---

25 | Eliezer is understood to have been a prominent servant of Avram.

26 | Alternatively, Avram recognized the righteousness of God.

27 | This was a covenant ceremony (cf., e.g., Jer. 34:18).

28 | The accumulated guilt of the inhabitants of Canaan does not yet warrant their displacement.

17 And when the sun set and it was very dark, a smoking furnace appeared
18 and a blazing torch passed between these pieces. On that day the LORD
made a covenant with Avram: "To your descendants I will give this land,
19 from the River of Egypt to the great river Euphrates, the land of the Kenites,
20 the Kenizzites, the Kadmonites, the Hittites, the Perizzites, the Refaim,
21 the Amorites, the Canaanites, the Girgashites, and the Jebusites."

16 1 Sarai, Avraham's wife, had borne him no children; but she had an Egyptian
2 maidservant named Hagar. Sarai said to Avram, "The LORD has kept me
from having children. Come now to my maid. Perhaps through her I
3 might build a family." And Avram listened to Sarai. So it was that, after
living in Canaan for ten years, Avram's wife Sarai took Hagar, her Egyptian
4 maidservant, and gave her to her husband Avram to be his wife. He came
to Hagar and she conceived. And when she realized that she was pregnant,
5 she began to look upon her mistress with contempt. Sarai said to Avram,
"The abuse I suffer is your fault. I laid my servant in your arms and now
that she knows she is pregnant, she looks upon me with contempt. Let the
LORD judge between me and you!"

6 Avram said to Sarai, "Your maid is in your own hands. Do with her whatever
you think best." Sarai treated her harshly – and Hagar ran away from her.

7 An angel of the LORD found her near a spring of water in the desert, the
8 spring by the road to Shur. He said, "Hagar, maidservant of Sarai, where
have you come from and where are you going?" She said, "I am running
away from my mistress Sarai."

9 The angel of the LORD said to her, "Go back to your mistress; submit
yourself under her hand."

10 And the angel of the LORD added: "I will greatly multiply your descendants;
11 they will be too many to count." Said the angel of the LORD:

"You are pregnant
and will give birth to a son.
You shall name him Yishmael,
for the LORD has heard your affliction.[29]

12 "He will become a wild donkey of a man;
his hand will be against everyone,
and everyone's hand against him.
He will live up against all his brothers."

13 She gave a name to the LORD who had spoken to her: "You are the God
14 who sees me," for she said: "Have I not here seen Him who sees me?" That
is why the well is called Be'er Laḥai Ro'i.[30] It is still there between Kadesh
and Bered.

---

29 | The name Yishmael means "God hears."

30 | Meaning "Well of the Living One Who Sees Me."

15 So Hagar bore Avram a son, and Avram gave the name Yishmael to the
16 son that she had borne. Avram was eighty-six years old when Hagar bore
him Yishmael.

17 1 When Avram was ninety-nine years old, the LORD appeared to him and
2 said, "I am El Shaddai. Walk before Me in integrity, and I will establish
My covenant between Me and you, and make you exceedingly numerous."
3 4 Avram fell facedown. And God said to him, "As for Me – this is My
5 covenant with you: you shall be father to a multitude of nations. No longer
shall you be called Avram. Your name will be Avraham, for I have made
6 you father to a multitude of nations.[31] I will make you exceptionally fertile,
7 I will turn you into nations; kings will come from you. I will establish My
covenant between Me and you and your descendants after you throughout
the generations: an eternal covenant. I will be God to you and your
8 descendants after you, and I will give you and your descendants after you
the land where you now live as strangers, the whole land of Canaan, an
everlasting possession, and I will be their God."

9 Then God said to Avraham, "As for you, you shall keep My covenant, you
10 and your descendants after you throughout their generations. This is My
covenant, kept between Me and you and your descendants after you: every
11 male among you shall be circumcised. You must circumcise the flesh of
your foreskin – this shall be the sign of the covenant between Me and you.
12 Throughout the generations, every male among you shall be circumcised
at the age of eight days, including the slave born in your household,
13 including one acquired from a stranger not descended from you. All must
be circumcised – those born in your household, those acquired with your
14 money – and My covenant in your flesh will be a covenant everlasting. Any
uncircumcised male, whose foreskin has not been circumcised, shall be
severed from his people; he has broken My covenant."

15 God then said to Avraham, "As for Sarai your wife, you shall no longer
16 call her Sarai. Her name will be Sara.[32] I will bless her and give you a son
by her. I will bless her so that she shall birth nations; kings of peoples
17 shall descend from her." Avraham fell on his face and laughed. "Can a
hundred-year-old man become a father?" he said to himself. "Can Sara, at
18 ninety, bear a child?" To God Avraham said, "If only Yishmael might live
before you!"

19 God said, "Nonetheless, Sara your wife will bear you a son, and you
shall name him Yitzḥak.[33] I will establish My covenant with him as an
20 everlasting covenant for his descendants after him. As for Yishmael – I
have heard you.[34] I will bless him and make him fertile and multiply him

31 | The name Avraham resonates with *av hamon* (father of a multitude).

32 | Meaning "noblewoman."

33 | The name Yitzḥak derives from the verb *vayitzḥak* (to laugh), referring to Avraham's mirth in verse 17.

34 | The name Yishmael means "God hears" (cf. 16:10).

exceedingly. He will become father of twelve princes, and I will make of
21 him a great nation. But I will establish My covenant[35] with Yitzḥak, whom
Sara will bear to you this time next year."

22 23 When He finished speaking with him, God went up from Avraham. On
that very day, Avraham took his son Yishmael, along with all those born
in his house or acquired with money, every male in Avraham's household,
and circumcised the flesh of their foreskins as God had instructed him.
24 25 Avraham was ninety-nine years old when he was circumcised, and
26 his son Yishmael was thirteen. That very day, Avraham and his son
27 Yishmael were circumcised; and all the men of his household, whether
home-born or acquired from strangers, were circumcised together with
him.

VAYERA 18 1 The LORD appeared to him by the Oaks of Mamre as he was sitting at the
2 entrance to his tent in the heat of the day. Avraham looked up and saw
three men standing nearby. The moment he saw them, he ran from the
opening of his tent to greet them, and bowed down low to the ground.

3 He said, "My lords, if I have found favor in your sight, please do not pass
4 your servant by. Let a little water be brought so that you can wash your
5 feet and rest under the tree. Since you are passing by your servant, let me
bring a morsel of bread so that you can be refreshed before you go on
your way."

They replied. "Do just as you say."

6 Avraham rushed to Sara in the tent and said, "Hurry – three *se'a*[36] of fine
flour; knead it and bake bread."

7 Avraham himself ran to the herd and took a tender choice calf and gave it
8 to the young man, who hurried to prepare it. He brought curds and milk
and the calf that had been prepared, and set them before them, standing
by them as they ate, under the tree.

9 They asked him, "Where is your wife Sara?"

"There, in the tent," he replied.

10 Then one of them said, "I will return to you this time next year, and your
wife Sara will have a son." Sara was listening at the opening of the tent
11 behind him. Avraham and Sara were already old, advanced in years; the
12 way of women no longer visited Sara. So Sara laughed to herself, saying,
"Now that I am worn out, can I have this pleasure? With my lord an old
man?"

---

35 | The covenant affirming that Avraham's progeny will take possession of the land of Canaan.

36 | See note on 1 Kings 18:32.

13 Then the Lord said to Avraham, "Why did Sara laugh and say, 'Can I really
14 have a child, now that I am old?' Is anything beyond the Lord's powers?
At the due time next year I will return to you, and Sara will have a son."

15 Sara, because she was afraid, denied it: "I did not laugh," she said. But He
said, "Not so. You laughed."

16 The men got up to leave and looked down toward Sedom. Avraham
17 accompanied them to see them on their way. The Lord said, "Shall I hide
18 from Avraham what I am about to do? Avraham is about to become a great
and mighty nation, and through him all the nations on earth will be blessed.
19 For I have chosen him so that he may direct his children and his household
after him to keep the way of the Lord by doing what is right and just, that
the Lord may bring about for Avraham what He spoke of for him."

20 Then the Lord said, "The outcry against Sedom and Amora is great, and
21 their sin is very grave. I shall go down now and see if they have really done
as much as the outcry that has reached Me. If not, I will know."

22 The men turned from there and went toward Sedom, while Avraham still
23 stood before the Lord. Then Avraham stepped forward and said: "Would
24 You really sweep away the righteous with the wicked? What if there are fifty
righteous people in the city? Would You really sweep it away and not spare the
25 place for the sake of the fifty righteous people in it? Far be it from You to do
such a thing to kill the righteous with the wicked, treating the righteous like
the wicked. Far be it from You! Shall the judge of all the earth not do justice?"

26 The Lord said, "If I find fifty righteous people in the city of Sedom, I will
spare the whole place for their sake."

27 Then Avraham spoke up again and said, "Now that I have dared to speak to
28 the Lord, though I am mere dust and ashes, what if the righteous are five
less than fifty? Will You destroy the whole city for the lack of five people?"

He said, "If I find forty-five there, I will not destroy it."

29 He spoke to Him yet again, saying, "What if only forty are found there?"

He said, "I will refrain for the sake of the forty."

30 Then he said, "Please, may the Lord not be angry, but let me speak. What
if only thirty are found there?"

He answered, "I will refrain if I find thirty there."

31 "Now that I have dared to speak to the Lord," he said, "what if only twenty
are found there?"

He said, "I will not destroy, for the sake of the twenty."

32 Then he said, "Please, may the Lord not be angry, but let me speak just
once more. What if only ten are found there?"

He said, "I will not destroy, for the sake of the ten."

33 When the Lord had finished speaking with Avraham, He left. And Avraham
went back to his place.

19 1 The two angels arrived at Sedom in the evening, while Lot was sitting in
the city gate. Lot saw them, and rose to greet them, bowing with his face
2 to the ground. He said, "Please, my lords, turn aside to your servant's
house, stay the night, wash your feet, and then go on your way early in
the morning."

"No," they said, "we will spend the night in the square."

3 But he was so insistent that they followed him to his house and came in. He
4 made a feast for them and baked unleavened bread, and they ate. They had
not yet gone to bed when all the townsmen, the men of Sedom – young
5 and old, all the people from every quarter – surrounded the house. They
called to Lot, "Where are the men who came to you tonight? Bring them
out to us so that we may know them."[37]

6 7 Lot went out to speak to them, shutting the door behind him, and said,
8 "My brothers, please do not do this evil. I have two daughters who have
never known a man. Let me bring them out to you; you may do what you
like with them. But do not do anything to these men, for they have come
under the protection of my roof."

9 "Get out of our way," they replied. "This fellow came here as a migrant
and now he is setting himself up as a judge! We will treat you worse than
them." They pressed hard against Lot and moved forward to break down
the door.

10 But the men inside reached out and pulled Lot back into the house and
11 shut the door behind him. Then they struck the men at the door, young
and old, with blindness so that they wore themselves out trying in vain
to find the door.

12 The visitors said to Lot, "Who else do you have here – children-in-law,
13 sons, daughters, or anyone else in the city? Bring them out of here, because
we are about to destroy this place. So great is the outcry against them
before the Lord that He has sent us to destroy it."

14 Lot went out and spoke to his sons-in-law, the men who were betrothed
to his daughters, and told them, "Get up and leave this place: the Lord is
about to destroy the city!" But his sons-in-law thought him laughable.

15 As dawn was breaking, the angels hurried Lot. "Get up," they said. "Take
your wife and your two daughters here, or you will be swept away amid
the city's sin."

---

37 | That is, violate them.

16 Still he hesitated. So the men seized him, his wife, and his two daughters
by the hand and led them safely outside the city, for the Lord had mercy
17 upon him. As soon as they had brought them out, one said, "Run for your
life. Do not look back. Do not stop anywhere in the plain. Flee to the
mountains or you will be swept away."

18 19 But Lot said to them, "No, my lords, please. Your servant has found favor
in your eyes, and you have done me great kindness in saving my life. But I
cannot flee to the mountains; the disaster would overtake me, and I would
20 die.[38] There is a town here close enough for refuge. It is small. Let me flee
there – is it not small? – so that I might survive."

21 "Very well," he said, "I will grant this request also; I will not overthrow
22 the town of which you speak. But hurry. Flee there, because I cannot do
anything until you reach it." That is why the town is called Tzoar.[39]

23 24 By the time Lot reached Tzoar, the sun had risen over the land. Then
the Lord rained down sulfur and fire on Sedom and Amora. Out of the
25 heavens it came from the Lord. He overthrew those cities, and the whole
26 plain, and all the cities' inhabitants, and the vegetation on the land. But
Lot's wife looked back – and she was turned into a pillar of salt.

27 Avraham rose early the next morning and returned to the place where he
28 had stood before the Lord. He looked down toward Sedom and Amora
and all the land of the plain, and he saw thick smoke rising from the land
like smoke from a kiln.

29 So it was, that when God destroyed the cities of the plain, He remembered
Avraham and brought Lot out of the overthrow that overturned the cities
where Lot had lived.

30 Lot went up from Tzoar and settled in the hills together with his two
daughters because he was afraid to stay in Tzoar. He and his two daughters
31 settled in a cave. The elder said to the younger, "Our father is old, and there
32 is no man left on earth to come to us in the normal way of the world. Let
us get our father drunk with wine and then sleep with him, so that we may
raise a new generation through our father."

33 That night they gave their father wine to drink. Then the elder daughter
went in and slept with him. He was unaware when she lay down and when
she arose.

34 The next day, the elder said to the younger, "Last night I slept with my
father. Let us get him to drink wine again tonight, then you go in and
sleep with him. So may we preserve our family line through our father."
35 So that night they got their father to drink wine again, and the younger

38 | Lot does not regard the mountains as a safe haven from the impending source of destruction.

39 | Tzoar resonates with *mitzar* (small) in verse 20.

went and slept with him. And he was unaware when she lay down and
when she arose.

36 37 And so both of Lot's daughters became pregnant by their father. The elder
had a son, whom she named Moav.[40] He is the ancestor of the Moabites
38 of today. The younger also had a son, whom she named Ben Ami.[41] And
he is the ancestor of the Amonites of today.

20 1 Avraham then journeyed on to the Negev region, settling between Kadesh
2 and Shur. For a while he lived as a stranger in Gerar. There Avraham said
of his wife Sara, "She is my sister." Avimelekh, king of Gerar, sent for Sara
and took her as his own.

3 But God came to Avimelekh in a dream one night and told him, "You
will die because of the woman you have taken. She is already married."
4 Avimelekh had not gone near her, so he said, "LORD, would You destroy an
5 innocent nation?Did he not tell me, 'She is my sister'? Did she not say, 'He
is my brother'? I have acted from an innocent heart, with clean hands."

6 Then, in the dream, God said to him, "I too knew that you acted from an
innocent heart, and so I kept you from sinning against Me. That is why
7 I did not let you touch her. But now, give back the man's wife. He is a
prophet. He will pray for you and you will live. But if you do not give her
back, know that you and all your people are to die."

8 Early the next morning, Avimelekh summoned all his servants and told
9 them all this – they were very afraid. Then Avimelekh summoned Avraham
and said, "What have you done to us? What wrong have I done you? Why
have you brought such onerous guilt upon me and my kingdom? You have
10 done to me that which should never be done. What were you thinking of,"
asked Avimelekh, "that you did such a thing?"

11 Avraham replied, "I thought, 'There is no fear of God in this place. They
12 will kill me because of my wife.' Besides, she really is my sister. She is the
daughter of my father though not of my mother, and she became my wife.
13 When God made me wander from my father's house, I said to her, 'Do me
this kindness: wherever we go, say of me: He is my brother.'"

14 Avimelekh gave Avraham sheep, cattle, and male and female slaves, and
15 returned his wife Sara to him. Avimelekh said, "Here is my land. Live
wherever you wish."

16 To Sara he said, "I am giving your brother a thousand pieces of silver.
This will allay the suspicions of everyone who is with you. You are fully
vindicated."

17 Then Avraham prayed to God, and God healed Avimelekh, his wife, and
18 his female slaves so they could again have children, for the LORD had

---

40 | The name Moav resonates with *me'av* (from father).

41 | Literally "son of my kin."

prevented all the women in Avimelekh's household from bearing children,
because of Sara, Avraham's wife.

21 1 The LORD remembered Sara as He had said He would, and acted for Sara
2 as He had promised. Sara became pregnant and bore a son to Avraham
3 in his old age at the very time God had promised. Avraham named his
4 newborn son, whom Sara had borne him, Yitzḥak. And when Yitzḥak his
son was eight days old, Avraham circumcised him as God had commanded.
5 Avraham was one hundred years old when his son Yitzḥak was born to
him.

6 Sara said,

"God has brought me laughter;
all those who hear will laugh with me."[42]

7 Then she said,

"Who would have told Avraham,
'Sara will nurse children'?
Yet I have borne a son in his old age."

8 The child grew and was weaned; on the day Yitzḥak was weaned, Avraham
9 held a great feast. But Sara saw the son whom Hagar the Egyptian had
10 borne Avraham mocking.[43] She said to Avraham, "Drive out that slave
woman and her son, for the son of that slave woman must not share the
inheritance with my son, with Yitzḥak."

11 12 This distressed Avraham greatly because of his son. But God told Avraham,
"Do not be distressed about the boy or about your slave. Listen to whatever
Sara tells you, because it is through Yitzḥak that your descendants will be
13 reckoned. But I will make the slave's son too into a nation, because he is
your child."

14 Early the next morning Avraham took bread and a skin of water and gave
them to Hagar. He placed them on her shoulder, and together with the
child, he sent her away. She went wandering in the Be'er Sheva desert.

15 When the water in the skin was all gone, she cast the child away under
16 one of the bushes and went and sat down at a distance, about a bowshot
away, saying, "I cannot watch the child die." Sitting there, at a distance, she
raised her voice and wept.

17 God heard the boy crying, and an angel of God called to Hagar from the
heavens and said to her, "Hagar, what is wrong? Fear not. God has heard
18 the boy's cry there, where he is. Go, raise up the boy and take him by the
hand, for I will make of him a great nation."

---

42 | The name Yitzḥak derives from the verb denoting laughter (cf. 17:17–19, 18:12–14).

43 | Hebrew *metzaḥek* – again bearing a connection to the name Yitzḥak.

19 Then God opened her eyes and she saw a well of water. She went and filled
the skin with water and gave the boy to drink.

20 God was with the boy as he grew. He lived in the desert and became an
21 expert with the bow. In the Paran desert he lived, and his mother took
him a wife from Egypt.

22 At that time, Avimelekh and Pikhol, commander of his troops, said to
23 Avraham, "God is with you in all you do. Now swear to me here before God
that you will not deal falsely with me or with my children or grandchildren.
Show me and the land where you have lived as a stranger the same kindness
I have shown to you."[44]

24 Avraham said, "I swear."

25 Then Avraham rebuked Avimelekh for the well of water that Avimelekh's
26 servants had seized. But Avimelekh said, "I do not know who has done
this. You did not tell me; I had not heard about it until today."

27 Avraham then brought sheep and cattle and gave them to Avimelekh, and
the two of them forged a covenant.

28 29 Avraham set apart seven ewe lambs from the flock. Avimelekh asked him,
"What is the meaning of these seven ewe lambs you have set apart?"

30 He replied, "Accept these seven lambs from me as testimony that I dug
this well."

31 That is why that place is called Be'er Sheva, because there the two men
swore an oath.[45]

32 Thus they made a pact at Be'er Sheva. And then Avimelekh and Pikhol,
33 commander of his troops, returned to the land of the Philistines. Avraham
planted a tamarisk tree in Be'er Sheva, and there he called on the name of
the Lord, the Everlasting God.

34 Avraham stayed on in the land of the Philistines for many days.

22 1 After these things, God tested Avraham. "Avraham!" He said.

And Avraham replied, "Here I am."

2 Then God said, "Take your son, your only one, the one whom you
love – Yitzḥak – and go to the land of Moria. There, offer him up as a burnt
offering on one of the mountains, the one that I will show you."

3 Early the next morning Avraham rose and saddled his donkey. With him
he took two of his young men and Yitzḥak his son. He cut wood for the
4 offering and set out toward the place of which God had told him. On the
5 third day Avraham looked up and, in the distance, he saw the place. He

44 | See 20:14–16.

45 | The name Be'er Sheva resonates with both *sheva* (seven) and *nishbe'u* (swore).

told his young men, "Stay here with the donkey. I and the boy will go there and worship. Then we will come back to you."

6 Avraham took the wood for the offering and placed it on Yitzḥak his son. He himself took the fire and the knife. The two of them walked together.
7 Then Yitzḥak said to his father, Avraham, "Father?"

Avraham said, "Here I am, my son."

Yitzḥak said, "Here is the fire and the wood, but where is the lamb for the burnt offering?"

8 And Avraham replied, "God will see to a lamb for an offering, my son." The two of them walked on together.

9 They came to the place of which God had spoken. There Avraham built
an altar and arranged the wood. Then he bound Yitzḥak his son and laid
10 him on the altar on top of the wood. Avraham reached out his hand and
11 took hold of the knife to slay his son. But an angel of the Lord called out
to him from the heavens, "Avraham! Avraham!"

He said, "Here I am."

12 "Do not lift your hand against the boy; do nothing to him, for now I know that you fear God: for you have not withheld from Me your son, your only one."

13 Avraham looked up and saw a ram caught in a thicket by its horns. Avraham
went, took hold of the ram, and offered it up as a burnt offering in place of
14 his son. And Avraham named the place The Lord Will See.[46] To this day
it is said, "On the mountain of the Lord, He will be seen."

15 Then the angel of the Lord called to Avraham from the heavens a second
16 time and said, "By My own Self I swear, says the Lord, that because you
17 have done this and have not withheld your son, your only one, I will
bless you greatly and make your descendants as many as the stars of the
heavens, as the sand on the seashore. Your descendants will possess their
18 enemies' gate,[47] and through your descendants will all nations of the earth
be blessed, because you have listened to My voice."

19 Avraham returned to his young men, and together they set out and went to Be'er Sheva, and Avraham stayed on in Be'er Sheva.

20 Some time later, Avraham was told, "Milka too has had children with your
21 brother Naḥor: Utz, his firstborn, his brother Buz, Kemuel, father of Aram,
22 Kesed, Ḥazo, Pildash, Yidlaf, and Betuel."

23 Betuel had a daughter Rivka. Milka bore these eight sons to Avraham's
24 brother Naḥor. His concubine, named Reuma, also had children: Tevaḥ,
Gaḥam, Taḥash, and Maakha.

---

46 | Cf. verse 8: "God will see to a lamb for an offering."

47 | That is, their cities.

ḤAYEI SARA

23 1 Sara's lifetime – the years of Sara's life – were one hundred and twenty-
2 seven. Sara died in Kiryat Arba – that is, Ḥevron – in the land of Canaan.
And Avraham came to mourn for Sara and to weep for her.

3 Then Avraham rose from beside his dead and spoke to the Hittites. He
4 said, "I am a migrant and a visitor among you. Sell me a burial site here so
that I can bury my dead."

5 6 The Hittites answered Avraham, "Hear us, my lord. You are a prince of
God in our midst. Bury your dead in the choicest of our tombs. None of
us will refuse you his tomb to bury your dead."

7 Avraham rose and bowed down to the Hittites, the people of the land,
8 and said to them, "If you are willing to allow me to bury the dead that lies
before me, then hear me and intercede on my behalf with Efron son of
9 Tzoḥar. Let him sell me the cave of Makhpela that he owns, at the edge
of his field. Ask him to sell it to me at the full price as a burial site in your
midst."

10 Efron was sitting among the Hittites. Efron the Hittite answered Avraham
in the hearing of all the Hittites who had come to the city gate. He said,
11 "No, my lord, hear me. I give you the field and I give you the cave that is
in it. In the presence of my people, I give it to you. Bury your dead."

12 13 Avraham bowed down again before the people of the land and said to Efron
in their hearing, "Please, would that you would hear me. I give you the
money for the field. Take it from me so that I can bury my dead there."

14 15 Efron answered Avraham and said to him, "My lord, hear me. A piece of
land worth four hundred silver shekel – what is that between you and me?
Bury your dead."

16 Avraham heard Efron.[48] He weighed out for him the price he had mentioned
in the Hittites' hearing: four hundred silver shekel at the merchants' standard
rate.

17 So Efron's field in Makhpela near Mamre – the field, its cave, and all the
18 trees within the field's borders – passed to Avraham as his possession, in
the presence of all the Hittites who had come to the city gate.

19 Avraham then buried Sara his wife in the cave in the field of Makhpela
20 near Mamre – that is, Ḥevron – in the land of Canaan. Thus the field and
its cave passed from the Hittites to Avraham as a burial site.

24 1 Avraham was old, advanced in years, and the Lord had blessed him in
2 all things. And Avraham said to the senior servant of his household, who
3 was in charge of all he had, "Place your hand under my thigh.[49] I want you
to swear by the Lord, God of heaven and earth, that you will not take

48 | Avraham discerned Efron's real intention: that he be paid the specified amount.

49 | An act sometimes performed in conjunction with an oath.

a wife for my son from among the daughters of the Canaanites among
4 whom I live. Instead, go to my land and birthplace, and there find a wife
for Yitzḥak my son."

5 The servant asked, "What if the woman does not want to come back with
me to this land? Shall I bring your son back to the land from which you
came?"

6 7 Avraham said to him, "Be sure not to take my son back there. The Lord,
God of the heavens, took me from my father's house and from the land of
my birth. He spoke to me and swore to me, 'To your descendants I will
give this land.' He will send His angel before you, and there you will find
8 a wife for my son. But if the woman does not want to come back with you,
then you will be released from this oath to me. Just do not take my son
9 back there." So the servant placed his hand under his master Avraham's
thigh and swore this by an oath to him.

10 The servant then took ten of his master's camels, laden with all his master's
11 bounty, and set out to Aram Naharayim, to the city of Naḥor. By the
well outside the city, he had the camels kneel. It was evening, the time
12 when the women came out to draw water. "Lord, God of my master
Avraham," he said, "please, grant me success today and show kindness to
13 my master Avraham. I am standing here by the spring and the daughters of
14 the townspeople are coming out to draw water. If I say to a young woman,
'Please lower your jar so that I can drink,' and she replies, 'Drink, and I will
water your camels also,' let her be the one You have chosen for Your servant
Yitzḥak. By this I will know that You have shown kindness to my master."

15 Before he had even finished speaking, Rivka, daughter of Betuel son of
Milka, the wife of Avraham's brother Naḥor, came out with her jar on her
16 shoulder. The young woman was very beautiful, a virgin whom no man
17 had known. She went down to the spring, filled her jar, and came up. The
servant ran to meet her and said, "Please let me sip a little water from your
18 jar." She said, "Drink, my lord," and quickly lowered her jar to her hand
19 and let him drink. When she had let him drink his fill, she said, "I will draw
20 water for your camels, too, until they have had enough to drink." Quickly
she emptied her jar into the trough and ran back to the well to draw more
21 water; she drew for all his camels. The man stood gazing at her, silently
wondering whether the Lord had made his journey successful.

22 When the camels had finished drinking, the man took a gold ring weighing
23 a half shekel and two gold bracelets for her arms weighing ten shekel, and
he asked, "Whose daughter are you? Please tell me, is there room in your
24 father's house for us to spend the night?" She answered him, "I am the
25 daughter of Betuel, the son Milka bore to Naḥor." She added, "We have
26 plenty of straw and fodder, as well as room for you to spend the night." The
27 man bowed low, prostrating himself to the Lord. He said, "Blessed be the
Lord, God of my master Avraham, who has not withheld His kindness

and faithfulness from my master. As for me – the LORD has guided me on
the way to the house of my master's close family."

28 The young woman ran and told all this to her mother's household. Rivka
29
30 had a brother named Lavan; he ran outside to the man at the spring. He
had seen the ring, and the bracelets on his sister's arms, and had heard
his sister Rivka tell what the man had said to her. He came up to the man
31 who was still standing by the camels at the spring, and said, "Come. The
LORD bless you! Why are you standing outside? I have made room in the
32 house and prepared a place for the camels." So the man entered the house,
the camels were unloaded, straw and fodder were brought for the camels,
33 and water was brought for him and his men to wash their feet. Food was
set before him to eat, but he said, "I will not eat until I have said what I
have to say."

"Speak, then," said Lavan.

34 "I am Avraham's servant," he said. "The LORD has blessed my master
35
greatly, and he has prospered. He has given him sheep and cattle, silver
36 and gold, male and female servants, camels and donkeys. My master's wife
Sara bore my master a son in her old age, and he committed to his son all
37 that is his. My master made me swear, saying, 'You must not take a wife for
my son from among the daughters of the Canaanites in whose land I live.
38 Instead you must go to my father's house and family and there find a wife
39 for my son.' I asked my master, 'What if the woman does not want to come
40 back with me?' He answered, 'The LORD before whom I have walked will
send His angel with you to make your journey a success, so that you may
41 find a wife for my son from my family and father's house. You are released
from this vow only if you come to my family and they refuse to give her to
you. Then you are released from my vow.'

42 "Today, when I came to the spring, I said, 'LORD, God of my master
Avraham, if You will, please grant success to this journey on which I have
43 come. I am standing here by a spring of water. The woman who comes out
to draw water, to whom I say, "Please let me sip a little water from your jar,"
44 and who says to me, "Drink, and I will also draw for your camels" – let her
be the one the LORD has chosen for my master's son.'

45 "Before I had even finished speaking to myself, Rivka came out with her jar
on her shoulder. She went down to the spring and drew water, and I asked
46 her, 'Please, let me drink.' She immediately lowered her jar and said, 'Drink,
and I will also water your camels.' So I drank, and she gave the camels
47 water too. I asked her, 'Whose daughter are you?' She said, 'The daughter
of Betuel son of Naḥor, whom Milka bore to him.' So I placed a ring on her
48 nose and bracelets on her arms. I bowed low and prostrated myself to the
LORD, and blessed the LORD, God of my master Avraham, who led me on
49 the right way to take the daughter of my master's brother for his son. Now,

if you are willing to show kindness and faithfulness to my master, tell me; and if not, tell me that, so that I may move on, right or left."

50 Lavan and Betuel answered, "This is surely from the LORD: there is nothing
51 for us to say to you, bad or good. Here is Rivka in front of you. Take her;
go. Let her be the wife of your master's son, as the LORD has spoken."

52 When Avraham's servant heard these words, he bowed down to the ground
53 before the LORD. The servant brought out gold and silver jewelry and
clothes and gave them to Rivka. He also gave costly gifts to her brother
54 and her mother. Then he and his men ate and drank and spent the night
there. When they got up the next morning he said, "Send me on my way
to my master."

55 But her brother and her mother replied, "Let the young woman stay with us a year or ten months. Then she may go."

56 "Do not delay me," he said, "now that the LORD has made my journey a success. Let me leave so that I may go back to my master."

57 58 They replied, "Let us call the young woman and ask her." So they called
Rivka and asked her, "Will you go with this man?"

She replied, "I will."

59 So they sent their sister Rivka on her way, together with her nurse and
60 Avraham's servant and his men. They blessed Rivka and said to her, "Our
sister, may you grow into thousands of myriads, and may your descendants
possess their enemies' gates."

61 Then Rivka set off with her maids, riding on camels and following the man. The servant took Rivka and went.

62 Yitzḥak was just coming back from the direction of Be'er Laḥai Ro'i, for he
63 was then living in the Negev. He had gone out in the field toward evening
64 to meditate. Looking up, he saw – there were camels approaching. Rivka
65 too looked up – and saw Yitzḥak. She jumped down from the camel and
asked the servant, "Who is that man walking in the field toward us?" The
servant replied, "That is my master." And she took her veil and covered
66 67 herself. The servant told Yitzḥak all he had done. And Yitzḥak brought her
into the tent of his mother Sara. He took Rivka as his wife, and he loved
her. And Yitzḥak was comforted after his mother's death.

25 1 2 Avraham took another wife, whose name was Ketura. She bore him
3 Zimran, Yokshan, Medan, Midyan, Yishbak, and Shuaḥ; Yokshan was the
father of Sheva and Dedan. The sons of Dedan were Ashurim, Letushim,
4 and Leumim. The sons of Midyan were Eifa, Efer, Ḥanokh, Avida, and
5 Eldaa; all these were descendants of Ketura. Avraham left all that was
6 his to Yitzḥak – while he was still living he gave gifts to the sons of his

concubines and sent them eastward, away from his son Yitzḥak, to the
land of the East.

7 These are the days, the years of Avraham's life: he lived one hundred and
8 seventy-five years. Avraham breathed his last and died in his ripe old age,
9 aged and satisfied, and was gathered to his people. His sons, Yitzḥak and
Yishmael, buried him in the cave of Makhpela, near Mamre, in the field of
10 Efron son of Tzoḥar the Hittite – the field Avraham had bought from the
11 Hittites. There Avraham was buried with Sara his wife. After Avraham's death,
God blessed Yitzḥak his son, who was then living near Be'er Laḥai Ro'i.

12 These are the descendants of Avraham's son Yishmael, whom Sara's maid-
13 servant, Hagar the Egyptian, bore to Avraham. The names of Yishmael's
sons, in the order of their birth, are: Nevayot – Yishmael's firstborn, Kedar,
14 15 Adbe'el, Mivsam, Mishma, Duma, Massa, Ḥadad, Teima, Yetur, Nafish, and
16 Kedma. These were Yishmael's sons, and these are their names by their
17 villages and encampments: twelve princes and their tribes. These were the
years of Yishmael's life: he lived one hundred and thirty-seven years. He
18 breathed his last and died, and was gathered to his people. The Ishmaelites
dwelt from Ḥavila to Shur, up against Egypt, all the way to Assyria, settling
up against all their brothers.

TOLEDOT

19 This is the story of Yitzḥak, son of Avraham: Avraham was Yitzḥak's father.
20 When Yitzḥak was forty he married Rivka, daughter of Betuel the Aramean
of Padan Aram, sister of Lavan the Aramean.

21 And Yitzḥak pleaded with the Lord on behalf of his wife, for she was
22 childless. The Lord granted his plea and Rivka became pregnant. But the
children clashed within her. She said, "If this is so, why am I living?" So
23 she went to inquire of the Lord. The Lord said to her,

"Two nations are inside your womb;
two peoples are to part from you.
People will overpower people,
and the greater shall the younger serve."[50]

24 When the time came for her to give birth, there were twins in her womb.
25 The first came out red. His whole body was like a hairy cloak, so they
26 named him Esav.[51] Then his brother emerged, his hand grasping Esav's
heel, so he named him Yaakov.[52] Yitzḥak was sixty years old when they
were born.

27 The boys grew up. Esav became a skilled hunter, a man of the field, while
28 Yaakov was an innocent man who stayed among the tents. Yitzḥak loved
Esav because he ate of his game, but Rivka loved Yaakov.

---

50 | The ambiguity as to who will serve whom reflects the Hebrew.

51 | The name Esav may bear the sense of "covered" or "concealed" (cf. Ob. 1:6). The word *se'ar* (hair) resonates with Se'ir, the land inhabited by Esav's descendants.

52 | The name Yaakov resonates with *akev* (heel).

29 Once when Yaakov was cooking a stew, Esav came in exhausted from the
30 field. He said to Yaakov, "Let me gulp down some of that red stuff. I am
starved!" – that is how he came to be named Edom.[53]

31 32 Yaakov said, "First sell me your birthright." And Esav said, "Look, I am
about to die. What use to me is a birthright?"

33 But Yaakov said, "Swear to me first." So he swore, and sold Yaakov his
34 birthright. Yaakov then gave Esav bread and lentil stew. He ate, drank, got
up, and left. Thus – Esav disdained his birthright.

26 1 Another famine afflicted the land, apart from the earlier famine in Avraham's
days, and Yitzḥak went to Avimelekh, king of the Philistines, in Gerar.
2 The Lord had appeared to him: "Do not go down to Egypt," He had
3 said. "Stay in the land I tell you of. Bide in this land and I will be with
you and bless you, for I am going to give all these lands to you and your
4 descendants, fulfilling the oath I swore to Avraham your father. I will make
your descendants as many as the stars of the heavens, and I will give them
all these lands. All the nations of the earth will bless themselves by your
5 descendants, because Avraham listened to My voice and kept My charge:
My commandments, My statutes, and My laws."

6 7 So Yitzḥak now settled in Gerar. The men of the place inquired after his
wife; "She is my sister," he said. He was terrified to say "She is my wife."
"The men of the place might kill me for Rivka," he thought, "she is so
8 beautiful." When he had already been there for some time, Avimelekh, king
of the Philistines, looked down from a window and saw Yitzḥak enjoying
9 himself with his wife Rivka. Avimelekh summoned Yitzḥak. "She is your
wife," he said. "Why did you say, 'She is my sister'?"

Yitzḥak replied, "I thought I might die because of her."

10 "What is this you have done to us?" said Avimelekh. "One of the people
might have slept with your wife, and you would have brought guilt upon
11 us." Avimelekh then issued an order to all the people: "Whoever touches
this man or his wife shall be put to death."

12 Yitzḥak planted crops in that land, and that year he reaped a hundredfold
13 because the Lord had blessed him. The man became rich; he prospered
14 more and more until he became very wealthy. He had flocks and herds
15 and a large retinue of servants, and the Philistines envied him. So the
Philistines stopped up all the wells that his father's servants had dug in
16 the time of his father Avraham, filling them with earth. Avimelekh said to
Yitzḥak, "Move away from us. You have become much too powerful for us."

17 18 So Yitzḥak left and camped in the valley of Gerar and settled there. And
he reopened the wells that had been dug in the time of his father Avraham,

53 | The name Edom resonates with *adom* (red) here, as well as with *admoni* (red) in verse 25.

which the Philistines had stopped up after Avraham died, and gave them
19 the same names his father had given them. Yitzḥak's servants dug in the
20 valley and discovered a well of fresh water, but the shepherds of Gerar
quarreled with Yitzḥak's shepherds, claiming that the water was theirs. So
21 he called the well Esek,[54] because they contended with him there. They
dug another well, and there was a quarrel about that too; so he called it
22 Sitna.[55] He moved on from there and dug another well, and this time they
did not quarrel over it; so he named this one Reḥovot.[56] "Now the Lord
has given us space," he said, "and we will flourish in the land."

23 24 From there he went up to Be'er Sheva. That night the Lord appeared to
him and said, "I am the God of your father Avraham. Do not be afraid, for I
am with you. I will bless you and multiply your descendants for the sake of
25 Avraham My servant." Yitzḥak built an altar there and called on the name
of the Lord. There he pitched his tent, and there his servants dug a well.

26 Avimelekh came to him from Gerar, with Aḥuzat his advisor and Pikhol
27 the commander of his troops. Yitzḥak said to them, "Why have you come
28 to me? You hate me; you sent me away from you." They said, "We have
seen clearly that the Lord is with you, so we say: Let there be a pact
29 between you and us. Let us make a covenant with you that you will do us
no harm, just as we did not touch you, just as we have done you nothing
but good and we sent you on your way in peace. And now – the Lord
30 31 bless you." Yitzḥak made them a feast, and they ate and drank. Early in
the morning they rose and exchanged oaths, and Yitzḥak sent them on
32 their way. They parted from him in peace. That day, Yitzḥak's servants
came and told him about the well that they had dug; they said, "We have
33 found water." He named it Shiva,[57] which is why the town is called Be'er
Sheva to this day.[58]

34 When Esav was forty years old, he married Yehudit daughter of Be'eri the
35 Hittite, and Basmat daughter of Eilon the Hittite. These were a source of
bitter sorrow to Yitzḥak and Rivka.

27 1 When Yitzḥak had grown old, when his eyes had grown so dim that he
could not see, he summoned his elder son Esav. "My son," he said.

Esav replied, "Here I am."

2 3 He said, "I am old, and I do not know when I will die. So now, take your
weapons, your quiver and bow, and go out into the field and hunt me some
4 game. Then make me delicious food, prepared in the way that I love, and
bring it to me to eat so that my soul may bless you before I die."

---

54 | Meaning "contention."

55 | Meaning "hostility."

56 | Meaning "wide spaces."

57 | The name Shiva resonates with *vayishave'u* (exchanged oaths) in verse 31.

58 | Be'er denotes a well, and Sheva resonates with Shiva and *vayishave'u*.

5 When Yitzḥak was speaking to Esav his son, Rivka was listening. Esav
6 went out into the field to hunt game to bring back. And Rivka said to her
7 son Yaakov, "I overheard your father say to your brother Esav, 'Fetch me
some game and make me delicious food so that I may eat and give you
8 my blessing before the LORD before I die.' Now, my son, listen carefully
9 to my instructions. Go to the flock and bring me two choice young goats.
10 I will make them into delicious food, in the way he loves. Then take it to
your father to eat so that he may give you his blessing before he dies."

11 Yaakov said to Rivka his mother, "My brother Esav is hairy, but I have
12 smooth skin. What if my father touches me? I will look to him like a fraud
and bring upon myself not a blessing but a curse."

13 But his mother replied, "Your curse will be on me, my son. Do as I say. Go;
fetch them for me."

14 So he went, took the goats, and brought them to his mother, and his
15 mother prepared delicious food in the way his father loved. Then Rivka
took her elder son Esav's best clothes, which were with her in the house,
16 and put them on Yaakov, her younger son. She put the goatskins on his
17 hands and the smooth part of his neck. She then handed her son Yaakov
the delicious food and bread that she had prepared.

18 He went in to his father; "My father," he said.

His father replied, "Here I am. Who are you, my son?"

19 Yaakov said to his father, "I am Esav your firstborn. I have done as you
asked. Please sit up and eat some of my game so that your soul may bless
me."

20 Yitzḥak asked his son, "How did you find it so quickly, my son?"

He replied, "The LORD your God brought it about for me."

21 Then Yitzḥak said to Yaakov, "Come close and let me feel you, my son, to
know – are you really my son Esav?"

22 Yaakov came close to Yitzḥak his father, who felt him and said, "The voice
23 is the voice of Yaakov, but the hands are the hands of Esav." He did not
recognize him, because his hands were hairy like those of his brother Esav.
And he blessed him.

24 "Are you really my son Esav?" he asked.

He replied, "I am."

25 "Then serve me and let me eat some of my son's game so that my soul may
bless you."

26 He served him food and he ate, he brought him wine and he drank. Then
27 Yaakov's father Yitzḥak said to him, "Come close and kiss me, my son." So

he came close and kissed him, and Yitzḥak smelled the smell of his clothes
and blessed him, saying:

"The smell of my son
is the smell of a field
the LORD has blessed.
28 God endow you
with dew of heaven,
the cream of the land,
much grain and wine.
29 May peoples serve you;
may nations bow down to you.
Be lord over your brothers,
and may your mother's sons bow down to you.
A curse on those who curse you;
on those who bless you, blessing."

30 Yitzḥak had finished blessing Yaakov, and Yaakov had just left his father
31 Yitzḥak, when his brother Esav came back from the hunt. He too had
prepared delicious food and brought it to his father. And he said to his
father, "Let my father sit up and eat some of his son's game so that your
soul may bless me."

32 "Who are you?" asked his father Yitzḥak.

"I am your son, your firstborn, Esav," he replied.

33 Yitzḥak was seized with a violent fit of trembling. "Who then was it that
hunted game and brought it to me? I ate it all before you came, and I
blessed him – and he will be blessed."

34 When Esav heard his father's words, he burst into a loud and bitter cry. He
said to his father, "Bless me, me too, my father!"

35 "Your brother came in deceit and took your blessing," he replied.

36 Esav said, "Is he not rightly named Yaakov? Twice he has supplanted me.[59]
He took my birthright and now he has taken my blessing." And then, "Do
you not have any blessing left for me?"

37 Yitzḥak answered Esav, "I have made him lord over you and given him all
his brothers as servants. I have endowed him with grain and wine. What
then can I do for you, my son?"

38 Esav said to his father, "Have you only one blessing, father? Bless me, me
too, my father!" And Esav wept aloud.

39 His father Yitzḥak answered him and said:

---

59 | Hebrew *vayakeveni*, resonating with the name Yaakov.

"Of the cream of the land your home shall be,
of the dew of heaven above.
40 By your sword you will live,
and your brother you will serve;
but when you break loose,
you will throw off his yoke from your neck."

41 Esav resented Yaakov because of the blessing his father had given him.
"The days of mourning for my father are approaching," he said to himself,
42 "and then I will kill my brother Yaakov." When Rivka was told what her
elder son Esav had said, she summoned her younger son Yaakov and said,
"Your brother Esav is consoling himself with the thought of killing you.
43 44 Now, my son, listen to me. Flee at once to my brother Lavan in Ḥaran. Stay
45 with him a while, until your brother's rage subsides. When your brother is
no longer angry with you and has forgotten what you did to him, I will send
word to you to come back. Why should I lose you both in one day?"

46 Rivka then said to Yitzḥak, "I loathe my life because of these Hittite
women. If Yaakov marries a Hittite woman like them, one of the women
of the land, why should I go on living?"

28 1 So Yitzḥak called Yaakov to him. He blessed him and charged him: "You
2 are not to marry a Canaanite woman. Go at once to Padan Aram, to the
house of your mother's father Betuel, and there marry a daughter of your
3 mother's brother Lavan. May El Shaddai bless you, make you fertile, and
4 multiply you so that you become a community of peoples. May He grant
Avraham's blessing to you and your descendants, that you may possess
the land where of your wayfaring you live as a stranger, which God gave
to Avraham."

5 Then Yitzḥak sent Yaakov on his way. He went toward Padan Aram, to
Lavan son of Betuel the Aramean, brother of Rivka, Yaakov and Esav's
mother.

6 Esav learned that Yitzḥak had blessed Yaakov and sent him to Padan Aram
to find a wife, and that when he blessed him, he commanded him not to
7 marry a Canaanite woman, and that Yaakov had obeyed his father and
8 mother and had gone to Padan Aram. Esav realized then that the Canaanite
9 women displeased his father Yitzḥak. So Esav went to Yishmael and took
Maḥalat, daughter of Avraham's son Yishmael, a sister of Nevayot, to be
his wife, with his other wives.

10 11 Yaakov left Be'er Sheva and journeyed toward Ḥaran. In time he chanced VAYETZE
upon a certain place and decided to spend the night there, because the sun
had set. He took some stones of the place and put them under his head, and
12 in that place lay down to sleep. And he dreamed: He saw a ladder set upon
the ground, whose top reached the heavens. On it, angels of God went up
13 and came down. The LORD stood over him there and said, "I am the LORD,

the God of Avraham your father, and the God of Yitzḥak. The land on
14 which you lie I will give to you and your descendants. Your descendants
shall be like the dust of the earth, and you will spread out to the west, the
east, the north, and the south. Through you and your descendants, all
15 the families of the earth will be blessed. I am with you. I will protect you
wherever you go and I will bring you back to this land, for I will not leave
you until I have done what I have spoken of to you."

16 Then Yaakov awoke from his sleep and said, "Truly, the LORD is in this
17 place – and I did not know it!" He was afraid and said, "How full of awe
is this place! This is none other than the House of God, and this the gate
of the heavens!"

18 Yaakov rose early the next morning, took the stone he had placed under
19 his head, set it up as a pillar, and poured oil on top of it. He named the
20 place Beit El;[60] the town was originally called Luz. Yaakov then made a
vow. "If God will be with me," he said, "protecting me on this journey I
21 am taking, giving me bread to eat and clothes to wear, and if I return in
22 peace to my father's house, then the LORD will be my God. This stone I
set up as a pillar will become a house of God, and of all that You give me
I will dedicate a tenth to You."

29 1 Yaakov began traveling again and came to the land of the people of the
2 East. There he saw a well in a field. Three flocks of sheep were lying beside
it because this was the well from which the flocks were watered. The top
3 of it was covered with a large stone. When all the flocks were gathered
there, the stone would be rolled from the mouth of the well and the sheep
watered. The stone would then be put back in place on top of the well.

4 Yaakov asked the shepherds, "Brothers, where are you from?"

"We are from Ḥaran," they replied.

5 He asked, "Do you know Lavan son of Naḥor?"

"We know him," they said.

6 He asked, "Is he well?"

"He is well," they said, "and look, here is his daughter Raḥel coming with
the sheep."

7 "Look," he said, "it is still broad daylight. It is not yet time to gather in the
animals. Water the flocks and take them back to pasture."

8 But they said, "We cannot do that until all the flocks are gathered and the
stone is rolled from the top of the well. Only then can we water the flocks."

9 While he was still talking with them, Raḥel came with her father's sheep;
10 she was a shepherdess. When Yaakov saw Raḥel, daughter of his mother's

60 | Meaning "House of God."

brother Lavan, with Lavan's sheep, he stepped forward, rolled the stone
11 from the top of the well, and watered his uncle's sheep. And Yaakov kissed
12 Raḥel – and wept aloud. And Yaakov told Raḥel that he was related to her
13 father: he was Rivka's son. She ran to tell her father. When Lavan heard
the news about Yaakov, his sister's son, he ran to meet him. He embraced
and kissed him and brought him to his house. Yaakov told Lavan all that
14 had happened. Lavan said to him, "You are truly of my own bones, my own
flesh." And Yaakov stayed with him for a month.

15 Then Lavan said to him, "If you are my brother, does that mean you should
work for me for nothing? Tell me what your hire should be."

16 Lavan had two daughters. The elder was called Leah and the younger
17 18 Raḥel. Leah had sensitive eyes; Raḥel was beautiful and lovely. And Yaakov
was in love with Raḥel, so he said, "I will work for you seven years for your
younger daughter Raḥel."

19 Lavan replied, "Better that I give her to you than to some other man. Stay
on with me."

20 So Yaakov worked for Raḥel seven years. But so great was his love for her
that they seemed to him but a few days.

21 Then Yaakov said to Lavan, "Give me my wife – my time is done, let me
22 come to her." So Lavan brought together all the local people and made a
23 feast. In the evening he took his daughter Leah and brought her in to him,
24 and he came to her. Lavan also gave his servant Zilpa to his daughter Leah
25 as her maid. Then came morning – and it was Leah.

Yaakov said to Lavan, "What is this you have done to me? I served you for
Raḥel, did I not? Why did you deceive me?"

26 Lavan said, "This is not done in our country – to marry off the younger
27 before the firstborn. Wait until the bridal week of this one is over and then
we will give you the other one also, in return for your serving me another
seven years."

28 Yaakov did so. He completed Leah's bridal week; then Lavan gave him
29 his daughter Raḥel as a wife. Lavan gave his servant Bilha to his daughter
30 Raḥel as her maid. And Yaakov came also to Raḥel; and he loved Raḥel
more than Leah. And he served him for another seven years.

31 When the Lord saw that Leah was unloved, He opened her womb, but
32 Raḥel was barren. Leah became pregnant and had a son. She named him
Reuven, saying, "The Lord has seen my affliction. Now my husband
33 will love me."[61] She became pregnant again and had a son. She said, "The
Lord has heard that I am unloved, so He has given me this son also," and
34 she named him Shimon.[62] She became pregnant again and had a son and

61 | The name Reuven resonates with *raa* (has seen) and *ben* (son).

62 | The name Shimon resonates with *shama* (has heard).

said, "Now that I have borne him three sons, my husband will walk with
35 me." That is why he was named Levi.[63] She became pregnant again and
had a son. She said, "This time I will praise the LORD," so she named him
Yehuda.[64] Then she ceased having children.

30 1 Aware that she had borne Yaakov no children, Raḥel became envious of
her sister. To Yaakov she said, "Give me children! If not, let me die!"

2 Yaakov grew angry with Raḥel, and said, "Am I in place of God, who has
kept you from having children?"

3 "Here is Bilha my slave," she said. "Come to her. Let her give birth on my
knees[65] so that I too can build a family through her."

4 5 So she gave him her maid Bilha as a wife. Yaakov came to her, and she
6 became pregnant and bore Yaakov a son. Then Raḥel said, "God has
vindicated me. He has listened to my voice and given me a son." So she
named him Dan.[66]

7 Bilha, Raḥel's maid, became pregnant again and bore Yaakov a second son.
8 And Raḥel said, "I have struggled hard with my sister and I have won." So
she named him Naftali.[67]

9 Leah realized that she was no longer having children, so she took her maid
10 Zilpa and gave her to Yaakov as a wife. And Leah's maid Zilpa bore Yaakov
11 a son. Leah said, "Good fortune has come!" So she named him Gad.[68]

12 13 Then Zilpa, Leah's maid, bore Yaakov a second son. Leah said, "How
blessed I am; young girls will call me blessed." So she named him Asher.[69]

14 During the wheat harvest, Reuven went for a walk and found mandrakes in
the field. He brought them to his mother Leah. Raḥel said to Leah, "Please
give me some of your son's mandrakes."

15 She replied, "Is it not enough that you have taken away my husband? Now
you want to take my son's mandrakes too!"

"Very well," said Raḥel. "Let him sleep with you tonight in exchange for
your son's mandrakes."

16 When Yaakov came back from the field that evening, Leah went out to
meet him and said, "You are to come to me, for I have hired you with my
son's mandrakes." So that night he slept with her.

63 | The name Levi resonates with *yillaveh* (will walk with).

64 | The name Yehuda resonates with *odeh* (I will praise).

65 | Meaning "I will raise the child as my own."

66 | The name Dan resonates with *dananni* (has vindicated me).

67 | The name Naftali resonates with *niftalti* (I have struggled hard).

68 | *Gad* is the word used to denote "good fortune."

69 | The name Asher resonates with *be'oshri* (how blessed I am).

17 God listened to Leah, and she became pregnant and bore Yaakov a fifth
18 son. Leah said, "God has rewarded me for giving my maid to my husband,"
so she named him Yissakhar.[70]

19 20 Leah became pregnant again and bore Yaakov a sixth son. "God has given
me a precious gift," said Leah. "This time my husband will honor me, for
21 I have borne him six sons," so she named him Zevulun.[71] Later she gave
birth to a daughter and named her Dina.

22 Then God remembered Raḥel and listened to her and enabled her to
23 conceive. She became pregnant and gave birth to a son. She said, "God
24 has taken away my shame," and she named him Yosef, saying, "May the
LORD grant me another son also."[72]

25 After Raḥel had given birth to Yosef, Yaakov said to Lavan, "Release me to
26 go home to my own land. Give me my wives and my children for whom I
have worked for you, and let me go. You know very well how much work
27 I have done for you." But Lavan said to him, "If you will allow me to say
so, I have learned by divination that it is because of you that the LORD has
28 blessed me." He added, "Name your hire and I will pay it."

29 Yaakov said, "You know well how I have worked for you and how your
30 livestock have fared under my care. You had little before I came, but it has
swelled into much. The LORD has blessed you wherever I have been. Now,
when can I do likewise for my own household?"

31 Lavan asked, "What shall I give you?"

Yaakov replied, "Do not give me anything. If you do this one thing for
32 me, I will continue to shepherd and guard your flocks. Let me go through
all your flocks today and remove every speckled or spotted sheep, every
dark-colored lamb, and every spotted or speckled goat. They shall be my
33 hire. Let my honesty testify for me in the future, whenever you come to
check the wages you have paid me. Any goat not speckled or spotted or
any lamb not dark colored in my possession shall be considered stolen."

34 Lavan said, "Agreed. Let it be as you have said."

35 That day Lavan removed the streaked or spotted goats, all the speckled
or spotted female goats – every one that had a trace of white – and every
36 dark-colored lamb. These he placed in the care of his sons. Then he put a
three-day-journey's distance between him and Yaakov. Yaakov tended the
rest of Lavan's flock.

37 Yaakov took fresh shoots of poplar, almond, and plane trees and peeled
38 white strips in them, exposing the white of the shoots. Then he set the

70 | The name Yissakhar resonates with *natan sekhari* (has rewarded me).

71 | The name Zevulun resonates with *zeved* (gift) and *yizbeleni* (will honor me).

72 | *Yosef* is the word used by Raḥel to denote "grant." The name also resonates with *asaf* (has taken away, v. 23).

peeled shoots in all the water troughs so that they would be in front of
the flocks when they came to drink. They would mate when they came to
39 drink, and since they mated by the shoots, they bore streaked, speckled,
40 and spotted young.[73] Yaakov set apart the young of the flock, and he made
the others belonging to Lavan face the streaked and dark-colored animals.
Thus he bred separate flocks for himself, and he did not let them breed with
41 Lavan's flocks. Whenever the stronger animals were mating, Yaakov would
place the shoots in the troughs facing them so that they mated facing the
42 shoots. But the weaker animals he did not put there, so the weaker went
43 to Lavan and the stronger to Yaakov. Thus the man's wealth swelled into
a fortune. He had large flocks, female and male servants, camels and
donkeys.

31 1 Yaakov heard that Lavan's sons were saying, "Yaakov has taken everything
our father owned; of what belonged to our father, he has made all these
2 riches." And Yaakov saw that Lavan's manner toward him was not what it
3 had been. The Lord said to Yaakov, "Go back to the land of your fathers
where you were born; I will be with you."

4 So Yaakov sent word to Raḥel and Leah to come out to the field where his
5 flock was. He said to them, "I see that your father's manner toward me is
6 not what it used to be. But the God of my father has been with me. You
7 well know how I have worked for your father with all my strength. Your
father cheated me, changing my wages ten times, but God has not let him
8 harm me. If he said, 'The speckled animals shall be your hire,' then all the
flock would give birth to speckled young. If he said, 'The streaked animals
shall be your hire,' then all the flock would give birth to streaked young.
9 God has taken your father's livestock and given it to me.

10 "Once, during the breeding season, I had a dream: I saw that the rams
11 mounting the flock were streaked, speckled, or spotted. And in the dream
an angel of God said to me, 'Yaakov.'

"I replied, 'Here I am.'

12 "He said, 'Look up and see that all the rams mounting the flock are streaked,
13 speckled, or spotted, for I have seen all that Lavan is doing to you. I am
the God of Beit El, where you anointed a pillar and made a vow to Me.
Now – leave this land at once and return to the land where you were
born.'"

14 Raḥel and Leah answered him, "Do we still have a share in the inheritance
15 of our father's estate? He treats us like strangers. He has sold us and spent
16 the money. All the wealth that God has taken from our father belongs to
us and our children. So do whatever God has told you."

---

73 | The animals produced offspring that exhibited the designs seen during the mating process.

17 18 So Yaakov put his children and wives on camels and drove all the livestock
and wealth he had accumulated – the livestock he had acquired in Padan
Aram – heading for his father Yitzḥak in the land of Canaan.

19 Meanwhile, when Lavan had gone to shear his sheep, Raḥel had stolen
20 her father's household gods. Yaakov deceived Lavan the Aramean by not
21 telling him that he was running away. He fled with all he had, crossed the
Euphrates, and headed for the hill country of Gilad.

22 23 On the third day, Lavan was told that Yaakov had fled. Taking his kinsmen
with him, he pursued him for seven days, catching up with him in the hill
24 country of Gilad. That night God came to Lavan the Aramean in a dream
and said to him, "Take care not to say anything to Yaakov for good or for
bad."

25 When Lavan overtook him, Yaakov had pitched his tent in the hill country,
and Lavan and his kinsmen too encamped in the hill country of Gilad.
26 Lavan said to Yaakov, "What have you done? You have deceived me, and
27 carried off my daughters like captives of the sword. Why did you leave
secretly? Why did you deceive me by not telling me? I would have sent
28 you off with celebration and song, with tambourines and harps. You did
not even let me kiss my grandchildren and daughters goodbye. You have
29 behaved foolishly. I have the power to harm you, but last night your father's
God spoke to me and said, 'Take care not to say anything to Yaakov for
30 good or for bad.' I realize you left because you longed so much for your
father's house. But why did you steal my gods?"

31 Yaakov answered Lavan, saying, "I was afraid; I thought you would take
32 your daughters away from me by force. But if you find your gods with
anyone here, they shall not live. In the presence of our kinsmen, see if there
is anything of yours here, and take it." Yaakov did not know that Raḥel was
the one who had stolen them.

33 So Lavan went into Yaakov's tent, Leah's tent, and the tents of the two
female slaves, but found nothing. Leaving Leah's tent, he entered Raḥel's.
34 But Raḥel had taken the household gods and put them inside a camel
cushion, and was sitting on them; and Lavan rummaged through the tent
35 but found nothing. She said to her father, "Do not be angry, my lord, but
I cannot get up for you, for the way of women is with me now." So he
36 searched but did not find his household gods. Yaakov became indignant
and confronted Lavan. "What is my crime?" he asked Lavan. "What wrong
37 did I do that you come chasing after me? You have rummaged through all
my possessions. What have you found that belongs to your house? Put it
here in front of my kinsmen and yours and let them decide between the
38 two of us! For the twenty years I was with you, your sheep and goats did
39 not miscarry. Not once did I take a ram from your flock as food. I never
brought you an animal torn by wild beasts. I bore the loss myself. Whether

40 it was stolen by day or by night you demanded payment from me. By day I
was ravaged by the heat; at night by the freezing cold. Sleep fled from my
41 eyes. Twenty years I spent working in your household – fourteen for your
two daughters and six for your flock – and ten times you changed my wages.
42 Had the God of my father – the God of Avraham, the Fear of Yitzḥak – not
been with me, you would have sent me away empty-handed. But God saw
my plight and the toil of my hands, and He rebuked you last night."

43 Then Lavan spoke up and said to Yaakov, "The daughters are my daughters.
The children are my children. The flocks are my flocks. All that you see
is mine. But what can I do now about my daughters or the children they
44 have borne? Come now, let us make a covenant, you and I, and let it be a
witness between us."

45 46 So Yaakov took a stone and set it up as a pillar. Yaakov said to his kinsmen,
"Gather stones." They took stones and made a mound, and there by the
47 mound they ate. Lavan called it Yegar Sahaduta, while Yaakov called it
Galed.[74]

48 Lavan said, "This mound is a witness between me and you this day." That
49 is why it is called Galed. It is also called Mitzpa because he said, "May
the Lord keep watch between me and you when we are out of each
50 other's sight.[75] If you mistreat my daughters or take other wives besides
my daughters, even though no one else is present, remember that God is
the witness between me and you."

51 Lavan said to Yaakov, "Here is the mound and here is the pillar I have set
52 up between us. This mound is a witness, and the pillar is a witness, that
I will not go past this mound on your side and that you will not go past
53 this mound and pillar on my side with intent to do harm. May the God
of Avraham, the god of Naḥor, and the god of their father be our judge."
54 Yaakov swore by the Fear of his father Yitzḥak. He offered a sacrifice on
the hill and invited his kinsmen to break bread. And they ate and spent
the night upon that hill.

55 Lavan rose early the next morning. He kissed his grandchildren and
daughters goodbye and blessed them. Lavan then left to return home.

32 1 2 Yaakov continued on his way – and angels of God encountered him. When
he saw them, Yaakov said, "This is God's own camp," and he named the
place Maḥanayim.[76]

VAYISHLAḤ 3 Yaakov sent messengers ahead of him to his brother Esav in the land of
4 Se'ir, the country of Edom. He instructed them, "Say the following to my
lord Esav: 'Your servant Yaakov says: I have been staying with Lavan; until

74 | Both names mean "mound of testimony," the former in Aramaic, the latter in Hebrew (cf. also the name Gilad in v. 25).

75 | The name Mitzpa derives from the same root as *yitzef* (keep watch).

76 | Literally "two camps."

5 now I have remained there. And I have acquired cattle, donkeys, sheep,
and male and female servants. I am sending this message to my lord to
find favor in your eyes.'"

6 And when the messengers returned to Yaakov, they said, "We came to your
brother Esav. He is on his way to meet you, and with him, four hundred
men."

7 Yaakov was acutely afraid and distressed. He divided the people with him
8 into two camps,[77] along with the flocks, the cattle, and the camels. "If
Esav comes and attacks one camp," he thought, "the other camp may still
survive."

9 Then Yaakov prayed, "God of my father Avraham and God of my father
Yitzḥak, Lord, You who said to me, 'Go back to the land where you were
10 born and I will deal well with you,' I am unworthy of all the kindnesses
and the faithfulness that You have bestowed upon Your servant. When I
crossed the Jordan I had only my staff, and now I have become two camps.
11 Rescue me, I pray, from my brother's hand, from the hand of Esav. I am
12 afraid he will come and kill us all, mothers and children alike. Yet You
said, 'I will deal well with you and make your descendants countless, like
the sand of the sea.'"

13 He spent the night there. Then, from what he had at hand, he selected a gift
14 for his brother Esav: two hundred female goats, twenty male goats, two
15 hundred ewes, twenty rams, thirty milk camels and their young, forty cows,
16 ten bulls, twenty female donkeys, and ten male donkeys. He put them in
the care of his servants, each herd by itself, and he told the servants, "Go
17 on ahead of me. Keep a space between the herds." He instructed the first,
"When my brother Esav meets you and asks, 'To whom do you belong?
18 Where are you going? Who owns all these animals ahead of you?' you must
say, 'They belong to your servant Yaakov; they are a gift sent to my lord
19 Esav – and he is coming behind us.'" He likewise instructed the second
and third and all the others who followed the herds, "You shall say the
20 same thing to Esav when you meet him. Also say, 'Your servant Yaakov is
coming behind us.'" He thought, "I will pacify him with these gifts I am
21 sending on ahead. Then I will face him. Perhaps he will accept me." So the
gifts went on ahead of him, while he remained in the camp that night.

22 That night Yaakov got up and took his two wives, two maidservants, and
23 eleven sons and crossed the ford of the Yabok. He took them and crossed
24 the stream with them and then brought across all that he had. And Yaakov
25 was left alone. And a man wrestled with him until dawn. When he saw that
he could not overpower him, the man wrenched Yaakov's hip in its socket
so that the socket of Yaakov's hip was strained as he wrestled with the man.
26 "Let me go," said the man, "for dawn is breaking."

77 | Cf. previous note.

But he replied, "I will not let you go unless you bless me."

27 "What is your name?" asked the man.

"Yaakov," he replied.

28 "No longer will your name be Yaakov, but Yisrael," said the man, "for you
have struggled with God and with men and have prevailed."[78]

29 Yaakov asked, "Please tell me your name."

But he said, "Why do you ask my name?" and he blessed him there.[79]

30 Yaakov named the place Peniel, "for I have seen God face-to-face and yet
31 my life has been spared."[80] The sun was rising on him as he moved on from
32 Penuel, limping on his thigh. That is why, to this day, the Israelites do not
eat the sciatic nerve by the hip socket: because he wrenched Yaakov's hip
socket at the sciatic nerve.

33 1 Yaakov looked up – and saw Esav coming with his four hundred men. So
2 he divided the children among Leah, Raḥel, and the two maidservants. He
put the maidservants and their children first, Leah and her children behind,
3 and Raḥel and Yosef at the rear. And he went ahead of them, bowing
4 down to the ground seven times until he came close to his brother. Esav
ran to meet him and embraced him. He threw his arms around his neck
5 and kissed him, and they wept. Esav looked up and saw the women and
children. He asked, "Who are these with you?"

Yaakov answered, "They are the children God has graciously given your
servant."

6 Then the maidservants and their children came forward and bowed down.
7 Leah and her children came forward and bowed down. And last, Yosef and
Raḥel approached and bowed down.

8 Esav asked, "What did you mean by all the procession that I met before?"

He said, "To find favor in your eyes, my lord."

9 But Esav said, "I have plenty, my brother. Let what is yours remain yours."

10 "No, please," said Yaakov. "If I have found favor in your eyes, accept this
gift from me, for seeing your face is like seeing the face of God, and you
11 have shown me favor. Please accept my blessing that was brought to you,
for God has been gracious to me, and I have everything." Yaakov pressed
him, and he accepted.

12 Then Esav said, "Let us be on our way. I will go beside you."

---

78 | The first part of the name Yisrael resonates with *sarita* (you have struggled). The ending "el" is a divine name.

79 | This response implies that the "man" is an angel; cf. Judges 13:18.

80 | The first part of the name Peniel resonates with *panim* (face). The ending "el" is a reference to God.

13 But Yaakov said, "My lord knows that the children are fragile, and I must
care for the nursing sheep and cattle. If they are driven hard even for one
14 day, all the flocks will die. Let my lord go on ahead of his servant, and I
will go slowly at the pace of the livestock before me and the pace of the
children until I come to my lord in Se'ir."

15 Esav said, "Let me leave some of my people with you."

"Why do that?" he said. "Just let me find favor in the eyes of my lord."

16 So that day Esav started back on his way to Se'ir, and Yaakov journeyed on
17 to Sukkot. There he built himself a house and made huts for his livestock;
18 that is why he named the place Sukkot.[81] Thus Yaakov, having come from
Padan Aram, arrived safely at the town of Shekhem in Canaan, and he set
19 up camp within sight of the town. He bought the plot of ground where
he pitched his tent from the sons of Ḥamor, father of Shekhem, for one
20 hundred *kesita*[82] of silver. There he erected an altar and named it El Elohei
Yisrael.[83]

34 1 Dina, the daughter whom Leah had borne to Yaakov, went out to see the
2 daughters of the land. When Shekhem son of Ḥamor the Hivite, prince of
3 the land, saw her, he took hold of her, lay with her, and violated her. He
became deeply drawn to Dina, Yaakov's daughter, and, in love with the
4 young woman, he spoke to her heart. Shekhem said to his father Ḥamor,
"Take this girl as a wife for me."

5 When Yaakov heard that he had defiled his daughter Dina, his sons were in
the field with his livestock, and so he stayed silent until they came home.
6 Shekhem's father Ḥamor came to Yaakov to speak with him. Meanwhile,
7 Yaakov's sons, having heard what had happened, came back from the field.
They were shocked and furious, for Shekhem had committed an outrage
in Israel by sleeping with Yaakov's daughter. Such a thing cannot be done!
8 But Ḥamor spoke with them and said, "My son Shekhem has his heart set
9 upon your daughter. Please give her to him as his wife. Intermarry with us.
10 Give us your daughters and take our daughters for yourselves. Settle with
us. The land is open to you. Live here, trade here, acquire property here."

11 Then Shekhem said to Dina's father and brothers, "Let me but find favor
12 in your eyes and I will give whatever you ask. Set the bridal price and gifts
as high as you like. I will give whatever you ask of me; only give me the
young woman as my wife."

13 Yaakov's sons responded to Shekhem and his father Ḥamor, and they
14 spoke deceptively: he had, after all, defiled their sister Dina. They told
them, "We cannot do this. To give our sister to an uncircumcised man
15 would be a disgrace to us. Only on one condition will we agree with you:

81 | Meaning "huts."

82 | Apparently a unit of silver.

83 | Meaning "God, the God of Yisrael."

16 If you become like us, circumcising all your males, then we will give you
our daughters and take your daughters for ourselves. We will live with you
17 and become one people. If you do not agree to be circumcised, we will
take our daughter and go."

18
19 Their words gratified Ḥamor and his son Shekhem. The young man, the
most honored of his father's family, lost no time in doing it, because he
20 longed for Yaakov's daughter. Ḥamor and his son Shekhem came to the
21 town gate and spoke to their fellow townsmen. "These people are friendly
toward us," they said. "Let them live in the land and trade in it. We have
space enough for them. We can marry their daughters and they can marry
22 ours. But only on one condition will they agree to dwell with us as one
23 people. Every male among us must be circumcised as they are. Will not
their livestock, property, and all their animals be ours? Let us, then, agree
to their terms and let them settle among us."

24 All the people who went out by the town gate listened to Ḥamor and
his son Shekhem, and all the males who went out by the town gate were
25 circumcised. On the third day, when the people were weak from pain, two
of Yaakov's sons, Shimon and Levi, Dina's brothers, took their swords,
26 entered the unsuspecting town, and killed every single male. They killed
Ḥamor and his son Shekhem by the sword, took Dina from Shekhem's
27 house and left. Yaakov's sons came upon the dead and plundered the
28 town that had defiled their sister. They took their flocks, their cattle, their
donkeys, and everything else of theirs in the town and out in the field.
29 Their wealth, their children, and their women they took captive and looted,
and all that was in the houses.

30 Yaakov said to Shimon and Levi, "You have brought trouble upon me – you
have made me odious to the inhabitants of the land, the Canaanites and
Perizzites. I am few in number, and if they join forces and attack me, I and
my household will be destroyed."

31 But they said, "Should our sister be treated like a whore?"

35 1 God said to Yaakov, "Arise, go up to Beit El. Stay there, and there build an
altar to God, who appeared to you as you fled your brother Esav."

2 Yaakov told his household and everyone with him, "Be rid of the alien gods
3 you have with you. Purify yourselves and change your clothes. Then come,
let us go up to Beit El, and there I will make an altar to God, who answered
me in my time of trouble and who has been with me wherever I have gone."
4 They gave Yaakov all the alien gods they had, and even the rings in their
5 ears,[84] and Yaakov buried them under a terebinth near Shekhem. As they set
out, the terror of God fell on the surrounding towns so that no one pursued
6 Yaakov's sons. Yaakov and all the people with him came to Luz – that is, Beit
7 El – in the land of Canaan. There he built an altar and called the place El Beit

84 | Earrings may have been associated with idol worship (cf. Ex. 32:2–4).

El,[85] because it was there that God had revealed Himself to him as he fled his
8 brother. Devora, Rivka's nurse, died and was buried under the oak outside
Beit El. And so it was named Oak of Weeping.

9 After Yaakov had returned from Padan Aram God appeared to him again
10 and blessed him. God said to him, "Your name is Yaakov; no longer shall
you be called Yaakov; Yisrael shall be your name." Thus He named him
11 Yisrael. God said to him:

"I am El Shaddai.
Be fertile and multiply.
A nation, a community of nations
will come to be from you.
Of your loins, kings shall come forth.
12 The land I gave to Avraham and Yitzḥak
I surely give to you;
to your descendants after you
I will give the land."

13 14 God went up from him at the place where He had spoken with him. Yaakov
set up a stone pillar at the place where God had talked with him, and on it
15 he offered a libation and poured oil. And Yaakov named the place where
God had spoken to him Beit El.[86]

16 From Beit El they moved on. While they were still some distance from Efrat,
17 Raḥel began to give birth; her labor pains were intense. When her labor was
at its worst, the midwife said to her, "Don't be afraid. You have another son."
18 But she was dying. With her last breath, she named him Ben Oni;[87] but his
father called him Binyamin.[88]

19 So Raḥel died and was buried on the road to Efrat – that is, Beit Leḥem.
20 Yaakov erected a pillar at her grave. To this day, that pillar marks Raḥel's
21 22 grave. Yisrael traveled on, pitching his tent beyond Migdal Eder. While
Yisrael was staying in that region, Reuven went and lay with his father's
concubine Bilha. And Yisrael heard –[89]

23 Yaakov had twelve sons. The sons of Leah were Reuven, Yaakov's firstborn,
24 Shimon, Levi, Yehuda, Yissakhar, and Zevulun. The sons of Raḥel were
25 Yosef and Binyamin. The sons of Raḥel's maid Bilha were Dan and Naftali.
26 The sons of Leah's maid Zilpa were Gad and Asher. These were the sons
of Yaakov, born to him in Padan Aram.

27 Yaakov came home to his father Yitzḥak at Mamre, near Kiryat Arba – that
28 is, Ḥevron – where Avraham and Yitzḥak had lived as strangers. Yitzḥak

85 | Literally "God, the House of God."

86 | Meaning "House of God."

87 | Meaning "son of my sorrow," but it may also denote "son of my strength."

88 | Meaning "son of the right side." The right side signifies strength.

89 | A break appears here in the middle of the verse, implying that the ensuing passage bears a connection to the present one.

29 lived one hundred and eighty years. Then he breathed his last, and died,
and was gathered to his people, aged, satisfied with his years. His sons Esav
and Yaakov buried him.

36 1 2 These are the descendants of Esav – that is, Edom. Esav took wives from
among the daughters of Canaan: Ada daughter of Eilon the Hittite, and
3 Oholivama daughter of Ana, granddaughter of Tzivon the Hivite – and
4 also Basmat, daughter of Yishmael and sister of Nevayot. Ada bore Elifaz
5 to Esav, and Basmat bore Reuel. Oholivama bore Yeush, Yalam, and Koraḥ.
6 These were the sons of Esav, born in the land of Canaan. Esav took his wives,
sons and daughters, and all the members of his household, together with
his livestock, his other animals, and all the possessions he had acquired in
Canaan, and he moved to another region, away from his brother Yaakov,
7 for their possessions were too great for them to remain together; because
of all their livestock, the land where they were living could not support
8 them both. So Esav settled in the hill country of Se'ir. Esav is Edom.

9 These, then, are the descendants of Esav, ancestor of the Edomites, in the
10 hill country of Se'ir. These are the names of Esav's sons: Elifaz, son of Esav's
11 wife Ada, and Reuel, son of Esav's wife Basmat. The sons of Elifaz were
12 Teiman, Omar, Tzefo, Gatam, and Kenaz. Timna, a concubine of Esav's
son Elifaz, bore him Amalek. These are the descendants of Esav's wife
13 Ada. The sons of Reuel were Naḥat, Zeraḥ, Shama, and Miza. These were
14 the descendants of Esav's wife Basmat. The sons of Oholivama, daughter
of Ana and granddaughter of Tzivon, Esav's wife, whom she bore to Esav,
were Yeush, Yalam, and Koraḥ.

15 These were the tribal chiefs among Esav's descendants. The sons of Elifaz,
16 Esav's firstborn, were the chiefs Teiman, Omar, Tzefo, Kenaz, Koraḥ,
Gatam, and Amalek. These were the chiefs descended from Elifaz in Edom;
17 they were grandsons of Ada. The sons of Esav's son Reuel were the chiefs
Naḥat, Zeraḥ, Shama, and Miza. These were the chiefs descended from
18 Reuel in Edom; they were grandsons of Esav's wife Basmat. The sons of
Esav's wife Oholivama were the chiefs Yeush, Yalam, and Koraḥ. These
were the chiefs descended from Esav's wife Oholivama daughter of Ana.
19 These were the sons of Esav – that is, Edom – and these were their chiefs.

20 These are the sons of Se'ir the Horite who were settled in the land: Lotan,
21 Shoval, Tzivon, Ana, Dishon, Etzer, and Dishan. These were the chiefs of
22 the Horites, descendants of Se'ir in the land of Edom. Lotan's sons were
23 Ḥori and Heimam. Timna was Lotan's sister. Shoval's sons were Alvan,
24 Manaḥat, Eival, Shefo, and Onam. Tzivon's sons were Aya and Ana. This
is the Ana who discovered hot springs in the desert while pasturing the
25 donkeys of his father Tzivon. Ana's children were Dishon and Oholivama
26 daughter of Ana. Dishon's sons were Ḥemdan, Eshban, Yitran, and Keran.
27 28 Etzer's sons were Bilhan, Zaavan, and Akan. Dishan's sons were Utz and
29 Aran. These were the tribal chiefs of the Horites: chiefs Lotan, Shoval,

30 Tzivon, Ana, Dishon, Etzer, and Dishan. These were the Horite chiefs by
their divisions in the land of Se'ir.

31 These were the kings who reigned in Edom before any king reigned over
32 the Israelites. Bela son of Beor became king in Edom. His city was named
33 Dinhava. When Bela died, Yovav son of Zeraḥ from Botzra succeeded
34 him as king. When Yovav died, Ḥusham from the land of the Temanites
35 succeeded him as king. When Ḥusham died, Hadad son of Bedad, who
defeated Midyan in the country of Moav, succeeded him as king. His city
36 was named Avit. When Hadad died, Samla from Masreka succeeded him
37 as king. When Samla died, Sha'ul from Reḥovot HaNahar succeeded him
38 as king. When Sha'ul died, Baal Ḥanan son of Akhbor succeeded him as
39 king. When Baal Ḥanan son of Akhbor died, Hadar succeeded him as king.
His city was named Pa'u, and his wife's name was Meheitavel, daughter of
Matred, daughter of Mei Zahav.

40 These were the chiefs descended from Esav, by their clans, localities, and
41 42 names: the chiefs Timna, Alva, Yetet, Oholivama, Ela, Pinon, Kenaz,
43 Teiman, Mivtzar, Magdiel, and Iram. These were the chiefs of Edom – of
Esav, ancestor of the Edomites – each with their own settlements in the
land that they held.

37 1 Yaakov settled where his father had lived as a stranger, in the land of Canaan. VAYESHEV
2 This is the story of Yaakov. Yosef, seventeen years old, was shepherding the
flock with his brothers, an assistant to the sons of his father's wives Bilha
3 and Zilpa. And Yosef brought his father bad reports of them. Now, Yisrael
loved Yosef more than all his other sons, for he was a child of his old age;
4 he made him an ornately colored robe. But when his brothers saw that
their father loved him more than any of them, they hated him and could
not say a peaceful word to him.

5 Then Yosef had a dream, and when he told it to his brothers, they hated
6 7 him still more. "Listen to this dream I had," he said. "We were binding
sheaves in the field when my sheaf rose and stood upright and your sheaves
gathered around mine and bowed down to it."

8 His brothers said to him, "Do you mean to be king over us? Do you mean
to rule over us?" Then they hated him even more for his dreams and for
what he said.

9 Then he had another dream and told it to his brothers. "I had another
dream," he said. "This time, the sun, moon, and eleven stars were bowing
down to me."

10 When he told his father as well as his brothers, his father rebuked him and
said, "What kind of dream is this that you have had? Shall we really come,
I and your mother and your brothers, to bow to the ground before you?"
11 His brothers were jealous of him; but his father kept the matter in mind.

12 When his brothers had gone to pasture their father's flock near Shekhem,
13 Yisrael said to Yosef, "Come, your brothers are pasturing the flocks near
Shekhem; I will send you to them."

Yosef said, "Here I am."

14 He said to him, "Go and see how your brothers and the flocks are doing,
and bring me back word," and he sent him from the Hevron Valley, from
15 where he walked to Shekhem. A man found him wandering lost among
the fields and asked him, "What are you looking for?"

16 He replied, "I'm looking for my brothers. Can you tell me where they are
pasturing the sheep?"

17 "They have moved on from here," said the man. "I heard them say, 'Let us
go to Dotan.'"

18 So Yosef went after his brothers and found them at Dotan. They saw him
in the distance, and by the time he reached them, they had plotted to kill
19 20 him. "Here comes the dreamer!" they said to one another. "Now let us kill
him and throw him into one of the pits – we can say that a wild animal ate
him – then we shall see what will come of his dreams!"

21 When Reuven heard this, he tried to save him from them. "Let us not kill
22 him," he said. "Do not shed blood," said Reuven. "Throw him into this pit
in the desert, but do not lay hands on him." His plan was to rescue him
23 and bring him back to his father. So when Yosef came to his brothers, they
24 stripped him of his robe, the ornately colored robe he was wearing, and
they took him and threw him into the pit. The pit was empty; there was
25 no water in it. And they sat down and ate their meal.

Looking up, they saw a caravan of Ishmaelites coming from Gilad, their
26 camels laden with spices, balm, and myrrh, to be taken to Egypt. Yehuda
said to his brothers, "What do we gain by killing our brother and covering
27 his blood? Let's sell him to the Ishmaelites and not harm him with our
own hands. After all, he is our brother, our own flesh and blood." His
brothers agreed.

28 Some Midianite traders passed by and they pulled Yosef up out of the pit,
and they sold him to the Ishmaelites for twenty pieces of silver. They then
29 brought Yosef to Egypt. Reuven returned to the pit – and Yosef was not
30 there. He tore his clothes, went back to his brothers, and said, "The boy is
gone, and I – where can I turn?"

31 They took Yosef's robe, slaughtered a goat, and dipped the robe in the
32 blood. They had the ornately colored robe brought to their father, and
they said, "We found this. Try to identify it. Is it your son's robe or not?"
33 He recognized it and said, "It is my son's robe! A wild animal must have
eaten him! Yosef has been torn limb from limb!"

34 Yaakov tore his clothes, put sackcloth on his loins, and mourned for his
35 son for many days. All his sons and daughters tried to comfort him, but
he refused to be comforted and said, "I will go down to Sheol[90] mourning
for my son." His father wept for him.

36 Meanwhile, the Medanites had sold him in Egypt to Potifar, one of Pharaoh's
officials, captain of the guard.

38 1 Around that time, Yehuda left his brothers and camped near an Adulamite
2 named Ḥira. There, Yehuda met the daughter of Shua, a Canaanite, and
3 he married her and came to her. She became pregnant and had a son,
4 whom he named Er. She became pregnant again and had another son,
5 and she named him Onan. She had yet another son and named him Shela;
6 Yehuda was in Keziv when she gave birth to him. Yehuda took a wife for his
7 firstborn, Er; her name was Tamar. But Er, Yehuda's firstborn, was wicked
in the LORD's sight, and the LORD took his life.

8 Yehuda then said to Onan, "Go in to your brother's wife and fulfill your
9 duty as her brother-in-law.[91] Provide children for your brother." But Onan
knew that the children would not be considered his. Whenever he came
to his brother's wife, he let his seed go to waste on the ground so as not to
10 have children in his brother's name. What he did was wicked in the LORD's
11 sight, and so He took his life also. Then Yehuda said to his daughter-in-law
Tamar, "Live as a widow in your father's house until my son Shela grows
up" – for he thought he too might die like his brothers. So Tamar went to
live in her father's house.

12 A long time passed, and Yehuda's wife, Shua's daughter, died. When he had
completed his time of mourning, he and his neighbor Ḥira the Adulamite
13 went to join his sheepshearers in Timna. Tamar was told, "Your father-in-
14 law is going to Timna to shear his sheep." And she took off her widow's
clothes and covered herself with a veil. Disguised, she sat at the entrance
to Einayim on the road to Timna, for she had seen that Shela was now
15 grown up and yet she had not been given to him as a wife. Yehuda saw her
16 and thought she was a prostitute, because she had covered her face. Not
realizing that she was his daughter-in-law, he turned aside to her on the
road and said, "Come, let me sleep with you."

She said, "What will you give me to sleep with you?"

17 He said, "I will send you a young goat from my flock."

"Only if you give me something as a pledge until you send it," she said.

18 "What pledge should I give you?" he asked.

90 | The netherworld.

91 | On levirate marriage, see Deuteronomy 25:5–10.

She answered, "Your seal and cord, and the staff in your hand." He gave
them to her and went in to her – and she became pregnant by him.

19 She got up and left, removed her veil, and put on her widow's clothes again.
20 And Yehuda sent the young goat by his neighbor the Adulamite, to recover
21 the pledge from the woman, but he could not find her. He asked the local
men, "Where is the cult prostitute,[92] the one by the roadside at Einayim?"
They said, "No cult prostitute has been here."

22 So he went back to Yehuda and said, "I could not find her. Besides, the
local men said that there was no cult prostitute there."

23 Yehuda said, "Let her keep what she has or we will become a laughingstock.
I tried to send her this young goat, but you could not find her."

24 About three months later, Yehuda was told, "Your daughter-in-law Tamar
has behaved as a loose woman; in fact she has become pregnant by her
harlotry."

"Take her out and let her be burned," Yehuda said.

25 As she was being brought out, she sent her father-in-law a message: "I am
pregnant by the man to whom these belong." She added, "Please identify
to whom this seal and cord and staff belong."

26 Yehuda recognized them and said, "She is more righteous than I. It was
because I did not give her to Shela my son." He did not know her intimately
again.

27 When the time came for her to give birth, there were twins in her womb.
28 As she was in labor one child put out a hand, so the midwife took a crimson
29 thread and tied it to his wrist, saying, "This one came out first." But he
pulled his hand back and then his brother came out. She said, "How you
have burst through!" So he was named Peretz.[93]

30 Then his brother came out with the crimson thread on his wrist. He was
namedZeraḥ.[94]

39 1 Meanwhile, Yosef had been brought down to Egypt. Potifar, an Egyptian,
one of Pharaoh's officials and captain of the guard, had bought him from
2 the Ishmaelites who had brought him there. The Lord was with Yosef,
and he became a successful man. He lived in the house of his Egyptian
3 master. And his master saw that the Lord was with him and that the Lord
4 granted him success in all he did; Yosef found favor in his eyes and became
his personal attendant. Potifar put him in charge of his household, giving
5 him responsibility for all he owned. From the moment he put him in
charge of his household and all he owned, the Lord blessed the Egyptian

---

92 | A type of prostitute associated with religious worship.

93 | Meaning "bursting through."

94 | The term *zeraḥ* means "shining," an apparent reference to the color of the thread.

because of Yosef. The LORD's blessing was in all he owned, in house and
6 field. And so he left all he had in Yosef's hands and, with him there, he had
no concern for anything but the food he ate.[95] Now, Yosef was well built
7 and handsome, and after a while, his master's wife cast her eyes on Yosef.
"Lie with me," she said.

8 But he refused. "With me here," he told her, "my master does not concern
himself with the running of the house; he has entrusted me with all that he
9 owns. No one in this house has greater authority than I. He has withheld
nothing from me except you, because you are his wife. How could I do so
10 great a wrong? It would be a sin against God!" And though she spoke to
Yosef day after day, he would not consent to lie with her or be with her.

11 One day he came into the house to do his work and none of the other
12 servants were there. She caught him by his cloak and said, "Lie with me!"
13 He ran away from her and fled outside. When she saw that he had left
14 his cloak in her hand and had run out of the house, she called out to her
servants and said to them, "Look! He brought us a Hebrew to mock[96] us!
15 He came to me to lie with me, but I screamed. And when he heard me
16 scream and cry for help, he left his cloak with me and ran outside." She
17 kept his cloak beside her until his master came home. Then she told him
the same story: "The Hebrew slave you brought us came to me to mock
18 me. I screamed and called for help, and he left his cloak with me and ran
outside."

19 When his master heard the story his wife told him – "This is what your
20 servant did to me!" – he was incensed. Yosef's master had him put in
prison, where the king's prisoners were confined. He remained there in
21 prison. But the LORD was with Yosef and showed him kindness, granting
22 him favor in the eyes of the prison warden. The warden put Yosef in
charge of all the prisoners in the jail. Everything done there was under his
23 direction. The warden did not need to pay attention to anything he had
entrusted to him, because the LORD was with him, giving him success in
all he did.

40 1 Some time later, the Egyptian kings' cupbearer and baker gave offense to
2 their master, the king of Egypt. Pharaoh was angry with the two officials,
3 his chief cupbearer, and his chief baker, and he placed them in custody
in the house of the captain of the guard, in the very place where Yosef
4 was confined. The captain of the guard assigned them to Yosef and it
was he who attended them. When they had been in custody for some
5 time, the two of them – the imprisoned cupbearer and baker of the king
of Egypt – each had a dream on the same night, each dream seeming to
6 carry its own meaning. When Yosef came to them the next morning, he
7 saw that they were both distressed. He asked Pharaoh's officials who

95 | Possibly a euphemism for his wife (cf. v. 9).

96 | This verb (*letzaḥek*) can have sexual connotations (cf., e.g., v. 17, 21:9, 26:8; Ex. 32:6).

were in custody with him in his master's house, "Why are you looking so
8 troubled today?" "We both had dreams," they told him, "but there is no
one to interpret them." Yosef replied, "Interpretation belongs to God. Tell
me your dreams."

9 So the chief cupbearer told his dream to Yosef and said to him, "In my
10 dream I saw a vine in front of me. The vine had three branches. As soon
11 as it budded, it blossomed, and its clusters ripened into grapes. Pharaoh's
cup was in my hand; I took the grapes and squeezed them into Pharaoh's
cup, and I placed the cup in his hand."

12 13 "This is what it means," Yosef said. "The three branches are three days. In
three days Pharaoh will lift your head and restore you to your position.
You will place Pharaoh's cup in his hand again, as you did when you were
14 his cupbearer. When it goes well with you, remember me and do me this
15 kindness: mention me to Pharaoh so as to free me from this place. The
truth is that I was kidnapped from the land of the Hebrews. Here too, I
have done nothing to deserve being placed in this pit."

16 The chief baker saw that he had given a favorable interpretation, so he said
to Yosef, "I too had a dream. There were three baskets of white bread on
17 my head. In the top basket were all sorts of baked food that Pharaoh eats,
but birds were eating them out of the basket above my head."

18 19 "This is what it means," Yosef said. "The three baskets are three days. In
three days Pharaoh will lift your head from your body; he will hang you
from a stake, and birds will eat your flesh."

20 The third day was Pharaoh's birthday. He made a feast for all his servants,
and from among them he singled out his chief cupbearer and chief baker.
21 He restored the chief cupbearer to his position so that, as before, he placed
22 the cup in Pharaoh's hand. But he hung up the chief baker, as Yosef had
23 predicted. Still, the chief cupbearer did not remember Yosef; he forgot him.

MIKETZ 41 1 Two years passed. Then Pharaoh had a dream: he was standing by the Nile
2 when seven handsome, healthy cows came up out of the river and grazed
3 among the reeds. Then seven other cows came up from the river after them,
4 ugly and gaunt, and stood beside them by the riverbank. The ugly, gaunt
cows ate up the seven handsome, healthy cows. Pharaoh awoke.

5 Falling back to sleep, he had a second dream: he saw seven ears of grain,
6 ripe and robust, growing on a single stalk. Suddenly, seven other ears
7 sprouted after them, thin and scorched by the east wind. The thin ears
swallowed up the seven ripe, full ears. Pharaoh awoke – and realized it
had been a dream.

8 In the morning his mind was troubled, so he sent for all the magicians and
sages of Egypt. Pharaoh told them his dream, but no one could offer an
interpretation that satisfied him.

9 Then the chief cupbearer said to Pharaoh, "I must recall my sins today.
10 Once, Pharaoh was angry with his servants and placed me and the chief
11 baker in custody in the house of the captain of the guard. One night he and
12 I each had a dream, and each dream seemed to have its own meaning. With
us was a young Hebrew, a slave of the captain of the guard. We told him
our dreams and he interpreted them for us, telling each of us the meaning
13 of his dream. Things turned out exactly as he interpreted them to us. I was
restored to my position, and the baker was hung up."

14 So Pharaoh sent for Yosef. He was rushed from the dungeon, had his hair
15 cut, changed his clothes, and came before Pharaoh. Pharaoh said to Yosef,
"I had a dream and no one can interpret it; I have heard that when you hear
a dream you can interpret it."

16 "Not I," replied Yosef to Pharaoh. "God will give Pharaoh the answer that
he needs."

17 Pharaoh told Yosef: "In my dream, I was standing by the bank of the Nile
18 when seven handsome, healthy cows came up out of the river and grazed
19 among the reeds. Then after them came seven other cows, scrawny, very
20 sickly, and thin – I never saw such sickly cows in all Egypt. Then the thin,
21 sickly cows ate up the first seven healthy cows. But when they had eaten
them you could not tell that they had eaten them, for they still looked
22 as bad as before. Then I awoke. In my dream I then saw seven ears of
23 grain, ripe and full, growing on a single stalk. Suddenly, seven other ears
24 sprouted after them, shriveled, thin, and scorched by the east wind, and
the thin ears swallowed the seven good ears. I told this to the magicians,
but none could explain it to me."

25 Yosef said to Pharaoh, "The two dreams of Pharaoh are one and the same.
26 God has told Pharaoh what He is about to do. The seven good cows are
seven years, and so too the seven good ears are seven years. It is one and
27 the same dream. The seven thin, sickly cows that came up after them are
seven years, as are the seven empty ears scorched by the east wind. They
28 are seven years of famine. It is as I have told Pharaoh: God has shown
29 Pharaoh what He is about to do. Seven years are coming when there will be
30 great abundance throughout the land of Egypt. But after them will come
seven years of famine, when all the abundance in Egypt will be forgotten.
31 Famine will ravage the land. So devastating will the famine be that no one
in the land will know anything of abundance anymore.

32 "As for Pharaoh having the same dream twice, this means that the matter
33 has already been decided by God, and He is soon to bring it about. So
now let Pharaoh seek out an astute, wise man and set him over the land of
34 Egypt. Let Pharaoh appoint overseers across the land and take a fifth of
35 Egypt's harvest during the seven years of abundance. Let them gather all
that food in these coming good years, storing the grain under Pharaoh's
36 aegis so that there is food under guard in all the cities. The food should be

held in reserve for the land when the seven years of famine come to Egypt,
so that the country is not ruined by the famine."

37 38 The plan seemed good to Pharaoh and all his officials. Pharaoh said to
them, "Could we find another like him, a man who has within him the
39 spirit of God?" So Pharaoh said to Yosef, "Since God has made all this
40 known to you, there can be no one else as astute or as wise as you. You
shall be in charge of my court, and by your command shall all my people
be directed. Only the throne itself will make me greater than you."

41 Then Pharaoh said to Yosef, "I hereby place you in charge of all the land
42 of Egypt." Pharaoh removed his signet ring from his hand and placed it
on Yosef's. He had him robed in garments of the finest linen, and placed a
43 gold chain around his neck. He had him ride in the chariot of his second-
in-command, and ahead of him people proclaimed, "*Avrekh*."[97] Thus was
44 he given authority over all Egypt. Pharaoh told Yosef, "I am Pharaoh,
45 but without your consent no one will lift hand or foot in all Egypt." And
Pharaoh gave Yosef the name Tzafenat Paneaḥ[98] and gave him Asnat,
daughter of Potifera, priest of On, as his wife. Thus Yosef went out to
oversee Egypt.

46 When he entered the service of Pharaoh, king of Egypt, Yosef was thirty
years old. Leaving Pharaoh's presence, Yosef traveled throughout the land
47 of Egypt. During the seven years of plenty the land produced in profusion.
48 He gathered all the grain produced during the seven years of plenty in
Egypt and stored it in the cities. In each city he stored the grain grown
49 in the surrounding fields. Yosef stored so much grain that it was like the
sand of the sea. They had to stop keeping records because it was beyond
measure.

50 Before the years of famine came, two sons were born to Yosef by Asnat
51 daughter of Potifera, priest of On. Yosef named his firstborn Menashe,
saying, "God has made me forget all my troubles and all my father's
52 family."[99] The second son he named Efrayim, saying, "God has made me
fruitful in the land of my affliction."[100]

53 54 The seven years of abundance in Egypt came to an end, and the seven years
of famine began, just as Yosef had said they would. There was famine in
55 all the other lands, but throughout Egypt there was food. When all Egypt
began to feel the famine, the people cried to Pharaoh for food. Pharaoh
told all the Egyptians, "Go to Yosef. Whatever he tells you – do."

56 The famine spread over the entire country. Yosef then opened all the
storehouses and sold grain to the Egyptians, for the famine was worsening

97 | Possibly meaning "bow" or "kneel," or in Egyptian "make way."

98 | Possibly "interpreter of secrets," or in Egyptian related to a word meaning "life."

99 | The name Menashe resonates with *nashani* (made me forget).

100 | The name Efrayim resonates with *hifrani* (made me fruitful).

57 throughout Egypt. People from all over the region came to Egypt to buy
grain from Yosef, because all across the land the famine was devastating.

42 1 Knowing that there was grain in Egypt, Yaakov said to his sons, "Why
2 do you keep looking at one another?" He said, "I have heard that there is
grain in Egypt. Go down there and buy some for us so that we may live
3 and not die." So ten of Yosef's brothers went down to buy grain in Egypt.
4 But Yaakov did not send Yosef's brother Binyamin with them, for he was
5 afraid that harm might come to him. So Yisrael's sons were among those
who came to buy grain, the famine having reached as far as the land of
Canaan.

6 Yosef was the governor of the land; it was he who dispensed food to all
its people. When Yosef's brothers arrived, they bowed down to him, their
7 faces to the ground. Yosef recognized his brothers as soon as he saw them,
but he acted like a stranger and spoke harshly to them. "Where have you
come from?" he asked.

8 They replied, "From the land of Canaan – to buy food." Yosef recognized
9 his brothers, but they did not recognize him. Then Yosef remembered the
dreams he had dreamed about them. "You are spies!" he said. "You have
come to see where our land is exposed."

10 11 "No, my lord," they said. "Your servants have come to buy food. We all are
sons of the same man. We are honest men. Your servants are not spies."

12 "Lies," he said. "You have come to see where our land is exposed."

13 "We were once twelve brothers," they replied, "sons of one man in Canaan.
The youngest is now with our father, and one is gone."

14 15 But Yosef said, "It is as I said to you – you are spies. This is how you will be
tested. By Pharaoh's life, you will not leave this place unless your youngest
16 brother comes here. Let one of you go and fetch your brother. The rest of
you will remain confined here. This will test whether or not you are telling
the truth. If not, by Pharaoh's life, you are spies."

17 18 He had them placed in custody for three days. On the third day, Yosef said
19 to them, "If you do this you will live, for I am a God-fearing man. If you
are honest, let one of your brothers stay here in prison while the rest of
20 you go and take back grain for your starving households. Then bring your
youngest brother to me so that your words can be verified and you will
not die." They agreed.

21 And they said to one another, "We are guilty, guilty because of what we
did to our brother. We saw his suffering when he pleaded with us but we
did not listen. That is why this trouble has come upon us."

22 Then Reuven spoke up: "Did I not tell you not to sin against the boy? But
you would not listen. Now comes the reckoning for his blood."

23 They did not realize that Yosef could understand them, for a translator
24 stood between them. And Yosef turned away from them and wept.

Then he turned back to them and spoke again. He had Shimon taken from
25 them and placed in chains before their eyes. Yosef gave orders to fill their
bags with grain and put each man's money back in his sack. They were to
26 be given provisions for the journey. After this was done for them, they
27 loaded their grain on their donkeys and left. As one of them was opening
his sack to feed his donkey at the place where they stopped for the night,
28 he saw his money right there at the top of his pack. "My money has been
returned!" he told his brothers. "There it is in my pack!"

Their hearts sank. Trembling, they turned to one another, saying, "What
is this that God has done to us?"

29 When they came to their father Yaakov in the land of Canaan, they told
30 him all that had happened to them. They said, "The man who is the lord of
31 the land spoke to us harshly. He accused us of spying on the land. We said
32 to him, 'We are honest men; we are not spies. We were twelve brothers,
sons of the same father. One is gone, and the youngest is now with our
33 father in Canaan.' Then the man who is lord of the land said to us, 'This
is how I will know that you are honest men. Leave one of your brothers
34 with me, take something for your starving households, and go. Then bring
your youngest brother to me. Then I will know that you are not spies but
honest men. And then I will give you back your brother, and you can trade
in the land.'"

35 They began emptying their sacks, and there in each one's sack was his
money bag. When they and their father saw the money bags, they were
36 afraid. Their father Yaakov said to them, "You have taken my children away
from me. Yosef is gone. Shimon is gone. Now you want to take Binyamin?
All this I must suffer!"

37 Reuven said to his father, "You may kill my two sons if I do not bring him
back to you; entrust him to my care and I will bring him back to you."

38 "My son will not go down with you," said Yaakov. "His brother is dead, and
he is all I have left. If any harm comes to him on the way, you will bring
down my gray head in grief to Sheol."

43 1 2 The famine in the land continued to be severe. When they had eaten all
the grain they had brought from Egypt, their father said to them, "Go back
and buy us some more food."

3 But Yehuda said to him, "The man warned us, 'Do not appear before me
4 unless your brother is with you.' If you agree to send our brother with us,
5 we will go and buy you food. But if you will not send him, we cannot go.
The man told us, 'Do not appear before me unless your brother is with
you.'"

6 Yisrael said, "Why did you bring this trouble on me by telling the man you had another brother?"

7 They replied, "The man kept asking about us and our family: 'Is your father still alive?' he asked. 'Do you have a brother?' We simply answered his questions. How could we know that he would say, 'Bring your brother here'?"

8 And Yehuda said to his father Yisrael, "Send the boy with me. Let us be on
9 our way so that we, you, and our children may live and not die. I myself am
the guarantee for his safety: you may hold me personally responsible. If I
do not bring him back and set him before you, I will have sinned against
10 you for all time. We could have been there and back twice if we had not
hesitated so long."

11 And then their father Yisrael said to them, "If that is how it must be, then do
this. Take some of the best produce of the land in your bags, and bring them
to the man as a gift – a little balm and a little honey, some spices and myrrh,
12 pistachio nuts and almonds. Take with you double the money. Return the
13 money that was put back into your sacks. Perhaps it was a mistake. And
14 take your brother. Go back to the man at once. May El Shaddai grant you
mercy before the man, that he may send your other brother forth to you,
and Binyamin. And as for me, if I am to be bereaved, I will be bereaved."

15 So the men took the gift and double the money and set out with Binyamin.
16 They went to Egypt and presented themselves to Yosef. When Yosef saw
Binyamin with them, he said to his house steward, "Take these men to
my house. Slaughter an animal and prepare a meal, for they will dine with
me at noon."

17 18 The man did as Yosef said and brought them to Yosef's house. The men
were frightened that they were being brought to Yosef's house. They said,
"We have been brought here because of the money that was put back in
our sacks the first time. He wants to attack us, seize us as slaves, and take
our donkeys."

19 So they went up to Yosef's steward and spoke to him at the entrance to the
20 house. "If you please, my lord," they said, "we came here once before to buy
21 food. But at the place where we stopped for the night, we opened our bags
and each of us found his money, in its exact weight, in the mouth of his
22 bag. So we have brought it back with us. We have also brought additional
money to buy food. We do not know who put our money in our bags."

23 He replied, "All is well. Do not be afraid. Your God, the God of your father, must have placed a hidden gift in your bags. I received the money you paid." Then he brought Shimon out to them.

24 He brought the brothers into Yosef's house, gave them water to bathe their
25 feet, and had fodder brought for their donkeys. They set out their gifts in

preparation for Yosef's arrival at noon, because they had heard that they
26 were going to eat there. When Yosef entered the house, they presented
him with the gifts they had brought and bowed low to the ground before
him.

27 He asked them how they were. Then he asked, "How is the elderly father
about whom you spoke? Is he still alive?"

28 They said, "Your servant our father is alive and well." They bowed down and
29 prostrated themselves. Then he looked up and saw his brother Binyamin,
his mother's son, and asked, "Is this your youngest brother, the one you
30 mentioned to me?" And he said, "God be gracious to you, my son." At
that, he hurried out, for he was overcome with feeling toward his brother
and was on the verge of tears. He went into a private room and there he
wept.

31 He washed his face and came out, controlling himself. "Serve the food,"
32 he said. They served him apart, them apart, and the Egyptians who ate
with him apart, for the Egyptians could not eat with Hebrews, since to
33 Egyptians that was considered abhorrent. Seated by his direction in order
34 of age, oldest to youngest, they looked at one another in amazement. He
sent them portions from his table, giving Binyamin five times as much as
anyone else. And they drank and grew merry with him.

44 1 Then Yosef instructed his steward, "Fill the men's bags with as much food
2 as they can carry, and put each one's money in the mouth of his bag. Then
put my chalice – the silver chalice – in the mouth of the youngest one's bag,
along with the money for his grain." He did as Yosef told him.

3 As morning showed its first light, the men were sent on their way with
4 their donkeys. They had not gone far from the city when Yosef said to his
steward, "Go after the men at once. When you catch up with them, say to
5 them, 'Why have you repaid good with evil? Is it not from this that my
master drinks and that he uses for divination? It is a wicked thing you
have done.'"

6 7 He caught up with them and repeated those words to them. But they said
to him, "How can my lord say such things? Heaven forbid that we should
8 do such a thing! Look, we brought back to you from Canaan the money
we found in the mouths of our bags. Why would we steal silver or gold
9 from your master's house? If any of your servants is found with it, he shall
die, and the rest of us will become my lord's slaves."

10 "Let it be as you say," he replied, "but only the one with whom it is found
11 shall be my slave. The rest of you can go free." Each of them quickly lowered
12 his bag to the ground, and each opened his bag. He searched, beginning
with the oldest and ending with the youngest. The chalice was found in
13 Binyamin's bag. The brothers tore their clothes. Each loaded his donkey
again, and they returned to the city.

14 Yehuda and his brothers came to Yosef's house – he was still there – and
15 they threw themselves on the ground before him. Yosef said to them,
"What is this thing you have done? Do you not know that a man like me
16 can find out the truth by divination?" Yehuda replied, "What can we say
to my lord? What can we speak? How can we prove our innocence? God
has uncovered your servants' guilt! We are now my lord's slaves – we and
the one in whose possession the chalice was found."

17 "Heaven forbid that I should do such a thing," he said. "The man in whose
possession the chalice was found will become my slave. As for the rest of
you, go back to your father in peace."

18 But Yehuda stepped forward to him. "If you please, my lord," he said, "let VAYIGASH
your servant speak a word in my lord's hearing. Do not be angry with me,
19 you who are the equal of Pharaoh. My lord asked his servants, 'Do you have
20 a father or a brother?' And we told my lord, 'We have an elderly father and
there is a young son, a child of his old age. When his brother died, he was
21 the only one of his mother's sons left, and his father loves him.' Then you
22 said to your servants, 'Bring him to me that I may set eyes on him.' But we
said to my lord, 'The boy cannot leave his father. If he left him, his father
23 would die.' Then you told your servants, 'Unless your youngest brother
comes with you, you shall not see my face again.'

24 "When we went back to your servant my father, we told him what my lord
25 had said. Then our father said, 'Go back and buy a little more food.'

26 "We said, 'We cannot go. We can go only if our youngest brother is with
us. If he is not with us, we cannot see the man's face.'

27 "Then your servant, my father, said to us, 'You know that my wife bore me
28 two sons. One is gone from me, and I said, "He must have been torn to
29 pieces." I have not seen him since. If you take this one from me and harm
30 befalls him, you will bring down my gray head in grief to Sheol.' So now, if
the boy is not with us when I go back to your servant my father, so bound
31 together are their lives that when he sees that the boy is not with us, he will
die. Your servants will have brought down the gray head of your servant,
32 our father, in grief to Sheol. Your servant offered himself to my father as a
guarantee for the boy. I said, 'If I do not bring him back to you, I will have
33 sinned against my father for all time.' So, please, let your servant stay as my
lord's slave in place of the boy, and let the boy go back with his brothers.
34 For how can I go back to my father if the boy is not with me? I could not
bear to see the misery that would overwhelm my father!"

45 1 Yosef could no longer control himself in the company of all his attendants.
He cried out, "Have everyone leave my presence!" So no one else was with
2 Yosef when he revealed himself to his brothers. He wept so loudly that
the Egyptians could hear him, and the news reached Pharaoh's palace.

3 Yosef said to his brothers, "I am Yosef. Is my father really still alive?"

His brothers were so bewildered at his presence that they could not answer
4 him. "Come close to me, please," said Yosef to his brothers. They came
close, and he said, "I am your brother Yosef, whom you sold into Egypt.
5 And now, do not be distressed or angry with yourselves that you sold me
6 here, for God sent me ahead of you to save lives. For two years now there
has been famine in the land, and for another five years there will be no
7 plowing or reaping. So God sent me ahead of you to ensure your survival
8 in the land, and to save your lives by a great deliverance. So then, it was
not you who sent me here, but God. He has made me a father to Pharaoh,
9 lord of his whole household and ruler of all Egypt. Hurry back to my father
and tell him, 'This is what your son Yosef says: God has made me lord of
10 all Egypt. Come down to me without delay. You may live in the region
of Goshen where you will be close to me, you, your children, and your
11 grandchildren, your flocks and herds and all that is yours. I will provide for
you there, for there are still five years of famine to come. Otherwise you,
12 your household, and all who belong to you will be destitute.' You and my
brother Binyamin can see with your own eyes that it is I who am speaking
13 to you. Tell my father about all the honor accorded to me in Egypt and
about everything you have seen. Hurry now – bring my father here."

14 Then he threw his arms around his brother Binyamin's neck and wept, and
15 Binyamin wept on his neck; he kissed all his brothers and wept over them.
Only after that could his brothers speak to him.

16 When the news reached Pharaoh's palace that Yosef's brothers had come,
17 Pharaoh and his officials were gratified. Pharaoh said to Yosef, "Tell your
18 brothers, 'Do this: Load your animals and go back to Canaan. Bring your
father and your families and come to me. I will give you the best of the land
19 of Egypt; you shall live off the cream of the land. You are also instructed
to do this: Take wagons from Egypt for your children and wives. Bring
20 your father and come. Do not trouble yourselves about your belongings,
for the best of all Egypt will be yours.'"

21 Yisrael's sons did so. Yosef gave them wagons as Pharaoh had ordered, and
22 gave them provisions for the journey. To each he gave new clothes, but to
23 Binyamin he gave three hundred pieces of silver and five sets of clothes. To
his father he sent the following: ten donkeys loaded with the best things
of Egypt and ten female donkeys loaded with grain, bread, and food for
24 his father's journey. He sent his brothers on their way; and as they were
leaving, he said to them, "Do not quarrel on the way."

25 So they went up out of Egypt and came to their father Yaakov in Canaan.
26 They told him, "Yosef is still alive; in fact, he is ruler over all Egypt."

27 His heart stood still; he did not believe them. But when they told him
everything Yosef had said to them, and when he saw the wagons that
Yosef had sent to carry him back, Yaakov's spirit was filled with new life.

28 Yisrael said, "It is enough: Yosef my son is still alive. I must go and see
him before I die."

46 1 So Yisrael set out with all he had. When he reached Be'er Sheva, he offered
2 up sacrifices to the God of his father Yitzḥak. And God spoke to Yisrael in
a night vision: "Yaakov, Yaakov."

He replied, "Here I am."

3 "I am God, the God of your father," He said. "Do not be afraid to go down
4 to Egypt, for there I will make of you a great nation. I Myself will go down
to Egypt with you, and I Myself will also bring you back; and Yosef's hand
will close your eyes."

5 Then Yaakov left Be'er Sheva. Yisrael's sons took their father Yaakov and
their children and wives in the wagons that Pharaoh had sent to carry
6 him. They took their livestock and all the possessions they had acquired
7 in Canaan. So Yaakov and all his descendants came to Egypt. He brought
with him to Egypt his sons and grandsons, daughters and granddaughters,
and all his descendants.

8 These are the names of the children of Israel – Yaakov and his descen-
9 dants – who came to Egypt: Reuven, Yaakov's firstborn, and Reuven's
10 sons, Ḥanokh, Palu, Ḥetzron, and Karmi. Shimon's sons were Yemuel,
Yamin, Ohad, Yakhin, Tzoḥar, and Sha'ul, son of the Canaanite woman.
11 12 Levi's sons were Gershon, Kehat, and Merari. Yehuda's sons were Er, Onan,
Shela, Peretz, and Zeraḥ – but Er and Onan had died in Canaan.[101] Peretz's
13 sons were Ḥetzron and Ḥamul. Yissakhar's sons were Tola, Puva, Yov, and
14 15 Shimron. Zevulun's sons were Sered, Elon, and Yaḥliel. These were the
sons whom Leah bore to Yaakov in Padan Aram, besides his daughter Dina.
In all, male and female, they numbered thirty-three.

16 17 Gad's sons were Tzifyon, Ḥagi, Shuni, Etzbon, Eri, Arodi, and Areli. Asher's
sons were Yimna, Yishva, Yishvi, and Beria. Their sister was Seraḥ. Beria's
18 sons were Ḥever and Malkiel. These were the children of Zilpa, whom
Lavan had given to his daughter Leah; these she bore to Yaakov – sixteen
in all.

19 20 The sons of Yaakov's wife Raḥel were Yosef and Binyamin. In Egypt
Menashe and Efrayim were born to Yosef; Asnat, daughter of Potifera
21 priest of On, bore them to him. Binyamin's sons were Bela, Bekher, Ashbel,
22 Gera, Naaman, Eḥi, Rosh, Mupim, Ḥupim, and Ard. These are the children
Raḥel bore to Yaakov – fourteen in all.

23 24 Dan's son was Ḥushim. Naftali's sons were Yaḥtze'el, Guni, Yetzer, and
25 Shilem. These were the sons born to Yaakov by Bilha, whom Lavan had
26 given to his daughter Raḥel – seven in all. So the number of people who

101 | See 38:7–10.

came to Egypt with Yaakov – his direct descendants, not including his sons'
27 wives – were sixty-six in all. Yosef's sons, born to him in Egypt, were two
in number. Thus the total number of Yaakov's family who came to Egypt
was seventy.

28 He sent Yehuda ahead of him to Yosef to show him the way to Goshen.
29 When they came to the region of Goshen, Yosef harnessed his chariot
and rode to Goshen to greet his father Yisrael. He presented himself to
him, threw his arms around his neck, and wept on his shoulder for a long
30 time. "Now I can die," said Yisrael to Yosef. "I have seen your face! You
are still alive!"

31 Yosef said to his brothers and his father's household, "I will go and speak
to Pharaoh. I will tell him, 'My brothers and my father's household have
32 come to me from Canaan. The men are shepherds. They tend livestock.
33 They have brought their sheep and cattle and all they have.' When Pharaoh
34 summons you and asks, 'What is your occupation?' you should say, 'We
and our fathers have tended livestock all our lives.' Then you will be allowed
to settle in the region of Goshen, because the Egyptians abominate all
who keep sheep."[102]

47 1 So Yosef went and told Pharaoh. He said, "My father and brothers, together
with their flocks, herds, and all they have, have come from Canaan and are
now in the region of Goshen."

2 3 He chose five of his brothers and presented them to Pharaoh. Pharaoh
asked the brothers, "What is your occupation?" They replied, "Your
servants are shepherds, as our fathers were before."

4 And they said to Pharaoh, "We have come to stay for a while in your land
because the famine is severe in Canaan and there is no pasture for your
servants' flocks. Please, then, let your servants settle in the region of
Goshen."

5 6 Pharaoh said to Yosef, "Your father and brothers have come to you. The
land of Egypt is open before you. Settle your father and brothers in the
best part of the land. Let them live in the region of Goshen, and if there are
able men among them, you may give them charge of my own livestock."

7 Then Yosef brought his father Yaakov and presented him before Pharaoh.
8 Yaakov blessed Pharaoh, and Pharaoh asked Yaakov, "How old are you?"
9 Yaakov said to Pharaoh, "The years of my wandering are one hundred and
thirty. Few and hard have been the years of my life, and I have not reached
10 the age my fathers reached in their own wanderings." Yaakov blessed
Pharaoh and left his presence.

102 | In other words, because of this consideration, Pharaoh will agree to have you live in a peripheral location such as Goshen.

11 Yosef settled his father and brothers, giving them holdings in the best part
12 of Egypt, in the region of Ramesses,[103] as Pharaoh had instructed. And
Yosef provided his father, his brothers, and all his father's household with
food, befitting the numbers of their dependents.

13 And there was no food across the land, because the famine was so severe.
14 Egypt and Canaan languished because of the famine. Yosef collected all
the money that was to be found in Egypt and Canaan in payment for the
grain the people were buying, and he brought it into Pharaoh's palace.
15 When the money in Egypt and Canaan was gone, all the Egyptians came
to Yosef, saying, "Give us food. Why should we die before your eyes just
because there is no more money left?"

16 "Bring your livestock," said Yosef, "and I will sell you food in exchange for
your livestock since there is no more money left."

17 So they brought their livestock to Yosef, and he gave them food in exchange
for horses, sheep, cattle, and donkeys. He supplied them with food that
year in exchange for all their livestock.

18 That year passed, and they came to him the following year and said, "We
cannot hide from my lord that the money is gone and the livestock belongs
to you. There is nothing left for my lord except our bodies and our land.
19 Why should we and our land die before your eyes? Acquire us and our
land in exchange for food, and we with our land will be slaves to Pharaoh.
Give us seed so that we can live and not die and so that the land does not
become desolate."

20 Thus Yosef acquired all the land of Egypt for Pharaoh. Each Egyptian sold
his field, because the famine had become too much for them. So the land
21 became Pharaoh's. As for the people, he transferred them town by town
22 from one end of Egypt to the other.[104] The only land he did not acquire
was that of the priests, because they received an allotment of food from
Pharaoh; they were able to live on the allotment that Pharaoh gave them,
and so they did not sell their land.

23 Yosef said to the people, "Today I have acquired you and your land for
24 Pharaoh. Here is seed for you to sow the land. When the harvest comes,
give one-fifth to Pharaoh. Four-fifths shall be yours as seed for your fields
and as food for you, your households, and your children."

25 "You have saved our lives," they said. "May we find favor in the eyes of
26 my lord – we shall be slaves to Pharaoh." So Yosef made it a law, as it is to
this day, governing land in Egypt, that one-fifth of all produce belongs to
Pharaoh. Only the land of the priests did not become Pharaoh's.

---

103 | Ramesses evidently comprised all or part of Goshen.

104 | To help ensure that the people would not try to reclaim their land.

27 Thus Yisrael settled in the land of Egypt, in the region of Goshen. They
acquired holdings in it and were fertile and greatly increased in number.

VAYEḤI 28 Yaakov lived in Egypt for seventeen years; the years of his life were one
29 hundred and forty-seven. As the time of his death drew near, he summoned
his son Yosef and said to him, "If I have found favor in your eyes, place your
hand under my thigh[105] and promise to deal kindly and truly with me: do
30 not bury me in Egypt. Let me lie with my fathers. Carry me from Egypt
and bury me where they are buried."

31 "I will do as you say," he replied. Yaakov said, "Swear to me," and Yosef
swore. Then, at the head of the bed, Yisrael bowed.

48 1 Some time later, Yosef was told, "Your father is ill." He brought with him
2 his two sons, Menashe and Efrayim. And when Yaakov was told, "Your son
Yosef has come to see you," Yisrael summoned his strength and sat up in
the bed.

3 Yaakov said to Yosef, "El Shaddai appeared to me in Luz in the land of Canaan.
4 He blessed me and said to me, 'I will make you fruitful and increase your
numbers. I will make you a community of peoples, and I will give this land to
5 your descendants as an everlasting possession.' Now, the two sons who were
born to you in Egypt before I came here shall be considered mine: Efrayim
6 and Menashe will be like Reuven and Shimon to me. Any child born to you
after shall be yours; in any inheritance they will be reckoned under the names
7 of their brothers.[106] For I – as I was returning from Padan, Raḥel died beside
me in Canaan while we were still on the way, a short distance from Efrat.
And I buried her there beside the road to Efrat – that is, Beit Leḥem."

8 Then Yisrael looked at Yosef's sons and said, "Who are these?"

9 Yosef told his father, "They are my sons God has given me here."

10 "Please bring them to me," Yaakov said, "so that I can bless them." Yisrael's
eyes were heavy with age and he could not see. So Yosef brought them
11 close to him, and he kissed and embraced them. Yisrael said to Yosef, "I
never expected to see you again, and now God has shown me your children
as well."

12 Yosef then took them from between his knees and bowed low, his face to
13 the ground. Yosef took both of them, Efrayim on his right to Yisrael's left,
14 and Menashe on his left to Yisrael's right, and brought them close. Yisrael
reached out his right hand and put it on Efrayim's head, even though he
was the younger. And, crossing his hands, he put his left hand on Menashe's
head even though he was the firstborn.

15 He blessed Yosef and said,

---

105 | Sometimes performed in conjunction with an oath (cf. 24:2).

106 | Descendants of Yosef through any other sons would thus be incorporated into the tribes of Efrayim and Menashe.

"God before whom my fathers walked –
Avraham and Yitzḥak –
God who has been my shepherd
all my life to now,
16 the angel who has delivered me from all harm,
may He bless the boys.
Through them may my name be recalled,
and the names of my fathers, Avraham and Yitzḥak.
May they grow to a multitude upon the land."

17 When Yosef saw that his father had placed his right hand on Efrayim's
head, he was displeased. He took hold of his father's hand to move it from
18 Efrayim's head to Menashe's head. Yosef said to his father, "Not so, father.
This is the firstborn. Put your right hand on his head."

19 But his father refused: "I know, my son, I know. He too will be a people,
and he too will become great, but his younger brother will become even
greater, and his descendants will become an abundance of nations."

20 On that day, he blessed them: "By you shall Israel bless,[107] saying:
May God make you like
Efrayim and Menashe."

21 He put Efrayim before Menashe. Then Yisrael said to Yosef, "I am about to
die, but God will be with you and will bring you back to the land of your
22 fathers. And to you I give one portion more than your brothers, which I
took from the Amorites by my sword and my bow."

49 1 Then Yaakov called for his sons and said, "Gather together so that I can
tell you what will happen to you in the days to come.

2 "Assemble and listen, Yaakov's sons.
Listen to your father Yisrael.
3 Reuven, you are my firstborn,
my strength, first fruit of my manhood,
excelling in rank, excelling in power.
4 Unstable as water, you shall not excel,
for you went up onto your father's bed
and defiled it – went up onto my couch.[108]

5 "Shimon and Levi are brothers;
weapons of violence their wares.[109]
6 Let me never join their council,
nor my honor be of their assembly.
For in their anger they killed men;
at their whim they hamstrung oxen.

107 | When the Israelites offer blessings, they will invoke Efrayim and Menashe.

108 | See 35:22.

109 | See 34:25–26.

7 Cursed be their anger, for it is most fierce,
and their fury, for it is most cruel.
I will divide them up in Yaakov,
and scatter them in Israel.[110]

8 "Yehuda, your brothers shall praise you.
Your hand will be on the neck of your foes.
To you will your father's sons bow.[111]
9 Yehuda is a lion's cub.
From the prey, my son, you have risen.
Like a lion he crouches, lies down,
like a lioness; who dares to rouse him?
10 The scepter shall not pass from Yehuda,
nor the staff from between his feet,
so that tribute will come to him
and the homage of nations be his.
11 He tethers his donkey to vines,
to the vine bough his donkey's colt;
he washes his clothes in wine,
his robe in the blood of grapes.[112]
12 His eyes are darker than wine,
and his teeth whiter than milk.[113]
13 "Zevulun will live by the seashore;
he will be a haven for ships.
To Sidon his border will reach.

14 "Yissakhar is a strong-boned donkey,
lying down among the sheep pens.
15 Seeing how good is his resting place,
and how pleasant is the land,
he will bend his shoulder to the load,
and work like a slave in harness.

16 "Dan will seek justice[114] for his people
as one of Israel's tribes.
17 Dan: a snake by the roadside,
a viper upon the path
that bites the horse's heel,
so that its rider falls backward.[115]
18 I wait for Your salvation, LORD.

---

110 | Neither tribe would receive a contiguous portion of territory in the Land of Israel.
111 | The tribe of Yehuda would later give rise to King David and his dynasty.
112 | These images suggest luxuriant wealth.
113 | From the abundance of wine and milk.
114 | The word *yadin* (seek justice) plays on the name Dan.
115 | This image suggests a type of military prowess.

19 "Gad will be raided by raiders,
but he then will raid at their heels.[116]

20 "From Asher will come rich food,
he will proffer the king's delights.

21 "Naftali is a deer set free,
bearing loveliest fawns.

22 "Yosef is a fruitful vine,
a fruitful vine by a spring,
whose branches spread over a wall.
23 Archers attacked him with bitterness,
shot at him, harassed him.
24 But his bow stopped steady,
and his arms held firm
because of the hand of the Mighty One of Yaakov,
the Shepherd, Yisrael's Rock,
25 because of the God of your father who will help you,
because of Shaddai who will bless you
with blessings of heaven above,
blessings of the deep that lies under,
blessings of breast and of womb.
26 May your father's blessing surpass
even the blessings of my forebears –
to the bounds of the everlasting hills.
May they rest on the head of Yosef,
on the brow of the elect of his brothers.

27 "Binyamin is a ravening wolf,
devouring prey in the morning,
and by evening dividing the plunder."

28 All these are the twelve tribes of Israel, and this is what their father said to
29 them when he blessed them, giving each his particular blessing. Then he
gave them instruction, saying, "I am about to be gathered to my people.
30 Bury me with my fathers in the cave in the field of Efron the Hittite, the
cave in the field of Makhpela near Mamre in Canaan, which Avraham
bought, together with the field, from Efron the Hittite as a burial place.[117]
31 There Avraham and his wife Sara are buried, there Yitzḥak and his wife
32 Rivka are buried, and there I buried Leah. The field and the cave in it were
33 bought from the Hittites." There Yaakov finished instructing his sons. And
he drew his feet back onto the bed, breathed his last, and was gathered to
his people.

116| The phrase *gedud yegudenu* (will be raided by raiders) and the word *yagud* (will raid) play on the name Gad.

117| See 23:16–18.

50 1 2 Yosef fell on his father's face and wept over him and kissed him. Then
Yosef instructed his servants the physicians to embalm his father. So the
3 physicians embalmed Yisrael. It took them forty days; that was the time
required for embalming. The Egyptians mourned him for seventy days.

4 When the period of mourning was over, Yosef spoke to Pharaoh's court:
"If I have found favor in your eyes, please speak to Pharaoh on my behalf.
5 Tell him, 'My father made me swear an oath, saying, "I am about to die.
Bury me in the grave I prepared for myself in the land of Canaan." Now let
me go up and bury my father; then I will return.'"

6 Pharaoh said, "Go and bury your father as he had you swear."

7 So Yosef went up to bury his father. With him went all Pharaoh's officials,
8 the elders of his palace, and all the other elders of Egypt, together with
all Yosef's household, his brothers, and his father's household. They left
9 only their children and flocks and herds in Goshen. With them too went
a chariot brigade and horsemen; it was a very large retinue.

10 When they reached the threshing floor of Atad, beyond the Jordan, they
held a great and solemn lamentation, and Yosef observed a seven-day
11 period of mourning for his father. When the Canaanites who lived there
saw the mourning at the threshing floor of Atad they said, "Egypt is in
deep mourning here"; that is why the place beyond the Jordan was called
12 13 Avel Mitzrayim.[118] So his sons did as he had instructed them. They carried
him to Canaan and buried him in the cave of the field of Makhpela, near
Mamre, which Avraham had bought as a burial site from Efron the Hittite.
14 After burying his father, Yosef returned to Egypt together with his brothers
and all those who had accompanied him to his father's burial.

15 When Yosef's brothers knew that their father was dead, they said, "What
if Yosef really hates us and decides to pay us back for all the wrong we
16 did to him?" So they sent word to Yosef saying, "Your father gave these
17 instructions before his death: 'This is what you are to say to Yosef: "Please
forgive the crime and sin of your brothers who inflicted such harm upon
you."' That being so, please forgive the crime of these servants of your
18 father's God." Yosef wept as they spoke to him. Then his brothers came
and threw themselves down before him and said, "We are your slaves."

19 20 But Yosef said to them, "Do not be afraid. Am I in place of God? You
intended to harm me, but God intended it for good, to bring about what
21 is now being done: the saving of many lives. So, do not be afraid. I myself
will provide for you and your children." And he comforted them and spoke
to their hearts.

22 Yosef remained in Egypt together with his father's family, and he lived one
23 hundred and ten years. Yosef saw the third generation of Efrayim's children,

118 | Meaning "mourning of Egypt."

and the children of Menashe's son Makir were also born on Yosef's knees.[119]
24 Yosef said to his brothers, "I am about to die. But God will surely take note
of you and bring you out of this land to the land He promised to Avraham,
25 Yitzḥak, and Yaakov." Then Yosef bound the children of Israel by an oath:
26 "When God takes note of you, carry my bones up from this place." Yosef
died at the age of one hundred and ten. He was embalmed and placed in
a coffin there, in Egypt.

119| That is, they were born during Yosef's lifetime.

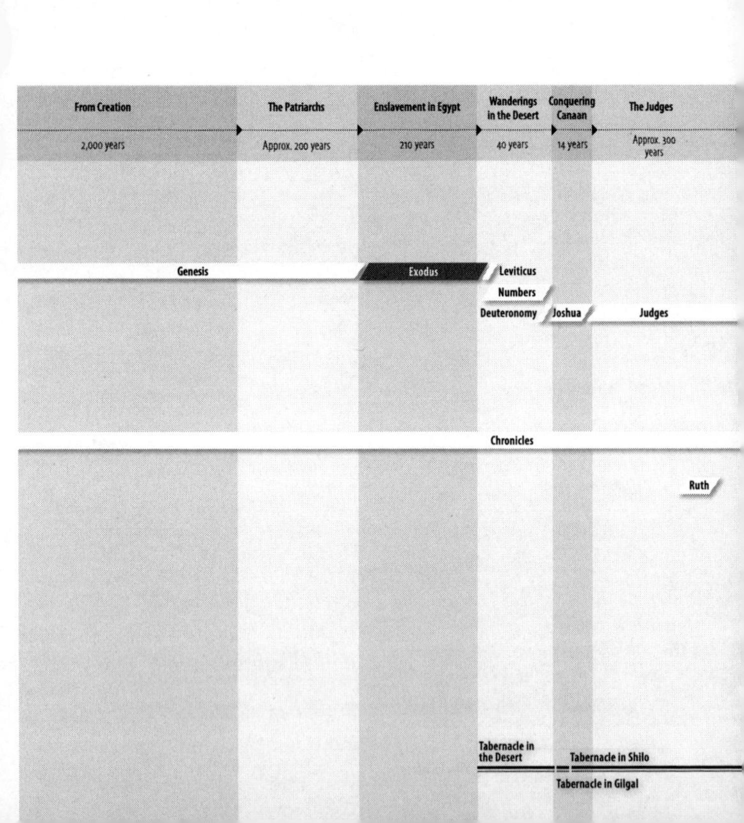

From Creation
2,000 years
The Patriarchs
Approx. 200 years
Enslavement in Egypt
210 years
Wanderings in the Desert
40 years
Conquering Canaan
14 years
The Judges
Approx. 300 years
Genesis
Exodus
Leviticus
Numbers
Deuteronomy
Joshua
Judges
Chronicles
Ruth
Tabernacle in the Desert
Tabernacle in Shilo
Tabernacle in Gilgal

EXODUS/SHEMOT

EXODUS	Suffering in Egypt and the arrival of Moshe	The exodus from Egypt	The assembly at Mount Sinai	The Tabernacle
	Chs. 1–2	3–17	18–24	25–40

1 1 And these are the names of the sons of Yisrael who came to Egypt with SHEMOT
2 Yaakov, each with his household: Reuven, Shimon, Levi and Yehuda;
3 4 Yissakhar, Zevulun and Binyamin; Dan and Naftali; Gad and Asher.
5 The descendants of Yaakov were seventy in all, and Yosef was already in
Egypt.

6 7 Then Yosef died, and all his brothers, and all that generation. But the
Israelites were fruitful and burgeoned; they multiplied and became
exceptionally strong, until the land was filled with them.

8 9 Then a new king arose over Egypt, who had not known Yosef. And he
said to his people, "You see that the Israelite people are many and more
10 powerful than we. Come, let us deal wisely with them in case they increase,
and if war breaks out they may join our enemies and fight against us and
escape from the land."

11 So they placed slave masters over the Israelites to oppress them with forced
12 labor; they built supply cities for Pharaoh: Pitom and Ramesses. But the
more they were oppressed, the more they increased and spread; and the
13 Egyptians came to dread the Israelites. The Egyptians imposed back-
14 breaking labor on the Israelites, embittering their lives with harsh work in
mortar and brick and all field labors; all the work they forced upon them
was intended to break them.

15 Then the king of Egypt said to the midwives of the Hebrews – one named
16 Shifra, the other Puah – "When you help a Hebrew woman give birth,
look on the birth stool. If it is a boy, kill him, and if it is a girl, let her live."
17 But the midwives feared God, and did not do as the king of Egypt ordered
them. They let the babies live.

18 Then the king of Egypt summoned the midwives and demanded, "Why
19 have you done this; why have you let the children live?" But "Hebrew
women," the midwives replied, "are not like Egyptians. They are full of
20 vigor, and have already given birth by the time the midwife arrives." God
was good to the midwives; and the people multiplied and grew very strong.
21 And because the midwives feared God, He granted them households.[1]

22 Then Pharaoh commanded his entire people, saying, "Throw every boy
that is born into the Nile, and let all the girls live."

2 1 2 A man of the house of Levi went and married a daughter of Levi. And she
became pregnant and gave birth to a son. She saw what a fine child he was, and
3 for three months she kept him hidden. And when she could no longer hide
him, she took a papyrus basket and coated it with tar and pitch. She laid the
4 child in it and placed it among the reeds by the bank of the Nile, and his sister
stood by at a distance to see what would happen to him.

1 | As generally understood, this means that they were blessed with progeny.

5 Pharaoh's daughter came down to bathe in the Nile, while her attendants
walked by the riverbank. She saw the basket among the reeds and sent her
6 maid to fetch it. When she opened it she saw him there, the child; the boy was
crying, and she was moved to pity for him: "This must be one of the Hebrew
7 boys." Then his sister asked Pharaoh's daughter, "Shall I go and fetch one of
the Hebrew women to nurse the child for you?"

8 "Go," said Pharaoh's daughter. So the girl went away and called the child's
9 mother. "Take this child," Pharaoh's daughter told her. "Nurse him for me, and
10 I will pay you your wage." So the woman took the child and nursed him. The
child grew, and she brought him to Pharaoh's daughter and he became her son.
She named him Moshe, "because," she said, "I drew him out of the water."[2]

11 One day, when Moshe had grown up, he went out to his people and saw
their forced labor. And he noticed an Egyptian striking a Hebrew: one of his
12 brothers. Looking this way and that and seeing no one, he struck down the
Egyptian and hid his body in the sand.

13 The next day he went out and saw two Hebrews fighting. He asked the guilty
14 one, "Why are you striking your own neighbor?" The man said, "Who made
you a ruler and judge over us? Do you intend to kill me as you killed the
Egyptian?" Then Moshe was afraid. "Surely," he thought, "the thing has
15 become known." Word reached Pharaoh and he sought to kill Moshe. But
Moshe fled his presence and went to live in the land of Midyan. There he sat
down beside a well.

16 The priest of Midyan had seven daughters; they came to draw water and
17 filled the troughs to water their father's flock. Then the shepherds arrived and
started to drive the young women away. But Moshe stood up to defend them,
18 and then watered their flock. When the sisters returned to Reuel their father,
19 he asked them, "How is it that you have come back so quickly today?" They
said, "An Egyptian rescued us from the shepherds. He even drew water for us
20 and watered the flock." "Where is he?" he asked his daughters. "Why did you
leave him there? Invite him in to have something to eat."

21 Moshe accepted an invitation to stay with the man, and he gave Moshe his
22 daughter Tzipora in marriage. She gave birth to a son, and Moshe named him
Gershom, saying, "I have been a stranger in an alien land."[3]

23 Years passed, and the king of Egypt died. The Israelites sighed in their
enslavement and cried out, and from their servitude their plea for help rose
24 up to God. And God heard their groaning, and remembered His covenant
25 with Avraham, with Yitzḥak, and with Yaakov. God saw the Israelites, and
God knew.[4]

---

2 | The name Moshe resonates with *meshitihu* (I drew him out).

3 | The name Gershom resonates with *ger sham* (a stranger there).

4 | God noted their suffering and took it to heart.

3 1 One day Moshe was tending the flock of his father-in-law Yitro, priest
of Midyan. He led the flock to the far side of the wilderness and came
2 to Ḥorev, the mountain of God. Then an angel of the LORD appeared to
him in flames of fire from the midst of a bush – and he saw – the bush was
3 ablaze with fire but was not consumed. Moshe said, "I must turn aside to
see this wonder. Why does the bush not burn up?"

4 The LORD saw that he had turned aside to look, and God called to him
5 from within the bush:[5] "Moshe, Moshe." He answered, "Here I am." Then
God said, "Do not come close. Remove the shoes from your feet, for the
place where you stand is holy ground.

6 "I," He said, "am the God of your father, the God of Avraham, the God
of Yitzḥak, and the God of Yaakov." Then Moshe hid his face, for he was
afraid to look at God.

7 The LORD continued, "I have seen My people's suffering in Egypt; I have
8 heard them cry out amid their oppressors; I know their anguish. So I have
come to rescue them from the hand of the Egyptians and bring them up
from that land to one that is good, spacious, a land flowing with milk and
honey, the place of the Canaanites, Hittites, Amorites, Perizzites, Hivites,
9 and Jebusites. Now the cry of the Israelites has reached Me; I have seen
10 the oppression the Egyptians subject them to. So go: I am sending you to
Pharaoh to bring My people, the Israelites, out of Egypt."

11 But "who am I," said Moshe to God, "to go to Pharaoh, to bring the
Israelites out of Egypt?"

12 God replied, "I will be with you. Proof that I have sent you will come
when, having brought the people out of Egypt, you come to serve God
upon this mountain."

13 Moshe said to God, "When I go to the Israelites and tell them, 'Your
fathers' God has sent me to you,' they will ask me, 'What is His name?'
What shall I say?"

14 God replied to Moshe, "I will be what I will be."[6] He said, "This is what
you shall tell the Israelites: I will be sent me to you."

15 Then God said to Moshe, "You shall say this to the Israelites: The LORD[7]
God of your fathers, the God of Avraham, the God of Yitzḥak, and the God
of Yaakov, has sent me to you. This is My name forever, and this is how I
will be remembered through the ages.

---

5 | When describing divine interaction with a human being, the text may variously refer to an "angel," as in verse 2, or to "God," as in the present verse.

6 | Several other translations are possible, for example, "I am who I am." The name seems to relate to being or eternity.

7 | This is the four-letter name of God (the tetragrammaton), which essentially means "He will be." This name is commonly represented in English by the phrase "the LORD."

16 "Go, gather the elders of Israel and tell them: The LORD God of your fathers
appeared to me – the God of Avraham, Yitzḥak, and Yaakov – saying: I
have taken note of you and I have seen what is being inflicted upon you in
17 Egypt. And I promise to bring you out of the misery of Egypt to the land
of the Canaanites and Hittites, the Amorites and Perizzites, the Hivites
and Jebusites, to a land flowing with milk and honey.

18 "They will listen to you. Then you and the elders of Israel shall go to
the king of Egypt and tell him, 'The LORD God of the Hebrews has
revealed Himself to us. Send us forth now for a three-day journey into
19 the wilderness to sacrifice to the LORD our God.' But I know that even by
20 a mighty hand the king of Egypt would not send you forth. So I will stretch
out My hand and strike Egypt with all the wonders I will do there. After
21 that, he will send you forth. And I will grant this people favor in the eyes
of the Egyptians, so that when you leave, you will not leave empty-handed.
22 Every woman shall ask her neighbor, ask any woman lodging with her, for
objects of silver and gold, and clothing, and you shall put these on your
sons and daughters, and despoil the Egyptians."

4 1 But Moshe replied, "They will not believe me. They will not listen to me.
They will say, 'The LORD has not appeared to you.'"

2 "What is that in your hand?" asked the LORD. "A staff," he replied.

3 "Throw it to the ground." He threw it, and it turned into a snake; and
Moshe fled back from it.

4 The LORD told Moshe, "Reach out your hand and take hold of its tail." He
reached out his hand and grasped it, and in his hand it turned back into
a staff.

5 "This is so that they will believe that the LORD God of their fathers, the
God of Avraham, Yitzḥak, and Yaakov, appeared to you."

6 The LORD spoke to him again: "Put your hand inside your cloak." He put
his hand inside his cloak; when he took it out it was as white as snow.[8]

7 "Put it back inside your cloak," He said. Moshe put his hand back inside
his cloak, and when he took it out the skin color had returned.

8 "If they do not believe you and are not persuaded by the first sign, they
9 will believe the evidence of the second sign. And if they do not believe
either of these signs, and will not listen to you, then take some water from
the Nile and spill it on the ground. The water you take from the Nile will
become blood on the ground."

10 Then Moshe said to the LORD, "Please, my LORD, I am not a man of words;
I was not yesterday, nor the day before, and still I am not since You spoke
to Your servant. I am slow of speech and tongue."

---

8 | The Hebrew denotes a scale disease associated with a white discoloration of the skin.

11 "Who gives man speech?" said the LORD to him. "Who makes people
dumb or deaf? Who gives them sight or blindness? Is it not I, the LORD?
12 Now go. I will help you speak and I will teach you what to say."

13 But "Please, my LORD," he said, "send someone else."

14 Then the LORD's anger blazed against Moshe. "Have you not a brother,
Aharon the Levite? He, I know, is able to speak. Even now he is setting out
15 to meet you, and when he sees you his heart will rejoice. You shall speak
to him and place words in his mouth. I will help you both to speak, and I
16 will teach you what to do. He will speak on your behalf to the people – he
17 will be your voice; and you will be his access to God.[9] Take this staff in
your hand. With it, you shall perform the signs."

18 Moshe left and returned to Yeter his father-in-law. He said to him, "Let me
go back to my brothers in Egypt, to see if they are still alive." Yitro said to
him, "Go in peace."

19 While Moshe was still in Midyan, the LORD said to him, "Go, return to
Egypt. All those who sought your life have died."

20 So Moshe took his wife and sons and put them on a donkey, and he set out
to return to Egypt, taking in his hand the staff of God.

21 The LORD said to Moshe, "When you return to Egypt, see that you perform
for Pharaoh all the wonders I have placed in your power. But still I will
22 strengthen his heart and he will not send the people forth. Tell Pharaoh:
23 This is what the LORD says, 'Israel is My son, My firstborn. I have told you:
Send forth My son, so that he may serve Me. If you refuse to let him go, I
will kill your son, your firstborn.'"

24 At a lodging place on the way, the LORD confronted Moshe and was about
25 to kill him. But Tzipora took a flint knife and cut off her son's foreskin,
throwing it down at his feet, and said, "You are a bridegroom of blood to
26 me." So He let him go. Then "A bridegroom of blood," she said, "because
of circumcision."[10]

27 The LORD said to Aharon, "Go and meet Moshe in the wilderness." And
28 he went and met him at God's mountain, and kissed him. And Moshe told
Aharon all that the LORD had said about his mission, and all the miraculous
signs He had commanded him to perform.

29 30 So Moshe and Aharon went and gathered all the elders of Israel. Aharon
told them everything the LORD had said to Moshe, and he performed the
31 signs before the people. And the people believed. When they heard that
the LORD was watching over the Israelites, and that He had seen their
misery, they bowed their heads and prostrated themselves.

9 | Literally "you will be to him as God," i.e., you will instruct him what to convey. Cf. 7:1.

10 | Tzipora's statements here, as well as their intended address, are cryptic in the Hebrew; interpretations vary.

5 1 After this, Moshe and Aharon came to Pharaoh; they said, "Thus says the
LORD, God of Israel: Send My people forth so that they may hold a festival
2 for Me in the wilderness." But Pharaoh said, "Who is this LORD that I
should obey Him and send Israel forth? I do not know the LORD, and I
will not send Israel forth."

3 "The God of the Hebrews has revealed Himself to us," they said. "Let us
take a three-day journey into the wilderness and sacrifice to the LORD our
God, or He may strike us with the plague or with the sword."

4 The king of Egypt said to them, "Why, Moshe and Aharon, would you take
5 the people from their work? Get back to your labor! Look," said Pharaoh,
"how numerous the people of the land have become; and yet you would
have them rest from their labors."

6 7 That day, Pharaoh gave orders to the people's taskmasters and foremen:
"Do not give the people straw for bricks as before. Let them go and gather
8 their own straw. But require them to make the same quota of bricks as
before. Do not reduce it. They are lazy. That is why they are crying out,
9 'Send us forth to sacrifice to our God.' Make the work harder for the people;
and make sure they do it instead of listening to lies."

10 So the taskmasters and foremen went out and told the people, "This is what
11 Pharaoh says: I will no longer give you straw. You must go and get your
own straw wherever you can find it. Your production must not fall short
12 of what it was." So the people spread out all over Egypt to collect stubble
13 for straw. The taskmasters kept pressuring them, saying, "Complete your
14 daily work quota just as when there was straw." And the Israelite foremen
whom Pharaoh's slave drivers had appointed were flogged. "Why have you
not fulfilled your quota of bricks," they were asked, "either yesterday or
today as you did before?"

15 The Israelite foremen came and protested to Pharaoh, "Why are you
16 treating your servants like this? Your servants are given no straw, yet they
17 tell us, 'Make bricks!' We are being flogged for your people's failing." But he
said, "Lazy, that is what you are – lazy! That is why you keep saying, 'Send
18 us forth to sacrifice to the LORD.' Now go. Get to work. Straw will not be
given you, and you must complete your count of bricks."

19 When the Israelite foremen saw that they were not to reduce each day's
20 quota, they knew that harm was coming to them. Leaving Pharaoh, they met
21 Moshe and Aharon, who stood awaiting them. They said to them, "May the
LORD look on you and judge, because you have made us repellent in the eyes
of Pharaoh and his officials; you have put a sword in their hands to kill us."

22 Then Moshe returned to the LORD and said, "Why, LORD, have You
23 brought harm to this people? Is this why You sent me? Ever since I came
to Pharaoh to speak in Your name, he has dealt worse with this people;
and You have done nothing to deliver Your people."

6 1 But the Lord said to Moshe, "Now you are about to see what I will do to
Pharaoh. By a mighty hand he will send them forth, and by a mighty hand
he will drive them from his land."

2 3 Then God spoke to Moshe. "I am the Lord," He said to him. "As El Shaddai VAERA
I appeared to Avraham, Yitzḥak, and Yaakov – but by My name the Lord[11]
4 I did not make Myself known to them. And I made a covenant with them
to give them the land of Canaan, the land where they lived as strangers.
5 And now, I have heard the groaning of the Israelites whom the Egyptians
6 are holding as slaves, and I remember My covenant. Therefore, say to the
Israelites: I am the Lord, and I will free you from the forced labor of the
Egyptians, I will rescue you from slavery. I will liberate you with an arm
7 stretched forth and with great acts of judgment. I will take you as My
people and I will be your God. Then you will know that I am the Lord
8 your God, freeing you from Egyptian forced labor. And I will bring you
to the land that I promised to give to Avraham, Yitzḥak, and Yaakov; to
9 you I will give it as a possession. I am the Lord." Moshe told this to the
Israelites, but in the brokenness of their spirit and the brutal labor they
did not listen to him.

10 11 Then the Lord said to Moshe, "Go, tell Pharaoh, king of Egypt, to send the
12 Israelites forth from his land." But Moshe said to the Lord, "The Israelites,
You see, have not listened to me. How then will Pharaoh listen? And I am
a man of uncircumcised lips."[12]

13 The Lord spoke to Moshe and Aharon; and He charged them with regard
to the Israelites and to Pharaoh, king of Egypt, to bring the Israelites out
of the land of Egypt.

14 These were the heads of their ancestral houses. The sons of Reuven,
Yisrael's firstborn, were Ḥanokh, Palu, Ḥetzron, and Karmi; these were
15 the families of Reuven. Shimon's sons were Yemuel, Yamin, Ohad, Yakhin,
Tzoḥar, and Sha'ul, son of a Canaanite woman; these are the families of
16 Shimon. These are the names of Levi's sons by their lineage: Gershon,
17 Kehat, and Merari. Levi lived one hundred thirty-seven years. The sons of
18 Gershon were Livni and Shimi, by their families. The sons of Kehat were
Amram, Yitzhar, Ḥevron, and Uziel. Kehat lived one hundred thirty-three
19 years. The sons of Merari were Maḥli and Mushi. These are the families of
the Levites by their lineage.

20 Amram married Yokheved, his father's sister, who bore him Aharon and
21 Moshe. Amram lived one hundred thirty-seven years. The sons of Yitzhar
22 were Koraḥ, Nefeg, and Zikhri. The sons of Uziel were Mishael, Eltzafan,
23 and Sitri. Aharon married Elisheva, daughter of Aminadav and sister of
24 Naḥshon, and she bore him Nadav and Avihu, Elazar and Itamar. The sons of

---

11 | See note on 3:15.

12 | This seems to denote some difficulty in speaking; cf. 4:10.

Koraḥ were Asir, Elkana, and Aviasaf; these are the families of the Korahites.
25 Elazar, Aharon's son, married one of the daughters of Putiel, and she bore
him Pinḥas. These were the heads of the Levite clans by their families.

26 These were the Aharon and Moshe to whom the LORD said, "Bring the
27 Israelites out of Egypt, by their battalions." It was they who spoke up to
Pharaoh, king of Egypt, to bring the Israelites out of Egypt – this same
28 Moshe and Aharon. So it came to pass on the day the LORD spoke to
Moshe in Egypt.

29 The LORD said to Moshe, "I am the LORD. Tell Pharaoh, king of Egypt, all
30 that I am telling you." But Moshe replied to the LORD, "You know that I
have uncircumcised lips.[13] How then will Pharaoh listen to me?"

7 1 Then the LORD said to Moshe, "I am making you now like a god to Pharaoh,
2 and your brother Aharon will be your prophet.[14] All that I command you,
you are to speak, and your brother Aharon to convey to Pharaoh, that he
3 send the Israelites forth from his land. But I will harden Pharaoh's heart
4 and multiply My signs and wonders in the land of Egypt. Still Pharaoh
will not listen to you. Then I will set My hand against Egypt and, with
great acts of judgment, bring My battalions, My people the Israelites, forth
5 out of the land of Egypt. When I stretch out My hand against Egypt and
bring the Israelites out from among them, the Egyptians will know that
6 I am the LORD." Moshe and Aharon did so; they did exactly as the LORD
7 commanded them. Moshe was eighty years old, and Aharon eighty-three,
when they spoke to Pharaoh.

8 9 Then the LORD said to Moshe, and to Aharon, "When Pharaoh says to
you, 'Perform a miracle,' tell Aharon: Take your staff and throw it down
10 before Pharaoh and it will become a crocodile." So Moshe and Aharon
went to Pharaoh and did just as the LORD had commanded. Aharon
threw down his staff before Pharaoh and his officials, and it became a
11 snake. Pharaoh then summoned his sages and sorcerers, and the Egyptian
12 magicians did the same thing by their sorcery. Each threw down his staff,
13 and they became snakes – but Aharon's staff swallowed up theirs. Pharaoh,
nonetheless, was obstinate, and he would not listen to them, just as the
LORD had predicted.

14 Then the LORD said to Moshe, "Pharaoh's heart is unyielding. He refuses to
15 send the people forth. So go to Pharaoh in the morning as he goes out to
the water. Place yourself by the bank of the Nile where you will encounter
16 him, taking in your hand the staff that turned into a snake. Say to him: The
LORD, God of the Hebrews, has sent me to tell you: Send My people forth,
so that they may serve Me in the wilderness. So far, you have not listened.
17 This is what the LORD says: This will make it known to you that I am the
LORD. With the staff in my hand I will strike the water in the Nile and it

13 | See note on verse 22.

14 | See note on 4:16.

18 will become blood. The fish in the Nile will die; the Nile will stink and
19 the Egyptians will be unable to drink its water." Then the LORD said to
Moshe, "Tell Aharon: Take your staff and stretch out your hand over the
waters of Egypt, their rivers, canals, ponds, and reservoirs, and they will
turn into blood. There will be blood throughout Egypt, even inside vessels
of wood and of stone."

20 Moshe and Aharon did just as the LORD commanded. Aharon raised his
staff, in full view of Pharaoh and his officials, and struck the water of the
21 Nile, and all the Nile's water turned into blood. The Nile fish died, and the
river stank so that the Egyptians could not drink its water. Throughout the
22 land of Egypt, blood appeared. But the Egyptian magicians did the same
thing by their sorcery. So Pharaoh's heart remained adamant, and he would
not listen to them, just as the LORD had predicted.

23 Pharaoh turned and went back into his palace and did not take even this to
24 heart. The Egyptians all dug along the Nile to get drinking water, unable
25 to drink of the waters of the Nile. And seven days went by after the LORD's
striking of the Nile.

26 Then the LORD said to Moshe, "Go to Pharaoh and say to him: This is
what the LORD says: Send My people forth, so that they may serve Me.
27 And if you should refuse to send them forth – I will scourge your land
28 with frogs from end to end. The Nile will teem with frogs. They will come
up into your palace, into your bedroom and up onto your bed, into the
houses of your officials and of all your people, into your ovens and your
29 kneading pans. The frogs shall climb up onto you and your people and all
your officials."

8 1 The LORD said to Moshe, "Speak to Aharon: Stretch out your hand that
holds your staff over the rivers, the canals, and the pools, and cause frogs
2 to climb up and out onto the land of Egypt." So Aharon stretched out
his hand over the waters of Egypt, and frogs climbed up and covered the
3 Egyptian land. But the magicians used their sorcery and did the same,
making frogs climb up over the land of Egypt.

4 Then Pharaoh called for Moshe and Aharon and said, "Pray to the LORD
to take the frogs away from me and from my people, and I will send your
people forth to sacrifice to the LORD."

5 Moshe said to Pharaoh, "Gloat over me:[15] you name the time when I
should pray that the frogs be removed, for you and your officials, and your
people, from you and your homes, remaining only in the Nile."

6 "Tomorrow," he replied. Moshe said, "It will be as you say. Then you will
7 know that there is none like the LORD our God. The frogs will depart from

---

15 | Interpretations of the phrase vary. According to this rendering, Moshe challenges Pharaoh to set a time when God would be unable to stop the plague. Should the plague persist then, Pharaoh would be able to "gloat."

you and from your homes, your officials, all your people. They will only
remain in the Nile."

8 Moshe and Aharon departed Pharaoh's presence, and Moshe cried out to
9 the Lord about the frogs He had brought upon Pharaoh. The Lord did as
10 Moshe said, and the frogs in the houses, courtyards, and fields died; they
gathered them up into heaping piles, and the stench filled the whole land.
11 But when Pharaoh saw that respite had come, he hardened his heart and
would not listen, just as the Lord had predicted.

12 Then the Lord said to Moshe, "Tell Aharon: Extend your staff and strike
the dust of the earth; all over Egypt it will be transformed into lice."

13 They did so. Aharon extended the hand that held his staff and struck the
dust of the earth, and suddenly there were lice on the people, on the
animals. The dust of the earth was turned to lice all across Egypt.

14 The magicians tried to produce lice with their sorcery, but they could
15 not. Meanwhile the lice still infested people and animals alike. "This," the
magicians told Pharaoh, "is the finger of God." But Pharaoh's heart was
toughened, and – as the Lord had predicted – he would not listen to
them.

16 Then the Lord said to Moshe, "Rise up early in the morning and confront
Pharaoh as he goes out to the water; tell him: This is what the Lord says:
17 Send My people forth, so that they may serve Me. If you refuse to send
them forth, I will send swarms of insects[16] onto you, your officials, your
people, and your houses. The Egyptians' houses will be filled with swarms
of insects; the ground they stand upon will be covered by them.

18 "On that day, I will set the land of Goshen, where My people live, apart –
there, there will be no swarms – and then you will know that I am the
19 Lord, here on earth. Between My people and yours I will mark out a
separation; tomorrow, this sign will come to be."

20 The Lord did so. Great swarms of insects infested Pharaoh's palace and
the houses of his officials. All across Egypt, swarms of insects devastated
the land.

21 Pharaoh called for Moshe and Aharon. "Go," he said, "and sacrifice to your
God here in the land."

22 But Moshe replied, "That would not be right for us to do; our sacrifice
to the Lord our God is an abomination to the Egyptians. If, before the
Egyptians' eyes, we offer the sacrifice they consider an abomination, will
23 they not stone us to death?[17] Send us forth, three days' journey into the

16 | Alternatively "wild animals."

17 | The sense seems to be that sheep, goats, and cattle were sacred to the Egyptians, and it would have offended them to witness the Israelites slaughtering them for their own rites.

wilderness, to sacrifice there to the Lord our God, as He will instruct us."

24 Pharaoh said, "I will send you forth; you shall sacrifice to the Lord your God in the wilderness. Just do not go far away. Pray for me."

25 Moshe said, "I am going to leave you and pray to the Lord. Tomorrow, the swarms of insects will move on from Pharaoh, his officials, and his people. But let Pharaoh no more deceive us, refusing to send the people forth to make their sacrifice to the Lord."

26 27 Moshe left Pharaoh and prayed to the Lord. And the Lord did what Moshe asked. He diverted the swarms of insects from Pharaoh, his officials, his people – not one was left behind.

28 But this time too, Pharaoh hardened his heart and did not send the people forth.

9 1 Then the Lord said to Moshe, "Go to Pharaoh. Tell him: This is what the
2 Lord, God of the Hebrews, says: Send My people forth to serve Me. If you
3 refuse to send them forth, if you continue to hold them back, the Lord's
hand will turn against your livestock in the field. A deadly epidemic will
4 strike horses, donkeys, and camels, cattle and flocks. But the Lord will
set Israel's livestock apart from Egypt's; none belonging to the Israelites
5 will die. The Lord has set His appointed time; tomorrow the Lord will
6 bring this about in the land." And the next day, the Lord brought it to be.
All the livestock of the Egyptians perished, but of the Israelites' livestock,
7 not one creature died. Pharaoh investigated the matter and discovered
that not one among Israel's livestock had died. But still Pharaoh's heart
remained hard, and he would not send the people forth.

8 Then the Lord said to Moshe and Aharon, "Take a handful of soot from
9 a furnace and throw it up in the air before Pharaoh's eyes. It will become a
cloud of dust over all the land of Egypt, and on people and animals it will
become a rash, breaking out into boils on people and animals throughout
10 the land of Egypt." So they took soot from the furnace and stood before
Pharaoh. Moshe threw it up in the air, and it became a rash that broke into
11 boils on people and animals. The magicians could not stand before Moshe
because of their boils; for the boils had affected them as they had the rest of
12 the Egyptians. But the Lord strengthened Pharaoh's heart, and he would
not listen to them, just as the Lord had told Moshe.

13 Then the Lord said to Moshe, "Rise up early in the morning and confront
Pharaoh. Tell him: This is what the Lord, God of the Hebrews, says:
14 Send My people forth to serve Me, or this time I will set the full force
of My plagues upon you, your officials, and your people so that you will
15 know that there is none like Me in all the world. By now I could have
stretched out My hand and struck you and your people with an epidemic
16 that would have wiped you off the face of the earth. But I have let you

survive for this purpose – to show you My power, and to have My name
17 known throughout the land. You are still abusing your power over My
18 people, refusing to let them go. And so this time tomorrow I will bring a
hailstorm on Egypt heavier than any it has suffered, from the day Egypt
19 was established until now. Give an order now to bring in your livestock
and all else you have in the field. Anyone or any animal in the open, any
20 not brought under shelter, will die when the hail beats down." Those of
Pharaoh's officials who feared the Lord's word hurried to bring in their
21 slaves and livestock. And those who set no stock in the Lord's word kept
their slaves and livestock where they were in the fields.

22 The Lord said to Moshe, "Reach your hand out to the sky, that hail may
fall on all the land of Egypt, on the people and the animals and everything
23 growing in Egypt's fields." Moshe raised his staff toward the sky; the Lord
sent thunderclaps and hail. Fire struck the ground, and the Lord rained
24 down hail on the land of Egypt. The hail, with fire blazing inside it, battered
so hard that there had been nothing like it anywhere in Egypt since it first
25 became a nation. The hail struck everything in the open field throughout
all Egypt: people, animals, and everything growing in the fields, and it
26 smashed asunder every tree. Only in Goshen, where the Israelites lived,
no hail fell.

27 Then Pharaoh sent for Moshe and Aharon and said to them, "This time I
28 have sinned. The Lord is in the right, and I and my people are guilty. Pray
to the Lord. Enough of God's thunder and hail – I will send you forth.
You need not wait any longer."

29 Moshe said to him, "As I leave the city, I will spread out my hands to the
Lord. The thunder will stop and there will be no more hail. You will then
30 know that the world belongs to the Lord. But I know that you and your
officials still do not hold the Lord God in awe."

31 By then the flax and barley had been destroyed, because the barley was
32 ripe and the flax in bud. But the wheat and emmer had not been destroyed,
33 because they ripen later. Moshe left Pharaoh and the city and spread out
his hands to the Lord. The thunder and hail stopped; the rain did not
34 pound the earth anymore. But when Pharaoh saw that the rain, hail, and
thunder had stopped, he once more turned to sinfulness. He hardened
35 his heart; his officials likewise. Pharaoh's heart was strengthened and
he refused to send the Israelites forth, just as the Lord had predicted at
Moshe's hand.

BO 10 1 Then the Lord said to Moshe, "Go to Pharaoh. I have hardened his heart
2 and his officials', that I may display these My signs before him, and so that
you may tell your children and grandchildren how I made the Egyptians
a laughingstock by the signs I revealed among them; and know that I am
the Lord."

3 Moshe and Aharon came to Pharaoh and said to him, "Thus says the
LORD, God of the Hebrews: How much longer will you refuse to submit
4 to Me? Send My people forth to serve Me. For if you refuse to send My
5 people forth, tomorrow I bring locusts to your land. They will cover the
landscape so that you will not be able to see the ground. They will eat what
little remains after the hail, including all the trees that grow up from your
6 soil. They will fill your palaces, your officials' houses, and all the houses of
Egypt. Your parents and grandparents never saw anything like this, from
the day they arrived upon this earth until today." Then Moshe turned and
left Pharaoh.

7 Pharaoh's officials then said to him, "How long must we leave this man to
ensnare us? Send the people forth to serve the LORD their God. Do you
not yet know that Egypt is being destroyed?"

8 Moshe and Aharon were summoned back to Pharaoh, and he said to them,
9 "Go and serve the LORD your God. Who exactly will be going?" "With our
youths and our elderly folk we will go," said Moshe, "with our sons and
our daughters, our sheep and our cattle, we all must go, for it will be our
festival of the LORD."

10 He replied, "The LORD be with you if I let you and your children go!
11 Look – evil is staring you in the face.[18] No! Let the men go and serve the
LORD. That is what you are asking for." Then Pharaoh had Moshe and
Aharon expelled from his presence.

12 The LORD said to Moshe, "Reach out your hand over Egypt so that locusts
swarm over the land and eat everything growing there, all that is left after
13 the hail." So Moshe stretched out his staff over Egypt, and the LORD
caused an east wind to blow across the land all that day and night. By
14 morning, the east wind had brought the locusts. They invaded all of Egypt
and settled throughout its land in a dense swarm. Never before had there
15 been such a plague of locusts, nor will there ever be again. They covered
all the landscape until the ground was black. They ate all that was left after
the hail: all the plants and all the fruit. Nothing green remained on trees
or plants throughout all Egypt.

16 In haste, Pharaoh summoned Moshe and Aharon and said, "I have sinned
17 against the LORD your God and you. Forgive my sin now, one more time.
Pray to the LORD your God to take this death away from me."

18 19 Moshe left Pharaoh's presence and prayed to the LORD. And the LORD
turned the wind, westerly and very strong, and lifted the locusts and swept
them into the Sea of Reeds.[19] Not one locust remained anywhere in Egypt.

18 | Explanations of this verse vary widely. According to this rendering, which is close to the original Hebrew, Pharaoh's words are defiant and threatening.

19 | The popular translation "Red Sea" is now regarded as incorrect.

20 But the LORD strengthened Pharaoh's heart and he would not send the
Israelites forth.

21 Then the LORD said to Moshe, "Reach out your hand toward the sky to
bring darkness down over Egypt – darkness so deep it can be felt."

22 Moshe reached out his hand toward the sky, and all across Egypt it was
23 pitch dark for three days. For three days, no one could see anyone else or
even move. But in the Israelites' homes, they had light.

24 Then Pharaoh summoned Moshe and said, "Go, serve the LORD. Just leave
your flocks and herds. Your children may go with you."

25 "Then give us sacrifices and burnt offerings to present to the LORD our
26 God," said Moshe. "Our livestock must go with us. Not a hoof can be left
behind. We must take them to serve the LORD our God, for until we arrive,
we will not know what we must use to serve the LORD."

27 But the LORD strengthened Pharaoh's heart, and he would not agree to
28 send the people forth. "Leave my presence," said Pharaoh. "Take care never
to see my face again, because on the day you do, that day you will die!"
29 Moshe replied, "As you say: I will not see your face again."

11 1 Then the LORD said to Moshe, "One last plague will I send against Pharaoh,
against Egypt. After that, he will send you forth from here, and when he
2 does, he will drive you out completely. Now tell the people, men and
women, to ask of their neighbors articles of silver and of gold."

3 The LORD granted the people favor in the eyes of the Egyptians. And the
man Moshe, too, was held in high regard in the land of Egypt, among both
Pharaoh's officials and the people.

4 Moshe said, "This is what the LORD says: Around midnight I will move
5 throughout Egypt, and every firstborn son in Egypt will die, from
Pharaoh's firstborn presiding on his throne to the firstborn of the slave
6 girl at her hand mill; the firstborn of the cattle as well. A scream will ring
out across Egypt, unlike any that has been before, or any that will be again.
7 But among the Israelites not a dog will bare its tongue at man or beast.[20]
8 Then you will know that the LORD is setting Israel apart from Egypt. And
all these officials of yours will come and bow down to me, saying, 'Leave,
you and all the people behind you.' After that, I will leave." He turned and
left Pharaoh, blazing with anger.

9 The LORD said to Moshe, "Pharaoh will not listen to you, that My wonders
may be multiplied in Egypt."

10 Moshe and Aharon had produced all these wonders before Pharaoh, but
the LORD strengthened Pharaoh's heart, and he did not let the Israelites
leave his land.

20 | The Israelites will not face any threat of harm.

12 1 Then the LORD spoke to Moshe and Aharon in the land of Egypt. He said,
2 "This month shall be to you the beginning of months; the opening of the
3 year, this month will be for you.[21] Speak to the entire community of Israel
and say: On the tenth of this month each man must take a lamb for his
4 family; one for every household. If the household is too small for a lamb,
let him and a close neighbor take a lamb together, to suit the number of
people involved; they shall be counted for the lamb in proportion to their
5 eating. A one-year-old male shall you take, flawless, from among the sheep
6 or goats. You shall guard it until the fourteenth day of this month. And
7 then, in the afternoon, all the community of Israel shall slaughter it. They
shall then take some of the blood and put it on the two sides and top of the
8 doorframes of the houses where they are to eat the lamb. They shall eat the
meat that night, roasted over a fire; with unleavened bread and bitter herbs
9 they shall eat it. Do not eat it raw or boiled in water; it must be roasted
10 over fire with its head, its legs, and its inner parts. Do not leave any of it
11 until morning; any left over until morning you shall burn with fire. This is
how you shall eat it: your belt secured, the sandals on your feet, your staff
in your hand. Eat it in haste. It is the LORD's Passover.[22]

12 "I will pass through the land of Egypt that night, and will kill every
firstborn in Egypt, man and beast. Against all the gods of Egypt I will
13 execute judgments. I am the LORD. The blood will be your sign on the
houses where you are. I will see the blood and I will pass over you.[23] No
deadly plague will touch you when I strike the land of Egypt.

14 "This day will become a memorial for you; you will celebrate it as a festival
to the LORD for all generations, a celebration that will be an everlasting
15 law. For seven days you shall eat unleavened bread. By the first day you
shall have removed leaven from your houses, for the soul of anyone who
eats leavened bread from the first day to the seventh will be severed from
Israel.[24]

16 "The first day shall be a sacred assembly and the seventh day shall be a
sacred assembly. On them no work may be done but preparing the food
17 for everyone to eat. That alone may you do. Safeguard the unleavened
bread,[25] because on this very day I will have brought your battalions out
of Egypt. You shall observe this day for all generations; it is an everlasting
18 law. From the fourteenth day of the first month in the evening until the
twenty-first day of the month in the evening, you may eat only unleavened
19 bread. During these seven days, leaven must not be found in your houses.

21 | The month in question – Nisan on the later Jewish calendar – coincides with the early part of spring. See note on 13:4.

22 | Cf. verse 13: "I will pass over you."

23 | Others translate "I will protect you." Cf. Isaiah 31:5.

24 | This punishment appears frequently in the Torah and is interpreted in various ways. According to this rendering, God warns of a spiritual dissolution.

25 | That is, ensure that it does not become leavened, or more generally, scrupulously observe the commandment.

Anyone, whether newcomer or native born, who eats leavened food will
20 have his soul severed from the community of Israel. Eat nothing leavened.
Wherever you may live, you shall eat unleavened bread."

21 Then Moshe called together all the elders of Israel and instructed them,
"Each select or acquire one of the flock for yourselves, for your families
22 and slaughter the Passover sacrifice. Take a bunch of hyssop, dip it in the
blood in the bowl, and put some of the blood on the top and two sides
of the doorframe. None of you shall leave by the doors of your houses
23 until morning. When the Lord passes through to strike Egypt and sees
the blood on the top and sides of a doorframe, He will pass over that
doorway and will not let the destroyer enter your houses to strike you
24 down. Keep this as a law for you and for your children forever. When
25 you enter the land the Lord will give you as He has promised, you shall
26 keep this ceremony. And when your children say to you, 'What does this
27 ceremony mean to you?' you shall say, 'It is the Passover sacrifice to the
Lord who passed over the houses of the Israelites in Egypt, for He struck
the Egyptians; but our homes, He spared.'" Then the people bowed down
28 and prostrated themselves. The Israelites proceeded to do exactly as the
Lord had commanded Moshe and Aharon.

29 It happened at midnight: the Lord struck down all the firstborn in Egypt,
from the firstborn of Pharaoh, presiding on his throne, to the firstborn of
30 the prison captives, and all the firstborn cattle. Pharaoh arose that night, he
and all his officials and all Egypt – for a great scream rang out across Egypt,
31 for there was no house without its dead. That night, Pharaoh summoned
Moshe and Aharon and said, "Get up, get out from among my people, you
32 and the Israelites. Go. Serve the Lord exactly as you requested; take your
sheep and cattle also, just as you said. Just go. But bless me too."

33 The Egyptians too urged the people to make haste and leave the land. "All
34 of us will die," they said. The people took their dough before it could rise,
carrying it on their shoulders in kneading pans wrapped in their clothing.
35 As Moshe had told them, the Israelites had requested items of silver and
36 gold, and clothing, of the Egyptians, and the Lord had given the people
favor in the eyes of the Egyptians and they had granted their request. Thus
they despoiled Egypt.

37 The Israelites traveled from Ramesses to Sukkot. There were about six
38 hundred thousand men on foot, quite apart from the children. And a
great variety of other people went up with them, as well as large droves of
39 livestock, flocks and cattle. With the dough they had brought from Egypt,
they baked cakes of unleavened bread, not risen. They had been driven out
of Egypt and could not delay, and had prepared no other provisions.

40 The Israelites had lived in Egypt for four hundred thirty years. At the end
41 of four hundred thirty years, to the very day, all the Lord's battalions left
42 Egypt. All that night, the Lord watched over them to bring them out of

Egypt; and still this night is kept as one of watchfulness for the LORD[26]
throughout the generations of Israel.

43 The LORD said to Moshe and Aharon, "This is the law of the Passover
44 sacrifice. No foreigner may eat of it. But any slave who has been acquired
45 for money and circumcised may eat it. No gentile resident or hired laborer
46 may eat of it. It should be eaten in a single house; bring none of the meat
47 outside the house. Do not break any of its bones. All the community of
Israel shall observe this.

48 "If a stranger lives among you and wishes to offer a Passover sacrifice to
the LORD, every male in his household must be circumcised. Then he may
join in observing it and be like a native born. But no uncircumcised man
49 may eat of it. There shall be one and the same law for the native born and
the stranger who lives among you."

50 All the Israelites did exactly as the LORD had commanded Moshe and
51 Aharon. And on that very day the LORD brought the Israelites out of Egypt
in their battalions.

13 1 The LORD said to Moshe, "Consecrate every firstborn to Me. Man and
2 beast, the first to emerge from every womb among the Israelites is Mine."

3 Moshe said to the people, "Remember this day, the day you left Egypt, the
house of slaves, when with a mighty hand the LORD rescued you from here.
4 No leaven may be eaten. Today, in the month of Aviv,[27] you are leaving.
5 And when the LORD brings you into the land of the Canaanites, Hittites,
Amorites, Hivites, and Jebusites, the land that He promised your ancestors
He would give you – one flowing with milk and with honey – you shall
keep this ceremony in this month.

6 "For seven days you shall eat unleavened bread; the seventh day shall be
7 a festival to the LORD. Unleavened bread shall be eaten for those seven
8 days; no bread or leavening shall be seen in all your land. On that day you
must tell your child, 'This is because of what the LORD did for me when I
9 left Egypt.' It shall be a sign on your arm, a reminder between your eyes,[28]
so that the LORD's teaching be on your tongue, for with a mighty hand
10 the LORD brought you out of Egypt. Celebrate this law each year at its
set time.

11 "When the LORD brings you to the land of the Canaanites, as He promised
12 you and your ancestors, and He gives it to you,you shall give over to the
LORD the first to emerge from every womb. Every male firstborn of your

---

26 | Meaning watchful observance of the prescribed ritual. Alternatively, "watchfulness *by* the LORD," i.e., a night of special divine protection.

27 | In early spring, when certain crops begin to form – equivalent to Nisan on the later Jewish calendar. *Aviv* literally means kernels of ripening grain.

28 | An idiom meaning something constantly remembered. Traditionally it is understood as a reference to tefillin, which are worn on the arm and just above the forehead.

13 animals shall be His. You shall redeem every firstborn donkey with a lamb;
otherwise, you must break the donkey's neck. You must redeem every
firstborn among your sons.

14 "And in the future, when your children ask, 'What is this?' you shall answer,
'With a mighty hand the Lord brought us out of Egypt, the house of
15 slaves. And when Pharaoh was obstinate and refused to set us free, the
Lord killed all the firstborn sons in Egypt, man and beast alike. That is
why I sacrifice every male firstborn animal to the Lord, and redeem all
my firstborn sons.'

16 "It shall be a sign on your arm and an emblem between your eyes – with
a mighty hand the Lord rescued us from Egypt."

BESHALAḤ 17 When Pharaoh let the people go, God did not lead them through the land
of the Philistines, though it was the shorter way. "If the people face war,"
18 thought God, "they will change their minds and go back to Egypt." So He
led them on a roundabout course, by way of the wilderness, to the Sea of
19 Reeds.[29] The Israelites left Egypt armed for battle. And Moshe took with
him the remains of Yosef, who had bound the Israelites by oath: "When
God comes to your aid, bring my remains with you out of here."

20 They set out from Sukkot and camped at Etam, at the edge of the desert.
21 The Lord went ahead of them by day in a column of cloud to guide them,
and at night in a column of fire to give them light, so that they might travel
22 day and night. Neither the column of cloud by day nor that of fire by night
once departed from the people.

14 1 2 Then the Lord said to Moshe, "Speak to the Israelites and tell them to
turn back and camp in front of Pi HaḤirot, between Migdol and the sea,
3 before Baal Tzefon. Encamp facing it, by the sea. Pharaoh will think that
4 the Israelites are lost across the land, that they are trapped in the desert. I
will toughen Pharaoh's heart, and he will pursue them. I will be glorified
over Pharaoh and all his force, and the Egyptians will know that I am the
Lord."

And so they did.

5 When the king of Egypt was told that the Israelites had escaped, he and
his officials changed their minds about the people: "What have we done,
releasing the Israelites from serving us?"

6 7 So the king harnessed his chariot and brought out his army. He took six
hundred elite chariots and all the other chariots of Egypt, with officers
8 over them all. The Lord strengthened the heart of Pharaoh, king of Egypt,
9 and he pursued the Israelites, who were leaving in defiance of them. The
Egyptians, with all the king's horses and chariots, cavalry and infantry,

29 | See note on 10:19.

chased and caught up with them as they were encamped by the sea near
Pi HaḤirot, before Baal Tzefon.

10 Pharaoh drew near – the Israelites looked up: there were the Egyptians
thundering after them. They were terrified and cried to the LORD for help.
11 "Were there no graves in Egypt?" they asked Moshe. "Is that why you
brought us here to die in the desert? What have you done to us, bringing
12 us out of Egypt? Did we not tell you in Egypt: Leave us alone – let us
serve the Egyptians. Better a life in servitude to Egypt than death in the
desert."

13 But Moshe told the people, "Fear not. Stand firm and see the deliverance
the LORD will bring you today. The Egyptians you see today, you shall
14 never see again. The LORD will fight for you. You stay silent."

15 The LORD said to Moshe, "Why are you crying out to Me? Speak to the
16 Israelites; have them move forward. Raise your staff, stretch out your hand
over the sea and divide it, and the Israelites will walk through the sea on
17 dry land. I will strengthen the Egyptians' hearts and they will go after them.
Then will My glory bear down hard upon Pharaoh and his entire army, his
18 chariots and cavalry. And when My glory bears down upon Pharaoh, his
chariots and cavalry, the Egyptians will know that I am the LORD."

19 Then the angel of God who had been traveling ahead of the Israelite camp
moved and went behind them, and the column of cloud moved from in
20 front of them to their rear. It came between the Egyptian and Israelite
camps, as cloud and darkness for one, but lighting the night for the other,
keeping the two apart all night.

21 Then Moshe stretched out his hand over the sea, and the LORD drove the
sea back by a strong east wind all night, turning it to dry land and dividing
22 the waters. So the Israelites walked through the sea on dry land. To their
right and left, the water was like a wall.

23 The Egyptians chased after them. All Pharaoh's horses, chariots, and
24 cavalry followed them into the sea. During the last watch of the night,[30]
the LORD looked down at the Egyptian army from a column of fire and
25 cloud and threw them into a panic, clogging their chariot wheels so that
it was hard for them to move. The Egyptians said, "Let us flee from the
Israelites. The LORD is fighting for them against Egypt."

26 Then the LORD said to Moshe, "Stretch out your hand over the sea. The
waters will flow back over the Egyptians and their chariots and cavalry."
27 Moshe stretched out his hand over the sea, and at daybreak the water came
back in full force. The Egyptians fled at its approach but the LORD swept
28 them into the sea. The waters returned, covering the chariots, the cavalry,
and the whole Egyptian army that had followed the Israelites into the sea.

30 | The night was divided into three sections, each one called a watch.

29 Not one of them remained. But the Israelites had walked through the sea
on dry land, with a wall of water to their right and left.

30 That day, the Lord saved the Israelites from the Egyptians. And when
31 the Israelites saw the Egyptians dead on the seashore, and witnessed
the wondrous power the Lord had unleashed against the Egyptians, the
people were in awe of the Lord, and they believed in Him and in Moshe
His servant.

15 1 And then, Moshe and the Israelites sang this song to the Lord:

I will sing to the Lord, for He has triumphed in glory;
horse and horseman He hurled into the sea.
2 The Lord is my strength and song –
and now my salvation.
This is my God, I will glorify Him,
my father's God, I will exalt Him.
3 The Lord is a Master of war;
the Lord is His name.
4 Pharaoh's chariots and army
He hurled into the sea;
the best of his officers
drowned in the Sea of Reeds.
5 The deep waters covered them;
they sank to the depths like a stone.
6 Your right hand, Lord, majestic in power,
Your right hand, Lord, shatters the enemy.
7 In the greatness of Your majesty, You overthrew those who rose against You.
You sent forth Your rage; it consumed them like stubble.
8 By the blast of Your nostrils the waters heaped;
the surge stood upright as a wall;
the deeps congealed at the heart of the sea.
9 The enemy said, "I will give chase, will overtake,
I will divide the spoils.
My desire shall gorge its fill of them.
I will draw my sword,
and my hand destroy them."
10 You blew with Your wind; the sea covered over them.
They sank like lead in mighty waters.
11 Who is like You, Lord, among the mighty?
Who is like You – majestic in holiness,
awesome in glory, working wonders?
12 You reached out Your right hand –
the earth swallowed them up.
13 In Your love, You guided out the people You redeemed.
In Your strength, You led them to Your holy abode.

14 Nations heard and they trembled;
terror seized the Philistines.
15 The chiefs of Edom were dismayed, then,
Moav's leaders were seized with trembling,
the people of Canaan melted away.
16 Dread, terror fell upon them;
by Your arm's power they were stilled as stone –
until Your people crossed, LORD,
until the people You acquired crossed over.
17 You will bring them, You will plant them on the mountain, Your heritage –
the place, LORD, that You made for Your dwelling,
the Sanctuary, LORD, that Your hands established.
18 The LORD will reign for ever and all time.

19 This they sang when Pharaoh's horses, chariots, and cavalry had gone into the sea
and the LORD had brought the waters of the sea back over them
while the Israelites had walked on dry land through the sea.
20 Then Miriam, the prophetess, sister of Aharon, took a tambourine in her
21 hand, and all the women followed her with tambourines and dance. And
Miriam led them in song:
Sing to the LORD, for He has triumphed in glory;
horse and horseman He hurled into the sea.

22 Moshe then led the Israelites from the Sea of Reeds out into the desert
of Shur. For three days, they journeyed across the desert without finding
23 water. Eventually they came to Mara, but they could not drink the water
24 there because it was bitter; because of this it was named Mara.[31] The people
railed against Moshe – "What are we to drink?"

25 Moshe cried out to the LORD. And the LORD showed him a piece of wood,
which he threw into the water – and the water became sweet.

It was there that the LORD gave His people decree and law; it was there
26 that He put them to the test.[32] He said, "If you listen faithfully to the
voice of the LORD your God, doing what is right in His eyes, heeding His
commands and keeping His decrees, I will not bring on you any of the
sicknesses I brought on the Egyptians, for I am the LORD – your Healer."

27 And then they arrived at Eilim, where there were twelve springs and
seventy date palms. They encamped there by the water.

16 1 They set out from Eilim, and on the fifteenth day of the second month after
leaving Egypt, the congregation of Israel all arrived at the desert of Sin,

31 | *Mara* means "bitter."

32 | This "test" apparently refers to the challenge that follows. Opinions vary regarding the "decree and law" – a phrase that the text does not clarify.

2 between Eilim and Sinai. In the desert, all the community started railing
3 against Moshe and Aharon. The Israelites said to them, "If only we had
died by the LORD's hand in Egypt, when we sat by the fleshpots and ate
our fill of bread. Instead, you have brought us out into this desert to kill
the entire assembly by starvation."

4 Then the LORD said to Moshe, "I am going to rain down bread from heaven.
Let the people go out and gather enough for each day; I will test them to
5 see whether they will follow My law or not. On the sixth day, they will
have to prepare what they bring in. It will be twice as much as they gather
on all other days."

6 So Moshe and Aharon told all the Israelites, "At evening you will know that
7 it was the LORD who brought you out of Egypt, and by morning you shall
see the LORD's glory, for He has heard you railing against Him. As for us,
8 what are we that you rail against us?" Then Moshe said, "In the evening,
the LORD will give you meat to eat, and in the morning bread to fill you,
for He has heard you railing against Him. We – what are we? It is not us
you rail against, but the LORD."

9 Then Moshe said to Aharon, "Tell all the community of Israel to come
10 before the LORD, because He has heard your railing." As soon as Aharon
had spoken to the whole community of Israel, they looked toward the
desert – and the glory of the LORD appeared in the midst of cloud.

11 12 The LORD spoke to Moshe and said, "I have heard the Israelites' railing.
Tell them: At twilight you shall eat meat, and in the morning your fill of
bread. Then you will know that I am the LORD your God."

13 That evening a flock of quail flew in and covered the camp; next morning
14 a layer of dew surrounded the camp. When the dew covering lifted, fine
15 flakes covered the floor of the desert like fine frost on the ground. When
the Israelites saw it, they asked one another, "What[33] is it?" for they did not
recognize it. Moshe said to them, "This is the bread the LORD has given
16 you to eat. This is what the LORD has instructed: Each of you gather as
much as you need, an omer[34] for every person; each take enough for all
17 the people in your tent." The people of Israel did so. Some gathered more,
18 others less. But when they measured it with an omer measure, those who
had gathered much had none left over, and those who gathered but little
19 did not fall short. All had gathered as much as they could eat. "Let no
20 one leave any over for the morning," said Moshe; but they did not listen
to Moshe. Some of them left part of it till morning, and it became worm
21 infested and stank. Moshe was enraged with them. Every morning they
gathered it, all as much as they could eat, and when the sun grew hot, it
melted away.

---

33 | Hebrew *man*; cf. verse 31: "The House of Israel named it *man* (manna)."

34 | A solid measure somewhat larger than the equivalent of two liters or half a gallon.

22 When the sixth day came, they gathered a double portion, two omer each.
23 All the leaders of the community came and reported this to Moshe. "This,"
he told them, "is what the LORD has said: Tomorrow is a day of rest, a holy
Sabbath to the LORD. Bake now what you need to bake and cook what you
24 need to cook. Whatever is left, keep carefully aside for the morning." So
they put it aside until the morning, as Moshe had instructed them, and
25 it did not stink, nor did worms infest it. And Moshe said, "Today, eat
this, for today is a Sabbath to the LORD; today you will not find it on the
26 ground. Six days shall you gather it, but on the seventh day, the Sabbath,
it will not be there."

27 Some people did go out to gather it on the seventh day; but they found
none.

28 Then the LORD said to Moshe, "How long will you refuse to keep My
29 commandments and laws? Understand that the LORD has given you a
Sabbath – that is why He gave you two days' bread on the sixth day. You
shall each rest where you are: let no man depart from where he is on the
30 seventh day." So the people rested on the seventh day.

31 The House of Israel named it manna.[35] It looked like white coriander
32 seeds, and tasted like wafers made with honey. Moshe said, "This is what
the LORD commands: Let an omer of it be kept carefully aside for your
descendants, that they may see the bread I fed you in the desert when I
33 brought you out of Egypt." Moshe said to Aharon, "Take an urn, put an
omer of manna in it, and place it before the LORD to be kept for future
34 generations." As the LORD commanded Moshe, so Aharon placed it before
35 the Ark of Testimony[36] to be kept with care. The Israelites ate manna for
forty years, until they came to the land where they could settle down.
36 They ate the manna until they came to the border of Canaan. An omer is
a tenth of an ephah.[37]

17 1 All the community of Israel moved on after that from the desert of Sin,
traveling from place to place as the LORD guided them, and they camped
2 at Refidim, but there was no water there for the people to drink. The people
started to wrangle with Moshe. "Give us water to drink," they raged. "Why do
3 you wrangle with me?" asked Moshe. "Why are you testing the LORD?" But
the people were thirsty for water. They railed against Moshe, "Why did you
bring us out of Egypt? Was it to kill me, my children, and all my livestock by
thirst?"

4 "What shall I do with this people?" Moshe cried to the LORD. "Another
5 moment and they will stone me." The LORD answered Moshe, "Walk out to
face the people taking some of the elders of Israel with you. Take the staff with

35 | See note on verse 15.

36 | Literally "before the Testimony." See 25:22, 32:15. It would seem that Aharon performed this action only after the construction of the Ark.

37 | See note on verse 16.

6 which you struck the Nile in your hand, and go. I will be there before you by
the rock at Ḥorev. Strike the rock; water will come out of it and the people
will drink." And that is what Moshe did, before the eyes of the elders of Israel.
7 He named the place Masa and Meriva, because the people had quarreled[38]
and had tested[39] the LORD, demanding, "Is the LORD among us or not?"

8
9 Then, at Refidim, Amalek came and attacked Israel. Moshe said to
Yehoshua, "Choose men for us, and go out and do battle against Amalek.
Tomorrow I will stand on top of the hill with the staff of God in my hand."
10 Yehoshua fought the Amalekites as Moshe had directed him, while Moshe,
11 Aharon, and Ḥur climbed to the top of the hill. Whenever Moshe held
his hand high, the Israelites prevailed, but whenever he let his hand drop,
12 the Amalekites prevailed. But Moshe's hands grew heavy. So they took a
stone and placed it under him and he sat, while Aharon and Ḥur held up
13 his hands, one on each side, so that his hands held true until sunset. And
Yehoshua overcame Amalek and his people by the sword.

14 Then the LORD said to Moshe, "Write this as a memorial on a scroll, and
commit it to Yehoshua's ears: I will erase the memory of Amalek, utterly,
15 from under the heavens." Moshe built an altar and named it "The LORD Is
16 My Banner," saying, "There is a hand on the LORD's throne.[40] The LORD
will be at war with Amalek throughout the ages."

YITRO 18 1 Moshe's father-in-law Yitro, priest of Midyan, heard about all that God
had done for Moshe and for His people Israel when the LORD brought
2 Israel out of Egypt. Yitro had received Moshe's wife Tzipora after he had
3 sent her home, together with her two sons. One was named Gershom, for
4 Moshe had said, "I have been a stranger in a foreign land,"[41] and the other,
Eliezer, for he had said, "My father's God has helped me, saving me from
Pharaoh's sword."[42]

5 And now Moshe's father-in-law Yitro came to Moshe in the desert, bringing
his sons and his wife, to where he was encamped by the mountain of
6 God. Yitro sent word to Moshe, "I am coming to you – your father-in-law
Yitro – together with your wife and both of your sons."

7 Moshe went out to greet his father-in-law and bowed down and kissed
him. Each asked after the other's welfare, and they went inside the tent.
8 And Moshe told his father-in-law all that the LORD had done to Pharaoh
and the Egyptians, for Israel's sake, all the hardship they had encountered
9 along the way, and how the LORD had rescued them. Yitro delighted in all

38 | *Meriva* means "quarrel."

39 | *Masa* means "test."

40 | Interpretations of this proclamation vary. Many commentaries understand the image of a raised hand as symbolizing an oath; cf. Genesis 24:2; Deuteronomy 32:40.

41 | See note on 2:22.

42 | *Eliezer* literally means "God has helped."

the good that the LORD had done for Israel, in His liberating them from
10 the Egyptians, and said, "Blessed be the LORD who has rescued you from
Egypt and Pharaoh and liberated the people from the Egyptians' hands.
11 Now I know that the LORD is greater than all gods – for He brought upon
12 them what they schemed against others." Then Yitro brought a burnt
offering and sacrifices to God. And Aharon and all the elders of Israel came
to break bread with Moshe's father-in-law before God.

13 The next day Moshe sat to serve the people as judge. From morning to
14 evening the people stood before him. When Moshe's father-in-law saw
everything Moshe did for the people, he asked, "What is this that you do
for the people? Why do you sit alone while all the people stand over you
from morning to evening?"

15 16 "The people come to me to inquire of God," Moshe replied. "When they
have a dispute, they come to me and I judge between one neighbor and
another, and I make God's laws and teachings known."

17 18 Moshe's father-in-law said to him, "What you are doing is not good. You
will be worn away, and this people along with you. It is too heavy a burden
19 for you. You cannot carry it alone. Now listen to me, let me advise you; and
may God be with you. You speak for the people before God, and bring their
20 concerns to Him. And you must acquaint them with His precepts and laws,
and make known to them the path they are to walk and the way they must
21 act. You, as well, must seek out among the people capable men – God-
fearing, trustworthy men, who despise corruption; and appoint them over
22 the people as leaders of thousands, hundreds, fifties, and tens. Have them
serve as daily judges for the people; let them bring the major cases to you,
but judge the minor ones themselves. In this way they will lighten your
23 load, and bear it together with you. If you do this, and God so commands,
then you will endure, and all these people will be able to go home in
peace."

24 25 Moshe listened to his father-in-law and did all that he said. Moshe chose
capable men from all Israel and made them chiefs over the people, leaders
26 of thousands, hundreds, fifties, and tens. They judged the people every
day. Any major case they brought to Moshe, but they decided every minor
27 matter themselves. Then Moshe parted from his father-in-law, and the
latter went forth, back to his own land.

19 1 On the first day of the third month after the Israelites had left Egypt they
2 came to the Sinai Desert. Setting out from Refidim they had arrived at the
Sinai Desert, encamping in the wilderness, and there Israel camped, facing
3 the mountain, while Moshe went up to God.

And the LORD called to him from the mountain: "This is what you shall
4 say to the House of Yaakov, what you shall tell the people of Israel: You
yourselves have seen what I did to the Egyptians: how I lifted you up

5 on eagles' wings and brought you to Me. Now, if you faithfully heed
My voice and keep My covenant, you will be My treasure among all the
6 peoples, although the whole earth is Mine. A kingdom of priests and a
holy nation you shall be to Me. These are the words you must speak to
the Israelites."

7 So Moshe came and summoned the elders of the people, and set before
8 them all that the LORD had commanded him. And the people answered
as one – "All that the LORD has spoken we will do." Moshe brought their
9 answer back to the LORD. Then the LORD said to Moshe, "I will come to
you in a dense cloud, that the people may hear Me speaking to you. They
will then believe you forever."

10 When Moshe reported the words of the people to the LORD, the LORD
said to Moshe, "Go to the people and consecrate them today and tomor-
11 row; let them wash their clothes and be ready for the third day, for on
that third day the LORD will descend on Mount Sinai before all the
12 peoples' eyes. Set a boundary for the people around the mountain; tell
them to take care not to ascend to it, nor even touch its edge. Anyone
13 who touches the mountain must be put to death. No hand shall touch
him: he shall be stoned or shot with arrows; beast or man, he shall not
live. When the ram's horn sounds a long blast – only then may they go
up on the mountain."

14 So Moshe came down from the mountain to the people; he consecrated
15 them and they cleansed their clothes. "Be ready for the third day," he told
them, "and do not draw close to your wives."

16 The third day came; and that morning there was thunder and lightning and
a dense cloud on the mountain and the sound of a ram's horn, intensely
17 loud, and all the people in the camp shook. Then Moshe led the people
out of the camp to meet God, and they stood at the foot of the mountain.
18 Mount Sinai was enveloped in smoke because the LORD had descended
on it in fire. Smoke billowed up from it as if from a furnace, and the
19 mountain shook violently as one. As the sound of the ram's horn grew
20 louder and louder, Moshe spoke and God answered him aloud. And the
LORD descended on Mount Sinai, to the top of the mountain, and called
Moshe to the mountaintop, and Moshe ascended.

21 The LORD told Moshe, "Go back down – warn the people not to force
22 their way through to look at the LORD, or many will die. Even priests who
come near to the LORD must first consecrate themselves, or the LORD will
23 break out against them." Moshe replied to the LORD, "The people cannot
climb Mount Sinai. You Yourself warned us to set a boundary around the
24 mountain and consecrate it." The LORD said to him, "Go down, and come
back together with Aharon. But do not let the priests or people force their
way through to come up to the LORD, or He will break out against them."
25 So Moshe went down to the people and told them.

20 1 Then God spoke all these words:
2 "I am the LORD your God who brought you out of the land of Egypt, out
of the house of slaves.
3 Have no other gods than Me.
4 Do not make for yourself any carved image or likeness of any creature in
the heavens above or the earth beneath or the water beneath the earth.
5 Do not bow down to them or worship them, for I the LORD your God
demand absolute loyalty. For those who hate Me, I hold the descendants
6 to account for the sins of the fathers to the third and fourth generation, but
to those who love Me and keep My commands – I shall act with faithful
love for thousands.
7 Do not speak the name of the LORD your God in vain, for the LORD will
not hold guiltless those who speak His name in vain.
8 9 Remember the Sabbath to keep it holy. Six days you shall work, and carry
10 out all your labors, but the seventh is a Sabbath to the LORD your God.
On it, do no work – neither you, nor your son or daughter, your male or
11 female servant, your livestock, or the migrant within your gates. For in six
days the LORD made heaven and earth, the sea, and all that they contain,
and He rested on the seventh day. And so the LORD blessed the Sabbath
day and made it holy.
12 Honor your father and mother. Then you will live long in the land that the
LORD your God is giving you.
13 Do not murder.
Do not commit adultery.
Do not steal.
Do not bear false witness against your neighbor.
14 Do not crave your neighbor's house. Do not crave your neighbor's wife,
his male or female servant, his ox, his donkey, or anything else that is your
neighbor's."

15 Every one of the people witnessed the thunder and lightning and the
sound of the ram's horn and the smoke-covered mountain; they saw and
16 they shook – and they stood at a distance, and said to Moshe, "Speak to us
yourself and we will listen, but let not God say any more to us, or we will
17 die." "Do not be afraid," said Moshe to the people, "God has come to lift
you up, so that the awe of Him will be with you always, keeping you from
18 sin." But the people remained at a distance while Moshe approached the
thick darkness where God was.

19 Then the LORD said to Moshe, "This is what you shall tell the Israelites: You
20 yourselves have seen that I, from the heavens, have spoken to you. Have
no others alongside Me; make yourselves no silver gods, no golden gods.
21 Make for Me an altar of earth and on that sacrifice your burnt offerings and
peace offerings, your sheep and your cattle. Wherever I cause My name to
22 be invoked, I will come to you and I will bless you. If you make Me an altar
of stones, do not build it of hewn stone, for in wielding a sword upon it,

23 you profane it. Do not ascend to My altar with steps, for your nakedness
must not be exposed on it.[43]

MISHPATIM

21 1 2 "And these are the laws that you shall set before them. If you buy a Hebrew
slave, he shall serve for six years, but in the seventh he shall go forth free,
3 without paying anything. If he came alone, he shall leave alone. But if he
4 was a married man, his wife shall leave with him. If his master gave him a
wife and she bore him sons or daughters, the woman and her children shall
5 remain her master's, while he shall leave alone. But if the slave declares, 'I
6 love my master, my wife, and my children; I do not want to go free,' then
his master shall bring him before the judges. He shall take him to the door
or to the doorpost and pierce his ear with an awl; after that he shall then
remain his slave forever.

7 "If a man sells his daughter as a maidservant, she does not go free in the
8 usual way of slaves. If her master, who intended to wed her, finds that he
dislikes her, he must let her be redeemed. He has no right to sell her to
9 foreigners, because he has broken faith with her. If he intends her for his
10 son, he shall grant her all the rights of a daughter. If he marries another
woman alongside her, he shall not reduce her food, her clothing, or marital
11 rights. If he fails her in any of these three things, she shall go forth free
without paying anything.

12 13 "One person who strikes another so that he dies shall be put to death. If
he did not lie in wait to harm him, but it came about by an act of God – I
am setting apart a place where he may find refuge.[44]

14 "But if someone schemes against another and kills him by stealth, you shall
take him even from My altar[45] and he shall die.

15 "One who wounds his father or mother shall be put to death.

16 "One who kidnaps a person shall be put to death, whether the victim has
been sold or found in his possession.

17 "One who curses his father or mother shall be put to death.

18 "If two people fight and one strikes another with a stone or with his fist – if
19 the victim does not die but is confined to bed, and afterward he gets up
and walks outdoors even leaning on a cane, the assailant is absolved, but
he must pay for the victim's loss of time and provide for his cure.

20 "If a man strikes his slave, male or female, with a rod and the slave dies
21 there and then, the death shall be avenged. But if the slave survives a day,
two days – since the money lost is the master's, the death shall not be
avenged.

---

43 | Most Israelites wore only loose clothing, and spreading the feet apart could expose one's genitalia.

44 | That is, from a vengeful relative of the victim.

45 | The altar was considered a place of sanctuary; cf. I Kings 1:51, 2:28.

22 "If two men fight and one of them hits a pregnant woman, and she
miscarries but suffers no irreparable injury herself, the offender must be
23 fined, as the woman's husband demands and as the judges rule. But if she
24 suffers an irreparable injury, he must compensate life for life, eye for eye,
25 tooth for tooth, hand for hand, foot for foot, burn for burn, wound for
wound, bruise for bruise.[46]

26 "If a man should strike the eye of his slave, male or female, and maim it,
27 he must send the slave out free on account of his eye. If he knocks out
the tooth of his slave, male or female, he must send the slave out free on
account of his tooth.

28 "If an ox gores a man or a woman to death, the ox shall be stoned, and its
29 flesh not eaten, but the owner of the ox shall not be liable. But if the ox has
already gored in the past, and its owner was warned but failed to guard it,
and it kills a man or a woman, the ox shall be stoned, and its owner also
30 shall be put to death. If a ransom is imposed on his life, then he shall pay
31 whatever is imposed on him and redeem his life. This rule also applies if
32 the ox gores a minor son or daughter, but if the ox gores a slave, male or
female, the owner shall give thirty shekels of silver to the master, and the
ox must be stoned.

33 "If a man uncovers a hole or digs one and fails to cover it, and an ox or a
34 donkey falls into it, the one responsible for the pit shall make restitution.
He shall give its owner its full value, and the dead animal shall be his.

35 "If one man's ox injures another's so that it dies, they shall sell the live ox
36 and share the money. The dead animal they shall also share. If, however,
it is known that the ox had gored in the past, and still the owner failed to
guard it, he shall pay an ox for an ox, and the dead animal shall be his.

37 "If a man steals an ox or a sheep and kills it or sells it, he shall pay five oxen
for an ox, four sheep for a sheep.

22 1 "If a burglar is caught tunneling in, and is struck and killed, there is no
2 bloodguilt on his account.[47] But if the sun has risen on him, there is
bloodguilt on his account. A thief must make restitution; if he lacks
3 the means, he shall be sold as a slave to repay his debt. If what he
stole – an ox, ass, or sheep – is found alive in his possession, he shall pay
double.

4 "If a person lets a field or vineyard be damaged, either by letting his
livestock loose or by letting them graze in someone else's field, he must
repay the best of his field or vineyard.

---

46 | According to rabbinic interpretation (Bava Kama 83b), the punishments in verses 24–25 are monetary.

47 | That is, one who kills him is not culpable for murder, because the thief poses a mortal threat.

5 "If a fire is started and spreads to thorns, so that grain is destroyed, stacked
or standing or growing in the field, the person who started the fire must
redress the damage.

6 "If one person entrusts another with money or goods, and they are stolen
7 from his house, then if the thief is found he must pay double. If the thief
is not found, then the owner of the house must swear before the court
8 that he has not laid hands on his neighbor's goods himself. In every case
of betrayal of trust, whether concerning an ox, donkey or sheep, clothing,
or any loss that one can point to and say, 'This is it,' – both parties' claims
shall be brought to the court. The one the court finds guilty shall pay the
other double.

9 "If one person entrusts another with a donkey, ox, sheep, or any animal,
10 for safekeeping, and it dies or is injured or is carried away unseen, an oath
before the LORD shall settle between them; if the second man swears that
he did not lay his hands on his charge, then the owner must accept this,
11 and no restitution need be made. But if the charge was stolen from him,
12 he must make restitution to the owner. If it was torn by a wild animal and
the second man brings the remains as evidence, he need not make good
the loss.

13 "If one person borrows a creature from his neighbor, and it is injured or
14 dies while the owner is not there, he must make restitution. But if the
owner was present, he need not make restitution; if the animal was hired,
only the hiring fee is due.

15 "If a man seduces a virgin who is not betrothed, and lies with her, he must
16 pay her bride price and marry her. If her father refuses to let him marry
her, he must still pay out the full bride price for virgins.

17 18 "Do not allow a witch to live. And any person who lies with an animal
shall be put to death.

19 "Whoever sacrifices to any other deity shall be utterly destroyed.

20 "Do not oppress a stranger or exploit him, for you yourselves were
strangers in the land of Egypt.

21 22 "Do not abuse a widow or an orphan. For if you do abuse them, if they cry
23 out to Me, I will unquestionably heed their cry. My anger will flare and I
will kill you by the sword – and then your wives will be widows and your
children orphans.

24 "If you lend money to one of My people who is poor, do not act with
25 him as a harsh creditor, and do not charge him interest. If you take your
neighbor's garment as collateral, return it to him before the sun sets,
26 because it is his only clothing, the sole covering for his skin. What else
does he have in which to sleep? And if he cries out to Me, I will be listening:
I am gracious.

27 “Do not curse a judge, and do not deride a leader of your people. Do not
28 delay offerings from your harvest of grain or wine. The firstborn of your
29 sons you must give to Me.[48] Likewise with your oxen and sheep; let them
stay with their mothers for seven days, and on the eighth, give them over
30 to Me. You are to be My holy people. Do not eat flesh torn by beasts in
the wild. Throw it to the dogs.

23 1 “Do not accept a false report. Do not join with an unscrupulous person to
2 bear corrupt witness. Do not follow the crowd to do evil. When you give
testimony in a lawsuit, do not pervert justice by siding with the crowd.
3 Do not show favoritism even to a poor man in a dispute.

4 “If you come across your enemy’s ox or donkey going astray – bring it back
5 to him. If you see the donkey of someone who hates you, fallen under its
load, resist the impulse to leave it there. Help him to release it.

6 “Do not subvert the rights of the needy when they come to court. Keep
7 far from a false charge. Do not bring death on the innocent and righteous,
8 for I will not acquit the wrongdoer. Take no bribe, for bribes blind the
sighted and subvert the cause of the just.

9 “Do not oppress a stranger. You know what it is to be a stranger, for you
yourselves were strangers in the land of Egypt.

10 “For six years, sow your land and gather its crops, but in the seventh let
11 it rest and lie fallow. Let the needy of your people eat from it, and what
they leave, let the wild animals eat. Do the same with your vineyards and
olive groves.

12 “For six days carry out your work, but on the seventh you must cease, so
that your ox and donkey may rest, and even the children of maidservants
and strangers be revived.

13 “Take care in all that I have said to you. Never invoke the names of other
gods; let them never pass your lips.

14 “Three times a year, celebrate a festival for Me. Keep the Festival of
15 Unleavened Bread. For seven days, eat unleavened bread as I commanded
you, at the time appointed, in the month of Aviv,[49] for at that time you
16 left Egypt. Do not appear before Me empty-handed. Likewise, keep the
Festival of the Harvest, of the first fruits of the produce that you sowed in
the field.[50] Keep the Festival of Ingathering at the end of the year, when
17 you gather in the fruit of your labor from the field.[51] Three times a year, all
the males among you shall appear before the Master, the Lord.

48 | Meaning redeem them from the priest; see 13:13.

49 | See note on 13:4.

50 | The Festival of Shavuot; cf. 34:22.

51 | The Festival of Sukkot; cf. Leviticus 23:33–43.

18 "Do not offer the blood of My sacrifice together with anything leavened.
19 Do not let the fat of My festive offering remain until morning. Bring the
best first fruits of your land to the House of the LORD your God. Do not
boil a kid in the milk of its mother.

20 "I am sending a messenger ahead of you to guard you on the way and to
21 bring you to the place that I have prepared. Heed his presence and listen
to his voice. Do not rebel against him, for he will not let your transgression
22 pass, because My name is with him. But if you listen carefully to him and
do all that I tell you, then I will be an enemy to your enemies, a foe to
your foes.

23 "When My messenger goes ahead of you and brings you to the Amorites,
Hittites, Perizzites, Canaanites, Hivites, and Jebusites, and I wipe them
24 out, do not bow down to their gods or worship them, and do not do as
25 they do. Demolish their gods and shatter their worship pillars. Serve the
LORD your God, and He will bless your bread, your water. I will banish all
sickness from your midst.

26 "No woman in your land will suffer miscarriage or barrenness. I will fill out
27 the full measure of your years. I will send My terror before you, throwing
into panic all the people you come upon. All you will see of your enemies
28 will be their fleeing backs. I will send hornets ahead of you, and they will
29 drive the Hivites, Canaanites, and Hittites out before you. I will not drive
them out in a single year, lest the land become desolate and the wild
30 animals too numerous for you. No – little by little I will drive them out
31 before you, as you burgeon and come to take possession of the land. I will
set your borders from the Sea of Reeds to the Sea of the Philistines, and
from the wilderness to the Euphrates, for I will deliver the inhabitants of
32 the land into your hands: you will drive them out before you. Make no
33 covenant with them and their gods. They must not stay in your land, for
they would make you sin against Me. If you worship their gods, it will be
a trap for you."

24 1 Then He said to Moshe, "Ascend to the LORD, you and Aharon, Nadav and
2 Avihu, and seventy of Israel's elders and bow down from afar. Moshe alone
shall approach the LORD. The others must not come close, nor shall the
people come up with him."

3 Moshe came and told the people all the LORD's words and laws, and the
people all responded with one voice, "All that the LORD has spoken we
4 shall do." Then Moshe wrote down all the LORD's words. Early the next
morning he rose and built an altar at the base of the mountain, and also
5 twelve pillars for the twelve tribes of Israel. Then he sent young men of
Israel, and they sacrificed bulls as burnt offerings and peace offerings to
6 the LORD. Moshe took half the blood and put it in bowls. The other half he
7 sprinkled on the altar. Then he took the book of the covenant and read it

aloud to the people. They replied, "All that the Lord has spoken we shall
do and we shall heed."

8 Then Moshe took the blood, sprinkled it on the people, and said, "This
is the blood of the covenant that the Lord is making with you regarding
all these words."

9 Then Moshe went up with Aharon, Nadav, Avihu, and seventy of Israel's
10 elders. They saw a vision of the God of Israel, and beneath His feet what
11 looked like a lapis lazuli pavement as clear as the sky itself. And He did
the leaders of Israel no harm – and they looked upon God and they ate
and they drank.

12 The Lord said to Moshe, "Ascend to Me on the mountain, and as
you stand there I will give you the stone tablets with the teaching and
commandments that I have written to instruct the people."

13 So Moshe set out with Yehoshua, his disciple, and ascended the mountain
14 of God. He told the elders, "Wait for us here until we return to you. Aharon
and Ḥur will stay here with you; whoever has a dispute shall go to them."
15 16 As Moshe climbed the mountain, it was covered in a cloud. The glory of the
Lord rested on Mount Sinai, and the cloud covered it for six days. On the
17 seventh, He called to Moshe from within the cloud. To the Israelites the
appearance of the Lord's glory on the mountaintop was like consuming
18 fire. Moshe entered the cloud and climbed the mountain, and he stayed
there for forty days and forty nights.

25 1 2 The Lord spoke to Moshe, saying, "Tell the Israelites to take an offering TERUMA
3 for Me; take My offering from all whose heart moves them to give. These
4 are the offerings you shall receive from them: gold, silver and bronze; sky-
5 blue, purple, and scarlet wool; linen and goats' hair; rams' hides dyed red
6 and fine leather;[52] acacia wood; oil for the lamps; spices for the anointing
7 oil and the fragrant incense; and rock crystal together with other precious
stones for the ephod[53] and breast piece.

8 9 "They shall make Me a Sanctuary and I will dwell in their midst. Form
the Tabernacle and form all of its furnishings following the patterns that
I show you.

10 "Make an Ark of acacia wood, two and a half cubits long, a cubit and a half
11 wide, and a cubit and a half high. Overlay it with pure gold, inside and out,
12 and around it make a gold rim. Cast four gold rings for it and place them
13 on its four corners, two rings on one side and two on the other. Make
14 staves of acacia wood and overlay them with gold; place these staves in

52 | Literally "*taḥash* hides." The term has been interpreted as referring to some sort of rare animal or to a way of processing leather.

53 | An apron-like garment.

15 the rings on the sides of the Ark so that the Ark may be carried. The staves
16 must stay in the rings of the Ark; they must not be removed. Inside the
17 Ark, place the tablets of the Covenant that I will give you. Make an Ark
cover of pure gold, two and a half cubits long and a cubit and a half wide.
18 Make two cherubim[54] of beaten gold and place them at the two ends of
19 the cover: one cherub at one end and one at the other; the cherubim shall
20 be made of one piece with the cover. These cherubim should have wings
spread upward, sheltering the cover. They should face one another, and
21 look toward the cover. Place the cover on top of the Ark, and inside the Ark
22 place the tablets of the Covenant that I will give you. There, from above
the cover, between the two cherubim, above the Ark of the Testimony, I
will meet with you and speak with you, and give you all My commands
to the Israelites.

23 "Make a table of acacia wood, two cubits long, a cubit wide, and a cubit
24 and a half high. Overlay it with pure gold and around it make a gold rim.
25 Make a frame a handbreadth wide all around, and around the frame also
26 make a gold rim. Make for it four gold rings, and place the rings on the
27 four corners where the four legs are. The rings should be attached next to
28 the frame as holders for staves to carry the table. Make the staves of acacia
29 wood and overlay them with gold; by these the table shall be carried. You
must also make, out of pure gold, its bowls, spoons, pitchers, and jars for
30 pouring libations. On this table the showbread must be placed before Me
at all times.

31 "Make a candelabrum of pure gold. Its base and shaft, cups, knobs, and
32 flowers shall be hammered from a single piece. Six branches shall extend
33 from its sides, three on one side, three on the other. On each branch there
shall be three finely crafted cups, each with a knob and a flower. All six
34 branches extending from the candelabrum shall be like this. The shaft of
the candelabrum shall have four finely crafted cups, each with a knob and
35 a flower. For the six branches that extend from the candelabrum, there
36 must be a knob at the base of each pair of branches. The knobs and their
branches shall be of one piece with it, the whole of it a single, hammered
piece of pure gold.

37 "Make its seven lamps and mount them so that they light the space in
38 39 front of it. Make its tongs and pans of pure gold. All these items shall be
40 made from a talent of pure gold.[55] Take care to make them according to
that design that is shown to you on the mountain.

26 1 "As for the Tabernacle itself, make it with ten sheets of finely spun linen
and sky-blue, purple, and scarlet wool, with a design of cherubim worked

---

54 | Opinions differ as to the appearance of the cherubim, which had a human or animal likeness.

55 | A talent in this context equals three thousand shekels; see note on 30:13.

2 into them. Each sheet shall be twenty-eight cubits long and four cubits
3 wide; all the sheets should be the same size. Five of the sheets should be
4 sewn together; the other five likewise. Make loops of sky-blue wool on
the upper edge of the end sheet in the first set, and likewise on the upper
5 edge of the outermost sheet in the second set. Make fifty loops on each
sheet on one side and fifty on the upper edge of the corresponding sheets
6 in the other set, with the loops opposite one another. And make fifty gold
clasps. With the clasps, join the sheets together so that the Tabernacle
becomes one whole.

7 "Make sheets of goats' hair as a tent over the Tabernacle; make eleven of
8 these sheets. Each sheet shall be thirty cubits long and four cubits wide,
9 all eleven sheets the same size. Join five of the sheets by themselves, and
the other six by themselves. Fold the sixth sheet over the front of the tent.
10 Make fifty loops on the edge of the end sheet of one set, and fifty on the
11 edge of the end sheet of the other. Make, also, fifty bronze clasps. Put the
clasps through the loops, joining the tent together so that it becomes one
12 whole. As for the additional length of the tent sheets, the extra half sheet
13 is to hang down at the rear of the Tabernacle. The extra cubit at either end
of each of the tent sheets should hang over the sides of the Tabernacle to
14 cover it on both sides. Make a covering for the tent from rams' hides dyed
red. Above it make a covering of fine leather.

15 16 "Make the upright boards for the Tabernacle of acacia wood. Each board
17 shall be ten cubits long and one and a half cubits wide. Each board should
have two matching tenons; all the Tabernacle's boards should be made in
18 19 this way. Make twenty boards for the southern side of the Tabernacle, and
forty silver sockets under the twenty boards, two sockets under the first
20 board for its two tenons, and two under the next. For the second side of
21 the Tabernacle, the northern side, there should be twenty boards, along
with their forty silver sockets, two under the first board and two under
22 each of the others. Make six boards for the west side of the Tabernacle,
23 24 and two additional boards for the Tabernacle's rear corners. These should
adjoin each other at the bottom, and be joined together at the top by a
25 ring. So it should be for both sides; they shall form the two corners. So
there should be eight boards and sixteen silver sockets, two sockets under
each board.

26 "Make crossbars, too, of acacia wood, five for the boards of the first side
27 of the Tabernacle, five for the boards of the second side of the Tabernacle,
and five for the boards of the western side of the Tabernacle at the rear.
28 The central crossbar should go through the middle of the boards from
29 one end to the other. Overlay the boards with gold, and make gold rings
30 for the crossbars. The crossbars too should be overlaid with gold. So shall
you set up the Tabernacle, according to the plan you were shown on the
mountain.

31 "Make a curtain of sky-blue, purple, and scarlet wool, and finely spun linen
32 with a design of cherubim worked into it. Hang it on four gold-covered
33 posts of acacia wood with gold hooks, set on four sockets of silver. Hang
the curtain under the clasps and bring the Ark of the Testimony behind it,
34 so that the curtain separates the holy place from the Holy of Holies. Put
35 the cover on the Ark of the Testimony in the Holy of Holies. The table shall
be placed on the north side of the Tabernacle outside the curtain, and the
candelabrum on the south side, opposite the table.

36 "Make a screen for the entrance to the tent, embroidered with sky-blue,
37 purple, and scarlet wool and finely spun linen. Make five posts of acacia
wood for the screen and overlay them with gold; their hooks, also, shall
be of gold. Cast for them, too, five sockets of bronze.

27 1 "Make the altar from acacia wood. It should be square, five cubits long, five
2 cubits wide, and three cubits high. Make horns for it on its four corners,
3 the horns being of one piece with it, and overlay it with bronze. Make pots
for removing its ashes, together with shovels, basins, forks, and pans. Make
4 all of these of bronze. Make a grate of bronze mesh for it, and on the mesh
5 make four bronze rings at its four corners. The grate should be set below,
under the ledge of the altar, so that the mesh reaches the middle of the
6 altar. And make staves of acacia wood for the altar, and overlay them with
7 bronze. Place the poles in the rings, so that the poles will be on the two
8 sides of the altar when it is carried. Make it hollow, with planks; make it
as it was shown to you on the mountain.

9 "Make the courtyard of the Tabernacle thus: on the south side there should
be hangings a hundred cubits long of finely spun linen, all the length of the
10 courtyard on that side, with twenty posts and their twenty bronze sockets.
11 The hooks and bands of the posts shall be of silver. Likewise on the north
side; the hangings shall be a hundred cubits long, with twenty posts and
their twenty corresponding bronze sockets, with hooks and bands of silver.
12 The width of the hangings at the western end of the courtyard shall be fifty
cubits, and it should have ten posts and their ten corresponding sockets.
13 The width of the courtyard at the front, facing east, shall be fifty cubits:
14 fifteen cubits of hangings with three posts and three sockets on one side,
15 and fifteen cubits of hangings with three posts and three sockets on the
16 other, and for the gate of the courtyard there shall be an embroidered
screen of twenty cubits of sky-blue, purple, and scarlet wool and finely
spun linen, with four posts and four sockets.

17 "All the posts around the courtyard should be banded with silver. Their
18 hooks shall be of silver, and their sockets of bronze. The courtyard shall be
a hundred cubits long, fifty cubits wide, and five cubits high, with hangings
19 of finely spun linen and sockets of bronze. All the Tabernacle utensils, for
every use, as well as all its tent pegs and the tent pegs of the courtyard,
shall be of bronze.

TETZAVEH

20 "Command the Israelites to bring you pure oil from crushed olives for
21 light, to kindle the lamp, every night. From evening to morning, before the
LORD, Aharon and his sons shall set it up to burn in the Tent of Meeting,[56]
outside the curtain that veils the Ark of the Testimony. This shall be a rule
for all time for the Israelites, throughout their generations.

28 1 "From among the Israelites, draw your brother Aharon and his sons close
to you to serve Me as priests – Aharon and his sons Nadav and Avihu,
2 Elazar and Itamar. Make sacred vestments for your brother Aharon, for
3 glory and for splendor. Speak to all the skilled craftsmen whom I have
endowed with a spirit of wisdom, and have them make Aharon's vestments;
4 these will consecrate him to serve Me as priest. These are the garments
they shall make: a breast piece, an ephod,[57] a robe, a quilted tunic, a miter
and a sash; sacred vestments shall they make, for your brother Aharon and
5 his sons to serve Me in. They should use gold, and sky-blue, purple, and
scarlet wool, and fine linen.

6 "They are to make the ephod of finely spun linen embroidered with gold,
7 and sky-blue, purple, and scarlet wool. It should have two shoulder pieces
8 attached to its two edges so that it can be joined together. The decorated
waistband on it shall be like it and of one piece with it, made of gold, of
sky-blue, purple, and scarlet wool and finely spun linen.

9 "Take two rock crystal stones and engrave on them the names of Yisrael's
10 sons: six names on one stone and the remaining six names on the other,
11 in the order of their birth. Engrave the two stones with the names of
Yisrael's sons as a gem cutter engraves a seal, then mount them in gold
12 filigree settings. Place the two stones on the shoulder pieces of the ephod
as remembrance stones for the sons of Yisrael. Thus will Aharon carry their
13 names on his shoulders as a remembrance before the LORD. Make gold
14 filigree settings and two sets of pure gold chains braided into cords, and
attach the cords of chains to the settings.

15 "Make a breast piece for judgment. Make it with the same skilled craftsmanship as the ephod: of gold, of sky-blue, purple, and scarlet wool, and
16 of finely spun linen. It shall be square and folded double, a span long and
17 a span wide. Mount four rows of precious stones onto it: the first row a
18 carnelian,[58] an olivine, and a garnet; the second row an emerald, a lapis
19 lazuli, and a green quartz; the third row an amber, a jet, and a sardonyx;
20 and the fourth an aquamarine, a rock crystal, and a jasper or opal. Mount
21 them in gold filigree settings. The stones shall correspond to the names of
Yisrael's sons. Each stone should be engraved like a seal, with one of the
names of the twelve tribes.

56 | That is, the Tabernacle, the locus of divine communication; cf. 25:22, 29:43.

57 | See note on 25:7.

58 | Identifications of these stones vary.

22 "Make chains of pure gold, braided into cords, for the breast piece. Make
23
24 the breast piece two gold rings and attach them to its two corners. Then
fasten the two gold chains to the two gold rings at the corners of the breast
25 piece. Attach the other ends of the chains to the two settings. They will
26 thus be joined to the ephod's shoulder pieces at the front. Make two gold
rings and place them at the two other corners of the breast piece on the
27 edge, inside, next to the ephod. Make two more gold rings and attach them
to the bottom of the ephod's two shoulder pieces facing its front, close to
28 its seam and above the ephod's woven waistband. The breast piece shall be
held in place by a cord of sky blue from its rings to the rings of the ephod,
so that the breast piece remains secured above the ephod's waistband, and
does not come loose from the ephod.

29 "Thus will Aharon carry the names of Yisrael's sons on the breast piece of
judgment at his heart whenever he enters the Sanctuary, as a remembrance
30 before the Lord at all times. Place the Urim and Tumim[59] in the breast
piece of judgment so that they too will be at Aharon's heart when he comes
before the Lord. Aharon will then always be carrying at his heart Israel's
means of judgment, before the Lord.

31 "Make the robe of the ephod entirely of sky-blue wool. It should have an
32
opening for the head in the middle with a woven border around it like the
33 neck of a coat of mail, so that it does not tear. Around the hem of the robe
make pomegranates of sky-blue, purple, and scarlet wool, and between
34 them put gold bells, so that gold bells and pomegranates alternate around
35 the hem of the robe. Aharon shall wear this robe whenever he ministers,
and its sound will be heard when he enters the Sanctuary before the Lord
and when he leaves, so that he will not die.

36 "Make a headplate of pure gold and engrave on it, as on a seal: Holy to
37 the Lord. Attach a cord of sky blue to it, so that it can be fixed to the
38 miter, affixed to the miter's front. It shall remain on Aharon's forehead,
that Aharon may bear away all guilt that arises from the holy offerings the
Israelites consecrate, from all their sacred gifts;[60] it shall be on his forehead
always, that they may find favor in the Lord's sight.

39 "Quilt the tunic of fine linen. Make a miter out of fine linen, and an
40 embroidered sash. Make tunics, sashes, and caps for Aharon's sons, for
41 glory and for splendor. Put these on your brother Aharon and his sons;
42 then anoint, ordain, and consecrate them to serve Me as priests. Make
them linen trousers to cover their nakedness, reaching from waist to
43 thigh. They must be worn by Aharon and his sons whenever they enter
the Tent of Meeting or approach the altar to minister in the Sanctuary so

59 | Explanations of the nature of this item vary. Numbers 27:21 makes clear that it is a conduit for divine communication.

60 | As generally understood, this means that the diadem atones for certain deviations from the rules that govern offerings.

that they do not incur guilt and die. This shall be a law for Aharon and his
descendants for all time.

29 1 "This is what you must do to consecrate them to serve Me as priests. Take
2 a young bull, two unblemished rams, and unleavened bread, unleavened
loaves mixed with oil, and unleavened wafers brushed with oil – all made
3 of fine wheat flour. Place these in a basket and bring them in the basket
4 together with the young bull and two rams. Bring Aharon and his sons
to the entrance of the Tent of Meeting, and you shall wash them with
5 water. Then take the vestments and dress Aharon in the tunic, the robe
of the ephod, the ephod itself, and the breast piece. Fasten the ephod on
6 him by its woven waistband. Put the miter on his head and on the miter
7 place the sacred diadem. Take the anointing oil, pour it on his head, and
8 anoint him. Then bring his sons forward and dress them with the tunics.
9 Gird Aharon and his sons with the sashes and fasten their headdresses.
The priesthood shall be theirs as a law for all time. Thus you shall ordain
Aharon and his sons.

10 "Then bring the young bull in front of the Tent of Meeting, and have
11 Aharon and his sons lay their hands on its head. Slaughter the bull before
12 the Lord at the entrance of the Tent of Meeting. Take some of the bull's
blood and put it on the horns of the altar with your finger. Pour out the rest
13 of the blood at the base of the altar. Take all the fat that covers the entrails,
the diaphragm of the liver, and the two kidneys with the fat around them,
14 and burn them on the altar. Burn the bull's flesh, its hide, and its waste
outside the camp; it is a purification offering.

15 "Then take one of the rams and have Aharon and his sons lay their hands
16 upon its head, then slaughter it; let them take its blood and sprinkle it
17 on all the sides of the altar. Cut the ram into pieces, wash its entrails and
18 legs, and put them with its pieces and its head. Burn the entire ram on the
altar. It is a burnt offering to the Lord, a pleasing aroma, a fire offering
to the Lord.

19 "Then take the second ram, and have Aharon and his sons lay their hands
20 on its head. Slaughter the ram, take some of its blood and put it on the
ridges of the right ears of Aharon and his sons, and on the thumbs of their
right hands and on the big toes of their right feet. Sprinkle the rest of the
21 blood on the sides of the altar. Collect some of the blood on the altar and
some of the anointing oil and sprinkle it on Aharon and his vestments, and
on his sons and his sons' vestments. Then he, and his sons with him, and
their vestments, will be consecrated.

22 "From the ram take its fat parts – the broad tail, the fat that covers the
entrails, the diaphragm of the liver, and the two kidneys with the fat on
23 them – and the right thigh, for this is the ram of ordination. From the
basket of unleavened bread before the Lord, take one loaf of bread, one
24 loaf of oil bread, and one wafer. Place all of these on the palms of Aharon

and his sons, and have them wave them as a wave offering before the Lord.
25 Then take them from their hands and burn them on the altar with the
burnt offering, for a pleasing aroma before the Lord. It is a fire offering
to the Lord.

26 "Take the breast of Aharon's ram of ordination and wave it as a wave
27 offering before the Lord; it shall be your portion. From Aharon and his
sons' ram of ordination, consecrate the breast, the wave offering and the
28 thigh, the upraised gift. These parts shall be the Israelites' due to Aharon
and his sons for all time. They are the Israelites' gift from their peace
offerings, their gift to the Lord.

29 "Aharon's sacred vestments shall pass on to his sons after him. In them
30 they shall be anointed and ordained. The son who succeeds him as priest,
entering the Tent of Meeting to minister in the Sanctuary, shall wear them
for seven days.

31 "Take the ram of ordination and, in the sacred precinct, cook its flesh.
32 Aharon and his sons shall eat the meat of the ram, and the bread in the
33 basket, near the entrance of the Tent of Meeting. They shall eat these
things, through which atonement will be made, to be ordained and
34 consecrated. Because they are consecrated no layman may eat of them. If
any of the meat of the ordination ram or any of the bread is left over until
morning, you shall burn what remains with fire. It must not be eaten, for
it is consecrated.

35 "This is what you must do for Aharon and his sons, just as I have com-
36 manded you. Their ordination shall take seven days. Each day, offer a
bull as a purification offering for atonement. Purify the altar by making
37 atonement for it, and consecrate it by anointing it. For seven days, make
atonement for the altar and consecrate it, so that the altar becomes holy
of holies – and anything that touches it will become holy.

38 "This is what you shall offer on the altar: two yearling lambs each day,
39 with constancy. Offer one lamb in the morning, and the other in the
40 afternoon. With the first lamb offer a tenth measure of fine flour mixed
with a quarter of a hin[61] of beaten oil, and a quarter of a hin of wine
41 as a libation. Offer the other lamb in the afternoon together with a
grain offering and libation as in the morning, as a pleasing aroma, a fire
42 offering to the Lord. This shall be the regular burnt offering throughout
your generations at the entrance of the Tent of Meeting before the Lord.
43 There I will meet with you, there I will speak to you, and there I will meet
44 with the Israelites. It will be sanctified by My glory. I will consecrate
the Tent of Meeting and the altar. I will also consecrate Aharon and his
45 sons to serve Me as priests. I will have My Presence dwell among the
46 Israelites and I shall be their God. Then they will know that I am the

61 | A liquid measure, equivalent to approximately 4 liters or 1 gallon.

Lord their God, who brought them out of Egypt to dwell among them.
I am the Lord their God.

30 1 2 "Make an altar on which to burn incense; make it of acacia wood. It shall
be square, a cubit long, a cubit wide, and two cubits high, its horns of one
3 piece with it. Overlay it with pure gold on its top, all around its sides, and
4 on its horns, and around it make a gold molding. Make two gold rings for
5 it under its molding on both sides to hold the staves used to carry it. Make
6 the staves of acacia wood and overlay them with gold. Put it in front of
the screen that veils the Ark of the Testimony, in front of the cover above
7 the Ark, where I will meet with you. Aharon should burn incense on it
8 every morning when he tends the lamps, and before evening when he
lights the lamps. It shall be a perpetual incense offering before the Lord
9 throughout your generations. Offer no unauthorized incense on it, or any
10 burnt offering, grain offering, or libation. Once a year Aharon shall make
atonement on its horns; once a year, with the blood of the purification
offering of atonement, he shall make atonement on it, throughout your
generations. It is holy of holies to the Lord."

11 12 The Lord said to Moshe, "When you take the census of the Israelites, KI TISA
as you count, each must give ransom for his life to the Lord, so that no
13 plague strikes them when you count them.[62] Everyone numbered in the
census shall give half a shekel according to the Sanctuary weight,[63] where
the shekel is twenty gerah.[64] This half shekel is an offering to the Lord.
14 Every male over twenty is to be included in the census and must give the
15 Lord's offering. The rich shall not give more, and the poor shall not give
less, than this half shekel. It is an offering to the Lord to redeem your
16 lives. Take this redemption money from the Israelites and assign it for the
service of the Tent of Meeting. It shall be a remembrance for the Israelites
before the Lord, to redeem your lives."

17 18 The Lord said to Moshe, "Make a bronze laver with a bronze base for
washing. Place it between the Tent of Meeting and the altar, and put water
19 20 in it, for Aharon and his sons to wash their hands and feet. When they
enter the Tent of Meeting or approach the altar to minister by presenting
a food offering to the Lord, they must wash with water, so that they do
21 not die. They must wash their hands and feet so that they do not die; it
shall be an eternal law for them, for Aharon and his offspring, throughout
the generations."

22 23 Then the Lord said to Moshe, "Take the finest spices: five hundred shekel
of liquid myrrh, and half as much, two hundred fifty, of fragrant cinnamon,
24 as well as two hundred fifty of aromatic cane, and five hundred shekel

62 | Taking a census posed the threat of a plague; cf. II Samuel, chapter 24.

63 | Sanctuary weights differed from standard weights.

64 | The gerah and the shekel are units of weight and currency. A shekel is close to 20 grams or three-quarters of an ounce.

of cassia – all according to the Sanctuary weight – and a hin of olive oil.
25 Make from these a sacred anointing oil, blended as by a perfumer; it shall
26 be a sacred anointing oil. With it, anoint the Tent of Meeting and the Ark
27 of the Testimony, the table and all its utensils, the candelabrum and its
28 utensils, the incense altar, the sacrificial altar with all its utensils, and the
29 laver and its base. You shall consecrate them and they will become holy
30 of holies, and whatever touches them will become holy. You shall anoint
31 Aharon and his sons and consecrate them to serve Me as priests. And you
shall tell the Israelites: This shall be My sacred anointing oil throughout
32 the generations. Do not pour it on anyone else's body, and do not make
any other oil with the same formula. It is sacred, and shall remain sacred
33 to you. Whoever makes perfume like it or applies it to a layperson shall
be severed from his people."

34 The Lord said to Moshe, "Take sweet spices, equal parts of stacte, onycha,
35 galbanum, and pure frankincense and make them into incense, blended
36 as by a perfumer, salted, pure and sacred. Beat some of it into powder
and put part of it before the covenant in the Tent of Meeting where I will
37 meet with you. It shall be holy of holies to you. Do not make any incense
with this formula for yourselves. It must, for you, remain sacred to the
38 Lord. The person who makes any incense like it to use as perfume shall
be severed from his people."

31 1 2 The Lord said to Moshe, "See, I have called by name Betzalel, son of Uri,
3 son of Ḥur from the tribe of Yehuda, and I have filled him with a divine
4 spirit, with wisdom, understanding, and knowledge in every craft. He
5 will fashion works of art in gold, silver, and bronze. He will cut stones
6 for setting, carve wood, and work in every craft. I have assigned to him
Oholiav, son of Aḥisamakh from the tribe of Dan. I have also put wisdom
into the heart of all the wise-hearted, so that they will be able to make all I
7 have commanded you: the Tent of Meeting, the Ark of the Testimony and
8 its cover, and all other furnishings of the Tent; the table and its utensils,
9 the pure candelabrum and all its utensils, the incense altar, the sacrificial
10 altar with all its utensils, the laver and its base, the service vestments, the
sacred vestments for Aharon the priest and the vestments for his sons for
11 when they serve as priests, the anointing oil and the fragrant incense for
the Sanctuary; they shall make them exactly as I have commanded you."

12 13 Then the Lord said to Moshe, "Speak to the Israelites and say: Nevertheless,
you shall keep My Sabbaths. It is a sign between Me and you throughout
14 the generations, that you may know that I, the Lord, make you holy. Keep
the Sabbath, for it is holy to you. Whoever profanes it shall be put to death.
15 Whoever does work on it shall be severed from his people. Six days shall
work be done, but the seventh day is a Sabbath of complete rest, sacred to
the Lord. Whoever does any work on the Sabbath shall be put to death.
16 The Israelites shall keep the Sabbath, making it a day of rest throughout
17 their generations as a covenant forever. It is an eternal sign between Me

and the Israelites that in six days the LORD made heaven and earth, and on the seventh day He ceased and was revived."

18 When He had finished speaking to Moshe on Mount Sinai, He gave him the two tablets of the covenant, stone tablets, inscribed by the finger of God.

32 1 When the people saw that Moshe was long delayed in coming down the
mountain, they gathered around Aharon and said to him, "Get up, make us
gods to go before us. This man Moshe who brought us out of Egypt – we
2 have no idea what has become of him." So Aharon said to them, "Remove
the gold rings from the ears of your wives, your sons and your daughters
3 and bring them to me." So all the people took the gold rings from their ears
4 and brought them to Aharon. He took the gold from them and, fashioning
it with a chisel, made a molten calf. And they said, "These, Israel, are your
5 gods who brought you out of Egypt!" Seeing this, Aharon built an altar
in front of it and announced, "Tomorrow will be a festival to the LORD."
6 The next day, they rose early and sacrificed burnt offerings and brought
peace offerings. The people sat down to eat and drink and then stood up
to engage in revelry.

7 The LORD said to Moshe, "Quick – go down. Your people, whom you
8 brought out of Egypt, are acting ruinously. They have deviated swiftly
from the way I commanded them; they have made themselves a molten
calf and are bowing down and sacrificing to it, saying, 'These, Israel, are
9 your gods who brought you out of Egypt!'" Then the LORD said to Moshe,
10 "I have seen this people; it is a stiff-necked people. So do not try to stop Me
when My anger burns against them. I will put an end to them and make
of you a great nation."

11 Moshe implored the LORD his God, "Why, O LORD, unleash Your anger
against Your people, whom You brought out of Egypt with such vast
12 power and mighty force? Why should the Egyptians be able to say that
You brought them out with evil intent, to kill them in the mountains and
purge them from the face of the earth? Turn from Your fierce anger and
13 relent from doing evil to Your people. Remember Avraham, Yitzhak, and
Yisrael, Your servants, to whom You swore by Your very Self, telling them,
'I will make your descendants as many as the stars of the heavens, and
14 give them this land of which I spoke, to inherit forever.'" Then the LORD
relented from the evil He had spoken of doing to His people.

15 Then Moshe turned and came down the mountain with the two tablets of
16 testimony in his hand, inscribed on both sides, front and back. The tablets
were the work of God, and the writing was God's writing, engraved on the
17 tablets. When Yehoshua heard the noise of the people shouting, he said
18 to Moshe, "The sound of war is coming from the camp." But Moshe said,
"It is neither the sound of triumph nor the wailing of defeat. What I hear
19 is the sound of revelry." As he approached the camp and saw the calf and

the dancing, Moshe's anger blazed, and he flung the tablets from his hands
20 and smashed them at the foot of the mountain. Then he took the calf that
they had made, burned it with fire, ground it to fine powder, scattered it
on the water, and made the Israelites drink it.

21 "What did this people do to you," said Moshe to Aharon, "that you should
22 have brought so great a sin upon it?" Aharon replied, "Do not be angry
23 with me. You know that the people are set on evil. They said to me, 'Make
us gods to go before us. This man Moshe who brought us out of Egypt – we
24 have no idea what has become of him.' So I told them, 'Who has gold? Take
it off.' They gave it to me, I threw it into the fire – and out came this calf."

25 Moshe saw that the people were running wild, for Aharon had let them run
26 beyond control and become a laughingstock to their enemies. So Moshe
stood at the gate of the camp and said, "Who is for the Lord? Come to me."
27 All the Levites rallied round him. He said to them, "This is what the Lord
God of Israel says: Let each of you put sword on thigh and go back and
forth from gate to gate throughout the camp – slaying brother, neighbor,
28 kinsman." The Levites did as Moshe had ordered. Some three thousand
29 people fell that day. Moshe said, "Dedicate yourselves to the Lord today.
You have been willing to act even against your son or brother. May He
bestow a blessing on you this day."

30 On the following day, Moshe said to the people, "You have committed a
grievous sin. Now I must go back up to the Lord. Perhaps I can secure
31 atonement for your sin." So Moshe went back to the Lord and said, "I
beg of You. This people has committed a grievous sin. They made gods
32 of gold for themselves. But now, if only You would forgive their sin – but
33 if not, please blot me out of the book You have written." The Lord said
to Moshe, "I will blot out of My book those who have sinned against Me.
34 Now go and lead the people to the place about which I have spoken to
you. My messenger shall go before you. But when the time comes for Me
to punish, I will punish them for their sin."

35 Thus the Lord struck the people with a plague for what they had done
with the calf Aharon had made.

33 1 The Lord said to Moshe, "Go. Set out from here – you and the people you
brought out of Egypt – to the land I promised to Avraham, Yitzḥak, and
2 Yaakov, saying, 'I will give this to your descendants.' I will send a messenger
ahead of you and drive out the Canaanites and Amorites, the Hittites
3 and the Perizzites, the Hivites, and the Jebusites. You will come to a land
flowing with milk and honey, but I will not go among you, because you
are a stiff-necked people; I might destroy you on the way."

4 When the people heard this distressing news, they were grief-stricken.
5 None put on their finery; for the Lord had said to Moshe, "Tell the
Israelites: You are a stiff-necked people. If for one moment I were to go

among you, I might destroy you. So now take off your finery; and I will
6 consider what to do with you." So the Israelites stripped themselves of
their finery from Mount Ḥorev onward.

7 Moshe took the tent and pitched it at a distance outside the camp, calling
it the Tent of Meeting. Whoever sought the Lord would go to the Tent
8 of Meeting, outside the camp. And when Moshe went out to the Tent, all
the people would rise, standing at the openings of their tents, and watch
9 Moshe until he had entered the Tent. When Moshe entered the Tent, the
pillar of cloud would descend and stand at the Tent's opening while He
10 spoke with Moshe. When the people saw the pillar of cloud standing at
the Tent's opening, all the people would rise and bow down, each at the
11 opening of his own tent. The Lord would speak to Moshe face-to-face, as
one person speaks to his friend. And then Moshe would return to the camp,
but his young disciple, Yehoshua son of Nun, did not leave the Tent.

12 Moshe said to the Lord, "You told me to lead this people forth, but You
have not let me know whom You will send with me. And You said, 'I have
13 known you by name, and you have found favor in My sight.' So now, if I
have found favor in Your sight, please show me Your ways, so that I may
know You and continue to find favor in Your sight. And look upon this
14 nation: it is Your people." "My Presence," He replied, "will go with you,
15 and I will grant you rest."[65] Then Moshe said to Him, "If Your Presence
16 does not go with us, do not make us leave this place. For unless You go
with us, how shall it be known that I and Your people have found favor in
Your sight? That is how I and Your people are distinguished from every
other people on the face of the earth."

17 Then the Lord said to Moshe, "In this too I will do what you ask, for you
18 have found favor in My sight; for I know you by name." Then Moshe said,
19 "Show me, please, Your glory." And He said, "I will cause all My goodness
to pass before you and in your presence I will proclaim My name: The
Lord. But I will be gracious to whom I choose to be gracious, and will
20 show mercy to whom I decide to show mercy. Nor," He said, "can you see
21 My face. For no one can see Me and live." Then the Lord said, "Look, there
22 is a place by Me where you may stand on the rock, and while My glory
passes by I will put you in a cleft of the rock, and I will shield you with My
23 hand until I have passed. Then I will take My hand away, and you will see
My back, but My face may not be seen."

34 1 The Lord said to Moshe, "Carve two tablets of stone like the first, and I
will inscribe on them the words that were on the first tablets that you broke.
2 Be ready in the morning. Climb Mount Sinai in the morning and present
3 yourself to Me there on the mountaintop. Let no one come up with you.

65 | "Rest" here is subject to varying interpretations, such as peace of mind or military success.

No one else should be seen anywhere on the mountain, nor may flocks or
4 herds graze near the mountain." So Moshe carved two stone tablets like the
first. He rose early in the morning and climbed Mount Sinai, as the LORD
had commanded him. In his hand he took the two tablets of stone.

5 The LORD descended in a cloud and stood with him there, and proclaimed
6 the name: The LORD. And the LORD passed before him, and proclaimed,
"The LORD, the LORD, God compassionate and gracious, slow to anger,
7 abounding in kindness and truth, extending kindness for thousands of
generations, forgiving sin, rebellion, and error, but who does not acquit the
guilty, holding descendants to account for the sins of the fathers, children
8 and grandchildren to the third and fourth generation." Moshe quickly
9 bowed and prostrated himself, and he said, "If now I have found favor in
Your sight, O LORD, please, let my LORD go among us. Though this is a stiff-
necked people, pardon our sins and errors, and keep us as Your own."

10 The LORD said, "Now am I hereby making a covenant. Before your entire
people I will perform such wonders as never have been performed anywhere on earth, for any nation. All the peoples you live among shall see:
how awe-inspiring are the deeds that I the LORD will do for you.

11 "Be vigilant in what I am commanding you this day. I am going to drive
out before you the Amorites, Canaanites, Hittites, Perizzites, Hivites, and
12 Jebusites. Take care not to make a treaty with the inhabitants of the land
13 you are going to; for they would become a dangerous trap to you. Tear
down their altars, smash their worship pillars, and cut down their sacred
14 trees, for you must worship no other god. The LORD, known to demand
15 absolute loyalty, is your God who demands it indeed. You must not make a
treaty with the inhabitants of the land, for they will lust after their gods and
sacrifice to them; they will invite you to join them and you will eat of their
16 sacrifice, and you will take their daughters as wives for your sons, and their
daughters will lust after their gods and cause your sons to do as they do.

17 "Make for yourselves no molten gods.

18 "Keep the Festival of Unleavened Bread. For seven days, eat unleavened
bread as I commanded you, at the time appointed, in the month of Aviv,[66]
19 because in that month you left Egypt. The first to emerge from every womb
20 is Mine; among all your livestock, firstborn cattle, and sheep. Redeem each
firstborn donkey with a sheep; if you do not redeem it, you must break
its neck. Also redeem all your firstborn sons. Do not appear before Me
empty-handed.

21 "Six days you shall work, but on the seventh day you shall rest, ceasing
22 from labor even at plowing time and harvest time. Observe the Festival
of Weeks, of the first fruits of wheat harvest, as well as the Festival of

66 | See note on 13:4.

23 Ingathering[67] at the close of the year. Three times a year all the males
24 among you shall appear before the Master, the LORD, God of Israel. For
I will banish nations before you and enlarge your territory. No one will
covet your land when you go up, three times a year, to appear before the
LORD your God.

25 "Do not offer the blood of My sacrifice with anything leavened. Do not let
26 any of the Passover festival sacrifice remain until morning. Bring the best
first fruits of your land to the House of the LORD your God. Do not cook
a kid in the milk of its mother."

27 Then the LORD said to Moshe, "Write down these words, for in accordance
28 with these words I have made a covenant with you and with Israel." He
stayed there with the LORD for forty days and forty nights, eating no
bread and drinking no water. And on the tablets, He wrote the words of
the covenant, the Ten Commandments.

29 When Moshe came down from Mount Sinai with the two tablets of
testimony in his hand, he was unaware that the skin of his face shone with
30 light, because he had been speaking with God. When Aharon and all the
Israelites saw the light that shone from the skin of Moshe's face, they were
31 afraid to come close to him. But Moshe called them, and Aharon and all
32 the community leaders came back to him, and Moshe spoke. After that, all
the Israelites approached, and he instructed them in all that the LORD had
33 spoken to him on Mount Sinai. And when Moshe had finished speaking
to them, he veiled his face.

34 Whenever Moshe came before the LORD to speak with Him, he would
remove the veil until he came out. When he came out and told the Israelites
35 what he had been commanded, the Israelites would see how the skin of
Moshe's face shone with light, and he would veil his face again until he
went back in to speak with Him.

35 1 Moshe assembled all the community of Israel and said to them, "These are VAYAK'HEL
2 the things the LORD has commanded you to do. For six days, let work be
done, but the seventh must be sacred to you. It is a Sabbath of complete
rest dedicated to the LORD. Whoever does work on it shall be put to death.
3 Do not light a fire in any of your dwellings on the Sabbath day."

4 Then Moshe said to all the community of Israel, "This is what the LORD has
5 commanded. Bring of what is yours an offering to the LORD. Let everyone
whose heart moves him bring an offering to the LORD: gold, silver, and
6 7 bronze; sky-blue, purple, and scarlet wool; linen and goats' hair; rams'
8 hides dyed red and fine leather; acacia wood; oil for the lamp; spices for
9 the anointing oil and the fragrant incense; and rock crystal together with
other precious stones for the ephod and breast piece.

67 | See notes on 23:16.

10 "And let all among you who are skilled come and make the things that the
11 Lord has commanded: the Tabernacle, its tent and covering, its hooks
12 and frames, its bars, posts, and sockets; the Ark and its staves, the cover
13 and the curtain for the screen; the table, its staves and all its utensils, and
14 the showbread; the candelabrum for light, together with its utensils, lamps,
15 and the oil for lighting; the incense altar with its staves, the anointing
oil and the fragrant incense, and the entrance screen for the entrance of
16 the Tabernacle; the sacrificial altar, its bronze grate, its staves and all its
17 utensils, the laver and its base; the hangings of the courtyard, its posts
18 and its sockets, and the screen for the gate of the court; the tent pegs of
19 the Tabernacle and of the courtyard and their ropes; the vestments for
ministering in the Sanctuary, and the sacred vestments for Aharon the
priest and for his sons for their priestly service."

20 21 So all the community of Israel left Moshe's presence. And they came,
everyone whose heart inspired him and whose spirit moved him, and
brought an offering for the Lord, to be used for the Tent of Meeting
22 and all its service, and for the sacred vestments. All whose hearts moved
them – the men with the women – brought brooches, earrings, signet
rings and pendants, all kinds of gold ornaments, together with all those
23 who gave gold as a wave offering to the Lord. Everyone who had sky-
blue, purple, or scarlet wool, linen or goats' hair, rams' hides dyed red or
24 fine leather brought them. Whoever could make an offering of silver or
bronze brought it as an offering to the Lord, as did everyone who had
25 acacia wood that could be used for the work. Every skilled woman spun
with her own hands, and brought what she had spun: sky-blue, purple, and
26 scarlet wool and fine linen. All the women whose hearts inspired them
27 used their skill to spin the goats' hair. The leaders brought rock crystal
stones and other precious stones for setting in the ephod and the breast
28 piece, together with spices and oil for the light, the anointing oil and the
29 fragrant incense. So the Israelites – all the men and women whose hearts
moved them to bring anything for the work that the Lord, through Moshe,
had commanded – brought it as a freewill offering to the Lord.

30 Then Moshe said to the Israelites, "Know that the Lord has summoned
31 by name Betzalel, son of Uri, son of Ḥur, of the tribe of Yehuda, and has
filled him with a divine spirit of wisdom, understanding, and knowledge in
32 33 every craft, to devise designs, working in gold, silver, and bronze, as well as
cutting stones for setting, carving wood, and working in every other craft.
34 He has also given him the ability to teach others, together with Oholiav,
35 son of Aḥisamakh of the tribe of Dan. He has filled them with the skill
to do all kinds of work, as engravers, designers, embroiderers in sky-blue,
purple, or scarlet wool or fine linen, and as weavers. They will be able to
carry out all the necessary work and design.

36 1 "And so Betzalel and Oholiav shall carry out everything the Lord has
commanded, together with all the skilled people to whom the Lord has

granted expertise and acumen to do all the work necessary for the service
of the Sanctuary."

2 Then Moshe summoned Betzalel and Oholiav and all the skilled craftsmen
to whom God had given expertise and who were inspired to dedicate
3 themselves and come to carry out the work. From Moshe they received
all the offerings the Israelites had brought for the work of the Sanctuary.
4 And the people kept bringing him additional gifts every morning. So all the
craftsmen engaged in the work of the Sanctuary left what they were doing,
5 and said to Moshe, "The people are bringing more than is necessary for the
6 work God has commanded us to do." Moshe ordered an announcement
to be made throughout the camp: "Let no man or woman make anything
more as an offering for the Sanctuary." So the people brought no more;
7 for what they already had was more than enough for all the work that was
to be done.

8 All the skilled craftsmen among those engaged in the work made the
Tabernacle with ten sheets of fine linen and sky-blue, purple, and scarlet
9 wool, with a woven design of cherubim. All the sheets were of the same
10 size: twenty-eight cubits long and four cubits wide. Five sheets were sewn
11 together, and likewise the second five. He made loops of sky-blue wool
on the edge of the outermost sheet of the first set and likewise on the
12 outermost sheet of the second set: fifty loops on the first sheet and fifty on
the edge of the end sheet of the other set, so that the loops were opposite
13 one another. He made fifty gold clasps and used them to fasten the two
sets of sheets together so that the Tabernacle was all of one piece.

14 He made sheets of goats' hair for a tent over the Tabernacle. There were
15 eleven such sheets. All eleven were the same size: thirty cubits long and
16 four cubits wide. He joined five of the sheets into one set and six into
17 another. He made fifty loops on the edge of the outermost sheet of the
18 first set, and fifty loops on the edge of the second set. He made fifty bronze
19 clasps to join the tent together into a single piece. And for the tent he made
a covering of rams' skins dyed red, with a covering of fine leather above.

20 Then he made the upright boards for the Tabernacle from acacia wood.
21 22 Each was ten cubits long and a cubit and a half wide. Each board had
two matching tenons; all the Tabernacle's boards were made in this way.
23 24 He made twenty boards for the south side, and forty silver sockets to
go under them, two sockets under each board, one under each tenon.
25 For the second side of the Tabernacle, the north side, he made twenty
26 27 boards and their forty silver sockets, two under each board. For the rear
28 of the Tabernacle on the west side he made six boards, along with two
29 boards for each of the rear corners of the Tabernacle. They were even
at the bottom, and joined at the top by a ring. This was so for the other
30 corner also. So there were eight boards and sixteen silver sockets, two
under each board.

31 He made crossbars of acacia wood, five for the boards of the first side of
32 the Tabernacle, five for the boards of the second, and five for those of the
33 rear of the Tabernacle on the west side. He made the central crossbar to go
34 across the middles of the boards from one end to the other. He overlaid the
boards with gold, and made gold rings to hold the crossbars; he overlaid
the crossbars themselves with gold.

35 He made the curtain of sky-blue, purple, and scarlet wool and finely spun
36 linen, with a design of cherubim worked into it. He also made four posts
of acacia wood for it and overlaid them with gold. Their hooks were of
37 gold, and he cast for them four sockets of silver. He made an embroidered
screen for the entrance of the Tent, of sky-blue, purple, and scarlet wool
38 and finely spun linen, as well as five posts with their hooks. He overlaid
their tops and bands with gold, but their five sockets were of bronze.

37 1 Betzalel made the Ark of acacia wood, two and a half cubits long, a cubit
2 and a half wide, and a cubit and a half high. He overlaid it with pure gold
3 inside and out, and encircled it around with a gold rim. He cast four gold
4 rings for its four corners, two rings on one side and two on the other. He
5 made staves of acacia wood and overlaid them with gold. He then placed
the staves in the rings on the Ark's sides so that it could be carried.

6 He made a cover of pure gold, two and a half cubits long and a cubit and
7 a half wide. He made two cherubim of beaten gold for the two ends of
8 the cover, one cherub at one end and one at the other. He made them
9 of one piece with the cover, and the wings of the cherubim were spread
upward, sheltering the cover. They faced each other, their faces toward
the cover.

10 He made a table of acacia wood, two cubits long, a cubit wide, and a cubit
11 and a half high. He overlaid it with pure gold and around it made a gold rim.
12 He also made a frame a handbreadth wide around it and made a gold rim
13 for the frame. He cast four gold rings and placed the rings on the corners
14 of its four legs. The rings were close to the frame to hold the staves used to
15 carry the table. He made the staves for carrying the table of acacia wood
16 overlaid with gold. The articles for the table – the bowls, spoons, jars, and
pitchers for pouring libations – he made of pure gold.

17 He made the candelabrum of pure beaten gold. Its base and shaft, cups,
18 knobs, and flowers were hammered from a single piece. Six branches
19 extended from its sides, three on one side, three on the other. On each of
the six branches extending from the candelabrum were three finely crafted
20 cups, each with a knob and a flower. On the candelabrum itself there were
four finely crafted cups, each, also, with a knob and a flower.

21 At the base of each of the three pairs of branches extending from the
22 candelabrum there was a knob of one piece with it; their knobs and
branches were of one piece with it, so that the whole of it was a single

23 piece of pure beaten gold. Its seven lamps and its tongs and pans were of
24 pure gold; it and all its utensils were made from a talent of pure gold.[68]

25 He made the incense altar of acacia wood, square, a cubit long, a cubit wide,
26 and two cubits high, with horns of one piece with it. He overlaid its top,
its sides all around, and its horns with pure gold and around it he made a
27 gold molding. Under the molding he made two gold rings on the two sides,
28 to hold the staves by which it was carried. The staves themselves were
29 made of acacia wood, overlaid with gold. As well as this, with the skill of a
perfumer, he prepared the sacred anointing oil and the fragrant incense.

38 1 He made the sacrificial altar of acacia wood, square, five cubits long, five
2 cubits wide, and three cubits high. He made horns on its four corners, of
3 one piece with it, and then overlaid it with bronze. He made all the altar's
4 utensils: pots, shovels, basins, forks, and pans, out of bronze. He made
a grate of bronze mesh beneath the ledge, extending downward to the
5 middle of the altar. Four rings were cast for the four corners of the bronze
6 mesh, to hold the staves, which were made of acacia wood and overlaid
7 with bronze. He placed the staves in the rings on the sides of the altar so
that it could be carried. The altar itself was hollow, made of planks.

8 He made the bronze laver and its bronze base from the mirrors of the
women who served at the entrance of the Tent of Meeting.

9 On the south side, the hangings were of finely spun linen, a hundred cubits
10 long, with twenty posts and their twenty bronze sockets. The posts' hooks
11 and bands were of silver. Likewise on the north side: the hangings were
a hundred cubits long, with twenty pillars and their bronze sockets, and
12 hooks and bands of silver. On the west side the hangings were fifty cubits
long, with ten posts and ten sockets, and hooks and bands of silver.

13 14 The east side was also fifty cubits long: fifteen cubits of hangings with
15 three posts and three sockets on one side, and fifteen cubits of hangings
16 with three posts and three sockets on the other. All the hangings of the
17 courtyard were of finely spun linen. The sockets for the posts were of
bronze, the posts' hooks and bands were of silver, and their tops were
overlaid with silver; all the posts had silver bands.

18 At the entrance of the courtyard there was an embroidered screen of
sky-blue, purple, and scarlet wool and finely spun linen, twenty cubits
19 long and five cubits wide, like the hangings of the courtyard. It had four
posts with four bronze sockets and with hooks and bands of silver; their
20 tops were overlaid with silver. All the tent pegs for the Tabernacle and the
surrounding courtyard were of bronze.

21 These are the accounts of the Tabernacle, the Tabernacle of testimony, PEKUDEI
recorded at Moshe's command by the Levites under Itamar, son of Aharon

68 | See note on 25:39.

22 the priest. Betzalel, son of Uri, son of Ḥur, from the tribe of Yehuda, made
23 everything that the Lord had commanded Moshe. He was assisted by
Oholiav, son of Aḥisamakh, from the tribe of Dan, an engraver, designer,
and embroiderer in sky-blue, purple, and scarlet wool and fine linen.

24 All the gold used in all the sacred work, donated as wave offerings, came
to twenty-nine talents and 730 shekels according to the Sanctuary weight.
25 The silver of those recorded in the census came to a hundred talents and
26 1,775 shekels, according to the Sanctuary weight. One beka – half a shekel
according to the Sanctuary weight – was given by each of the 603,550
27 men aged twenty or over included in the census. A hundred talents of
silver were used for casting the sockets of the Sanctuary and the curtain,
28 one talent for each socket: a hundred talents for the hundred sockets. Of
1,775 shekels he made the hooks and bands of the posts and their silver-
29 plated tops. The bronze given as an offering came to seventy talents
30 and 2,400 shekels. With this were made the sockets for the entrance
of the Tent of Meeting, the bronze altar with its bronze mesh, and all
31 the utensils of the altar, the sockets around the courtyard, the sockets
at the courtyard gate, and all the tent pegs for the Tabernacle and the
surrounding courtyard.

39 1 From the sky-blue, purple, and scarlet wool they made woven garments for
ministering in the Sanctuary. They also made sacred vestments for Aharon,
as the Lord commanded Moshe.

2 He made the ephod of gold, with sky-blue, purple, and scarlet wool
3 and finely spun linen. They hammered out thin sheets of gold and cut
strands to be worked into the sky-blue, purple, and scarlet wool and fine
4 linen – highly skilled work. They made fixed shoulder pieces for the ephod;
5 these were affixed to its two ends. Its decorated waistband was like it and
of one piece with the ephod, made with gold, with sky-blue, purple, and
scarlet wool and finely spun linen, as the Lord commanded Moshe.

6 They mounted the rock crystal stones in gold filigree settings and engraved
7 them as a seal with the names of Yisrael's sons. He fastened them on the
shoulder pieces of the ephod as remembrance stones for Yisrael's sons, as
the Lord commanded Moshe.

8 He made the breast piece with the same skilled craftsmanship as the
ephod: of gold, of sky-blue, purple, and scarlet wool, and of finely spun
9 10 linen. It was square and folded double, a span long and a span wide. Then
they mounted four rows of precious stones on it. The first row was a
11 carnelian, an olivine, and a garnet; the second row was an emerald, a lapis
12 lazuli, and a green quartz; the third row was an amber, a jet, and a sardonyx;
13 and the fourth was an aquamarine, a rock crystal, and a jasper or opal. They
14 were mounted in gold filigree settings. There were twelve stones, one for
each of the names of Yisrael's sons. Each was engraved like a seal with the
name of one of the twelve tribes.

15 For the breast piece they made chains of pure gold, braided like cords.
16 They made two gold filigree settings and two gold rings, and attached the
17 rings to two of the corners of the breast piece. They fastened the two gold
18 chains to the rings at the corners of the breast piece, and the other ends
of the chains to the two settings, attaching them to the ephod's shoulder
19 pieces at the front. They made two gold rings and placed them at the two
other corners of the breast piece on the edge, inside, next to the ephod.
20 Then they made two more gold rings and attached them to the bottom of
the ephod's two shoulder pieces facing the priest's front, close to the seam
21 and above the ephod's woven waistband. They tied the rings of the breast
piece to the rings of the ephod with a sky-blue cord, connecting it to the
waistband so that the breast piece would remain secured to the ephod, as
the LORD had commanded Moshe.

22 23 They made the robe of the ephod woven entirely of sky-blue wool, with
an opening in the center like the neck of a coat of mail, with a woven
24 border around it so that it would not tear. They made pomegranates
of sky-blue, purple, and scarlet wool and finely spun linen around the
25 hem of the robe. And they made bells of pure gold and attached them
26 around the hem between the pomegranates. The bells and pomegranates
alternated around the hem of the robe worn for ministering, as the LORD
commanded Moshe.

27 28 For Aharon and his sons, they made tunics woven from fine linen, together
29 with a linen miter, linen headdresses, and trousers of finely spun linen. The
sash was embroidered out of finely spun linen and sky-blue, purple, and
scarlet wool, as the LORD commanded Moshe.

30 They made the headplate, the holy diadem, of pure gold and engraved on
31 it, as on a seal: Holy to the LORD. Then they attached a sky-blue cord to it
to affix it to the miter, as the LORD had commanded Moshe.

32 Thus all the work on the Tabernacle, the Tent of Meeting, was completed.
The Israelites did everything exactly as the LORD had commanded Moshe.
33 They brought the Tabernacle to Moshe: the Tent and all its furnishings,
34 its clasps, frames, crossbars, posts, and sockets; the covering of reddened
rams' hides and the covering of fine leather and the curtain that covered
35 the screen; the Ark of the Testimony and its carrying staves; the Ark cover;
36 37 the table with all its utensils; the showbread; the pure gold candelabrum
with its row of lamps and all its accessories, together with the oil for
38 lighting; the gold altar, the anointing oil, the fragrant incense, and the
39 curtain for the entrance to the Tent; the bronze altar with its bronze
40 mesh, its staves, and all its utensils; the laver with its base; the hangings
for the courtyard, its posts and sockets, and the screen for the courtyard
gate; the ropes and tent pegs for the courtyard; all the furnishings for the
41 service of the Tabernacle, the Tent of Meeting; and the woven garments
for ministering in the Sanctuary, both the sacred vestments for Aharon the
priest and the vestments for his sons to wear when serving as priests.

42 The Israelites had completed all the work exactly as the LORD commanded
43 Moshe. Moshe saw that all the work had been done just as the LORD had
commanded – and Moshe blessed them.

40 1 2 Then the LORD spoke to Moshe, saying, "On the first day of the first month
3 you shall set up the Tabernacle of the Tent of Meeting. Put in it the Ark
4 of the Testimony, and screen the Ark with the curtain. Bring in the table
5 and set it. Bring in the candelabrum and light its lamps. Put the golden
incense altar in front of the Ark of the Testimony, and hang the screen for
6 the Tabernacle's entrance. Put the sacrificial altar in front of the entrance of
7 the Tabernacle of the Tent of Meeting. Place the laver between the Tent of
8 Meeting and the altar, and put water in it. Arrange the courtyard all around,
and put in place the screen for the courtyard gate.

9 "Take the anointing oil and anoint the Tabernacle and everything in it.
10 Consecrate it and all its furnishings so that it becomes holy. Anoint the
sacrificial altar and all its utensils, consecrating it so that it becomes holy
11 of holies. Anoint the laver with its base, making it holy.

12 "Then bring Aharon and his sons to the entrance of the Tent of Meeting,
13 and cleanse them with water. Robe Aharon with the sacred vestments and
14 anoint him, that he may serve Me as priest. Then bring his sons forward,
15 robe them with tunics, and anoint them as you anointed their father, that
they may serve Me as priests. Through this anointing, theirs will become
an everlasting priesthood throughout the generations."

16 17 Moshe did exactly as the LORD had commanded him. On the first day
18 of the first month of the second year[69] the Tabernacle was set up. Moshe
set up the Tabernacle, placed its sockets, erected its frames, inserted its
19 bars, and put up its posts. He spread the tent over the Tabernacle and
20 placed the covering over the tent, as the LORD had commanded him. He
took the covenant and put it in the Ark. He inserted the carrying staves
21 into the Ark and placed the cover on top of it. He brought the Ark into
the Tabernacle and hung the cloth curtain, screening off the Ark of the
22 Testimony, as the LORD had commanded him. He put the table in the Tent
23 of Meeting, outside the curtain on the north side of the Tabernacle, and
arranged the bread on it before the LORD, as the LORD had commanded
24 him. He placed the candelabrum in the Tent of Meeting, opposite the
25 table, on the Tabernacle's south side, and lit the lamps before the LORD,
26 as the LORD had commanded him. He placed the golden altar in the Tent
27 of Meeting, in front of the curtain, and on it he burned fragrant incense,
28 as the LORD had commanded him. He hung the curtain at the entrance of
29 the Tabernacle. He put the sacrificial altar at the entrance of the Tabernacle
of the Tent of Meeting, and on it sacrificed a burnt offering and a grain
30 offering, as the LORD had commanded him. He placed the laver between
the Tent of Meeting and the altar, and in it he put water for washing.

69 | Since the exodus from Egypt.

31 Moshe, Aharon, and his sons would wash their hands and feet there, for
32 they washed themselves whenever they went into the Tent of Meeting or
33 approached the altar, as the LORD had commanded Moshe. Then he set up
the courtyard around the Tabernacle and the altar, and hung the curtain
for the courtyard gate.

And so Moshe completed the work.

34 Then the cloud covered the Tent of Meeting, and the glory of the LORD
35 filled the Tabernacle. Moshe could not now enter the Tent of Meeting,
because the cloud had settled on it, and the glory of the LORD filled the
36 Tabernacle. In all the journeys of the Israelites, when the cloud rose from
37 the Tabernacle, they would set out. But if the cloud did not lift, they did
38 not move on; they waited until it had lifted. The LORD's cloud was over
the Tabernacle by day, and fire was in it at night, in view of all the House
of Israel through all their journeys.

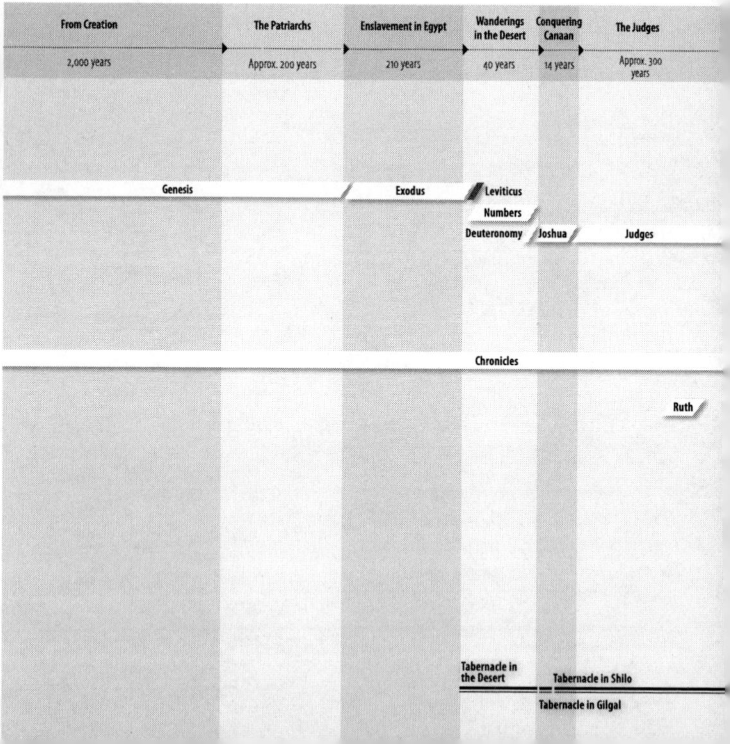

From Creation	The Patriarchs	Enslavement in Egypt	Wanderings in the Desert	Conquering Canaan	The Judges
2,000 years	Approx. 200 years	210 years	40 years	14 years	Approx. 300 years

Genesis

Exodus

Leviticus

Numbers

Deuteronomy

Joshua

Judges

Chronicles

Ruth

Tabernacle in the Desert

Tabernacle in Shilo

Tabernacle in Gilgal

LEVITICUS/VAYIKRA

LEVITICUS	Offerings	Initiation of the priests and their service	Ritual purity and impurity	Laws of sanctity
	Chs. 1–7	8–10	11–16	17–27
	Approx. 1 month			

VAYIKRA

1 1 The LORD called to Moshe. From the Tent of Meeting He spoke to him
2 and said, "Speak to the Israelites. Say: When one of you brings an animal
offering to the LORD, you may bring it either from the herd or from the
flock.

3 "If the offering is a burnt offering from the herd, one must offer a male
animal without blemish. The one making the offering shall bring it to the
entrance to the Tent of Meeting to be accepted on his behalf before the
4 LORD; and, that it be accepted on his behalf, to make his atonement, he
5 shall lay his hand on the head of the burnt offering and shall have the bull
slaughtered before the LORD. And Aharon's sons the priests shall present
the blood, dashing it against each side of the altar at the entrance to the
6 Tent of Meeting. The burnt offering shall then be skinned and cut into
7 pieces. The sons of Aharon the priest shall arrange wood on the fire they
8 will have placed upon the altar. Then Aharon's sons the priests shall arrange
the pieces of the sacrifice, with the head and the fat, upon the wood on the
9 altar fire; the inner organs and legs shall first be washed with water. The
priest shall then burn it all on the altar as a burnt offering, an offering of
fire, a pleasing aroma to the LORD.

10 "If the offering is a burnt offering from the flock, whether a sheep or a goat,
11 one must offer a male without blemish. The one making the sacrifice shall
have it slaughtered on the north side of the altar before the LORD, and
Aharon's sons the priests shall dash its blood against each side of the altar.
12 The sacrifice shall be cut into pieces, including the head and the fat, and
13 the priest shall arrange these upon the wood on the altar fire, the inner
organs and legs having been washed with water. The priest shall then offer
it all, sending it up in smoke upon the altar as a burnt offering, an offering
of fire, a pleasing aroma to the LORD.

14 "If the offering for the LORD is to be a burnt offering of fowl, one may offer
15 doves or pigeons. The priest shall bring the offering to the altar, sever its
neck, and burn it on the altar; its blood shall be drained against the altar
16 wall: the priest shall remove the crop with its feathers and throw that to
17 the east side of the altar, to the place where the ashes are gathered. Then
he shall tear the bird open by its wings, without dividing it completely.
The priest shall then send it up in smoke upon the altar, on the wood of
the altar fire. It is a burnt offering, an offering of fire, a pleasing aroma to
the LORD.

2 1 "When one brings a grain offering to the LORD, it shall be of fine flour.
The one who brings the sacrifice shall pour oil over it, then place incense
2 upon it, and bring it to Aharon's sons, the priests. From this, the priest shall
scoop out a handful of its fine flour and oil, together with all its incense,
and send this remembrance[1] up in smoke upon the altar as an offering of

---

1 | A part of the offering sent up in smoke, prompting the Lord to "remember" the individual in a favorable way.

3 fire, a pleasing aroma to the Lord. What remains of the grain offering shall
belong to Aharon and his sons; it is holy of holies among the fire offerings
to the Lord.[2]

4 "When you bring a grain offering baked in an oven, it shall be of fine flour:
unleavened loaves mixed with oil or unleavened wafers spread with oil.

5 "If your offering is grain prepared on a griddle, it shall be of fine flour mixed
6 with oil, and unleavened. Crumble it into pieces and pour oil over it; this
is a grain offering.

7 "If your offering is grain prepared in a pan, it shall be of fine flour in oil.
8 You shall bring the grain offering made in one of these ways to the Lord,
9 presenting it to the priest, who will bring it to the altar. The priest shall lift
a remembrance from the grain offering and send it up in smoke upon the
10 altar as an offering of fire, a pleasing aroma to the Lord. What is left of
this grain offering shall belong to Aharon and his sons; it is holy of holies
11 among the fire offerings to the Lord. No grain offering that you bring to
the Lord shall be made with leaven, for no leaven or honey may be used
12 in a fire offering to the Lord, sent up in smoke. You may bring them as
offerings of first produce to the Lord, but they may not be offered on the
altar as a pleasing aroma.[3]

13 "You shall season all your grain offerings with salt; do not omit from your
grain offering the salt of your covenant with God. You shall offer salt with
all your offerings.

14 "If you bring a grain offering of first produce to the Lord, it shall be
brought as soon as it ripens on the stalk. Roasted in fire, crushed from
15 fresh kernels; thus shall you bring the grain offering of first produce. You
16 shall put oil and incense on it; it is a grain offering. The priest shall send
its remembrance up in smoke – some of the crushed new grain and oil
together with all of the incense – as a fire offering to the Lord.

3 1 "If one's sacrifice is a peace offering, and brought from the herd, whether
male or female, the animal one offers before the Lord must be without
2 blemish. The one bringing the offering shall lay his hand on its head and
have it slaughtered at the entrance to the Tent of Meeting. Aharon's sons
3 the priests shall dash the blood against each side of the altar. A priest shall
present of the peace offering a fire offering to the Lord: the fat that covers
4 the entrails and all the fat surrounding them; the two kidneys and the fat
that is on them at the loins; and the diaphragm of the liver, which should
5 be removed with the kidneys. Aharon's sons shall send all these up in

2 | Offerings in the category of "holy of holies" bear greater restrictions and may be eaten only by the priests.

3 | See, for example, Deuteronomy 26:2.

smoke upon the altar, along with the burnt offering[4] on the wood on the
altar fire – a fire offering, a pleasing aroma to the LORD.

6 "If one's offering is a peace offering from the flock, whether male or female,
7 it must be without blemish. If one brings a sheep as his offering, he shall
8 present it before the LORD. He shall lay his hand on the head of the offering
and have it slaughtered at the entrance to the Tent of Meeting. Aharon's
9 sons the priests shall dash the blood against each side of the altar. The
priest shall present the fat from the peace offering as a fire offering to the
LORD: the whole broad tail, removed close to the backbone; the fat that
10 covers the entrails and all the fat surrounding them; the two kidneys and
the fat that is on them at the loins; and the diaphragm of the liver, which
11 should be removed with the kidneys. The priest shall send these up in
smoke upon the altar: foodstuffs – a fire offering to the LORD.

12 "If the sacrifice is a goat, the one bringing it shall present it before the LORD.
13 He shall lay his hand on the head of the offering and have it slaughtered
at the entrance to the Tent of Meeting. Aharon's sons the priests shall
14 dash the blood against each side of the altar. The priest shall present of
the offering a fire offering to the LORD: the fat that covers the entrails and
15 all the fat surrounding them; the two kidneys and the fat that is on them
at the loins; and the diaphragm of the liver, which should be removed
16 with the kidneys. The priest shall send these up in smoke upon the altar:
foodstuffs – a fire offering to the LORD. All the fatty parts belong to the
17 LORD: this is an everlasting statute throughout your generations in all your
dwellings: you shall not eat either that fat or blood."

4 1 2 The LORD spoke to Moshe: "Tell the Israelites: If a person sins
unintentionally with regard to any of the LORD's commands, doing what
3 should not be done; any transgression – if it is the anointed priest who
sins, bringing guilt upon his people, he shall bring an unblemished young
bull to the LORD as a purification offering for the sin he has committed.
4 He shall bring the bull before the LORD at the entrance to the Tent of
Meeting, lay his hand upon the bull's head, and slaughter the bull before
5 the LORD. The anointed priest shall take some of the bull's blood and bring
6 it into the Tent of Meeting. The priest shall dip his finger into the blood
and sprinkle of it seven times before the LORD in front of the Sanctuary's
7 inner curtain. Then the priest shall apply some of the blood to the horns
of the altar of fragrant incense, which is in the Tent of Meeting before the
LORD.[5] The rest of the bull's blood he shall pour out at the base of the altar
8 of burnt offerings, at the entrance to the Tent of Meeting.[6] He shall remove
all the fat from the bull of the purification offering: the fat that covers the
9 entrails and all the fat surrounding them; the two kidneys and the fat that
is on them at the loins; and the diaphragm of the liver, which should be

4 | Apparently the burnt offering that was brought every morning (see Ex. 29:38–42).

5 | See Exodus 30:1–10.

6 | See Exodus 27:1–7.

10 removed with the kidneys, just as it is removed from the ox of the peace
offering.[7] The priest shall send these up in smoke upon the altar of burnt
11 offerings. But the bull's skin and all its flesh, together with its head, legs,
12 entrails, and dung – all the rest of the bull – he shall take to a ritually pure
place outside the camp, to the ash heap, and burn upon a wood fire; at the
ash heap it shall be burned.

13 "If it is the entire community of Israel that commits an unintentional
sin, the congregation unwittingly violating one of the LORD's commands,
14 doing what must not be done, when the sin that they committed becomes
known, the community shall bring a young bull as a purification offering,
15 presenting it before the Tent of Meeting. The community elders shall lay
their hands on the bull's head before the LORD and, before the LORD, the
16 bull shall be slaughtered. The anointed priest shall take some of the bull's
17 blood into the Tent of Meeting. The priest shall dip his finger into the
blood and sprinkle it seven times before the LORD in front of the curtain.
18 Then he shall apply some of the blood to the horns of the altar before the
LORD in the Tent of Meeting, and pour out all the rest at the base of the
19 altar of burnt offerings, at the entrance to the Tent of Meeting. Then he
20 shall remove all its fat and send it up in smoke upon the altar. He shall do
the same with this bull as he does with the bull of his purification offering;[8]
he shall do the same with this. So shall the priest make atonement for
21 the people, and they shall be forgiven. The priest shall then take the bull
outside the camp and burn it just as he burns the first bull.[9] This is the
community's purification offering.

22 "When a leader sins unintentionally with regard to any of the LORD's
23 commands, doing what must not be done and thus incurring guilt, when
the sin that he has committed is made known to him, he shall bring an
24 unblemished male goat as his offering. He shall lay his hand upon the goat's
head, and it shall be slaughtered in the place where burnt offerings are
25 slaughtered before the LORD. It is a purification offering. The priest shall
take some of the blood from the purification offering with his finger, and
apply it to the horns of the altar of burnt offerings. The rest of the blood
26 he shall pour out at the base of the altar of burnt offerings. He shall send
up all its fat in smoke upon the altar, like the fat of the peace offerings.[10]
So shall the priest make atonement for that leader for his sin, and he will
be forgiven.

27 "If an individual among the people sins unintentionally with regard to
any of the LORD's commands, doing what should not be done and thus
28 incurring guilt, when the sin he has committed is made known to him, he
shall bring an unblemished female goat as his offering to atone for the sin

---

7 | See 3:3–4.
8 | Above, verses 5–10.
9 | Above, verses 11–12.
10 | See 3:3–5.

29 that he committed. He shall lay his hand on the head of the purification
offering, and it shall be slaughtered in the same place as the burnt offerings.
30 The priest shall take some of its blood with his finger, and apply it to the
horns of the altar of burnt offerings. The rest of the blood he shall pour
31 out at the base of the altar. The priest shall remove all its fat, just as the fat
is removed from a peace offering, and send it up in smoke upon the altar
as a pleasing aroma to the Lord. So shall the priest make atonement for
that person, and he will be forgiven.

32 "If one brings a sheep as a purification offering,[11] it shall be an unblemished
33 female. One shall lay one's hand upon the head of the purification
offering, and it shall be slaughtered in the place where burnt offerings are
34 slaughtered. The priest shall take some of its blood with his finger, and
apply it to the horns of the altar of burnt offerings. The rest of the blood
35 he shall pour out at the base of the altar. He shall remove all its fat, as the
fat of a sheep is removed from a peace offering. The priest shall send it up
in smoke upon the altar with the other fire offerings to the Lord. So shall
the priest make atonement for that person for the sin that he committed,
and he will be forgiven.

5 1 "If a person sins by failing to testify after hearing a public adjuration to
do so: if he knows or has seen something, yet does not speak up, and thus
2 bears his guilt; or sins through touching an impure thing – the carcass of an
impure beast, or a carcass of impure livestock, or the carcass of an impure
creeping creature – and it escapes his notice, and while impure, he incurs
3 guilt;[12] or sins by touching human impurity of any kind that makes him
4 impure, and it escapes his notice, but later he realizes his guilt; or sins by
making a verbal oath to do something, bad or good – whatever one might
carelessly swear – and it escapes his attention, but later he realizes his
5 guilt;[13] in any one of these ways – when he realizes the guilt he has incurred
6 in any of these ways, he shall confess the sin he has committed, and bring
the amends of his guilt to the Lord for the sin he has committed: a female
sheep or goat as a purification offering. So shall the priest make atonement
for that person for his sin.

7 "If he cannot afford a sheep,[14] he shall bring two doves or two pigeons as
his guilt offering to the Lord, one as a purification offering and the other
8 as a burnt offering. He shall bring them to the priest, who will offer the first
as a purification offering, severing its neck at the back without detaching
9 the head. Then he shall sprinkle some of the blood of the purification
offering against the side of the altar; the rest of the blood shall be drained
10 out at its base. This is the purification offering. He shall then offer the
second bird as a burnt offering in the prescribed way. So shall the priest

11 | Meaning as an alternative to the goat mentioned in verse 28.

12 | For example, by entering the Sanctuary while impure.

13 | In that he has violated his oath.

14 | The word *seh*, here translated "sheep," can denote either a sheep or a goat; see verse 6.

make atonement for that person for the sin he has committed, and he will
be forgiven.

11 "If he cannot afford two doves or two pigeons, he shall bring the purification
offering of a tenth of an ephah of fine flour as the sacrifice for his sin. He
shall not put any oil on it, nor place on it any incense, for it is a purification
12 offering. He shall bring it to the priest, and the priest shall lift a handful
from it – its remembrance – and send it up in smoke upon the altar with
13 the LORD's fire offerings. It is a purification offering. Thus shall the priest
make atonement for that person for whichever one of these sins he has
committed, and he will be forgiven. The rest of the offering, as in the case
of a grain offering,[15] shall belong to the priest."

14 15 And the LORD spoke to Moshe: "If a person commits a trespass, sinning
unintentionally with respect to any of the LORD's sacred objects, he shall
bring an unblemished ram from the flock, valued in silver shekel by the
Sanctuary weight,[16] as his guilt offering to the LORD; it is a guilt offering.
16 He shall make restitution for his trespass against the sacred object, adding
one-fifth to its value and giving it to the priest. The priest shall make his
atonement with the ram of the guilt offering, and he will be forgiven.

17 "If a person sins without realizing it, doing any of the things that the LORD
commanded not to be done, he incurs guilt and is subject to punishment.
18 He shall bring an unblemished ram from the flock, of the appropriate
value, as a guilt offering to the priest. The priest shall atone for him for that
19 unintentional sin, committed unknowingly, and he will be forgiven. This
is a guilt offering, for he had incurred guilt before the LORD."

20 21 The LORD spoke to Moshe: "If a person sins, committing a trespass against
the LORD by lying to his neighbor about a deposit or pledge, or by robbery,
22 or by defrauding his neighbor, or by finding lost property and lying about
it; if he swears falsely about anything he does in any of the ways a person
23 sins, afterward acknowledging guilt for the sin, he shall return what he
took by robbery or fraud, or the deposit left with him for safekeeping, or
24 the lost property that he found, or anything else about which he swore
falsely. He shall repay its value and add to that a fifth; he shall pay this to
25 its owner on the day he presents his guilt offering. And as his guilt offering
to the LORD he shall bring the priest an unblemished ram from the flock
26 of the appropriate value. The priest shall make his atonement before the
LORD, and he will be forgiven for whatever he did to incur this guilt."

TZAV 6 1 2 The LORD spoke to Moshe: "Instruct Aharon and his sons: This is the law
of the burnt offering.[17] The burnt offering shall remain on the altar hearth
all night until the morning, and the altar fire shall be kept alight upon it.

15 | See 2:3.

16 | Sanctuary weights differed from standard weights.

17 | The passages that follow concentrate on the responsibilities of the priests with regard to each type of offering.

3 The priest shall dress in his linen vestments, with linen undergarments
against his skin. He shall lift the ashes of the burnt offering that the fire
4 consumed on the altar, and place them by the altar's side. Then he shall take
off his vestments, put on other garments, and take the ashes to a ritually
5 pure place outside the camp. The altar fire shall be kept alight; it shall not
go out. Every morning the priest shall add wood to it, lay out the burnt
offering upon it, and send the fat parts of the peace offering up in smoke
6 upon it. A daily fire shall be kept alight on the altar; it shall not go out.

7 "This is the law of the grain offering. Aharon's sons shall bring these before
8 the LORD in front of the altar. The priest shall lift a handful of the fine
flour and oil from the grain offering, and all the incense on it, and send
this remembrance up in smoke upon the altar as a pleasing aroma to the
9 LORD. Aharon and his sons shall eat what is left of it. It shall be eaten as
unleavened bread in a holy place; in the courtyard of the Tent of Meeting
10 shall they eat it. It shall not be baked with any leaven. I have given it as
their portion of My fire offerings; it is holy of holies, like the purification
11 offering and the guilt offering. Any male among Aharon's descendants may
eat it as their eternal share of the LORD's fire offerings throughout their
generations; anything that touches it is sanctified."

12 13 The LORD spoke to Moshe: "This is the offering of Aharon and his sons that
each shall present to the LORD on the day when he is anointed: one-tenth
of an ephah of fine flour as a continual grain offering, half in the morning
14 and half in the evening. It shall be made on a griddle with oil. You shall
bring it well mixed, and offer it in pieces like a crumbled grain offering,
15 as a pleasing aroma to the LORD. The priest among Aharon's sons who is
anointed to succeed him shall prepare it; it is the LORD's perpetual share,
16 to be sent up in smoke in its entirety. Any grain offering from a priest shall
be wholly burned; it shall not be eaten."

17 18 The LORD spoke to Moshe: "Tell Aharon and his sons: This is the law of
the purification offering. The purification offering shall be slaughtered
before the LORD at the place where burnt offerings are slaughtered; it is
19 holy of holies. The priest who offers it as a purification offering shall eat of
it. It shall be eaten in a holy place, in the courtyard of the Tent of Meeting.
20 Anything that touches its flesh is sanctified; if any of its blood splashes
21 on a garment, you shall wash that part in a holy place. An earthen vessel
in which it was cooked shall be broken, but if it was cooked in a bronze
22 vessel, that shall be scoured and rinsed with water. Any male among the
23 priests may eat of it; it is holy of holies. But no purification offering shall
be eaten from which blood is brought inside the Tent of Meeting to make
atonement within the Sanctuary;[18] that shall be burned with fire.

7 1 2 "And this is the law of the guilt offering; it is holy of holies. The guilt offering
shall be slaughtered at the place where burnt offerings are slaughtered, and

18 | See, e.g., 4:3–21.

3 its blood dashed against each side of the altar. All its fat shall be offered: the
4 broad tail, the fat covering the entrails, the two kidneys and the fat around
them at the loins, and the diaphragm of the liver, which shall be removed
5 with the kidneys. The priest shall turn these into smoke on the altar as a
6 fire offering for the LORD; it is a guilt offering. Any male priest may eat of
it and it shall be eaten in a holy place; it is holy of holies.

7 "The guilt offering follows the same law as the purification offering: it
8 belongs to the priest who makes atonement with it. The priest who offers
any person's burnt offering shall keep the skin of the burnt offering that
9 he has offered. Any grain offering baked in an oven or prepared in a pan
10 or griddle also belongs to the priest who offers it, while every other grain
offering, whether mixed with oil or dry, shall belong equally to all of
Aharon's sons.

11 12 "This is the law of the peace sacrifice that one may offer to the LORD: If it
is offered for thanksgiving, one offers unleavened loaves mixed with oil
with the thanksgiving sacrifice, and unleavened wafers spread with oil, and
13 loaves of fine flour mixed with oil. This offering, together with loaves of
leavened bread, he shall present with the peace sacrifice of thanksgiving.
14 Of these he shall offer one of each kind as a gift raised up to the LORD. This
shall belong to the priest who dashed the blood of the peace offering.

15 "The flesh of the peace sacrifice of thanksgiving shall be eaten on the day
16 it is offered; you may not leave any of it to the morning. If the sacrifice is
to fulfill a vow, however, or is a freewill offering, it shall be eaten on the
day when one offers the sacrifice, while what is left over may be eaten the
17 next day. Whatever of the flesh of the sacrifice is left over on the third day
18 shall be burned with fire. If any of the flesh of the peace sacrifice is eaten
on the third day, it shall not be accepted, nor shall it be credited to the
one who offered it. It is offensive, and anyone who eats of it is liable to
punishment.

19 "Flesh that touches any impure thing shall not be eaten; it shall be burned
20 with fire. As for other flesh, any ritually pure person may eat it, but one who
eats the flesh of a peace sacrifice to the LORD in a state of impurity shall be
21 severed from his people. When anyone touches any impure thing – human
impurity, or an impure animal, or any impure, detested creature – and then
eats flesh from the LORD's peace sacrifice, that person shall be severed
from his people."

22 23 The LORD spoke to Moshe: "Tell the Israelites: Do not eat the fat of an ox,
24 sheep, or goat. The fat of one of these that died naturally or was killed by
25 another animal may be put to other use, but you may not eat it. For anyone
who eats the fat of an animal of which a fire offering could be offered to
26 the LORD – he is severed from his people. Do not eat any blood, whether
27 that of a bird or of an animal, in any of your dwellings. Anyone who eats
any blood shall be cut off from his people."

28 29 And the LORD spoke to Moshe: "Tell the Israelites: One who brings a
peace sacrifice to the LORD is to bring the offering of his peace sacrifice
30 before the LORD himself; with his own hands he shall present the LORD's
fire offerings. He shall bring the animal's fat and breast so that the breast
can be displayed, this way and that, as a wave offering before the LORD.
31 The priest shall send the fat up in smoke upon the altar, but the breast
32 shall go to Aharon and his sons. The right thigh of your peace offering
33 you shall give as an upraised gift to the priest.[19] The one among the sons
of Aharon who offers the blood and fat of the peace offering shall receive
34 the right thigh as his portion. For I have taken from the peace sacrifices of
the Israelites the breast of the wave offering and the thigh of the upraised
gift, and given them to Aharon the priest and to his sons as their perpetual
share from the Israelites.

35 "This is the anointed right of Aharon and his sons from the LORD's fire
36 offerings from the day they are presented to serve the LORD as priests; when
the LORD anointed them as priests He commanded that these be given them
by the Israelites as their perpetual share throughout the generations."

37 This, then, is the law for the burnt offering, the grain offering, the purification offering, the guilt offering, the ordination offering,[20] and the peace
38 offering, which the LORD commanded Moshe at Mount Sinai when he
commanded the Israelites to bring their offerings to the LORD, in the
Wilderness of Sinai.

8 1 2 The LORD said to Moshe:[21] "Take Aharon, and his sons with him, the
vestments, the anointing oil, a bull for the purification offering, two rams,
3 and a basket of unleavened bread, and assemble the whole community at
4 the entrance to the Tent of Meeting." Moshe did as the LORD commanded
him; and the community was assembled at the entrance to the Tent of
5 Meeting. And Moshe told the community, "This is what the LORD has
commanded us to do."

6 Then Moshe brought Aharon and his sons close, and he washed them with
7 water. He put the tunic on Aharon, tied the sash around him, clothed him
in the robe, and placed the ephod on him. He bound the ephod's decorated
8 belt about him, securing the ephod to him.[22] Then he put the breast piece
9 on him, and inside the breast piece he placed the Urim and Tumim. On his
head he placed the miter, and on the miter in front, he placed the golden
head plate, the holy diadem, as the LORD had commanded him.

10 Then Moshe took the anointing oil and anointed the Tabernacle and
11 everything in it; thus he consecrated them. He sprinkled some of the oil
on the altar seven times. He anointed the altar and all its vessels, and the

19 | The term *teruma* – here translated "upraised gift" – commonly denotes a sanctified gift.
20 | See Exodus, chapter 29.
21 | This passage recounts the performance of the priestly ordination ritual.
22 | See Exodus, chapter 28, for descriptions of the priestly vestments.

12 laver and its base, thus consecrating them. Some of the anointing oil he
13 poured on Aharon's head, anointing him, consecrating him. Then Moshe
brought close Aharon's sons, dressed them in their tunics, bound sashes
about them, and placed their headdresses on them, just as the LORD had
commanded him.

14 Moshe drew close the bull for the purification offering, and Aharon and
15 his sons laid their hands on its head. It was slaughtered, and Moshe took
the blood and applied it with his finger to all the altar's horns, purifying
the altar. The rest of the blood he poured out at the altar's base. Thus he
16 consecrated it so that, upon it, atonement could be made. Moshe removed
all the fat around the entrails, the diaphragm of the liver, the two kidneys
17 and their fat, and sent them up in smoke upon the altar. But the rest of the
bull, its skin, its flesh, and its dung, he burned with fire outside the camp
as the LORD had commanded him.

18 Then Moshe drew close the ram for the burnt offering, and Aharon and
19 his sons laid their hands on its head. Moshe slaughtered it and dashed the
20 blood against each side of the altar. He cut the ram into pieces and sent
21 the head, pieces, and suet up in smoke. After washing the entrails and legs
with water, Moshe sent the entire ram up in smoke upon the altar. It was
a burnt offering for a pleasing aroma: a fire offering to the LORD, as the
LORD had commanded Moshe.

22 Moshe then drew close the second ram, the ram of ordination. Aharon and
23 his sons laid their hands upon its head. It was slaughtered; and Moshe took
some of its blood and applied it to the ridge of Aharon's right ear, to his
24 right thumb, and to his right big toe. He drew Aharon's sons close and put
some of the blood on the ridges of their right ears, on their right thumbs,
and on their right big toes. Moshe dashed the rest of the blood against each
25 of the altar's sides. Then he took the fat, the broad tail, all the fat around
the entrails, the diaphragm of the liver, and the two kidneys with their
26 fat, as well as the right thigh. He took a loaf of unleavened bread from the
basket, before the LORD, and also one loaf of oil bread, and one wafer, and
27 placed them on the fat and on the right thigh. All of this he placed on the
palms of Aharon and of his sons, and displayed them this way and that
28 as a wave offering before the LORD. Then Moshe took them from their
hands and burnt them upon the altar with the burnt offering. This was the
29 ordination offering, a pleasing aroma, a fire offering to the LORD. Moshe
then took the breast and waved it as a wave offering before the LORD. This
was Moshe's portion of the ordination ram, as the LORD had commanded
30 him. Moshe took some of the anointing oil and some of the blood from
the altar and sprinkled it on Aharon and on his vestments, and on his sons
and theirs. Thus Moshe consecrated Aharon and his vestments, and his
sons and their vestments.

31 Then Moshe said to Aharon and his sons: "Cook the meat at the entrance
to the Tent of Meeting and eat it there together with the bread in the basket

of the ordination offering, as I have charged you: Aharon and his sons
32 shall eat it. Whatever is left over of the meat and the bread, burn with fire.
33 Do not leave the entrance to the Tent of Meeting for seven days, until the
days of your ordination are complete, for your ordination will take seven
34 days, each like today. This is what the LORD has commanded to be done
35 to make your atonement. Stay, then, at the entrance to the Tent of Meeting
for seven days, day and night, keeping the LORD's charge – and you will
not die. This is what I have been commanded."

36 And Aharon and his sons did everything that the LORD had commanded
through Moshe.

9 1 On the eighth day, Moshe called to Aharon and his sons, and to the SHEMINI
2 elders of Israel. "Take a bull calf for yourself as a purification offering," he
told Aharon, "and a ram for a burnt offering, both without blemish, and
3 offer them up before the LORD. Then tell the Israelites: Take a goat for a
purification offering, and a calf and a lamb, both yearlings without blemish,
4 for a burnt offering, a bull and a ram for a peace offering to offer up before
the LORD, and a grain offering mixed with oil – for on this day the LORD
will be revealed to you."

5 They brought what Moshe had commanded to the space before the Tent
of Meeting, and all the community drew near and stood before the LORD.
6 Moshe said, "This is what the LORD has commanded you to do so that
7 the LORD's glory be revealed to you." Moshe said to Aharon, "Approach
the altar, prepare your purification offering and burnt offering, and make
atonement for you and for the people. Then prepare the people's offering
to make atonement for them, as the LORD has commanded."

8 Aharon drew close to the altar and slaughtered the calf of his purification
9 offering. Aharon's sons presented him with the blood, and he dipped his
finger into it and applied the blood to the horns of the altar; the rest of the
10 blood he poured out at the altar's base. Then he sent the fat, the kidneys,
and the diaphragm of the liver from the purification offering up in smoke
11 upon the altar as the LORD had commanded Moshe, and he burned the
flesh and skin with fire outside the camp.

12 Then he slaughtered the burnt offering. Aharon's sons presented him with
13 the blood, and he dashed it on each side of the altar. Then they presented
him with the burnt offering in its pieces, with its head, and he sent them
14 up in smoke upon the altar. Having washed the entrails and legs, he sent
them up in smoke upon the altar with the burnt offering.

15 Then he brought close the people's offering. He took the goat of
the people's purification offering, slaughtered it, and prepared it as a
16 purification offering like the first. He presented the burnt offering and
17 sacrificed it in the prescribed way. He then presented the grain offering,
took a handful from it, and sent this portion up in smoke upon the altar,
with the morning's burnt offering.

18 He slaughtered the ox and the ram: the people's peace sacrifice. Aharon's
sons presented him with the blood, and he dashed it against each side of
19 the altar, and the fat parts of the ox and ram:[23] the broad tail, the covering
20 fat, the kidneys, and the diaphragm of the liver. They laid the fat parts over
21 the breasts, and he sent them up in smoke upon the altar. But the breasts
and right thigh Aharon displayed, this way and that, as a wave offering
before the LORD, as Moshe had commanded.

22 Then Aharon raised his hands to the people and blessed them. And,
having presented the purification offering, the burnt offering, and the
23 peace sacrifice, he stepped down. Moshe and Aharon entered the Tent
of Meeting; when they came out, they blessed the people, and the glory
24 of the LORD was revealed to all the people. And from before the LORD,
fire came forth. It consumed the burnt offering and the fat pieces on the
altar; and all the people saw it, and cried out for joy, and threw themselves
facedown upon the ground.

10 1 Aharon's sons Nadav and Avihu took their fire pans, put fire in them, and
placed incense upon it, and they offered unauthorized fire before the
2 LORD: fire He had not commanded. And fire came forth from before the
LORD and consumed them. They died before the LORD.

3 Moshe said to Aharon, "Of this the LORD spoke when He said: I will be
sanctified through those close to Me, and before all the people I will be
honored."[24] And Aharon was silent.

4 Moshe called to Mishael and Eltzafan, sons of Uziel, Aharon's uncle;
"Draw near," he said, "carry your kinsmen from the Sanctuary and take
5 them outside the camp." They approached and, as Moshe had instructed
them, they carried Nadav and Avihu out by their tunics to a place outside
6 the camp. Moshe said to Aharon and to Elazar and Itamar his sons, "Do
not dishevel your hair or tear your clothes[25] or you will die and bring fury
down upon the whole community. Your brothers, the whole House of
7 Israel, may mourn the burning that the LORD has brought about. But you
must not leave the entrance to the Tent of Meeting or you will die, for the
LORD's anointing oil is upon you." They did as Moshe had told them.

8 And the LORD spoke to Aharon: "You and your sons must not drink wine
9 or strong drink when you enter the Tent of Meeting, so that you do not
10 die. This is an everlasting statute throughout your generations, to enable
you to distinguish between sacred and profane, and between impure and
11 pure, and to teach the Israelites all the statutes that the LORD has spoken
to them through Moshe."

12 Moshe told Aharon, and Elazar and Itamar, the two sons left to him, "Take

23 | In addition to the blood, Aharon's sons also presented him with the fat.

24 | Explanations of this statement and when it was uttered vary.

25 | Acts that a mourner would typically have performed.

the grain offering left over after the fire offerings to the LORD and eat it
13 unleavened beside the altar, for it is holy of holies. You must eat it in a holy
place because it is your share, and that of your sons, from the LORD's fire
offerings, for so I have been commanded.

14 "But you and your sons and daughters may eat the breast of the wave
offering and the thigh of the upraised gift in any ritually pure place, for
these have been given to you from the peace sacrifices of Israel as your
15 portion and the portion of your children. The thigh for the upraised gift
and the breast for the wave offering are to be brought, with the fat of
the fire offering, to be waved as a wave offering before the LORD. These
are to be your share and that of your children forever, as the LORD has
commanded."

16 Moshe inquired about the goat for the purification offering, and discovered
that it had been burned. He was furious with Elazar and Itamar, the two
17 sons left to Aharon. "Why did you not eat the purification offering in the
holy area?" he asked. "It is holy of holies, and it has been given to you to
remove the guilt of the community and atone for them before the LORD.
18 Because its blood was not to be brought into the inner Sanctuary, you
should have eaten it in the Sanctuary, as I commanded."[26]

19 It was Aharon who replied to Moshe, "They offered their purification
offering and their burnt offerings before the LORD today – but such things
have happened to me. Would it really have been right in the LORD's eyes
20 if I had eaten a purification offering today?" Moshe listened; and it was
right in his eyes.

11 1 2 The LORD spoke to Moshe and Aharon, saying to them: "Tell the Israelites:
3 These are the creatures that you may eat among the land mammals: You
may eat any animal that has divided hoofs, fully split, and chews the cud.
4 Among those that chew the cud or have divided hoofs you must not eat
the following: the camel, because though it chews the cud, it does not
5 have divided hoofs, and so it is impure for you; the hyrax, though it chews
6 the cud, does not have divided hoofs and so it is impure for you; the hare,
though it chews the cud, does not have divided hoofs and so it is impure
7 for you; the pig, though it has fully divided hoofs, does not chew the cud
8 and so it is impure for you. You may not eat the flesh of these animals or
touch their carcasses; they are impure for you.

9 "These you may eat among the creatures of the water: anything in the
water, whether in sea or in stream, that has fins and scales may be eaten,
10 whereas anything in the sea or the stream that does not have fins and scales,
whether one of the swarming creatures of the water or any other of living
11 creature there, is detestable to you and will remain so. You may not eat

26 | See 6:23.

12 their flesh, and you shall detest their carcasses. Anything in the water that
does not have fins or scales is detestable to you.

13 "Among the birds, the following you shall regard as detestable – being
detested they shall not be eaten:[27] the griffon vulture, the bearded vulture,
14 15 the lappet-faced vulture, the kite, any kind of buzzard, any kind of raven,
16 17 the ostrich, the swift, the gull, any kind of sparrow hawk, the little owl, the
18 19 fish owl, the short-eared owl, the barn owl, the pelican, the vulture, the
stork, any kind of heron, the hoopoe, and the bat.

20 "All swarming, flying creatures that crawl on fours are detestable to you,
21 but you may eat those swarming, flying creatures that crawl on four legs,
22 with legs jointed above their feet with which they hop on the ground. Of
these you may eat the following: any kind of locust, bald locust, cricket,
23 or grasshopper. Every other swarming, flying, crawling creature on fours
is detestable to you.

24 "You become impure through these: whoever touches their carcasses shall
25 be impure until evening, and whoever moves their carcasses shall immerse
26 his clothes and be impure until evening. All livestock with divided hoofs
that are not completely split, or that do not chew the cud, are impure for
27 you; whoever touches them becomes impure. Among four-footed animals,
all those that walk on their paws are impure for you; anyone touching their
28 carcasses shall be impure until evening. One who moves their carcasses
shall immerse his clothes and be impure until evening; these animals are
impure for you.

29 "Among the creatures that creep along the ground, the following are
impure for you:[28] the marten, the mouse, every kind of spiny-tailed lizard,
30 the legless lizard, the chameleon, the lizard, the skink, and the mole rat.
31 Of all the creatures that creep along the ground, these are impure for you;
whoever touches them when they are dead shall be impure until evening.
32 And if any of these dies and falls on something – a wooden vessel, clothing,
leather goods or sackcloth, any utensil with which work is done – it renders
it impure. The article must be immersed in water and then remains impure
33 until evening, when it will become pure again. If any of these falls into a
pottery jar, everything inside it becomes impure; you must smash the pot.
34 Edible food becomes impure in such a jar if water has been poured over;
any drinkable beverage in such a jar becomes impure.

35 "Anything on which a part of one of their dead bodies falls becomes
impure. If it is an oven or stove, it must be broken into pieces; it is impure
36 for you and will remain so. A spring or cistern holding water remains pure,
37 but anyone who touches one of their dead bodies in it becomes impure. If
any part of their dead bodies falls on seed that has been planted, the seed

27 | The identities of many of these birds are subject to debate.

28 | The identities of these animals are debated.

38 remains pure. But if water has been poured over the seed and afterward
any part of their dead bodies falls upon it, it is rendered impure for you.

39 "If an animal of a kind that you are allowed to eat dies naturally, one who
40 touches its carcass shall be impure until evening. Anyone who eats of its
carcass must immerse his clothes, and he remains impure until evening.
Anyone who moves the carcass must immerse his clothes, and he remains
impure until evening.

41 "All creatures that swarm on the earth are detested; they shall not be eaten.
42 Of these swarming things you shall not eat any, those that move on their
bellies or crawl on all fours or on many feet – for they are all detestable.
43 Do not make yourselves detestable by contact with any of these swarming
44 creatures. Do not defile yourselves with them or be defiled by them. I am
the Lord your God. Consecrate yourselves and be holy, for I am holy.
Do not defile yourselves with any swarming creature that crawls on the
45 ground. I am the Lord, who brought you up out of Egypt to be your God.
Be holy, for I am holy."

46 This is the law concerning animals, birds, all creatures that live in water
47 and all that swarm on the earth, to distinguish between the impure and the
pure and between creatures that may be eaten and those that may not.

12 1 The Lord spoke to Moshe: "Tell the Israelites: If a woman conceives and TAZRIA
2 gives birth to a son, she shall be impure for seven days, as she is during
3 her menstrual period. On the eighth day, the child's foreskin shall be
4 circumcised. For thirty-three days she shall wait, bleeding pure blood, but
until her time of purification is completed, she must not touch anything
5 holy or enter the Sanctuary. If she gives birth to a daughter, she shall be
impure – as she is during her menstrual period – for two weeks, and bleeds
in purity for sixty-six days.

6 "When the days of her purification are complete, whether for a son or a
daughter, she shall bring a yearling sheep to the priest at the entrance to the
Tent of Meeting as a burnt offering and a pigeon or dove as a purification
7 offering. The priest shall present it before the Lord and make atonement
for her; so shall she be purified of her source of blood."

This is the law for a woman who bears a child, male or female.

8 "But if she cannot afford a sheep, she may bring two doves or two
pigeons – one for the burnt offering and the other for the purification
offering. The priest will then make atonement for her, and she shall be
pure."

13 1 The Lord spoke to Moshe and Aharon: "When a person has a swelling,
2 a rash, or a bright patch on his skin, and it develops on his skin into what
seems to be an impure blight, he shall be brought to the priests, to Aharon
3 or one of his sons. The priest shall examine the disease on his skin. If hair

in the diseased part has turned white and the disease appears to be deeper
than the skin, then it is the disease of an impure blight. When the priest
4 sees this, he shall declare the person impure. But if the bright patch on the
skin is white but does not appear to be deeper than the skin and the hair
in it has not turned white, the priest shall quarantine the patient for seven
5 days. On the seventh day the priest shall examine him again. If the disease
has remained the same in appearance and not spread on the patient's skin,
6 the priest shall quarantine him for another seven days. On the seventh
day the priest shall examine it again. If the diseased area has receded and
not spread over the skin, the priest shall declare the patient pure; it was
7 only a rash. He shall immerse his clothes, and he shall be pure. But if the
rash does spread over the skin after he has appeared before the priest
8 for purification, he must appear before the priest again. If the priest sees
that the rash has indeed spread over the skin, he shall declare the person
impure; it is a blight.

9 "When a person has a blight-like disease, he shall be brought to the priest,
10 and the priest shall look. If there is a white swelling in the skin that has
11 turned the hair white, and within the swelling there is healthy flesh, it is a
chronic blight on the skin of his body, and the priest shall pronounce the
patient impure; he need not quarantine him, for he is definitely impure.
12 If, however, the blight has spread over the skin, so that it covers all of the
13 patient's skin from head to foot, wherever the priest can see, the priest shall
make an examination, and if the blight has covered all his body, he shall
pronounce him pure of the disease; if he has turned completely white, he is
14 15 pure. But as soon as healthy flesh appears, the patient is impure. The priest
shall examine the healthy flesh and pronounce him impure; the healthy
16 flesh is impure, for it indicates a blight.[29] But if the healthy flesh turns white
17 again, the patient shall come back to the priest. The priest shall examine
him, and if the disease has indeed whitened, the priest shall pronounce
the patient pure, and he shall be pure.

18 19 "When one has a boil on his skin and it heals, and in the place of the boil
there comes a white swelling or a bright patch of white and reddish color,
20 this shall be shown to the priest. The priest shall then make an examination,
and if the area appears lower than the rest of the skin and its hair has turned
white, the priest shall declare the patient impure: it is a case of blight that
21 has broken out in the boil. But if the priest examines it and there is no
white hair in it and it does not appear lower than the skin, but it has not
22 receded, then the priest shall quarantine the patient for seven days. If it
23 spreads in the skin, the priest shall declare him impure; it is a blight. But if
the bright patch remains in one place and does not spread, it is scar tissue
from the boil, and the priest shall declare the patient pure.

24 "When one has a burn on his skin and the raw flesh of the burn becomes

29 | In conjunction with the surrounding blight, the healthy flesh renders the individual impure.

25 a bright patch, either white and reddish or only white, the priest shall
examine it, and if the hair in the bright patch has turned white and it
appears to be deeper than the skin, then it is a blight. It has broken out in
the burn, and the priest shall pronounce the patient impure: it is a blight.
26 But if the priest examines it and there is no white hair in the spot and it
appears no deeper than the skin, but it has not receded, the priest shall
27 quarantine him for seven days. The priest shall examine him on the seventh
day. If the disease is spreading on the skin, then the priest shall declare him
28 impure; it is a blight. But if the spot remains in its place and has not spread
on the skin, but has receded, then it was a swelling from the burn, and the
priest shall pronounce him pure; it is merely scar tissue from the burn.

29 30 "When a man or woman has a disease on the scalp or beard,[30] and the
priest examines the disease and finds that it appears to be deeper than
the skin, and has fine blond hairs in it, the priest shall declare the person
31 impure. It is a scaling eruption, a blight of the head or beard. If the priest
examines the scaling and it appears no deeper than the skin but there is
no black hair in it, then the priest shall quarantine the person with the
32 scaling eruption for seven days, and on the seventh day the priest shall
examine the disease. If the scaling has not spread, and there is no blond
33 hair among it, and the scaling appears to be no deeper than the skin, then
the patient shall shave himself, but shall not shave the scaled part; and the
priest shall quarantine the person with the scaling eruption for a further
34 seven days. On the seventh day the priest shall examine the scaling, and
if it has not spread in the skin and it appears to be no deeper than the
skin, then the priest shall pronounce the patient pure; he shall immerse
35 his clothes and be pure. But if the scaling spreads in the skin after he is
36 declared pure, and when the priest examines him, if the scaling has spread
37 in the skin, the priest need not seek the blond hair; he is impure. But if it
appears to him that the scaling is unchanged and if black hair has grown
in among it, the eruption is healed and is pure, and the priest shall declare
the person pure.

38 "When a man or a woman has white patches on the skin of his or her body,
39 the priest shall examine them, and if the patches on the skin are dull white,
it is merely a rash breaking out on the skin; the person is pure.

40 41 "If a man loses the hair on his head, it is merely baldness; he is pure. If he
loses the hair from his forehead, it is merely a receding hairline; he is pure.
42 But if there is a white and reddish diseased area on his bald spot or receding
hairline, it is a blight erupting in his bald spot or at his receding hairline.
43 The priest shall examine him, and if the diseased swelling is a white and
reddish area on his bald spot or receding hairline, resembling a blight in
44 the skin of the body, he is a blighted person; he is impure. The priest shall
declare him impure; he has a blight on his scalp.

30 | Meaning on the area where a beard grows.

45 "And a blighted person, one bearing the disease – his clothes shall be torn
and the hair of his head disarrayed. And he shall cover his upper lip as he
46 cries out, 'Impure, impure.' He shall be in a state of impurity for as long
as he has the disease; he is impure. He shall live apart; outside the camp
shall be his dwelling.

47 "When a blight appears in a garment, whether the garment is of wool or
48 of linen, or in the warp or in the weft of the linen or wool cloth, in leather
49 or anything made of leather, if the infection shows as green or red in the
garment, the leather, the warp or the weft, or the article of leather, it is a
50 case of the impure blight and shall be shown to the priest. And the priest
shall examine the disease and quarantine the diseased article for seven
51 days. He shall examine the disease on the seventh day. If the disease has
spread in the garment, the warp or the weft, or the leather, whatever the
leather is used for, the infection is a malignant disease blight; it is impure.
52 The garment shall be burned – or the warp or weft, wool or linen, or any
article of leather that is infected – for it is a malignant disease blight; it
must be burned in fire.

53 "If, however, the priest examines it and the disease has not spread in the
54 garment, the warp or the weft, or the article of leather, then the priest shall
command the article in which the disease appears to be washed, and he
55 shall quarantine it for another seven days. After this washing the priest
shall once more examine the diseased article. If the diseased area has
not changed color, though the disease has not spread, it is impure. You
shall burn it in fire, whether the mark of decay is on the inside or on the
outside.

56 "But if the priest examines it and the diseased area has faded after washing,
he shall tear it out of the garment or the leather or the warp or the weft.
57 If it appears again in the garment, in the warp or weft, or in the leather
article, it is erupting. Whatever has the disease, you shall burn with fire.
58 But the garment, or the warp or weft, or the leather article from which the
disease departs after you have washed it shall be washed a second time
and then be pure."

59 This is the law concerning the disease blight in a garment of wool or of
linen, in warp or in weft, or in any article made of leather, to determine
whether it is pure or impure.

METZORA 14 1 2 The Lord spoke to Moshe: "This shall be the law of the person with an
impure blight on the day he is to be purified. He shall be brought to see
3 the priest, and the priest shall go out of the camp to examine him. If the
4 disease is healed in the blighted person, the priest shall command two
living ritually pure birds, and cedarwood, scarlet wool, and hyssop to be
5 brought for the one who is to be purified. The priest shall command one of
6 the birds to be slaughtered into an earthen vessel, over living water.[31] Then

31 | Water that is taken from a flowing source.

he shall take the living bird, together with the cedarwood, the scarlet wool,
and the hyssop, and dip them and the living bird in the blood of the bird
7 that was killed over living water. With these he shall sprinkle seven times
over the one who is to be purified of the blight to purify him; and he shall
set the living bird free into the open field.

8 "The one who is to be purified shall then wash his clothes, shave off all his
hair, and immerse himself in water; then he shall be purified. After that he
may come into the camp, but he shall dwell outside his tent for seven days.
9 On the seventh day he shall shave all the hair from his head, his beard, and
his eyebrows. When he has shaved off all his hair, he shall wash his clothes
and immerse his body in water, and he shall be pure.

10 "On the eighth day he shall take two unblemished male lambs and one
unblemished ewe lamb in its first year, with three-tenths of an ephah of
11 fine flour mixed with oil as a grain offering, and one *log* of oil. The priest
who purifies shall present the one to be purified, together with these, to
the LORD at the entrance to the Tent of Meeting.

12 "The priest shall take one of the male lambs and offer it as a guilt offering,
along with the *log* of oil; he shall display these, this way and that, as a wave
13 offering before the LORD. He shall slaughter the lamb in the place where
purification offerings and burnt offerings are slaughtered within the holy
place. For the guilt offering, like the purification offering, belongs to the
14 priest and is holy of holies. The priest shall take some of the blood of the
guilt offering and apply it to the ridge of the right ear, to the right thumb,
15 and to the right big toe of the one who is to be purified. The priest shall
16 pour some of the *log* of oil into his own left palm, dip his right finger into
the oil in his left hand, and sprinkle of the oil with his finger seven times
17 before the LORD. The priest shall apply some of the remaining oil in his
hand to the ridge of the right ear, to the right thumb, and to the right big
18 toe of the one who is to be purified, over the guilt offering blood. What
remains of the oil in his hand the priest shall pour on the head of the one to
be purified. Thus shall the priest make his atonement before the LORD.

19 "Then the priest shall offer the purification offering to make atonement
for the one to be purified of his defilement. Then he shall slaughter the
20 burnt offering.[32] The priest shall offer the burnt offering and the grain
offering on the altar.[33] Thus shall the priest make his atonement, and he
shall be purified.

21 "If, however, the person is poor and cannot afford so much, he shall take
one male lamb as a guilt offering to be made a wave offering[34] to make his
atonement, and one-tenth of an ephah of fine flour mixed with oil as a

---

32 | Verse 10 refers to three animals, which are used for a guilt offering, a purification offering, and a burnt offering.

33 | Most parts of the other offerings, by contrast, are eaten by the priests.

34 | The Torah clarifies this procedure in the next passage.

22 grain offering, and a *log* of oil, and two doves or two pigeons, such as he can
afford; one shall be a purification offering and the other a burnt offering.

23 "On the eighth day of his purification, he shall bring them to the priest
24 at the entrance to the Tent of Meeting before the Lord. The priest shall
take the lamb of the guilt offering, together with the *log* of oil, and move
25 them this way and that as a wave offering before the Lord. Then he shall
slaughter the guilt offering lamb. The priest shall take some of the blood
of the guilt offering and apply it to the ridge of the right ear, to the right
26 thumb, and to the right big toe of the one who is to be purified. The priest
27 shall then pour some of the oil into his own left palm, and, using his right
finger, shall sprinkle of the oil that is in his left hand seven times before
28 the Lord. He shall apply some of the oil remaining in his hand to the
ridge of the right ear, to the right thumb, and to the right big toe of the
29 person to be purified, over the guilt offering blood. What remains of the
oil in his hand the priest shall pour on the head of the one to be purified,
30 to make his atonement before the Lord. He shall then offer up one of the
31 doves or pigeons the person could afford; whatever he can afford, one as
a purification offering, and the other as a burnt offering, together with the
grain offering; and thus shall the priest make atonement for the person
who is to be purified before the Lord."

32 This is the law for a person who has an impure blight and cannot afford
the regular offerings for his purification.

33 34 The Lord spoke to Moshe and to Aharon: "When you enter the land of
Canaan that I am giving you as a possession, and I afflict a house in the
35 land you possess with an impure blight, the owner of the house shall come
and tell the priest, 'It looks to me as if there were some disease in the
36 house.' The priest shall instruct them to empty the house before he goes
to examine the disease, to prevent everything in the house from becoming
37 impure. After that, the priest shall go to examine the house. He shall look
at the disease. If the disease is in the walls of the house with greenish or
38 reddish spots that appear to go deep into the wall, the priest shall go out to
39 the door of the house and shut the house up for seven days. On the seventh
day, the priest shall return; he shall examine the disease and, if it has spread
40 in the walls of the house, the priest shall order the stones in which the
disease appears to be removed and thrown into a ritually impure place
41 outside the town. He shall have the inside of the house scraped all around,
and the plaster that they scrape off shall be poured out in an impure place
42 outside the city. They shall take other stones and put them in the place of
those stones, and take new plaster and replaster the house.

43 "If the disease breaks out again in the house after the stones have been
44 removed and the house has been scraped and plastered, the priest shall
come back and examine it. If the disease has spread, then there is malignant
45 blight in the house; it is impure. He shall have the house torn down, its
stones, timber, and all the plaster from the house, and have them all taken

46 outside the town to an impure place. Anyone who entered the house while
47 it was shut up shall be impure until the evening. Anyone who slept in the
house shall wash his clothes; anyone who ate in the house shall wash his
clothes.

48 "If, however, the priest comes and examines it and the disease has not
spread in the house after its plastering, then the priest shall pronounce the
49 house pure; the disease is healed. He shall take two birds, and cedarwood,
50 scarlet wool, and hyssop to purify the house. He shall slaughter one of the
51 birds in an earthen vessel over living water. He shall take the cedarwood,
the hyssop, the scarlet wool, and the living bird and dip them in the blood
of the slaughtered bird, in the living water, and sprinkle the house seven
52 times. He shall purify the house with the blood of the bird and the living
water, with the living bird, the cedarwood, the hyssop, and the scarlet
53 wool. And he shall send the living bird forth free outside the city, into the
open field. Thus shall he make atonement for the house,[35] and it shall be
purified."

54 This is the law for every impure blight of disease, for a scaling eruption,
55 56 for blight of a garment or a house, and for swellings, eruptions, and bright
57 patches on the skin, to determine when they are impure and when they
are pure. This is the law of the blight.

15 1 2 The Lord spoke to Moshe and Aharon: "Speak to the Israelites. Say:
3 When any man has a genital discharge,[36] he is rendered impure. This is the
impurity brought about by his discharge: whether his member allows the
discharge to flow or whether it blocks it, the discharge renders him impure,
4 so that any bed he lies upon and any object he sits upon becomes impure.
5 Anyone who touches his bed shall wash his clothes, immerse in water, and
6 remain impure until evening. Anyone who sits on something he has sat
upon shall wash his clothes, immerse in water, and remain impure until
7 evening. Anyone who touches his body shall wash his clothes, immerse in
8 water, and remain impure until evening. If the man with the discharge spits
on a person who is pure, that person shall wash his clothes, immerse in
9 water, and remain impure until evening. Any saddle on which the man with
10 the discharge rides becomes impure. Anyone who touches anything that
was underneath him shall be impure until evening. Anyone who moves[37]
such an item shall wash his clothes, immerse in water, and be impure until
11 evening. If the man with the discharge touches someone without first
washing his hands with water, that person shall wash his clothes, immerse
12 in water, and remain impure until evening. Any earthen vessel that the man

35 | Perhaps for the sins of the house's owner. Others render the formulation in the sense of "purification" instead of "atonement"; cf. 12:7.

36 | Generally identified as gonorrhea. Verses 16–17 assign a different law to the emission of semen.

37 | Literally "carries." In rabbinic law, however, this rule applies to one who moves the object even without lifting it.

with the discharge touches shall be broken, any wooden vessel immersed
in water.

13 "When the man with the discharge is purified of it, he shall count seven
days for his purification. Then he shall wash his clothes and immerse his
14 body in flowing water; then he is pure. On the eighth day he shall take
two doves or two pigeons before the LORD to the entrance of the Tent of
15 Meeting and give them to the priest. The priest shall offer them, one as
a purification offering, the other as a burnt offering. Thus shall the priest
make the man's atonement before the LORD after his discharge.

16 "If a man has an emission of semen, he shall immerse his entire body
17 in water, and he remains impure until evening. Any clothing or leather
on which there is an emission of semen shall be washed in water and
18 shall be impure until evening. And any woman with whom a man lies
carnally – both partners shall immerse in water and remain impure until
evening.

19 "When a woman has a discharge of blood that is her usual bodily discharge,
she retains her menstrual status for seven days. Any person who touches
20 her then shall be impure until evening. Anything on which she lies or
21 sits during her menstrual time becomes impure. Whoever touches her
bed shall wash his clothes, immerse in water, and remain impure until
22 evening. Whoever touches any object she has sat upon shall wash his
23 clothes, immerse in water, and remain impure until evening. Whether it be
a bed or any object she sits upon, when one touches it he shall be impure
24 until evening. If a man has sexual relations with her, her menstrual status
is extended to him; he too shall be impure for seven days, and any bed he
lies upon is rendered impure.

25 "Whenever a woman has a discharge of blood for many days at a time other
than her menstrual period, or if she has a discharge beyond her menstrual
period, she shall be impure as long as she has the discharge, as she is in
her menstrual time.

26 "Any bed she lies upon while she has this discharge shall be treated like
the bed she uses during her menstruation, and any object she sits upon
27 becomes impure, as during her menstrual time. Whoever touches these
things is rendered impure; he shall wash his clothes, immerse in water, and
remain impure until evening.

28 "When the woman's discharge ends,[38] she shall count seven days; after
29 that, she will be purified. On the eighth day she shall take two doves or
two pigeons and bring them to the priest at the entrance to the Tent of
30 Meeting. The priest shall prepare one as a purification offering and the
other as a burnt offering. Thus shall the priest make her atonement before
the LORD following her impure discharge.

38 | Referring to the extended, unnatural discharge mentioned in verse 25.

31 "You must separate the Israelites from their own impurity so that they
do not die in their impurity by making My Tabernacle impure in their
midst."

32 This is the law concerning the man who is impure because of a discharge
33 or seminal emission, the woman during her menstrual period, the man or
woman who has a discharge, and the man who has sexual relations with a
woman who is impure.

AHAREI MOT

16 1 After the deaths of Aharon's two sons – when they came close to the LORD
2 and died – the LORD spoke to Moshe. "Tell your brother Aharon," said the
LORD to Moshe, "that he may not come at any time[39] into the holy place
inside the inner curtain in front of the cover on the Ark, or he will die – for
3 in a cloud above the cover I appear. This is how Aharon is to enter the holy
place: with a young bull as a purification offering and a ram as a burnt
4 offering; he shall put on the sacred linen tunic with linen undergarments
covering his body. He shall bind the linen sash around himself and wrap a
linen turban about his head. These are sacred vestments; he shall immerse
5 himself in water and only then put them on. From the community of
Israel he shall take two male goats for a purification offering and a ram for
a burnt offering.

6 "And Aharon shall bring close the bull for his purification offering, to make
7 atonement for him and for his family. He shall take the two goats and set
8 them before the LORD at the entrance to the Tent of Meeting. Aharon shall
cast lots over the two goats, one lot marked 'For the LORD,' the other 'For
9 Azazel.'[40] The goat on which the lot for the LORD fell, Aharon should bring
10 close and offer up as a purification offering. But the goat on which the lot
fell for Azazel shall be presented alive before the LORD; atonement shall be
made over it; it shall be sent forth, away into the wilderness to Azazel.

11 "Aharon shall bring close the bull for his purification offering to make
atonement for him and for his family; he shall slaughter the bull as his
12 purification offering. He shall then take a pan full of burning coals from
the altar, from before the LORD, and two handfuls of finely ground fragrant
13 incense, and bring them inside the inner curtain. He shall place the incense
on the fire before the LORD so that the cloud of incense conceals the cover
14 on top of the Ark of the Testimony, so that he does not die.[41] He shall take
some of the bull's blood and sprinkle it with his finger on the cover on the
east side. Then, in front of the cover, he shall sprinkle some of the blood
15 with his finger seven times. He shall then slaughter the goat for the people's
purification offering, bring its blood inside the inner curtain, and do with
it as he did with the blood of the bull, sprinkling it on the cover and before

39 | Meaning except under the circumstances described below. Alternatively, "any time he wants."

40 | The word "Azazel" and the purpose of this ritual are subject to varying interpretations.

41 | As punishment for looking at the Divine Presence. See, e.g., verse 2; Exodus 25:22.

16 the cover. In this way, he shall make atonement for the Sanctuary – from
the impurity of the Israelites, from their rebellions and all their sins. And
he shall do the same for the Tent of Meeting, which is with them in the
17 midst of their impurity. No one shall be in the Tent of Meeting from the
time Aharon enters to make atonement in the Sanctuary until he comes
out. Thus he shall make atonement for himself, for his house, and for the
whole assembly of Israel.

18 "He shall then go out to the altar that is before the Lord and make its
atonement. He shall take some of the bull's blood and some of the goat's
19 blood and apply it to each of the altar's horns. He shall sprinkle some of
the blood upon it with his finger seven times, to purify it and sanctify it
from the impurity of the Israelites.

20 "When he has finished making atonement for the Sanctuary, the Tent
21 of Meeting and the altar, he shall bring close the live goat. Aharon shall
lay both his hands on the head of the live goat and confess over it all the
Israelites' iniquities and rebellions, all of their sins, putting them on the
head of the goat and then sending it away into the wilderness with the
22 person designated for the task. The goat shall carry all their iniquities
upon itself to a desolate place, and then the goat shall be sent forth into
the wilderness.

23 "Then Aharon shall enter the Tent of Meeting, take off the linen vestments
24 he was wearing when he entered the Sanctuary, and leave them there. He
shall immerse his body in water in a holy place and put on his vestments.
Then he shall come out and offer his burnt offering and the burnt offering
25 of the people, to make atonement for himself and for the people. And
he shall send the fat of the purification offering up in smoke upon the
26 altar. The man who sent forth the goat for Azazel shall wash his clothes
and immerse his body in water; after that he may return to the camp.
27 The purification offering bull and the purification offering goat, whose
blood was brought in to make atonement in the inner Sanctuary, shall be
removed from the camp. Their skin, flesh, and dung shall be burned with
28 fire. The one who burns them shall wash his clothes and immerse his body
in water. After that, he too may return to the camp.

29 "This shall be an everlasting statute for you: on the tenth day of the
seventh month, you must afflict yourselves. You shall perform no work at
30 all – neither the native born nor the migrant living among you. On this
day, atonement shall be made for you to purify you; of all your sins you
31 shall be purified before the Lord. It shall be a Sabbath of complete rest for
you, and on it you shall afflict yourselves. This is an everlasting statute.

32 "The priest who is anointed and ordained to succeed his father and serve as
priest[42] shall perform the atonement, wearing the sacred linen vestments.

42 | That is, the High Priest.

33 He shall make atonement for the innermost Sanctuary, for the Tent of
Meeting, and for the altar. He shall make atonement for the priests and
34 for all the people of the community. This shall be an everlasting statute
for you, making atonement for the Israelites once a year for all their sins."
And as the LORD commanded Moshe, so it was done.

17 1 2 The LORD spoke to Moshe: "Speak to Aharon, his sons, and all the Israelites.
3 Say: This is what the LORD has commanded: Any Israelite who slaughters
4 an ox, sheep, or goat inside or outside the camp without then bringing it
to the entrance of the Tent of Meeting to bring close an offering to the
LORD before the LORD's Tabernacle will be considered guilty of bloodshed.
5 He has shed blood; he shall be severed from his people. For the Israelites
must bring the sacrifices they have been offering in the open fields – to the
LORD, to the priest at the entrance of the Tent of Meeting, and offer them
6 as peace sacrifices to the LORD. The priest shall dash the blood against the
LORD's altar at the entrance to the Tent of Meeting and send the fat up
7 in smoke as a pleasing aroma to the LORD; and no more may they offer
sacrifices to the goat demons to whom they prostitute themselves. This
8 shall be an everlasting statute for them throughout their generations. And
you shall tell them: Anyone of the House of Israel or any migrant living
9 among you who offers up a burnt offering or other sacrifice and does not
bring it to the entrance of the Tent of Meeting to offer it to the LORD shall
be severed from his people.

10 "Anyone of the House of Israel, or any migrant living among you, who eats
blood – I will set My face against that person who eats blood and will sever
11 him from his people, for the life of a creature is in its blood. I have given it
to you to make atonement for your lives on the altar, for blood, which is
12 bound up with life, atones. That is why I have told the Israelites: None of
you may eat blood, nor may any migrant living among you eat blood.

13 "Any Israelite or migrant living among you who hunts an animal or bird
14 that may be eaten shall pour out its blood and cover it with earth, for the
life of all flesh – its blood is its life. That is why I have said to the Israelites:
You must not eat any creature's blood, because the life of every creature is
bound up with its blood. All who eat it will be severed.

15 "Anyone, native born or migrant, who eats an animal that has died of itself
or been torn by beasts shall wash his clothes, immerse in water, and remain
16 impure until evening; then he shall be purified. If he does not wash or
immerse his body, he shall bear his guilt."

18 1 2 The LORD spoke to Moshe: "Speak to the Israelites. Say: I am the LORD
3 your God. You shall not do as they do in the land of Egypt where you lived.
Nor shall you do as they do in the land of Canaan where I am bringing
4 you; do not follow their practices. Observe My laws, keep My statutes and
5 follow them; I am the LORD your God. Keep My statutes and laws, for by
them a person shall live; I am the LORD.

6 "No one among you shall draw close to any near relative to expose their
nakedness;[43] I am the Lord.
7 You shall not expose your father's and mother's nakedness. She is your
mother; you shall not expose her nakedness.
8 You shall not expose the nakedness of your father's wife; it is your father's
nakedness.
9 You shall not expose the nakedness of your sister – whether she is your
father's daughter or your mother's, whether born into the household or
outside, you shall not expose her nakedness.
10 You shall not expose the nakedness of your son's daughter or your
daughter's daughter; it is your own nakedness.[44]
11 The nakedness of your father's wife's daughter, born to your father[45] – she
is your sister; do not expose her nakedness.
12 You shall not expose the nakedness of your father's sister; she is of your
father's flesh.
13 You shall not expose the nakedness of your mother's sister, for she is of
your mother's flesh.
14 You shall not expose the nakedness of your father's brother – do not draw
close to his wife; she is your aunt.
15 You shall not expose the nakedness of your daughter-in-law: she is
16 your son's wife; do not expose her nakedness. You shall not expose the
nakedness of your brother's wife; it is your brother's nakedness.
17 You shall not expose the nakedness of a woman and her daughter, nor
shall you marry her son's daughter or her daughter's daughter, exposing
18 her nakedness; they are of the same flesh; it would be depravity. Do not
marry a woman to be a rival to her sister,[46] exposing her nakedness while
her sister is alive.

19 "Do not draw close to a woman to expose her nakedness while she bears
20 the impurity of her menstruation. Do not have carnal relations with your
21 neighbor's wife, becoming impure through her. Do not give any of your
children over to be sacrificed to Molekh,[47] profaning the name of your
22 God; I am the Lord. Do not lie with a male as with a woman; this is an
23 abhorrent act. Do not have carnal relations with any animal, through it
making yourself impure; nor may a woman give herself to an animal to
mate with it – this is perversion.

24 "Do not make yourselves impure in any of these ways, for it is by all these
25 that the nations I am casting out before you made themselves impure. And
so the land itself became impure, and I held it to account for its sins, and
26 the land vomited out its inhabitants. But you shall keep My statutes and
My laws and do none of these abhorrent acts, neither the native born nor

43 | This expression is a euphemism for sexual relations.
44 | Meaning they are your own blood relatives.
45 | This verse seems to repeat a case already mentioned in verse 9. Interpretations vary.
46 | Meaning to be a rival wife to her sister, to whom you are already married.
47 | A Canaanite ritual (see, e.g., Jer. 32:35).

27 the migrant living among you. The people who lived in the land before
28 you committed all these abhorrent acts and the land became impure. Let
the land not vomit you out for making it impure, as it vomited out the
29 nation there before you, for anyone who performs any of these abhorrent
30 acts shall be severed from his people. Keep My charge and do not follow
any of these abhorrent practices that were followed before you; do not by
them make yourselves impure; I am the LORD your God."

19 1 2 The LORD spoke to Moshe: "Speak to all the community of Israel. Say: Be KEDOSHIM
3 holy, for I am holy; I, the LORD your God. Each one of you, revere your
4 mother and father and keep My Sabbaths; I am the LORD your God. Do
5 not turn to idols or cast yourselves gods; I am the LORD your God. When
you offer a peace sacrifice to the LORD, offer it in such a way that it may
6 be accepted for you. It shall be eaten on the day you sacrifice it or on the
7 following day; what is left on the third day shall be burned with fire. If
any of it is eaten on the third day, it is repugnant; it will not be accepted.
8 Anyone who eats it shall bear his guilt, for he has desecrated what is holy
9 to the LORD; he shall be severed from his people. When you reap the
harvest of your land, do not reap all the way to the edge of your field or
10 gather the gleanings[48] of your harvest. Do not harvest your vineyard bare
or gather the grapes that have fallen there. Leave them for the poor and
for the migrant; I am the LORD your God.

11 12 "Do not steal; do not deceive; do not lie to one another. Do not swear
13 falsely by My name, desecrating the name of your God; I am the LORD. Do
not defraud or rob[49] your neighbor. Do not hold back the wages of a hired
14 worker until the morning. Do not curse the deaf or put a stumbling-block
before the blind. Fear your God; I am the LORD.

15 "Do not pervert justice: do not show partiality to the poor or deference to
16 the great; judge your fellow man fairly. Do not go around as a gossipmonger
among your people. Do not stand by while your neighbor's life is in danger;
17 I am the LORD. Do not hate your brother in your heart. Admonish your
18 fellow and do not bear guilt on his account. Do not take revenge or bear
a grudge against any one among your people, but love your neighbor as
your own self; I am the LORD.

19 "Keep My decrees. Do not crossbreed different kinds of animal, do not
plant your field with two kinds of seed intermixed, and do not wear
clothing made from two materials combined.

20 "If a man has carnal relations with a woman who is a slave designated
for another man, and who has not been redeemed or given her freedom,
there shall be punishment but they shall not be put to death since she has
21 not been freed. The man shall bring his guilt offering to the LORD at the

48 | Individual stalks that fall from the bundle.

49 | Whereas "stealing" (*geneva*, v. 11) denotes taking by stealth, "robbery" (*gezela*) denotes taking by force.

22 entrance of the Tent of Meeting: a ram for a guilt offering. The priest shall
make his atonement before the LORD with the ram of the guilt offering for
the sin that he committed, and the sin he committed shall be forgiven.

23 "When you enter the land and plant any tree for food, you shall regard
its fruit as forbidden. For three years it shall be forbidden to you; it must
24 not be eaten. In the fourth year, all its fruit shall be holy, to give praise
25 to the LORD. In the fifth year you may eat its fruit – and so shall its yield
proliferate for you; I am the LORD your God.

26 "Do not eat any creature with its blood. Do not practice divination or
27 seek omens. Do not cut off the hair on the sides of your head or destroy
28 the edges of your beard. Do not gash your body for the dead or put tattoo
29 marks on yourself; I am the LORD. Do not profane your daughter by
making her a prostitute, that the land shall not be prostituted, the land
30 filled with depravity. Keep My Sabbaths, revere My Sanctuary; I am the
31 LORD. Do not turn to ghosts or inquire of spirits, rendering yourself
32 impure; I am the LORD your God. Stand up in the presence of the white-
haired and show respect to the elderly; revere your God; I am the LORD.

33 34 "When a stranger lives with you in your land, do not wrong him. The
stranger living with you shall be like one of your native born to you: love
him as your own self, for you yourselves were strangers in the land of
35 Egypt; I am the LORD your God. Do not falsify measures – not of length,
36 nor of weight, nor of volume. You shall have honest scales, honest weights,
an honest ephah, and an honest hin.[50] I am the LORD your God, who
37 brought you out of the land of Egypt. Keep all My decrees and laws and
fulfill them; I am the LORD."

20 1 2 The LORD spoke to Moshe: "Tell the Israelites: Any person – any Israelite
or any migrant residing among Israel – who sacrifices any of his children to
3 Molekh[51] shall be put to death. The people of the land shall stone him, and I
Myself will set My face against that person; I will sever him from his people
because, in sacrificing his children to Molekh, he defiles My Sanctuary; he
4 desecrates My holy name. If the people of the land close their eyes to a man
5 as he sacrifices his children to Molekh – if they do not put him to death – I
Myself will set My face against him and his family; I will sever him from
his people, and with him all who follow him in going astray after Molekh.
6 And anyone who turns to ghosts or spirits, going astray after them – I will
set My face against him and sever him from his people.

7 8 "Consecrate yourselves and be holy, for I am the LORD your God. Keep My
9 decrees and fulfill them; I am the LORD, who makes you holy. One who
curses his father or mother shall be put to death. Since he has cursed his
10 father or mother, his bloodguilt is upon him. If a man commits adultery
with a married woman, another man's wife, both the adulterer and the

50 | An ephah is a solid measure, and a hin is a liquid measure.

51 | See note on 18:21.

11 adulteress shall be put to death. If a man lies with his father's wife, he has
exposed his father's nakedness;[52] both of them[53] shall be put to death;
12 their bloodguilt is upon them. If a man lies with his daughter-in-law, both
of them shall be put to death. They have committed perversion; their
13 bloodguilt is upon them. If a man lies with a male as he would with a
woman, both have performed an abhorrent act; they shall be put to death;
14 their bloodguilt is upon them. If a man marries a woman and also her
mother, it is depravity. He and they shall be burned by fire; there must be
15 no depravity among you. If a man lies with an animal, he shall be put to
16 death and you shall kill the animal. If a woman approaches an animal to
mate with it, you shall kill the woman and the animal; they shall both be
17 put to death; their bloodguilt is upon them. If a man takes his sister – his
father's daughter or his mother's daughter – and they see one another's
nakedness, it is a deep disgrace; they shall be severed in the sight of their
18 people. He has exposed his sister's nakedness; he shall bear his guilt. If a
man lies with a menstruating woman and exposes her nakedness, he has
laid her hidden source bare; she has exposed the source of her blood; both
19 of them shall be severed from their people. Do not expose the nakedness of
your mother's sister or your father's sister, because that is to lay bare your
20 own near relative; both shall bear their guilt. If a man lies with his aunt, he
has exposed his uncle's nakedness. Both parties shall bear their guilt; they
21 shall die childless. For a man to marry his brother's wife – that is taboo.
He has exposed his brother's nakedness; both parties shall be childless.

22 "Keep all My decrees and all My laws and fulfill them, so that the land to
23 which I am bringing you to settle will not vomit you out. Do not follow the
practices of the nation I am driving out before you, for they did all these
24 things and I was disgusted with them. I have told you: You shall possess
their land; I am giving it to you to possess. It is a land that flows with milk
and with honey. I am the LORD your God, who has set you apart from all
25 other peoples. You, then, shall set pure apart from impure animals, pure
from impure birds. Do not make yourselves detestable by an animal or bird
or anything that creeps upon the ground that I have set apart from you
26 to regard as impure.[54] Be holy to Me, for I the LORD am holy, and I have
27 set you apart from all other peoples to be My own. A man or woman who
seeks ghosts or spirits shall be put to death. They shall be stoned; their
bloodguilt is on them."

21 1 The LORD said to Moshe, "Speak to the priests, Aharon's sons. Say: No EMOR
one of you shall render himself impure for any dead person among his
2 people except for his nearest relatives: his mother, father, son, daughter,
3 or brother; or his virgin sister who has remained close to him because
4 she has not married – for her, he may render himself impure. But he shall

52 | See 18:6–8.

53 | Both participants in the act.

54 | See chapter 11.

not become impure for those he is related to by marriage, and so become
profane.

5 "Priests shall not make bald patches on their heads, or shave off the edges
6 of their beards, or gash wounds into their flesh. They shall be holy to their
God and not profane God's name, for they bring close the LORD's fire
offerings, foodstuff offerings to their God; therefore they shall be holy.
7 They may not marry a woman made profane by immorality,[55] nor may
they marry a woman divorced from her husband, for they are holy to their
8 God. You shall treat a priest as holy, for he brings close the offerings of
foodstuffs to your God. And he shall be holy to you, because I, the LORD,
9 am holy and make you holy. If the daughter of a priest profanes herself by
immorality, she profanes her father also; she shall be burned with fire.

10 "The priest, the highest among his brothers, on whose head the anointing
oil has been poured and who has been ordained to wear the vestments,
11 shall not dishevel his hair or tear his clothes. He shall not go near the dead;
12 even for his father or mother he shall not render himself impure. He shall
not leave the Sanctuary, profaning his God's Sanctuary, for the crown of
13 his God's anointing oil rests upon him; I am the LORD. He may marry a
14 woman only in her virginity. He may not marry a widow, a divorcée, or
one profaned by immorality. He may marry only a virgin from his own
15 people, so that he will not profane his children among his people, for I,
the LORD, sanctify him."

16 17 The LORD spoke to Moshe: "Tell Aharon: Any of your future descendants
who has a physical blemish may not draw close to present foodstuff
18 offerings to his God. No one with a blemish shall approach: this includes
19 one who is blind, lame, disfigured, or deformed; or who has a broken foot
20 or hand; or who is a hunchback or a dwarf, or who has a growth in his eye,
21 a severe rash, scabs, or crushed testicles. No descendant of Aharon the
priest who has a physical blemish shall draw near to present the LORD's
fire offerings; because of his blemish, he shall not approach to present an
22 offering of foodstuffs to his God. He may eat the foodstuff offerings of his
23 God, the holy of holies as well as the holy.[56] But he may not come close to
the inner curtain or approach the altar, because of his blemish; he shall not
profane My Sanctuary; I am the LORD who makes them holy."

24 Moshe told this to Aharon, his sons, and all the Israelites.

22 1 2 The LORD spoke to Moshe: "Tell Aharon and his sons to take great care
with the sacred offerings that the Israelites consecrate to Me, so that they
3 do not profane My holy name: I am the LORD. Tell them: If any descendant
of yours throughout the generations comes near the sacred offerings that
the Israelites have consecrated to the LORD while in an impure state, he

55 | Referring to forbidden sexual relations.

56 | Offerings designated as "holy of holies" are eaten exclusively by the priests and bear other restrictions. See, e.g., 6:10–11, 22, 24:9.

4 shall be severed from My presence; I am the LORD. Any descendant of
Aharon who has a defiling blight of the skin or a discharge may not eat of
the sacred offerings until he becomes pure. One who touches anything
made impure by contact with the dead, or who has had a seminal emission,
5 or who has touched any swarming thing or any person who renders him
6 impure – whatever his impurity – the one who touches these things shall
be impure until the evening, and shall not eat of the sacred offerings until
7 he has washed his body in water. When the sun sets, he shall become
8 pure again and may eat of the sacred offerings, for they are his food. He
may not eat an animal found dead or one that was torn by wild animals,
9 becoming impure by doing so; I am the LORD. They shall keep My charge
and not bear guilt and die through it, having profaned it. I am the LORD,
who makes them holy.

10 "No layman may eat of the sacred offerings,[57] nor may a priest's visitor or
11 hired laborer eat of them. But if a priest acquires a slave for money, the
slave may eat of them, and those born into his household also may eat his
12 food. If a priest's daughter marries a layman, she may no longer eat of the
13 sacred gifts. If a priest's daughter is a widow or a divorcée, has no children,
and returns to live in her father's house as when she was young, she may
eat her father's food again; but no layperson may do so.

14 "If someone eats of the sacred gift unintentionally, he shall make restitution
15 to the priest, adding an extra fifth to its value. The people must not profane
16 the sacred meats that Israelites bring as offerings to the LORD or incur the
penalty of iniquity by eating their sacred offerings; for I, the LORD, make
them holy."

17 18 The LORD spoke to Moshe: "Speak to Aharon, his sons, and all the Israelites.
Say: When anyone of the House of Israel or of the migrants living in
Israel presents an offering to the LORD as a burnt offering – whether in
19 fulfillment of a vow or as a freewill offering – to be acceptable on your
behalf, it must be an unblemished male from the herd, or of the sheep or
20 goats. Do not offer anything that has a blemish, for it will not be accepted
21 on your behalf. When someone presents a peace sacrifice to the LORD
from the herd or flock – whether because of a spoken vow or as a freewill
offering – it must be unblemished to be acceptable; there shall be no
22 blemish on it. Do not present to the LORD anything blind, injured, or
maimed, or with warts, a severe rash, or scabs. Do not place any of these on
23 the altar as a fire offering to the LORD. You may offer as a freewill offering
an ox or sheep with a limb deformed or uncloven, but they will not be
24 accepted in fulfillment of a vow. Do not offer to the LORD an animal whose
testicles are bruised, crushed, torn, or cut off; and do not do such things
25 in your land. Do not accept such animals from a migrant as an offering of

57 | The sacred gifts designated for the priests.

foodstuffs to your God. Because they are mutilated and blemished, they
will not be accepted on your behalf."

26 27 The LORD spoke to Moshe: "When an ox or sheep or goat is born, it shall
remain with its mother for seven days. From the eighth day it is acceptable
28 as a sacrifice, a fire offering to the LORD, but do not slaughter an ox or
29 sheep and its young on the same day. When you sacrifice a thanksgiving
offering for the LORD, sacrifice it so that it will be acceptable on your
30 behalf. It shall be eaten on the same day – leave none of it to the morning;
31 32 I am the LORD. Keep My commands and fulfill them; I am the LORD. Do
not profane My holy name – that I may be sanctified in the midst of the
33 Israelites. I am the LORD, who makes you holy, who brought you out of
Egypt to be your God: I am the LORD."

23 1 2 The LORD spoke to Moshe: "Speak to the Israelites. Say: These are the
LORD's appointed times that you shall proclaim as sacred assemblies;
3 these are My appointed times. Work shall be done through six days, but
the seventh day shall be a Sabbath of complete rest, a sacred assembly.
You shall perform no work at all; it shall be a Sabbath for the LORD in all
your dwellings.

4 "These are the LORD's appointed times, sacred assemblies, which you
5 shall proclaim at their appointed times. In the first month, the fourteenth
of the month in the afternoon is the time for the Passover sacrifice to the
6 LORD. The fifteenth day of this month is the LORD's Festival of Unleavened
7 Bread; for seven days you shall eat unleavened bread. The first day shall be
8 a sacred assembly for you; you shall perform no laborious work. And you
shall present a fire offering for the LORD for seven days; on the seventh day
there shall be a sacred assembly; you shall perform no laborious work."

9 10 The LORD spoke to Moshe: "Speak to the Israelites. Say: When you come
to the land that I am giving you and reap its harvest, bring the first sheaf
11 of your harvest to the priest. He shall display the sheaf this way and that
before the LORD for your acceptance; on the day after the day of rest the
12 priest shall display it. On the day you display the sheaf this way and that,
you shall offer a yearling sheep without blemish as a burnt offering to the
13 LORD. Its grain offering shall be two-tenths of an ephah of fine flour mixed
with oil, a fire offering for the LORD, a pleasing aroma; and its libation shall
14 be a quarter of a hin of wine. Until that day, until you bring this sacrifice to
your God, you shall eat no bread or roasted grain or ripe grain. This is an
everlasting statute throughout your generations, in all your dwellings.

15 "And from the day you bring the sheaf of the wave offering, the day after
16 the day of rest, you shall count for yourselves seven complete weeks. To
the day after the seventh week, you shall count fifty days; and then you
17 shall present a new grain offering to the LORD. You shall bring two loaves of
bread from your dwellings made with two-tenths of an ephah of fine flour
18 baked with leaven, as a wave offering: first produce to the LORD. Together

with the bread, you shall present seven unblemished yearling male lambs,
one young bull, and two rams – these shall be a burnt offering for the Lord
with their grain offering and their libations, a fire offering, a pleasing aroma
19 to the Lord. And you shall offer one he-goat as a purification offering and
20 two yearling male sheep as peace sacrifices. The priest shall display them
this way and that with the bread of the first produce as a wave offering
before the Lord together with the two sheep; they shall be holy to the
21 Lord and belong to the priest. On that day you shall make a proclamation;
it shall be a sacred assembly for you; you shall perform no laborious
work. This is an everlasting statute throughout your generations in all your
22 dwellings. And when you reap the harvest of your land, do not reap to the
edge of your field or gather the gleanings of your harvest. Leave them for
the poor and for the migrant; I am the Lord your God."

23 24 Then the Lord spoke to Moshe: "Tell the Israelites: On the first day of the
seventh month, you shall observe a day of rest, a commemoration with
25 the sounding of the ram's horn, a sacred assembly. You shall perform no
laborious work, and you shall bring close a fire offering to the Lord."

26 27 The Lord spoke to Moshe: "Hear: the tenth day of this seventh month is
the Day of Atonement. It shall be a sacred assembly for you, and you shall
28 afflict yourselves and bring a fire offering to the Lord. You shall perform
no work at all during this entire day, for it is the Day of Atonement, there
29 to make atonement for you before the Lord your God. Anyone who does
30 not afflict himself for this whole day shall be severed from his people, and
if anyone performs any work during this whole day, I will annihilate that
31 person from among his people. No work at all may you perform; this is an
32 everlasting statute throughout your generations in all your dwellings. It is
a Sabbath of complete rest for you, and you shall afflict yourselves from
the evening of the ninth day of the month: from evening to evening shall
you observe your Sabbath."

33 34 The Lord spoke to Moshe: "Tell the Israelites: From the fifteenth day of
this seventh month, for seven days shall be the Festival of Tabernacles to
35 the Lord. The first day shall be a sacred assembly; on it, you shall perform
36 no laborious work. For seven days you must bring close a fire offering to
the Lord. The eighth day shall be a sacred assembly for you, and you shall
present a fire offering to the Lord. It is an assembly; you shall perform
no laborious work.

37 "These are the Lord's festivals, which you shall proclaim, sacred
assemblies to present a fire offering to the Lord: burnt offering, grain
38 offering, sacrifice, and libations, each on its appointed day; in addition to
the Lord's Sabbaths,[58] and in addition to your gifts and all your offerings
in the fulfillment of vows and all the freewill offerings that you give to the
Lord.

---

58 | Meaning the special Sabbath offerings.

39 "Hear: on the fifteenth day of the seventh month, when you have harvested
the land's produce, you shall celebrate a festival to the LORD for seven
days. The first day shall be a day of rest; the eighth day shall be a day of
40 rest. On the first day you shall take for yourselves fruit of the majestic
tree, branches of palm trees, boughs of the leafy tree, and willows of the
41 brook, and rejoice before the LORD your God for seven days. You shall
celebrate it as a festival to the LORD for seven days in the year. It shall be
an everlasting statute throughout your generations; celebrate this in the
42 seventh month. For seven days you shall live in huts. All those native born
43 in Israel must live in huts, so that future generations may know that I had
the Israelites live in huts when I brought them out of the land of Egypt; I
am the LORD your God."

44 Thus Moshe announced the LORD's appointed times to the Israelites.

24 1 2 The LORD spoke to Moshe: "Command the Israelites to bring you pure
3 oil from crushed olives for the light, to kindle the lamp, every night. From
evening to morning, before the LORD, Aharon shall set it up outside the
curtain of the testimony in the Tent of Meeting to burn each night. This
4 shall be a rule for all time, throughout your generations. Aharon shall set
out the lamps on the pure candelabrum each day before the LORD.

5 "And you shall take fine flour and bake twelve loaves, two-tenths of an
6 ephah for each loaf. You shall place them in two columns, six to each
7 column, on the pure table[59] before the LORD. Lay pure incense on each
stack, as a remembrance[60] for the bread, as a fire offering to the LORD.
8 Every Sabbath he shall set it out, always, before the LORD on behalf of
9 the Israelites: an everlasting covenant. It shall belong to Aharon and his
sons. They shall eat it in a holy place because it is holy of holies among the
LORD's fire offerings, their perpetual share."

10 A man went out among the Israelites, the son of an Israelite woman and
an Egyptian man. And a fight broke out in the camp between this son
11 of an Israelite woman, and an Israelite man. The Israelite woman's son
blasphemed the Name and cursed – his mother's name was Shlomit,
daughter of Divri, of the tribe of Dan – and they brought him before
12 Moshe. They placed the man in custody until the LORD's verdict would
be pronounced to them.

13 14 And the LORD spoke to Moshe: "Take the one who cursed outside the
camp. All the people who heard him shall lay their hands on his head – and
15 then the whole community shall stone him. Tell the Israelites: Anyone
16 who curses his God shall bear the sin, and anyone who blasphemes the
LORD's name shall be put to death: the whole community shall stone him.
Migrant and native born alike: one who blasphemes the LORD's name
shall be put to death.

59 | That is, of pure gold, referring to the overlay (see Ex. 25:24).

60 | See note on 2:2. This incense, unlike the bread, was burned on the altar.

17 18 "One who takes the life of any human being shall be put to death. One who
19 takes the life of an animal shall make restitution for it: life for life. One
who injures his fellow man shall be penalized in proportion to the injury
20 inflicted:[61] the cost of[62] a broken bone for a broken bone, of an eye for an
eye, of a tooth for a tooth. Just as he inflicted injury on another human
21 being, so shall he suffer the loss.[63] One who kills an animal shall make
restitution for it; but one who kills a human being shall be put to death.
22 There shall be one law for you, for migrant and for native born alike, for I
am the LORD your God."

23 Moshe told this to the Israelites, and so they took the blasphemer outside
the camp and stoned him. Thus the Israelites did as the LORD had
commanded Moshe.

25 1 2 On Mount Sinai the LORD spoke to Moshe: "Speak to the Israelites. Say: BEHAR
When you enter the land that I am giving you, the land shall keep a Sabbath
3 to the LORD. For six years you may plant your fields, prune your vineyards,
4 and harvest their crops. But the seventh year shall be to the land a Sabbath
of complete rest, a Sabbath to the LORD. You shall not sow your fields or
5 prune your vineyards; you shall not harvest what grows of itself or gather
6 the grapes of your unpruned vine; it is a year of rest for the land. You may
eat the land's Sabbath yield: you, your male and female servants, and the
7 hired worker and resident worker who live with you, your livestock and
the wild animals in your land – whatever the land produces is there to be
eaten.

8 "And you shall count off seven Sabbaths of years – seven times seven
9 years – so that the seven Sabbath cycles total forty-nine years. Then you
shall sound the ram's horn. On the tenth day of the seventh month, on
10 the Day of Atonement, you shall sound the horn all across your land. You
shall consecrate the fiftieth year and proclaim liberty throughout the land
to all its inhabitants. This shall be your Jubilee; each person shall return to
11 his hereditary home, each to his family. The fiftieth year shall be a Jubilee
for you. Do not sow, or reap what grows of itself, or harvest the unpruned
12 vines, for it is a Jubilee; it shall be holy to you. You shall eat only directly
13 from the field. And in this Jubilee year, each person shall return to his
hereditary home.

14 "But when you sell land to your fellow or buy it from him, brother must
15 not cheat brother: you shall buy from your neighbor by the number of
years since the Jubilee; he shall sell to you by the number of years left for
16 harvesting. You shall increase the price if the remaining years are many,
and lower it if they are few; what is being sold to you is the number of

---

61 | Literally "shall have done to him the same thing that he did." The translation follows the rabbinic interpretation.

62 | This phrase is not explicit in the Hebrew; see previous note.

63 | Literally "so shall it be inflicted on him."

17 harvests. You shall not cheat one another; you shall hold your God in awe;
18 I am the LORD your God. You shall fulfill My statutes, and keep and act
19 in accordance with My laws – then you will live securely on the land. The
20 land will yield its fruit and you will eat your fill and live securely there. If
you should ask, 'What shall we eat in the seventh year? We may not sow
21 and may not harvest our crops' – I will send My blessing over you in the
22 sixth year and it will yield three years' harvest. As you sow in the eighth
year, you will eat of the old harvest; you will still be eating of the old when
the crop of the ninth year comes.

23 "And the land shall not be sold in perpetuity, for the land is Mine. You are
24 merely migrants and visitors to Me. Throughout the land that you possess,
you must allow land to be redeemed.

25 "If your brother grows poor and sells part of his hereditary land, his closest
26 redeeming relative shall come and redeem what his kinsman has sold. If
the person lacks a relative to redeem it, but later prospers and can afford to
27 buy it back, he shall calculate the years since its sale and refund the balance
to the one to whom he sold it, and return to his hereditary home.

28 "If he cannot afford to recover it, what was sold shall remain in the
possession of the buyer until the Jubilee year; but at the Jubilee it shall be
released, and he shall return to his possession.

29 "One who sells a house in a walled city retains the right to redeem it until
30 a year after its sale. This is the period of redemption. If it is not redeemed
before a full year has passed, the house in the walled city shall belong
permanently to the buyer and his descendants forever; it is not released
31 at the Jubilee. Houses in villages without surrounding walls, however, are
considered as if they were open country. They may be redeemed, and they
are released at the Jubilee.

32 "In the Levitical towns – Levites always retain the right to redeem houses
33 in their ancestral towns. Levite property that can be redeemed – houses
sold in towns belonging to them – shall be released at the Jubilee, because
the houses in Levitical towns are their ancestral possession among the
34 Israelites. But the pastureland around their towns can never be sold,
because that is their permanent possession.

35 "If your brother becomes poor and is struggling, extend him support – a
36 migrant or visitor also – that he may live among you. Do not take advance
or accrued interest from him; fear your God so that your brother can live
37 with you. Do not lend him your money at interest or provide him with
38 food at a profit. I am the LORD your God, who brought you out of the land
of Egypt to give the land of Canaan to you, to be your God.

39 "If your brother becomes poor and sells himself to you, do not work him as
40 a slave. He shall abide with you like a hired worker or a resident worker and
41 work for you until the Jubilee year. Then he and his children shall be free to

42 leave you and return to their family and their ancestral land. For they are
My servants whom I brought out from Egypt: they cannot be sold as slaves.
43 Do not rule them harshly with backbreaking labor; fear your God.

44 "As for male or female slaves that you may have: from the nations around
45 you, you may acquire a male or female slave. You may also acquire them from
among the migrants residing with you and from their families among you who
46 were born in your land; they may be yours, in your possession. They become
hereditary property that you can bequeath to your children; they may be
your slaves, but over your brother Israelites you may not rule so harshly.

47 "If a migrant or temporary resident prospers among you, and your fellow
Israelite becomes poor and is sold to a migrant residing among you or to a
48 branch of a foreign family, the Israelite has the right, subsequent to the sale,
49 to be redeemed; one of his relatives may redeem him. His uncle or cousin
or any other blood relative may redeem him, or if he can afford to do so, he
50 may redeem himself. Together with his owner, he shall calculate the time
from the year he was sold until the Jubilee year. The price of his release
shall be based on that number of years, as if he had been there as a hired
51 laborer. If many years remain, he shall pay that proportion of his purchase
52 price for his redemption. If only a few years remain until the Jubilee year,
53 he shall calculate that and pay for the redemption accordingly. He shall be
with him like a worker hired year by year; and never shall he be oppressed
54 in his labors while you look on. And if he is not redeemed in any of these
55 ways, he and his children shall be released in the Jubilee year. For it is to
Me that the Israelites are servants. They are My servants whom I brought
out of the land of Egypt; I am the Lord your God.

26 1 "You shall make no idols, nor may you erect any divine image or worship
pillar.[64] Do not set up any carved stone in your land and bow down to it,
2 for I am the Lord your God. Keep My Sabbaths, revere My Sanctuary; I
am the Lord.

BEḤUKOTAI

3 4 "If you follow My decrees, keep My commands, and fulfill them, then I
shall give you rain in its due time. The land shall yield its crops and the
5 trees of the field shall yield their fruit. Your threshing season shall last until
the grape harvest; the grape harvest shall last until sowing time. You shall
6 eat your bread to the full and live securely in your land. And I will grant
peace in the land; when you lie down, no one will make you afraid. I will
cause dangerous animals to cease in the land, and through that land no
7 sword shall pass. You shall chase your enemies, and they shall fall before
8 you by the sword. Five of you shall chase away a hundred, and a hundred
of you shall put ten thousand to flight; your enemies shall fall before you
9 by the sword. I will turn to you and make you fruitful, make you numerous,
10 and I will uphold My covenant with you. You shall eat the grain of long
11 ago and take the old grain out to make space for all the new. I shall set My

64 | Pillars were a feature of certain forms of ancient worship (see also Ex. 23:24).

12 dwelling among you, and I shall not despise you; I shall walk among you.
13 I shall be your God, and you shall be My people. I am the LORD your God,
who brought you out of Egypt, to be their slaves no more. I broke the bars
of your yoke and led you to walk with your heads held high.

14 "But if you do not listen to Me and do not carry out all these commands – if
15 you spurn My decrees and despise My laws, not keeping all My commands;
16 violating My covenant – then I will do this to you: I will appoint over
you terror, consumption, and fever, which make your eyes fail and your
spirit languish. In vain shall you sow your seed, for your enemies will eat
its yield.

17 "I shall set My face against you. You will be struck down before your
enemies. Those who hate you will rule over you; you will flee, though no
one chases you.

18 "And if, in spite of all this, you still will not listen to Me, I shall punish
19 you seven times over for your sins. I will break down the majesty of your
20 power. I will make your sky like iron, your land like brass. Your strength
will be spent in vain. Your land will not yield its produce, nor the trees of
the land their fruit.

21 "If you still walk contrary to Me and refuse to listen to Me, I will strike you
22 seven times over for your sins: I will send wild animals against you. They
will bereave you of your children and annihilate your cattle. They will make
you few in number and your roads will be deserted.

23 "If, despite all this, you still do not accept My discipline and still you walk
24 contrary to Me, then I too will walk contrary to you and strike you seven
25 times over for your sins. I will bring a sword against you to avenge the
broken covenant. If you retreat into your cities, I shall send pestilence
26 against you, and you will be delivered up into your enemy's hand. When I
cut off your supply of bread, ten women shall bake bread in a single oven.
They will ration it out by weight, and you will eat but not be full.

27 "If, despite all this, you still do not listen to Me – if still you walk contrary
28 to Me – then I, in My fury, will walk contrary to you. I will punish you
29 seven times more for your sins: you shall eat the flesh of your own sons; the
30 flesh of your own daughters you shall eat. I will destroy your high shrines,
cut down your incense altars, and heap your corpses on the corpses of your
31 idols. I shall despise you. I will turn your cities into ruins and make your
32 sanctuaries desolate. I will not savor your pleasing aromas. I Myself will
devastate the land, so that your enemies who settle there will be appalled.
33 I shall scatter you among the nations; I will draw My sword against you.
Your land will be desolate; your cities, ruins.

34 "Then shall the land make appeasement for its Sabbaths[65] for as long as it

65 | Referring to those described in 25:1–24. If the Israelites do not observe these Sabbaths, they will be banished and the land will finally be allowed to lie fallow in their absence.

lies desolate and you are in your enemies' lands. Then the land will rest and
35 make appeasement for its Sabbaths. In its desolation, the land will have the
rest it did not have during the Sabbaths when you were dwelling there.

36 "As for the survivors, I will bring such insecurity into their hearts in their
enemies' lands that the sound of a windblown leaf will make them run as
if they fled the sword; and they will fall, though no one is chasing them.
37 They will stumble over one another as if fleeing the sword, when no one
38 chases them. You will have no power to stand before your enemies. You
39 will perish among the nations; your enemies' lands will devour you. Those
of you who survive will waste away in their enemies' lands because of their
sins – for their ancestors' sins also, they will waste away.

40 "But if they confess their sins and those of their ancestors – their trespass
41 against Me and their walking contrary to Me, which made Me walk contrary
to them, bringing them into their enemies' lands – if their obstinate[66]
42 hearts are humbled and they atone for their sin, then I will remember My
covenant with Yaakov; and My covenant with Yitzḥak and My covenant
43 with Avraham I will also remember, and I will remember the land. The land
will be deserted, making appeasement for its Sabbaths, lying desolate of
them, while they will be making appeasement for their sins, because they
44 rejected My laws, because they despised My statutes. Yet even then, when
they are in the land of their enemies, I will not reject them nor despise
them and annihilate them, will not break My covenant with them, for I
45 am the LORD their God. I will remember for them the covenant with their
ancestors whom I brought out of Egypt in the sight of the nations, to be
their God; I am the LORD."

46 These are the statutes, laws, and instructions that the LORD established
between Himself and the Israelites, through Moshe, on Mount Sinai.

27 1 2 The LORD spoke to Moshe: "Speak to the Israelites. Say: When a person
makes a spoken vow to the LORD to give the equivalent of the value of
3 a person – if it is a male from twenty to sixty years old, his equivalent is
4 fifty silver shekel by the Sanctuary weight. If it is a female, the equivalent
5 is thirty shekel. If the person's age is between five and twenty years, the
6 equivalent for a male is twenty shekel, and for a female, ten shekel. If the
age is between one month and five years, the equivalent for a male is five
7 silver shekel; for a female, three silver shekel. If the age is sixty years or
more, the equivalent for a male is fifteen shekel, and for a female, ten shekel.
8 But if the person is too poor to pay the full amount, he shall be presented
to the priest, who will assess him. The priest shall assess him with reference
to the means of the person making the vow.

9 "If the vow concerns an animal of a type that may be offered to the LORD,
10 any such animal given to the LORD becomes sacred. One may not exchange

66 | Literally "uncircumcised."

it or offer a substitute for it, either better for worse or worse for better; and
if one animal is substituted for another, both it and the substitute become
11 holy. If the vow involves any type of impure animal, which cannot be
offered to the LORD, the animal shall be brought to stand before the priest.
12 The priest shall assess it, whether good or bad, and its value shall accord
13 to the priest's assessment. If the donor wishes to redeem it, a fifth shall be
added to its valuation.

14 "When someone consecrates his house to be sacred to the LORD, the
priest shall assess it, whether good or bad, and its value shall accord to the
15 priest's assessment. If the donor wishes to redeem it, he shall add a fifth to
its valuation, and it shall be his again.

16 "If someone consecrates part of his hereditary land to the LORD, its value
shall be set in relation to the seed needed to sow it: fifty silver shekel
17 for each homer[67] of barley seed. If the person consecrates his field from
18 the Jubilee year, the value that has been set stands.[68] But if the person
consecrates the field after the Jubilee, the priest shall calculate its value
in relation to the number of years left until the next Jubilee year, and the
19 valuation shall be reduced accordingly. If the person who consecrated the
field wishes to redeem it, he shall add a fifth to its valuation, and it shall
20 be his again. But if he does not redeem the field, or if it has been sold to
21 someone else, it can no longer be redeemed. When the field is released in
the Jubilee, it shall be holy to the LORD like devoted land; it comes into
22 the priest's possession. If the person consecrates to the LORD a field he
23 has purchased – not part of his hereditary land – the priest shall calculate
its proportionate value until the Jubilee year, and the donor shall pay its
24 valuation on that day,[69] as a sacred donation to the LORD. In the Jubilee
year the field shall return to the person from whom it was bought, whose
25 hereditary land it was. All assessments shall follow the Sanctuary standard,
by which a shekel is twenty gerah.

26 "A person cannot consecrate a firstborn animal, whether ox or sheep,
27 because, being a firstling, it already belongs to the LORD. If it is an impure
animal, it may be redeemed for its valuation with a fifth added. If it is not
redeemed, it shall be sold at its assessed value.[70]

28 "Nothing that a person owns that has been devoted to the LORD – be it
a person, an animal, or inherited land – may be sold or redeemed. Every
29 devoted thing is holy of holies to the LORD.[71] And no person condemned
to utter destruction may be ransomed; he must be put to death.

---

67 | A homer is a solid measure equivalent to roughly 50 liters.

68 | That is, if he consecrates it at the onset of the Jubilee cycle and wishes to redeem it immediately, he pays a full fifty shekel per homer of barley seed.

69 | Meaning the proportionate value calculated as of that day.

70 | That is, with no fifth added.

71 | This verse introduces a new type of consecrated entity called *Ḥerem* (devoted thing), which is not subject to redemption.

30 "All tithes from the land, whether seed from the ground or fruit of the
31 tree, belong to the LORD; they are sacred to the LORD. If a person wishes
32 to redeem part of his tithe, he shall add a fifth to its value. All tithes from
the herd or flock – every tenth animal that passes under the shepherd's
33 staff – shall be sacred to the LORD. One should not pick out the good
from the bad or make any substitution. But if a substitution is made, both
the item and its substitute shall be sacred; they cannot be redeemed."

34 These are the commands that the LORD gave Moshe, on Mount Sinai, for
the people of Israel.

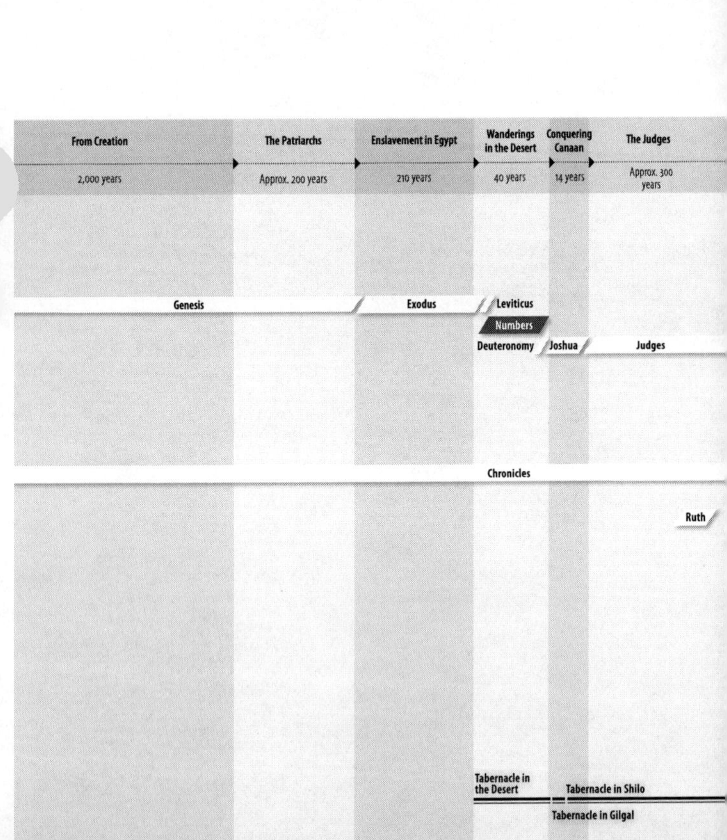
From Creation
2,000 years
The Patriarchs
Approx. 200 years
Enslavement in Egypt
210 years
Wanderings in the Desert
40 years
Conquering Canaan
14 years
The Judges
Approx. 300 years
Genesis
Exodus
Leviticus
Numbers
Deuteronomy
Joshua
Judges
Chronicles
Ruth
Tabernacle in the Desert
Tabernacle in Shilo
Tabernacle in Gilgal

NUMBERS/BEMIDBAR

NUMBERS	Preparations for the journey to the land of Israel	Crises during the second year of the journey	Events of the fortieth year of the journey	Preparations for entering the land
	Chs. 1–10	11–19	20–25	26–36
	38 years and 9 months			

1 1 The Lord spoke to Moshe in the Sinai Desert, in the Tent of Meeting, on BEMIDBAR
the first of the second month, in the second year since their coming out
2 from the land of Egypt. He said: "Take a census of the entire community
of Israel by their clans and their ancestral houses, listing every male by
3 name individually, twenty years of age and upward: everyone in Israel who
is capable of active service. You and Aharon shall number them by their
4 divisions.[1] And one man from each tribe shall join you in the task, each the
5 head of his ancestral house. These are the names of the men who will assist
6 you: from Reuven, Elitzur son of Shedeiur; from Shimon, Shelumiel son
7 8 of Tzurishadai; from Yehuda, Naḥshon son of Aminadav; from Yissakhar,
9 10 Netanel son of Tzuar; from Zevulun, Eliav son of Ḥelon. For the sons of
Yosef: from Efrayim, Elishama son of Amihud; from Menashe, Gamliel son
11 12 of Pedatzur. From Binyamin, Avidan son of Gidoni; from Dan, Aḥiezer
13 14 son of Amishadai; from Asher, Pagiel son of Okhran; from Gad, Elyasaf
15 16 son of Deuel; and from Naftali, Aḥira son of Einan." These were the ones
chosen from the community, princes of their ancestral tribes; they are the
heads of Israel's clans.

17 Moshe and Aharon took these men, those who had been marked out
18 by name, and they convened the entire community on the first day of
the second month. And the people declared themselves by their clans
and their ancestral houses. All those over twenty years old were counted
19 individually by name, as the Lord had commanded Moshe; so it was that
he counted them in the Sinai Desert.

20 The children of Reuven, Yisrael's firstborn – his descendants by their clans
and their ancestral families – the tally of their names, each male aged
twenty years and above: everyone capable of active service, all counted
21 individually – those counted from the tribe of Reuven numbered 46,500.

22 Of the children of Shimon – his descendants by their clans and their
ancestral families – the tally of their names, each male aged twenty years and
23 above: everyone capable of active service, all counted individually – those
counted from the tribe of Shimon numbered 59,300.

24 Of the children of Gad – his descendants by their clans and their ancestral
families – the tally of their names, each male aged twenty years and above:
25 everyone capable of active service, all counted individually – those counted
from the tribe of Gad numbered 45,650.

26 Of the children of Yehuda – his descendants by their clans and their ancestral
families – the tally of their names, each male aged twenty years and above:
27 everyone capable of active service, all counted individually – those
counted from the tribe of Yehuda numbered 74,600.

28 Of the children of Yissakhar – his descendants by their clans and their
ancestral families – the tally of their names, each male aged twenty years and

1 | That is, military divisions. Chapter 2 assigns a division to each tribe.

29 above: everyone capable of active service, all counted individually – those
counted from the tribe of Yissakhar numbered 54,400.

30 Of the children of Zevulun – his descendants by their clans and their
ancestral families – the tally of their names, each male aged twenty years and
31 above: everyone capable of active service, all counted individually – those
counted from the tribe of Zevulun numbered 57,400.

32 Of the children of Yosef: of the children of Efrayim – his descendants
by their clans and their ancestral families – the tally of their names, each
male aged twenty years and above: everyone capable of active service, all
33 counted individually – those counted from the tribe of Efrayim numbered
40,500.

34 Of the children of Menashe – his descendants by their clans and their
ancestral families – the tally of their names, each male aged twenty years and
35 above: everyone capable of active service, all counted individually – those
counted from the tribe of Menashe numbered 32,200.

36 Of the children of Binyamin – his descendants by their clans and their
ancestral families – the tally of their names, each male aged twenty years and
37 above: everyone capable of active service, all counted individually – those
counted from the tribe of Binyamin numbered 35,400.

38 Of the children of Dan – his descendants by their clans and their ancestral
families – the tally of their names, each male aged twenty years and
39 above: everyone capable of active service, all counted individually – those
counted from the tribe of Dan numbered 62,700.

40 Of the children of Asher – his descendants by their clans and their ancestral
families – the tally of their names, each male aged twenty years and
41 above: everyone capable of active service, all counted individually – those
counted from the tribe of Asher numbered 41,500.

42 The children of Naftali – his descendants by their clans and their ancestral
families – the tally of their names, each male aged twenty years and
43 above: everyone capable of active service, all counted individually – those
counted from the tribe of Naftali numbered 53,400.

44 These were the ones counted by Moshe, Aharon, and the twelve princes
45 of Israel, one from each ancestral house. Thus the total number of the
Israelites counted, by their ancestral houses, aged twenty years and
46 47 above – everyone in Israel capable of active service – was 603,550. The
ancestral house of the Levites, however, was not counted among them.

48 49 For the Lord had spoken to Moshe and said, "You shall not count the
50 tribe of Levi, nor take a census of them among the Israelites. Instead, you
shall appoint the Levites over the Tabernacle of the Testimony, over all its
utensils and all that belongs to it. For they are to carry the Tabernacle and
all its utensils; they are to tend to it, and around the Tabernacle they shall

51 encamp. When the Tabernacle is to move onward, the Levites shall take
it down, and when the Tabernacle is to encamp, the Levites shall erect it.
Any outsider who draws close to it shall be put to death.

52 The Israelites shall encamp in their respective camps, each by his own
53 banner, in his division. But the Levites shall encamp around the Tabernacle
of the Testimony, so that fury does not engulf the community of the
Israelites; the Levites shall keep watch faithfully over the Tabernacle of
54 the Testimony."[2] The Israelites did so; all that the LORD had commanded
Moshe, they fulfilled.

2 1 The LORD spoke to Moshe and Aharon: "The Israelites shall camp, each by
2 his banner, the ensign of his ancestral house, positioned around the Tent
of Meeting at a distance.

3 "Camping to the east, toward the sunrise, shall be the divisions under the
banner of Yehuda. The leader of Yehuda's descendants is Naḥshon son of
4 Aminadav. And his division numbers 74,600.

5 "Camping next to them shall be the tribe of Yissakhar. The leader of
6 Yissakhar's descendants is Netanel son of Tzuar. And his division numbers
54,400.

7 "Then the tribe of Zevulun. The leader of Zevulun's descendants is Eliav
8 son of Ḥelon. His division numbers 57,400.

9 "The total number in Yehuda's camp, in their divisions, is 151,450. They
shall be the first to set out.

10 "The divisions under the banner of Reuven's camp shall be to the south.
11 The leader of Reuven's descendants is Elitzur son of Shedeiur. And his
division numbers 46,500.

12 "Camping next to them shall be the tribe of Shimon. The leader of
13 Shimon's descendants is Shelumiel son of Tzurishadai. His division
numbers 59,300.

14 "Then the tribe of Gad: the leader of Gad's descendants is Elyasaf son of
15 Reuel. And his division numbers 45,650.

16 "The total number in Reuven's camp, in their divisions, is 186,400. They
shall set out second.

17 "And the Tent of Meeting and the Levite camp shall set out in the midst
of the camps. All shall set out as they encamp, each in his own place under
his banner.

18 "The divisions under the banner of Efrayim shall be to the west. The leader
19 of Efrayim's descendants is Elishama son of Amihud. And his division
numbers 40,500.

---

2 | The verse implies that unauthorized entry into the Tabernacle may provoke God's wrath.

20 "Next to them shall be the tribe of Menashe. The leader of Menashe's
21 descendants is Gamliel son of Pedatzur. His division numbers 32,200.

22 "Then the tribe of Binyamin: the leader of Binyamin's descendants is
23 Avidan son of Gidoni. His division numbers 35,400.

24 "The total number of men in Efrayim's camp, in their divisions, is 108,100.
They shall set out third.

25 "The divisions under the banner of Dan shall be to the north. The leader
26 of Dan's descendants is Aḥiezer son of Amishadai. His division numbers
62,700.

27 "Camping next to them shall be the tribe of Asher. The leader of Asher's
28 descendants is Pagiel son of Okhran. His division numbers 41,500.

29 "Then the tribe of Naftali: the leader of Naftali's descendants is Aḥira son
30 of Einan. His division numbers 53,400.

31 "The total number in Dan's camp, in their divisions, is 157,600. They shall
set out last, by their banners."

32 These were the numbers of the Israelites by their ancestral houses. The
33 total number in the camps by their divisions was 603,550. As the Lord
had commanded Moshe, the Levites were not counted among the other
Israelites.

34 And so the Israelites did all that the Lord had commanded Moshe. Thus
they camped by their banners, and thus they set out, each amid his clan
and his ancestral house.

3 1 These were the descendants of Aharon and Moshe at the time when the
Lord spoke to Moshe at Mount Sinai.

2 The names of Aharon's sons were Nadav, the firstborn, Avihu, Elazar,
3 and Itamar. These were the names of Aharon's sons, the anointed priests,
4 ordained for priestly service. But Nadav and Avihu died before the Lord
when, before the Lord, they offered unauthorized fire in the Wilderness
of Sinai;[3] they had had no sons. And Elazar and Itamar served as priests
while their father Aharon lived.[4]

5 6 The Lord said to Moshe, "Bring close the tribe of Levi and set them
7 before Aharon the priest to assist him. They shall keep his charge and that
of the whole community at the Tent of Meeting, carrying out the service
8 of the Tabernacle. Theirs shall be the charge of all the utensils of the
Tent of Meeting, and they shall keep, too, the charge of the Israelites by
9 performing the service of the Tabernacle. Give the Levites over to Aharon
and his sons; they among the Israelites are to be dedicated wholly to him.

3 | See Leviticus 10:1–2.

4 | In other words, only these two remaining sons served during Aharon's lifetime.

10 Appoint Aharon and his sons to attend to the priestly duties; any outsider
who draws close[5] will die."

11 12 And the LORD spoke to Moshe: "In place of the firstborn, the first to
emerge from every womb among the Israelites, I have taken the Levites
13 from among the Israelites; the Levites shall be Mine, for all the firstborn
are Mine. On the day I struck down all the firstborn in Egypt, I consecrated
every firstborn in Israel to Myself, man and animal. They are to be Mine;
I am the LORD."

14 15 Then the LORD spoke to Moshe in the Sinai Desert: "Count the Levites
by their ancestral houses and their clans. Count every male a month
16 old or more." So Moshe counted them at the LORD's word as he was
commanded.

17 These were the names of Levi's sons: Gershon, Kehat, and Merari.

18 These were the names of Gershon's sons with their clans: Livni and Shimi.

19 Kehat's sons with their clans: Amram, Yitzhar, Ḥevron, and Uziel.

20 Merari's sons with their clans: Maḥli and Mushi.

These were the Levite clans by their ancestral houses.

21 Gershon encompassed the clans of Livni and Shimi; these were the
22 Gershonite clans. Their total number of males a month old and upward
23 was 7,500. The Gershonite families were to camp behind the Tabernacle
24 to the west. And the leader of the Gershonite families was Elyasaf son of
25 Lael. The charge of the sons of Gershon at the Tent of Meeting was the
Tabernacle and the tent, its covering,[6] the screen at the entrance to the
26 Tent of Meeting, the curtains of the courtyard, the screen at the entrance
to the courtyard surrounding the Tabernacle and altar, and its ropes – and
all the service related to these.

27 Kehat encompassed the clans of Amram, Yitzhar, Ḥevron, and Uziel; these
28 were the Kohatite clans. Their total number of males a month old and
29 upward was 8,600; these kept the charge of the Sanctuary. The Kohatite
30 families were to camp on the south side of the Tabernacle. The leader of
the ancestral house of the Kohatite families was Elitzafan son of Uziel.
31 Their charge was the Ark, the table, the candelabrum, the altars, and
the sacred utensils used in their service, and the screen and everything
32 pertaining to it. Chief of the leaders of the Levites was Elazar son of
Aharon the priest; he was appointed over those responsible for keeping
charge of the Sanctuary.

---

5 | See note on 1:53.

6 | The Tabernacle, the tent, and the covering represent different layers of the structure; see Exodus 26:1–14. For components of the Tabernacle generally, see Exodus, chapters 25–27.

33 Merari encompassed the clans of Maḥli and Mushi; these were the
34 Merarite families. The total number of their males a month old and upward
35 was 6,200. The leader of the ancestral house of the Merarite families was
Tzuriel son of Aviḥayil; and they were to camp on the north side of the
36 Tabernacle. The Merarites were appointed to take care of the frames, bars,
37 posts, and bases of the Tabernacle, all its utensils and accessories, as well as
the posts of the surrounding courtyard with their bases, pegs, and ropes.

38 Those who were to camp to the east of the Tabernacle in front of the Tent
of Meeting toward the sunrise were Moshe, Aharon, and his sons. They
were charged, on the Israelites' behalf, to keep faithful watch over the
Sanctuary. Any outsider who drew close would die.

39 The total number of Levites counted by Moshe and Aharon at the LORD's
command, by their clans, all the males a month old and upward, was
22,000.

40 Then the LORD said to Moshe, "Count all the firstborn Israelite males a
41 month of age and upward, taking a census of their names. Take the Levites
for Me – I am the LORD – in place of all the firstborn of the Israelites, and
the livestock of the Levites in place of all the firstborn of the Israelites'
livestock."

42 So Moshe counted all the firstborn of the Israelites, as the LORD had
43 commanded him. The total number of firstborn males a month of age and
upward, the full tally of their names, was 22,273.

44 45 Then the LORD spoke to Moshe: "Take the Levites in place of all the
firstborn of Israel, and the livestock of the Levites in place of their livestock.
46 The Levites shall be Mine; I am the LORD. As for the redemption of the
47 273 firstborn Israelites who exceed the number of the Levites, collect five
shekel for each, according to the Sanctuary weight – a shekel being twenty
48 gerah.[7] Give the money to Aharon and his sons as a redemption for the
additional Israelites."

49 Moshe took the redemption money from those who were over and above
50 those redeemed by the Levites; from the firstborn of the Israelites he
51 took silver weighing 1,365 shekel by the Sanctuary weight. Moshe gave
the redemption money to Aharon and his sons, at the LORD's word, as the
LORD had commanded Moshe.

4 1 2 The LORD spoke to Moshe and Aharon: "Take a census of the Kohatites
3 among the Levites, by their families and their ancestral houses, from thirty
to fifty years old: all those able to go into service to perform the work of
4 the Tent of Meeting. This will be the service of the Kohatites in the Tent

7 | The gerah and the shekel are units of weight and currency, of which Sanctuary weights differed from the standard measure. A shekel was close to 20 grams or three-quarters of an ounce.

5 of Meeting: the most sacred objects; when the camp is about to set out,
Aharon and his sons shall come and take down the screening curtain
6 and cover the Ark of the Testimony with it. Then they shall put over it a
covering of fine leather, and over that a cloth of pure blue, and then they
shall insert its poles.

7 "On the table of the showbread they shall spread a blue cloth, and on it
place the bowls, spoons, jars, and the libation pitchers; and the bread of
8 the Presence shall be on it constantly. They shall spread over them a scarlet
cloth, and then cover it with a covering of fine leather; and then they shall
insert its poles.

9 "They shall take a blue cloth and cover the candelabrum and its lamps,
10 tongs, pans, and all the oil vessels used in its service. Then they must put
it and all its utensils into a covering of fine leather, and place them on a
carrying frame.

11 "They shall spread a blue cloth on the golden altar, and cover it with a
12 covering of fine leather; and then they shall insert its poles. Then they shall
take all the service utensils, with which they serve in the Sanctuary, put
them into a blue cloth, cover them with a covering of fine leather, and place
13 them on a carrying frame. They shall remove the ashes from the altar and
14 spread a purple cloth over it. Then they shall place upon it all the special
implements with which they serve there – the pans, the forks, the shovels,
the basins, and all the altar's utensils – and spread over it all a covering of
fine leather, and then insert its poles.

15 "When Aharon and his sons have finished covering the Sanctuary and
all the furnishings of the Sanctuary, when the camp is ready to set out,
then the Kohatites shall come to carry them; but they must not touch the
sacred objects lest they die. These are what the Kohatites must carry for
the Tent of Meeting.

16 "The responsibility of Elazar son of Aharon the priest is for the lighting
oil, the fragrant incense, the daily grain offering, and the anointing oil.
He is also responsible for the whole Tabernacle and all that is in it, for the
Sanctuary and all its utensils."

17 18 Again the LORD spoke to Moshe and Aharon: "Do not let the tribe of the
19 clans of Kehat be cut off from among the Levites. So that they may live
and not die when they come close to the most sacred things, they must
do this: let Aharon and his sons go in and assign each man his duties and
20 what he must carry; but they themselves must not go in and watch while
the holy things are being covered, for they would die."

21 22 Then the LORD spoke to Moshe: "Take a census too of the Gershonites, by NASO
23 their clans and their ancestral houses, from thirty years old to fifty: all who
24 go into service to carry out the work of the Tent of Meeting. This will be
25 the service of the clans of Gershon, serving and carrying: they shall carry

the curtains of the Tabernacle and the Tent of Meeting, its covering, the
covering of fine leather that is over it, the screen at the entrance to the Tent
26 of Meeting, the hangings for the courtyard, the curtain for the entrance
of the gate to the courtyard around the Tabernacle and the altar, and their
ropes, together with all the utensils for their service and everything made
for them; and they will serve.

27 "All the carrying and service of the Gershonites shall be performed at
Aharon and his sons' command; you shall assign to their charge all that
28 they are to carry. This is the service of the families of the Gershonites for
the Tent of Meeting. Their charge will be under the authority of Itamar
son of Aharon the priest.

29 "As for the sons of Merari, you shall number them by their clans and
30 ancestral houses, from thirty years old to fifty, all who go into service to
31 carry out the work of the Tent of Meeting. This is what they are charged
to carry as the whole of their service in the Tent of Meeting: the boards
32 of the Tabernacle, its crossbars, its posts, its sockets; and the posts of the
surrounding courtyard with their sockets, pegs, and ropes, together with
all their furnishings and everything for their service. You shall assign each
33 object by name to the man charged with carrying it. This is the service
of the families of the Merarites, the whole of their service for the Tent of
Meeting, under the authority of Itamar son of Aharon the priest."

34 So Moshe and Aharon and the leaders of the community counted the
35 Kohatites by their clans and their ancestral houses, from thirty years old
36 to fifty, all who went into the service of the Tent of Meeting; and those
37 numbered by their clans were 2,750. These were the ones numbered from
the clans of Kehat, all who served in the Tent of Meeting, whom Moshe
and Aharon numbered at the Lord's command through Moshe.

38 Those numbered of the Gershonites, by their families and ancestral houses,
39 from thirty years old to fifty: all who went into the service of the Tent of
40 Meeting – those numbered by their clans and ancestral houses were 2,630.
41 These were the ones numbered from the families of the Gershonites, all
who served in the Tent of Meeting, whom Moshe and Aharon numbered
at the command of the Lord.

42 Those numbered from the clans of the Merarites, by their clans and
43 ancestral houses, from thirty years old to fifty, all who went into the service
44 45 of the Tent of Meeting – those numbered by their clans were 3,200. These
were the ones numbered from the clans of the Merarites, whom Moshe
and Aharon numbered at the Lord's command through Moshe.

46 All the Levites, whom Moshe, Aharon, and the leaders of Israel numbered
47 by their clans and ancestral houses, from thirty years old to fifty: all who
entered to do the work of service and the work of carrying relating to the
48 49 Tent of Meeting – those numbered were 8,580. At the command of the

LORD they were listed, and by the authority of Moshe, each according to
his service and to what he was to carry; thus was each one numbered as
the LORD had commanded Moshe.

5 1 2 Then the LORD spoke to Moshe: "Command the Israelites to send away
from the camp anyone who has an impure blight,[8] or has had a discharge,[9]
3 or anyone made impure by contact with the dead. Male or female, you
must send them away – send them away outside the camp, so that they do
4 not defile their camps, in the midst of which I dwell." The Israelites did
so: outside the camp they sent them. As the LORD spoke to Moshe, so
the Israelites did.

5 6 And the LORD spoke to Moshe: "Tell the Israelites: When one man or
woman commits any sin against another, breaking faith with the LORD and
7 incurring guilt, then he or she shall confess the sin committed and make
restitution, adding a fifth to its value, and giving it all to the one whom
8 he has wronged.[10] But if there is no relative to whom restitution can be
made for the wrong,[11] the restitution for that wrong shall go to the LORD,
to the priest, in addition to the ram of atonement by which atonement is
9 made on his behalf. All gifts the Israelites present to the priest as sacred
10 offerings shall be his. Each priest's sacred offerings will be his; whatever
anyone gives him shall be his."

11 12 The LORD spoke to Moshe: "Speak to the Israelites and tell them: If any
13 man's wife goes astray and is unfaithful to him; if another man has sexual
relations with her, and this happens without the husband's knowledge
because she defiled herself in secret, there were no witness against her,
14 and she was not caught in the act – if a fit of jealousy overcomes him,
making him jealous over his wife who has defiled herself, or a fit of jealousy
overcomes him, making him jealous over his wife who has not defiled
15 herself[12] – then the man shall bring his wife to the priest together with the
prescribed offering for her, one-tenth of an ephah[13] of barley flour. He shall
not pour oil on it or place frankincense upon it, for it is a grain offering of
jealousy, a grain offering of remembrance, calling attention to a wrong.

16 "The priest shall bring the woman close and have her stand before the
17 LORD. He shall then take sacred water in an earthenware vessel, and pick
up some earth from the floor of the Tabernacle and place it in the water.
18 He shall have the woman stand before the LORD, and loosen the hair of

8 | See Leviticus, chapter 13.

9 | See Leviticus, chapter 15.

10 | Cf. Leviticus 5:20–26; one who takes a false oath denying theft or embezzlement must add a fifth when making restoration.

11 | According to the traditional understanding, this means that the victim is a since-deceased convert, who has no Israelite heirs.

12 | In other words, the husband does not know for sure whether his wife has "defiled herself."

13 | An ephah is a solid measure equivalent to approximately 25 liters.

the woman's head, placing on her palms the grain offering of remembrance,
the grain offering of jealousy. His hand shall hold the bitter water that gives
19 rise to a curse. And the priest shall administer an oath to her, saying to
the woman, 'If no man has had sexual relations with you, and if you have
not gone astray, letting yourself be defiled while married to your husband,
20 may your innocence be established by this bitter, cursing water. But if
you have gone astray while married to your husband, and if you have let
yourself be defiled and a man other than your husband has had relations
21 with you' – the priest shall here put the woman under the oath of the curse,
and say to her – 'the LORD make you a curse and an oath among your
22 people, when the LORD makes your thigh sag and your belly swell;[14] may
this curse-causing water enter your intestines and make your belly swell
and your thigh sag.' And the woman shall say, 'Amen, Amen.'

23 "Then the priest shall write these curses on a scroll and wash them off
24 into the bitter water. He shall make the woman drink the bitter water
that causes a curse, and the curse-causing water will enter into her and
25 turn bitter. The priest shall take the grain offering of jealousy from the
woman's hand, wave the grain offering before the LORD, and bring it close
26 to the altar. Then the priest shall take a handful of the grain offering as
a token, and burn it on the altar, after which he shall make the woman
27 drink the water. He having given her the water to drink, then, if she has
let herself be defiled and behaved unfaithfully toward her husband, the
curse-causing water will turn bitter, her belly will swell, her thigh will sag,
28 and the woman will become a curse among her people. But if the woman
has not let herself be defiled and is pure, then she shall be cleared and will
conceive children."

29 This is the law for cases of jealousy, when a woman goes astray with
30 someone in place of her husband and becomes defiled, or when a fit of
jealousy overcomes a man and he grows jealous over his wife.[15] He shall
have the woman stand before the LORD, and the priest will deal with her
31 as all this law prescribes. No guilt will attach to the husband,[16] but the
woman in question will bear the punishment of her offense.

6 1 Then the LORD spoke to Moshe: "Speak to the Israelites. Say: When a man
2 or a woman takes a special vow, the vow of a nazirite,[17] to separate him or
3 herself to the LORD, he must separate himself from wine and strong drink.
He must drink neither vinegar made from wine nor vinegar made from
any other strong drink, nor may he drink any juice made with grapes, nor

14 | Opinions vary regarding the precise nature and implications of this physical reaction.

15 | That is, even though she in fact did not defile herself.

16 | According to rabbinic interpretation, the husband may initiate the process only if there is testimony that his wife, despite being warned, secluded herself with a particular man. The husband therefore does not bear responsibility for subjecting her to the procedure without cause.

17 | Literally "one who is separated." *Nezer* can also mean "crown"; see verse 7 below.

4 eat fresh grapes or raisins. All the days of his separation he must not eat
anything that comes from the grapevine, from seed to skin.

5 "All the days of his separation vow, no razor shall touch his head. Until the
completion of the time for which he separated himself to the LORD, he
shall be holy, and must let the locks of his hair grow long.

6 "All the days of his separation to the LORD, he must not come near a dead
7 body. Even for his father or mother or brother or sister, if they die, he must
8 not defile himself, for his vow of separation to his God is on his head.[18] All
the days of his separation he is holy to the LORD.

9 "If someone dies suddenly beside him, defiling his consecrated head, he
shall shave his head on the day of his purification; on the seventh day he
10 shall shave it. Then, on the eighth day, he shall bring two turtledoves or
two young pigeons to the priest, to the entrance of the Tent of Meeting.
11 The priest will offer one as a purification offering and the other as a burnt
offering, and make atonement for him for the guilt he incurred through
contact with the dead body. He shall consecrate his head anew on that day.
12 He must rededicate himself to the LORD for the full term of his vow, and
bring a yearling lamb as a guilt offering. The former days are discounted
because his separation was defiled.

13 "This is the law of the nazirite: On the day that the term of his nazirite vow
is completed, he shall be brought to the entrance to the Tent of Meeting.
14 He shall present his offering to the LORD: one male yearling lamb without
blemish for a burnt offering, one yearling ewe lamb without blemish for a
15 purification offering, one ram without blemish for a peace offering, and a
basket of unleavened bread, loaves of fine flour mixed with olive oil, and
unleavened wafers smeared with olive oil, along with their grain offering
and libations.

16 "The priest shall present these before the LORD and offer up his purification
17 offering and his burnt offering. He shall then offer the ram as a sacrifice, a
peace offering to the LORD, together with the basket of unleavened bread.
The priest shall also offer his grain offering and his libation.

18 "The nazirite shall shave his consecrated hair at the entrance to the Tent of
Meeting and take the hair of his consecrated head and place it on the fire
19 beneath the peace offering. The priest shall take the boiled foreleg of the
ram, one unleavened loaf from the basket, and one unleavened wafer, and
place them on the hands of the nazirite after he has shaved his consecrated
20 head. The priest shall wave them as a wave offering before the LORD. It is a
sacred gift for the priest, together with the breast of the wave offering and
the thigh of the upraised gift.[19] After this the nazirite may drink wine."

---

18 | The phrase can simultaneously be understood to mean: "the crown (*nezer*) of his God is on his head."

19 | See Leviticus 7:28–34.

21 This is the law of the nazirite who vows offerings to the LORD as a nazirite. Whatever he can afford further and vows to give, beyond what the law of the nazirite obliges him to, that too shall he fulfill.

22 23 The LORD spoke to Moshe: "Tell Aharon and his sons: This is how you
are to bless the Israelites. Say to them:

24 'May the LORD bless you and watch over you.
25 May the LORD make His face shine upon you
and be gracious to you.
26 May the LORD raise His face toward you
and grant you
peace.'

27 They shall set My name upon the Israelites,[20] and I will bless them."

7 1 On the day when Moshe finished establishing the Tabernacle, he anointed
it and consecrated it. He anointed and consecrated the altar, too, and all its
2 utensils. And the princes of Israel, leaders of their ancestral houses, drew
close. They were the princes of the tribes, the ones who had directed the
3 census. And they brought their offerings before the LORD: six covered
wagons and twelve oxen – a wagon for every two leaders, and for each one
an ox. They presented them before the Tabernacle.

4 5 The LORD said to Moshe, "Accept these from them and use them for
service in the Tent of Meeting. Give them to the Levites, to each according
to his service."

6 Moshe took the wagons and the oxen, and he gave them to the Levites.
7 He gave two wagons and four oxen to the Gershonites as their service
8 required. He gave four wagons and eight oxen to the Merarites for their
9 service under the supervision of Itamar son of Aharon the priest. But to
the Kohatites he gave none, for their responsibility was for the sacred
10 articles that had to be carried on their shoulders. The princes presented
their dedication offering for the altar at the time when it was anointed. The
princes brought their offerings before the altar.

11 The LORD said to Moshe, "Each day one prince is to bring close his offering
for the dedication of the altar."

12 The one who presented his offering on the first day was Naḥshon son
13 of Aminadav, from the tribe of Yehuda. His offering was one silver bowl
weighing one hundred and thirty shekel and one silver basin weighing
seventy shekel according to the Sanctuary weight, both filled with fine
14 flour mixed with oil for a grain offering; one golden spoon weighing ten
15 shekel, full of incense; one young bull, one ram, and one yearling sheep
16 17 for a burnt offering; one goat for a purification offering; and for the peace

20 | By invoking God's name during the blessing.

sacrifice two oxen, five rams, five male goats, and five yearling sheep. This
was the offering of Naḥshon son of Aminadav.

18 On the second day Netanel son of Tzuar, prince of Yissakhar, presented
19 his offering. He presented as his offering one silver bowl weighing one
hundred and thirty shekel and one silver basin weighing seventy shekel
according to the Sanctuary weight, both filled with fine flour mixed with
20 oil for a grain offering; one golden spoon weighing ten shekel, full of
21 incense; one young bull, one ram, and one yearling sheep for a burnt
22 23 offering; one goat for a purification offering; and for the peace sacrifice
two oxen, five rams, five male goats, and five yearling sheep. This was the
offering of Netanel son of Tzuar.

24 25 On the third day came Eliav son of Ḥelon, prince of the Zebulunites: His
offering was one silver bowl weighing one hundred and thirty shekel and
one silver basin weighing seventy shekel according to the Sanctuary weight,
26 both filled with fine flour mixed with oil for a grain offering; one golden
27 spoon weighing ten shekel, full of incense; one young bull, one ram, and
28 one yearling sheep for a burnt offering; one goat for a purification offering;
29 and for the peace sacrifice two oxen, five rams, five male goats, and five
yearling sheep. This was the offering of Eliav son of Ḥelon.

30 On the fourth day came Elitzur son of Shedeiur, prince of the Reubenites:
31 His offering was one silver bowl weighing one hundred and thirty shekel
and one silver basin weighing seventy shekel according to the Sanctuary
32 weight, both filled with fine flour mixed with oil for a grain offering; one
33 golden spoon weighing ten shekel, full of incense; one young bull, one
34 ram, and one yearling sheep for a burnt offering; one goat for a purification
35 offering; and for the peace sacrifice two oxen, five rams, five male goats,
and five yearling sheep. This was the offering of Elitzur son of Shedeiur.

36 On the fifth day came Shelumiel son of Tzurishadai, prince of the Simeonites:
37 His offering was one silver bowl weighing one hundred and thirty shekel
and one silver basin weighing seventy shekel according to the Sanctuary
weight, both filled with fine flour mixed with oil for a grain offering;
38 39 one golden spoon weighing ten shekel, full of incense; one young bull,
40 one ram, and one yearling sheep for a burnt offering; one goat for a
41 purification offering; and for the peace sacrifice two oxen, five rams, five
male goats, and five yearling sheep. This was the offering of Shelumiel son
of Tzurishadai.

42 43 On the sixth day came Elyasaf son of Deuel, prince of the Gadites: His
offering was one silver bowl weighing one hundred and thirty shekel and
one silver basin weighing seventy shekel according to the Sanctuary weight,
44 both filled with fine flour mixed with oil for a grain offering; one golden
45 spoon weighing ten shekel, full of incense; one young bull, one ram, and
46 one yearling sheep for a burnt offering; one goat for a purification offering;

47 and for the peace sacrifice two oxen, five rams, five male goats, and five
yearling sheep. This was the offering of Elyasaf son of Deuel.

48 On the seventh day came Elishama son of Amihud, prince of the Efraimites:
49 His offering was one silver bowl weighing one hundred and thirty shekel
and one silver basin weighing seventy shekel according to the Sanctuary
50 weight, both filled with fine flour mixed with oil for a grain offering; one
51 golden spoon weighing ten shekel, full of incense; one young bull, one
52 ram, and one yearling sheep for a burnt offering; one goat for a purification
53 offering; and for the peace sacrifice two oxen, five rams, five male goats, and
five yearling sheep. This was the offering of Elishama son of Amihud.

54 On the eighth day came Gamliel son of Pedahtzur, prince of the Manassites:
55 His offering was one silver bowl weighing one hundred and thirty shekel
and one silver basin weighing seventy shekel according to the Sanctuary
56 weight, both filled with fine flour mixed with oil for a grain offering; one
57 golden spoon weighing ten shekel, full of incense; one young bull, one
58 ram, and one yearling sheep for a burnt offering; one goat for a purification
59 offering; and for the peace sacrifice two oxen, five rams, five male goats, and
five yearling sheep. This was the offering of Gamliel son of Pedahtzur.

60 On the ninth day came Avidan son of Gidoni, prince of the Benjaminites:
61 His offering was one silver bowl weighing one hundred and thirty shekel
and one silver basin weighing seventy shekel according to the Sanctuary
62 weight, both filled with fine flour mixed with oil for a grain offering; one
63 golden spoon weighing ten shekel, full of incense; one young bull, one
64 ram, and one yearling sheep for a burnt offering; one goat for a purification
65 offering; and for the peace sacrifice two oxen, five rams, five male goats,
and five yearling sheep. This was the offering of Avidan son of Gidoni.

66 On the tenth day came Aḥiezer son of Amishadai, prince of the Danites:
67 His offering was one silver bowl weighing one hundred and thirty shekel
and one silver basin weighing seventy shekel according to the Sanctuary
68 weight, both filled with fine flour mixed with oil for a grain offering; one
69 golden spoon weighing ten shekel, full of incense; one young bull, one
70 ram, and one yearling sheep for a burnt offering; one goat for a purification
71 offering; and for the peace sacrifice two oxen, five rams, five male goats, and
five yearling sheep. This was the offering of Aḥiezer son of Amishadai.

72 On the eleventh day came Pagiel son of Okhran, prince of the Asherites:
73 His offering was one silver bowl weighing one hundred and thirty shekel
and one silver basin weighing seventy shekel according to the Sanctuary
weight, both filled with fine flour mixed with oil for a grain offering;
74 75 one golden spoon weighing ten shekel, full of incense; one young bull,
76 one ram, and one yearling sheep for a burnt offering; one goat for a
77 purification offering; and for the peace sacrifice two oxen, five rams, five
male goats, and five yearling sheep. This was the offering of Pagiel son of
Okhran.

78 79 On the twelfth day came Aḥira son of Einan, prince of the Naftalites: His
offering was one silver bowl weighing one hundred and thirty shekel and
one silver basin weighing seventy shekel according to the Sanctuary weight,
80 both filled with fine flour mixed with oil for a grain offering; one golden
81 spoon weighing ten shekel, full of incense; one young bull, one ram, and
82 one yearling sheep for a burnt offering; one goat for a purification offering;
83 and for the peace sacrifice two oxen, five rams, five male goats, and five
yearling sheep. This was the offering of Aḥira son of Einan.

84 All this was the dedication offering from the princes of Israel for the altar
at the time it was anointed: There were twelve silver bowls, twelve silver
85 basins, and twelve golden spoons, each silver bowl weighing one hundred
and thirty shekel and each basin seventy shekel – so all the silver in the
utensils weighed two thousand four hundred shekel according to the
86 Sanctuary weight. There were twelve gold spoons full of incense weighing
ten shekel each according to the Sanctuary weight – so all the gold of the
87 spoons weighed one hundred and twenty shekel. The total number of the
animals for the burnt offerings was twelve bulls, twelve rams, and twelve
yearling sheep, along with their grain offerings. There were also twelve
88 goats for the purification offerings. The total number of all the animals
for the peace sacrifices was twenty-four bulls, sixty rams, sixty goats, and
sixty yearling sheep. This was the dedication offering for the altar after it
was anointed.

89 When Moshe entered the Tent of Meeting to speak with the LORD, he
would hear the Voice speaking to him from above the cover over the Ark
of the Covenant, from between the two cherubim. Thus did He speak to
him.

8 1 2 And the LORD spoke to Moshe: "Speak to Aharon; say to him: When you BEHAALOTEKHA
raise up the lamps, the seven lamps shall light the space in front of the
candelabrum."[21]

3 Aharon did so; he mounted the lamps toward the front of the candelabrum
4 as the LORD had commanded Moshe. This is how the lampstand was made:
of hammered gold, hammered from its base to its flowers. According to the
vision that the LORD had shown Moshe, so was the lampstand made.

5 6 The LORD spoke to Moshe: "Take the Levites from among the Israelites
7 and purify them. This is what you shall do to them to purify them: Sprinkle
upon them the water of purification,[22] and have them shave their whole
8 bodies and wash their clothes; then they will be purified. They shall
take a young bull with its grain offering of fine flour mixed with oil. You,
9 meanwhile, shall take a second young bull for a purification offering. You
shall bring the Levites before the Tent of Meeting and assemble all the
10 community of Israel. Then you shall bring the Levites forward before the

21 | Concerning the candelabrum, see Exodus 25:31–40.

22 | Cf. the ritual described in chapter 19.

11 LORD, and the Israelites shall lay their hands upon the Levites. Aharon
shall then present the Levites before the LORD like a wave offering from
12 the Israelites, so that they may perform the LORD's service. The Levites
shall then lay their hands upon the heads of the bulls, and Aharon shall
offer one as a purification offering and the other as a burnt offering to the
LORD, to make atonement for the Levites.

13 "You shall have the Levites stand before Aharon and his sons, and then
14 present them like a wave offering to the LORD. Thus you shall separate
the Levites from among the other Israelites; the Levites shall become
15 Mine. After that, the Levites shall enter to perform the service of the Tent
of Meeting, once you have purified them and presented them as a wave
16 offering. They are wholly given over to Me from among the Israelites. I
have taken them for Myself in place of the first to emerge from every womb,
17 the firstborn of all the Israelites. For all the firstborn among the Israelites,
man and beast alike, are Mine; on the day that I struck down the firstborn
18 in Egypt, I consecrated them to Myself. But I have now taken the Levites in
19 place of all the firstborn among the Israelites, and I have given the Levites
to Aharon and his sons from among the Israelites, to perform the service
of the Israelites in the Tent of Meeting and to make atonement for the
Israelites, so that no plague will come among the Israelites for drawing
too close to the Sanctuary."

20 Moshe, Aharon, and all the community of Israel did this for the Levites; all
that the LORD commanded Moshe with regard to the Levites, so the Israelites
21 did. The Levites purified themselves and washed their clothes. Aharon
presented them as a wave offering before the LORD, and made atonement for
22 them in order to purify them. And after that, the Levites went in to perform
their service in the Tent of Meeting before Aharon and his sons. As the LORD
had commanded Moshe regarding the Levites, so they did for them.

23 24 And the LORD spoke to Moshe: "The Levites: From twenty-five years
25 upward they shall go into the service of the Tent of Meeting. At fifty years
26 old they shall retire from the service and serve no longer. They may assist
their fellow Levites in carrying out their duties in the Tent of Meeting,
but shall not perform the service itself. This is how you shall conduct the
Levites with regard to their duties."

9 1 The LORD spoke to Moshe in the Sinai Desert in the first month of the
2 second year after they had left Egypt: "Let the Israelites offer the Passover
3 sacrifice at its appointed time. On the fourteenth day of this month in the
afternoon you shall offer it at its appointed time. Bring it in accordance
with all its decrees and laws."[23]

4 5 And so Moshe instructed the Israelites to offer the Passover sacrifice. On
the afternoon of the fourteenth day of the first month they offered the

23 | See Exodus, chapter 12.

Passover sacrifice in the Sinai Desert. Just as the LORD commanded Moshe,
so the Israelites did.

6 But there were people who were impure because of contact with the dead,
and they were unable to offer the Passover sacrifice on that day. That
7 very day they approached Moshe and Aharon: "We have become impure
because of contact with the dead," these people said to him, "but must
we be debarred from presenting the LORD's offering at its appointed time
among all the Israelites?"

8 "Wait," Moshe replied, "and let me hear what the LORD commands concerning you."

9 10 And the LORD spoke to Moshe: "Tell the Israelites: When any of you or
your future descendants are impure because of contact with the dead, or
away on a journey, they may still offer a Passover sacrifice to the LORD.
11 They shall offer it in the afternoon of the fourteenth day of the second
12 month; then shall they eat it with unleavened bread and bitter herbs. They
shall not leave any of it over until morning, nor shall they break any of its
bones. They shall offer it in compliance with all the rules of the Passover
13 sacrifice. But anyone who is ritually pure and not on a journey, but still
fails to offer the Passover sacrifice, that person shall be severed from his
people, because he did not offer the LORD's sacrifice at its appointed time;
14 he will bear his guilt. If there is a migrant living among you and he offers
a Passover sacrifice to the LORD, he shall do so in compliance with all its
rules and laws. You shall have one law for migrant and native born alike."

15 On the day when the Tabernacle was erected, the cloud covered the
Tabernacle, the Tent of the Testimony, and from evening until morning
16 it hung over the Tabernacle with the appearance of fire. It was always
17 there; the cloud covered the Tent, appearing at night as fire. Whenever
the cloud rose above the Tent, the Israelites would set out, and wherever
18 the cloud settled, the Israelites would encamp. At the LORD's command,
the Israelites set out, and at the LORD's command they would encamp;
for as long as the cloud rested on the Tabernacle, they continued to camp
19 there. Even when the cloud lingered over the Tabernacle for many days,
20 the Israelites kept the LORD's charge and did not journey on. Sometimes
the cloud would be over the Tabernacle for just a few days; at the LORD's
command they would camp, and at the LORD's command they would set
21 out. Sometimes the cloud stayed only from evening to morning, and in the
morning it rose, and they set out. Day or night, they would set out when
22 the cloud rose. Whether it was two days, or a month, or for many days
together, the Israelites would camp as long as the cloud rested over the
Tabernacle, and would not move on. They journeyed only when the cloud
23 rose. At the LORD's command they camped, and at the LORD's command
they set out. And they kept the LORD's charge, the LORD's word through
Moshe.

10 1 2 The Lord spoke to Moshe: "Make two silver trumpets; make them of
hammered metal. Use them for summoning the community and for
3 having the camps set out. When both are blown with a long note, the
entire community shall assemble before you at the entrance to the Tent of
4 Meeting. If only one is blown, the princes, leaders of Israel's divisions, shall
5 assemble before you. When you blow a series of short blasts, the camps
6 on the east side shall march, and when you blow a second series of short
blasts, the camps on the south side will march; thus shall a series of short
blasts signal them to move on.

7 "To assemble the community, blow a long blast, not a series of short blasts.
8 Aharon's sons the priests shall blow the trumpets. This shall be for you an
everlasting decree throughout your generations.

9 "When you go to war against an enemy who is attacking you in your land,
you shall blow short blasts on the trumpets to be remembered before the
Lord your God, to be delivered from your enemies.

10 "And on your days of rejoicing, your festivals and New Moons, you shall
blow the trumpets over your burnt offerings and your peace offerings. They
will be a reminder of you before your God. I am the Lord your God."

11 On the twentieth day of the second month in the second year, the cloud
12 rose above the Tabernacle of the Covenant. The Israelites set out on
their journey from the Sinai Desert, and the cloud came to rest in the
13 Wilderness of Paran. For the first time, at the Lord's command through
14 Moshe, they set out. The divisions of Yehuda's camp set out first, under
15 their banner. Leading that division was Naḥshon son of Aminadav. Netanel
16 son of Tzuar was in charge of the division of the tribe of Yissakhar. Eliav
17 son of Ḥelon was in charge of the division of the tribe of Zevulun. The
Tabernacle was taken down, and the Gershonites and the Merarites, who
carried it, set out.

18 The divisions of the camp of Reuven set out next, under their banner.
19 Leading that division was Elitzur son of Shedeiur. Shelumiel son of
20 Tzurishadai was in charge of the division of the tribe of Shimon. Elyasaf
21 son of Deuel was in charge of the division of the tribe of Gad. Then the
Kohatites, who carried the sacred objects, set out. By the time they arrived,
the Tabernacle would have been erected.

22 The divisions of the camp of Efrayim set out next, under their banner.
23 Leading that division was Elishama son of Amihud. Gamliel son of
24 Pedahtzur was in charge of the division of the tribe of Menashe. Avidan
son of Gidoni was in charge of the division of the tribe of Binyamin.

25 Then, at the rear of the whole camp, the divisions of the camp of Dan
set out under their banner. Leading that division was Aḥiezer son of
26 Amishadai. Pagiel son of Okhran was in charge of the division of the
27 tribe of Asher. Aḥira son of Einan was in charge of the division of the

28 tribe of Naftali. This was the order in which the Israelites set out in their
divisions.

29 Moshe said to Ḥovav son of Reuel the Midianite, Moshe's father-in-law,[24]
"We are setting out to the place that the Lord said He would give us. Come
with us and we will be good to you, for the Lord has promised good
things to Israel."

30 But he replied, "I will not come; I must go back to my own land and my
own people."

31 "Please do not leave us," said Moshe, "for you know where we should camp
32 in the wilderness; you would be our eyes. If you come with us, whatever
good the Lord does for us, we will do for you."

33 They journeyed from the Lord's mountain for three days; and the Ark
of the Lord's Covenant went ahead of them for those three days to find
34 a resting place for them. The Lord's cloud was over them by day as they
journeyed from the camp.

35 When the Ark set out, Moshe would say, "Arise, Lord; let Your enemies be
36 scattered, and Your foes flee before You." When it came to rest, he would
say, "Bring back, O Lord, the myriad thousands of Israel."[25]

11 1 The people began to rail bitterly in the Lord's presence. And the Lord
heard and was incensed; fire from the Lord blazed against them, consuming
2 at the edge of the camp. The people cried out to Moshe – Moshe prayed
3 to the Lord – and the fire subsided. And so that place was named Tavera,[26]
because the Lord's fire had blazed against them.

4 The rabble in their midst began to have strong cravings, and once again
5 the Israelites began to weep, saying, "Who will give us meat to eat? We
remember the fish we ate in Egypt at no cost, the cucumbers, and the
6 melons, and the leeks, and the onions, and the garlic. But now our throats
are dry. There is nothing at all but this manna to look at."

7 8 The manna was like coriander seed, and like bdellium in color.[27] The
people went around gathering it. Then they would grind it in a mill or
crush it in a mortar. They cooked it in a pot and they made cakes from it;
9 it tasted like cakes made with oil. When the dew fell over the camp at night,
the manna would fall upon that.

10 Moshe heard the people weeping clan by clan, each one at his tent's
opening. The Lord's anger blazed intensely, and Moshe was distressed.
11 "Why have You treated Your servant so badly?" asked Moshe of the Lord.

---

24 | Cf. Exodus 2:18; Judges 4:11.

25 | Perhaps referring to Israelite fighters. According to this approach, these verses invoke the military function of the Ark, which represented God's presence in battle.

26 | Literally "burning."

27 | That is, of exquisite taste and beauty.

"Why have I found so little favor in Your sight that You lay all the burden
12 of this people upon me? Was it I who conceived all this people? Was it I
who gave birth to them all, that You should say to me, 'Carry them in your
bosom, as a nursemaid carries a baby,' to the land that You swore to their
13 fathers? Where am I to get meat to give all this people when they come
14 wailing to me, 'Give us meat to eat'? I cannot bear all this people alone;
15 the burden is too heavy for me. If this is how You treat me, kill me now, if
I find any favor in Your sight, and let me not see my own misery."

16 Then the LORD said to Moshe, "Gather for Me seventy of Israel's elders,
whom you know to be the people's elders and officers, and bring them to
17 the Tent of Meeting. Let them stand there with you. I will come down
and speak with you there, and I will take some of the spirit that is on you
and place it upon them; they will share the burden of the people with you,
18 and you will not have to bear it alone. And say to the people: Consecrate
yourselves for tomorrow; you will then have meat to eat, for you have been
wailing in the presence of the LORD, 'Who will give us meat to eat? It was
19 better for us in Egypt.' The LORD will give you meat, and you will eat. You
will eat it not just for one day, or two days, or five, or ten, or twenty days,
20 but for a whole month, until it comes out at your nostrils and becomes
nauseating to you; for you have rejected the LORD who is among you and
have come wailing in His presence, 'Why ever did we leave Egypt?'"

21 But Moshe said, "Here I am among six hundred thousand men on foot, and
22 You say, 'I will give them meat to eat for a whole month'! If whole flocks
and herds were slaughtered for them, would there be enough? If all the fish
of the sea were caught for them, would there be enough?!"

23 The LORD said to Moshe, "Does the LORD's hand fall short? Soon you shall
see whether what I say comes true or not."

24 Moshe went out and told the people what the LORD had said. He gathered
seventy of the people's elders and had them stand surrounding the Tent.
25 Then the LORD came down in the cloud and spoke to him, and took some
of the spirit that was upon him and placed it on the seventy elders. When
the spirit rested upon them, they prophesied – but they did not do so
again.[28]

26 Two men, one named Eldad and the other Meidad, had remained in the
camp, yet the spirit rested upon them. Though they were among those
listed, they had not gone out to the Tent – and they spoke prophecy in the
27 camp. A young man ran and told Moshe, "Eldad and Meidad are speaking
prophecy in the camp!"

28 Yehoshua son of Nun, who had been Moshe's disciple since his youth, said,
"My lord Moshe, stop them!"

---

28 | That is, sustained prophetic capacity was not essential to these elders' leadership function.

29 But Moshe replied, "Are you jealous for me? Would that all the Lord's
people were prophets, that the Lord would put His spirit upon them all!"
30 And Moshe returned to the camp together with the elders of Israel.

31 Then a wind from the Lord sprang up, sweeping quail in from the sea and
letting them fall near the camp, about a day's journey on one side and a day's
journey on the other, around the camp and piled up two cubits above the
32 ground. All that day, all night, and all the next day, the people went out and
gathered quail. Even those who gathered least gathered ten omer,[29] and they
33 spread them out all around the camp. While the meat was still between their
teeth, before it was eaten, the Lord's anger blazed against the people, and the
Lord struck the people with a very great plague.

34 The place was named Kivrot HaTaava, because there they buried the people
35 who had craved.[30] And from Kivrot HaTaava the people journeyed to Ḥatzerot,
and at Ḥatzerot they stayed.

12 1 Once, Miriam and Aharon spoke against Moshe because of his Kushite
2 wife; he had married a Kushite woman. "Has the Lord spoken only
through Moshe?" they said. "Has He not spoken through us also?" The
3 Lord heard this. Now the man Moshe was very humble, more so than
any other man on earth.

4 And suddenly the Lord said to Moshe and Aharon and Miriam: "All three
of you, come out to the Tent of Meeting." So the three of them went.

5 The Lord came down in a column of cloud, and, standing at the entrance
to the Tent, called, "Aharon and Miriam." The two of them came forward.
6 The Lord said: "Now listen to My words: When there is a prophet among
you, I make Myself known to him in a vision, I speak to him in a dream.
7 8 Not so with Moshe My servant: he is trusted in all My House: With him I
speak mouth to mouth, clearly, never in riddles. He sees the Lord's form.
9 Why, then, are you not afraid to speak against My servant Moshe?" The
Lord's anger flared against them; and He departed.

10 When the cloud withdrew from the Tent, Miriam had been struck with an
impure blight, white as snow. Aharon turned toward Miriam and saw that she
11 was blighted. Aharon said to Moshe, "Please, my lord, do not hold against
12 us the sin that we have foolishly committed! Let her not be like a stillborn
child emerging from its mother's womb with half its flesh eaten away!"[31]

13 And Moshe cried out to the Lord, "Please, God, heal her now!"

14 But the Lord said to Moshe: "If her father had spat in her face, would she
not be shamed for seven days? Let her be shut out of the camp for seven
days; after that, she may be brought back."

29 | An omer is a solid measure equal to one-tenth of an ephah; see 5:15 and note.
30 | The name literally means "graves of craving."
31 | Apparently a description of the disease that afflicted Miriam.

15 So Miriam was shut out of the camp for seven days, and the people did
not move on until Miriam was brought back.

16 After that, the people set out from Ḥatzerot and encamped in the Wilderness of Paran.

SHELAḤ 13 1 2 Then the Lord spoke to Moshe: "Send out men to scout the land of
Canaan, which I am going to give to the Israelites, one man from each of
3 their ancestral tribes, each a leader among them." So Moshe sent them
at the Lord's command from the Wilderness of Paran. They were all
4 leading men among the Israelites. These were their names: from the tribe
5 of Reuven, Shamua son of Zakur; from the tribe of Shimon, Shafat son
6 7 of Ḥori; from the tribe of Yehuda, Kalev son of Yefuneh; from the tribe
8 of Yissakhar, Yigal son of Yosef; from the tribe of Efrayim, Hoshe'a son
9 10 of Nun; from the tribe of Binyamin, Palti son of Rafu; from the tribe of
11 Zevulun, Gadiel son of Sodi; from the tribe of Yosef, from the tribe of
12 Menashe, Gadi son of Susi; from the tribe of Dan, Amiel son of Gemali;
13 14 from the tribe of Asher, Setur son of Mikhael; from the tribe of Naftali,
15 16 Naḥbi son of Vofsi; from the tribe of Gad, Geuel son of Makhi. These were
the names of the men Moshe sent to scout the land. And Moshe named
Hoshe'a son of Nun Yehoshua.

17 When Moshe sent them to scout the land of Canaan, he told them, "Ascend
18 there into the Negev; then go up into the hill country. See what the land
19 is like. Are the people who live there strong or weak, few or many? Is the
land in which they live a good place or bad? Are the cities in which they
20 live open or fortified? Is the soil rich or poor? Are there trees in it or not?
Take courage and bring back some of the fruit of the land" – it was the
season of the first ripe grapes.

21 So they went up and scouted the land from the Wilderness of Tzin to
22 Reḥov, near Levo Ḥamat.[32] They went up through the Negev and came to
Ḥevron, where Aḥiman, Sheshai, and Talmai, descendants of Anak, were
dwelling. Ḥevron had been built seven years before the Egyptian city of
Tzoan.

23 Then they came to the Eshkol Ravine and there they cut down a vine
branch, and on it one cluster of grapes, which they carried on a pole
24 between two men. They also took some pomegranates and figs. That place
was named the Eshkol Ravine, because of the cluster that the Israelites
cut there.[33]

25 26 They returned from scouting the land when forty days had passed. As soon
as they arrived they came to Moshe and Aharon and to all the community
of Israel at Kadesh in the Wilderness of Paran, and brought their report
to them and to all the community, and showed them the fruit of the land.

---

32 | The southern and northern reaches of Canaan, respectively; cf. chapter 34.

33 | *Eshkol* denotes a cluster of fruit.

27 They told Moshe, "We came to the land you sent us to, and it is indeed
28 flowing with milk and with honey, and this is its fruit. But the people who
live in the land are fierce, and the cities are fortified and very large indeed.
29 We even saw the descendants of Anak there.[34] In the Negev region, Amalek
lives; the Hittites, Jebusites, and Amorites live in the hill country, and the
Canaanites live by the sea and by the Jordan."

30 But Kalev silenced the people around Moshe and said, "Let us go up at
once and take possession of it, for certainly we are able."

31 The men who had gone up with him said, "We cannot go up against
32 those people, for they are stronger than us." So they gave the Israelites an
adverse report of the land that they had scouted: "The land which we have
journeyed through and scouted is a land that consumes its inhabitants;
33 the people we saw in it were tall and broad to a man. There we saw the
Nefilim – the descendants of Anak are from the Nefilim.[35] We looked to
our own eyes like grasshoppers, and so we were in theirs."

14 1 All the community lifted their heads and cried out – that night the people
2 wept. And all the Israelites railed against Moshe and Aharon; all the
community said to them, "If only we had died in Egypt, if only we had
3 died in this wilderness! Why is the LORD bringing us as far as this land
only to fall by the sword? Our wives and children will be made plunder.
Would it not be better for us to go back to Egypt?"

4 So they said to one another, "Let us appoint a leader and go back to Egypt."

5 Moshe and Aharon fell facedown before all the assembled community of
6 Israel. Yehoshua son of Nun and Kalev son of Yefuneh, who were among
7 those who scouted the land, tore their clothes and said before the entire
community of Israel: "The land we journeyed through and scouted is a very,
8 very good land. If the LORD favors us, He will bring us into this land, a land
9 flowing with milk and with honey, and He will give it to us. Do not rebel
against the LORD, and do not be afraid of the people of the land, for they
are no more than bread for us. They have been stripped of their protection
and the LORD is with us. Do not be afraid of them!"

10 The community, all, threatened to stone them to death – but then the
LORD's glory was revealed to all the Israelites at the Tent of Meeting.

11 The LORD said to Moshe, "How long will these people provoke Me? How
long will they fail to have faith in Me in spite of all the signs I have performed
12 among them? I will strike them with a plague now and disinherit them,
and make you into a nation greater and mightier than they."

13 But Moshe said to the LORD, "The Egyptians will hear about it, for by Your
14 power You brought this people up from among them, and they will tell the

34 | The Anakites were of giant stature; see verse 33.

35 | See Genesis 6:4.

inhabitants of this land. They have heard that You, LORD, are among these
people, that You, LORD, are seen face-to-face, that Your cloud stands over
them, that You go before them in a pillar of cloud by day and in a pillar of
15 fire by night. If You kill this people like a single man, the nations that have
16 heard of Your fame will say, 'It was because the LORD was unable to bring
this people into the land He swore to them; that is why He slaughtered
them in the wilderness.'

17 "So now, let my LORD's power be great, as You declared when You said:[36]
18 'The LORD is slow to anger and abounding in kindness, forgiving sin and
rebellion, though He does not acquit the guilty, but holds the descendants
to account for the sins of the fathers; children and grandchildren to the
19 third and fourth generation.' Please – pardon the sin of this people in Your
great kindness, as You have forgiven this people from the time of Egypt
until now."

20 21 And the LORD said, "I have forgiven them at your word. Yet as surely as I
22 live and as the LORD's glory fills the whole earth, none of those who have
seen My glory and the signs I performed in Egypt and in the wilderness,
23 and have tested Me these ten times and not obeyed Me, shall see the land
I swore to their fathers. None of those who have provoked Me will see it.
24 But My servant Kalev, because he was filled with a different spirit and has
followed Me wholeheartedly – him I will bring into the land he came to,
25 and his descendants will inherit it. The Amalekites and Canaanites are
living in the valleys; so turn tomorrow and head for the wilderness by way
of the Sea of Reeds."[37]

26 27 Then the LORD spoke to Moshe and Aharon: "How long shall this wicked
community keep railing against Me? I have heard the Israelites' complaints
28 with which they rail against Me. Tell them: 'As surely as I live,' says the
29 LORD, 'I will do to you the very thing I heard you say. In this wilderness
your corpses will fall, all of your number, all those listed in the census,
from twenty years old and upward: all those who have railed against Me.
30 None of you will enter the land that I promised to settle you in, except
31 for Kalev son of Yefuneh and Yehoshua son of Nun. I will bring in Your
children, whom you said would be taken captive, and they will know the
32 land you rejected. But as for you, your corpses will fall in this wilderness.
33 Your children will shepherd in the wilderness for forty years, suffering for
your faithlessness until the last of your corpses lies here in the wilderness.
34 For the number of the days in which you scouted the land, forty days,
you shall bear your sins – for every day a year: forty years. You will know
35 what it is to oppose Me. I, the LORD, have spoken.' This will I do to this
entire wicked community that has gathered together against Me. In this
wilderness they shall come to their end, and there they shall die."

---

36 | See Exodus 34:6–7.

37 | That is, toward the southwest, away from the land of Israel and its hostile peoples.

36 So the men Moshe sent to scout the land, and who came back and caused
all the community to rail against him by giving an adverse report of the
37 land – those men who gave the adverse report of the land died by a plague
before the LORD.

38 And only Yehoshua son of Nun and Kalev son of Yefuneh remained alive
of all those men who went to scout the land.

39 When Moshe reported these words to all the Israelites, the people were
40 overcome with grief. They rose early the next morning and climbed up to
the heights of the hill country, saying, "We are ready to go up to the place
that the LORD spoke of; we were wrong."

41 But Moshe said, "Why are you transgressing the LORD's command? It will
42 not work. Do not go up; the LORD is not with you. Do not be struck down
43 by your enemies. Ahead of you are the Amalekites and Canaanites, and
you will fall by the sword. Because you have turned away from following
the LORD, the LORD will not be with you."

44 Defiantly, they went up to the heights of the hill country. Neither the Ark
45 of the LORD's Covenant nor Moshe left the camp. And the Amalekites and
Canaanites who lived in that hill country came down, and fought them,
and crushed them, all the way to Ḥorma.[38]

15 1 2 The LORD spoke to Moshe: "Speak to the Israelites. Say: When you come
3 to the land that I am giving you to live in, and you present a fire offering
from the herd or from the flock for a pleasing aroma to the LORD – whether
it be a burnt offering or a sacrifice to fulfill a spoken vow, or brought as a
4 freewill offering, or a festival offering – the one who brings this offering to
the LORD shall bring with it a grain offering of a tenth of a measure[39] of fine
5 flour mixed with a quarter of a hin[40] of oil, and with the burnt offering or
6 the sacrifice, a quarter of a hin of wine as a libation for every lamb. In the
case of a ram, you shall bring a grain offering of two-tenths of a measure of
7 fine flour mixed with a third of a hin of oil. You shall also offer a third of a
8 hin of wine as a libation, for a pleasing aroma to the LORD. If, however, you
offer an animal from the herd as a burnt offering or as a sacrifice to fulfill a
9 spoken vow, or as a peace offering to the LORD, then you shall bring with
each animal a grain offering of three-tenths of a measure of fine flour mixed
10 with half a hin of oil. You shall also offer half a hin of wine as a libation; it
11 is a fire offering, a pleasing aroma to the LORD. So shall it be with each ox,
12 each ram, and with any sheep or goat. However many you offer, you shall
do the same for each.

13 "Every native-born person, presenting a fire offering as a pleasing aroma to
14 the LORD, shall perform them in this way. And whensoever, through the

38 | The name of this place literally means "destruction."

39 | That is, of an ephah. This measure is identical to an omer; see notes on 5:15 and 11:32.

40 | A hin is a liquid measure equal to approximately 4 liters.

generations, a migrant joins you or lives among you, and he too prepares a
15 fire offering for a pleasing aroma to the Lord, he shall do just as you do. There
shall be one law for the congregation: as for you, so for any migrant. It shall be
an eternal decree throughout the generations: you and the migrant shall be
16 the same before the Lord. One law and one rule for you and for the migrant
who lives among you."

17 18 The Lord spoke to Moshe: "Speak to the Israelites. Say: When you come
19 to the land to which I am bringing you, and eat the bread of the land, you
20 shall set some aside as an offering to the Lord. As the first portion of
your kneading, you shall set aside a loaf as an offering, like the offering
21 you present from the threshing floor. You shall present to the Lord an
offering from the first of your kneading throughout your generations.

22 "If, without intention, you fail to perform any of these command-
23 ments that the Lord gave to Moshe, anything that the Lord has commanded you through Moshe from the day the Lord commanded it and
24 onward – in all generations to come – if it is done unintentionally by
the community, the entire community must offer one bull from the herd
as a burnt offering, a pleasing aroma to the Lord, with its prescribed
25 grain offering and libation, and one goat as a purification offering. The
priest shall then make atonement for all the community of Israel and
they will be forgiven, because it was an accidental failing, and because
they brought their sacrifice, a fire offering to the Lord and the purifica-
26 tion offering for their error before the Lord. The community of Israel
and the migrants living among them will all be forgiven, because all the
people acted in error.

27 "If it is an individual who sins inadvertently, he shall offer a year-old female
28 goat as a purification offering. The priest shall make atonement before
the Lord for the person who sinned inadvertently, to atone for his sin,
29 and he will be forgiven. There shall be one law for one who inadvertently
commits a sin, whether he is a native-born Israelite or a migrant living
among them.

30 "However, if a person commits a sin high-handedly, whether he is native
born or a migrant, he reviles the Lord and shall be severed from the people.
31 Because he despises the Lord's word and violates His commandments, he
will be severed utterly and must bear his guilt."

32 When the Israelites were in the wilderness, they encountered a man
33 gathering wood on the Sabbath. Those who found him gathering wood
brought him before Moshe and Aharon, and before the whole community,
34 and he was placed in custody, because it had not been specified what should
be done to him.

35 And the Lord said to Moshe, "The man shall be put to death. The whole
community must stone him outside the camp."

36 And so, as the LORD had commanded Moshe, the whole community took
him outside the camp and stoned him to death.

37 38 The LORD said to Moshe: "Speak to the Israelites; tell them to make fringes
on the corners of their garments throughout the generations. To the fringe
39 on each corner they should attach a blue cord. And this shall be your
fringe: seeing it, you shall remember all the LORD's commands and keep
them. You will not then go astray, following the lusts of your heart or of
40 your eyes. This is to remind you to keep all My commands, to remain holy
41 to your God. I am the LORD your God, who brought you out of Egypt to
be your God. I am the LORD your God."

16 1 Koraḥ, son of Yitzhar son of Kehat son of Levi, together with Datan and KORAḤ
Aviram sons of Eliav and On son of Pelet – descendants of Reuven – took
2 two hundred fifty Israelite men, leaders of the community, chosen from
3 the assembly, men of repute, and confronted Moshe and Aharon together.
They said to them, "You have gone too far. All the community is holy,
every one of them, and the LORD is in their midst. Why then do you set
yourselves above the LORD's people?"

4 5 When Moshe heard this, he fell upon his face. Then he spoke to Koraḥ
and all his company. "In the morning," he said, "the LORD will make
known who is His and who is holy, and will bring that one close to Him.
6 The one He chooses will be the one He will allow to come close. Do this:
7 Let Korah and his company take censers. Tomorrow light fire in them
and place incense upon them before the LORD. The man whom the LORD
chooses – he is holy. It is you, sons of Levi, who have gone too far!"

8 9 Moshe said to Koraḥ, "Listen now, you sons of Levi. Is it not enough for
you that the God of Israel has separated you from the Israelite community,
enabling you to come close to Him, to serve in the LORD's Tabernacle,
10 and stand in the presence of the community to minister to them? He has
brought you, and with you all your fellow Levites, to be close to Him, and
11 yet you seek the priesthood also? And so you and all your company have
assembled to defy the LORD. Aharon – who is he that you should have
grievances against him?"

12 After this, Moshe sent for Datan and Aviram, sons of Eliav. But they said,
13 "We will not come up. Is it not enough that you have brought us out of a
land flowing with milk and with honey to kill us in the desert, that you
14 insist on lording it over us? And more: you have not brought us to a land
flowing with milk and with honey, nor have you given us an inheritance
of cropland and vineyard. Would you pull out these people's eyes?! We
will not come up!"

15 Moshe became very angry and said to the LORD, "Pay no attention to their
offering. I have not taken a single donkey from them, nor have I wronged
any one of them."

16 Moshe said to Koraḥ, "You and your entire company shall appear before
17 the Lord tomorrow: you, they, and Aharon. Each one shall take his censer,
place incense upon it, and present it before the Lord, each holding his
censer, two hundred fifty censers in all, and you and Aharon likewise
18 with yours." Each took his censer, placed fire in it, put incense upon it,
and stood at the entrance to the Tent of Meeting, as did Moshe and
19 Aharon. Koraḥ gathered all his company against them to the entrance
to the Tent of Meeting. Then the glory of the Lord was revealed to the
entire community.

20 21 The Lord spoke to Moshe and Aharon: "Separate yourselves from this
community and let Me consume them in a moment."

22 They fell on their faces and said, "God, the God of the spirit of all flesh, if
one man sins, will You rage against the entire community?"

23 24 The Lord spoke to Moshe: "Tell the community to move away from the
dwellings of Koraḥ, Datan, and Aviram."

25 Moshe rose and went to Datan and Aviram. Israel's elders followed him.
26 He spoke to the community, saying: "Turn away now from the tents of
these wicked men. Do not touch anything of theirs, lest you be swept away
27 for all their sins." So they moved away from around the dwellings of Koraḥ,
Datan, and Aviram. Datan and Aviram came out and stood at the openings
of their tents with their wives, children, and infants.

28 Moshe said, "By this you will know that the Lord sent me to do these
29 deeds; it was not my idea. If all these men die as others do, and share the
30 common fate of all humanity, then the Lord has not sent me. But if the
Lord creates something entirely new, so that the ground opens its mouth
and swallows them and all they have, and they go down alive to Sheol,[41]
then you will know that these men have provoked the Lord."

31 As soon as he had finished speaking these words, the ground beneath
32 them split open. The earth opened its mouth and swallowed them and
their households, with all the people who pertained to Koraḥ and all their
33 possessions – they and all that was theirs descended alive to Sheol – the
earth closed over them – and they perished from the midst of the assembly.
34 At their cry, all the Israelites around them fled, for they said, "The earth
could swallow us."

35 And fire came forth from the Lord and consumed the two hundred fifty
men who were offering incense.

17 1 2 Then the Lord spoke to Moshe: "Tell Elazar son of Aharon the priest to
remove the censers from the fire, for they have become holy. Scatter the
3 burning coals far and wide. And the censers of those who committed a
mortal sin – make them into hammered plates as a covering for the altar.

41 | The netherworld.

Having been offered before the LORD, they have become holy. And they
will be a sign for the Israelites."

4 Elazar the priest took the bronze censers that the men consumed by fire
5 had presented, and hammered them into a covering for the altar, as the
LORD had said to him through Moshe – a reminder for the Israelites that
no outsider, no one not descended from Aharon, should offer incense
before the LORD, and become like Koraḥ and his company.

6 The next day the entire Israelite community complained to Moshe and
Aharon, "You have killed the LORD's people!"

7 As the community assembled against Moshe and Aharon, they turned
toward the Tent of Meeting. A cloud was covering it, and the glory of
8 the LORD appeared. Moshe and Aharon came to the front of the Tent of
9 10 Meeting. And the LORD spoke to Moshe: "Get away from this community;
11 let Me consume them in an instant." They fell on their faces, and Moshe
said to Aharon, "Take the censer, put fire from the altar into it, place
incense upon it, and go quickly to the community and make atonement
for them. Fury has come forth from the LORD; the plague has begun."

12 Aharon took it as Moshe said and ran into the midst of the assembly, for
the plague had already begun among the people. He offered incense and
13 made atonement for the people; he stood between the dead and the living,
14 and the plague was halted; 14,700 died from that plague, in addition to
15 those who died on account of Koraḥ. And Aharon returned to Moshe at
the entrance to the Tent of Meeting – for the plague had stopped.

16 17 Then the LORD spoke to Moshe: "Speak to the Israelites and take from
them twelve staffs, one for each ancestral house, from all the leaders
18 of their ancestral houses. Write each man's name on his staff, and on
Levi's staff write Aharon's name, for there shall be one staff for the head
19 of each ancestral house. Place them in the Tent of Meeting in front of
20 the Ark of the Covenant, where I meet with you. The staff of the man
I choose – that will give flower. Thus I will rid myself of the incessant
railings of the Israelites against you."

21 Moshe spoke to the Israelites, and each of their leaders gave him a staff,
one for each leader, according to their ancestral houses, twelve staffs
with Aharon's staff among them.

22 Moshe placed the staffs before the LORD in the Tent of the Testimony.
23 And the following day Moshe entered the Tent of the Testimony, and
Aharon's staff, representing the House of Levi, had given flower. It had
24 budded, produced blossoms, and was now bearing almonds. Moshe
brought out all the staffs from before the LORD to all the Israelites. They
saw. And each man took back his staff.

25 Then the LORD said to Moshe, "Put back Aharon's staff in front of the Ark
of the Covenant to serve as a sign to rebels so that their railings against

26 Me end, and they will not die." Moshe did so. As the Lord commanded
him, so he did.

27 The Israelites said to Moshe, "We are going to die. We are lost; all of us
28 are lost. Whoever approaches the Lord's Tabernacle is to die. Will we die
out completely?"

18 1 The Lord said to Aharon: "You, your sons, and your ancestral house shall
bear any guilt connected with the Sanctuary, and you and your sons will
2 bear any guilt connected with your priesthood. Bring with you also your
brothers from the tribe of Levi, your father's tribe. Let them join you and
3 minister to you and your sons before the Tent of the Testimony. They shall
discharge their duties to you and to the Tent as a whole, but they must not
draw close to the utensils of the Sanctuary or the altar, or both they and
4 you will die. They will join you in discharging the duties of the Tent of
5 Meeting for all the service of the Tent; no outsider shall draw near you. You
shall discharge the duties of the Sanctuary and the altar, so that fury may
6 never again fall upon the Israelites. I have singled out your brothers, the
Levites, from among the Israelites as a gift to you, dedicated to the Lord
7 to perform the service of the Tent of Meeting. You and your sons shall take
care to perform the duties of your priesthood in all matters pertaining to
the altar and inside the curtain. I give you your priestly service as a gift,
but any outsider who draws close will die."

8 The Lord spoke to Aharon: "I place in your charge the offerings made to
Me, all the sacred gifts of the Israelites. I give them to you and your sons
9 as an anointed right; this is an everlasting decree. This is what belongs
to you among the holiest offerings, from the fire: all their offerings, their
grain offerings, their purification offerings, and their guilt offerings. The
10 holiest offerings that they bring to Me will be yours and your sons'. You
shall eat them in the way of the holiest things. All your males may eat it;
it is holy to you.

11 "This too will be yours: as an everlasting statute I give the upraised gifts
of all the Israelites' wave offerings to you,[42] together with your sons and
daughters. Anyone who is ritually pure in your household may eat of them.
12 All the best of the oil, wine, and grain, the choice produce that they give to
13 the Lord, I give to you. The first fruits of all that is in their land that they
bring to the Lord will be yours. Anyone who is pure in your household
14 15 may eat it. Everything that is set aside in Israel shall be yours. All the first
to emerge from the womb of any creature, human or animal, that is offered
to the Lord shall be yours. You must, however, redeem firstborn boys and
16 the firstborn of impure animals.[43] Their redemption price from the age of

42 | That is, the priests shall receive portions from offerings whose procedures include elevating and waving.

43 | The Israelites must redeem them with the priests' involvement, as the passage proceeds to clarify.

one month shall be set at five shekel of silver according to the Sanctuary
17 weight: twenty gerah per shekel. You must not redeem the firstborn of an
ox, sheep, or goat; they are sacred. You must dash their blood on the altar
18 and send their fat up in smoke for a pleasing aroma to the LORD. But their
meat is yours. It shall be yours like the breast of the wave offering and the
19 right thigh. All the sacred gifts that the Israelites raise up to the LORD I
give to you, your sons, and your daughters as an everlasting statute. It is
an everlasting covenant of salt[44] before the LORD, for you and for your
descendants."

20 The LORD said to Aharon: "You will have no inheritance in their land, nor
shall you have any share among them. I am your share, your inheritance,
among the Israelites.

21 "And I give to the Levites all tithes in Israel as an inheritance in return for
22 the service they perform, the service in the Tent of Meeting. From now
the Israelites shall no longer come close to the Tent of Meeting, or they
23 will incur guilt and die. Instead, the Levites will perform the service of
the Tent of Meeting, and they will bear responsibility for their own sins;
this is an everlasting decree through all your generations. But among the
24 Israelites they will not inherit land, because I have given as an inheritance
to the Levites the tithe of the Israelites which they have lifted up to the
LORD as an upraised gift. That is why I have said of them that they shall
have no land inheritance among the Israelites."

25 26 The LORD spoke to Moshe: "Speak to the Levites and say to them: When
you receive from the Israelites the tithe that I have given you from them as
your inheritance, you shall lift up a tenth of it as an offering to the LORD,
27 a tithe of the tithe. It will be considered your own upraised gift, like the
28 grain of the threshing floor or the flow from the winepress.[45] So shall you
set aside an offering to the LORD from all the tithes that you take from the
Israelites, and you shall give it as an upraised gift to the LORD for Aharon
29 the priest. From all your gifts, you shall set aside an offering to the LORD;
of each the finest portion shall be consecrated.

30 "Say to the Levites: When you have presented the best portion of it, it will
be reckoned to you as the yield of the threshing floor and the winepress.[46]
31 You and your household may eat of it anywhere, because this is your
32 payment for your service in the Tent of Meeting. You will not bear guilt
for it once you have separated out the finest portion; then you will not be
profaning the sacred offerings of the Israelites, and will not die."

19 1 2 The LORD spoke to Moshe and Aharon: "This is the decree of the Law that HUKAT
the LORD commands. Tell the Israelites to bring you a cow, completely red,

44 | Salt, which is used for preservation, signifies Israel's enduring covenant with God.

45 | Meaning this tithe is comparable to the tithe taken by a landowner from his produce.

46 | Meaning the Levites may then partake of what remains as though it is their own produce.

3 without blemish, on which no yoke has been laid. Give this to Elazar the
priest; it shall be taken outside the camp and slaughtered in his presence.
4 Elazar the priest shall take some of its blood with his finger and sprinkle it
5 seven times toward the front of the Tent of Meeting. The cow shall then be
burned in front of him; its skin, flesh, and blood shall be burned, together
6 with its dung. The priest shall take cedarwood, hyssop, and scarlet cloth
7 and throw them into the fire where the cow is burning. Then the priest
shall wash his clothes and bathe his body in water. Afterward he may
8 enter the camp, but he will remain impure until that evening. The one
who burned it shall wash his clothes in water and bathe his body in water,
9 but he too will remain impure until evening. Meanwhile, one who is pure
shall gather up the ashes of the cow and place them outside the camp in a
pure place. And they shall be kept by the Israelite community for the water
10 of lustration, as a purification offering. The one who gathers the ashes of
the cow shall likewise wash his clothes but remains impure until evening.
This shall be an everlasting decree for the Israelites and for any migrant
living among them.

11 "Whoever touches the dead body of any person shall be impure for seven
12 days. He must purify himself with the water on the third and seventh days
to become pure. If he does not purify himself on the third and seventh
13 days, he will not be pure. Whoever touches a corpse of a person who has
died, and fails to purify himself, defiles the Lord's Tabernacle. He shall be
severed from Israel because, since the water of lustration was not sprinkled
on him, he remains impure; his impurity is still with him.

14 "This is the law: when a person dies in a tent, whoever enters that tent
15 and whoever is in it shall remain impure for seven days. Any open vessel
16 not sealed with a cover shall be impure. Anyone in the open field who
touches a person killed by the sword, or who died naturally, or a human
17 bone or a grave, shall be impure for seven days. For this impure person
they shall take some of the ashes of the burnt purification offering, and
18 place living water[47] along with it into a vessel. A person who is pure shall
then take hyssop, dip it into the water, and sprinkle it on the tent, on all
the vessels, on the people who were there, and on anyone who touched
19 the bone, the slain person, or any other corpse, or a grave. On the third
day and seventh day the person who is pure shall sprinkle it on the one
who is impure, thus purifying him on the seventh day. He shall then wash
20 his clothes and immerse in water, and at evening he will be pure. Anyone
who becomes impure and fails to purify himself shall be severed from the
assembly, for he has defiled the Lord's Sanctuary. Since water of lustration
was not sprinkled on him, he is impure.

21 "This is an everlasting decree for them. The one who sprinkles the water
of lustration shall wash his own clothes. Anyone who had contact with

47 | Water taken from a flowing source.

22 the water of lustration shall remain impure until evening. Anything the
impure person touches is rendered impure, and one who touches him
remains impure until evening."

20 1 The Israelites, all the community, arrived at the Wilderness of Tzin in the
first month, and the people stayed at Kadesh. There Miriam died and was
2 buried. And there was no water for the community, and together they
3 confronted Moshe and Aharon. The people contended with Moshe: "If
4 only we had died when our brothers died before the LORD! Why have
you brought the LORD's assembly into this wilderness only for us and our
5 livestock to die here? Why did you take us up out of Egypt to bring us to
this dreadful place with no grain, no figs, no vines or pomegranates – there
is no water to drink!"

6 Moshe and Aharon went away from the assembly to the entrance of the
Tent of Meeting. They fell on their faces, and the LORD's glory was revealed
to them.

7 8 And the LORD spoke to Moshe: "Take the staff, you and your brother
Aharon, and assemble the community. Speak to the rock before their eyes
and it will give forth water. You shall bring forth water for them from the
rock, giving the community and their animals to drink."

9 Moshe took the staff from before the LORD, as He had commanded him.
10 And Moshe and Aharon gathered the assembly together before the rock.
He said to them, "Listen now, rebels! Shall we produce water for you from
11 this rock?" Then Moshe raised his hand and struck the rock twice with his
staff. Water gushed out, and the community and their animals drank.

12 But the LORD said to Moshe and Aharon, "Because you did not put your
trust in Me to demonstrate My holiness in the Israelites' eyes, you shall
13 not bring this assembly into the land that I am giving them." These were
the waters of Meriva,[48] where the Israelites quarreled with the LORD and
where He showed them His holiness.[49]

14 Moshe sent messengers from Kadesh to the king of Edom: "This is what
your brother Israel says: 'You know all the hardship we have encountered,
15 how our ancestors went down to Egypt and lived in Egypt for a long time.
16 And the Egyptians oppressed us and our forebears, and we cried out
to the LORD. He heard our voice, sent a messenger, and He brought us
out of Egypt. Now here we are in Kadesh, a town adjoining your border.
17 Please, let us pass through your land. We will not pass through any field
or vineyard, nor will we drink water from any well. We will go along the
King's Highway and not turn from it to the right or the left until we have
passed through your territory.'"

48 | Literally "quarrel."

49 | "He showed them His holiness," Hebrew *vayikadesh*, resonates with the place-name Kadesh.

18 But Edom said to him, "You shall not pass through, or I will come out
against you with the sword."

19 The Israelites said, "We will keep to the beaten track. If we or our livestock
drink any of your water, we will pay for it. It is such a small matter; we only
want to pass through on foot."

20 But they said, "You will not pass through." And Edom came out against
21 them with a large fighting force, heavily armed. Edom refused to let Israel
pass through their territory, and Israel turned away.

22 They set out from Kadesh, and all the Israelite community arrived at Mount
23 Hor. There at Mount Hor, by the border of the land of Edom, the LORD said
24 to Moshe and Aharon, "Aharon is to be gathered to his people. He shall not
enter the land that I have given to the Israelites, because you disobeyed My
25 command at the waters of Meriva. Take Aharon and his son Elazar, and
26 bring them up onto Mount Hor. Strip Aharon of his vestments and put
them on his son Elazar. There will Aharon be gathered in and he will die."

27 Moshe did as the LORD commanded. They ascended Mount Hor in the
28 sight of all the community. Moshe stripped Aharon of his vestments and
put them on his son Elazar. And there, Aharon died, at the top of the
29 mountain; and Moshe and Elazar came down from the mountain. When
all the community saw that Aharon had perished, the whole House of
Israel wept for Aharon for thirty days.

21 1 When the Canaanite king of Arad, dwelling in the Negev, heard that the
Israelites were coming by the way of Atarim, he attacked the Israelites
2 and took captives. And the Israelites vowed to the LORD: "If You give this
3 people over into our hands, we will utterly destroy[50] their towns." The LORD
listened to Israel's plea and gave over the Canaanites. They completely
destroyed them and their cities; and so the place was named Ḥorma.[51]

4 They set out from Mount Hor by the way to the Reed Sea, going around
5 the land of Edom. But the people became restive along the way. The people
spoke out against God and Moshe: "Why did you bring us up from Egypt
to die in the desert? There is no bread, there is no water; we detest this
miserable food!"

6 The LORD sent venomous snakes among the people; they bit the people,
and many Israelites died.

7 The people came to Moshe and said, "We sinned when we spoke against
the LORD and you. Pray to the LORD to take the snakes away from us."
Moshe prayed for the people.

---

50 | The Israelites employ the root *ḥ-r-m* (ח־ר־ם), indicating devotion of the towns to God. The present translation adopts the view that the devotion of these towns implies their destruction.

51 | Literally "destruction" or "devotion"; see previous note.

8 The LORD then said to Moshe, "Fashion a snake and place it on a pole.
Anyone who is bitten shall look at that and live."

9 Moshe fashioned a bronze snake and placed it on a pole. When anyone was
bitten by a snake, he would look at the bronze snake and live.

10 11 The Israelites moved on and camped at Ovot. Then they moved on from
Ovot, and camped at Iyei HaAvarim in the wilderness bordering Moav to
12 13 the east. From there they moved on and camped at the Zered Stream. From
there they moved on and camped beyond the Arnon, in the wilderness
that extends from the border of the Amorites, for the Arnon marks the
14 border of Moav, between Moav and the Amorites. That is why the Book
of the Wars of the LORD[52] records:

"Vahev in Sufa and the wadis,
15 Arnon and the wadi slopes
that lead to the settlement of Ar
and lie along the border of Moav."

16 And from there to Be'er, the well where the LORD said to Moshe, "Gather
17 the people, and I will give them water."[53] Then the Israelites sang this
song:

"Spring up, well – sing to her –
18 that the nobles of the people carved out
with their scepter and their staffs."

19 They went from the desert to Matana, from Matana to Naḥaliel, from
20 Naḥaliel to Bamot, and from Bamot to the valley in the fields of Moav, to
the top of Pisga, overlooking the wasteland.

21 22 Then the Israelites sent messengers to Siḥon, king of the Amorites: "Let us
pass through your land. We will not turn aside into any field or vineyard,
nor will we drink water from any well. We will walk on the king's highway
until we have passed through your territory."

23 But Siḥon would not allow the Israelites to pass through his territory.
He gathered all his people and went out to confront the Israelites in the
wilderness. When he arrived at Yahatz, he launched an attack on the Israelites.
24 The Israelites struck him down with their swords and took possession of
his land from the Arnon to the Yabok, as far as the Amonites, for the border
25 of the Amonites was strong. The Israelites took all these cities, and they
settled in all the cities of the Amorites, in Ḥeshbon and all its surrounding
settlements.

26 Ḥeshbon was the city of Siḥon, king of the Amorites, who had fought
against the former king of Moav and had taken all his land from him as far
as the Arnon.

---

52 | The book in question has not survived.

53 | *Be'er* means "well."

27 That is why the ballad singers sing:

"Come to Ḥeshbon,
build and refound the town of Siḥon.
28 For fire went forth from Ḥeshbon,
a flame from the town of Siḥon.
It consumed Ar of Moav the
masters of Arnon's high shrines.
29 Woe for you, Moav!
You are destroyed, men of Kemosh![54]
He made his sons fugitives,
his daughters fugitives,
to Siḥon the Amorite king.
30 Yet we – we threw them wholly down,
from Ḥeshbon to Divon,
laid waste as far as Nofaḥ,
as far as Meideva."

31 32 So Israel settled in the land of the Amorites. And Moshe sent spies to
Yazer. And Israel captured its surrounding settlements and dispossessed
33 the Amorites who were there. Then they turned and journeyed along the
road toward Bashan. Og, king of Bashan, with all his people came out to
34 Edrei to engage them in battle. But the Lord said to Moshe: "Do not be
afraid of him, for I have given him into your hand, with all his people and
his land. Do to him what you did to Siḥon, king of the Amorites, who
lived in Ḥeshbon."

35 So they struck him down, together with his sons and all his people until
there were no survivors, and they took possession of his land.

22 1 The Israelites moved on and encamped in the plains of Moav across the
Jordan from Yeriḥo.

BALAK 2 And Balak son of Tzipor had seen all that the Israelites had done to the
3 Amorites. The Moabites were in deep dread of the people because they
4 were so numerous. Fearful of the Israelites, the Moabites said to the elders
of Midyan, "This horde will now lick up everything around us, as an ox
licks up grass in the field." Balak son of Tzipor was king of Moav at that
5 time. He sent messengers to summon Bilam son of Beor who was at Petor
near the River[55] in his native land: "A people has come out of Egypt, and
now they cover the face of the land – and they have settled down alongside
6 me. Please, come now and curse this people for me, for they are stronger
than I. Perhaps then I will be able to defeat them and drive them from the
land, for I know that whomsoever you bless is blessed and whomsoever
you curse is cursed."

54 | Kemosh was the Moabite deity.

55 | Referring to the Euphrates.

7 So the elders of Moav and Midyan went, carrying with them payment for
8 divination. They came to Bilam and repeated Balak's words to him. "Spend
the night here," he said, "and I will give you your reply that the Lord
speaks to me." So the princes of Moav stayed the night with Bilam.

9 God came to Bilam and said, "Who are these men with you?"

10 And Bilam replied to God, "Balak son of Tzipor, king of Moav, has sent me
11 a message: 'A people has come out of Egypt and covers the face of the land.
Now come and curse them for me. Perhaps I will be able to fight against
them and drive them away.'"

12 "Do not go with them," said God to Bilam. "Do not curse this people, for
they are blessed."

13 Then Bilam arose in the morning and said to Balak's princes, "Go back to
your land, because the Lord has refused to let me go with you."

14 The princes of Moav rose and went to Balak and said, "Bilam refuses to
go with us."

15 Balak then sent other princes, yet more numerous and eminent than the
16 first. They came to Bilam and said to him, "This is what Balak son of Tzipor
17 says: 'Do not let anything prevent you from coming to me, for I will do
you great honor, and whatever else you ask of me. Please – come and curse
this people for me.'"

18 Bilam replied to Balak's servants, "Even if Balak were to give me his palace
full of silver and gold, I could not do anything, small or great, to transgress
19 the word of the Lord my God. But now, you too remain here tonight so
that I may know what else the Lord may tell me."

20 God came to Bilam that night and said to him, "If the men have come to
summon you, you may get up and go with them; but do only what I tell
21 you to do." So Bilam rose in the morning, saddled his donkey, and went
along with the princes of Moav.

22 God was furious at his going, and an angel of the Lord stood in the road
to oppose him as he was riding on his donkey, his two servants with him.
23 The donkey saw the angel of the Lord standing in the road, drawn sword
in hand, and she swerved from the road into a field. And Bilam beat the
24 donkey to urge her back onto the road. Then the angel of the Lord was
standing in a narrow path between vineyards with a wall on either side.
25 When the donkey saw the angel of the Lord, she pressed against the wall,
crushing Bilam's foot against it. He beat her once again.

26 And the angel of the Lord went ahead and stood in a narrow place where
27 there was no room at all to turn right or left. When the donkey saw the
angel of the Lord, she lay down under Bilam. Bilam was furious and beat
28 the donkey with his stick. Then the Lord opened the donkey's mouth

and – "What have I done to you," she said to Bilam, "that you have struck me these three times?"

29 "You are playing games with me," said Bilam to the donkey. "If only I had a sword in my hand, I would kill you here and now."

30 But the donkey said to Bilam, "Am I not your donkey on whom you have always ridden to this day? Have I been in the habit of doing this to you?"

"No," he replied.

31 Then the LORD uncovered Bilam's eyes, and he saw the angel of the LORD
standing in the road, drawn sword in hand. He bowed and prostrated
32 himself facedown. The angel of the LORD said to him, "Why have you
beaten your donkey these three times? It was I who came out here to
33 oppose you, because your way is perverse to me. The donkey saw me and
turned away from me these three times. If she had not turned away from
me, I would certainly have killed you by now and let her live."

34 Bilam said to the angel of the LORD, "I have sinned, for I did not know that you were standing against me in the road. Now, if you consider it wrong, I will go back."

35 The angel of the LORD said to Bilam, "Go with the men, but say nothing except what I tell you." So Bilam continued on with Balak's princes.

36 When Balak heard that Bilam was coming, he went out to meet him at the
37 city of Moav, at the Arnon border on the edge of his territory. Balak said
to Bilam, "Did I not send to summon you? Why did you not come to me?
Am I really not able to offer you any honor?"

38 Bilam replied to Balak, "Well, I have come to you now. But can I speak any words I choose? I can only say the word God puts into my mouth."

39 40 Then Bilam went with Balak and they came to Kiryat Ḥutzot. Balak
sacrificed oxen and sheep and sent them to Bilam and the princes who
41 were with him. In the morning Balak took Bilam up to Bamot Baal, where
he could see part of the people.

23 1 Bilam said to Balak, "Build me seven altars here and prepare for me seven bulls and seven rams."

2 Balak did as Bilam said, and Balak and Bilam offered a bull and a ram on
3 each altar. Then Bilam said to Balak, "Stand by your offerings and I will
go; perhaps the LORD will come to meet me. Whatever He shows me, I
will tell you." And he went off alone.

4 God met Bilam, who said to Him, "I have prepared seven altars; on each altar I have offered a bull and a ram."

5 And the LORD put a word in Bilam's mouth, "Go back to Balak and say this."

6 He went back to him, and found him standing by his offering together
7 with all the princes of Moav. And Bilam took up his oracle and said:

"Balak brought me from Aram,
the king of Moav from the eastern hills.
'Go: curse Yaakov for me;
go: denounce Israel.'
8 How can I curse
whom God has not cursed?
How can I denounce
whom the Lord has not denounced?
9 From the tops of crags I see him;
from the hills I gaze down:
a people that dwells alone;
not reckoning itself among nations.
10 Who can number the dust of Yaakov,
count even a fourth of Israel?
Let me die the death of the upright,
and let my end be like his."

11 And Balak said to Bilam, "What have you done to me? I brought you to
curse my enemies, and you have blessed them."

12 He answered, "Am I not obliged to speak strictly the words the Lord puts
in my mouth?"

13 Then Balak said to him, "Come with me to another place where you will
see them. You will see only part of them; you will not see them all. Curse
them for me from there."

14 He took him to the field of Tzofim, to the top of Pisga. He built seven altars
and on each altar offered a bull and a ram.

15 Then Bilam said to Balak, "Stand here beside your offering, while I seek
a meeting there."

16 The Lord met Bilam and put a word in his mouth. "Go back to Balak," He
said, "and tell him this."

17 He came to him and found him standing by his offering together with the
princes of Moav. Balak asked him, "What did the Lord say?"

18 So he took up his oracle and said:

"Stand up, Balak, listen;
pay attention, son of Tzipor.
19 Not man is God, to lie;
no mortal, to change His mind.
Would He speak and not fulfill, would He
promise and not keep?

20 I received an order to bless.
He has blessed; I cannot revoke it.
21 He has glimpsed no wrong in Yaakov,
He has seen no sin in Israel.
The LORD their God is with them,
in them the King's horn blasts sounds.
22 God, who freed them from Egypt,
is like the oryx's proud horn for them.
23 There is no divination over Yaakov,
no spell against Israel can hold.
It will now[56] be said of Yaakov,
of Israel, "See what God has done."
24 A people – see – rises like a lioness,
lifts itself up like a lion.
It will not lie down until it eats its meat
and drinks the blood of the slain."

25 Balak said to Bilam, "Do not curse or bless them."

26 But Bilam answered, "Did I not tell you, 'I must do whatever the LORD
says'?"

27 Then Balak said to Bilam, "Come now and I will take you to another place.
Perhaps God will deem it right to let you curse them for me there."

28 29 So Balak took Bilam to the top of Peor, overlooking the wasteland. Bilam
said to Balak, "Build me seven altars here and prepare for me seven bulls
30 and seven rams." Balak did as Bilam had said, and offered a bull and a ram
on each altar.

24 1 When Bilam saw that it pleased the LORD to bless the Israelites, he did
not go as at other times to seek omens. Instead, he turned toward the
2 wilderness. And Bilam raised his eyes and saw Israel encamped there
3 tribe by tribe, and God's spirit came upon him. He took up his oracle and
said:

"The word of Bilam, son of Beor;
the word of the man whose eye is opened.
4 The word of one who hears God's speech,
who sees a vision of Shaddai,
who falls, but with eyes unveiled.[57]
5 How good are your tents, Yaakov,
your homes, O Israel.
6 Like palm groves stretching forth,
like gardens by the river,

56 | That is, after God's salvation of Israel.

57 | Perhaps this line describes Bilam prophesying in a fallen position; cf., for example, Genesis 17:3.

like aloes the LORD planted,
 like cedars by the waters.
7 Water will drip from his branches;
 his seed has abundant water;
his king will be higher than Agag,[58]
 his kingdom exalted.
8 God, who freed him from Egypt,
 is the oryx's proud horn to him.
He will devour enemy nations,
 break their bones, pierce them with arrows.
9 Like a lion he crouches, lies down,
 like a lioness; who dares to rouse him?
Blessing on all who bless you,
 on those who curse you, curse."

10 Balak was furious with Bilam. He struck his hands together. Balak said to
Bilam, "I summoned you to curse my enemies. Instead you have blessed
11 them these three times over. Now get away from here and go home. I said
that I would honor you, but the LORD has denied you all honor."

12 Bilam replied to Balak, "Did I not tell the messengers whom you sent to
13 me, 'Even if Balak were to give me his palace full of silver and gold, I could
not do anything to transgress the word of the LORD, doing either good or
bad of my own accord. What the LORD says is what I must say.'

14 "So now that I am going back to my people, let me advise you what this
15 people will do to your people in days to come." He took up his oracle,
saying:

"The word of Bilam son of Beor,
 the word of a man whose eye is opened.
16 The word of one who hears God's speech,
 and has knowledge from the Most High,
who sees a vision of Shaddai,
 who falls, but with eyes unveiled.
17 I see him,[59] but not now;
 I gaze upon him, though not near:
A star will shoot forth from Yaakov;
 a scepter will arise from Israel,
and smash the brow of Moav,
 and devastate all children of Shet.
18 Edom will become a possession,
 Se'ir the possession of its foes.
 But Israel will act valiantly.
19 From Yaakov will come forth a ruler

58 | Agag was an Amalekite king; see I Samuel, chapter 15.

59 | This apparently refers to a future king of Israel.

and empty the city[60] of survivors."

20 He looked at Amalek; he took up his oracle and said:
"Amalek is first among nations,[61]
but its end will be death forever."

21 He looked at the Kenites; he took up his oracle and said:
"Invincible your dwelling,
your nest set in the rock.
22 Yet Kayin is destined for burning,
when Assyria seizes you captive."

23 And he took up his oracle and said,
"Alas! Who will live when God does this?
24 Ships from the coast of Kitim
will afflict Assyria, afflict Ever;
they too will perish for all time."

25 Then Bilam rose and returned home, and Balak also set off upon his way.

25 1 Israel was dwelling at Shitim. And the men began to consort with Moabite
2 women, who invited the people to join the sacrifices to their god; the men
3 ate, and then they worshipped the women's god. Israel allied itself with
4 Baal Peor,[62] and the LORD was filled with fury against Israel. "Take all the
people's leaders," said the LORD to Moshe, "and have them impaled before
the LORD in broad daylight, so that the LORD's fury with Israel may be
5 allayed." Moshe said to Israel's judges, "Each of you kill those of your men
who have allied themselves with Baal Peor."

6 At that moment, an Israelite man brought a Midianite woman to his
friends before the eyes of Moshe and the entire Israelite community, who
7 were weeping at the entrance to the Tent of Meeting. When Pinḥas son
of Elazar son of Aharon the priest saw this, he rose from the midst of the
8 community, took a spear in his hand, went after the Israelite man into the
tent, and stabbed both of them, the Israelite man and the woman, through
9 the stomach – and the plague among the Israelites ended. Those who had
died by the plague numbered twenty-four thousand.

PINḤAS

10 11 The LORD spoke to Moshe: "Pinḥas son of Elazar son of Aharon the priest
has allayed My rage against the Israelites. Because he was passionate on
My behalf among you, I did not destroy the Israelites in My own passion.
12 13 Therefore, say this: I grant him My covenant of peace. For him and for
his descendants, it shall be a covenant of everlasting priesthood, because
he was passionate for his God and made atonement on the part of the
14 Israelites." The name of the slain Israelite man who was killed with the
Midianite woman was Zimri son of Salu, leader of the ancestral House

60 | Perhaps an unspecified Edomite city, or the region of Edom generally.

61 | Amalek was the first group to attack Israel after the exodus from Egypt; see Exodus 17:8.

62 | A local deity.

15 of Shimon. The name of the Midianite woman who was killed was Kozbi,
daughter of Tzur the tribal leader of a Midianite ancestral house.

16 17 And the LORD spoke to Moshe: "Attack the Midianites and defeat them,
18 for they attacked you by the deception they practiced against you in the
Peor affair, and in the affair of their sister Kozbi, daughter of a Midianite
leader, who was killed on the day of the plague in the Peor affair."[63]

26 1 After the plague –

2 the LORD said to Moshe and Elazar son of Aharon the priest: "Take a
census of the entire Israelite community, from twenty years of age and
upward, by their ancestral houses: everyone in Israel capable of active
service."

3 Moshe and Elazar the priest spoke to them in the plains of Moav by the
4 Jordan opposite Yeriḥo: "Take a census of those twenty years of age and
upward just as the LORD commanded Moshe and the Israelites who came
out of Egypt."

5 Reuven was Yisrael's firstborn. Reuven's descendants: of Ḥanokh, the clan
6 of Ḥanokh; of Palu, the clan of Palu; of Ḥetzron, the clan of Ḥetzron; of
7 Karmi, the clan of Karmi. These are the Reubenite clans. Their tally was
43,730.

8 Palu's descendants: Eliav.

9 Eliav's descendants: Nemuel, Datan, and Aviram. These were the same
Datan and Aviram, elect of the community, who rebelled against Moshe
and Aharon in the company of Koraḥ, when they rebelled against the
10 LORD.[64] The earth opened its mouth and swallowed them, along with
Koraḥ, when the company died and fire consumed the two hundred fifty
11 men; and they became a sign. But the sons of Koraḥ did not die.

12 Shimon's descendants by their clans: of Nemuel, the clan of Nemuel; of
13 Yamin, the clan of Yamin; of Yakhin, the clan of Yakhin; of Zeraḥ, the
14 clan of Zeraḥ; of Sha'ul, the clan of Sha'ul. These are the Simeonite clans:
22,200.

15 Gad's descendants by their clans: of Tzefon, the clan of Tzefon; of Ḥagi,
16 the clan of Ḥagi; of Shuni, the clan of Shuni; of Ozni, the clan of Ozni; of
17 Eri, the clan of Eri; of Arod, the clan of Arod; of Areli, the clan of Areli.
18 These are the Gadite clans. Their tally was 40,500.

19 Among Yehuda's sons were Er and Onan; Er and Onan died in the land of
20 Canaan.[65] Yehuda's descendants by their clans: of Shela, the clan of Shela;
of Peretz, the clan of Peretz; of Zeraḥ, the clan of Zeraḥ.

63 | The account of the attack itself appears in chapter 31.

64 | See chapter 16.

65 | See Genesis, chapter 38.

21 Peretz's descendants: of Ḥetzron, the clan of Ḥetzron; of Ḥamul, the clan
22 of Ḥamul. These are the clans of Yehuda. Their tally was 76,500.

23 Yissakhar's descendants by their clans: of Tola, the clan of Tola; of Puva,
24 the clan of Puva; of Yashuv, the clan of Yashuv; of Shimron, the clan of
25 Shimron. These are the clans of Yissakhar. Their tally was 64,300.

26 Zevulun's descendants by their clans: of Sered, the clan of Sered; of Elon,
27 the clan of Elon; of Yaḥle'el, the clan of Yaḥle'el. These are the Zebulunite
clans. Their tally was 60,500.

28 Yosef's descendants by their clans: Menashe and Efrayim –

29 Menashe's descendants: of Makhir, the clan of Makhir. Makhir had a son
30 Gilad. Of Gilad, the clan of Gilad. These are Gilad's descendants: of I'ezer,
31 the clan of I'ezer; of Ḥelek, the clan of Ḥelek; of Asriel, the clan of Asriel;
32 of Shekhem, the clan of Shekhem; of Shemida, the clan of Shemida;
33 and of Ḥefer, the clan of Ḥefer. But Tzelofḥad son of Ḥefer had no sons,
only daughters. The names of Tzelofḥad's daughters were Maḥla, Noa,
34 Ḥogla, Milka, and Tirtza.[66] These are the clans of Menashe. Their tally
was 52,700.

35 These are Efrayim's descendants by their clans: of Shutelaḥ, the clan of
36 Shutelaḥ; of Bekher, the clan of Bekher; of Taḥan, the clan of Taḥan. These
37 are Shutelaḥ's descendants: of Eran, the clan of Eran. These are the clans
of Efrayim. Their tally was 32,500. All these are Yosef's descendants by
their clans.

38 Binyamin's descendants by their clans: of Bela, the clan of Bela; of Ashbel,
39 the clan of Ashbel; of Aḥiram, the clan of Aḥiram; of Shefufam, the clan
40 of Shefufam; of Ḥufam, the clan of Ḥufam. Bela's descendants were Ard
41 and Naaman: the clan of Ard; of Naaman, the clan of Naaman. These are
the clans of Binyamin. Their tally was 45,600.

42 These are Dan's descendants by their clans: of Shuham, the clan of Shuham.
43 These are the clans of Dan; all the Shuhamite clans according to their tally
were 64,400.

44 Asher's descendants by their clans: of Yimna, the clan of Yimna; of Yishvi,
45 the clan of Yishvi; of Beria, the clan of Beria. Of Beria's descendants: of
46 Ḥever, the clan of Ḥever; of Malkiel, the clan of Malkiel. The name of
47 Asher's daughter was Seraḥ. These are the clans of Asher; their tally was
53,400.

48 Naftali's descendants by their clans: of Yaḥtze'el, the clan of Yaḥtze'el; of
49 Guni, the clan of Guni; of Yetzer, the clan of Yetzer; of Shilem, the clan of
50 Shilem. These are all the clans of Naftali. Their tally was 45,400.

51 The total number of those Israelite men was 601,730.

---

66 | See 27:1–11.

52 The LORD spoke to Moshe: "The land shall be apportioned to them for
53
54 inheritance by the tally of their names. To those who are many, give a large
inheritance; to those who are few, a small inheritance. Let each be given
55 its inheritance in keeping with its number. The land must be apportioned
56 by lot. By the names of their ancestral tribes they shall inherit. Whether
large or small, each tribe will inherit by means of the lot."

57 These are the numbers of the Levites by their clans: of Gershon, the clan
of Gershon; of Kehat, the clan of Kehat; of Merari, the clan of Merari.

58 These are the Levite clans: the clan of Livna, the clan of Ḥevron, the clan
of Maḥli, the clan of Mushi, and the clan of Koraḥ. Kehat had a son Amram.
59 The name of Amram's wife was Yokheved daughter of Levi; she had been
born to Levi in Egypt. She bore to Amram Aharon, Moshe, and their sister
60 Miriam. To Aharon were born Nadav, Avihu, Elazar, and Itamar. Nadav
61
and Avihu died when they offered unauthorized fire before the LORD.[67]
62 Their number was 23,000, this including every male one month of age and
upward. They were not numbered along with the Israelites because no land
inheritance was given to them in the Israelites' midst.

63 This was the census that Moshe and Elazar the priest took of the Israelites
64 on the plains of Moav by the Jordan opposite Yeriḥo. It contained not one
man who had been counted by Moshe and Aharon the priest when they
65 took the census of the Israelites in the Sinai Desert. For the LORD had said
of those, "They shall die in the wilderness." Not one of them was left now
except for Kalev son of Yefuneh and Yehoshua son of Nun.[68]

27 1 Then the daughters of Tzelofḥad son of Ḥefer son of Gilad son of Makhir
son of Menashe, of the clans of Menashe son of Yosef, came forward; the
2 daughters' names were Maḥla, Noa, Ḥogla, Milka, and Tirtza. And they
stood before Moshe, Elazar the priest, the princes, and all the community
3 at the entrance to the Tent of Meeting, and said, "Our father died in
the wilderness. He was not among the company of those who gathered
together against the LORD in the company of Koraḥ; he died in his own sin,
4 and had no sons. Why should our father's name be lost to his family only
because he had no son? Give us a portion of land along with our father's
5 brothers." Moshe brought their case before the LORD.

6 And the LORD said to Moshe: "What Tzelofḥad's daughters say is right.
7
You must certainly give them a heritable portion of land along with their
8 father's kin. Transfer their father's portion to them. Speak to the Israelites;
tell them: If a man dies and has no son, you shall transfer his property to
9 his daughters. If he does not have a daughter, you shall give his property
10 to his brothers. If he has no brothers, you shall give his property to his
11 father's brothers. If his father had no brothers, give his property to the

67 | See Leviticus 10:1–2.

68 | See 14:30.

closest relative in his clan, and that person shall inherit it." This shall be a
decree of law for the Israelites, as the LORD commanded Moshe.

12 The LORD said to Moshe, "Ascend this mountain of Avarim, and gaze upon
13 the land that I have given to the Israelites. After you have seen it, you too
14 will be gathered to your people, like Aharon your brother, because when
the community rebelled in the Wilderness of Tzin, you disobeyed Me,
failing to affirm My sanctity in their eyes through the water." These were
the waters of Merivat Kadesh in the Wilderness of Tzin.[69]

15 16 Moshe spoke to the LORD: "Let the LORD, God of the spirit of all flesh,
17 appoint a man over the community who will go out before them and come
in before them, who will lead them out and bring them home. Let not the
LORD's community be like sheep without a shepherd."

18 The LORD said to Moshe, "Take Yehoshua son of Nun, a man infused with
19 My spirit, and lay your hand upon him. Have him stand before Elazar
the priest and the entire community, and in their sight, give him this
20 charge. Give over to him some of your majesty, so that the entire Israelite
21 community will obey him. Let him stand before Elazar the priest, who
shall seek the decision of the Urim before the LORD on his behalf. By this
word they will go out and by this word they will return, he and all Israel,
the entire community."

22 Moshe did as the LORD commanded him. He took Yehoshua and had
23 him stand before Elazar the priest and the entire community. And he laid
his hands upon him and commissioned him, as the LORD had spoken
through Moshe.

28 1 2 The LORD spoke to Moshe: "Command the Israelites; say to them: Take
care to present My offering of foodstuffs – fire offerings of pleasing aroma
to Me – at its appointed times.

3 "Say to them: This is the fire offering you must present to the LORD: two
4 yearling lambs without blemish as a regular burnt offering each day. Offer
5 one lamb in the morning and the second in the afternoon, with a tenth of
an ephah of fine flour as a grain offering mixed with a quarter of a hin of
6 beaten oil. This is the regular burnt offering instituted at Mount Sinai, as
7 a pleasing aroma, a fire offering to the LORD. Its libation shall be a quarter
of a hin for each lamb, to be poured out in the Sanctuary as a libation
8 of fermented drink to the LORD. Offer the other lamb in the afternoon
together with a grain offering and libation as in the morning; a fire offering,
a pleasing aroma to the LORD.

9 "On the Sabbath day: two yearling lambs without blemish and two-tenths
of a measure of fine flour as a grain offering, mixed with oil, and its libation.

---

69 | See above, 20:1–13.

10 This is the burnt offering for every Sabbath, to be brought in addition to
the regular daily burnt offering and its libation.

11 "On your New Moons you shall present a burnt offering to the Lord: two
12 young bulls, one ram, and seven yearling lambs, all without blemish. There
shall be a grain offering of three-tenths of a measure of fine flour mixed
with oil for each bull, a grain offering of two-tenths of fine flour mixed
13 with oil for each ram, and a grain offering of one-tenth of fine flour mixed
with oil for each lamb. This shall be a burnt offering of pleasing aroma, a
14 fire offering to the Lord. Their libations shall be half a hin of wine for a
bull, a third of a hin of wine for a ram, and a quarter of a hin of wine for a
lamb. This is the monthly burnt offering for each New Moon of the year.
15 One male goat shall be brought as a purification offering to the Lord, in
addition to the regular burnt offering and its libation.

16 "On the fourteenth day of the first month, a Passover sacrifice shall be
17 brought to the Lord. And the fifteenth day of this month will be a festival.
18 For seven days unleavened bread shall be eaten. The first day shall be a
19 sacred assembly; you shall perform no laborious work. You shall offer
a burnt fire offering to the Lord: two young bulls, one ram, and seven
20 yearling lambs, all unblemished. Their grain offering shall be fine flour
mixed with oil: three-tenths of a measure for each bull, two-tenths for the
21 22 ram, and one-tenth for each of the seven lambs, together with one male
23 goat as a purification offering to make your atonement. These you shall
offer in addition to the morning burnt offering, the regular daily offering.
24 In the same way you shall offer daily for seven days the foodstuffs of a fire
offering, a pleasing aroma to the Lord. It shall be offered in addition to
25 the regular burnt offering and its libation. The seventh day shall be for you
a sacred assembly; you shall perform no laborious work.

26 "The day of first produce, when you bring an offering of new grain[70] to the
Lord on your Festival of Weeks, shall be a sacred assembly for you. On it
27 you shall perform no laborious work. You shall present a burnt offering as a
pleasing aroma to the Lord: two young bulls, one ram, and seven yearling
28 lambs. Their grain offering shall be fine flour mixed with oil: three-tenths
29 of a measure for each bull, two-tenths for the one ram, and one-tenth for
30 31 each of the seven lambs. Offer one male goat to atone for you. These you
shall offer in addition to the regular burnt offering, its grain offering and
libations. They shall be without blemish.

29 1 "The first day of the seventh month shall be a sacred assembly for you;
you shall perform no laborious work on it. It shall be for you a day of the
2 horn's sounding. You shall present a burnt offering as a pleasing aroma to
the Lord: one young bull, one ram, and seven yearling lambs, all without
3 blemish. Their grain offering shall be fine flour mixed with oil, three-tenths

70 | See Leviticus 23:16.

4 of a measure for the bull, two-tenths for the ram, and one-tenth for each of
5 the seven lambs; and there shall be one male goat as a purification offering
6 to atone for you. This will be in addition to the monthly burnt offering
with its grain offering, and the regular burnt offering with its grain offering
and libations as prescribed. It shall be a pleasing aroma, a fire offering to
the Lord.

7 "The tenth day of this seventh month shall be a sacred assembly for you;
8 you shall afflict yourselves on it and perform no work at all.[71] You shall
present a burnt offering to the Lord for a pleasing aroma: one young
9 bull, one ram, and seven yearling lambs, all without blemish. Their grain
offering shall be fine flour mixed with oil, three-tenths of a measure for
10 the bull, two-tenths for the single ram, and one-tenth for each of the seven
11 sheep. There shall be one male goat as a purification offering, in addition
to the special purification offering of atonement and the regular burnt
offering with its grain offering and libations.

12 "The fifteenth day of the seventh month shall be a sacred assembly for you;
you shall perform no laborious work on it; you shall celebrate a festival
13 to the Lord for seven days.[72] And you shall present a burnt offering, a
fire offering, for a pleasing aroma to the Lord: thirteen young bulls, two
14 rams, and fourteen yearling lambs, all without blemish. Their grain offering
shall be fine flour mixed with oil: three-tenths of a measure for each of
15 the thirteen bulls, two-tenths for each of the two rams, and one-tenth for
16 each of the fourteen lambs. There shall be one male goat as a purification
offering, in addition to the regular burnt offering with its grain offering
and libation.

17 "On the second day: twelve young bulls, two rams, and fourteen yearling
18 lambs, all without blemish. The grain offering and libations for the bulls,
19 rams, and sheep shall be as prescribed for their number. There shall be
one male goat as a purification offering, in addition to the regular burnt
offering with its grain offering and libations.

20 "On the third day: eleven bulls, two rams, and fourteen yearling lambs, all
21 without blemish. The grain offering and libations for the bulls, rams, and
22 lambs shall be as prescribed for their number. There shall be one male goat
as a purification offering, in addition to the regular burnt offering with its
grain offering and libation.

23 "On the fourth day: ten bulls, two rams, and fourteen yearling lambs, all
24 without blemish. The grain offering and libations for the bulls, rams, and
25 sheep shall be as prescribed for their number. And there shall be one male
goat as a purification offering, in addition to the regular burnt offering with
its grain offering and libation.

---

71 | Cf. Leviticus 23:26–32.

72 | Cf. Leviticus 23:33–43

26 "On the fifth day: nine bulls, two rams, and fourteen yearling lambs, all
27 without blemish. The grain offering and libations for the bulls, rams, and
28 lambs shall be as prescribed for their number. And there shall be one male
goat as a purification offering, in addition to the regular burnt offering with
its grain offering and libation.

29 "On the sixth day: eight bulls, two rams, and fourteen yearling lambs, all
30 without blemish. The grain offering and libations for the bulls, rams, and
31 lambs shall be as prescribed for their number. And there shall be one male
goat as a purification offering, in addition to the regular burnt offering with
its grain offering and libations.

32 "On the seventh day: seven bulls, two rams, and fourteen yearling lambs,
33 all without blemish. The grain offering and libation for the bulls, rams, and
34 lambs shall be as prescribed for their number. And there shall be one male
goat as a purification offering, in addition to the regular burnt offering with
its grain offering and libation.

35 "On the eighth day you shall hold an assembly; you shall perform no
36 laborious work on it. You shall present a burnt offering, a fire offering, for
a pleasing aroma to the LORD: one bull, one ram, and seven yearling lambs,
37 all without blemish. The grain offering and libations for the bull, ram, and
38 lambs shall be as prescribed for their number. And there shall be one male
goat as a purification offering, in addition to the regular burnt offering with
its grain offering and libation.

39 "These you shall offer to the LORD on your festivals, in addition to your
vows and freewill offerings: your burnt offerings, grain offerings, libations,
and peace offerings."

30 1 And Moshe told the Israelites all that the LORD had commanded him.

2 Moshe spoke to the tribal heads of the Israelites: This is what the LORD MATTOT
3 has commanded: When a man makes a vow to the LORD or takes an oath
binding himself to an obligation, he must not break his word; whatever he
speaks, that he must fulfill.

4 "When a woman makes a vow to the LORD or takes an oath binding herself
5 to an obligation while still a girl in her father's house, and her father hears
of her vow or self-imposed obligation and remains silent, then all her vows
6 and self-imposed obligations stand. But if her father restrains her[73] on the
day he hears her, none of her vows or self-imposed obligations shall stand.
The LORD will forgo them for her, because her father has restrained her.

7 8 "If she marries, having made vows or verbally bound herself, and her
husband hears of it and on the day he does so keeps silent, then her vow
9 or any pledge by which she has bound herself shall stand. But if, on the
day her husband hears of it, he restrains her, he can annul her vow or the

73 | That is, he nullifies the vow or oath.

pledge by which she has bound herself, and the LORD will forgo them for her.

10 "The vow of a widow or a divorcée – whatever she binds herself by – stands.

11 "If, while in her husband's house, a woman makes a vow or takes an oath
12 binding herself to an obligation and her husband hears and keeps silent,
and does not restrain her, then all her vows and the obligations by which
13 she binds herself shall stand. But if her husband annuls them on the day
when he hears them, then the words she spoke as a vow or the obligation
by which she bound herself will not stand. Her husband has annulled them,
and the LORD will forgo them for her.

14 "Every vow or binding by oath may be upheld by her husband or else
15 annulled by her husband. But if her husband keeps silent from that day
to the next, then he has upheld all her vows and the obligations by which
she has bound herself. He has upheld them by remaining silent on the day
16 when he heard them. If he nullifies them some time after he has heard of
them, he shall bear her guilt."[74]

17 These are the decrees that the LORD issued to Moshe, between a husband and his wife and between a father and his daughter while she is a girl in her father's home.

31 1 2 The LORD spoke to Moshe: "Take revenge for the Israelites against the Midianites;[75] after that you will be gathered in to your people."

3 Moshe spoke to the people: "Equip men from among you for active service,
to go out against Midyan, to execute the LORD's vengeance against Midyan.
4 For this service, call up one thousand from each of Israel's tribes."

5 And so, of the thousands of Israel, one thousand men were selected
6 from each tribe, twelve thousand in all, all armed for battle. Moshe sent
them, a thousand from each tribe, into service, together with Pinḥas
son of Elazar the priest, who was in charge of the sacred utensils and the
7 trumpets for sounding the blast. And they did battle against Midyan as
8 the LORD had commanded Moshe, and killed every male. And, among
the slain, they killed the kings of Midyan: Evi, Rekem, Tzur, Ḥur, and
Reva – all five kings of Midyan. At the sword's edge they also killed
Bilam son of Beor.

9 The Israelites took captive the Midianite women and children, and took as
10 booty all their cattle, flocks, and wealth. They burned all the towns where
11 they lived and their encampments. They gathered all the spoil and plunder,
12 people and animals, and they brought the captives and the plunder and

74 | In other words, if she violates her obligation because she thinks that he successfully nullified it, it is he who bears responsibility.

75 | See above, chapter 25.

spoil to Moshe, Elazar the priest, and the Israelite community, at the camp
on the plains of Moav by the Jordan across from Yeriḥo.

13 Moshe, Elazar the priest, and all the community princes went to meet
14 them outside the camp. And Moshe grew furious with the commanders of
the forces, the officers of thousands and of hundreds, now returned from
15 the service of war. "Have you left all the women alive?" Moshe demanded.
16 "These were the very ones who, on Bilam's advice, induced the Israelites
to betray the Lord during the Peor affair, so that a plague struck down
17 the Lord's community. Now, therefore, kill every male child and kill every
18 woman who has had relations with a man. All the young girls who have
19 not had relations with any man – them you may spare alive. You must stay
outside the camp for seven days. Every one among you or your captives
who has killed a person or touched a corpse must purify himself or herself
20 on the third and seventh days. You must also purify every garment, as well
as every article of leather, goats' hair, or wood."

21 Elazar the priest said to the soldiers returning from war, "This is the Law's
22 decree that the Lord commanded Moshe: Gold, silver, bronze, iron, tin,
23 and lead – anything that can withstand fire – you shall pass through the
fire and it will be purified, though it must also be purified with the water
of lustration. Anything that cannot withstand fire, you must immerse in
24 water. You shall wash your clothes on the seventh day and you will then
be pure, and may enter the camp."

25 26 The Lord said to Moshe: "Together with Elazar the priest and the family
heads of the community, you must make an inventory of the plunder that
27 was taken, people and animals, giving half to the soldiers who went into
28 battle and half to the rest of the community. Levy a tribute to the Lord.
From the soldiers who took part in the battle, take one part of every five
29 hundred, be it of people, oxen, donkeys, or flocks. Take this from their half
30 and give it to Elazar the priest as an upraised gift to the Lord. From the
Israelites' half, take one out of every fifty, be it of people, cattle, donkeys,
or flock – all the animals – and give them to the Levites who carry out the
duties of the Lord's Tabernacle."

31 32 Moshe and Elazar the priest did as the Lord commanded Moshe. The
plunder, aside from the spoil the troops had taken, was 675,000 sheep,
33 34 72,000 oxen, 61,000 donkeys, and 32,000 women who had not had
35 36 relations with a man. The half share of those who had served in battle
37 38 was 337,500 sheep, of which the Lord's tribute was 675. The cattle were
39 36,000, of which the Lord's tribute was 72. The donkeys were 30,500, of
40 which the Lord's tribute was 61. There were 16,000 people, of which the
41 Lord's tribute was 32 persons. Moshe gave the tribute, an upraised gift for
the Lord, to Elazar the priest, as the Lord had commanded Moshe.

42 The half share that Moshe took for the Israelites from those who had
43 44 served in battle as the community's half consisted of 337,500 sheep, 36,000

45 46 heads of cattle, 30,500 donkeys, and 16,000 people. Moshe took from the
47 Israelites' half one out of every 50 humans and animals. These he gave to
the Levites who keep the charge of the Lord's Tabernacle, as the Lord
had commanded Moshe.

48 The commanders over the thousands of the warriors – officers over
49 thousands and officers over hundreds – approached Moshe and said to
him, "Your servants have counted the warriors in our charge; not one
50 of us is missing. And so we make an offering to the Lord of the gold
articles each man found – anklets, bracelets, signet rings, earrings, and
51 pendants – to make our atonement before the Lord." Moshe and Elazar
52 the priest took all the gold from them, all the crafted objects. All the gold
for the upraised gift presented to the Lord by the officers of thousands
53 and the officers of hundreds was worth 16,750 shekel. Yet the men of the
54 army each kept plunder for themselves.[76] Moshe and Elazar the priest
took the gold from the officers of thousands and of hundreds, and brought
it to the Tent of Meeting as a remembrance for the Israelites before the
Lord.

32 1 The people of Reuven and Gad had much cattle – in this they were very
rich. And seeing the lands of Yazer and Gilad they noticed that this was
2 cattle country. So the people of Gad and Reuven came to Moshe, Elazar
3 the priest, and the princes of the community and said: "Atarot, Divon,
4 Yazer, Nimra, Ḥeshbon, Elaleh, Sevam, Nevo, and Beon, the land that the
Lord struck down before the community of Israel, is good cattle country,
and your servants keep cattle."[77]

5 They said, "If we have found favor with you, let this land be given to your
servants as our possession. Do not make us cross the Jordan."

6 But Moshe asked the Gadites and Reubenites, "Are your brothers to go to
7 war while you stay here? Why would you discourage the Israelites from
8 crossing into the land the Lord has given them? That is what your fathers
9 did when I sent them from Kadesh Barne'a to see the land.[78] They went
as far as the Eshkol Ravine and saw the land, but they discouraged the
10 Israelites from entering the land the Lord had given them, and on that day
11 the Lord's rage burned, and He swore: None of the men twenty years of
age or above who left Egypt will see the land that I swore to give Avraham,
12 Yitzḥak, and Yaakov, because they did not follow Me wholeheartedly – none
except Kalev son of Yefuneh the Kenizzite and Yehoshua son of Nun,
13 because they wholeheartedly followed the Lord. The Lord was incensed
at Israel, and He made them wander in the wilderness for forty years until
14 the whole generation that had done evil in the Lord's sight was gone. And

76 | That is, only the commanders offered their plunder to the Lord.

77 | Although this request appears after the Midianite war, the areas in question include those conquered earlier; see chapter 21.

78 | See chapter 13.

here you are, a brood of sinners, taking your fathers' places and bringing
15 yet more of the LORD's burning rage down upon Israel. If you turn back
from following Him, He will once again leave them in the wilderness, and
you will destroy this entire people."

16 Then they set forward and said to him, "Let us build sheep pens here for
17 our livestock and towns for our children. But we will arm ourselves and
go ahead of the Israelites until we have seen them safely to their place.
Meanwhile, our children will remain in the fortified towns, protected from
18 the inhabitants of the land. We will not return to our homes until every
19 one of the Israelites has taken possession of his inheritance. We, however,
will not take possession with them on the far side of the Jordan, for our
inheritance will be on the east side of the Jordan."

20 Moshe replied to them, "If you do this – if you arm yourselves for battle
21 before the LORD, and each of your armed men crosses the Jordan before
22 the LORD until He has driven out His enemies before Him, and the
land has been subdued before the LORD – then you may return and be
clear before the LORD and before Israel, and this land will be yours as a
23 possession before the LORD. But if you do not do this, you will have sinned
24 against the LORD, and know that your sin will find you. Build towns for
your children and pens for your flocks, but do what you have promised."

25 The people of Gad and Reuven replied to Moshe, "Your servants will
26 do just as my lord charges us. Our children, wives, livestock, and all our
27 animals will remain here in the towns of Gilad, but your servants, all
equipped for war, will cross over to do battle before the LORD, as my lord
has said."

28 Moshe gave instructions concerning them to Elazar the priest, Yehoshua
29 son of Nun, and the family heads of the Israelite tribes. Moshe said to them,
"If the men of Gad and Reuven cross the Jordan with you, each equipped
for battle before the LORD, and the land is subdued before you, then you
30 shall give them the land of Gilad as a possession. But if they do not cross
with you, equipped for war, then they must have their possession with you
in the land of Canaan."

31 The Gadites and the Reubenites answered, "What the LORD has spoken to
32 your servants, we will do. We will cross into the land of Canaan equipped
for war before the LORD, and we shall then have our hereditary land across
the Jordan."

33 So Moshe gave to them – the people of Gad and Reuven, and half the
tribe of Menashe son of Yosef – the kingdom of Siḥon, king of the
Amorites, and the kingdom of Og, king of Bashan, the land along with
34 its towns and the territory of the surrounding towns. The Gadites rebuilt
35 36 Divon, Atarot, Aroer, Atrot Shofan, Yazer, Yogbeha, Beit Nimra, and
37 Beit Haran, as fortified towns and enclosures for flocks. The Reubenites
38 built Ḥeshbon, Elaleh, Kiryatayim, Nevo and Baal Meon – the names of

which were changed – and Sivma. They named the cities that they built up.
39 The descendants of Makhir son of Menashe went to Gilad and captured
40 it, driving out the Amorites who were there. So Moshe gave Gilad to
41 Makhir son of Menashe, and he settled there. Yair son of Menashe went
42 and captured their villages, naming them Hamlets of Yair. Novaḥ went
and captured Kenat and its surrounding villages, renaming it Novaḥ after
himself.

MASEI 33 1 These were the journeys of the Israelites when they left Egypt by their
2 divisions under the leadership of Moshe and Aharon. Moshe recorded the
places of their setting out on every journey at the LORD's command. These
are their journeys, by the places from which they set out.

3 They set out from Ramesses on the fifteenth day of the first month. On
the day after the Passover the Israelites went out defiantly, before all the
4 Egyptians' eyes, while the Egyptians were burying their firstborns, whom
the LORD had struck down, every one. The LORD had executed judgments
even against their gods.
5 The Israelites set out from Ramesses and camped at Sukkot.
6 They set out from Sukkot and camped at Etam on the edge of the
wilderness.
7 They set out from Etam and turned back to Pi HaḤirot, which faces Baal
Tzefon, and camped before Migdol.
8 They set out from Pi HaḤirot and passed through the sea into the
wilderness – and they made a three-day journey through the Wilderness
of Etam and camped at Mara.
9 They set out from Mara and came to Eilim. At Eilim there were twelve
springs and seventy date palms, and they encamped there.
10 They set out from Eilim and camped by the Sea of Reeds.
11 They set out from the Sea of Reeds and camped in the Wilderness of
Sin.
12 They set out from the Wilderness of Sin and camped at Dofka.
13 They set out from Dofka and camped at Alush.
14 They set out from Alush and camped at Refidim, where there was no water
for the people to drink.
15 They set out from Refidim and camped in the Sinai Desert.
16 They set out from the Sinai Desert and camped at Kivrot HaTaava.
17 They set out from Kivrot HaTaava and camped at Ḥatzerot.
18 They set out from Ḥatzerot and camped at Ritma.
19 They set out from Ritma and camped at Rimon Peretz.
20 They set out from Rimon Peretz and camped at Livna.
21 They set out from Livna and camped at Risa.
22 They set out from Risa and camped at Kehelata.
23 They set out from Kehelata and camped at Mount Shefer.
24 They set out from Mount Shefer and camped at Ḥarada.
25 They set out from Ḥarada and camped at Mak'helot.

26 They set out from Mak'helot and camped at Taḥat.
27 They set out from Taḥat and camped at Teraḥ.
28 They set out from Teraḥ and camped at Mitka.
29 They set out from Mitka and camped at Ḥashmona.
30 They set out from Ḥashmona and camped at Moserot.
31 They set out from Moserot and camped at Benei Yaakan.
32 They set out from Benei Yaakan and camped at Ḥor HaGidgad.
33 They set out from Ḥor HaGidgad and camped at Yotvata.
34 They set out from Yotvata and camped at Avrona.
35 They set out from Avrona and camped at Etzyon Gever.
36 They set out from Etzyon Gever and camped in the Wilderness of Tzin,
that is, Kadesh.
37 They set out from Kadesh and camped at Mount Hor, at the edge of the
38 land of Edom. And Aharon the priest ascended Mount Hor at the Lord's
command, and he died there in the fortieth year, on the first day of the
39 fifth month after the Israelites left Egypt. Aharon was one hundred and
40 twenty-three years old when he died on Mount Hor. And the Canaanite
king of Arad, who lived in the Negev in the land of Canaan, heard that the
Israelites were coming.[79]
41 They set out from Mount Hor and camped at Tzalmona.
42 They set out from Tzalmona and camped at Punon.
43 They set out from Punon and camped at Ovot.
44 They set out from Ovot and camped at Iyei HaAvarim in the territory of
Moav.
45 They set out from Iyim and camped at Divon Gad.
46 They set out from Divon Gad and camped at Almon Divlatayma.
47 They set out from Almon Divlatayma and camped in the Mountains of
Avarim, before Nevo.
48 They set out from the Mountains of Avarim and camped in the plains of
49 Moav by the Jordan across from Yeriḥo. And they camped by the Jordan
from Beit HaYeshimot to Avel HaShitim in the plains of Moav.

50 And the Lord spoke to Moshe on the plains of Moav by the Jordan across
51 from Yeriḥo: "Speak to the Israelites. Say: When you cross the Jordan
52 into the land of Canaan, you shall drive out all the inhabitants of the land
before you. You shall destroy all their carved images and all their molten
53 idols and demolish all their high shrines. You shall take possession of
54 the land and settle there, for I have given you the land to possess. You
shall divide up the land by lot among your clans: to a large clan give a
large inheritance, and to a small one a small inheritance. Whatever falls
to them by lot will be theirs. According to your ancestral tribes you shall
55 inherit. But if you do not drive the inhabitants out of the land before you,
then those you allow to remain will be barbs in your eyes and thorns in

79 | See 21:1–3.

56 your sides. They will harass you in the land where you settle. Then, what I
intended to do to them, I will do instead to you."

34 1 2 The LORD said to Moshe: "Command the Israelites. Say to them: As you
enter the land of Canaan – this is the land that will become your possession,
the land of Canaan with its borders:

3 "Your southern sector shall extend from the Wilderness of Tzin alongside
Edom; your southern border to the east begins at the end of the Dead Sea.
4 The border shall then turn south of Scorpion Ascent and cross toward Tzin.
Its outer limit shall be south of Kadesh Barne'a, extending to Ḥatzar Adar
5 and continuing toward Atzmon. The border shall then turn from Atzmon
to the Ravine of Egypt and end at the sea.

6 "Your western border will be the Great Sea and its coast; this shall be your
western border.

7 "This shall be your northern border: from the Great Sea, mark a line to
8 Mount Hor. From Mount Hor mark a line to Levo Ḥamat. The outer limit
9 of the border shall be at Tzedad; the border shall then extend to Zifron,
and its outer limit shall be Ḥatzar Einan. This shall be your northern
border.

10 11 "Mark your eastern border from Ḥatzar Einan to Shefam. The border
will run down from Shefam to Rivla on the east side of Ayin. It will then
12 continue down to reach the eastern slope of the Sea of Galilee. From there
the border will run down along the Jordan, ending at the Dead Sea. This
is to be your land with its borders on all sides."

13 Moshe commanded the Israelites: "This is the land of which you take
possession by lot, which the LORD has commanded to give to the nine and
14 a half tribes – for the tribe of Reuven by its ancestral houses, and the tribe
of Gad by its ancestral houses, and half the tribe of Menashe have taken
15 their possession. The two and a half tribes have taken their possession
across the Jordan from Yeriḥo to the east as the sun rises."

16 17 And the LORD spoke to Moshe: "These are the names of the men who shall
apportion the land to you for possession: Elazar the priest and Yehoshua
18 son of Nun. And you shall also take one leader from each tribe to apportion
19 the land. These are the names of the men: for the tribe of Yehuda, Kalev
20 son of Yefuneh; for the tribe of the Simeonites, Shmuel son of Amihud;
21 22 for the tribe of Binyamin, Elidad son of Kislon; for the tribe of the Danites,
23 a leader, Buki son of Yogli. For the descendants of Yosef: for the tribe of
24 the Manassites a leader, Ḥaniel son of Efod; for the tribe of the Efraimites
25 a leader, Kemuel son of Shiftan. For the tribe of the Zebulunites a leader,
26 Elitzafan son of Parnakh. For the tribe of the Issakharites a leader, Paltiel
27 son of Azan. For the tribe of the Asherites a leader, Aḥihud son of Shelomi.
28 29 For the tribe of the Naftalites a leader, Pedahel son of Amihud." These were

the ones whom the Lord commanded to apportion the possession for the
Israelites in the land of Canaan.

35 1 The Lord spoke to Moshe in the plains of Moav by the Jordan across
2 from Yeriḥo: "Command the Israelites to grant the Levites towns to live
in, among the inheritance they will possess. Grant them also pasturelands
3 around the towns. The towns shall be theirs to live in, and the pasturelands
4 shall be for their cattle, all that they own, and all their animals. The
pasturelands of the towns that you shall give to the Levites shall extend
5 from the town wall outward for a thousand cubits in all directions; you
shall measure out from the town, two thousand cubits on the east side, two
thousand cubits on the south side, two thousand cubits on the west side,
and two thousand cubits on the north side, with the town in the middle,
and this shall belong to them as pastureland for their towns.

6 "Six of the towns that you give to the Levites shall be towns of refuge,
which you will designate as places to which a manslayer may flee. In
7 addition to these, you shall give them forty-two more towns. Thus the
total number of towns you shall give to the Levites shall be forty-eight,
8 along with their pastureland. As for the towns that you give from the
possession of the Israelites, take more from the larger tribes and fewer
from the smaller so that each grants towns to the Levites in proportion to
its own inheritance."

9 10 The Lord spoke to Moshe: "Speak to the Israelites. Tell them: When you
11 cross the Jordan into the land of Canaan, select towns to be your refuge
12 cities, to which a person who kills another unintentionally may flee. The
cities shall be a refuge for you from avengers,[80] so that no person who has
13 killed another may die without standing trial before the community. The
14 towns that you designate shall be six cities of refuge for you; you shall
designate three towns across the Jordan and three in the land of Canaan
15 as cities of refuge. These six towns shall be a place of refuge for Israelites,
migrants, and temporary residents alike, so that anyone who kills a person
unintentionally may flee there.

16 "If a person strikes another with an iron object,[81] however, and he dies,
17 that person is a murderer; the murderer must be put to death. If he strikes
him with a hand held stone that could cause death and he dies, that person
18 is a murderer; the murderer must be put to death. Likewise, if he strikes
him with a wooden tool that could cause death and he dies, that person is
19 a murderer; the murderer must be put to death. The blood avenger shall
put the murderer to death; whenever he meets him, he may put him to
20 death. So too if one person pushes another in hate, or throws something
21 at him with prior intent, he shall be put to death. If in enmity someone

80 | Referring to the victim's next of kin.

81 | An iron object is considered a deadly weapon.

strikes a person with his hand and he dies, the one who struck the blow
is a murderer and shall be put to death. The blood avenger shall put the
murderer to death whenever they meet.

22 "If, however, one person pushes another suddenly, without enmity, or
23 throws an object at him unintentionally, or drops a fatal stone on him
without seeing him and he dies – they were not enemies, he intended him
24 no harm – then the community must judge between the killer and the
25 blood avenger in accordance with these laws.[82] And the community must
protect the manslayer from the avenger of blood and return him to the
refuge city to which he fled. There he shall live until the death of the High
26 Priest anointed with the sacred oil. But if the manslayer ever goes outside
27 the limits of the city of refuge to which he fled and the blood avenger
finds him outside the limits of his city of refuge and kills him, the avenger
28 is not liable for murder; the manslayer must stay in his city of refuge until
the High Priest dies. After the death of the High Priest the manslayer may
return to his own hereditary land.

29 "These shall be a decree of law for you throughout your generations,
wherever you should live.

30 "If anyone kills a human being, the murderer shall be put to death on the
evidence of eyewitnesses. No one shall be put to death on the testimony of
31 one witness alone. You may not accept a ransom for the life of a murderer
32 found guilty of a capital crime; he must be put to death. Nor may you
accept a ransom for someone who has fled to his city of refuge, to allow
33 him to return and live on his land before the priest dies. You shall not
pollute the land in which you live; blood pollutes the land. And the land
can have no atonement for the blood that is shed in it – except through
34 the blood of the one who shed it. Do not defile the land in which you live,
and in the midst of which I dwell – for I the Lord dwell in the midst of
Israel."

36 1 The heads of the ancestral houses of the descendants of Gilad son of
Makhir son of Menashe, one of the families of Yosef's sons, came forward
and spoke before Moshe and the leaders, the heads of the ancestral
2 houses of the Israelites. "The Lord," they said, "commanded my lord to
give the land as an inheritance to the Israelites by lot. But my lord was
also commanded by the Lord to give the inheritance of our brother
3 Tzelofḥad to his daughters. If they marry men from another Israelite
tribe, their share will be taken away from our ancestral inheritance and
given to the tribe into which they marry. It will be taken away from the
4 allotted portion of our inheritance. When the Israelites observe the
Jubilee, their inheritance will be added to that of the tribe into which

82 | In other words, they must carefully determine that the killing was in fact unintentional.

they married; their inheritance will be taken away from the inheritance
of our forefathers' tribe."[83]

5 Then Moshe, at the LORD's word, commanded the Israelites: "What the
6 tribe of Yosef's descendants say is right. This is the word that the LORD
has commanded to Tzelofḥad's daughters: They may marry whomever
7 they wish as long as they marry within a clan of their father's tribe, so that
the Israelites' inheritance does not pass from one tribe to another. Thus
the Israelites will each stay attached to the inheritance of their ancestral
8 tribes. Every daughter among the Israelite tribes who inherits land must
marry a member of her father's tribe, so that the Israelites may possess
9 the inheritance of their ancestors. No inheritance may pass from one
tribe to another; each Israelite tribe shall remain attached to its own
inheritance."

10 11 Tzelofḥad's daughters did as the LORD commanded Moshe. Maḥla, Tirtza,
Ḥogla, Milka, and Noa, Tzelofḥad's daughters, were each married to men
12 who were their cousins. They thus married into the families of Menashe
son of Yosef, and their inheritance remained within the tribe of their
father's clan.

13 All these are the commandments and laws that the LORD gave through
Moshe to the Israelites on the plains of Moav, by the Jordan, across from
Yeriḥo.

83 | At the Jubilee year, land goes back to its original owner (see Lev. 25:7–13), and each tribe thereby ought to retain its allotment. But if these women were to marry men from other tribes, the land inherited from Tzelofḥad would enter the possession of those men permanently.

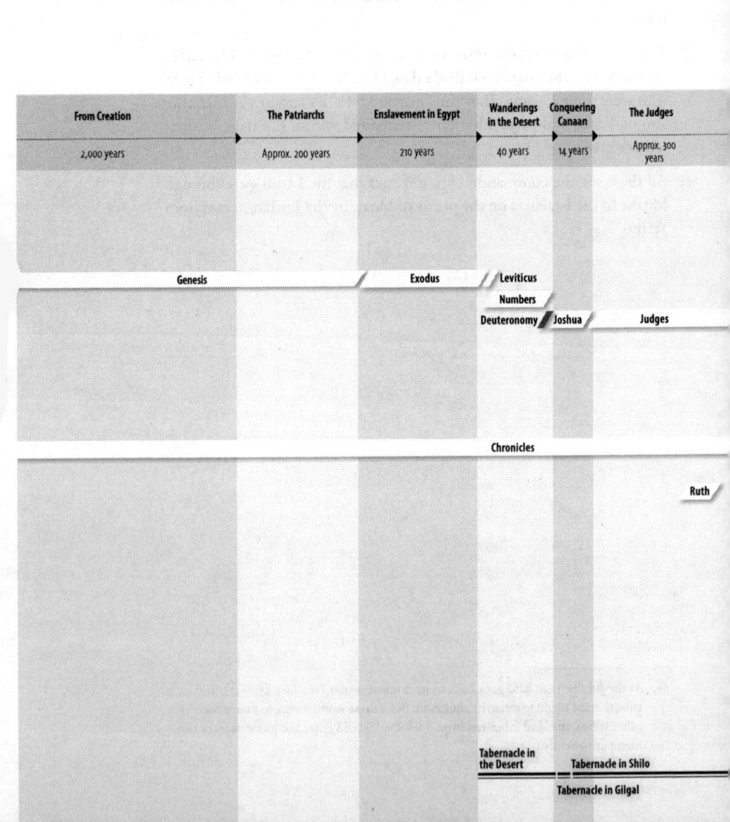

From Creation
2,000 years
The Patriarchs
Approx. 200 years
Enslavement in Egypt
210 years
Wanderings in the Desert
40 years
Conquering Canaan
14 years
The Judges
Approx. 300 years
Genesis
Exodus
Leviticus
Numbers
Deuteronomy
Joshua
Judges
Chronicles
Ruth
Tabernacle in the Desert
Tabernacle in Shilo
Tabernacle in Gilgal

DEUTERONOMY/ DEVARIM

DEUTERONOMY	The historical address	The address about the commandments	The covenantal address	Moshe's departure
	Chs. 1–4	5–26	27–30	31–34

DEVARIM

1 1 These are the words that Moshe spoke to all Israel east of the Jordan, in the
wilderness; in the Arava across from Suf, between Paran and Tofel, Lavan,
2 Ḥatzerot, and Di Zahav. By way of Mount Se'ir, it takes eleven days to cross
from Ḥorev to Kadesh Barnea.[1]

3 In the fortieth year,[2] on the first day of the eleventh month, Moshe spoke to
4 the Israelites exactly as the Lord had commanded him regarding them, after
he had defeated Siḥon, king of the Amorites, who lived in Ḥeshbon, and Og,
5 king of Bashan, who lived in Ashtarot and in Edre'i.[3] On the east bank of the
Jordan, in the land of Moav, Moshe began to expound this Law:[4]

6 "The Lord our God spoke to us at Ḥorev; He said: You have settled long
7 enough at this mountain. Start out and advance into the hill country of the
Amorites and all the neighboring regions – the Arava, the hill country, the
lowlands, the Negev, and the seacoast – the land of the Canaanites and the
8 Lebanon, as far as the Euphrates River. See: I have set the land before you.
Go in and take possession of the land that the Lord swore He would give to
your ancestors – to Avraham, Yitzḥak, and Yaakov – and to their descendants
after them.

9 10 "At that time[5] I said to you, 'I cannot bear the burden of you alone. The Lord
your God has increased your numbers: today you are as numerous as the stars
11 of the heavens. May the Lord, God of your ancestors, multiply you again a
12 thousandfold and bless you, as He has promised. But how can I bear alone
13 all your problems, your burdens, your disputes? Choose for yourselves men
who are wise, discerning, and known to your tribes, and I will appoint them
as your leaders.'

14 15 "You answered me, 'The plan you propose is a good one.' So I took the leaders
of your tribes, wise men and well known, and appointed them to be leaders
over you, chiefs of thousands, chiefs of hundreds, chiefs of fifties, chiefs of
16 tens, and officials, for your tribes. I charged your judges at that time: 'Hear the
disputes among your people and judge fairly, between one person and another,
17 whether Israelite or migrant. Do not show partiality in judgment: listen equally
to the small and the great. Do not be intimidated by any man, for judgment
belongs to God. Any case that is too difficult for you, bring to me, and I will
18 hear it.' I charged you at that time, with all the things you are to do.

19 "Then we set out from Ḥorev and journeyed through all that vast and fearful
wilderness that you have seen, toward the hill country of the Amorites, as the
20 Lord our God had commanded us, until we reached Kadesh Barnea. I said

1 | Ḥorev is the same as Sinai. These two verses seem to convey that much of the contents of the following orations (from v. 5), delivered in Moav, were originally communicated to the people earlier in the wilderness, in the area that extends from Sinai to Kadesh Barnea south of Canaan.

2 | After the exodus from Egypt.

3 | See Numbers 21:21–35.

4 | The legal portions of Moshe's presentation appear later, beginning in chapter 12.

5 | This probably refers to the episode recounted in Exodus 18:13–26.

to you, 'You have reached the hill country of the Amorites, which the LORD
21 our God is giving us. See, the LORD your God has laid the land out before you.
Go up, take possession, as the LORD, God of your ancestors, has promised. Do
not fear and do not be dismayed.'

22 "Then all of you drew close to me and said, 'Let us send men ahead of us to
explore the land and bring back a report to us about the route by which we
should go up and the towns we will come to.'[6]

23 "The plan seemed good to me, so I selected twelve of you, one man from
24 each tribe. They set out and went up into the hill country. And, arriving at
25 the Eshkol Ravine, they spied it out. They took some of the fruit of the land,
which they brought down to us, and they brought us back a report: 'The land
that the LORD our God is giving us is good.'

26 "But you were unwilling to go up, and you rebelled against the word of the
27 LORD your God. You grumbled in your tents and said, 'It is because the LORD
hates us that He has brought us out of the land of Egypt, to hand us over to
28 the Amorites to destroy us. Where can we go? Our brothers have melted
all the bravado from our hearts by telling us, "The people are stronger and
taller than we are. The cities are large and walled to the sky; we even saw the
Anakites there."'[7]

29 30 "And I said to you, 'Do not be terrified and have no fear of them. The LORD
your God, who is going before you, He will fight for you, just as He did for
31 you in Egypt before your eyes, and in the wilderness, where you saw the LORD
your God carry you as a man carries his child, all along the way you traveled
32 until you reached this place. And yet despite all this, you show no faith in the
33 LORD your God, who goes ahead of you on your journey – in fire by night,
and cloud by day – to seek out a place for you to camp and show you the way
you should go.'

34 35 "Hearing your words, the LORD became furious and swore an oath: 'Not one
man of this evil generation shall see the good land that I swore to give your
36 ancestors, except for Kalev son of Yefuneh. He will see it, and to him and his
descendants I will give the land on which he set foot, because he followed the
37 LORD wholeheartedly.'[8] And because of you, the LORD was enraged even with
38 me, and said, 'You also shall not enter it. Yehoshua son of Nun, who stands
before you – he shall enter there. Encourage him, for he will give Israel their
39 possession. As for your little ones, whom you thought would be taken captive,
and your children who do not yet know good from bad, they shall enter, and I
40 will give it to them, and they will take possession of it. But you – turn around
and set out into the wilderness by way of the Sea of Reeds.'

6 | Cf. Numbers, chapters 13–14.

7 | The Anakites were of giant stature; see Numbers 13:33.

8 | Kalev, although one of the spies, did not participate in the discouraging report. The same is true of Yehoshua son of Nun who, as verse 38 affirms, not only would enter the land but also would succeed Moshe as Israel's leader.

41 "And you answered me: 'We have sinned against the Lord! We will go up
and fight, as the Lord our God commanded us.' So each of you strapped on
your weapons thinking that it would be easy to go up into the hill country.

42 "The Lord said to me, 'Tell them: Do not go up and do not fight, for I will not
be with you. Do not be struck down by your enemies.'

43 "And I told you, but you would not listen. You rebelled against the word of the
44 Lord and willfully went up into the hill country. The Amorites who lived in
those hills came out against you and chased you like a swarm of bees. In Se'ir
45 they struck you down, as far as Ḥorma.[9] You came back and wept before the
46 Lord, but the Lord would not listen to you, nor pay you any heed. And so
you remained at Kadesh for a long time – all that time that you were there.

2 1 "Then we turned and journeyed back into the wilderness, by way of the Sea
of Reeds, as the Lord had told me and, for a long time, made our way around
Mount Se'ir.

2 3 "Then the Lord said to me: 'You have circled about this hill country long
4 enough now. Turn to the north. And give the people these orders: You are
about to pass through the territory of your kinsmen, the descendants of Esav,
5 who live in Se'ir. They will be afraid of you, but be very careful. Do not provoke
them, for I will not give you even a foot of their land; I have given Mount Se'ir
6 to Esav as his possession. You shall pay them in silver for the food you eat, pay
7 them silver for the water that you buy from them and drink. For the Lord
your God has blessed you in all the work of your hands. He has watched over
your wanderings through this vast wilderness. These forty years the Lord your
God has been with you: you have lacked for nothing.'

8 "So we passed by, away from our kinsmen, the descendants of Esav who live
in Se'ir. We turned from the route of the Arava, away from Eilat and Etzyon
Gever, and journeyed in the direction of the Wilderness of Moav.

9 "Then the Lord said to me: 'Do not mistreat the Moabites or provoke them
to war, for I will not give you any of their land as a possession: I have given Ar
to the descendants of Lot for a possession.'"[10]

10 The Emim lived there originally – a strong and numerous people, as tall as the
11 Anakites. Like the Anakites, they are considered Refaim, but the Moabites
12 call them Emim. Horites used to live in Se'ir, but the descendants of Esav
dispossessed them, destroying them and settling in their place, as Israel did in
the land that the Lord gave them as a possession.

13 "'Now, get up and cross the Zered Stream.' So we crossed the Zered Stream.
14 From the time we left Kadesh Barnea to the time we crossed the Zered Stream
was thirty-eight years – until the entire generation of warriors had perished

---

9 | *Ḥorma* literally means "destruction."

10 | Ar is the equivalent of Moav; see, e.g., Numbers 21:28. The Moabites and the Amonites descended from Lot; see Genesis 19:36–38.

15 from the camp – as the LORD had sworn to them. And the LORD's hand was
against them to trouble them from the camp until they had all perished.

16 17 "When all those warriors among the people had died, the LORD spoke to me:
18 19 'Today you are going to cross the border of Moav at Ar. When you come to the
Amonites, do not harass them or provoke them to war, for I will not give you
any of the land of the Amonites as a possession: I have given it as a possession
to the descendants of Lot.'"

20 This too was considered a land of Refaim. Refaim lived there originally,
21 although the Amonites call them Zamzumim – a strong and numerous people,
as tall as the Anakites. The LORD destroyed them so that the Amonites could
22 dispossess them and settle in their place, just as He did for the descendants of
Esav, who live in Se'ir, by destroying the Horites before them so that they could
dispossess them and settle in their place to this day, where they still remain;
23 likewise the Avim, who had lived in villages as far as Aza – the Caftorites,
emerging from Caftor, destroyed them and settled in their place.

24 "'Set out and cross the Arnon Stream. I have given over Siḥon, the Amorite
king of Ḥeshbon, with his land, into your hands. Begin to take possession
25 of it; enter into battle with him.[11] This day I am beginning to put the terror
and fear of you upon the peoples everywhere under the skies. When they
hear reports of you, they will tremble in dread of you.'

26 "So I sent messengers from the Kedemot wilderness to Siḥon, king of
27 Ḥeshbon, with an offer of peace: 'Let us pass through your land. We
will stay on the main road, turning aside neither to the right nor to the
28 left. Provide us with food and we will pay for it in silver and eat; give us
water and we will pay for it in silver and drink. Only let us pass through
29 on foot – just as the descendants of Esav living in Se'ir and the Moabites
living in Ar did for us – until we cross the Jordan into the land that the
30 LORD our God is giving us.' But Siḥon, king of Ḥeshbon, refused to let us
pass through, for the LORD your God had hardened his spirit and made
his heart defiant in order to give him over into your hands, as He has now
done.

31 "The LORD said to me, 'I have begun to give Siḥon and his land over to
you. Go: begin to conquer and possess his land.'

32 33 "Then Siḥon and all his people came out to meet us in battle at Yahatz. The
LORD our God gave him over to us, and we struck him down, together
34 with his sons and all his people. At that time we captured all his towns
and completely destroyed them, men, women, and children alike, leaving
35 not a single survivor. Only the livestock and the spoil of the cities we
36 captured did we keep as booty for ourselves. From Aroer on the banks of
the Arnon Stream, including the town in the ravine, as far as Gilad, not

11 | Concerning the battles with Siḥon and Og recounted in this passage, cf. Numbers 21:21–35.

one city was unattainable to us. The LORD our God gave us all of them.
37 But you did not touch the land of the Amonites, not the land around the
Yabok Stream, nor the towns of the hill country that the LORD our God
commanded us to leave.

3 1 "After this, we turned and journeyed along the road toward Bashan. Og,
king of Bashan, with all his people came out to Edre'i to engage us in battle.
2 But the LORD said to me, 'Do not be afraid of him, for I have given him
into you hand, with all his people and his land. Do to him what you did
3 to Siḥon, king of the Amorites, who lived in Ḥeshbon.' So the LORD our
God also gave over to us Og, king of Bashan, and all his people. We struck
4 him down until not a single survivor remained. We captured all his towns
at that time; there was not a single town we did not take from them – sixty
5 towns, the entire region of Argov, Og's kingdom in Bashan. And these were
all fortress towns with high walls, gates, and bars – there were a great many
6 unwalled towns besides. And we utterly destroyed them, as we had done
to Siḥon, king of Ḥeshbon, in each town utterly destroying them: men,
7 women, and children. All the livestock and the spoil of the towns we kept
as booty for ourselves.

8 "At that time, then, we took from the two kings of the Amorites the land
9 beyond the Jordan, from the Arnon Stream to Mount Ḥermon" – the
10 Sidonians call Ḥermon Siryon, and the Amorites call it Senir – "all the
towns of the plateau, the whole of Gilad, and the whole of Bashan, as far
as Salkha and Edre'i, towns of Og's kingdom in Bashan."

11 Only Og, king of Bashan, was left then of the remaining Refaim. His bed,
made of iron, is still there, in Raba of the Amonites: it is nine cubits long
and four cubits wide, as measured by a man's forearm.

12 "Of the land that we took possession of at that time, I gave to the Reubenites
and Gadites the territory from Aroer on the edge of the Arnon Stream, as
13 well as half the hill country of Gilad with its towns.[12] To the half tribe of
Menashe I gave the rest of Gilad and all of Bashan, Og's kingdom – the whole
region of Argov: all that portion of Bashan that used to be known as the land
14 of the Refaim." Yair of Menashe took the whole region of Argov – that is,
Bashan – as far as the border of the people of Geshur and of Maakha – and
named it after himself, hamlets of Yair, as it is called to this day.

15 16 "To Makhir I gave Gilad, and to the Reubenites and the Gadites I gave
the territory from Gilad as far as the Arnon Stream, with the middle of the
ravine as a border, and up to the Yabok Stream and the Amonites' border.
17 It included also the Arava, with the Jordan and its banks, from the Sea
of Galilee down to the Arava Sea, the Dead Sea, with the lower slopes of
Pisga on the east.

---

12 | Cf. Numbers, chapter 32.

18 "At that time, I charged you:[13] 'The LORD your God has given you this
land to possess, but all your troops must cross over armed before your
19 fellow Israelites. Only your wives, children, and cattle – I know that you
20 have much cattle – shall stay behind in the towns I have given you, until
the LORD gives rest to your fellows as to you, and they too have taken
possession of the land that the LORD your God is giving them beyond the
21 Jordan. Then you may each return to the land that I have given to you.' And
I charged Yehoshua also at that time: 'Your own eyes have seen all that the
LORD your God has done to these two kings; so will the LORD do to all
22 the kingdoms into which you are about to cross. Do not fear them, for it
is the LORD your God who is fighting for you.'

VAETHANAN 23 24 "At that time, I pleaded with the LORD: 'O LORD GOD, You have begun
to show Your servant Your greatness and Your mighty hand; what force
25 in heaven or earth can do deeds and mighty acts like Yours! Please let
me cross over and see the good land beyond the Jordan, that good hill
26 country and the Lebanon.' But the LORD was enraged with me because
of you,[14] and would not listen to me. 'It is enough!' the LORD said to me.
27 'Never speak to Me about this again! Go up to the top of Pisga and gaze
around you to the west, to the north, to the south, and to the east. See it
28 with your eyes, for you will not cross this Jordan. But charge Yehoshua,
make him strong and determined, for he will be the one to cross over at
the head of this people and who will secure their possession of the land
that you may only see.'

29 "And we came to rest in the valley beside Beit Peor.

4 1 "And now, Israel, listen to the decrees and laws that I am teaching you to
keep, so that you may live to enter and take possession of the land that the
2 LORD, God of your ancestors, is giving to you. Do not add anything to that
which I command you, or subtract from it; keep the commandments of
3 the LORD your God with which I am charging you. You saw with your own
eyes what the LORD did in the affair of Baal Peor[15] – how the LORD your
4 God wiped out from among you everyone who followed Baal Peor, while
you, who held firmly to the LORD your God, are all here living today.

5 "See: I have taught you decrees and laws as the LORD my God commanded
me, for you to keep in the land that you are about to enter and possess.
6 Take care to keep them, for this will be your wisdom and understanding
in the eyes of the peoples: when they hear all these decrees they will say,
7 'Surely this great nation is a wise and understanding people!' For what
other great nation has God so close to it as the LORD our God is to us
8 whenever we call out to Him? And what other great nation has decrees
and laws as just as this entire Torah that I am setting before you today?

13 | "You" refers to the Reubenites and Gadites.

14 | See 1:37.

15 | See Numbers, chapter 25.

9 "But take care and be very vigilant not to forget the things that your eyes
have seen, nor to let them fade from your mind, as long as you live. Make
10 known to your children and your children's children, how you once
stood before the LORD your God at Ḥorev,[16] when the LORD said to me,
'Assemble the people for Me, and I will let them hear My words so that
they may learn to be in awe of Me as long as they live on earth, and teach
their children likewise.'

11 "And you came close and stood at the foot of the mountain while the
12 mountain was ablaze to high heaven and shrouded in dark clouds. Then
the LORD spoke to you out of the fire. You heard the sound of words but
13 saw no image; there was only a voice. He announced to you His covenant,
which He charged you to keep – the Ten Commandments – and He wrote
14 them on two tablets of stone. And the LORD charged me at that time to
teach you decrees and laws for you to keep in the land that you are about
to cross into and possess.

15 "You saw no image when the LORD spoke to you at Ḥorev out of the fire,
16 and so take great care for your own sake not to act in self-destruction,
making yourselves any idol, an image of any shape, any form of man or of
17 woman, or in the form of any animal of the land, or any winged bird that
18 flies in the sky, or in the form of anything that crawls on the ground, or of
19 any fish in the waters below the earth. And when you raise your eyes to the
heavens and see the sun, moon, and stars, all the heavenly array, do not be
led astray to bow down to them and worship them; the LORD your God
20 has allotted them to all the other peoples beneath the sky. But you, the
LORD took, and He brought you out of the iron crucible that was Egypt,
to become the people of His heritage, as you are on this day.

21 "The LORD was incensed with me because of your words, and He vowed
that I would not cross the Jordan nor enter the good land that the LORD
22 your God is giving you as a heritage. I will die in this land without crossing
the Jordan – but you will cross over and take possession of that good land.
23 Take care not to forget the covenant that the LORD your God has forged
with you. Do not make yourselves an idol in any form: the LORD your
24 God has forbidden it. For the LORD your God is a consuming fire, an
impassioned God.

25 "When you have had children and grandchildren, and have lived long in the
land, if you act destructively, forming an idol in any image, wreaking evil in
26 the sight of the LORD your God and provoking Him to anger, I call heaven
and earth to witness against you today – to bear witness that you will quickly
perish from the land that you are crossing the Jordan to take possession
of. You will not live long there; you will be utterly destroyed. The LORD
27 will scatter you among the peoples. Only a few of you will remain among
28 the nations that the LORD will drive you away to. There you will worship

16 | Sinai; see Exodus, chapters 19–20.

man-made gods of wood and of stone, ones that do not see, do not hear, do
29 not eat or smell. Yet there, if you seek the LORD your God, you will find Him:
30 if you search after Him with all your heart and all your soul. In your distress,
when all these things have happened to you, in the days to come, you will
31 finally return to the LORD your God and heed His voice. For the LORD your
God is a merciful God. He will not forsake or destroy you. He will not forget
the covenant that He forged on oath with your ancestors.

32 "For ask now about earliest times, times long before your own, from the
day God created humans on the earth; ask from one end of heaven to the
other: Has anything as great as this ever happened before? Has anyone
33 heard of anything like this? Has any people ever heard the voice of God
34 speaking out of fire, as you have, and lived? Has God ever taken one nation
to Himself, by miracles, from the midst of another, by trials, signs, wonders,
and war, with a mighty hand and an arm stretched forth and terrifying
displays of power, as the LORD your God did for you in Egypt before your
35 eyes? To you this was shown – so that you may know that the LORD is God;
36 besides Him, there is no other. From heaven He let you hear His voice to
discipline you. On earth He showed you His great fire, and from within
37 the fire you heard His words. And because He loved your ancestors and
chose their descendants after them He brought you out of Egypt with His
38 own presence and by His great power, driving out from before you nations
greater and mightier than you, to bring you in and give you their land as a
39 possession, as it is on this day. Know today and take to heart that the LORD
40 is God in heaven above and on the earth beneath; there is no other. Keep
His decrees and commandments, with which I am charging you today, so
that it may be well for you and your children after you, and that you may
live long in the land that the LORD your God is giving you for all time."

41 42 Then Moshe designated three cities to the east side of the Jordan to which
a manslayer could flee, someone who had killed a fellow human being
43 without intent or prior enmity.[17] He could flee to one of these cities and live:
Betzer in the wilderness plateau for the people of Reuven, Ramot in Gilad
for the people of Gad, and Golan in Bashan for the people of Menashe.

44 45 This is the Law that Moshe set before the people of Israel. These are the
testimonies, decrees, and laws that Moshe spoke to the Israelites when
46 they had come out of Egypt and were beyond the Jordan in the valley
opposite Beit Peor, in the land of Siḥon, king of the Amorites, who reigned
at Ḥeshbon, whom Moshe and the Israelites defeated when they came out
47 of Egypt. They had taken possession of his land and the land of Og, king of
48 Bashan, the two Amorite kings east of the Jordan: from Aroer on the edge
49 of the Arnon Stream, as far as Mount Siyon – that is, Ḥermon – together
with all the Arava on the east bank of the Jordan as far as the Arava Sea,
below the slopes of Pisga.

---

17 | See Numbers 35:10–15.

5 1 Moshe summoned all Israel, and said to them: "Listen, Israel, to the
decrees and laws that I shall declare in your hearing today; learn them
and carefully observe them.

2 3 "The Lord our God forged a covenant with us at Ḥorev. Not with our
ancestors did the Lord forge this covenant,[18] but with us who are here
today, all of us, alive.

4 5 "Face-to-face from amid the fire the Lord spoke to you at the mountain. I
was standing between the Lord and you at that time to tell you the word
of the Lord, because you were afraid of the fire and did not go up the
mountain. He said:

6 "I am the Lord your God, who brought you out of the land of Egypt, out
of the house of slaves.
7 Have no other gods than Me.
8 Do not make for yourself a carved image or likeness of any creature in the
9 heavens above or the earth beneath or the water beneath the earth. Do not
bow down to them or worship them, for I the Lord your God demand
absolute loyalty. For those who hate Me, I hold the descendants to account
10 for the sins of the fathers to the third and fourth generation, but to those
who love Me and keep My commands – I shall act with faithful love for
thousands.
11 Do not speak the name of the Lord your God in vain, for the Lord will
not hold guiltless those who speak His name in vain.
12 Guard the Sabbath to keep it holy, as the Lord your God has commanded
13 14 you. Six days you shall work and carry out all your labors, but the seventh is
a Sabbath to the Lord your God. On it, do no work at all – neither you, nor
your son or daughter, your male or female servant, your ox, your donkey,
nor any of your livestock, or the migrant within your gates, so that your
15 male and female servants may rest as you do. Remember that you were
slaves in Egypt, and the Lord your God brought you out of there with a
mighty hand and an arm stretched forth. That is why the Lord your God
has commanded you to keep the Sabbath day.
16 Honor your father and mother, as the Lord your God has commanded
you, so that you may live long and that it may be well for you in the land
that the Lord your God is giving you.
17 Do not murder.
Do not commit adultery.
Do not steal.
Do not bear false witness against your neighbor.
18 Do not crave your neighbor's wife.
Do not set your desire on your neighbor's house, or field, or male or female
servant, his ox, his donkey, or anything else that is your neighbor's.

18 | That is, not with our ancestors exclusively.

19 "The LORD spoke these words with a loud voice to your whole assembly
at the mountain from amid the fire, cloud, and thick darkness, and He
added no more. And He wrote them on two stone tablets, and gave them
20 to me. When you heard the voice out of the darkness, while the mountain
21 was ablaze with fire, your tribal leaders and elders came to me; they said,
'The LORD our God has shown us His glory and greatness – we have heard
His voice from within the fire. Today we have seen that God may speak
22 to a person and that person still live. But now, must we die? For this great
fire will consume us. If we hear the voice of the LORD our God for any
23 longer, we will die. For what mortal has heard the voice of the Living God
24 speaking from within the fire, as we have, and yet lived? You go near and
listen to all that the LORD our God says. Then tell us all that the LORD our
God tells you, and we will heed and do it.'

25 "The LORD heard your words when you spoke to me, and to me the LORD
said: 'I have heard the words this people have spoken to you; they did well
26 to speak as they did. If only they would have such a mind as this always, to
hold Me in awe and to keep all My commandments, so that it might be well
27 for them and for their children forever! Go, tell them to go back to their
28 tents. But you stay here by Me, and I will tell you all the commandments,
decrees, and laws that you shall teach them, so that they may keep them
in the land that I am giving them to possess.'

29 "Take care to do as the LORD your God has commanded you; do not turn
30 aside – neither to the right nor to the left. Follow only the path that the
LORD your God has commanded you, so that you may live and it may be
well for you, and your years may be long in the land you are to possess.

6 1 "This is the command – the decrees and the laws – that the LORD your
God charged me to teach you to keep in the land that you are about to
2 cross over into and take possession of, so that you and your children and
grandchildren may remain in awe of the LORD your God as long as you
live, keeping all His decrees and commandments that I am commanding
3 you and so that your years may be long. Listen, Israel, and take care to keep
them, so that it may be well for you, and so that you may be abundantly
fertile in a land flowing with milk and with honey, as the LORD, the God
of your ancestors, promised you.

4 5 "Listen, Israel: the LORD our God – the LORD is one.[19] You shall love the
LORD your God with all your heart, with all your soul, and with all your
6 might. Let these words that I charge you with today remain impressed
7 upon your heart. Teach them to your children, speaking of them when
you sit at home and when you travel on the way, when you lie down and
8 when you rise. Bind them as a sign upon your hand, and have them as an

---

19 | There is only one God. The Hebrew could equally be translated "Listen, Israel, the LORD is our God, the LORD alone," stressing Israel's exclusive loyalty to God.

9 emblem between your eyes. Write them on the doorposts of your houses
and on your gates.

10 "When the LORD your God brings you into the land that he swore to
your ancestors Avraham, Yitzhak, and Yaakov that He would give to you,
11 a land with great and goodly towns you did not build, houses full of all
good things that you did not provide, hewn cisterns you did not hew, and
vineyards and olive groves that you did not plant – and you eat and are
12 satisfied, take care that you do not forget the LORD who brought you out
13 of Egypt, out of the house of slaves. It is the LORD your God you must
revere, Him you must serve, and only by His name that you must swear.
14 15 Do not walk after other gods, after gods of the peoples around you, for
the LORD your God in your midst demands absolute loyalty. The anger of
the LORD your God would burn against you and He would annihilate you
from the face of the earth.

16 17 "Do not test the LORD your God as you tested Him at Masa.[20] Be very
vigilant to keep the commandments of the LORD your God, and the
18 testimonies and decrees with which He has charged you. Do what is right
and what is good in the LORD's eyes, so that it may go well with you, and
you may go in and take possession of the good land that the LORD swore
19 to your ancestors to give you, driving out all your enemies before you, as
the LORD promised.

20 "And in the future, when your child asks you, 'What is the meaning of the
testimonies, decrees, and laws that the LORD our God has commanded
21 you?' tell him, 'We were slaves to Pharaoh in Egypt, but the LORD brought
22 us out of Egypt with a mighty hand. Before our eyes the LORD sent great
and awesome signs and wonders against Egypt and Pharaoh and his whole
23 household. And He freed us from there, to bring us in and give us the land
24 that He promised on oath to our ancestors. The LORD commanded us
to keep all these decrees, to revere the LORD our God, so that we might
25 always prosper; to keep us alive, as we are today. And if we carefully keep
all this command before the LORD our God, as He has charged us, this
will be our righteousness.'

7 1 "When the LORD your God brings you into the land that you are about to
enter and possess, when you drive out many nations before you – the Hittites,
Girgashites, Amorites, Canaanites, Perizzites, Hivites, and Jebusites, seven
2 nations larger and stronger than you – and the LORD your God gives them
over to you and you defeat them, you must utterly destroy them. Make no
3 covenant with them and grant them no mercy. Do not intermarry with them;
do not give your daughters to their sons in marriage or take their daughters
4 for your sons. For they will turn your children away from walking after Me,
and bring them to serve other gods. The LORD's anger will burn against you,
5 and He will quickly destroy you. Instead, this is what you must do to them:

20 | See Exodus 17:1–7.

tear down their altars, smash their worship pillars, cut down their sacred
6 trees,[21] and burn their idols with fire. For you are a holy people to the LORD
your God. The LORD your God has chosen you, of all the peoples on earth,
to be His treasured people.

7 "It is not because you were more numerous than other peoples that the
LORD desired you and chose you, for you are the smallest of all peoples.
8 It was because of the love the LORD had for you, because of the oath He
kept, that He swore to your ancestors, that the LORD freed you with a
mighty hand and redeemed you from the house of slaves, from the grip of
9 Pharaoh, king of Egypt. Know therefore that only the LORD your God is
God, the faithful God who keeps His covenant and the love to a thousand
10 generations of those who love Him and keep His commandments, and
who instantly repays with destruction those who reject Him, requiting
11 them in a moment. Therefore, carefully keep the command – the decrees
and the laws – that I am charging you with today.

EKEV 12 "If, indeed, you heed these laws, always vigilant to keep them, the LORD your
God will keep with you the covenant and the love He forged on oath with your
13 ancestors. He will love you, bless you, and multiply you. He will bless the fruit
of your womb and the fruit of your land, your grain and wine and oil, the calves
of your herds and the lambs of your flock, in the land that He swore to your
14 ancestors to give you. You shall be blessed above all other peoples, and no male
15 or female among you or your livestock will be barren or childless. The LORD
will keep you free from all sickness. All the terrible diseases of Egypt that you
knew, He will not inflict upon you, but He will lay them upon all those who
16 hate you. You shall devour all the peoples that the LORD your God is giving
over to you. Do not show them pity, and do not worship their gods – for that
would be a snare to you.

17 "You might say to yourself, 'These nations are more numerous than I. How can
18 I possibly dispossess them?' Do not be afraid of them. Remember well what the
19 LORD your God did to Pharaoh and to all Egypt. Your own eyes saw the great
trials, the signs and wonders, the mighty hand and the arm stretched forth, with
which the LORD your God brought you out. The LORD your God will do the
20 same to all the peoples you fear. The LORD your God will send the hornet,[22] too,
21 against them until even the survivors who hide from you are destroyed. Do not
be terrified of them, for the LORD your God, a great and awesome God, is in
22 your midst. The LORD your God will drive out these nations before you, little
by little. You may not put an end to them at once, or the wild beasts would
23 become too numerous for you.[23] But the LORD your God will give them
24 over to you, throwing them into great panic until they are destroyed. He
will give their kings over to your hands and you shall wipe out their name

21 | Literally "Asheras": trees, wooden posts, or images representing the Canaanite fertility goddess Ashera.

22 | This may refer to actual hornets or to a different means of destruction.

23 | That is, the desolation would allow a proliferation of wild animals.

from under heaven. No one will be able to stand against you, until you
25 have destroyed them. You shall burn the images of their gods with fire.
Do not covet the silver or gold on them and take it for yourself, because
26 you would be ensnared by it, for it is abhorrent to the LORD your God. Do
not bring any abhorrent thing into your house, or you, like it, will be set
apart for utter destruction. Detest and abhor it utterly, for it is set apart
for utter destruction.

8 1 "Take care to keep every command that I am charging you with on this day,
so that you may survive and thrive, go in, and take possession of the land
that the LORD swore He would give to your ancestors.

2 "Remember that the LORD your God has led you through all this journey
of forty years in the wilderness, to humble you and to test you, and to
know what was in your heart: to know whether you would keep His
3 commandments or whether you would fail to. He humbled you by leaving
you hungry, then feeding you manna, which neither you nor your ancestors
had ever known – to teach you that one does not live by bread alone, but
4 by all that comes forth from the mouth of the LORD. Your clothes did not
5 wear out, nor did your feet swell these forty years. Know then in your heart
that just as a parent disciplines his child, so the LORD your God disciplines
6 you. And so keep the commandments of the LORD your God, walking in
7 His ways and revering Him. For the LORD your God is bringing you into
a good land, a land of streams and springs and deep waters gushing out
8 to the valleys and the hills, a land of wheat and barley, vines, fig trees and
9 pomegranates, a land of olive oil and honey, a land where bread will not
be scarce, where you will lack nothing, a land where the rocks are iron
10 and where you can hew bronze from her hills. And when you eat and are
satisfied, you shall bless the LORD your God for the good land that He
has given you.

11 "Take care not to forget the LORD your God, failing to keep His
commandments, laws, and decrees, with which I am charging you this
12 day. Otherwise, when you have eaten and been satisfied, and have built
13 fine houses and lived in them, when your herds and flocks have grown
abundant, and your silver and gold is abundant, and all that you have has
14 grown abundant, your heart may become proud, forgetting the LORD
15 your God who brought you out of Egypt, the house of slaves, who led
you through the vast and terrifying wilderness, an arid wasteland with
venomous snakes and scorpions, who brought forth water from flint rock
16 for you, and fed you manna in the wilderness, something your ancestors
did not know, to humble and to test you – so that in the end it would
17 be well for you. You might be tempted to say to yourself, 'My power,
18 the strength of my own hand, have brought me this great wealth.' But
remember the LORD your God, for it is He who gives you the power to
do great things, upholding the covenant that He swore to your ancestors,
as He is doing on this day.

19 "If you do forget the LORD your God and follow other gods, serving and
worshipping them, I solemnly warn you today that you will be altogether
20 lost. Like the nations that the LORD will cause to die before you, so shall
you be lost, because you would not listen to the voice of the LORD your
God.

9 1 "Listen, Israel! You are now about to cross the Jordan, to go in and
dispossess nations larger and mightier than you, with great cities, fortified
2 to high heaven. The people are strong and lofty – Anakites. You know
of them; you have heard it said of them, 'Who can stand up against the
3 descendants of Anak?' Know then today that it is the LORD your God, who
is crossing over before you like a consuming fire: He will wipe them out,
subduing them before you, so that you may rapidly dispossess and destroy
them, as the LORD promised you.

4 "When the LORD your God drives them out before you, do not say to
yourself, 'It is because of my righteousness that the LORD has brought me
in to take possession of this land.' The LORD is dispossessing these nations
5 before you because of their own wickedness. Not for your righteousness
or rectitude are you coming to take possession of their land; it is for
these nations' wickedness that the LORD your God is driving them out
before you and to fulfill the promise that the LORD made on oath to your
ancestors, Avraham, Yitzḥak, and Yaakov.

6 "Know, then, that it is not for your righteousness that the LORD your God
is giving you this good land to possess, for you are a stiff-necked people.
7 Remember and never forget how you provoked the LORD your God to
fury in the wilderness. From the day you left Egypt until you arrived here,
you have always been rebellious against the LORD.

8 "At Ḥorev you provoked the LORD to fury:[24] so incensed was the LORD
9 that He was ready to destroy you. I had ascended the mountain to receive
the stone tablets, the tablets of the Covenant the LORD made with you.
I remained on the mountain forty days and forty nights; I ate no bread
10 and I drank no water. The LORD gave me two stone tablets inscribed by
the finger of God. And upon them were all the words that the LORD had
spoken to you at the mountain out of the fire, on the day of that assembly.
11 And when the forty days and forty nights were at an end, the LORD gave
me the two stone tablets, the tablets of the Covenant.

12 "And then the LORD said to me, 'Get up; go down from here immediately,
because your people whom you brought from Egypt have acted
disastrously; how rapidly they strayed from the path that I commanded
13 them to follow – they have made a molten image for themselves.' The LORD
said to me, 'I have seen this people, and they are a stiff-necked people.
14 Stand back from Me and I will destroy them and erase their name from

24 | See Exodus, chapter 32.

under the heavens, and I will make of you a nation mightier and more
numerous than they.'

15 "I turned and went down from the mountain while it was still ablaze with
16 fire, and the two tablets of the Covenant were in my two hands. When I
looked, I saw that you had indeed sinned against the LORD your God. You
had made for yourselves a molten calf; you had strayed rapidly indeed from
17 the path that the LORD had commanded you to follow. So I took hold of
the two tablets and flung them from my hands, smashing them to pieces
18 before your eyes. Then I threw myself down before the LORD as before, for
forty days and forty nights; I ate no bread and I drank no water, because
of the great sin you had committed, angering the LORD by doing what
19 was evil in His eyes. I was terrified of the LORD's blazing fury and rage
against you, ready to destroy you. But the LORD listened to me that time
20 also. The LORD was so enraged with Aharon that He was ready to destroy
21 him, but I prayed for Aharon also at that time. Then I took that thing of
sin you had made, the calf, and burned it in fire. I crushed it and ground it
thoroughly, until it was as fine as dust, and I threw the dust into a stream
running down the mountain.

22 "At Tavera also,[25] and at Masa[26] and Kivrot HaTaava,[27] you provoked the
23 LORD. And when the LORD sent you from Kadesh Barnea, saying, 'Go
up and take possession of the land that I have given you,' you rebelled
against the command of the LORD your God.[28] You did not have faith in
24 Him and did not obey Him. You have rebelled against the LORD as long
as I have known you.

25 "I threw myself down before the LORD, and as I lay prostrate those forty
26 days and forty nights, when the LORD had said He would destroy you, I
prayed to the LORD – 'LORD GOD,' I said, 'do not destroy the people, Your
heritage, those whom You redeemed in Your greatness and brought out
27 of Egypt with a mighty hand. Remember Your servants Avraham, Yitzhak,
and Yaakov; do not attend to the stubbornness of this people, to their
28 wickedness or sinfulness; otherwise the nation from which You brought
us will say, "It was because the LORD was unable to bring them into the
land that He promised them, and because He hated them, that He took
29 them out to kill them in the wilderness." But they are Your people, Your
possession, whom You freed by Your great power and Your arm stretched
forth.'

10 1 "And then the LORD said to me, 'Carve two tablets of stone like the first,
2 and come up to Me on the mountain. Make, as well, a wooden ark. I will

25 | See Numbers 11:1–3.

26 | See Exodus 17:1–7.

27 | See Numbers 11:4–34.

28 | See above, 1:19–46.

inscribe upon these tablets the words that were on the first, which you
smashed, and you shall place them in the ark.'

3 "So I made an ark of acacia wood and carved two tablets of stone like the
4 first. I ascended the mountain with these two tablets in my hand. And He
inscribed on the tablets the same words as before, the Ten Commandments
that the LORD had proclaimed to you on the mountain out of the fire on
5 the day of the assembly; and the LORD gave them to me. I turned, came
down from the mountain, and put the tablets in the ark that I had made.
And there they have remained, as the LORD commanded me.

6 "And the Israelites journeyed from Be'erot Benei Yaakan to Mosera. There
7 Aharon died and was buried. Elazar, his son, succeeded him as priest. From
there they journeyed to Gudgod, and from Gudgod to Yotvat, a region of
8 flowing streams. At that time the LORD set the tribe of Levi apart to carry
the Ark of the LORD's Covenant, to stand before the LORD to minister to
9 Him, and to give blessing in His name, as they do to this day. This is why
the Levites have no share or inheritance among their fellow Israelites. The
LORD is their inheritance, as the LORD your God promised them.

10 "I stayed on the mountain forty days and forty nights, as I had the first time.
And this time too, the LORD listened to me; the LORD did not choose to
11 destroy you. Then the LORD said to me, 'Rise and resume your journey at
the head of the people, so that they may go in and take possession of the
land that I swore to their ancestors to give to them.'

12 "So now, Israel, what does the LORD your God ask of you? Only this: to
revere the LORD your God, to walk in all His ways and love Him; to serve
13 the LORD your God with all your heart and all your soul, and to keep the
commandments and decrees of the LORD your God that I am commanding
14 you today, for your own good. Look: the heavens, even the highest heavens,
15 belong to the LORD your God, with the earth and all it contains. Yet it was
on your ancestors alone that the LORD set His heart in love, and it was
you, their descendants after them, that He chose among all the peoples, as
16 He does to this day. And so remove the hardness[29] of your heart, and be
17 stiff-necked no longer. For the LORD your God is God of gods and LORD
of lords, the great, mighty, and awesome God, who shows no partiality
18 and accepts no bribe, who executes justice for the orphan and the widow,
19 and who loves the stranger, giving him food and clothing. You too must
love the stranger, for you yourselves were strangers in the land of Egypt.
20 Revere the LORD your God and worship Him. Hold fast to Him and swear
21 by His name. He is your praise;[30] He is your God, who has done these
22 great and awesome things for you that your own eyes have seen. When
your ancestors went down to Egypt, they were but seventy souls. Now
the LORD your God has made you as many as the stars of the heavens.

29 | Literally "circumcise the foreskin."

30 | In other words, the proper object of your praise, or the source of your pride.

11 1 "And so – love the LORD your God and keep His charge: His decrees, His
2 laws, and His commands through all your days. Know today that it was
not your children who knew or saw the LORD your God's lesson – His
3 greatness, His mighty hand, and His arm stretched forth, the signs and
the acts that He performed in Egypt against Pharaoh, Egypt's king, and
4 all his land; what He did to the Egyptian fighting force, their horses and
their chariots, how He made the Reed Sea's water flood over them as they
5 pursued you, so that the LORD destroyed them forever; what He did for
6 you in the wilderness until you came to this place; and what he did to
Datan and Aviram, sons of Eliav son of Reuven, in the midst of all Israel,
how the earth opened its mouth and swallowed them, their families, tents,
7 and every living thing in their households: it is your own eyes that have
seen all these immense acts, all that the LORD did.

8 "And so – keep all of this command with which I charge you on this day,
so that you may be empowered to go in and take possession of the land
9 that you are crossing over to possess, and so that your years may be long in
the land that the LORD swore to your ancestors to give to them and their
descendants, a land flowing with milk and with honey.

10 "For the land that you are about to go into and take possession of is not
like the land of Egypt you left behind, where you could sow your seed and
11 irrigate by foot as in a vegetable garden. The land that you are crossing over
12 to possess is a land of hills and valleys; it is watered by the sky's rains. It is a
land the LORD your God watches over; the eyes of the LORD your God are
always upon it, from the year's opening to its end.

13 "And if you heed My commands, with which I charge you on this day, to love
the LORD your God and to serve Him with all your heart and with all your
14 soul, I will grant your land's rain in its season, the early and the late rain; you
15 shall gather in your grain, your wine, your oil. I will grant your fields grass
16 for your cattle, and you will eat and be satisfied. Be vigilant lest your heart
be seduced and you go astray and serve other gods and worship them. Then
17 the LORD's rage will blaze against you, and He will close the skies; there will
be no rain. The land will not yield its crops, and you will swiftly perish from
18 the good land that the LORD is giving you. Therefore set these words of
Mine upon your heart and upon your soul. Bind them as a sign upon your
19 hand, and have them as an emblem between your eyes. Teach them to your
children, speaking of them when you sit at home and when you travel on the
20 way, when you lie down and when you rise. Write them on the doorposts of
21 your house and on your gates, so that you and your children may live long
years in the land that the LORD swore to your ancestors to give to them for
as long as the sky endures above the land.

22 "If you carefully keep all of this command with which I am charging you,
loving the LORD your God, walking in all His ways, and holding fast to
23 Him, then the LORD will drive all these nations out before you, and you will
24 dispossess nations larger and mightier than you. Every place where you set

foot shall be yours. Your territory shall stretch from the wilderness to the
25 Lebanon, from the Euphrates River to the Western Sea.[31] No one will be able
to stand against you. The LORD your God will put the fear and dread of you
over all the land you set foot upon, just as He promised you.

RE'EH 26 "See this: I am setting before you on this day a blessing and a curse: the
27 blessing, if you obey the commandments of the LORD your God that I am
28 commanding you today; and the curse, if you do not obey the commandments
of the LORD your God, and instead stray from the way I am commanding
you this day to follow, to walk after other gods that you have not known.

29 "When the LORD your God has brought you into the land that you are
entering to possess, you shall proclaim the blessing on Mount Gerizim and
30 the curse on Mount Eival.[32] They are across the Jordan, westward toward
the setting sun, near the Oaks of Moreh, in the territory of the Canaanites
who live in the Arava, near Gilgal.

31 "You are about to cross the Jordan, to go into and take possession of the land
that the LORD your God is giving you. When you have possession of it and
32 live there, you must be vigilant to keep all the decrees and laws that I am
setting before you on this day.

12 1 "These are the decrees and laws that you must take care to keep in the land
that the LORD, God of your ancestors, has given you to possess for as long
as you live on this earth.

2 "Demolish completely all the shrines where the nations you are about
to dispossess served their gods: on the high mountains, on the hills, and
3 under every leafy tree. Tear down their altars, smash their worship pillars,
burn their sacred trees with fire, and cut down the statues of their gods,
4 obliterating their names from that place. Do not make such things for the
5 LORD your God; instead, seek the place that the LORD your God will choose
from among all your tribes to set His name there, to be His dwelling. Go
6 there, bringing your burnt offerings and peace offerings, your tithes and your
offerings, your gifts in fulfillment of vows and your freewill offerings, and the
7 firstborns of your herds and flocks. There you and your families shall eat in
the presence of the LORD your God, rejoicing in all your endeavors in which
the LORD your God has granted blessing.

8 "Do not behave as we have been behaving here, now, everyone doing what
is right in his own eyes.

9 "For you have not yet reached the resting place and inheritance that the
10 LORD your God is giving you. But you will cross the Jordan and live in the
land that the LORD your God is giving you as an inheritance. When He gives
11 you rest from all the enemies around you so that you are living in safety, then
you shall bring everything that I command you to the place that the LORD

31 | The Mediterranean.

32 | See below, 27:11–26; Joshua 8:30–35.

your God will choose as a dwelling for His name: your burnt offerings and
peace offerings, your tithes and your offerings, and all the choice gifts that
12 you commit by vow to the LORD. And you shall rejoice before the LORD your
God, along with your sons and daughters, your male and female servants,
and the Levites living in your towns, for they have no share or inheritance
with you.

13 14 "Take care not to offer your burnt offerings in any place you may see. Only
in the place that the LORD will choose of one of your tribes – there you shall
offer your burnt offerings and there do all that I command you.

15 "Whenever you desire, you may slaughter and eat meat in any of your towns,
according to the blessing that the LORD your God gives you. People both
16 impure and pure may eat of it, as they would of gazelle or of deer.[33] The blood,
17 however, you must not eat. Pour it out on the ground like water. You may not
eat the tithe of your grain, wine, and oil within your towns, or the firstlings
of your herds and flocks, or any of the gifts that you commit by vow, your
18 freewill offerings, or your gifts.[34] These you must eat in the presence of the
LORD your God at the place that the LORD your God will choose, along with
your sons and daughters, your male and female servants, and the Levites
living in your towns, rejoicing in all your endeavors in the presence of
19 the LORD your God. Take care not to neglect the Levite in all your years
living in your land.

20 "When the LORD your God has enlarged your territory as He has promised,
and you say, 'I shall eat some meat,' because you have the urge to eat it,
21 you may eat meat whenever you desire it. If the place where the LORD
your God chooses to place His name is too distant from you, you may
slaughter animals from the herds and flocks the LORD has given you, as
I have commanded you. These you may eat within your towns whenever
22 you wish. Eat them as you would eat gazelle or a deer;[35] the impure may
23 eat together with the pure. But make sure that you do not eat the blood,
24 for blood is life, and you must not eat the life with the meat. Do not eat
25 it; pour it out onto the ground like water; do not eat it, so that all may be
well for you and your children after you, because you do what is right in
26 the LORD's eyes. But your sacred offerings and the gifts you commit by
27 vow you must bring to the place that the LORD will choose. Present your
burnt offerings – the meat and the blood – on the altar of the LORD your
God. Of your other sacrifices, the blood shall be poured out on the altar
of the LORD your God, but you may eat the meat.

28 "Take care to heed all these words that I command you today, so that it may

33 | Wild animals not used for sacrifices at all.

34 | Various types of consecrated food and offerings. According to rabbinic tradition, this last term refers to first fruits.

35 | See note on verse 15.

be well for you and for your children after you forever, because you will be
doing what is good and right in the LORD your God's eyes.

29 "When the LORD your God has cut down before you the nations that you
are about to come to and dispossess, after you have dispossessed them
30 and live in their land, beware being tempted into their ways after they have
been destroyed before you. Do not inquire about their gods, saying, 'How
31 did these nations worship their gods? Let me do the same.' You must not
worship the LORD your God in their way, because they have done for their
gods every abhorrent thing that the LORD hates. They even offer their sons
13 1 and daughters up in fire to their gods. Take care: fulfill all that I command
you. Neither add to it nor subtract from it.

2 "If a prophet rises up among you, or one who divines by dreams, and he
3 tells you of some sign or omen, and the sign or omen of which he spoke
is realized – and he had said, 'Let us walk after other gods and worship
4 them' – gods you have not known – do not listen to the words of that
prophet or dream diviner. The LORD your God will be testing you, to
know whether you really love the LORD your God with all your heart and
with all your soul.

5 "Follow the LORD your God, revere Him, keep His commandments, and
6 listen to His voice. Worship Him; stay close to Him. And that prophet or
dream diviner – he shall be put to death for inciting rebellion against the
LORD your God who brought you out of Egypt and redeemed you from
the house of slaves, seeking to make you stray from the path the LORD your
God commanded you to walk. You must purge the evil from your midst.

7 "If anyone, even your brother, your mother's son, or your own son or
daughter, the wife of your embrace, or the friend who is like your own self
to you, secretly tempts you: 'Let us go and worship other gods' – whom
8 neither you nor your ancestors have known, gods of the peoples around
9 you, near or far, end to end of the earth – do not acquiesce, do not listen to
10 him, do not show him pity or compassion, or cover up for him. You must
put him to death. Your own hand shall be first against him to kill him, and
11 after yours, the hand of all the people. Stone him to death for seeking to
make you abandon the LORD your God who brought you out of Egypt,
12 the house of slaves. And all Israel shall hear, and fear, and never commit
such an evil again.

13 "If you hear it said about one of the towns that the LORD your God is giving
14 you to live in that depraved men among you have gone out and led the
people of the town astray, saying, 'Let us go and worship other gods' – gods
15 you have not known – you shall seek the truth, investigate, and inquire
thoroughly abroad. If it is true and is confirmed that this abhorrent thing
16 has been done among you, you shall put the inhabitants of that town to
the sword, destroying it and everything in it; put even its animals to the
17 sword. Gather all its spoil into its public square, then burn with fire the

town and all its spoil, in its entirety, to the LORD your God. It shall be an
eternal ruin, never to be rebuilt.

18 "Let nothing that has been banned remain in your hands, so that the LORD
may turn away from His flaming rage, show you compassion, and in His
19 compassion increase your numbers, as He swore to your ancestors, for
you will have heeded the voice of the LORD your God, keeping all His
commandments that I am giving you today and doing what is right in the
LORD your God's eyes.

14 1 "You are children of the LORD your God. Do not lacerate yourselves or
2 make bald patches in the middle of your heads for the dead. For you are a
people sacred to the LORD your God. The LORD has chosen you of all the
peoples on earth to be to Him a treasured people.

3 4 "Do not eat any abhorrent thing. These are the animals you may eat: the
5 ox, the sheep, the goat, the deer, the gazelle, the hartebeest, the ibex, the
6 white antelope, the wild ox, and the giraffe. You may eat any animal that
7 has divided hoofs, fully split in two, and chews the cud. Of those that chew
the cud or that have a cleft hoof, these you shall not eat: the camel, the
hare, and the hyrax, because they chew the cud but do not have a divided
8 hoof – they are impure for you; and the pig, because it has a divided hoof
but does not chew the cud – it is impure for you. You may not eat their
flesh or touch their carcasses.

9 "These you may eat among the creatures of the water: anything that has
10 fins and scales. Whatever does not have fins and scales you may not eat;
it is impure for you.

11 12 "You may eat any pure species of bird. These you may not eat:[36] the
13 griffon vulture, the bearded vulture, the lappet-faced vulture, the glede,
14 15 the buzzard, the kite of any kind, any kind of raven, the ostrich, the swift,
16 the gull, any kind of sparrow hawk, the little owl, the short-eared owl, the
17 18 barn owl, the pelican, the vulture, the fish owl, the stork, any kind of heron,
19 the hoopoe, and the bat. All swarming, flying creatures are impure for you;
20 they may not be eaten. You may, however, eat any pure flying creature.

21 "Do not eat any creature that has died of itself. Give it to the migrant in
your town to eat, or you may sell it to a foreigner. For you are a people
holy to the LORD your God.

"Do not boil a kid in the milk of its mother.

22 "Each year, set aside a tenth of the yield of all you have sown in the field.
23 You shall eat the tithe of your grain, wine, and oil, as well as the firstborn
of your herds and flocks in the presence of the LORD your God in the place
that He will choose as a dwelling for His name, so that you may learn to
24 hold the LORD your God in awe always. But if the distance is too great for

36 | The identities of many of these birds are subject to debate.

you to carry them, because the place where the Lord your God chooses to
set His name is far from you and because the Lord your God has blessed
25 you, then you may exchange the tithe for money. Wrap up the money in
26 your hand, go to the place that the Lord your God will choose, and spend
the money on whatever you choose: cattle, sheep, wine, strong drink, or
whatever else you like. There you shall eat it in the presence of the Lord
27 your God, and rejoice together with your household. As for the Levites
living in your towns, do not neglect them, because they have no share or
inheritance as you do.

28 "At the end of every third year, bring out the full tithe of your produce for
29 that year, and leave it within your towns, so that the Levites, who have
no share or inheritance as you have, together with the migrants, orphans,
and widows in your towns, may come and eat and be satisfied, so that the
Lord your God will grant you blessing in all the work of your hands.

15 1 2 "At the end of every seventh year, you shall grant a remission of debts. This
is how the remission is carried out: every creditor shall relinquish any
debt owed by his fellow. He shall not exact it from his brother, his fellow,
3 because the Lord's remission has been proclaimed. You may require
payment from a foreigner, but you must remit any debt owed to you by
4 a brother. There should be no poor among you, because the Lord will
bless you in the land that the Lord your God is giving you to possess as
5 your inheritance, if only you obey the Lord your God, staying vigilant
6 to keep all the command with which I am charging you this day. For the
Lord your God will bless you as He has promised you. You will lend to
many nations, but will not borrow. You will rule over many nations, and
they will not rule over you.

7 "If there be a poor person among your kinsfolk in any of your towns
in the land that the Lord your God is giving you, do not harden your
8 heart or close your hand toward your brother in need. Open your hand
9 generously and freely lend him enough to answer all his needs. Be vigilant:
let your heart not whisper a depraved thought: 'The seventh year, the year
of remission, is close,' making you miserly toward your brother in need,
giving him nothing. He will cry out to the Lord about you, and you will
10 be held guilty. Give to him generously, and do not let your heart begrudge
it, for by merit of this the Lord your God will grant you blessing in all
11 your work and all your hands' endeavors. There will never cease to be poor
people in the land. And so I command you: open your hand generously to
your kinsmen, your poor and needy, who share your land.

12 "If a fellow Hebrew, man or woman, is sold to you, he or she shall work for
13 you for six years; in the seventh year you shall send him or her forth free. And
14 when you send one forth free, do not send him empty-handed. Provide for
him liberally from your flock, your threshing floor, and your winepress, giving
him a share in the things with which the Lord your God has blessed you.

15 Remember: you were a slave in Egypt and the LORD your God redeemed you;
and so I give you this command today.

16 "But if he says to you, 'I do not want to leave you' – because he loves you and
17 your household and he fares well with you, then take an awl and put it through
his ear into the door, and he will be your slave for all time; you shall do the
same with a female slave.

18 "Do not consider it a hardship when you set him free, because for six years he
has given you twice the service of a hired laborer; and the LORD your God
will bless you in all your work.

19 "Every firstborn male among your herd and flock you shall consecrate
to the LORD your God. Do not work your firstborn ox or shear your
20 firstborn sheep. You and your household shall eat them year by year in the
21 presence of the LORD your God in the place that the LORD will choose. If
the animal has a blemish, a serious blemish such as lameness or blindness,
22 you shall not sacrifice it to the LORD your God. The impure as well as the
pure among you shall eat it within your towns, as you would a gazelle or a
23 deer. Its blood, however, you must not eat. You must pour it out onto the
ground like water.

16 1 "Observe the month of Aviv[37] by offering a Passover sacrifice to the LORD
your God; for in the month of Aviv the LORD your God brought you out of
2 Egypt by night.[38] You shall offer up the Passover sacrifice to the LORD your
God, from the flock and the herd, at the place that the LORD will choose as
3 a dwelling for His name. You must not eat anything leavened with it. For
seven days, eat unleavened bread – the bread of affliction – because you
left Egypt in haste. This is for you to remember the day you left Egypt all
4 the days of your life. For seven days no leaven shall be found with you in all
your land. And do not let any of the meat that you sacrificed on the evening
5 of the first day remain until morning. You may not slaughter the Passover
6 sacrifice in any of the towns that the LORD your God is giving you. Only
at the place that the LORD your God chooses as a dwelling for His name,
there shall you slaughter the Passover sacrifice in the evening;[39] at sunset,[40]
7 at the time appointed to leave Egypt, you shall cook and eat it at the place
that the LORD your God will choose, and on the following morning you
8 may set out to your tents. For six days you shall eat unleavened bread and,
on the seventh day, you shall hold an assembly for the LORD your God
and perform no work.

9 "You shall count seven weeks. At the time when you first put sickle to

37 | See note on Exodus 13:14.

38 | According to Exodus 12:29–42, the Israelites began to leave Egypt at night.

39 | See Exodus 12:33–34.

40 | As traditionally understood, the sacrifice is slaughtered before sunset and consumed after sunset; cf. Exodus 12:6–8.

10 standing grain, begin your count of seven weeks. And then celebrate the
Festival of Weeks to the Lord your God, bringing a freewill offering,
tribute proportionate to the blessing the Lord your God has granted you.
11 And rejoice before the Lord your God – you and your sons and daughters,
your male and female slaves, and the Levites living in your towns, together
with the migrants, orphans, and widows among you – at the place that
12 the Lord your God will choose as a dwelling for His name. Remember
that you were a slave in Egypt, and so take care to fulfill these decrees.

13 "You shall keep the Festival of Tabernacles for seven days, after you have
14 gathered the produce from your threshing floor and winepress. Rejoice
in your festival, you and your sons and daughters; your male and female
servants; the Levites; and the migrants, orphans, and widows living in
15 your towns. For seven days, celebrate before the Lord your God at the
place that the Lord will choose, for the Lord your God will grant you
blessing in all your harvest and in all the work of your hands, and you shall
be wholly joyful.

16 "Three times a year, all the males among you shall appear before the Lord
your God in the place that He will choose: on the Festival of Unleavened
Bread, the Festival of Weeks, and the Festival of Tabernacles. They shall not
17 appear before the Lord empty-handed; each shall bring a gift, in keeping
with the blessing that the Lord your God has given you.

SHOFETIM 18 "Appoint judges and officials for your tribes in all the towns that the Lord
19 your God is giving you, to govern the people with equitable justice. Do
not pervert justice or show partiality. Do not take bribes, for bribes blind
20 the eyes of the wise and subvert the cause of the just. Pursue justice, only
justice, so that you may live and possess the land that the Lord your God
is giving you.

21 "Do not plant a sacred tree of any kind beside the altar that you make for
22 the Lord your God, and do not erect a worship pillar, for these are things
that the Lord your God hates.[41]

17 1 "Do not sacrifice an ox or a sheep that has any blemish, any serious
defect, to the Lord your God, for that to the Lord your God would be
abhorrent.

2 "If a man or woman living among you in one of the towns the Lord your
God is giving you is found doing what is evil in the Lord your God's eyes,
3 breaking His covenant by going off to serve or bow to other gods – the
4 sun or moon or any of the heavenly host, which I have forbidden – if
you have been told of this or have heard about it, then you must make
thorough inquiry. If it is true and is confirmed that this abhorrent deed
5 has been done in Israel, then you shall take the man or woman who has

41 | See 7:5 and the note there.

done this evil act out to the town gates and stone that man or that woman
6 to death. The accused shall be put to death only on the testimony of two
or three witnesses; no one shall be put to death on the evidence of one
7 witness alone. The hand of the witnesses shall be the first against him to
kill him, and after theirs, the hand of all the people. You must purge the
evil from your midst.

8 "If a case is beyond your judgment, be it a conflict over bloodshed, over
civil claims or over injury – any dispute in your town courts – then you
9 shall go up to the place that the LORD your God will choose. There you
shall approach the Levitical priests or the judge who is in office at that
10 time. Inquire of them and they will give you the verdict. You must act in
accordance with the ruling they give you from the place that the LORD
11 will choose, taking care to do exactly as they instruct you. You shall act in
accord with the Law as they interpret it for you and the judgment as they
tell you, not deviating from their declaration to the right or to the left.
12 Should anyone act in wickedness, refusing to listen to the priest appointed
to minister there to the LORD your God, or the judge, that person shall be
13 put to death. You must purge the evil from Israel. All the people will hear
and fear and will not act in such wickedness again.

14 "When you enter the land that the LORD your God is giving you, and have
taken possession of it and settled in it, should you say, 'I will set a king
15 over me, like all the surrounding nations,' set over you a king whom the
LORD your God chooses. The king you set over you must be one of your
own people. You may not set a foreigner over you, who is not your brother.
16 Further, he must not acquire many horses for himself, he must not make
the people return to Egypt to acquire more horses, since the LORD has told
17 you: You must not go back that way again. He must not accumulate wives
and let his heart be led astray, nor should he amass large amounts of silver
18 and gold. As he presides upon his royal throne, he must inscribe a copy of
this Law for himself upon a scroll in the presence of the Levitical priests.
19 It must always be with him, and he shall read from it all the days of his
life, so that he may learn to revere the LORD his God, taking care to keep
20 all the words of this commandment and these decrees, not considering
himself superior to his people, or straying from the commandments to
the right or to the left. Then he and his descendants will reign long in the
midst of Israel.

18 1 "The Levitical priests, the whole tribe of Levi, will have no share or
inheritance with Israel. They will eat the LORD's fire offerings as their
2 inheritance, but will have no inheritance among their kinsfolk. The LORD
is their inheritance, as He has promised them.

3 "This shall be the priests' due from the people: those offering a sacrifice – an
ox or a sheep – shall give to the priest the shoulder, the cheeks, and the
4 stomach. You shall give him the first yield of your grain, wine, and oil, and

5 the first wool from the shearing of your sheep. For the Lord your God
has chosen him out of all your tribes to stand and minister in the name of
the Lord – him and his sons for all time.

6 "If a Levite leaves any of your towns throughout Israel where he has been
living, and comes to the place that the Lord will choose – he may do so
7 whenever he wishes – then he may minister in the name of the Lord his
God, alongside any of his brother Levites who serve there before the Lord.
8 They shall have equal portions to eat, regardless of income they may have
from the sale of family possessions.

9 "When you come into the land that the Lord your God is giving you,
do not learn to partake in the abhorrent practices those nations carry
10 out. Let no one be found among you who makes a son or daughter pass
through fire,[42] or who casts spells, or is an augur or diviner or soothsayer,
11 or who practices sorcery, or consults ghosts or spirits, or seeks oracles
12 from the dead. For anyone who does these things is abhorrent to the
Lord; it is because of such abhorrent acts that the Lord your God is
13 driving them out before you. You must be wholly loyal to the Lord your
14 God. The nations that you are driving out listen to augurs and to those
who cast spells. But as for you – the Lord your God does not permit
you these.

15 "The Lord your God will raise up another prophet like me from among
16 your own people. To him you must listen. For this is what you asked of the
Lord your God at Ḥorev on the day of the assembly when you said: 'If I
hear the voice of the Lord my God any more, or continue to see this great
17 18 fire, I will die.' The Lord said to me: They have spoken well. I will raise up
for them a prophet like you from among their own people. I will put My
words in the prophet's mouth and he will tell them all that I command.
19 Anyone who does not listen to My words that he speaks in My name, I
20 Myself will call him to account. But a prophet who acts in wickedness,
speaking anything I have not commanded in My name, or speaking in
21 the name of other gods – that prophet shall die. You may say to yourself,
22 'How can we recognize a message that the Lord has not spoken?' If what
a prophet proclaims in the name of the Lord does not take place or come
true, that is a message that the Lord has not spoken. The prophet has
proclaimed it in wickedness. Do not be afraid of him.

19 1 "When the Lord your God has cut down the nations whose land the Lord
your God is giving you, and you have driven them out and are living in
2 their towns and in their houses, you shall set aside three cities in that land
3 that the Lord your God gives you to possess. Determine the distances
and divide the land that the Lord your God is giving you as a heritage

42 | This is traditionally equated with Molekh worship; see Leviticus 18:21 and the note there.

into three equal parts – so that any manslayer will be able to flee to one
of these cities.[43]

4 "This is the rule for a manslayer who may flee to one of these and live: it is
one who has killed another person unintentionally, without prior hatred.
5 For instance, a man may go into the forest with a neighbor to cut wood,
and as he swings the ax to cut down a tree, the ax-head may fly off the
handle and strike the neighbor and kill him; that man may flee to one of
6 these cities and live. Should the distance be too great, the avenger of blood[44]
might pursue him in hot anger, overtake, and kill him even though he did
not deserve to die, there having been no prior enmity between the two.
7 That is why I charge you thus: three cities must you set aside.

8 "If the LORD your God enlarges your territory, as He swore to your
ancestors, and gives you all of that land that He promised to give your
9 ancestors,[45] if you vigilantly observe all of this commandment with which
I charge you today, loving the LORD your God and walking in all His ways,
10 then you shall add to these three, three cities more so that innocent blood
is not shed, bringing bloodguilt upon you, in the land that the LORD your
God is giving you as a possession.

11 "But if one person hates his fellow, lies in wait for him, and attacks and kills
12 him, and then flees to one of these cities, the elders of his town shall have
him brought back from there and handed over to the avenger of blood to
13 die. Show him no pity. You must purge the guilt of innocent blood from
Israel, so that it may be well for you.

14 "Do not move back your neighbor's boundary marker, set up by those long
ago in the allotted land that the LORD your God is giving you to possess.

15 "One witness alone is not enough to convict a person of any crime or
wrongdoing. A case is to be established only on the evidence of two or
16 three witnesses. If a corrupt witness comes forward to accuse someone
17 of wrongdoing, both parties to the dispute shall appear before the LORD,
18 before the priests and judges in office in that time. The judges shall make a
thorough investigation. If the man who testified proves to be a false witness,
19 having testified falsely against his fellow, then inflict upon the false witness
what the false witness had intended to inflict upon his fellow; you must
20 purge the evil from your midst. Others will hear and fear, and such an evil
21 will not be committed again in your midst. Show no pity: life for life, eye
for eye, tooth for tooth, hand for hand, foot for foot.[46]

20 1 "When you go out to battle your enemies, and see horses and chariots,
an army greater than yours, do not be afraid of them; for the LORD your

43 | Three parallel cities east of the Jordan had already been designated by Moshe in 4:41–43.

44 | That is, the victim's vengeful relative.

45 | See the expansive borders promised to Avraham in Genesis 15:18.

46 | See notes on Exodus 21:23 and Leviticus 24:19–20.

2 God, who brought you out of Egypt, He will be with you. Before you
3 engage in battle, the priest shall come forward and address the men. 'Listen,
Israel,' he shall say to them, 'this day you are going into battle against your
4 enemies. Do not lose heart or be afraid, do not panic or dread them; for
it is the LORD your God who goes with you, to fight against your enemies
for you, to bring you victory.'

5 "Then the officers shall address the men: 'Is there a man here who has built
a new house but not yet dedicated it? Let him go back home, or he may
6 die in battle and someone else will dedicate it. Is there a man here who
has planted a vineyard but not yet harvested it? Let him go back home,
7 or he may die in the battle and someone else will harvest it. Is there a
man here who has betrothed a woman but not yet married her? Let him
go back home, or he may die in battle and someone else will marry her.'
8 And further, 'Is there a man here,' the officers shall say to the men, 'who
is afraid or fainthearted? Let him go back home so that his comrades do
9 not become fainthearted along with him.' When the officers have finished
addressing the men, they shall appoint the commanders to lead them.

10 11 "When you approach a town to fight against it, first offer it peace. If it
accepts your terms of peace and lets you in, all the people found there
12 shall serve you a tribute of forced labor. If it rejects your peace offer and
13 wages war against you, you shall lay siege. When the LORD your God gives
14 it over into your hands, you shall put all its males to the sword. You may,
however, take as your plunder the women, children, livestock, and all else
in the town, all its spoil; you may use the spoil of your enemies, which
15 the LORD your God has given you. This is how you are to treat all the
towns that are distant from you and do not belong to the nations nearby.
16 However, in the towns of the nations that the LORD your God is giving
17 you as an inheritance, let nothing that breathes remain alive. These, the
Hittites and Amorites, Canaanites and Perizzites, Hivites and Jebusites,
18 you must utterly destroy as the LORD your God has commanded you, so
that they cannot teach you to do all the abhorrent things that they do for
their gods, causing you to sin against your God, the LORD.

19 "When you lay siege to a town and wage war against it for a long time to
capture it, do not destroy its trees; do not wield an ax against them. You
may eat from them; you must not cut them down. Are trees of the field
20 human beings that you should besiege them too? Only trees that you know
do not produce food may you cut down for use building siege works until
the town that has made war against you falls.

21 1 "If a person is found lying slain in a field on the land that the LORD your
2 God is giving you to possess, and it is not known who killed him, your
elders and judges must go out and measure the distances from the slain
3 person to each of the surrounding towns. The elders of the town nearest
the body shall take a female calf that has never been worked or drawn a
4 load with a yoke, and lead it to a valley with a flowing stream that has not

been plowed or planted, and there in the valley the elders of that town shall
5 break the calf's neck. The priests, sons of Levi, shall step forward, for it is
them the LORD your God has chosen to minister to Him, to give blessing
6 in the LORD's name, and to decide all cases of dispute and assault. Then
all the elders of the town nearest the slain person shall wash their hands
7 over the calf whose neck was broken in the valley and declare: 'Our hands
8 did not shed this blood[47] and our eyes did not witness it. Absolve Your
people Israel, whom You redeemed, LORD, and do not leave the guilt of
innocent blood among Your people Israel.' So shall atonement be made
9 for the bloodshed, and so will you purge the guilt of innocent blood from
yourselves, by doing what is right in the LORD's eyes.

10 "When you wage war against your enemies, and the LORD your God gives KI TETZEH
11 them into your hand and you take captives, if you see a beautiful woman
12 among the captives, and you desire her and wish to marry her, bring her
13 to your house. Have her shave her head, pare her nails, and remove her
captive's garb. She shall sit in your house mourning for her father and
mother for a full month. Only after that may you go in to her and be her
14 husband, and she shall be your wife. But if you no longer desire her, you
must let her go free. You may not sell her for money or treat her as a slave,
since you have dishonored her.

15 "If a man has two wives, and loves one but not the other, and if both the
loved and the unloved bear him sons, but the firstborn is the son of the
16 one unloved, then on the day he bequeaths his possessions to his sons, he
may not give the rights of the firstborn to the son of the loved in preference
17 to the son of the unloved, the true firstborn. He must acknowledge the
son of his unloved wife as the firstborn, giving him a double portion of all
that he has. He is the first fruit of his manhood; the right of the firstborn
belongs to him.

18 "If a man has a wayward and rebellious son who does not listen to his father
19 and mother and, though they discipline him, still will not listen, his father
and his mother shall take hold of him and bring him out to the elders at the
20 town gate. They shall say to the town elders, 'This son of ours is wayward
and rebellious. He does not listen to us. He is a glutton and a drunkard.'
21 Then all the men of the town shall stone him to death. Thus you shall purge
the evil from your midst, and all Israel will hear, and be afraid.[48]

22 "When someone is convicted of a capital crime and is executed and you
23 hang him from a post, do not let his corpse remain all night upon that post.
You must bury him that same day, because a man left hanging is a slur upon
God, and you must not defile the land that the LORD your God is giving
you as your possession.

---

47 | Meaning the blood of the slain individual.

48 | As with other death sentences in the Torah, the Sages listed numerous qualifications, leading to the opinion that this case and the one above in 13:13–19 "never happened and never will" (Sanhedrin 71a).

22 1 "If you see your kinsman's ox or sheep straying away, do not ignore it; you
2 must return it to its owner. If the owner does not live nearby or you do
not know who the owner is, you must bring it home with you and keep it
3 until the owner claims it; then you must return it. You must do the same
with his donkey, the same with his garment, the same with anything your
kinsman loses and you find. You cannot ignore it.

4 "You shall not see your kinsman's donkey or ox fallen on the road and
ignore it. Help him to lift it.

5 "Men's clothing shall not be seen on a woman, nor shall a man wear
women's dress. Whoever does such things is abhorrent to the LORD your
God.

6 "If you come across a bird's nest containing fledglings or eggs by the
roadside, in a tree, or on the ground, and the mother is sitting on the
7 fledglings or the eggs, do not take the mother with the young. Let the
mother go; only then may you take the young, so that it may be well for
you and you may live long.

8 "When you build a new house, erect a parapet for your roof. Otherwise
you may bring bloodguilt on your house should anyone fall from it.

9 "Do not sow your vineyard with a second kind of seed,[49] or the whole
yield – both the crop you have sown and the yield of the vineyard – will
have to be forfeited.

10 "Do not plow with an ox and a donkey yoked together.

11 "Do not wear clothes made of wool and linen woven together.

12 "Make tassels on the four corners of the garment with which you cover
yourself.

13 14 "If a man takes a wife and, after sleeping with her, he dislikes her, and he
makes up charges against her, sullying her name, saying, 'I married this
15 woman, but when I lay with her, I did not find her to be a virgin,' the girl's
father and mother shall produce the evidence of the girl's virginity before
16 the town elders at the gate. The girl's father shall say to the elders: 'I gave
17 my daughter in marriage to this man but he dislikes her. Now he has made
up charges against her, saying, "I did not find your daughter to be a virgin."
But here is the evidence of my daughter's virginity.' They shall spread out
18 the cloth before the town elders.[50] And then the town elders shall take the
19 man and flog him. They shall fine him one hundred shekel of silver, and
give it to the girl's father, because he has sullied the name of an Israelite
virgin. She shall remain his wife; he does not have the choice to divorce
her as long as he lives.

---

49 | That is, apart from the grape seed.

50 | Tradition assigns a metaphorical meaning to this formulation.

20 "If, however, the charge is true, no evidence being found that the girl was
21 a virgin, then the girl shall be brought to the entrance of her father's house
and the men of her town shall stone her to death, for she committed an
outrage in Israel by acting immorally while in her father's house. You shall
purge the evil from your midst.

22 "If a man is caught lying with the wife of another, both shall die, the man
and the woman with whom he lay. You shall purge the evil from Israel.

23 "If a virgin is betrothed to be married, and a man encounters her within
24 a town and lies with her, you shall bring them both to the town gate and
stone them to death, the girl because she did not cry for help in the town,
and the man because he violated the wife of his fellow. You shall purge the
evil from your midst.

25 "But if the man encounters the betrothed woman in the open country,
26 forces her and lies with her, only the man who did this shall die. You shall
do nothing to the girl; she did not commit the capital offense. Just as one
27 man at times attacks and murders his fellow man, so too here; he came
upon her in open country. The betrothed woman may have cried out for
help, but no one was there to rescue her.

28 "If a man encounters a virgin who is not betrothed and rapes her, and they
29 are caught in the act, the man who lay with her shall pay the girl's father
fifty shekel of silver, and she shall become his wife. Because he violated her
he does not have the choice to divorce her as long as he lives.

23 1 "A man cannot marry his father's wife; he must not dishonor his father's
bed.

2 "No one whose testicles have been crushed or whose member is severed
shall be admitted to the congregation of the LORD.[51]

3 "No one born of an illicit union[52] shall be admitted to the congregation of the
LORD; even to the tenth generation, no descendant of such a union may be
admitted to the congregation of the LORD.

4 "No Amonite or Moabite shall be admitted to the congregation of the LORD;
even to the tenth generation, none of their descendants shall be admitted to
5 the congregation of the LORD, for they would not greet you with food and
water on your way when you came out of Egypt; and in hostility against you
they hired Bilam son of Beor from Petor of Aram Naharayim to curse you.[53]
6 But the LORD your God chose not to listen to Bilam; the LORD your God
turned the curse into a blessing for you, because the LORD your God loves
7 you. Do not seek their ease or welfare as long as you live.

8 "Do not despise an Edomite, for he is your kin. Do not despise an Egyptian,

51 | That is, such people may not marry an Israelite.

52 | According to tradition, an adulterous or incestuous relationship.

53 | See Numbers, chapters 22–24.

9 for you lived as a stranger in his land. Children born to them may be admitted,
in the third generation, to the congregation of the Lord.

10 "When you are encamped against your enemies, guard against any impropriety.
11 If one of the men becomes impure because of a nocturnal emission, he shall
12 go outside the camp and not reenter it. As evening approaches, he shall bathe
in water, and at sunset he may reenter the camp.

13 "You must designate an area outside the camp where you may relieve yourself.
14 Among your gear you shall have a trowel. When you relieve yourself outside,
15 you shall dig a hole with it and cover up your excrement. The Lord your
God travels with your camp, to protect you and to deliver your enemies to
you. Therefore your camp must be holy; He must not find any indecent thing
among you and turn away from you.

16 "If a slave seeks refuge with you from his master, do not hand him back to his
17 master. He shall live with you in the place he chooses, in whichever of your
towns he likes. Do not ill-treat him.

18 "No woman of Israel shall be a cult prostitute;[54] no man of Israel shall be a
19 male cult prostitute. Do not bring wages of prostitution or the payment for a
dog[55] into the house of the Lord your God in fulfillment of any vow, for both
are abhorrent to the Lord your God.

20 "Do not charge interest on loans to your kinsmen, whether on money or
21 food or anything that could earn interest. You may charge interest on loans
to a foreigner, but on loans to your kinsmen do not charge, so that the Lord
your God may bless you in all your endeavors in the land you are entering to
possess.

22 "When you make a vow to the Lord your God, do not delay in fulfilling it, for
23 the Lord your God will certainly require it of you; you will incur guilt. But
24 if you refrain from vowing you will not incur guilt. Whatever your lips utter,
take care to do, since you have voluntarily vowed to the Lord your God, with
your own mouth.

25 "When you enter your neighbor's vineyard,[56] you may eat as many grapes as
you wish; eat your fill, but do not put any in a container.

26 "When you enter your neighbor's field of standing grain, you may pluck ears
with your hand, but you may not put a sickle to your neighbor's grain.

24 1 "If a man takes a wife and becomes her husband, but begins to dislike her
because he finds something indecent in her; if he writes her a bill of divorce,
2 puts it in her hand, and sends her from his house, she may leave his house
3 and become another man's wife. However, if the second husband rejects her,
writes her a bill of divorce, puts it in her hand, and sends her from his house,

54 | Referring to a prostitute at a place of worship.

55 | "Dog" may refer to a male prostitute.

56 | According to tradition, this refers to a laborer employed in the field.

4 or the second husband dies, her first husband, who sent her away, is not
permitted to take her again to be his wife after she has been defiled,[57] for that
would be abhorrent to the LORD, and you must not bring sin into the land
that the LORD your God is giving you for your possession.

5 "When a man is newly married, he shall not go out with the army or have any
related duty laid on him. He shall be exempt for one year, to be with his home
and bring happiness to the woman he has married.

6 "Do not take an upper or lower millstone as security for a debt, for that would
be taking a person's livelihood as security.

7 "If someone is found to have kidnapped another Israelite, enslaving or
selling him, the kidnapper shall die. You must purge the evil from your
midst.

8 "Take great care in cases of impure blight. Carefully do whatever the Levitical
9 priests instruct you, as I have commanded them. Remember what the LORD
your God did to Miriam on your way when you left Egypt.[58]

10 "When you make your neighbor a loan of any kind, do not go into his house
11 to take his pledge. Wait outside while the person to whom you are making
12 the loan brings the pledge out to you. If the person is poor, do not go to sleep
13 with the pledge in your possession. You must return his pledge by sunset, so
that he may sleep in his cloak[59] and bless you. This will be accounted to you
as a righteous act before the LORD your God.

14 "Do not take advantage of a poor and destitute laborer, whether he is a
15 kinsman or a migrant living in one of the towns in your land. Pay him his
wages on the same day, before sunset, because he is poor and his livelihood
depends on it. Otherwise he will cry out to the LORD against you, and you
will bear your guilt.

16 "Parents shall not be put to death for their children, nor shall children be put to
death for their parents. A person shall be put to death only for his own sin.

17 "Do not deprive a migrant or an orphan of justice. Do not take a widow's
18 garment as a pledge. Remember that you were a slave in Egypt and the LORD
your God redeemed you from there. And so I command you in this.

19 "When you reap the harvest in your field and forget a sheaf in the field, do not
go back to get it. Leave it for the migrant, the orphan, and the widow, so that
the LORD your God may grant you blessing in all the work of your hands.

20 "When you beat the fruit from your olive trees, do not go over them again.
Leave what remains for the migrant, the orphan, and the widow.

---

57 | That is, the second relationship makes a return to her first husband improper. The word "defiled" does not imply any indecency inherent in the second marriage.

58 | See Numbers, chapter 12.

59 | The pledge in question is evidently a garment worn at night; cf. Exodus 22:24–26.

21 "When you gather the grapes of your vineyard, do not go over the vines
again. Leave what remains for the migrant, the orphan, and the widow.
22 Remember that you were a slave in the land of Egypt. And so I command
you in this.

25 1 "When two people have a dispute they shall go to the court of justice
and the judges shall decide between them, acquitting the innocent and
2 condemning the guilty. If the guilty person is to be flogged, the judge shall
make him lie down and have him flogged there in his presence with the
3 requisite number of lashes. He may be given as many as forty lashes but
no more; if he is given more lashes than this, an excessive flogging, your
kinsman will be degraded in your eyes.

4 "Do not muzzle an ox while it is treading out the grain.

5 "When brothers live together, and one of them dies without a son, his
widow shall not be married to a stranger outside the family. Her husband's
brother shall come to her and take her in marriage, fulfilling the duty of
6 a brother-in-law. The firstborn son whom she bears will perpetuate the
7 name of the dead brother, so that his name is not erased from Israel. But
if the man does not wish to marry his brother's widow, she shall go up to
the elders at the gate and say, 'My husband's brother refuses to perpetuate
his brother's name in Israel. He does not care to perform the duty of a
8 brother-in-law for me.' The elders of the town shall summon him and
they must talk to him. If he persists in saying, 'I have no desire to marry
9 her,' then his brother's widow shall go up to him in the presence of the
elders, pull the sandal from his foot, spit in his face, and say, 'This is what
10 is done to the man who will not build up his brother's house.' Throughout
Israel his family shall be known as 'the house of the one whose sandal was
pulled off.'

11 "If two men fight, and the wife of one comes to defend her husband from
the one who does him harm by reaching out and seizing the man's genitals,
12 you shall cut off her hand: show no pity.[60]

13 "Do not have two different weights in your bag, one large and the other
14 small. Do not have in your house two different measures, one large and
15 other small. You must have a full and honest weight and a full and honest
measure, so that your days may be long on the land that the Lord your
16 God is giving you. Whoever does such things, whoever acts dishonestly,
is abhorrent to the Lord your God.

17 18 "Remember what Amalek did to you on your way as you left Egypt,[61] how
he attacked you on the way, when you were tired and exhausted, striking
19 down all the stragglers in your rear, with no fear of God. And so, when
the Lord your God gives you rest from all the enemies around you in the

60 | According to rabbinic interpretation, the actual punishment is monetary.

61 | See Exodus 17:8–16.

land that the LORD your God is giving you as an inheritance to possess,
you shall blot out the memory of Amalek from beneath the sky. Do not
forget.

26 1 "When you have come into the land that the LORD your God is giving you KI TAVO
2 as a possession, and have taken possession and settled in it, you shall take
some of every first fruit of the soil, which you harvest from the land that
the LORD your God is giving you. Put it in a basket and go to the place that
3 the LORD your God will choose as a dwelling for His name. You shall go
to the priest officiating at that time and say to him, 'I declare today to the
LORD your God that I have come into the land that the LORD swore to our
4 ancestors to give us.' The priest shall take the basket from your hand and
5 set it down before the altar of the LORD your God. You shall then make
this declaration before the LORD your God:

"'My ancestor was a wandering Aramean.[62] He went down into Egypt and
lived there as a stranger, just a handful of souls, and there he became a
6 nation – large, mighty, and great. And the Egyptians dealt cruelly with
7 us and oppressed us, subjecting us to harsh labor. We cried out to the
LORD, God of our ancestors. And the LORD heard our voice and He saw
8 our oppression, our toil, and our enslavement. The LORD brought us out
of Egypt with a mighty hand and His arm stretched forth, with terrifying
9 power, with signs, and with wonders. He brought us into this place and
10 He gave us this land, a land flowing with milk and with honey. And now
I am bringing the first fruit of the land that You, O LORD, have given me.'
Set the basket down before the LORD your God, and then bow down low
11 before the LORD your God. Then you, with the Levites and the migrants
who live among you, shall rejoice in all the good that the LORD your God
has bestowed on you and on your household.

12 "When you have finished setting aside a tenth of all your produce in the
third year, the year of the tithe,[63] and have given it to the Levites, the
migrants, the orphans, and the widows, so that they may eat in your towns
13 and be satisfied, you shall declare before the LORD your God:

"'I have removed the consecrated portion from my house, and I have given
it to the Levites and the migrants, the orphans, and the widows, just as
You commanded me. I have not transgressed or forgotten any of Your
14 commandments. I have not eaten of it while in mourning. I have not
removed any of it while impure. I have not offered any of it to the dead. I
15 have obeyed the LORD my God, doing just as You commanded me. Look
down from Your holy habitation, from heaven, and bless Your people Israel
and the land that You have given us, as You swore to our ancestors – a land
flowing with milk and with honey.'

62 | Apparently a reference to Yaakov, whose mother Rivka was Aramean and who lived for a time in Aram (Gen. 27:41–28:5).

63 | See 14:28–29.

16 "The Lord your God is commanding you this day to keep these decrees
and laws. Take care to keep them with all your heart and with all your soul.
17 Today you have proclaimed the Lord to be your God, and that you will
walk in His ways, keep His decrees, commandments, and laws, and listen to
18 His voice. And today the Lord has proclaimed you to be, as He promised
19 you, His treasured people who guard His commands; He will set you high
above all the nations He has made, in praise, fame, and honor. You will be
a people holy to the Lord your God, just as He has promised."

27 1 Then Moshe and the elders of Israel charged the people: "Keep all of the
2 command that I charge you with this day. On the day that you cross the
Jordan to the land that the Lord your God is giving you, set up large
3 boulders, and coat them with plaster, and write on them all the words of
this Law when you cross over, that you may enter the land that the Lord
your God is giving you, a land flowing with milk and with honey, as the
4 Lord, God of your ancestors, promised you. When you cross the Jordan,
set up these stones, as I command you today, on Mount Eival,[64] and coat
5 them with plaster. And there, build an altar to the Lord your God, an altar
6 of stones. Do not take any iron tool to them: of uncut stones[65] you shall
build the altar of the Lord your God. On it, offer burnt offerings to the
7 Lord your God. You shall also sacrifice peace offerings and eat them there,
8 rejoicing before the Lord your God. On the boulders you shall write very
clearly all the words of this Law."

9 Then Moshe and the Levitical priests spoke to all Israel: "Be still and
listen, Israel. Today you have become the people of the Lord your God.
10 Therefore listen to the Lord your God, keeping His commandments and
decrees, with which I charge you on this day."

11 12 On that day Moshe charged the people: "When you have crossed the
Jordan, these shall stand on Mount Gerizim to bless the people: Shimon,
13 Levi, Yehuda, Yissakhar, Yosef, and Binyamin. And these shall stand on
Mount Eival for the curse: Reuven, Gad, Asher, Zevulun, Dan, and Naftali.
14 The Levites shall then recite to all the Israelites in a loud voice:

15 "'Cursed be one who makes a graven or molten image, abhorrent to the
Lord, the work of a craftsman, and secretly sets it up.'
And all the people shall respond and say, 'Amen!'
16 'Cursed be one who degrades his father or mother.'
And all the people shall say, 'Amen!'
17 'Cursed be one who moves back his neighbor's boundary marker.'
And all the people shall say, 'Amen!'
18 'Cursed be one who leads a blind person astray along his way.'
And all the people shall say, 'Amen!'

64 | See Joshua 8:30–35.
65 | Cf. Exodus 20:22.

19 'Cursed be one who deprives the migrant, orphan, or widow of justice.'
And all the people shall say, 'Amen!'
20 'Cursed be one who lies with his father's wife, dishonoring his father's bed.'
And all the people shall say, 'Amen!'
21 'Cursed be one who lies with any animal.'
And all the people shall say, 'Amen!'
22 'Cursed be anyone who lies with his sister, whether she is the daughter of
his father or of his mother.'
And all the people shall say, 'Amen!'
23 'Cursed be one who lies with his mother-in-law.'
And all the people shall say, 'Amen!'
24 'Cursed be one who strikes down his fellow in secret.'
And all the people shall say, 'Amen!'
25 'Cursed be one who accepts a bribe to execute an innocent man.'
And all the people shall say, 'Amen!'
26 'Cursed be one who does not uphold the words of this Law by keeping
them.'
And all the people shall say, 'Amen!'

28 1 "If you listen faithfully to the LORD your God, taking care to keep all His
commandments, which I am commanding you today, the LORD your God
2 will set you above all the nations of this earth. All these blessings will come
upon you – overtake you – if you listen to the voice of the LORD your God:

3 "Blessed shall you be in the town,
and blessed shall you be in the field.
4 Blessed shall be the fruit of your womb,
the fruit of your land, and the fruit of your cattle,
the calves of your herd,
the lambs of your flock.
5 Blessed shall be your basket
and your kneading pan.
6 Blessed shall you be when you enter,
and blessed shall you be when you leave.

7 "The LORD will cause your enemies who rise against you to be vanquished
before you. They will come at you from one direction, but flee from you
in seven.

8 "The LORD will send you blessing in your barns and in all your endeavors.
9 He will bless you in the land that the LORD your God is giving you. The
LORD will establish you as His holy people, just as He has sworn to you, if
10 you keep the LORD your God's commandments and walk in His ways. All
the peoples of earth shall see that you are called by the LORD's name, and
11 they shall hold you in awe. The LORD will make you abound in prosperity,
in the fruit of your womb, the fruit of your cattle, and the fruit of your soil
in the land that the LORD swore to your ancestors to give you.

12 "The Lord will open for you His treasury of good, the heavens, to give
your land rain in its season, to bless all the work of your hands. You will
13 lend to many nations, and borrow from none. The Lord will make you
the head, never the tail. You shall be always above, and never beneath – if
you obey the commandments of the Lord your God that I am charging
14 you with on this day, taking care to keep them, and if you do not stray from
any of the words that I am commanding you today, either to the right or
to the left, to follow other gods and serve them.

15 "But if you do not listen to the voice of the Lord your God, taking care to
keep all His commandments and decrees that I am charging you with on
this day, all these curses will come upon you and overtake you:

16 "Cursed shall you be in the town,
and cursed shall you be in the field.
17 Cursed shall be your basket
and your kneading pan.
18 Cursed shall be the fruit of your womb,
the fruit of your land,
the calves of your herd,
the lambs of your flock.
19 Cursed shall you be when you enter,
and cursed shall you be when you leave.

20 "The Lord will send upon you curse, panic, and thwarting in every
endeavor you undertake, until you are destroyed and come to sudden
21 ruin because of the evil you have done in forsaking Me. The Lord will
make disease cling to you until it consumes you entirely in the land you
22 are coming into to possess. The Lord will afflict you with consumption,
fever, inflammation, scorching heat and drought, blight and mildew. They
23 will pursue you until you die. The sky over your head will be like bronze,
24 and the earth beneath you iron.[66] The Lord will turn the rain of your
land into powder and dust. It will descend upon you from the sky until
you are destroyed.

25 "The Lord will cause you to be vanquished before your enemies. You will
come at them from one direction but flee before them in seven. You will be
26 an object of horror to all the kingdoms on earth. Your corpses will be food
for all the birds of the sky, for the beasts of the earth; there will be no one
27 to make them afraid. The Lord will afflict you with the boils of Egypt,[67]
with hemorrhoids, rashes, and scabs, from which you shall never recover.
28 29 The Lord will afflict you with insanity, blindness, confusion of mind. You
will grope at noon as a blind man gropes in darkness. Your way will not
prosper. Day after day, you will be abused and looted, and no one will be
30 there to rescue you. You will betroth a woman and some other man will

66 | That is, the sky will not give rain, and the earth will not yield produce.

67 | See Exodus 9:9–10.

lie with her. You will build a house, but will not live there. You will plant a
31 vineyard, but not harvest its fruit. Your ox will be slaughtered before your
eyes, but you will not eat of it. Your donkey will be stolen in front of you,
and never return. Your sheep will be given to your enemies, and no one
32 will be there to rescue you. Your sons and daughters will be given over to
another people. You will see it with your own eyes and pine for them all
33 through the day but have no power to act. A people that you do not know
will eat the fruit of your land and of your labor. You will be incessantly
34 abused and crushed. The sights you see will drive you to insanity. The
35 LORD will strike your knees and thighs with incurable infection, spreading
from the sole of your foot to the crown of your head.

36 "The LORD will bring you and the king you set over you to a nation that
neither you nor your ancestors have known. There you will worship other
37 gods, of wood and of stone. You will become an object of horror, a proverb,
and a byword among all the peoples into whose midst the LORD will lead
you.

38 "You will carry much seed into the field but gather little, because locusts
39 will eat it. You will plant vineyards and cultivate them, but you will not
drink the wine or gather the grapes, because worms will devour them.
40 You will have olive trees throughout your country, but you will have no
41 oil for anointing, because the olives will fall away. You will bear sons and
daughters, but they will not remain yours, for they will be taken into
42 captivity. Crickets will take over all your trees and the fruit of your land.
43 Strangers in your midst will rise ever higher above you, while you descend
44 ever further beneath. They will lend to you but you will be unable to lend
to them. They will be the head and you will be the tail.

45 "All these curses will come upon you; they will pursue and overtake you,
until you are destroyed – because you did not listen to the voice of the
LORD your God, keeping the commandments and decrees with which He
46 charged you. They will be a sign and portent to you and your descendants
forever.

47 "Because you did not serve the LORD your God with joy and with a heart
48 content in the abundance of all things, you shall serve the enemies whom
the LORD will send against you, in hunger and thirst, in nakedness and
the lack of all things. He will lay an iron yoke upon your neck until He has
49 destroyed you. The LORD will bring against you a nation from afar, from
the end of the earth, and it will dart down on you like an eagle; a nation
50 whose language you do not understand, a fierce-faced nation with no
51 respect for the old, no mercy for the young. They will eat the fruit of your
cattle and the fruit of your land until you are destroyed. They will leave
you no grain, wine, or oil, no calves of your herd or lambs of your flock,
52 until they have brought you to death. They will lay siege to you in all the
towns throughout your land until the high, fortified walls in which you

placed your trust have fallen. In all your towns throughout the land the
LORD your God has given you, they will lay siege to you.

53 "And you will eat the fruit of your womb. When your enemies besiege you,
so fiercely will they crush you that you will eat the flesh of your own sons
54 and daughters whom the LORD your God has given you. Even the most
gentle and sensitive of men among you will begrudge food to his own
55 brother, his beloved wife, those of his children who survive, and give none
of them any of the flesh of his own children when he eats them, because
he has nothing else left, so fiercely will the besieging enemy crush you in
56 all your towns. The most gentle and sensitive of women among you, so
sensitive and gentle that she would not venture to set the sole of her foot
on the ground, will begrudge food to the husband she loves, and to her
57 own son and daughter, the afterbirth from her womb and the children she
bears – she will eat them in secret for lack of anything else, so fiercely will
the besieging enemy crush you in your towns.

58 "If you do not take care to keep all the words of this Law, written in this
59 scroll, to revere this glorious, awesome name, the LORD your God, then
the LORD will overwhelm you and your descendants with terrible and
60 relentless plagues, and malignant and chronic diseases. He will bring back
on you all the diseases of Egypt that you dreaded, and they will cling to
61 you. Every other sickness and plague – even those not recorded in this
scroll of the Law – the LORD will inflict upon you until you are destroyed.
62 Though you were once as numerous as the stars in the sky, you will be left
but a handful of souls, because you did not listen to the LORD your God.
63 And as the LORD once delighted in making you prosperous and numerous,
so will the LORD delight in bringing you to ruin and destruction. You will
64 be torn away from the land that you are now coming into to possess. The
LORD will scatter you among all nations, from one end of the earth to the
other, and there you will serve other gods, of wood and of stone, which
65 neither you nor your ancestors have known. Yet even among those nations
you shall find no ease, no resting place for the sole of your foot. There
the LORD will give you a trembling heart, pining eyes, and a languishing
66 spirit. Your life will hang suspended before you; you will dread both night
67 and day, never sure you will survive. In the morning you will say, "Would
that it were evening!" In the evening you will say, "Would that it were
morning!" – because of the dread in your heart that you will dread, the
68 scenes in your eyes that you will see. The LORD will send you back in ships
to Egypt, by a route that I told you that you would never see again. You
will offer yourselves to your enemies for sale as male and female slaves,
but none will buy you."

69 These are the words of the covenant that the LORD commanded Moshe to
make with the Israelites in the land of Moav, alongside the covenant that
He had made with them at Ḥorev.

29 1 Moshe summoned all Israel and said to them: "You have seen all that the
LORD did before your eyes in the land of Egypt, to Pharaoh, all his officials,
2 and all of his land. Your own eyes saw the great trials, the signs, and the
3 great wonders. But to this day the LORD has not given you a mind that
4 understands, or eyes that see, or ears that hear. For forty years I[68] brought
you through the wilderness. The clothes on your back did not wear out,
5 nor the sandals on your feet. You ate no bread and drank no wine or strong
6 drink, so that you might know that I am the LORD your God. When you
came to this place, Siḥon, king of Heshbon, and Og, king of Bashan, came
7 out to meet us in warfare, but we defeated them. We took their land and
gave it as a heritage to the Reubenites, the Gadites, and half the tribe of
8 Menashe. Therefore take great care to keep the words of this covenant, that
you may succeed in all you undertake.

NITZAVIM

9 "All of you are standing today before the LORD your God – the leaders
10 among you, the tribes, the elders and officials, all the men of Israel, the
children, the women, the strangers in your camp, from woodcutter to water
11 drawer – to enter into the covenant of the LORD your God, and the oath
12 the LORD your God is making with you today, to establish you today as
His people, that He may be your God, as He promised you and swore to
13 your ancestors, Avraham, Yitzḥak, and Yaakov. Not with you alone am I
14 making this covenant and oath; with you who are standing here with us
today before the LORD our God I make it, and with those, too, who are
not with us here today.

15 "You yourselves know what it was like when we lived in Egypt, and when
16 we passed through the nations we encountered. You saw their detestable
17 things, their abominations of wood and stone, of silver and gold. Let there
be among you no man or woman, family or tribe, whose heart turns away
from the LORD our God to serve the gods of those nations. Let there be
18 among you no root whose fruit is poison and wormwood. When such a
person hears the words of this oath, he may think himself immune, saying,
'I will be safe even if I go my own stubborn way, sweeping away the moist
19 and dry alike,'[69] but the LORD will not be willing to pardon him. Instead,
the LORD's anger and passion will smolder against him; all the curses
written in this scroll will fall on him, and the LORD will erase his name
20 from under the sky. The LORD will single him out for disaster – from all the
tribes of Israel – in line with all the curses of the covenant written in this
21 scroll of the Law. A future generation – your descendants who rise after
you, and foreigners from distant lands – will see the land's devastation and
22 the sicknesses with which the LORD has afflicted it, all its soil a burning
waste of sulfur and salt, nothing planted, nothing sprouting, no vegetation

68 | The voice now is that of God.

69 | This phrase is interpreted by traditional commentators to mean "sinning casually or lustfully."

growing on it, like the ruins of Sedom and Amora, Adma and Tzevoyim,
23 which the LORD overturned in His fierce rage.[70] All the nations will ask,
'Why did the LORD do this to the land? Why this great, blazing anger?'
24 They will say, 'It is because they abandoned the covenant of the LORD, God
of their ancestors, which He made with them when He brought them out
25 of Egypt. They went and served other gods and worshipped them, gods
26 they did not know and whom He had not allotted to them. So the LORD's
anger burned against that land, bringing on it every curse that is written
27 in this scroll. The LORD uprooted them from their land in anger, rage, and
28 great fury, and threw them into another land, as we now see them.' Hidden
things belong to the LORD our God, but as for overt acts – it is for us and
our children to eternity to keep all the words of this Law.

30 1 "When all these things have come upon you, the blessings and the curses
I have set before you, and you – amidst all the nations where the LORD
2 your God has driven you – take them to heart, and return, you and your
children, to the LORD your God, obeying Him with all your heart and all
3 your soul, just as I am commanding you today, then the LORD your God
will bring your captives back and show you compassion. He will bring you
back together from all the nations among whom the LORD your God has
4 scattered you. If you should be expelled to the furthest of horizons, even
from there the LORD your God will gather you, from there He will take
5 you back. The LORD your God will bring you into the land that belonged
to your ancestors, and you will possess it. He will make you yet more
prosperous and numerous than your ancestors were.

6 "The LORD your God will circumcise your heart and the hearts of your
descendants,[71] so that you may love the LORD your God with all your
7 heart, with all your soul, that you may live. The LORD your God will inflict
all these curses on your enemies and on those who hate and persecute
8 you. Then you shall turn and heed the LORD's voice, keeping all His
9 commandments with which I am charging you this day, and the LORD
your God will grant you abundant prosperity in all the work of your hands,
in the fruit of your womb, the fruit of your cattle, and the fruit of your land.
The LORD will again delight in your well-being as He did in your ancestors',
10 when you heed the LORD your God, keeping His commandments and
decrees that are written in this book of the Law, and have returned to the
LORD your God with all your heart and with all your soul.

11 "For this commandment that I am giving you today is not unattainable
12 to you, neither is it distant. It is not in heaven, that you should say, 'Who
will go up to heaven for us and bring it to us that we may hear it and keep
13 it?' Nor is it beyond the sea, that you should say, 'Who will cross to the
far side of the sea for us, and bring it to us that we may hear it and keep

70 | See Genesis 19:24–25.

71 | That is, He will soften their hearts, allowing them to devote themselves to Him.

14 it?' This word is very close to you. It is in your mouth and in your heart
for you to keep it.

15 16 "See: I have set before you today life and goodness, and death and evil. For
I charge you on this day to love the LORD your God, walk in His ways, and
keep His commandments, decrees, and laws. Then you will survive and
thrive and the LORD your God will bless you in the land you are coming
17 into to possess. But if your heart turns away and you do not listen and are
18 led astray, and bow down to other gods and worship them, then I declare
to you today that you will certainly perish; you will not live long in the
19 land that you are crossing the Jordan to enter and possess. I call heaven and
earth as witnesses against you today: I have set before you life and death,
the blessing and the curse. Choose life – so that you and your children may
20 live, loving the LORD your God, heeding His voice and holding fast to Him,
for this is your life and the length of your days, living in the land that the
LORD swore to give to your ancestors, to Avraham, Yitzḥak, and Yaakov."

31 1 2 Moshe went and spoke these words to all Israel. He told them, "I am a VAYELEKH
hundred and twenty years old now, and no longer able to enter and to leave.
3 And the LORD has told me, 'You shall not cross this Jordan.' The LORD
your God Himself will cross ahead of you. He will destroy these nations
before you, and you shall take possession in their place. It is Yehoshua who
4 will lead you across, as the LORD has spoken. The LORD will do to those
nations as He did to Siḥon and to Og, kings of the Amorites, and to their
5 land, when He destroyed them. The LORD will deliver them to you and
6 you shall deal with them just as I have commanded you. Be strong and be
determined. Do not fear or dread them, for the LORD your God is going
with you. He will not fail you or forsake you."

7 Then Moshe summoned Yehoshua and said to him in the sight of all Israel:
"Be strong and be determined, for it is you who will come with this people
into the land that the LORD has sworn to their ancestors to give them, and
8 you will allocate it to them for an inheritance. The LORD Himself will go
before you. He will be with you. He will not fail you or forsake you. Do
not fear and do not be dismayed."

9 Then Moshe wrote down this Law and gave it to the priests, descendants
of Levi, who carried the Ark of the Covenant of the LORD, and to all
10 the elders of Israel. Moshe then commanded them: "At the end of every
seventh year, the year of remission,[72] during the Festival of Tabernacles,
11 when all Israel comes to appear before the LORD your God at the place that
He will choose, you shall read out this Law in the presence of all Israel, for
12 them to hear. Assemble the people – men, women, and children, including
the migrants living in your towns – so that they may listen and learn to fear
13 the LORD your God and carefully keep all the words of this Law, and so
that their children, who do not know it, may listen and learn to be in awe

72 | See 15:1–2.

of the Lord your God, as long as you live in the land that you are crossing
the Jordan to possess."

14 The Lord said to Moshe, "Your time to die draws near. Call Yehoshua and
come and stand in the Tent of Meeting, so that I may give him his charge."
15 So Moshe and Yehoshua went and stood in the Tent of Meeting. The Lord
appeared in the Tent in a pillar of cloud; and the pillar of cloud stood at
the entrance to the Tent.

16 Then the Lord said to Moshe, "Soon, you are going to rest with your
ancestors. And this people will begin to stray after the foreign gods of
the land into which they are going. They will forsake Me and break the
17 covenant I have made with them. My rage will flare against them at that
time. I will abandon them and hide My face from them. They will become
easy prey, and many evils and troubles will come upon them. On that day
they will ask, 'Have not these troubles come upon us because our God is
18 not in our midst?' And I – I will hide My face at that time because of all
19 the evil they have done by turning to other gods. So now write down this
song and teach it to the Israelites. Place it in their mouths, so that this
20 song may be My witness against them. When I have brought them into
the land that flows with milk and with honey, which I promised on oath
to their ancestors, they will eat their fill and grow fat, and they will turn
to other gods and worship them, rejecting Me and breaking My covenant.
21 And when they are beset by many evils and troubles, this song will testify
as a witness against them, for it will not be forgotten by their descendants.
For I know what they are inclined to do even now, before I have brought
22 them into the land that I promised them on oath." So, that day, Moshe
wrote down this song and taught it to the Israelites.

23 And He charged Yehoshua son of Nun: "Be strong, be determined, because
you shall bring the Israelites into the land that I promised them – and I
will be with you."

24 Moshe finished writing down in a scroll the words of this Law to the very
25 end; and then Moshe instructed the Levites who carried the Ark of the
26 Covenant of the Lord: "Take this scroll of the Law and place it beside the
Ark of the Covenant of the Lord your God. Let it remain there as a witness
27 to you. For I know how rebellious and stiff-necked you are. Even now, while
I am still living among you, you have been rebellious toward the Lord; how
28 much more so will you be after my death! Gather to me all the elders of your
tribes and your officials, so that I may proclaim these words in their hearing
29 and call heaven and earth to witness against them. For I know that after my
death you will act in self-destruction, turning away from the path that I have
commanded you. In the days to come evil will befall you, because you will do
evil in the sight of the Lord, angering Him with the work of your hands."

30 Then Moshe proclaimed the words of this song in the hearing of the entire
assembly of Israel, to the very end.

HAAZINU

32 1 "Listen, heavens, I will speak;
let the earth hear the words of my mouth.
2 May my teaching pour down like rain,
let my speech fall like the dew;
like gentle rain on tender plants,
like showers upon the grasses.
3 As I call out the name of the LORD –
come, praise the greatness of our God.
4 The Rock, His work is whole,
and all His ways are justice.
A God of faith who does no wrong,
just is He and upright.
5 Did He act ruinously? No, with His children lies the fault,
a warped and twisted generation.
6 Is this how you repay the LORD,
you foolish, unwise people?
Is not He your Father, your Maker,
who formed you and set you on your feet?
7 Remember the days of old,
consider the years of ages past;
ask your father, and he will tell you;
your elders, and they will speak.
8 When the Highest gave nations their heritage,
when He divided humankind,
He fixed the boundaries of peoples
by the number of Israel's sons.[73]
9 The LORD's own share is His people,
Yaakov His allotted place.
10 He found him in a desert land,
in a barren, howling waste;
He encircled him, watched over him,
guarded him close like the apple of His eye.
11 As an eagle stirs up its nest,
and hovers over its young;
as it spreads its plumes and takes them,
bearing them aloft on its wings,
12 just so, the LORD alone led him –
no strange god at His side –
13 He set him astride the heights of the earth,
and fed him the bounty of meadows;
He nursed him with honey from the crag,
and oil from flinty rock;

73 | Explanations of this phrase vary, e.g., the seventy nations parallel the seventy descendants of Yaakov (Rashi), or Kenaan and his eleven descendants parallel the twelve sons of Israel (Bekhor Shor).

14 with curds from the herd, milk from the flock,
and the fat of lambs and goats,
choice rams of Bashan,
and the fattest buds of wheat –
you drank fine wine from blood-red grapes.
15 Yeshurun[74] grew fat, and kicked;[75]
you grew fat, grew gross, grew coarse.
They abandoned God who made them,
rejected the Rock of their rescue.
16 They provoked Him with strange gods,
and angered Him with abominations.
17 They sacrificed to demons, no-gods,
to deities they never knew,
new ones, lately arisen,
whom your forebears never feared.
18 You deserted the Rock that bore you;
you forgot the God who gave you birth.
19 The LORD saw this and He in turn rejected
the sons and daughters who angered Him so.
20 He said: I will hide My face from them,
and see what their end will be;
for they are a perverse generation,
children with no faithfulness.
21 They incensed Me with a no-god,
they angered Me with their vanities;
I will incense them with a no-people,
enrage them with a fool nation.
22 For a fire My anger has kindled,
it burns to the depths of Sheol,[76]
will devour the land and its harvests,
and set fire to the hills' foundations.
23 I will heap evils upon them,
exhaust My arrows on them:
24 consuming famine, flaming fever, bitter plague,
and fanged beasts will I send against them,
and venomous vipers crawling in the dust.
25 Sword outside and terror within
will claim young men and women,
nursing infants, and the gray-haired old.
26 I thought I would scatter them,
erasing their memory from man,
27 were it not for fear of the enemy's taunts,

---

74 | A name for Israel, derived from a term denoting uprightness.

75 | Became ungrateful and rebellious.

76 | The netherworld.

lest their adversaries misunderstand
and say, 'Our hand has triumphed;
it was not the LORD who did all this.'
28 They are a nation devoid of sense;[77]
they have no understanding.
29 If they were wise, they would contemplate this,
and know what their end would be.[78]
30 How could one man pursue a thousand,
and two put ten thousand to flight,
unless their Rock had sold them,
the LORD had handed them over?[79]
31 For their rock[80] is not like our Rock;
even in our enemies' judgment.
32 Their vine is from Sedom,
from the vineyards of Amora;[81]
their grapes are grapes of poison,
their clusters bitter;
33 their wine is serpents' venom,
cruel poison of the viper.
34 Is this not kept in My reserve,
sealed away in My treasury?
35 Vengeance is Mine; I will repay:
in time, their foot will slip;
their day of disaster is near,
their destiny hastens to meet them.
36 For the LORD will vindicate His people,
bring solace to His servants,
when He sees their strength has slipped away,
no one remains, no bond nor free.
37 He will say: Where are these gods of theirs,
the rock they went to for refuge,
38 that ate their sacrificial fat
and drank their wine of libation?
Let those rise up and help you now,
let them be your protection!
39 See now that I, I alone, am He;
there is no god apart from Me.
I deal death and I bring life;
I wounded but will heal;

---

77 | This refers to the enemy nation.

78 | That is, they would anticipate the consequences of oppressing Israel.

79 | In other words, a nation that defeats Israel ought to realize that it is God who enables such an outcome.

80 | Referring to the enemy's deity.

81 | Verses 32–33 describe the punishment that awaits the enemy, as the subsequent verses make clear.

and there is no rescue from My hand.
40 For I lift My hand skyward and swear:
as sure as I live forever,
41 when I whet My flashing sword,
and My hand grasps justice;
I will wreak vengeance on My foes,
and repay those who hate Me.[82]
42 I will make My arrows drunk with blood,
while My sword devours flesh,
the blood of the slain and the captives,
leaders of the long-haired foe.
43 O nations, sing out of His people,
for He will avenge His servants' blood,
take vengeance upon His foes,
and cleanse His land and His people."

44 Moshe came and proclaimed all the words of this song in the hearing of the
45 people, he and Hoshea son of Nun. When Moshe had finished speaking
46 all these words to all Israel, he said to them: "Take to heart all the words I
testify to you today, and charge your children with them, so that they may
47 take care to keep all the words of this Law. For these are not idle words for
you; they are your very life. By this word you may live long in the land that
you are crossing over the Jordan to possess."

48
49 On that very day the Lord spoke to Moshe: "Ascend this mountain of
Avarim, Mount Nevo, in the land of Moav, facing Yeriḥo, and gaze upon
50 the land of Canaan, which I am giving to the Israelites as a holding. There,
on the mountain that you ascend, you will die and be gathered to your
people, as your brother Aharon died on Mount Hor and was gathered to
51 his people;[83] because both of you broke faith with Me in the midst of the
Israelites at the waters of Merivat Kadesh in the Wilderness of Tzin, failing
52 to affirm My holiness among the Israelites.[84] You will see the land from
afar, but you shall not enter it – the land that I am giving to the people of
Israel."

VEZOT HABERAKHA

33 1 This is the blessing with which Moshe, man of God, blessed the Israelites
2 before he died. Moshe said:

"The Lord came from Sinai,
He shone upon them from Se'ir,
He appeared over the crest of Paran
and came among myriads of holy ones:[85]

82 | Referring to the enemies mentioned above.
83 | See Numbers 20:22–29.
84 | See Numbers 20:1–12.
85 | Meaning angels.

at His right hand, darting fire.
3 He is a lover of peoples,
all His holy ones are in Your hand;[86]
they place themselves at Your feet,
upholding Your words.
4 Moshe charged us with the Law,
heritage of Yaakov's assembly.
5 He became king in Yeshurun,[87]
when the heads of the people gathered[88] –
the tribes of Israel together.

6 "May Reuven live, and not die,
even though his men are few."

7 And this he said of Yehuda:

"Listen, LORD, to Yehuda's voice,
and bring him home to his people;[89]
strengthen his hands,
be his support against his foes."

8 And of Levi he said:

"Let Your Tumim and Urim[90] be with Your faithful,
the one You tested at Masa,
and challenged at the Meriva waters;[91]
9 who said of his father and mother,
'I do not regard them,'
ignored his brothers,
and did not acknowledge his children[92] –
instead keeping Your word,
and guarding close Your covenant.
10 They shall teach Your laws to Yaakov,
and Your instruction to Israel;
they shall place incense before You,
and whole offerings on Your altar.
11 Bless, O LORD, his vigor,
and accept the work of his hands;
crush the loins of his foes;
let his enemies rise no more."

---

86 | The varying second-person and third-person references to God are a feature of biblical poetry. The "holy ones" here are traditionally understood to refer to Israel.

87 | See note on 32:15.

88 | Perhaps a reference to the Revelation at Sinai.

89 | That is, from the battlefield.

90 | See note on Exodus 28:30.

91 | See Exodus 17:1–7.

92 | See Exodus 32:26–29.

12 Of Binyamin he said:

"Beloved of the Lord,
may he dwell in safety with Him –
He protects him all day long
as he rests between His shoulders."[93]

13 And of Yosef he said:

"Blessed by the Lord be his land,
with the bounty of heaven, with dew,
and the deep waters that lie below;
14 with the bounty brought forth by the sun,
and the bounteous yield of the moon;
15 with the best from the age-old mountains,
and the bounty of the everlasting hills;
16 with the bounty of earth and its fullness,
and the will of Him who dwelt in the bush.[94]
May these rest on Yosef's head,
on the brow of the prince among brothers.
17 His glory is that of a firstborn bull,
his horns the grand horns of the wild ox;
with them he gores the peoples,
all, to the ends of the earth.
These are the myriads of Efrayim,
these the thousands of Menashe."

18 And of Zevulun he said:

"Rejoice, Zevulun, as you set out;
and Yissakhar, in your tents.
19 They summon peoples to the mountain;[95]
there they offer righteous sacrifice;
they will feast on the plenty of oceans
and the hidden, buried riches of the sands."

20 And of Gad he said:

"Blessed be He who enlarges Gad!
He lives like a lion,
he tears at arm and scalp.[96]
21 He chose the first portion for himself,[97]

---

93 | Traditionally, this is understood to mean that the Sanctuary would ultimately stand in Benjaminite territory.

94 | See Exodus, chapter 3.

95 | Traditionally understood to mean Mount Zion, where the Temple eventually stood.

96 | In battle.

97 | The tribe of Gad settled east of the Jordan, in land that the Israelites conquered first; see Numbers, chapter 32.

for there the lawgiver's portion is reserved,[98]
where the heads of the people come.
He executed the LORD's justice,
and His ordinances for Israel."

22 And of Dan he said:

"Dan is a lion's whelp
springing forth from Bashan."

23 And of Naftali he said:

"Naftali, sated with favor,
filled with the LORD's blessing,
west and south possess."

24 And of Asher he said:

"Most blessed of sons is Asher;
may he win his brothers' favor,
and bathe his feet in oil.
25 Your bars are iron and bronze;[99]
may your strength be equal to your days.

26 "There is none like the God of Yeshurun,
riding the skies to help you,
the heavens, in His grandeur.
27 Your refuge the God of time immemorial,
you rest in eternal arms.
Dispelling every enemy before you,
He spoke: 'Destroy!'
28 So Israel dwells in safety;
Yaakov takes refuge alone
in a land of grain and wine,
where the skies drop their dew.
29 Happy are you, Israel. Who is like you,
a people rescued by the LORD?
He is your shield of help,
your sword of triumph.
Your enemies will cower before you,
and you shall tread their high places."

34 1 Then Moshe went up from the plains of Moav to Mount Nevo, to the
summit of Pisga, facing Yeriḥo. The LORD showed him all the land: from
2 Gilad to Dan, all of Naftali, the land of Efrayim and Menashe, all the land
3 of Yehuda as far as the Westward Sea, the Negev, and the plain – the Valley
4 of Yeriḥo, city of palm trees – as far as Tzoar. The LORD said to him, "This

98 | Often understood to refer to the burial place of Moshe.

99 | That is, you will live in security.

is the land I promised Avraham, Yitzḥak, and Yaakov, saying, 'I will give
this to your descendants'; I have let you see it with your eyes, but to that
place you will not cross over."

5 Then Moshe, the LORD's own servant, died there in the land of Moav, at the
6 LORD's word. He buried him in Moav, in a valley opposite Beit Peor, and to
7 this day no one knows his burial place. Moshe was a hundred and twenty
years old when he died; his eyes had not grown dim, nor his vitality fled.
8 The Israelites wept for Moshe in the plains of Moav for thirty days, until
the time of weeping and mourning for him was over.

9 Yehoshua son of Nun was filled with the spirit of wisdom, for Moshe had
laid his hands upon him, and the Israelites listened to him, and did as the
LORD had commanded Moshe.

10 There has never arisen a prophet in Israel like Moshe, whom the LORD
11 knew face-to-face, in all the signs and wonders the LORD sent him to
perform in Egypt, against Pharaoh, all his officials, and all of his land,
12 and in all the acts of a mighty hand and of terrifying power that Moshe
performed before the eyes of all Israel.

PROPHETS/NEVI'IM

JOSHUA / YEHOSHUA

JUDGES / SHOFETIM

SAMUEL / SHMUEL

KINGS / MELAKHIM

ISAIAH / YESHAYA

JEREMIAH / YIRMEYA

EZEKIEL / YEḤEZKEL

THE TWELVE PROPHETS /

SHENEIM ASAR

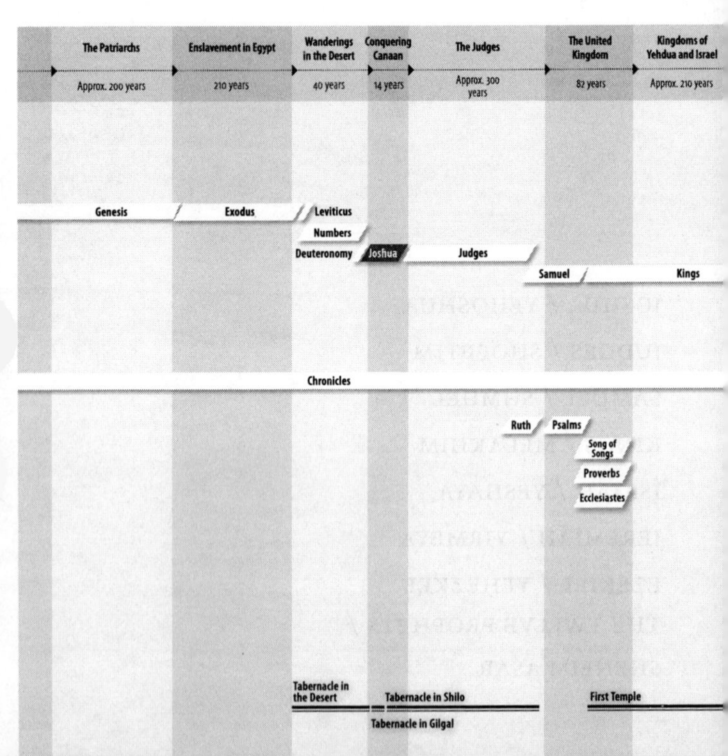
The Patriarchs
Enslavement in Egypt
Wanderings in the Desert
Conquering Canaan
The Judges
The United Kingdom
Kingdoms of Yehdua and Israel
Approx. 200 years
210 years
40 years
14 years
Approx. 300 years
82 years
Approx. 210 years
Genesis
Exodus
Leviticus
Numbers
Deuteronomy
Joshua
Judges
Samuel
Kings
Chronicles
Ruth
Psalms
Song of Songs
Proverbs
Ecclesiastes
Tabernacle in the Desert
Tabernacle in Shilo
Tabernacle in Gilgal
First Temple

JOSHUA/YEHOSHUA

JOSHUA	From the Plains of Moav to the camp at Gilgal Chs. 1–5	Wars with the nations of Canaan 6–12	From the camp in Gilgal to the settlement of the land 13–21	The altar at the Jordan and Yehoshua's farewell speeches 22–24
	7 years		7 years	

1 1 After the death of Moshe, the LORD's servant, the LORD said to Moshe's
2 disciple, Yehoshua son of Nun: "Moshe, My servant, is dead; now arise,
cross the Jordan here – you and all this people – to the land that I am
3 giving to the Israelites. I have given you every place your foot will tread,
4 just as I promised Moshe. Your territory shall stretch from the wilderness
and Lebanon here to the Great River, the Euphrates River, and all the
5 land of the Hittites, to the Great Sea where the sun sets. No one will be
able to stand against you for as long as you live; just as I was with Moshe,
6 I will be with you. I will never let you go, and I will never leave you. Be
strong and brave, for you will bring this people into possession of the
7 land I swore to their ancestors to give them. But you must be strong and
brave indeed to uphold faithfully all the Torah that Moshe My servant
commanded you; do not stray from it – neither right nor left – so that you
8 may triumph wherever you go. This book of Torah must never leave your
lips; contemplate it day and night, so that you will faithfully uphold all
that is written within it. For then your course will succeed; then you will
9 triumph. Hear now – I have charged you to be strong and brave. Do not
be frightened or dismayed, for the LORD your God is with you wherever
you go."

10 11 Yehoshua commanded the officers of the people: "Cross through the camp
and instruct the people: 'Prepare provisions for yourselves, for in three
days' time you are to cross the Jordan here, to come and take possession
of the land that the LORD your God is giving you as your own.'"

12 Yehoshua then told the Reubenites, the Gadites, and half the tribe of
13 Menashe: "Remember what Moshe, the LORD's servant, commanded you:[1]
14 The LORD your God has granted you rest and given you this land. Your
wives and little ones and your cattle shall dwell in the land that Moshe gave
you across the Jordan, but all your warriors shall cross over armed to join
15 your brothers and assist them, until the LORD grants rest like yours to your
brothers and they too take possession of the land that the LORD your God
is giving them. Then you shall return to your own land, which Moshe, the
LORD's servant, gave you on the eastern side of the Jordan – and you shall
16 17 take possession of it." They answered Yehoshua, "As we obeyed Moshe,
so we will obey you as long as the LORD your God is with you, as He was
18 with Moshe. Whoever rebels against your word or disobeys anything you
command shall be put to death; only be strong and brave."

2 1 Yehoshua son of Nun had sent two men as spies from Shitim, in secret:
"Go forth and survey the land and the region of Yeriḥo." So the men had set
out, arriving at the house of a harlot named Raḥav, where they lay down
2 for the night. And word reached the king of Yeriḥo: "Listen, people have
3 come here tonight – Israelites – to probe the land." The king of Yeriḥo sent
word to Raḥav: "Bring out those men who came to you, who arrived at

1 | See Numbers, chapter 32.

4 your house, for they have come to probe the land." Now, the woman had
taken the two men and hidden them, and she replied, "Yes, men came to
5 me, but I did not know where they were from. Just as the gate was being
closed at nightfall, the men left, and I do not know where they went. Go
after them quickly, for you can overtake them."

6 She had taken the spies up to the roof and hidden them amongst the stalks
7 of flax she had laid out on the roof. The king's men ran after them toward
the Jordan route, over the river fords; and the moment the pursuers left,
the gate was closed behind them.

8 9 They were not yet asleep when she went up to them on the roof. "I know
that the LORD has given you the land," she said to the men, "and that dread
of you has fallen upon us; for all the inhabitants of the land quake before
10 you. For we have heard that the LORD dried up the waters of the Sea of
Reeds before you when you left Egypt, and we have heard what you did to
the two Amorite kings across the Jordan – how you utterly destroyed Siḥon
11 and Og. We heard it and our hearts dissolved; no one has the spirit to face
12 you, for the LORD your God is God of heaven above and earth below. Now,
please swear to me by the LORD – for I have shown you loyalty – that you,
13 too, will be loyal to my father's house. Give me a true sign that you will
spare my father and mother and my brothers and sisters and all that is
theirs. Please, save our souls from death!"

14 The men replied to her, "We pledge to die in your place, if you speak no
word of this, and when the LORD gives us the land, we will show you true
15 loyalty." She let them down by a rope through the window, for her house
16 was built into the city wall; she lived inside the wall. "Flee toward the hills,"
she said to them, "lest the pursuers run into you. Hide there for three days
17 until the pursuers have returned; only then be on your way." They said to
18 her, "We will be free of this oath you have sworn us to unless, when we
come back to the land, you tie this scarlet thread in the window you let
us down from. Bring your father, your mother, your siblings, and all your
19 father's household into your home. If anyone ventures outside the doors
of your house, his blood will be upon his own head – we will be free of
blame – while if a hand is laid on anyone who remains in the house with
20 you, his blood shall be upon ours. But if you speak a word of this, we shall
21 be free of the oath we swore to you." "As you say, so be it," she said, and she
sent them away. They left, and she tied the scarlet thread in the window.

22 They set out and arrived at the hills. They stayed there for three days until
the pursuers turned back, for the pursuers had searched the entire route
23 but failed to find them. The two men then went back, descended the hills,
and crossed over. They came to Yehoshua son of Nun and reported all
24 that had befallen them. "The LORD has delivered the whole land into our
hands," they said to Yehoshua, "and what is more, all the people of the
land quake before us."

3 1 Early the next morning, Yehoshua rose and journeyed on from Shitim
together with all the people of Israel. They arrived at the Jordan, where
2 they stayed before crossing. Three days had passed, and the officers crossed
3 through the camp, commanding the people, "When you see the Ark of the
Covenant of the LORD your God, and the Levite priests bearing it, set out
4 from where you are and follow it. But keep a distance between you and it,
about two thousand cubits – do not come any closer. You will then know
the way to go, for you have never traveled this way before."

5 And Yehoshua told the people, "Sanctify yourselves, for tomorrow the
LORD will perform wonders in your midst."

6 "Raise up the Ark of the Covenant," said Yehoshua to the priests, "and
cross before the people." So they raised up the Ark of the Covenant and
7 advanced to the front of the people. And the LORD said to Yehoshua,
"Today I shall begin to exalt you in the eyes of all Israel so that they may
8 know that I shall be with you as I was with Moshe. Instruct the priests who
bear the Ark of the Covenant: when you reach the verge of the Jordan's
waters, stand still there in the Jordan."

9 And Yehoshua called out to the Israelites, "Draw near to hear the words
of the LORD your God."

10 "By this you shall know," Yehoshua continued, "that the living God is in
your midst, and that He will dispossess the Canaanites, the Hittites and the
Hivites, the Perizzites and the Girgashites, the Amorites and the Jebusites,
11 before you. Behold, the Ark of the Covenant of the Master of all the earth
12 is about to pass before you into the Jordan. Now, take twelve men from
13 the tribes of Israel, one from each tribe. As soon as the feet of the priests
who bear the Ark of the LORD, Master of all the earth, come to rest in the
waters of the Jordan, the waters of the Jordan will be cut off, and the water
flowing from upstream will stand still in one mound."

14 When the people set out from their tents to cross the Jordan, the priests
15 bearing the Ark of the Covenant went before them. When the bearers of
the Ark reached the Jordan, and the feet of the priests who bore the Ark
dipped into the water's edge – for the Jordan's banks had been overflowing
16 throughout harvest season – the waters flowing from upstream rose up in
one mound far away at Adam, the city beside Tzartan, while those flowing
downstream toward the Arava Sea – the Dead Sea – were cut off completely,
17 and the people crossed opposite Yeriḥo. The priests bearing the Ark of the
LORD's Covenant stood firmly on dry land in the midst of the Jordan until
all the nation had finished crossing the Jordan.

4 1 And when all the nation had finished crossing the Jordan, the LORD said to
2 3 Yehoshua: "Select twelve men, one from each tribe, and instruct them as
follows: Lift twelve stones from here, from the midst of the Jordan where
the priests' feet stand firm. Carry them with you and set them down at the
campsite where you will stay tonight."

4 Yehoshua summoned the twelve men he had chosen from the Israelites,
5 one from each tribe. "Pass before the Ark of the LORD your God," Yehoshua
said to them, "into the Jordan, and let each one of you lift one stone upon
6 his shoulder, corresponding to the number of Israelite tribes. This will be
a sign among you. In the future, when your children ask you, 'What do
7 these stones mean to you?' you shall answer them that the Jordan's waters
were cut off before the Ark of the LORD's Covenant; when it crossed
the Jordan, the Jordan's waters were cut off, so that these stones shall
8 be a memorial for the Israelites forever." The Israelites did as Yehoshua
commanded and lifted twelve stones from the Jordan's midst – as the
LORD had bidden Yehoshua – corresponding to the number of the Israelite
tribes. They carried these with them to the campsite and set them down
9 there. Yehoshua then erected twelve stones within the Jordan where the
feet of the priests who bore the Ark had stood. There they remain to this
10 day. The priests who bore the Ark remained standing in the midst of
the Jordan until the very end of the message that the LORD had ordered
Yehoshua to relate to the people – in accordance with what Moshe had
11 bidden Yehoshua – and the people hastened across. When all the people
had finished crossing, the Ark of the LORD and the priests crossed to the
12 front of the people. Ahead of the Israelites, the Reubenites, the Gadites,
and half the tribe of Menashe had crossed, armed, as Moshe had instructed
13 them. Around forty thousand armed warriors crossed before the LORD to
the plains of Yeriḥo, ready for war.

14 On that day, the LORD exalted Yehoshua in the eyes of all Israel, and they
revered him as they had revered Moshe all the days of his life.

15 16 The LORD said to Yehoshua, "Order the priests bearing the Ark of
17 Testimony to come up from the Jordan." And so Yehoshua ordered the
18 priests, "Come up from the Jordan." As the priests bearing the Ark of the
Covenant of the LORD came up from the Jordan – as soon as the soles of
the priests' feet stepped up onto dry land – the waters of the Jordan rushed
back to their place, overflowing its banks as before.

19 The people came up from the Jordan on the tenth of the first month, and
20 they encamped at Gilgal, on the eastern edge of Yeriḥo. As for the twelve
stones they had taken from the Jordan, Yehoshua erected them at Gilgal
21 and said to the Israelites, "In the future, when your children ask their
22 fathers, 'What are these stones?' make sure your children know: 'On dry
23 land Israel crossed this Jordan.[2] For the LORD your God dried up before
you the waters of the Jordan until you crossed over, just as the LORD your
God did to the Sea of Reeds, which He dried up before us until we crossed.
24 All the peoples of the land shall know the might of the LORD's hand, and
you shall revere the LORD your God forever.'"

5 1 When all the Amorite kings on the western side of the Jordan and all the

2 | See Numbers 32:20–22.

Canaanite kings by the sea heard how the LORD had dried up the waters of the Jordan before the Israelites until they crossed over, their hearts dissolved, and no spirit was left in them to face the Israelites.

2 At that time, the LORD said to Yehoshua, "Make yourselves knives of flint
3 and circumcise the Israelites a second time." So Yehoshua made knives
4 of flint and circumcised the Israelites at the Hill of Foreskins. This is why
Yehoshua circumcised them: all the men who left Egypt – all the males
fit for battle – had died in the wilderness during the journey, as they
5 came away from Egypt. And while all the men who left there had been
circumcised, all those who were born in the wilderness during the journey
6 away from Egypt had not been circumcised. For forty years the Israelites
had wandered in the wilderness until those among the nation who had
left Egypt fit for battle had perished. They disobeyed the voice of the
LORD, and the LORD swore not to show them the land He had sworn to
our ancestors that He would give us – a land flowing with milk and honey.
7 Yehoshua circumcised those children that He raised in their stead, for they
still had their foreskins, not having been circumcised during the journey.
8 When the whole nation's circumcision was over, they remained in place
in the camp until they recovered.

9 The LORD said to Yehoshua, "Today, I have rolled the shame of Egypt away
10 from you."[3] He has named that place Gilgal,[4] as it is known to this day. The
Israelites encamped at Gilgal and performed the Passover sacrifice on the
11 fourteenth day of the month at dusk on the plains of Yeriḥo. On the day
after the Passover sacrifice, they ate of the yield of the land – unleavened
12 bread and roasted grain – that very day. The manna stopped falling the
day after they had eaten from the yield of the land. The Israelites never
had manna again; from that year on they ate from the crops of the land
of Canaan.

13 When Yehoshua was near Yeriḥo, he looked up and suddenly saw a man
standing opposite him, drawn sword in hand. Yehoshua approached him
14 and asked, "Are you for us or for our enemies?" He said, "No, for I am the
commander of the LORD's hosts. Now I have come!" Yehoshua flung his
face to the ground and prostrated himself, asking him, "What does my lord
15 bid his servant?" The commander of the LORD's hosts said to Yehoshua,
"Remove the shoes from your feet, for the place where you stand is holy."[5]
And Yehoshua did so.

6 1 Yeriḥo was barred and bolted against the Israelites; no one came out, and
no one went in.

2 The LORD said to Yehoshua, "Behold, I have delivered Yeriḥo and its king
3 into your hands, though they are mighty warriors. March around the city

3 | Evoking the physical act of circumcision.

4 | Echoing the Hebrew *galloti*, "rolled away," in the previous verse.

5 | Cf. Exodus 3:5.

until all your fighting men have circled the city once. Do this for six days
4 while seven priests bear seven rams' horns before the Ark. And on the
seventh day, march around the city seven times as the priests blow on the
5 rams' horns. As the ram's horn resounds – when you hear the sound of the
ram's horn – all the people must give a mighty shout. Then the city wall
will come crashing down, and the people will rise up, each man charging
straight ahead."

6 Yehoshua son of Nun summoned the priests. "Lift up the Ark of the
Covenant," he said to them, "and let seven priests bear seven rams' horns
7 before the Ark of the LORD." Then Yehoshua said to the people, "Advance
and march around the city, and let the vanguard pass before the Ark of
8 the LORD." As Yehoshua spoke to the people, seven priests bearing seven
rams' horns before the LORD advanced and sounded the rams' horns, with
9 the Ark of the LORD's Covenant following behind them. The vanguard
marched before the priests who blew the rams' horns, and the rearguard
10 marched behind the Ark, with the rams' horns blasting all the while. But
Yehoshua had instructed the people: "Do not shout; do not make a sound;
do not let a word out of your mouth – until the day when I tell you to
11 shout. Then you will shout!" The Ark of the LORD was marched around
the city, circling it once. Then they arrived back at the camp and spent
the night there.

12 Yehoshua rose early in the morning, and the priests lifted up the Ark of the
13 LORD. The seven priests bearing the seven rams' horns marched before the
Ark of the LORD, sounding the rams' horns, with the vanguard marching
before them, the rearguard marching behind the Ark of the LORD, and the
14 rams' horns blasting all the while. They marched around the city once on
15 the second day and returned to the camp; this they did for six days. And
on the seventh day, they rose early, as dawn broke, and marched around
the city in this way seven times; only on that day did they circle it seven
16 times. And on the seventh circuit, as the priests blasted the rams' horns,
Yehoshua said to the people, "Shout out, for the LORD has given you the
17 city! The city and everything in it shall be placed under a ban and shall
belong to the LORD;[6] only Raḥav the harlot shall live, she and everyone in
18 her home, for she hid the messengers we sent. But beware of the ban lest
you be subject to utter destruction; if you take anything banned, you will
19 subject the camp of Israel to a scourge and to utter destruction.[7] All the
silver and gold and all the bronze and iron vessels are sacred to the LORD;
20 to the LORD's treasury they shall be taken." The people shouted and blasted
the rams' horns – and when the people heard the sound of the ram's horn,
they raised a mighty roar, and the wall came crashing down. Then the
people charged up to the city, each man running straight ahead, and they

---

6 | That is, the Israelites were prohibited from partaking of the spoils.

7 | Both "ban" and "utter destruction" correspond to the same Hebrew word: *ḥerem*. The verse thus describes a punishment in kind.

21 captured the city. They destroyed everything in the city with the sword:
22 man and woman; young and old; ox, lamb, and donkey. Yehoshua said to
the two men who had scouted out the land, "Go to the house of the harlot
and rescue the woman and all that is hers, as you swore to her that you
23 would." So the young spies went and rescued Raḥav, her father, her mother,
her siblings, and all that was hers; they rescued her entire family and set
24 them down outside the Israelite camp. The city and everything in it was
burned with fire – only the silver and gold and the bronze and iron vessels
25 were delivered to the treasury of the LORD's House – but the harlot Raḥav,
her father's household, and all that was hers were spared by Yehoshua; and
she dwells among Israel to this day, for she hid the messengers Yehoshua
sent to scout out Yeriḥo.

26 At that time, Yehoshua pronounced this oath: "Cursed by the LORD is the
man who attempts to rebuild this city, Yeriḥo:

"He shall lay down his firstborn with its foundations;
with his youngest he will set its gates!"

27 The LORD was with Yehoshua, and his fame rang out across the land.

7 1 But the Israelites broke the ban. It was Akhan son of Karmi son of Zavdi
son of Zeraḥ, of the tribe of Yehuda, who took of what was banned; and
the LORD's wrath raged against the Israelites.

2 Yehoshua sent men from Yeriḥo to Ai, which is near Beit Aven, east of Beit
El, bidding them, "Go up and spy out the land." The men went up and spied
3 on Ai. When they returned to Yehoshua, they said to him: "All the people
need not go up; let two thousand or three thousand men go up to attack
the Ai. Do not wear out all the fighters there, for the men of Ai are few."
4 So about three thousand fighters marched up there – but they fled before
5 the men of Ai. The men of Ai struck down about thirty-six of their men,
chasing them from the gate to the crags; they smote them at the descent,
and the people's hearts dissolved and turned to water.

6 Yehoshua rent his clothes and flung his face to the ground before the Ark
of the LORD. Lying prostrate until dusk, he and the elders of Israel smeared
7 dust upon their heads. "Alas, LORD God," Yehoshua said, "why did you
bring this people across the Jordan to give us over into Amorite hands
to be destroyed? If we had only been content to stay beyond the Jordan!
8 Please, LORD, what have I left to say now that Israel has turned tail before
9 its enemies? The Canaanites and all the inhabitants of the land will hear
and turn on us and sever our very name from the earth; what, then, will
You do about Your great name?"

10 The LORD said to Yehoshua, "Stand up! Why have you fallen on your face?
11 Israel has sinned; they have violated My covenant, which I charged them
to obey. They have taken from what was banned; they have stolen; they
12 have deceived; they have hidden it away among their vessels. The Israelites

will not be able to rise up before their enemies – they shall turn tail to
their enemies – for they have become subject to utter destruction.[8] I will
no longer be with you unless you purge from your midst what is banned.
13 Arise; sanctify the people; say: Sanctify yourselves for tomorrow, for thus
says the LORD, God of Israel: Something banned is among you, Israel; you
shall not be able to rise up against your enemies until you purge what has
14 been banned from among you. Come forward in the morning, grouped
according to your tribes. The tribe singled out by the LORD shall come
forward grouped by clan; the family singled out by the LORD shall come
forward grouped by house; the house singled out by the LORD shall come
15 forward man by man. The one caught with that which was banned shall
be burned with fire, he and all that is his; for he has violated the LORD's
covenant – he has committed an outrage in Israel."

16 Early the next morning, Yehoshua rose and had Israel come forward tribe
17 by tribe; and the tribe of Yehuda was singled out. He had the clans of
Yehuda come forward, and he singled out the family of Zeraḥ; he had the
male heads of the family of Zeraḥ come forward, and Zavdi was singled
18 out. He then had the males of the house come forward – and Akhan son of
Karmi son of Zavdi son of Zeraḥ, of the tribe of Yehuda, was singled out.

19 "My son," Yehoshua said to Akhan, "please – give glory to the LORD, God
of Israel, and make your confession to Him. Please: tell me what you did;
20 do not hold back from me." Akhan answered Yehoshua and said, "Truly,
21 I have sinned against the LORD, God of Israel. This is what I did: I saw
among the spoils a fine Shinar mantle and two hundred shekel of silver and
a golden ingot weighing fifty shekel. I coveted them and I took them. They
are buried in the ground inside my tent, with the silver underneath."

22 Yehoshua sent messengers who ran to the tent, and there it was, buried
23 in his tent, with the silver underneath. Taking them out of the tent, they
brought them to Yehoshua and all the Israelites and poured them out
24 before the LORD. Then Yehoshua took Akhan son of Zeraḥ, the silver, the
mantle, the golden ingot, his sons and daughters, his ox, his donkey, his
tent, and all that was his – and brought them, accompanied by all of Israel,
25 up to the Valley of the Scourge.[9] Yehoshua said, "A scourge have you been
to us! Now, on this day, the LORD will bring a scourge upon you." All of
Israel pelted him with stones, burned them with fire, and stoned them
26 with stones, and erected a great heap of stones over him – it endures there
to this day. Then the raging wrath of the LORD subsided. To this day that
place is called the Valley of the Scourge.

8 1 The LORD said to Yehoshua, "Do not fear or hesitate; take all the fighting
men with you and march up against Ai. Behold: I have delivered the king
2 of Ai, his people, his city, and his land, all into your hands. You shall do to

8 | Hebrew *ḥerem* (see note on 6:18).
9 | Hebrew *akhor*, resonating with the name Akhan.

Ai and to her king as you did to Yeriḥo and hers – but you may plunder her
spoil and livestock. Lay an ambush to the west of the city."

3 Yehoshua and all the fighting men marched up to Ai. Yehoshua selected
4 thirty thousand warriors and sent them off at night. "You are to lay an
ambush west of the city," he instructed them. "Do not stray too far from
5 the city, and all of you – be at the ready. I and all the men with me will
approach the city. When they come out toward us, as they did last time,
6 we will flee. They will chase us until we have lured them away from the
city – for they will think, 'They are fleeing before us as they did last time.'
7 But as we flee them, you will rise up from ambush and seize the city, and
8 the LORD will deliver it into your hands. When you capture the city, set
9 it on fire; do what the LORD has said; I have commanded you." Then
Yehoshua sent them off; they proceeded to the ambush site, taking up a
position between Beit El and Ai to the west of Ai. Yehoshua spent that
night among the men.

10 Early the next morning Yehoshua rose and mustered the men, and he
11 and the elders of Israel marched up toward Ai ahead of the people. All
the fighting men with him made their way up, advancing until they faced
the city. They laid their camp to the north of Ai, with the ravine dividing
12 them from Ai. Then he took about five thousand men and stationed them
13 in ambush between Beit El and Ai to the west of the city so that the main
camp of men was located to the north of the city while its rear guard stood
to the west. That night Yehoshua patrolled the valley.

14 As soon as the king of Ai saw the Israelites, the men of the city swiftly
rose and charged out to meet Israel in combat – he and all his men – on
the spot they had planned for before the plain; he did not know of the
15 ambush lurking behind the city. Yehoshua and all Israel feigned defeat and
16 fled toward the wilderness. And all the people of the city were alerted to
pursue them; they went after Yehoshua and so were lured away from the
17 city. Not a man remained in Ai or Beit El who did not go after Israel; they
left the city open and ran in pursuit of the Israelites.

18 The LORD said to Yehoshua, "Stretch out the javelin in your hand toward Ai,
for I have delivered it into your hand," and Yehoshua stretched the javelin
19 in his hand toward the city. With the thrust of his hand, the ambushers rose
swiftly from their position and ran; they reached the city and captured it,
20 then swiftly set it alight. The men of Ai turned to look behind them – all of
a sudden, the smoke of the city rose skyward! Their hands were tied – they
had nowhere to flee – and the people fleeing from them desertward had
21 turned into their pursuers! When Yehoshua and all of Israel saw that the
ambush had captured the city, and that smoke rose from the city, they
22 turned around and attacked the men of Ai. Then the other Israelites came
out of the city toward them so that they were hemmed in on both sides by
Israel, who struck them down until neither survivor nor fugitive remained.
23 But the king of Ai they seized alive and brought forward to Yehoshua.

24 When Israel had finished killing all the inhabitants of Ai who had chased
them toward the open wilderness, and every last one of them had fallen
25 by the sword, all of Israel returned to Ai and put it to the sword. All the
fallen on that day – man and woman, Ai's entire population – numbered
26 twelve thousand. Yehoshua did not draw back the hand that stretched
27 forth the javelin until he had utterly destroyed all the people of Ai. And
Israel plundered the livestock and spoil for themselves, just as the LORD
28 had commanded Yehoshua. Yehoshua burned down Ai, rendering it an
29 eternal ruin, a wasteland to this day. He hung the king of Ai on a tree until
evening time; when the sun set, Yehoshua gave orders for the corpse to be
lowered from the tree. They flung it outside the gated entrance to the city
and raised a great heap of stones on top; it endures to this day.

30 Then Yehoshua built an altar to the LORD, God of Israel, on Mount Eival,
31 as Moshe, God's servant, had commanded the Israelites – as is written in
the book of Moshe's teaching: an altar of uncut stones upon which no iron
tool had been wielded.[10] They offered up burnt offerings to the LORD and
32 sacrificed peace offerings. And there, upon the stones, he inscribed a copy
33 of the teaching that Moshe had written before the Israelites. All Israel and
its elders, officers, and judges stood on either side of the Ark, opposite
the Levitical priests bearing the Ark of the LORD's Covenant. To bless
the people of Israel, half of the citizens and strangers alike faced Mount
Gerizim and half of them faced Mount Eival, just as Moshe, the LORD's
34 servant, had originally commanded. He then read out all the words of
the Torah, blessing and curse, exactly as written in the book of the Torah.
35 There was not a single word Moshe had commanded that Yehoshua failed
to read before the whole congregation of Israel, including the women, the
children, and the strangers who walked among them.

9 1 When all the kings across the Jordan heard – those in highlands and
lowlands; those all along the coast of the Great Sea facing Lebanon;
2 the Hittites, Amorites, Perizzites, Hivites, and Jebusites – they gathered
together, of one accord, to fight against Yehoshua and the Israelites.

3 The inhabitants of Givon heard what Yehoshua had done to Yeriḥo and Ai.
4 So they, too, acted with guile; they went and disguised themselves and took
worn sackcloth for their donkeys; worn wineskins, cracked and stitched;
5 worn, patched shoes on their feet, and worn clothes to wear; and all their
6 bread provisions were dry and speckled with mold. They went to Yehoshua
at the camp at Gilgal.

"We have come from a distant land," they said to him and the men of Israel. "Please, form a pact with us."

10 | See Deuteronomy 27:5.

7 "Perhaps you live among us," the men of Israel replied to the Hivites.[11]
"How, then, can we form a pact with you?"[12]

8 "We are your servants," they responded to Yehoshua.

"Who are you?" Yehoshua said. "And where do you come from?"

9 "Your servants have come from a faraway land," they told him, "because
of the LORD your God's name, for we have heard of His fame and of all
10 He did in Egypt, and of all He did to the two Amorite kings on the other
side of the Jordan: to Siḥon, king of Ḥeshbon, and Og, king of Bashan,
11 in Ashtarot. Our elders and all the people of our land said to us, 'Take
supplies for the journey and go out to meet them; tell them, "We are your
12 servants."' Now, form a pact with us! This bread of ours – it was hot when
we packed it at home on the day we set out to meet you; now, look – it is
13 dry and speckled with mold! These wineskins were new when we filled
them; now, look how cracked they are! And these clothes and sandals of
ours are worn out from the sheer length of the journey."

14 The men took of their supplies; they did not seek the LORD's word.
15 Yehoshua made peace with the Gibeonites and formed a pact with them to
spare their lives, and the leaders of the community gave them their oath.

16 Three days after they had formed a pact with them, they heard that they
17 were nearby, living among them. The Israelites set out and arrived at their
cities on the third day; their cities were Givon, Kefira, Be'erot, and Kiryat
18 Ye'arim. The Israelites did not attack them, for their community leaders had
sworn to them by the LORD, God of Israel, although the whole community
19 railed against the leaders. The leaders all answered the community, "We
swore to them by the LORD, God of Israel, and now we cannot touch
20 them. This we shall do for them: we will spare them, so that there will not
21 be wrath upon us for the oath we swore to them." The leaders said to the
people, "Let them live." They became woodcutters and water drawers for
the entire community, as the leaders decreed.

22 But Yehoshua summoned them and charged them: "Why did you deceive
23 us, claiming, 'We are so distant from you' when you live among us? Now
you are cursed; you shall never cease to be slaves, woodcutters, and water
24 drawers for the House of My God!" They countered Yehoshua, "We your
servants were gravely warned of what the LORD your God commanded
Moshe His servant: to give you the entire land and annihilate all the
inhabitants of the land before you. We feared greatly for our souls before
25 you, and so we did this thing. Now we are in your hands; do to us whatever
26 seems good and fit in your eyes." So he did; he saved them from the hands
27 of the Israelites, who did not kill them. On that day, Yehoshua designated

11 | See 11:19: "the Hivites who lived in Givon."

12 | See Deuteronomy 7:2.

them as woodcutters and water drawers for the community and for the altar of the LORD – as they are to this day – in the place He would choose.

10 1 When Adoni Tzedek, king of Jerusalem, heard that Yehoshua had captured
Ai and utterly destroyed it – doing to Ai what he had done to Yeriḥo and
its king – and that the people of Givon had made peace with Israel and
2 dwelled among them, they were terrified. For Givon was as mighty as any
3 of the royal cities[13] – mightier than Ai – and all its men were warriors. So
Adoni Tzedek, king of Jerusalem, summoned Hoham, king of Ḥevron;
Piram, king of Yarmut; Yafia, king of Lakhish; and Devir, king of Eglon,
4 saying, "Come up and help me attack Givon, for they have made peace
5 with Yehoshua and the Israelites." The five Amorite kings – the king of
Jerusalem, the king of Ḥevron, the king of Yarmut, the king of Lakhish, and
the king of Eglon – assembled all their forces and marched up together.
6 They set up camp near Givon and attacked it. The Gibeonites reached out
to Yehoshua, to the camp at Gilgal: "Do not abandon your servants; come
up to us quickly! Deliver us and save us, for all the Amorite kings of the
7 highlands have gathered against us." Yehoshua marched up from Gilgal
together with all his fighting men – all his most valiant warriors.

8 The LORD said to Yehoshua, "Do not fear them, for I have delivered them
9 into your hands; not one of their men shall withstand you." Yehoshua
10 took them by surprise, having marched up from Gilgal all night. The LORD
threw them into a frenzy before Israel, and they dealt them a mighty blow
in Givon, chasing them along the Beit Ḥoron Ascent and striking them
11 up to Azeka and Makeda. As they fled before Israel along the Beit Ḥoron
Descent and up to Azeka, the LORD hurled great stones down from the
sky, and they died; more died from the hailstones than the Israelites slew
with the sword.

12 Then Yehoshua spoke to the LORD on the day the LORD delivered the
Amorites to the Israelites, and said before the eyes of Israel:

"O Sun, halt in Givon,
and Moon, in the Ayalon Valley!"
13 And the sun halted and the moon stood still
until a nation had wreaked vengeance on its foes.
Is it not written in the Book of the Upright?
How the sun stood still in the midst of the sky,
not rushing to set as in a natural day.
14 Never before and never again was there such a day
when the LORD listened to the voice of a man,
for the LORD was fighting for Israel's sake.

15 16 Yehoshua, and all of Israel with him, returned to camp at Gilgal, and those
17 five kings escaped and hid in a cave. Yehoshua was informed, "The five

13 | Cities where local kings resided, whose domain included the city and surrounding towns.

18 kings have been found hiding in a cave in Makeda." "Roll large stones over
the mouth of the cave," Yehoshua said, "and post men by it to guard them.
19 As for you, do not delay; chase after your enemies and attack them from
behind – do not let them reach their cities, for the LORD has delivered
20 them into your hand!" After Yehoshua and the Israelites had defeated them
in a deadly attack that finished them off, only a few survivors reached the
21 fortified cities. All the men made their way back to Yehoshua in the camp
at Makeda in safety; no one even dared sneer at the Israelites.

22 Then Yehoshua said, "Open the mouth of the cave and bring those five
23 kings out of the cave to me." They obeyed and brought those five kings
out of the cave – the king of Jerusalem, the king of Ḥevron, the king of
24 Yarmut, the king of Lakhish, and the king of Eglon. As the kings were being
brought out to Yehoshua, he summoned all the men of Israel and said
to the captains of the fighting men who had marched with him, "Come
forward and place your feet upon these kings' necks." They came forward
25 and placed their feet upon their necks. "Do not fear or hesitate," Yehoshua
said to them. "Be strong and determined, for this is what the LORD shall
26 do to all the enemies you fight against." And Yehoshua struck them down,
killed them, and hung them on five trees; they hung from the trees until
27 dusk. Toward sunset, Yehoshua gave orders; they took them down from
the trees and flung them into the cave where they had hidden. Over the
mouth of the cave they placed the large stones, which remain there to
this day.

28 Yehoshua also captured Makeda on that day and struck it down by sword;
its king he destroyed, together with every living soul there – leaving no
survivor. He did to the king of Makeda what he had done to the king of
Yeriḥo.

29 Then Yehoshua and all of Israel with him proceeded from Makeda to
30 Livna and fought with Livna. The LORD delivered it, too, into the hand
of Israel, along with its king. He put it to the sword together with every
living soul there, leaving no survivor. He did to its king what he did to the
king of Yeriḥo.

31 Then Yehoshua and all of Israel with him proceeded from Livna to Lakhish;
32 he encamped and fought against it, and the LORD delivered Lakhish into
Israel's hand. He conquered it on the second day and put it to the sword
together with every living soul there – just as he had done to Livna.

33 Then Horam, king of Gezer, marched up to assist Lakhish; but Yehoshua
34 struck him and his people down until no survivor was left. Then Yehoshua
and all of Israel with him proceeded from Lakhish to Eglon; they encamped
35 and fought against it. They captured it that same day, putting it to the sword
and destroying every living soul there – just as he had done to Lakhish.

36 Then Yehoshua and all of Israel with him marched up from Eglon to
37 Ḥevron and fought against it. He captured it and put it to the sword, its

king and all its towns and every living soul there, leaving no survivor – just
as he had done to Eglon. He utterly destroyed it, along with every living
soul there.

38 Then Yehoshua and all of Israel with him turned back to Devir and fought
39 against it. He captured its king and all its towns and put them to the
sword; they destroyed every living soul there, leaving no survivor. They
did to Devir and its king just as they had done to Ḥevron and to Livna
and its king.

40 Thus Yehoshua conquered the entire land – the hill country, the Negev,
the lowlands, the slopes – and all their kings; he left no survivor and
destroyed everyone who drew breath, just as the Lord, God of Israel, had
41 commanded. Yehoshua defeated them from Kadesh Barnea to Aza, and
42 the entire land of Goshen up to Givon. Every one of these kings and all
their lands were captured by Yehoshua in a single campaign, for the Lord,
43 God of Israel, fought for Israel. Then Yehoshua and all of Israel with him
returned to the camp at Gilgal.

11 1 When Yavin, king of Ḥatzor, heard, he sent word to Yovav, king of Madon,
2 to the king of Shimron, to the king of Akhshaf; to the kings of the north
in the hills, in the plains south of Kinerot, in the lowlands, and in the
3 district of Dor to the west; to the Canaanites to the east and west; to the
Amorites, Hittites, Perizzites, and Jebusites in the hills; and to the Hivites
4 at the foot of Ḥermon in the Mitzpa region. Out they marched with all
their forces, a horde of men as boundless as the sand on the shore, with
5 abundant horses and chariots. All these kings convened; they arrived and
set up camp together by the Merom waters to wage war against Israel.

6 The Lord said to Yehoshua, "Do not fear them, for by this time tomorrow,
I will have rendered them into corpses before Israel. Maim their horses and
7 burn their chariots with fire." Yehoshua, with all his fighting men, caught
8 them by surprise at the Merom waters, swooping down upon them. The
Lord delivered them into Israel's hand; they attacked them and chased
them to Greater Sidon, the Salt Pits, and as far as the Mitzpeh Valley to
9 the east, striking them down until no survivor remained. Yehoshua did to
them exactly what the Lord had bidden him: he maimed their horses and
burned their chariots with fire.

10 Then Yehoshua headed back and captured Ḥatzor. He put its king to the
11 sword, for until then, Ḥatzor had been the head of all those kingdoms. They
put every living soul there to the sword, utterly destroying them – nothing
12 breathing remained – and set Ḥatzor on fire. As for all those royal cities
and their kings, Yehoshua put them to the sword, utterly destroying them
13 as Moshe, the Lord's servant, had commanded. But Israel did not burn all
the cities mounted on their hilltops, only Ḥatzor alone, which Yehoshua
14 did burn. As for all the spoils and livestock of these cities, the Israelites
plundered them, but they put every person to the sword until they had

15 annihilated them; they left alive no one who drew breath. Just as the
LORD had commanded His servant Moshe, so Moshe had commanded
Yehoshua, and so Yehoshua did; he omitted nothing that the LORD had
commanded Moshe.

16 Yehoshua conquered this entire land: the hill country and all the Negev
and all the land of Goshen; the lowlands and the plain, the hill country of
17 Israel and its valleys; from the bare mountain rising up toward Se'ir as far as
Baal Gad in the Lebanon Valley at the foot of Mount Ḥermon. He captured
18 all their kings, struck them down, and put them to death. Yehoshua waged
19 war against all these kings for a long time. Except for the Hivites who
lived in Givon, no city made peace with the Israelites, who conquered
20 all in battle. For the LORD determined that their enemies' hearts would
be obdurate when waging war against Israel, so that Israel might destroy
them without mercy – so that they might annihilate them as the LORD
had commanded Moshe.

21 At that time, Yehoshua went and obliterated Anakites from the hill
country, Ḥevron, Devir, Anav – all the hill country of Yehuda and all
the hill country of Israel. Yehoshua destroyed them together with their
22 cities. No Anakites were left in the land of the Israelites; they remained
23 only in Aza, Gat, and Ashdod. Yehoshua conquered the entire land, just
as the LORD had promised Moshe. Yehoshua assigned it to Israel as their
inheritance, allotted according to their tribal divisions. And the land rested
from war.

12 1 These are the kings whom the Israelites defeated and the lands that they
took possession of on the eastern side of the Jordan, from the Arnon
Stream to Mount Hermon and the entire plain to the east:

2 King Siḥon of the Amorites, who resided at Ḥeshbon, ruling from Aroer
on the banks of the Arnon Stream and within the streambed and half of
3 the Gilad to the Yabok Stream, the Amonite border; and over the Arava
up to east of the Sea of Galilee and east of the Arava Sea, the Dead Sea,
toward Beit HaYeshimot; and his southern border was at the lower slopes
of Pisga.

4 And the region of Og, king of Bashan, last of the Refaim, who resided at
5 Ashtarot and Edre'i and ruled over Mount Ḥermon and Salkha, the entire
Bashan up to the Geshurite and Maakhatite borders, and half of the Gilad
6 to the border of Siḥon, king of Ḥeshbon. Moshe, the LORD's servant, and
the Israelites had defeated them, and Moshe, the LORD's servant, had
assigned the region as an inheritance to the Reubenites, the Gadites, and
half the tribe of Menashe.

7 These are the kings of the land whom Yehoshua and the Israelites defeated
on the western side of the Jordan, from Baal Gad in Lebanon Valley up
to the bare mountain rising up toward Se'ir. Yehoshua assigned it as an
8 inheritance to the tribes of Israel according to their divisions: the hill

country and the lowlands, the plains and the slopes, the wilderness and
the Negev; that of the Hittite, the Amorite, the Canaanite, the Perizzite,
the Hivite, and the Jebusite:

9 The king of Yeriḥo – one;
the king of Ai, near Beit El – one;
10 the king of Jerusalem – one;
the king of Ḥevron – one;
11 the king of Yarmut – one;
the king of Lakhish – one;
12 the king of Eglon – one;
the king of Gezer – one;
13 the king of Devir – one;
the king of Geder – one;
14 the king of Ḥorma – one;
the king of Arad – one;
15 the king of Livna – one;
the king of Adulam – one;
16 the king of Makeda – one;
the king of Beit El – one;
17 the king of Tapuaḥ – one;
the king of Ḥefer – one;
18 the king of Afek – one;
the king of Sharon – one;
19 the king of Madon – one;
the king of Ḥatzor – one;
20 the king of Shimron Meron – one;
the king of Akhshaf – one;
21 the king of Tanakh – one;
the king of Megiddo – one;
22 the king of Kedesh – one;
the king of Yokne'am of Carmel – one;
23 the king of Dor of the district of Dor – one;
the king of the Gilgal peoples – one;
24 the king of Tirtza – one;
thirty-one kings in all.

13 1 Now Yehoshua was old, advanced in years.

"You have grown old," the Lord said to him, "you have advanced in
2 years, and so much of the land is yet to be possessed. This is the land that
remains:

3 "All the districts of the Philistines; all of the Geshurites' from the Shiḥor,
which is close to Egypt, to the border of Ekron to the north, which are
considered Canaanite; of the five chieftains of the Philistines – the Gazite,
the Ashdodite, the Ashkelonite, the Gittite, and the Ekronite; of the Avite

4 to the south; all the land of the Canaanites and Sidonian Maara up to
5 Afeka and the Amorite border; the land of the Giblite and all Lebanon to
6 the east of Baal Gad at the foot of Mount Ḥermon up to Levo Ḥamat; all
the people of the hills from Lebanon to the Salt Pits; all the Sidonians – I
Myself will dispossess them all before the Israelites. Now, allot them to
7 Israel as estates as I have commanded you; divide up this land into estates
for the nine tribes and half the tribe of Menashe."

8 Now, the Reubenites and Gadites had already received the estates that
Moshe had assigned to them on the eastern side of the Jordan, exactly as
they were assigned by Moshe, the LORD's servant:
9 From Aroer on the banks of the Arnon Stream and the city located within
the streambed and all the Meideva Plains up to Divon;
10 all the cities of King Siḥon of the Amorites, who had ruled in Ḥeshbon, to
the Amonite border;
11 the Gilad, the territory of the Geshurites and Maakhatites, all of Mount
Ḥermon, and all the Bashan up to Salkha.
12 The entire kingdom of Og of Bashan, who had ruled in Ashtarot and
Edre'i – he was the last of the remaining Refaim. Moshe had struck them
down and dispossessed them.
13 The Israelites did not dispossess the Geshurites and the Maakhatites, and
Geshur and Maakhat dwell among Israel to this day.

14 Only to the Levite tribe he did not grant an estate; the fire offerings of
the LORD, God of Israel, were to be their share, as He had ordained for
them.

15 Moshe had assigned the Reubenite tribe its estate according to its clans,
16 granting them:
the territory from Aroer on the banks of the Arnon Stream
and the city located within the streambed
and the entire plain of Meideva;
17 Ḥeshbon and all its towns on the plain;
Dibon, Bamot, Baal, and Beit Baal Meon;
18 Yahtza, Kedemot, and Mefaat;
19 Kiryatayim, Sivma, and Tzeret HaShaḥar in the hill of the valley;
20 Beit Peor, the Pisga slopes, and Beit HaYeshimot;
21 all the cities of the plain and the entire kingdom of Siḥon, king of the
Amorites, who ruled in Ḥeshbon, whom Moshe had defeated along with
the princes of Midyan: Evi, Rekem, Tzur, Ḥur, and Reva, who had resided
22 in the land as princes of Siḥon. As for the sorcerer Balaam son of Beor,
Israel had put him to the sword along with all the rest of their slain.
23 The Reubenites' border was the Jordan; this territory was the estate of the
Reubenites by their clans – the cities with their villages.

24 Moshe had assigned an estate to the tribe of Gad according to its clans,
25 granting them:

the territory of Yazer and all the cities of Gilad;
half the land of the Amonites up to Aroer, facing Raba;
26 from Ḥeshbon to the Heights of Mitzpeh and Betonim;
from Maḥanayim to the border of Lidvir;
27 in the valley, Beit HaRam, Beit Nimra, Sukkot, and Tzafon – the rest of
the kingdom of King Siḥon of Ḥeshbon;
the Jordan and its border to the edge of the Sea of Galilee on the eastern
side of the Jordan.
28 This was the estate of the Gadites by their clans – the cities with their
villages.

29 Moshe had assigned an estate to half the tribe of Menashe – they were half
of the tribe of Menashe by their clans:
30 the territory extending from Maḥanayim,
the entire Bashan – the entire kingdom of King Og of Bashan –
and all the hamlets of Yair in the Bashan, sixty cities;
31 half of the Gilad;
Ashtarot and Edrei, Og's royal cities in Bashan –
he granted this to the sons of Makhir son of Menashe, to half the clans of
the Makhirites.

32 These had been allotted by Moshe in the plains of Moav, on the eastern side
33 of the Jordan by Yeriḥo. Moshe had not assigned an estate to the tribe of
Levi; the Lord, God of Israel, is their share, as He ordained for them.

14 1 And this is what the Israelites inherited in the land of Canaan, as allotted
by the priest Elazar, Yehoshua son of Nun, and the clan leaders of the
2 Israelite tribes; the estates by lot, as the Lord had commanded through
3 Moshe, for the nine and a half tribes. For Moshe had assigned estates
to the two and a half tribes across the Jordan, but he had assigned no
4 estate to the Levites among them because the sons of Yosef, Menashe
and Efrayim, counted as two tribes. They gave no share to the Levites in
the land besides towns to live in and pasture for their cattle and space for
5 their possessions. The Israelites did as the Lord had commanded Moshe
and divided up the land.

6 The Judahites approached Yehoshua at Gilgal, and Kalev son of Yefuneh
the Kenizzite said to him, "You know what the Lord told Moshe, man of
7 God, concerning me and concerning you, in Kadesh Barnea. I was forty
years old when Moshe, the Lord's servant, sent me from Kadesh Barnea to
8 scout out the land, and I brought back an honest report. But my comrades
who went up with me dissolved the heart of the people, while I fulfilled
9 the will of the Lord my God. So that day, Moshe swore: 'The land upon
which your foot trod shall become yours and your children's estate forever,
10 for you fulfilled the will of the Lord my God.' Now look – the Lord has
sustained me, as He promised, for the past forty-five years, ever since the
Lord spoke those words to Moshe while Israel wandered the wilderness,
11 and here I am today, eighty-five years old. I am still as able as on the day

Moshe sent me; my strength now is the same as it was then to enter and
12 to leave. Now give me this mountain, the one the Lord spoke of on that
day. You heard on that day of the Anakites and great fortified cities there.
Perhaps the Lord will be with me, and I shall dispossess them as the
Lord promised."

13 Yehoshua blessed him and gave Ḥevron to Kalev son of Yefuneh as an estate.
14 Ḥevron has remained the estate of Kalev son of Yefuneh the Kenizzite to
15 this day, for he fulfilled the will of the Lord, God of Israel. The name of
Ḥevron was previously Kiryat Arba, who was the mightiest of the Anakites.
And the land rested from war.

15 1 The allotment of the Judahite tribe by their clans extended southward to
the border of Edom, to the wilderness of Tzin at the furthest south.
2 Their southern border ran from the end of the Dead Sea, from the tongue
projecting southward,
3 and extended to the south of Scorpion Ascent, continuing past Tzin and
rising up to the south of Kadesh Barnea;
then it passed to Ḥetzron, rising up toward Adar and turning toward
Karka;
4 then it passed through Atzmon, extended toward the Ravine of Egypt, and
ended at the sea; "that shall be your southern border."
5 The eastern border was the Dead Sea up to the mouth of the Jordan.
The corner of the northern border ran from the tongue of sea at the Jordan's
mouth;
6 the border rose up toward Beit Ḥogla, passed north of Beit HaArava,
then rose up to Even Bohan, son of Reuven;
7 the border then rose up toward Devir from the Valley of the Scourge and
turned north toward Gilgal, opposite the Ascent of Adumim, south of
the wadi;
the border then continued to the waters of the Shemesh Spring and ended
at the Rogel Spring;
8 the border then rose up to the Valley of Ben Hinom to the southern slope
of the Jebusites – that is, Jerusalem;
then the border rose up to the mountaintop overlooking the Valley of Ben
Hinom to the west, at the northern edge of the Refaim Valley;
9 the border then curved from the mountaintop toward the waters of
the Fountainhead of Neftoaḥ and extended toward the cities of Mount
Efron;
then the border curved toward Baala – that is, Kiryat Ye'arim;
10 the border turned west from Baala toward Mount Se'ir, passing north of
the slope of Mount Ye'arim – that is, Kesalon –
and descended toward Beit Shemesh and continued to Timna;
11 the border extended toward the northern slope of Ekron,
then curved toward Shikron, continuing toward Mount Baala and extending to Yavne'el; the border ended at the sea.
12 The western border was the Great Sea;

this was the border all around the territory of the Judahites, rendered by
their clans.

13 Kalev son of Yefuneh was given a share among the Judahites because
of the LORD's word to Yehoshua: Kiryat Arba, who was father of the
14 Anakites – that is, Ḥevron. Kalev dispossessed the three sons of the giant
15 from there: Sheshai, Aḥiman, and Talmai, the descendants of Anak. From
there he marched up against the people of Devir,[14] the previous name of
16 which was Kiryat Sefer. Kalev declared: "Whoever defeats Kiryat Sefer and
17 captures it – I shall give him my daughter Akhsa for a wife." Otniel son of
Kenaz, Kalev's kinsman, captured it, and he gave him his daughter Akhsa
18 for a wife. When she arrived, having urged him to ask her father for the
field, she dismounted rapidly from the donkey.

"What is the matter?" Kalev said to her.

19 "Give me a blessing," she replied, "for you have given me desert land, and
you should give me springs of water." So he gave her the upper springs and
the lower springs.

20 This is the estate of the Judahite tribe by their clans:
21 The cities at the edge of the tribe of Yehuda, by the Edomite border in the
Negev, were:
Kavtze'el, Eder, and Yagur,
22 Kina, Dimona, and Adada,
23 Kedesh, Ḥatzor, and Yitnan,
24 Zif, Telem, and Be'alot,
25 Ḥatzor Ḥadata, Keriyot, and Ḥetzron – that is, Ḥatzor,
26 Amam, Shema, and Molada,
27 Ḥatzar Gada, Ḥeshmon, and Beit Pelet,
28 Ḥatzar Shual, Be'er Sheva, and Bizyotya,
29 Baala, Iyim, and Etzem,
30 Eltolad, Kesil, and Ḥorma,
31 Tziklag, Madmana, and Sansana,
32 Levaot, Shilḥim, Ayin, and Rimon;
twenty-nine cities in all, with their villages.[15]
33 In the Shefela: Eshtaol, Tzora, and Ashna,
34 Zanoaḥ, Ein Ganim, Tapuaḥ, and the Einam,
35 Yarmut, Adulam, Sokho, and Azeka,
36 Shaarayim, Aditayim, the Gedera, and Gederotayim; fourteen cities in all,
with their villages.
37 Tzenan, Ḥadasha, and Migdal Gad,
38 Dilan, Mitzpeh, and Yokte'el,

14 | Cf. Judges 1:11–15.

15 | Explanations vary as to why more than twenty-nine cities are listed here; either some of these cities were taken by the tribe of Shimon (19:2–7), or only twenty-nine are cities and the rest are villages.

39 Lakhish, Botzkat, and Eglon,
40 Kabon, Laḥmas, and Kitlish,
41 Gederot, Beit Dagon, Naama, and Makeda; sixteen cities in all, with their villages.
42 Livna, Eter, and Ashan,
43 Yiftaḥ, Ashna, and Netziv,
44 Ke'ila, Akhziv, and Maresha; nine cities in all, with their villages.
45 Ekron, with its dependencies and villages.
46 From Ekron westward, all that was near Ashdod, with their villages:
47 Ashdod, its dependencies and its villages; Aza, its dependencies and its villages, up to the Ravine of Egypt – the Great Sea was its border.
48 And in the hill country: Shamir, Yatir, and Sokho,
49 50 Dana, Kiryat Sana – that is, Devir – Anav, Eshtemoa, and Anim,
51 Goshen, Ḥolon, and Gilo; eleven cities, with their villages.
52 Arav, Duma, and Eshan,
53 Yanum, Beit Tapuaḥ, and Afeka,
54 Ḥumta, Kiryat Arba – that is, Ḥevron – and Tzior; nine cities, with their villages.
55 Maon, Carmel, Zif, and Yuta,
56 Yizre'el, Yokde'am, and Zanoaḥ,
57 Kain, Giva, and Timna; ten cities, with their villages.
58 Ḥalḥul, Beit Tzur, and Gedor,
59 Maarat, Beit Anot, and Eltekon; six cities, with their villages.
60 Kiryat Baal – that is, Kiryat Ye'arim – and Rava; two cities, with their villages.
61 In the wilderness: Beit HaArava, Midin, Sekhakha,
62 Nivshan, City of Salt, and Ein Gedi; six cities, with their villages.

63 As for the Jebusites, the inhabitants of Jerusalem, the Judahites, could not dispossess them; the Jebusites dwell with the Judahites in Jerusalem to this day.[16]

16 1 The allotment of the Josephites extended from the Jordan at Yeriḥo
eastward to the Yeriḥo waters, to the wilderness rising from Yeriḥo, toward
2 the hill country of Beit El; it extended from Beit El to Luz and crossed
3 through the territory of the Arkites at Atarot; descended to the west
into the territory of the Jafletites to Lower Beit Ḥoron, up to Gezer, and
4 ended at the Sea. The sons of Yosef, Menashe and Efrayim, received their
estates.

5 This was the territory of the Efraimites by their clans: the eastern border of their estate ran from Atarot Adar to Upper Beit Ḥoron;
6 it extended westward toward Mikhmetat to the north,
then it turned eastward to Taanat Shilo, passed through it to the east of Yanoaḥ,

16 | Cf. Judges 1:21.

7 descended from Yanoaḥ to Atarot and Naarat, touched Yeriḥo, and
extended to the Jordan;
8 from Tapuaḥ, the border ran westward to the Kana Ravine, ending at the
Sea.
9 This was the Efraimites' estate by their clans, except for the cities reserved
for the Efraimites within the Manassites' estate, all the cities with their
villages.

10 But they did not dispossess the Canaanites who live in Gezer; the
Canaanites became forced laborers and live among the Efraimites to this
day.

17 1 The tribe of Menashe was allotted a territory, for he was Yosef's firstborn;
as Makhir, firstborn of Efrayim and ruler of Gilad, was a valiant warrior,
2 the Gilad and the Bashan became his. And Efrayim's remaining sons were
assigned territory by their clans: the sons of Aviezer, the sons of Ḥelek,
the sons of Asriel, the sons of Shekhem, the sons of Ḥefer, and the sons
of Shemida – these are the male descendants of Efrayim, son of Yosef,
3 by their clans. Tzelofḥad son of Ḥefer son of Gilad son of Makhir son of
Efrayim had no sons, only daughters. These are the names of his daughters:
4 Maḥla, Noa, Ḥogla, Milka, and Tirtza. They approached Elazar the priest,
Yehoshua son of Nun, and the leaders, saying, "The Lord instructed
Moshe to grant us an estate among our brothers."[17] In accordance with the
5 Lord's word, he granted them an estate among their father's brothers. Ten
districts fell to Menashe besides the land of Gilad and the Bashan beyond
6 the Jordan, for the daughters of Efrayim inherited an estate along with his
sons, while the land of Gilad went to the remaining sons of Efrayim.

7 Menashe's border ran from Asher to the Mikhmetat, which is by Shekhem,
then continued southward toward the dwellers of Ein Tapuaḥ.
8 The Tapuaḥ region belonged to Menashe, while Tapuaḥ itself, on Menashe's
border, belonged to the Efraimites.
9 The border then descended to the Kana Ravine. The cities south of the
wadi there belonged to Efrayim, enclaved among the cities of Menashe.
10 Menashe's border ran north of the wadi and ended at the Sea; the south
belonged to Efrayim and the north to Menashe, with the Sea their border;
they touched Asher on the north and Yissakhar on the east.
11 Within Yissakhar and Asher, Menashe possessed Beit She'an and its
dependencies,
Yivle'am and its dependent towns,
the people of Dor and its dependent towns,
the people of Ein Dor and its dependent towns,
the people of Tanakh and its dependent towns,
the people of Megiddo and its dependent towns – three districts.[18]

17 | See Numbers 27:1–7.

18 | Megiddo, Tanakh, and Yivle'am were located near each other in the eastern part of the Yizre'el Valley, and together probably constituted one district.

12 The Manassites were unable to dispossess these cities, and the Canaanites
13 were determined to stay in that land. When the Israelites grew stronger,
they imposed tributes on the Canaanites, but they never dispossessed
them.

14 The Josephites protested to Yehoshua, "Why have you given me a single
estate – a single district – when I am so vast a people, so blessed by the
Lord?"

15 "If you are so vast a people," Yehoshua said to them, "then go up to the
forest and cut it down for yourselves there in the land of the Perizzites and
the Refaim, if the Efrayim hills are too confined for you."

16 "The hill country is not enough for us," replied the Josephites, "but all the
Canaanites living in the lowlands have iron chariots – both those in Beit
She'an and its dependencies and those in the Yizre'el Valley."

17 Yehoshua said to the House of Yosef, to Efrayim and Menashe, "You are a
18 vast people, and you have great power; you shall not have a single lot. The
hill country shall be yours; it may be forest, but you may cut it down and
what comes out of it shall be yours, and you shall dispossess the Canaanites
despite their iron chariots and despite their strength."

18 1 The entire community of Israelites assembled at Shilo, where they set
2 up the Tent of Meeting, and the land lay conquered before them. There
remained seven Israelite tribes whose estates had not yet been distributed.
3 Yehoshua said to the Israelites, "How long will you be slack about coming
to inherit the land given to you by the Lord, God of your forefathers?
4 Provide three men from each tribe; I will send them to travel around the
land and map it out for apportionment; then they will come back to me.
5 Divide it up into seven parts, Yehuda retaining its borders in the south and
6 the House of Yosef retaining its borders in the north. Map out the land into
seven parts and bring it here to me; I shall then cast lots for you here before
7 the Lord our God. For there is to be no share among you for the Levites
since the Lord's priesthood is their estate, and Gad, Reuven, and half the
tribe of Menashe took their estates on the east side of the Jordan – those
that Moshe, the Lord's servant, had assigned to them."

8 So the men rose and set out, and Yehoshua commanded those who were
traveling to map out the land: "Go and travel the land and map it out,
and return to me; I will cast lots for you here before the Lord at Shilo."
9 The men set out and traveled across the land, mapping out its cities into
seven parts on a scroll. They came back to Yehoshua, to the camp at Shilo.
10 Yehoshua cast lots in Shilo before the Lord, and there Yehoshua divided
the land for the Israelites by their tribal divisions.

11 The first lot fell to the tribe of Binyamin by its clans. Their allotment lay
between the Judahites and the Josephites.
12 The northern edge of their border began at the Jordan;

then the border rose to the northern slope of Yeriḥo, rose westward to the
hills, and reached the wilderness of Beit Aven;
13 from there, the border continued toward Luz, to the southern slope of
Luz – that is, Beit El;
the border then descended to Aterot Adar on the hill south of Lower Beit
Ḥoron.
14 The border then curved, turning to the west, southward from the hill facing
Lower Beit Ḥoron, and ended at Kiryat Baal – that is, Kiryat Ye'arim, a
Judahite city. This was its western edge.
15 Its southern edge ran from the edge of Kiryat Ye'arim and continued west,
reaching the spring of the Fountainhead of Neftoaḥ;
16 the border then descended to the foot of the hill by the Valley of Ben
Hinom at the northern end of the Refaim Valley; it descended through the
Hinom Valley toward the Jebusite slope to the south, descending toward
17 the Rogel Spring; curving northward, it continued to the Shemesh Spring
and then on to Gelilot, by Maaleh Adumim, and descended to Even Bohan,
18 son of Reuven; continuing northward to the slope facing the Arava, it then
descended to the Arava;
19 the border then continued northward to the Beit Ḥogla slope and ended
at the northern tongue of the Dead Sea, at the southern end of the Jordan.
20 This was its southern border. The Jordan bordered it on the eastern edge.
This was the Benjaminites' estate, defined by its borders all around, divided
according to its clans.

21 The cities of the tribe of Benjamin by its clans were:
Yeriḥo, Beit Ḥogla, and Emek Ketzitz,
22 Beit HaArava, Tzemarayim, and Beit El,
23 Avim, Para, and Ofra,
24 Kefar HaAmona, Ofni, and Geva; twelve cities with their villages.
25 Givon, Rama, and Be'erot,
26 Mitzpeh, Kefira, and Motza,
27 Rekem, Yirpe'el, and Tarala,
28 Tzela, Elef, and the Jebusite – that is, Jerusalem –
Givat, Kiryat; fourteen cities with their villages.
This was the estate of the Benjaminites by their clans.

19 1 The second lot fell to Shimon, to the tribe of the Simeonites by their clans.
Their estate lay within the Judahites' estate.
2 Their estate included Be'er Sheva with Sheva, and Molada,
3 Ḥatzar Shual, Bala, and Etzem,
4 Eltolad, Betul, and Ḥorma,
5 Tziklag, Beit HaMarkavot, and Ḥatzar Susa,
6 Beit Levaot and Sharuḥen; thirteen cities with their villages.
7 Ayin, Rimon, Eter, and Ashan; four cities with their villages,
8 as well as all the villages surrounding these cities up to Baalat Be'er and
Ramat Negev – this was the tribe of Shimon's estate, divided according
9 to its clans. Shimon's estate was within Yehuda's district: because the

Judahites' share was too large for them, the Simeonites settled within Yehuda's estate.

10 The third lot fell to the Zebulunites by their clans; the borders of their estate ran to Sarid.
11 Their border rose up westward to Marala, touched Dabeshet, and reached
12 the wadi facing Yokne'am, then turned back from Sarid to the east, where the sun rises, up to the border of Kislot Tavor, continuing on to Davrat and rising up to Yafia;
13 from there, it turned eastward to Gat Ḥefer and to Et Katzin and reached Rimon, where it curved toward Ne'a;
14 the border then swung around north of Ḥanaton and ended in the Yiftaḥ El Valley.
15 With Katat, Nahalal, Shimron, Yidala, and Beit Leḥem, there were twelve cities with their villages.
16 This was the Zebulunites' estate, divided by their clans – these cities with their villages.

17 The fourth lot fell to Yissakhar, to the Issacharites by their clans.
18 Their territory comprised Yizre'el, Kesulot, and Shunem,
19 Ḥafarayim, Shion, and Anaḥarat,
20 Rabit, Kishyon, and Evetz,
21 Remet, Ein Ganim, Ein Ḥada, and Beit Patzetz.
22 Their border reached Tavor, Shahatzima, and Beit Shemesh, and ended at the Jordan; sixteen cities with their villages.
23 This was the tribe of Yissakhar's estate, divided by their clans – the cities and their villages.

24 The fifth lot fell to the tribe of the Asherites by their clans.
25 Their border encompassed Ḥelkat, Ḥali, Beten, and Akhshaf,
26 Alamelekh, Amad, and Mishal,
then touched Carmel on the west and Shiḥor Livnat;
27 it turned back to the east toward Beit Dagon and reached Zevulun and the Yiftaḥ El Valley to the north, Beit HaEmek and Ne'iel, and continued on
28 to Kabul on the north, Evron, Reḥov, Ḥamon, and Kana, up to Greater Sidon;
29 the border then turned back toward Rama to the fortified city of Tyre;
then the border turned back toward Ḥosa and ended at the sea by the Akhziva district.
30 With Uma, Afek, and Reḥov, there were twenty-two cities with their villages.
31 This was the tribe of Asher's estate, divided by their clans; these cities and their villages.

32 The sixth lot fell to Naftali, to the tribe of the Naftalites by their clans.
33 Their border ran from Ḥelef, Elon in Tzaananim, Adami HaNekev, and Yavne'el, to Lakum, and ended at the Jordan;
34 the border then turned back westward to Aznot Tavor and from there

continued toward Ḥukok, reaching Zevulun at the south, Asher at the
west, and Yehuda at the Jordan to the east.
35 Its fortified cities were Tzidim, Tzer, Ḥamat, Rakat, and Kinneret,
36 Adama, Rama, and Ḥatzor,
37 Kedesh, Edre'i, and Ein Ḥatzor,
38 Yiron, Migdal El, Ḥorem, Beit Anat, and Beit Shemesh: nineteen cities
with their villages.
39 This was the tribe of Naftali's estate, divided according to its clans – the
cities and their villages.

40 41 The seventh lot fell to the tribe of Dan by their clans. The borders of their
estate ran through Tzora, Eshta'ol, and Ir Shemesh,
42 Shaalabin, Ayalon, and Yitla,
43 Eilon, Timna, and Ekron,
44 Eltekeh, Gibeton, and Baalat,
45 Yehud, Benei Berak, and Gat Rimon,
46 and the waters of the Yarkon and Rakon, including the shoreline facing
Jaffa.
47 But the Danite territory was not sufficient for them, so the Danites marched
up to Leshem, captured it, and put it to the sword. They took possession
of it and settled it, renaming Leshem as Dan after their ancestor Dan.
48 This was the tribe of Dan's estate, divided by their clans; these cities and
their villages.

49 When they had finished allotting the land, with all its borders, the Israelites
50 bestowed an estate on Yehoshua son of Nun among them. At the Lord's
word, they gave him the city he requested: Timnat Seraḥ in the hill country
of Efrayim. He built up the city and settled it.

51 These are the estates that the priest Elazar, Yehoshua son of Nun, and
the clan leaders allotted to the Israelite tribes at Shilo, before the Lord,
at the entrance to the Tent of Meeting. And so they finished dividing up
the land.

20 1 2 The Lord spoke to Yehoshua, saying, "Tell the Israelites: assign yourselves
3 the cities of refuge I bid you through Moshe,[19] so that an accidental,
unwitting killer – a manslaughterer – may flee there; they shall give him
4 refuge from the blood avenger. When he flees to one of these cities, he
shall stand by the entrance of the city gate and plead his case before the
city elders, and then they will receive him into the city and give him a
5 place to live among them. If the blood avenger pursues him, they will not
hand the killer over to him, for he struck his fellow man unintentionally;
6 he never hated him before. He shall dwell in that city until he stands trial
before the court. Upon the death of the High Priest of that time, and only
then, the killer may return to his hometown and home, to the city from
which he fled."

19 | See Numbers, chapter 35, and Deuteronomy 5:41–49.

7 So they dedicated Kedesh in the Naftali hills in the Galilee, and Shekhem
in the Efrayim hills, and Kiryat Arba – that is, Ḥevron – in the Judean hills.
8 Across the Jordan, east of Yeriḥo, they assigned Betzer in the wilderness on
the plain of the tribe of Reuven, Ramot in Gadite Gilad, and Golan in the
9 Manassite Bashan. In any case of accidental manslaughter, any Israelite – or
stranger staying among them – could flee to any of these designated cities
so that they would not die at the hand of the blood avenger before standing
trial before the court.

21 1 The ancestral heads of the Levites approached the priest Elazar, Yehoshua
2 son of Nun, and the ancestral heads of the tribes of Israel and spoke to
them at Shilo in the land of Canaan: "The Lord commanded, through
Moshe, that you give us cities to live in and pastureland for our livestock."
3 So, at the Lord's word, the Israelites gave the Levites these cities and
pasturelands from their own estates.

4 The first lot fell to the Kehatite clan, and the sons of Aharon the priest of
the Levites received thirteen cities, by lot, from the tribe of Yehuda, the
tribe of Shimon, and the tribe of Binyamin.

5 The remaining Kehatites received ten cities by lot from clans of the tribe
6 of Efrayim, the tribe of Dan, and half of the tribe of Menashe. The sons
of Gershon received thirteen cities by lot from the clans of the tribe of
Yissakhar, the tribe of Asher, the tribe of Naftali, and half the tribe of
7 Menashe in the Bashan. The Merarites by their clans received twelve cities
from the tribe of Reuven, the tribe of Gad, and the tribe of Zevulun.

8 The Israelites gave these cities and their pasturelands to the Levites by lot,
as the Lord had commanded through Moshe.

9 The Judahite tribe and the Simeonite tribe gave these cities, listed below by
10 name, to the sons of Aharon, of the Levite Kehatites, for the lot fell to them
11 first. They gave them Kiryat Arba,[20] who was father of the Anakites – that
12 is, Ḥevron – in the Judean hills, and all the pastureland around it; but the
fields within the city and its villages were given to Kalev son of Yefuneh
as his property.[21]

13 To the sons of the priest Aharon, they gave the killers' city of refuge – that
is, Ḥevron – and its pasturelands, and Livna and its pasturelands,
14 Yatir and its pasturelands, Eshtemoa and its pasturelands,
15 Ḥolon and its pasturelands, Devir and its pasturelands,
16 Ayin and its pasturelands, Yuta and its pasturelands, and Beit Shemesh and
its pasturelands; nine cities from these two tribes.

20 | Meaning the City of Arba.

21 | The *migrash*, here translated "pastureland," refers to the band of land around the city and adjacent to its walls, used for sheep and goat pens and for other agricultural installations and equipment. The fields (*sadeh*) of the city were farther away, beyond the pasturelands.

17 From the tribe of Binyamin:
Givon and its pasturelands, Geva and its pasturelands,
18 Anatot and its pasturelands, and Almon and its pasturelands; four cities.
19 In all, the cities of Aharon's sons numbered thirteen cities with their pasturelands.

20 As for the Levite Kehatite clans – the remaining Kehatites – the cities that fell to them by lot were from the tribe of Efrayim.
21 They were given the killers' city of refuge Shekhem and its pasturelands in the Efrayim hills, Gezer and its pasturelands,
22 Kivtzayim and its pasturelands, and Beit Ḥoron and its pasturelands – four cities.

23 From the tribe of Dan:
Eltekeh and its pasturelands, Gibeton and its pasturelands,
24 Ayalon and its pasturelands, and Gat Rimon and its pasturelands – four cities.

25 From half the tribe of Menashe:
Tanakh and its pasturelands and Gat Rimon and its pasturelands – two cities.

26 Ten cities in all and their pasturelands for the remaining Kehatites.

27 As for the Gershonite clan of the Levites, from half the tribe of Menashe:
the killers' city of refuge Golan in Bashan and its pasturelands, and Be'eshtera and its pasturelands – two cities.

28 From the tribe of Yissakhar:
Kishyon and its pasturelands, Daverat and its pasturelands,
29 Yarmut and its pasturelands, and Ein Ganim and its pasturelands – four cities.

30 From the tribe of Asher:
Mishal and its pasturelands, Avdon and its pasturelands,
31 Ḥelkat and its pasturelands, and Reḥov and its pasturelands – four cities.

32 From the tribe of Naftali:
the killers' city of refuge Kedesh in Galilee and its pasturelands, Ḥamot Dor and its pasturelands, and Kartan and its pasturelands – three cities.

33 In all, the cities of the Gershonite clan numbered thirteen cities with their pasturelands.

34 As for the Merarite clan, the remaining Levites:
from the tribe of Zevulun:
Yokne'am and its pasturelands, Karta and its pasturelands,
35 Dimna and its pasturelands, and Nahalal and its pasturelands – four cities.[22]

22 | A parallel list of Levitical cities in 1 Chronicles, chapter 6, includes a description of

36 From the tribe of Gad:
the killers' city of refuge Ramot in Gilad and its pasturelands, Maḥanayim
and its pasturelands,
37 Ḥeshbon and its pasturelands, and Yazer and its pasturelands – four cities
in all.

38 In all, the Merarite clans – the remaining Levites – were allotted twelve
cities.

39 In all, the Levite cities in the midst of the Israelite territories numbered
40 forty-eight cities with their pasturelands. These were the cities; each city
was surrounded by its pasturelands, and so it was with every one of these
cities.

41 The LORD gave Israel the entire land He had sworn to give their ancestors;
42 they took possession of it and settled in it. The LORD granted them rest on
all sides, just as He had sworn to their ancestors. Not a single one of their
enemies withstood them – the LORD delivered all their enemies into their
43 hands. Not one of the good things the LORD had promised the House of
Israel was wanting; everything came to pass.

22 1 Then Yehoshua summoned the Reubenites, the Gadites, and half the tribe
2 of Menashe and said to them, "You have performed everything that Moshe,
the LORD's servant, commanded you, and you have obeyed me in all that I
3 commanded you. You have not abandoned your brothers all this time – to
this very day – and you have fulfilled the charge of the LORD your God's
4 command. Now the LORD your God has granted rest to your brothers, as
He promised them, so turn now and make your way home to the lands of
your holding, which Moshe, the LORD's servant, assigned to you beyond
5 the Jordan. Only take great care to fulfill the laws and teachings that Moshe,
the LORD's servant, commanded you to follow, to love the LORD your God,
to walk in all His ways, to keep His commandments, to cling to Him, and
to serve Him with all your heart and all your soul."

6 Yehoshua blessed them and sent them off, and they made their way
home.

7 Moshe had assigned the Bashan to half the tribe of Menashe, while to the
other half Yehoshua had assigned land with their brothers on the western
8 side of the Jordan. Yehoshua also sent them off and blessed them. "Go back
home with great wealth," he said to them, "with great wealth in cattle, silver
and gold, bronze and iron, and a great many garments. Share the spoils of
your enemies with your brothers."

---

cities from the tribe of Reuven, which can be seen in smaller font in the Hebrew text on the facing page. Mention of these cities in Joshua does not appear in most manuscripts, and our English translation does not include this description (cf. 1 Ch. 6:63–64), which reads as follows: "Beyond the Jordan at Yeriḥo, on the east side of the Jordan, from the tribe of Reuven: Betzer in the wilderness with its pasturelands, Yahtza with its pasturelands, Kedemot with its pasturelands, and Meifaat with its pasturelands."

9 So the Reubenites, the Gadites, and half the tribe of Menashe returned,
setting out from the Israelites at Shilo in the land of Canaan toward the land
of the Gilad to the land of their holding, where they had taken possession
10 because of the LORD's word transmitted through Moshe. They arrived at
the Jordan region in the land of Canaan, and there beside the Jordan, the
Reubenites, the Gadites, and half the tribe of Menashe built an altar – an
altar mighty to behold.

11 Word reached the Israelites: "The Reubenites, the Gadites, and half the
tribe of Menashe have built an altar facing the land of Canaan in the
12 Jordan region beyond the border of the Israelites!" When the Israelites
heard this, the entire Israelite assembly gathered together at Shiloh to go
to war against them.

13 The Israelites then sent Pinḥas, son of Elazar the priest, to the Reubenites,
14 the Gadites, and half the tribe of Menashe in the land of Gilad, along
with ten leaders, one head of an ancestral family for each of the Israelite
tribes; each was the head of his ancestral house of thousands of Israelites.
15 They reached the Reubenites, the Gadites, and half the tribe of Menashe
16 in the land of Gilad and accused them: "Thus says the entire community
of the LORD: Why have you broken faith with the God of Israel, turning
away from the LORD today by building yourselves an altar to rebel today
17 against the LORD? Was the sin of Peor – from which we have not yet
purified ourselves to this day – not enough for us, when the plague ravaged
18 the LORD's community?[23] If you turn away from the LORD today and
rebel against the LORD today, tomorrow He shall rage against the entire
19 community of Israel! If the land of your holding is unclean, then cross over
to the land of the LORD's holding where the LORD's Tabernacle dwells,
and take possession among us. But do not rebel against the LORD or rebel
against us by building yourselves any altar besides an altar for the LORD
20 our God. When Akhan the Zeraḥite broke faith and broke the ban, there
was rage against the entire community of Israel – he was not the only one
who perished for his sin!"[24]

21 The Reubenites, the Gadites, and half the tribe of Menashe answered,
speaking to the heads of Israel's thousands:

22 "O LORD, God of gods! O LORD, God of gods! He knows, and Israel shall
23 know. If we rebelled or broke faith with the LORD, do not save us today! If
we had built an altar to turn away from the LORD, to offer up burnt offerings
and grain offerings, or to offer up peace offerings – then the LORD would
24 seek us out. No – we were moved by concern that one day, your children
will say to our children, 'What have you to do with the LORD, God of
25 Israel? The LORD placed a boundary between you and us, Reubenites and
Gadites – the Jordan! You have no share in the LORD!' Your children will

---

23 | See Numbers 25:1–9.
24 | See chapter 7.

26 prevent our children from fearing the LORD. So we said, let us now build
27 an altar – not for burnt offerings, and not for sacrifices, but as testimony
between us and you, and all future generations, that we remain entitled to
perform services to the LORD before Him with our burnt offerings and our
sacrifices and our peace offerings; so that your children will not say to our
28 children tomorrow, 'You have no share in the LORD!' We thought that if
they say this to us or to our future generations, we will reply, 'Look at this
replica of the LORD's altar that our ancestors made – not for burnt offerings
29 or sacrifices but as testimony between us and you.' Far be it from us to rebel
against the LORD and turn away from the LORD today by building an altar
for burnt offerings, grain offerings, or sacrifices other than the altar of the
LORD our God before His Tabernacle!"

30 Pinḥas the priest, along with the community leaders and the heads of
Israel's thousands, heard the Reubenites', Gadites', and Manassites' speech
31 and approved. Pinḥas son of Elazar the priest said to the Reubenites,
Gadites, and Manassites, "Now we know that the LORD is among us, for
you have not broken faith with the LORD; you have saved the Israelites
from the LORD's hand!"

32 Then Pinḥas son of Elazar the priest and the leaders returned from the
Reubenites and Gadites in the land of Gilad to the Israelites in the land
33 of Canaan and reported back to them. The Israelites approved of the
report and blessed God, and no longer spoke of going to war against the
34 Reubenites and Gadites in order to destroy the land where they lived. The
Reubenites and Gadites referred to the altar as Witness,[25] "for it is a witness
among us that the LORD is God."

23 1 Many years after the LORD had granted Israel rest from all their surrounding
2 enemies, when Yehoshua was old, advanced in years, he summoned all of
Israel – its elders, leaders, judges, and officers – and said to them, "I have
3 grown old, advanced in years. You have seen all that the LORD your God
has done to all these nations before you, for the LORD your God is the
4 One who has fought for you. Look – I have allotted to you the lands of
the remaining nations as estates by your tribes, along with those of all the
nations that I have cut off, from the Jordan to the Great Sea where the sun
5 sets. The LORD your God will drive them out before you and dispossess
them, and you shall inherit their land as the LORD your God promised
6 you. But you must be strong enough to keep faithfully all that is written in
7 the book of Moshe's Torah; not to stray from it, neither right nor left; not
to mingle[26] with these nations left among you – do not utter the names
of their gods or swear by them or worship them or bow down to them.
8 9 Cling only to the LORD your God, as you have done up to this day. The

25 | The name "Witness" (*Ed*) is not explicitly stated in the Hebrew but is implied. See also Genesis 31:48 for the name Galed (Gal-Ed), likely related to the area of Gilad, where both stories occur.

26 | See Deuteronomy 7:3.

LORD has dispossessed great, mighty nations from before you, and no one
10 has withstood you to this day. A single one of you shall put a thousand to
flight, for the LORD your God Himself is fighting for you, as He promised
11 you. Take great care, though, for your own sakes, to love the LORD your
12 God. For if you regress and cling to these remaining nations who live in
your midst and marry among them, mingling with them and they with
13 you, know with certainty that the LORD your God will not continue to
dispossess these nations before you. They shall become a snare and an
obstacle for you, a whip for your sides and thorns in your eyes[27] until you
perish from this good land that the LORD your God has granted you.

14 "Today I am going the way of all the earth. Know with all your heart and
all your soul that not a single thing is wanting among all the good things
the LORD your God promised you – everything has been fulfilled for
15 you; no, not a single thing is wanting. But just as all the good things the
LORD your God promised have come, the LORD can bring all the evils,
too, until He has eliminated you from this good land that the LORD your
16 God granted you. If you violate the covenant of the LORD your God that
He commanded you, and if you follow and worship other gods and bow
down to them, then the LORD's wrath will rage against you, and you will
swiftly perish from the good land He has granted you."

24 1 Yehoshua gathered all the tribes of Israel at Shekhem. He summoned
the elders of Israel, its leaders, judges, and officers, and they presented
2 themselves before God. Yehoshua said to the entire people:

"Thus says the LORD, God of Israel:

"From time immemorial, your ancestors – Teraḥ, the father of Avraham and
3 the father of Naḥor – dwelled across the river and worshipped other gods. I
took your forefather Avraham from across the river, and I led him all about
4 the land of Canaan and multiplied his seed and granted him Yitzḥak. To
Yitzḥak I granted Yaakov and Esav. I granted Mount Se'ir as the inheritance
5 to Esav, while Yaakov and his sons went down to Egypt. I sent Moshe and
Aharon and devastated Egypt with plagues in its midst; then I took you out.
6 I took your ancestors out of Egypt, and you came to the sea; the Egyptians
7 chased your ancestors with chariots and cavalry to the Sea of Reeds. They
cried out to the LORD, and He put a veil of darkness between you and the
Egyptians, and He brought the sea upon them, entombing them. Your own
eyes have seen what I did in Egypt.

8 "You dwelled in the wilderness for many years, then I brought you to the
land of the Amorite, who live on the banks of the Jordan. They fought
with you, and I delivered them into your hand; you inherited their land,
9 and I annihilated them before you. Then Balak son of Tzipor, king of
Moav, rose up to fight against Israel. He sent for Bilam son of Beor and

27 | Cf. Deuteronomy 33:55.

10 directed him to curse you,[28] but I was not willing to listen to Bilam, and
11 he was compelled to bless you – I saved you from his hand. You crossed
the Jordan and arrived at Yeriḥo. The citizens of Yeriḥo fought against you,
and the Amorites, Perizzites, Canaanites, Hittites, Girgashites, Hivites, and
12 Jebusites; and I delivered them into your hand. I sent the plague of hornets
ahead of you,[29] and it drove out the two Amorite kings before you – it was
13 not by your sword or your bow. I granted you a land that you did not toil
for and cities that you did not build, to live in; you eat from vineyards and
14 olive groves that you did not plant. Now fear the LORD and serve Him
fully and truly. Remove the gods your ancestors served across the river
15 and in Egypt, and worship the LORD! If serving the LORD seems evil in
your eyes, then choose whom to worship today: the gods your ancestors
served across the river or the gods of the Amorites whose land you live in.
But as for me and my household – we shall serve the LORD!"

16 "Far be it from us to abandon the LORD and serve other gods!" the people
17 answered. "For the LORD our God is the One who brought us and our
ancestors up from the land of Egypt, from the house of slavery; who
performed these great wonders before our eyes; who watched over us all
along the way we traveled and amidst all the peoples through whom we
18 passed. The LORD drove out all the peoples – even the Amorites, dwellers
of the land – before us. We too shall serve the LORD, for He is our God!"

19 "You cannot serve the LORD," said Yehoshua to the people, "for He is a
holy God, a jealous God – He will not tolerate your crimes and your sins.
20 If you abandon the LORD and serve alien gods, He will turn on you, harm
you, and cause you to perish after dealing so kindly with you."

21 "No," the people said to Yehoshua, "we will serve the LORD!"

22 Yehoshua said to the people, "You are your own witnesses that you,
yourselves, have chosen the LORD, to serve Him," and they confirmed,
23 "Witnesses!" "Now, purge the alien gods from your midst and direct your
24 hearts toward the LORD, God of Israel!" The people said to Yehoshua, "The
25 LORD our God we shall serve, and His voice we shall obey!" Yehoshua
formed a covenant with the people on that day and instituted law and order
26 in Shekhem. Yehoshua then inscribed these words in the book of God's
Torah; he took a large stone and erected it there under the terebinth by
27 the LORD's Sanctuary. Then Yehoshua said to the entire people, "Behold,
this stone shall be our witness, for it has heard all the LORD's words that
He spoke to us; it shall be a witness against you lest you deny your God."
28 And Yehoshua sent the people away, each to his estate.

29 After these events, Yehoshua son of Nun, the LORD's servant, died at the

---

28 | See Numbers, chapters 22–24.

29 | Cf. Exodus 23:28.

30 age of one hundred and ten.[30] They buried him at the border of his estate
at Timnat Seraḥ in the hill country of Efrayim, north of Mount Gaash.

31 Israel served the LORD all the days of Yehoshua and all the days of the
elders who lived on after Yehoshua and who knew of all the deeds the
32 LORD had done for Israel. As for Yosef's bones, which the Israelites brought
up from Egypt,[31] they were buried at Shekhem in the field which Yaakov
had purchased from the sons of Ḥamor, the father of Shekhem, for one
hundred *kesita*,[32] and they became the Josephites' heritage.

33 And when Elazar son of Aharon died, they buried him on the hill
of his son Pinḥas, which had been given to him in the hill country of
Efrayim.

---

30 | Cf. Judges 2:7–9.

31 | See Exodus 13:19.

32 | See Genesis 33:19.

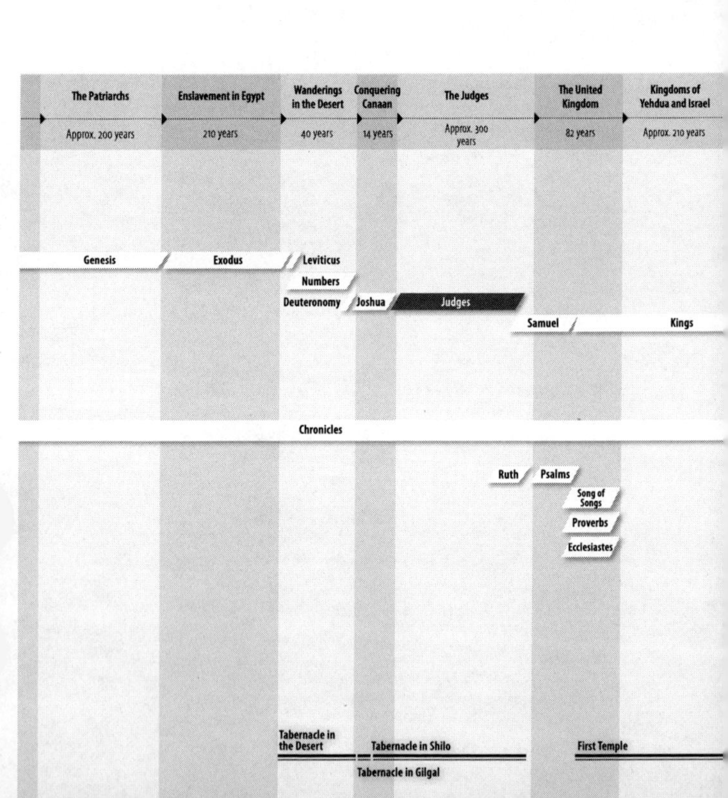

The Patriarchs
Approx. 200 years
Enslavement in Egypt
210 years
Wanderings in the Desert
40 years
Conquering Canaan
14 years
The Judges
Approx. 300 years
The United Kingdom
82 years
Kingdoms of Yehdua and Israel
Approx. 210 years
Genesis
Exodus
Leviticus
Numbers
Deuteronomy
Joshua
Judges
Samuel
Kings
Chronicles
Ruth
Psalms
Song of Songs
Proverbs
Ecclesiastes
Tabernacle in the Desert
Tabernacle in Shilo
Tabernacle in Gilgal
First Temple

JUDGES/SHOFETIM

JUDGES	Tribal inheritances and relations with neighbors and Canaanites Chs. 1:1–3:6	Judges, saviors, and their actions 3:7–16:31	Mikha's idol and the migration of the tribe of Dan 17–18	The concubine at Giva and the wars of Israel and Binyamin 19–21
	Approx. 300 years			

1 1 After the death of Yehoshua, the Israelites inquired of the LORD, asking,
"Who should be the first to go up against the Canaanites and fight them?"

2 "Yehuda shall go up," said the LORD. "Behold, I will now deliver the land
into their hands."

3 "Advance with us to our allotment," Yehuda said to their brother-
tribe, Shimon, "and we will fight the Canaanites together. Then we will
4 accompany you to your allotment." So Shimon joined them. Yehuda went
up, and the LORD delivered the Canaanites and the Perizzites into their
5 hands; they struck down ten thousand men in Bezek. They found Adoni
Bezek in Bezek and fought against him and defeated the Canaanites and
6 the Perizzites. Adoni Bezek fled, but they chased after him; they seized him
7 and severed his thumbs and big toes. "Seventy kings with severed thumbs
and big toes have gathered the scraps under my table," said Adoni Bezek.
"As I have done, so God has requited me." They brought him to Jerusalem,
and there he died.

8 The Judahites attacked Jerusalem and captured it, then they put it to the
9 sword and set the city alight. After that, the Judahites went down to attack
the Canaanites who lived in the hill country, the Negev, and the lowlands.
10 Yehuda marched against the Canaanites of Ḥevron – its previous name
was Kiryat Arba – and they struck down Sheshai, Aḥiman, and Talmai.
11 From there, they set out against the people of Dvir, the previous name of
12 which was Kiryat Sefer. Kalev declared: "Whoever defeats Kiryat Sefer
13 and captures it – I shall give him my daughter Akhsa for a wife." Otniel
son of Kenaz, Kalev's younger brother, captured it, and he gave him his
14 daughter Akhsa for a wife. When she arrived, having urged him to ask her
father for the field, she dismounted rapidly from the donkey. "What is the
matter?" Kalev said to her.

15 "Grant me blessing," she replied, "for you have given me desert land, and
you should give me springs of water." So he gave her the upper springs and
the lower springs.[1]

16 Now, the descendants of the Kenite, Moshe's father-in-law, ascended from
the City of Palms with the Judahites to the Wilderness of Yehuda in the
17 Negev region near Arad; they came and settled among the people. Yehuda
joined its brother-tribe Shimon, and they attacked the Canaanites of
18 Tzefat; they laid it to waste and renamed the city Ḥorma.[2] Yehuda captured
Aza and its surroundings, Ashkelon and its surroundings, and Ekron and
19 its surroundings. The LORD was with Yehuda, and they seized the hills, but
they did not dispossess the people of the valley, for they had iron chariots.
20 As Moshe had promised, they gave Ḥevron to Kalev, who dispossessed
21 from there the three sons of Anak. As for the Jebusites, the inhabitants of

1 | Cf. Joshua 15:13–19.

2 | Literally "waste" or "destruction."

Jerusalem, the Benjaminites did not dispossess them; the Jebusites dwell
with the Benjaminites in Jerusalem to this day.[3]

22 The House of Yosef also advanced to Beit El, and the Lord was with them.
23 24 As they scouted out Beit El – previously called Luz – the sentries saw a
man leaving the city. "Show us the way into the city," they said to him, "and
25 we will show you loyalty." He showed them the way into the city, and they
26 attacked the city by sword, but they let the man and all his family go. The
man made his way to the Hittite country. He built a city and named it Luz,
which is its name to this day.

27 Menashe did not dispossess Beit She'an and its dependencies, Tanakh and
its dependencies, the people of Dor and its dependencies, Yivle'am and
its dependencies, or Megiddo and its dependencies; the Canaanites were
28 determined to stay in that land. When Israel grew strong, they taxed the
Canaanites with forced labor, but they never dispossessed them.

29 Efrayim did not dispossess the Canaanites who lived in Gezer, and the
30 Canaanites lived among them in Gezer. Zevulun did not dispossess the
people of Kitron or the people of Nahalol, and the Canaanites lived among
31 them and were taxed with forced labor. Asher did not dispossess the
people of Akko, nor the people of Sidon, Aḥlav, Akhziv, Ḥelba, Afik, and
32 Reḥov. The Asherites lived among the Canaanite inhabitants of the land,
33 for they did not dispossess them. Naftali did not dispossess the people of
Beit Shemesh or the people of Beit Anat; they lived among the Canaanites,
the inhabitants of the land, and the people of Beit Shemesh and Beit Anat
became forced laborers for them.

34 The Amorites forced the people of Dan into the hills; they would not
35 allow them to descend into the valley. The Amorites were determined to
stay in Mount Ḥeres, Ayalon, and Shaalvim, but the hand of the House
of Yosef weighed heavily upon them and taxed them with forced labor.
36 The Amorite border extended from Scorpion Ascent, upward from the
Rock.

2 1 Once, an angel of the Lord ascended from Gilgal to Bokhim and declared:

"I raised you up out of Egypt and brought you to the land that I promised
2 your forefathers, saying, 'I will never break My Covenant with you, and
you must never form a covenant with the inhabitants of this land – you
must smash their altars,' but you have not obeyed Me. What have you
3 done? Therefore, I said, 'I shall not drive them out from your midst; they
4 will be thorns in your sides, their gods will be a snare for you.'" As the
angel of the Lord uttered these words to all the Israelites, the people
5 raised their voices and wept. They named that place Bokhim,[4] and they
sacrificed there to the Lord.

---

3 | Cf. Joshua 15:63.

4 | Meaning "weepers."

6 Then Yehoshua sent the people away, and each of the Israelites went to
7 his estate, taking possession of the land. And the people served the LORD
all the days of Yehoshua and all the days of the elders who lived on after
Yehoshua and who had seen all the mighty deeds that the LORD had
8 done for Israel. Yehoshua son of Nun, the LORD's servant, died at the age
9 of one hundred and ten.[5] They buried him at the border of his estate, at
10 Timnat Ḥeres in the Efrayim hills, north of Mount Gaash. And when all
of that generation, too, were gathered to their fathers, a new generation
arose after them, who did not know the LORD or the deeds He had done
for Israel.

11 Then the Israelites did what was evil in the eyes of the LORD, and they
12 worshipped the Be'alim. They abandoned the LORD, the God of their
ancestors who had taken them out of the land of Egypt, and embraced
other gods – gods of the peoples around them – and bowed to them,
13 angering the LORD. They abandoned the LORD and served Baal and
14 Ashtarot. The LORD's wrath raged against Israel, and He abandoned them
to the hands of marauders who oppressed them. He handed them over
to the foes that surrounded them – no longer could they withstand their
15 foes. Wherever they went, the LORD's hand moved to harm them, as the
LORD had warned them and as the LORD had sworn to them, and they
suffered terribly.

16 So the LORD appointed judges who saved them from the hands of their
17 oppressors. But they did not obey their judges either, for they strayed after
other gods and worshipped them. They swiftly slipped away from the path
that their ancestors had followed in order to obey the LORD's command;
18 they did not do what was right. Yet when the LORD appointed a judge for
them, the LORD would side with that judge. He would save them from
their enemies' hands throughout the judge's life, for the LORD was moved
19 by their moaning under their oppressors and tormentors. But with the
judge's death, they would relapse into worse corruption than their fathers,
following other gods, serving and bowing down to them, and they would
20 not relinquish their practices or their harsh ways. So the LORD's wrath
raged against Israel, and He said, "This nation has violated the Covenant
21 with which I charged their ancestors, and has not obeyed Me; I will no
longer dispossess before them any of the nations that Yehoshua left upon
22 his death in order to test whether or not Israel will keep following the
23 path of the LORD as their ancestors did." The LORD had let these nations
be rather than swiftly dispossessing them, and He did not give them over
into Yehoshua's hands.

3 1 These are the nations that the LORD left behind to test Israel – all those
2 who had not experienced the Canaanite wars – for the Israelite generations
3 to gain experience of warfare, which they had not known before. The five

5 | Cf. Joshua 24:29–30.

Philistine chieftains,[6] and all the Canaanites, Sidonians, and Hivites living
4 in the Lebanon Mountains, from Mount Baal Ḥermon to Levo Ḥamat – they
served to test Israel, to determine whether or not they would obey the
Lord's commandments which He had transmitted to their ancestors
5 through Moshe. The Israelites lived among the Canaanites, the Hittites,
6 the Amorites, the Perizzites, the Hivites, and the Jebusites. They took their
daughters as wives, gave their own daughters to their sons, and worshipped
their gods.

7 Israel did what was evil in the eyes of the Lord; they forgot the Lord their
8 God and worshipped the Be'alim and the Asherot. The Lord's wrath raged
against Israel, and He handed them over to King Kushan Rishatayim of
Aram Naharayim. The Israelites served Kushan Rishatayim for eight years.
9 Then the Israelites cried out to the Lord, and the Lord appointed a savior
10 to rescue them: Otniel son of Kenaz, Kalev's younger brother. The spirit of
the Lord was upon him, and he judged Israel. He went out to war, and the
Lord delivered Kushan Rishatayim, king of Aram, into his hand; against
11 Kushan Rishatayim his hand prevailed. And the land was quiet for forty
years; then Otniel son of Kenaz died.

12 Then the Israelites resumed doing what was evil in the eyes of the Lord,
and the Lord inspired Eglon, king of Moav, to overcome Israel, for they had
13 done evil in the eyes of the Lord. He rallied the Amonites and Amalek to
14 him, and they launched an attack on Israel and seized the City of Palms. The
15 Israelites served Eglon, king of Moav, for eighteen years. Then the Israelites
cried out to the Lord, and the Lord appointed a savior for them: Ehud son
of Gera the Benjaminite, a left-handed man.

16 When the Israelites sent tribute to Eglon, king of Moav, through him, Ehud
made himself a two-edged dagger a cubit long and fastened it under his
17 uniform onto his right thigh. He presented the tribute to Eglon, king of
18 Moav, an exceedingly portly man. When Ehud had finished presenting the
19 tribute, he sent the men who had carried it on their way, but he himself
doubled back from the carved images near Gilgal and said, "I have a secret
message for you, O king."

"Silence!" said the king, and all his attendants left him.

20 Ehud drew near him – he was lounging alone in his private cooling chamber.
"I have a message for you from God," said Ehud.

21 The king heaved himself up from the throne. Ehud thrust out his left hand,
22 seized the sword from his right thigh, and drove it into Eglon's belly. The
hilt was sucked in after the blade, and the fat closed over the blade, for he
23 did not withdraw the dagger from his belly – and the filth oozed out. Ehud
slipped out to the corridor, closed the chamber doors behind him, and

6 | As in Joshua 13:1 and 1 Samuel 6, these are the leaders of Aza, Ashkelon, Ashdod, Ekron, and Philistine Gat.

24 locked them. As he left, the servants came back and saw that the chamber
doors were locked. "He must be relieving himself in the cooling chamber,"
25 they thought. They waited until it grew late, but he had still not opened
the chamber doors, so they took the key and opened them up – and there,
sprawled on the floor, lay their master, dead.

26 Ehud had escaped while they tarried; he passed by the carved images and
27 fled toward Se'ira. As soon as he arrived, he blasted the ram's horn on
Mount Efrayim, and the Israelites marched with him down the hills; he
28 took the lead. "Follow me," he said to them, "for the LORD has delivered
your enemies – Moav – into your hands!"

They marched down after him, captured the Jordan fords bordering on
29 Moav, and let no one cross. They defeated Moav on that day – about ten
30 thousand men, each one robust and valiant, and not a man escaped. On
that day, Moav surrendered to Israel's hand. And the land was quiet for
eighty years.

31 After him came Shamgar son of Anat, who defeated six hundred Philistines
with an ox-goad; he, too, rescued Israel.

4 1 The Israelites resumed doing what was evil in the eyes of the LORD once
2 Ehud had died. So the LORD handed them over to Yavin, king of Canaan,
who reigned in Ḥatzor; his general was Sisera, who ruled at Ḥaroshet
3 HaGoyim. The Israelites cried out to the LORD, for he had nine hundred
iron chariots, and he oppressed Israel fiercely for twenty years.

4 Devora was a prophetess, the wife of Lapidot; she was judging Israel at
5 that time. She sat beneath Devora's palm between Rama and Beit El in the
Efrayim hills; the Israelites would go up to her for judgment.

6 One day, she summoned Barak son of Avinoam from Kedesh Naftali and
said to him,

"The LORD, God of Israel, has commanded: Go, take ten thousand men of
7 the people of Naftali and Zevulun and lead them to Mount Tavor. And at
the Kishon Stream I shall lead to you to Sisera, Yavin's general, along with
his chariots and his hordes, and deliver him into your hands."

8 Barak said to her, "If you go with me, I will go; if not, I will not."

9 "Then I shall go with you," she said, "but you will find no glory on the
path you are taking, for the LORD will deliver Sisera into the hands of
10 a woman." So Devora arose and accompanied Barak to Kedesh. Barak
mustered Zevulun and Naftali at Kedesh and advanced with ten thousand
men behind him, and Devora went up with him.

11 Ḥever the Kenite had parted ways from the Kenites, who were descended
from Ḥovav, Moshe's father-in-law. He had pitched his tent at Elon
BeTzaananim, which was by Kedesh.

12 Sisera was informed that Barak son of Avinoam had advanced to Mount
13 Tavor. And Sisera mustered all his chariots – nine hundred iron chariots –
and all his warriors from Ḥaroshet HaGoyim to Kishon Stream.

14 "Rise up!" Devora said to Barak. "For on this day, the LORD will deliver
Sisera into your hands – the LORD marches before you!" Barak charged
15 down Mount Tavor with ten thousand men behind him. And the LORD
threw Sisera, all his chariots, and his entire force into panic before Barak's
16 swords. Sisera dismounted from his chariot and fled on foot. Barak chased
the chariots and warriors to Ḥaroshet HaGoyim, and all of Sisera's army
fell by the sword; not a single man survived.

17 Now Sisera had fled on foot to the tent of Yael, the wife of Ḥever the Kenite,
for there was peace between Yavin, king of Ḥatzor, and Ḥever's family.
18 Yael went out to meet Sisera. "Turn aside, my lord," she said to him, "turn
aside to me – do not fear." He turned aside into her tent, and she covered
him with a blanket.

19 "Give me a little water, please," he asked her, "for I am thirsty." She opened
a skin of milk, gave him some to drink, and covered him once again.

20 "Stand at the entrance to the tent," he told her, "and if anyone comes and
21 asks you if someone is here, say, 'No.'" Then Yael, wife of Ḥever, picked
up a tent peg, grasped a mallet, crept up to him – he had fallen asleep,
exhausted – and hammered the tent peg through his temple until it sunk
22 into the ground and he died. Now Barak was chasing Sisera, and Yael went
out to meet him. "Come," she said to him, "I will show you the man you
seek." He came to her, and there was Sisera, sprawled out dead, with the
23 tent peg through his temple. On that day, God subdued Yavin, king of
24 Canaan, before the Israelites. And the hand of the Israelites grew harsher
and harsher against Yavin, king of Canaan, until they had destroyed him.

5 1 And Devora sang –
    and Barak son of Avinoam with her –
        on that day:

2 When chaos was loosed in Israel,
    when people offered themselves willingly[7] –
        bless the LORD!

3 Hear, O kings,
    give ear, O rulers,
I – to the LORD I will sing,
    I will chant to the LORD, God of Israel.

4 O LORD, when You left Se'ir,
    when You marched from the fields of Edom,
the earth shook,
    the heavens poured –
        rain poured from the clouds,

7 | Devora praises the volunteering spirit of the Israelite warriors.

5 the mountains melted before the LORD,
Sinai itself before the LORD, God of Israel!
6 In the days of Shamgar son of Anat,
in the days of Yael,
there were no caravans;
wayfarers walked roundabout paths.
7 There were no unwalled cities in Israel,
none –
until you arose, Devora,
until you arose, a mother in Israel!
8 When they chose new gods,
there was war at the gates –
but no shield or spear was seen
amid forty thousand of Israel!
9 My heart is with Israel's leaders,
the people who offer themselves willingly –
bless the LORD!
10 O riders of white she-donkeys,
mounted on fine saddles,
O wayfarers:
speak out –
11 louder than the sound of archers
by the watering places;
there they shall recount the LORD's graces,
how He graced the unwalled cities in Israel;
then, down to the gates
marched the people of the LORD!
12 Awake, awake, Devora –
awake, awake, burst into song!
Arise, Barak –
seize your captives, son of Avinoam;
13 then the remnant ruled over the mighty people,
the LORD ruled over the warriors for me!
14 From Efrayim, rooted in Amalek:
"After you, Binyamin, with your people!"
From Makhir marched down leaders,
from Zevulun, wielders of the scribal staff.[8]
15 Yissakhar's chiefs were with Devora,
Yissakhar, like Barak, charged into the valley,
while amongst the clans of Reuven
was great soul-searching.
16 Why did you linger among the sheepfolds
to hear the whistling for the flocks?

8 | This and the following verses alternately praise the Israelite tribes that came to war and castigate those who did not.

Amongst the clans of Reuven
was great soul-searching.
17 Gilad stayed put across the Jordan,
and why did Dan stay by the ships?
Asher lingered by the seashore,
staying put by its harbors.
18 Zevulun, a people who risked their lives for death
with Naftali on the open heights;
19 then came the kings to do battle,
then Canaan's kings did battle
at Tanakh, by the waters of Megiddo –
but they took no spoil of silver!
20 From the heavens they fought;
the stars from their courses fought against Sisera!
21 Kishon Stream swept them away,
the ancient stream, the Kishon Stream –
march on, my soul, with might!
22 The hooves of horses hammered
with the gallop, the gallop of the steeds!
23 "Curse Meroz," said the Lord's angel,
"curse its people harshly,
for they did not come to the aid of the Lord,
to the aid of the Lord amidst the warriors."
24 Blessed beyond women be Yael,
wife of Ḥever the Kenite,
blessed beyond women in tents!
25 Water he asked for, milk she gave;
in a princely bowl she offered cream.
26 Her hand shot out for the tent peg,
her right hand for the workman's hammer,
and hammered Sisera
and crushed his head
and smashed and pierced his temple!
27 Between her legs he lay slumped, sprawled,
between her legs he slumped, sprawled,
where he slumped, there he sprawled, slain!
28 Through the window she peered,
Sisera's mother wailed through the lattice,
"Why does his chariot tarry so?
Why so late, the clank of his chariots?"
29 The wisest of her ladies reply –
she even answers herself –
30 "Why, they are dividing up the spoil they found,
a womb or two for every man,
a haul of colors for Sisera,

a haul of colors of embroidery,
colored embroidery, two apiece, for the spoilers' throats."
31 Thus may all Your enemies perish, O LORD,
and may His friends be like the risen sun!
And the land was quiet
for forty years.

6 1 The Israelites did what was evil in the eyes of the LORD, so the LORD
2 handed them over to Midyan for seven years. And Midyan's hand grew
harsh against Israel; because of Midyan, the Israelites made themselves
the tunnels that are in the mountains, and the caves, and the mountain
3 strongholds. Whenever Israel would sow, Midyan, Amalek, and the
4 peoples of the East would come up and raid them. They attacked them and
destroyed the land's produce all the way to Aza; they left no sustenance in
5 Israel, no sheep, no ox, no donkey. For they would ascend with their cattle
and tents like a swarm of locusts; they and their camels were innumerable,
6 and they raided the land to ravage it. Israel was reduced to destitution
7 by Midyan, and the Israelites cried out to the LORD. When the Israelites
8 cried out to the LORD because of Midyan, the LORD sent a prophet to the
Israelites.

He said to them, "Thus says the LORD, God of Israel: I brought you out
9 of Egypt and freed you from the house of bondage. I delivered you from
Egypt's hand and from the hands of all your oppressors; I drove them out
10 before you and gave you their land. I said to you, 'I am the LORD your God;
you shall not revere the gods of the Amorites whose land you live in' – but
you did not listen to My voice."

11 An angel of the LORD came and sat beneath the terebinth in Ofra of Yoash
the Aviezrite.[9] His son Gidon was threshing wheat in the winepress to hide
12 it from Midyan. The LORD's angel appeared to him and said to him: "The
LORD is with you, valiant warrior!"

13 "If you please, my Lord," Gidon said to him, "if the LORD is with us, then
why has all this befallen us? Where are all the wonders our ancestors have
told us about, saying, 'The LORD brought us out of Egypt'? But now the
14 LORD has forsaken us and given us over to the clutches of Midyan." The
LORD turned to Gidon and said, "Go with this power of yours and save
Israel from Midyan's hand: I hereby send you."

15 "Please, my Lord," Gidon replied to Him, "how am I to save Israel? Look,
my clan is the poorest among Menashe, and I am the youngest of my
father's household."

16 "Because I shall be with you," the LORD said to him, "and you shall strike
Midyan down as if they were a single man."

---

9 | Aviezer was one of the clans of Menashe (presumably identical with I'ezer in Num. 26:30).

17 "Please," he said to Him, "if I have found favor in Your eyes, give me a sign
18 that You are indeed speaking to me. Please do not move from here until I
come back to You, produce my offering, and set it down before You." He
replied, "I will remain here until your return."

19 Gidon went in and prepared a young goat and unleavened bread from an
ephah of flour. He placed the meat in a basket and poured the broth into
a pot. He brought it out to Him under the terebinth and served it.

20 The angel of God said to him, "Take the meat and the unleavened bread;
place them on that crag over there, and pour out the broth," and he did so.
21 The angel of the LORD extended the tip of the staff in his hand and touched
the meat and unleavened bread; fire flared up from the rock and consumed
the meat and the unleavened bread, and the angel of the LORD vanished
22 before his eyes. Gidon realized that he was indeed an angel of the LORD.

"Alas, O Lord GOD," said Gidon, "I have seen an angel of the LORD face-to-face!"

23 "All is well with you," the LORD said to him. "Fear not; you will not die."

24 Gidon built an altar there for the LORD and called it ADONAI Shalom. To
this day, it is still in Ofra of the Aviezrites.

25 That night, the LORD said to him, "Take your father's special bull and
the second one, the seven-year-old bull. Destroy the altar of Baal which
26 belongs to your father, and cut down the Ashera over it. Then build an altar
to the LORD your God on the level surface on top of this stronghold. Take
the second bull and offer it up as a burnt offering, using the wood of the
27 Ashera that you cut down." So Gidon took ten of his servants and did as
the LORD had told him. Since he was afraid to act during the day because
28 of his father's household and the townspeople, he acted at night. Early the
next morning, the townspeople rose to see that the altar of Baal had been
shattered, the Ashera over it cut down, and the second bull offered up on
29 the newly built altar! "Who did this deed?" they asked one another, and
inquired and investigated until they determined that Gidon son of Yoash
had done this deed.

30 "Bring out your son," the townspeople said to Yoash, "he must die, for
31 he has smashed the altar of Baal and cut down the Ashera over it." Yoash
replied to all those who confronted him, "Why should you contend for
Baal? Do you have to save him? Whoever contends for him shall be put to
death by morning. If he is a god, let him contend for himself if someone
32 smashes his altar." On that day, Yoash called Gidon "Yerubaal" – "let Baal
contend with him" – for he had smashed his altar.

33 All of Midyan, Amalek, and the peoples of the East gathered together,
34 crossing over and encamping at Yizre'el Valley. The spirit of the LORD
swathed Gidon, and he blasted the ram's horn, rallying Aviezer next to

35 him. He sent messengers throughout Menashe to rally them as well; he
sent messengers to Asher, Zevulun, and Naftali, and they marched up
36 to meet them. Then Gidon said to God, "If You indeed wish to deliver
37 Israel through me, as You said – here, I have placed a woolen fleece on
the threshing floor. If there will be dew on the fleece alone, while the
surrounding ground is dry, then I shall know that You will save Israel
38 through me, as You said." So it was; he rose early the next day, wrung out
the fleece, and squeezed dew from the fleece – a whole bowlful of water.
39 Then Gidon said to God, "Do not be angry with me – let me speak just
once more. Please, let me test the fleece just once more: let the fleece
40 alone remain dry, but let there be dew all over the ground." That night
God made it so: the fleece alone remained dry, while there was dew all
over the ground.

7 1 Early the next morning, Yerubaal – that is, Gidon – rose, along with all his
men. They encamped by Ḥarod Spring. The Midianite camp was to their
north, in the valley by the Heights of Moreh.

2 The Lord said to Gidon, "There are too many men with you for Me to
deliver Midyan into their hands – Israel might glorify themselves instead
3 of Me, thinking, 'My own hands saved me.' Now, call out in the people's
hearing, 'If any of you are fearful or anxious, let them go back and take
flight from the hill country of Gilad.'" Twenty-two thousand troops
returned, and ten thousand remained.

4 "There are still too many men," the Lord said to Gidon. "Take them down
to the water; I will select them for you there. Whoever I tell you shall go,
5 shall go. Whoever I tell you shall not go, shall not go." He brought the
people down to the water, and the Lord said to Gidon, "Separate all those
who lap at the water with their tongues, as a dog laps, from all those who
6 kneel down to drink water."[10] The number of men who lapped from their
hands into their mouths came to three hundred, while all the rest of the
7 men kneeled down to drink water.The Lord said to Gidon, "With these
three hundred men who lapped, I will save you and deliver Midyan into
8 your hand; let all the other men return home." Keeping hold of the men's
provisions as well as their rams' horns, he sent all the rest of the men
of Israel back to their tents, retaining only the three hundred men. The
Midianite camp was below them in the valley.

9 That night the Lord said to him, "Get up and head down to the camp, for
10 I have delivered it into your hand. If you are afraid to march down, then go
11 down to the camp with your lad Pura. When you hear what they speak of,
you will be encouraged – then you will march down to the camp." So he
and his lad Pura went down to the outposts of the camp, where the armed

10 | Kneeling down to drink like a dog was degrading and may have had idolatrous connotations. God selected only those who raised the water to their mouths with their hands like dignified human beings, without kneeling and bending over.

12 sentries were. Midyan, Amalek, and all the people of the East sprawled
throughout the valley, swarming like locusts; their camels were without
13 number, as boundless as the sand of the seashore. Gidon arrived just as a
man was recounting a dream to another.

"I dreamed a dream," he said. "A loaf of barley bread came rolling through
the Midianite camp – it came up to a tent, struck it, knocked it down,
14 turned it upside down – and the tent collapsed." His friend answered,
"That can only be the sword of Gidon son of Yoash the Israelite – God has
delivered Midyan and all its forces into his hand."

15 When Gidon heard the tale of the dream and its interpretation, he bowed
down low and went back to the Israelite camp. "Get up," he announced,
16 "for the LORD has delivered the Midianite camp into your hands!" He split
the three hundred men into three groups and gave each of them rams'
17 horns and empty jars, with torches inside the jars. "Watch me and do as I
do," he said to them. "As soon as I reach the edge of the camp, do as I do.
18 When I blast the ram's horn – along with all those who are with me – you
too will blast the ram's horn all around the camp and cry, 'For the LORD
and for Gidon!'"

19 Gidon and the hundred men with him reached the edge of the camp as the
middle watch began, just after the sentries had been posted. They blasted
20 the rams' horns and smashed the jars in their hands. Then all three groups
blasted the rams' horns and broke the jars, holding the torches in their left
hands and the rams' horns in their right to blast, and called out, "A sword
21 for the LORD and for Gidon!" Each one stood in position all around the
22 camp, and the whole camp ran off, shrieking as they fled. As the three
hundred rams' horns blasted, the LORD set everyone's swords against
each other all across the camp. The forces fled toward Beit HaShita, in the
direction of Tzerera, and farther toward Avel Meḥola, which is by Tabat.[11]
23 The men of Israel were alerted – Naftali, Asher, and all of Menashe, who
24 chased after Midyan. Gidon sent messengers throughout the Efrayim
hills, bidding them, "March down toward Midyan and seize control of the
water sources from them as far as Beit Bara and the Jordan." Every man in
Efrayim was rallied, and they seized control of the water sources as far as
25 Beit Bara and the Jordan. They captured two Midianite leaders, Orev and
Ze'ev. They killed Orev at the Rock of Orev and Ze'ev at the Winepress of
Ze'ev, and they chased Midyan away. They brought the heads of Orev and
Ze'ev across the Jordan to Gidon.

8 1 The men of Efrayim said to him, "Why have you done this to us, not
calling us when you went to fight against Midyan?" They contended with
him fiercely.

---

11 | These are apparently two different locations at which it was possible to ford the Jordan River.

2 "Why, what have I done compared to you?" he said to them. "Efrayim's
3 gleanings are better than Aviezer's finest vintage! It was into your hand
that God delivered the leaders of Midyan, Orev and Ze'ev – what could I
have done compared to you?" As he spoke to them in this way, their rage
against him abated.

4 Gidon reached the Jordan and crossed over, but the three hundred men
5 with him were weary from the chase. He said to the people of Sukkot,
"Please, provide loaves of bread for the men following me, for they are
weary and I am pursuing Zevaḥ and Tzalmuna, the kings of Midyan."

6 "Are Zevaḥ or Tzalmuna already in your hands," the leaders of Sukkot
replied, "that we should supply bread for your army?"

7 "If not," Gidon said, "when the Lord does deliver Zevaḥ and Tzalmuna
into my hands, I shall thresh your flesh against the desert thorns and briars."
8 From there he marched up to Penuel and asked them the same, but the
people of Penuel answered him as the people of Sukkot had answered
9 him. So he retorted to the people of Penuel, saying, "Upon my safe return,
I shall smash down this tower."

10 Zevaḥ and Tzalmuna were in Karkor with their forces – about fifteen
thousand were all that remained of the camp of the peoples of the East;
11 one hundred twenty thousand swordsmen had fallen. Gidon marched up
through the tent dwellers' route, east of Novah and Yogbeha, and attacked
12 the camp which was unsecured. When Zevaḥ and Tzalmuna fled, he chased
after them; he captured the two Midianite kings, Zevaḥ and Tzalmuna, and
terrified their entire army.

13 14 Gidon son of Yoash returned from the battle via the Ascent of Ḥeres. He
captured a boy from among the people of Sukkot and interrogated him; he
had him dictate a list of the leaders of Sukkot and its elders, who numbered
15 seventy-seven men. When he came to the people of Sukkot, he said, "Here
are Zevaḥ and Tzalmuna, about whom you taunted me! You said, 'Are Zevaḥ
and Tzalmuna already in your hands, that we should give bread to your weary
16 men?'" He seized the elders of the city along with desert thorns and briars and
17 taught the people of Sukkot a lesson. As for the Tower of Penuel, he smashed
it down and killed the townspeople.

18 He then said to Zevaḥ and Tzalmuna, "What kind of men did you kill at
Tavor?"

"They were just like you," they replied. "Each had the bearing of a king's son."

19 "They were my brothers," he said, "my mother's sons! As the Lord lives, if you
had let them live, I would not have killed you."

20 He then said to Yeter, his firstborn, "Get up; kill them!" But the boy did not
draw his sword; he was frightened, for he was still a boy.

21 "You get up!" said Zevaḥ and Tzalmuna. "You strike us down, for strength

comes with manhood." So Gidon got up and killed Zevaḥ and Tzalmuna and
took the crescents from their camels' necks.

22 The men of Israel said to Gidon, "Rule over us, you and your son and the son
of your son – for you have saved us from Midyan's hand!"

23 "I shall not rule over you," Gidon said to them, "nor shall my son rule over
you – the LORD shall rule over you."

24 Gidon then said to them, "Let me make a request of you – let each man
give me an earring from his spoil." They had gold earrings, for they were
25 Ishmaelites. "Of course we will," they said, and spread out a garment where
26 each man tossed an earring from his spoil. The mass of the golden earrings
he had asked for came to one thousand seven hundred in gold – besides the
crescents, pendants, and purple robes of the Midianite kings, and besides the
collars on their camels' necks.

27 Gidon made it into an ephod[12] and mounted it in his own city, in Ofra. All of
Israel lusted after it there, and it became a snare for Gidon and his household.
28 Midyan submitted to the Israelites and did not rear their heads again. And the
land was quiet for forty years, throughout the days of Gidon.

29 30 Yerubaal son of Yoash went home and settled down. Gidon had seventy sons
31 of his own issue, for he had many wives. His concubine in Shekhem also bore
32 him a son, and he established his name as Avimelekh. Gidon son of Yoash
died at a ripe old age and was buried in the tomb of his father Yoash, in Ofra
of the Aviezrites.

33 After Gidon died, the Israelites relapsed and strayed after the Be'alim; they
34 established Baal Brit as their own god. No longer did the Israelites remember
the LORD their God, who had saved them from all their surrounding enemies.
35 And they showed no loyalty to the house of Yerubaal-Gidon in return for all
the good he had done for Israel.

9 1 Avimelekh son of Yerubaal went to Shekhem, to his mother's kinsmen, and
addressed them along with the whole clan of his mother's father.

2 "Speak up now to all the citizens of Shekhem: What is better for you? For
seventy men to rule over you – all the sons of Yerubaal – or for a single man to
3 rule over you? Remember that I am your own bones and flesh!" His mother's
brothers repeated all this on his behalf to all the citizens of Shekhem, and they
4 were won over by Avimelekh, for they thought: "He is our brother." They gave
him seventy pieces of silver from the temple of Baal Brit, which Avimelekh
5 used to hire worthless, reckless men to follow him. He arrived at his father's
house in Ofra and killed his brothers, the sons of Yerubaal – seventy men
upon a single stone. Only Yotam, Yerubaal's youngest son, was left, for he
had hidden.

12 | An outer garment worn by the priests (see Ex. 28).

6 All the citizens of Shekhem and Beit Milo assembled and proclaimed
7 Avimelekh king at the Monumental Oak at Shekhem. When they informed
Yotam, he went and stood at the top of Mount Gerizim. He raised his voice
and cried out,

"Listen to me, citizens of Shekhem,
so that God may listen to you.
8 Once, the trees set out
to anoint themselves a king.
They said to the olive tree,
'Rule over us!'
9 But the olive tree replied,
'Have I ceased to yield my oil,
which honors God and men,
to go waving over the trees?'
10 So the trees said to the fig tree,
'Come, rule over us!'
11 But the fig tree replied,
'Have I ceased to yield my sweetness,
my good fruit,
to go waving over the trees?'
12 So the trees said to the grapevine,
'Come, rule over us!'
13 But the grapevine replied,
'Have I ceased to yield my wine,
which cheers God and men,
to go waving over the trees?'
14 So all the trees said to the thornbush,
'Come, rule over us!'
15 The thornbush replied to the trees,
'If you are truly anointing me as king over you,
then come, take shelter in my shade.
But if not, then may fire flare from the thornbush
and consume the cedars of Lebanon!'

16 "If you have acted truly and sincerely in appointing Avimelekh as king;
if you have treated Yerubaal and his household well; if you have treated
17 him as he deserves – for my father fought for you, risking his life to save
18 you from the hand of Midyan, yet today you have risen against my father's
house and killed his sons, seventy men upon a single stone, and appointed
Avimelekh, the son of his handmaiden, king over the citizens of Shekhem,
19 just because he is your kin! – if you have dealt truly and sincerely with
Yerubaal and his house today, then rejoice in Avimelekh, and may he, too,
20 rejoice in you. But if not, may fire flare from Avimelekh and consume the
citizens of Shekhem and Beit Milo, and may fire flare from the citizens of
Shekhem and Beit Milo and consume Avimelekh!"

21 With that, Yotam fled, escaping toward Be'er, where he stayed because of
his brother Avimelekh.

22 Avimelekh ruled over Shekhem for three years. Then God stirred up an ill
23 wind between Avimelekh and the citizens of Shekhem, and the citizens
24 of Shekhem betrayed Avimelekh. This was in order to turn the violence
against and the blood of the seventy sons of Yerubaal toward their brother
Avimelekh, who killed them, and toward the citizens of Shekhem, who
25 empowered him to kill his brothers. The citizens of Shekhem lay ambushes
against him on the hilltops and robbed everyone who passed by them on
the road, but Avimelekh was informed of this.

26 Gaal son of Eved and his brothers passed through Shekhem, and the
27 citizens of Shekhem placed their confidence in him. They went out to the
fields, harvested and trampled the vintage of their vineyards, and held
celebrations; they went to the temple of their gods and feasted, drank, and
cursed Avimelekh.

28 "Who is this Avimelekh compared to Shekhem, that we need serve him?"
said Gaal son of Eved. "He is but the son of Yerubaal, and Zevul is but his
deputy. We should serve the descendants of Ḥamor, Shekhem's father – why
29 should we be serving him? If only this people were in my hands – I would get
rid of Avimelekh!" And he addressed Avimelekh, "Muster your full forces
and come forth!"

30 Zevul, the city governor, heard Gaal's speech and grew furious. He sent a
31 secret message to Avimelekh: "Beware – Gaal son of Eved and his brothers
32 have arrived in Shekhem, and they are inciting the city against you. Take
action tonight, you and the men on your side, and lay ambush in the field.
33 Early in the morning, at daybreak, raid the city – he and the troops on
his side will charge at you, and you will do to him what you find in your
power."

34 So Avimelekh and all the men on his side rose at night: they set up four
35 large groups in ambush against Shekhem. When Gaal son of Eved went
out and stood by the entrance to the city gate, Avimelekh and his men
36 rose from ambush. Gaal saw the men and said to Zevul, "Look – men are
coming down from the mountaintops!" Zevul replied, "The shadows of
the mountains look like people to you."

37 But Gaal spoke up again. "Look," he said, "men are coming down from the
uplands, and another large group is coming from the Augurs' Oak Road."
38 Zevul said to him, "Where, then, is that bold mouth of yours, boasting,
'Who is Avimelekh, that we should serve him?' Aren't those the men you
39 scorned? Go on, now – go fight him!" So Gaal went out before the citizens
40 of Shekhem and fought with Avimelekh. Avimelekh pursued him, and
Gaal fled before him. Many fell slain all the way up to the entrance gate.
41 Avimelekh remained in Aruma while Zevul drove Gaal and his kinsmen
away and kept them out of Shekhem.

42 The next day, the men marched out to the field, and Avimelekh was informed.
43 He took his men, split them into three large groups, and lay an ambush in
the field. When he saw the men marching out of the city, he pounced on
44 them and attacked them. Avimelekh and the group with him rushed ahead
and stationed themselves by the entrance gate of the city while the other
two companies charged against everyone in the field and struck them down.
45 Avimelekh fought in the city that entire day and captured the city; he slew
everyone in it, razed the city, and sowed it with salt.

46 All the citizens of Tower of Shekhem heard, and they made for the
47 stronghold of the El Brit temple. When Avimelekh was informed that all
48 the citizens of Tower of Shekhem had gathered, he marched up Mount
Tzalmon together with all his men. Taking hold of an ax, Avimelekh
chopped off a branch, lifted it up, and placed it on his shoulder. He told
49 the troops, "What you saw me do – quickly, do as I did!" So each of the
men chopped off a branch and followed Avimelekh; they placed them
against the walls and used them to set the stronghold on fire. And all the
people of Tower of Shekhem died, around a thousand men and women.

50 Avimelekh then marched to Tevetz; he set up camp at Tevetz and captured
51 it. There was a stronghold in the town where all the town's citizens, men
and women, had fled; they locked themselves in and went up to the roof
52 of the tower. Avimelekh reached the tower and attacked it. Just as he was
53 approaching the entrance of the tower to set it alight, a woman dropped
54 an upper millstone on Avimelekh's head and shattered his skull. He called
urgently to the boy who bore his arms.

"Draw your sword and put me to death," he said to him, "lest they say of
55 me, 'A woman killed him.'" So his boy stabbed him, and he died. When
the people of Israel saw that Avimelekh had died, they all went back to
their own places.

56 Thus God requited the evil Avimelekh had done to his father by murdering
57 his seventy brothers. As for the evil of the people of Shekhem, God
requited it upon their own heads; the curse of Yotam son of Yerubaal
overcame them.

10 1 After Avimelekh, Tola son of Puah son of Dodo, a man of Yissakhar, arose
2 to rescue Israel. He lived in Shamir in the Efrayim hills. He judged Israel
for twenty-three years. He died and was buried in Shamir.

3 After him, Yair the Gileadite arose; he judged Israel for twenty-two years.
4 He had thirty sons who rode on thirty donkeys and owned thirty villages;[13]
they are called the Hamlets of Yair[14] to this day in the land of the Gilad.
5 Yair died and was buried in Kamon.

6 The Israelites resumed doing evil in the eyes of the Lord; they worshipped

13 | "Donkeys," *ayarim*, and "villages," *ayarim*, are homonyms in Hebrew.

14 | Cf. Numbers 32:41.

the Be'alim, the Ashtarot, the gods of Aram, the gods of Sidon, the gods
of Moav, the gods of the Amonites, and the gods of the Philistines. They
7 abandoned the LORD and did not worship Him. The LORD's wrath
raged against Israel, and He handed them over to the Philistines and the
8 Amonites. They harassed and suppressed the Israelites that year and for
the next eighteen years – all the Israelites across the Jordan in the land of
9 the Amorites in the Gilad region. Then the Amonites crossed the Jordan
to attack Yehuda, Binyamin, and the House of Efrayim as well; Israel was
in desperate straits.

10 The Israelites cried out to the LORD, wailing, "We have sinned against You,
for we abandoned You our God and served the Be'alim."

11 The LORD said to the Israelites, "Indeed, Egypt and the Amorites and the
12 Amonites and the Philistines and the Sidonites and Amalek and Maon
oppressed you; then you cried out to Me, and I saved you from their hands.
13 But you abandoned Me and worshipped other gods – I will save you no
14 longer. Go and cry out to the other gods you chose – let them save you in
your times of trouble."

15 "We have sinned," the Israelites said to the LORD. "Do to us as You see
16 fit – but please, save us this very day." They purged the alien gods from
their midst and worshipped the LORD, and He could not bear Israel's
misery any longer.

17 The Amonites mustered and encamped in Gilad, and Israel gathered
18 and encamped at Mitzpa. The leaders of the men of Gilad said among
themselves, "Whoever launches the first attack against the Amonites shall
become the head of all the people of Gilad."

11 1 Yiftaḥ the Gileadite was a valiant warrior. He was the son of a harlot; Gilad
2 sired Yiftaḥ, but Gilad's wife bore him sons as well. When the wife's sons
grew up, they drove Yiftaḥ away, telling him, "You shall have no share in
3 our father's estate, for you are the son of another woman." So Yiftaḥ fled
from his brothers; he settled in the land of Tov. Worthless men were drawn
to him and went out raiding with him.

4 5 Time passed, and the Amonites waged war upon Israel. When the Amonites
attacked Israel, the elders of Gilad set out to bring Yiftaḥ back from the
6 land of Tov. "Come with us," they said to Yiftaḥ, "and be our commander,
so that we can fight against the Amonites."

7 "But you despised me," Yiftaḥ said to the elders of Gilad, "and drove me
away from my father's house. Why do you come to me now, when you are
in trouble?"

8 "For that reason we ourselves have come back to you now," the elders of
Gilad said to Yiftaḥ. "You shall march out with us and fight the Amonites,
and you shall be the leader of all the people of Gilad."

9 "If you bring me back to fight against the Amonites," Yiftaḥ replied to the
elders of Gilad, "and the LORD delivers them to me, then I shall be your
leader."

10 The elders of Gilad said to Yiftaḥ, "The LORD shall bear witness between
11 us if we do not comply with your words." So Yiftaḥ went with the elders
of Gilad, and the people made him their head and commander. Yiftaḥ
repeated all his terms before the LORD at Mitzpa.

12 Yiftaḥ sent messengers to the king of the Amonites:

"What do you have against us, that you came to attack our land?"

13 The king of the Amonites replied to Yiftaḥ's messengers, "Israel seized my
lands when they came out of Egypt – from the Arnon to the Yabok and
up to the Jordan. Now hand them back peacefully."

14 Once again Yiftaḥ sent messengers to the king of the Amonites. "Thus says
15 Yiftaḥ," they said. "Israel did not seize the land of Moav nor the land of the
16 Amonites. For when they came out of Egypt, Israel trekked through the
17 wilderness to the Sea of Reeds, then they arrived at Kadesh. And Israel
sent messengers to the king of Edom, saying, 'Please let us pass through
your land,' but the king of Edom would not listen; they also reached out to
the king of Moav, but he would not comply. So Israel remained in Kadesh.
18 They trekked through the wilderness, making their way around the land
of Edom and the land of Moav until they reached the eastern side of the
land of Moav, where they encamped across the Arnon. They did not enter
Moabite territory, for the Arnon is the Moabite border.

19 "Then Israel sent messengers to Siḥon, king of the Amorites, the king of
Ḥeshbon. Israel said to him, 'Please, let us pass through your land to our
20 own place.' But Siḥon did not trust Israel to pass through his territory. And
Siḥon assembled all his troops, encamped at Yahtza, and attacked Israel.
21 The LORD, God of Israel, delivered Siḥon and all of his people into Israel's
hands; they defeated them, and the Israelites took possession of the entire
22 land of the Amorites, who lived in that land. They took possession of all
the Amorite territory from Arnon to the Yabok, and from the wilderness
to the Jordan.

23 "Now, the LORD, God of Israel, dispossessed the Amorites before His
24 people, Israel – why should you possess it? You take possession of what
Kemosh, your god, grants you, and we will take possession of everything
25 the LORD, our God, grants us. Now, are you any better than Balak son
of Tzipor, king of Moav? Did he pick a quarrel with Israel? Did he wage
26 war against them? Israel has been dwelling in Ḥeshbon and its boroughs,
Aroer and its boroughs, and in all the towns near Arnon, for three hundred
years – why have you not reclaimed them all this time?

27 I have never offended you, yet you do me wrong by fighting against me.

May the LORD, who judges, judge between the Israelites and the Amonites today."

28 But the king of the Amonites did not listen to the words Yiftaḥ delivered to him.

29 The spirit of the LORD settled upon Yiftaḥ, and he crossed through Gilad
and Menashe; he crossed Mitzpeh Gilad; and from Mitzpeh Gilad he
30 crossed over to the Amonites. Then Yiftaḥ swore a vow to the LORD.
31 He said, "If You deliver the Amonites into my hand, then whatever
comes out of the doors of my home to meet me when I return safely
from the Amonites shall be for the LORD, and I shall offer it up as a burnt
offering."

32 Yiftaḥ crossed over to the Amonites and attacked them, and the LORD
33 delivered them into his hand. He defeated them from Aroer to Minit,
twenty towns, all the way to Avel Keramim – a crushing defeat – and the
Amonites were conquered by the Israelites.

34 Yiftaḥ arrived home in Mitzpa – and there was his daughter, coming out
to meet him, drumming and dancing! She was his one and only – he had
35 no son or daughter besides her. When he saw her, he rent his clothes.

"O, O, my daughter," he said, "you have brought me down low – you have become my scourge! I have gone and opened up my mouth to the LORD, and I cannot go back."

36 "O, Father," she said to him, "If you opened your mouth up to the LORD, do to me whatever it was that came out of your mouth – after what the LORD has done for you, defeating your enemies the Amonites.

37 "Only grant me this one thing," she said to her father. "Let me go for two months so that I may roam the hills and weep for my maidenhood, my friends and I."

38 "Go," he said to her, and sent her off for two months; she and her friends
39 went and wept for her maidenhood upon the hills. At the end of two
months, she returned to her father. He did to her what he had vowed to
do. She never knew a man.[15]

40 It became a custom in Israel: every year, the daughters of Israel would go and lament the daughter of Yiftaḥ the Gileadite for four days a year.

12 1 The men of Efrayim mustered and crossed over, moving northward. They said to Yiftaḥ, "Why did you cross over to attack the Amonites without calling us to march with you? We will burn down your house around you!"

15 | Commentators are divided over whether Yiftaḥ made his daughter live a solitary life or actually sacrificed her.

2 "My troops and I were in fierce combat with the Amonites," Yiftaḥ said
to them. "I summoned you, but you did not rescue me from their hands.
3 I saw that you were not coming to my aid, so I took my life in my hands
and crossed over to the Amonites, and the LORD delivered them into my
hands. Why have you come up to fight me now?"

4 Yiftaḥ assembled all the men of Gilad and attacked Efrayim. The men of
Gilad struck Efrayim down for saying, "You are merely fugitives within
5 Efrayim – Gilad is within Efrayim and within Menashe!"[16] Gilad captured
the Jordan fords that belonged to Efrayim. When a fugitive from Efrayim
would say, "Let me pass," the men of Gilad would say to him, "Are you
6 an Efraimite?" If he denied it, they would order him, "Say Shibolet," and
he would instead say "Sibolet," unable to pronounce the word properly.[17]
Then they would seize him and slay him by the Jordan fords. Forty-two
thousand from Efrayim fell victim during that time.

7 Yiftaḥ judged Israel for six years. Yiftaḥ the Gileadite then died, and he was
buried in the Gilad region.

8 9 After him, Ivtzan of Beit Leḥem judged Israel. He had thirty sons, he
married off thirty daughters, and he had thirty young women brought in
10 for his sons from outside. He judged Israel for seven years. Then Ivtzan
died and was buried in Beit Leḥem.

11 After him, Eilon the Zebulunite judged Israel; he judged Israel for ten
12 years. Eilon the Zebulunite died and was buried in Ayalon, in the land of
Zevulun.

13 14 After him, Avdon son of Hillel the Piratonite judged Israel. He had forty
sons and thirty grandsons who rode on seventy donkeys; he judged Israel
15 for eight years. Then Avdon son of Hillel the Piratonite died and was
buried in Piraton, in the Amalekite hills in the land of Efrayim.

13 1 The Israelites resumed doing evil in the eyes of the LORD, and the LORD
handed them over to the Philistines for forty years.

2 There was a man of Tzora whose name was Manoaḥ, from the family of
3 Dan. His wife was barren and had never given birth. An angel of the LORD
appeared to the woman and said to her: "Look! Though you have been
4 barren and have never given birth, you shall conceive and bear a son. Take
5 care: drink neither wine nor strong drink, and eat nothing unclean. For
indeed, you shall be with child; you shall bear a son. Let no razor touch
his head, for the boy shall be a nazirite to God from the womb.[18] He will
begin to save Israel from the hands of the Philistines."

---

16 | Apparently, a taunt denying Gilad's status within these tribes.

17 | Due to the difference in pronunciation between the dialect of the Gileadites and that of the Israelites of the west bank of the Jordan.

18 | See Numbers, chapter 6.

6 The woman went and told her husband, "A man of God came to me; he
looked like an angel of God – dazzling, awe-inspiring. I did not ask him
7 where he was from, and he did not tell me his name. He said to me, 'You
shall be with child, and you shall bear a son; drink neither wine nor strong
drink and eat nothing unclean, for the boy will be a nazirite to the Lord
from the womb until his dying day.'"

8 Then Manoaḥ appealed to the Lord. "Please, my Lord," he said, "let the
man of God whom You sent come to us again and teach us what to do with
9 the boy who will be born." God heard Manoaḥ's voice, and God's angel
came to the woman once more. She was sitting in the field, her husband
10 Manoaḥ not with her. The woman rushed to tell her husband.

"Look!" she said to him. "The man who came to visit me that day has
11 appeared!" Manoaḥ rose and followed his wife. When he reached the man,
he said to him, "Are you the man who spoke to this woman?"

"I am," he said.

12 "Now," said Manoaḥ, "may your words come to pass. How should the boy
13 be properly dealt with?" The Lord's angel replied to Manoaḥ, "The woman
14 must be kept from all that I said to her. She must eat nothing derived
from the grapevine, drink neither wine nor strong drink, and eat nothing
unclean; she must follow all my instructions."

15 Manoaḥ said to the Lord's angel, "Please let us detain you, and we will
prepare a young goat for you."

16 "Even if you detain me, I will not eat your food," the Lord's angel said to
Manoaḥ, "but if you prepare a burnt offering, offer it to the Lord." For
Manoaḥ did not realize that he was an angel of the Lord.

17 "What is your name," Manoaḥ asked the Lord's angel, "so that when your
words come to pass, we may honor you?"

18 "Why should you ask my name?" the Lord's angel replied to him. "For it
is wondrous."

19 Manoaḥ took the young goat and the grain offering and offered them
up on the rock to the Lord. As Manoaḥ and his wife were watching, He
20 performed wonders: as the flames flared up from the altar to the heavens,
the Lord's angel ascended in the altar's flames while Manoaḥ and his
wife were watching. They threw themselves down with their faces to the
21 ground. When the Lord's angel did not appear again to Manoaḥ and his
wife, Manoaḥ realized that he had been an angel of the Lord.

22 "We will surely die!" Manoaḥ said to his wife, "for it was God we saw!"

23 "Had the Lord wanted to kill us," his wife said to him, "He would not have
accepted burnt offerings or grain offerings from us. And He would not have
shown us all that we saw or made this announcement."

24 The woman bore a son and named him Shimshon. The boy grew up and
25 the Lord blessed him. The spirit of the Lord first stirred him in the Dan
encampment between Tzora and Eshtaol.

14 1 Shimshon went down to Timna and noticed a woman in Timna among the
2 daughters of the Philistines. He went up and told his father and mother.

"I noticed a woman in Timna among the Philistines," he said. "Now, acquire
3 her as a wife for me." His father and mother replied, "Are there no women
among your kin or among all my people that you must go and take a wife
from the uncircumcised Philistines?"

"Take her for me," Shimshon said to his father, "for in my eyes, she is the right one."

4 His father and mother did not know that this was from the Lord, for He
was seeking a pretext against the Philistines. At that time, the Philistines
were ruling over Israel.

5 Shimshon and his father and mother went down to Timna, and when
they reached the vineyards of Timna, a young lion suddenly came roaring
6 toward him. The spirit of the Lord seized him, and he ripped the lion apart
with his bare hands as if ripping apart a kid. But he did not tell his father
7 or mother what he had done. He went down and spoke with the woman,
and in Shimshon's eyes, she seemed right.

8 Some time later, he returned to marry her. He made a detour to see the fallen
9 lion – and there, in the lion's carcass, was a swarm of bees – with honey! He
scooped the honey up in his hands and continued on, eating as he walked.
He went to his father and mother and gave them some, and they ate, but he
did not tell them that he had scooped the honey out of a lion's carcass.

10 His father went down to the woman, and Shimshon made a feast there
11 as the young men used to do. When they saw him, they assigned thirty
companions to be with him.

12 "Let me riddle you a riddle," Shimshon said to them. "If you can answer
correctly during the seven days of the feast, then I will give you thirty
13 blankets and thirty sets of clothing. But if you cannot tell me, then you
must give me thirty blankets and thirty sets of clothing."

14 "Riddle us your riddle," they said to him. "Let us hear it." And he said to them,

"From the predator came meat;
from the fierce came something sweet."

15 They could not solve the riddle for three days. On the seventh day[19] they
said to Shimshon's wife, "Lure your husband into telling us the answer, or

19 | Perhaps the Sabbath, which was the fourth of the seven feast days (Radak).

we will set you and your father's house on fire. Did you invite us here to ruin us?"

16 So Shimshon's wife whined to him:

"You only hate me," she said. "You never loved me. You told my countrymen a riddle, but you never told me the answer."

"Look," he said to her, "I have not even told my father and mother – why should I tell you?"

17 She whined at him for the rest of the seven days of the feast they had; on
the seventh day he told her, for she had nagged him so, and she told the
18 answer to her countrymen. The townspeople said to him on the seventh
day before sundown,

"Honey: What more sweet?
Lion: What terror more complete?"

He said to them,

"Had you not plowed with my young cow,
You would not have guessed my riddle now!"

19 Then the spirit of the Lord seized him; he marched down to Ashkelon,
struck down thirty of their men, stripped their robes, and gave the
garments to the riddle solvers. Furiously, he went up to his father's house.
20 And Shimshon's wife was given to the groomsman who had been assigned
as his companion.

15 1 It was some time later, during the time of the wheat harvest, that Shimshon visited his wife with a young goat. He said, "Let me enter my wife's chamber," but her father would not let him in.

2 "I was sure that you hated her," her father said, "so I gave her to your
companion. But her younger sister is better than she is, is she not? Let her
3 be yours instead now." "This time," Shimshon told them, "the Philistines
cannot hold me accountable for the harm I am about to do them."

4 Shimshon went and snared three hundred foxes. Turning them tail to
5 tail, he took torches and placed a torch between each pair of tails. He set
the torches alight and let them loose into the Philistines' standing grain,
setting fire to the stacked sheaves, the standing grain, and even the olive
groves.

6 "Who did this?" said the Philistines, and they were told, "Shimshon, the son-in-law of the Timnite who took his wife away and gave her to his companion." The Philistines stormed up and burned her and her father with fire.

7 "Now that you have done that," Shimshon told them, "I will not back down
8 until I have taken revenge upon you!" With a fierce beating, he brought

them to their knees; then he made his way down and stayed in a cave of the rock at Eitam.

9 The Philistines marched up and encamped at Yehuda, deploying at Leḥi.[20]

10 "Why have you marched up against us?" said the men of Yehuda.

"We have marched up to bind Shimshon," they replied, "to do to him as he
11 did to us." Three thousand men of Yehuda went down to the cave of the
rock at Eitam.

"You know the Philistines rule over us," they said to Shimshon. "What have you done to us?"

He said to them, "I did to them as they did to me."

12 "We came down to bind you," they told him, "to give you over to the Philistines." And Shimshon said to them, "Swear to me that you will not harm me yourselves."

13 "We will not," they said. "We will only bind you and hand you over to
them; we will certainly not kill you." They bound him with two new cords
14 and brought him up from the rock. When he reached Leḥi, the Philistines
shouted out to him, and the spirit of the Lord seized him. The cords
around his arms became like flax singed by fire; his bonds melted off his
15 hands. He spotted the fresh jawbone of a donkey and shot out his hand to
seize it; with it, he then struck down a thousand men.

16 Shimshon declared:

"With a donkey's jaw –
a mound and still more –
with a donkey's jaw,
I brought down a thousand men."

17 As he finished speaking, he tossed the jawbone from his hand. And he called that place Heights of Leḥi.[21]

18 But he grew desperately thirsty and called out to the Lord: "You granted
this great victory to Your servant's hand," he said, "but shall I now die
19 from thirst and fall into heathen hands?" So God split the crater at Leḥi
and water flowed forth. He drank and his spirit was restored; he revived.
Therefore, he called it Spring of the Caller at Leḥi,[22] and that has been its
name to this day.

20 And he judged Israel during the Philistine era for twenty years.

---

20 | *Leḥi* means jawbone; the name is given based on the subsequent story.

21 | Literally "heights of the jawbone."

22 | Literally "spring of the caller at jawbone."

16 1 Shimshon went to Aza. He noticed a harlot woman there and slept with
2 her. When the people of Aza were told, "Shimshon has come here," they
surrounded the city gate and lay in wait for him all night long. And all
3 night long, they remained silent, thinking, "We will kill him at dawn." But
Shimshon slept only until midnight. He rose at midnight, grasped the
doors of the city gate and both its gateposts, and pried them loose – bolt
and all. He hoisted them onto his shoulders and carried them off to the
top of the hill facing Ḥevron.

4 Afterward it happened that he fell in love with a woman from Sorek Stream
5 whose name was Delila. The Philistine chieftains approached her.

"Lure him," they said to her, "and find out why he is so strong, and how we can overcome him and bind him in order to subdue him. Then each of us will give you eleven hundred pieces of silver."

6 So Delila said to Shimshon, "Tell me now, how are you so strong, and what
might be used to bind you in order to subdue you?"

7 If they bind me up with seven fresh bowstrings that have not yet dried,"
Shimshon replied to her, "I would become as frail as any other man."

8 So the Philistine chieftains supplied her with seven fresh bowstrings that
9 had not yet dried, and she bound him up with them. As the ambush lay
in wait in her chamber, she said to him, "The Philistines are upon you,
Shimshon!" He snapped the bowstrings the way a thread of tow snaps near
fire; the secret of his strength was not revealed.

10 "Oh, you have mocked me and told me lies!" Delila said to Shimshon.
"Now tell me, with what can you be bound?"

11 "If they bind me with new cords that have never been used," he said to her,
12 "then I would become as frail as any other man." So Delila took new cords
and bound him with them. She said to him, "The Philistines are upon you,
Shimshon!" – for the ambush lay in wait in the chamber – and he snapped
them off his arms like thread.

13 Delila said to Shimshon, "Until now you have mocked me and told me lies.
Tell me how you can be bound!"

He replied to her, "Weave the seven locks of my hair into the web."

14 Fastening it around the shuttle, she said to him, "The Philistines are upon
you, Shimshon." He stirred from his sleep and pried loose the shuttle,
loom, and web.

15 "How can you say you love me when your heart is not with me?" she
said to him. "You have mocked me three times now, but you have not
16 told me how you are so strong." She nagged him and pestered him with
17 her talk day after day until he longed to die. Then he poured out his
heart to her.

"No razor has ever touched my head," he told her, "for I have been a nazirite
to God from my mother's womb. If I were to be shaved, my strength would
slip away from me, and I would become as frail as any other man."

18 Delila realized that he had poured out his heart to her, and she summoned
the Philistine chieftains, saying, "Come up, for this time he has poured
out his heart to me." The Philistine chieftains went up to her, bringing the
19 money in hand. She soothed him to sleep on her lap, called to the man,
and had him shave the seven locks of his hair. As she began to subdue him,
20 his strength slipped away from him. She said, "The Philistines are upon
you, Shimshon!" and he stirred from his sleep, thinking, "I will break free
and shake myself loose as before," not knowing that the Lord had turned
21 away from him. The Philistines seized him and gouged out his eyes. They
brought him down to Aza and bound him in bronze shackles, and he
22 became a grinder in the prison. But the hair on his head began to grow
back as soon as it had been shaved.

23 The Philistine chieftains gathered to offer great sacrifices to their god
Dagon and to celebrate. They declared, "Our god has delivered Shimshon,
24 our enemy, into our hands." The people saw him and praised their gods,
declaring,

"Our gods delivered into our hands
our foe, destroyer of our lands,
who left so many dead."

25 As their hearts grew merry, they said, "Call for Shimshon and let him
amuse us!" They summoned Shimshon from prison, and he performed
before them. They positioned him between the pillars.

26 "Leave me," Shimshon said to the boy who held his hand, "but help me feel
27 out the pillars the temple rests upon, so I can lean on them." The temple
was full of men and women, and all the Philistine chieftains were there,
and from the roof about three thousand men and women were watching
Shimshon perform.

28 Shimshon called out to the Lord: "O Lord God," he said, "remember
me – please – and strengthen me – please! Just this once, God, let me
take revenge against the Philistines – just one act of vengeance for both
of my eyes!"

29 Shimshon gripped the two central pillars that the temple rested upon and
30 leaned against them, one with his right arm and one with his left. And
Shimshon cried, "Let me die with the Philistines!"

He thrust with all his might, and the temple collapsed on the chieftains
and all the people inside. The dead he killed as he died outnumbered those
he had killed throughout his life.

31 His brothers and all his father's house went down and carried him back

up. They buried him between Tzora and Eshtaol in the tomb of his father
Manoaḥ. He had judged Israel for twenty years.

17 1 2 There was a man from the Efrayim hills by the name of Mikhayehu. He
said to his mother, "About the eleven hundred pieces of silver that were
taken from you, about which you uttered a curse[23] and echoed it in my
hearing – look, I have the silver. I took it." His mother replied, "Blessed is
3 my son to the LORD!" As he returned the eleven hundred pieces of silver
to his mother, his mother said, "I hereby devote the silver to the LORD
from my own hand for the sake of my son, to make a statue and a cast
4 image; let me return it to you." But he returned the silver to his mother,
and his mother took two hundred pieces of silver and gave them to the
silversmith, who made them into a statue and a cast image. They remained
in Mikhayehu's house.

5 That man, Mikha, owned a temple. He had made an ephod[24] and household
6 idols and had appointed one of his sons to become a priest for him. In
those days, there was no king in Israel; each one did what was right in his
own eyes.

7 There was a young man from Beit Leḥem of Yehuda, which belonged to
8 a clan of Yehuda; he was a Levite who was staying there. The man had
traveled from the city, from Beit Leḥem of Yehuda, to settle wherever he
could; as he made his way through the Efrayim hills, he reached the house
of Mikha.

9 "Where are you from?" Mikha said to him.

"I am a Levite from Beit Leḥem of Yehuda," he said to him, "and I am
traveling to settle wherever I can."

10 "Stay with me," Mikha said to him. "Be my father and priest, and I will
give you ten pieces of silver a year, a clothing allowance, and board." The
11 Levite went along with this; he agreed to stay with him, and the young
12 man became like one of his own sons to him. Mikha ordained the Levite,
and the young man became his priest and stayed in the house of Mikha.
13 Mikha thought, "Now I know that the LORD will be good to me, for the
Levite has become a priest for me."

18 1 In those days, there was no king in Israel; in those days, the Danite tribe
sought out territory to live in, for before that day, no estate had fallen to
2 them among the tribes of Israel. Out of their clan, the Danites sent five of
their number, valiant warriors from Tzora and Eshtaol, to scout out the
land and explore it.

"Go," they said to them, "explore the land." They traveled as far as the house
3 of Mikha in the Efrayim hills, and there they spent the night. While they

---

23 | Either on the thief, or on anyone who withheld its whereabouts from you (cf. Lev. 5:1).
24 | See note on 8:27.

were passing the house of Mikha, they recognized the voice of the Levite
boy, so they made a detour and said to him, "Who brought you here?
4 What have you been doing here, and what is your business here?" "This
is what Mikha has done for me," he told them, "and he hired me, and I
5 have become his priest." They said to him, "Please inquire of God – we
6 want to know whether the path we are taking will be successful." "Go in
peace," the priest said to them. "The LORD is watching the path that you
are following."

7 The five men moved on and arrived in Layish. They saw the people there
dwelling in security as the Sidonians do, tranquil and unsuspecting, with
no one troubling them in the area and no heir to the throne. They were
8 far removed from the Sidonians and had nothing to do with anyone. They
came back to their kinsmen at Tzora and Eshtaol.

"How did you fare?" their kinsmen said to them.

9 "Rise up, and let us attack them," they said. "We saw the land, and look – it
is very good, yet you do nothing! Do not delay; go and attack and seize
10 possession of the land. When you arrive, you will meet an unsuspecting
people. The land is spacious, for God has given it into your hands – a
11 place where nothing on earth is lacking." They set out from there, from
the Danite clan of Tzora and Eshtaol, six hundred men armed with battle
12 gear. They marched up and encamped at Kiryat Ye'arim in Yehuda; hence
that place, west of Kiryat Ye'arim, has been called Camp Dan to this day.
13 From there, they passed onward to the Efrayim hills and reached the house
of Mikha.

14 The five men who had gone to scout the land of Layish observed to their
kinsmen, "Did you know that there are an ephod, household idols, a
statue, and a cast image in these buildings? Now, you know what to do!"
15 They turned off there, and when they reached the quarters of the Levite
16 boy in the house of Mikha, they greeted him. The Danites – six hundred
17 men, armed with their battle gear – stood at the entrance gate, while the
five men who went up to scout the land went inside to seize the statue,
the ephod, the household idols, and the cast image. The priest stood at
18 the entrance gate by the six hundred men armed with battle gear. As they
entered Mikha's temple and seized the statue, the ephod, the household
idols, and the cast image, the priest asked them, "What are you doing?"

19 "Be quiet!" they said to him. "Put your hand over your mouth, come with
us, and be our father and priest. Would you rather be the priest of one
20 man's household or the priest of a whole tribal clan in Israel?" The priest
was very pleased; he took the ephod, household idols, and statue and
21 joined the people. They turned and left, placing the little ones, the cattle,
22 and the goods in front of them. They had already distanced themselves
from the house of Mikha when the people in the homes near Mikha's
23 house mustered and caught up with the Danites. They called out to the

Danites, who turned their heads and said to Mikha, "What happened to
you that caused you to muster?"

24 "My gods," he said, "the ones I made – you took them, along with the priest,
and left! What else do I have? How can you ask me, 'What happened to
you?'"

25 "Do not raise your voice at us," the Danites said to him, "or bitter-souled
men might attack you, and you will squander your own lives and the lives
of your household."

26 The Danites continued on their way. When Mikha realized that they were
27 stronger than he, he turned and went back to his house. Having seized
what Mikha had made along with the priest that had been his, they reached
Layish, a tranquil and unsuspecting people. They put them to the sword
28 and set the city on fire. No one came to the rescue, for they were far away
from Sidon and had nothing to do with anyone, situated as they were in the
29 valley by Beit Reḥov. The Danites built up the city and settled in it. They
named the city Dan after their ancestor Dan who was born to the man
30 Yisrael – whereas Layish was the city's former name. The Danites set up
the statue as their own, and Yehonatan son of Gershom son of Menashe,[25]
along with his sons, served as priests of the Danite tribe until the day of
31 their exile from the land. They maintained the statue that Mikha had made
as their own throughout the time that God's House remained at Shilo.

19 1 Back then, when there was no king in Israel, a Levite man who lived on
the outskirts of the Efrayim hills took for himself a concubine from Beit
2 Leḥem of Yehuda. His concubine betrayed him and left him for her father's
house in Beit Leḥem of Yehuda. She stayed there for a while – for four
3 months. Then her husband got up and followed her to implore her to
return; his servant boy was with him, along with a pair of donkeys. She
brought him into her father's house, and the girl's father was glad to see
4 him. His father-in-law, the girl's father, pressured him into staying with
5 him for three days, and they feasted, drank, and slept there. On the fourth
day, they rose early in the morning and got up to leave, but the girl's father
6 said to his son-in-law, "Eat your fill of bread before you go." So the two of
them sat down to eat together, and then they drank.

"Please," the girl's father said to the man, "stay for the night! Enjoy yourself!"
7 The man got up to leave, but when his father-in-law urged him, he turned
back and spent the night there.

8 On the fifth day, he rose early in the morning to leave, but the girl's father
said to him, "Please, just eat your fill." But they lingered past noon, with the
9 two of them eating. The man then got up to leave – he and his concubine
and his servant boy.

25 | The *nun* of Menashe is written suspended in the Masoretic Text. Without this *nun*, the word "Menashe" could be read as "Moshe."

"Look now, the day is dwindling to evening," his father-in-law, the girl's
father, said to him. "Stay over today; stay here and enjoy yourself. Then
10 be on your way early tomorrow and go home." But the man would not
agree to stay; he got up and left and reached the vicinity of Yebus – that is,
Jerusalem – with his pair of loaded donkeys and his concubine.

11 They were near Yebus, and the day was fading fast. The servant boy said
to his master, "Come now – let us turn off to this Jebusite city and spend
12 the night there." But his master said, "We will not turn off to a foreign city
where there are no Israelites. We will continue toward Giva."

13 "Come," he said to his servant boy, "let us move closer to one of the places,
14 and we will spend the night in Giva or Rama." They kept going, but the
15 sun went down on them by Giva of Binyamin. So they turned off there and
sought to spend the night in Giva. He reached the town square and stopped,
16 but no one was taking them in to spend the night. Just then, an old man was
coming back from his work in the field in the evening – the man was from the
17 Efrayim hills, but he was living in Giva; the locals were Benjaminites – and
he looked up and noticed the traveler in the town square.

18 "Where are you going?" asked the old man. "And where are you from?" He
said to him, "We are passing through from Beit Leḥem of Yehuda to the
outskirts of the Efrayim hills – I am from there. I have journeyed from
Beit Leḥem of Yehuda, and I am going to the House of the Lord, but no
19 one has taken me in. We have straw and fodder for our donkeys as well
as food and wine for myself, your handmaiden, and your servant's boy;
nothing at all is lacking."

20 "Welcome," said the old man, "everything you lack is on me – just don't
spend the night in the square."

21 He brought him into his home and mixed fodder for the donkeys; they
22 washed their feet and ate and drank. As they were enjoying themselves,
some townspeople – depraved men – suddenly surrounded the house,
pounding on the door. They said to the elderly host, "Bring out the man
23 who came to your house so that we can get to know him intimately." The
host went out to them and said to them, "No, my brothers, please do
no harm since this man has entered my home – do not commit such an
24 outrage. Look, here are my virgin daughter and his concubine. I will bring
them out now; torment them and do to them as you please, but do not
25 commit such an outrage with this man." But the men would not listen to
him, so the man seized his concubine and forced her out to them. They
raped her and abused her all night long, until dawn approached, and sent
26 her off at daybreak. As dawn rose, the woman came back to the entrance
of the man's house where her master was, and she collapsed there as it
grew light.

27 Her master got up in the morning and opened the doors of the house to
set out and continue on his way – and there was his concubine, sprawled

28 at the entrance of the house with her hand upon the threshold. "Get up,
let's go," he said to her, but there was no answer. Having lifted her onto
29 the donkey, the man mounted and proceeded to his destination. When he
reached his house, he took a knife, seized hold of his concubine and hacked
her up, limb by limb, into twelve pieces, and he sent one to each and every
30 region of Israel. And all who saw said, "Nothing like this has ever happened
or been witnessed from the day the Israelites came out of Egypt until this
very day; bear this in mind, take counsel, and speak out!"

20 1 All the Israelites marched forth. From Dan to Be'er Sheva and the Gilad
2 region, the entire gathering assembled before the Lord at Mitzpa. All the
leaders of the people, of all the tribes of Israel, presented themselves at
3 the assembly of God's people: four hundred thousand swordsmen. And
the Benjaminites heard that the Israelites had marched up to Mitzpa.

"Speak up," said the Israelites. "How did this evil come to pass?"

4 The Levite man, husband of the murdered woman, answered. "To Giva of
5 Binyamin," he said, "my concubine and I came to stay. The citizens of Giva
attacked me and surrounded the house at night; me they meant to kill, and
6 as for my concubine – they tortured her to death. So I seized hold of my
concubine, cut her in pieces, and sent them out to each and every estate
7 in Israel, for they committed a foul, outrageous thing in Israel. Now look,
all you Israelites – devise a plan of action, here and now!"

8 The entire people rose as one, saying, "We will not go back to our tents,
9 and we will not turn back home. Now, this is what we will do to Giva. We
10 will draw lots; we will take ten out of every hundred men from all the
tribes of Israel; a hundred out of every thousand; a thousand out of every
ten thousand, to collect supplies for the fighters in preparation for their
arrival at Geva of Binyamin – because of the outrage they committed in
11 Israel." Every single man in Israel gathered near the city, united as one.

12 The tribes of Israel sent men to all the tribal clans of Binyamin, saying,
13 "Why has such evil transpired among you? Hand over those depraved
men from Giva. We will put them to death and purge evil from Israel."
14 But Binyamin would not comply with their Israelite brothers. So the
Benjaminites gathered from their towns at Giva to wage war against the
15 Israelites. On that day, the Benjaminites mustered twenty-six thousand
swordsmen from the towns, besides the people of Giva, who mustered
16 seven hundred elite warriors. Out of all these men, seven hundred elite
warriors were left-handed; each one could sling a stone at a hair without
missing.

17 The men of Israel mustered; without Binyamin, their troops were four
18 hundred thousand swordsmen, all of them ready for battle. They set out
and marched up to Beit El, where they consulted God. The Israelites
asked, "Who of us should lead the attack against the Benjaminites?" The

19 LORD responded, "Yehuda should lead." So the Israelites set out in the
20 morning and set up camp at Giva. The Israelite troops set out for battle
21 against Binyamin, and the Israelite troops took up positions at Giva. The
Benjaminites charged out of Giva and struck down twenty-two thousand
Israelite troops that day.

22 Then the Israelite troops rallied and set out for battle once more where
23 they had fought the first day. The Israelites had gone up to weep before the
LORD until dusk; they had inquired of the LORD, asking, "Shall we once
again meet our brothers, the Benjaminites, in battle?" And the LORD had
said, "March up against them."

24 The Israelites advanced toward the Benjaminites on the second day.
25 Binyamin charged out toward them from Giva on the second day and laid
waste to another eighteen thousand Israelite troops, every one of them a
26 swordsman. Then all the Israelites and all their men went up and arrived
at Beit El, and weeping, they sat there before the LORD. On that day, they
fasted until dusk and offered burnt offerings and peace offerings before
27 the LORD. Then the Israelites inquired of the LORD, for the Ark of God's
28 Covenant was there in those days; in those days, Pinḥas son of Elazar son
of Aharon was stationed before it.

"Shall we persevere in battle with the Benjaminites, our brothers, or shall we withdraw?"

The LORD said, "March up, for tomorrow I shall deliver them into your hands."

29 30 Israel set up ambushes around Giva.The Israelites advanced toward the
31 Benjaminites on the third day and took up positions at Giva, as before. The
Benjaminites, having been lured away from the city, charged out toward the
men and began striking them down as before on the highways, one leading
to Beit El and the other in the field toward Giva; there were about thirty
32 Israelite casualties. The Benjaminites thought: "They are being routed
by us as they were last time" – but the Israelites had made plans: "We
33 will flee and lure them away from the city to the highways." All the main
Israelite forces rose from their positions and regrouped at Baal Tamar; the
34 Israelite ambush burst out from its position by the Plain of Geva.[26] In the
thick of battle, ten thousand elite Israelite troops arrived across from Giva,
35 and before Binyamin realized that disaster had befallen them, the LORD
routed them before Israel. On that day, the Israelites slaughtered 25,100
36 from Binyamin, everyone a swordsman, and the Benjaminites realized
that they had been routed.

Now, the Israelite men had given ground to Binyamin, for they were relying
37 on the ambush they had set up at Giva. The ambushers swiftly spread out
38 toward Giva, advanced, and put the entire city to the sword. The main

26 | This likely refers to Giva (cf. v. 10).

Israelite army and the ambushers had agreed on a signal: when they sent up
39 a great column of smoke from the city, the Israelite men would turn around
and attack. Binyamin had begun striking at the Israelite men – inflicting
about thirty casualties – leading them to think: "They are being routed
40 by us again, as in the previous battles." When the pillar of smoke began to
rise from the city, Binyamin turned around – the entire city had suddenly
41 flared up to the heavens! The Israelite troops then turned on them, and the
Benjaminite troops panicked, for they realized that disaster had befallen
42 them. They retreated before Israel along the wilderness route, but the
battle caught up with them at the same time that those in the cities were
massacring them from within.

43 They surrounded Binyamin, hunted them down, and easily crushed
44 them at Menuḥa, by the eastern front of Giva. Eighteen thousand fell
45 among Binyamin, all of them valiant warriors. They retreated and fled to
the wilderness, to Pomegranate Rock, but the Israelites picked off five
thousand men along the highway; they caught up with them at Gidom and
46 struck down two thousand more men. In all, Binyamin's casualties on that
day totaled twenty-five thousand swordsmen, all of them valiant warriors.
47 Six hundred men who had retreated and fled toward the wilderness hid
48 out at Pomegranate Rock for four months. As for the Israelite men, they
headed back to the Benjaminites and put them to the sword – town, man,
beast – everything in sight; they set fire to every city that remained.

21 1 Now, the Israelites had pronounced this oath at Mitzpa: "Not one of us
2 shall give his daughter as a wife to Binyamin." But when the people arrived
at Beit El, they sat there before God until dusk and raised their voices,
weeping bitterly.

3 "Why, O Lord, God of Israel," they said, "did this happen in Israel? Now
4 one tribe from Israel is missing." The next morning, the people rose early,
built an altar there, and offered up burnt offerings and peace offerings.

5 Then the Israelites said, "Who among all the tribes of Israel did not go up to
the assembly before the Lord?" For a solemn oath had been pronounced
against anyone who did not go up to the Lord at Mitzpa: "He is doomed
6 to die." But the Israelites felt remorse toward their brother Binyamin and
7 said, "Today, a tribe has been severed from Israel. How can we provide
wives for those who are left when we have sworn by the Lord not to give
8 them our daughters as wives?" So they said, "Was there anyone among
the tribes of Israel who did not go up to the Lord at Mitzpa?" Now, no
9 one from Yavesh Gilad had come to the camp and to the assembly, and
when the men were counted, not a man from the people of Yavesh Gilad
was there.

10 The assembly dispatched twelve thousand warriors, instructing them, "Go
and put the people of Yavesh Gilad to the sword – including women and
11 children. This is the course of action you should take: every male and every

12 woman who has lain with a man – utterly destroy them." Out of the people
of Yavesh Gilad, they found four hundred maidens who had never lain with
a man, and they brought them to the Shilo camp in the land of Canaan.

13 The whole congregation sent word to the Benjaminites at Pomegranate
14 Rock, declaring peace with them. The Benjaminites immediately returned,
and they gave them as wives the women they had spared from the women
15 of Yavesh Gilad, but there were not enough of them. And the people felt
remorse toward Binyamin, for the Lord had caused a rift in the tribes of
16 Israel. The community elders asked, "How can we provide wives for those
17 who are left when the women of Binyamin have been annihilated? There
must be a surviving remnant for Binyamin," they continued, "so that a
18 tribe of Israel will not be wiped out. But we cannot give them wives from
our daughters, for the Israelites have sworn, 'Cursed is he who gives a wife
to Binyamin.'"

19 Then they said, "Look – the annual festival to the Lord is now being held
at Shilo," which is north of Beit El, east of the highway leading from Beit
20 El to Shekhem, and south of Levona. They instructed the Benjaminites
21 as follows: "Go and lie in wait in the vineyards. When you see the girls of
Shilo come out to dance, come out of the vineyards. Each of you should
snatch a wife for himself from the daughters of Shilo, then head for the
22 land of Binyamin. When their fathers or brothers arrive to contend with
us, we shall tell them, 'Be gracious to them, for we could not provide each
man with a wife through war; because you did not give your daughters to
them, now you will not be held guilty.'"

23 So the Benjaminites did so; they took as many women as they needed from
the dancers they had seized and headed back to their estate. They rebuilt
24 their cities and settled in them. Soon after, the Israelites went their own
separate ways, each man back to his own tribe and his own clan; from there,
each man left for his own estate.

25 In those days, there was no king in Israel; everyone did what was right in
his own eyes.

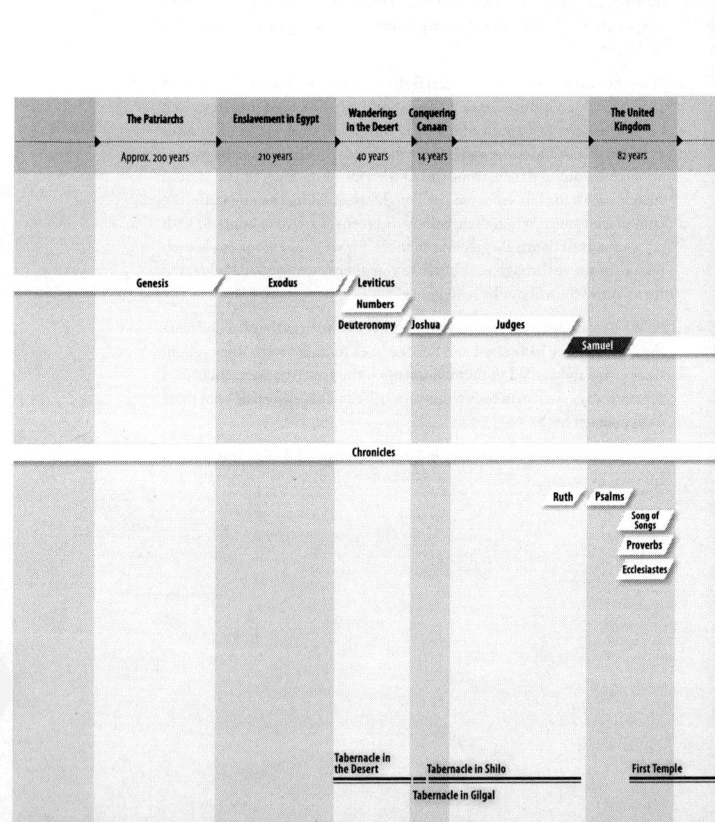
The Patriarchs
Approx. 200 years
Enslavement in Egypt
210 years
Wanderings in the Desert
40 years
Conquering Canaan
14 years
The United Kingdom
82 years
Genesis
Exodus
Leviticus
Numbers
Deuteronomy
Joshua
Judges
Samuel
Chronicles
Ruth
Psalms
Song of Songs
Proverbs
Ecclesiastes
Tabernacle in the Desert
Tabernacle in Shilo
Tabernacle in Gilgal
First Temple

SAMUEL/SHMUEL

SAMUEL	Shmuel's life – from the period before his birth through his initiation as a prophet and judge	Laying the foundations of the monarchy in Israel, through Sha'ul's death and eulogy	David's reign in Ḥevron and the collapse of the house of Sha'ul	David's reign in Jerusalem	David's sin with Batsheva and its ramifications	The Gibeonites, David's warriors, David's song, the census, and the plague
	I Samuel Chs. 1–7	I Samuel 8– II Samuel 1	II Samuel 2–4	II Samuel 5–10	II Samuel 11–20	II Samuel 21–24
			7 years	Approx. 33 years		

1 1 There was once a man from Ramatayim, of the Zufite clan in the hill
country of Efrayim, whose name was Elkana son of Yeroḥam son of
2 Elihu son of Toḥu son of Zuf of Efrayim. He had two wives: the first was
named Ḥana, and the second Penina. Penina had children, but Ḥana had
3 none. Year after year, that man would make a pilgrimage from his town to
worship and sacrifice to the Lord of Hosts in Shilo, where the two sons
4 of Eli, Ḥofni and Pinḥas, were priests to the Lord. On the day of Elkana's
sacrifice, he would give portions to his wife Penina and all her sons and
5 daughters. And to Ḥana he would give a single portion, but choice, for it
6 was Ḥana whom he loved, though the Lord had closed her womb. Then
her rival, to provoke her, would taunt her fiercely, for the Lord had closed
7 up her womb. The same thing would happen year in, year out – whenever
she went up to the Lord's House, Penina would torment her, and she wept
and would not eat.

8 One year, her husband, Elkana, said to her, "Ḥana, why do you weep? Why
do you never eat, and why are you so heartsore? Am I not better to you
than ten sons?"

9 Ḥana rose after the meal at Shilo and after the drinking. Eli the priest sat
10 stationed by the doorpost of the Lord's Sanctuary. Wretched and bitter,
11 she prayed to the Lord, weeping all the while. She then swore a vow:
"Lord of Hosts, if You look down with sympathy on the misery of Your
handmaid and recognize me; if You do not forget Your handmaid and grant
Your handmaid a son, I will then give him to the Lord all the days of his
12 life, and a razor will never pass over his head." As she prayed on and on
13 before the Lord, Eli was watching her mouth. Ḥana was speaking in her
heart; only her lips were moving, and her voice could not be heard, so Eli
thought her drunk.

14 "How long will you act the drunkard?" he said to her. "Deny yourself
wine!"

15 "No, sir," Ḥana answered, "I am a woman of troubled spirit. Neither wine
nor beer have I drunk, but I have poured out my soul before the Lord.
16 Do not think your handmaid depraved, for it was my overwhelming worry
and my torment that moved me to pray just now."

17 "Go in peace," Eli answered, "and may the God of Israel grant what you
seek of Him."

18 "May I, your servant, find favor in your eyes," she said. And the woman
went on her way, and ate, and was downcast no longer.

19 They rose early in the morning and bowed down before the Lord, then
headed back and arrived home in Rama. Elkana was intimate with his
20 wife Ḥana, and the Lord remembered her. At the turn of the year, Ḥana

conceived and bore a son, and she named him Shmuel,[1] "for I sought him
from the LORD."

21 The man Elkana and all his household went up to offer the yearly sacrifice
22 to the LORD and fulfill his vow. But Ḥana did not go up, for she said to
her husband, "When the boy is weaned, I shall bring him; he will appear
23 before the LORD, and he will stay there forever." Her husband Elkana said
to her, "Do what seems best to you; stay behind until you wean him. May
the LORD only keep His word." And so she stayed behind and nursed her
son until she weaned him.

24 Once she had weaned him, she brought him up with her, along with three
bulls, an ephah[2] of flour, and an amphora of wine, and presented him at
25 the LORD's House at Shilo, though the boy was young. They slaughtered
26 the bull and presented the boy to Eli. She said, "If you please, my lord; as
you live, my lord, I am the woman who stood here beside you, praying to
27 the LORD. This is the boy I prayed for – the LORD gave me what I sought
28 from Him. I, in turn, give him over[3] to the LORD – he has been given over
to the LORD for all his days." And they bowed down there to the LORD.

2 1 Then Ḥana prayed. She said:

"My heart exults in the LORD;
 my horn is raised up[4] by the LORD;
my mouth opens wide against my enemies,
 for I rejoice in Your salvation!
2 There is no holy being like the LORD,
 for there are none besides You,
  no Rock like our God.
3 Do not drone on in pride;
 let no insolence cross your lips,
for the LORD is an all-knowing God;
 by Him deeds are weighed.
4 Heroes' bows are shattered
 while the feeble are girded with power.
5 Those once sated hire out for bread,
 while those once hungry grow fat.
By the time the barren has borne seven,
 the mother of many has withered.
6 The LORD deals out death and grants life,
 casts down into Sheol[5] and lifts up.

---

1 | Evoking the Hebrew *sha'ul me'el* (sought from God).

2 | About 23 liters or, alternatively, 40 liters.

3 | The use of *hishil*, "to give over," mirrors that which Ḥana says she "sought" (*shaal*) from Him in the previous verse.

4 | Meaning "I am strengthened."

5 | The netherworld.

7 The Lord impoverishes and enriches,
humbles and exalts.
8 He lifts the poor from the dust,[6]
raises the needy from the refuse heap
and seats them beside nobility,
bequeaths them the seat of honor.
For the pillars of the earth are the Lord's,
and He set the world upon them.
9 He guards the steps of His faithful
while the wicked perish in darkness,
for man does not prevail by power.
10 The Lord's foes shall be shattered;
He thunders the heavens above them;
the Lord shall judge to the ends of the earth.
May He grant might to His king
and raise up the horn of His anointed!"

11 Elkana went home to Rama, while the boy became a servant of the Lord
under the priest Eli's supervision.

12 Eli's sons were depraved men who would not acknowledge the Lord.
13 This was how the priests would deal with the people: Whenever someone
offered a sacrifice, the priest's boy would come along as the meat was
14 boiling, a three-pronged fork in his hand. He would stab it into the
cauldron, kettle, pot, or vat, and the priest would snatch whatever came
up on the fork. This was how they treated every Israelite who came there
15 to Shilo. Even before they burned off the fat, the priest's boy would come
and say to the person who was sacrificing, "Hand over some meat to roast
16 for the priest – he won't accept boiled meat from you, only raw." And if the
man would say to him, "Let them first burn off the fat, then take as much
as you want," he would reply, "No, hand it over at once – if not, I will take
17 it by force." The young men's offense was very grave before the Lord, for
the men showed contempt for the Lord's offerings.

18 Now Shmuel was serving before the Lord – a boy clad in a linen ephod[7]
19 and a little robe that his mother made for him; she brought one up for him
year after year when she made pilgrimage with her husband to offer the
20 yearly sacrifice. And Eli would bless Elkana and his wife and say, "May the
Lord grant you seed from this woman in place of the gift she has given
21 to the Lord," and they would return home. As the Lord took note of
Ḥana, she conceived; she bore three sons and two daughters, while young
Shmuel grew up with the Lord.

22 Now Eli was very old. When he heard about all that his sons had done to
all of Israel, and how they lay with the women who served at the entrance

6 | Cf. Psalms 113:7–8.

7 | An outer garment worn by the priests (see Ex., ch. 28).

23 of the Tent of Meeting, he said to them, "How could you do such things?
24 I hear of your terrible deeds from so many people. No, my sons – the
25 rumors I hear spreading among the LORD's people are not good. If a man
commits an offense against another man, God might intercede for him,
but if a man commits an offense against the LORD – who will intercede for
him?" But they would not heed their father's voice, for the LORD wanted
to put them to death.

26 Meanwhile, young Shmuel was growing in stature and favor with the LORD
and with people alike.

27 A man of God came to Eli. "Thus says the LORD," he said to him. "Did I
not reveal Myself to your ancestor when they were in Egypt, serving in
28 Pharaoh's house? Did I not choose him out of all the tribes of Israel as My
priest – to ascend My altar, to burn incense, to bear the ephod before Me? I
29 granted your ancestral house every one of the Israelites' fire offerings. Why,
then, do you spurn My sacrifices and My offerings, those I commanded
at My dwelling? You honor your sons more than Me, fattening yourselves
30 from the first pick of every offering of Israel – of My people! Therefore,
declares the LORD, God of Israel, I indeed said: Your house and your
father's house shall walk before Me forever. But now, declares the LORD,
far be it from Me; I shall honor those who honor Me, while those who
31 scorn Me shall be slighted. Behold, a time is coming when I shall sever
your arm and the arm of your father's house; there shall be no elder in
32 your house. You shall gaze upon all the good your rival for My dwelling
will do for Israel, but never again will there be an elder in your own house.
33 I shall not cut off every one of you from My altar, but to wear out your
eyes and sadden your soul, all the children born to your family will die
34 in their prime. And this will be the sign for you that will befall your two
35 sons, Ḥofni and Pinḥas: the two of them will die in a single day. And I shall
appoint a faithful priest for Myself who will act according to My own heart
and soul; I shall build him a faithful house, and he will accompany My
36 anointed one for all time. But everyone left in your house will come and
pay homage before him for a pittance and a loaf of bread, pleading, 'Please,
add me to one of the priestly groups, just for a crust of bread to eat.'"

3 1 Now young Shmuel served the LORD under Eli's supervision. In those
days, the LORD's word was scarce; visions were far from common.

2 On that fateful day, Eli was lying in his usual place. His eyes had begun to
3 grow dim, and he could no longer see. The lamp of God had not yet gone
out, and Shmuel was lying in the LORD's Sanctuary where the Ark of God
4 5 was when the LORD called out to Shmuel, who said, "Here I am!" He ran
to Eli and said, "Here I am; you called me." "I did not call you," he said.
"Go back to sleep." So he went back in and lay back down.

6 And the LORD called out to Shmuel once more. Shmuel rose and went to
Eli. "Here I am," he said, "for you called me."

"I did not call, my son," he said. "Go back to sleep."

7 Shmuel did not yet know the LORD; the word of the LORD had not yet
8 been revealed to him. And once again, the LORD called out to Shmuel – for
the third time. He rose and went to Eli. "Here I am," he said, "for you called
me." And Eli realized that the LORD was calling to the boy.

9 "Go lie down," Eli said to Shmuel. "If He calls out to you, say, 'Speak, O
LORD, for Your servant is listening.'" So Shmuel went and lay down in
10 his place. The LORD came and stood there, and called as before, "Shmuel,
Shmuel."

"Speak," Shmuel said, "for Your servant is listening."

11 The LORD said to Shmuel, "Now, whoever hears of the deed I am about
12 to do in Israel – why, both his ears will ring. On that day, I will bring upon
13 Eli all that I have warned of against his house, from beginning to end. I
shall tell him that I have sentenced his house forever, for he was aware of
a crime: his sons have been blasphemous, but he failed to rebuke them.
14 Therefore, I have sworn to the house of Eli that the crime of the house of
Eli shall never be expiated by sacrifice or offering."

15 And Shmuel lay there until morning, when he opened the doors of the
16 LORD's house. Shmuel was afraid to tell Eli about the vision, but Eli called
Shmuel and said, "Shmuel, my son," and he replied, "Here I am."

17 "Of what did He speak to you?" he asked. "Hide nothing from me; so may
18 God do to you – and more – if you hide any part of all He told you." So
Shmuel told him everything and hid nothing from him. "He is the LORD,"
he said. "He will do as He sees fit."

19 Shmuel grew up, and the LORD was with him; He let none of his words go
20 unfulfilled. And all of Israel, from Dan until Be'er Sheva, knew that Shmuel
21 was a faithful prophet of the LORD.The LORD continued to appear at Shilo,
for at Shilo the LORD revealed the LORD's word to Shmuel.

4 1 Shmuel's word became the word of all Israel.

Israel went out to war against the Philistines. They encamped at Help
2 Stone while the Philistines encamped at Afek. The Philistines drew up
their lines against Israel, and when battle erupted, Israel was routed before
the Philistines, who struck down about four thousand men upon the
3 battlefield. When the men reached the camp, the elders of Israel said,
"Why has the LORD routed us today before the Philistines? Let us take the
Ark of the LORD's Covenant with us from Shilo; when it comes among our
4 ranks, it will save us from the hands of our enemies." The men sent to Shilo
and carried out from there the Ark of the Covenant of the LORD of Hosts
Enthroned upon the Cherubim; from there the two sons of Eli, Ḥofni and
5 Pinḥas, accompanied the Ark of God's Covenant. When the Ark of the
LORD's Covenant arrived at the camp, all of Israel burst into a mighty roar,
and the earth resounded.

6 The Philistines heard the roaring sound and said, "What is that great
roaring sound in the Hebrew camp?" When they learned that the Ark of
7 the LORD had come to the camp, the Philistines were frightened, for they
thought, "God has come to the camp." And they said, "Woe to us, for this
8 has never happened before! Woe to us! Who will save us from the hands
of these mighty gods – the very same gods who struck down Egypt with
9 every kind of plague in the wilderness! Muster your strength and be men,
Philistines, lest you become slaves to the Hebrews as they were slaves to
you; be men and fight!"

10 And oh, the Philistines fought, and Israel was routed, and every man fled
11 back to his tent. The defeat was devastating; thirty thousand foot soldiers
of Israel fell. And the Ark of God was captured, and both of Eli's sons
12 died – Ḥofni and Pinḥas. A Benjaminite soldier ran from the battle lines
and reached Shilo that same day, his uniform torn and earth upon his
13 head.[8] He arrived and there was Eli, seated on a chair by the lookout road,
for his heart was trembling over the Ark of God. The man came to town
to announce the news, and the whole city cried out.

14 When Eli heard the sound of screaming, he asked, "What is that cacoph-
15 ony?" and the man rushed over and broke the news to Eli. Eli was nine-
ty-eight years old, and his eyes stared out sightlessly.

16 "I am the one who has come from the battle lines," the man said to Eli. "I
fled the battle lines just now."

"What happened, my son?" he asked.

17 The news-bearer replied, "Israel has fled before the Philistines, and the
men were ravaged terribly. What is more, your two sons died – Ḥofni and
18 Pinḥas – and the Ark of God was taken." As soon as he mentioned the
Ark of God, Eli fell out of his chair backward by the gate post; his neck
snapped and he died, for the man was old and heavy. He had judged Israel
for forty years.

19 Now his daughter-in-law, Pinḥas's wife, was about to give birth. When
she heard the news that God's Ark had been taken and that her father-
in-law and husband had died, she crouched down to give birth, for her
20 birth pangs overwhelmed her. As she lay dying, the women standing over
her spoke to her. "Do not fear, for you have given birth to a son." But she
21 neither answered nor cared. And she called the boy Ikhavod,[9] saying,
"Glory is gone from Israel," referring to the taking of the Ark of God, her
father-in-law, and her husband.

22 "Glory is gone from Israel," she said, "for the Ark of God has been taken."

---

8 | In mourning.

9 | Literally "no glory."

5 1 Meanwhile, the Philistines had taken the Ark of God and brought it from
2 Help Stone to Ashdod. The Philistines took hold of the Ark of God and
3 brought it into the temple of Dagon, placing it next to Dagon. But when
the men of Ashdod rose the next day, there lay Dagon, sprawled on the
ground before the Ark of the Lord. They took hold of Dagon and set him
4 back in his place. But when they rose the next morning, there lay Dagon,
sprawled on the ground before the Ark of the Lord – and Dagon's head
and both his hands had been chopped off on the threshold; only Dagon's
5 torso was intact. That is why to this day, the priests of Dagon or anyone
who comes to Dagon's temple will not tread upon the threshold of Dagon
in Ashdod.

6 The hand of the Lord bore heavily against the Ashdodites, and He
devastated them, plaguing Ashdod and its territories with hemorrhoids.
7 When the people of Ashdod saw it was so, they said, "The Ark of Israel's
God must not remain among us, for His hand is harsh against us and
8 against our god Dagon." So they sent and summoned all the Philistine
chieftains to them, asking, "What shall we do about the Ark of Israel's
God?"

"Let the Ark of Israel's God be removed to Gat," they determined.

9 So they relocated the Ark of Israel's God. Once they had removed it, the
Lord's hand caused a mortifying panic in the city, plaguing the people
of the city – young and old – with hemorrhoids bursting open on them.
10 So they sent the Ark of God on to Ekron, but as soon as the Ark of God
reached Ekron, the Ekronites cried out in protest, "They have removed
11 the Ark of Israel's God to us to kill us and our people." And they sent and
summoned all the Philistine chieftains and said to them, "Send the Ark
of Israel's God back to its place so that it will not kill me and my people."
For a deadly panic had seized the city, God's hand bore down so heavily
12 there. The people who had not died were plagued with hemorrhoids, and
the shrieks of the city flared up to the heavens.

6 1 The Ark of the Lord had remained in Philistine territory for seven months
2 when the Philistines summoned the priests and diviners, asking them,
"What shall we do with the Ark of the Lord? Tell us, how should we send
it back to its place?"

3 "If you are sending the Ark of Israel's God back," they said, "do not send it
empty-handed; be sure to recompense Him with a guilt offering. Only
then will you be cured – when you acknowledge why He would not turn
His hand away from you."

4 "With what guilt offering shall we compensate Him?" they replied.

"Five, according to the number of Philistine chieftains," they said, "five
golden hemorrhoids and five golden mice, for one plague befell all of you
5 and your chieftains. Make images of your hemorrhoids and those mice

of yours that are ravaging the land, and give honor to the God of Israel;
perhaps then He will lighten His hand from upon you, your gods, and your
6 land. Why should you harden your hearts, as Egypt and Pharaoh hardened
their hearts; after all, when He dealt harshly with them, did they not send
7 them off to go free? Now prepare a new cart and two nursing cows that
have never borne a yoke. Hitch the cows to the cart, but bring their calves
8 back inside behind them. Then take the Ark of the Lord, place it on the
cart, and put the gold objects that you are paying Him as compensation
9 in a saddlebag beside it. Send it off and let it go. Then watch: if it makes its
way up to its own territory, to Beit Shemesh, then it was He who inflicted
this great evil upon us; but if not, we shall know that it was not His hand
that afflicted us; what befell us was mere chance."

10 And so the men did; they took two nursing cows, hitched them to a cart,
11 and shut their calves up indoors. Then they placed the Ark of the Lord
onto the cart, along with the saddlebag, the golden mice, and the images of
12 their hemorrhoids. The cows made their way straight to the Beit Shemesh
road and walked along that one highway; though they lowed as they went,
they veered neither right nor left, and the Philistine chieftains followed
them until the Beit Shemesh border.

13 At Beit Shemesh, they were reaping the wheat harvest in the valley. When
14 they looked up and noticed the Ark, they rejoiced at the sight. The cart
reached the field of Yehoshua the Beit Shemeshite and came to a halt there,
where there was an enormous stone. They split the wood of the cart to offer
the cows as a burnt offering to the Lord.

15 The Levites had unloaded the Ark of the Lord and the saddlebag
containing the golden objects and placed them on the enormous stone.
Then the people of Beit Shemesh offered up burnt offerings and made
16 sacrifices to the Lord on that day. The five Philistine chieftains watched,
then returned to Ekron that same day.

17 These are the golden hemorrhoids that the Philistines paid as compensation
to the Lord: one for Ashdod, one for Aza, one for Ashkelon, one for Gat,
18 and one for Ekron, while the golden mice represented the number of all the
Philistine towns belonging to the chieftains, from the fortified cities to the
open hamlets. And to this day, the enormous stone where they placed the
Ark of the Lord remains in the field of Yehoshua the Beit Shemeshite.

19 But He struck down the people of Beit Shemesh, for they had looked upon
the Ark of the Lord – He struck down seventy as well as fifty thousand of
the people. And the people mourned, for the Lord had struck the people
20 a grave blow. "Who can stand before the Lord, this holy God," said the
people of Beit Shemesh, "and to whom will it depart from us?"

21 They sent messengers to the inhabitants of Kiryat Ye'arim, saying, "The
Philistines have returned the Ark of the Lord; come down and bring it
up to you."

7 1 So the men of Kiryat Ye'arim came and brought up the Ark of the Lord.
They conveyed it to the house of Avinadav on the hill and appointed his
2 son Elazar to guard the Ark of the Lord. From the time the Ark came to
dwell in Kiryat Ye'arim, the days slipped by into twenty years, and all the
House of Israel yearned for the Lord.

3 Shmuel said to all the House of Israel, "If you mean to return to the Lord
with all your heart, then remove the alien gods from among you, along
with the Ashtarot, and direct your hearts to the Lord, and serve Him
4 alone; then He will save you from the hand of the Philistines." So the
Israelites removed the Baalim and the Ashtarot and served the Lord
alone.

5 Then Shmuel said, "Assemble all of Israel at Mitzpa, and I will pray to the
6 Lord on your behalf." They assembled at Mitzpa and drew water and
poured it out before the Lord. On that day they fasted, declaring there,
"We have sinned against the Lord," and Shmuel judged the Israelites at
Mitzpa.

7 When the Philistines heard that the Israelites had gathered at Mitzpa, the
Philistine chieftains marched up toward Israel. And when the Israelites
8 heard, they were frightened of the Philistines, and the Israelites said to
Shmuel, "Do not be deaf and dumb to us, not crying out to the Lord our
9 God – let Him save us from the hand of the Philistines!" Shmuel took a
suckling lamb and offered it up as a whole burnt offering to the Lord. And
Shmuel cried out to the Lord for Israel's sake, and the Lord answered him.
10 For just as Shmuel was offering up the burnt offering, and the Philistines
advanced to attack Israel, the Lord thundered with a mighty voice against
the Philistines at that moment, throwing them into a panic, and they were
11 routed before Israel. The men of Israel charged out of Mitzpa and chased
12 the Philistines, striking them down as far as below Beit Kar. And Shmuel
took a single stone and placed it between Mitzpa and Shen, naming it Help
Stone: "For thus far," he said, "the Lord has helped us."

13 The Philistines were crushed and no longer ventured into Israel's territory,
and the Lord's hand bore down against the Philistines for the rest of
14 Shmuel's life. And the cities that the Philistines had seized from Israel,
from Ekron to Gat, were restored to Israel; Israel recovered their territory
from Philistine control, and there was peace between Israel and the
15 16 Amorites. Shmuel judged Israel all the days of his life. Year after year, he
would make his rounds from Beit El to Gilgal to Mitzpa, judging Israel
17 in all those places before returning to Rama; for there was his home, and
there he judged Israel, and there he built an altar to the Lord.

8 1 2 When Shmuel grew old, he appointed his sons to be Israel's judges. The
name of his elder son was Yoel, and the name of his second was Aviya; they
3 were judges in Be'er Sheva. But his sons did not follow his path; they were
bent on gain, and they took bribes, and they bent justice.

4 5 All the elders of Israel gathered and came to Shmuel at Rama. "Look, you
have grown old," they said to him, "and your sons have not followed in your
6 path. Now appoint a king for us to govern us like any other nation." When
they said, "Give us a king to govern us," the idea displeased Shmuel, and
Shmuel prayed to the LORD.

7 The LORD said to Shmuel, "Heed the voice of the people in all they say
to you. For it is not you they have rejected – it is Me they have rejected,
8 from reigning over them. All the deeds they have done since the day I
brought them up from Egypt to this day – forsaking Me and serving other
9 gods – they are doing to you as well. So now, heed their voice; but you
must solemnly warn them, informing them of the royal rights of the king
who will reign over them."

10 Shmuel relayed all the words of the LORD to the people who were asking
him for a king.

11 "These will be the royal rights of the king who will reign over you," he
said. "He will seize your sons and assign them as his charioteers and riders
12 to run before his chariot; and assign them as his officers of thousands
and his officers of fifty, and to till his soil, and reap his harvest, and to
13 manufacture his weapons and his chariots. He will seize your daughters as
14 perfumers and cooks and bakers. He will seize your best fields, vineyards,
15 and olive groves and give them to his servants. He will tithe your seeds and
16 vineyards and give them to his officials and his staff. He will seize your best
servants, maidservants, and young workers, and your donkeys, and he will
17 use them for his own work. He will tithe your flocks, and you yourselves
18 shall become his slaves. And on that day, you will cry out because of your
own king, whom you yourselves chose, but the LORD will not answer you
on that day."

19 20 But the people refused to heed the voice of Shmuel. "No," they declared,
"we must have a king over us, so we, too, will be like all the other nations.
21 Our king shall govern us and go out before us and fight our battles." So
Shmuel heeded all the words of the people and repeated them before the
22 LORD.And the LORD replied to Shmuel, "Heed their voice and appoint a
king over them." Shmuel then said to the men of Israel, "Go back, each to
his own town."

9 1 There was a man of Binyamin whose name was Kish son of Aviel son of
Tzeror son of Bekhorat son of Afiaḥ; a Benjaminite, he was a powerful
2 man. He had a son whose name was Sha'ul. He was a fine young man,
and no one in Israel was finer than he; he was head and shoulders above
everyone else.

3 Once, some donkeys belonging to Kish, Sha'ul's father, went missing,
and Kish said to Sha'ul, his son, "Now, take one of the stewards and go
4 out to search for the donkeys." So he traveled through the Efrayim hills

and crossed through the Shalisha region, but they did not find them;
they crossed through the Shaalim region, but nothing; and they crossed
5 through the territory of Binyamin, but they did not find them. As they
reached the Zuf region, Sha'ul said to the steward with him, "Come, let us
go back, or my father might give up on the donkeys and begin to worry
about us."

6 "Look now," he said to him, "there is a man of God in this town, and the
man is highly esteemed – whatever he says comes to pass. Let us go there
now – perhaps he will advise us about the journey we have undertaken."

7 "If we do go," Sha'ul said to his steward, "then what can we bring for the
man? The bread in our packs is finished, and there is no gift to present to
the man of God – what do we have?"

8 "Here," replied the steward to Sha'ul again, "I find I have a quarter shekel
of silver with me. If I give it to the man of God, he might advise us about
our journey."

9 Formerly in Israel, when someone went to inquire of God, he would say,
"Let us go to the seer," for today's prophet was then referred to as a "seer."

10 "Well said," Sha'ul said to his steward. "Come, let us go." And they made
their way to the town where the man of God was.

11 As they were traveling up the ascent to the town, they met some girls going
out to draw water and asked them, "Is the seer here?"

12 "Oh yes, he is," they answered him, and added, "Look – he is just ahead
of you. Hurry, now – he just came to town today, for the people have a
13 sacrifice today at the high shrine. When you reach the town, you will find
him about to go up to the high shrine to eat – for the people will not eat
until he arrives; he must bless the sacrifice, and only then will the guests
14 eat. Now go up, for this is the right moment to find him." So they went up
to the town, and just as they entered the city, there was Shmuel coming
out toward them, going up to the high shrine.

15 Now, the Lord had revealed the following to Shmuel on the day before
16 Sha'ul's arrival: "At this time tomorrow, I will send a man from the land of
Binyamin to you, and you shall anoint him as ruler over My people, Israel.
He shall rescue My people from the hand of the Philistines, for I have taken
17 notice of My people – their cries have reached Me." As Shmuel noticed
Sha'ul, the Lord answered him, "Here is the man I told you about – the
one who will rule over My people."

18 Then Sha'ul approached Shmuel inside the gate. "Please tell me," he asked,
"where is the house of the seer?"

19 "I am the seer," Shmuel answered Sha'ul. "Go up to the high shrine before
me – you shall eat with me today. I will send you off in the morning when

20 I have told you about whatever is on your mind. As for the donkeys lost
to you these three days – do not be concerned about them, for they have
been found, while whom do all of Israel long for but you and all your
father's house?"

21 "But I am a Benjaminite," Sha'ul answered, "of the smallest of Israel's tribes.
And my family is the most junior of all the clans of the tribe of Binyamin.
Why do you speak to me in this way?"

22 But Shmuel took Sha'ul and his steward and brought them to the hall. He
gave them places among the guests of honor, who numbered about thirty.
23 Shmuel said to the carver, "Fetch the portion I gave you – the one I told
24 you to set aside." When the carver had served up the thigh and the fat
around it and set it before Sha'ul, he said, "Here, what was reserved has
been set before you. Eat, for it was kept for you for this occasion when I
25 said I had invited the people." So Sha'ul ate with Shmuel on that day. They
descended from the high shrine to the town, and he spoke with Sha'ul on
the roof.

26 They awoke early; when dawn rose Shmuel called Sha'ul to the roof. "Arise,"
he said, "and I will send you off." Sha'ul arose and the two of them – he
27 and Shmuel – went outside. As they made their way down to the edge of
the city, Shmuel said to Sha'ul, "Tell the steward to go on ahead of us," and
he went on ahead. "As for you, stay here for a moment, and I will let you
hear the word of God."

10 1 And Shmuel took the juglet of oil and poured it over his head and kissed
him. And he said, "The Lord hereby anoints you as ruler over His estate.

2 "Now, when you leave me today, you will meet two men near Raḥel's
tomb on the border of Binyamin, in Tzeltzaḥ. They will tell you, 'The
donkeys you set out to search for have been found – by now, your father
has dropped the matter of the donkeys and is worried about you, saying,
3 "What shall I do about my son?"' Pass on swiftly from there until you reach
the Oak of Tavor. There, three men making pilgrimage to God at Beit El
will find you: one bearing three kid goats, one bearing three loaves of bread,
4 and one bearing an amphora of wine. They will greet you and give you two
5 loaves of bread; you shall accept them from their hands. After that, you
will come to Givat HaElohim where the Philistine garrisons are. When
you reach the city, you will walk right into a band of prophets coming
down from the high shrine, with harp and drum and flute and lyre before
6 them, caught up in prophetic frenzy. And the spirit of the Lord will seize
you, and you will be caught up in their prophetic frenzy, and you will be
7 transformed into a different person. Then, once all these signs have come
to pass for you, do what you find in your power to do, for God is with you.
8 You shall go down before me to Gilgal – I will soon come down to you
to offer up burnt offerings and to sacrifice peace offerings. Wait for seven
days until I come to you; then I will inform you what you are to do."

9 And just as he turned away to leave Shmuel, God transformed his heart,
and all these signs came to pass that very day.

10 When they arrived there at Giva, there was the band of prophets coming
toward him – and the spirit of God seized him, and he was caught up in
11 their prophetic frenzy. And when all those who knew him from before saw
him – there he was, in a prophetic frenzy along with the prophets – the
people asked one another, "What happened to the son of Kish? Is Sha'ul,
12 too, among the prophets?" Then one man from there retorted, "Well, who
is their father?" Thus the saying came about: "Is Sha'ul, too, among the
13 prophets?" When the prophetic frenzy had worn off, he arrived at the
high shrine.

14 Sha'ul's uncle said to him and his steward, "Where have you been?" "To
search for the donkeys," he said, "but when we saw they were nowhere to
be found, we came to Shmuel."

15 "Tell me, now," said Sha'ul's uncle, "what did Shmuel say to you?"

16 "Sure enough, he told us that the donkeys had been found," Sha'ul said to
his uncle, but he told him nothing of the matter of kingship that Shmuel
had mentioned.

17 18 Shmuel summoned the people to the Lord at Mitzpa. "Thus says the
Lord, God of Israel," he proclaimed to the Israelites, "I have brought
Israel out of Egypt, and I have delivered you from the hand of Egypt and
19 from the hands of all the kingdoms who oppress you. But today you have
rejected Your God, who is your Savior from all your troubles and all your
crises; you have said to Him, 'Set a king over us.' Now, present yourselves
20 before the Lord by your tribes and by your clans." And Shmuel had all
the tribes of Israel come forward, and the tribe of Binyamin was singled
21 out by lot. Then he had the tribe of Binyamin come forward, clan by clan,
and the Matrite clan was singled out; then Sha'ul son of Kish was singled
22 out. And they searched for him, but he was nowhere to be found. So they
inquired of the Lord again, "Is the man even here?" And the Lord said,
"There he is – hiding among the baggage."

23 They ran and took him from there, and when he presented himself
among the people, he towered head and shoulders above everyone else.
24 And Shmuel said to all the nation, "Have you seen whom the Lord has
chosen – for there is none like him among all the people!" And all the
people cheered and shouted, "Long live the king!"

25 Shmuel announced the royal rights to the people and recorded them in a
scroll that he placed before the Lord. Then Shmuel sent everyone back,
26 each to his own home. And Sha'ul, too, went back home to Giva, escorted
27 by the throngs whose heart had been touched by God. But some depraved
men said, "How is that one going to save us?" They scorned him and did
not bring him any gifts, but he feigned indifference.

11 1 Now, Naḥash the Amonite advanced and set up camp against Yavesh Gilad.
All the men of Yavesh said to Naḥash, "Form a pact with us, and we will
2 serve you." But Naḥash the Amonite replied to them, "This is how I will
form a pact with you: by gouging out every one of your right eyes, thus
3 casting disgrace upon all of Israel." "Grant us seven days' respite," the
elders of Yavesh said to him, "and we will send messengers throughout
all of Israel's borders. If no one comes to our rescue, then we shall come
out to you."

4 The messengers arrived at Givat Sha'ul and conveyed the message in the
5 people's hearing, and all the people lifted their voices and wept. Just then,
Sha'ul came in after the oxen from the field. "What happened, that the
people weep so?" Sha'ul asked, and they told him the message of the men
6 of Yavesh. The spirit of God rushed upon Sha'ul as he heard these words,
7 and his wrath flared up fiercely. And he took a pair of oxen and hacked
them up and sent them out to every border of Israel with the messengers,
saying, "Whoever does not follow after Sha'ul and after Shmuel – this will
be done to his oxen!" And the fear of the LORD fell upon the people, and
they charged out as one man.

8 He marshaled them at Bezek; the Israelites totaled three hundred
9 thousand, and the men of Yehuda were thirty thousand. He told the
messengers who had just arrived, "This is what you should say to the men
of Yavesh Gilad: tomorrow, victory will be yours as the sun grows hot."
When the messengers arrived and told the men of Yavesh, they rejoiced.
10 Then the men of Yavesh said, "Tomorrow we will come out to you; do to
us whatever is best in your eyes."

11 The next day, Sha'ul arranged the men into three companies, and they
infiltrated the camp during the morning watch. They struck at Amon until
the heat of the day; by then, all those who were left had scattered; no two
12 remained together. And the people said to Shmuel, "Who was it that said,
'Should Sha'ul reign over us?' Hand the men over, and we will put them to
13 death." But Sha'ul said, "No one will be put to death on this day, for today,
the LORD has granted victory in Israel."

14 And Shmuel said to the people, "Come, let us go to Gilgal, and we will
15 renew the kingship there." All the people went to Gilgal, and they crowned
Sha'ul king there at Gilgal before the LORD. They sacrificed peace offerings
before the LORD, and Sha'ul rejoiced greatly along with all the men of
Israel.

12 1 Then Shmuel addressed all of Israel. "Now, I have heeded your voices in
2 all you said to me, and I have crowned a king over you – and now, here is
the king, walking before you. I have grown old and gray, but my sons are
here with you; I have been walking before you from my youth until this
3 day. Here I am – testify against me in front of the LORD and in front of
His anointed – whose ox have I seized, and whose donkey have I seized?

Whom have I cheated, and whom have I oppressed, and from whose hand
have I taken a bribe and averted my eyes from him? Let me repay you."

4 And they said, "You have not cheated us, nor oppressed us, nor taken
anything from anyone."

5 "The LORD is witness against you," he said to them, "and His anointed is
witness on this day, that you have found nothing in my possession." And
6 it was declared, "The witness is…the LORD," Shmuel said to the people,
"who appointed Moshe and Aharon and brought your ancestors out of
7 the land of Egypt. Now take your stand, and I will plead my case with you
before the LORD: all the LORD's acts of loyalty that He has done for you
8 and your ancestors. When Yaakov arrived in Egypt and your ancestors
cried out to the LORD, the LORD sent Moshe and Aharon to take them
9 out of Egypt, and they settled them in this place. But they forgot the
LORD their God, and He sold them into the hands of Sisera, the general
of Ḥatzor, and into the hands of the Philistines, and into the hands of the
10 king of Moav, who attacked them. Then they cried out to the LORD. 'We
have sinned,' they said, 'for we left the LORD and served the Baalim and the
Ashterot – oh, save us from the hands of our enemies, and we will serve
11 You.' So the LORD sent Yerubaal and Bedan and Yiftaḥ and Shmuel and
saved you from the hands of the enemies around you, and you dwelled in
12 safety. But when you saw that King Naḥash of the Amonites came upon
you, you told me, 'No, we must have a king to reign over us,' though the
13 LORD your God is your King. And now, here is the king that you yourselves
have chosen – that you yourselves demanded – here, the LORD has set a
14 king over you! If you fear the LORD, then serve Him and heed His voice,
and do not spurn the word of GOD; both you and the king who reigns over
15 you must follow the LORD your God. But if you do not heed the LORD's
voice and rebel against the LORD's word, then the LORD's hand shall bear
down against you and your ancestral houses.

16 "And now, stand by and see what a tremendous feat the LORD is about to
17 perform before your very eyes: Is it not the wheat harvest today? I will
call out to the LORD, and He will unleash thunder and rain. Then you will
know, and then you will see, how great an evil you have committed in the
eyes of the LORD by asking for a king for yourselves."

18 Then Shmuel called out to the LORD, and the LORD unleashed thunder
and rain on that day. All the people were struck with terror of the LORD,
19 and of Shmuel as well. And all the people said to Shmuel, "Pray on your
servants' behalf to the LORD your God so that we will not die; for we
have added yet another evil to all our offenses by asking for a king for
ourselves."

20 "Do not fear, though you have done all this evil," Shmuel said to the people,
"so long as you do not turn away from the LORD; serve the LORD with all
21 your heart. But do not turn away to follow futilities that neither help nor

22 save, for they are futile. For the LORD will not desert His people for the
sake of His great name, because the LORD has undertaken to make you His
23 people. As for me – far be it from me to sin against the LORD by ceasing to
24 pray on your behalf; I will teach you the good and the straight path. But
you must revere the LORD and serve Him truly with all your heart – just
25 look at how well He has treated you. But if you lapse into evil, then both
you and your king shall be swept away."

13 1 A year passed before Sha'ul became king, and he had been reigning over
2 Israel for two years when he selected three thousand men from Israel.
Two thousand were with Sha'ul at Mikhmas in the hills of Beit El, and a
thousand were with Yonatan at Giva of Binyamin. As for the rest of the
men, he sent them back to their tents.

3 Yonatan struck down the Philistine governor at Geva, and the Philistines
heard. And Sha'ul blasted the ram's horn throughout the land, declaring,
4 "Let the Hebrews hear." When all of Israel heard how Sha'ul had struck
down the Philistine governor, and how Israel had become odious to the
5 Philistines, the people rallied to Sha'ul at Gilgal. But then the Philistines
gathered to fight with Israel – thirty thousand chariots and six thousand
riders and men as innumerable as the sand on the shore – and they
6 advanced and set up camp at Mikhmas, east of Beit Aven. When the
men of Israel saw that they were in dire straits, for the men were hard-
pressed, the people hid in caves, and among the crevices and the rocks,
7 and in tunnels and pits. And some Hebrews crossed the Jordan to the land
of Gad and the Gilad, while Sha'ul remained at Gilgal with all the men
8 trembling behind him. He waited seven days until Shmuel's appointed
time, but Shmuel did not arrive at Gilgal, and the men began to disperse.
9 So Sha'ul said, "Bring the burnt offering and peace offerings to me," and he
10 offered up the burnt offering. Just as he finished offering up the burnt
offering, Shmuel suddenly arrived, and Sha'ul went out toward him to
greet him.

11 "What have you done?" said Shmuel.

"When I saw that the men were beginning to disperse from me," Sha'ul said,
"but you had not come on the designated day, though the Philistines were
12 gathering at Mikhmas, I thought, 'Now the Philistines will swoop down on
me at Gilgal, but I have not yet invoked the LORD's presence.' So I spurred
myself to offer up the burnt offering."

13 "You have acted foolishly," Shmuel said to Sha'ul. "You have not kept the
commandment that the LORD, your God, commanded you. Though the
14 LORD would have established your dynasty over Israel forever, now your
dynasty will not endure. The LORD will seek out a man after His own heart,
and the LORD will charge him as ruler over His people, for you have not
done what the LORD commanded you."

15 And Shmuel arose and made his way up from Gilgal to Giva of Binyamin

while Sha'ul mustered the men who were with him, around six hundred men.

16 Sha'ul, his son Yonatan, and the men with them were stationed at Giva
17 of Binyamin while the Philistines camped at Mikhmas. And the sortie
marched out of the Philistine camp in three divisions; one division headed
18 for the Ofra road that led to the land of Shual; one division headed for
the Beit Ḥoron road; and one division headed for the frontier road
overlooking the Valley of the Hyenas, toward the wilderness.

19 There was no smith to be found anywhere in the land of Israel, for the
Philistines were concerned that the Hebrews would make swords or
20 spears. All of Israel needed to go down to the Philistines to sharpen their
21 plowshares, mattocks, axes, and sickles. The sharpening fee was a *pim*[10]
for plowshares, mattocks, three-pronged pitchforks, axes, or setting the
22 goad. So on the day of battle, neither sword nor spear was to be found
among Sha'ul and Yonatan's men; they could be found only for Sha'ul and
23 Yonatan his son. Meanwhile, the Philistine garrison had set out toward
the Mikhmas pass.

14 1 Soon after, Yonatan son of Sha'ul said to his armor-bearer, "Come, let us cross over to the Philistine garrison on the other side." But he did not tell his father.

2 Now Sha'ul was stationed on the outskirts of Giva, under the pomegranate
tree in Migron, and the men with him numbered around six hundred.
3 Aḥiya son of Aḥituv, the brother of Ikhavod, who was the son of Pinḥas
son of Eli, the Lord's priest at Shilo, bore the ephod.[11] The men did not
know that Yonatan had gone.

4 Between the passes through which Yonatan planned to reach the Philistine
garrison, there was a rocky crag on one side and a rocky crag on the other;
5 one was called Botzetz and the other was called Seneh. One crag rose to
a crest on the north, facing Mikhmas, while the other was south, facing
Geva.

6 Yehonatan said to his armor-bearer, "Come – let us cross over to the garrison of these heathens; perhaps the Lord will act on our behalf, for nothing can stop the Lord from achieving victory through many or few."

7 "Do whatever your heart tells you," his armor-bearer said to him. "Lead on; I am with you wholeheartedly."

8 "Look," said Yehonatan, "we will cross over to the men and show ourselves
9 to them. If they say to us, 'Halt until we reach you,' we will stay where we
10 are and not go up to them, and if they say to us, 'Come up to us,' then let
us go up, for the Lord has delivered them into our hands – that will be the

10 | Two-thirds of a shekel, about 10 grams of silver.

11 | See note on 2:18.

11 sign." And the two of them showed themselves to the Philistine garrison.
"Look!" said the Philistines. "Hebrews have come crawling out of the holes
12 where they were hiding." The garrison men called out to Yonatan and his
armor-bearer. "Come up to us!" they said, "and we will teach you a thing
or two."

"Come up after me," Yonatan said to his arms-bearer, "for the LORD has
delivered them into Israel's hands."

13 Yonatan made his way up on his hands and knees, with his arms-bearer
right behind him; they fell before Yonatan while his arms-bearer finished
14 them off behind him. The first attack launched by Yonatan and his arms-
bearer was against about twenty men over about half a furrow of an acre
15 of land. And terror seized the camp in the field and all the men – the
garrison and the raiders trembled too – and the very earth shuddered in
holy terror.

16 The lookouts for Sha'ul, who was in Giva of Binyamin, saw that the horde
17 was scattering, rushing back and forth. Sha'ul said to the men with him,
"Muster now, and see who has left us"; they mustered and saw that Yonatan
18 and his arms-bearer were missing. And Sha'ul said to Aḥiya, "Bring the Ark
19 of God over," for the Ark was among the Israelites that day. But as Sha'ul
was speaking to the priest, the commotion in the Philistine camp kept
20 rising, and Sha'ul said to the priest, "Withdraw your hand." Sha'ul and the
men with him rallied and reached the battle – to find that each man's sword
21 slashed his fellow in utter pandemonium. And the Hebrews previously on
the Philistines' side, who had gone up with them to the camp, changed
sides, and they too joined the Israelites who were with Sha'ul and Yonatan.
22 And when all the men of Israel who had been hiding in the Efrayim hills
heard that the Philistines had fled, they too caught up with them in battle.
23 And the LORD delivered Israel on that day.

24 But meanwhile, the battle spread past Beit Aven, and the men of Israel were
hard-pressed. For Sha'ul had placed the men under oath, saying, "Cursed
be the man who eats food until evening, when I have avenged myself on
25 my enemies," so none of the men had tasted food. Now, the whole area had
26 deepened to forest, where there was honey on the ground's surface. The
men reached the forest, and there was an oozing puddle of honey – but
27 no one dared touch his hand to his lips, for the men feared the oath. But
Yonatan had not heard that his father placed the men under oath, and he
extended the tip of the staff in his hand and dipped it in the honeycomb.
And when he brought his hand back to his mouth, his eyes brightened.
28 One of the men spoke up and said, "Your father placed the men under
oath, declaring, 'Cursed is the man who eats food today.' So the men are
famished."

29 "My father has brought a scourge upon the land," said Yonatan. "Just look
30 how my eyes brightened when I tasted a bit of this honey. If only the men

had eaten from their enemies' spoil that they found – for so far, the blow
against the Philistines has not been great."

31 On that day, they defeated the Philistines from Mikhmas to Ayalon, and
32 the men were utterly famished. The men pounced upon the spoil; they
seized sheep, cattle, and calves and slaughtered them over the ground, and
33 the men ate them with the blood.[12] When they informed Sha'ul, saying,
"Look – the men are sinning to the LORD by eating with the blood," he
34 said, "You have shown disloyalty. Roll a large stone over to me now." Then
Sha'ul said, "Spread out among the men, and tell them, 'Each one of
you – bring his ox and sheep to me, and slaughter them on this; eat, but
do not offend the LORD by eating with the blood.'" And every one of the
men brought forth the ox in his possession that night, and slaughtered it
35 there. And Sha'ul built an altar to the LORD; it was the first altar he built
to the LORD.

36 Then Sha'ul said, "Let us descend upon the Philistines by night and ravage
them until the light of morning – we shall not leave a man among them,"
and they said, "Do whatever is best in your eyes." But the priest said, "Let
37 us approach God here." So Sha'ul inquired of God, "Should I go down after
the Philistines? Will You deliver them into Israel's hand?" But He did not
answer him on that day.

38 "All troop leaders, come forward," said Sha'ul, "and determine how such
39 an offense transpired today. For as the LORD lives – He who delivers
Israel – even if it is through Yonatan, my son, he will surely die." But none
40 of the men would answer him. So he addressed all of Israel, "Stay on one
side, and I and Yonatan, my son, will be on the other."

"Do what is best in your eyes," the men said to Sha'ul.

41 "Produce the Tumim,"[13] Sha'ul said to the LORD, God of Israel; Yonatan
and Sha'ul were singled out, ruling out the men.

42 "Cast the lots between myself and my son Yonatan," Sha'ul said, and
Yonatan was singled out.

43 "Tell me, what have you done?" Sha'ul said to Yonatan, and Yonatan told
him.

"I indeed tasted a bit of honey from the very tip of the staff in my hand," he
said. "I am ready to die."

44 "So may God do – and more," Sha'ul said, "for you will surely die,
Yonatan!"

45 But the men said to Sha'ul, "Shall Yonatan die – he who brought this great
victory to Israel? Never! As the LORD lives, not a hair from his head shall

12 | Prohibited in Leviticus 19:26.

13 | The oracle possessed by the High Priest (see Ex. 28:30; Num. 27:21).

fall to the ground – for he acted together with God on this day." And the
men came to Yonatan's rescue, and he did not die.

46 And Sha'ul went back up, desisting from the Philistines, and the Philistines
returned to their place.

47 When Sha'ul won the kingship over Israel, he battled against all his
surrounding enemies: against Moav, the Amonites, Edom, the kings of
48 Tzova, and the Philistines; wherever he turned, he brought doom. He
valiantly struck down Amalek and saved Israel from the hands of their
oppressors.

49 Sha'ul's sons were Yonatan, Yishvi, and Malki Shua, and as for the names
of his two daughters – the elder was named Merav and the younger was
50 named Mikhal. The name of Sha'ul's wife was Aḥinoam, daughter of
Aḥimaatz, and the commander of his army was named Aviner son of Ner,
51 Sha'ul's uncle; Kish, Sha'ul's father, and Ner, Avner's father, were sons of
52 Aviel. There was fierce war against the Philistines all the days of Sha'ul,
and whenever Sha'ul saw any strong man or valiant warrior, he would
recruit him.

15 1 Shmuel said to Sha'ul, "It was I whom the LORD sent to anoint you as king
2 over His people, over Israel; now, heed the words of the LORD. Thus says
the LORD of Hosts: I have taken note of what Amalek did to Israel; how
3 they set upon them on the way as they came out of Egypt. Now, go and
strike down Amalek; you must utterly destroy all that is theirs – spare
nothing. You must slay man and woman; child and infant; ox and sheep;
camel and donkey."

4 Sha'ul summoned the men and mustered them at Telaim; two hundred
5 thousand infantrymen and ten thousand men from Yehuda. Sha'ul reached
6 the city of Amalek and lay in wait in the wadi. And Sha'ul said to the
Kenites, "Leave; turn and withdraw from among the Amalekites lest I
destroy you together with them; you dealt loyally with all the Israelites
7 when they left Egypt," and the Kenites departed from Amalek. Then Sha'ul
8 struck down Amalek from Ḥavila up to Shur, which is east of Egypt. He
captured King Agag of Amalek alive and utterly destroyed the entire
9 people by the sword. But Sha'ul and the men spared Agag and the best
of the sheep, cattle, fat calves, and lambs – the very best of everything;
they were not willing to destroy them. As for all the spurned, worthless
property – that, they utterly destroyed.

10 11 Then the word of the LORD reached Shmuel: "I regret that I crowned
Sha'ul as king, for he has turned away from following Me and he has failed
to fulfill My words." This enraged Shmuel, and he cried out to the LORD
12 all night long. And Shmuel set out early in the morning toward Sha'ul, and
Shmuel was told, "Sha'ul has gone to Carmel, where he set up a monument
13 for himself; then he turned off and made his way down to Gilgal." When

Shmuel reached Sha'ul, Sha'ul said to him, "Blessed are you to the LORD! I have fulfilled the LORD's word."

14 "Then what is this bleating of sheep in my ears," said Shmuel, "and the lowing of cattle that I hear?"

15 "They brought them from the Amalekites," said Sha'ul, "for the men spared the best of the sheep and cattle for sacrificing to the LORD, your God – but we utterly destroyed the rest."

16 "Stop," said Shmuel, "and let me tell you what the LORD told me last night."

"Speak," he said to him.

17 And Shmuel said, "Though you may seem small in your own eyes, you are
the head of the tribes of Israel, and the LORD anointed you as king over
18 Israel. The LORD sent you on a mission, bidding, 'Go and utterly destroy
the offenders – Amalek – and fight them until you have destroyed them.'
19 But why did you fail to heed the voice of the LORD, pouncing on the spoil
and doing evil in the eyes of the LORD?"

20 "But I did heed the voice of the LORD," Sha'ul said to Shmuel. "I set out on
the mission the LORD assigned me, and I brought Agag, king of Amalek,
21 and utterly destroyed Amalek. And the men took of the spoil – the choicest
sheep and cattle from what was banned – to sacrifice to the LORD, your
God, at Gilgal."

22 And Shmuel said,
"Does the LORD delight in burnt offerings and sacrifices
as much as obedience to the LORD's voice?
Behold – obedience is better than sacrifice,
and compliance than the fat of rams.
23 For rebellion is as bad as the sin of divination,
and presumption as corruption and idolatry.
Because you rejected the word of the LORD,
He has rejected you as king."

24 "I have sinned," Sha'ul said to Shmuel, "for I violated the LORD's command
25 and your word, because I feared the people and heeded their voice. But
now, please forgive my sin and return with me, so I may worship before
the LORD."

26 "I will not return with you," Shmuel said to Sha'ul, "for you have rejected
the word of the LORD – and the LORD has rejected you from being king
27 over Israel." And Shmuel turned to go, but Sha'ul grabbed the corner of
his robe, and it tore.

28 "The LORD has torn the kingship of Israel away from you today," Shmuel
29 said to him, "and has granted it to your peer, who is better than you. What

is more, Israel's Eternal will not betray or waver, for He is not a mere
wavering human."

30 "I have sinned," he said. "Now please honor me in front of the elders of
my people and in front of Israel; return with me and I will worship the
31 Lord your God." So Shmuel followed Sha'ul back, and Sha'ul worshipped
the Lord.

32 Shmuel then gave the order, "Bring Agag, king of Amalek, to me." Agag
walked up to him with stately steps.

"So," said Agag, "the bitterness of death is upon me."

33 And Shmuel said,
"As your sword has made women childless,
so your mother shall be childless among women!"

And Shmuel hacked Agag to pieces before the Lord at Gilgal.

34 Then Shmuel went to Rama while Sha'ul made his way up to his home in
35 Givat Sha'ul. Shmuel never saw Sha'ul again to his dying day, yet Shmuel
grieved for Sha'ul, for the Lord regretted appointing Sha'ul over Israel.

16 1 The Lord said to Shmuel, "For how long will you grieve over Sha'ul when
I have rejected him from reigning over Israel? Fill your horn with oil and
set off; I am sending you to Yishai, the Bethlehemite, for I have seen a king
for Me among his sons."

2 "How can I go?" said Shmuel. "If Sha'ul hears, he will kill me!"

The Lord said, "Take a heifer with you and say, 'I have come to sacrifice
3 to the Lord.' Then summon Yishai to the sacrifice, and I will let you know
what to do; you shall anoint for Me the one I reveal to you."

4 Shmuel did as the Lord bid and arrived in Beit Leḥem. The elders of the
city came trembling out to meet him and said, "Have you come in peace?"

5 "Peace," he replied. "I have come to sacrifice to the Lord. Sanctify
yourselves and come with me to the sacrifice." Then he sanctified Yishai
and his sons and summoned them to the sacrifice.

6 When they arrived, he saw Eliav and thought, "Surely the Lord's anointed
7 is before Him." But the Lord said to Shmuel, "Do not look upon his
appearance or his tall bearing, for I have rejected him, not seeing as man
does; for man sees what the eyes see, but the Lord sees into the heart."
8 Then Yishai called to Avinadav and passed him before Shmuel, who said,
9 "The Lord has not chosen this one either." And when Yishai had Shama
10 pass, he said, "The Lord has not chosen this one either." Yishai had his
seven sons pass before Shmuel, but Shmuel said to Yishai, "The Lord has
not chosen any of these."

11 Then Shmuel asked Yishai, "Are there no other boys?"

"There is still the youngest," he said. "Right now, he is shepherding the flock."

"Send out to fetch him," Shmuel said to Yishai, "for we will not move on until he comes here."

12 He sent out and brought him; he was ruddy, with beautiful eyes, and handsome. And the LORD said, "Arise, anoint him – for he is the one."

13 Shmuel took the horn of oil and anointed him in the midst of his brothers, and the spirit of the LORD seized David from that day onward. Then Shmuel rose and set out for Rama.

14 Now the spirit of the LORD had slipped away from Sha'ul, while a dark
15 spirit from the LORD began to haunt him. Sha'ul's servants said to him,
16 "Look, a dark spirit from God is haunting you. Perhaps our lord should
bid the servants before you, 'Seek out a man who knows how to play the
lyre,' so that when the dark spirit from God settles upon you, with the
17 strumming of his fingers, you will feel well." And Sha'ul said to his servants,
"Seek out someone for me who plays well, and bring him to me."

18 One of the servant boys answered, "I have noticed that Yishai the
Bethlehemite has a son who knows how to play," he said. "He is a powerful
man, a seasoned warrior, wise of word and attractive – and the LORD is
19 with him." So Sha'ul sent messengers to Yishai, saying, "Send me your son
David, the one who is with the flock."

20 Yishai loaded a donkey with bread, a skin of wine, and a young goat, and
21 sent it to Sha'ul along with his son David. David came to Sha'ul and
22 attended him; he loved him dearly, and he became his armor-bearer. Sha'ul
sent word to Yishai, "Let David attend me, for he has found favor in my
23 eyes." Whenever the spirit of God would settle upon Sha'ul, David would
take up his lyre and play; then Sha'ul would feel relieved and well, and the
dark spirit would leave him.

17 1 Now, the Philistines rallied their forces for war; they rallied at Sokho of
2 Yehuda; they set up camp between Sokho and Azeka, at Efes Damim. And
Sha'ul and the men of Israel rallied and set up camp in the Valley of the
3 Terebinth and arrayed for battle against the Philistines. The Philistines
were stationed on a hill on this side, Israel were stationed on a hill on that
4 side, and the valley lay between them. Then the champion of the Philistine
forces came forth; his name was Golyat, of Gat, and he was six cubits and a
5 span tall. A bronze helmet was on his head, and he was clad in scale armor;
6 the armor weighed five thousand shekel of bronze. Bronze greaves were on
7 his legs, and a bronze javelin was slung between his shoulders. The shaft
of his spear was like a weaver's beam, the blade of his spear weighed six
8 hundred shekel of iron, and a shield-bearer marched before him. He stood
and called out to the ranks of Israel.

"Why should you march out to wage battle?" he said to them. "I represent

the Philistines and you are Sha'ul's subjects; select a man, and let him come
9 down to me! If he beats me in combat and strikes me down, then we will
become your subjects; but if I beat him and strike him down, then you
10 shall become our subjects and serve us." And the Philistine concluded, "I
11 challenge the ranks of Israel today: give me a man, and let us duel!" When
Sha'ul and all of Israel heard the Philistine's speech, panic and terror seized
them.

12 Now David was the son of a certain Efratite from Beit Leḥem of Yehuda;
his name was Yishai, and he had eight sons. By Sha'ul's time, the man had
13 grown old, senior among men, so Yishai's three oldest sons had gone out
to follow Sha'ul in battle. The names of the three sons who had left for
the war were Eliav, the oldest; his second was Avinadav, and the third
14 was Shama. David was the youngest, while only the three oldest had left
15 to follow Sha'ul; David was going back and forth between Sha'ul and
16 shepherding his father's flock in Beit Leḥem. Meanwhile, the Philistine
had been looming every morning and evening, flaunting himself, for forty
days.

17 Yishai said to his son David, "Please take an ephah of this toasted grain
and ten loaves of this bread for your brothers, and rush them over to
18 your brothers in the camp. As for these ten cheeses, bring them to the
commander of the thousand. Take note of your brothers' welfare, and
19 bring some token from them. Sha'ul and they, and all the men of Israel, are
in the Valley of the Terebinth, at war with the Philistines."

20 David rose early in the morning, left the sheep with a keeper, and set out,
taking what Yishai had instructed him to. He arrived at the entrenchment
just as the force was marching out toward the battle lines and sounding the
21 22 war cry. And Israel and the Philistines deployed, line against line. David
left the baggage with him in the baggage-keeper's care, ran to the battle
23 line, and arrived and greeted his brothers. As he was speaking to them,
the champion came marching up from the Philistine ranks – Golyat the
Philistine was his name, from Gat – and gave his usual speech, and David
24 heard. When all the men of Israel saw the man, they retreated before him
25 in utter terror. And the men of Israel were saying, "Did you see that man,
the one marching up? To challenge Israel – that is why he marches up!
Whoever defeats him – the king will reward him with great riches and
give him his daughter, and his father's house will be granted exemption in
26 Israel." David said to the men who were standing with him, "What will be
done for the man who defeats that Philistine and clears Israel's disgrace?
For who is this heathen Philistine to dare to taunt the ranks of the Living
27 God?" And the people repeated to him what would be done for the man
who defeated him.

28 When his older brother Eliav heard him speaking to the men, he grew
furious with David. "Why have you come down here," he said, "and with

whom did you leave that measly flock in the wilderness? I know your
presumption and your dark intentions – you just came down to see the
battle, did you not?"

29 "What have I done now?" said David. "It was only a question."

30 But he turned away from him toward someone else and asked the same
31 thing, and the people gave the same answer as the first. And the words
David spoke were heard and reported to Sha'ul, and he took him aside.
32 David said to Sha'ul, "Let no one lose heart. Your servant will go and fight
with that Philistine."

33 "You cannot go and fight against this Philistine," Sha'ul said to David, "for
you are just a boy, while he has been a warrior from his youth."

34 "Your servant has been tending the sheep for his father," David said to
Sha'ul, "and whenever a lion or a bear came and carried off a sheep from
35 the flock, I went after it, struck it down, and rescued the sheep from its jaws.
36 And if it charged at me, I seized its mane, struck it down, and killed it. Your
servant has defeated both lion and bear – and this heathen Philistine is
37 just like them, for he has taunted the ranks of the Living God." And David
continued, "The Lord who has rescued me from the lion and the bear will
rescue me from this Philistine."

"Go," Sha'ul said to David, "and the Lord will be with you."

38 And Sha'ul dressed David in his own uniform, placed a bronze helmet on
39 his head, and clad him in armor. David girded himself with his sword over
the uniform and tried to walk, but he was not used to it.

"I cannot walk in this," David said to Sha'ul, "for I am not used to it," and
40 David took them off. He took hold of his sling stick and chose five smooth
stones from the wadi bed, placing them in the pouch of his shepherd's
41 bag. Then, sling in hand, he approached the Philistine. The Philistine was
drawing closer and closer to David, with the man bearing the shield before
42 him, and when the Philistine looked down and saw David, he scorned him,
for he was young and ruddy with a handsome look.

43 "Am I a dog," the Philistine asked David, "that you come at me with sticks?"
44 And the Philistine cursed David by his gods. "Come here," the Philistine
then said to David, "and I will dole out your flesh to the birds of the sky
and the beasts of the field."

45 And David replied to the Philistine, "You come at me with sword and spear
and javelin. But I come at you in the name of the Lord of Hosts, the God
46 of the ranks of Israel, whom you taunted. This very day, the Lord will
deliver you into my hands, and I will strike you down and sever your head
from your body. And I will dole out the corpses of the Philistine camp for
the birds of the sky and the beasts of the land, on this very day. Then all

47 the land will know that there is a God over Israel; and all this crowd will
know that the LORD does not grant victory by sword or by spear – for the
battle is the LORD's, and He will deliver you into our hands."

48 And when the Philistine rose up and drew closer to David, David rushed
49 to the battle line toward the Philistine. David thrust his hand into the bag,
took out a stone, slung, and hit the Philistine in his forehead; the stone
50 sank into his forehead, and he toppled face down to the ground. David
overpowered the Philistine with sling and stone; he struck the Philistine,
51 and then he killed him. There was no sword in David's hand, so he ran and
stood over the Philistine; seized his sword and drew it from its sheath, and
killed him, cutting off his head. When the Philistines saw that their hero
52 was dead, they fled, but the men of Israel and Yehuda rose up, sounding
the battle cry, and chased the Philistines to the valley, all the way up to the
gates of Ekron; Philistine corpses littered the way to Shaarayim as far as
53 Gat and Ekron. Then the Israelites returned from their hot pursuit of the
54 Philistines and plundered their camp. And David seized the Philistine's
head and brought it to Jerusalem, but as for his weapons, he placed them
in his tent.

55 As Sha'ul watched David charging out toward the Philistine, he said to his
army commander, Avner, "Whose son is that boy again, Avner?"

"By your life, O King," said Avner, "I do not know."

56 The king replied, "Find out whose son that youth is."

57 So when David returned from defeating the Philistine, Avner took him and
brought him before Sha'ul, with the head of the Philistine in his hand.

58 "Whose son are you, young man?" Sha'ul asked him, and David replied,
"The son of your servant, Yishai the Bethlehemite."

18 1 By the time he had finished speaking to Sha'ul, Yehonatan's very soul
became bound up with David's, and Yehonatan loved him as his own
2 self. Sha'ul took him in on that day and did not allow him to return to
3 his father's house. And Yehonatan and David formed a pact; because he
4 loved him as himself, Yehonatan stripped off the robe he wore and gave
it to David, along with his uniform, his sword, his bow, and his belt.

5 When David set out, he was successful in every mission on which Sha'ul
sent him, so Sha'ul appointed him over the military force. This pleased all
the men and even Sha'ul's officials.

6 Once, when they arrived after David returned from defeating the
Philistines,

the women came out from all the towns of Israel to sing,
the dancers to meet Sha'ul the king,
to the joyful accompaniment of timbrels and lutes.

7 The laughing women echoed each other, chanting,
"Sha'ul has struck down thousands,
and David – myriads!"

8 This infuriated Sha'ul, and the affair seemed ominous to him. "They
credited myriads to David," he said, "and credited me with just thousands.
9 Only the kingship is yet to be his!" And Sha'ul kept a close eye on David
from that day onward.

10 The next day, a dark spirit from God seized Sha'ul, and he began to rave in
the house. Now, David was strumming away as usual – while the spear was
11 in Sha'ul's hand. Sha'ul hurled the spear, thinking, "I will pin David to the
12 wall," but David turned away from him twice. And Sha'ul became afraid of
David, for the LORD was with him, while He had grown distant from Sha'ul.
13 So Sha'ul had him distanced from him; he appointed him as a commander
of a thousand, and he went out and came in at the head of the people.

14 15 David was successful in every way, and the LORD was with him. When
16 Sha'ul saw how successful he was, he shrank away from him, but all of Israel
17 and Yehuda loved David, for he went out and came in before them. So
Sha'ul said to David, "Here is my elder daughter, Merav; her I shall give you
for a wife on the condition that you be a valiant man for me and fight the
LORD's battles," for Sha'ul thought, "I need not deal with him myself – let
the Philistines deal with him."

18 "Who am I," David said to Sha'ul, "and how worthy is my father's kin in
19 Israel, that I should become son-in-law to the king?" So at the time that
Merav, Sha'ul's daughter, was supposed to be given to David, she was given
to Adriel the Meholatite for a wife.

20 But Mikhal, Sha'ul's daughter, loved David, and when Sha'ul was told of
21 this, the matter pleased him. "If I give her to him," Sha'ul thought, "she
will be a distraction for him, and the Philistines will deal with him." So
Sha'ul said to David for the second time, "This time, you will become
22 my son-in-law." And Sha'ul commanded his servants, "Speak to David
privately, saying, 'Now, the king is delighted with you, and all his servants
23 love you; now you should become the king's son-in-law.'" Sha'ul's servants
repeated these words in David's hearing, and David said, "Is it a trivial
matter in your eyes, to become the king's son-in-law? I myself am but a
24 poor, trivial man." When Sha'ul's servants told him, "This was David's
25 answer," Sha'ul said, "Tell David the following: the only bride-price the
king desires is a hundred Philistine foreskins, to wreak vengeance upon
the king's enemies," for Sha'ul intended to have David fall into the hands
26 of the Philistines. When Sha'ul's servants repeated these words to David,
the idea of becoming the king's son-in-law pleased David. And before the
27 set time was up, David rose and set out, together with his men, and struck
down two hundred Philistine men. David brought their foreskins, fulfilling

the king's conditions for becoming the king's son-in-law, and Sha'ul gave
28 him his daughter Mikhal for a wife. And Sha'ul realized and acknowledged
that the LORD was with David, and that Mikhal, Sha'ul's daughter, loved
29 him. Yet Sha'ul grew still more afraid of David, and Sha'ul became David's
lifelong enemy.

30 The Philistine officers launched attacks, and whenever they launched an
attack, David was the most successful of all of Sha'ul's servants. And his
reputation soared high.

19 1 Sha'ul spoke to Yehonatan and to all his servants about having David
2 killed, but Yehonatan, the son of Sha'ul, stuck by David. So Yehonatan told
David, "Sha'ul, my father, seeks to kill you. Now be on your guard in the
3 morning – stay hidden in a secret place. I will go out and stand with my
father in the field where you are, and I will speak about you to my father.
Then I will see what there is to tell you."

4 And Yehonatan spoke well of David to Sha'ul, his father. "Do not let the
king wrong his servant, David," he said to him, "for he has not wronged
5 you – in fact, his deeds are highly advantageous for you. He took his life
in his hands and defeated the Philistine, and the LORD granted a great
victory for Israel – when you saw it, you rejoiced. Why should you sin by
shedding innocent blood and kill David without cause?"

6 Sha'ul heeded Yehonatan's voice, and Sha'ul swore, "As the LORD lives, he
7 shall not be killed." Yehonatan called to David, and Yehonatan told him
everything. Then Yehonatan brought David to Sha'ul, and he remained in
8 his presence as before. War raged once more, and David charged out to
fight against the Philistines; he dealt them a mighty blow, and they fled
before him.

9 But a dark spirit from the LORD settled on Sha'ul while he was sitting at
10 home with his spear in his hand as David strummed away. Sha'ul attempted
to pin David to the wall with the spear, but he eluded Sha'ul, who rammed
the spear into the wall, and David bolted and escaped that very night.
11 Sha'ul sent messengers to David's house to keep watch over him so that
12 they could kill him in the morning. Mikhal, David's wife, told him, "If you
do not run for your life tonight, tomorrow you will be killed." Mikhal let
13 David down through the window; he managed to flee and escaped. Mikhal
then took the household gods and placed them on the bed, arranging a
goat-hair quilt around the head, and covering it with a sheet.

14 15 When Sha'ul sent messengers to arrest David, she said, "He is ill." But Sha'ul
sent the messengers to see David, insisting, "Bring him up to me in his bed
16 to kill him!" The messengers arrived, and there were the household gods
upon the bed, with the goat-hair rug at its head.

17 "Why have you deceived me like this," Sha'ul said to Mikhal, "letting my
enemy escape?"

Mikhal replied to Sha'ul, "He said to me, 'Let me go – why should I have to kill you?'"

18 David fled, and escaped, and came to Shmuel in Rama. He told him all that
19 Sha'ul had done to him, then he and Shmuel left and stayed in Nayot. But
20 Sha'ul was informed, "Now David is in Nayot BaRama." When Sha'ul sent
messengers to arrest David, they saw a band of prophets in a prophetic frenzy,
with Shmuel standing over them. And the spirit of God settled on Sha'ul's
21 messengers, and they, too, were thrown into a prophetic frenzy. When they
informed Sha'ul, he sent other messengers, but they, too, were caught up in
a prophetic frenzy; Sha'ul sent messengers again, a third time, but they, too,
22 were caught up in a prophetic frenzy. So he himself made his way to Rama.
When he reached the great cistern by Sekhu, he asked, "Where are Shmuel
23 and David?" and someone said, "There – in Nayot BaRama." As he was
making his way there, to Nayot BaRama, the spirit of God settled on him
24 as well, and he went raving along until he reached Nayot BaRama. Then he,
too, stripped off his clothes, and he, too, was caught up in a prophetic frenzy
before Shmuel and sprawled naked all that day and all night long. And that
is why they say, "Is Sha'ul, too, among the prophets?"

20 1 Meanwhile, David had fled from Nayot BaRama, and he came to Yehonatan. "What have I done?" he said. "How have I sinned or offended your father, that he seeks my life?"

2 "May it never come to pass," he said. "You shall not die. Look, my father has never done anything, great or small, without revealing it to me; why should my father hide this matter from me? It cannot be."

3 But David swore once more. "Your father surely knows that I have your favor," he said, "so he must think, 'Yehonatan must not know of this, lest he be grieved.' But as the Lord lives, and as you live, there is but a step between me and death."

4 And Yehonatan said to David, "Whatever you have in mind, I will do for you."

5 "Now, tomorrow is the New Month," David said to Yehonatan, "and I am
supposed to sit with the king to feast. But let me go, and I will hide in the
6 field until the third evening. If your father takes note of my absence, then
say, 'David asked an urgent favor of me: to run back to his hometown, Beit
Leḥem, as the yearly sacrificial feast for the entire clan is being held there.'
7 If he says, 'Fine,' then all is well with your servant, but if he becomes furious,
8 know that he has determined to do harm. Show loyalty to your servant, for
you have entered into a covenant of the Lord together with your servant.
If I am indeed at fault, then kill me yourself; but your father – why should
you hand me over to him?"

9 "May it never happen to you," Yehonatan said, "for if I indeed learn that my father is determined that harm will befall you, would I not tell you?"

10 "Who will tell me if your father answers you harshly?" David asked
Yehonatan.

11 "Come, let us go out to the field," said Yehonatan. And the two of them
went out to the field.

12 And Yehonatan said to David, "By the LORD, God of Israel: by this time
tomorrow or the next day, I will determine whether my father is pleased
13 with David. If not, then I will send word to you and let you know. So may
the LORD do to Yehonatan – and more – if my father is pleased at the evil
befalling you but I do not let you know or let you go, and you do not go in
14 peace. And may the LORD be with you as He was once with my father. Now,
15 if I remain alive, show me the LORD's loyalty;[14] and if I die, never sever
Your loyalty from my house – never – even when the LORD has severed
16 every one of David's enemies from the face of the earth. Thus Yehonatan
has sealed a pact with the House of David, and may the LORD hold David's
17 enemies[15] responsible." And Yehonatan made David swear once more by
his love for him, for he loved him as he loved his own self.

18 Yehonatan then said to David, "Tomorrow is the New Month,[16] and you
19 shall be missed, for your seat will be empty. Now wait three days, then
on the day people go back to work, make your way swiftly down to your
20 hiding place, and stay close to the Ezel Stone.[17] As for me – I will shoot
21 three arrows to its side, as though aiming at a target. Now, when I send the
boy off to find the arrows, if I say to him, 'Look, the arrows are just past you,
come take them,' then come, for all is well with you, and there is nothing
22 wrong – as the LORD lives. But if I say to the boy, 'Look, the arrows are far
23 past you,' then go, for the LORD has sent you away. As for the matter we
spoke of, you and I – the LORD is between me and you forever."

24 David hid out in the field. The New Month came around, and the king sat
25 down at the feast to eat. When the king sat in his usual seat by the wall,
Yehonatan rose, and Avner sat by Sha'ul's side while David's seat remained
26 empty. Sha'ul did not mention anything that day. "It must be by chance
that he is not clean," he thought; "he must be unclean."

27 But the next day, on the second day of the New Month, David's seat was
still empty, and Sha'ul asked Yehonatan, his son, "Why did the son of
Yishai fail to come to the feast – both yesterday and today?"

28 "David urgently asked me for leave to Beit Leḥem," Yehonatan answered
29 Sha'ul. "He said, 'Please let me go, for we have a family feast in the city,
and my brother has bid me – so now, if I have gained your favor, please

14 | See verse 8 above; compare II Samuel 9:3.

15 | Possibly a euphemism for David himself.

16 | Observed with a feast at the beginning of every lunar month.

17 | Sometimes translated as "Traveler's Stone."

let me get away to see my brothers.' That is why he has not come to the
king's table."

30 Sha'ul burst into a rage at Yehonatan. "Son of a perverse, wayward woman!"
he said. "Oh, I knew you would side with the son of Yishai – to your own
31 disgrace and the disgrace of your mother's nakedness! But as long as the
son of Yishai lives on this earth, you and your kingship will not endure – so
bring him to me now, for he is a dead man!"

32 But Yehonatan answered Sha'ul, his father. "Why should he be killed?" he
33 said to him. "What has he done?" And Sha'ul hurled the spear toward him
to strike him down, and Yehonatan realized that his father was determined
34 to kill David. Furious, Yehonatan rose up from the table; he ate no food on
the second day of the New Month out of anguish for David, for his father
had humiliated him.

35 In the morning, Yehonatan went out to the field for the rendezvous with
36 David, a young boy with him. He said to his boy, "Now, run and find the
arrows I am about to shoot." The boy ran off, and he shot the arrows past
37 him. When the boy reached the place where Yehonatan's arrows had
fallen, Yehonatan called out after the boy, "Oh – the arrows are far past
you." Then Yehonatan called out after the boy, "Quick – hurry, do not
38 linger." When Yehonatan's boy gathered up the arrows and came back
39 to his master – the boy knew nothing; only Yehonatan and David knew
40 about the arrangement – Yehonatan gave his gear to his boy and said
41 to him, "Go – bring these back to town." When the boy had left, David
emerged from the southern side of the stone, flung his face to the ground,
and bowed three times. And they kissed each other and wept with each
other until David's sobs reached a crescendo.

42 "Go in peace," Yehonatan said to David, "for the two of us have sworn in the
name of the Lord, 'May the Lord be between me and you, and between
my seed and your seed, forever.'"

21 1/2 He got up and went on his way while Yehonatan came back to town. And
David came to Nov to the priest Aḥimelekh. Aḥimelekh came trembling
out toward David and asked him, "Why are you alone, with no one with
you?"

3 "The king charged me with a mission," David said to the priest Aḥimelekh,
"and said to me, 'Let no one know anything about the mission on which
I have sent you, that I charged you with.' So I dismissed the servants to
4 a certain place. Now, what do you have on hand? Provide me with five
5 loaves of bread or whatever there is." The priest answered David, "There is
no ordinary bread on hand, but there is sacred bread, as long as the young
men have kept themselves away from women."

6 "Certainly – women have been kept from us, as always," David replied to
the priest, "for whenever I set out, the men's vessels are consecrated, even

7 on an ordinary mission, so their vessels are certainly sacred today." So
the priest gave him what was sacred, for there was no bread there but the
showbread that had been removed from the LORD's presence and replaced
with hot, fresh bread as soon it was taken away.

8 Meanwhile, one of Sha'ul's servants had been detained there before the
LORD; his name was Doeg the Edomite, and he was the chief of Sha'ul's
patrolmen.

9 David then said to Aḥimelekh, "Do you have any spear or sword on hand
here? For I took neither my sword nor any of my weapons with me due to
the urgency of the king's mission."

10 "The sword of Golyat the Philistine, whom you defeated in the Valley
of the Terebinth," said the priest, "here it is, wrapped in a cloth, behind
the ephod.[18] If you wish to take it, then take it, for there is nothing here
besides it."

11 "There is none like it," said David. "Give it to me."

And David set out and fled from Sha'ul on that very day and reached
12 Akhish, the king of Gat. But Akhish's servants said to him, "Isn't that
David, king of the land? Isn't that the one they sang and danced about,
chanting,
'Sha'ul has struck down thousands,
and David – myriads!'?"

13 David took these words to heart and became very wary of King Akhish
14 of Gat. So he acted as if he had lost his reason in their eyes; he ranted and
raved at them and scribbled on the doors of the gate and drooled into
15 his beard. And Akhish said to his servants, "Just look at that lunatic; why
16 have you brought him to me? Do I lack lunatics so that you brought this
one here to play the lunatic before me? Should this one be let into my
house?"

22 1 David made his way out of there and escaped to the cave of Adulam.
When his brothers and all his father's household heard, they went down
2 to him there. And everyone who was distressed, and everyone in debt,
and every wretched, bitter soul gathered to him, and he became their
3 leader; about four hundred men were with him. From there, David went
to Mitzpeh Moav. He said to the king of Moav, "Please let my father and
mother remain out here with you until I know what God has in store for
4 me." He led them before the king of Moav, and they stayed with him for as
5 long as David was in the stronghold. When the prophet Gad said to David,
"Do not remain in the stronghold; set out for the land of Yehuda," David
traveled until he reached the Ḥeret Forest.

6 When Sha'ul heard that David and his men had been discovered, Sha'ul

---

18 | See note on 2:18.

was stationed at Giva beneath the tamarisk at Rama, with his spear at the
ready and all his servants attending him.

7 "Now listen, Benjaminites," Sha'ul said to his officials, who were attending
him, "will the son of Yishai also give fields and vineyards to you? Will all
of you be appointed as captains of thousands and captains of hundreds?
8 For you have all conspired against me; no one let me know that my son
formed a pact with the son of Yishai. And not one of you felt sorry enough
for me to let me know that my son set my own servant as a trap against
me this very day."

9 And Doeg the Edomite, who was standing by Sha'ul's servants, answered.
"I saw the son of Yishai – he came to Nov, to Aḥimelekh son of Aḥituv,"
10 he said, "who made an inquiry of the LORD for him and gave him provisions – he even gave him the sword of Golyat the Philistine."

11 So the king summoned the priest Aḥimelekh son of Aḥituv and all the
priests of his father's house, who were in Nov; and they all came to the
12 king. Sha'ul said, "Now listen, son of Aḥituv."

"Here I am, my lord," he said.

13 "Why did you conspire against me, you and the son of Yishai," Sha'ul said
to him, "by giving him bread and a sword, and making an inquiry of God
for him – that he may rise up against me in ambush this very day?"

14 "But out of all your servants, who is as faithful as David?" Aḥimelekh
answered the king. "The king's son-in-law and captain of your bodyguard,
15 so honored in your house? Have I begun to make inquiries of God for
him? Absolutely not! Let the king not accuse his servant or any of my
father's house of anything, for your servant knew absolutely nothing of
all this – not the slightest hint."

16 But the king said, "You will surely die, Aḥimelekh – you and all your
father's house."

17 And the king said to the couriers attending him, "Go around and kill the
priests of the LORD, for they, too, side with David – they knew that he was
fleeing, but they did not let me know." But the servants of the king were
18 not willing to raise their hands to strike the priests of the LORD. So the
king said to Doeg, "You go around and strike down the priests." And Doeg
the Edomite went around and struck down the priests himself; that same
19 day he slaughtered eighty-five men who were clad in the linen ephod. And
he put Nov, the city of priests, to the sword – man and woman, child and
infant, ox, donkey, and sheep to the sword.

20 A single son of Aḥimelekh son of Aḥituv escaped; his name was Evyatar,
21 and he ran away to David. Evyatar told David that Sha'ul had murdered
the priests of the LORD.

22 "I knew on that day – when Doeg was there – that he would surely inform

Sha'ul," David said to Evyatar. "I am responsible for all the lives of your
23 father's household. Stay with me and do not fear; though the one who
seeks my life seeks your life, you are safe with me."

23 1 David was informed, "There are Philistines attacking Ke'ila, and they are
2 plundering the threshing floors." David asked the Lord, "Shall I go and
strike down these Philistines?"

And the Lord said, "Go, strike down the Philistines, and save Ke'ila."

3 But David's men said to him, "Even here in Yehuda we are afraid – must
4 we really go to Ke'ila, to the ranks of the Philistines?" So David asked the
Lord once more,and the Lord answered him. "Arise and go down to
Ke'ila," He said, "for I shall deliver the Philistines into your hand."

5 David and his men marched on Ke'ila. They fought against the Philistines,
led away their cattle, and dealt them a great blow; and David saved the
people of Ke'ila.

6 Now, when Evyatar son of Aḥimelekh had fled to David in Ke'ila, he
7 brought the ephod[19] down with him. When Sha'ul was informed that
David had come to Ke'ila, Sha'ul said, "God has cast him away into my
8 hands, for he has shut himself in by entering a gated, bolted city." And
Sha'ul rallied all the men for war, to march down to Ke'ila and besiege
9 David and his men. But David knew that Sha'ul was scheming evil against
him, and he said to Evyatar, the priest, "Bring the ephod forth."

10 David said, "O Lord, God of Israel, Your servant has heard that Sha'ul
11 intends to come to Ke'ila to ravage the city because of me. Will the citizens
of Ke'ila hand me over to him? Will Sha'ul march down as Your servant
has heard? O Lord, God of Israel, please tell Your servant." And the Lord
12 said, "He will march down." And David asked, "Will the citizens of Ke'ila
hand me over to Sha'ul?"

And the Lord said, "They will hand you over."

13 So David and his men arose, around six hundred men; they made their way
out of Ke'ila, and they wandered wherever they could. When Sha'ul was
informed that David has escaped from Ke'ila, he abandoned the mission.
14 David settled in the strongholds of the wilderness; he settled in the hills of
the Wilderness of Zif. Sha'ul constantly hunted for him, but God did not
15 let him fall into his hands. David learned that Sha'ul had set out to hunt
16 him down while David was in the Wilderness of Zif, at Ḥoresh. Yehonatan,
Sha'ul's son, rose and made his way to David at Ḥoresh, to strengthen his
commitment to God.

17 "Do not fear," he said to him, "for the hand of Sha'ul, my father, will
not find you. You will be king over Israel, and I will be your second in

19 | The ephod of the High Priest held the Urim and Tumim. See note on 14:41.

18 command – even Sha'ul, my father, knows this is so." Then the two of
them formed a pact before the LORD. And David stayed in Ḥoresh while
Yehonatan went back home.

19 But the Zifites went up to Sha'ul at Giva, saying, "David is hiding among us
in the strongholds of Ḥoresh, in the Heights of Ḥakhila south of Yeshimon.
20 Now, if you so wish to come down, O king, come down; and we shall be
the ones to hand him over to the king."

21 22 "May the LORD bless you for taking pity on me," said Sha'ul. "Now go and
confirm once more; make sure you know every place where his foot treads.
23 Who has seen him there? For I have been told that he is very sly. Make sure
you know of all his possible hiding places; come back to me when you are
sure, and I shall set out with you. If he is in the area, I shall search for him
24 in all the clans of Yehuda." And they arose and went to Zif ahead of Sha'ul.
Meanwhile, David and his men were in the Wilderness of Maon, in the
plains south of Yeshimon.

25 When Sha'ul and his men set out to search, David was informed. He
climbed down the rock and settled in the Wilderness of Maon. When
26 Sha'ul heard, he chased after David in the Wilderness of Maon. Sha'ul
made his way along one side of the mountain while David and his men
were on the other side; David was desperately running away from Sha'ul,
27 but Sha'ul and his men were closing in to trap David and his men. Just
then, a messenger came to Sha'ul and announced, "Hurry, go, for the
28 Philistines have invaded the land." Sha'ul turned back from chasing David
and headed out toward the Philistines. Therefore, they called that place
29 Sela HaMaḥlekot.[20] Then David climbed up from there and settled in the
strongholds of Ein Gedi.

24 1 When Sha'ul returned from pursuing the Philistines, they informed him,
2 "David is now in the Wilderness of Ein Gedi." Sha'ul took three thousand
elite fighters from all of Israel and set out to search for David and his men
3 along the rocks of the wild goats. When they reached the sheepfolds by
the road, there was a cave there, and Sha'ul went inside to relieve himself;
David and his men were sitting in the depths of the cave.

4 David's men said to him, "Now is the very moment that the LORD spoke
of to you: 'Now, I am handing your enemies over to you.' Do to him as
you see fit!" And David got up and stealthily cut off the corner of Sha'ul's
5 robe. Later on, though, David's heart ached for having cut Sha'ul's hem.

6 "LORD forbid that I should do such a thing to my master – to the LORD's
own anointed!" he said to his men. "To raise my hand against him when
7 he is the LORD's anointed?" David restrained his men with words and did
not allow them to rise against Sha'ul. And Sha'ul rose out of the cave and
went on his way.

20 | Literally "rock of the parting."

8 David then rose, went out of the cave, and called after Sha'ul, "O my lord
king!"

Sha'ul looked behind him, and David bowed down with his face to the
9 ground in homage. And David said to Sha'ul, "Why do you listen to the
words of people who say, 'Look, David seeks to harm you?'

10 "Now, right now, see for yourself how the LORD handed you over to me
in the cave –
though I was urged to kill you, I showed you mercy.
And I said,
'I will not raise my hand against my lord,
for he is the LORD's own anointed.'
11 O my father, look –
look closely at the corner of your robe in my hand;
when I cut off the corner of your robe, I did not kill you.
Realize that I have no intention of harm, or crime, or offending you –
yet you pursue my life to snatch it away.
12 May the LORD judge between me and you,
and may the LORD avenge me on you –
my own hand will never touch you.
13 As the ancient proverb says,
'Evil is as evil does' –
my own hand will never touch you.
14 After whom, exactly, has the king of Israel set out?
After whom, exactly, are you chasing?
After a dead dog!
After a single flea!
15 May the LORD be Judge,
and judge between me and you.
May He witness and contend on my behalf
and defend me from you!"

16 When David had finished speaking these words to Sha'ul, Sha'ul said, "Is
that your voice, my son David?"

And Sha'ul broke down and wept.

17 "You are more just than I," he said to David, "for you have shown me
18 good while I have shown you evil. Now you have just told me how you
have acted toward me with good, for the LORD handed me over to you,
19 but you did not kill me. When a man finds his enemy, does he send him
away with good? May the LORD repay you with good for how you acted
20 toward me today. I now know that you will surely become king and that
21 the kingdom of Israel will be established through you. So now, swear to
me by the LORD that you will not cut off my seed after me, nor wipe out
my name from my father's house."

22 And David swore to Sha'ul. And Sha'ul went back to his house while David
and his men ascended to the stronghold.

25 1 Shmuel died, and all of Israel gathered to mourn him. They buried him at
his home in Rama.

Meanwhile, David had gone down to the Wilderness of Paran.

2 Now, there was a man in Maon whose business was in Carmel. The man
was very wealthy; he owned three thousand sheep and one thousand goats.
3 At the time, he was shearing his flock in Carmel. The man's name was Naval,
and his wife's name was Avigayil; the woman was intelligent and beautiful,
but the man, a Calebite, was coarse and vicious.

4 When David, out in the wilderness, heard that Naval was shearing his flock,
5 David sent out ten lads.

"Go up to Carmel," David said to the lads, "and when you reach Naval, ask
6 about his welfare in my name. Say,

"'To life! Peace unto you, and peace to your household, and peace to all that
7 is yours. I have heard that you are presently holding your shearing. Now,
the shepherds who belong to you have been with us; we have not shamed
them, nor did anything of theirs go missing throughout the time they were
8 in Carmel – ask your lads, and they will tell you. May the lads find favor
in your eyes, for we have come during a festive time. Please give whatever
you can to your servants and to your son, David.'"

9 So David's lads came and related all these words to Naval in David's name.
10 When they paused, Naval answered David's lads. "Who is David, and
who is the son of Yishai? Today, so many servants break away from their
11 masters; should I take my own bread and my own water and my own meat
that I slaughtered for my shearers and give it to people who come from I
don't know where?"

12 So David's lads turned back around, and as soon as they arrived, they
reported everything to him.

13 "Everyone, gird your swords!" David said to his men, and each man girded
his sword. David, too, girded his sword, and they marched up after David,
about four hundred men, while two hundred stayed with the baggage.

14 Meanwhile, one of the lads had told Avigayil, Naval's wife, "David just
sent messengers from the wilderness to greet our master, and he shouted
15 at them. But the men were very good to us; we were not shamed, and we
missed absolutely nothing throughout the time we went about with them
16 while we were in the field. They were a wall over us, both night and day,
17 for as long as we were with them tending the sheep. Now, consider what
to do, for harm has been determined for our master and all his household;
and he is too depraved to speak to."

18 Avigayil quickly grabbed two hundred loaves of bread, two amphorae of
wine, five prepared lambs, five *se'a* of toasted grain, one hundred cakes of
raisins, and two hundred cakes of figs, and loaded them onto the donkeys.
19 "Go on before me," she said to her servants, "I am coming right after you,"
but she did not tell Naval, her husband.

20 As she was riding her donkey down the shaded mountain trail, David and
21 his men came down toward her, and she met them. Now, David had been
saying, "It was only in vain that I guarded everything that belonged to this
one; absolutely nothing of his went missing, but he has paid me back with
22 evil for good. So may God do to David's enemies[21] – and more – if I leave a
23 single male[22] of his alive by the morning light." When Avigayil saw David,
she swiftly alighted from her donkey, flung herself face down before David,
24 and bowed to the ground. Then she flung herself at his feet.

"It is my own fault, my lord," she said.
"Please let your handmaiden speak to you; listen to the words of your handmaiden.
25 Let my lord not take this depraved man, Naval, to heart,
for he is just like his name – 'fool' is his name, and a fool he is indeed;
but I, your handmaiden, never saw my lord's lads whom you sent.
26 Now, my lord, as the Lord lives, and as you yourself live,
the Lord has prevented you from being tainted by blood by taking matters into your own hands;
and now may your enemies and those who wish evil upon my lord be like Naval.
27 As for this gift, which your maidservant brought for my lord,
let it be given to the lads who accompany my lord.
28 Please forgive your handmaiden's offense,
for the Lord will surely grant my lord an enduring house – as my lord fights the Lord's battles –
and no evil should be found in you all your days.
29 If anyone should arise to pursue you and seek your life,
may the life of my lord be tucked away in the pouch of life of the Lord your God
as He slings away your enemy's life as from the hollow of the sling.
30 And when the Lord has fulfilled for my lord all the good He has promised you
and has appointed you as ruler over Israel,
31 my lord will have no qualms or pangs of conscience for having spilled innocent blood through my lord's taking charge himself.
And when the Lord deals well with my lord,
may you remember your handmaiden."

32 And David said to Avigayil, "Blessed is the Lord, God of Israel, for having

21 | A euphemism for David himself, common in such oaths.

22 | Literally "one who urinates against a wall." The same phrase occurs in verse 34 below.

33 sent you to meet me today. And blessed is your sense of reason, and blessed
are you, who restrained me from being tainted with blood and taking
34 matters into my own hands. For as the LORD lives – the God of Israel, who
prevented me from harming you – had you not rushed out to meet me,
not a single male of Naval's would have been left by the morning light."

35 And David took what she had brought for him from her hands.

"Go up to your home in peace," he said to her. "See, I have heeded your
voice and granted your request."

36 When Avigayil came to Naval, the feast he was holding at his house was a
feast fit for a king; he was in high spirits, enormously drunk. So she told
37 him nothing at all until the morning light, but in the morning, when the
wine had seeped out of Naval, his wife related these things to him. And
38 his heart died within him, and he stiffened like a stone. And ten days later,
the LORD struck Naval and he died.

39 When David heard that Naval had died, he said, "Blessed is the LORD, who
has contended on my behalf against Naval's insults; he kept His servant
from evil and brought the evil of Naval back down on his own head." Then
40 David sent a proposal to Avigayil to take her as a wife; David's servants
came to Avigayil at Carmel and spoke to her, saying, "David has sent us
41 to you to take you for him as a wife." She rose, then bowed, face down, to
the ground, and said, "Here is your handmaiden as maidservant, to wash
42 the feet of my lord's servants." Then Avigayil swiftly rose and mounted her
donkey, with her five maids following at her heels; she followed David's
43 messengers and became his wife. David also took Aḥinoam from Yizre'el in
44 marriage, and both of them became his wives. Meanwhile, though, Sha'ul
had given his daughter Mikhal, David's wife, to Palti son of Layish, who
was from Galim.

26 1 Now the Zifites came to Sha'ul at Giva, reporting, "David is hiding in the
2 Heights of Ḥakhila facing Yeshimon." And Sha'ul set out and went down
to the Wilderness of Zif, together with three thousand elite fighters of
3 Israel, to track David down in the Wilderness of Zif. Sha'ul set up camp
by the road in the Heights of Ḥakhila, facing Yeshimon; and David, who
was staying in the wilderness, realized that Sha'ul had followed him to
4 the wilderness. So David sent out spies, and confirmed that Sha'ul had
5 indeed come. David rose and reached the site where Sha'ul was encamped,
and David could see exactly where Sha'ul and Avner son of Ner, his army
commander, were lying; Sha'ul lay within the circle, while the men were
6 encamped around him. David spoke up and asked Aḥimelekh the Hittite
and Avishai son of Tzeruya, Yoav's brother, "Who will go down with me
to Sha'ul, to the camp?" and Avishai said, "I will go down with you."

7 David and Avishai came to the camp at night, and there was Sha'ul, lying
asleep within the circle, with his spear thrust into the ground at his head,
and Avner and the men lying around him.

8 "Today God has delivered your enemy into your hands," Avishai said
to David. "Now let me pin him to the ground with a single thrust of the
9 spear – I will not need to strike him twice." But David said to Avishai, "Do
no violence to him, for who can strike against the anointed one of the
Lord and be pardoned?"

10 And David continued, "As the Lord lives, only the Lord shall strike
him – either his time will come and he will die, or he will go down to
11 battle and perish. The Lord forbid that I raise my hand against the Lord's
anointed. And now, take the spear by his head and the water jar, and let us
12 be off." And David took the spear and the water jar from next to Sha'ul's
head, and they made their way out. No one saw, no one knew, and no one
stirred, as all were fast asleep; for a deep sleep from the Lord had fallen
upon them.

13 Then David crossed over to the other side and stood upon a distant hilltop;
14 vast space stretched between them. And David called out to the men and
to Avner son of Ner, "Won't you answer, Avner?"

And Avner answered, "Who are you, calling out to the king?"

15 "You are quite a man, Avner," David said to Avner. "Who is quite like you
in all of Israel? So why did you fail to guard your master the king, when
16 one of the people came to destroy the king your master? You have not done
your job well – as the Lord lives, you are dead men – for failing to guard
your master, the Lord's anointed. Now, look around: Where are the king's
spear and the water jar that were by his head?"

17 And Sha'ul recognized David's voice and said, "Is that your voice, my son
David?"

18 "It is my voice, my lord the king," said David, and continued, "Why does
my lord chase after his servant so? What have I done; what guilt is on my
19 hands? Now, may my lord the king please listen to the words of his servant.
If the Lord has incited you against me, may He savor an offering, but if it
was mere men, then may they be cursed before the Lord, for they have
driven me out today from sharing in the Lord's estate, saying, 'Go serve
20 other gods.' Now do not let my blood spill to the ground far from the
Lord's presence. For the king of Israel has set out to hunt a single flea, just
as he would chase after a partridge in the hills."

21 And Sha'ul said, "I have sinned. Come back, my son David, for I will never
harm you again, as my life was so precious in your eyes today. Oh, I have
been foolish and have strayed so far."

22 "Here is the king's spear," answered David. "Let one of the lads come over
23 and take it. May the Lord repay each man for his virtue and faith; though
the Lord handed you over to me today, I was not willing to raise my hand
24 against the anointed one of the Lord. Now, just as I valued your life so
highly today, may the Lord value my life and rescue me from all danger."

25 "Bless you, my son," said Sha'ul. "You will surely succeed in whatever you
do."

And David went on his way while Sha'ul returned home.

27 1 Now David thought to himself, "One day soon, I might perish at Sha'ul's
hand; I have no better option than to escape to the land of the Philistines.
Then Sha'ul might despair of hunting me within the entire border of
2 Israel, and I shall escape his clutches." So David set out, together with
the six hundred men who were with him, and crossed over to Akhish son
3 of Maokh, king of Gat. And David stayed with Akhish in Gat, together
with his men, each with his own household and David with his two wives,
Aḥinoam the Jezreelite and Avigayil the Carmelite, the wife of Naval.
4 When Sha'ul was informed that David had fled to Gat, he never hunted
him down again.

5 David said to Akhish, "If I have found favor in your sight, let me be given
a place in one of the rural towns, and I will live there; why should your
6 servant be living in the royal city together with you?" Soon after, Akhish
granted him Tziklag; therefore Tziklag has belonged to the kings of Yehuda
7 to this day. The amount of time David remained in the Philistine country
was a year and four months.

8 David and his men would march up and raid the Geshurites and the
Gezerites and the Amalekites, for these were the age-old inhabitants of
9 the land leading from Shur up to the land of Egypt. David would attack
the land, never leaving man or woman alive, and he would take sheep,
cattle, donkeys, camels, and garments before returning and coming back
10 to Akhish. Akish would ask, "Where did you go raiding today?" and David
would answer, "The Negev of Yehuda" or "The Negev of the Jerahmeelites"
11 or "The Negev of the Kenites."[23] David never left any men or women alive
to bring to Gat, for he thought, "They might inform on us, saying, 'This is
what David was doing.'"

This was his practice throughout the time he remained in the Philistine
12 country. Akhish trusted David, saying, "He must have become odious
among his own people, Israel, so he has become my vassal forever."

28 1 It was around that time that the Philistines gathered their forces for battle
to fight against Israel. Akhish said to David, "You know, of course, that you
and your men are to march out to battle with me."

2 "Well," David said to Akhish, "then you must know just what your servant
will do."

"Well," Akhish said to David, "then I shall appoint you as my bodyguard
forever."

3 Shmuel had died, and all of Israel had mourned him and buried him in his

23 | Israelite localities.

hometown of Rama. And Sha'ul had already purged the necromancers and mediums from the land.

4 The Philistines gathered, and they came and set up camp in Shunem, while
5 Sha'ul gathered all of Israel and encamped at Gilboa. When Sha'ul saw the
6 Philistine camp, his heart shuddered with fear. And Sha'ul inquired of the
Lord, but the Lord did not answer him, neither in dreams nor through
7 the Urim[24] nor through prophets. So Sha'ul said to his servants, "Seek out
a necromancer for me, and I shall go to her and consult through her." His
8 servants replied to him, "There is a necromancer in Ein Dor." So Sha'ul
disguised himself and donned different clothing. Then he set out with two
of his servants, and they came to the woman by night.

"Please cast a spell for me by necromancy," he said, "and bring up for me the one I bid you."

9 "You must know what Sha'ul has done and how he cut off the necromancers and the mediums from the land," the woman said to him, "so why do you lay such a trap for me, to have me killed?"

10 And Sha'ul swore to her by the Lord. "As the Lord lives," he said, "no punishment will befall you for this act."

11 "Whom should I bring up for you?" said the woman.

"Bring up Shmuel for me," he said.

12 When the woman saw Shmuel, she screamed out loud. "Why have you deceived me?" she said to Sha'ul. "You are Sha'ul!"

13 "Do not be frightened," the king said to her, "but what have you seen?"

And the woman said to Sha'ul, "I saw divine beings rising up from the earth."

14 "What form does he have?" he asked her, and she replied, "An old man is rising up, and he is cloaked in a robe." And Sha'ul knew that it was Shmuel, and he bowed down with his face to the ground in homage.

15 And Shmuel said to Sha'ul, "Why have you disturbed me by bringing me up?"

"I am in grave danger," said Sha'ul. "The Philistines are fighting against me, but God has turned away from me and no longer answers me, neither through prophets nor in dreams – so I summoned you to tell me what to do."

16 "Why should you ask me," said Shmuel, "when the Lord has turned away
17 from you and has become your adversary? The Lord has executed what
He spoke of through me; the Lord has torn the kingship from your hands

---

24 | See note on 14:41.

18 and given it to your peer, to David. Because you failed to heed the voice of
the LORD and failed to execute His burning fury against Amalek, the LORD
19 will therefore execute this against you this very day: the LORD will deliver
Israel, together with you, into the hand of the Philistines. Tomorrow, you
and your sons shall be with me. And what is more, the LORD will deliver
the forces of Israel into the hands of the Philistines!"

20 At once, Sha'ul fell to the ground from his full stately height, terrified of
Shmuel's words. Nor did he have any strength left in him, for he had eaten
nothing all day and all night.

21 The woman came up to Sha'ul, and seeing how aghast he was, said to him,
"Look, your servant heeded your voice, and I took my life in my hands
22 and heeded the words that you spoke to me. Now, please, you yourself
should heed the voice of your servant. I will set a morsel of food before
23 you; eat it so that you will have the strength to go on your way." And Sha'ul
refused and said, "I will not eat," but when his servants – along with the
woman – urged him, he heeded their voice and got up from the ground and
24 sat on the bed. The woman had a fattened calf at home, which she quickly
25 slaughtered; she took flour, kneaded it, and baked unleavened bread. Then
she served Sha'ul and his servants, and they ate before rising and setting
out that same night.

29 1 The Philistines mustered all their forces to Afek, while Israel were
2 encamped by the spring at Yizre'el. The Philistine chieftains advanced in
their hundreds and their thousands while David and his men marched in
3 the rear with Akhish. And the Philistine chieftains said, "What are those
Hebrews?"

"Why, that is David, the servant of King Sha'ul of Israel," Akhish said to
the Philistine chieftains. "He has been with me for a while – over a year
now – and I have found nothing wrong with him from the day he defected
4 to this day." But the Philistine officials were furious with him.

"Send the man back, and let him go back to the place you assigned him," the
Philistine officials said to him. "He must not march down to battle with us;
he must not oppose us[25] in battle! How can this one reconcile himself with
5 his master? With the heads of these men, of course – isn't this the David
they sang and danced about, chanting, 'Sha'ul has struck down thousands,
and David – myriads!'?"

6 So Akhish summoned David and said to him, "As the LORD lives, you are
certainly honest, and I approve of your marching in and out of battle with
me, for I have found no fault with you from the day you came to me until
7 this very day. But in the eyes of the chieftains, you are not acceptable. Now
return, and go in peace, so as not to offend the Philistine chieftains."

---

25 | Cf. Numbers 22:22, 32.

8 "But what have I done," David said to Akhish, "and of what did you
disapprove in your servant – from the day I entered your service to this
day – that I should not come and fight against the enemies of my lord, the
king?"

9 "I know that in my eyes, you are as good as an angel of God," Akhish
answered David, "but the Philistine lords said, 'He must not march up with
10 us in battle.' Now set out early in the morning together with your lord's
servants who came with you; rise early in the morning, and leave as soon
11 as it is light." So David and his men rose and set out early in the morning
to return to the land of the Philistines, while the Philistines advanced
toward Yizre'el.

30 1 But by the time David and his men had reached Tziklag, on the third day,
the Amalekites had raided the Negev, including Tziklag; they had attacked
2 Tziklag and set it ablaze. They had taken the women there captive, from
young to old, though they had not killed anyone – they had led them
3 off and gone on their way. David and his men reached the town to find
it burned down, with their wives and sons and daughters taken captive.
4 And David and the men with him raised their voices and wept until they
5 had no strength left to weep. David's two wives, Aḥinoam the Jezreelite
and Avigayil, the wife of Naval the Carmelite, had been taken captive.
6 And David was in grave danger, for the men were all ready to stone him,
wretched and bitter as every man was about his sons and daughters; but
David drew strength from the LORD, his God.

7 David said to the priest Evyatar son of Aḥimelekh, "Bring the ephod[26] out
8 to me," and Evyatar brought out the ephod to David. And David inquired
of the LORD, asking, "Shall I pursue this band? Can I overtake them?"

"Pursue," He said to him, "for you will surely overtake, and you will surely
rescue."

9 David set out along with the six hundred men who were with him. When
they reached the Besor Stream, those who would stay behind came to a
10 halt. David led the chase with four hundred men, while two hundred men
who were too exhausted to cross the Besor Stream came to a halt.

11 They found an Egyptian man in the field and took him to David. They gave
12 him food, and he ate, and they gave him water to drink; they gave him a
slice of pressed figs and two cakes of raisins. When he had eaten, his spirits
revived, for he had not eaten food or drunk water for three days and three
13 nights. David then said to him, "To whom do you belong, and where are
you from?"

"I am an Egyptian boy," he said, "a slave to an Amalekite man. My master
14 abandoned me when I fell ill three days ago; we were raiding the south of

26 | See note on 23:6.

the Keretites, next to Yehuda, and the south of Kalev, and as for Tziklag, we set it alight."

15 "Can you lead us down to this band?" David asked him.

"If you swear to me by God that you will not kill me or hand me over to my master," he said, "then I will lead you down to this band."

16 He led them down, and there they were, all sprawled across the ground;
feasting and drinking and reveling in all the masses of spoil they had seized
17 from the land of the Philistines and the land of Yehuda. David attacked
them the next day from dawn until dusk, and not a man escaped, save four
18 hundred young fighters who fled on camelback. David rescued all that the
Amalekites had seized, and as for his own two wives, David rescued them.
19 Nothing of theirs was missing, from the youngest to the oldest; neither
sons nor daughters nor any of the spoil nor anything they had taken from
20 them; David recovered everything. Then David took all the sheep and
cattle they were driving ahead of the other livestock, and they declared,
"This is David's spoil."

21 When David reached the two hundred men who had been too exhausted to
follow him – those who had been left in the Besor Stream – they went out
toward David and the men who were with him. David approached the men
22 and greeted them. But every spiteful, depraved man among the people
who had gone with David reacted. "Because they did not come with us,"
they said, "we shall not give them any of the spoil we recovered except
for each man's wife and children – they can lead them away and be off."

23 But David said, "You shall not do so, my brothers, considering what the
Lord has given us and how He watched over us and handed over to us
24 the band that attacked us. Who would listen to you in this matter? For
the share of those who remain with the baggage should be the same as
25 the share of those who go down to battle; they will share together." And
from that day onward, he established it as law and order in Israel, which
endures to this day.

26 When David reached Tziklag, he distributed some of the spoil to the elders of Yehuda, his allies, saying, "Here is a gift for you from the spoil of the enemies of the Lord":

27 for those in Beit El,
for those in Ramot Negev,
for those in Yatir,
28 for those in Aroer,
for those in Sifemot,
for those in Eshtemoa,
29 for those in Rakhal,
for those in the Jerahmeelite towns,
for those in the Kenite towns,

30 for those in Ḥorma,
for those in Bekhor Ashan,
for those in Atakh,
31 for those in Ḥevron; for all the places where David and his men had
roamed.

31 1 Meanwhile, the Philistines were fighting against Israel; the men of Israel
2 fled before the Philistines and fell slain on Mount Gilboa.[27] And the
Philistines closed in on Sha'ul and his sons; the Philistines struck down
3 Yehonatan and Avinadav and Malki Shua, the sons of Sha'ul. And the battle
weighed heavily upon Sha'ul, and when the archer-men found him, he
shook, terrified by the archers.

4 "Draw your sword and stab me with it," Sha'ul said to his arms-bearer, "lest
these heathens come and stab me and torture me," but his arms-bearer was
not willing because of his great reverence, so Sha'ul took the sword and
5 fell upon it. When his arms-bearer saw that Sha'ul was dead, he too fell
6 upon his sword and died along with him. Sha'ul, his three sons, and his
arms-bearer died on that day, together with all his men.

7 When the men of Israel on the other side of the valley, and on the other
side of the Jordan, realized that the men of Israel had fled and that Sha'ul
and his sons were dead, they abandoned the cities and fled. And Philistines
came and settled in them.

8 The next day, when Philistines came to strip the corpses, they found
9 Sha'ul and his three sons fallen on Mount Gilboa. They cut off his head
and stripped off his armor and sent word throughout the land of the
Philistines, bringing tidings to the temples of their idols and to the people.
10 They deposited his armor in the temple of Ashtarot, and as for his corpse,
they impaled it on the wall of Beit Shan.

11 Now when the inhabitants of Yavesh Gilad heard of it – what the Philistines
12 had done to Sha'ul – all their boldest men set out and trekked all night
long. They took down Sha'ul's corpse and his sons' corpses from the wall
13 of Beit Shan and came back to Yavesh, where they burned them. Then
they took their bones and buried them under the tamarisk in Yavesh and
fasted for seven days.

II SAMUEL 1 1 After the death of Sha'ul, David returned from defeating the Amalekites.
2 David had been staying in Tziklag for two days when, on the third day, a
man suddenly came from Sha'ul's camp, his clothes torn and earth on his
head. When he came to David, he flung himself to the ground and bowed
down low.

3 "Where have you come from?" David asked him.

"I have escaped from the camp of Israel," he said to him.

---

27 | Cf. 1 Chronicles 10:1–12.

4 "What has happened?" David asked him. "Tell me now!"

"The troops fled from the battle," he said, "and so many of the troops fell and died; Sha'ul and his son Yehonatan died as well."

5 David asked the youth who was reporting to him, "How do you know that Sha'ul and his son Yehonatan have died?"

6 "I happened to be on Mount Gilboa," said the youth who was reporting
to him, "and there was Sha'ul, leaning upon his spear, and there were the
7 chariots and riders closing in on him. He turned around, saw me, and
8 called out to me, and I said, 'Here I am.' 'Who are you?' he asked me, and
9 I said, 'I am an Amalekite.' Then he said to me, 'Stand over me and finish
10 me off, for I am wracked with convulsions, but my life still lingers.' So I
stood over him and finished him off, for I knew that he would not live after
his collapse. And I took the crown upon his head and the armlet upon his
arm and brought them here to my lord."

11 And David grasped hold of his clothes and rent them, and all the men with
12 him did as well. They grieved and wept and fasted until dusk; for Sha'ul,
and for his son Yehonatan, and for the men of the LORD, and for the House
of Israel, for they had fallen by the sword.

13 Then David asked the youth who was reporting to him, "Where are you from?" "I am the son of a sojourner," he said, "an Amalekite."

14 And David said to him, "How did you dare raise your hand to destroy the LORD's anointed?"

15 David summoned one of the lads and said, "Here! Fall upon him." He struck him and he died.

16 "Your blood is on your own head," David said to him, "for your own mouth testified against you, declaring, 'I put the LORD's anointed to death.'"

17 Then David lamented over Sha'ul and over Yehonatan his son with this
18 lament. He ordered that the Judahites be instructed in archery, as is
recorded in the Book of the Upright.

19 "The glory, O Israel, lies slain on your heights;
oh, how heroes have fallen!
20 Say nothing in Gat,
proclaim nothing in the streets of Ashkelon,
lest the daughters of Philistines rejoice,
lest the daughters of heathens gloat.
21 O hills of Gilboa,
let there be no dew
nor rain
nor bountiful fields upon you,
for there the shield of heroes was defiled –
the shield of Sha'ul, unanointed with oil.

22 From the blood of the slain,
from the fat of warriors,
Yehonatan's bow never retreated,
and Sha'ul's sword never withdrew empty.
23 Sha'ul and Yehonatan,
beloved and dear,
never parted in life or in death!
Swifter than eagles! Stronger than lions!
24 O daughters of Israel, weep over Sha'ul,
who clothed you in scarlet, in finery;
who draped golden jewelry over your dresses.
25 How heroes have fallen in the thick of battle!
Yehonatan lies slain on your heights –
26 I ache for you, my brother, Yehonatan,
you were so dear to me.
More wondrous was your love for me
than the love of women.
27 Oh, how heroes have fallen,
and the weapons of war are lost."

2 1 Sometime later, David inquired of the LORD, asking, "Shall I go up to one
of the cities of Yehuda?" And the LORD said to him, "Go up."

"Where shall I go up?" asked David.

"To Ḥevron," He said.

2 So David went up there, along with his two wives, Aḥinoam the Jezreelite
3 and Avigayil, wife of Naval the Carmelite. And David brought up the men
who were with him, each man with his household, and they settled in the
4 towns of Ḥevron. The people of Yehuda came, and there they anointed
David as king over the House of Yehuda.

They informed David about the men of Yavesh Gilad, who had buried
5 Sha'ul. So David sent messengers to the men of Yavesh Gilad, declaring to
them, "Blessed are you by the LORD for showing such loyalty to your lord,
6 to Sha'ul, and burying him. Now, may the LORD show you true loyalty;
7 I too will reward you for having done this deed. Now, be determined,
valiant warriors, for your lord Sha'ul is dead while the House of Yehuda
has appointed me as king over them.

8 "Meanwhile, Avner son of Ner, Sha'ul's army commander, had taken Ish
9 Boshet,[28] Sha'ul's son, and conveyed him to Maḥanayim. He appointed
him over the Gilad, the Ashurites, Yizre'el, Efrayim, and Binyamin – over
10 all of Israel. Ish Boshet, Sha'ul's son, was forty years old when he reigned

28 | In 1 Chronicles 8:33, this character is called Eshbaal. *Boshet*, literally "shame," was a derogatory epithet commonly substituted for the name of the Canaanite god Baal. Cf. Jeremiah 11:13.

over Israel, and he reigned for two years, but the House of Yehuda followed
11 David. The length of time that David reigned in Ḥevron over the House
of Yehuda was seven years and six months.

12 Avner son of Ner and the men of Ish Boshet son of Sha'ul marched out
13 from Maḥanayim toward Givon. So Yoav son of Tzeruya and David's
men marched out, and they confronted each other at the pool of Givon;
they positioned themselves on one side of the pool, and they positioned
themselves on the other.

14 "Let the lads get up and sport before us," Avner said to Yoav.

"Let them," said Yoav.

15 They got up, crossed over, and counted off – twelve for Binyamin and Ish
16 Boshet son of Sha'ul and twelve of David's men. Each man grasped hold
of his opponent's head, with his sword in his opponent's side, and they
fell together. And that place was called Ḥelkat HaTzurim,[29] which is in
Givon.

17 And the fighting grew brutally fierce that day, and Avner and the men of
18 Israel were routed before David's subjects. Now the three sons of Tzeruya
were there – Yoav, Avishai, and Asael; Asael was as swift-footed as a gazelle
19 in the field. Asael chased after Avner, veering neither right nor left behind
20 Avner. Avner looked back and called, "Is that you, Asael?"

"It is I," he said.

21 "Veer to your right or to your left," Avner said to him. "Grab hold of one
of the lads and seize his gear for yourself."

22 But Asael would not turn away from him. So Avner called out again to
Asael, "Turn away from me – why should I strike you to the ground? How
will I look your brother Yoav in the face?"

23 But he refused to turn away, and Avner struck him in the stomach with
the butt of his spear; the spear burst out of his back, and he fell down and
died on the spot. And everyone who reached the place where Asael had
fallen down and died came to a halt there.

24 But Yoav and Avishai chased after Avner. By the time the sun was setting,
they had gone as far as Heights of Ama overlooking Giaḥ on the road to
25 the Givon wilderness. And all the Benjaminites gathered behind Avner,
26 formed a single band, and positioned themselves on a single hilltop. Then
Avner called out to Yoav:

"Must the sword consume forever? You know how bitter the end will
be – when will you order the troops to cease pursuing their brothers?"

29 | Literally "field of the swords"; cf. *ḥarvot tzurim* in Joshua 5:2.

27 "As God lives," said Yoav, "if you had not spoken – why, since this morning
the people would have moved on, each man away from his brother."

28 Yoav blasted the ram's horn, and all the troops came to a halt; they left off
29 their pursuit of Israel and did not continue fighting. Avner and his men
trudged through the plain all that night, crossed the Jordan, and trudged
30 all morning long until they reached Maḥanayim. And Yoav ceased his
pursuit of Avner and gathered all the troops. Nineteen men of David's
31 subjects – as well as Asael – were missing, while David's subjects had
defeated Binyamin and Avner's men; three hundred and sixty men were
32 dead. They carried Asael and buried him in his father's tomb, which was in
Beit Leḥem; then Yoav and his men marched all night, and light dawned
on them at Ḥevron.

3 1 The war between the house of Sha'ul and the House of David proved long
and drawn out; David grew stronger while the house of Sha'ul grew weaker.
2 Sons were born to David at Ḥevron; his firstborn was Amnon, by Aḥinoam
3 the Jezreelite. His second born was Kilav, by Avigayil, the wife of Naval the
Carmelite, while his third was Avshalom, the son of Maakha, who was the
4 daughter of King Talmai of Geshur. The fourth was Adoniya, son of Ḥagit,
5 and the fifth was Shefatya, the son of Avital. The sixth was Yitre'am, by Egla,
the wife of David; these were born to David at Ḥevron.

6 As hostilities between the House of Sha'ul and the House of David
7 continued, Avner was gaining power within the house of Sha'ul. Now
Sha'ul had a concubine by the name of Ritzpa, daughter of Aya, and
Avner was accused: "Why have you slept with my father's concubine?"
8 Ish Boshet's words made Avner furious, and he said, "Am I but a dog's head
of Yehuda? To this day, I have shown loyalty to the house of your father,
Sha'ul, and his friends in not handing you over to David, yet you dare
9 charge me with guilt over this woman today? So may God do to Avner, and
10 more, if I do not fulfill for David what the LORD swore to him: to transfer
the kingdom from the house of Sha'ul and establish David's throne over
Israel and Yehuda, from Dan to Be'er Sheva."

11 And he could not answer Avner back because of his fear of him.

12 Avner secretly sent messengers to David, saying, "To whom does the land
belong?" and further, "Form a pact with me, then my hand will be with
you, guiding all of Israel toward you."

13 "Good," he replied, "I shall form a pact with you – but I require one thing
of you: you shall not be allowed in my presence unless you bring Mikhal,
Sha'ul's daughter, when you come to see me."

14 Then David sent messengers to Ish Boshet, son of Sha'ul, declaring, "Give
me my wife, Mikhal, for whom I paid a bride-price of a hundred Philistine
15 foreskins." So Ish Boshet sent and had her taken from her husband, from

16 Paltiel son of Layish. And her husband went with her, weeping as he
walked behind her, until Baḥurim.

"Go back," Avner said to him, and he went back.

17 Now Avner had been conferring with the elders of Israel, saying, "You
18 have long sought out David as your king. Now take action, for the Lord
has said to David, 'Through the hand of My servant David, I will save My
people from the hand of the Philistines and the hands of all their enemies.'"
19 Avner made the same speech in Binyamin's hearing. Then Avner went to
David in Ḥevron to report all the decisions of Israel and the whole House
20 of Binyamin. Avner came to David in Ḥevron accompanied by twenty
men, and David held a feast for Avner and the men who had accompanied
him.

21 "I will rise and set out to gather all of Israel to my lord, the king," Avner
said to David. "They will form a pact with you, and you shall rule over
everything your heart desires." David then dismissed Avner, who set out
and departed in peace.

22 Just then, David's officials and Yoav arrived from a raid, bringing a wealth
of spoil with them. Avner was no longer with David in Ḥevron, for he had
23 dismissed him, and he had set out and departed in peace. Yoav and all the
troops with him arrived, and they informed Yoav: "Avner son of Ner came
to the king, and he dismissed him, and he set out and departed in peace."
24 Then Yoav went to the king.

"What have you done?" he said. "Look, Avner came to you – why did you
25 just dismiss him, so that he went off? You know Avner son of Ner – he
came to lure you and learn of your maneuvers and learn of all you do."

26 And Yoav left David's presence and sent messengers after Avner, who
brought him back from the cistern of Sira without David's knowledge.
27 When Avner came back to Ḥevron, Yoav took him aside, within the gate,
as if to talk with him privately; but there he struck him in the stomach, and
he died for the blood of Asael, Yoav's brother.

28 When David heard of this afterward, he declared: "I and my kingdom are
29 forever blameless before the Lord for the blood of Avner son of Ner – may
it fall upon the head of Yoav and all his family. May Yoav's household never
lack one who suffers from a discharge, or a leper, or one who clings to a
30 crutch, or a victim of the sword, or one who lacks bread." Yoav and Avishai,
his brother, had murdered Avner because he killed their brother Asael
during the battle at Givon.

31 Now David said to Yoav and to all the troops who were with him, "Tear
your clothes, don sackcloth, and wail before Avner," while King David
32 himself walked after the bier. They buried Avner in Ḥevron, and the king
33 raised his voice and wept over Avner's grave, as all the people wept. And
the king lamented Avner and uttered:

"How could Avner have died
such a lowly death?
34 Your hands were not bound,
and your feet were not fettered;
yet you fell as one falls
before violent men."

And all the people continued to weep over him.

35 When all the troops came to serve David bread that same day, David
swore, "So may God do to me – and more – if I taste bread, or anything
36 at all, before sunset." All the troops acknowledged and approved of it, just
37 as the troops approved of everything else the king had done. And on that
day all the troops – and all of Israel – knew that it was not the king who
had put Avner son of Ner to death.

38 Then the king announced to his subjects, "You certainly know that a noble
39 man, a great man, has fallen this day in Israel. And I am mild and only just
anointed king, while these men – the sons of Tzeruya – are harsher than
me; may the Lord repay the evildoer according to his evil."

4 1 When Sha'ul's son heard that Avner had died in Ḥevron, he lost his grip,
2 and all of Israel became anxious. Now the son of Sha'ul had two men,
leaders of raiding parties. One was called Baana and the other Rekhav;
they were sons of Rimon the Be'erotite, of the Benjaminites, for Be'erot
3 was considered part of Binyamin. The Be'erotites fled to Gitayim, and they
live there to this day.

4 Yehonatan son of Sha'ul had a son who was lame. He had been five years
old when the news of Sha'ul and Yehonatan arrived from Yizre'el. When
his nurse picked him up and fled, in her rush to flee she dropped him, and
he became lame. His name was Mefivoshet.[30]

5 The sons of Rimon the Be'erotite – Rekhav and Baana – set out and reached
the house of Ish Boshet in the heat of the day, when he was lying down
6 for his midday rest. They entered the inner part of the house as though to
fetch wheat and struck him in the stomach; then Rekhav and Baana his
7 brother escaped – when they entered the house, he had been lying on his
bed in his bedchamber, and they had struck him, killed him, and cut off
his head. They seized his head, and then, all through the night, they made
their way across the Arava.

8 They brought the head of Ish Boshet to David at Ḥevron. "Here is the head
of Ish Boshet, son of your enemy Sha'ul, who sought your life," they said
to the king. "On this day the Lord has granted vengeance to my lord the
king against Sha'ul and his seed."

9 But David retorted to Rekhav and Baana his brother, the sons of Rimon

30 | See note on 2:8 and cf. 1 Chronicles 8:34.

the Be'erotite, "As the Lord lives – He who saved my life from every
10 danger," he said to them, "when the one who told me, 'look – Sha'ul is dead,'
thought he was bringing me good news, I seized hold of him and killed
11 him in Tziklag – that was his reward for the news. So when evil men have
murdered an innocent man in his own house in his own bed – now, will I
not demand his blood from your hands and purge you from the land?"

12 David gave the order to his lads; they killed them and severed their arms
and legs and hung them over the cistern in Ḥevron. As for the head of Ish
Boshet, they took it and buried it in Avner's grave in Ḥevron.

5 1 Now all the tribes of Israel came to David at Ḥevron.

2 "Here we are, your own flesh and blood. All along, even when Sha'ul was
king over us, you were the one who led Israel out and brought them back.[31]
And the Lord said to you, 'You shall shepherd My people Israel, and you
3 shall be the ruler over Israel.'" All the elders of Israel came to the king at
Ḥevron. King David formed a covenant with them at Ḥevron before the
Lord, and they anointed David as king over Israel.

4 David was thirty years old when he became king, and he reigned for forty
5 years. In Ḥevron, he reigned over Yehuda for seven years and six months,
and in Jerusalem, he reigned over all of Israel and Yehuda for thirty-three
years.

6 The king and his men set out for Jerusalem against the Jebusites, who
inhabited the land. David was told, "You shall not enter here; surely even
our blind and lame will repel you" – meaning, "David will not enter here."
7 8 But David captured the stronghold of Zion, that is, the City of David. And
David declared on that day, "Whoever attacks the Jebusites, as well as their
blind and lame, whom David despises with his very soul, and reaches the
water shaft..."[32] – for this reason, they say, "The blind and the lame may not
9 enter the House." David settled in the stronghold and named it "The City
of David"; he then built up the surrounding area from the Milo[33] inward.
10 And David grew in greatness; the Lord, God of Hosts, was with him.

11 King Ḥiram of Tyre sent envoys to David with cedar logs, and carpenters
12 and stonemasons, who built a palace for David. And David knew that
the Lord had established him as the king over Israel and had exalted his
kingship for the sake of His people, Israel.

13 David took more concubines and wives from Jerusalem after his arrival
14 from Ḥevron, and more sons and daughters were born to David. These
are the names of those born to him in Jerusalem: Shamua, Shovav, Natan,
15 16 and Shlomo; Yivḥar, Elishua, Nefeg, and Yafia; Elishama, Elyada, and
Elifelet.

31 | In battle; cf. I Samuel 8:20.

32 | See I Chronicles 11:6.

33 | Probably a terraced fortifying structure.

17 When the Philistines heard that they had appointed David as king over
Israel, all the Philistines marched up to hunt David down. When David
18 heard, he descended into the stronghold. The Philistines came and spread
out in the Refaim Valley.

19 David inquired of the LORD, "Shall I go up to the Philistines? Will You
deliver them into my hand?"

"Go up," the LORD replied to David, "for I will surely deliver the Philistines
into your hands."

20 David reached Baal Peratzim, and there David defeated them. And he said,
"The LORD has blasted my enemies away before me like a blast of water." For
21 that reason, he named that place Baal Peratzim.[34] They abandoned their
idols there, and David and his men carried them off.

22 But the Philistines marched up once more and spread out in the Refaim
23 Valley. David inquired of the LORD, who said, "Do not go up; turn around
24 to their rear, and advance upon them opposite the baca trees. As soon as
you hear the sound of marching echoing across the tops of the baca trees,
act swiftly, for then the LORD will go out before you to strike down the
25 Philistine force." And David did as the LORD commanded him, and he
defeated the Philistines from Geva all the way up to Gezer.

6 1 2 David mustered all of Israel's elite once more, thirty thousand. Then
David, along with all the troops with him, set out from Baalim of Yehuda.
From there they brought up the Ark of God, which is called by a name:
The Name of the LORD of Hosts Enthroned upon the Cherubim is upon
3 it. They mounted the Ark of God upon a new cart and conveyed it from
the house of Avinadav in Giva, with Uza and Aḥyo, the sons of Avinadav,
4 driving the new cart. They conveyed it from the house of Avinadav in
5 Giva – the Ark of God, Aḥyo walking before the Ark, and David and all
the House of Israel reveling before the LORD with all kinds of instruments
6 of cypress wood, lyres, harps, timbrels, sistra, and cymbals. When they
reached the threshing floor of Nakhon, Uza reached out toward the Ark
7 of God and grasped hold of it, for the oxen had stumbled. And the LORD's
rage flared up against Uza, and God struck him down on the spot for his
8 impudence; he died there with the Ark of God. David was enraged that
the LORD had burst out against Uza, and that place has been called Peretz
9 Uza[35] to this day. David feared the LORD on that day, and he said, "How
will the Ark of the LORD come to me?"

10 And David was not willing to have the Ark of the LORD removed to him
in the City of David; David had it redirected to the house of Oved Edom,
11 the Gittite. The Ark of the LORD remained at the house of Oved Edom,

34 | From the Hebrew *peretz*, meaning "blast."

35 | Literally "outburst [against] Uza."

the Gittite, for three months, and the LORD blessed Oved Edom and his
whole household.

12 When it was reported to King David that the LORD had blessed Oved
Edom's household and all that was his because of the Ark of God, David
went and brought up the Ark of God from the house of Oved Edom to
13 the City of David, with joy. When the bearers of the Ark of the LORD had
14 advanced six paces, he sacrificed an ox and a fatling. And David danced
15 with all his might before the LORD; David was clad in a linen ephod.[36] So
David and all the House of Israel led the Ark of the LORD up with joyous
16 shouting and the sound of the ram's horn. As the Ark of the LORD entered
the City of David, Mikhal, Sha'ul's daughter, was watching through the
window; when she saw David – the king! – leaping and dancing before
the LORD, she felt a rush of contempt for him.

17 They brought the Ark of the LORD and set it in its place within the tent
David had pitched for it, and David offered burnt offerings and peace
18 offerings before the LORD. When David had finished offering the burnt
offering and the peace offerings, he blessed the people in the name of the
19 LORD of Hosts. He then distributed a ring of bread, a share of meat, and a
cake of raisins to all the people – to all the multitudes of Israel, every single
man and woman. Then all the people, every one, made their way home.

20 When David returned to bless his own household, Mikhal, Sha'ul's
daughter, came out to meet him.

"How dignified the king of Israel was today," she said, "exposing himself before all the eyes of his servants' slave girls just as one of the rabble might expose himself!"

21 "It was before the LORD, who chose me instead of your father and all
his household and appointed me as ruler over the LORD's people, Israel,"
22 David said to Mikhal. "I danced before the LORD. And I would have
lowered myself even further and been humiliated in my own eyes – but to
the slave girls you speak of, I would still be dignified."

23 And Mikhal, Sha'ul's daughter, never had a child – to her dying day.

7 1 Once the king had settled in his palace, and the LORD had granted him
2 repose from all his surrounding enemies, the king said to the prophet
Natan, "Look now – I am dwelling in a cedarwood palace while the Ark
of God is dwelling in a tent."

3 "Go – do whatever you have in mind," Natan said to the king, "for the
LORD is with you."

4 But that same night,the word of the LORD came to Natan.

5 "Go, and say to My servant David: Thus says the LORD: Shall you be

36 | See note on I Samuel 2:18.

6 the one to build a house for Me, for My abode? For I have not dwelt in
a house from the day I brought the Israelites out of Egypt to this day; I
7 have roamed in tent and tabernacle. But wherever I roamed, among all the
Israelites, have I ever spoken a word to any of the tribes of Israel whom
I charged to shepherd My people Israel, saying, 'Why have you not built
Me a cedarwood palace?'

8 "Now you shall say so to My servant David: Thus says the LORD of Hosts:
I took you out of the pastures, from following the sheep, to be ruler over
9 My people Israel. I have been with you wherever you went, and I have cut
down all your enemies before you. I will make your name great – one of
10 the greatest names on earth. I will set aside a place for My people Israel and
let them take root and settle down within it, and they will be disturbed no
11 longer; violent men will no longer oppress them as they once did in the
days when I appointed judges over My people Israel. To you I will grant
repose from all your enemies; moreover, the LORD declares that the LORD
12 will establish a house for you. For when your days are done and you lie
with your ancestors, I will raise up your own seed after you – the issue of
13 your own loins – and I will establish his kingdom. He will build a house
14 in My name, and I will firmly establish his royal throne forever. I will be a
father to him, and he will be a son to Me; and should he do wrong, I will
15 berate him with the rod of mortals and with human afflictions. But My
loyalties shall not move from him, as I removed them from Sha'ul, whom
16 I removed before you. And your house and your kingdom will be ever
steadfast before you, and your throne will be secure forever."

17 Natan related all these words and all this vision to David.

18 Now King David came and sat before the LORD.
"Who am I, O LORD GOD, and who is my house," he said,
"that You have brought me so far?
19 And yet even this is small in Your eyes, O LORD GOD,
as You also speak of Your servant's house in the distant future –
why, this is a revelation to humanity, O LORD GOD.
20 But what more can David say to You;
You know Your servant, O LORD GOD.
21 It is for the sake of Your own word, and Your own will,
that You brought about this greatness
and made it known to Your servant.
22 How great You are, O LORD God;
there is no one like You, and no god besides You,
as we have heard all along.
23 And who is like Your people Israel –
the only nation on earth
God went to redeem as His own people,
making a name for Himself
and performing great and wondrous deeds

to the nations and gods in Your land
before the people You redeemed for Yourself from Egypt.
24 You have established Your people Israel
as Your own people forever,
and You, O LORD, have become their God.
25 Now, O LORD God,
fulfill the promise You made regarding Your servant,
and regarding his house, forever;
do as You have promised.
26 May Your name be exalted forever;
let them say,
'The LORD of Hosts is God of Israel,'
and may the house of David be established before You.
27 As You, O LORD of Hosts, God of Israel,
have revealed this to Your servant,
saying 'I will build a house for you,'
Your servant has found the heart
to offer this prayer before You.
28 And now, O LORD GOD –
You are God,
and Your words are truth,
and You have promised this favor to Your servant
29 and now –
please bless Your servant's house
to be before You forever,
as You promised, O LORD GOD,
and by Your blessing,
may Your servant's house be blessed forever."

8 1 Sometime later, David defeated the Philistines and subjugated them; and
2 David seized Meteg HaAma from the hand of the Philistines. He defeated
Moav and measured them out with a cord; he made them lie on the ground
and measured out two cord-lengths for execution, and one full length to
be kept alive. And Moav became David's tribute-bearing vassals.

3 David defeated Hadadezer son of Reḥov, the king of Tzova, who had set
4 out to extend his dominion to the Euphrates. David captured a thousand
seven hundred of his riders and twenty thousand infantrymen; David
hamstrung all the chariot horses, retaining one hundred chariot horses.
5 Aram of Damascus came to King Hadadezer of Tzova's aid, but David
6 struck down twenty-two thousand of Aram's men. And David posted
governors in Aram of Damascus, and the Arameans became David's
tribute-bearing vassals. And the LORD granted David victory wherever
7 he went. David took the golden quivers that had belonged to Hadadezer's
8 officials and brought them to Jerusalem, and from Betaḥ and Berotai,
Hadadezer's cities, David confiscated a vast amount of bronze.

9 When King To'i of Ḥamat heard that David had defeated all of Hadadezer's
10 forces, To'i sent his son Yoram to King David to greet him and congratulate
him for having conquered Hadadezer in battle, for Hadadezer had been
11 at war with To'i. He bore vessels of silver, gold, and bronze. King David
devoted those, too, to the LORD, in addition to all the silver and gold he
12 had devoted from all the nations he had conquered; from Aram, Moav, the
Amonites, the Philistines, Amalek, and the spoil from Hadadezer son of
Reḥov, King of Tzova.

13 David made a name for himself when he returned from defeating the
14 Arameans in the Valley of Salt – eighteen thousand of them.[37] He stationed
governors in Edom – throughout Edom, he stationed governors, and all
of Edom became David's vassals. And the LORD granted David victory
wherever he went.

15 David reigned over all of Israel, and David upheld justice and righteousness
16 for all his people. Yoav son of Tzeruya was the commander of his army;
17 Yehoshafat son of Aḥilud was royal herald; Tzadok son of Aḥituv, and
18 Aḥimelekh son of Evyatar, were priests; Seraya was royal scribe; Benayahu
son of Yehoyada commanded the Keretites and Peletites; and David's sons
were priests.

9 1 Now David said, "Is there anyone still left from the house of Sha'ul? I will
show him kindness for Yehonatan's sake."

2 There was a servant of the house of Sha'ul whose name was Tziva; they
summoned him to David, and the king said to him, "Are you Tziva?"

"At your service," he said.

3 "Is there anyone at all who is still left from the house of Sha'ul?" said the
king. "I will show him God's own loyalty."

"There is still a son of Yehonatan's, who is lame," Tziva said to the king.

4 "Where is he?" the king said to him, and Tziva replied to the king,

"He is there in the house of Makhir son of Amiel, in Lo Devar."

5 King David sent and had him brought from the house of Makhir son of
6 Amiel, in Lo Devar. And Mefivoshet son of Yehonatan son of Sha'ul came
before David and flung himself on his face in homage.

"Mefivoshet," David said.

"Here, at your service," he replied.

7 "Do not be afraid," David said to him, "for I will show you nothing but
kindness, for the sake of Yehonatan, your father. I will restore all the fields
of your grandfather Sha'ul to you, and as for you – you will always dine
at my table."

37 | Cf. Psalms 60:2; I Chronicles 18:12.

8 He prostrated himself and said, "What is your servant, that you should
have turned to a dead dog like me?"

9 The king summoned Tziva, Sha'ul's lad, and said to him, "I have given all
10 that belonged to Sha'ul and all his household to the son of your master. Now,
you shall work his land – you and your sons and your slaves – and bring in
food, so that the son of your master will have sustenance; but Mefivoshet,
son of your master, will always dine at my table." Now Tziva had fifteen
11 sons and twenty slaves. And Tziva replied to the king, "Whatever the king
commands his servant – so your servant shall do."

"Yes, Mefivoshet shall dine at my table, like one of the king's sons."

12 Mefivoshet had a small son whose name was Mikha; and all the members
13 of Tziva's household were Mefivoshet's servants. But Mefivoshet lived
in Jerusalem, for he always dined at the king's table. Both his feet were
crippled.

10 1 Sometime later, the king of the Amonites died, and Ḥanun, his son, reigned
in his place.

2 "I will show loyalty to Ḥanun son of Naḥash," said David, "just as his father
showed loyalty to me." David sent his condolences for his father through
3 his officials, and David's officials reached the land of the Amonites. But
the ministers of the Amonites said to their master Ḥanun, "Do you really
think that David honors your father because he sent you condolences?
No – David sent his officials to you to scout and spy out the city to
overthrow it."

4 So Ḥanun had David's officials seized; he shaved half their beards, cut off
half of their uniforms – until their buttocks – and sent them off.

5 They reported this to David, and he sent word out to them, for the men
were utterly humiliated. "Remain in Jericho until your beards grow," said
the king, "and then return."

6 When the Amonites realized that they had become odious to David, the
Amonites sent and hired twenty thousand infantrymen from Aram of Beit
Reḥov and Aram Tzova, a thousand men from the king of Maakha, and
7 twelve thousand men from Tov. When David heard, he sent Yoav together
8 with his entire military force. The Amonites advanced and deployed for
battle by the entrance of the gate, while the Arameans of Tzova and Reḥov,
the men of Tov, and Maakha were stationed separately, in the open field.
9 Yoav saw that he was faced with battle before him and behind him, so he
10 selected all of Israel's elite troops and deployed against Aram. He handed
command of the remaining troops to his brother Avshai and deployed
them against the Amonites.

11 "If Aram overpowers me, come to my aid," he said, "and if the Amonites
12 overpower you, I will come to your aid. Let us be strong and remain strong

for the sake of our people and the cities of our God – and may the Lord
13 do as He sees fit." Then Yoav and all the troops with him charged out to
battle against Aram, who fled before them.

14 When the Amonites saw that Aram had fled, they fled before Avishai and
entered the city, so Yoav withdrew his attack on the Amonites and came
15 to Jerusalem. But when Aram saw that it had been defeated by Israel, they
16 regrouped their forces. Hadadezer sent and summoned Aram from across
the Euphrates, and their forces marched out with Shovakh, Hadadezer's
17 army commander, at their head. When this was reported to David, he
mustered all of Israel and crossed the Jordan; and when he reached Ḥelam,
18 the Arameans charged out toward David and fought against him. But Aram
fled before Israel, and David killed seven hundred charioteers and forty
thousand riders of Aram, and as for Shovakh, their army commander, he
struck him down, and he died on the spot.

19 When all the kings who were subject to Hadadezer realized that they had
been routed before Israel, they surrendered to Israel and became subject to
them. And Aram was too frightened to come to the Amonites' aid again.

11 1 The next spring – when kings launch campaigns – David sent out Yoav
together with his officers and all of Israel. They ravaged the Amonites and
besieged Raba – while David remained in Jerusalem.

2 As dusk was falling, David rose from his bed and went for a stroll upon the
roof of the palace. And from the roof, he saw a woman bathing, and the
woman was absolutely beautiful.

3 David sent and made inquiries about the woman and was told, "She
4 is Batsheva, daughter of Eliam, wife of Uriya the Hittite." David sent
messengers to fetch her. She came to him, and he lay with her – she had
5 just cleansed herself from her impurity. Then she returned home. The
woman conceived and sent word to David.

"I am pregnant," she said.

6 So David sent a message to Yoav, "Send Uriya the Hittite to me," and Yoav
7 sent Uriya to David. When Uriya came to him, David asked how Yoav was
faring, how the troops were faring, and how the war was faring.

8 "Go down to your home," David then said to Uriya, "and bathe your
feet."

When Uriya left the king's palace, royal provisions were brought out after
9 him. But Uriya lay at the entrance of the king's palace along with all his
lord's servants and did not go down to his own home.

10 When they told David, "Uriya has not gone down to his home," David said
to Uriya, "You have just come from a journey; why do you not go down
to your home?"

11 "The Ark and Israel and Yehuda are dwelling in huts," Uriya said to David,
"and my lord Yoav and my lord's officers are camping in the open field – how
can I come to my own home, to eat and drink and lie with my wife? By
your life – by your very life – I will not do such a thing."

12 "Stay here today as well," David said to Uriya, "and tomorrow I will send
13 you off." And Uriya stayed in Jerusalem that day and the next. David
summoned him to eat and drink in his presence, and he got him drunk.
But he left in the evening to lie on his bed with his lord's servants – he did
not go down to his own home.

14 In the morning, David wrote a letter to Yoav and sent it by Uriya's hand.
15 The letter he wrote said, "Position Uriya in the front line where the battle
is thickest, and then retreat, so he will be struck down and killed."

16 And when Yoav was keeping watch over the city, he assigned Uriya a
17 position where he knew the seasoned warriors would be. The men of the
city charged out and fought against Yoav, and some of the troops, David's
men, fell; Uriya the Hittite was among the dead.

18 19 Yoav sent a message to David, giving him a full report of the war. He
instructed the messenger as follows: "When you have finished giving the
20 full report of the war to the king, if the king's fury is roused, and he says
to you, 'Why did you approach the city to fight – were you not aware
21 that they would shoot over the wall? Who struck down Avimelekh son of
Yerubeshet?[38] It was a woman who hurled an upper millstone over the wall,
so that he died in Tevetz![39] Why did you approach the wall?' – then say,
'Your servant, Uriya the Hittite, was among those who died.'"

22 The messenger set out and came to David, to deliver Yoav's full report.

23 "First the men were overpowering us, and they charged out at us toward
the open ground," the messenger said to David, "and then we drove them
24 back to the entrance of the gate. But then the archers shot at your servants
from the wall, and some of the king's servants were killed. Your servant,
25 Uriya the Hittite, was among the dead." "This is what you must say to Yoav,"
David told the messenger, "'Do not take this affair so gravely; the sword
consumes one way or another. Battle on against the city even more fiercely,
and destroy it!' Encourage him."

26 Uriya's wife heard that her husband Uriya was dead, and she mourned over
27 her husband. When the mourning period passed, David sent and had her
brought to his palace. She became his wife, and she bore him a son. But
what David had done was grave in the eyes of the LORD.

---

38 | That is, Gidon, also called Yerubaal; see Judges 6:32. *Boshet* is a substitute for *baal*; see note on 2:8.

39 | See Judges 9:53.

12 1 The Lord sent the prophet Natan to David, and he came to him.

"There were two men in the same city," he said to him. "One was rich and
2 3 the other poor. The rich man had a great wealth of sheep and cattle, but the
poor man had nothing but one small lamb that he had bought. He nurtured
her, and she grew up together with him and his children; she would eat
from his own crusts of bread and drink from his own cup and sleep curled
up in his embrace – she was like his own daughter.

4 "But a traveler came to the house of the rich man, and it seemed a pity to
him to take from his own flock and herd to prepare food for the guest who
had come to him. So he took the poor man's lamb and prepared it for the
man who had come to him."

5 David's fury blazed hot against the man.

"As the Lord lives," he said to Natan, "the man who did this is a dead man.
6 As for the lamb – he must pay for it four times over for doing such a deed
and for having no pity."

7 "You are the man!" Natan said to David. "Thus says the Lord, God of
Israel: I anointed you as king over Israel, and I saved you from the hand of
8 Sha'ul. I gave you your master's house and your master's wives into your
embrace, and I gave you the House of Israel and Yehuda, and if that would
9 be too little, I would give you even twice as much. Why, then, have you
scorned the word of the Lord, doing such evil in His eyes? You put Uriya
the Hittite to the sword and took his wife as your own wife; you killed him
with the sword of the Amonites.

10 "And now, the sword will never turn away from your house because you
11 scorned Me and took Uriya the Hittite's wife as your own wife. Thus
says the Lord: I am about to raise up evil against you from within your
own house; I will take your wives before your very eyes and give them to
12 another who will lie with your wives in broad daylight. You acted in secrecy,
but I shall make this come to pass before all of Israel, in broad daylight."

13 And David said to Natan, "I have sinned against the Lord."

"The Lord has suspended your sin; you shall not die," Natan said to David.
14 "However, because through this affair you have scorned the enemies of the
15 Lord,[40] the son who has just been born to you will surely die." And with
this, Natan went home.

The Lord struck the child that Uriya's wife had borne to David, and he
16 became mortally ill. David pleaded with God for the boy's sake; he fasted
17 and came in and spent the night lying on the ground. The elders of his
house stood over him and urged him to get up from the ground, but he
18 would not agree and would not eat with them. And on the seventh day,

40 | A euphemism used to avoid blasphemy, meaning that he had scorned God Himself.

when the child died, David's servants were afraid to tell him that the child was dead.

"When the child was alive, we spoke to him and he would not listen to us," they said, "so how can we possibly tell him that the child has died? He might do harm."

19 But David saw that his servants were whispering among themselves, and David understood that the child had died.

"Is the child dead?" David asked his servants.

"He is dead," they said.

20 David got up from the ground. When he had washed, anointed himself, and changed his clothes, he came to the House of the LORD to worship. Then he went back home; at his request they set food before him, and he ate.

21 His servants asked him, "Why have you acted in this way? While the child was still alive, you fasted and wept, but now that the child is dead, you get up and eat food."

22 "While the child was still alive," he said, "I fasted and wept, for I thought,
'Who knows; perhaps the LORD will be gracious to me, and the child will
23 live.' But now he is dead – why should I fast? Will I be able to bring him
back again? I shall go to him, but he will never come back to me."

24 And David comforted Batsheva, his wife; he came to her and lay with her,
25 and she bore a son. She named him Shlomo, and the LORD loved him. And
He sent a message through the prophet Natan, naming him Yedidya,[41] for
the LORD's sake.

26 Meanwhile, Yoav was fighting against Raba of the Amonites, and he
27 captured the royal city. Yoav sent messengers to David, reporting, "I have
28 attacked Raba and seized control of the city's water supply. Now muster
the rest of the troops and encamp against the city to capture it; otherwise
29 I will capture the city myself, and my name will be associated with it." So
David mustered all the troops and set out for Raba; he fought against it
30 and captured it. And he took their king's crown from upon his head – it
weighed a talent of gold and was set with jewels – and it was placed on
31 David's head. And he brought out great masses of spoil from the city. As
for its people, he brought them out and set them to work with saws and
iron picks and iron axes and made them toil away at the kilns; so he did
for all the Amonite towns. Then David and all the troops returned to
Jerusalem.

13 1 Sometime later, this came to pass: Avshalom, David's son, had a beautiful
2 sister whose name was Tamar, and Amnon, David's son, loved her. Amnon

41 | Literally "the LORD's beloved."

grew obsessed to the point of sickness with his sister Tamar, for she was a virgin, and it seemed impossible to Amnon that he would ever do anything to her.

3 Now, Amnon had a friend whose name was Yonadav son of Shima, David's brother, and Yonadav was a very shrewd man.

4 "Why do you grow so haggard from morning to morning, O son of the king?" he asked him. "Won't you tell me?"

"It is Tamar, Avshalom's sister, whom I love," Amnon said to him.

5 "Lie on your bed and feign sickness," Yehonadav said to him, "and when your father comes to see you, say to him, 'Let my sister Tamar come to me and serve me food – let her prepare the fare before me, and I will eat from her hand.'"

6 So Amnon lay down and feigned sickness. When the king came to see him,
Amnon said to the king, "Let my sister Tamar come now and form two
7 heart-cakes before me, and I will take nourishment from her hand." And
David sent for Tamar at home, saying, "Now go to your brother Amnon's
8 house and prepare nourishment for him." Tamar went to her brother
Amnon's house; he was lying down. She took the dough and kneaded it
9 and formed it in his sight and cooked the heart-cakes. She took the pan
and set it before him, but he refused to eat.

"Have everyone leave my presence!" Amnon said, and everyone left his
10 presence. "Bring the nourishment into the inner chamber," Amnon said
to Tamar, "and I will take nourishment from your hand."

So Tamar took the heart-cakes she had prepared and brought them to
11 Amnon, her brother, into the inner chamber. But when she served them
to him, to eat, he grasped hold of her and said to her, "Come, lie with me,
my sister."

12 "No, my brother," she said to him, "do not violate me – such things are not
13 done in Israel. Do not commit such an outrage. As for me – where will I
drive my shame? While you – you will be considered a vile man in Israel!
Speak to the king now, for he will not hold me back from you."

14 But he would not heed her voice, and he overpowered her and violated her and lay with her.

15 Then Amnon hated her with a fierce hatred; his hatred for her was fiercer than the love he had felt toward her. And Amnon said to her, "Get up! Be gone!"

16 "Don't!" she said to him. "This great wrong – to send me away – would be
even worse than what you did to me before." But he would not heed her.
17 He called his servant boy and said to him, "Send this away from me now,
outside, and lock the door behind her."

18 She wore an ornate tunic, for the virgin daughters of the king wore such
robes. But when his servant boy put her outside and locked the door
19 behind her, Tamar put ashes on her head and tore the ornate tunic that
she wore; she put her hand to her head and went off, screaming as she
20 went. And Avshalom, her brother, said to her, "Has your brother Amnon
been with you? For now, my sister, be silent; he is your brother. Do not
take this affair to heart." And Tamar remained, forlorn, in the house of her
brother Avshalom.

21 22 When King David heard all about this affair, he was absolutely livid. And
Avshalom would not speak a word to Amnon, neither good nor bad, for
Avshalom despised Amnon for having violated Tamar, his sister.

23 But two years later, when Avshalom held a sheep-shearing at Baal Hatzor
24 in Efrayim, Avshalom invited all the king's sons. And Avshalom came to
the king and said, "Now, your servant is holding a sheep-shearing. Let the
king and his servants accompany your servant."

25 "No, my son," the king said to Avshalom, "we must not all come together,
and impose upon you."

He pressed him, but he would not agree to go and bade Avshalom farewell.

26 "If not," said Avshalom, "let my brother Amnon accompany us."

"Why should he go with you?" asked the king.

27 But Avshalom pressed him, and he sent Amnon with him along with all
the king's sons.

28 Avshalom then instructed his lads, saying, "Now look. When Amnon's
heart is merry with wine, and I say to you, 'Strike Amnon down,' then kill
him; do not fear, for I am the one giving you the order. Act boldly, like
29 warriors." And when Avshalom's lads did to Amnon just as Avshalom had
instructed, all the king's sons rose, mounted their mules, and fled.

30 They were on their way when the rumor reached David: "Avshalom has
31 struck down all of the king's sons, and not a single one is left. "And the
king got up and rent his clothes and lay down on the ground, while all his
32 servants stood around him with their garments rent. But Yonadav son of
Shima, David's brother, spoke up.
"My lord must not think that they have killed all of the young men, the
king's sons; for Amnon alone is dead – this has been determined by
33 Avshalom since the day he violated his sister Tamar. Now, my lord king
must not take the idea to heart that all the king's sons are dead, for Amnon
alone is dead."

34 Meanwhile, Avshalom had fled.

And the lookout boy raised his eyes and suddenly saw a great crowd

35 coming from the rear road by the hillside. And Yonadav said to the king,
"Look – the king's sons have come, just as your servant said they would."
36 And as he finished speaking, the king's sons arrived and burst out weeping,
and the king and all his servants wept too, heaving with sobs.

37 Now Avshalom had fled; he went to Talmai son of Amihud, king of Geshur,
38 while David mourned his son all the while. Avshalom had fled and gone
39 to Geshur and was there for three years. Then David was no longer driven
to march out against Avshalom, for he had grown reconciled to Amnon's
death.

14 1 Now, Yoav son of Tzeruya knew that the king's mind was on Avshalom.
2 And Yoav sent to Tekoa and fetched a wise woman from there.

"Now pretend you are mourning," he said to her. "Don mourning garb, do
not anoint yourself with oil, and act like a woman who has been mourning
3 the dead for a long time. When you come to the king, this is what you must
say...," and Yoav put the words in her mouth.

4 When the Tekoite woman spoke to the king, she flung her face to the
ground and bowed down low.

"Help, O king!" she said.

5 "What is the matter?" the king asked her.

6 "I am but a widow woman," she said. "My husband died. Your servant had
two sons, but they brawled in the field with no one to come between
7 them, and one struck the other and killed him. And now, the whole family
has risen against your servant, saying, 'Give over the one who struck his
brother, so we can put him to death for ending his brother's life – we will
destroy the heir as well.' They would extinguish my last remaining ember,
leaving my husband without name or remnant on the face of the earth."

8 "Go back home," the king said to the woman, "and I will issue a command
for you."

9 "My lord the king," the Tekoite woman said to the king, "may the guilt lie
with me and my father's house; the king and his throne are blameless."

10 "If anyone speaks to you," said the king, "bring him to me, and he shall
harass you no longer."

11 "Please," she said, "may the king keep the Lord your God in mind and the
blood avenger from too much corruption; let them not destroy my son!"

"As the Lord lives," he said, "not a hair of your son shall fall to the ground."

12 And the woman said, "Let your servant now speak a word to my lord the
king." "Speak," he said.

13 "Why, then, have you determined such a thing for God's people?" said the
woman. "By making this pronouncement, it is as if the king is guilty for

14 not having brought back the king's own banished one. For die we must,
like water spilled to the earth that cannot be gathered up, and God will
not hold a soul accountable for determining that none of his own shall
be banished.

15 "Now I came to speak of this to my lord the king because the people
have frightened me, and your servant thought, 'Let me speak to the king;
16 perhaps the king will do as his handmaid asks. For the king might pay heed
and save his handmaid from the hands of the man who would destroy both
17 me and my son from God's heritage.' And your servant thought, 'May the
word of my lord the king grant relief,' for my lord the king is like an angel
of God, understanding good and evil, and may the LORD your God be
with you."

18 And the king responded. "Please," he said to the woman, "do not hide
anything from me of what I am about to ask you."

"Please," said the woman, "let my lord the king speak."

19 "Does Yoav have a hand in all this along with you?" asked the king.

"As you live, my lord the king," the woman answered, "there is no turning
right or left from all the king has said! For indeed, your servant Yoav was
the one who gave me the orders, and he was the one who put all these
20 words in the mouth of your servant. Your servant Yoav arranged this
scheme to turn matters around, but my lord is as wise as an angel of God
and is aware of all that goes on in the land."

21 Then the king said to Yoav, "Look, I will fulfill this word: go, bring back
the boy Avshalom."

22 Yoav flung his face to the ground and bowed down low and blessed the king.
"Today," Yoav said, "I, your servant, know that I have found favor in your
sight, my lord the king, for the king has granted his servant's request."

23 24 Yoav proceeded straight to Geshur and brought Avshalom to Jerusalem. But
the king said, "Let him turn off to his house; he will not be admitted to
my presence." So Avshalom turned off to his house and was not admitted
to the king's presence.

25 Now there was no one in all of Israel who was admired for his beauty as
26 Avshalom was; he was flawless from head to toe. When he cut his hair – he
would have it cut once a year when it grew too heavy for him – the hair of
his head weighed two hundred shekel by royal weight.

27 Three sons were born to Avshalom, and one daughter, whose name was
Tamar; she became a beautiful woman.

28 Avshalom lived in Jerusalem for two years without being admitted into
29 the king's presence. And Avshalom sent for Yoav, to send him to the king,
but he would not come to him; he sent for him again, a second time, but

30 he would not come. So he said to his servants, "Do you see Yoav's field
over there, next to mine? He has barley there. Go and set it on fire." And
Avshalom's servants set the field on fire.

31 Yoav went straight to Avshalom's house. "Why have your servants set my
field on fire?" he asked.

32 "Look," Avshalom said to Yoav, "I sent for you, asking you to come here so
I could send you to the king with the message, 'Why did I come back from
Geshur – had I stayed there, I would have been better off. Now admit me
into the king's presence; if I am guilty, then put me to death.'"

33 So Yoav went to the king and told him, and he summoned Avshalom. He
came before the king and bowed down low before the king with his face
to the ground, and the king kissed Avshalom.

15 1 It was after this that Avshalom procured for himself a chariot and horses
2 and fifty men to run before him. Avshalom would rise early and stand by
the road to the main gate, and whenever anyone had a dispute that was
to come before the king in judgment, Avshalom would call out to him.
"Where are you from?" he would say, and when he replied, "Your servant
3 is from one of the tribes of Israel," Avshalom would answer, "Look, your
words are fair and frank – but there is no one from the king to hear you
out.

4 "If only someone would appoint me as judge in the land," Avshalom would
continue, "everyone with a legal dispute would come to me, and I would
treat him justly."

5 And if someone approached him to bow to him, he would extend his hand
6 and take hold of him and kiss him. Avshalom acted in this way toward all
the Israelites who came to the king for justice, and Avshalom deceived
the people of Israel.

7 At the end of forty years,[42] Avshalom said to the king, "I will now go and
8 fulfill the vow that I pledged to the Lord in Ḥevron. For your servant
pledged a vow when I was staying in Geshur of Aram, saying, 'If the Lord
will bring me back to Jerusalem, then I will serve the Lord.'"

9 "Go in peace," said the king, and he arose and set out for Ḥevron.

10 Then Avshalom sent spies throughout every tribe of Israel, communicat-
ing: "When you hear the sound of the ram's horn, announce, 'Avshalom
11 has become king in Ḥevron.'" Avshalom was accompanied by two hundred
men of Jerusalem who had been invited and went along with him, unsus-
12 pecting; they knew nothing. And Avshalom sent Aḥitofel the Gilonite,
David's advisor, from his hometown of Gilo as he offered the sacrifices.

---

42 | Aware of the chronological difficulties in this phrase, the major commentators, following talmudic sources, suggest that the reference here is to the forty years since the Israelites initially demanded a king of Samuel.

The conspiracy gained power, and the people's support for Avshalom
increased.

13 An informant came to David reporting that the men of Israel's hearts were
14 being drawn to Avshalom. And David said to all the subjects who were
with him in Jerusalem, "Rise – we must flee, or none of us will escape
from Avshalom. Hurry, leave, in case he is faster and manages to overtake
us, bringing ruin to us and putting the city to the sword."

15 And the king's subjects replied to the king, "Whatever our lord the king
16 decides – your servants are here." So the king set out on foot along with
all his household, save for ten concubines whom the king left to mind the
17 palace. The king set out with all the people at his heels, and they stopped
18 by the farthest house while all his subjects passed him, all the Keretites
and Peletites and all the Gittites – six hundred men who had followed him
from Gat passed ahead of the king.

19 King David said to Itai the Gittite,
"Why should you, too, come with us? Go back; stay with the king, for
20 you are a foreigner as well as an exile from your own place. Just yesterday
you arrived; why should I make you wander about with us today while I
myself go wherever I can? Go back and take your brothers with you in
true loyalty."

21 "As the Lord lives," Itai answered the king, "and by the life of my lord the
king, wherever my lord the king may be – for death or for life – there will
be your servant."

22 "Go, pass ahead," David said to Itai, and Itai the Gittite passed with all his
men, and all the little ones who were with him.

23 And all the land wept aloud as all the troops passed by; the king crossed
Kidron Valley, and all the troops passed along the road to the wilderness.
24 And now Tzadok and all the Levites were with him as well, bearing the
Ark of God's Covenant; they set down the Ark of God until all the troops
had passed over from the city and Evyatar came up.

25 Then the king said to Tzadok, "Bring the Ark of God back to the city; if I
find favor in the Lord's sight, He will bring me back and let me see it and
26 its abode. But if He says thus, 'I take no pleasure in you,' I am ready; let
Him do to me as He sees fit.

27 "Now, do you see?" the king continued to the priest Tzadok. "Go back to
the safety of the city, along with both of your sons – your son Aḥimaatz,
28 and Yehonatan son of Evyatar. Look, I will linger in the wilderness steppes
until your word reaches me and informs me."

29 So Tzadok and Evyatar brought the Ark of God back to Jerusalem and
30 stayed there. But David made his way up Maaleh HaZeitim, weeping as
he climbed; his head was covered, and he walked barefoot. And all the

troops with him each covered their heads and made their way up, weeping
as they climbed.

31 When David was informed that Aḥitofel was part of Avshalom's conspiracy,
32 David said, "O LORD, make Aḥitofel's counsel foolish." And as David
reached the summit, where he was about to worship before God, there
was Ḥushai the Arkite coming toward him, his robe rent and earth upon
his head.

33 "If you cross over with me, you will be a burden to me," David said to
34 him, "but if you go back to town and say to Avshalom, 'I am your servant,
O king – I was always your father's servant, but from now on I am your
35 servant,' then you will be able to thwart Aḥitofel's counsel for me. The
priests Tzadok and Evyatar will be there with you, so report anything
36 you hear in the palace to the priests Tzadok and Evyatar. Both their sons
are there with them – Tzadok's Aḥimaatz, and Evyatar's Yehonatan; send
anything you hear to me through them."

37 So Ḥushai, David's friend, reached the city just as Avshalom reached
Jerusalem.

16 1 David had passed only a short distance from the summit when Tziva,
Mefivoshet's servant, suddenly approached him with a pair of saddled
donkeys loaded with two hundred loaves of bread, a hundred clusters of
raisins, a hundred summer fruit, and an amphora of wine.

2 "Why have you brought all this?" the king asked Tziva.

"The donkeys are for the royalty to ride," said Tziva, "and the bread and summer fruit are for the young men to eat, while the wine is for the weary to drink in the wilderness."

3 "And where is the son of your master?" asked the king.

"Oh, he is staying in Jerusalem," Tziva said to the king, "for he says, 'Today, the House of Israel will restore my father's throne to me.'"

4 "Now, all that belongs to Mefivoshet belongs to you," the king said to
Tziva.

"I bow down low!" said Tziva. "May I find favor in your sight, my lord the king."

5 King David had reached Baḥurim when a member of the house of Sha'ul,
whose name was Shimi son of Gera, suddenly charged out from there,
6 cursing as he came. He hurled stones at David and at all King David's
7 subjects, and at all the troops and warriors to his right and to his left. And
this was the curse Shimi uttered: "Get out, get out, you man of blood, you
8 depraved man! The LORD has brought all the blood of the house of Sha'ul
back upon you for ruling in his place, and the LORD has given the kingship

over to Avshalom, your son! Now you languish in your own evil, for you
are a man of blood."

9 Avishai son of Tzeruya said to the king, "Why should this dead dog curse
my lord the king? Let me pass, please, and I will cut off his head."

10 "What do I have to do with you, sons of Tzeruya?" said the king. "Let him
curse – perhaps the LORD told him to curse David; who is to say, 'Why
did you do so?'

11 "Look, my own son, the issue of my own loins, seeks my life," David
continued to Avishai and all his subjects, "and now the Benjaminite does,
12 all the more so. Let him be and let him curse, as the LORD bid him. Perhaps
the LORD will look upon my suffering and the LORD restore my favor in
place of his curses on this day.

13 "So David and his men went on their way as Shimi walked along the
opposite hillside, hurling curses and stones toward them as he went, and
14 flinging dust. The king and all the troops with him were exhausted when
they arrived, and there they paused for breath.

15 Meanwhile, Avshalom and all the people, the men of Israel, had entered
16 Jerusalem, and Aḥitofel with him. And when Ḥushai the Arkite, David's
friend, came to Avshalom, Ḥushai declared to Avshalom, "Long live the
king! Long live the king!"

17 "Is this loyalty toward your friend?" Avshalom asked Ḥushai. "Why haven't
you followed your friend?"

18 "No," Ḥushai said to Avshalom. "Should I not be with the one whom the
LORD and this people and all the men of Israel have chosen? With him I
19 shall remain. Besides, whom shall I serve if not his son? As I was at your
father's service, I am at yours."

20 Avshalom then said to Aḥitofel, "Let us have your counsel; what shall we
do?"

21 "You should go to bed with your father's concubines, the ones he left
to mind the palace," Aḥitofel said to Avshalom, "and when all of Israel
hears that you have become odious to your father, the hand of all your
supporters will be strengthened."

22 So they erected a tent for Avshalom on the roof, and he bedded his father's
concubines in full view of all Israel.

23 In those days, the counsel Aḥitofel gave was considered tantamount to
the word sought from God; that was how all of Aḥitofel's counsel was to
David as well as Avshalom.

17 1 Now Aḥitofel said to Avshalom, "Let me select twelve thousand men, and
2 I will set out and pursue David this very night. I will come upon him when

he is weary and weak and throw him into a panic, and all the troops with
3 him will flee – then I will strike down just the king. And I will bring all the
troops back to you, and when all have come back but the man you seek, all
the people will have peace."

4 This idea pleased Avshalom, and it pleased all the elders of Israel. But
5 Avshalom said, "Summon Ḥushai the Arkite, and let us hear what he, too,
6 has to say." Ḥushai came to Avshalom, and Avshalom said to him, "This is
what Aḥitofel said; shall we follow his idea? If not, speak up."

7 "This time," Ḥushai answered Avshalom, "the counsel Aḥitofel has given
8 you is not good. You know that your father and his men are seasoned
warriors," Ḥushai continued, "and they are as wretched and bitter as a
bereaved bear in the wild. Your father is a veteran of war; he will not be
9 spending the night with the troops – even now, he must be hiding in some
hollow or some other place. And as soon as any of them fall, rumor will
spread that there has been a massacre among the supporters of Avshalom,
10 and even the hearts of brave, lion-hearted men will surely melt, for all of
Israel knows that your father is a seasoned warrior, and that the men with
11 him are brave. And so I advise you: have all of Israel – from Dan to Be'er
Sheva – gather to you, as innumerable as the sand upon the seashore, and
12 you yourself must go forth in battle. When we come upon him – wherever
he may be – we will descend upon him as the dew settles on the earth, and
13 not a single one will be left of all the men who are with him. And should
he withdraw into a city, all of Israel will bring ropes to that city, and we will
drag it away to the wadi until not even a pebble remains."

14 And Avshalom and all the men of Israel declared, "The counsel of Ḥushai
the Arkite is better than the counsel of Aḥitofel." For the Lord had
determined that Aḥitofel's good counsel would be thwarted, in order for
the Lord to bring evil upon Avshalom.

15 Then Ḥushai said to the priests Tzadok and Evyatar, "This is what Aḥitofel
16 advised Avshalom and the elders of Israel, and this is what I advised. Now,
send word quickly, informing David, 'Do not spend the night on the
wilderness steppes; cross over at once, or the king and everyone with him
will be engulfed.'"

17 Now, Yehonatan and Aḥimaatz were stationed in the Rogel Spring; a
servant girl would go and inform them, and they would go and inform King
18 David, as they could not be seen coming into the city. But when a boy saw
them and informed Avshalom, the two of them left in a hurry. They came
to the house of a man in Baḥurim who had a well in his courtyard, and
19 they climbed down inside it. The man's wife then took a cloth, stretched
it over the mouth of the well, and spread groats over it, so nothing was
revealed.

20 Avshalom's officials came to the woman's house and said, "Where are
Aḥimaatz and Yehonatan?"

"They have crossed over the river fords," the woman said to them. They searched but found nothing, and they went back to Jerusalem.

21 After they had left, they climbed out of the well and went to inform King David. "Set out and cross over the water at once," they said to David, "for this is how Aḥitofel advised to deal with you."

22 David set out at once along with all the troops who were with him, and they crossed the Jordan; by the light of morning, every last one of them had crossed the Jordan.

23 When Aḥitofel saw that his counsel had not been taken, he saddled his donkey and went straight to his home in his hometown. He issued orders for his household, then he hanged himself. And he was buried in his ancestral tomb.

24 Meanwhile, David had reached Maḥanayim, while Avshalom crossed the
25 Jordan along with all the men of Israel. Avshalom had appointed Amasa as
army commander in Yoav's place. Amasa was the son of a man named Yitra
the Israelite, who had lain with Avigayil, the daughter of Naḥash and the
26 sister of Tzeruya, mother of Yoav. And Israel and Avshalom set up camp
in the land of Gilad.

27 When David arrived in Maḥanayim, Shovi son of Naḥash of Raba of the
Amonites, Makhir son of Amiel of Lo Devar, and Barzilai the Gileadite of
28 Rogelim had set up couches and basins and earthenware; wheat, barley,
29 meal and toasted grain; beans and roasted lentils and grain. They served
honey and curds from the flock and cheese from the herd for David and
his troops to eat, for they thought, "The troops must have grown hungry,
weary, and thirsty in the wilderness."

18 1 Now David mustered the troops who were with him and appointed officers
2 of thousands and officers of hundreds over them. He sent a third of the
troops with Yoav, a third with Avishai son of Tzeruya, Yoav's brother, and
a third with Itai the Gittite.

"And I, of course, will also march out with you," the king proclaimed to the troops.

3 But the troops said, "Do not march out, for if we must retreat, they will pay us no heed; even if half of us die, they will pay us no heed – for you are worth ten thousand of us. Right now, it is best if you help us from the city."

4 "Whatever seems best in your eyes, I will do," the king said to them. And the king stood by the gate as all the troops marched out, in their hundreds and their thousands.

5 The king then gave orders to Yoav, Avishai, and Itai. "For my sake," he said, "deal gently with young Avshalom." And the troops all heard the king's orders about Avshalom to all of his officials.

6 The troops marched out to the field toward Israel, and battle took place in
7 the forest of Efrayim. There, the Israelite troops were routed before David's
8 men – there was a devastating loss that day of twenty thousand. Battle
broke out all over the land, and on that day, the forest itself consumed
more troops than the sword.

9 Meanwhile, Avshalom encountered David's men. Avshalom was riding
on his mule when the mule passed beneath the tangled branches of a
great oak; the hair of his head caught fast in the oak, and he was left
dangling between heaven and earth as the mule beneath him continued on.
10 Someone saw and reported this to Yoav. "Look!" he said. "I saw Avshalom
hanging from an oak."

11 "What, you just saw that?" Yoav said to the man reporting to him. "Why
didn't you cut him down to the ground on the spot? I would have owed
you ten measures of silver and a belt."

12 "Even if I felt the weight of a thousand silver pieces in my hands, I would
not dare make a move against the son of the king," said the man to
Yoav, "for we heard ourselves how the king charged you, Avishai and Itai,
13 'Whoever it may be – watch over young Avshalom.' But if I had betrayed
myself – and nothing can be hidden from the king – why, you would have
stood aloof."

14 "I'll wait for you no longer," said Yoav, and he seized three darts and thrust
them into the heart of Avshalom, who was still alive in the heart of the oak.
15 16 Ten of Yoav's arms-bearers closed in and struck Avshalom to death. Then
Yoav blasted the ram's horn and the troops ceased their pursuit of Israel, for
17 Yoav held back the troops. They took Avshalom and flung him into a deep
pit in the forest and set up a great heap of stones over him; meanwhile, all
of Israel fled back to their tents.

18 Now, during his lifetime, Avshalom had taken over the monument in the
Valley of the King and set it up for himself, for he thought, "I have no son
to commemorate my name," and he named the monument for himself,
calling it Avshalom's Monument, as it is called to this day.

19 Aḥimaatz son of Tzadok then said, "I will now run and bring news to the
king, for the LORD has defended him from his enemies' hands."
20 "No, you will not be the bearer of news today," Yoav said to him. "Perhaps
another day you will bring news. But today you will not bring news, for
the king's son is dead."

21 And Yoav said to the Kushite, "Go – report what you have seen to the
king."

22 The Kushite bowed to Yoav and ran off. But Aḥimaatz persisted and said to
Yoav, "Come what may – let me run as well after the Kushite."

"Why should you run, my son," said Yoav, "when your news will not be welcomed?"

23 "Come what may, I will run."

"So run," he said to him, and Aḥimaatz ran by the way of the plain, and overtook the Kushite.

24 Now David was sitting between the two gates. The lookout had gone up to
the roof of the gate, to the wall, when he looked up and suddenly saw a man
25 running by himself. The lookout called out and reported to the king.

26 "If he is alone," the king said, "he has news to tell," as he came closer. Then the lookout saw another man running, and the lookout called out to the gate.

"Look – a man running by himself," he said.

"He, too, has news," said the king.

27 "It seems to me that the first one runs like Aḥimaatz son of Tzadok," said the lookout. "That one is a good man," said the king. "He must be coming with good news."

28 Aḥimaatz called out to the king, "All is well," and bowed to the king with his face to the ground. "Blessed is the Lord your God," he said, "who has handed over the men who raised their hands against my lord the king."

29 "Is all well with young Avshalom?" asked the king.

"I saw a great crowd when the king's servant, Yoav, was sending your servant off," said Aḥimaatz, "but I know not what…"

30 "Turn aside," said the king, "and stand by," and he turned aside and stood by.

31 Just then, the Kushite arrived.

"Let it be known to my lord the king," said the Kushite, "that today the Lord has defended you against all those who rose against you."

32 "But is all well with young Avshalom?" the king said to the Kushite, and the Kushite replied, "May all my lord the king's enemies, and all those who have risen against you to harm you, fare like that young man."

19 1 The king shuddered, made his way up to the chamber above the gate, and wept. And this is what he cried as he went:

"My son, Avshalom! O my son, my son Avshalom! If only I had died instead of you, O Avshalom, my son, my son!"

2 Yoav was told, "Look, the king is weeping and mourning for Avshalom."
3 And that day's victory turned into mourning for all the troops, for on that
4 day, the troops heard that the king was grieving for his son. And on that day,

the troops stole into the city when they arrived, as disgraced troops steal
5 in when they flee from battle. And the king hid his face, and cried out at
the top of his voice, "My son, Avshalom! O Avshalom, my son, my son!"

6 But Yoav entered the king's quarters.

"Today," he said, "you have humiliated your own supporters, who saved
your life – and the lives of your sons and daughters, and the lives of your
7 wives, and the lives of your concubines – by showing love for those who
hate you and hatred for those who love you.

"Today, you have made it clear that your officers and subjects are nothing to you.

"Today, I realize that were Avshalom alive and all of us dead right now – why, then, you would be pleased.

8 "Now get up, and go out, and make a heartfelt speech to your servants. For
by the LORD, I swear that if you do not go out, not a single man will be on
your side by tonight, and that would be a worse evil for you than all the
evil that has befallen you from your youth until now."

9 And the king got up and sat by the gate. All the troops were told, "The
king is now sitting at the gate." And all the troops came before the king.

10 Meanwhile, the Israelites had fled back to their homes. And all the people
were arguing throughout the tribes of Israel. "The king delivered us from
the hands of our enemies," they said, "and he saved us from the clutches
of the Philistines, and now he has fled from the land because of Avshalom.
11 But Avshalom, whom we anointed over us, died in battle. So now, why have
you done nothing to bring the king back?"

12 King David sent to Tzadok and Evyatar the priests, saying, "Speak to the
elders of Yehuda, asking, 'Why should you be the last ones to bring the
king back to his palace? The word of all Israel has already reached the king
13 in his quarters. You are my brothers, my own flesh and blood – why should
you be the last ones to bring the king back?'

14 "And to Amasa, say, 'You are of my own flesh and blood; so may God do to
me – and more – if you will not be the commander of my army in Yoav's
place from now on.'"

15 And he drew the hearts of every man in Yehuda as if they were a single
man, and they sent a message to the king: "Come back, you and all your
16 supporters." So the king turned back, and when he reached the Jordan, the
contingent from Yehuda had come to Gilgal to meet the king and escort
the king across the Jordan.

17 Shimi son of Gera, the Benjaminite from Baḥurim, hurried down to meet
18 David together with the men of Yehuda. A thousand men from Binyamin
accompanied him along with Tziva, the servant of the house of Sha'ul, his

fifteen sons, and twenty slaves. They rushed down to the Jordan before the
19 king, crossing back and forth to bring the royal household across, to gain
favor in his sight. And Shimi son of Gera flung himself before the king as
he was crossing the Jordan.

20 "Let my lord not consider me guilty," he said to the king, "and do not hark
back to the crime your servant committed on the day my lord the king left
21 Jerusalem; let the king not take it to heart. For your servant knows that
I have sinned, and now I have come down here today, the first of all the
House of Yosef, to meet my lord the king."

22 Avishai son of Tzeruya spoke up. "Just for that, will Shimi be pardoned
from death?" he asked. "He cursed the LORD's anointed one!"

23 "What have I to do with you, sons of Tzeruya, that you should oppose
me today?" said David. "Today, should any man of Israel be put to death?
Today, am I not aware that I am king of Israel?

24 "You shall not die," the king said to Shimi, and he gave him his oath.

25 And Mefivoshet, grandson of Sha'ul, had made his way down to meet the
king. He had not tended to his feet, trimmed his mustache, or washed his
clothes from the day of the king's departure to the day of his safe return.
26 When he arrived from Jerusalem to meet the king, the king asked him,
27 "Why did you fail to accompany me, Mefivoshet?" "My lord the king," he
said, "my servant deceived me, for your servant planned, 'I will saddle a
donkey for me to ride upon and accompany the king, as your servant is
28 lame.' But he slandered your servant to my lord the king. Now, my lord
29 the king is like an angel of God – do whatever is best in your eyes. For all
of my father's household was doomed to death by my lord the king, yet
you set your servant among those who dine at your table, so what further
right do I have to cry out to the king?"

30 "Speak no further," the king said to him. "I have decided that you and Tziva
shall divide the land."

31 "He can take it all," Mefivoshet said to the king, "now that the king has
come home safely."

32 And now Barzilai the Gileadite came down from Rogelim and crossed over
33 the Jordan with the king, to see him across the Jordan. Barzilai was very
old, eighty years old, yet he had provided the king with sustenance upon
his return to Maḥanayim, for he was a very great man.

34 "Cross over with me," the king said to Barzilai, "and I will provide for you
in Jerusalem, together with me."

35 "How many years of my life are left that I should go up to Jerusalem with
36 the king?" Barzilai said to the king. "I am now eighty years old; can I
still tell the difference between good and bad when your servant tastes
food or drink or hears the voices of men and women singing? Why, then,

37 should your servant remain a burden to my lord the king? Your servant
barely managed to cross the Jordan with the king, so why should the king
38 repay me with this favor? Let your servant stay behind, and I will die in
my hometown where my mother and father are buried. But here – your
servant Kimham will cross over with my lord the king; treat him as you
see fit."

39 "Kimham will cross over with me," said the king, "and I will treat him as
you see fit. Whatever you wish me to do, I will do for you."

40 Then all the troops crossed the Jordan, and the king crossed over. The
41 king kissed Barzilai and blessed him, and he went back home. Then the
king crossed over toward Gilgal, and Kimhan crossed over with him. All
the men of Yehuda crossed over with the king, as well as half of the men
of Israel.

42 And now all the men of Israel reached the king, and they said to the king,
"Why have our brothers, the men of Yehuda, stolen you away, bringing
the king and his household across the Jordan together with all of David's
men?"

43 "The king is our kin," the men of Yehuda answered the men of Israel, "so
why should this matter infuriate you so? Have we eaten anything at the
king's expense? Have we been given any gifts?"

44 "Why, we have ten shares in the king, so we have more in David than you,"
the men of Israel retorted to the men of Yehuda. "Why have you slighted
us so when we first had the idea to bring our king back?"

But the men of Yehuda's word was harsher than the men of Israel's word.

20 1 Now a depraved man happened to be there; his name was Sheva son of
Bikhri, a Benjaminite. He blasted the ram's horn and declared,

"We have no portion in David and no share in the son of Yishai! Back to
your tents, men of Israel!"

2 And all the men of Israel deserted David to follow Sheva son of Bikhri, but
the men of Yehuda stood by their king from the Jordan to Jerusalem.

3 David arrived at his palace in Jerusalem. The king took the ten concubine
women he had left to mind the palace and placed them in a house under
watch. He provided for them, but he did not come to bed with them, and
until their dying day, they were shut up in living widowhood.

4 The king then said to Amasa, "Rally the men of Yehuda within three days,
5 then stop off here." Amasa set out to rally Yehuda, but he missed the
deadline that had been set for him.

6 "Now Sheva son of Bikhri will be worse for us than Avshalom was," David

said to Avishai. "Take your master's servants and pursue him before he
reaches the fortified cities and we lose sight of him."

7 Yoav's men set off along with the Keretites and Peletites and all the warriors,
8 and they left Jerusalem to pursue Sheva son of Bikhri. They were by the
great stone in Givon when Amasa came before them. Yoav was clad in his
battle garb with a sword strapped to his waist in its sheath; and as he came
forward, it slipped out.

9 "Is all well with you, my brother?" Yoav asked Amasa as Yoav took hold
10 of Amasa's beard with his right hand, as if to kiss him. Amasa was caught
off guard by the sword in Yoav's hand. He struck him in the stomach;
his insides spilled out to the ground – he did not need to strike him
twice – and he died.

As Yoav and his brother Avishai continued in pursuit of Sheva son of Bikhri,
11 one of Yoav's men stood by him and called out, "Whoever favors Yoav, and
12 whoever is for David – after Yoav!" Meanwhile, Amasa lay wallowing in
his blood in the middle of the road, and the man saw that all the troops
were coming to a halt. When he realized that everyone who reached him
came to a halt, he dragged Amasa off the road to the field and flung a
13 garment over him. Once he had been removed from the road, all the troops
14 marched ahead, following Yoav in his pursuit of Sheva son of Bikhri, who
had passed through all the tribes of Israel to Avel of Beit Maakha. All the
Berites[43] gathered to join him and followed him inside.

15 All the troops who were with Yoav came and besieged him within Avel of
Beit Maakha; they heaped up a mound against the city, and it stood against
16 the rampart. As they bombarded the wall to bring it down, a wise woman
called out from the city, "Listen! Listen! Please tell Yoav to come over here,
and I will speak with him."

17 Yoav went over to her, and the woman asked, "Are you Yoav?"

"I am," he said.

"Listen to the words of your handmaid," she said to him, and he said, "I
am listening."

18 "There used to be a saying, 'Let them ask in Avel, and all will be settled,'"
19 she said. "I am a faithful peacekeeper of Israel. But you seek to kill a mother
city in Israel – why should you engulf the LORD's heritage?"

20 21 "Far be it! Far be it from me to engulf or destroy," answered Yoav. "That
is not the case, for a man from the hill country of Efrayim – Sheva son of
Bikhri is his name – has raised his hand against King David. If you hand
him over – just him – then I will leave the city alone."

---

43 | Meaning of Hebrew uncertain.

"Here!" said the woman. "His head is about to be flung over the wall to you."

22 The woman came to all the people with her wise advice, and they cut off Sheva son of Bikhri's head and flung it to Yoav. He blasted the ram's horn and the troops dispersed, each back to his own tent, while Yoav headed back to the king in Jerusalem.

23 Yoav was in charge of all of Israel's army, while Benaya son of Yehoyada
24 oversaw the Keretites and Peletites. Adoram was in charge of taxation, and
25 Yehoshafat son of Aḥilud was royal herald. Sheva was a royal scribe, and
26 Tzadok and Evyatar were priests; Ira the Yairite was also priest to David.

21 1 Now famine struck in David's time for three years – year after year – and
David sought the presence of the Lord. And the Lord said, "It is on account
2 of Sha'ul and his house of bloodshed for having killed the Gibeonites." So
the king summoned the Gibeonites to speak to them.

Now the Gibeonites were not part of the Israelites; they were of the remaining Amorites. Though the Israelites had given them their oath, Sha'ul had hunted them down in his zeal for the people of Israel and Yehuda.

3 David asked the Gibeonites, "What shall I do for you, and how can I make amends so that you may bless the Lord's heritage?"

4 "We have no interest in the silver and gold of Sha'ul and his house," the Gibeonites said to him, "or in killing any of the people of Israel."

"Whatever you say, I will do for you," he said.

5 "There is a man who massacred us and who plotted against us," they said
to the king. "Why, we have been wiped out from existence throughout
6 Israel's borders. Let seven of his male descendants be handed over to us,
and we will impale them before the Lord at Givat Sha'ul, the chosen one
of the Lord."

"I will hand them over," said the king.

7 The king took pity on Mefivoshet son of Yehonatan, Sha'ul's son, because
of the Lord's oath between them, between David and Yehonatan, Sha'ul's
8 son. So the king took the two sons that Ritzpa daughter of Aya had borne
to Sha'ul, Armoni and Mefivoshet, and the five sons that Mikhal,[44] Sha'ul's
9 daughter, had borne to Adriel son of Barzilai the Meholatite, and handed
them over to the Gibeonites. They impaled them on the hill before the
Lord, the seven of them in one fell swoop. They were put to death during
the first days of harvest time, at the beginning of the barley harvest.

10 Then Ritzpa daughter of Aya took sackcloth and stretched it out for herself
on a rock from the beginning of the harvest season until water poured

44 | Cf. 1 Samuel 18:19, which reads "Merav."

down on them from the sky. She would not let the birds of the sky settle
on them by day, nor the wild beasts by night.

11 When David was told what Ritzpa daughter of Aya, Sha'ul's concubine, had
12 done, David went and took the bones of Sha'ul, along with the bones of
his son Yehonatan, from the citizens of Yavesh Gilad. They had recaptured
them from the Beit Shan square where the Philistines had hung Sha'ul on
13 the day the Philistines defeated Sha'ul at Gilboa. He brought up Sha'ul's
bones from there, along with the bones of his son Yehonatan, and gathered
14 up the bones of the impaled. They buried the bones of Sha'ul and his son
Yehonatan at Tzela in the Binyamin region, in the tomb of his father Kish,
and carried out all of the king's orders. And after that, God responded to
the plea of the land.

15 War broke out once again between the Philistines and Israel. David
marched down with his officials, and they fought against the Philistines,
16 but David grew weary. And Yishbi Benov, a descendant of the Rafa[45] – his
spear weighed three hundred weights of bronze, and he was clad in new
17 armor – was determined to strike David down. But Avishai son of Tzeruya
came to his aid, struck down the Philistine, and killed him.

Right then, David's men swore to him: "You will never go out to war with us again; you must not extinguish the lamp of Israel!"

18 Some time after that, another war broke out against the Philistines, at Gov,
this time, Sibekhai the Hushatite defeated Saf, a descendant of the Rafa.

19 Yet another war broke out against the Philistines, at Gov, and Elḥanan son
of Yaarei-Oregim[46] of Beit Leḥem defeated Golyat the Gittite, whose spear
shaft was like a weaver's beam.

20 Yet another war broke out, at Gat. There was a man of gigantic proportions
who had six fingers and six toes on his hands and feet, twenty-four in all;
21 he, too, was descended from the Rafa. When he taunted Israel, Yehonatan
22 son of Shima, David's brother, struck him down. All four of these were
descendants of the Rafa in Gat, and they fell at the hands of David and
his subjects.

22 1 David uttered these words of song to the Lord
on the day that the Lord saved him
from the hands of all his enemies and from the hand of Sha'ul.[47]

2 He said:

The Lord is my Rock and my fortress, my own rescuer;
3 my God is the Rock of my refuge

45 | A giant; see Deuteronomy 2:11.

46 | A compound family name, *oregim* meaning "weavers." Elḥanan was from a family of weavers located in Beit Leḥem. Cf. 1 Chronicles 20:5.

47 | Cf. Psalm 18.

my shield, the horn of my salvation, my haven,
my refuge, my savior who delivers me from violence.

4 Praise! When I call on the LORD,
I am saved from my enemies.

5 For when waves of death assailed me,
deadly torrents engulfed me,
6 the cords of Sheol[48] entangled me,
snares of death confronted me,

7 in my distress I called on the LORD;
I called out to my God;
He heard my voice from His temple,
and my cry rang in His ears.

8 Then the earth shook and shuddered;
the foundations of heaven trembled;
they shuddered from His wrath.

9 Smoke issued from His nostrils;
devouring flames flared from His mouth;
from Him gleaming coals blazed forth.

10 He bent the heavens and descended,
dense cloud beneath His feet;
11 He mounted a cherub and flew,
appearing on wings of wind.

12 He surrounded Himself with a shelter of darkness,
of heavy storm clouds dense with rain.

13 From the brilliant glow of His presence
blazed fiery coals.

14 The LORD thundered from the heavens;
the Most High raised His voice;
15 He shot arrows to scatter them,
lightning bolts to rout them.

16 The ocean bed was exposed,
the foundations of the world laid bare
by the onslaught of the LORD,
by the blast of His breath.

17 From on high He reached down and took me;
He drew me out of the mighty waters.

18 He saved me from my fierce enemy,
from foes too strong for me.

48 | The grave or netherworld.

19 They confronted me on my direst day,
but the LORD was my support.

20 He brought me out to freedom;
He rescued me because He delighted in me.

21 The LORD rewarded me as I deserved;
as my hands were clean, He repaid me,
22 for I kept the ways of the LORD
and did not betray my God,

23 for all His laws are before me;
I will not turn away from His statutes.
24 I am blameless to Him
and keep myself from sin.
25 So the LORD repaid me as I deserved
as I was pure in His sight.

26 You deal loyally with those who are loyal,
to the blameless warrior You show Yourself blameless;
27 You are pure with those who are pure,
but with the crooked, You are shrewd.
28 You bring salvation to a humble people;
You cast Your eyes down on the haughty.

29 For You are my lamp, LORD;
the LORD lights up my darkness.
30 With You I can rush a ridge;
with my God I can leap over a wall.

31 God's ways are blameless;
the LORD's words are pure;
He is a shield to all who take refuge in Him.

32 For who is a god besides the LORD;
who is a Rock besides our God?
33 God is my powerful stronghold;
He frees my way so it is sound.
34 He makes my legs like a deer's
and stands me on the heights.
35 He trains my hands for battle
so that my arms can bend a bow of bronze.

36 You gave me the shield of Your victory;
Your battle cry stirred me with power.
37 You made my steps broad and firm;
my feet never faltered.
38 I pursued my enemy to destroy them,
never turning back until they perished.

39 I cut them down and crushed them, and they did not rise;
they fell beneath my feet.
40 You girded me with power for battle
and sunk my adversaries far beneath me;
41 You made my enemies turn tail before me;
my foes, too, I destroyed.
42 They looked wildly about, but there was no savior –
called out to the LORD, but He did not answer them –
43 while I ground them up like dust of the earth;
I crushed and pounded them like street-mud.

44 You rescued me from civil strife;
you kept me as the head of nations;
peoples I never knew of serve me.
45 Foreign peoples come cringing before me;
they merely hear me and obey;
46 foreign peoples lose heart
and come trembling out of their forts.

47 The LORD lives!
Blessed is my Rock;
exalted is God, Rock of my rescue!
48 God who grants vengeance to me,
who subjugates people under me,
49 my redeemer from my enemies,
You raise me above those who rise against me;
You save me from violent men.

50 So I praise You, LORD, among the nations,
and sing to Your name.

51 He is a tower of victory for His king
and shows loyalty to His anointed,
to David and his seed forever.

23 1 And these are the last words of David:
"Thus spoke David, son of Yishai;
thus spoke the man raised on high,
anointed of the God of Yaakov,
sweet singer of Israel.
2 The spirit of the LORD has spoken through me;
His word is on my tongue.
3 The God of Israel has declared,
the Rock of Israel has said of me:
He who rules men justly,
he who rules in awe of God
4 is like morning light at sunrise,

like a cloudless morning,
more radiant than the gleam of rain
on the grass of the earth.
5 Is my house not so with God?
For an eternal covenant He formed with me,
all in order, guaranteed.
Will He not bring my every triumph,
my every desire, to bloom?
6 But as for the depraved,
they will be thrust away like thorns;
they cannot be grasped by hand;
7 whoever touches them
must be armed with iron and shaft of spear –
or must burn them with fire on the spot."

8 These are the names of David's warriors:
Yoshev Bashevet, a Tahkemonite, head of the Three, he is Adino the
Eznite – he wielded his spear[49] against eight hundred victims at once.
9 Next in rank was Elazar son of Dodo son of Aḥoḥi, one of the three
warriors with David who taunted the Philistines gathered there for battle.
10 The men of Israel retreated, but he stood his ground and struck down the
Philistines until his hand grew sore and his hand stuck fast to his sword.
The Lord granted a great victory on that day, and the troops came back
only to strip the slain.

11 Next in rank was Shama son of Ageh the Hararite. The Philistines had
gathered into a pack where there was a plot of land full of lentils, and the
12 troops fled from the Philistines. But he took his stand in the middle of
the field and defended it, defeating the Philistines, and the Lord granted
a great victory.

13 Once, during the harvest, the chief three of the Thirty came to David in the
cave of Adulam, when a pack of Philistines was encamped in the Refaim
14 Valley. At the time, David was in the stronghold while the Philistines were
15 then stationed at Beit Leḥem. David was seized with a craving and said,
"Oh, if only someone could give me water to drink from the well of Beit
16 Leḥem by the gate." So the three warriors infiltrated the Philistine camp,
drew water from the Beit Leḥem well by the gate, and carried it back. But
when they brought it to David, he would not drink it and poured it out in
a libation to the Lord.

17 "The Lord forbid that I do such a thing!" he said. "It is the blood of men
who risked their very lives by going." And he would not drink it. These
18 were the feats of the three warriors; Avishai, the brother of Yoav son of
Tzeruya, was the head of these three. He wielded his spear against three
19 hundred victims. He was famous among the Three and the most honored

49 | This phrase is missing here but is present in the parallel verse in I Chronicles 11:6.

of these three and so became their leader, though he never reached the
rank of the Three.[50]

20 Benayahu son of Yehoyada, from Kavtze'el, was a powerful man who
achieved great feats. He defeated the two leonine warriors of Moav, and
21 he climbed down into a pit and overpowered a lion on a snowy day. He
defeated an Egyptian, a formidable man; the Egyptian held a spear, and he
charged down at him with a pole, snatched the spear from the Egyptian's
22 hand, and killed him with his own spear. These were the feats of Benayahu
23 son of Yehoyada, and he was famous among the three warriors. He was
among the most honored of the Thirty though he never reached the rank
of the Three, and David appointed him over his bodyguard.

24 Among the Thirty were: Asael, Yoav's brother,
Elḥanan son of Dodo of Beit Leḥem,
25 Shama the Harodite, Elika the Harodite,
26 Ḥeletz the Paltite,
Ira son of Ikesh the Tekoite,
27 Aviezer the Anatotite,
Mevunai the Hushatite,
28 Tzalmon the Ahohite,
29 Mahrai the Netofatite, Ḥelev son of Baana the Netofatite,
Itai son of Rivai of Giva of the Benjaminites,
30 Benayahu the Piratonite,
Hidai of Naḥalei Gaash,
31 Avi Alvon the Arbatite,
Azmavet the Barhumite,
32 Elyaḥba the Shaalbonite,
sons of Yashen, Yehonatan,
33 Shama the Hararite,
Aḥiam son of Sharar the Ararite,
34 Elifelet son of Aḥasbai, son of the Maakhatite,
Eliam son of Aḥitofel the Gilonite,
35 Ḥezrai the Carmelite,
Paarai the Arbite,
36 Yigal son of Natan of Tzova,
Bani the Gadite,
37 Tzelek the Amonite,
Naḥrai the Be'erotite, arms-bearer to Yoav son of Tzeruya,
38 Ira the Itrite, Garev the Itrite,
39 Uriya the Hittite –
thirty-seven in all.

24 1 The LORD's fury flared against Israel once more, and He incited David
2 against them, saying, "Go, count Israel and Yehuda." The king said to

50 | Adino, Elazar, and Shama (vv. 8–12).

Yoav, commander of his force, "Now make your way around all the tribes
of Israel, from Dan up to Be'er Sheva, and take a census of the people to
inform me of the number of the population."

3 "May the LORD your God increase the number of the people a hundred
times over in my lord the king's sight," Yoav said to the king, "but why does
my lord the king desire such a thing?"

4 But the king's word prevailed over Yoav and the force commanders, and
Yoav and the force commanders left the king's presence to take a census
5 of the people, of Israel. They crossed the Jordan and camped by Aroer to
the south of the city, which is in the midst of the Gad Ravine, and by Yazer.
6 They came to Gilad and to the region of Taḥtim Ḥodshi, went on to Dan
7 Yaan, and made their way around to Sidon. They continued to the fortress
of Tyre and all the towns of the Hivites and Canaanites, and set out for
8 Be'er Sheva in southern Yehuda. They made their way all around the land
9 and reached Jerusalem at the end of nine months and twenty days. Yoav
delivered the census figures of the population to the king; Israel numbered
eight hundred thousand sword-wielding men of fighting age, and Yehuda
numbered five hundred thousand men.

10 But afterward, David's heart ached with remorse for having counted the
people."I have sinned gravely by doing this," David said to the LORD. "Now,
O LORD, please excuse Your servant's offense, for I have been so foolish."

11 By the time David rose in the morning, the word of the LORD had reached
12 the prophet Gad, David's seer: "Go and tell David – thus says the LORD:
I am holding three things over you; choose one of them, and I will bring
it upon you."

13 Gad came to David and told him.

"Will you suffer seven years of famine in your land," he said to him, "or will
you flee before your foes for three months as they pursue you, or will there
be three days of sickness in your land? Now, consider what reply I should
bring back to Him who sent me."

14 "I am in grave torment," David said to Gad. "Let us fall into the Hand of
the LORD, for His mercy is great; do not let me fall into human hands."

15 And the LORD sent a sickness against Israel from morning until the set
time, and from Dan up to Be'er Sheva, seventy thousand of the people died.
16 But as the angel raised his hand to destroy Jerusalem, the LORD regretted
the evil and said to the angel who was wreaking destruction among the
people, "Enough! Now, stay your hand." The angel of the LORD was then
by the threshing floor of Aravna the Jebusite.

17 When David saw the angel who was striking down the people, he spoke
to the LORD. "Look – I alone have sinned," he said, "and I alone offended.

But this flock – what have they done? Please, let Your hand move against
me and against my father's house."

18 On that same day, Gad came to David and said to him, "Go up; erect an
19 altar to the LORD by the threshing floor of Aravna the Jebusite." At Gad's
20 word, David went up, just as the LORD had charged. When Aravna looked
out and saw the king and his officials crossing over toward him, Aravna
went out and bowed before the king, his face to the ground.

21 "Why has my lord the king come to his servant?" asked Aravna.

"To purchase your threshing floor from you to build an altar to the LORD,"
said David, "so that the plague will cease among the people."

22 "Let my lord the king take and offer up as he sees fit," said Aravna. "Look,
oxen for a burnt offering and threshing boards and cattle gear for wood.
23 O King, Aravna has given it all to the king." And Aravna added to the king,
"May the LORD your God show you favor."

24 "No, I insist on buying it from you at a price," the king said to Aravna. "I
will not offer up burnt offerings to the LORD my God at no cost."

And David bought the threshing floor and the oxen for fifty shekel of silver.
25 David built an altar there for the LORD and offered up burnt offerings and
peace offerings. And the LORD responded to the plea of the land, and the
plague ceased in Israel.

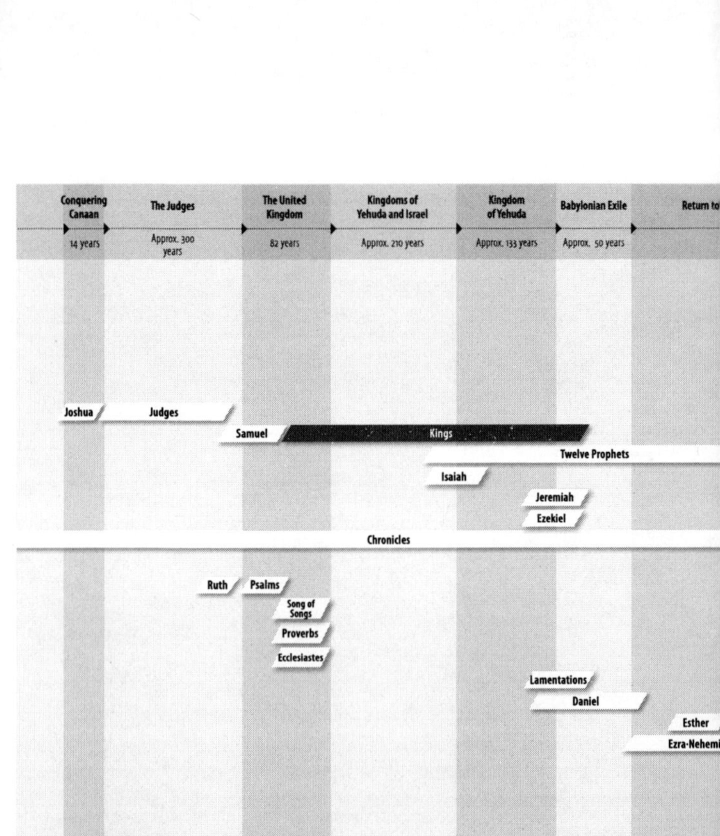

Conquering Canaan
The Judges
The United Kingdom
Kingdoms of Yehuda and Israel
Kingdom of Yehuda
Babylonian Exile
Return to
14 years
Approx. 300 years
82 years
Approx. 210 years
Approx. 133 years
Approx. 50 years
Joshua
Judges
Samuel
Kings
Twelve Prophets
Isaiah
Jeremiah
Ezekiel
Chronicles
Ruth
Psalms
Song of Songs
Proverbs
Ecclesiastes
Lamentations
Daniel
Esther
Ezra-Nehemi
Tabernacle in Shilo
Tabernacle in Gilgal
First Temple
Second Temple

KINGS/MELAKHIM

KINGS	From David's reign to Shlomo's reign	Shlomo's reign	Kings of Yehuda and Israel – from the division of the monarchy through the final days of the house of Omri	Kings of Yehuda and Israel – from Yehu's rebellion through the destruction of the Kingdom of Israel	Kingdom of Yehuda – from the destruction of the Kingdom of Israel through the destruction of Jerusalem
	I Kings Chs. 1–2	I Kings 3–11	I Kings 12 – II Kings 8	II Kings 9–17	II Kings 18–25
	40 years		98 years	143 years	Approx. 135 years

1 1 King David was old, advanced in years, and though they covered him
2 with bedclothes, he never felt warm. His servants said to him, "Let a
young virgin be sought out for our lord the king, to wait upon the king
and become his companion; when she lies in your embrace, our lord the
king will feel warm."

3 They searched throughout Israel's borders for a beautiful girl, found
4 Avishag the Shunamite, and brought her to the king. The girl was most
beautiful, and she became the king's companion and served him, but the
king was not intimate with her.

5 Meanwhile, Adoniya son of Ḥagit promoted himself, declaring, "I will
become king," and he procured a chariot and riders and fifty men to
6 run before him. Now his father had never disciplined him, saying, "Why
have you acted like that?" He was born after Avshalom, and he too was
devastatingly handsome.

7 He conspired with Yoav son of Tzeruya and Avyatar the priest, and they
8 lent their support to Adoniya. But Tzadok the priest, Benayahu son of
Yehoyada, Natan the prophet, Shimi and Rei, and David's warriors were
not on Adoniyahu's side.

9 Adoniyahu sacrificed sheep, oxen, and fatlings by the Zoḥelet Stone near
the Rogel Spring, and he invited all his brothers – the king's sons – and all
10 the men of Yehuda, the king's subjects. But he did not invite the prophet
Natan or Benayahu or the warriors, or his brother Shlomo.

11 And Natan said to Batsheva, Shlomo's mother, "Have you heard?
Adoniyahu the son of Ḥagit has become king without our lord David's
12 knowledge. Come now, let me give you advice – to save your own life and
13 the life of your son Shlomo. Go to King David at once and say to him, 'My
lord the king, did you not swear to your handmaid, "Your son Shlomo will
rule after me, and he will sit on my throne"? Why, then, has Adoniyahu
14 become king?' And while you are still speaking there with the king, I will
come in after you and confirm your words."

15 So Batsheva went to the king in the inner chamber – the king had aged
16 severely, and Avishag the Shunamite was tending to him – and Batsheva
bowed down low in homage to the king.

"What is the matter?" asked the king.

17 "My lord," she said to him, "you swore by the LORD your God to your
handmaid, 'Your son Shlomo will rule after me, and he will sit on my
18 throne.' But now, look – Adoniya has become king – and you, my lord the
19 king, did not even know! He has sacrificed a wealth of oxen and fatlings
and sheep and invited all the king's sons, the priest Avyatar, and the army
20 commander Yoav, but he did not invite your servant Shlomo. But all the
eyes of Israel look to you, my lord the king, to tell them who will succeed

21 my lord the king on his throne. Otherwise, when my lord the king lies
with his ancestors, my son Shlomo and I will be considered offenders."

22 And as she was still speaking with the king, Natan the prophet arrived.

23 "Here is Natan the prophet," they announced to the king, and he came
before the king and bowed to him with his face to the ground.

24 "My lord the king," said Natan, "Did you yourself say, 'Adoniyahu will be
25 king after me, and he will sit on my throne'? For he went down today and
sacrificed a wealth of oxen, fatlings, and sheep and invited all the king's
sons, the army officers, and Avyatar the priest. And now they are feasting
before him and toasting him and declaring, 'Long live King Adoniyahu!'
26 But he did not invite me, your servant, or the priest Tzadok, or Benayahu
27 son of Yehoyada, or your servant Shlomo. Could it be that my lord the
king has decided this without informing your servant who will succeed
my lord the king on his throne?"

28 "Summon Batsheva to me," King David said in response, and she came
before the king and stood in the king's presence.

29 And the king swore an oath. "As the Lord lives," he said, "who has
30 rescued me from every danger, what I swore to you by the Lord, God of
Israel – that Shlomo your son will rule after me, and that he will sit on my
throne in my place – I shall fulfill this very day."

31 And Batsheva bowed her face to the ground in royal homage and said,
"May my lord, King David, live forever!"

32 King David then said, "Summon Tzadok the priest to me, along with Natan
the prophet and Benayahu son of Yehoyada," and they came before the
king.

33 "Take your lord's servants with you," the king said to them, "and mount my
34 son Shlomo upon my own mule, and lead him down to Giḥon. There, the
priest Tzadok and the prophet Natan will anoint him as king over Israel;
and you will sound the ram's horn and declare, 'Long live King Shlomo!'
35 Then you will go up after him; he will enter and sit on my throne and
reign in my place, for it is him whom I have charged as ruler over Israel
and Yehuda."

36 "Amen," Benayahu son of Yehoyada answered the king. "May the Lord,
37 God of my lord the king, deem it so. Just as the Lord has been with my
lord the king, so may He be with Shlomo, and may He make his throne
even greater than the throne of my lord, King David."

38 So Tzadok the priest, the prophet Natan, and Benayahu son of Yehoyada
and the Keretites and Peletites[1] went down. They mounted Shlomo on

---

1 | Armed forces loyal to David, perhaps of foreign origin; see, e.g., II Samuel 8:18, 15:18, 20:23.

39 King David's mule and led him to Giḥon. Then Tzadok the priest took
the horn of oil from the Tent and anointed Shlomo. They sounded the
40 ram's horn, and all the people cried, "Long live King Shlomo!" And all the
people marched up after him, with the people piping away on pipes and
rejoicing with such great joy that the very earth split from the sound.

41 As Adoniyahu and all the guests who were with him finished eating, they
heard. When Yoav heard the sound of the ram's horn, he asked, "Why is
42 there the sound of commotion in the city?" And as he was still speaking,
Yonatan, the priest Avyatar's son, arrived. "Come in," said Adoniyahu, "for
you are a worthy man, and you surely bring good news."

43 "Alas," Yonatan answered Adoniyahu, "our lord, King David, has made
44 Shlomo king. And with him, the king sent Tzadok the priest, Natan the
prophet, and Benayahu son of Yehoyada with the Keretites and Peletites,
45 and they mounted him on the king's own mule. The priest Tzadok and
the prophet Natan anointed him as king at Giḥon; they paraded up from
there in celebration, and commotion swept the city – that is the sound
46 47 you heard. And what is more, Shlomo now sits on the royal throne, and
the king's subjects have come to bless our lord, King David, saying, 'May
God make Shlomo's name more famous than your own name, and may He
make his throne even greater than your own throne,' and the king bowed
48 down from his bed. And the king even said, 'Blessed is the Lord, God
of Israel, who has granted an heir to my throne today while my own eyes
can witness it.'"

49 50 All of Adoniyahu's guests rose in alarm, and each went on his way, while
Adoniyahu, in fear of Shlomo, rose and made his way straight to the horns
51 of the altar and grasped hold of them. Shlomo was told, "Now, out of fear
of King Shlomo, Adoniyahu is clutching at the horns of the altar, saying,
'Let King Shlomo swear to me – right now – that he will not put his servant
to death by sword.'"

52 "If he will prove to be a worthy man, not a hair of his will fall to the ground,"
Shlomo said, "but if any fault will be found with him, he is dead."

53 And Shlomo sent and had him brought down from the altar, and he came and
bowed before King Shlomo.

And Shlomo said to him, "Go home."

2 1 The time of David's death was drawing near, and he gave instructions to his
son Shlomo.

2 "I am going the way of all the earth," he said. "You must be strong and prove
3 yourself a man. You must keep the charge of the Lord your God, following
His ways and keeping His laws and commandments, His rulings and decrees,
as written in the teaching of Moshe. For then you will succeed in whatever
you do, wherever you turn.

4 "For then, the LORD will fulfill the promise He made to me, saying: If your sons
keep to their path and walk before Me truly, with all their heart and all their
soul, then no one of your lineage will be cut off from the throne of Israel.

5 "Now you know what Yoav son of Tzeruya did to me – how he dealt with the
two commanders of Israel's forces, Avner son of Ner and Amasa son of Yeter.
By killing them, he shed the blood of war in peacetime and tainted the belt
6 around his waist and the shoes upon his feet with the blood of war.[2] Use your
wisdom – do not let his gray-haired head go down to Sheol[3] in peace.

7 "As for the sons of Barzilai the Gileadite, show them loyalty and let them dine
at your table,[4] for they befriended me when I was fleeing from Avshalom your
brother.[5]

8 "Now, look – though Shimi son of Gera the Benjaminite from Baḥurim is
with you, he cursed me with a vehement curse on the day I left Maḥanayim.
When he came down to meet me by the Jordan, I swore to him by the LORD
9 that I would not put him to death by sword[6] – but now, do not let him go free.
You are a wise man, and you will know how to deal with him – bring his gray-
haired head down in blood to Sheol."

10 11 And David slept with his ancestors and was buried in the City of David. The
length of time that David had reigned over Israel was forty years; he reigned
in Ḥevron for seven years, and he reigned in Jerusalem for thirty-three
12 years. Now Shlomo sat on his father David's throne, and his kingdom was
firmly established.

13 Adoniya son of Ḥagit came to Batsheva, Shlomo's mother. "Do you come
in peace?" she asked, and he said, "Yes, in peace."

14 "May I have a word with you?" he continued, and she said, "Speak."

15 "You know that the kingship was meant to be mine," he said, "and that
all of Israel expected me to reign. But the kingship was transferred to my
16 brother, for the LORD determined that it should be his. Now I have but a
single request of you – do not turn me away."

"Speak," she said to him.

17 "Please ask King Shlomo," he said, "for he will not turn you away: let him
give me Avishag the Shunamite as a wife."

18 "Very well," said Batsheva. "I will speak to the king on your behalf."

19 Batsheva came to King Shlomo to speak to him on Adoniyahu's behalf.

---

2 | The murder of Avner is recounted in II Samuel 3:27 and the murder of Amasa in II Samuel 20:10.

3 | The netherworld.

4 | Provide for their maintenance.

5 | See II Samuel 19:32–40.

6 | See II Samuel 16:5–13, 19:16–24.

The king rose to greet her and bowed to her before sitting down on his throne. He had a throne set out for the queen mother, and she sat down on his right.

20 "I have one small request of you," she said. "Do not turn me away."

"Make your request, Mother," the king said to her, "for I will not turn you away."

21 "Let Avishag the Shunamite be given to your brother Adoniya as a wife," she said.

22 "And why do you request Avishag the Shunamite for Adoniyahu?" King Shlomo countered his mother. "You might as well request the kingship for him – as he is my older brother – and for Avyatar the priest, and for Yoav son of Tzeruya as well."

23 And King Shlomo swore by the LORD, "So may God do to me – and more,"
24 he said, "if this affair has not cost Adoniyahu his life. And now, as the LORD
lives – who set me firmly on the throne of my father David, and who made
a house for me as He promised – on this very day, Adoniyahu will be put to
25 death." And King Shlomo sent orders to Benayahu son of Yehoyada, who
struck him down, and he died.

26 As for Avyatar the priest, the king said, "Go to your fields in Anatot. Though you deserve to die, I will not have you killed at this time because you bore the Ark of the LORD GOD before my father David and because you suffered along with my father throughout all his suffering."

27 And Shlomo dismissed Avyatar from the role of priest to the LORD, fulfilling what the LORD had pronounced for the house of Eli at Shilo.[7]

28 And the news reached Yoav, and Yoav fled to the Tent of the LORD
and grasped hold of the horns of the altar, for Yoav had sided with
29 Adoniya – though he had not sided with Avshalom. When King Shlomo
was informed that Yoav had fled to the Tent of the LORD and that he was
by the altar, Shlomo sent Benayahu son of Yehoyada, ordering him, "Go,
strike him down."

30 When Benayahu reached the Tent of the LORD, he said to him, "By order of the king, come out!"

"No!" he said. "I will die right here!"

Benayahu reported back to the king, saying, "This is what Yoav said to me in response."

31 "Do as he says," the king said to him. "Strike him down and bury him
and remove the innocent blood that Yoav spilled from upon me and my
32 father's house. The LORD will bring his bloodguilt back upon his own

7 | See 1 Samuel 2:27–36.

head for having struck down two men who were more righteous and
better than he – he put them to the sword without my father David's
knowledge – Avner son of Ner, the army commander of Israel, and Amasa
33 son of Yeter, the army commander of Yehuda. May their bloodguilt be
brought back upon Yoav's own head and upon the head of his descendants
forever; and may David and his descendants, and his house and his throne,
forever have peace from the LORD."

34 And Benayahu son of Yehoyada advanced and struck him down and put
35 him to death, and he was buried in his home in the wilderness. The king
appointed Benayahu son of Yehoyada in charge of the army in his place,
and the king appointed the priest Tzadok instead of Avyatar.

36 Now the king sent for and summoned Shimi. "Build yourself a house in
Jerusalem and settle there," he said to him, "but you must not leave there
37 for anywhere else. For from the very moment you leave, once you cross
the Kidron Valley, know that you are doomed to die, and your blood will
be upon your own head."

38 "Very well," Shimi said to the king. "Whatever my lord the king says, your
servant will do."

39 Shimi remained in Jerusalem for a long time, but three years later, two of
Shimi's servants ran away to Akhish son of Maakha, the king of Gat. When
40 Shimi was told, "Look – your servants are in Gat," Shimi set out, saddled
his donkey, and went to Akhish in Gat to find his slaves; he went to bring
his slaves from Gat.

41 When Shlomo was informed that Shimi had gone from Jerusalem to Gat
42 and back, the king sent and summoned Shimi and said to him, "Did I not
make you swear to the LORD and warn you that from the moment you left
and went anywhere else, you would know that you would be doomed to
43 death? And you said to me, 'Very well, I accept.' Why did you fail to keep
the LORD's oath and the command I charged you with?"

44 The king then continued to Shimi, "You are aware of all the evil you
harbored in your heart; of what you did to my father David. Now the LORD
45 has brought your own evil back on your own head. But King Shlomo will
be blessed, and the throne of David will be established before the LORD
forever."

46 The king gave orders to Benayahu son of Yehoyada, and he set out and
struck him down, and he died. Thus the kingdom was secured in Shlomo's
hand.

3 1 Shlomo formed a marriage alliance with King Pharaoh of Egypt; he took
Pharaoh's daughter in marriage and brought her to the City of David until
he had finished building his palace, the House of the LORD, and the wall
2 around Jerusalem. But the people were sacrificing at the high shrines, for
at that time a House for the LORD's name had not yet been built.

3 Shlomo loved the LORD and followed the laws of his father David, but he
4 still offered sacrifices and incense at the high shrines. And the king went
to Givon to sacrifice there, for it was the greatest of the high shrines, and
Shlomo offered up a thousand burnt offerings on that altar.

5 At Givon the LORD appeared to Shlomo in a dream. And God said,
"Ask – what shall I give you?"

6 And Shlomo said, "You treated Your servant David, my father, with great
kindness, for he walked before You in truth and in justice, and with a
sincere heart toward You. And You have maintained this great kindness for
7 him by granting him a son and heir to his throne, as is now the case. And
now, O LORD, my God, You made Your servant king in my father David's
8 place, but I am a young boy; I have no experience as a leader. Yet Your
servant is among Your own people, whom You have chosen, a people too
9 vast to be numbered or counted. Grant Your servant an understanding
heart to judge Your people, to distinguish between good and evil, for who
can judge this immense people of Yours?"

10 11 And it pleased the LORD that Shlomo had made this request, and God said
to him, "Because this is the request you made – you did not ask for long life,
or for wealth, or for the lives of your enemies, but you asked for wisdom
12 to discern in judgment – I have fulfilled your words. Here, I am granting
you a wise, discerning heart – no one like you has ever been before you,
13 and no one like you will ever rise again after you. But what is more, I am
granting you what you did not ask for, both wealth and honor – not a man
14 among kings will compare to you for as long as you live. And if you follow
in My ways and keep My laws and commandments, as your father David
did, then I shall grant you long life."

15 Then Shlomo awoke – it had all been a dream! When he came to Jerusalem,
he stood before the Ark of the LORD's Covenant and offered up burnt
offerings and presented peace offerings, and he held a feast for all his
servants.

16 17 Then two harlot women came before the king and stood before him. "If
you please, my lord," said the first woman, "this woman and I live in one
18 house, and I gave birth while she was in the house. On the third day after I
gave birth, this woman also gave birth. The two of us live together – there
was no one else in the house besides us, just the two of us in the house.
19 20 The son of this woman died in the night, for she lay on him. But she got
up during the night and took my own son from me while your handmaid
was sleeping and lay down with him in her embrace, and laid her own dead
21 son in my embrace. I woke up in the morning to nurse my son to find that
he was dead! But when I looked at him closely in the morning, why – it
wasn't my own son, the one I had borne!"

22 "No!" said the other woman. "My son is the one who is alive, and your son
is the one who died!"

"No," she said, "your son is dead, and my son is alive!" and they continued
arguing before the king.

23 "This one says, 'This is my son, who is alive, and your son is dead,'" said
the king, "and this one says, 'No, your son is dead, and my son is alive.'"

24 And the king said, "Fetch me a sword," and they brought a sword before
the king.

25 "Cut the living child into two," the king declared, "and give half to one and
half to the other."

26 But the woman whose son was alive spoke up, for she burned with
compassion for her son. "Please, my lord," she said, "give her the living
child; do anything but kill him!" while the other one said, "Neither of us
will have him – cut him up."

27 And the king spoke up. "Give her the living child," he said, "and make no
move to kill him. She is his mother."

28 When all of Israel heard about the case that the king had judged, they
held the king in awe, for they saw that divine wisdom was within him to
do justice.

4 1 King Shlomo was king of all Israel. These were the names of his officials:
2 Azariya son of Tzadok the priest.
3 Elihoref and Aḥiya, sons of Shisha, scribes,
Yehoshafat son of Aḥilud, royal herald.
4 Benayahu son of Yehoyada, in charge of the army,
5 Tzadok and Avyatar, priests. Azariya son of Natan, in charge of the
prefects,
Zavud son of Natan the priest, the king's companion.
6 Aḥishar, in charge of the palace,
Adoniram son of Avda, in charge of the forced labor.

7 Shlomo had twelve prefects over all of Israel who provided for the king
and his household; each one was responsible for provision for one month
8 of the year. And these are their names:
Ben Ḥur in the Efrayim hills;
9 Ben Deker in Makatz, Shaalvim, Beit Shemesh, and Eilon Beit Ḥanan;
10 Ben Ḥesed in Arubot – he oversaw Sokho and all the region of Ḥefer;
11 Ben Avinadav, all the region of Dor – Tafat, Shlomo's daughter, was his
wife;
12 Baana son of Aḥilud in Ta'nakh, Megiddo, and all of Beit She'an near
Tzartan below Yizre'el, from Beit She'an to Avel Meḥola to the other side
of Yokme'am;
13 Ben Gever in Ramot Gilad – he oversaw the hamlets of Yair son of Menashe
in the Gilad and the Argov region in the Bashan – sixty great towns, walled,
with bolts of bronze;

14 Aḥinadav son of Ido in Maḥanayim;
15 Aḥimaatz in Naftali – he, too, took a daughter of Shlomo's in marriage, Basmat;
16 Baana son of Ḥushai in Asher and Be'alot;
17 Yehoshafat son of Paruaḥ in Yissakhar;
18 Shimi son of Ela in Binyamin;
19 Gever son of Uri in the land of Gilad, the land of Siḥon, king of the Amorites, and Og, king of the Bashan.
And one prefect was in the land.

20 Yehuda and Israel were as boundless as the sand upon the seashore, eating and drinking and content.

5 1 Shlomo ruled over all the kingdoms from the River[8] to the land of the Philistines, up to the border of Egypt. They offered tribute and served Shlomo all his life.

2 Shlomo's fare for a single day was thirty *kor*[9] of fine flour, sixty *kor* of
3 meal, ten fattened oxen, twenty pasture-raised oxen, and a hundred sheep,
4 besides deer, gazelle, antelope, and fattened geese. For he had dominion
over the whole region to the west of the River[10] – from Tifsaḥ up to
Aza – and over all the kings to the west of the River. He had peace on
5 every surrounding border; from Dan to Be'er Sheva, Yehuda and Israel
dwelled in safety, each person beneath his grapevine and fig tree, all the
days of Shlomo.

6 Shlomo had forty thousand stalls for his cavalry horses and twelve thou-
7 sand riders. During their assigned month, the aforementioned prefects
would provide for King Shlomo and all who were received at King Shlo-
8 mo's table, and they let nothing fall short. As for the barley and straw for
the horses and steeds, they would deliver it to the place where they were
stationed according to their schedule.

9 God had granted wisdom to Shlomo, and deep understanding, and a
10 mind as broad as the sand upon the seashore. Shlomo's wisdom surpassed
the wisdom of all the peoples of the East and all the wisdom of Egypt.
11 He was wiser than any other man – than Eitan the Ezrahite and Heiman,
than Kalkol and Darda, the sons of Maḥol – and he was famous among
12 all the surrounding nations. He composed three thousand proverbs, and
13 his songs numbered a thousand and five. And he spoke of the trees, from
the cedar in Lebanon to the hyssop that grows out of walls; and he spoke
14 of the beasts and the birds and the creeping creatures and the fish. People
from all nations came to hear Shlomo's wisdom on behalf of all the kings
of the earth who had heard of his wisdom.

---

8 | The Euphrates; cf. Genesis 15:18.

9 | A single *kor* is the equivalent of 60 gallons or 230 liters.

10 | Literally "the other side of the River," a widely used term referring to the part of the Fertile Crescent west and south of the Euphrates.

15 Ḥiram, king of Tyre, sent his officials to Shlomo when he heard that
he had been anointed king in his father's place, for Ḥiram had always
16 17 respected David. And Shlomo sent a message to Ḥiram: "You know that
my father David was not able to build a house for the name of the LORD
his God, given how battle surrounded him, until the LORD brought them
18 to heel beneath him. But now, the LORD my God has granted me respite
19 all around; there is no adversary or misfortune. And so I intend to build a
House for the name of the LORD my God, just as the LORD promised my
father David, saying, 'Your son, whom I will enthrone in your stead, will
be the one to build the House for My name.'[11]

20 "And now, order them to cut down cedars for me from Lebanon; my
servants will work with your servants, and I will provide whatever wages
you demand for your servants, for as you know, we have no one as skilled
in cutting timber as the Sidonians."

21 When Ḥiram heard Shlomo's words, he was delighted and exclaimed,
"Blessed is the LORD today, for having given David such a wise son over
22 this great people." And Ḥiram sent word to Shlomo: "I have received your
message; I will supply all the cedarwood and cypress wood you require.
23 My servants will bring them down from Lebanon to the sea, and by the
sea I will form them into rafts, to go to whatever place you tell me. And
there, I will dismantle them for you to carry away. You, for your part, will
supply the food I require for my household."

24 And so Ḥiram supplied Shlomo with all the cedarwood and cypress wood
25 he required, while Shlomo supplied Ḥiram with twenty thousand *kor*
of wheat as provision for his household, and twenty *kor* of fine-pressed
26 oil; those were the quantities Shlomo supplied to Ḥiram every year. The
LORD had endowed Shlomo with wisdom, as He had promised him. There
was peace between Ḥiram and Shlomo, and the two of them formed an
alliance.

27 King Shlomo began to levy forced labor upon all of Israel; the levy was
28 thirty thousand men. He had ten thousand men sent to Lebanon every
month, in shifts; they would spend a month in Lebanon and two months
29 at home. Adoniram was in charge of the forced labor. And Shlomo had
seventy thousand porters and eight thousand quarriers in the mountains,
30 besides Shlomo's three thousand and three hundred prefect officers in
charge of the labor, who supervised the people who performed the labor.
31 At the king's command, they quarried enormous blocks of prime stone
32 so that the foundations of the House would be laid with hewn stone. And
Shlomo's builders, together with Ḥiram's builders and the Gevalites,[12]
carved the wood and the stone in preparation for the construction of the
House.

---

11 | See II Samuel 7:12–13.

12 | Skilled workers from the Phoenician port city of Byblos; cf. Ezekiel 27:9.

6 1 In the four hundred and eightieth year after the Israelites left Egypt, in the
month of Ziv[13] – the second month – of the fourth year of Shlomo's reign
2 over Israel, he began to build the House for the LORD. The House that
King Shlomo built for the LORD was sixty cubits long, twenty cubits wide,
3 and thirty cubits high. The Hall leading up to the Sanctuary of the House
was twenty cubits long along the width of the House, and ten cubits wide
leading up to the House.

4 He made recessed, paned windows for the House.

5 Around the outer wall of the House – the outer walls around the Sanctuary
and Inner Sanctuary[14] – he built a tiered structure and made side chambers
6 all around. The lowest tier was five cubits wide, the middle tier was six
cubits wide, and the third tier was seven cubits wide, as he had designed
recesses around the outside of the House to avoid making grooves in the
walls of the House.

7 The House was entirely built of finished stones that had been cut at the
quarry; no hammer, ax, or iron tool was heard in the House during its
construction.

8 There was an entrance through the central alcove on the southern side of
the House; a winding staircase led to the middle tier and from the middle
tier to the third one.

9 When he finished building the House, he paneled the House with beams
10 and planks of cedar. He built the tiered structure against the whole
house, each story five cubits high, so that the House was encased with
cedarwood.

11 12 And the word of the LORD came to Shlomo: "Concerning this House that
you are building: if you follow My laws and uphold My rulings and keep
all My commandments by following them, then I will fulfill My promise
13 through you, the promise that I made to your father David. I will dwell in
the midst of the Israelites, and I will never abandon My people Israel."

14 15 Shlomo completed the construction of the House. He paneled the inside
of the walls of the House with boards of cedar – from the floor of the
House to the ceiling, he overlaid the interior with wood; and he overlaid
the floor of the House with boards of cypress.

16 Twenty cubits from the end of the House, he built up boards of cedar from
the floor to the ceiling and built the Inner Sanctuary, the Holy of Holies,
17 on the inside. The front part of the House, the Sanctuary, measured forty
cubits.

18 And cedar, the interior was all cedar, with carvings of bulbs and blossoming
flowers; there was no visible stone.

13 | The second month, known by Jews as Iyar after the Babylonian exile.

14 | Also called the Holy of Holies in verse 16 and elsewhere.

19 In the innermost part of the House, he furnished the Inner Sanctuary to
20 place the Ark of the LORD's Covenant. The interior of the Inner Sanctuary
was twenty cubits long, twenty cubits wide, and twenty cubits high; he
overlaid it and overlaid the cedar altar with solid gold.

21 Shlomo overlaid the interior of the House with solid gold; he fastened
golden chains in front of the Inner Sanctuary, which he overlaid with
gold.

22 He overlaid the whole House with gold, every last part of the House; and
he overlaid the whole altar within the Inner Sanctuary with gold.

23 Within the Inner Sanctuary, he formed two cherubim of olive wood, ten
24 cubits high. One cherub wing measured five cubits, and the second cherub
25 wing measured five cubits: ten cubits from wingtip to wingtip. The other
cherub also measured ten cubits, as the two cherubim were both of the
26 same size and shape – one cherub was ten cubits tall, and so was the
27 second cherub. He placed the cherubim within the innermost part of
the House.[15] Their wings were spread so that the tip of one cherub's wing
touched one wall, and the tip of the other cherub's wing touched the other
28 wall; and their inner wings touched wing to wing. And he overlaid the
cherubim with gold.

29 All over the walls, within and without, he made carvings all around –
carvings of cherubim and palms and blossoming flowers.

30 He overlaid the floor of the House with gold, within and without.

31 He made olive wood doors for the entrance to the Inner Sanctuary; the
32 lintel and doorposts were five-sided. The double doors were of olive wood,
and on them he carved cherubim and palms and blossoming flowers and
overlaid them with gold; he hammered the gold down over the cherubim
and the palms.

33 For the entrance to the Sanctuary, too, he made olive wood doorposts,
34 which were four-sided. The double doors were of cypress wood, with two
35 folding leaves for one door and two folding leaves for the other door. He
carved cherubim and palms and blossoming flowers, and he overlaid the
reliefs evenly with gold.

36 He built the inner courtyard with three rows of hewn stone and a row of
cut cedar beams.

37 In the fourth year, in the month of Ziv, the foundations for the House of
38 the LORD were laid. And in the eleventh year, in the month of Bul[16] – that
is, the eighth month – the House was finished down to every last detail
and every last design. He had spent seven years to complete it.

---

15 | The Inner Sanctuary, or Holy of Holies.

16 | The eighth month, known by Jews as Marḥeshvan after the Babylonian exile.

7 1 Shlomo spent thirteen years building his own house, until his house was
2 completely finished. He built the House of the Lebanon Forest[17] with
four rows of cedar columns, with cut cedar beams on top of the columns;
3 it was a hundred cubits long, fifty cubits wide, and thirty cubits high. It
was paneled over in cedar, with boards atop the columns, forty-five in all;
4 fifteen in every row. There were three rows of frames, with three sets of
5 windows facing each other. All the entrances and doorframes had square
frames, with the three sets of windows facing each other.

6 He made the hall of columns fifty cubits long and thirty cubits wide; there
was a hall in front with columns and a canopy in front of them.

7 He made the throne room where he was to sit in judgment the Hall of
8 Judgment and paneled its floor with cedar from floor to floor. The house
of his actual residence, in the rear courtyard behind the Hall, was of similar
design; and the house Shlomo made for Pharaoh's daughter, whom he had
married, was similar to that Hall.

9 All these were of prime stone – hewn to size and smoothed with a file
on every side – from foundation to coping, extending to the great court-
10 yard on the outside. The foundations were of prime stone, enormous
stones – stones measuring ten cubits and stones measuring eight cubits;
11 12 and above were prime stones hewn to size, and cedar. The surrounding
great courtyard had three rows of hewn stone and a row of cut cedar beams,
the same as the inner courtyard of the House of the LORD and the Hall
of the House.

13 14 King Shlomo sent and had Ḥiram fetched from Tyre. He was the son
of a widow from the tribe of Naftali, and his father had been a Tyrian
coppersmith. He was brimming with the talent, expertise, and skill to craft
15 any work in bronze; he came to King Shlomo and crafted all his work. He
formed the two pillars of bronze; each pillar was eighteen cubits high, and
16 the circumference of both pillars was twelve cubits. He crafted two capitals,
cast in bronze, to place atop the pillars – the height of each capital was
17 five cubits – as well as fronds of meshwork and garlands of chainwork for
18 the capitals atop the pillars, seven for each of the two capitals. He crafted
the pillars with two rows around one mesh to cover the capitals that were
above the pomegranates, and he did the same with the second capital.
19 The capitals atop the pillars in the Hall were crafted in the form of a lily
20 four cubits high; the capitals atop both pillars bulged out through the
meshwork over the rows of two hundred pomegranates encircling both
21 capitals. He erected the pillars by the Hall of the Sanctuary; he set up the
right pillar and named it Yakhin, and he set up the left pillar and named it
22 Boaz. Atop each pillar was the form of a lily; thus the work of the pillars
was complete.

---

17 | This was apparently inspired by the large number of cedar columns and beams utilized in its construction.

23 He made the Molten Sea,[18] ten cubits across from rim to rim and perfectly
24 round. It was five cubits high and thirty cubits in circumference. There
were bulb-shaped knobs beneath its rim, encircling it all around, clustered
around the Sea ten to a cubit; the two rows of bulbs were cast together
25 with it. It stood upon twelve oxen, three facing north, three facing west,
three facing south, and three facing east; the Sea was on top of them, and
26 their haunches were all turned inward. It was a handbreadth thick, and its
rim was like the rim of a cup, like the petals of a lily; its capacity was two
thousand *bat*.[19]

27 He made ten stands of bronze; each stand was four cubits long, four cubits
28 wide, and three cubits high. This is how the stands were constructed: They
29 consisted of panels; the panels were joined by frames. On the panels in
between the frames were lions, oxen, and cherubim; there was a base
30 above the frames, and hammered spirals beneath the lions and oxen. There
were four bronze wheels on every stand, with bronze axles. Its four legs
had brackets underneath the laver; the brackets were cast with spirals on
31 each side. Its spout rose a cubit above the capital; the spout was shaped
like a cylindrical base, a cubit and a half across. On the spout, too, there
32 were carvings; its panels were square, not round. The four wheels were
beneath the panels, with the wheel sockets fixed into the stand; each
33 wheel was a cubit and a half high. The wheels were designed like chariot
34 wheels; their sockets, rims, spokes, and hubs were all of cast metal. The
four brackets reached the four corners of each stand; the brackets were
35 part of the stand. A cylinder rose half a cubit above the top of the stand;
36 its handles and panels were part of the top of the stand. On the surface of
its handles, and on its panels, he engraved cherubim, lions, and palms in
the available space, with spirals all around.

37 This was how he crafted the ten stands: all of them were cast alike, of
38 uniform size and shape. And he made ten lavers of bronze, each laver with
a capacity of forty *bat*, each laver four cubits across; one laver for each of
39 the ten stands. He positioned five stands to the right side of the House,
and five stands to the left side of the House; and he positioned the Sea to
the right side of the House, in the southeast corner.

40 Ḥiram crafted the lavers and the shovels and the basins. And so Ḥiram
completed all the work for the House of the LORD as commissioned by
King Shlomo:
41 two pillars and two globe-shaped capitals for the pillar tops;
two pieces of meshwork to cover the two globe-shaped capitals for the
pillar tops;
42 four hundred pomegranates for the two pieces of meshwork – two rows of
pomegranates for each piece of meshwork, which covered the two globe-
shaped capitals on top of the pillars;

18 | A large tank made of cast metal.

19 | A single *bat* is the equivalent of 6 gallons or 23 liters.

43 ten stands and ten lavers for the stands;
44 one Sea with twelve oxen beneath the Sea;
45 pots, shovels, and basins.

All these vessels, which Ḥiram crafted for King Shlomo, for the House
46 of the LORD, were of burnished bronze. The king had them cast in clay
47 molds on the Jordan plain between Sukkot and Tzartan. Due to their sheer
abundance, Shlomo left all the vessels out of account; the weight of the
bronze was not determined.

48 Shlomo made all the vessels for the House of the LORD: the altar was of
49 gold, and the table for the showbread was of gold. The candelabra – five
on the right and five on the left, in front of the Inner Sanctuary – were of
50 solid gold; the flowers, the lamps, and the tongs were all of gold. The bowls,
shears, basins, spoons, and firepans were of solid gold. The hinges of the
doors to the inner House, to the Holy of Holies, and of the doors of the
House to the Sanctuary, were of gold.

51 When all the work that King Shlomo did for the House of the LORD was
finished, Shlomo brought what David his father had dedicated – the silver,
the gold, and the vessels[20] – and placed them in the treasury of the House
of the LORD.

8 1 Then Shlomo assembled the elders of Israel – all the heads of the tribes,
the ancestral leaders of the Israelites – before King Shlomo in Jerusalem,
to bring up the Ark of the LORD's Covenant from the City of David, Zion.
2 All the men of Israel assembled before King Shlomo in the month of
3 Etanim,[21] the seventh month, at the festival.[22] When all the elders of Israel
4 had arrived, the priests lifted up the Ark and brought up the Ark of the
LORD, the Tent of Meeting, and all the sacred vessels in the Tent. While
5 the priests and the Levites brought them up, King Shlomo and the whole
community of Israel, who had met him before the Ark, sacrificed sheep
and oxen – far too many to number or count.

6 The priests brought the Ark of the LORD's Covenant to its place – to the
House's Inner Sanctuary, the Holy of Holies, to under the shade of the
7 wings of the cherubim. For the wings of the cherubim were spread over
the place of the Ark so that the cherubim sheltered the Ark and its poles
8 from above. The poles extended so that the ends of the poles were visible
from the Holy Place[23] in front of the Inner Sanctuary, but they could not
9 be seen from the outside, and they are there to this day. The Ark contained
nothing but the two stone tablets Moshe placed there at Ḥorev when the
LORD made a covenant with the Israelites as they left the land of Egypt.[24]

20 | See II Samuel 8:9–12.

21 | The seventh month, known by Jews as Tishrei after the Babylonian exile.

22 | The Festival of Tabernacles; cf. Leviticus 23:34.

23 | The main Sanctuary.

24 | See Deuteronomy 10:1–5.

10 And as the priests left the Holy Place, a cloud filled the House of the Lord;
11 the priests could not stand and serve because of the cloud, for the glory of
12 the Lord had filled the House of the Lord. Then Shlomo declared:
"The Lord promised that He would dwell in deep mist;
13 I have now built You an exalted House,
a permanent place for Your abode."

14 And the king turned his face and blessed the whole assembly of Israel,
while the whole assembly of Israel stood.

15 "Blessed is the Lord, God of Israel," he said, "who made a promise to my
father David with His own mouth and has now fulfilled it with His own
hand, saying:

16 "From the day I brought My people, Israel, out of Egypt, I never chose a
city from among all the tribes of Israel, to build a House where My name
would be; but I chose David to be over My people Israel.[25]

17 "My father David had his heart set on building a House for the name of
18 the Lord, God of Israel. But the Lord said to my father David: Though
you have set your heart on building a House for My name, and though
19 you have set your heart well, you will not be the one to build the House.
But your son, the issue of your own loins – he will be the one to build the
House for My name.[26]

20 "The Lord has fulfilled the promise He made; I have risen in my father's
stead, and I sit upon Israel's throne, as the Lord promised. I have built
21 the House for the name of the Lord, God of Israel. And there I have set a
place for the Ark, which contains the covenant that the Lord made with
our ancestors when He brought them out of the land of Egypt."

22 Shlomo stood before the Altar of the Lord, facing the whole assembly of
Israel, and he raised his palms heavenward.

23 "O Lord, God of Israel," he cried,
"there is no God like You in the heavens above or the earth below.
O keeper of the covenant and the love for Your servants, who walk before
You with all their heart,
24 You kept what You promised to my father David; You made him a promise
with Your own mouth, and You have fulfilled it with Your own hand this
very day.
25 Now, O Lord, God of Israel, keep the promise You made to Your servant
David, my father, saying, 'No one of your lineage shall be cut off from
sitting on the throne of Israel before Me, but only if your sons keep to their
path before Me as you walked before Me.'
26 Now, O God of Israel, let the promise You made to Your servant David,
my father, be realized.

25 | See II Samuel 7:6–7.
26 | See II Samuel 7:12–13.

27 For will God truly dwell on earth? If the heavens – the highest heavens – cannot contain You, how will this House that I have built?

28 Yet – turn to the prayer of Your servant, O LORD my God, and to his plea;
listen to the cry and the prayer your servant offers before you today.

29 Let Your eyes be open to this House, night and day;
to the place of which You said, 'There, My name will be.'
Listen to the prayer Your servant offers at this place.

30 Listen to the plea of Your servant; of Your people, Israel, who pray at this place;
listen from Your heavenly abode; listen and forgive.

31 Should a person wrong another who then imposes an oath upon him and
he thus becomes cursed, and he comes before Your altar in this House with
32 the curse – listen from the heavens, take action, and judge Your servant.
Condemn the wicked by bringing his own ways upon his own head, and
vindicate the righteous by rewarding him as befits his righteousness.

33 "Should Your people Israel be defeated by an enemy because they have
sinned against You, and they come back to You, acknowledging Your name
34 in prayer and pleading to You in this House – listen from the heavens,
forgive the sin of Your people Israel, and bring them back to the land You
gave to their ancestors.

35 "When the heavens are stopped up and there is no rain because they have
sinned against You, and they pray at this place and acknowledge Your name,
36 repenting from their sins so that You will answer them – listen from the
heavens and forgive the sin of Your servants and Your people Israel, having
taught them the proper path to follow. Shower rain upon the land You gave
to Your people as their share.

37 "Should there be famine in the land; should there be sickness; should
there be blight, mildew, locust, or larvae; should the enemy harass them
38 in the land within their own gates – oh, any suffering, or any disease! – and
anyone from Your people, Israel, offers any prayer or any plea, moved by the
39 suffering of his own heart, and raises his palms toward this House – listen
from Your heavenly abode, forgive, and take action. Treat each person
according to his ways, for You know his heart – for You alone know the
40 hearts of all humanity – so that they will revere You for as long as they live
upon the soil that You gave to our ancestors.

41 "Should the foreigner, too, not of Your people Israel, come from a distant
42 land for the sake of Your name, having heard of Your great name and Your
mighty hand and Your outstretched arm; should he come and pray at this
43 House, listen from Your heavenly abode and fulfill all that the foreigner
calls out to You. For then all the peoples of the land will know Your name
and revere you as Your people Israel does; for then they will know that it
is Your name that is proclaimed over this House.

44 "Should Your people go out to war against their enemy, wherever You
might send them, and they pray to the LORD toward the city You have
45 chosen and the House I built for Your name, listen from the heavens to
their prayer and plea, and uphold their cause.

46 "Should they sin against You – for there is no person who does not sin –
and You rage against them and deliver them over to their enemy, who drags
47 them off as captives to the enemy's land, whether far or near, but they take it
to heart in the land where they are being held captive, and they repent and
offer pleas to You in the land of their captors, declaring, 'We have sinned
48 and offended and done evil,' and they come back to You with all their heart
and all their soul in the land of their enemy captors, and they pray to You,
toward their own land which You gave to their ancestors, to the city that You
49 chose and the House I built for Your name, listen from Your heavenly abode
50 to their prayer and their plea, and uphold their cause. Forgive Your people
who sinned against You, and all the transgressions they committed against
You; grant them mercy before their captors so that they will have mercy
51 on them. For they are Your people and Your share, whom You brought out
from Egypt, from the midst of the iron crucible.[27]

52 "Let Your eyes be open to the plea of Your servant and the plea of Your
53 people Israel; listen to them whenever they call out to You. For You set
them apart from all the other peoples of the land as Your own share,[28]
as You promised through Moshe, Your servant, when You brought our
ancestors out of Egypt, O LORD GOD."

54 When Shlomo had finished offering the whole of this prayer and plea to
the LORD, he rose from before the Altar of the LORD, where he had been
55 kneeling on his knees with his palms raised heavenward. And he stood and
blessed the whole assembly of Israel in a loud voice:

56 "Blessed is the LORD, who has granted rest to His people Israel, fulfilling
all His promises," he said. "Not one thing is unfulfilled from all the good
57 promises He made through Moshe, His servant. May the LORD our God
be with us as He was with our ancestors; may He never leave us or abandon
58 us. May He sway our hearts toward Him so that we follow in all His ways
and keep His commandments, laws and rulings that He commanded our
59 ancestors. May these words of mine, which I have pleaded before the LORD,
stay close to the LORD our God day and night, to uphold the cause of His
60 servant and the cause of His people Israel as each day's needs arise – so
that all the peoples of the land will know that the LORD is God, and there
61 is no other. May your hearts be fully with the LORD our God, following
His laws and keeping His commandments, as today."

62 And the king, together with all of Israel, offered sacrifices before the LORD;
63 Shlomo sacrificed the peace sacrifices he offered to the LORD – twenty-two

27 | Cf. Deuteronomy 4:20; Jeremiah 11:4.

28 | Cf. Leviticus 20:24, 26.

thousand cattle and one hundred twenty thousand sheep – and thus the
64 king and all of Israel dedicated the House of the LORD. On that day, the
king consecrated the center of the courtyard in front of the House of
the LORD, for it was there that he prepared the burnt offering, the grain
offering, and the fats of the peace offerings. The bronze altar before the
LORD was too small to contain the burnt offering, the grain offering, and
the fats of the peace offerings.

65 At that same time, Shlomo celebrated the festival[29] together with all of
Israel; they were a great assembly, from Levo Ḥamat to the Wadi of Egypt,[30]
before the LORD our God for seven days and seven days more – fourteen
66 days in all.[31] On the eighth day[32] he sent the people off, and they blessed
the king; they went back to their homes joyful and glad at heart for all
the goodness the LORD had shown to David, His servant, and Israel, His
people.

9 1 When Shlomo had finished building the House of the LORD and the
2 king's own house, and fulfilled every desire he wished to fulfill, the LORD
appeared to Shlomo a second time as He had appeared to him at Givon.[33]
3 And the LORD said to him, "I have listened to the prayer and the plea that
you offered before Me. I have consecrated this House, which you built
to set My name there forever; My eyes and My heart will be there for all
time.

4 "As for you – if you walk before Me as your father David did, wholeheartedly and sincerely fulfilling all I have commanded you, and if you
5 keep My laws and My rulings, then I will establish your royal throne over
Israel forever, as I promised your father David: No one of your lineage
6 will be cut off from the throne of Israel. But if you and your sons dare
turn away from Me and do not keep the commandments and laws I
7 set before you, and serve other gods and worship them, then I will cut
Israel off from the face of the land that I gave them, and I will cast away
from My presence the House I have sanctified for My name; and Israel
will become but a proverb and a byword among all the nations. And
8 whoever passes by this once-exalted House will reel and hiss[34] and say,
9 'Why did the LORD do such a thing to this land and this House?' and
they will answer, 'Because they left the LORD, their God, who brought
heir ancestors out of the land of Egypt, and they embraced other gods
and worshipped them and served them. For this the LORD brought all
this evil upon them.'"

29 | See note on verse 2.

30 | The northern and southern borders of the country.

31 | One week for the dedication of the altar and one week for the Festival of Tabernacles; cf. II Chronicles 7:9.

32 | Cf. II Chronicles 7:9–10.

33 | See 3:4–15.

34 | An expression of dismay.

10 This came to pass at the end of the twenty years that Shlomo had spent
building the two houses, the House of the Lord and the king's own
11 house. Ḥiram, king of Tyre, had supplied Shlomo with all the cedarwood,
cypress wood, and gold that he required, and in return, King Shlomo gave
12 Ḥiram twenty towns in the region of Galil. But when Ḥiram set out from
Tyre to survey the towns that Shlomo had given him, they did not please
13 him. "What kind of towns have you given me, my brother?" he asked, and
14 named them the land of Kavul,[35] as they are called to this day. Nonetheless,
Ḥiram sent the king one hundred twenty talents of gold.[36]

15 For these purposes, King Shlomo imposed forced labor: to build the
House of the Lord and his own house, the Milo,[37] the wall of Jerusalem,
16 Ḥatzor, Megiddo, and Gezer. Pharaoh, king of Egypt, had marched up
and captured Gezer – he burned it with fire and killed the Canaanite
inhabitants of the city – and he gave it as a wedding gift to his daughter,
17 18 Shlomo's wife. Shlomo built Gezer, lower Beit Ḥoron, Baalat, and Tadmor
19 in the wilderness in the region, as well as all of Shlomo's store towns,
chariot towns, and cavalry towns – all that Shlomo desired to build in
20 Jerusalem, Lebanon, and throughout the land of his dominion. As for all
the people who remained among the Amorites, the Hittites, the Perizzites,
21 the Hivites, and the Jebusites, who were not of the Israelites – their
remaining descendants in the land, whom the Israelites had been unable to
22 destroy – Shlomo drafted them for forced labor to this day. Shlomo never
reduced the Israelites to slavery, for they were military men, his servants,
23 ministers, officials, and the officers of his chariots and cavalry. These were
the ministers of prefects in charge of Shlomo's work: five hundred fifty
supervised the people who executed the work.

24 As soon as Pharaoh's daughter went up from the City of David to the palace
he had built for her, he built the Milo.[38]

25 Three times a year, Shlomo would offer up burnt offerings and peace
offerings on the altar he had built for the Lord, and he would burn incense
upon it before the Lord; in this way he made the House complete.

26 Shlomo built a fleet at Etzyon Gever, which is by Elot[39] on the shore of
27 the Red Sea, in the land of Edom. Ḥiram sent his servants with the fleet,
28 skilled seamen familiar with the sea, to be with Shlomo's servants, and
they traveled to Ofir.[40] There they collected gold – four hundred twenty
talents – and brought it to King Shlomo.

---

35 | Perhaps deriving from the Phoenician, meaning "worthless."

36 | One talent is the equivalent of three thousand shekel and weighs about 34 kilograms.

37 | Apparently a fortification.

38 | See note on verse 15.

39 | Eilat.

40 | An unknown location, sometimes identified with ports or regions in East Africa or the Arabian Peninsula.

10 1 Now the Queen of Sheba[41] had been hearing of Shlomo's fame through
2 the name of the LORD, and she came to test him with riddles. She came to
Jerusalem with a vast entourage: with camels bearing spices, an immense
wealth of gold, and precious stones. She came to Shlomo and told him
3 all that she had in mind. Shlomo addressed all of her words; there was
nothing that remained hidden from the king, and there was nothing he
4 failed to address. When the Queen of Sheba saw all of Shlomo's wisdom
5 and the House he had built, and the fare of his table and how his subjects
were seated and his servants' attendance and attire, and his cupbearers
and the burnt offerings he offered up in the House of the LORD, she was
left breathless.

6 "What I heard in my land about your deeds and your wisdom was true!"
7 she said to the king. "I never believed it until I came and saw it with my own
eyes – and I was not told even the half of it! Your wisdom and wealth far
8 exceeds the rumors I heard. How fortunate are your men – how fortunate
are these attendants of yours, who are always in your presence, hearing
9 your wisdom. Blessed be the LORD your God, who delighted in you and set
you upon the throne of Israel; because of the LORD's eternal love of Israel,
He has appointed you as king to uphold justice and righteousness."

10 She gave the king one hundred twenty talents of gold and a wealth of
spices and precious stones; never again has there been a wealth of spices
11 as vast as the Queen of Sheba's gift to King Shlomo – Hiram's fleet, which
conveyed gold from Ofir, also brought a vast wealth of sandalwood and
12 precious stones. The king had the sandalwood made into banisters for the
House of the LORD and the royal house, and harps and lyres for the singers;
never again has such a wealth of sandalwood arrived, or even been seen, to
13 this day. He gave the Queen of Sheba all that she desired, besides what he
had already bestowed upon her with the generous hand of King Shlomo.
Then, together with her servants, she took her leave and journeyed back
to her own land.

14 The weight of gold that Shlomo received in a single year was 666 talents,
15 beside what came from traveling merchants and the business of traders,
16 all the Arabian kings, and the governors of the land. King Shlomo made
two hundred shields of beaten gold – six hundred pieces of gold went into
17 each shield – and three hundred bucklers of beaten gold – three mina[42] of
gold went into each buckler – and the king placed them in the House of the
Lebanon Forest.[43]

18 The king made an enormous ivory throne and overlaid it with the finest
19 gold. Six steps led up to the throne; the back of the throne was rounded at
the top, and there were armrests on both sides of the seat. Two lions were

41 | Sabea, in the southwestern Arabian Peninsula.

42 | One mina is the equivalent of fifty shekel and weighs 570 grams.

43 | See note on 7:2.

20 positioned by the armrests, and twelve lions stood there on the six steps
on either side. Nothing like it was ever made in any other kingdom.

21 All of the king's drinking vessels were of gold, and all the utensils of the
House of the Lebanon Forest were of solid gold. There was no silver; it
22 counted for nothing in the days of Shlomo. For the king had a Tarshish[44]
fleet at sea with Hiram's fleet; every three years, the Tarshish fleet would
come back loaded with gold and silver, ivory, monkeys, and peacocks.

23 King Shlomo surpassed all the kings of the earth in wealth and in wisdom;
24 from all over the world they sought audience with Shlomo to hear the
25 wisdom that God had granted him. And each one brought his tribute:
vessels of silver and vessels of gold, garments, weapons, spices, horses, and
mules, according to the yearly due.

26 Shlomo amassed chariots and horsemen; he had one thousand four
hundred chariots and twelve thousand horsemen. He stationed them in
27 the chariot towns and with the king in Jerusalem. The king made silver
as common in Jerusalem as stones, while cedars were as common as
28 sycamores in the lowlands. Shlomo's horses were procured from Egypt
and Keveh; the king's traders would import them from Keveh at a set price.
29 The cost of importing a chariot from Egypt was six hundred pieces of silver,
while a horse was one hundred fifty; these, in turn, were exported to all
the kings of the Hittites and all the kings of Aram.

11 1 King Shlomo loved many foreign women besides the daughter of
Pharaoh – Moabite women, Amonite women, Edomite women, Sidonian
2 women, Hittite women – from the nations of which the Lord had warned
the Israelites: "You must not join with them, nor must they join with you,
for they will turn your hearts astray after their own gods."[45] Shlomo clung
3 to these in love. He had seven hundred wives of royal rank and three
4 hundred concubines, and his wives turned his heart astray.[46] By the time
Shlomo grew old, his wives had turned his heart to other gods, and his
heart was not entirely with the Lord, his God, as his father David's heart
5 had been. Shlomo went after Ashtoret, the god of the Sidonians, and after
6 Milkom, the abomination of the Amonites. Shlomo did what was evil
in the Lord's sight and was not fully with the Lord, as his father David
was.

7 It was then that Shlomo built a high shrine to Kemosh, the abomination of
Moav, on the hill overlooking Jerusalem,[47] and to Molekh, the abomination
8 of the Amonites. He did the same for all his foreign wives, who offered
9 incense and sacrifices to their gods. Then the Lord raged against Shlomo,

44 | Referring either to the destination of the fleet (perhaps Tarsus in Asia Minor), or to a type of ship.

45 | See Deuteronomy 7:3–4.

46 | Cf. Deuteronomy 17:17.

47 | The Mount of Olives.

for his heart had turned away from the LORD, God of Israel, who had
10 appeared to him twice[48] and commanded him about this very matter – not
to follow after other gods. But he failed to keep the LORD's command.

11 And the LORD said to Shlomo, "Because this has been your will, and you
failed to keep My covenant and My laws, which I commanded you – I will
surely tear the kingdom away from you, and I will give it to your servant.
12 But for the sake of your father David, I will not do this in your own lifetime;
13 I will tear it away from the hand of your son. And even so, I will not tear the
whole kingdom away; I will grant a single tribe to your son for the sake of
My servant David and for the sake of Jerusalem, which I have chosen."

14 The LORD raised up an adversary for Shlomo: Hadad the Edomite, who
15 was of the royal line of Edom. When David had been in Edom, Yoav had
gone up to bury the slain, for he had struck down every male in Edom
16 during the six months that Yoav and all of Israel had stayed there, until
17 they had wiped out every last male in Edom. But Hadad, together with
some Edomite men who were his father's servants, had fled toward Egypt;
18 Hadad had been a young boy. They left Midyan and reached Paran, taking
men with them from Paran, and when they reached Egypt, Pharaoh, king
of Egypt, provided him with a house, arranged for his provisions, and
19 granted him land. Hadad found great favor with Pharaoh, and he gave him
20 his wife's sister in marriage: the sister of Taḥpenes, the queen mother. The
sister of Taḥpenes bore him a son, Genuvat, and Taḥpenes weaned him in
Pharaoh's palace; Genuvat lived in Pharaoh's palace with Pharaoh's own
21 sons. When Hadad heard in Egypt that David slept with his ancestors, and
that Yoav, the army commander, had died, Hadad said to Pharaoh, "Give
me leave, and I will go to my own land."

22 "But what do you lack here with me?" Pharaoh asked him. "Why do you
ask to go back to your own land?"

"Nothing," he said, "but please, permit me to leave."

23 And God raised up Rezon son of Elyada as his adversary. He had fled from
24 King Hadadezer of Tzova, his master, when David massacred them. He
rallied men to him and became the troop leader. They went to Damascus
25 and settled there and established rule in Damascus. He was an adversary
to Israel all the days of Shlomo beyond the trouble Hadad wrought; he
was hostile toward Israel and reigned over Aram.

26 Yorovam son of Nevat was an Efraimite from Tzereda; his mother was a
widow by the name of Tzerua. He was a servant of Shlomo, but he raised
27 his hand against the king. This is how he came to raise his hand against the
king: Shlomo built the Milo[49] to repair a breach in the City of David, his
28 father. Yorovam was a capable man, and when Shlomo saw how the young

48 | See 3:5, 9:2.

49 | See note on 9:15.

man performed his work, he appointed him over all the forced labor of
the House of Yosef.

29 Around that time, Yorovam was leaving Jerusalem when Aḥiya the
Shilonite, the prophet, met him on the way. He was dressed in a new robe,
30 and the two of them were alone in the field. Aḥiya grasped hold of the new
robe he wore and tore it into twelve pieces.

31 "Take ten of the pieces," he said to Yorovam, "for thus says the Lord, God
of Israel: I am about to tear the kingdom from the hand of Shlomo, and
32 I will give ten tribes over to you. A single tribe will be his for the sake of
my servant David and for the sake of Jerusalem, the city I have chosen out
33 of all the tribes of Israel. For they have abandoned Me and bowed down
to Ashtoret, god of the Sidonians, and to Kemosh, god of Moav, and to
Milkom, god of the Amonites; they have failed to follow in My path, doing
what is right in My eyes, keeping My laws and My rulings like David, his
father.

34 "But I will not take the whole kingdom from his hands; I will let him
remain as ruler for as long as he lives, for the sake of My servant David,
35 whom I chose – he kept My commandments and laws. I will take the
kingship from the hand of his son and give it to you – over the ten tribes.
36 I will give a single tribe to his son, so there will always be a lamp for My
servant David's sake before Me in Jerusalem, the city where I chose to
establish My name.

37 "But it is you that I will take to reign over all you desire; you will become
38 king over Israel. If you obey all that I command you and follow in My path
and do what is right in My eyes, keeping My laws and My commandments
as My servant David did – then I will be with you, and I will build you
a dynasty as lasting as I built for My servant David, and I will give Israel
39 over to you. And I will humble David's descendants for this purpose, but
not forever."

40 Shlomo sought to put Yorovam to death, but Yorovam fled straight to
Egypt, to King Shishak of Egypt, and he remained in Egypt until Shlomo's
death.

41 As for the rest of Shlomo's history, and all his deeds, and his wisdom – they
42 are recorded in the Book of the History of Shlomo. The length of Shlomo's
43 reign in Jerusalem, over all of Israel, was forty years. And Shlomo slept
with his ancestors and was buried in the City of David, his father. And his
son Reḥavam reigned in his place.

12 1 Reḥavam went to Shekhem, for all of Israel had come to Shekhem for his
2 coronation. Yorovam son of Nevat heard this when he was still in Egypt,
3 for he had escaped from King Shlomo and settled in Egypt. They sent for
and summoned him, and Yorovam came with the whole assembly of Israel,
who made the following speech to Reḥavam:

4 "Your father made our yoke heavy – now, relieve the heavy workload and the harsh yoke your father placed upon us, and we will serve you."

5 "Leave for three days," he said to them, "and then come back to me," and the people left.

6 King Reḥavam consulted with the elders who had served his father Shlomo during his lifetime. "How would you advise to answer this people's request?" he said.

7 "If you become this people's servant today," they told him, "and serve them and respond to them by speaking kind words, then they will become your servants forever."

8 But he rejected the advice that the elders gave him and consulted with the
9 youngsters who had grown up with him, who now served him. "What do
you advise?" he asked them. "How should we answer this people's request? They told me, 'Relieve the yoke your father placed upon us.'"

10 The youngsters who had grown up with him said, "This is what you should
say to this people, who told you, 'Your father made our yoke heavy – you
should relieve us.' Tell them this: 'My little finger is thicker than my father's
11 loins. Now, my father burdened you with a heavy yoke, but I will increase
your yoke; my father flogged you with whips, but I will flog you with
scorpions.'"

12 Yorovam and all the people came to Reḥavam on the third day, just as
13 the king had told them, saying, "Come back to me on the third day." The
king answered the people harshly, rejecting the advice that the elders had
14 given him. He answered them as the youngsters had advised, saying, "My
father burdened you with a heavy yoke, but I will increase your yoke. My
15 father flogged you with whips, but I will flog you with scorpions!" The king
would not listen to the people, for it was part of the Lord's plan to fulfill
the promise that the Lord had made to Yorovam son of Nevat through
Aḥiya the Shilonite.

16 When all Israel saw that the king would not listen to them, the people retorted to the king,

"We have no part in David
 nor any share in the son of Yishai!
To your tents, O Israel!
 Now look to your own house, O David!"

17 And Israel went back to their tents. But as for the Israelites who lived in the towns of Yehuda, Reḥavam ruled over them.

18 King Reḥavam sent out Adoram, who was in charge of the forced labor,
but all of Israel pelted him with stones, and he died. At that, Reḥavam
19 forced his way onto his chariot, to flee to Jerusalem. And the Israelites
have rebelled against the House of David ever since.

20 When all of Israel heard that Yorovam had returned, they sent and
summoned him to the assembly and made him king over all Israel.
21 Only the tribe of Yehuda followed the House of David. When Reḥavam
reached Jerusalem, he assembled all the House of Yehuda and the tribe of
Binyamin – one hundred eighty thousand elite fighters – to fight against
22 the House of Israel, to restore the kingship to Reḥavam son of Shlomo. But
23 the word of God came to Shemaya, man of God: "Say to Reḥavam son of
Shlomo, king of Yehuda, and to all the House of Yehuda and Binyamin and
24 the rest of the people: Thus says the LORD: Do not advance, and do not fight
with your brothers, the Israelites. Let every man go back home, for it is
through Me that this has come about." And they heeded the word of the
LORD and turned back, following the LORD's word.

25 Yorovam built Shekhem in the Efrayim hills and settled there; later, he left
there and built Penuel.

26 "Now the kingdom will revert to the House of David," Yorovam said to
27 himself. "If this people makes pilgrimage to offer sacrifices in the House
of the LORD in Jerusalem, then the heart of this people might turn back to
their lord – to Reḥavam, king of Yehuda. They might kill me and go back
to Reḥavam, king of Yehuda."

28 So the king took counsel and made two calves of gold. "You have been
making pilgrimage to Jerusalem long enough," he said to them. "Here are
29 your gods, O Israel, who brought you up from the land of Egypt."[50] He
30 placed one in Beit El and set up the other in Dan.[51] This resulted in grave
sin; the people went to worship before the one or before the other in Dan.
31 He made buildings for the high shrines and made priests out of an array
32 of people who were not Levites. And Yorovam established a festival in the
eighth month, on the fifteenth day of the month, similar to the festival[52] in
Yehuda, and he ascended the altar. The sacrifice to the calves he had made
took place in Beit El; he stationed at Beit El the priests he had appointed
33 in the shrines. He ascended the altar that he had made in Beit El on the
fifteenth day of the eighth month – on a date of his own invention – to
establish a festival for the Israelites. And he stepped up to the altar to offer
a sacrifice.

13 1 Just then, a man of God from Yehuda arrived at Beit El at the LORD's
command; Yorovam was standing on the altar about to offer a sacrifice
2 when he called out against the altar with a message from the LORD:

"Altar, O altar," he said, "thus says the LORD: A son will be born to the
House of David, Yoshiyahu by name. Upon you, he will slaughter the
shrine priests who sacrifice upon you; upon you, human bones will be
3 burnt." And he gave a sign that same day, declaring, "This is the sign the

50 | Cf. Exodus 32:4.

51 | Respectively, the southern and northern limits of his realm.

52 | Referring to the Festival of Tabernacles, which took place one month earlier.

Lord has decreed: The altar will suddenly split apart, and the ashes upon it will be spilled."

4 When the king heard the message that the man of God called out against
the altar in Beit El, Yorovam thrust out his hand over the altar, shouting,
"Seize him!" but the hand he thrust against him froze, and he could not
5 draw it back again. And the altar split apart, and the ashes from the altar
spilled – the very sign that the man of God had given at the Lord's
command.

6 "Please!" the king cried out to the man of God. "Entreat the Lord your
God and pray on my behalf that my hand will be restored to me." The
man of God entreated the Lord, and the king's hand was restored to its
usual state.

7 "Come home with me and dine," the king told the man of God, "and I will
give you a gift."

8 "Were you to give me half your house, I would not come with you," the
man of God said to the king. "I will not eat any food nor drink any water
9 in this place. For thus I was charged by the word of the Lord: Do not eat
any food, do not drink any water, and do not retrace the road you have
10 traveled." And he set out on a different road; he did not return by the road
he had taken to Beit El.

11 There was an old prophet who lived in Beit El. His sons came and told him
all about the feats that the man of God had performed that day in Beit El;
they told their father all about the words he had spoken to the king.

12 "By which road did he leave?" their father asked them, and his sons had
noticed the road taken by the man of God who had come from Yehuda.

13 "Saddle the donkey for me," he said to his sons, and they saddled the
14 donkey for him. He mounted it and followed after the man of God, and
he found him sitting beneath a terebinth. "Are you the man of God who
came from Yehuda?" he asked him.

"I am," he said.

15 "Come home with me and have some food," he said to him.

16 "I cannot return with you and come with you," he said, "I will not eat food
17 or drink water with you in this place. For I was told by the word of the
Lord: Do not eat food or drink water there, and do not retrace the road
you have traveled."

18 "I too am a prophet, just like you," he said to him, "and an angel spoke to
me with the word of the Lord, saying: Bring him back with you to your
home, and let him eat food and drink water." But he was lying to him.

19 20 He went back with him and ate food in his house, and drank water. But as
they sat at the table, the word of the Lord came to the prophet who had

21 brought the other back, and he called out to the man of God who had come
from Yehuda, "Thus says the LORD: Because you have violated the word
of the LORD and failed to keep the instructions that the LORD your God
22 charged you with – you came back and ate food and drank water in the
place where He told you: Do not eat food, and do not drink water – your
corpse will not reach the grave of your ancestors."

23 After he had eaten food, and drunk, he saddled the donkey for him – for
24 the prophet he had brought back. He set out, but a lion found him on the
road and killed him. His corpse was left flung down on the road while the
25 donkey stood close by; the lion, too, stood by the corpse. Just then some
people passed by, and they saw the corpse flung down on the road with the
lion standing by the corpse. They reached the town where the old prophet
26 lived and spread word about it. When the prophet who had brought him
back from the road heard about it, he said, "He is the man of God who
violated the word of the LORD. The LORD gave him over to the lion that
27 mauled him to death, fulfilling the word that the LORD spoke to him." And
he told his sons, "Saddle the donkey for me," and they saddled it.

28 He set out and found his corpse flung down on the road, with the donkey
and the lion still standing by the corpse; the lion had not eaten the corpse,
29 nor had it mauled the donkey. The prophet lifted the corpse of the man
of God, placed it on the donkey, and brought it back – it went to the old
30 prophet's town for lament and burial. He placed the corpse in its grave, and
31 they lamented over it: "Alas, my brother!" After he had buried him, he said
to his sons, "When I die, bury me in the grave where the man of God is
32 buried – lay my bones to rest next to his bones. For the word of the LORD
he pronounced against the altar in Beit El, and against all the buildings
of the high shrines in the towns of Shomron, will surely come to pass."

33 Even after this incident, Yorovam did not turn back from his evil ways. He
continued appointing an array of people as the priests of the high shrines;
34 he ordained anyone who so desired as a priest of the high shrines. This
counted as a grave sin for the house of Yorovam – leading to their total
obliteration from the face of the earth.

14 1 2 Around that time, Aviya, Yorovam's son, fell ill. Yorovam said to his wife,
"Set out now and disguise yourself so that no one will know that you are
the wife of Yorovam. Go to Shilo, where the prophet Aḥiya is; he was the
3 one who foretold I would be king over this people. Take ten loaves of bread,
some cakes, and a jar of honey with you, and go to him. He will tell you
what will become of the boy."

4 Yorovam's wife did just that: she set out toward Shilo and reached the
house of Aḥiya. Aḥiyahu could no longer see, for his eyes had dimmed
5 with old age. But the LORD had said to Aḥiyahu, "The wife of Yorovam
will soon come to inquire about her son through you, for he is ill. Thus
and thus you shall speak to her. When she arrives, she will be in disguise."

6 When Aḥiyahu heard the sound of her footsteps approaching the door,
he said:

"Come in, wife of Yorovam. Why are you in disguise? I have a harsh message
7 for you. Go and say to Yorovam, 'Thus says the LORD, God of Israel: I
raised you up from among the people and appointed you ruler over My
8 people Israel. But though I tore the kingdom away from the House of
David and gave it to you, you have not been like My servant David, who
kept My commandments and followed Me with all his heart, doing only
9 what is right in My eyes; you have acted worse than all those before you.
You have made yourself other gods – molten images – to anger Me, while
10 as for Me – you have cast Me behind your back. Therefore, I am about
to bring evil to the house of Yorovam. I will cut off every last male[53] of
Yorovam in Israel, bond and free, and I will burn up the house of Yorovam
11 as a person burns every last trace of dung. Those of Yorovam's who die in
the city will be devoured by dogs, and those who die in the field will be
devoured by the birds of the sky, for the LORD has spoken.'

12 "Now, go straight to your house; as soon as you set foot in the city, the
13 child will die. All of Israel will lament him and bury him, and he alone of
Yorovam will reach his grave, for the LORD, God of Israel, has found good
14 in him alone out of all the house of Yorovam. The LORD will appoint a
king for Himself over Israel, who will wipe out the house of Yorovam this
15 very day – yes, even now. And the LORD will strike Israel like a reed that
swishes in the water. He will uproot Israel from this good soil that He gave
to their ancestors, and He will scatter them beyond the Euphrates because
16 they have made their own sacred trees,[54] angering the LORD. He will hand
Israel over because of the sins that Yorovam committed, and because he
led Israel to sin."

17 Yorovam's wife set out immediately and came to Tirtza. As soon as she
18 reached the threshold of the house, the boy died. All of Israel buried him
and lamented him, just as the LORD had pronounced through His servant,
the prophet Aḥiyahu.

19 As for the rest of Yorovam's history – how he fought and how he reigned – it
20 is recorded in the Book of the History of the Kings of Israel. The length
of Yorovam's reign was twenty-two years. And he slept with his ancestors,
and his son Nadav reigned in his place.

21 Meanwhile, Reḥavam son of Shlomo reigned in Yehuda. Reḥavam was
forty-one years old when he became king, and for seventeen years he
reigned in Jerusalem, the city where the LORD had chosen to establish His

53 | Literally "one who urinates against a wall." This phrase appears also in 16:11, 21:21; II Kings 9:8; and I Samuel, chapter 25.

54 | Hebrew *asherim*: trees, wooden posts, or images representing the Canaanite fertility goddess Ashera.

name out of all the tribes of Israel. His mother's name was Naama the
Amonite.

22 Yehuda did what was evil in the eyes of the Lord; the sins they committed
23 enraged Him more than all that their ancestors had ever done. They, too,
built their own high shrines and worship pillars and sacred trees on every
24 high hill and under every shady tree; there were even male ritual prostitutes
in the land. They committed all the horrors of the nations that the Lord
had dispossessed before the Israelites.

25 In the fifth year of Reḥavam's reign, King Shishak of Egypt launched an
26 attack on Jerusalem. He seized the treasures of the House of the Lord and
the treasures of the royal palace; he seized everything. He even seized all
27 the golden shields that Shlomo had made.[55] King Reḥavam had bronze
shields made in their place and entrusted them to the chief sentry, who
28 guarded the entrance of the palace. Whenever the king went to the House
of the Lord, the sentry would carry them and then return them to the
sentry armory.

29 As for the rest of Reḥavam's history and all his deeds – they are recorded
30 in the Book of the History of the Kings of Yehuda. There was ongoing war
31 between Reḥavam and Yorovam. And Reḥavam slept with his ancestors
and was buried with his ancestors in the City of David. His mother's name
was Naama the Amonite, and his son Aviyam reigned in his place.

15 1 In the eighteenth year of King Yorovam son of Nevat, Aviyam became king
2 over Yehuda. For three years he reigned in Jerusalem, and his mother's
3 name was Maakha daughter of Avishalom. He followed in all the sinful
ways his father had practiced before him, and his heart was not fully with
4 the Lord his God as his ancestor David's heart had been. Yet for the
sake of David, the Lord his God granted him a lamp[56] in Jerusalem by
5 establishing his son after him, and by upholding Jerusalem. For David had
done what was right in the eyes of the Lord and never turned away from
all He commanded him throughout his life – except in the matter of Uriya
the Hittite.[57]

6 Hostility that had begun between Reḥavam and Yorovam continued
7 throughout his life. As for the rest of Aviyam's history and all his
deeds – they are recorded in the Book of the History of the Kings of
8 Yehuda. Hostility continued between Aviyam and Yorovam. And Aviyam
slept with his ancestors and was buried in the City of David. And his son
Asa reigned in his place.

9 In the twentieth year of King Yorovam of Israel, Asa became king over
10 Yehuda. For forty-one years he reigned in Jerusalem, and his mother's

55 | See 10:17.

56 | Cf. 11:36.

57 | See II Samuel 11:15–17.

11 name was Maakha daughter of Avishalom. Asa did what was right in the
12 eyes of the LORD like his ancestor David. He banished the male ritual
prostitutes from the land, and he removed all the idols that his ancestors
13 had made. He even deposed his mother Maakha from the position of queen
mother because she had made a monstrous image for Ashera;[58] Asa cut
14 down her monstrous image and burned it by the Kidron Valley. Though the
high shrines were not removed, Asa's heart was fully with the LORD all the
15 days of his life. He brought his father's sacred items and his own[59] sacred
items into the House of the LORD: silver, gold, and vessels.

16 There was ongoing war between Asa and Basha, king of Israel, all their
17 days. Basha, king of Israel, advanced against Yehuda and fortified Rama to
18 prevent Asa, king of Yehuda, from marching out into battle. So Asa took
all the silver and gold that remained in the treasury of the House of the
LORD and the treasury of the royal palace, and entrusted it to his officials.
Then King Asa sent them to Ben Hadad son of Tavrimon son of Ḥezyon,
the king of Aram, who resided in Damascus, with this message:
19 "There is an alliance between me and you, between my father and your
father. Look, I have sent you an incentive of silver and gold; go, break your
alliance with Basha, king of Israel, so that he will withdraw from me."

20 Ben Hadad complied with King Asa and sent his military officers against
the towns of Israel; he attacked Iyon, Dan, Avel Beit Maakha, all of Kinerot,
21 and all the region of Naftali. When Basha heard, he ceased construction in
22 Rama and remained in Tirtza. Then King Asa rallied all of Yehuda – no one
was exempt – and they seized the stones and wood Basha had been using
to build up Rama, and with them, King Asa fortified Geva of Binyamin
and Mitzpa.

23 As for the rest of Asa's history and all his exploits and all his deeds and
the towns he built – they are recorded in the Book of the History of the
Kings of Yehuda. In his old age, however, he suffered from a foot disease.
24 And Asa slept with his ancestors and was buried with his ancestors in the
City of David his father. And his son Yehoshafat reigned in his place.

25 Meanwhile, Nadav son of Yorovam became king over Israel in the second
26 year of Asa, king of Yehuda. He reigned over Israel for two years. He did
what was evil in the eyes of the LORD and followed in his father's ways;
27 with his sin he led Israel to sin. Then Basha son of Aḥiya, of the house of
Yissakhar, formed a conspiracy against him; Basha struck him down in
Gibeton of the Philistines while Nadav and all of Israel were besieging
28 Gibeton. Basha killed him in the third year of King Asa of Yehuda, and he
29 reigned in his place. When he became king, he struck down all the house
of Yorovam – he left not a single soul to Yorovam – until he had destroyed
it, fulfilling the LORD's word that He had pronounced through His servant

58 | See note on 14:15.

59 | See II Chronicles 15:18, as well as Targum and Radak here.

30 Aḥiya the Shilonite. This was on account of the sins that Yorovam had
committed, through which he led Israel to sin; he had provoked the LORD,
God of Israel, to anger.

31 As for the rest of Nadav's history and all his deeds – they are recorded in
32 the Book of the History of the Kings of Israel. There was ongoing hostility
between Asa and Basha, king of Israel, all their days.

33 In the third year of Asa, king of Yehuda, Basha son of Aḥiya became king
34 over all Israel in Tirtza for twenty-four years. He did what was evil in the
eyes of the LORD, and he followed in Yorovam's ways; through his sin he
led Israel to sin.

16 1 The word of the LORD came to Yehu son of Ḥanani concerning Basha:
2 "Though I raised you up from the dust and appointed you ruler over My
people Israel, you followed in Yorovam's ways and led My people Israel to
3 sin, angering Me with their sins. Therefore I am about to burn up every
last trace of Basha and his house; I will make your house like the house of
4 Yorovam son of Nevat. Those of Basha who die in the city will be devoured
by dogs, and those of his who die in the field will be devoured by the birds
of the sky."

5 As for the rest of Basha's history and his deeds and his exploits – they are
6 recorded in the Book of the History of the Kings of Israel. And Basha slept
with his ancestors, and he was buried in Tirtza. And his son Ela reigned
7 in his place. But through the prophet Yehu son of Ḥanani, the word of
the LORD was against Basha and his house for all the evil he had done in
the eyes of the LORD, angering Him with his deeds: for striking down the
house of Yorovam but acting just like them.

8 In the twenty-sixth year of Asa, king of Yehuda, Ela son of Basha became
9 king over Israel in Tirtza for two years. His servant Zimri, commander of
half the chariotry, formed a conspiracy against him. While he was in Tirtza,
drinking himself into a stupor in the house of Artza, who was in charge of
10 the palace at Tirtza, Zimri entered, struck him down, and killed him. It was
the twenty-seventh year of Asa, king of Yehuda, when he became king in
11 his place. As soon as he became king and took the throne, he struck down
all the house of Basha, not leaving a single male of his kin or his friends.
12 Zimri wiped out all the house of Basha, fulfilling the LORD's word that He
13 had promised to Basha through the prophet Yehu. This was on account of
all of Basha's sins and the sins of his son Ela; they sinned and led Israel to
14 sin, angering the LORD, God of Israel, with their worthless idols. As for
the rest of Ela's history and all his deeds – they are recorded in the Book
of the History of the Kings of Israel.

15 In the twenty-seventh year of Asa, king of Yehuda, Zimri became king
in Tirtza for seven days while the troops were encamped at Gibeton of
16 the Philistines. When the encamped troops heard, "Zimri has formed a

conspiracy and assassinated the king," all of Israel made Omri, the army
17 commander, king over Israel that very day in the camp. Then Omri marched
18 up from Gibeton, together with all Israel, and besieged Tirtza. When Zimri
saw that the city had been captured, he went into the citadel of the royal
19 palace, set the palace on fire over himself, and died on account of the sins
he had sinned, doing what was evil in the eyes of the LORD. He followed
in the ways of Yorovam and the sin he had committed, which led Israel to
20 sin. As for the rest of Zimri's history and the conspiracy he formed – they
are recorded in the Book of the History of the Kings of Israel.

21 Then the people of Israel were divided into factions; half the people
supported Tivni son of Ginat, to make him king, while the other half
22 supported Omri. The people who supported Omri overpowered the
people who supported Tivni son of Ginat; Tivni died, and Omri became
king.

23 In the thirty-first year of King Asa of Yehuda, Omri became king over Israel
24 for twelve years; he reigned in Tirtza for six years. Then he purchased
Mount Shomron from Shemer for two talents of silver. He built up the hill
25 and named the city Shomron, after Shemer, the owner of the hill. Omri
did what was evil in the eyes of the LORD; he was worse than all who
26 came before him. He followed in all the ways of Yorovam son of Nevat
and his sins, leading Israel to sin, angering the LORD, God of Israel, with
27 their worthless idols. As for the rest of Omri's history, his deeds, and his
exploits – they are recorded in the Book of the History of the Kings of
28 Israel. And Omri slept with his ancestors and was buried in Shomron. And
his son Aḥav reigned in his place.

29 Aḥav son of Omri became king of Israel in the thirty-eighth year of Asa,
king of Yehuda. Aḥav son of Omri ruled over Israel in Shomron for twenty-
30 two years. Aḥav son of Omri did what was evil in the eyes of the LORD,
31 more than all who came before him. Following in the footsteps of Yorovam
son of Nevat was the slightest of his sins; he married Izevel, daughter of
King Etbaal of the Sidonians, and went and served Baal[60] and worshipped
32 him. He erected an altar for Baal in the temple of Baal he built in Shomron.
33 And Aḥav made a sacred tree; he did more to anger the LORD, God of Israel,
than any of the kings of Israel before him.

34 In his time, Ḥiel of Beit El rebuilt Yeriḥo; he lay down his firstborn, Aviram,
with its foundations, and with Seguv, his youngest, he set its gates, fulfilling
the word of the LORD that He had pronounced through Yehoshua son of
Nun.[61]

17 1 Eliyahu the Tishbite, from the people of Gilad, said to Aḥav, "By the life of
the LORD, God of Israel, whom I serve – there will be no dew or rain these
years, except by my word."

60 | A Canaanite storm god.

61 | See Joshua 6:26.

2 3 Then the word of the Lord came to him: "Get away from here; turn and
make your way to the east and hide in the Kerit Stream, which is east of
4 the Jordan. You will be able to drink from the stream, and I have bid the
ravens to provide you with sustenance there."

5 He went and did as the Lord told him; he went and stayed in the Kerit
6 Stream, which faces the Jordan. The ravens brought him bread and meat
each morning and bread and meat each evening, and he drank from the
7 stream. But after some time, the stream dried up because no rain fell in
8 9 the land. And the word of the Lord came to him: "Go straight to Tzarfat
of Sidon and stay there; I have bid a certain widow to provide you with
10 sustenance there." He went straight to Tzarfat, and as he reached the
entrance of the town, there was a widow gathering wood, and he called out
to her. "Please," he said, "fetch a little water in a vessel for me to drink."

11 As she was fetching it, he called to her and added, "Please bring a piece of
bread along for me."

12 "By the life of the Lord your God," she said, "I have nothing baked; just a
handful of flour in the jar and a little oil in the jug. Here I am, gathering a
few sticks so I can go and prepare it for my son and me; we will eat it, and
then we will die."

13 "Do not fear," Eliyahu said to her. "Do as you say, but first make me a little
cake from it, and bring it out for me; prepare something for you and your
14 son afterward. For thus says the Lord, God of Israel: The jar of flour will
not run out, and the jug of oil will never be empty until the day that the
Lord sends rain upon the face of the earth."

15 She went and did as Eliyahu told her, and she, he, and her household
16 had food for some time. The jar of flour did not run out, and the jug of
oil was never empty, fulfilling the word the Lord had promised through
Eliyahu.

17 Some time later, the son of the woman, the head of the household, fell ill;
his illness was so severe that he stopped breathing.

18 "What have I to do with you, man of God?" she said to Eliyahu. "Did you
come to me just to draw attention to my sin and to kill my son?"

19 "Give me your son," he said to her, and he pried him from her embrace
and brought him up to the roof chamber where he was staying and laid
20 him out on his bed. And he called out to the Lord. "O Lord, my God,"
he cried, "must You even bring harm to the widow with whom I stay by
killing her son?"

21 He stretched out over the child three times and called out to the Lord.
"O Lord, my God," he cried, "please – let this child's life stir again within
him!"

22 And the LORD heeded Eliyahu's voice; the child's life stirred again within
23 him, and he revived. Eliyahu took the child, brought him down from
the roof chamber to the house, and gave him to his mother. "Look," said
Eliyahu, "your son is alive."

24 "Now I know that you are a man of God," the woman said to Eliyahu, "and
that the word of the LORD is truly on your lips."

18 1 A long time passed. In the third year,[62] the word of the LORD came to
Eliyahu: "Go, present yourself to Aḥav, and I will send down rain on the
2 face of the earth." So Eliyahu set out to present himself to Aḥav. By then,
famine was raging fiercely in Shomron.

3 Aḥav summoned Ovadyahu, who was in charge of the palace – Ovadyahu
4 had deep reverence for the LORD; when Izevel was annihilating the prophets
of the LORD, Ovadyahu had taken one hundred prophets and hidden them,
fifty men to a cave, and provided them with food and water.

5 "Go about the land to every spring and every wadi," Aḥav said to Ovadyahu.
"Perhaps we will find some grass to keep the horses and mules alive so that
6 our animals will not be annihilated." They divided up the land between
them for exploration; Aḥav set out alone in one direction, while Ovadyahu
set out alone in another.

7 As Ovadyahu was on the road, he was suddenly met by Eliyahu. He
recognized him at once and fell on his face. "Is that you, my lord Eliyahu?"
he said.

8 "It is I," he said to him. "Go and tell your lord: Eliyahu is here."

9 "How have I offended you, that you hand your servant over to Aḥav to
10 be killed?" he said. "As the LORD your God lives – is there a single nation
or kingdom where my lord has not sent and looked for you? And when
they said, 'He is not here,' he had every kingdom and every nation swear
11 that you were nowhere to be found. Now you say, 'Go, tell your lord that
12 Eliyahu is here,' but as soon as I leave you, the spirit of the LORD will carry
you off – to where, I know not – and when I go to tell Aḥav and he does
not find you, he will kill me, though I, your servant, have revered the LORD
13 from my youth. Has my lord not been told what I did when Izevel was
killing the LORD's prophets, how I hid one hundred of the LORD's prophets,
14 fifty men to a cave, and provided them with food and water? Now you say,
'Go, tell your lord that Eliyahu is here' – but he will kill me."

15 "As the LORD of Hosts lives, whom I serve," said Eliyahu, "Today I will
present myself to him."

16 So Ovadyahu set out toward Aḥav and told him, and Aḥav went to meet

62 | That is, since the drought began.

17 Eliyahu. When Aḥav saw Eliyahu, Aḥav said to him, "Is that you, O scourge
of Israel?"

18 "I have not brought a scourge upon Israel," he said, "but you and your
father's house have by abandoning the LORD's commandments and by
19 following the Baalim.[63] Now summon all of Israel to gather to me at Mount
Carmel, together with the four hundred fifty prophets of Baal and the four
hundred prophets of Ashera, those who dine at Izevel's table."[64]

20 Aḥav summoned all the Israelites and gathered the prophets to Mount
21 Carmel. And Eliyahu drew close to all the people and said, "How long will
you sway from one side to another?[65] If the LORD is God, then follow Him,
and if Baal, follow him!" But the people had no reply.

22 "I am the only prophet left to the LORD," Eliyahu said to the people, "while
23 the prophets of Baal are four hundred fifty men. Let two bulls be given
to us; let them choose one bull for themselves, cut it up, and position it
on the wood without setting it alight, while I prepare the other bull and
24 place it on the wood without setting it alight. You will invoke your god by
name, while I will invoke the LORD by name, and the God who answers
with fire – He is God."

And all the people answered, "We accept."

25 "Choose one bull for yourselves, and go first," Eliyahu said to the prophets
of Baal, "for you are the majority. Do not set it alight yourselves; invoke
your god by name."

26 They took the bull that was given to them and prepared it, then invoked
Baal by name from morning to noon, crying, "O Baal, answer us," but
there was no sound and no reply, and they swayed around the altar that
had been prepared.

27 At noon, Eliyahu began to mock them: "Shout louder," he said, "for he is
a god – he may be in conversation, or busy, or out traveling; he may be
asleep – he might wake!"

28 And they shouted louder and gashed themselves with swords and spears,
29 as was their custom, until blood streamed down them. Noon passed by,
and they raved until the time of the grain offering, but there was no sound
and no answer and no response.

30 Then Eliyahu said to all the people, "Draw close to me." All the people drew
31 close, and he began to repair the LORD's ruined altar. Eliyahu took twelve
stones, corresponding to the number of the tribes of the sons of Yaakov,
32 who received the word of the LORD: "Yisrael shall be your name."[66] With

63 | The deity seems to have had multiple manifestations.

64 | See note on 2:7.

65 | Literally "hop between the two boughs."

66 | See Genesis 35:10.

the stones he built an altar for the name of the Lord and made a trench
33 large enough for two *se'a*[67] of seed all around the altar. He arranged the
wood, cut up the bull, and placed it on the wood.

34 "Fill four jugs with water," he said, "and pour it over the offering and the
wood.

"Now do it a second time," he said, and they did it a second time.

35 "Do it a third time," he said, and they did it a third time. The water flowed
around the altar; he even filled the trench with water.

36 At the time of the grain offering, the prophet Eliyahu drew close and said,
"O Lord, God of Avraham, Yitzḥak, and Yisrael, let it be known today that
You are the God in Israel and that I am Your servant, and it was by Your
37 word that I have done all these things. Answer me, Lord, answer me, so
that this people will know that You, O Lord, are God; it was You who
turned their hearts backward."

38 And fire from the Lord flared down and consumed the offering, the wood,
39 the stones, and the dirt, and licked up the water in the trench. And all the
people saw, and they fell on their faces and cried, "The Lord – He is God!
The Lord – He is God!"

40 "Seize the prophets of Baal!" Eliyahu said to them. "Let none of them
escape!" They seized them, then Eliyahu led them down to the Kishon
Stream and slaughtered them there.

41 "Go up to eat and drink," Eliyahu then said to Aḥav, "for here comes the
42 sound of roaring rain." And Aḥav went up to eat and drink while Eliyahu
went up to the top of Mount Carmel. He crouched down on the ground
and pressed his face between his knees.

43 "Go up now," he said to his boy, "and look out to sea."

He went up and looked out. "Nothing is there," he said. Seven times he
said, "Go back."
44 The seventh time, he said, "A tiny cloud, the size of a man's hand, is rising
up from the sea."

"Go up," he said, "and say to Aḥav, 'Harness up and make your way down
so that the rain will not hold you back.'"

45 And all the while, the skies grew dark with clouds and wind, and heavy
46 rain began to fall. Aḥav mounted his chariot and rode out to Yizre'el. The
hand of the Lord settled on Eliyahu, and he hitched up his tunic and ran
before Aḥav until he reached Yizre'el.

19 1 When Aḥav told Izevel all that Eliyahu had done and how he had put all
2 the prophets to the sword, Izevel sent a messenger to Eliyahu: "So may the

67 | A single *se'a* is the equivalent of 7.7 liters.

gods do to me and more if by this time tomorrow, I have not treated your
life like one of theirs."

3 Frightened, he understood and fled for his life at once, and he reached
4 Be'er Sheva of Yehuda and left his servant boy there. But he continued a
day's journey into the wilderness, then came and sat under a certain broom
tree and prayed that he might die. Enough!" he said. "O LORD, take my
5 life now, for I am no better than my ancestors." Then he lay down and fell
asleep beneath that broom tree.

6 Suddenly, an angel was touching him, urging him, "Get up; eat." He looked
up and there, at his head, was a stone-baked cake and a flask of water. He
7 ate and drank and lay back down. The angel of the LORD came back a
second time and touched him. "Get up; eat," it said, "or the long journey
will prove too much for you."

8 He got up and ate and drank, and by the strength of that food, he walked
9 forty days and forty nights to the mountain of God, Ḥorev.[68] There he
reached a cave, and there he spent the night. Suddenly, the word of the
LORD came to him and said to him, "Why are you here, Eliyahu?"

10 "I acted out of fervor, out of passion for the LORD, God of Hosts," he said,
"for the Israelites have abandoned Your covenant, destroyed Your altars,
and put Your prophets to the sword. I am the only one left, and they seek
to take my life."

11 "Go out and stand on the mountain before the LORD," He said, "for the
LORD is about to pass by."

And a great, powerful wind split mountains and shattered rocks before
the LORD –
but the LORD was not in the wind.
And after the wind, an earthquake –
but the LORD was not in the earthquake.
12 And after the earthquake, fire –
but the LORD was not in the fire.
And after the fire –
a faint sound of silence.

13 And when Eliyahu heard, he wrapped his face in his cloak and went out
and stood by the entrance of the cave. And suddenly a voice came to him
and said, "Why are you here, Eliyahu?"

14 "I acted out of fervor, out of passion for the LORD, God of Hosts," he said,
"for the Israelites have abandoned Your covenant, destroyed Your altars,
and put Your prophets to the sword. I am the only one left, and they seek
to take my life."

---

68 | Mount Sinai.

15 And the Lord answered him, "Set back out on your way to the Wilderness
16 of Damascus. When you arrive, anoint Ḥazael as king over Aram. As for
Yehu son of Nimshi, anoint him as king over Israel; and as for Elisha son
17 of Shafat of Avel Meḥola, anoint him as a prophet in your place. Whoever
escapes the sword of Ḥazael will be killed by Yehu, and whoever escapes
18 the sword of Yehu will be killed by Elisha. I will leave but seven thousand
of Israel: every knee that has not bowed to Baal and every mouth that has
not kissed him."

19 He set out from there and found Elisha son of Shafat. He was plowing
with twelve pairs of oxen before him, and he was with the twelfth. When
20 Eliyahu reached him, he tossed his cloak over him. He left the oxen and
went running after Eliyahu. "Let me just kiss my father and mother," he
said, "and I will follow you."

"Go back, then," he said to him. "What have I done to you?"[69]

21 He turned back from him and took the pair of oxen; he slaughtered them
and, using the oxen gear,[70] he boiled their meat and gave it out to the people
to eat. Then he set out and followed Eliyahu and became his attendant.

20 1 Ben Hadad, king of Aram, gathered all his forces; thirty-two kings were
with him, with horses and chariots. He advanced, laid siege to Shomron,
2 and launched an attack; he then sent messengers to Aḥav, king of Israel,
3 inside the city, saying, "Thus says Ben Hadad: 'Your silver and gold are
mine, and the finest of your women and children are mine.'"

4 "As you say, my lord the king," the king of Israel answered, "I and all I have
are yours."

5 But the messengers returned, saying, "Thus says Ben Hadad: 'I have sent
word to you that you must hand over your silver, your gold, your women,
6 and your children to me. At this time tomorrow, I will send my servants
to you; they will search your house and the houses of your servants, and
they will seize all that you hold dear and carry it away.'"

7 And the king of Israel summoned all the elders of the land. "Be aware, now,
and consider the evil this one seeks," he said. "He sent to me for my wives
and my children, my silver and my gold, and I have not refused him."

8 And all the elders and all the people said, "Do not listen, and do not
consent!"

9 So he said to Ben Hadad's messengers, "Say to my lord the king, 'I will do
all that you first demanded of your servant, but this I cannot do.'" And the
messengers went and brought the message back.

10 And Ben Hadad sent to him and said, "So may the gods do to me, and more,

69 | That is, I am not preventing you.

70 | To fuel the fire.

if there is dust enough in Shomron for each of the troops at my heels to take a handful."

11 "Tell him," the king of Israel retorted, "that one who girds should not boast like one who ungirds."

12 He was drinking with the other kings at Sukkot when he heard this message, and he ordered his servants, "Charge!"

And they charged against the city.

13 Just then, a prophet came forward to Aḥav, king of Israel. "Thus says the Lord," he said. "Have you seen all these great hordes? I am about to hand them over to you today so that you will know that I am the Lord."

14 "Through whom?" asked Aḥav.

"Thus says the Lord," he said. "Through the servants of the district officers."

"Who will launch the battle?" he asked.

And he replied, "You."

15 So he mustered the servants of the district officers – they numbered
232 – and afterward, he mustered all the troops; the Israelites numbered
16 seven thousand in all. They marched out at noon while Ben Hadad was
drinking himself into a stupor in Sukkot together with the kings – the
17 thirty-two kings who had come to his aid. The servants of the district
officers marched out first. Ben Hadad had sent scouts, who told him, "Men
have marched out of Shomron."

18 "If they have come out to surrender," he said, "capture them alive! And if tey have come out to fight – capture them alive!"

19 Meanwhile, the junior district officers had marched out of the city,
20 followed by the troops, and each one struck down his man. Aram fled, and
Israel pursued them, but Ben Hadad, king of Aram, escaped on horseback
21 along with some riders. The king of Israel charged out and attacked the
22 horses and chariots and dealt Aram a crushing blow. Then the prophet
approached the king of Israel. "Go, and keep up your strength," he said,
"and consider what course of action to take, for at the turn of the year, the
king of Aram will advance upon you."

23 Meanwhile, the servants of the king of Aram said to him, "Their God is a
God of mountains; that is why they overpowered us. But if we fight them
24 in the plain, we will surely overpower them. This is what you should
do: Depose every king from his position and appoint governors in their
25 place. Then you must amass a force, the same as your fallen force – horse
for horse, chariot for chariot – and we will fight them in the plain. We
will surely overpower them." And he listened to their advice and did just
that.

26 It was the turn of the year, and Ben Hadad mustered Aram and marched
27 up to Afek to do battle with Israel. And the Israelites were rallied and
provisioned, and they set out toward them. When the Israelites set up
camp opposite them, they seemed like two vulnerable flocks of goats,
28 while Aram filled the land. But the man of God approached and said to
the king of Israel, "Thus says the LORD: Because Aram said that the LORD
is a God of mountains and not a God of valleys, I will hand all these vast
hordes over to you. And you will know that I am the LORD."

29 They encamped opposite each other for seven days. On the seventh day,
battle broke out, and the Israelites struck down one hundred thousand
30 Aramean foot soldiers in a single day. The survivors fled to Afek, to the
city, but the wall came crashing down on the twenty-seven thousand men
who had survived. Ben Hadad managed to flee, and he entered an inner
31 chamber within the city. His officials said to him, "Look, we have heard
that the kings of the House of Israel are benevolent kings. Let us place
sackcloth around our waists and ropes around our heads, and let us go out
32 before the king of Israel; perhaps he will spare our lives." So they girded
their waists with sackcloth and placed ropes around their heads, and they
came to the king of Israel.

"Your servant, Ben Hadad, asks, 'Please, spare my life,'" they said.

"Is he still alive?" he said. "He is my brother."

33 The men took it as a good omen and quickly seized their chance. "Ben
Hadad is indeed your brother," they said.

"Come, fetch him," he said. Ben Hadad went out to him, and he had him mount the chariot.

34 "I will give back the cities that my father seized from your father," he said
to him, "and you may set up markets in Damascus, as my father did in
Shomron."

"Under this pact, I will set you free."

And he formed a pact with him and set him free.

35 Now a certain man from the brotherhood of the prophets said to another,
by the word of the LORD, "Now strike me," but the man refused to strike
him.

36 "Because you did not obey the voice of the LORD," he said, "as soon as you
leave me, you will be attacked by a lion." And as soon as he left him, a lion
found him and attacked him.

37 He found another man and said to him, "Now strike me," and the man
38 struck him a blow and wounded him. The prophet went and stood by the
road waiting for the king, and he disguised himself with a wrapping over
his eyes.

39 When the king passed by, he shouted out to the king, "Your servant went
out into the thick of battle. Suddenly, a man turned around and brought
someone to me and said to me, 'Guard this man – if he goes missing, it will
40 be yor life for his life, or you will have to weigh out a talent of silver.' But
your servant was busy with this and that, and he got away."

"Well, that is your sentence," the king of Israel said to him. "You yourself pronounced it."

41 He quickly removed the wrapping from his eyes, and the king of Israel
42 recognized him as one of the prophets. "Thus says the LORD," he said to
him. "Because you freed the man I had marked for destruction, your life
will be in place of his life, and your people instead of his people."

43 And the king of Israel went home, dour and sullen, and he came to
Shomron.

21 1 Some time passed after these events. Now Navot the Jezreelite owned a
2 vineyard in Yizre'el next to the palace of Aḥav, king of Shomron. Aḥav told
Navot, "Give me your vineyard so that I can use it as a vegetable garden,
for it is right next to my home. I will give you a better vineyard in its place,
or, if you prefer, I will give you its worth in silver."

3 But Navot said to Aḥav, "The LORD forbid that I should give up my
ancestral share to you."

4 Aḥav came home, dour and sullen over what Navot the Jezreelite had told
him: "I will not give up my ancestral share to you." He lay down on his bed
5 and turned his face away and would not eat. Izevel, his wife, came to him.
"What is this dour mood of yours?" she asked him. "You won't even eat."

6 "I spoke to Navot the Jezreelite," he told her, "and I said to him, 'Give me
your vineyard for silver, or, if you prefer, I will give you a vineyard in its
place,' but he said, 'I will not give you my vineyard.'"

7 "Why, you must now exercise your royal rights over Israel," his wife Izevel
said to him. "Get up and eat, and take heart. I will give you the vineyard
of Navot the Jezreelite."

8 She wrote letters in Aḥav's name and sealed them with his own seal. Then
she sent the letters out to the elders and the nobles who lived in the same
9 town as Navot. "Proclaim a fast, and seat Navot in front of the people,"
10 she had written in the letters. "Seat two depraved men opposite him, and
have them testify against Navot, declaring, 'You have "blessed"[71] God
11 and the king!' Then take him out, and stone him to death." And the men
of his town – the elders and nobles who lived in his town – did as Izevel
12 directed them, just as she had written in the letters she sent to them. They
13 proclaimed a fast and seated Navot in front of the people. Then came

71 | "Bless" is a euphemism for "curse"; cf. Job 2:5, 9.

two men – depraved men – who sat opposite him, and the depraved men
testified against Navot in front of the people, saying, "Navot has 'blessed'
God and the king!" Then they took him outside the city and stoned him
14 to death and sent to Izevel, "Navot has been stoned to death."

15 When Izevel heard that Navot had been stoned to death, Izevel said to
Aḥav, "At once – take possession of Navot the Jezreelite's vineyard, which
he refused to sell to you for silver, for Navot is no longer alive; he is dead."
16 When Aḥav heard that Navot was dead, he went straight down to the
vineyard of Navot the Jezreelite to take possession of it.

17 18 And the word of the LORD came to Eliyahu the Tishbite. "Go straight
down to meet Aḥav, king of Israel, who is in Shomron. He is now in the
19 vineyard of Navot; he went down there to take possession of it. Tell him,
'Thus says the LORD: Have you murdered, and also seized possession?
Thus says the LORD: In the very place that the dogs lapped up the blood
of Navot, the dogs will lap up your own blood, too.'"

20 "So, you have found me, my enemy?" Aḥav said to Eliyahu.

"Yes, I have found you," he said. "Because you have sold yourself to what is
21 evil in the eyes of the LORD, I am about to bring evil upon you, and I will
burn up every last trace of you. I will cut off every last male of Aḥav in Israel,
22 bond and free, and I will make your house like the house of Yorovam son
of Nevat and like the house of Basha son of Aḥiya because of the anger
you have provoked by leading Israel to sin."

23 And the LORD has also spoken against Izevel: "The dogs will devour Izevel
24 within the bounds of Yizre'el. Those of Aḥav's who die in the city will be
devoured by dogs, and those of his who die in the field will be devoured
by the birds of the sky."

25 Never again was there anyone like Aḥav, who sold himself to what was
26 evil in the eyes of the LORD, goaded on by Izevel his wife. Deeply corrupt,
he followed after idols just as the Amorites did, whom the LORD had
27 dispossessed before the Israelites. But when Aḥav heard these words,
he rent his clothes and put sackcloth on his body; he fasted and lay in
sackcloth and stumbled about in despair.

28 29 Then the word of the LORD came to Eliyahu the Tishbite: "Have you
seen how Aḥav has humbled himself before Me? Because he has humbled
himself before Me, I will not bring the evil about in his own time; I will
bring the evil upon his house during his son's time."

22 1 For three years there was a respite, with no war between Aram and Israel.
2 But in the third year, Yehoshafat, king of Yehuda, went down to the king
of Israel.

3 "Are you aware that Ramot Gilad is ours," the king of Israel said to his
servants, "yet we have done nothing to take it back from the king of Aram's
hands?

4 Will you go out to battle with me at Ramot Gilad?" he asked Yehoshafat.

"I am ready, as you are," Yehoshafat said to the king of Israel. "My troops are
5 your own troops; my horses are your own horses." Then Yehoshafat said
to the king of Israel, "Please, inquire of the LORD today."

6 So the king of Israel gathered the prophets, about four hundred men, and said to them, "Shall I go to battle over Ramot Gilad, or should I refrain?"

"Advance!" they said, "and the LORD will deliver them to the king's hand."

7 "Is there no other prophet of the LORD here?" said Yehoshafat. "Let us inquire through him."

8 "There is another man through whom we could inquire of the LORD," the king of Israel said to Yehoshafat, "but I despise him; he has never prophesied good for me, only evil – Mikhayehu son of Yimla."

"Do not say such a thing, O king," said Yehoshafat.

9 So the king of Israel summoned one of the eunuchs and said, "Bring Mikhayehu son of Yimla at once."

10 The king of Israel and Yehoshafat, king of Yehuda, each sat upon their
thrones, attired in robes, at the threshing floor at the entrance of the
Shomron Gate, and all the prophets were prophesying before them.
11 Tzidkiya son of Kenaana had made himself horns of iron. "Thus says the
12 LORD," he said. "With these you shall gore Aram until their demise." And
all the prophets echoed his prophecy: "Advance to Ramot Gilad, and be
victorious," they were saying. "The LORD will deliver it to the king's hand."

13 Then the messenger who had gone to summon Mikhayehu told him, "Look here – the words of the prophets are unanimous; they favor the king. May your words be like theirs – speak favorably."

14 "As the LORD lives," said Mikhayehu, "I will speak only what the LORD says to me."

15 He came up to the king, and the king said to him, "Mikhayehu – shall we go to battle over Ramot Gilad, or should we refrain?"

"Advance and be victorious," he said, "and the LORD will deliver it to the king's hand."

16 "How many times must I have you swear?" the king said to him. "You must speak only the truth to me, by the name of the LORD."

17 "I saw all of Israel scattered over the hills," he said, "like sheep without a shepherd. And the LORD said: These have no masters. Let each man return home in peace."

18 "Did I not tell you?" the king of Israel said to Yehoshafat. "He never prophesies good for me – only evil!

19 "Therefore, listen to the word of the LORD," he continued. "I saw the LORD
sitting on His throne, with all the heavenly hosts standing in attendance,
20 to His right and to His left. And the LORD said, 'Who will lure Aḥav so
that he will advance and fall at Ramot Gilad?' This one said this and that
21 one said that. Then a spirit came forward and stood before the LORD and
said, 'I will lure him.'

"'How?' said the LORD.

22 "'I will go out and become a false spirit in the mouths of all his prophets,'
it said. 'Lure him – you will succeed.' He said: 'Go out and do so.'

23 "And now, look – the LORD has placed a false spirit in the mouths of all
these prophets of yours, and the LORD has pronounced evil for you."

24 Tzidkiyahu son of Knaana came forward and slapped Mikhayehu across
the cheek. "How did the spirit of the LORD pass from me to speak to you?"
he said.

25 "Oh, you will see on that day," Mikhayehu said, "when you enter the
innermost room to hide."

26 "Seize Mikhayehu!" said the king of Israel. "Hand him over to Amon, the
27 city governor, and to Yoash, the king's son, and say, 'Thus says the king:
Put this one in prison, and feed him only scant bread and scant water until
28 my safe arrival.'" "If you indeed return safely, then the LORD did not speak
through me," said Mikhayehu. And he added, "Listen, all peoples!"[72]

29 So the king of Israel and Yehoshafat, king of Yehuda, advanced to Ramot
Gilad.

30 "I will disguise myself and go into battle," the king of Israel said to Yehoshafat,
"while you should wear your robes." And the king of Israel disguised himself
31 and went into battle. Now the king of Aram had instructed his chariot
commanders – they numbered thirty-two – as follows: "Do not attack
32 anyone, great or small, except for the king of Israel." When the chariot
commanders saw Yehoshafat, they thought, "Look: he must be the king of
33 Israel." They charged toward him to attack, but Yehoshafat cried out, and
when the chariot commanders realized that he was not the king of Israel,
they turned back away from him.

34 But one man drew his bow at random, and he struck the king of Israel
between the joints of his armor. He called out to his chariot driver, "Steer
35 back around and get me out of the camp, for I am wounded." As the battle
raged that day, the king was propped up in his chariot facing Aram. The
blood from his wound trickled down into the hollow of the chariot, and he
36 died that evening. At sundown, the cry echoed through the camp: "Every
man back to his hometown; every man back to his own land."

72 | In his opening prophecy, the later prophet Mikha the Morashtite echoes these closing words of Mikhayehu son of Yimla; cf. Micah 1:2.

37 But the king was dead and was brought to Shomron. They buried the king
38 in Shomron, and they rinsed out the chariot at the pool of Shomron; the
dogs lapped up his blood, and the whores bathed, fulfilling the word that
the Lord had spoken.[73]

39 As for the rest of Aḥav's history and all his deeds and the ivory palace that
he built and all the cities that he built – they are recorded in the Book of
40 the History of the Kings of Israel. And Aḥav slept with his ancestors, and
his son Aḥazya reigned in his place.

41 Yehoshafat son of Asa became king over Yehuda in the fourth year of Aḥav,
42 king of Israel. Yehoshafat was thirty-five years old when he became king,
and for twenty-five years he reigned in Jerusalem. His mother's name was
43 Azuva daughter of Shilḥi. He followed in all the ways of his father Asa
and did not turn away from them, doing what was right in the eyes of the
44 Lord. Only the high shrines were not removed; the people continued to
45 offer sacrifices and incense at the high shrines. Yehoshafat made peace
with the king of Israel.

46 As for the rest of Yehoshafat's history, his exploits, and his battles – they
47 are recorded in the Book of the History of the Kings of Yehuda. He purged
every last trace of the male ritual prostitutes who remained from the time
48 of his father Asa. There was no king in Edom; a governor served as king.
49 Yehoshafat built a Tarshish[74] fleet to set sail to Ofir for gold, but the ships
50 were wrecked at Etzyon Gever, and he never set sail. Then Aḥazyahu son of
Aḥav proposed to Yehoshafat, "Let my servants set out with your servants
51 in the ships," but Yehoshafat would not give his consent. And Yehoshafat
slept with his ancestors and was buried with his ancestors in the City of
David, his ancestor. And his son Yehoram reigned in his place.

52 Aḥazyahu son of Aḥav became king over Israel in Shomron in the
seventeenth year of Yehoshafat, king of Yehuda, and he reigned over Israel
53 for two years. He did what was evil in the eyes of the Lord and followed
in the ways of his father, the ways of his mother, and the ways of Yorovam
54 son of Nevat, who led Israel to sin. He served the Baal and worshipped him
and angered the Lord, God of Israel, just as his father did.

II KINGS 1 1 After Aḥav's death, Moav rebelled against Israel.

2 Aḥazya fell through the lattice in his upper chamber at Shomron and was
injured. He sent messengers, instructing them, "Go, inquire of Baal Zevuv,
the god of Ekron, whether I will recover from this injury."

3 But an angel of the Lord spoke to Eliyahu the Tishbite, "Arise and go up
to meet the messengers of the king of Shomron and tell them, 'Is it for lack
of a God in Israel that you go to inquire of Baal Zevuv, the god of Ekron?'

73 | See 21:19.

74 | See note on 10:22.

4 Therefore, thus says the LORD: You will never rise from your sickbed again – you will surely die!" And Eliyahu set out.

5 When the messengers returned to him, he said, "Why have you returned?"

6 "A man came up to meet us," they said to him, "and he said to us, 'Go back to the king who sent you, and tell him, Thus says the LORD: Is it for lack of a God in Israel that you sent to inquire of Baal Zevuv, god of Ekron? Therefore, you will never rise from your sickbed again – you will surely die!'"

7 "What kind of man came up to meet you and told you these words?" he asked them.

8 "A hairy man," they said to him, "with a leather belt tied around his waist."

"Why," he said, "it must be Eliyahu the Tishbite!"

9 And he sent his officer of fifty to him, together with his company of fifty. He climbed up to him – for there he was, sitting on the hilltop. "O man of God," he said to him, "the king has spoken: 'Come down!'"

10 "If I am a man of God," Eliyahu answered the officer of fifty, "let fire flare down from heaven and consume you and your company of fifty."

And fire flared down from heaven and consumed him and his company of fifty.

11 So again, he sent another officer of fifty, together with his company of fifty, and he addressed him. "O man of God," he said, "thus says the king: 'Come down at once.'"
12 "If I am a man of God," Eliyahu answered them, "let fire flare down from heaven and consume you and your company of fifty."

And a divine fire flared down from heaven and consumed him and his company of fifty.

13 So again, he sent a third officer of fifty, together with his company of
fifty. But when the third officer of fifty arrived, he dropped down on his
knees before Eliyahu and pleaded with him. "O man of God," he said,
"please – may my life and the lives of these fifty servants of yours have
14 some worth in your eyes. Look – fire has just flared down from heaven and
consumed the first two officers of fifty, together with their companies of
fifty. But now, may my life have some worth in your eyes."

15 Then an angel of the LORD spoke to Eliyahu, "Go down with him; do
not fear his presence." So he arose and accompanied him down to the
16 king. And he declared to him, "Thus says the LORD: Because you sent
messengers to inquire of Baal Zevuv, the god of Ekron – was it for lack
of a God in Israel whose word you could seek? – you will never rise from
your sickbed again; you will surely die!"

17 And he died, fulfilling the word of the LORD that Eliyahu had pronounced.
Yehoram[75] reigned in his place in the second year of King Yehoram son
18 of Yehoshafat of Yehuda, for he did not have a son. As for the rest of
Aḥazyahu's history and deeds – they are recorded in the book of the
History of the Kings of Israel.

2 1 When the LORD was about to take Eliyahu up to heaven in a whirlwind,
2 Eliyahu and Elisha had just set out from Gilgal. "Stay here for now," Eliyahu
said to Elisha, "for the LORD has sent me to Beit El."

"As the LORD lives, and by your own life," said Elisha, "I will not leave you."
3 So they went down to Beit El. The brotherhood of the prophets in Beit El
came out to Elisha and said to him, "Do you know that the LORD will take
your master away from you today?"

"Of course I know," he said. "Be silent!"

4 Then Eliyahu said to him, "Elisha, stay here for now, for the LORD has sent
me to Yeriḥo."

"As the LORD lives, and by your own life," he said, "I will not leave you."
5 So they came to Yeriḥo. The brotherhood of the prophets in Yeriḥo
approached Elisha and said to him, "Do you know that the LORD will
take your master away from you today?"

"Of course I know," he said. "Be silent!"

6 Then Eliyahu said to him, "Stay here for now, for the LORD has sent me
to the Jordan."

"As the LORD lives, and by your own life," he said, "I will not leave you." So
7 the two of them went on. Fifty men from the brotherhood of the prophets
followed and stood by at a distance while the two of them stood by the
8 Jordan. Eliyahu took his cloak, rolled it up, and struck the waters; they split
9 down the middle, and the two of them crossed over on dry land. As they
were crossing, Eliyahu said to Elisha, "Ask what I may do for you before I
am taken from you."

"Oh, if only twice of your spirit would rest upon me," said Elisha.

10 "You have made a difficult request," he said. "If you see me as I am taken
from you, then it will be granted for you, but if not, then it will not."

11 And as they were walking along, speaking to each other, a fiery chariot with
fiery horses suddenly appeared and parted the two of them, and Eliyahu
12 rose up to heaven in a whirlwind. As Elisha watched, he screamed, "Father!
Father! The chariots of Israel and its riders!" and then he saw him no more.
13 Then he grasped hold of his clothes and rent them in two. He picked up
Eliyahu's cloak, which had fallen from him, and he turned back and stood

75 | Aḥazya's brother.

14 by the bank of the Jordan. Grasping Eliyahu's cloak, which had fallen
from him, he struck the waters. "Oh, where is the Lord, God of Eliyahu?"
he said. When he, too, struck the waters, they split down the middle, and
Elisha crossed over.

15 When the brotherhood of the prophets in Yeriḥo saw him from the other
side, they said, "The spirit of Eliyahu has settled on Elisha!" They came
out toward him and bowed low before him.

16 "Please – your servants have fifty able men here with them," they said
to him. "Let them go and look for your master. Perhaps the spirit of the
Lord has carried him off and cast him upon some mountain or into some
valley."

17 "Do not send them," he said. But they pressed him until it grew late, and
he said, "Send them!" They sent fifty men, and they searched for him for
18 three days, but they did not find him. He was staying in Yeriḥo when they
came back to him. "Well, I told you not to go," he said.

19 Now the townspeople said to Elisha, "Look, the town is a good place to
live in, as my lord can see, but the water is bad, and the land brings grief."

20 "Fetch me a new dish and put salt in it," he said, and they brought it to him.
21 He went out to the water source and flung the salt there. "Thus says the
Lord," he said, "I have healed these waters; no longer will death or grief
22 issue from there." And the waters have remained fresh ever since, fulfilling
the word that Elisha pronounced.

23 From there, he went up to Beit El. As he was making his way up, some
young boys came out of the town and began to taunt him. "Go away, baldy!"
they said to him. "Go away, baldy!"

24 He turned around, and when he saw them, he cursed them in the name of
the Lord – and two bears came out of the forest and mauled forty-two of
25 the children. From there, he went on to Mount Carmel, and from there,
he went back to Shomron.

3 1 Yehoram son of Aḥav became king over Israel in Shomron in the eighteenth
2 year of Yehoshafat, king of Yehuda, and he reigned for twelve years. He did
what was evil in the eyes of the Lord – though not to the same extent as
his father and mother, and he removed the pillar of Baal that his father had
3 made. But he clung to the sins of Yorovam son of Nevat, who led Israel to
sin, and did not turn away from them.

4 Mesha, king of Moav, was a sheep breeder, and he would pay tribute
to the king of Israel with one hundred thousand lambs and the wool
5 of one hundred thousand rams. But when Aḥav died, the king of Moav
6 rebelled against the king of Israel. So at that time King Yehoram set out
7 from Shomron and rallied all of Israel. Then he went and sent word to

Yehoshafat, king of Yehuda: "The king of Moav has rebelled against me. Will you go to war with me against Moav?"

"I will," he said. "I am ready, as you are; my troops are your own troops; my horses are your own horses."

8 "By which route shall we go up?" he asked.

"By the road through the wilderness of Edom," he said.

9 So the king of Israel, the king of Yehuda, and the king of Edom set out, but
by the time they had made a circuit of seven days' journey, there was no
water for the camp or for the animals at their heels.

10 "Alas!" said the king of Israel. "The Lord has summoned these three kings
to hand them over to Moav."

11 "Is there no prophet of the Lord here?" said Yehoshafat. "Let us inquire
of the Lord through him."

One of the king of Israel's officials spoke up. "Elisha son of Shafat is here," he said, "the one who poured water on the hands of Eliyahu."[76]

12 "He must have the word of the Lord," said Yehoshafat, and the king of
13 Israel, Yehoshafat, and the king of Edom went down to him. But Elisha
said to the king of Israel, "What have I to do with you? Go to the prophets
of your father and to the prophets of your mother."

"No," the king of Israel said to him, "for the Lord has summoned these three kings to hand them over to Moav."

14 "As the Lord of Hosts lives, whom I serve," said Elisha, "were it not for
my regard for Yehoshafat, king of Yehuda, I would not look at you or even
15 glance at you. Now fetch me a musician."

And as the musician played, the hand of the Lord settled upon him.

16 "Thus says the Lord," he said. "This wadi shall fill up with pool after pool.
17 For thus says the Lord: You will see no wind and you will see no rain, yet
the wadi shall be filled with water, and you and your livestock and your
18 animals shall drink. But this is nothing in the eyes of the Lord, for He
19 will also hand Moav over to you. You will defeat every fortified city and
every illustrious city; you will fell every good tree and stop up every spring,
20 and you will wreck every good field with stones." And in the morning, at
the time of the grain offering, water suddenly came from the direction of
Edom, and the land was filled with water.

21 When all of Moav heard that the kings had marched up to fight them,
everyone old enough to bear arms rallied and stationed themselves at the

76 | That is, who served as an attendant to Eliyahu.

22 border. When they rose early in the morning, the sun rose over the water,
and to the Moabites, the water in the distance seemed as red as blood.

23 "That's blood!" they said. "The kings must have fought among themselves
and slaughtered each other – now to the spoil, Moav!"

24 But when they reached the camp of Israel, Israel charged and attacked
Moav, and they fled from them. They advanced, constantly on the attack
25 against Moav, and destroyed their cities; each man flung stones at every
good field until it was filled up, and they stopped up every spring of water
and felled every good tree, leaving only the stone wall of Kir Ḥareset,
which the slingers then surrounded and attacked.

26 When the king of Moav saw that the battle was too fierce for him, he took
seven hundred swordsmen with him to break through to the king of Edom,
27 but they could not. So he took his firstborn son, who was to reign in his
place, and he offered him up as a burnt offering on the wall. Then there
was great wrath against Israel, and they withdrew from him and returned
to the land.

4 1 A woman – the wife of one of the brotherhood of the prophets – cried out
to Elisha, "Your servant, my husband, is dead! You know that your servant
always feared the Lord. Now a creditor has come to take my two children
away to be his slaves."

2 "What can I do for you?" said Elisha. "Tell me, what do you have in the
house?"

"Your servant has nothing at all at home," she said, "except for a jar of oil."

3 "Go out and borrow vessels from all your neighbors," he said to her, "empty
4 vessels – as many as you can. When you come back in, close the door
behind you and your sons. Then pour away into all those vessels, setting
them aside when they are full."

5 And so she left him. When she closed the door behind her and her sons,
6 they kept bringing vessels to her while she kept pouring. When the vessels
were full, she said to her son, "Bring me another vessel," and he said to her,
7 "There are no more vessels" – and the oil stopped flowing. She came and
told the man of God, and he said, "Go, sell the oil and pay off your debt,
and you and your sons can live on the rest."

8 One day, Elisha was passing through Shunem, and a wealthy woman there
urged him to have something to eat. So whenever he passed through, he
9 would stop there for some food. She said to her husband, "Look, I am
sure that the man who passes through here regularly is a holy man of God.
10 Let us make him a small enclosed upper chamber and provide him with
a bed, table, chair, and lamp there, so that whenever he comes to us, he
can turn in there."

11 One day, he came by; he turned in to the upper chamber and lay down
12 there. He said to Geḥazi, his servant, "Call the Shunamite woman." He
13 called her, and she stood before him. He said to him, "Please say to her,
'You have shown us so much concern. What can we do for you? Shall I
speak to the king on your behalf, or to the army commander?'"

"I live among my own people," she said.

14 "Then what can be done for her?" he said.

"Well, she is childless," said Geḥazi, "and her husband is old."

15 "Call her," he said, and he called her, and she stood in the entrance.

16 "At this time next year," he said, "you will be embracing a son."

"No, my lord, man of God," she said. "Do not delude your servant."

17 But the woman did conceive, and she bore a son at that time during the
following year, just as Elisha had promised her.

18 The child grew up. One day, he went out to his father, who was with the
reapers.

19 "My head! My head!" he said to his father, who said to the servant, "Carry
20 him to his mother." He carried him over and brought him to his mother;
he sat on her lap until noon, and then he died.

21 She went up and laid him on the man of God's bed, closed the door behind
22 him, and went out. Then she called to her husband. "Send me one of the
servants and one of the donkeys at once," she said. "I must rush over to
the man of God and come right back."

23 "Why are you going to him today?" he said. "It is not the New Moon, nor
the Sabbath."

"All is well," she said.

24 She saddled the donkey and said to her servant, "Drive! Be off! Do not
stop riding on my account unless I tell you."

25 She set out and reached the man of God at Mount Carmel. When the man
of God saw her in the distance, he said to Geḥazi, his servant, "Look, there
26 is that Shunamite woman. Run to meet her straightaway and say to her, 'Are
you well? Is your husband well? Is your child well?'"

"All is well," she said.

27 But she came up to the man of God at the mountain and grasped his feet.
Geḥazi came forward to push her away, but the man of God said, "Leave
her be, for she is bitter of spirit, and the Lord has hidden this from me
and did not tell me."

28 "Did I ask my lord for a son?" she said. "Did I not say, 'Do not lead me on?'"

29 "Hitch up your tunic," Elisha said to Geḥazi. "Take my staff in your hand, and set out. If you meet anyone, do not greet them, and if anyone greets you, do not answer them. Place my staff on the boy's face."

30 "As the Lord lives, and by your own life," said the boy's mother, "I will not leave you." So he followed straight behind her.

31 Geḥazi went on ahead of them and placed the staff on the boy's face, but
there was no sound and no response. He went back to meet him and told
32 him, "The boy did not wake." Elisha entered the house, and there was the
33 boy laid out on his bed – dead. He entered and closed the door behind
34 the two of them, and he prayed to the Lord. Then he mounted the bed
and lay on top of the boy; he placed his mouth on his mouth and his eyes
on his eyes and his palms on his palms, and he bent down over him, and
35 the child's body became warm. He went back down and paced about the
house, back and forth, then he climbed up and crouched down over him.
And the boy sneezed – seven times – and the boy opened his eyes.

36 He called to Geḥazi and said to him, "Call the Shunamite woman." He called her, and she came to him.

37 "Pick up your son," he said. And she came and fell at his feet and bowed to the ground. Then she picked up her son and went out.

38 When Elisha returned to Gilgal, there was famine in the land. As the
brotherhood of the prophets sat before him, he said to his servant, "Set up
39 the large pot and cook a stew for the brotherhood of the prophets." One
of them went out to the field to gather herbs, and he found a wild vine.
He plucked its wild gourds and filled up his garment, then he came and
diced them into the pot of stew, for they did not realize what they were.
40 They poured it out for the people to eat, but as they were eating from the
stew, they began to shout, "There is death in the pot, O man of God!" and
they could not eat.

41 "Fetch some flour," he said, and flung it into the pot. "Pour it out for the people and let them eat," he said, and there was no longer anything harmful in the pot.

42 A man came from Baal Shalisha and brought the man of God bread made of the first grain: twenty loaves of barley bread and some fresh grain in his sack. "Give it to the people and let them eat," he said.

43 "How can I set this before a hundred people?" asked his attendant.

"Give it to the people and let them eat," he said, "for thus says the Lord:
44 They will eat and leave some over." So he set it before them and they ate,
and there was some left over, fulfilling the word of the Lord.

5 1 Naaman, the commander of the king of Aram's army, was highly esteemed
by his master and held in favor, for the LORD had granted victory to Aram
through him. But this powerful man suffered from an impure blight.

2 Once, when the Arameans were out raiding, they captured a young girl
3 from the land of Israel, and she became a servant of Naaman's wife. She
said to her mistress, "If only my master would present himself to the
4 prophet in Shomron, he would cure him of his blight." Naaman then went
and told his own master about what the girl from the land of Israel had
said.

5 "Prepare to set out," said the king of Aram, "and I will send along a letter
to the king of Israel." He set out, taking ten talents of silver, six thousand
6 pieces of gold, and ten sets of clothing with him. And he brought the letter
to the king of Israel, which read: "Now, as this letter reaches you, I have
sent my servant Naaman to you, that you may cure him of his blight."

7 When the king of Israel read the letter, he rent his clothes. "Am I God,
dealing death and granting life, that this one sends me a man to cure his
blight?" he said, "Be aware now, look – he must be provoking a quarrel
with me."

8 When Elisha, the man of God, heard that the king of Israel had rent his
clothes, he sent to the king, saying, "Why have you rent your clothes? Let
him come to me now, and he will know that there is a prophet in Israel."
9 So Naaman came with his horses and chariots and halted at the entrance
10 of Elisha's house. And Elisha sent a messenger to him, saying, "Go and
bathe in the Jordan seven times; your skin will be restored to you, and
you will be cleansed."

11 Naaman was furious and walked away. "I was certain he would come out
to me," he said, "and stand and invoke the name of the LORD, his God,
12 and wave his hand toward the affected area and cure my blight. Why,
Amana and Parpar, the rivers of Damascus, are better than all the waters
of Israel – if I bathe in them, will I not be cleansed?" And he turned and
stormed off in a rage.

13 But his servants approached him and spoke to him. "Father,"[77] they said,
"had the prophet given you more difficult instructions, would you not
carry them out? All the more so when he has only said to you, 'Bathe and
14 be cleansed.'" So he went down and immersed in the Jordan seven times,
fulfilling the instruction of the man of God, and his skin became like the
skin of a young boy, and he was cleansed.

15 He went back to the man of God along with all his company, and he came
and stood before him. "Now I know that there is no God in all the world
except in Israel," he said. "Now, please accept your servant's gift."

77 | A term of respect.

16 "As the LORD lives, whom I serve," he said, "I will not accept it." He urged
him to accept, but he refused.

17 "If not," said Naaman, "may your servant be given two mule loads' worth
of soil, for your servant will no longer offer burnt offering or sacrifice to
18 other gods, but only to the LORD. But may the LORD forgive your servant
this: when my master comes to the temple of Rimon[78] to bow down there,
he leans on my hand so that I must bow down in the temple of Rimon. So
when I bow down in the temple of Rimon, may the LORD forgive your
servant for this."

19 "Go in peace," he said to him.

20 When he had traveled some distance away from him, Geḥazi, the servant
of the man of God, Elisha, thought, "Look, my master has let that Aramean
Naaman off without taking what he brought with him. As the LORD lives, I
21 will run after him and take something from him." And Geḥazi chased after
Naaman. When Naaman saw him running behind him, he alighted from
his chariot toward him.

"Is all well?" he said.

22 "All is well," he said. "My master has sent me, saying, 'Two lads from the
brotherhood of the prophets in the Efrayim Hills have just come to me;
please let them have a talent of silver and two sets of clothing.'"

23 "Please," said Naaman, "be so kind as to accept two talents." He urged him
and tied two talents of silver in two bags with two sets of clothing and gave
24 them to two of his servants to bear before him. When he reached the Ofel,
he took it off their hands and deposited it inside. Then he dismissed the
men and they left.

25 When he came to attend to his master, Elisha said to him, "Where have
you been, Geḥazi?"

"Your servant has not gone anywhere," he said.

26 "Was I not with you there in spirit when a man came down from his chariot
to meet you?" he said to him. "Is now the time to take silver and to take
clothes, and olive groves and vineyards, and sheep and cattle, and servants
27 and maidservants? Now, the blight of Naaman will cling to you and your
descendants forever."

And he left his presence as a leper, as white as snow.

6 1 The brotherhood of the prophets said to Elisha, "Look – the place where
2 we live under your charge is too cramped for us. Let us go to the Jordan,
and each one of us will take a beam from there, and there we will build a
meeting place for us."

78 | Another name for Hadad, the Aramean god of storm and thunder.

"Yes, go," he said.

3 "Please, be so kind as to accompany your servants," one said.

4 "I will come," he said, and he accompanied them. When they reached the
5 Jordan, they began to cut the wood. But as one of them was felling a beam,
the ax-head fell into the water.

"Oh, no, Master!" he cried, "it was borrowed."

6 "Where did it fall?" asked the man of God. When he showed him the place,
he chopped off a stick and flung it in, and it made the ax-head float.

7 "Pick it up," he said, and he reached out and took it.

8 Now the king of Aram was at war with Israel, and he took counsel with his
officials. "I will set up camp in a certain hidden place," he said.

9 The man of God sent word to the king of Israel: "Beware of passing through
10 that place, for the Arameans have set up camp there." So the king of Israel
sent warning to the place that the man of God specified to him, and time
11 and again he took precautions there. This made the king of Aram seethe,
and he summoned his officials. "Tell me," he said to them, "who among
us has defected to the king of Israel?"

12 "No, my lord the king," said one of his officials, "for it is Elisha, the prophet
in Israel, who has been informing the king of Israel of the words you speak
in your private chamber."

13 "Go and find out where he is," he said, "and I will send and seize him."

14 When he was informed, "He is in Dotan," he sent out horses and chariots
15 and vast forces there. They arrived at night and surrounded the city. The
man of God's attendant rose early and went outside, to find that a force
with horses and chariots was surrounding the city.

"Oh, no, Master," his servant said to him, "what shall we do?"

16 "Do not be afraid," he said, "for there are many more with us than with
them."

17 And Elisha prayed. "O Lord," he said, "open his eyes now, so he may
see."

The Lord opened the boy's eyes, and suddenly, the hill was full of horses
18 and fiery chariots all around Elisha. As they came down to him, Elisha
prayed to the Lord, "Strike this nation with a blindness." And He struck
them with a blindness, just as Elisha said.

19 "This is not the way, and this is not the city," Elisha said to them. "Follow
me, and I will lead you to the man you seek." And he led them to Shomron.
20 When they reached Shomron, Elisha said, "O Lord, open the eyes of these
men and let them see." And the Lord opened their eyes, and they found

21 themselves inside Shomron. When the king of Israel saw them, he said to
Elisha, "Shall I attack, Father?[79] Shall I attack?"

22 "Do not attack," he said. "Did you capture those you wish to attack with
your own sword and bow? Place bread and water before them, and let
23 them eat and drink and go to their master." So he prepared a great feast for
them, and they ate and drank; then he sent them off, and they went back
to their master. And Aramean bands stopped raiding the land of Israel.

24 But some time later, Ben Hadad, king of Aram, gathered all his forces and
25 marched up to lay siege to Shomron. Famine grew fierce in Shomron as
the siege went on, until a donkey's head fetched eighty pieces of silver,
26 and a quarter kab of doves' droppings[80] fetched five pieces of silver. Once,
as the king of Israel was passing along the wall, a woman screamed out to
him, "Save me, O lord the king!"

27 "If the Lord has not saved you, how can I save you?" he said. "From the
28 threshing floor, or from the winepress?" Then the king said to her, "What
is the matter?"

"That woman said to me, 'Give me your son, and we will eat him today; we
29 will eat my son tomorrow,'" she said, "so we cooked my son and ate him.
But when I said to her the next day, 'Give me your son and let us eat him,'
she had hidden her son."

30 When the king heard the woman's words, he rent his clothes; and as
he passed along the wall, the people saw that he was wearing sackcloth
underneath.

31 "So may the Lord do to me – and more," he said, "if the head of Elisha
32 son of Shafat remains on his shoulders today." And he sent a man ahead
of him.

Elisha was sitting in his house, and the elders were sitting with him. Before
the messenger arrived, he said to the elders, "Do you see? That son of a
murderer has ordered my decapitation! Look, when the messenger arrives,
shut the door and hold the door fast against him – for no doubt, the sound
33 of his master's footsteps is close behind." And as he was still speaking with
them, the messenger descended upon him.

"This evil is from the Lord,"[81] he said. "How can I still have hope in the
Lord?

7 1 "And Elisha said, "Hear the word of the Lord. Thus says the Lord: By this
time tomorrow, a *se'a*[82] of fine flour will sell for a shekel, and two *se'a* of
barley will sell for a shekel at the gate of Shomron."

---

79 | See note on 5:13.

80 | A popular term for carob husks.

81 | According to Rashi, Radak, and others, it is the king now speaking.

82 | See note on 1 Kings 18:32.

2 The adjutant upon whose arm the king leaned spoke up and said to the
man of God, "Even if the LORD were to make floodgates in the heavens,
how could this possibly come to pass?"

"You will see it with your own eyes," he said, "but you will not eat of it."

3 There were four men, who were lepers, at the entrance to the gate, and they
4 said to one another, "Why should we sit here until we die? If we decide to
enter the city when there is famine in the city, we will die there; and if we
stay here, we will die. So let us now defect to the Aramean camp; if they let
5 us live, we will live, and if they kill us, we will die." They set out at dusk to
reach the Aramean camp, but when they reached the edge of the Aramean
6 camp, there was no one there. For the LORD had caused the Aramean
camp to hear the sound of chariots, the sound of horses, the sound of
a vast army – and the men had said to one another, "Look, the king of
Israel must have hired the Hittite kings and the kings of Egypt against us,
7 to attack us!" They rose and fled at dusk, leaving their tents, their horses
and their donkeys, and the camp as it was, and they ran for their lives.

8 When those lepers reached the edge of the camp, they entered one tent
and ate and drank. Then they carried off silver and gold and garments
from there and went and hid them. When they came back, they went into
9 another tent, carried off what was in it, and went and hid it. But then one
man said to another, "We are not doing what is right. This is a day of good
news, yet we are silent. If we wait until the light of morning, we will be
10 found guilty. We must go and report to the royal palace right now." When
they arrived, they called out to the city gatekeepers and reported to them,
"We came to the Aramean camp, but there was not a man or a human voice
there, with the horses still tied up and the donkeys still tied up and the
11 tents just as they were." The gatekeepers called out, and it was reported
inside the royal palace.

12 The king rose in the night and said to his servants, "Let me tell you what
the Arameans are doing to us. They know we are starving, so they have
left the camp to hide in the field, planning, 'When they leave the city, we
will catch them alive and enter the city.'"

13 One of his servants spoke up. "Let them take five of the remaining horses
that are still here," he said. "Look, either they will be like all the masses of
Israelites who remain or like all the masses of Israelites who have perished.
14 Let us send and find out." So they took two chariots with horses, and the
king sent them after the Aramean camp, ordering them, "Go and find out."
15 They followed them as far as the Jordan to find that the whole road was
full of garments and vessels that Aram had cast aside in their haste, and
the messengers went back and reported to the king.

16 Then the people went out and ransacked the Aramean camp, so that a
se'a of fine flour fetched a shekel, and two *se'a* of barley fetched a shekel,
17 fulfilling the word of the LORD. Meanwhile, the king had stationed the

adjutant on whose arm he leaned by the gate, and the people trampled
him to death by the gate – just as the man of God had pronounced when
18 the king came down to him. For when the man of God had told the king,
"Two *se'a* of barley will fetch a shekel, and a *se'a* of fine flour will fetch a
19 shekel by this time tomorrow at the gate of Shomron," the adjutant had
retorted to the man of God, "Even if the Lord were to make floodgates
in the heavens, how could this possibly come to pass?"

"You will see it with your own eyes," he had said, "but you will not eat of
it."

20 And that is exactly what happened to him – the people trampled him to
death by the gate.

8 1 Now Elisha had told the woman whose son he had revived, "Leave with
your household right away and settle wherever you can, for the Lord has
2 decreed a seven-year famine on the land, and it has already begun." The
woman carried out the man of God's instructions at once; she set out with
3 her household and settled in the land of the Philistines for seven years. At
the end of seven years, the woman returned from the land of the Philistines,
and she went to appeal to the king about her house and her field.

4 Just then, the king was speaking with Geḥazi, the man of God's servant,
saying, "Please, tell me all about the great deeds that Elisha has done."
5 And as he was telling the king about how he had revived the dead, the
woman whose son he had revived came to appeal to the king about her
house and field.

6 "My lord the king," said Geḥazi, "this is the very woman, and this is her
son whom Elisha revived."

The king questioned the woman, and she told him her story; then the king
assigned a eunuch to her, ordering: "Restore all that belongs to her and
all the revenue from her field from the day she left the land until now."

7 Elisha arrived in Damascus while Ben Hadad, king of Aram, was ill. When
8 he was informed, "The man of God has arrived here," the king said to
Ḥazael, "Take a gift with you, and go out to meet the man of God, and
inquire of the Lord through him, asking, 'Will I recover from this illness?'"
9 Ḥazael went to meet him, taking a gift with him: forty camel loads of all
of Damascus's finest, and he came and stood before him. "Your son Ben
Hadad, king of Aram, has sent me to you to ask, 'Will I recover from this
illness?'"

10 "Say to him, 'You will certainly recover,'" said Elisha, "though the Lord
11 has shown me that he will certainly die." He managed to keep a stoic face
for a long time, but then the man of God began to weep.

12 "Why does my lord weep?" asked Ḥazael.

"Because I know the evil you will inflict on Israel," said Elisha. "You will

set their fortresses on fire and put their young men to the sword and dash
their little ones to pieces and slash open their pregnant women."

13 "But how could your mere dog of a servant do such mighty deeds?" said
Ḥazael.

"The LORD has shown me," said Elisha, "that you will be king over Aram."

14 He left Elisha and came to his lord. "What did Elisha say to you?" he asked
him.

"He said to me, 'You will certainly recover,'" he said.

15 But the next day, he took a cloth, dipped it in water, and spread it over his
face, and he died. And Ḥazael reigned in his place.

16 In the fifth year of Yoram son of Aḥav, king of Israel – Yehoshafat had been
king of Yehuda – Yehoram son of Yehoshafaṭ became king over Yehuda.
17 He was thirty-two years old when he became king, and for eight years he
18 reigned in Jerusalem. He followed in the ways of the kings of Israel, as the
house of Aḥav had done, for Aḥav's daughter was his wife; he did what
19 was evil in the eyes of the LORD. But the LORD was not willing to destroy
Yehuda for the sake of His servant David, for He had promised to grant
him a lamp for his descendants for all time.[83]

20 In his time Edom rebelled against Yehuda and appointed their own king.
21 Yoram crossed over to Tza'ir with all his chariots; he advanced at night to
attack Edom, who had surrounded him and his chariot officers, but the
22 troops fled back to their homes. And Edom has rebelled against Yehuda
ever since; Livna, too, rebelled at that time.

23 As for the rest of Yoram's history and all his deeds – they are recorded in
24 the Book of the History of the Kings of Yehuda. And Yoram slept with his
ancestors and was buried with his ancestors in the City of David. And his
son Aḥazyahu reigned in his place.

25 In the twelfth year of Yoram son of Aḥav, king of Israel, Aḥazyahu son of
26 Yehoram became king over Yehuda. Aḥazyahu was twenty-two years old
when he became king, and he reigned in Jerusalem for a single year; his
27 mother's name was Atalyahu daughter of Omri, the king of Israel.[84] He
followed in the ways of the house of Aḥav, doing what was evil in the eyes
of the LORD just like the house of Aḥav, for he was a son-in-law of the
28 house of Aḥav. Together with Yoram son of Aḥav, he went to war against
Ḥazael, king of Aram, at Ramot Gilad, but the Arameans defeated Yoram.
29 King Yoram went back to Yizre'el to recover from the wounds that the
Arameans had inflicted upon him in Ramah when he was fighting against
Ḥazael, king of Aram. And Aḥazyahu son of Yehoram, king of Yehuda,
went down to visit Yoram son of Aḥav in Yizre'el while he was injured.

83 | See I Kings 15:4.

84 | Cf. verse 18; the term "daughter" in this verse is likely intended to mean "granddaughter."

9 1 The prophet Elisha summoned one of the brotherhood of the prophets.

"Hitch up your tunic," he said to him, "take this flask of oil in your hand,
2 and go to Ramot Gilad. When you arrive there, you will see Yehu son of
Yehoshafat son of Nimshi there; go in and get him to leave his comrades,
3 and bring him into an inner room. Then take the flask of oil and pour it
on his head and say, 'Thus says the Lord: I have anointed you as king of
Israel.' Then open the door and flee; do not linger."

4 5 So the lad, the prophet's servant boy, set out for Ramot Gilad. When he
arrived, there were the army officers sitting together. "I have a message for
you, officer," he said.

"For which one of us?" asked Yehu.

"For you, officer," he said.

6 He got up and came inside, and he poured the oil on his head. "Thus says
the Lord, God of Israel," he said. "'I have anointed you as king of the
7 Lord's people – of Israel! You will strike down the house of Aḥav, your
master; thus I will take vengeance on Izevel for the blood of My servants
8 the prophets and the blood of all the Lord's servants. All the house of
Aḥav will be lost; I will cut off every last male of Aḥav in Israel, bond and
9 free, and I will make the house of Aḥav like the house of Yorovam son of
10 Nevat and like the house of Basha son of Aḥiya. As for Izevel – the dogs
will devour her in the plot of Yizre'el, with no one to bury her.'" And he
opened the door and fled.

11 When Yehu went out to his lord's officials, they said to him, "Is all well?
Why did that madman come to you?"

"Oh, you know the man and his talk," he said to them.

12 "Lies!" they said. "Tell us!"

"This is what he said to me," he said. "Thus says the Lord: I have anointed
you as king of Israel."

13 Each man quickly took his garment and placed it beneath him[85] on the top
14 step. They blasted the ram's horn and proclaimed, "Yehu is king!" Thus
Yehu son of Yehoshafat son of Nimshi formed a conspiracy against Yoram.
Yoram had been on the defense against Ḥazael, king of Aram, in Ramot
15 Gilad, together with all of Israel. But Yoram had come back to Yizre'el to
recover from the wounds the Arameans had inflicted upon him while he
was fighting against Ḥazael, king of Aram.

"If this is indeed your will," said Yehu, "let no one escape from town to
16 go and inform in Yizre'el." And Yehu mounted a chariot and set out for

85 | Beneath Yehu.

Yizre'el, for there Yoram lay, and Aḥazya, king of Yehuda, had gone down to visit Yoram.

17 The watchman stationed in the lookout tower in Yizre'el saw Yehu's company as they approached and called out, "I see a company."

"Fetch a rider and send him out toward them," said Yoram, "and have him ask, 'Is all well?'"

18 The rider set out toward him on horseback and asked, "Thus says the king: 'Is all well?'"

"Does it matter to you if all is well?" said Yehu. "Fall in behind me."

And the watchman reported, "The messenger has reached them, but he has not come back."

19 He sent out a second rider on horseback. When he reached them, he said, "Thus says the king: 'Is all well?'"

"Does it matter to you if all is well?" said Yehu. "Fall in behind me."

20 And the watchman reported, "He has reached them, but he has not come back. It looks like the driving of Yehu son of Nimshi – he drives like a madman."

21 "Harness up," said Yehoram, and he harnessed his chariot. Yehoram, king
of Israel, and Aḥazyahu, king of Yehuda, went out toward Yehu, each in
his own chariot, and they met him at the plot that belonged to Navot the
22 Jezreelite. When Yehoram saw Yehu, he asked, "Is all well, Yehu?"

"How can all be well," he said, "while the whoring and endless devilry of your mother Izevel continues?"

23 Yehoram steered back around and fled. "Treason, Aḥazya!" he called out
24 to Aḥazyahu. But Yehu had drawn a bow, and he struck Yoram between
his arms – the arrow pierced his heart, and he crumpled in his chariot.

25 "Pick him up," he said to his adjutant Bidkar, "and throw him in the field
plot of Navot the Jezreelite. Remember how you and I rode side by side
behind his father Aḥav when the Lord made this pronouncement against
26 him: 'I swear, having seen the blood of Navot and the blood of his children
last night,' declares the Lord, 'I will pay you back in this very plot,' declares
the Lord, so now pick him up and throw him in the plot, fulfilling the
word of the Lord."

27 When Aḥazya, king of Yehuda, saw, he fled by the Beit HaGan Road, and Yehu chased after him.

"Strike him as well!" said Yehu, and they struck him[86] in his chariot by the
28 Ascent of Gur near Yivle'am. He fled to Megiddo, and there he died. His

86 | The words "and they struck him" are not explicit in the Hebrew; see, e.g., Radak.

servants had him driven to Jerusalem and buried him in his ancestral grave in the City of David.

29 In the eleventh year of Yoram son of Aḥav, Aḥazya had become king over Yehuda.

30 Meanwhile, Yehu arrived in Yizre'el. When Izevel heard, she lined her
eyes with kohl and dressed her hair and looked out through the window.
31 When Yehu entered the gate, she said, "Is all well, Zimri, killer of his own
master?"[87]

32 He looked up to the window and said, "Who is with me? Who?" Two or three eunuchs looked out at him.

33 "Throw her down," he said, and they threw her down, and her blood spattered the walls and the horses, and he trampled her.

34 He came in and ate and drank and then said, "Take note of that cursed one,
35 and bury her. After all, she was the daughter of a king." But when they went
to bury her, all they found of her was her skull, her legs, and the palms of
36 her hands. When they went back to tell him, he said, "It is the word of the
Lord, which He pronounced through His servant Eliyahu the Tishbite: 'In
37 the plot of Yizre'el, the dogs will devour Izevel's flesh.' Now Izevel's corpse
shall be like dung on the ground in the plot of Yizre'el, so that none will
ever say, 'This was Izevel.'"

10 1 Now Aḥav had seventy sons in Shomron. Yehu wrote letters and sent them
to Shomron to the officers of Yizre'el, the elders, and the guardians of
2 Aḥav's sons, stating: "Now, when this letter reaches you, as the sons of your
lord are with you, and the chariots, horses, fortified cities, and weapons
3 are also with you, consider which is the best and worthiest of your lord's
sons, and set him on his father's throne. Then fight for the house of your
4 lord." They were absolutely terrified and said, "Look, if two kings could
5 not stand up to him, how can we take a stand?" Those in charge of the
palace, those in charge of the city, the elders, and the guardians replied to
Yehu, saying, "We are your servants, and whatever you say to us we will
6 do. We will not make anyone king; do as you please." So he wrote them a
second letter, stating: "If you are on my side, ready to obey my command,
then take the heads of the men, your master's sons, and come to me this
time tomorrow in Yizre'el." The king's sons numbered seventy men, and
7 the nobles of the city were raising them. When the letter reached them,
they seized the king's sons, massacred the seventy men, and placed their
8 heads in baskets, which they sent to him in Yizre'el. When the messenger
informed him, "They have brought the heads of the king's sons," he said,
"Place them in two heaps by the entrance to the gate until morning."

9 In the morning, he went out and stood by. "You are all innocent," he said

87 | See 1 Kings 16:8–10.

to all the people, "while it is I who formed a conspiracy against my lord
10 and killed him. Yet who killed all of these? Know, then, that not a word of
what the Lord pronounced for the house of Aḥav will fall through; the
11 Lord has fulfilled what He pronounced through His servant Eliyahu." And
Yehu struck down all who remained of the house of Aḥav in Yizre'el – all
its nobles, associates, and priests – until there were no survivors left.

12 He then set out toward Shomron, and on the way, at Beit Eked of the
13 shepherds, Yehu encountered the kinsmen of Aḥazyahu, the king of
Yehuda.

"Who are you?" he asked, and they said, "We are Aḥazyahu's kinsmen, and
we are going down to visit the king's sons and the queen mother's sons."

14 "Take them alive!" he said, and they took them alive, and he massacred
them by the Beit Eked pit – forty-two men; he did not leave a single one
of them.

15 They continued on from there. He met Yehonadav son of Rekhav coming
toward him and greeted him. "Is your heart truly with me, as my heart is
with you?" he said.

"It is indeed," said Yehonadav.

"If so, give me your hand."

He held out his hand, and Yehu hoisted him up into the chariot with him.
16 "Come with me and see my fervor for the Lord," he said, and drove him
17 in his chariot. When he arrived in Shomron, he struck down all those who
were left to Aḥav in Shomron until he had wiped him out, fulfilling the
word that the Lord had pronounced to Eliyahu.

18 Yehu then gathered all the people and said to them, "Aḥav hardly served
19 the Baal; Yehu will serve him fully! Now, summon all of Baal's prophets,
worshippers, and priests to me; let no one be absent, for I am making
a great sacrifice for Baal, and whoever is absent will not live." Yehu was
staging deceit in order to destroy the worshippers of Baal.

20 "Declare a holy assembly for Baal," said Yehu, and so it was proclaimed.
21 Yehu sent throughout Israel, and all the worshippers of Baal came; not a
single one failed to come. They came to the temple of Baal, and the temple
22 of Baal was packed from end to end. "Bring out the vestments for all the
worshippers of Baal," he said to the man in charge of the raiment, and he
23 brought vestments out for them. Then Yehu and Yehonadav son of Rekhav
entered the temple of Baal.

"Search carefully and make sure there are no worshippers of the Lord
here among you," he said to the worshippers of Baal. "There must only
24 be worshippers of Baal." And they went to offer sacrifices and burnt
offerings.

Now Yehu had stationed eighty men outside, and he had said to them, "If
a single person escapes among those I hand over to you, it will be your
25 life for his life." And as he finished presenting the burnt offering, Yehu
said to the sentry and the adjutants, "Come in and strike them down! Let
no man escape!" They put them to the sword, then the sentry and the
adjutants threw them out and proceeded to the Baal temple compound.
26 27 They brought out the pillars of the temple of Baal and burned them, and
they tore down the sacred pillar of Baal, and they tore down the temple
28 of Baal, and they have used it as latrines ever since. Thus Yehu wiped out
the Baal from Israel.

29 But as for the sins of Yorovam son of Nevat, who led Israel to sin through
the golden calves in Beit El and Dan – Yehu did not turn away from
30 them.The LORD said to Yehu, "Because you have accomplished what was
right in My eyes, executing all My intentions against the house of Aḥav,
31 four generations of your line will sit on the throne of Israel." But Yehu did
not follow the teaching of the LORD, God of Israel, with care, with all his
heart; he did not turn away from the sins of Yorovam, who led Israel to
sin.

32 In those days, the LORD began to weaken Israel at the edges. Ḥazael attacked
33 Israel on every front: from east of the Jordan, all the land of the Gilad – the
Gadites, the Reubenites, and the Manassites – from Aroer by the Arnon
34 Stream to the Gilad and the Bashan. As for the rest of Yehu's history and
all his deeds and all his heroic feats – they are recorded in the Book of the
35 History of the Kings of Israel. And Yehu slept with his ancestors, and they
36 buried him in Shomron. And his son Yehoaḥaz reigned in his place. Yehu
had reigned over Israel for twenty-eight years in Shomron.

11 1 When Atalya, the mother of Aḥazyahu, saw that her son was dead, she
2 swiftly destroyed all those of royal descent. But Yehosheva, the daughter of
King Yoram and the sister of Aḥazyahu, took Yoash, Aḥazya's son, and stole
him away from where the princes were being put to death to a bedchamber,
together with his nurse. They hid him from Atalya, so he was not put to
3 death. He stayed with her in the House of the LORD, hiding for six years,
while Atalya reigned over the land.

4 In the seventh year, Yehoyada[88] sent for the Keretite[89] officers of hundreds
and the sentry and had them come to him in the House of the LORD. He
made a pact with them and had them swear an oath in the House of the
5 LORD; then he showed them the king's son. "This is what you must do," he
instructed them. "A third of you on weekly duty will keep guard over the
6 royal palace, a third of you at the Sur Gate, and a third of you at the gate
7 behind the sentry post – maintain unrelenting watch over the House. As
for the two of your units who are off weekly duty – keep guard over the

88 | The High Priest and Yehosheva's husband; see verse 9 and II Chronicles 22:11, 24:6.

89 | See note on I Kings 1:38.

8 House of the LORD for the sake of the king. Surround the king on all sides,
and make sure every man's weapon is poised, and whoever breaks through
the ranks must be killed. And stay with the king when he comes or goes."

9 The officers of hundreds did all that the priest Yehoyada instructed them,
and each took their men – those on weekly duty and those off weekly
10 duty – and came to the priest Yehoyada. The priest gave the officers of
hundreds David's own spears and quivers, which were in the House of the
11 LORD. And the sentry – each man with his weapon poised – were stationed
from the south end of the House to the north end of the House, by the
12 altar and the House, all around the king. He brought out the king's son
and set the crown and the royal insignia upon him. They declared him as
king and anointed him and clapped their hands and shouted, "Long live
the king!"

13 Atalya heard the sound of the sentry, of the people, and she came to the
14 people at the House of the LORD. When Atalya looked up to find the king
standing on the platform, as was the custom, with officers with trumpets
beside the king and all the people of the land rejoicing and blowing the
trumpets, Atalya rent her clothes and called out, "Treason! Treason!"

15 But Yehoyada gave orders to the officers of hundreds, the force commanders.
"Take her out between the ranks," he said to them, "and put anyone who
follows to the sword," for the priest thought, "She should not be put to
16 death in the House of the LORD." They cleared the way for her, and she
entered the royal palace through the horses' entrance, and there she was
put to death.

17 Then Yehoyada reinstated the covenant between the LORD, the king, and
the people, to be the LORD's people; and between the king and the people.
18 All the people of the land came to the temple of Baal and tore it down and
shattered its altars and images through and through, and killed Matan, the
priest of Baal, in front of the altars.

19 The priest set watchmen over the House of the LORD, and he had the
officers of the hundreds, the Keretites, the sentry, and all the people of
the land escort the king down from the House of the LORD. They came
in through the sentry gate of the royal palace, and he took his seat upon
20 the royal throne. All the people of the land rejoiced, and calm settled over
the city. As for Atalya, they had put her to death by sword in the royal
palace.

12 1 2 Yehoash was seven years old when he became king; Yehoash became king
in the seventh year of Yehu, and for forty years, he reigned in Jerusalem.
3 His mother's name was Tzivya, of Be'er Sheva. Yehoash did what was right
in the eyes of the LORD all his days, as the priest Yehoyada had taught him.
4 Yet the high shrines were not removed; the people still offered sacrifices
and incense at the high shrines.

5 Yehoash said to the priests, "All the dedicated money brought to the
House of the LORD – the money from the census, the money equivalent
to a person's worth,[90] or any money that a person is moved to bring to the
6 House of the LORD – let the priests accept it, each from his donor, and
they will see to the repair of the House wherever damage may be found."
7 But by the twenty-third year of King Yehoash, the priests had not seen to
8 the repair of the House, and King Yehoash summoned the priest Yehoyada
and the priests.
"Why have you not kept the House in repair?" he said to them. "From now
on, do not take any money from your donors; rather, you must donate it
9 toward the repair of the House." The priests agreed that they would neither
10 take money from the people nor see to the House's repair. So the priest
Yehoyada took a chest, made a hole in its lid, and placed it to the right of
the altar, where people entered the House of the LORD. There, the priestly
guardians of the threshold placed all the money that was brought to the
11 House of the LORD. Whenever they saw that there was a considerable
amount of money in the chest, the royal scribe and the High Priest would
come up, tie it into a bundle, and count the money found in the House
12 of the LORD. They then gave the weighed-out money to the foremen in
charge of the House of the LORD, who would use it to pay the carpenters
13 and the builders who worked in the House of the LORD, and the masons
and stonecutters, and to purchase timber and quarry stones to keep the
House of the LORD in repair, and for any other expenses for maintenance
14 of the House. However, no silver bowls, shears, basins, or trumpets – or
any golden or silver vessels – were made from the money that was brought
15 to the House of the LORD, as it was given to the overseers, who used it
16 to keep the House of the LORD in repair. They did not need to keep track
of the men who received the money to pay out to the workers, for they
17 dealt honestly. Money from guilt offerings and money from purification
offerings was not brought to the House of the LORD; it belonged to the
priests.

18 At that time, Ḥazael, king of Aram, marched up and attacked Gat, and he
19 captured it; Ḥazael then set out to march up against Jerusalem. So Yehoash,
king of Yehuda, took all the sacred objects that had been dedicated by his
ancestors Yehoshafat, Yehoram, and Aḥazya, the kings of Yehuda, along
with his own sacred objects and all the gold found in the treasuries of the
House of the LORD and the royal palace. He sent them to Ḥazael, king of
Aram, and he withdrew from Jerusalem.

20 As for the rest of Yoash's history and all his deeds – they are recorded in
21 the Book of the History of the Kings of Yehuda. His officials rose up and
formed a conspiracy, and they struck Yoash down in Beit Milo where it
22 leads down to Sila; Yozakhar son of Shimat and Yehozavad son of Shomer
were the officials who struck him down and killed him. They buried him

90 | See Leviticus 27:1–8.

with his ancestors in the City of David, and his son Amatzya reigned in
his place.

13 1 In the twenty-third year of Yehoash son of Aḥazyahu, king of Yehuda,
Yehoaḥaz son of Yehu became king over Israel in Shomron for seventeen
2 years. He did what was evil in the eyes of the LORD, following after the
sins of Yorovam son of Nevat, who led Israel to sin; he did not turn away
3 from them. Then the LORD's rage flared against Israel, and He handed
them over to Ḥazael, king of Aram, and to Ben Hadad, Ḥazael's son, for a
4 long time. But Yehoaḥaz entreated the LORD, and the LORD heeded him,
for He saw Israel's oppression and how the king of Aram oppressed them.
5 So the LORD granted Israel a savior, and they were freed from the hand
6 of Aram, and the Israelites dwelled in their homes as before. But they did
not turn away from the sins of the house of Yorovam, who had led Israel to
sin – they followed them, and the sacred tree[91] still stood in Shomron.

7 Yehoaḥaz was left without an army save fifty riders, ten chariots, and ten
thousand foot soldiers, for the king of Aram had reduced them into dust
8 to be trampled. As for the rest of Yehoaḥaz's history and all his deeds and
heroic feats – they are recorded in the Book of the History of the Kings
9 of Israel. And Yehoaḥaz slept with his ancestors, and they buried him in
Shomron. And his son Yoash reigned in his place.

10 In the thirty-seventh year of Yoash, king of Yehuda, Yehoash son of
11 Yehoaḥaz became king over Israel in Shomron for sixteen years. He did
what was evil in the eyes of the LORD; he did not turn away from all the
sins of Yorovam son of Nevat, who had led Israel to sin; he perpetuated
12 them. As for the rest of Yoash's history and all his deeds and heroic feats,
and how he fought with Amatzya, king of Yehuda – they are recorded
13 in the Book of the History of the Kings of Israel. And Yoash slept with
his ancestors, and Yorovam ascended his throne. Yoash was buried in
Shomron with the kings of Israel.

14 Elisha had fallen ill with the illness of which he was to die, and Yoash, king
of Israel, went down to him. He wept in his presence and said, "Father!
Father! The chariots of Israel and its riders!"[92]

15 "Take a bow and some arrows," Elisha said to him, and he fetched him a
bow and some arrows.

16 "Position your hand on the bow," he said to the king of Israel, and he
positioned his hand, and Elisha put his hands over the king's hands.

17 "Open the window that faces east," he said, and he opened it. Then Elisha
said, "Shoot," and he shot.

---

91 | See I Kings 16:33.
92 | Cf. 2:12.

"An arrow of victory for the LORD; an arrow of victory over Aram," he said.
"You will defeat Aram at Afek – completely."

18 He then added, "Take the arrows," and he took them. "Now, strike the
ground!" he said to the king of Israel. He struck three times and stopped –

19 and the man of God grew furious with him. "Had you struck five or six
times, you would have defeated Aram completely," he said, "but now,
20 you will defeat Aram only three times." And Elisha died, and they buried
him.

21 Now Moabite bands would raid the land at the start of every year. Once, as
they were burying someone, they suddenly saw the band, and they flung
the man into Elisha's grave. The moment the man's body touched Elisha's
bones, he sprang to life and stood on his feet.

22 Ḥazael, king of Aram, oppressed Israel throughout the days of Yehoaḥaz.
23 But the LORD was gracious and compassionate toward them; He turned
to them for the sake of His covenant with Avraham, Yitzḥak, and Yaakov,
and He was unwilling to destroy them or cast them away from His
24 presence – for now. When Ḥazael, king of Aram, died, and his son Ben
25 Hadad reigned in his place, Yehoash son of Yehoaḥaz managed to take back
the cities from Ben Hadad son of Ḥazael – those that had been taken from
his father Yehoaḥaz in war. Yoash defeated him three times and recaptured
the cities of Israel.

14 1 In the second year of King Yoash son of Yoaḥaz of Israel, Amatzyahu son
2 of Yoash, king of Yehuda, became king. He was twenty-five years old when
he became king, and for twenty-nine years he reigned in Jerusalem. His
3 mother's name was Yehoadan, of Jerusalem. He did what was right in the
eyes of the LORD, though not to the extent of his ancestor David; he did
4 all that his father Yoash had done. Yet the high shrines were not removed;
the people still offered sacrifices and incense at the high shrines.

5 Once the kingdom was firmly in his grasp, he executed the officials who
6 had struck down the king his father. But he did not execute the sons of the
assassins, fulfilling what is written in the book of the teaching of Moshe, as
the LORD commanded: "Parents shall not be put to death for their children,
nor shall children be put to death for their parents. A person shall be put to
death only for his own sin."[93]

7 He defeated ten thousand of Edom in the Valley of Salt, and he captured
Sela in battle and renamed it Yokte'el, as it has been called ever since.

8 Then Amatzya sent messengers to Yehoash son of Yehoaḥaz son of Yehu,
9 king of Israel, saying, "Come, let us meet face-to-face." Yehoash, king
of Israel, sent a response to Amatzyahu, king of Yehuda: "The thistle in

93 | Deuteronomy 24:16.

Lebanon sent to the cedar in Lebanon, saying, 'Give me your daughter as
a wife for my son.' But a wild beast in Lebanon passed by and trampled the
10 thistle. Yes, you defeated Edom, but you have grown arrogant – revel in your
honor and stay at home. Why should you provoke disaster and fall down
together with Yehuda?"

11 But Amatzyahu paid no heed, and Yehoash, king of Israel, marched up
and met Amatzyahu, king of Yehuda, face-to-face in Beit Shemesh of
12 Yehuda. Yehuda was routed before Israel, and every man fled back to his
13 tent. As for Amatzyahu, king of Yehuda, the son of Yehoash, the son of
Aḥazyahu – Yehoash, king of Israel, captured him in Beit Shemesh and
then marched on Jerusalem. He broke down the wall of Jerusalem from the
14 Efrayim Gate up to the Corner Gate, a distance of four hundred cubits. He
seized all the gold and silver and all the vessels that were in the House of
the Lord and the royal treasuries of the palace, along with hostages, and
he returned to Shomron.

15 As for the rest of Yehoash's history, his deeds and his heroic feats and how
he fought with Amatzyahu, king of Yehuda – they are recorded in the Book
16 of the History of the Kings of Israel. And Yehoash slept with his ancestors
and was buried in Shomron with the kings of Israel. And his son Yorovam
reigned in his place.

17 Amatzyahu son of Yoash, king of Yehuda, lived for fifteen years after
18 the death of Yehoash son of Yehoaḥaz, king of Israel. As for the rest of
Amatzyahu's history – it is recorded in the Book of the History of the
19 Kings of Yehuda. They formed a conspiracy against him in Jerusalem, and
he fled to Lakhish, but they sent after him to Lakhish and assassinated him
20 there. They conveyed his body back by horse, and he was buried with his
21 ancestors in Jerusalem, in the City of David. Then all the people of Yehuda
took Azarya, who was sixteen years old, and made him king in place of
22 his father Amatzyahu. He was the one who rebuilt Eilat and restored it to
Yehuda once the king slept with his ancestors.

23 In the fifteenth year of Amatzyahu son of Yoash, king of Yehuda, Yorovam
son of Yoash, king of Israel, became king in Shomron for forty-one years.
24 He did what was evil in the eyes of the Lord; he did not turn away from
25 all the sins of Yorovam son of Nevat, who led Israel to sin. He was the one
who restored Israel's border from Levo Ḥamat to the Arava Sea, fulfilling
the word of the Lord, God of Israel, as He had promised through His
26 servant Yona son of Amitai, the prophet from Gat Ḥefer. For the Lord had
seen the depth of Israel's bitter suffering, with neither bond nor free left
27 and no helper for Israel. But the Lord had not decreed to blot out Israel's
name from under the heavens, so He delivered them through Yorovam
son of Yoash.

28 As for the rest of Yorovam's history and all his deeds and heroic feats in
battle, and how he restored Damascus and Ḥamat to Yehuda in Israel –

29 they are recorded in the Book of the History of the Kings of Israel. And
Yorovam slept with his ancestors, with the kings of Israel, and his son
Zekharya reigned in his place.

15 1 In the twenty-seventh year of Yorovam, king of Israel, Azarya[94] son of
2 Amatzya, king of Yehuda, became king. He was sixteen years old when he
became king, and for fifty-two years he reigned in Jerusalem. His mother's
3 name was Yekholyahu, of Jerusalem. He did what was right in the eyes
4 of the LORD, just as his father Amatzyahu had done. Yet the high shrines
were not removed; the people still offered sacrifices and incense at the
5 high shrines. The LORD struck the king with disease, and he became a leper
until his dying day. He remained in secluded quarters while Yotam, the
king's son, took charge of the palace and governed the people of the land.
6 As for the rest of Azaryahu's history and all his deeds – they are recorded
7 in the Book of the History of the Kings of Yehuda. And Azarya slept with
his ancestors, and they buried him with his ancestors in the City of David.
And his son Yotam reigned in his place.

8 In the thirty-eighth year of Azaryahu, king of Yehuda, Zekharyahu son
9 of Yorovam became king over Israel in Shomron for six months. He did
what was evil in the eyes of the LORD, as his ancestors did; he did not turn
10 away from the sins of Yorovam son of Nevat, who led Israel to sin. Then
Shalum son of Yavesh formed a conspiracy against him; he struck him
11 down before the people and assassinated him and reigned in his place.
As for the rest of Zekharya's history – it is recorded in the Book of the
12 History of the Kings of Israel. This was the word of the LORD as promised
to Yehu: "Four generations of your line will sit on the throne of Israel,"[95]
and it had come to pass.

13 Shalum son of Yavesh became king in the thirty-ninth year of Uziya,[96] king
14 of Yehuda, and for one month, he reigned in Shomron. Then Menaḥem
son of Gadi marched up from Tirtza and entered Shomron. He struck
down Shalum son of Yavesh in Shomron and assassinated him, and he
15 reigned in his place. As for the rest of Shalum's history and the conspiracy
that he formed – they are recorded in the Book of the History of the Kings
of Israel.

16 It was then that Menaḥem attacked Tifsaḥ and everything in it and its
territories from Tirtza; they would not yield, so he attacked – he even
17 slashed open its pregnant women. In the thirty-ninth year of Azarya, king
of Yehuda, Menaḥem son of Gadi became king over Israel, for ten years
18 in Shomron. He did what was evil in the eyes of the LORD; all his days, he
19 did not turn away from the sins of Yorovam son of Nevat. When Pul,[97] king

94 | Also referred to as Uziya; see, e.g., verses 13, 30, 32, 34.

95 | See 10:30.

96 | See note on verse 1.

97 | A nickname of the Assyrian king Tiglat Pileser III.

of Assyria, invaded the land, Menaḥem gave Pul one thousand talents of
20 silver to gain his support in maintaining control of the kingdom. Menaḥem
exacted the silver from Israel; every able man had to pay fifty shekel of
silver to the king of Assyria. Then the king of Assyria withdrew and did
21 not remain there in the land. As for the rest of Menaḥem's history and all
his deeds – they are recorded in the Book of the History of the Kings of
22 Israel. And Menaḥem slept with his ancestors, and his son Pekaḥya reigned
in his place.

23 In the fiftieth year of Azarya, king of Yehuda, Pekaḥya son of Menaḥem
24 became king over Israel in Shomron for two years. He did what was evil in
the eyes of the LORD; he did not turn away from the sins of Yorovam son
25 of Nevat, who led Israel to sin. Then Pekaḥ son of Remalyahu, his adjutant,
formed a conspiracy against him; he struck him down in the citadel of the
royal palace in Shomron. With him were Argov and Aryeh[98] and fifty men
26 of the Gileadites; they assassinated him, and he reigned in his place. As for
the rest of Pekaḥyahu's history and all his deeds – they are recorded in the
Book of the History of the Kings of Israel.

27 In the fifty-second year of Azarya, king of Yehuda, Pekaḥ son of Remalyahu
28 became king over Israel in Shomron for twenty years. He did what was evil
in the eyes of the LORD; he did not turn away from the sins of Yorovam
son of Nevat, who led Israel to sin.

29 In the days of Pekaḥ, king of Israel, Tiglat Pileser, king of Assyria, came
and seized Iyon, Avel Beit Maakha, Yanoaḥ, Kedesh, Ḥazor, the Gilad, the
30 Galil, and all the region of Naftali, and had them exiled to Assyria. Then
Hoshe'a son of Ela formed a conspiracy against Pekaḥ son of Remalyahu;
they struck him down and assassinated him, and he reigned in his place
31 in the twentieth year of Yotam son of Uziya. As for the rest of Pekaḥ's
history and all his deeds – they are recorded in the Book of the History
of the Kings of Israel.

32 In the second year of Pekaḥ son of Remalyahu, king of Israel, Yotam son
33 of Uziyahu, king of Yehuda, became king. He was twenty-five years old
when he became king, and for sixteen years he reigned in Jerusalem. His
34 mother's name was Yerusha daughter of Tzadok. He did what was right
35 in the eyes of the LORD, just as his father Uziyahu had done. Yet the high
shrines were not removed; the people still offered sacrifices and incense
36 at the high shrines. He built the upper gate of the House of the LORD. As
for the rest of Yotam's history and all his deeds – they are recorded in the
37 Book of the History of the Kings of Yehuda. At that time the LORD began
to rouse Retzin, king of Aram, and Pekaḥ son of Remalyahu against Yehuda.
38 And Yotam slept with his ancestors and was buried with his ancestors in
the City of David, his ancestor. And his son Aḥaz reigned in his place.

98 | Perhaps names of warriors or military units.

16 1 In the seventeenth year of Pekaḥ son of Remalyahu, Aḥaz son of Yotam,
2 king of Yehuda, became king. Aḥaz was twenty years old when he became
king, and for sixteen years he reigned in Jerusalem. But he did not do
what was right in the eyes of the Lord his God, like his ancestor David;
3 he followed in the ways of the kings of Israel and even passed his son
through the fire, imitating the horrors of the nations whom the Lord
4 had dispossessed before the Israelites. He offered sacrifices and incense
5 at the high shrines and on hilltops and under every shady tree. It was then
that Retzin, king of Aram, and Pekaḥ son of Remalyahu, king of Israel,
launched an attack on Jerusalem. They besieged Aḥaz, but they could not
6 conquer him. At that time, Retzin, king of Aram, restored Eilat to Aram,
and he drove out the Judahites from Eilat; Edomites came to Eilat and
have dwelled there ever since.

7 Then Aḥaz sent messengers to Tiglat Pileser, king of Assyria, saying, "I am
your servant and your son; come up and rescue me from the hand of the
8 king of Aram and the hand of the king of Israel, who threaten me." And
Aḥaz took the silver and gold that was in the House of the Lord and the
royal treasuries of the palace, and he sent them to the king of Assyria as
9 a bribe. The king of Assyria acceded to him; the king of Assyria launched
an attack on Damascus, captured it, and exiled its people to Kir. As for
Retzin – he put him to death.

10 King Aḥaz went to meet Tiglat Pileser, king of Assyria, in Damascus. When
he saw the altar in Damascus, King Aḥaz sent an image of the altar to Uriya
11 the priest with its design, down to every last detail of its construction. The
priest Uriya then built the altar exactly as King Aḥaz had instructed from
Damascus, and the priest Uriya completed it by the time that King Aḥaz
12 returned from Damascus. When the king arrived from Damascus and saw
13 the altar, he approached the altar and ascended it and offered up his burnt
offering and his grain offering, poured out his libation, and dashed the
blood of his peace offering against the altar.

14 As for the bronze altar before the Lord, he moved it from the front of the
House, between the new altar and the House of the Lord, and placed it
15 to the northern side of the new altar. King Aḥaz then instructed the priest
Uriya, "On the great altar, offer the morning burnt offering, the evening
grain offering, the royal burnt offering and grain offering, as well as the
burnt offering of all the people of the land and their grain offerings and
libations; and all blood from the burnt offerings and the blood from any
sacrifices should be dashed against it. As for the bronze altar, I have yet to
16 decide." And the priest Uriya did just as King Aḥaz instructed.

17 King Aḥaz then stripped off the frames of the washstands and removed
their lavers, and he took the Sea down from the bronze oxen that supported
18 it and placed it on a stone pavement. He also altered the Sabbath canopy
that they had built in the House, as well as the king's outer entrance to the
House of the Lord – all on account of the king of Assyria.

19 As for the rest of Aḥaz's history and his deeds – they are recorded in the
20 Book of the History of the Kings of Yehuda. And Aḥaz slept with his
ancestors and was buried with his ancestors in the City of David. And his
son Ḥizkiyahu reigned in his place.

17 1 In the twelfth year of Aḥaz, king of Yehuda, Hoshe'a son of Ela became king
2 over Israel in Shomron for nine years. He did what was evil in the eyes of
the LORD, though not to the extent of the kings of Israel who preceded
3 him. Shalmaneser, king of Assyria, marched up against him, and Hoshe'a
4 became his vassal and paid him tribute. But when the king of Assyria
discovered that Hoshe'a had betrayed him by sending envoys to So, king
of Egypt, and by failing to pay his annual tribute to the king of Assyria, he
5 had him seized and thrown into prison. Then the king of Assyria marched
against the whole land and marched up to Shomron and besieged it for
6 three years. In the ninth year of Hoshe'a, the king of Assyria captured
Shomron. He exiled Israel to Assyria and settled them in Ḥalaḥ, the Ḥavor,
the Gozan River, and the cities of Media.

7 This came to pass because the Israelites had sinned against the LORD
their God – who had brought them out from the land of Egypt and the
8 oppression of Pharaoh, king of Egypt – by revering other gods. They
followed the customs of the nations whom the LORD had dispossessed
9 before the Israelites and those that the kings of Israel had practiced. The
Israelites ascribed falsehoods to the LORD their God, and they built
themselves high shrines wherever they lived, from watchtower to fortified
10 city. They set up worship pillars and sacred trees for themselves on every
11 high hill and under every shady tree and made offerings there, at all the
shrines, like the nations whom the LORD had exiled before them. And they
12 did evil things to anger the LORD; they served idols though the LORD had
told them, "You must not do this thing."

13 The LORD warned Israel and Yehuda through every prophet and every seer,
declaring: "Turn back from your evil ways and keep My commandments
and laws according to all the teachings that I commanded your ancestors
14 and that I conveyed to you through My servants the prophets." But they
would not listen; they were as stubborn as their ancestors, who did not
15 believe in the LORD their God. They spurned His laws and the covenant
He had made with their ancestors and the warnings He had given them;
they went after futilities until they themselves grew futile, imitating the
nations around them that the LORD had commanded them not to imitate.
16 They abandoned all the commandments of the LORD their God and
made themselves molten images of two calves; they made a sacred tree;
they bowed down to all the heavenly hosts; they worshipped the Baal.
17 They passed their sons and daughters through the fire and cast spells and
practiced divination; they sold themselves to do what was evil in the eyes of
18 the LORD to anger Him. And the LORD raged fiercely against Israel, and He
banished them from His presence; the tribe of Yehuda alone remained.

19 Even Yehuda, though, failed to keep the commandments of the LORD their
20 God, and they followed the customs that Israel had practiced. And the
LORD rejected all of Israel's seed, and He tormented them by handing them
21 over to plunderers until He had cast them away from His presence. For
Israel had torn away from the House of David, and they made Yorovam son
of Nevat king. But Yorovam drove Israel away from the LORD and led them
22 to grave sin, and Israel followed all the sins that Yorovam had committed
23 and would not turn away from them. Finally, the LORD banished Israel
from His presence, as He had promised through all His servants the
prophets, and Israel was exiled from its own soil to Assyria to this day.

24 The king of Assyria brought in people from Babylon, Kuta, Ava, Ḥamat,
and Sefarvites, and he settled them in the towns of Shomron instead of the
25 Israelites. They took possession of Shomron and settled its cities. When
they first settled there, they had no reverence for the LORD, so the LORD
26 sent forth against them lions who killed some of them. They reported to
the king of Assyria, "The nations whom you exiled and settled in the towns
of Shomron do not know the customs of the local God, and He has sent
forth lions against them; they are now killing them because they do not
27 know the customs of the local God." So the king of Assyria commanded,
"Bring back one of the priests whom you exiled from there; let them go and
settle there to teach them the customs of the local God."

28 One of the priests who had been exiled from Shomron came and settled
29 in Beit El, and he taught them how to revere the LORD. Yet each nation
continued to make its own gods, and they placed them in the shrine
temples that the Samarians had made, each nation in the city where they
30 settled. The people of Babylon made Sukkot Benot; the people of Kut made
31 Nergal; the people of Ḥamat made Ashima; the Avites made Nivḥaz and
Tartak; the Sefarvites would burn their children with fire for Adramelekh
32 and Anamelekh, the gods of Sefarvites. Though they revered the LORD,
they appointed some of their own number as shrine priests, and they
33 would officiate for them in the shrine temples. Though they revered the
LORD, they served their own gods and followed the customs of the nations
34 from which they had been exiled. To this day, they follow their former
customs; they do not truly revere the LORD, and they do not follow the
laws, customs, teachings, and commandments that the LORD commanded
35 the children of Yaakov, whose name He changed to Yisrael. With them the
LORD had made a covenant, and He had commanded them, "Do not revere
other gods; do not bow down to them or serve them or make sacrifices
36 to them. You shall revere only the LORD who brought you out from the
land of Egypt with great might and an outstretched arm; to Him you shall
37 bow down, and to Him you shall make sacrifices. As for the laws, customs,
teachings, and commandments He wrote for you – keep them carefully
38 forever, and do not revere other gods. Never forget the covenant that I
39 made with you, and do not revere other gods. Revere only the LORD your

40 God, and He will save you from the hands of all your enemies." But they
did not listen; they continued to follow their former customs.

41 Now, although these nations revered the LORD, they continued to serve
their idols – and their children and their children's children do just as their
ancestors did to this day.

18 1 In the third year of Hoshe'a son of Ela, king of Israel, Ḥizkiya son of
2 Aḥaz, king of Yehuda, became king. He was twenty-five years old when
he became king, and for twenty-nine years he reigned in Jerusalem. His
3 mother's name was Avi daughter of Zekharya. He did what was right in
4 the eyes of the LORD just as his ancestor David did. He removed the high
shrines and tore down the worship pillars and cut down the sacred tree.
And he crushed the bronze serpent that Moshe had made, for until that
time the Israelites were making sacrifices to it and calling it Neḥushtan.[99]
5 In the LORD, God of Israel, he placed his trust; there were none like
him among all the kings of Yehuda who succeeded him or those who
6 came before him. He clung to the LORD and never turned away from him
and kept the commandments that the LORD had commanded Moshe.
7 And the LORD was with him; wherever he turned, he was successful. He
8 rebelled against the king of Assyria and did not serve him. He defeated
the Philistines up to Aza and its territories, from watchtower to fortified
city.

9 In the fourth year of King Ḥizkiyahu – which was the seventh year of
Hoshe'a son of Ela, king of Israel – Shalmaneser, king of Assyria, marched
10 up against Shomron and besieged it. He captured it three years later during
the sixth year of Ḥizkiya; it was during the ninth year of Hoshe'a, king of
11 Israel, that Shomron was captured. And the king of Assyria exiled Israel to
Assyria and transferred them to Ḥalaḥ, the Ḥavor, the Gozan River, and
12 the cities of Media. This was because they would not heed the voice of
the LORD their God, and they violated His covenant – all that Moshe, the
LORD's servant, had commanded. They would not obey, and they would
not comply.

13 In the fourteenth year of King Ḥizkiya, Sanḥeriv, king of Assyria, marched
14 up against all the fortified cities of Yehuda and seized them.[100] So Ḥizkiya,
king of Yehuda, sent to the king of Assyria at Lakhish, saying, "I have
offended. Withdraw from me, and I will bear whatever you impose on me."
So the king of Assyria charged Ḥizkiya, king of Yehuda, with three hundred
15 talents of silver and thirty talents of gold, and Ḥizkiya surrendered all
the silver that was to be found in the House of the LORD and in the royal
16 treasuries of the palace. It was then that Ḥizkiya stripped down the doors
of the LORD's Sanctuary and the doorposts that Ḥizkiya, king of Yehuda,
had overlaid himself, and he surrendered them to the king of Assyria.

99 | See Numbers 21:8–9.

100 | Cf. this story in Isaiah, chapters 36–39.

17 The king of Assyria then sent the Tartan, the Rav-Saris, and the Rav-
Shakeh[101] from Lakhish to King Ḥizkiyahu in Jerusalem, along with vast
forces; they marched up and came to Jerusalem, and when they arrived,
they stationed themselves by the conduit of the Upper Pool, by the Fuller's
18 Field Road. They summoned the king, and Elyakim son of Ḥilkiyahu,
who was in charge of the palace, Shevna the scribe, and Yoaḥ son of Asaf,
19 royal herald, went out to them. And the Rav-Shakeh said to them, "Now,
tell Ḥizkiyahu, 'Thus says the great king, the king of Assyria: What is this
20 display of trust? You talk as if mere chatter were counsel and might in war!
21 Now, in whom have you placed your trust, that you rebel against me? Have
you placed your trust in that crushed reed of a staff, in Egypt, who pierces
and punctures the palm of anyone who leans upon it? For that is Pharaoh,
king of Egypt, to all who place their trust in him.

22 And if you say to me, "We have placed our trust in the LORD, our God" – is
that not the one whose high shrines and altars Ḥizkiyahu removed, telling
Yehuda and Jerusalem, "Bow only before *this* altar, in Jerusalem"?

23 Come, now, make a wager with my lord, the king of Assyria: I will provide
you with two thousand horses if you are able to provide them with riders!
24 How dare you slight even one of the deputies of my lord's lesser servants
25 and place your trust in Egypt for chariots and riders! What is more – was it
without the LORD that I marched up to destroy this place? It was the LORD
Himself who said to me: March up against this land and destroy it.'"

26 Elyakim son of Ḥilkiyahu, Shevna, and Yoaḥ said to the Rav-Shakeh,
"Please, speak to your servants in Aramaic, for we understand it. Do not
speak with us in Hebrew[102] within earshot of the people who are on the
wall."

27 "Was it to you and your master that my lord sent me to speak these
words?" the Rav-Shakeh told them, "Oh, but it was to the very men who
are stationed on the wall, who will have to eat their own excrement and
28 drink their own urine along with you." And the Rav-Shakeh stood and
shouted out in Hebrew:

29 "Hear the word of the great king, the king of Assyria," he proclaimed. "Thus
says the king:

"Do not let Ḥizkiyahu deceive you, for he cannot save you from my hand.
30 Do not let Ḥizkiyahu convince you to place your trust in the LORD, saying,
'The LORD will surely save us, and this city will not be handed over to the
king of Assyria.'

31 "Do not listen to Ḥizkiyahu, for thus says the king of Assyria: Make peace
with me; come out to me, and each will eat from his own vine and his own
32 fig tree, and each will drink from his own cistern until I come and take

101 | Titles of Assyrian officials.

102 | *Yehudit*, literally the language of Judah.

you to a land like your own – a land of grain and wine, a land of bread and
vineyards, a land of olive oil and honey, and you shall live and not die. Do
not listen to Ḥizkiyahu, for he misleads you by saying, 'The LORD will save
33 us.' Have the gods of other nations managed to save their own lands from
34 the hand of the king of Assyria? Where are the gods of Ḥamat and Arpad?
Where are the gods of Sefarvites, Hena, and Iva – did they save Shomron
35 from my hand? Who among all the gods of the lands saved their own land
from my hands, that the LORD will save Jerusalem from my hand?"

36 And the people were silent and did not say a word, for the king's order was,
"Do not answer him."

37 Then Elyakim son of Ḥilkiya, who was in charge of the palace, Shevna the
scribe, and Yoaḥ son of Asaf, the royal herald, came to Ḥizkiyahu with their
clothes rent and reported what the Rav-Shakeh had said.

19 1 When King Ḥizkiyahu heard, he rent his clothes and covered himself in
2 sackcloth and came to the House of the LORD. He then sent Elyakim, who
was in charge of the palace, and Shevna the scribe, and the senior priests,
covered in sackcloth, to the prophet Yeshayahu son of Amotz.

3 "Thus says Ḥizkiyahu," they said to him. "'Today is a day of distress and
reproach and disgrace, for children are about to be born, but there is no
4 strength left for the birth.[103] Perhaps the LORD your God will hear all
the words of the Rav-Shakeh, whom the king of Assyria, his lord, sent to
taunt the living God, and will condemn the words that the LORD your
God heard – oh, offer a prayer for the sake of the surviving remnant!'"

5 6 Now, when the servants of King Ḥizkiyahu came to Yeshayahu, Yeshayahu
said to them, "This is what you should tell your lord. Thus says the LORD:
'Do not be afraid of the words you heard, which the king of Assyria's
7 servant boys used to revile Me. I will strike him with delusion so that he
will hear a rumor and return to his own land; then I will have him fall by
the sword in his own land.'"

8 The Rav-Shakeh withdrew, for he heard that the king of Assyria had moved
9 on from Lakhish, and he found the king of Assyria attacking Livna. When
the latter heard rumor that Tirhaka, king of Kush, had set out to fight
10 against him, he sent messengers to Ḥizkiyahu once more, saying: "This is
what you should tell Ḥizkiyahu, king of Yehuda: Do not let your God in
whom you trust deceive you, saying, 'Jerusalem will not be handed over
11 to the king of Assyria.' Look, you have heard what the kings of Assyria
have done to all the lands – they have utterly destroyed them. Will you
12 be saved? Did the gods of the nations that my ancestors destroyed save
13 them – Gozan and Ḥaran and Retzef and the Edenites of Telasar? Where
is the king of Ḥamat and the king of Arpad and the king of La'ir, Sefarvites,
Hena, and Iva?"

103 | A proverbial expression of distress and helplessness.

14 When Ḥizkiyahu received the letter from the messengers and read it, he
went up to the House of the LORD, and Ḥizkiyahu spread it open before
15 the LORD. Then Ḥizkiyahu prayed before the LORD:
"O LORD, God of Israel, Enthroned upon the Cherubim," he said,
"You alone are God of all the kingdoms of the earth;
You made both heaven and earth.
16 Incline Your ear, O LORD, and listen;
open Your eyes, O LORD, and see –
listen to the words of Sanḥeriv,
those he sent to revile the living God.
17 It is true, LORD,
that the kings of Assyria have laid the nations to waste,
together with their lands.
18 They have cast their gods to the fire –
for they are not gods but the work of human hands, wood and stone –
and destroyed them.
19 But now, LORD our God,
save us from his hand,
and all the kingdoms of the earth will see
that You alone, O LORD, are God."

20 And Yeshayahu son of Amotz sent word to Ḥizkiyahu: "Thus says the
LORD, God of Israel: What you prayed to Me about Sanḥeriv, king of
21 Assyria, I have heard. This is the word the LORD has spoken of him:
Virgin daughter Zion
scorns you, mocks you;
she shakes her head behind your back,
daughter Jerusalem.
22 Whom have you taunted, whom reviled;
against whom did you raise your voice,
lifting your eyes haughtily
against the Holy One of Israel?
23 By your messengers' hand
you taunted the LORD;
you said, 'With the wealth of my chariots
I climbed to the heights of the hills,
the ends of Lebanon,
and I cut down its tallest cedars,
its choicest junipers;
I have reached its farthest lodgings,
its richest forests.
24 I have dug down and drunk strange waters;
the passing soles of my feet have parched
all the rivers of Egypt.'
25 Did you not hear of this long ago?
I did this in ancient times; I formed the plan;

now I have brought it to be:
towns crash to heaps of rubble,
and the fortified cities are ruined.
26 The inhabitants are powerless,
frozen in fear and ashamed,
like the field grasses,
like green stalks,
the grass of rooftops,
blasted before ripening.
27 Your stops, your goings, your comings, I know them all,
and your raging against Me.
28 Because you have raged against Me,
your arrogance has reached My ears;
I shall put My ring in your nose,
My bit between your lips,
and drag you back along the road you came by.
29 And this will be your sign:
This year you will eat what grows of itself,
next year what grows from that,
and in the third year you will sow and harvest,
plant vineyards and eat of their fruit.
30 Once more, the remaining survivors of the House of Yehuda
will set down roots below,
bear fruits above.
31 For a remnant will emerge from Jerusalem,
survivors from Mount Zion;
the passion of the Lord of Hosts
will bring all this to be.
32 And so, thus says the Lord of the king of Assyria:
He will not enter this city;
he will not shoot one arrow there.
He will not advance upon her with the shield,
nor pile up a siege mound against her.
33 The way he came
he will return,
but this city he will not enter.
The Lord has spoken.
34 And I will protect this city, and deliver her,
for My own sake and for the sake of My servant David."

35 And that night, an angel of the Lord went out and struck down 185,000
in the Assyrian camp; by daybreak the next morning, they were all dead
36 bodies. And Sanḥeriv, king of Assyria, departed at once and retreated and
settled again in Nineveh.

37 He was worshipping in the temple of his god, Nisrokh, when his sons

Adramelekh and Saretzer put him to the sword. They fled to the land of
Ararat, and his son Esar Ḥadon reigned in his place.

20 1 At that time, Ḥizkiyahu fell deathly ill, and the prophet Yeshayahu son of
Amotz came to him. "Thus says the LORD," he said. "Issue orders for your
household, for you are dying; you will not recover."

2 And he turned his face to the wall and prayed to the LORD. "Please, O
3 LORD," he said, "please remember how I walked before You truly, with
all my heart, and how I did what is right in Your eyes." And Ḥizkiya wept
bitter tears.

4 Yeshayahu had not yet left the middle courtyard when the word of the
5 LORD came to him: "Go back and say to Ḥizkiyahu, leader of My people:
Thus says the LORD, the God of your ancestor David: I have heard your
prayer; I have seen your tears. Now I will heal you – on the third day, you
6 will go up to the House of the LORD. And I will add fifteen years to your
life; and I will save you and this city from the hand of the king of Assyria – I
will protect this city for My sake and for the sake of My servant David."

7 Then Yeshayahu said, "Fetch a cake of dried figs," and they fetched one and
placed it on the boils, and he recovered.

8 Ḥizkiyahu then said to Yeshayahu, "What is the sign that the LORD will
heal me so that I will go up to the House of the LORD on the third day?"

9 "Let this be a sign for you from the LORD that the LORD will fulfill the
promise He made," said Yeshayahu. "Shall the shadow advance ten steps
or recede ten steps?"

10 "The shadow can easily lengthen by ten steps," said Yeḥizkiyahu, "but it
11 cannot recede by ten steps." And the prophet Yeshayahu called out to the
LORD, and He made the shadow that had descended on the sundial of
Aḥaz recede by ten steps.

12 At that time, Berodakh Baladan son of Baladan, king of Babylon, sent
letters and a gift to Ḥizkiyahu, for he had heard that Ḥizkiyahu had fallen
13 ill. Ḥizkiyahu received them and showed them all around his treasure
house: the silver and gold, the spices and fine oil, his armory, and
everything that was kept in his treasuries, in his palace, and all his realm;
there was nothing that Ḥizkiyahu did not show them.

14 But the prophet Yeshayahu came to King Ḥizkiyahu and said to him,
"What did these people say, and from where did they come to you?"

"They came from a distant land," said Ḥizkiya, "from Babylon."

15 "What have they seen in your palace?" he asked.

"Why, they have seen everything in my palace," said Ḥizkiyahu. "There was
nothing in my treasuries that I did not show them."

16 "Hear the word of the Lord," Yeshayahu said to Ḥizkiyahu.
17 "Behold – the days are coming
when all that fills your palace
and all that your fathers amassed
until this day
will be borne away to Babylon,
and nothing will be left,"
the Lord has said,
18 "while sons of yours
who came forth from you,
who were born to you,
will be borne far away, castrated slaves
in the palace of the king of Babylon."

19 And Ḥizkiyahu said to Yeshayahu, "The word of the Lord you have spoken
is fair." For he thought, "At least peace and truth will reign in my own
time."

20 As for the rest of Ḥizkiyahu's history and all his heroic feats and how he
constructed the pool and the conduit to bring water into the city – they are
21 recorded in the Book of the History of the Kings of Yehuda. And Ḥizkiyahu
slept with his ancestors, and his son Menashe reigned in his place.

21 1 Menashe was twelve years old when he became king, and for fifty-five years
2 he reigned in Jerusalem. His mother's name was Ḥeftziva. He did what was
evil in the eyes of the Lord, imitating the horrors of the nations whom the
3 Lord had dispossessed before the Israelites. He rebuilt the high shrines
that his father Ḥizkiyahu had destroyed, and he erected altars for Baal and
made a sacred tree as Aḥav, king of Israel, had done; he bowed down to
4 all the heavenly hosts and served them. He even built altars in the House
of the Lord, of which the Lord had said, "In Jerusalem, I will establish
5 My name" – he built altars for all the heavenly hosts in both courtyards of
6 the House of the Lord. He passed his son through the fire and practiced
augury and divination and consulted ghosts and spirits; he did so much
7 that was evil in the eyes of the Lord, angering Him. He placed the statue
of Ashera that he had made in the very House of which the Lord said to
David and his son Shlomo: "In this House, and in Jerusalem, which I have
8 chosen out of all the tribes of Israel, I will establish My name forever. And
never again will I make the feet of Israel wander from the soil that I gave
to their ancestors – so long as they carefully observe all that I commanded
them, and all the teachings that My servant Moshe commanded them."

9 But they did not listen, and Menashe led them astray – to commit even
worse evil than the nations whom the Lord had destroyed before the
10 11 Israelites. So the Lord spoke through His servants the prophets: "Because
Menashe, king of Yehuda, has committed these abominations – worse than
all the Amorites did before him – and because he has led Yehuda to sin

12 with his idols, thus says the LORD, God of Israel: I am about to bring such
evil on Jerusalem and Yehuda that whoever hears of it – why, both his ears
13 will ring. I will stretch out the measuring line of Shomron and the plummet
of the house of Aḥav over Jerusalem, and I will wipe out Jerusalem as a dish
14 is wiped clean and turned upside down. I will abandon the remnant of My
share and hand them over to their enemies, and they will become plunder
15 and prey to all their enemies – because they have been doing what is evil in
My eyes, angering me from the day their ancestors left Egypt to this day."

16 And what is more, Menashe shed so much innocent blood until Jerusalem
was brimming from end to end; this was besides the sin of leading Yehuda
17 to sin, doing what was evil in the eyes of the LORD. As for the rest of
Menashe's history and all he did and the sins that he sinned – they are
18 recorded in the Book of the History of the Kings of Yehuda. And Menashe
slept with his ancestors and was buried in his palace garden, in the garden
of Uza. And his son Amon reigned in his place.

19 Amon was twenty-two years old when he became king, and for two years
he reigned in Jerusalem. His mother's name was Meshulemet, daughter
20 of Ḥarutz of Yotva. He did what was evil in the eyes of the LORD, as his
21 father Menashe had done; he followed in all the ways that his father had
followed, and he served the idols that his father had served and bowed
22 down to them. He left the LORD, the God of his ancestors, and he did not
follow in the ways of the LORD.

23 Then the servants of Amon formed a conspiracy against him, and they
24 assassinated the king in his palace. But the people of the land struck down
all those who had conspired against King Amon, and the people of the land
appointed his son Yoshiyahu king in his place.

25 As for the rest of Amon's history and his deeds – they are recorded in the
26 Book of the History of the Kings of Yehuda. They buried him in his burial
plot in the garden of Uza, and his son Yoshiyahu reigned in his place.

22 1 Yoshiyahu was eight years old when he became king, and for thirty-one
years he reigned in Jerusalem. His mother's name was Yedida daughter of
2 Adaya, from Botzkat. He did what was right in the eyes of the LORD and
followed in all the ways of his ancestor David, straying neither right nor
3 left. In the eighteenth year of King Yoshiyahu, the king sent the scribe
Shafan son of Atzalyahu son of Meshulam to the House of the LORD with
4 this message: "Go up to Ḥilkiyahu the High Priest and have him calculate
the silver that has been brought to the House of the LORD, which the
5 guardians of the threshold have collected from the people. Have them
give it to the foremen in charge of the House of the LORD, and they will
pay it out to the workers in the House of the LORD to keep the House in
6 repair – to the carpenters, builders, and masons – and to purchase wood
7 and quarry stones to repair the House. But there is no need to keep track
of the silver entrusted to them, for they deal honestly."

8 Then the High Priest Ḥilkiyahu said to Shafan the scribe, "I found a scroll
of the Torah in the House of the Lord." Ḥilkiya gave the scroll to Shafan,
and he read it.

9 Shafan the scribe came to the king, and reported back to the king, "Your
servants have melted down the silver found in the House, and they have
10 paid it out to the foremen in charge of the House of the Lord." Then
Shafan the scribe told the king, "The priest Ḥilkiya gave me a scroll," and
Shafan read it out before the king.

11 When the king heard the words of the Torah scroll, he rent his clothes.
12 And the king gave orders to Ḥilkiya the priest, Aḥikam son of Shafan,
Akhbor son of Mikhaya, Shafan the scribe, and Asaya, the king's servant:
13 "Go, inquire of the Lord on my behalf, and on behalf of the people, and
on behalf of all of Yehuda, about the words of this scroll that has just been
found. For great divine fury must have been kindled against us, because
our ancestors did not obey the words of this scroll and do all that was
prescribed for us."

14 The priest Ḥilkiyahu, Aḥikam, Akhbor, Shafan, and Asaya went to Ḥulda
the prophet, the wife of Shalum son of Tikva son of Ḥarḥas, keeper of the
wardrobe – she lived in Jerusalem in the Mishneh[104] – and they spoke to
15 her. She said to them, "Thus says the Lord, God of Israel: Say to the man
16 who sent you to me: Thus says the Lord: I am about to bring disaster upon
this place and its inhabitants – fulfilling all the words of the scroll that the
17 king of Yehuda read. Because they left Me and made sacrifices to other
gods to anger Me with all their practices, My fury has been kindled against
18 this place, and it will not be extinguished. And to the king of Yehuda, who
sent you to inquire of the Lord, say this: Thus says the Lord, God of
19 Israel: Concerning the words that you heard, because you softened your
heart and humbled yourself before the Lord when you heard My promise
that this place and its people will become a desolation and a curse, and
you rent your clothes and wept before Me, I too have heard. The Lord
20 has spoken. I will gather you to your ancestors, and you will be gathered
to your grave peacefully; your own eyes will not see all the disaster I will
bring upon this place." And they reported back to the king.

23 1 The king summoned all the elders of Yehuda and Jerusalem, who gathered
2 to him. And the king went up to the House of the Lord, along with all
the men of Yehuda and all the inhabitants of Jerusalem, the priests and
the prophets and all the people, from the smallest to the greatest. And he
read out to them all the words of the scroll of the covenant that had been
3 found in the House of the Lord. The king stood on the platform and
reinstated the covenant before the Lord: to follow the Lord and to keep
His commandments, decrees, and laws with all their heart and all their

104 | A quarter in the city.

soul; to fulfill the words of this covenant as written in this book. And all
the people pledged themselves to the covenant.

4 The king then commanded Ḥilkiyahu, the High Priest, the deputy priests,
and the guardians of the threshold to remove from the LORD's Sanctuary
all the vessels that had been made for Baal, Ashera, and all the heavenly
hosts. He burned them outside of Jerusalem in the fields of Kidron and
5 removed their ashes to Beit El. He shut down the idolatrous priests whom
the kings of Yehuda had appointed to offer sacrifices at the high shrines in
the towns of Yehuda and the area around Jerusalem as well as those who
offered sacrifices to Baal, to the sun and moon and stars, and to all the
6 heavenly hosts. He brought out the Ashera from the House of the LORD
to the Kidron Valley outside of Jerusalem, and he burned it in the Kidron
Valley and ground it to dust, then he scattered the dust over the common
7 burial ground. He tore down the booths of the male ritual prostitutes in the
House of the LORD, where the women would weave coverings for Ashera.
8 He brought in all the priests from the towns of Yehuda and defiled the high
shrines where the priests had offered sacrifices from Geva to Be'er Sheva.
And he tore down the high shrines by the gates, those by the entrance to
the gate of Joshua, the city governor; they were on a person's left at the
9 city gate. Though the shrine priests could not go up to the Altar of the
LORD in Jerusalem, they did eat of the unleavened bread along with their
10 kin. He defiled the Tofet in the Valley of Ben Hinom so that no one could
11 pass their son or daughter through the fire for Molekh. He put down the
horses that the kings of Yehuda had devoted to the sun from the entrance
of the House of the LORD to the chamber of the eunuch Natan Melekh in
12 the precincts; and as for the sun chariots, he burned them with fire. As for
the altars on the roof of Aḥaz's upper chamber that the kings of Yehuda
had made and the altars that Menashe had made in both courtyards of the
House of the LORD, the king tore them down, and from there he promptly
13 had the rubble scattered in the Kidron Valley. As for the high shrines facing
Jerusalem to the south of the Har HaMashḥit[105] – which Shlomo, king of
Israel, had built for Ashtoret, the abhorrence of the Sidonians, and for
Kemosh, the abhorrence of Moav, and for Milkom, the abomination of
14 the Amonites[106] – the king defiled them. He shattered the worship pillars
and cut down the sacred trees and covered their sites with human bones.
15 As for the altar in Beit El, the high shrine that Yorovam son of Nevat, who
led Israel to sin, had built – he tore down that altar and that high shrine as
well. He burned down the high shrine and ground it to dust and burned
down the sacred tree.

16 Yoshiyahu then turned to see the graves that were there on the hillside. He
had the bones dug out of the graves, and he burned them on the altar to

105 | Literally "mountain of the destroyer"; this is a disparaging wordplay on Har HaMishḥa (Mount of Ointment), i.e., the Mount of Olives.

106 | Cf. 1 Kings 11:5–7.

defile it, fulfilling the word of the LORD that was pronounced by the man
17 of God who foretold these events.[107] When he asked, "What is the marker
that I see over there?" the townspeople told him, "It is the grave of the man
of God who came from Yehuda and foretold the very things you just did
upon the altar of Beit El."

18 "Leave him be," he said. "Let no one disturb his bones." Thus they
spared his bones together with the bones of the prophet who came from
Shomron.[108]

19 As for all the shrine temples in the towns of Shomron, which the kings of
Israel had made for provocation, Josiah removed them as well and repeated
20 all the procedures he had carried out at Beit El. He slaughtered all the
priests of the high shrines there on the altars, and he burned human bones
on them; then he went back to Jerusalem.

21 The king then commanded all the people: "Make the Passover sacrifice to
22 the LORD your God, as it is written in this book of the covenant." Now no
such Passover sacrifice had been made since the days of the judges who
ruled Israel, nor throughout all the time of the kings of Israel or the kings
23 of Yehuda. But in the eighteenth year of King Yoshiyahu, such a Passover
sacrifice was made to the LORD in Jerusalem.

24 As for the necromancers, mediums, household gods, idols, and all the
detestable things that had appeared in the land of Yehuda and Jerusalem,
Yoshiyahu stamped them out in order to uphold the words of the teaching
written in the book that Ḥilkiyahu the priest had found in the House of
25 the LORD. There was none like him before him – a king who returned to
the LORD with all his heart, all his soul, and all his might, following all the
teaching of Moshe, and none like him ever arose after him.

26 Yet the LORD did not turn back from His great fury, the fury that raged
against Yehuda because of all of Menashe's provocations that angered Him.
27 And the LORD said, "I will also remove Yehuda from My presence, just as
I removed Israel. I have rejected this city I once chose, Jerusalem, and the
House where I said My name would be."

28 As for the rest of Yoshiyahu's history and all his deeds – they are recorded in
29 the Book of the History of the Kings of Yehuda. In his time, Pharaoh Nekho,
the king of Egypt, marched up against the king of Assyria at the Euphrates,
and King Yoshiyahu confronted him, but he killed him at Megiddo as soon
30 as he saw him. His servants had his body driven from Megiddo and brought
him to Jerusalem, and they buried him in his burial plot. Then the people
of the land took Yehoaḥaz son of Yoshiyahu, anointed him, and made him
king in his father's place.

31 Yehoaḥaz was twenty-three years old when he became king, and for three

---

107 | See I Kings 13:2.

108 | See I Kings 13:31–32.

months he reigned in Jerusalem. His mother's name was Ḥamutal daughter
32 of Yirmeyahu, of Livna. He did what was evil in the eyes of the Lord, just
33 as his ancestors had done. Pharaoh Nekho imprisoned him at Rivla in
the land of Ḥamat to prevent him from reigning in Jerusalem and placed
a penalty on the land of one hundred talents of silver and a talent of gold.
34 Then Pharaoh Nekho made Elyakim son of Yoshiyahu king in his father
Yoshiyahu's place and changed his name to Yehoyakim. As for Yehoaḥaz,
35 he seized him; and he came to Egypt, where he died. Yehoyakim paid the
silver and gold to Pharaoh by assessing the land to meet Pharaoh's demand
for money; he exacted the silver and gold from the people of the land
according to each man's worth to pay Pharaoh Nekho.

36 Yehoyakim was twenty-five years old when he became king, and for eleven
years he reigned in Jerusalem. His mother's name was Zevuda daughter
37 of Pedaya, of Ruma. He did what was evil in the eyes of the Lord, all that
his ancestors had done.

24 1 In his time, Nevukhadnetzar, king of Babylon, marched up, and Yehoyakim
became his vassal for three years before he turned and rebelled against
2 him. But the Lord sent forth bands of Chaldeans, bands of Arameans,
bands of Moabites, and bands of Amonites against him; He sent them
forth against Yehuda to destroy it, to fulfill the word of the Lord that He
3 had pronounced through His servants the prophets. This was the Lord's
will – to remove Yehuda from His presence because of all the sins Menashe
4 committed, and because of all the innocent blood he spilled; he filled
Jerusalem with innocent blood, and the Lord was not willing to forgive.
5 As for the rest of Yehoyakim's history and all his deeds – they are recorded
6 in the Book of the History of the Kings of Yehuda. And Yehoyakim slept
with his ancestors, and his son Yehoyakhin reigned in his place.

7 The king of Egypt no longer ventured out of his own land, for the king of
Babylon had seized all that belonged to the king of Egypt, from the Ravine
of Egypt to the Euphrates River.

8 Yehoyakhin was eighteen years old when he became king, and for three
months he reigned in Jerusalem. His mother's name was Neḥushta daughter
9 of Elnatan, of Jerusalem. He did what was evil in the eyes of the Lord,
10 just as his father had done. At that time, the subjects of Nevukhadnetzar,
king of Babylon, marched up against Jerusalem, and the city came under
11 siege, and Nevukhadnetzar, king of Babylon, came to the city while his
12 army laid siege to it. Yehoyakhin, king of Yehuda, surrendered to the king
of Babylon, together with his mother, his officials, his ministers, and his
eunuchs, and the king of Babylon took him captive in the eighth year of his
13 reign. From there he carried off all the treasures of the House of the Lord
and the treasures of the palace, and he stripped off all the golden vessels
that Shlomo, king of Israel, had made in the Sanctuary of the Lord, as
14 the Lord had foretold. He exiled all of Jerusalem, all its ministers and all
its warriors – ten thousand exiles – including all the artisans and smiths;

15 only the very poorest people of the land remained. He exiled Yehoyakhin
to Babylon while the queen mother, the king's wives and eunuchs, and the
16 notables of the land were led in exile from Jerusalem to Babylon. The king
of Babylon led all the powerful men, numbering seven thousand, and one
thousand artisans and smiths – all strong and fit for battle – as exiles to
17 Babylon. And the king of Babylon made Matanyahu, Yehoyakhin's uncle,
king in his place, and he changed his name to Tzidkiyahu.

18 Tzidkiyahu was twenty-one years old when he became king, and for eleven
years he reigned in Jerusalem.[109] His mother's name was Ḥamutal, daughter
19 of Yirmeyahu of Livna. He did what was evil in the eyes of the Lord, just
20 as Yehoyakim had done. And because of the Lord's fury against Jerusalem
and Yehuda, He cast them away from His presence.

Now Tzidkiyahu rebelled against the king of Babylon.

25 1 In the ninth year of his reign, on the tenth day of the tenth month,
Nevukhadnetzar, king of Babylon, and all his forces attacked Jerusalem.
2 He encamped against it and built a siege wall all around, and the city
3 remained under siege until the eleventh year of King Tzidkiyahu. By the
ninth of the month,[110] famine raged so fiercely in the city that there was no
4 food for the people of the land. The city was breached, and all the military
men fled by the dark of night through the gate between the double walls by
the royal garden, as the Chaldeans surrounded the city, and made toward
5 the Arava. But the Chaldean force pursued the king and caught up with
him on the plains of Yeriḥo, and all his forces scattered and deserted him.
6 They seized the king and hauled him up before the king of Babylon at Rivla,
7 and they spoke harshly to him. They slaughtered Tzidkiyahu's sons before
his eyes and blinded Tzidkiyahu; then they chained him in bronze fetters
and brought him to Babylon.

8 And on the seventh day of the fifth month, in the nineteenth year of
the reign of Nevukhadnetzar, king of Babylon, Nevuzaradan, chief of
9 the guard, the king of Babylon's official, entered Jerusalem. He burned
down the House of the Lord and the royal palace and all the houses in
10 Jerusalem; he set fire to every important building in Jerusalem. As for the
walls surrounding Jerusalem, all the Chaldean forces with the chief of the
11 guard tore them down. And as for the rest of the people who remained in
the city and those who defected to the king of Babylon and the rest of the
12 population, Nevuzaradan, chief of the guard, exiled them. But the chief
of the guard retained some of the poorest of the land as vinedressers and
field workers.

13 The Chaldeans broke down the bronze pillars from the House of the
Lord, the stands, and the Bronze Sea that was in the House of the Lord
14 and carried the bronze off to Babylon. They took the pots, shovels, shears,

109 | Cf. this story in Jeremiah, chapters 39 and 52.

110 | Referring to the fourth month; see Jeremiah 52:6.

15 and spoons and all the bronze vessels that had been used in service, while
the chief of the guard took the firepans and the basins – whatever was of
16 gold, and whatever was of silver. The two pillars, the Molten Sea, and the
stands that Shlomo had made for the House of the LORD – the weight in
17 bronze of all these vessels was incalculable. Each pillar was eighteen cubits
high, and its capital was of bronze – the capital was three cubits high – and
meshwork and pomegranates surrounded the capital, all of bronze; and
18 the same on top of the second pillar atop the meshwork. The chief of the
guard seized Seraya, the head priest, and Tzefanyahu, the deputy priest,
19 and the three guardians of the threshold. And from the city, he took one
official who was in charge of the military men and five men among the
king's personal attendants who were left in the city, and the scribe of the
army commander whose duty was to rally the people of the land, and sixty
20 of the people of the land who were left in the city. Nevuzaradan, the chief
21 of the guard, took them and led them to the king of Babylon in Rivla, and
the king of Babylon struck them down and put them to death in Rivla, in
the land of Ḥamat. Thus Yehuda was exiled from its own soil.

22 As for the people who remained in the land of Yehuda, whom
Nevukhadnetzar, king of Babylon, had left, he appointed Gedalyahu son
23 of Aḥikam son of Shafan over them.[111] But when all the army officers, they
and their men, heard that the king of Babylon had appointed Gedalyahu,
they came to Gedalyahu at Mitzpa – Yishmael son of Netanya, Yoḥanan son
of Kare'aḥ, Seraya son of Tanḥumet the Netofatite, and Yaazanyahu son of
the Maakhatite, they and their men.

24 "Do not fear the Chaldean officials," Gedalyahu promised them and their
men. "Stay in the land and serve the king of Babylon, and all will be well
for you."

25 But in the seventh month, Yishmael son of Netanya son of Elishama, of
royal descent, came with ten men and assassinated Gedalyahu, along with
26 the Judahites and Chaldeans who were with him in Mitzpa. Then all the
people – from the smallest to the greatest and the army officers – set out
and came to Egypt, for they were afraid of the Chaldeans.

27 In the thirty-seventh year following the exile of Yehoyakhin, king of
Yehuda, on the twenty-seventh of the twelfth month, Evvil Merodakh,
king of Babylon, in the year he became king, granted Yehoyakhin, king of
28 Yehuda, pardon from prison. He spoke kindly to him and set his throne
29 above the thrones of the kings who were with him in Babylon. He removed
30 his prison garb, and he dined in his presence for the rest of his life, and he
was granted a permanent allowance from the king – a daily allowance – for
the rest of his life.

111 | Cf. Jeremiah 40:7–41:18.

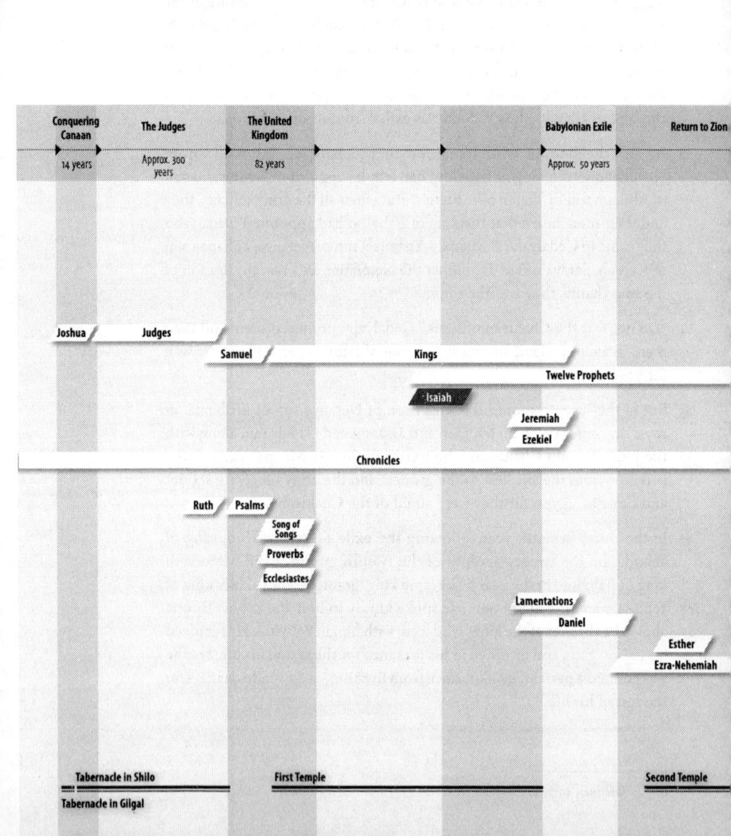
Conquering Canaan
14 years
The Judges
Approx. 300 years
The United Kingdom
82 years
Babylonian Exile
Approx. 50 years
Return to Zion
Joshua
Judges
Samuel
Kings
Twelve Prophets
Isaiah
Jeremiah
Ezekiel
Chronicles
Ruth
Psalms
Song of Songs
Proverbs
Ecclesiastes
Lamentations
Daniel
Esther
Ezra-Nehemiah
Tabernacle in Shilo
Tabernacle in Gilgal
First Temple
Second Temple

ISAIAH/YESHAYA

ISAIAH	Rebuke to a corrupt affluent society	Military and spiritual evaluation of the ascent of Assyria	Prophecies regarding the nations	Prophecies of cataclysm and redemption	Yeshaya and Ḥizkiya	Prophecies of consolation and redemption
	Chs. 1–6	7–12	13–23	24–35	36–39	40–66

1 1 The vision of Yeshayahu son of Amotz, which he saw regarding Yehuda and Jerusalem in the days of Uziyahu, Yotam, Aḥaz, and Ḥizkiyahu, kings of Yehuda:[1]

2 Listen, heavens,
hear, O earth:[2]
the LORD has spoken:
I brought up children, raised them;
they rebelled against Me.
3 Even an ox knows its owner,
an ass its master's trough.
Israel does not know;
My people does not try to understand.
4 Woe to the sinning nation,
a people weighed down with iniquity,
seed of the wicked,
vicious children,
they forsook the LORD,
defamed the Holy One
of Israel, fell away.
5 Why should you suffer more beatings?
Yet you spawn more defiance,
your head sickened, all,
your whole heart ailing.
6 From sole to crown –
nothing is sound;
laceration, bruise, and open wound
never squeezed or bandaged;
never eased with oil:
7 your land is laid waste,
your towns burned up in fire;
your own land – before your eyes
strangers consume it –
laid waste: a vision of strangers' overturning.[3]
8 Only daughter Zion stands
like the watchman's shack in a vineyard,
like the hut in a cucumber field –
a town besieged.
9 *Were it not for the LORD of Hosts,*
who left of us a bare remnant,

---

1 | This period saw the expansion of Assyria and its conquest of the Kingdom of Israel. The prophecies in most of the book are not arranged in chronological order, and it contains narrative accounts as well.

2 | Cf. Deuteronomy 32:1. This prophecy is best understood as a reference to the events of 701 BCE, in which Sanḥeriv, king of Assyria, destroyed many cities of Yehuda.

3 | Cf. the story of Sedom and Amora in Genesis, chapters 18–19.

we would have been like Sedom,
like Amora – gone.[4]

10 Listen to the LORD's word, you officers of Sedom;
hear the teaching of our God, you townsmen of Amora.
11 Why, says the LORD,
would I want all these offerings?
I am sated with burnt offerings, with rams
and fleshy creatures' fat,
the blood of bulls and sheep
and goats – I do not want them.
12 You come, appear before Me –
Who asked all this of you,
who asked you for all this: trampling My courtyards?
13 Bring no more your empty gifts –
they are foul incense to Me;
New Moon and Sabbath,
the feast days you proclaim –
I cannot endure
these sins and assemblies.
14 Your New Moons and festivals –
how I hate them;
they have become a burden to Me;
I am weary, I
cannot bear them.
15 When you spread your hands out skyward,
I must turn My eyes away;
when you pray with such verbosity,
I am not listening –
Your hands, they are covered in blood.
16 Wash them, be clean now,
remove your terrible deeds from My sight;
stop bringing about such evils.
17 Learn to do good.
Seek justice.
Correct what is cruel.
Rule justice for orphans.
Fight the widows' cause.

18 Come, let us argue this out;
so says the LORD.
Though your sins may be like scarlet,
they will grow whiter than snow.

---

4 | In Isaiah the translator has used italic font to indicate a change in voice or internal dialogue.

Though they redden you more than dye worms,
they will be clean wool again.
19 If you will it and listen,
the best of this earth is yours to eat,
20 but if you refuse and rebel against Me,
the sword will devour you –
the LORD has spoken.

21 How like a whore is she now,
the faithful metropolis.
How full she was of justice
once; righteousness lodged with her,
now murderers.
22 Your silver has turned into dross,
your wine is watered down,
23 your ministers are wayward,
friends to thieves,
loving corruption, all of them,
chasing bribes.
They do not judge an orphan's case;
a widow's claim
does not even come before them.

24 And so, says the Master,
the LORD of Hosts,
the Mighty One of Israel –
This woe! – I shall seek consolation, crush My foes,
wreak vengeance on My enemies.
25 I shall set My hand against you again, as if
smelting, refining away your dross;
all your lead will I remove.
26 I shall set up your judges again as first they were,
your counselors as long ago.
And then you shall be called
Righteous City,
Faithful Metropolis.
27 Zion will be redeemed by justice,
by righteousness – those who return to her;
28 rebels and sinners will all be broken,
those who forsook the LORD all gone.
29 How ashamed you will be of the oaks
that you longed for –
how mortified over
the gardens you chose.[5]

---

5 | See 65:3.

30 For you will be like an oak
with withered leaves,
like a garden that sees no water.
31 That mighty oak will become flax fibers
and the one who once carved them the spark –
the two will burn together, and
no one will be there
to quench the fire.

2 1 The vision of Yeshayahu son of Amotz
for Yehuda and Jerusalem:
2 This will be in days to come:
The mountain of the LORD's House will be
rooted firm, the highest of mountains,
raised high above all hills,
and all the nations will stream to it.
3 Many peoples will come, saying:
"Come, let us go up to the mount of the LORD,
to the House of Yaakov's God;
He will teach us of His ways;
we will walk in His pathways" –
for teaching will come forth from Zion,
from Jerusalem, the LORD's word.
4 He will judge among nations
and arbitrate for many peoples;
they shall beat their swords into plowshares,
their spears into pruning hooks.
Nation shall not raise sword against nation;
no more will they learn to make war.[6]

5 House of Yaakov, come,
let us walk
by the LORD's light.
6 For you have forsaken your people,
House of Yaakov,
full of what comes from the east,
full of auguries like the Philistines,
glutted with customs of strangers.
7 Their land is filled with silver and gold,
there is no end to their treasures;
8 their land is filled with horses,
there is no end to their chariots.
Their land is filled with false gods –
they bow to the works of their hands –
their own fingers formed them.

---

6 | Cf. Micah 4:1–3.

9 Man falls on his face;
a man degrades himself;
You would not lift Your judgment.
10 Climb into the rock face;
bury yourself in the dust
for dread of the LORD
before the loftiness of His majesty.
11 The proud eyes of man are fallen,
man's erect bearing bent low;
the LORD alone will be exalted
on that day.

12 It is the day of the LORD of Hosts
for each exalted, each proud man,
for each man who is raised – to be brought down.
13 For all the cedars of Lebanon,
high and exalted;
for all the oaks of Bashan;
14 for all the lofty mountains,
all the high hills;
15 for each tall tower,
each impenetrable wall;
16 for all the boats of Tarshish,[7]
all the ships of longing.
17 Man's arrogance will be thrown down,
the pride of men brought low;
the LORD alone will be exalted
on that day;
18 all false gods will cease to be.
19 And people will run to the caves among the rocks,
into the caverns of dust,
for fear of the LORD
and His dazzling majesty
as He comes to strike dread across the earth.
20 On that day, man will throw down
his gods of silver,
gods of gold,
that he made to worship –
to the moles and the bats;
21 he will go into the rocks' clefts,
the cliff's hidden places
for fear of the LORD
and His dazzling majesty
as He comes to strike dread across the earth.

7 | A seagoing people who were skilled shipbuilders.

22 Stop; leave man be
who breathes –
for what is his importance?

3 1 For behold: the Master, the Lord of Hosts,
is taking from Jerusalem, from Yehuda
all support, all sustenance;
all the bread they lean on, all the water;
2 all the heroes, men of war,
judges, prophets,
seers, elders,
3 captains of fifties,
and all who are respected,
advisors, artisans,
whisperers of spells.
4 I shall make children their princes;
infants will rule them.
5 The people will be oppressed,
one by another,
each by his friend;
children will lord it over old men,
and those who are contemptible
over those who merit honor.
6 A man will grasp hold of his brother
there in his father's house –
"You – you have a cloak:
be our leader;
let this ruin be in your charge."
7 And he, on that day, will raise his voice,
"How can I be the one to bandage you?
In my house no bread,
no cloak;
do not make me a leader of men."
8 For Jerusalem and Yehuda
have stumbled, fallen,
their words, their actions flouting the Lord,
defying His glorious eyes.
9 Their faces bear witness against them;
their sin is like that of Sedom.
They say it outright, deny nothing;
woe to their souls,
for they have done them wrong.
10 Tell the righteous that all is well,
for they shall eat the fruits of their deeds.
11 And woe to the wicked man, evil;

for what his hands have done
will be done to him.
12 My people – their tyrants are infants;
women rule over them.
My people, those who lead you lead awry,
confounding your pathways.

13 The LORD is ready for His case to be heard:
He stands up now to judge nations.
14 The LORD is coming to trial with
His people's elders, its princes:
"It is you who ravaged the vineyard;
the plunder of the poor is in your homes.
15 By what right do you crush My people,
grinding the faces of the poor?"
So speaks the LORD GOD of Hosts.

16 The LORD says:
Because the daughters of Zion are proud,
walking with their heads poised,
casting their eyes around them,
walking their dainty walk,
their feet ringing with anklets –
17 the LORD will scab over the skulls
of the daughters of Zion;
the LORD will lay their heads bare.

18 On that day,
the LORD will pull off the glory of those anklets,
those headbands and moon pendants,
19 earrings and bangles and scarves,
20 those headdresses, silver bands, and sashes,
the perfume boxes and amulets,
21 all those finger rings and nose rings,
22 the fine robes, the mantles,
the stoles and the purses,
23 the mirrors and shawls,
the turbans and veils.
24 And where there was perfume, there shall be stench,
and where there were fine girdles, rope.
Fine braided hair will fall away to baldness;
fine robes will fall to leave women wrapped in sacking;
this – where once there was beauty.
25 Your men will fall to the sword,
your valor killed in action.
26 Her gates will be weeping, lamenting –
and empty will she sit upon the ground.

4 1 Seven women will take hold of
any one man on that day; they will say,
"We will eat our own bread;
we will wear our own clothes –
only let us be called by your name;
only take away our disgrace."

2 On that day,
the LORD's shoot will flower
into beauty, into glory,
and the fruit of the land
will be majesty, magnificence,
for those of Israel who remain.
3 And those who are left in Zion,
surviving in Jerusalem –
"holy" will be said of them,
of all in Jerusalem
who are inscribed to live
4 after the LORD has cleaned
the filth from the women of Zion,
washed away Jerusalem's
staining blood
with a spirit of judgment,
a spirit that burns.
5 And the LORD has formed
over Mount Zion's foundation
and all her assemblies
a cloud by day and smoke,
brilliant light and burning fire by night,
for over all the glory, a canopy shields.
6 And that shelter will be shade
all day from searing heat
and a covering, a hiding place
from the deluge,
from the rain.

5 1 Let me sing a song for my friend –
my beloved's vineyard song:
My beloved had a vineyard
on the side of a rich hill.
2 He fenced it round, He cleared it,
He planted it with vines.
He built a watchtower in it
and hewed a winepress there.
He hoped it would yield grapes –
it grew them rotten.

3 "Now, man of Jerusalem, of Yehuda,
judge between Me and My vineyard.
4 What more could I do for My vineyard,
what, that I have not done?
Why did I hope to husband grapes
where they grew rotten?
5 I tell you here and now
what I must do to My vineyard.
Tear up the border hedge
and leave it to be ravaged.
Burst through the fence,
to let them trample it.
6 I must turn this into wasteland,
never pruned or hoed;
brambles and briars will take it over;
I forbid the clouds ever
to rain their rain upon it."

7 The LORD of Hosts' vineyard
is the House of Israel,
the people of Yehuda
His planting of joy;
He hoped for justice: instead, disease;
for kindness: instead, the scream.[8]

8 Woe to those who add house to house,
join field to field
until no space is left;
you are settled there alone
on the face of the land.
9 As My ears hear it, I swear –
I, the LORD of Hosts –
a wealth of homes will become desolation,
great ones, fine ones, left without people.
10 Ten *tzemed* of vineyard will yield but one *bat*;
ten omer of seed but one ephah.[9]

11 Woe to those who rise early to chase ale,
whom wine lights up through the night,
12 who feast on lute and harp music,
on timbrel, flutes, and wine,
never once turning to look at the LORD's workings,
never once noticing the work of His hands.

8 | The Hebrew for "disease" (*mispaḥ*) echoes "justice" (*mishpat*). Likewise with "scream" (*tze'aka*) and "kindness" (*tzedaka*).

9 | These amounts express an acute crop failure.

13 And so – My people are exiled for want of knowledge,
her glory shrunk to men of hunger,
her masses arid with thirst.
14 And so – Sheol[10] spreads herself wide;
her mouth gapes wide without limit.
And My people's glory, her crowds and her noise,
will all fall
with those who rejoice in her.
15 Humanity is humbled;
man is thrown down;
proud eyes fall.
16 For the LORD of Hosts rises up in judgment:
God most holy, made holy by justice.
17 Sheep will graze then, as if in their pasture,
while wayfarers eat
from the fat clans' ruins.[11]

18 Woe to those who draw iniquity
with ropes of nothingness,
pulling sin like a harnessed carriage.
19 "Let Him come quickly,"
they say.
"Let Him bring His works with haste,
that we may see;
let the plan of the Holy One of Israel
draw close and come to pass;
then we will know."

20 Woe to those who say of evil, "good";
of good, "evil";
those who call darkness light
and light darkness;
who consider sweetness bitter
and bitter things sweet.

21 Woe to those who are wise in their own eyes,
full of their own insight.

22 Woe to the mighty drinkers of wine –
heroes in the field of pouring liquor,
23 who vindicate the wicked for all they will pay
and strip the righteous of their rights.

24 Just as a tongue of flame consumes the straw
and chaff collapses beneath the blaze,

10 | The netherworld.

11 | That is, tranquility will return to the land after the exile and destruction described in verses 13–14.

so will their root grow fetid,
their flowers rising as dust,
for they reject the LORD of Hosts' teaching,
debasing the word of Israel's Holy One.
25 So the LORD's fury rages against His people,
and He stretches His hand out over them
and beats them,
and the mountains quake,
and their corpses will be
tossed aside like trash in the streets.
And still He has not turned away His rage,
and still He stretches forth His hand.
26 He will raise a signal to the nations from afar
and whistle them forth from the ends of the earth;
how swiftly they come.
27 None weary, none stumbling among them –
they do not slumber,
do not sleep;
no belt slips,
no sandal thong snaps,
28 their arrows sharp,
and every last bow drawn;
his[12] horses' hooves like flint
and the wheels like a storm wind.
29 His growl like a lion's;
like a young lion he growls,
roars, seizes his prey,
hauls it away,
and no one will be there
to rescue it.

30 On that day he roars
like the roaring of the sea,
and he looks down to earth
and sees – darkness,
pain, and light,
darkening, across her clouded skies.

6 1 In the year in which King Uziyahu died I saw the LORD sitting on a high,
2 raised throne, the hem of His clothing filling the Sanctuary. There were
seraphim standing above Him, each with six wings – with two they covered
their faces, with two they covered their feet, and with two they were flying.
3 And they called out one to another –

12 | The shift to the singular refers to the Assyrian king or to Assyria as an individual.

"Holy, holy, holy – the Lord of Hosts –
all the world's fullness His glory."

4 The door pillars shook with the voice of him who called –
5 and smoke filled the House. And I said,
"This ache – I am condemned,
for my mouth has been defiled,[13]
one man among a people with their mouths defiled –
and my eyes see
the King, the Lord of Hosts."

6 One of the seraphim flew to me,
and in his hand was a coal,
taken with tongs from the altar top.
7 With this he touched my lips and said,
"When this has touched your lips,
your iniquity is gone,
and all your sin forgiven."

8 I heard the voice of the Lord saying,
"Whom shall I send,
and who will go for us?"

And I said, "I am here.
Send me."

9 He said,
"Go – tell this people:
Hear, you shall hear but understand it not,
see it all but know it not.
10 Fatten the heart of this people;
make their ears heavy;
coat their eyes with plaster,
lest they see with their eyes
and hear with their ears,
and their hearts understand
and they return – and are healed."

11 I said,
"My Lord, how long?"
And He said,
"Until the towns are stripped of all who live in them,
houses left without people,
the land stripped bare,
12 and the Lord dispatches man far hence,
and swaths of land will be forsaken;

13 | That is, I have spoken impure words.

13 if a tenth there will survive,
it will return and will be burnt
like the terebinth and oak tree
that drop their leaves, and
yet the trunk remains –
and the trunk is holy seed."

7 1 In the days of Aḥaz[14] son of Yotam son of Uziyahu, king of Yehuda, Retzin,
king of Aram, and Pekaḥ son of Remalyahu, king of Israel, launched an
2 attack on Jerusalem, but they could not conquer it. The House of David[15]
was told, "Aram is allied with Efrayim." And his heart swayed, and the
hearts of his people, as trees of the forest will sway with the wind.

3 And the LORD said to Yeshayahu:
Go out now to meet Aḥaz,
you and She'ar Yashuv[16] your son,
to the end of the Upper Pool's conduit,
by the road to the Fuller's Field.
4 And say to him:
Be guarded, stay still,
do not fear,
and let your heart not soften
before these smoking
tails of firebrands,
before the rage of Retzin and Aram
and the son of Remalyahu.
5 For Aram has conspired to harm you,
along with Efrayim and Remalyahu's son:
6 "We shall go up to Jerusalem, bring about her end;
we shall break her walls open for ourselves
and set a new king over her: the son of Taval."[17]

7 Thus says the LORD GOD:
It will not come to pass;
it will not be.
8 For the head of Aram is Damascus,
and the head of Damascus, Retzin,
and in another five and sixty years
Efrayim will be shattered as a nation.
9 The head of Efrayim is Shomron,
the head of Shomron is Remalyahu's son –

14 | See II Kings 16:5.

15 | Aḥaz.

16 | The name means "a remnant will return." Symbolic names of sons appear also in verse 14 and 8:3.

17 | The "son of Taval" cannot be identified with certainty. The name might mean "someone good for us."

and if you have no faith,
you have no future.

10 The Lord spoke again to Aḥaz and said,
11 "Ask any sign of the Lord your God;
make it deep as Sheol
or high as the heights."
12 But Aḥaz replied,
"I shall not ask;
I shall not test the Lord."[18]
13 "Listen, House of David,"
Yeshayahu said.
"Is it not enough to weary men?
Must you weary my God also?
14 The Lord, then,
will give you His sign.
This maiden will conceive,[19]
and she will bear a son.
She will call that child Imanu El.[20]
15 Curds and honey will he eat[21]
when he knows to refuse what is evil
and choose the good.
16 For by the time he knows
to refuse what is evil,
to choose the good –
the lands of the two kings you dread
will all be forsaken,
17 and the Lord will bring upon you,
your people,
and your fathers' house,
the king of Assyria –
days such as never have been since
Efrayim left Yehuda."

18 On that day, the Lord will whistle
to a fly at the Egyptian Nile's edge,
to a bee in the land of Assyria,

---

18 | Aḥaz offers a pious explanation for his refusal to ask for a sign; cf. the prohibition in Exodus 17:2.

19 | The "maiden" could refer to the wife of Yeshayahu or of the king, or possibly to a different young woman present. The sign is not the birth of the child itself, but the unusual food he will consume.

20 | Meaning "God is with us."

21 | The sign initially sounds positive. However, as verses 21–25 explain, the background is troubling: cultivation of the land will cease, and only these good but simple foods will remain.

19 and they will swarm and come to rest everywhere –
in the crag ravines,
in the clefts of rock,
on every thorn,
in every pasture.
20 On that day
the LORD will take a hired razor
beyond the River – the king of Assyria –
and shave: head, nakedness,
beard – utterly.

21 On that day, each man will nurture
one calf, two goats;
22 yet they will yield so much milk
that he will live upon curds;
all those remaining on the land will live
on curds and on honey.
23 On that day,
in each place
where once there grew a thousand vines
worth a thousand silver coins,
briars and thorns will take over.
24 One will need a bow and arrow to pass through there,
for the land will be wild with briars and thorns.
25 But the hills that the hoe turns over –
no fear of briar or thorn will come there,
for oxen will wander there
and sheep will tread.

8 1 The LORD said to me:
Take a large scroll and write upon it
in common script:
Of Maher Shalal Ḥash Baz.[22]
2 I called faithful witnesses to witness it for me:
Uriya the priest and Zekharya son of Berakhya.
3 And so I came to my prophetess;[23]
she conceived and bore a son.
And the LORD said to me,
call him, name him,
Maher Shalal Ḥash Baz.
4 For before the child knows
how to call out

22 | Meaning "hasten plunder, speed booty."

23 | Called so either because she was the wife of a prophet (Yeshayahu), or a prophetess in her own right.

"Mother," "Father,"
the might of Damascus,
the plunder of Shomron,
will all be borne away
before the Assyrian king.

5 The Lord spoke to me again:
6 Because these people shun
the waters of Shiloaḥ,[24] flowing slow,
in their frenzy over Retzin and Remalyahu's son,
7 the Lord will bring upon them
the potent waters of the great river –
the king of Assyria in all his glory –
to flood all the wadis,
engulf all the banks,
8 to course over Yehuda,
flood it in passing,
steep it to the neck.
His wings spread over
all your land's breadth,
Imanu El.[25]

9 Blast, peoples, then fall apart –
listen, far-off places of this world;
gird yourselves, then fall apart,
gird, then fall apart.
10 Plot and plan – you will fail;
confer, conspire; it will not come to be:
Imanu El.[26]

11 For the Lord said to me, as if taking my hand,
instructing me not to walk the path of this people:
12 "Do not say 'Conspiracy,'
to all this people call conspiracy.
Do not fear all those they fear,
nor pay them homage."
13 The Lord of Hosts – it is Him you must sanctify,
Him that you fear;
to Him you owe homage.
14 And He is Sanctuary
and striking stone – stumbling block

---

24 | Jerusalem's only source of water, the modest Shiloaḥ pool, symbolized the city's self-sufficiency under God. The people, however, look to the brawn of Assyria, symbolized by the great Euphrates River.

25 | Meaning "God is with us"; this is the symbolic name given to the child in 7:14. Here it may refer to God's protection.

26 | See note to verse 8; here the term is not a name but a refrain.

to both houses of Israel,
trap and snare
to the people of Jerusalem.
15 And many will stumble on these,
and many will fall and be broken,
will be ensnared, be caught.

16 *Bind up the testimony;*
seal Teaching in My students[27] –
17 I wait for the Lord,
who hides His face from Yaakov;
I long for Him.
18 You see: I and all
the children the Lord gave me
are messages,
are signs – to Israel
from the Lord of Hosts,
who rests upon Mount Zion.

19 When they say to you,
"Ask of the necromancers,
of the mediums,
the chirpers and mutterers" –
say, "Does not a people ask its God;
why go to the dead for the living?"
20 For teaching, for testimony;
this is what they will say, words
the sun never rose upon.
21 And one will pass through, hardened, hungry,
and when he has grown hungry,
he will overflow with fury and will curse
his king, his God,
and turn to look upward;
22 he will look down at the land
and see:
pain and darkness,
dread dark of anguish,
and be thrust into the gloom.
23 And the one does not weary
who presses her to anguish.
The first lay light
on the land of Zevulun,
the land of Naftali,
and the last weighs heavy

27 | Yeshayahu's warnings are not heeded, nor are they vindicated in the short term. God has warned him of this frustration in 6:9.

by the road to the sea, across the Jordan,
to the Galilee of nations.[28]

9 1 The people who walked in darkness
have seen abounding light;
those who live in a land of death's shadow –
light now bathes them.
2 For You have made great Your nation,
have raised up its joy;
they rejoice before You,
like harvest joy,
as a people celebrates
dividing the spoils.
3 For You have broken the yoke of their suffering,
the rod over their shoulders,
the oppressor's staff,
as on Midyan's day.[29]
4 For every boot that tramps like thunder,
each mantle filthy with blood,
will be burned, will become
the bonfire's fodder.
5 For a child is born to us,
a son is given us;
leadership rests on his shoulders,
and he shall be called
Mighty God Is Planning Wonders,
Eternal Father, Prince of Peace.[30]
6 To instill great leadership,
peace without end,
on the throne of David,
and over his kingdom,
founding and supporting it
with justice and with righteousness
now and forever;
the passion of the Lord of Hosts
will bring all this to be.

7 The Lord has sent word to Yaakov;
it falls upon Israel,
8 and all the people know it,
Efrayim and the people of Shomron

28 | This is the route the conquerors would take in a campaign that would focus on the Galilee, which had a mixed population ("of nations"). This passage apparently refers to two separate invasions; see I Kings 15:20 and II Kings 15:29.

29 | See the victory described in Judges, chapters 6–8.

30 | The son mentioned in these verses may be Aḥaz's son Ḥizkiyahu or a future messianic leader; the verses may refer to his birth or to his coronation.

in their pride, in their
swollen-headedness, even as they say:
9 "Bricks have fallen;
we will rebuild in hewn stone;
they chop down sycamores;
we plant cedars in their place."
10 The LORD has raised Retzin's enemies high over him,
stirs up his foes to battle one another;
11 Aram from the East,
the Philistines west –
they eat up Israel, mouths agape,
and still He has not turned away His rage,
and still He stretches forth His hand.
12 And still the people do not turn to Him who beats them,
and do not seek to find the LORD of Hosts.

13 The LORD has cut off
head and tail of Israel,
palm and bulrush,
all in a day.
14 The elders and those who are honored –
they are the head,
and the tail are the prophets,
the teachers of lies.
15 Those who led this people – led awry,
and those who were led were confounded.
16 And so the LORD takes no joy in its young people,
nor shows any compassion
for its orphans, its widows.
For all of them are godless, evildoers,
the words of each one poisoned.
And still He has not turned away His rage,
and still He stretches forth His hand.
17 For evil burns like fire here,
consuming briars and brambles,
setting the forest undergrowth aflame,
sending them curling up in plumes of smoke.
18 By the rage of the LORD of Hosts, the land is blackened;
the people are nothing but fuel for the fire;
brother cares nothing for brother.
19 He on the right carves meat but stays hungry;
he on the left will eat but not feel full;
a man will eat the flesh of his own arm –
20 Menashe on Efrayim,
Efrayim on Menashe,

and the two together on Yehuda.[31]
And still He has not turned away His rage,
and still He stretches forth His hand.

10 1 Woe to the lawmakers who set abuse in stone,
for authors of unholy writ
2 who turn justice away from the needy,
stealing the judgments of My people's poor,
making widows their plunder
and orphans their spoils.
3 What will you do on the day of judgment
when, from far away, calamity comes?
To whom will you then flee for help;
where will you leave all your wealth behind?
4 What then but to buckle as captives,
among the fallen to fall?
And still He has not turned away His rage,
and still He stretches forth His hand.

5 Woe to Assyria, staff of My fury;
My rage is the rod in their hand.
6 I will set them loose upon a vile nation
and command them against the people of My wrath
to plunder for plunder,
to ravage for spoils,[32]
to leave them to be trampled
like street mud.
7 But this is not how he thinks of it;
his heart does not see it so;
his heart is set on destruction,
on cutting down not a few nations,
8 for he says, "Are not my ministers,
all of them, kings?[33]
9 Is Kalneh not the same as Karkemish,
Ḥamat like Arpad,
Shomron just like Damascus?[34]
10 As my hand grasped the kingdoms
of false gods, their idols more numerous
than Jerusalem's, Shomron's,
11 will I not do as I did
to Shomron and her gods,
Jerusalem and her images also?"

---

31 | This refers to internecine struggles that weakened both Israel and Yehuda and made it harder for them to withstand Assyrian attacks; see, e.g., II Kings 15:25, 16:5.

32 | This echoes the symbolic name of Yeshayahu's son in 8:1, 3.

33 | Referring to the Assyrian practice of replacing local kings with Assyrian governors.

34 | These cities were conquered by Assyria around the time of the conquest of Shomron.

12 It will be, when the LORD finishes His work
on Mount Zion and in Jerusalem –
I shall come to judge what grows
from the swollen head of the king of Assyria, from
the supremacy of his haughty eyes,
13 for he says, "By the power of my hands I act,
and in my wisdom, for I have insight;
sweep away the borders of peoples
and take their leaders for plunder;
like a wild bull I pull down all who preside.
14 As if in a nest my hand grasps
the wealth of peoples,
and as one might gather abandoned eggs,
I gather up all the world,
yet none moves her wing to stop me;
none opens a beak or chirrups."
15 Does the axe gloat over the one who wields it?
Would a saw place itself above the one who swings it?
Does a staff swing the one who lifts it?
Does a rod lift Him who is not wood?[35]

16 So the LORD God of Hosts
will send paucity to his fatness,
and under his frame a burning
will burn as fire burns.
17 The Light of Israel will be fire,
their Holy One the flame,
and it will burn and consume
the briars and thorns of him
all in a day.
18 All the glory of his forest and pasture,
man and beast, will be consumed,
the standard bearer melting away.
19 As for the remnant of his forest,
so few will be the trees,
a child could mark their tally.

20 On that day this will be:
No more will the remnant of Israel,
the fugitives of the House of Yaakov,
return to lean upon the one who beats them;
they will lean upon the LORD in truth,
the Holy One of Israel.
21 A remnant will return,[36]

35 | That is, the king of Assyria is merely a tool God wields.

36 | This is the symbolic name of Yeshayahu's son in 7:3. "Mighty God" similarly refers back to the symbolic name in 9:5.

the remnant of Yaakov,
to mighty God.
22 For though your people Israel may be
like sands of the sea for number,
but a remnant will return of them –
for annihilation is ordained,
sweeping through in justice,
23 for annihilation ordained,
the LORD of Hosts enforces
all across the earth.

24 And so, thus says the LORD GOD of Hosts:
Do not be afraid,
My people in Zion;
fear not Assyria;
they will beat you with the rod
and raise their staff against you
on their way to Egypt.
25 Let but a wisp of time pass by,
and the rage will be spent,
My fury – over their destruction.
26 And the LORD of Hosts will awaken against him
a whip – as when Midyan were lashed
at the Rock of Orev[37] –
and raise His staff over the sea,
bearing him away, as He did to Egypt.
27 On that day, this will be:
his burden will drop from your shoulders,
his yoke from your neck –
your heft will shatter the yoke.
28 He comes to Ayat,[38]
marches through Migron,
and stows His arms at Mikhmas.
29 They pass over the ford
and lodge at Geva;
Rama trembles;
Givat Sha'ul has fled.
30 Cry out, daughter Galim;
hear the cry, Laysha; scream, Anatot.
31 Madmena wanders;
the people of Gevim seek refuge –
32 this very day, he stands at Nov,
waving his hand toward the mount of daughter Zion,

37 | See Judges 7:25, and 9:3 above.

38 | This list maps an army's advance from the Assyrian province of Shomron southward toward Jerusalem.

Jerusalem's hill.

33 Behold the Master, the LORD of Hosts,
stirring dread, shearing off branches.
Those who held their heads high are brought down;
the exalted will be laid low.
34 He fells the forest groves with iron –
Lebanon falls
to the blows of majesty.

11 1 A new shoot will grow from the stem of Yishai;
from his roots a branch will bud.
2 And the spirit of the LORD will rest upon him –
a spirit of wisdom, of knowing,
a spirit of guidance and might,
a spirit of insight and awe of the LORD.
3 With awe of the LORD infusing his senses,
he will not judge by his eyes' perception,
nor rule by what his ears can grasp;
4 he will judge poor people justly,
render judgment rightly
for oppressed ones in the land;
he will strike the land
with the staff of his speech,
and the spirit that crosses his lips
will execute those who do evil.
5 He will gird his loins with righteousness:
his battle dress is truth.
6 Wolf will lie down beside lamb,
the leopard will lie beside the young goat;
calf, lion cub, fatted lamb together –
a little child will tend them.
7 The cow and the bear will graze
with their young lying down together,
and lion, like ox, will feed upon straw.
8 A baby will play at the cobra's hole,
and an infant's hand
will explore the viper's nest.
9 There will be no wrong or violence
on all My holy mountain,
for knowledge of the LORD will fill the earth
as waters cover the ocean.

10 On that day,
that offshoot of Yishai
that stands as a banner to all the peoples –

nations will come to seek him,
and his resting place will be glorious.

11 On that day this will be:
The LORD will stretch forth His hand again
to take back the remnant of His people,
those who remain, from Assyria and Egypt,
from Patros and from Kush,
from Eilam and from Shinar,
Ḥamat and the islands of the sea.[39]
12 He will lift up a banner to nations
and gather in the banished ones of Israel;
He will gather in the scattered ones of Israel
from all four edges of the world.
13 Efrayim's jealousy will fall away,
the enemies in Yehuda will be cut down,
Efrayim will no more be jealous of Yehuda;
Yehuda will bear toward Efrayim no more enmity.
14 They will fly west to the Philistines, shoulder to shoulder;
together they will sack the people of the East;
they will thrust their hand against Edom and Moav,
and the people of Amon will obey them.
15 The LORD will destroy the Egyptian Sea gulf
and wave His hand over the River through His fearsome wind –
He will beat it into seven separate streams
that people may cross in their shoes.
16 A path will be there for the remnant of His people,
those who remain, from Assyria,
as there was for the people of Israel
on the day they came up from the land of Egypt.
12 1 And you will say on that day:
I thank You, LORD
for You raged against me,
but You turned back Your rage,
and now You console me.
2 *Behold the God of my salvation;*
I trust and will not fear,
for God, the LORD, is my strength and song –
and now my salvation.
3 With joy you will draw water
from the flowing springs of rescue.
4 And you will say upon that day:
Give thanks to the LORD;

39 | Patros and Kush are in the south of modern-day Egypt, Eilam is in Iran, and Shinar is southern Mesopotamia. Ḥamat is in northern Syria. Jews had spread out to all these areas around the time of the destruction of the First Temple.

call on His name;
proclaim His acts among the peoples;
recount: His name is transcendent.
5 *Sing out to the Lord:*
He has performed grandeur;
all across the world this thing is known.
6 *Cry out, sing out joy, all you who dwell in Zion;*
for great in your midst
is the Holy One of Israel.

13 1 The burden of Babylon
seen by Yeshayahu son of Amotz:
2 Raise a banner upon the high mountain,
and lift your voice toward them –
gesture with your hand and
let them come
to the nobles' gates.
3 I command those I have consecrated
and call up the mighty men of My rage,
exuberant with My own pride.
4 The clamor of the horde fills the mountains,
the image of a mass of men,
the roar of whole kingdoms,
of nations called together:
the Lord of Hosts is gathering
a host for war.
5 They come from a distant land,
from the skies' edge,
the Lord and His armaments of fury,
to wreak violence across the world.
6 Wail, for the day of the Lord is nigh;
like assault from Shaddai it strikes,
7 so all hands give way,
so each mortal heart dissolves.
8 The throes take hold of them;
agony grips them;
they writhe like a woman in labor.
They stare in horror at each other
as at faces dragged through the flames.
9 Here it is coming: the day of the Lord,
cruel with fury,
with flaming rage,
turning the land to desolation,
routing out all her sinners,
10 for the stars of the sky in their patterns
will shine no more their light;

the sun will rise in darkness,
and the moon not beam its light.
11 I shall repay this earth its evil,
and the wicked ones their wrongs.
I shall halt the vicious ones' majesty
and fell the tyrants' pride.
12 Human life will be prized higher than gold;
I shall make it so: people scarcer than fine gold.
13 For this I shall jolt the heavens,
shake the land out of its resting place
through the fury of the LORD of Hosts
on the day His rage flames high.
14 And they will be like a hounded gazelle,
a flock with none to herd it;
each man will turn to his people
and flee back to his land.
15 Whoever is found will be run through
with the sword, they will fall, all
who are caught in flight.
16 Their little ones will be battered to death before their eyes,
their houses sacked,
their women raped.
17 I shall rouse Media against them,
who care not for silver, who
have no desire for gold.[40]
18 And their bows will crush children;
they will show infants no mercy,
their eyes spare no one's child.
19 Babylon: splendor among kingdoms,
crowning glory of Chaldean pride,
her end like God's overturning
of Sedom and Amora,
20 it will never again be inhabited,
and never be settled, in any generation,
nor any Arab nomad pitch his tent there,
nor shepherds lay their flocks down in that place.
21 Desert beasts will lie down there
and owls fill the houses.
Ostriches will make their homes,
and wild goats will dance.
22 Wild cats will scream in her palaces
and jackals in her pleasure halls.
Her time is coming close now;

40 | Koresh (Cyrus) of Persia, which had been a vassal state of the Median empire, conquered Babylon in 539 BCE.

her days draw to a close.

14 1 For the LORD will show compassion to Yaakov,
choose Israel again.
He will set them down upon their land,
and strangers will join them –
add themselves to the House of Yaakov –
2 while they will take of those peoples
and bring them to their place,
and the House of Israel will possess them
on the LORD's own land,
slaves and bondswomen;
be captors to their captors
and rule those who oppressed them.

3 On the day when the LORD lets you rest
from your pain and your turmoil,
and all the hard labor
to which you are subjected,
4 then you shall bear this speech
to the king of Babylon; say:
How could the oppressor be halted so,
the city of gold be halted?
5 The LORD has broken the staff of the wicked,
the tyrants' scepter,
6 the rod that beat peoples in fury,
beating and never letting up;
the one who ruled nations by wrath is now
pursued unrelentingly.
7 Now all the land rests, stilled –
then breaks out in song.
8 Even the juniper trees rejoice
over you; even cedars of Lebanon:
"Since you have fallen,
no one will rise again
to cut us down."
9 Sheol shakes below you,
waiting for your coming.
It rouses the shades to meet you,
all leaders of this earth,
commanding the kings of all nations
to rise up from their thrones.
10 Each one will speak up to you:
"Are you fallen like us now?
Are you like one of us?"

11 All your majesty has gone down to Sheol
along with the crooning of your harps;
grubs are laid as sheets beneath you;
worms are your covers.
12 How you have fallen from heaven now,
shining one, son of the dawn light;
how you are cut down to earth,
you who decided nations' fates.
13 You once said in your heart,
"I shall ascend to the sky,
raise my throne to the godly stars;
I shall sit on the mount where the gods meet,
at the farthest reach of the north.
14 I shall mount the clouds' summits
and be like the Most High."[41]
15 Instead you fell down into Sheol,
to the lowest depths of the pit.
16 Those who see it will gaze down;
they will scrutinize you well:
"Is this really the man who shook the world,
who overturned all kingdoms,
17 making the earth like a wasteland,
razing its towns,
his captives never to come home?"
18 All the kings of nations, each
lies down in glory in his home.
19 But you – you are cast out of your grave
like a rejected branch,
dressed in the dead
whom the sword cut through,
thrown down on the rocks of the pit,
a trampled carcass.[42]
20 No, you will not be one with kings in burial,
for you have destroyed your own land,
killed your own people;
let no child ever bear
your evil-wreaking name.
21 Prepare the slaughter for his sons
for their forefathers' iniquities;
let them not rise to inherit the earth;
let the world be filled again with towns.

41 | Hebrew "Elyon." This term is often used as an epithet for Israel's God, but here refers ambiguously to a Canaanite god of that name.

42 | Sargon II, king of Assyria, who deported Israelites from Shomron and then crowned himself king of Babylon, was killed on the battlefield in 705 BCE and not buried.

22 I rise up against them,
so says the LORD of Hosts,
and I shall cut off from Babylon
name and remnant,
child and child's child,
so says the LORD.
23 I shall make her the inheritance of wild owls
and water bogs,
sweep her with the broom of extinction:
the LORD of Hosts has spoken.

24 The LORD of Hosts swears an oath:
As I envisioned it, always,
has it not come to be?
Just as I decide it,
will it not always be?
25 *To break Assyria in My land,*
I shall bring them down from My hills;
I shall pull their yoke from this people,
their burden down from their shoulders:
26 this is the plan that is already
plotted out for all the world,
and this is the hand stretched forth
over all nations,
27 for what the LORD of Hosts has planned,
who can ever thwart it?
This His hand stretched forth,
who can ever turn it back?

28 In the year when King Aḥaz died, this burden was spoken:
29 Do not rejoice,
all of you in Philistia,
that the staff that beat you is broken.
From the snake's severed root a cobra will rise,
its fruit a flying serpent.
30 The firstborn of the poor will graze
as the powerless lie down in safety,
but I will kill your root by hunger,
and those who survive will be slain.
31 Wail at the gates;
cry out, O town;
melt, all of you in Philistia,
for smoke is billowing from the north,
and not one man breaks rank.
32 What message back to the nation's messengers?
That the LORD has laid Zion's foundation,

and there, the poor among His people
will shelter.

15 1 The burden of Moav:[43]
Massacre came to Ar in the night;
Moav is silenced.
For massacre came in the night;
Kir Moav was silenced.
2 The people of the House and of Divon
climb to their high shrines in tears
for Nevo and for Meideva –
Moav is wailing;
every head is shaven,
each beard shorn.[44]
3 They walk the streets in sackcloth;
on the rooftops, in the squares,
all is one great wailing,
poured out in tears.
4 Ḥeshbon cries out, and Elaleh,
and their voices reach Yahatz.
This is why Moav's warriors roar –
their souls are screaming for them.
5 My heart cries out for Moav;
the refugees reach Tzoar,
Eglat Shlishiya,
climbing the slope of Luḥit
weeping;
all along the Ḥoronayim Road
rise the wails of brokenness,
6 for the waters of Nimrim
will become a desolation;
for grass will wither
and plants will die:
all green gone.
7 And so, the wealth they have accumulated,
all that they have saved,
they carry away across the Stream of Willows.
8 Her cries rise all around the border of Moav,
her wails as far as Agalim,
her wails as far as Be'er Eilim.
9 The waters of Dimon are filled with blood;
I will spill out yet more upon Dimon,
set a lion upon Moav's fugitives;
those left will be swallowed by the ground.

43 | The locations mentioned in this passage were principle cities of Moav.
44 | Gestures of mourning or marks of enslavement.

16 1 Send a sheep, ruler of the land,
from Sela into the desert,
to the mount of daughter Zion:
2 Like a bird wandering,
banished from the nest –
the women of Moav
on the fords to Arnon.
3 Bring counsel;
act with judgment;
cast your shade like night
over the noon heat.
Hide these outcasts;
do not expose the wanderers.
4 Let the outcasts of Moav bide among you;
be their hiding place
from the invading mass
until the oppressor is gone,
the massacre over,
brutality is ended
all across the land.

5 There is a throne founded on kindness,
presided from in truth
in David's tent,
by a judge, a seeker of justice,
one who hastens righteousness.
6 We have all heard Moav's arrogance,
excessive arrogance:
his loftiness, his hubris,
his wrath;
his illusions came to naught.
7 So Moav wails for Moav,
all of her wailing,
for the grapes of Kir Ḥareshet
low moans sound,[45]
8 for the vineyards of Ḥeshbon are pitiful,
the vines of Sivma –
its grapes were fit for the masters of nations –
they reached Yazer,
wandered in the desert;
their tendrils spread
and crossed the sea.
9 So I weep the cries of Yazer
for the vine of Sivma;

45 | Cf. Jeremiah 48:29–33.

I would quench you with tears,
Ḥeshbon and Elaleh,
for over your summer fruits and reaping
the battle call has fallen.
10 Joy and celebration are
dispelled from the fruitful field;
no cheerful singing in vineyards;
no more trumpet song.
The treaders do not tread
the wine in the winepresses; I have
silenced those calls also.
11 And so, for Moav, my being
moans like a lute, and all
that is in me is with Kir Ḥareshet.
12 And it will be: when Moav
appears on the high shrine, when he is wearied,
he will climb to his sanctuary to pray –
and will not be able.

13 This is what the Lord spoke
of Moav long ago,
14 and now the Lord speaks – He says:
Three more years, three hired workers' years,
and Moav's glory will fall to shame
among all the vast multitude,
the remnant a thin trace,
all eminence gone.

17 1 The burden of Damascus:
Behold: Damascus is dismissed from the company of cities:
piled up rubble;
2 the Aroer towns abandoned,
left to the flocks
lying down with none to trouble them.
3 No more fortresses in Efrayim;
no more kingship in Damascus,
and Aram will be a remnant –
like the children of Israel's glory;
the Lord of Hosts has spoken.

4 On that day,
slender will grow Yaakov's glory,
the fat of his body grown lean – it is
5 as a man gathers up the standing corn at harvest,
and his arm slashes down the heads of grain,
as the heads are collected in the Refaim Valley –
6 yet some will remain;

as the olives are beaten down,
but two or three buds will be left
at the very top of the tree;
perhaps four or five
on the fruitful vine's limbs –
so says the LORD, God of Israel.

7 On that day,
man will turn to his Maker,
and his eyes will see the Holy One of Israel.
8 No more will he turn to the altars his hands build
to see what his own fingers formed,
the sacred trees and sun statues.

9 On that day,
his bastion cities will be
like fields forsaken, lapsed to groves and woods,
like those they forsook when Israel came;
it will be wasteland,
10 for you have forgotten God, your rescue –
you do not remember your bastion Rock.
So you sow these gorgeous shoots,
plant cuttings from a stranger's branch;
11 that day you bring your shoots to flourish,
by morning you see your seeds give flower;
the fruits will be waste
on the day of your sickness:
incurable pain.

12 Woe to the throngs of great peoples
that roar the roar of oceans,
that thunder the thunder of nations,
like the thunder of mighty waters.
13 Nations thunder, the thunder of great oceans –
a voice dispels the flood – it flees far away,
chased away like hill chaff by the wind,
like tumbleweed in a tempest –
14 at evening, horror;
by morning it will be gone.
This is the fate of those who plunder us,
the portion due to any
who take us for their spoils.

18 1 Woe to the land of buzzing insect wings,
far away beyond the Kushite rivers,
2 that sends its messengers out by sea –
reed vessels crossing the waters:

"Go now, swift messengers,
to a people pulled apart and mauled,
to a people always fearsome until now,
a nation trampled piece by piece,
despoiled by kings of the river land."[46]
3 All you who live upon this earth,
all dwellers on the land –
when the banner is raised up on the mountains you shall see;
when the horn sounds its blast –
then you shall hear.

4 For this is what the LORD has told me:
Still I rest in My residence, gaze down
as when pure heat rests on sunlight,
or on the harvest heat a cloud of dew,
5 for before harvest comes,
when the blossom is gone,
as the grape buds swell into young fruits,
the trembling stems shall fall to the pruning knife.
The branches will be cleared, cut down,[47]
6 abandoned to mountain eagles,
to beasts of the land.
And birds of prey will feed on this all summer,
and all beasts of the land
will see winter through on this.

7 At that time,
tribute shall be brought to the LORD of Hosts
from this people pulled apart and mauled,
from a people always fearsome until now,
a nation trampled piece by piece,
despoiled by the kings of the river land,
to the place of the LORD of Hosts, His name:
Mount Zion.

19 1 The burden of Egypt:
Behold the LORD,
riding upon swift
cloud and coming to Egypt.
The gods of Egypt all sway before Him;
the heart of Egypt will dissolve.
2 I shall make Egypt wrestle with Egypt;
brother will fight against brother,

46 | Verses 1–3 seem to refer to political leaders in upper Egypt who seek an alliance with Yehuda against Assyria.

47 | Possibly referring to the downfall of Assyria.

friend against friend,
city against city,
realm against realm.
3 Egypt will empty its spirit from within,
and I shall confound all its plans.
The people will seek after their false gods and mutterers,
necromancers, mediums.
4 I shall dam Egypt
through a hard-handed master;
a mighty king will tyrannize them,
so says the Master, LORD of Hosts.
5 The sea will be emptied of water;
the river will be scorched dry.
6 Rivers will be forsaken;
Egypt's canals will dwindle and dry,
and rush and reed wither.
7 Naked land on the Nile bed,
naked the bank of the Nile,
and all that seeds and grows in the Nile
will dry up, disperse, be gone.
8 The fishermen will lament;
all who throw hooks to the river will mourn,
all who spread nets over water left waste.
9 The many who work combed flax will be shamed
with all those who weave fine cotton;
10 Egypt's foundations – crushed,
its dam builders mired spirits.
11 The princes of Tzoan are fools;
the wisest of Pharaoh's advisors
give idiots' counsel.
How can you say to Pharaoh,
"I am a son of wise men,
heir to the ancient kings"?
12 Where, then – where are these wise men of yours?
Surely they would tell you,
surely they must know what
the LORD of Hosts has planned for Egypt.
13 The princes of Tzoan are fools;
the princes of Nof, deceived.
They have led Egypt astray, the very
mainstay of its tribes.
14 The LORD has poured into her a spirit of madness,
and they have led Egypt awry in all it does,
like a drunk man lurching through his vomit.
15 Nothing in Egypt will be done

that is done
by head or by tail,
by palm or by bulrush of them.[48]

16 On that day,
Egypt will be like women
who quake and fear
the Lord of Hosts' raised hand
brandished over them;
17 the land of Yehuda will be
the terror of Egypt.
Whoever may mention its name
will strike them with fear
of the Lord of Hosts' plan –
of what He has destined for them.

18 On that day,
five cities of Egypt
shall speak the language of Canaan
and swear their oaths by the Lord of Hosts.
City of Calamity, one shall be named.

19 On that day,
in Egypt's heartlands, an altar to the Lord
will stand; at her borders a pillar to the Lord.
20 They will be sign and testament
in the land of Egypt to the Lord of Hosts,
for the people shall cry out to the Lord
because of their oppressors;
He will send them a rescuer,
a fighter; he will save them.
21 The Lord will be made known to Egypt,
and Egypt will know the Lord
on that day.
And they will serve by sacrifice and offering;
they will make the Lord vows and honor them.
22 The Lord will plague Egypt –
plague it and heal.
They will come back to the Lord, and He will receive
their appeal
and heal.

23 On that day
a road will run

48 | Both the leadership and the masses will be rendered powerless, and Egyptian society will cease to function.

from Egypt to Assyria.
Assyria will come to Egypt.
Egypt will come to Assyria,
and Egypt with Assyria will worship.

24 On that day,
Israel will be one with
Egypt and Assyria,
a blessing on this earth.
25 For the LORD of Hosts has blessed him, saying:
Blessed are My people, Egypt;
Assyria, work of My hands;
and Israel, My own possession.

20 1 It was the year the Tartan[49] came to Ashdod – dispatched by Sargon, king
2 of Assyria – when he fought against Ashdod and captured the city. At that
time, the LORD spoke through Yeshayahu son of Amotz: "Go, undo the
sackcloth that covers your loins, and take off the sandals on your feet." And
that is what he did – naked and barefoot would he walk.

3 And the LORD said:
My servant Yeshayahu,
walking naked and barefoot for these three years,
is a message, a sign,
concerning Egypt and Kush.
4 Just so will it be
when the king of Assyria leads away
the captives of Egypt,
the exiles of Kush,
young and old,
naked, barefoot,
backsides bare,
that nakedness of Egypt,
5 full of dread and shame
for Kush, their hope;
for Egypt, their glory.
6 The ruler of this shore will be saying
on that day,
"Look where our hope is now:
the place we would flee to for aid,
to be saved from the king of Assyria –
now we – how will we escape?"

21 1 The burden of the Ocean Desert:[50]
As storm winds sweep on through the Negev,

49 | A title referring to the Assyrian king's second-in-command.

50 | Perhaps Babylon, where the banks of the Euphrates overflow into desert.

so from the wilderness it comes,
from the terrible land.
2 A fierce vision is spoken to me:
the traitors betraying,
the plunderers plunder –
Go up, Eilam;
Media, lay siege;
I have silenced all groaning.[51]
3 This is why my hips are seized with sickness,
why agonies take hold of me, like agonies of birth.
I writhe away from hearing,
shrink, horrified, from seeing;
4 my heartbeat strays;
I lurch with terror.
He has turned the twilight of my pleasure
into dread.
5 So lay a table now
and raise the lamp,
feast, drink.
Now get up, all you princes;
grease your shields.

6 For the LORD is saying to me:
Go now: set a watchman;
let him tell you what he sees.
7 He sees a chariot, a pair of horses,
a donkey rider, a camel rider;
he listens, closely listens.
8 A lion roars.
"At my post, LORD, always
I stand, daylong
at my watch, stationed through the nights."
9 And here they come:
a chariot of men,
a pair of horses.
Then He spoke and said:
Fallen, fallen is Babylon;
all the statues of her gods
are smashed into the ground.
10 My downtrodden one –
grain of my threshing floor –
what I hear from the LORD of Hosts, the God of Israel,
I have spoken now to you.

---

51 | The groans of Babylon, whom they are attacking. The italic font indicates God's voice, distinct from that of the prophet.

11 The burden of Duma:[52]
A voice calling to me from Se'ir:
"What news does night bring, watchman?
Watch, what news of night?"
12 The watch says,
"Morning comes –
and also night."
If you would ask it, ask;
turn back, return.

13 The burden of Arabia:
In the forest of Arabia you spend the night,
nomads on the trail from Dedan.[53]
14 People of Teima –
meet the thirsty with water,
greet the travelers with bread;
15 for they have fled the sword,
the drawn sword,
the taut bow,
the dead weight of war.

16 For so the Lord has said to me:
One more year, a hired worker's year,
and the glory of Kedar[54] will be all gone,
17 their bowmen a small remnant,
Kedar's mighty men left few;
the Lord, God of Israel, has spoken.

22 1 The burden of the Valley of the Vision:[55]
Why now, why have you all
climbed up onto the rooftops?
2 You, full of bustle, buzzing metropolis,
exuberant city?
Not for your fallen to fall to the sword,
not yours to perish in warfare.[56]
3 Now all Your commanders have strayed,
or been bound up by their bowstrings;
all those found in you were bound up together
or fled from what comes from the distance.
4 So I say: Turn your gaze away;

52 | A kindom in what is now the northern part of Saudi Arabia. Se'ir is on the northern border of Duma.

53 | A kingdom in the northwestern Arabian Peninsula.

54 | The Kedarites were nomads whose areas of habitation included Dedan and Duma; Assyria fought these nomads several times.

55 | Apparently a reference to Jerusalem.

56 | But rather ingloriously from starvation and disease.

the tears I weep are bitter.
Do not rush in to comfort me
for my maiden nation's ravaging.
5 For a day of turmoil, defeat, and shame
is come from the Lord God of Hosts
in the Valley of the Vision.
Kir cries carnage;[57]
the call reaches the hills.
6 Eilam bore ammunition
in horse-drawn chariots of men,
and Kir drew out its shields.
7 So it was: the best of your valleys filled with chariots,
and cavalry streamed to the gate.
8 They pulled away the city's cover:
on that day you viewed all
the weapons of the Forest House,[58]
9 the ruptures in the City of David – many –
and you gathered the waters to the Lower Pool
10 and numbered Jerusalem's houses,
then smashed those houses down
to reinforce the city wall.
11 Yes, you dug a channel between the walls
for the waters of the ancient pool[59]
and looked not once to the One who made it;
you saw not the One who, long since, formed it.
12 On that day, the Lord God of Hosts
called for tears and eulogies,
the baldness and sackcloth of grief;
13 but here: festivity and joy,
the butchering of cattle, the slaughter of flock.
"Eat your meat, drink your wine;
eat, drink; tomorrow we die."[60]
14 The Lord of Hosts' voice resounds in my ears:
See if this sin can ever be
atoned for
to the day you die,
says the Lord of Hosts.

15 So says the Lord God of Hosts:
Go – go to this minister,

57 | Men from Kir (of Moav) and Eilam joined the Assyrian fighting forces.
58 | The royal palace; cf. 1 Kings 7:2–5.
59 | King Ḥizkiyahu fortified Jerusalem by building the broad wall, which necessitated the demolition of houses to clear space for it, and a channel to divert water into the city.
60 | The slaughter of the flock is a response to the siege, in which food and water for people and animals are lacking.

to Shevna in charge of the palace:
16 Why? What is yours here,
and who here is yours
that you hew yourself a grave in this place?
Hewing his grave on high,
engraving his resting place into the rock.
17 See – the LORD will shake you, a masterful shake,
will put you on and wear you,
18 will wind you, bind you, turn you around
into an open-handed land.
It is there that you will die,
there that your chariots of glory
will curse your master's house.
19 I shall push you down from your high position,
destroy your standing.
20 It will be on that day:
I shall call upon my servant,
Elyakim son of Ḥilkiya.[61]
21 I shall dress him in your tunic,
with your breastplate will protect him.
I shall give over your rule into his hand,
and he shall be father
to the people of Jerusalem,
the House of Yehuda.
22 I shall put the key to the House of David upon his shoulder;
what he opens, none will close;
what he closes, none will open.
23 I shall set him as a peg in an enduring place
and make him a throne of glory to his father's house.
24 All the glory of his father's house will hang upon him,[62]
children and progeny,
small vessels, all,
from barrels to wine jars.
25 On that day, says the LORD of Hosts,
that peg, fixed in an enduring place, will shift
and be broken and fall,
and the burden it carries will fall,
for the LORD has spoken.

23 1 The burden of Tyre:
Wail, ships of Tarshish,
for she is sacked: no home, no harbor;
it was shown to them in the land of Kitim.

61 | Also mentioned in 36:3 and II Kings 18:18.

62 | This will apparently be his downfall – despite a promising beginning he will start giving undue favor to his own family members.

2 Stand silent, you, living on the island;[63]
the merchant of Sidon, the sea voyager
once filled you up.
3 Great waters bore the seed of the Shiḥor,
the River's crop her harvest,
making her merchant to nations.
4 Be humbled, Sidon, for the sea speaks,
the fortress sea – she says,
"No! I never labored,
never birthed;
I never brought up boys,
nor raised young ladies."[64]
5 When Egypt hear,
they will quake at the news of Tyre.
6 Cross over then, back to Tarshish.
Wail, you who live on the island.
7 Has it come to this, your exuberant city,
old as antiquity?
Her feet will carry her far to seek haven.
8 Who planned all this for
Tyre, who wore the crown?
Tyre, whose merchants are princes,
whose tradesmen are nobles of this earth.
9 It is the Lord of Hosts who planned it,
to desecrate all of splendor's eminence,
to degrade all nobles of this earth.
10 Pass through your land like the Nile,[65] daughter Tarshish;
there is no more landing.
11 He has stretched His hand out over the sea
and whipped nations to a ferment.
The Lord has commanded Canaan
to destroy her strongholds.
12 He says: No more
will you exult,
virgin daughter Sidon, downtrodden.
Kitim – rise and go there.
You will find no rest there either.
13 You see, land of Chaldeans,
this is the people that never was.
Assyria built this land for desert beasts.
They set up their watchtowers,

---

63 | Tyre was an island until Alexander the Great made it a peninsula.

64 | The sea is either disowning, or perhaps mourning, her Tyrian "children."

65 | Referring, seemingly, to the seasonal flooding of the Nile bank, which displaces those on the shore.

laid waste all her palaces,
turned them to rubble.
14 Now wail, ships of Tarshish;
your stronghold is sacked.

15 It will be on that day:
Tyre will be forgotten for seventy years,
the reign of a single king –
but at the end of seventy years,
the strain of a harlot's song will come to Tyre.
16 Take up your harp now;
circle the town,
forgotten harlot.
Play your music beautifully
and fill the place with song,
that you may be remembered.
17 So it will be, at the end of seventy years,
the LORD will return to Tyre;
she will go to hire again.
Now she can play harlot to
all kingdoms of the land
across the world.
18 But her merchandise, her hire,
will be sacred to the LORD;
it will not be put by,
will not be hoarded.
For to all those who live in the LORD's presence,
her merchandise will be
enough to eat their fill
and dress in finery.

24 1 Behold the LORD
pouring out the world, laying it waste,
warping its face,
scattering all its dwellers.
2 People and priest alike,
servant and master alike,
maid and mistress,
buyer, seller,
lender and debtor,
debtor and usurer
3 poured out – the world will be drained,
sacked, and ransacked –
for the LORD has spoken this.
4 The land has grieved and withered;
pitiful, withered, is the earth;

the exalted of this land –
pitiful.
5 The land has turned vile beneath its burden of humanity:
they flout the teachings, overturn the laws;
they violate the ancient covenant,[66]
6 so the country, a curse consumes it.
The guilt lies with her people,
and the people dry up upon the land,
humanity left a bare remnant.
7 New wine is mourning, the vine is pitiful,
the merry-hearted men are gone to groans.
8 The joy of drums is frozen,
the noise of exuberance silenced,
the joy of the harp is frozen.
9 No more will they drink their wine in song;
strong drink has turned bitter to the drinker.
10 The city of emptiness is broken,[67]
its homes shut off to all comers.
11 In the streets, they cry out for wine;[68]
all joy has darkened to grief,
the joy of the land in exile.
12 Desolation remains in the city,
its gate beaten down to ruin,
13 for so will it be:
in the midst of the earth,
the peoples
like the beatings of an olive tree,
like gleanings left at harvest's end.
14 They will raise their voices in joyful song,
singing out from the ocean
in the Lord's swelling majesty.
15 So: Out of the fires, glorify the Lord;
in the coastlands of the ocean, the name of the Lord,
of Israel's God.

16 From the edge of the world
we hear songs come:
"Glory to the good man."
But I say, "I am starving, starving,
aching" –
Traitors betray –
betrayal – traitors betray –

---

66 | That is, that the land will provide sustenance while people will not pollute it with evil behavior.

67 | Perhaps morally bankrupt, or empty of life after the calamity.

68 | The party has ceased and the celebrants are suffering hangovers.

17 terror, trench, entrapment[69]
for you who live on earth.
18 And he who flees the terror
will fall into the trench,
and he who rises from the trench
is caught up in the trap.
Windows are opening to the heights,[70]
and earth's foundations shake.
19 Shivering, shattering, the earth;
the land crumbles, crumbles,
collapses – the land – collapsed.
20 The land sways, sways like a drunkard,
shaking like a makeshift hut;
its sin rests heavy on it,
it is falling, falling, nevermore
to rise.

21 On that day, the LORD will take notice
in heaven of the heavenly host,
and on earth of the kings of earth;
22 they will be rounded up all together
as captives are gathered to the pit;
they will be shut in under lock –
but after many days they will be noticed.
23 The moon will be abashed,
the sun ashamed,
for the LORD of Hosts will rule –
on Mount Zion, Jerusalem,
before His elders – in glory.

25 1 LORD, You are my God,
and I exalt You, declare Your name,
for You have worked wonders;
commands issued long since
faithfully come true.
2 You have turned town to rubble heap,
walled city to ruin,
the palace of strangers to no more town,
never to be rebuilt.
3 So You are glorified by a fearsome people;
the cities of powerful nations fear You.
4 For You have been a stronghold to the vulnerable,
the stronghold of the poor man in his anguish,
shelter from the storm,

69 | The alliteration mirrors the Hebrew: *paḥad vafaḥat vafakh*.

70 | Cf. Genesis 7:12.

and shade from searing sun,
for the spirit of oppression
is a storm against the wall,
5 like searing heat in desert land:
You quell the roar of strangers.
Like searing heat behind clouds' shadows;
the tyrants' song will be subdued.

6 The LORD of Hosts – He will lay out
for all the nations on this hill[71]
a feast of fats,
a feast of wines;
of fats with the marrow,
of wine refined.
7 On this hill He will consume
the covering wrapped about
the faces of all peoples,
the weave that is woven
to shroud all nations.
8 He will swallow up death forever;
the LORD GOD, He will wipe every tear
from every face.
He will sweep His people's shame away
from all the earth.
The LORD has spoken.

9 It will be said on that day:
This – this is our God;
it is Him we waited for, and He has saved us.
This, the LORD we waited for,
we exult, we rejoice in His salvation,
10 for the hand of the LORD will rest upon
this hill.
Moav is trampled beneath Him
as straw is trampled in the dung heap;
11 He will spread His hands within her
as one spreads one's arms to swim;
her pride will be brought low
by the power of His hands.
12 The high defenses of your walls,
He has brought them down, has brought them low;
and they have fallen down
to earth,

71 | That is, Jerusalem.

to dust.

26 1 On that day, this song will be sung in the land of Yehuda:
How mighty – this our city:
He has turned wall and bulwark
to salvation.
2 Open wide the gates;
let a righteous nation in
that kept its faith;
3 for a faithful nature
You keep peace, peace,
for it trusts in You.
4 Trust in the LORD forever,
for in God, the LORD, you will find
a Rock everlasting,
5 for He has brought down those who dwelled on high.
Elevated city, He brought it low,
brought it down
to earth,
to dust.
6 Feet trample it –
poor men's feet,
the footsteps of the beaten.
7 The path is smooth for a righteous man,
and You level the straight road of the righteous.
8 But through all Your judgments, LORD,
we wait for You,
for Your name and Your memory,
for which the soul yearns.
9 My soul yearns for You by night,
and with the spirit that is in me
I rise to meet You early,
for when Your judgment comes
to this world, all earth's dwellers
will learn righteousness.
10 Will He have mercy on the wicked man
who will not learn righteousness?
Such a one contorts what is upright in this world
and never once sees
the LORD's grandeur.

11 LORD,
Your hand held high; they do not see it,
but let them see Your passion for a people – and be shamed;
let the fire of your foes consume them.
12 LORD,

set peace to warm[72] for us,
for all the evil we wrought, You brought back to us.
13 LORD our God –
other lords than You have mastered us,
but still it is Your name alone we speak.
14 Deceased, they will not live again –
shades that will not rise.
You have come, You will destroy them, and
will wipe away all memory.
15 You have added to this people, LORD;
You have added to the people; You are glorified;
You have pushed back all the borders of the land.

16 LORD – in anguish they came to You,
pouring out whispers to You even as You beat them.
17 Like a woman with child, about to give birth,
writhing, crying out in her agonies,
so have we been before You, LORD.
18 We carried, writhed,
gave birth – as to the wind.
We made no salvation in the world,
and those residing in the earth were not delivered.
19 Let Your dead ones live;
let my own bodies rise.
Wake up and rejoice,
inhabitants of dust,
for droplets of light are Your dewfall,
and You will fell the shades,
down to the earth.

20 Go now, My people,
into your inner chambers;
close the doors behind you
and wait there – but a moment –
until the rage has passed.
21 For here – the LORD –
He comes out of His place
to repay the land's dwellers for their sin.
The land is uncovering her blood now:
no longer will she hide her slain.

27 1 On that day,
the LORD will come
with His sword, broad and long and strong
upon the Leviathan, the Fleeing Serpent,

72 | The same Hebrew word appears in Ezekiel 24:3 and describes the act of placing food on a fire to cook.

upon the Leviathan, the Winding Serpent,
and slay the great beast of the sea.

2 On that day,
sing to her,
"Vineyard of red wine...."
3 I, the LORD, watch over her,
moment by moment will I water her,
that no one may come to do harm;
by night, by day I watch her.
4 There is no fury in Me now.
Would that I could be those
briars and brambles in battle:
in would I march and
set them on fire as one.
5 But let them grasp My stronghold –
then they will make peace with Me,
peace, will they make Me.
6 In days to come, Yaakov will take root,
Israel will put out buds and flower,
and all the land on all the earth
will be covered with the fruits.

7 Was he beaten as are beaten those who beat him?
Was his slaying like the slaying of their slain?
8 With a faithful measure, driving them out You fight them;
He blew them away with His blasting spirit
on the day of the gale.
9 This, then, is how the iniquity
of Israel may be atoned –
and that, all the fruit of removing his sin –
by rendering all his altar stones
smashed limestone,
no sacred trees or incense shrines rising again.
10 The fortress city will sit alone,
a shelter left behind, lonely as desert.
Calves will graze there,
there will they lie,
and eat up all their branches.
11 When their yield dries up they will be broken down.
Women will come and use them as firewood,
for this is not a wise people;
and so its Maker will have no compassion,
its Creator will grant it no grace.

12 On that day,
the LORD will beat the branches

from the Euphrates's surge
to the River of Egypt
and gather you up
one by one, you children of Israel.

13 It will be, on that day:
a great ram's horn will sound,
and they will come, all those lost
in the land of Assyria,
and those who are exiled
to the land of Egypt,
and bow low to the Lord
on the holy mount
in Jerusalem.

28 1 Woe to the proud garland
of Efrayim's drunkards,
for the withered lotus flower that was
the glorious supremacy
crowning the oiled valley
of the wine benumbed.
2 See what comes – something strong and determined of the Lord,
like pelting hail, like a cataclysmic storm,
like a river of great waters, flooding waters –
heavy-handed, casting people down to earth,
3 trampling underfoot
the garland pride
of Efrayim's drunkards.
4 Like a withered lotus flower it shall be, its
glorious supremacy
that crowned the fat valley
like the first fig before harvest;
the one that all who saw
would swallow up sooner than hold it.

5 On that day
the Lord of Hosts will be a garland of splendor,
the crown of supremacy,
to the remnant of His people,
6 He will be the spirit of justice
in those who preside over justice,
and of might in those who drive war
back from the gate.
7 For these men too[73] have gone astray with wine,
they have lost themselves in ale –

73 | The leaders of the Kingdom of Israel.

priest and prophet – gone astray with their ale,
been swallowed up in wine,
got lost by their ale,
gone astray in their vision,
fallen over in judgment –
8 the tables are soaked, all, in vomit and filth,
until there is no space left.

9 Whom would he teach knowledge,
whom bring
to comprehend his words?
Those barely weaned of milk, those
just taken from the breast?
10 *Law after law, law after law,*
line after line, line after line,
a little bit here, a little bit there –
11 in a babble of words, in a different tongue
he speaks to this people.
12 He told them, "This is rest: leave the weary be;
this is calm." They would not hear.[74]
13 So the word of the Lord is to them
law after law, law after law,
line after line, line after line,
a little bit here, a little bit there,
for them to walk and stumble on backward,
be broken, be beaten, be caught.

14 And so, hear the word of the Lord,
you cynics, you
leaders of this people in Jerusalem.
15 "We have forged a covenant with death,"
you say, "we have reached
a seers' agreement with Sheol.[75]
When the whip cracks over us
it will not touch us,
for we have delusion as a refuge;
we will hide away inside the lie."

16 And so, thus says the Lord God:
Behold: it is I who laid down a stone in Jerusalem,
a tested stele,
precious cornerstone,
foundation stone, and founded well;
one who believes will not act in haste.

74 | To heed the prophet's message would bring peace and security, but his audience are as children, unable or unwilling to understand his words. Cf. 6:9ff.

75 | Apparently referring to a futile alliance with some foreign power.

17 And I laid down law as the measuring line,
and justice as the plumb weight.
And the hail will sweep off that delusion of cover,
and water will wash away the hiding place.
18 Your covenant with death will be swept away;
your agreement with Sheol will not be honored.
The whip will crack and as it passes
you will be trampled down.
19 Ever as it passes it will take you,
and morning, early morning, it will pass,
all day, all night,
and only terror
comprehends what it hears.
20 For the sheet is too short to be stretched out upon,
and the shroud too narrow to gather up under.
21 For the Lord will rise up as on Mount Peratzim,
and will rage as in the Valley of Givon,[76]
to do what He shall do – and strange is what He does;
to work His work – and foreign is His work to you.
22 Now – no more cynical speeches,
lest your chains grip firmer;
for ordained annihilation, this is what I have heard
from the Lord God of Hosts
for all the land.

23 Listen now, and hear My voice;
heed and hear these words of Mine:
24 Does the plowman plow all day to plant,
opening and breaking up the clods?
25 Does he not then make the ground even
and scatter the black caraway,
throw down the cumin,
sow the wheat in line,
the barley in its place, the emmer in bounds?
26 This is the way his God trains him
in what is right, and teaches him;
27 you cannot thresh caraway with a board,
or roll a wagon wheel over cumin;
black caraway must be beaten with a rod,
and cumin with a staff,
28 and grain for bread must be ground fine –
and not forever does one thresh,
pounding with the wheel of his carriage,
crushing the seeds under his horsemen.

---

76 | Victories narrated in II Samuel 5:20 and Joshua 10:10.

29 This too, then, came forth from the LORD of Hosts
whose plans are wondrous,
and whose wisdom great.[77]

29 1 Oh Ariel, Ariel,[78]
the city where David camped,
add year to year,
the festivals circling round again,
2 and I shall torment Ariel,
and weeping and wailing there will be;
it will be like Ariel to Me.[79]
3 I shall camp like a ring around you,
besiege you with a palisade,
build the siege walls around you.
4 Brought low, you speak up from the ground –
words spoken up from the dust,
your voice a ghost rising up from the ground;
from the dust your speech gibbers.
5 But then your many invaders
will become like thinnest sand,
your many oppressors
like transient dust;
it will be so very sudden
6 from the LORD of Hosts, who will visit you
with thunder and earthquake and deafening voice,
storm and tempest,
and the flame of consuming fire.
7 It will all be as a dream, as a vision of the night:
all these, every nation, that mobbed Ariel,
all her invading hordes and entrapments
tormenting her.
8 It will be: as a hungry man dreams –
and there is food before him,
but he wakes to find himself empty;
as the thirsty man dreams –
he is drinking –
but he wakes and is faint and is yearning –
so will it be for all the nations
mobbing around Mount Zion.[80]

77 | Just as after a time, the plowman's preparation ends, so too will the time for the prophets' warnings. Then Israel must cease sinning or face the consequences.

78 | This term refers to the altar in the Temple and is a metonym for Jerusalem; cf. Ezekiel 43:15–16.

79 | Jerusalem will be like an altar of sacrifices.

80 | The siege will be but a dream. See chapters 37–38 and II Kings 18:17–19:37.

9 Stop for a moment dumbfounded –
blind yourselves, and be blind,
you who are drunk, but not with wine,
who sway, but not from ale;
10 the LORD has poured over you
a spirit of sleep
and closed your eyes;
your prophets, your leaders
who see visions – He covered their eyes.
11 The vision of everything will be
like the words of a sealed book to you;
you would give such a book to a man who can read:
"Read to us from this,"
but he would say, "No, I cannot,
because it is sealed."
12 Or give such a book to a man who cannot read:
"Read to us from this" –
and all he would say is
"I know not how to read."

13 The LORD says:
Because this people comes
with its mouth, with its lips gives Me honor
while its heart is far from Me,
and the awe in which they hold Me
is a precept people taught them,
14 I shall go on dazzling this people
by wonder upon wonder
until their wise ones lose their wisdom,
and the knowledge of their knowing ones
hides itself away.

15 Gone, those who think to go deeper than the LORD,
to hide their counsel
in the darkness of their deeds.
"Who sees us?" they say.
"Who will know?"

16 Oh, your reversals:
Is the potter to be viewed as clay?
Does a thing say to its maker,
"You did not make me,"
or the work of its artisan,
"He does not understand"?

17 Soon, do you see it? Just a little longer –
the Lebanon will turn to fertile land

and fertile land to forest.
18 On that day, the deaf will hear book words,
and out of the gloom and darkness,
blind men's eyes will see.
19 The humble will rejoice in the LORD, more and more;
the most pitiful of men
will celebrate the Holy One,
20 for the oppressors – they are gone, the cynical rulers
are done for, and those who lie in wait
to sin will all be severed,
21 those whose words bring men to sin,
who entrap the man rebuking at the gate
and lead the good astray to follow emptiness.

22 And so, this is what the LORD has said –
Avraham's redeemer – to the House of Yaakov:
No more will Yaakov be ashamed,
his face no more grow pale,
23 for when he sees his children,
the work of My hands, in his midst,
sanctifying My name,
it is Yaakov's Holy One they sanctify;
it is Israel's God they worship.
24 Hearts that go astray will know understanding,
and those who murmured bitterly
will lay themselves open to learn.

30 1 Woe to the wayward sons,
so says the LORD,
who live by a plan that is not Mine,
who pour out thoughts not of My spirit,
add sin upon sin –
2 who set out to go down to Egypt,
without having sought My word,
to seek refuge in Pharaoh's stronghold
and shelter in the shadow of Egypt.
3 That stronghold of Pharaoh will be your shame;
that shelter of Egypt's shade, your disgrace,
4 for his princes were at Tzoan;
his emissaries reached as far as Ḥanes;[81]
5 shameful, reeking affair, this leaning
on a people that brings no benefit,
no aid and no benefit,
but only debasement and shame.

81 | Tzoan and Ḥanes were important Egyptian cities.

6 The burden of the southern beasts,[82]
bound for a land of trouble and anguish,
of lions, great growling lions,
of viper and flying serpent:
They carry their wealth on the backs of donkeys,
their treasures on camels' humps,
to a nation that brings them no benefit.
7 Egypt will help like hot air and emptiness,
and so I called her Rahav,[83] that is they,
sitting still.
8 Now, come and write this on a stone with them
and etch it in a scroll
for it to be there to the very last day,
forever, for as long as there is time:
9 that this is a rebellious people,
children who deny,
children who refuse to hear
the teaching of the Lord,
10 who say to the seers, "Do not see,"
to the men of the visions,
"No visions for us of uprightness;
speak smooth words to us;
bring visions of deceit.
11 Turn, turn from the path,
go aside from that way,
and remove from our sight
the Holy One of Israel."

12 And so the Holy One of Israel says:
Because you have despised this word
to place your trust in oppression and strayed
and leaned upon that –
13 because of this, this sin shall be
like the crack lengthening, ready to bring down
your exalted wall –
the breaking of which will come
so very suddenly.
14 That break is like the shattering of a wine jar:
shattering; no mercy;
in its shattering you will not find
a shard big enough

82 | Yeshayahu here derides those who send the animals bringing Judahite tribute to Egypt in an attempt to obtain that country's support against Assyria.

83 | A play on words. "Hot air and emptiness" (*hevel varik*) echoes "Rahav," a mythical beast sometimes associated with Egypt; cf. Psalms 87:4.

to take fire from the hearth, nor
to scoop a little water from the pool.

15 For this is what the LORD GOD has said,
the Holy One of Israel:
In stillness and in peace shall you be saved;
in quiet and in trust, your might will be –
but you did not wish it.
16 You say,
"No, we will speed away on horses,"
and so you will flee.
"We will mount the swiftest steeds,"
and so, swift will your pursuers be.
17 A thousand will flee at one man's
harsh word, at the harsh word of five
until you are left like a flagpole at the hilltop,
like a banner on the mountain's peak.[84]
18 So the LORD waits, that He may show You grace;
He lifts Himself aloof, that He may find compassion –
for the LORD is a God of judgment,
and happy is the man who waits for Him.

19 For a people will live
in Zion, Jerusalem;
you will weep no more tears;
favor – favor will He show you
at the sound of your cries;
when He hears, He will answer you.
20 And though He feeds you bread of pain
and water of oppression,
your teacher will hide Himself no more –
your eyes will see your teacher,
21 your ears will hear
a word behind you:
"This is the path:
now walk it
whether right
or left."
22 You will defile your silver-plated statues,
the breastplates of your golden images.
You will cast them out like
a menstruating woman –
tell them, "Go!"
23 He will grant rain for your seedlings

84 | Erected to give the soldiers a landmark to return to, the flagpole is left alone when the army flees.

that you will plant upon the land,
the bread of the land's bounty;
it will become succulent, fat.
Your livestock will graze
on that day,
wide-open pasture.
24 The oxen and the donkeys,
the earth's workers,
seasoned hay they will eat,
winnowed with spade and with fork.
25 It will be: on each high mountain,
every elevated hill,
streams,
rivers of water[85] –
on the day of the terrible killing
when all towers fall.
26 The light of the moon will be
like the light of the sun,
and the sun's light seven times
the light of seven days,
on the day when the LORD bandages
the breaking of His people
and heals up the gash from their beating.

27 See: The LORD's name
coming from far hence,
His rage burning
and the heavy cloud of smoke.
His mouth is full of fury,
His tongue, consuming fire.
28 His breath a torrent overflowing,
crossing the land neck deep,
sifting all the nations
with a sieve of nothingness,[86]
with a false-leading bridle,
holding nations by the jaw.
29 How you will sing
as on the night when the festival begins;
joy that fills the heart
as when you walk out with your flute
to come to the LORD's mountain,
to the Rock of Israel,

85 | Geographical features will be transformed for the better, perhaps as a result of the earthquake that will quell the wicked.

86 | A sieve that lets nothing through; the enemy armies are not sifted but are completely wiped out.

30 when the Lord sounds
the glory of His voice,
shows His arm coming down
with blazing rage,
a flame of fire consuming,
cloudburst, torrent,
rocks of hail,
31 for at the Lord's voice
Assyria will tremble,
who once struck with their rod.
32 In every passage
where the Lord plants down
the staff, firmly,
drums will sound, and lutes,
and the brandished hands of warfare;
so will He fight them.
33 For the flaming valley[87] is prepared from yesterday,
ready to receive even a king;
its hearth is full of fire
and wood aplenty,
and the Lord's breath
like a river of sulfur
burns inside.

31 1 Woe to those who go down to Egypt for aid,
relying on horses,
placing their trust in chariots – so many –
and horsemen – how powerful they are;
and do not turn to Israel's Holy One,
do not seek after the Lord.
2 But He too is wise – He brings evil
and does not call back His words.
He rises up against a house of those who harm
and those who abet the workers of iniquity.
3 Egypt is human, not God,
and their horses are flesh, not spirit.
The Lord will stretch out His hand:
helper will trip, and helped will fall;
both together will be destroyed.

4 For so the Lord has said to me:
As a lion, a young lion, roars over his prey
even as a band of shepherds calls out over him,

87 | The Tofet altars in the Valley of Ben Hinom near Jerusalem are known from Jeremiah 7:31 as the location of abominable idolatrous practices. This location has become a metaphor for hell (*Gehinom*).

never pausing at their voice,
a multitude unanswered,
so will the Lord of Hosts come down
to camp over Mount Zion, her hill.
5 As a mother bird hovers above,
so will the Lord of Hosts defend Jerusalem,
defending and saving,
passing over and delivering.
6 Come back to the One whom
they have gone so deep to turn from,
Israel's children,
7 for on that day
each man will recoil from
his silver gods,
his golden gods,
those your hands made for you,
sinning.
8 Assyria will fall to a sword not of man;
a sword not of mortals will consume him.
He will flee the sword, and still
his youths will be bonded laborers.
9 His rock will fade away in terror,
his princes will freeze at the sight of the banner.[88]
So says the Lord,
who has a fire burning in Zion,
a furnace in Jerusalem.

32 1 Then kings will govern to bring goodness
and ministers rule to bring justice.
2 A man[89] will be
a hiding place from the gale,
from the winter storm shelter –
like streams of water in an arid place,
like the shade of a heavy rock
on weary land.
3 The eyes of those who see will not be blinded,
and the ears of those who hear –
they will be listening.
4 The hearts of the hasty
will understand and know;
each stammering tongue will swiftly
speak clear truth.

88 | The rock stele on which the king engraves a record of his accomplishments is a symbol of Assyrian power; the banner is a symbol of the Assyrian army's presence.

89 | Referring to the just leaders referenced in the previous verse, who do not rely on foreign aid but rather on God.

5 No more will fools be counted noble,
nor villains be named the elite,
6 for the fool speaks felony;
his heart works sin,
working vile deeds and speaking
falsehoods of the Lord,
emptying the hungry of their life's bread
and stealing all the thirsty have to drink.
7 The devices of the devious are wicked;
they plot out their plans
to do violence by lies to the oppressed ones,
talking the vulnerable out of their justice.
8 But one who is noble forms noble plans,
and on his nobility he stands.

9 Come, you sanguine ladies,
and listen to my words;
you women of security,
pay heed to what I say.
10 Mere days beyond a year
and the safe ones will be shaken,
for harvest is over,
and the crop will not come.
11 Tremble, sanguine ladies;
shake, women in safety;
strip yourselves bare
and tie sack about your waists.
12 Breasts are beaten in mourning
for the lovely meadows,
the fruitful vine.
13 All over My people's land
the sounds of thorn and briar rise
to reach all joyous homes
across the exuberant city,
14 for the palace is forsaken,
the crowded city, bleak;
citadel and tower
turned back to caves forever –
wild donkeys' joy,
pasture of flocks –
15 until, from above, the wind is bared to us,
turning the wilderness to fertile land
and fertile land to woods.
16 Justice will preside in the wilderness,
and righteousness rest across the fertile land.
17 The act of goodness will be repaid with peace

and the work of righteousness with calm and safety, always.
18 My people will reside in a shelter of peace,
in dwellings of safety,
in sanguine harbor.
19 Hail will fall as the forest comes down,
and low, low will the town then fall.
20 Happy you are who sow seeds by the water
and send forth hoof falls of ox and of ass.

33 1 Woe to one who plundered though he had not been plundered,
who betrayed though none betrayed him.
When you are done plundering, you too shall be plundered;
your betrayal at an end, you are betrayed.

2 LORD, be gracious to us –
it is You we waited for;
be the people's arm, morning
by morning, their rescue
in times of distress.
3 The sound of the throng sent peoples adrift,
nations scattered in the wake
of Your greatness.
4 The plunder is ingathered
as one would pluck up locusts,
spreading as locusts teem.
5 The LORD is exalted,
dwelling on high,
filling Zion
with justice, with righteousness.
6 He is constancy through time for you,
rescuing might,
wisdom, knowledge –
His treasure house
is fear of the LORD.

7 The mighty cry out in the streets,
and messengers of peace weep in bitterness.
8 The roads are desolate:
no passersby.
He has broken the covenant,
turned cities to scrap,
counted people as nothing.
9 The land is mourning – misery –
Lebanon disgraced and withered away,
the Sharon dried to desert,
Bashan and Carmel shaken clear of all life.

10 "Now I shall rise,"
says the LORD.
"Now shall I rise up, now
be exalted."
11 Conceive chaff;
give birth to straw;
your breath of fire will consume you.
12 The peoples around – they will be a lime furnace,
like broken thorns
gone up in flames.

13 You who are far away,
hear what I have done;
you who are close, know My might.
14 Sinners in Zion have feared this;
trembling catches hold of the vile.
"Who of us can abide through
consuming fire;
who of us can abide
through everlasting burning?"
15 One who walks in righteousness,
speaks the truth,
rejects oppression's profits,
and shakes his hands clear
of bolstering corruption,
blocks his ears from hearing violence,
and closes his eyes to the allure of wrong;
16 he will reside on high,
sheltered in strongholds of the rocks.
His bread is given to him;
his water flows faithfully.
17 Your eyes will see a king in his splendor,
will see his land from far away.
18 Your heart will speak of awe:
"Who can count, who can measure;
who can count the towers?"
19 You will not see a brazen people,
a people whose speech is beyond hearing,
a barbarian tongue without sense.
20 Look upon Zion,
the city of our meeting:
your eyes shall see Jerusalem,
sanguine shelter,
the tent that need not be shifted,
with stakes that will never be lifted,
none of its cords ever cut.

21 For there the Lord is our majesty
in a place of broad-handed rivers
where no sailing boat can pass,
and ships of majesty cannot cross –
22 for the Lord is our judge,
the Lord our lawgiver,
the Lord our King –
and He will rescue us.
23 Your ropes are abandoned;
they will not hold;
their masts will not
spread the banner.
Then will great plunder
be shared about in plenty;
those once limping will loot the hoard.
24 Her dwellers will not say,
"I am ill";
all those who live there –
their sins will be forgiven.

34 1 Come near, nations far away, and listen;
peoples, hear.
The earth and her fill will listen,
the world and all her children:
2 The Lord is filled with fury for all nations,
rage for all their armies;
He has damned them and
given them up to the slaughter.
3 Their fallen will be cast aside;
the stench will rise up from their corpses
as hills dissolve in their blood.
4 All the hosts of heaven will rot.
The scroll of the heavens will be rolled shut.
All its hosts will wither away
as leaves wither and fall from the vine,
like a fig that falls too soon,
5 for My sword has slaked its thirst from the skies –
see: it comes down upon Edom,
upon the people I have damned in judgment.
6 The Lord – His sword is sated with blood,
fleshed out with fat,
with the blood of rams and goats,
the fat parts of rams' livers,
for the Lord receives His offering in Botzra,
a great slaughter in the land of Edom.
7 The wild oxen go down with them,

bullocks along with wild bulls,
and all their land is slaked with blood,
their dust fleshed out with fat,
8 for the LORD has had His day of vengeance,
a year of repayment
for Zion's cause.
9 Her[90] streams will turn to pitch,
her dust to sulfur,
and all her land will be
burning tar.
10 Night and day the burning will not stop –
her smoke will rise forever;
from one generation to the next, she will be devastation;
from one age to the next,
no passersby.
11 The pelican and fish owl will take up possession;
the long-eared owl and raven will take up residence;
He will stretch out across her
a measuring line of chaos, hung down
with weights of emptiness.
12 Her nobles – they will not be there,
they will not be called royalty;
her ministers will turn to nothing.
13 Thorns will come up in her palaces –
milk thistle, oyster thistle filling her fortresses.
It will be a jackals' shelter,
the ostriches' pasture.
14 Desert beasts will meet there with the wildcats,
night birds will call out for each other,
and brown owls too will take their ease,
finally finding a resting place.
15 There will the great owl build her nest,
lay her eggs and hatch them
to warm in her shadow;
there will the kites gather too,
one to another.
16 Seek out the Book of the LORD and read:
not one will be missing.[91]
None will seek her neighbor in vain,
for it is My mouth that charged them,
My spirit that gathered them in.
17 He has cast the lots for them;

90 | Edom's.

91 | That is, all the animals predicted in the prophecy ("the Book") will indeed come to roost in Edom's ruins.

His hand has divided them up;
He has settled their legacy forever;
age after age they will live on there.

35 1 The desert, the parched land, will celebrate,
and the arid plain rejoice
and blossom like a dune flower,
2 flowering, blossoming, rejoicing –
rejoicing and singing –
she is given the glory of Lebanon,
the splendor of Carmel and Sharon,
that the LORD's glory may be seen,
the splendor of our God.

3 Sustain your weakened hands;
hold firm your failing knees.
4 Say to those whose pulse beats fast –
"Do not fear;
here is your God, coming for vengeance;
God's repayment comes; this will save you."
5 The eyes of the blind will be opened,
and the ears of the deaf will be unlocked.
6 Then will lame men skip like deer,
while the tongues of those who could not speak will sing.
For the desert will be split across with water,
streams across the arid plain.
7 Parched ground will turn to lakes
and thirst to springs of water.
In the shelter of jackals, where they lay:
grasses, reeds, and rushes.
8 There will a path, a road run by,
and Holy Road will they call it.
No impure person will pass along it –
it will be theirs, theirs who walk the road;
even fools will not mistake it.
9 No lion will be there;
no ravaging creature will dare ascend;
they will not be there –
and the redeemed ones will walk on.
10 Those the LORD has claimed will return,
arriving in Zion in song,
crowned with everlasting joy;
they will have found joy and happiness,
and sorrow and moaning will flee.

36 1 In the fourteenth year of King Ḥizkiyahu, Sanḥeriv, king of Assyria,
marched up against all the fortified cities of Yehuda and seized them.[92]
2 And the king of Assyria sent the Rav-Shakeh[93] from Lakhish to King
Ḥizkiyahu in Jerusalem, along with vast forces; they marched up and came
to Jerusalem, and stationed themselves by the conduit of the Upper Pool,
3 by the Fuller's Field Road. Elyakim son of Ḥilkiyahu, who was in charge of
the palace, Shevna the scribe, and Yoaḥ son of Asaf, royal herald, went out
4 to them. And the Rav-Shakeh said to them, "Now, tell Ḥizkiyahu: 'Thus
5 says the Great King, the king of Assyria: What is this display of trust? You
talk as if mere chatter were counsel and might in war! Now, in whom have
6 you placed your trust, that you rebel against me? Have you placed your
trust in that crushed reed of a staff, in Egypt, who pierces and punctures
the palm of anyone who leans upon it? For that is Pharaoh, king of Egypt,
to all who place their trust in him.

7 "'And if you say to me, "We have placed our trust in the LORD, our God," is
that not the one whose high shrines and altars Ḥizkiyahu removed, telling
Yehuda and Jerusalem, "Bow only before *this* altar"?

8 "'Come, now, make a wager with my lord, the king of Assyria: I will
provide you with two thousand horses if you are able to provide them
9 with riders! How dare you slight even one of the deputies of my lord's
lesser servants and place your trust in Egypt for chariots and riders!
10 What is more – was it without the LORD that I marched up to destroy
this land? It was the LORD Himself who said to me: March up against
this land and destroy it.'"

11 Elyakim, Shevna, and Yoaḥ said to the Rav-Shakeh, "Please, speak to your
servants in Aramaic, for we understand it. Do not speak to us in Hebrew
within earshot of the people who are on the wall."

12 "Was it to you and your master that my lord sent me to speak these words?"
the Rav-Shakeh said. "Oh, but it was to the very men who are stationed
on the wall, who will have to eat their own excrement and drink their own
13 urine along with you."[94] And the Rav-Shakeh stood and shouted out in
Hebrew:

"Hear the words of the Great King, the king of Assyria," he proclaimed.
14 "Thus says the king: Do not let Ḥizkiyahu deceive you, for he cannot save
15 you. Do not let Ḥizkiyahu convince you to place your trust in the LORD,
saying, 'The LORD will surely save us, and this city will not be handed over
to the king of Assyria.'

92 | Regarding chapters 36–39, cf. II Kings 18:13–20:19.

93 | The title of an Assyrian official.

94 | The translation follows the vocalized version, the *keri*. The terminology of the *ketiv* (written version) is more vulgar.

16 "Do not listen to Ḥizkiyahu, for thus says the king of Assyria: Make peace
with me; come out to me, and each will eat from his own vine and his
17 own fig tree, and each will drink from his own cistern until I come and
take you to a land like your own – a land of grain and wine, a land of bread
18 and vineyards, a land of olive oil and honey. Do not listen to Ḥizkiyahu,
for he misleads you by saying, 'The Lord will save us.' Have the gods of
other nations managed to save their own lands from the hand of the king
19 of Assyria? Where are the gods of Ḥamat and Arpad? Where are the gods
20 of Sefarvites? Did they save Shomron from my hand? Who among all the
gods of the lands saved their own land from my hands, that the Lord will
save Jerusalem from my hand?"

21 And the people were silent and did not say a word, for the king's order
was, "Do not answer him."

22 Then Elyakim son of Ḥilkiyahu, who was in charge of the palace, Shevna
the scribe, and Yoaḥ son of Asaf, the royal herald, came to Ḥizkiyahu with
their clothes rent and reported what the Rav-Shakeh had said.

37 1 When King Ḥizkiyahu heard, he rent his clothes and covered himself in
2 sackcloth and came to the House of the Lord. He then sent Elyakim, who
was in charge of the palace, and Shevna the scribe, and the senior priests,
covered in sackcloth, to the prophet Yeshayahu son of Amotz.

3 "Thus says Ḥizkiyahu," they said to him. "'Today is a day of distress and
reproach and disgrace, for children are about to be born, but there is no
4 strength left for the birth.[95] Perhaps the Lord your God will hear the
words of the Rav-Shakeh, whom the king of Assyria, his lord, sent to
taunt the Living God, and will condemn the words that the Lord your
God heard – Oh, offer a prayer for the sake of the surviving remnant!'"

5 6 Now, when the servants of King Ḥizkiyahu came to Yeshayahu, Yeshayahu
said to them, "This is what you should tell your lord. Thus says the Lord:
Do not be afraid of the words you heard, which the king of Assyria's servant
7 boys used to revile Me. I will strike him with delusion so that he will hear
a rumor and return to his own land; then I will have him fall by the sword
in his own land."

8 The Rav-Shakeh withdrew, for he heard that the king of Assyria had moved
9 on from Lakhish, and he found the king of Assyria attacking Livna. When
the latter heard rumor that King Tirhaka, king of Kush, had set out to fight
against him – when he heard, he sent messengers to Ḥizkiyahu, saying:
10 "This is what you should tell Ḥizkiyahu, king of Yehuda: Do not let your
God in whom you trust deceive you, saying, 'Jerusalem will not be handed
11 over to the king of Assyria.' Look, you have heard what the kings of Assyria
have done to all the lands – they have utterly destroyed them. Will you
12 be saved? Did the gods of the nations that my ancestors destroyed save

95 | A proverbial expression of distress and helplessness.

13 them – Gozan and Ḥaran and Retzef and the Edenites of Telasar? Where
is the king of Ḥamat and the king of Arpad and the king of La'ir, Sefarvites,
Hena, and Iva?"

14 When Ḥizkiyahu received the letter from the messengers and read it, he
went up to the House of the LORD, and Ḥizkiyahu spread it open before
the LORD.

15 Then Ḥizkiyahu prayed to the LORD.
16 "LORD of Hosts, God of Israel, Enthroned upon the Cherubim," he said,
"You alone are God of all the kingdoms of the earth;
You made both heaven and earth.
17 Incline Your ear, O LORD, and listen;
open Your eyes, O LORD, and see –
listen to the words of Sanḥeriv,
those he sent to revile the Living God.
18 It is true, LORD,
that the kings of Assyria have laid countries to waste,
with their lands.
19 They have cast their gods to the fire –
for they are not gods
but the work of human hands,
wood and stone
and destroyed them.
20 But now, LORD our God,
save us from his hand,
and all the kingdoms of the earth will see
that You alone are LORD."

21 And Yeshayahu son of Amotz sent word to Ḥizkiyahu: "Thus says the
LORD, God of Israel: Because you prayed to Me about Sanḥeriv, king of
22 Assyria, this is the word the LORD has spoken of him:

"Virgin daughter Zion
scorns you, mocks you;
she shakes her head behind your back,
daughter Jerusalem.
23 Whom have you taunted, whom reviled;
against whom did you raise your voice,
lifting your eyes haughtily
against the Holy One of Israel?
24 By your servants' hand
you taunted the LORD;
you said, 'With the wealth of my chariots
I climbed to the heights of the hills,
the ends of Lebanon,
and I cut down its tallest cedars,

its choicest junipers;
I attained its farthest reaches,
its richest forests.
25 I have dug down and drunk the waters;
the passing soles of my feet have parched
all the rivers of Egypt.'
26 Did you not hear of this long ago?
I did this in ancient times; I formed the plan;
now I have brought it to be:
towns crash to heaps of rubble,
and fortified cities are ruined.
27 The inhabitants are powerless,
frozen in fear and ashamed,
like field grasses, like
green stalks,
the grass of rooftops,
and fields before harvest.
28 Your stops, your goings, your comings, I know them all,
and your raging against Me.
29 Because you have raged against Me,
your arrogance has reached My ears;
I shall put My ring in your nose,
My bit between your lips,
and drag you back along the road you came by.
30 And this will be your sign:[96]
This year you will eat what grows of itself,
next year what grows from that,
and in the third year you will sow and harvest,
plant vineyards and eat of their fruit.
31 Once more, the remaining survivors of the House of Yehuda
will set down roots below,
bear fruits above.
32 For a remnant will emerge from Jerusalem,
survivors from Mount Zion;
the passion of the Lord of Hosts
will bring all this to be.
33 And so, thus says the Lord of the king of Assyria:
He will not enter this city;
he will not shoot one arrow there.
He will not advance upon her with the shield
nor pile up a siege mound against her.
34 The way he came
he will return,
but this city he will not enter.

96 | Ḥizkiyahu is now addressed.

The Lord has spoken.
35 And I will protect this city, and deliver her,
for My own sake and for My servant, David."

36 An angel of the Lord went out then and struck down 185,000 in the
Assyrian camp; by daybreak the next morning they were all dead bodies.
37 And Sanḥeriv, king of Assyria, departed at once and retreated and settled
again in Nineveh.

38 He was worshipping in the temple of his god, Nisrokh, when his sons
Adramelekh and Saretzer put him to the sword. They fled to the land of
Ararat, and his son Esar Ḥadon reigned in his place.

38 1 At that time, Ḥizkiyahu fell deathly ill, and the prophet Yeshayahu son of
Amotz came to him. "Thus says the Lord," he said. "Issue orders for your
household, for you are dying; you will not recover."

2 And Ḥizkiyahu turned his face to the wall and prayed to the Lord.

3 "Please, O Lord," he said, "please remember how I walked before You
truly, with all my heart, and how I did what is right in Your eyes." And
Ḥizkiyahu wept bitter tears.

4 And the word of the Lord came to Yeshayahu: "Go and say to Ḥizkiyahu,
5 leader of My people: Thus says the Lord, the God of your ancestor David:
I have heard your prayer; I have seen your tears. I will add fifteen years
6 to your life; and I will save you and this city from the hand of the king
7 of Assyria – I will protect this city. This will be a sign for you from the
8 Lord that the Lord will fulfill the promise He made: I shall turn back the
shadow that has fallen on the sundial of Aḥaz by ten steps" – and the sun
receded by ten steps on which it had cast its shadow.

9 The inscription of Ḥizkiyahu, king of Yehuda, when he was ill and survived
his illness:
10 In the full blood of my days, I said,
I must leave this place,
committed to the gates of Sheol
for all of my years that remained.
11 I said, I shall not see the Lord,
the Lord in the land of the living;
never again will I see a human face,
any one of those who live upon this mortal earth.
12 My generation wanders on;
they have moved away from me
like a shepherd's tent;
I cut off my life like a weaver –
cut it off the threads –
from day to night You finish me.
13 Until the dawn it was as though a lion

were breaking all my bones;
from day to night You will finish me.
14 Like a swift, like a swallow I chirp;
like a dove I call.
My eyes hang on the heights:
LORD, in my oppression,
be security to me.
15 What can I say?
He told me
it is He who did this.
I trudged through all my years
with the bitterness of my soul.
16 LORD, this is what a person lives upon,
and my life's spirit depends on this –
heal me and let me live.
17 Longing for peace, my life is bitter, bitter;
You willed My soul away
from destruction and oblivion,
throwing all my sins
behind Your back,
18 for Sheol does not acknowledge You;
death does not praise You;
those who have descended to the pit
will not look toward Your faithfulness.
19 The living, the living acknowledge You
as I do today;
a father of children, he
will speak Your truth.
20 The LORD is here to save me;
let us sing these songs of mine
all the days of our lives
in the House of the LORD.

21 Yeshayahu said, "Let them bring a cake of dried figs
and rub it over the boils,
and he will recover."
22 But Ḥizkiyahu said, "What is the sign to assure me
that I shall go up to the House of the LORD?"

39 1 At that time, Merodakh Baladan son of Baladan, king of Babylon, sent
letters and a gift to Ḥizkiyahu, for he had heard that he had fallen ill and
2 recovered. Ḥizkiyahu received them joyfully and showed them around his
treasure house: the silver and gold, the spices and fine oil, his armory, and
everything that was kept in his treasuries, in his palace, and all his realm;
there was nothing that Ḥizkiyahu did not show them.

3 But the prophet Yeshayahu came to King Ḥizkiyahu and said to him,
"What did these people say, and from where did they come to you?"

"They came to me from a distant land," said Ḥizkiyahu, "from Babylon."

4 "What have they seen in your palace?" he asked.

"Why, they have seen everything in my palace," said Ḥizkiyahu. "There was nothing in my treasuries that I did not show them."

5 "Hear the word of the LORD of Hosts," Yeshayahu said to Ḥizkiyahu.
6 "Behold – the days are coming
when all that fills your palace
and all that your fathers amassed
until this day
will be borne away to Babylon,
and nothing will be left,
the LORD has said it,
7 while sons of yours
who came forth from you,
who were born to you,
will be borne far away, castrated slaves
in the palace of the king of Babylon."
8 And Ḥizkiyahu said to Yeshayahu,
"The word of the LORD you have spoken is good."
For he thought,
"Truth and peace
will reign in my days."

40 1 Comfort, comfort, My people –
these are your God's words[97] –
2 speak to Jerusalem's heart and
call out to her
that her term is served,
her guilt appeased,
that she has received at the LORD's hand
twice over for all her sins.

3 A voice calls out:
"Clear the LORD's way in the desert:
smooth across the arid plain
a road for our God."
4 Every valley will be raised,
each hill and mountain leveled;
the twisted road will be made straight;
the mountain ranges, open land,

97 | The rest of the book of Isaiah relates to the period of the return to Zion, detailed in Ezra and Nehemiah.

5 to let the LORD's glory be revealed,
and all flesh see as one –
the voice of the LORD has spoken.

6 A voice speaks: "Call out!"
I say, "What shall I call?"
All life is nothing more than grass,
and all its love, green shoots upon the land.
7 And grass dries up; shoots wither,
when the LORD's breath blows over them
and yes – this people is but grass.
8 Grass dries up, and shoots will wither,
but the word of our God stands firm; always.

9 O lady, ascend the high mountain,
you who bear tidings to Zion;
raise your voice in strength,
with tidings to Jerusalem.
Raise it – do not fear – call out loud
to the cities of Yehuda:
"Behold: your God."
10 Behold: the LORD your God
coming in all His strength,
His mighty arm ruling.
Behold: with Him, His prize;
His reward walks before Him;
11 like a shepherd He pastures His flock,
gathering the lambs into His arms,
bearing them in His embrace,
guiding His young.

12 Who was it who measured out the waters in His palm
and gauged the skies by His handspan?
Who measured in His fingers all the dust of earth;
who weighed out the hills on His balance and
the mountains upon a hand scale?
13 Who could survey the wind? The LORD.
Who is the confidant He would tell?
14 To gain His insight, with whom did He hold counsel;
who taught Him the path of justice?
Who ever taught Him awareness; who
showed Him the way of insight?
15 Whole nations are like the drop left in His bucket,
as inconsequential as dust on the balance.
He sweeps up the distant isles like powder.
16 All Lebanon has not wood enough,
or animals, for the burnt offering.

17 All the nations are as nothing before Him,
less than absence, than emptiness, to Him –
18 And what will you liken to God;
what image will you draw of Him?
19 A smith molds a statue;
the jeweler plates it with gold
and fashions chains of silver for it.
20 Mulberry wood his offering,
he chooses a tree that will not rot;
he chooses a skilled craftsman
to build a statue that cannot fall.
21 Do you not know it, have you not heard,
was it not told to you long before?
Have you paid no attention
to the world's foundations?
22 He sits over the dome of the sky,
its dwellers like grasshoppers below;
He spreads out the skies like a canvas
and pulls them taut like a tent to dwell in.
23 He turns great rulers to nothing,
the judges of this earth to emptiness,
24 as if they were not planted, were not sown,
as if their stem had no root within the earth –
He breathes on them and they dry up to nothing;
the storm will sweep them all away
like straw.

25 Whom can you compare Me to –
so speaks the Holy One –
and find them equal?
26 Raise your eyes skyward
and see: Who created all these?
Who summons their legions by number
and calls each man by name?
In His great might, His adamantine strength,
not one of them is lost.

27 Why do you say, Yaakov;
Israel, why declare,
"My way is hidden from the LORD;
my God overlooks my claim"?
28 Do you not know this;
have you not heard?
The LORD is God eternal,
Creator of all horizons;
He does not weary, does not tire;

no one can plumb His understanding.
29 He gives the weary strength,
the helpless, power: more and more.
30 Youths will tire, grow weary;
young men will falter and fall,
31 but those who wait for the Lord –
their strength will be renewed;
they will rise on their wings like eagles,
will run and never grow weary,
will walk on and never grow tired.

41 1 Hush before Me, coastlands
and nations; renew your strength,
and then come forward, speak,
draw close; let us come into judgment.
2 Who roused the one from the east[98]
and called victory to his feet?
Who herded nations before him,
laid their kings low,
and made his swords numerous as dust,
his bowshots like chaff in the wind?
3 He pursued them and came through in peace
on paths that his feet never walked.
4 Who was it who acted and did this,
who called forth generations long before?
I, the Lord, am the first,
and I shall be,
I, with the last who will be.
5 Coastlands witness this and fear,
earth's horizons witness, tremble,
draw near, come.
6 *Each man helps his fellow*
and tells his brother, "Be strong."
7 *"Strong," says the wright to the goldsmith,*
the hammerman to him who beats.
He says of the glue, "This is good,"
and firms it up with nails, never to fall.[99]

8 And you, Israel, My servant,
Yaakov whom I chose,
children of Avraham who loved Me,
9 whom I lifted and brought from the ends of the earth,
calling you forth from its furthest corners,

98 | Koresh of Persia, who conquered Babylon and allowed the exiles to return to Yehuda.

99 | These verses appear to ridicule those who fashion idols. The message of the passage as a whole is that God alone gives power to kings.

telling you: You are My servant;
You have I chosen, and I will not reject you –
10 do not fear, for I am with you;
do not be afraid: I am your God;
I strengthen you and help you,
uphold you with My right hand of righteousness.
11 All who rage against you will
be shamed, debased; become
like nothing, lost,
all those who fight you.
12 Look for them then – you will not find them –
the men with whom you are wrestling,
adversaries in war –
like nothing, like no more.
13 For I am the Lord your God,
holding your right hand,
telling you: Do not fear,
for I am here: I help you.

14 Yaakov: worm,[100]
men of Israel,
do not fear;
I will help you,
so speaks the Lord,
the Holy One of Israel,
your redeemer.
15 You shall see: I have made you
a slotted threshing board,
new and razor edged;
you will thresh mountains, turn them to powder,
and hills into chaff.
16 As you winnow, the wind will lift them,
and the storm will spread them far;
you will rejoice in the Lord and will,
through the Holy One of Israel, be praised.

17 The oppressed, impoverished,
beg for water – there is none –
their tongues are seared with thirst.
I am the Lord; I will answer them –
Israel's God, I will not leave them.
18 Unlocking rivers upon the high mountains
and springs in the open land,
I shall turn the very desert into a lake of water;
parched land will bring forth water;

100 | A reflection of Israel's perception of its own weakness.

19 I will fill the desert with cedars, acacia trees,
with myrtle, pine,
and will plant the arid plain with
junipers, with cypress trees
and pencil pines together –
20 all this for people to see, to know,
to take to heart, growing aware
that the LORD's hand has done all this:
this, created by Israel's Holy One.

21 Bring forth your claim,
so says the LORD;
present your case,
says Yaakov's King.[101]
22 Let them lay it out
and tell us
what is yet to be.
The long-gone past – what happened then? Tell.
Let us listen closely and know their future also;
let us hear what is to come.
23 Tell over the signs
so that we know that you are gods,
know that you bring good and harm;
let us tell and confront one another.
24 You come from nowhere;
your works are nothing;
to choose you would be
contemptible.

25 I roused him from the north – he came; [102]
from the place of sunrise
he called My name,
and he walks over captains as if they were clay,
like the potter tramping, mixing muck.
26 Who said this would happen before; who let us know;
who, long ago? We would declare him victor.
But none were there to say, and none to voice,
and none to hear your words.[103]
27 I was first to speak to Zion: Here, these things are come;
I have sent one to break news
to Jerusalem.
28 No man could I see to speak,

---

101 | Here God presses His case against other gods, arguing they are powerless and cannot predict the future.

102 | A reference to Koresh.

103 | The opponents did not contest the case; they did not argue against God.

no counselor among all these
to question, that he might answer.
29 I see: all of them
worthless, nothing all their deeds,
cold wind and emptiness their molten images.

42 1 My servant, I uphold him,
the one I chose, I wanted.
I have placed My spirit over him
to draw justice out to nations;
2 he will not shout nor raise
his voice; in the street
he will not be heard;[104]
3 not one crushed reed will break beneath him,
no dimming wick be quelled –
he will open out judgment to truth,
4 never himself dimmed or crushed
until he has brought the world justice,
and all the distant coastlands
quake before his teaching.

5 So says God, the LORD,
who created the skies, who stretched them across
and set down the land and all her children,
and gave humanity upon her breath,
and spirit to those who walk her.
6 I, the LORD, call you forth in victory,
and I will hold your hand;
I shall form you and make you a covenant people,
make you a light unto nations,
7 to open blinded eyes,
to bring prisoners out of captivity,
and those who dwell in darkness from their jail.[105]
8 I am the LORD;
this is My name,
and I share not My glory with others,
My praise with idols.
9 What I said at the beginning: see, it has come,
and I tell you now what will be afresh
before it pushes through the earth;[106]
you will hear it first from Me.

104 | God's servant does not resort to shouted demagoguery. The appellation of God's "servant" can refer to many different characters, such as Koresh here and Israel in 42:18–25.

105 | Koresh claimed to have released the subjects of Babylon from their enslavement.

106 | God predicts the return to Zion before it happens, just as if He had predicted a plant's sprouting while it was still in the ground.

10 Sing out to the LORD a new song,
His praise from the ends of the earth,
You who go to sea, and all that fill it,
distant coastlands and you who live there.
11 Desert and its towns, raise your voices,
Kedarites in their scattered camps;
those who dwell in the rocks must sing out joy
from the mountaintops, shout
12 and give the LORD His glory;
His praise will be spoken in the distant coastlands.
13 The LORD sets out like a hero,
rousing His passion like a man of war;
He gives the war cry, bellows the war cry,
overthrows His enemies.

14 Always I held still and
was silent, held back –
I will bellow out like one giving birth,
breathing out, breathing in all together,
15 will vanquish hills and mountains and
will dry up all the green;
I shall turn the rivers into coastlands
and desiccate the lakes,
16 and lead the blind along a way they know not,
on paths unknown shall guide them;
I shall turn darkness to light before them,
the treacherous road to open highway;
these things I will perform,
and will not fail.
17 Those who trust in idols will step back
ashamed,
those who say to molded statuary,
"You – you are our gods."

18 All you deaf ones – listen,
and you who are blind – now see.
19 Who is blind if not My servant,
who deaf like the messenger I send?[107]
Who could be blind like him – who is devoted,
blind like this, the LORD's servant?
20 Many things seen, but you remember not,
with open ears, hear nothing.
21 Yet the LORD has desired them, that His righteousness be known –

---

107 | In verse 18, God addresses the people and accuses them of being deaf and blind, unable to realize that God is sending Koresh to return them to Zion. In verse 19, the people respond: they think it is not they but the prophet who is blind.

to raise aloft His teachings, to confer majesty.
22 He is with this plundered, this torn-apart people,
who are trapped away in pits,
hidden in prison,
plunder with none to save them,
given over to looters with none to cry, "Give back!"
23 Who among you will listen to this,
will hear it and heed for the future?
24 Who was it who gave Yaakov up for looting,
Israel for plunder –
was it not the LORD?
Him against whom we sinned;
whose ways they cared not to follow,
whose Law they did not heed.
25 He poured out the fire of His rage against them,
His terrible warfare,
and flames raged all around them, yet they did not know;
they burned but still they took it not to heart.

43 1 And now, Yaakov, so says
the LORD, your Creator,
the One who formed you, Israel:
Do not fear: I redeem you;
I name you: you are Mine.
2 Though you pass through waters – I am with you –
through rivers – they will not wash you away.
Though you walk right through the fire – you will not be burned,
and no flame will take hold of you,
3 for I am the LORD your God,
the Holy One of Israel, your rescuer.
I have paid Egypt as your ransom,
Kush and Seva in your place.[108]
4 Because you are valued in My eyes, you are honored –
I love you
enough to give up other men for you,
whole nations in your place.
5 Do not fear, for I am with you.
I will bring your children from the east,
will gather you back from the west.
6 To the north I will say, "Give over";
to the south, "Imprison no more."
Bring My sons from far away,
My daughters back from the ends of the earth –
7 all the people I called by My name,

108 | Three kingdoms along the Nile are here said to be given by God to the king of Persia in return for releasing Israel.

created for My glory;
I formed them, I made them.
8 He brought out a people – blind though they have eyes,
deaf though they have ears.[109]
9 Were all the nations to gather,
the peoples to come into session,
who of them could tell of this?
Who could speak of this before?
Let them bring their witnesses to vindicate them,
so that hearers may say, "This is truth."
10 No – you are My witnesses, so says the LORD,
My servants whom I chose,
so that you should know, and trust in Me
and understand that I am He –
before Me, no god was made,
and after Me – no other.
11 I, I am the LORD;
aside from Me there is no rescue;
12 I spoke, and I rescued; I gave voice;
no stranger stood among you;
you are My witnesses, so says the LORD,
and I am God.
13 And still from this day onward, I am He,
and from My hands there is no rescue;
I act, and what I do, who,
who can undo?

14 So says the LORD,
your redeemer, the Holy One of Israel:
for Your sake I sent one[110] to Babylon;
I will bring down all their bars
and the Chaldeans in the ships of their joy.
15 I am the LORD, your Holy One,
Creator of Israel, King.

16 So says the LORD,
who forges a way through the ocean,
who sets a path through raging waters,
17 who destroys mighty horse and
chariot of war,
to make them lie down
never to rise;
they died down like
a flaxen

109 | See 42:18.
110 | That is, Koresh.

wick, snuffed out.
18 Do not remember the earliest things
nor look upon the beginnings,
19 for I am making something new;
even now it grows,
and will you not know it?
I shall make a way through desert land
and rivers across the wilderness;
20 wild beasts will glorify Me,
jackals and ostriches,
for I have given the desert water
and rivers in the wilderness
to give My people, My chosen one, to drink –
21 the people I have formed for Me,
who are to tell My praises.
22 It is not Me you call for, Yaakov;
Israel, you wearied of Me.
23 You did not bring Me the lamb of your offering;
it was not Me your sacrifice honored;
I did not enslave you to My gifts
or weary you with frankincense.
24 You did not pay silver for calamus[111] for Me
or slake My thirst with fat of the sacrifice,
yet you enslaved Me to your iniquity
and wearied Me with your sins.
25 I am I, who expunge your offenses for My own sake
and will not keep your sins in mind.
26 Recall Me now; let us argue this out; tell Me
so that you may be vindicated.
27 Your first father sinned,
and those who spoke for you rebelled against Me,
28 so I desecrated your Sanctuary's ministers
and marked you for destruction, Yaakov; Israel,
to be denounced.

44 1 And now listen, Yaakov My servant,
Israel whom I chose;
2 so says the Lord who made you –
the One who made you in the womb, who helps you:
Do not fear, My servant Yaakov,
Yeshurun[112] whom I chose.
3 As I pour water on thirsty earth,
water upon parched land,
I shall pour forth My spirit upon your children,

111 | An element in the incense offering.
112 | An appellation for Israel; see, e.g., Numbers 23:10.

upon your offspring My blessing.
4 They will sprout among the grasses,
like willows on streams of water,
5 and a man will say, "I am the LORD's,"
while another invokes the name of Yaakov,
and a third one will inscribe on his hand, "The LORD's,"
to name himself Israel.

6 So says the LORD,
King of Israel, its rescue,
the LORD of Hosts:
I am the first and I the last;
beside Me is no God.
7 Who like Me calls the future forth
and tells it? Let them lay their claim before Me.
I have formed an eternal people,
so let them bring out signs and tell
what is to come.
8 Do not fear, do not lose faith –
have I not let you hear this from the start?
I told it, and you are My witnesses:
Is there any God but Me?
There is no rock I do not know.
9 All those makers of images – all emptiness,
their gorgeous objects useless,
and all their witnesses see nothing
and know not and are shamed.
10 Who has made a god
and molded an idol
to bring him no good?
11 All his company will be shamed –
craftsmen – they are human;
let them come together, all, and stand
and fear and feel their shame together,
12 for the craftsman in iron makes a chisel,
works it over the coals
and forms it with hammers,
works it with his arms' strength,
grows hungry and has no strength,
fails to drink water until he grows faint.
13 The carpenter stretches out his line
and marks it with a thread;
he forms it with his planes and
marks it with a compass.
He is making it into the form of a man,
a supreme human frame,

to sit in a house.
14 He cuts down cedars for his work
or chooses a cypress or oak
and sees it grow strong in the forest,
plants a bay laurel and lets rain
nourish it to grow.
15 These become firewood for a man;
he takes them and warms himself,
kindles them and bakes bread,
and works the rest into a god, and worships
a statue and prostrates himself before it.
16 Half of it he burns in the fire;
thanks to that half he eats meat,
roasts the roast, feels fullness,
warms himself, says, "Ah –
I am warmed; I have seen the flames."
17 And with what is left over, he makes a god, a statue
to prostrate himself in front of and to worship,
pray to, say, "Save me, please:
you are my god."
18 They know not; they do not comprehend,
for their eyes are smeared over, not to see,
not to let understanding into their hearts,
19 so they do not take it to heart,
nor find mind or wisdom to say,
"I burned half in the fire;
I baked bread on the coals;
I roasted meat and ate it;
with the rest should I make this disgusting thing,
this slab of wood, and bow down?"
20 He courts ashes; his deceived heart has misled him; he cannot
save himself; he cannot say,
"This in my right hand – it is a lie."

21 Hold these things in mind, Yaakov,
Israel, for you are My servant.
I made you – you are My servant –
do not forget Me, Israel.
22 I dispelled your offenses like mist,
like a cloud all your sins –
come back to Me, for I have redeemed you.

23 Sing out, heavens,
for the Lord has acted.
Sound the trumpets, lowest depths of earth;
hills, break out in song,

and forests, all their trees,
for the LORD has redeemed Yaakov;
in Israel is He glorified.

24 For so says the LORD, your redeemer,
the One who formed you in the womb:
"I the LORD am Maker of all,
stretching out the heavens alone,
firming the earth with My own power.
25 It is I who unravels the necromancers' signs,
who turns the sorcerers mad,
who turns the wise men back,
confounding their knowledge.
26 It is I who bring My servants' words to be,
My messengers' plans to be fulfilled,
who tells Jerusalem: Let her be settled,
and the cities of Yehuda: Let them be built up;
I shall raise up all her ruins;
27 I who say to the deeps: Be arid;
I shall dry up your rivers;
28 who says of Koresh: he is My shepherd,
fulfilling all My will,
that he should tell Jerusalem, 'She shall be built,'
and the Sanctuary, 'Let her be founded.'"

45 1 Thus says the LORD
to His anointed one, to Koresh,
into whose right hand I invested strength
to subjugate nations before him,
and I shall loosen the girdles of kings[113]
to unlock doors before him, open
city gates, never to be closed:
2 I walk before you;
I will level out mountain lands;
I will break through doors of bronze
and cut down iron bars.
3 I give to you treasures of darkness,
buried hoards in hidden places,
for you to know that it is I the LORD
who calls your name –
I, the God of Israel –
4 all for My servant Yaakov,
for Israel, My chosen.
For them I call you by your name
and give you your title though you know Me not.

113 | Weaken and hinder them before Koresh.

5 I am the LORD – there is no other,
no gods aside from Me –
and I gird you though you do not know Me
6 so that they all should know,
from the east of the sun's rising to the west of its dusk,
that there is none but I:
I am the LORD; there is no other,
7 forming light, creating darkness,
making peace, creating evil –
I, the LORD, make all of these.

8 Skies above, form drops, and let
the heavens rain down victory.
Land, open; let triumph bear
her fruit; let vindication flourish –
for I, the LORD, created this.

9 Woe to one who fights his Maker –
for this potsherd among shards upon the earth.
Does clay ask its maker, "What would you now do?
This work of yours
lacks handles"?

10 Woe to one who asks a father,
"Why did you conceive?"
Who asks a woman, "What then
did you labor so to birth?"

11 Thus says the LORD,
the Holy One of Israel, its Maker:
Would you ask Me for the signs; would you
command Me about My children,
about My own hands' work?
12 I made the earth, and I
created mankind on it.
I, My hands, stretched out the skies,
commanded all their armies forth.
13 I roused him[114] for victory
and will smooth out all his paths.
He will build My city;
he will send My exile forth,
not for silver, not for pay:
so speaks the LORD of Hosts.

14 Thus says the LORD:
The fruits of Egypt's labor,

114 | Koresh.

the wares of Kush,
and Sabeans,[115] lofty men,
will come to join you,
will be yours
and follow you,
pass across in chains
and pray through you:
"It is you that God resides in;
there are no more gods, none.
15 You are, indeed,
a hidden God,
God of Israel, rescuer."
16 They are all shamed, debased,
walking together debased,
all who crafted images.
17 Israel's rescue is in the LORD,
rescue everlasting.
They will not be shamed, will never be debased
to the end of time.

18 For thus says the LORD,
God, who created the skies,
who formed the earth, forged it,
sets its foundation;
He did not create it for emptiness;
He formed it for life:
I am the LORD – there is no other.
19 I did not speak in hiding
somewhere away in a land of darkness;
I did not say to the seed of Yaakov,
"Seek Me amid emptiness."
I am the LORD – I tell of justice,
speak clear truth.
20 Gather together, come,
draw near together,
survivors of nations.
They have no knowledge,
they who bear the wood of images
and pray to a god who affords no rescue.
21 Speak, bring your case
and make your plans together.
Who spoke of this long ago;
who told it from the beginning?
Was it not I, the LORD?

115 | Cf. 43:3.

There is no other god but Me –
righteous God, rescue,
and there is none beside Me.
22 Turn to Me; be saved
from all ends of the earth –
for I am God; there is no other.
23 By My own self I swore;
justice issued from My lips,
and not one word will be returned,
for every knee should bend before Me;
every tongue should swear its oath
24 and say, "In the LORD alone can I
find righteousness and power."
To Him they will come,
and all who rage against Him now be shamed.
25 In the LORD will be proved victorious,
all the seed of Israel, they will glorify themselves.
46 1 Bel is prostrate; Nevo falls;
their statues are loaded
on beasts, on cattle;[116]
your bearers are weighed down
beneath their weary burden.
2 The gods fell, were laid prostrate together;
they cannot deliver this burden;
they themselves are prisoners.

3 Listen to Me, House of Yaakov,
all of you remaining of the House of Israel,
you whom I bore from the womb,
whom I have carried since before your birth
4 and into your old age: I am He,
and in your white-haired years
I shall still bear you.
I made you; I shall carry
and bear you, shall deliver.

5 To whom will you compare and liken Me,
with whom match Me
and find us equal?
6 Men pour out gold from their pouches,
weigh silver in reed baskets,
hire a smith – he makes a god,
and they worship it, worship.
7 They carry it on their shoulders, bear it

116 | A description of the collapse of the Babylonian gods, who are here said to have fled Babylon when Koresh conquered the city.

away, then set it down, and there it stands;
it will not move an inch from its place;
when he cries out to it, it will not answer
and will not deliver him
from all his troubles.

8 Remember this: be strong,
transgressors; call this to your hearts.
9 Remember the first, the earliest things,
for I am God, there is no other –
God, there is none like Me,
10 telling of the end from the beginning,
telling long since of what was not yet made,
saying, "My plan, it will arise;
I shall bring about all that I desire,"
11 calling the kite from the east,
from a far-off land – the man who carries My design.
I have spoken, and I shall bring to be –
have formed and shall perform it.

12 Listen to Me, mighty hearts,
far away from righteousness;
13 I will bring close My victory;
it never will be far from you;
My rescue will not come too late.
I shall grant in Zion My rescue,
grant Israel My glory.

47 1 Go down, sit in the dust,
virgin daughter Babylon;
sit upon the ground, no throne,
Chaldean daughter,[117]
for no more will you be called
delicate lady, refined.
2 Take a millstone;
grind some flour;
expose your tresses,
lift your hem, and
show your legs
to cross the rivers.
3 Your nakedness will be exposed
and your abjection seen;
I shall take vengeance; I shall not
accept the prayers of man.

117 | The chapter is a mocking lament of Babylon on the occasion of its fall to Koresh. The Chaldeans were an ethnic group prominent around Babylon.

4 Our redeemer, His name is the LORD of Hosts,
Israel's Holy One.
5 Sit silent; come into the dark,
Chaldean daughter,
for no more are you to be called
a lady among kingdoms.
6 I raged against My people,
defiled My estate;
I gave them over to your hands –
you bore them
no compassion;
you laid your heavy yoke
upon the backs of aged men.
7 You thought, "I am, always, the lady,"
so you did not lay this on your heart, did not
consider that lady's future.

8 Listen now to this,
delicate lady,
living without cares,
saying in your heart,
"I: there is none but me;
I will not live a widow's life,
will not know the loss of children."
9 These two came to you all in a moment,
in one day: child grief, widowhood,
whole and pure, for all your witchcraft,
for the mighty force of your wizardry.
10 You felt secure in your evil:
"No one sees me," so you said.
It is your very wisdom, your
knowledge, that led you astray,
"I" – you said in your heart –
"there is no other."
11 Evil came to you;
you knew not how to meet it;
calamity fell on you
that you cannot cover over;
suddenly it came to you,
catastrophe you have not known.
12 Cling now to your magic,
to all the forms of witchcraft
that you have worked so hard at
perfecting since your youth;
perhaps you will do some good; perhaps

you can strike dread again.
13 How you have wearied of all your counsels;
let them stand up now and rescue you –
diviners by the skies, stargazers,
tellers of tidings by the shape of the moon –
let them save you from what will come.
14 No; they are become like straw
burned up in fire;
they cannot even save themselves
from the flames' hold.
No ember remains to warm yourself by,
no fire to sit before.
15 So did they become to you, those for whom you labored,
those who peddled spells from your first youth;
each has gone astray in his own way;
not one will be your rescue.

48 1 Listen, people of Yaakov, to this,
you who are called by the name Israel, you
who emerged from Judahite waters,
who swear by the name of the Lord,
calling on the name of Israel's God
but neither in truth nor in righteousness – know:
2 you are called from the holy city forth,
depend upon Israel's God,
the Lord of Hosts is His name.

3 From the first I told you all of this;
it issued from My mouth, resounded;
suddenly I brought these things about;
they came to be
4 from My own mind, for you are tough,
your neck an iron sinew,
your forehead bronze.
5 I told you from the start,
before they came to be, resounded them to you,
lest you say, "It was my idol
that did these things,
my statue, my cast image,
that issued the command."
6 You have heard; now see it all,
and now, will you not speak it?
I told you of this newness that now comes
and guarded secrets you knew not.
7 Now they have been made, and not before,
but yesterday you could not hear it –

lest you tell me, "This I knew."
8 You did not hear; you did not know;
even then your ears were opened not;
I knew you would betray Me –
you were named a rebel from the womb.
9 For My name's sake I shall hold back My rage;
for My praise I will hold back
and will not sever you from life.
10 I have refined you, not like silver;
in the furnace of oppression you are chosen.
11 For My sake shall I act, for Mine,
for how can I be profaned, and how could I
give over of My glory to another?

12 Listen to Me, Yaakov,
and Israel, named for Me.
It is I – I am the first,
and I shall be the last;
13 My hand laid down the land
and My right hand spread the heavens;
when I call to them,
they stand, all, to attention.
14 Gather, listen all –
who among you spoke of this?
It is the LORD who loved him:
He shall do his will in Babylon,
raise his arm over Kasdim.
15 I, it is I who spoke this,
I who called him forth,
who brought him and made his way prosper.
16 Come close to Me and hear this:
Long ago, and not in secret, did I speak;
ever since it began, I was there.
And now the LORD my God has sent me –
and His spirit.

17 Thus says the LORD, your redeemer,
Israel's Holy One:
I am the LORD your God,
who taught you in order to better you,
who showed you the path to walk.
18 Would you but heed My charge,
your peace would flow like a river,
your righteousness waves on the ocean.
19 Like sand would your children be,
the fruit of your womb abundant as its grains,

their name never severed,
never rendered extinct
before Me.

20 Go forth from Babylon;
flee Kasdim;
call out joyful song;
resound,
spread the word to the ends of the earth;
say it: "the LORD has redeemed
His servant Yaakov."[118]

21 They did not thirst –
He led them through dry ruins but
poured water from the rock.
The rock burst open, and out
coursed water.

22 There is
no peace,
the LORD says,
for the wicked.

49 1 Listen to me, distant coastlands;
hear me, nations far away:
From the womb the LORD called me;
when I was in my mother still, He spoke my name

2 and made my mouth a dagger, sharp,
concealed in the shadow of His hand.
He made me a sheer arrowhead
and hid me in His quiver.

3 He said to me: You are My servant,
Israel;
through you I am glorious.

4 And I say: I toiled for nothing;
in breath and emptiness I spent my strength,
but the LORD retains my rightful share;
my reward is with my God.

5 Now the LORD has spoken –
the One who made me in the womb to serve Him,
to bring Yaakov back to Him,
to gather Israel in to Him –
and in the LORD's eyes I found honor;
my God became my strength.

6 It is not enough, He said, that you serve Me,
raising up Yaakov's tribes,

118 | A reference to the moment the exiles departed from Babylon, headed for Yehuda.

restoring those of Israel
I protected;
I made you to be
a light unto nations;
My rescue must reach
the ends of this earth.

7 Thus says the Lord,
redeemer of Israel, his Holy One,
to a soul reviled,
a nation's abhorrence,
slave of rulers;
kings will see and rise to their feet,
ministers bow low
for the sake of the Lord who is faithful,
of Israel's Holy One
who chooses you.

8 Thus says the Lord:
At a time of favor I answered you;
on a day ripe for rescue I was there for your aid.
I guarded you and made you a covenant people,
ready to build up a land,
to take possession of a lost estate,
9 to say to prisoners, "Leave,"
and to people in darkness, "Come to light."
They will graze along the way,
with all the hills their pasture.
10 They will know no hunger, know no thirst;
searing heat and sun will never harm them,
for the One who cares for them will be their guide,
leading them by springs of water.
11 I shall make all mountains a path to walk
and build up My roads.
12 Here – from far away they come,
all of these, from the north, from the west,
all of these, from the land of Sinim.
13 Sing out, skies, and land, rejoice;
hills, break out in song,
for the Lord has brought His people comfort;
He will care for the oppressed ones who are His.

14 Zion speaks:
"The Lord has forsaken me;
my Lord, He has forgotten me."
15 Can a mother forget her own baby; can she
fail to care for the child of her womb?

These too may yet forget,
but I will not forget you.
16 I have etched you on My palms;
your walls are before My eyes
always.
17 Your children will run to you;
your destroyers, your demolishers,
will all be gone from you.
18 Raise your eyes; look around and see:
the children all gathered
and coming back to you.
As I live, so says the Lord,
you will wear them all as jewels,
which you will bind on like a bride.
19 For your ruins, for your wastelands,
for the land of your destruction,
for you will be too narrow for your dwellers,
while those who would destroy you will be far away from you.
20 You will yet hear
the children say,
of whom you were bereaved,
"The place is too tight for me;
make space for me to sit,"
21 while you say in your heart,
"Who bore these children, mine –
to me, bereft and left alone,
exiled and expelled –
these children – who has raised them?
I was left all alone, and
these – who can they be?"

22 So says the Lord God:
Behold: I shall raise My hands to nations,
lift My banner toward peoples;
they will bring your sons back in the folds of their robes,
bearing your daughters upon their shoulders;
23 kings will be your caregivers,
their princesses your nursemaids.
They will bow to the ground before you
and kiss the dust you tread upon,
and you will know: I am the Lord,
and those who wait for Me will not be shamed.

24 Can a mighty warrior be plundered;
can a victor's captives flee?
25 For so says the Lord:

The mighty man's captives may yet be taken,
the tyrant's plunder flee,
but I shall fight against those who fight you,
I will save your children.
26 To those who wrong you, I will feed their own flesh;
their blood will intoxicate them like wine,
and all flesh will know then
that I am the LORD, your rescue,
your redeemer, Mighty One of Yaakov.

50 1 So says the LORD:
Where is your mother's bill of divorce
with which I banished her?
Which one of My creditors
have I, then, sold you to?
No, it was for your sins that you were sold;
for your faithlessness your mother was sent hence.
2 Why is it that I came, and
no man was here –
I cried out, and
no one answered?
Does My arm fall short to redeem you;
have I not strength to rescue?
No – at My rebuke I dry the sea;
I turn whole rivers to desert land.
Their fish will stink for lack of water,
dead of thirst.
3 I will dress the skies in darkness
and make mourning sack their covering.

4 The LORD my God made me
a learning tongue
to sustain the weary with words;
morning, early morning, He wakens
my ears, He wakes them,
like students, to hear.
5 The LORD my God opened my ears,
and I did not reject Him;
I never shrank back –
6 I gave up my back to beating,
my cheeks to those who scratched them.
I never hid my face from
humiliations, spittle,
7 but the LORD my God will help me, and so
no humiliation;
I set my face as flint and know

I will not be ashamed.
8 He is near who shows me righteous –
Who, then, will contend with me?
Let us stand up opposing one another –
Who has a claim against me?
Let him come to me,
9 for the LORD GOD, He will help me;
who then can condemn me?
They will wear out like an old cloak;
moths will eat them.

10 Who of you reveres the LORD,
and listens to His servant's voice?
Let one who walked in darkness,
nothing shining for him,
trust in the LORD's name,
and lean on his God.
11 You – you light your fire
and gird yourselves with torchlight.
Walk by the light of your own fire,
by torches that you burn.
From My hand, all this came to you;
you will lie down in pain.

51 1 You who chase righteousness, listen to Me,
you who seek the LORD:
2 Look to the rock you are hewed from,
the quarry from which you were carved;
look to your father, Avraham,
to Sara who gave you birth,
for I called him, one alone,
and blessed him, made him many.
3 And the LORD has comforted Zion –
brought comfort to all her ruins;
He has made her desert like Eden,
her arid land like the LORD's garden;[119]
celebration, joy are found in her,
and thanks, and sounds of song.

4 My people, listen to Me –
heed Me, nation Mine,
for teaching will come forth from Me;
in a moment I bring My judgment,
light for all peoples;
5 My victory is close;

119 | Cf. Genesis 13:10.

My rescue has come forth;
My arms' strength brings judgment to peoples.
The coastlands wait for Me;
for My strong arm they long.
6 Lift your eyes to the heavens
and gaze at the earth below:
the heavens fade away like smoke;
like an old cloak, the land wears out,
and those who dwell upon her likewise die –
but My rescue is forever;
My justice will not be broken.

7 Listen to Me, you who know what is right,
people with My teaching at your heart:
do not fear disgrace from men,
nor break when they abuse you,
8 for moths will eat them up like cloth,
like wool, the grubs will eat them
while My justice, that will always be,
My rescue through all ages.

9 Rise, rise,
and don your dress of might,
the LORD's strong arm.
Rise as long ago
in the earliest time –
was it not You who cleaved Rahav,
beat the Serpent down?[120]
10 Was it not You who dried the ocean,
the waters of endless deeps,
making the depths of the ocean
a path for redeemed ones to travel?
11 They will return, those the LORD has claimed,
arriving in Zion in song,
crowned with everlasting joy;
they will have found joy and happiness,
and sorrow and moaning will flee.

12 It is I, I
who comfort you.
Who are you
to fear mortal man,
humanity, that ends like grass,
13 forgetting the LORD who made you,
who stretches out the skies,

120 | Rahav was a mythical monster of the sea (see 30:7 above and cf. Ps. 89:11; Job 9:13, 26:12).

lays down the earth?
All day you fear
the oppressor's rage
as he makes his schemes of violence –
yet where is the oppressor's rage?
14 The man bent under his burden – how fast will he be freed;
he[121] will not die into the pit,
nor will his bread be lacking.
15 I am the LORD your God –
I trouble the ocean;
its waves roar –
the LORD of Hosts is My name.
16 I have placed My words in your mouth
and covered you in My hand's shade,
planting the skies, laying down the earth,
and saying to Zion: "You are My people."

17 Rouse, rouse yourself
and rise, Jerusalem,
you who have drunk from the LORD's hand
His full cup of rage,
the poisoned goblet –
drunk and drained it.
18 No one will guide her back,
of all the children she has borne;
of all the sons she raised
there is none to hold her hand.[122]
19 Two things came to you,
but who is moved for you?
Massacre and breaking,
hunger and the sword –
through whom may I comfort you?
20 Your children fainted, fallen
at every street corner,
like netted wild oxen –
full of the LORD's rage,
your God's rebuke.
21 So listen, woman oppressed
and drunk but not with wine.

22 So says the LORD, your LORD;
so your God fights His people's cause:
Behold: I have taken

121 | The bent-over prisoner is a metaphor for Israel in exile.

122 | This may refer to the trope of a drunken parent whose children will not steady her but leave her helpless in her debasement; cf. Genesis 9:20–27.

the poisoned cup
from your hand,
the goblet of My rage;
you will drink from it no more.
23 I shall place it in the hands
of those who torment you,
who have said to your face,
"Bow down to let us pass" –
You made your back like earth, like
the road to be walked over.

52 1 Rise, rise, Zion,
and don your dress of might;
wear your garb of glory,
Jerusalem, holy town,
for no more will
uncircumcised, impure ones
enter you.
2 Shake yourself free of the dust;
rise up to take your place, Jerusalem.
Break free of the chains around your neck,
captive daughter Jerusalem.

3 For so says the LORD:
You were sold away for nothing,
and it is not for silver[123]
that you will be redeemed.

4 For so says the LORD GOD:
My people went down long ago
to Egypt, to live there for a time;
for nothing, Assyria oppressed them,
5 and now, what is there here for Me?
So says the LORD:
For nothing My people is taken captive,
its rulers baying.
So says the LORD:
Unceasingly, all day,
My name is defamed,
6 and so – My people will know My name,
and so – on that day –
they will know that it is I who spoke, that
I am here.

7 How lovely upon the mountains:
the steps of the bringer of tidings,

---

123 | They will be redeemed for free, which will restore God's dignity among nations.

resounding with peace,
tidings of good,
resounding of rescue,
saying to Zion:
"Your God has ascended the throne."
8 The voice of your watchmen –
their voices rise as one, singing,
for they will see with their own eyes
the LORD's return to Zion.
9 Break out in song; sing out together,
ruins of Jerusalem,
for the LORD has comforted His people,
redeemed His Jerusalem.
10 The LORD has uncovered His holy arm
before the eyes of all nations,
and all ends of this earth will see
rescue from our God.

11 Turn, turn aside – leave that place
without touching the defiled.
Go out from there; cleanse yourselves,
you who bear the LORD's vessels;[124]
12 this time you will not leave in haste,[125]
you will not leave in flight.
The LORD will go before you,
the God of Israel your rear guard behind.

13 My servant will prevail,[126]
be elevated, raised, attain great height.
14 As everyone was aghast at you –
racked beyond recognition as a man,
face no longer human –
15 just so: many nations leap in fear,
their kings silenced before him,
for they have seen what they were never told of
and witnessed what they never heard.
53 1 Who would believe what we have to tell?
To whom is the LORD's strong arm revealed?
2 He came up like a tender shoot before Him,
like a slip from a desert land;
he has no appearance or manifest glory,
no beauty for us to desire,

124 | Probably a reference to the carrying of the Temple vessels from Babylon to Jerusalem as ordered in Ezra 6:5.

125 | As you did from Egypt; cf. Deuteronomy 16:3.

126 | The servant described in this passage is the Jewish people, who made the difficult journey from Babylon to Yehuda, only to find suffering and poverty in their homeland.

3 scorned and forsaken by men,
a being of pain, schooled in sickness,
one whom we would hide our faces from,
scorned – we never considered him.
4 But yes: he has borne our own sickness,
has suffered our own pain,
and we thought him polluted,
God-beaten, abused –
5 but it was our betrayals that desecrated him,
our iniquities that crushed him down;
the anguish of our peace is on his shoulders,
and in his bruises – we are healed.
6 All of us have strayed like sheep,
each man turning his own way,
and the LORD has thrust upon him
the iniquity of us all.
7 He was battered and oppressed
and opened not his mouth;
led like a lamb to the slaughter,
mute as a ewe before the shearer,
he opened not his mouth.
8 Taken from imprisonment and judgment,
who of his time will talk to him?
For he is expelled from the land of life,
wounded for My people's sin.
9 His grave is with the sinners';
he will be with the wealthy in death[127]
for no violence at his hands,
for no deceit at his lips.[128]
10 The LORD has desired to crush him with sickness –
if you offer him up for guilt,[129]
then he shall see children, live long,
and the LORD's desire will flourish at his hand.
11 From his soul's very burden
he will see and feel fullness;
of his mind, My servant
will vindicate the righteous before many
and bear their iniquities himself.
12 And so I shall give him his share among the great;
with the mighty he will share the spoils,
for he has offered up his soul to death,

127 | This is a punishment because wealthy people's graves were more likely to be plundered by grave robbers.

128 | That is, he did not deserve this punishment.

129 | If you confess (following Rabbi Isaiah miTrani); cf. Numbers 5:6–7.

been numbered among sinners,
and borne the guilt of many
while pleading for the sinners' good.

54 1 Barren woman, never a mother,
rejoice;
break out in joyful song
though you have not given birth,
for the children of the forsaken woman
will outnumber those of the wife,
so says the Lord.
2 Broaden the site of your tent;
stretch out your canvas home;
do not hold back;
lengthen your tent cords,
and strengthen its pegs:
3 you shall overflow rightward and left,
your children possessing nations,
and filling forsaken towns with life.
4 Do not fear – you will not be shamed;
fear not, for none can disgrace you.
You will forget your youthful abjection;
the debasement of your widowhood
you will call no more to mind,
5 for your husband, He who made you –
the Lord of Hosts is His name,
and your redeemer, Israel's Holy One –
will be named God
of all the world,
6 for as a woman abandoned,
of sorrowful spirit,
the Lord has called to you:
Can the young bride ever be rejected?
says your God;
7 for one small moment I left you;
with infinite care shall I gather you back;
8 in the flash of My fury
I hid My face from you for just a moment,
and in everlasting love will I care for you now.
So speaks the Lord, your redeemer.

9 For these are the waters of Noaḥ to Me,
and I swore that the waters of Noaḥ would never
sweep again over the earth.
And so did I swear no more to
be furious with you,

no more to rebuke you.
10 For mountains may move,
hills may crumble away;
but My love for you will not be moved,
nor My pact of peace crumble.
So speaks the LORD,
who cares for you.

11 Oppressed and storm swept,
never comforted –
behold: I am paving your ground with garnet,
lapis lazuli your foundations.
12 I am fitting your windows with rubies,
your gates with glowing granite,
marking your borders with stones men covet.
13 All your children will be students of the LORD,
and great will be your children's peace.
14 On righteousness will you be founded;
stay far from oppression –
you will not fear,
and terror
will never come near you.
15 No strife can arise
without My assent;
who among you fears
one who could come upon you?
16 For I create the craftsman who blows the charcoal fire
and brings forth the tools of his trade;
I create also
the destroyer to do harm.
17 No weapon made to harm you
can prevail;
any tongue that calls you into judgment,
you will prove its fault.
This is the birthright of the LORD's servants,
for their innocence is Mine –
so says the LORD.

55 1 You who are thirsty, all –
come to water;
you who have no silver,
come, take food and eat;
come and take food without silver,
wine and milk without cost,
2 for why should you weigh out your silver for no bread,
your labor bringing you no fullness?

Listen – listen to Me:
let goodness nourish you, and let
your souls delight in plenty.
3 Turn your ear to Me and come;
listen, that your souls may live;
let Me forge an everlasting covenant with you –
like David's faithful promises,
4 for I make him a witness to nations,
a leader, a ruler of nations;
5 for you shall call out, call, to a people you know not,
and a people who know you not
will come running out to you
for the sake of the Lord your God,
the Holy One of Israel, your glory.

6 Seek out the Lord while He is to be found;
call to Him – now, when He is close.
7 Let the wrongdoer turn from his path,
the corrupt man abandon his thoughts
and return to the Lord, who shows compassion,
to our God, who forgives much,
8 for My thoughts, they are not your thoughts
and nor are your ways Mine –
so says the Lord.
9 As high as the sky is raised above the land,
so are My ways above yours,
My thoughts above your thoughts;
10 just as rain and snow fall from the skies
and will not there return before
quenching the earth's thirst, before
seeing her birth and flourish,
yielding seed to the sower
and bread to the one who eats,
11 just so My word, when it leaves My mouth,
will not come back to Me unanswered
without working My desire, without
bearing the fruit of My message,
12 for you will go forth in joy,
be led on in peace –
the mountains and the hills will
break out in song before you
as all the wild trees clap their hands.
13 In place of the thorn tree, juniper will grow,
and where there were nettles, myrtle.
This will be, for the Lord, a monument,
an everlasting sign,

that will not be severed.

56 1 So says the LORD:
Guard close the Law; do what is right.
My salvation is close at hand,
My righteousness will be revealed.
2 Happy the man who does this,
the person who clings to this:
guarding My Sabbath from being profaned,
guarding his hand from performing evil.
3 Let not the son of strangers say –
who has come to walk with the LORD –
"The LORD has separated me from His people."
Let the castrated slave not say,
"I am a tree dried up."

4 For thus says the LORD
of those castrated slaves who have guarded My Sabbath,
who chose what I desire
and hold fast to My covenant:
5 To these I am giving, in My house
between My walls,
a monument and name
better than sons and than daughters;
I give them a name everlasting
that will not be severed.

6 And the children of strangers
who have come to join the LORD, to serve Him,
to love the LORD's name
and be His servants,
all who guard the Sabbath from being profaned
and hold fast to My covenant,
7 I shall bring them to My holy mount,
show them joy in My house of prayer.
Their offerings and sacrifices
are desired on My altar,
for My House will be called a house of prayer
for all peoples.
8 So says the LORD GOD,
who gathers back the banished ones of Israel:
I shall gather yet more with those who have been gathered.
9 All the wild animals, come
and eat, you creatures of the forest.

10 All his watchmen[130] are blind,

130 | The people's leaders or false prophets.

do not know,
mute dogs all,
no bark,
full of dreams, lying down,
lovers of slumber,
11 like brazen dogs
who know no fullness.
These shepherds, who know not
how to understand –
each turns to his own way,
every man to his own profit:
12 *"Here: I bring the wine;*
let us get us drunk on ale;
let the morrow be like today,
and greater still."
57 1 The righteous man is gone;
none take it to heart;
all good people are gathered up,[131]
with none to understand:
it is this evil that causes
the righteous to be gathered up.
2 Yet peace will come:
they lie still in their resting place,
those who walked upright.

3 Now draw close, you
children of sorcery,
sons of a philanderer
and an adulterous wife.
4 To whom do you go for your delight;
to whom do you open wide your mouth
and make your mocking tongue long?
Are you not children of sin,
the offspring of lies,
5 in heat with the false gods
under every leafy tree,
slaughtering children in rivers
and under the crags of the rocks.
6 You took your share amid the riverbeds' smooth stones;
they are your destiny;
to them as well you poured out offerings,
brought sacrifices.
Am I to be comforted for that?
7 Upon the high and lofty mountains

131 | That is, they perish.

you laid down your bed;
there too you went up
to make your offerings.
8 Behind the door, the doorpost,
you mounted your keepsakes,
for you are uncovered and gone from Me;[132]
you made your bed broad,
forged your covenant with them;
you have loved to lie with them,
loved every hand you saw.[133]
9 Daubed in oils, you paid your court to kings;
how great your perfumery is;
you sent your messengers out afar
and lowered yourself as deep as Sheol –
10 you put great efforts into your path,[134]
never admitting despair.
Your hands made their livelihood
and did not give way to sickness;
11 whom did you regard or fear
throughout your deception?
Me you did not remember
or take to your heart.
I have held still, always,
and so you did not fear Me.
12 Let Me recount your righteousness ...[135]
Your actions do you no good.
13 When you call out, let them rescue you, the gods that you collected –
The wind will carry them all away;
empty breath will take them.
But those who shelter in Me
will possess the earth
and inherit My holy mountain;
14 they will say, "Mark, mark a road here;[136]
clear a way.
Lift out of My people's way
all that could make them fall."

15 Thus says the high, the exalted One,
abiding forever, whose name is holy:
High and holy I abide –

---

132 | The "wife" has gone from the marital bed to embrace her lovers.

133 | You looked favorably upon anyone who reached out to embrace you.

134 | The "path" and "livelihood" allude to prostitutes to the wealthy, whose custom was to advertise through messengers.

135 | This is said in irony.

136 | Stones would be cleared to the two sides of the dirt path, forming the road.

yet I am with the crushed and humbled,
giving life to the humbled,
giving life to crushed men's hearts.
16 I will not forever contend with you,
will not rage to the bitter end.
When the spirit faints before Me –
I created these souls.
17 I have raged at the sin behind their profits,
have struck them, have hidden My face and raged
as they went wayward
on the path their hearts beat out.
18 I have seen their ways and will heal them.
I will lead them, will reward them in comfort,
them and their mourners;
19 I form the words:
Peace, peace to those far away and near –
so the LORD speaks – I will heal them.
20 The wicked are like the ocean surging,
unable to be still;
its waters fling up mud and filth.
21 There is no peace, says my God,
for the wicked.

58 1 Shout out loud; do not hold back;
raise up your voice like a ram's horn.
Tell My people of their rebellion;
tell the House of Yaakov their sins.
2 Day after day they search for Me;
they desire to know My ways[137] –
like a nation that always did right
and never forsook its God's justice.
They ask for rulings in law.
They say that being close to God
is all that interests them.
3 "Why do we fast and You not see it,
oppress ourselves and You acknowledge it not?"
But even on your fast days you press your interests,
extort a profit on all that you own.
4 Contending and fighting each other, you fast
while you beat with the fist of evil.
The fast you perform today
will not carry your voice on high.
5 Is this the fast I have chosen –
a day for man to oppress himself?

137 | That is, they falsely claim to seek God's ways.

To bow his head like a rush in the wind,
to lay his bed with sackcloth and ashes?
Is this what you call a fast,
"a day for the LORD's favor"?
6 No! This is the fast I choose:
loosen the bindings of evil,
and break the slavery chain.
Those who were crushed, release to freedom,
and shatter every yoke of slavery.
7 Break your bread for the starving;
bring dispossessed wanderers home.
When you see a man naked, clothe him;
do not avert your eyes from your own flesh.[138]
8 Then will your light break forth like sunrise,
and healing will grow fast over your wound.
Your righteousness will go before you,
with the LORD's presence your rear guard behind.
9 Then you will call, and the LORD will answer;
when you cry out, He will say, "I am here";
10 if you give of your soul to the starving
and answer the hunger of souls oppressed –
then your light will shine out in darkness;
your very night will shine like noontide.
11 The LORD will fortify your bones.
You will be like a watered garden,
like a spring of waters
that will not fail.
12 Places ruined long ago will be rebuilt in you;
you will raise up houses from age-old foundations,
be known as mender of the ruptured wall,
as the one who restored the paths for living.
13 If you keep your feet from roving on the Sabbath,[139]
from pursuing your interests on My holy day,
if you call the Sabbath a delight,
the LORD's holy day to be honored,
if you honor it by not going your own way,
attending to your own affairs, or speaking idle words,
14 then you will find joy in the LORD;
I will set you astride the heights of the earth
to feast on the inheritance of your father Yaakov –
for the mouth of the LORD has spoken.

59 1 The LORD's hand does not fall short of rescue;
His ear is not so dull as not to hear –

138 | A play on words; as in English, "flesh" can refer to the naked body or to one's relatives.

139 | Following the instruction in Exodus 16:29.

2 It is your sins that separated
you from your God,
your iniquities that hid His face
from you, Him from your hearing,
3 the palms of your hands disgusting with blood,
your fingers with iniquity;
your lips have spoken lies,
and your tongue frames violence.
4 No one calls out in integrity; none
come honestly to be judged;
they trust in emptiness, speak hollow words,
pregnant with treachery, breeding sin.[140]
5 They hatch out adders' eggs and
weave spiders' webs.
Anyone eating those eggs will die;
kicked apart, they will hatch out vipers.
6 Those webs will not make them a garment,
nor will their actions hide them.
Their actions are acts of wickedness,
and violence is in their hands.
7 Their feet race toward evil;
they rush to spill
innocent blood;[141]
their thoughts are thoughts of wickedness,
with violent destruction strewn along their road.
8 They do not know the way of peace;
their byways know no justice;
their paths turn crooked before them:
no one who treads these
will ever know peace.
9 This is why justice is far from them,
and they will not reach goodness.
"We hope for light, and here is darkness;
for brightness, yet we walk in gloom.
10 We feel our way like blind men against the wall;
we stumble on as if eyeless.
We have fallen at noontime as if it were night;
we walk among the healthy as if dead.
11 All of us growl like bears,
moan like doves,
hope for judgment, but none comes;
for rescue, but it is far from us,
12 for our crimes in Your presence are many;

140 | Cf. Psalms 7:15; Job 15:35.
141 | Cf. Proverbs 1:16.

our sins have spoken against us.
Our crimes are with us always;
we know our iniquities well:
13 rebelling against the LORD, denying Him,
fleeing away from our God,
speaking oppression and waywardness,
conceiving and speaking a mind's lies.
14 Justice has fled back,
and righteousness stands distant,
for truth has fallen down in the town square,
and uprightness gains no entry;
15 truth is absent;
those who turn from evil
are gone away from us."
The LORD sees it all; it is evil in His eyes,
for there is no justice.
16 He sees there is no man here – aghast,
for there is none to intercede –
so His own arm brings rescue;
His righteousness brings strength.
17 He dons righteousness as armor,
with a helmet of rescue on His head;
He dons the clothes of vengeance
and His passion as a mantle.
18 A rightful punishment, rightly paid,
rage against His foes,
punishment of enemies,
punishment to far-off coastlands
He shall pay.
19 From the western horizon they will fear the LORD's name;
from the rising of the sun, revere His glory,
for the foe will come flooding like a river,
but from the spirit of the LORD he will flee.
20 A redeemer is coming to Zion,
to those among Yaakov who turn back from sin;
the LORD has spoken.
21 And I, this is My covenant with them –
so says the LORD –
My spirit, which is upon you,
My words, which I planted in your mouths,
will not fade from your mouths
or the mouths of your children
or of your children's children –
so speaks the LORD –
from now until the end of time.

60 1 Rise, give light,
for your light has come:
the glory of the Lord
shines over you,
2 for darkness may cover the earth,
and clouds shroud nations,
but over you, the Lord will be shining,
His glory manifest over you;
3 nations will walk toward your light,
and kings into the brilliance you shine forth.
4 Raise your eyes; look around and see –
all of them gathered in,
and come to you;
your sons have come from far away,
your daughters as if clinging to nursemaids' hips.[142]
5 Then you will see and shine;
your heart will fill with awe and open wide,
for the ocean's abundance will turn to you;
the wealth of nations will come to you;
6 herds of camels will cover your land,
young camels from Midyan and Eifa,
all having come to you from Sheba,
carrying gold and frankincense
and tidings of the Lord's praise.
7 All the flocks of Kedar will be gathered in to you;
the rams of Nevayot will be in your service.
Offered on My altar, they will be desired;
I shall glorify the House of My glory.
8 Who are these sailing like clouds,
like doves come back to their roosting cote?
9 It is Me the distant islands wait for;
ships of Tarshish come the first,[143]
to bring your children from far away,
their silver and gold with them,
for the name of the Lord your God,
the Holy One of Israel: He has glorified you.
10 The children of strangers will build your walls;[144]
their kings will be in your service,
for in My fury I beat you,
but, desiring you now, I show you mercy,
11 and your gates will be always open,

142 | As if carried by their nursemaids; cf. 49:23.

143 | A symbol of wealth and power; see note on 2:16 and 1 Kings 10:23.

144 | Rather than toiling over them yourselves while foreigners attempt to hinder you; contrast with Nehemiah 2:19–20, 4:1–17.

day and night, never closed,[145]
as the wealth of nations is brought in to you,
their kings led to you,[146]
12 for the nations and kingdoms that do not serve you
will be lost,
nations desolate, destroyed.
13 Lebanon's glory will come to you:
junipers, cypress trees, and pencil pines together,
to lend the place of My Sanctuary splendor;
I shall glorify the place of My footstool.[147]
14 The children of those who once oppressed you will
come before you prostrate,
bowing themselves to the soles of your feet;
all who once denounced you,
they will call you The LORD's City,
Zion of Israel's Holy One.
15 Where once you were forsaken, hated,
never even passed through,
I have made you everlasting majesty,
the joy of generations.
16 You shall suckle the milk of nations,
suckle at kings' breasts,[148]
and know that I am the LORD, your rescue,
your redeemer, the Mighty One of Yaakov.
17 Where once there was bronze, I shall bring gold,
and where there was iron, silver.
Where once there was wood, I shall bring bronze,
and where there was stone, now iron.
I shall make peace your commander,
your ruling class: righteousness.
18 No more will violence
be heard of in your land,
nor plunder or destruction
in your borders.
You shall name your walls Rescue,
and your gates, Praise.
19 No more, by day, will the sun be your light,
nor the moon's radiance shine for you,
for the LORD will be your light forever;
your God will be your glory.
20 Your sun will set no longer,

145 | A sign of prosperity and security.

146 | To bring tribute.

147 | That is, the Temple, where God's presence resides on earth.

148 | The Hebrew contains a wordplay between the similar words for "breast" (*shad*) and "loot" (*shod*).

nor your moon be gathered in,
for the LORD is your light forever;
the days of your mourning are done.
21 Your people, all of them righteous,
will inherit the land forever,
the shoots of My planting,
works of My hands, spreading branches in glory.[149]
22 The little son will become a thousand strong,
the youngest child a mighty nation;
I am the LORD:
when the time is right –
in a flash I will bring it all to be.

61 1 The spirit of the LORD GOD is with me:
the LORD has anointed me
to bring to oppressed ones tidings; has sent me
to bandage broken hearts,
to cry freedom to captives,
and to break the prisoners' bonds;
2 to call forth a year of the LORD's favor,
a day for the vengeance of our God,
to comfort all mourners;
3 to give to the mourners of Zion –
to crown them in splendor where once there was ash,[150]
where once there was mourning, oil of joy,
a mantle of praise where there were dark spirits,
calling them oaks of righteousness,
the LORD's planting, grown for His splendor.
4 Ancient ruins will be rebuilt,
from the first desolations will rise again;
deserted cities will be renewed,
those desolate age after age.
5 Foreigners will stand up to pasture your flocks,
children of strangers your farm and vineyard laborers.
6 You will be called the LORD's priests;
"These are our God's servants,"
will be said of you.
You will eat of the wealth of nations
and boast of their glory.
7 Where once you had shame, you will twice have goodness;
instead of disgrace, you will sing of your share.
And so, in their land, they will inherit twofold:
everlasting joy will be theirs,

149 | The verb *lehitpaer* means both "to spread branches" and "to be glorified."
150 | The word "splendor" (*pe'er*) is an anagram of "ash" (*efer*) in Hebrew.

8 for I the Lord love justice,
rejecting stolen offerings.
I shall give those who are true, return for their work;
I shall forge an everlasting covenant with them;
9 their children will be well known among the nations,
their offspring among peoples,
for all those who see them will know who they are:
children of the Lord's own blessing.

10 I shall rejoice, rejoice in the Lord;
my soul exults in my God;
He has wrapped me in garb of rescue,
on my shoulders the mantle of righteousness –
as a bridegroom attends in splendor,
and a bride puts on her jewels;
11 just as the land brings forth green life,
having all that is planted in her flower like a garden,
so will the Lord God bring forth
righteousness and glory
before all the nations.
62 1 For Zion's sake I cannot be silent,
for Jerusalem's I cannot be still
until righteousness bursts forth shining,
and rescue burns like a brand,
2 and all nations see your righteousness,
all the kings your glory.
They will call you by a new name
spoken from the Lord's own mouth.[151]
3 You will be a crown of glory in the Lord's hand,
a kingly diadem in your God's palms.
4 No more will they say of you, "Abandoned,"
"Desolate" of your land,
for you shall be called "My Desire,"
your land renamed "Embraced,"
for it is you the Lord desires,
and your land shall be embraced;
5 as a young man embraces a maid,
so will your children embrace you,
while the joy of a bridegroom over his bride
is the joy your God will take in you.
6 Over your walls, Jerusalem,
I have appointed watchmen,
all day, all night long, always,
and they will not keep silence;

151 | In place of the derogatory names that have been used by the nations until now.

you who call the LORD by name,
none of you be quiet,
7 and do not give Him quiet
until He has established, until He has raised Jerusalem
to be the glory of this earth.
8 The LORD has sworn by His right hand
and by His mighty arm:
never again to give away your grain
as your foes' food,
never to let strangers drink
the wine that you have labored for –
9 no – the ones who harvest it will eat
and sing out the LORD's praise,
and those He has gathered in will drink[152]
within My sacred courtyards.

10 Pass, pass through the gates,
and make way for the people.
Mark, mark a road here;
clear the stones;
raise a banner
above all peoples.
11 Behold: the LORD
resounding to the earth's ends –
tell daughter Zion,
your rescue is come,
and with Him, His prize:
His work walking before Him.[153]
12 They will call them a holy people,
redeemed ones of the LORD.
And you – you shall be called
the One Sought After,
the City That Will Never
Be Abandoned.

63 1 "Who is this, coming from Edom,
from Botzra, in reddened clothes?[154]
Who, His clothing glorious,
striding forth in might?"
It is I who speak with rectitude,
powerful to rescue.
2 "And why is Your clothing red,

---

152 | Referring to the consumption of tithes in Jerusalem; see Deuteronomy 14:22–27.
153 | Cf. 40:10.
154 | *Edom* means red (see Gen. 25:30); Botzra, a city in ancient Edom, derives from the root meaning "grape harvest."

your garments, as if You trod the winepress?"
3 I have trodden the vat alone;
no man of any nation was there with Me;
I trod them in My fury,
trampling them in rage,
until their lifeblood steeped My clothes,
befouling all My garments,
4 for today in My heart is a day of vengeance;
My year of redemption is come.
5 I look, and no one is there
to help;
with dismay I see – no aid;[155]
so My arm will bear My rescue;
My rage is My support.
6 My fury will tread peoples low;
in My rage I shall make them drunk
and pour down their lifeblood to earth.

7 Let me speak the LORD's acts of kindness,
praises of the LORD
for all the LORD has done for us,
for His great goodness to Israel,
performed in all compassion,
in all His loving-kindness.
8 He said: They, they are My people,
My children who would not lie to Me –
and He was their rescue.
9 Wherever they suffered, He too suffered,[156]
and His presence, its emissary
rescued them;
in His love, in His mercy
He redeemed them
and took them up and bore them
through all those long-past days.
10 And they rebelled and saddened
His holy spirit –
and He became their enemy;
He fought against them.
11 Then they remembered those long-past days,
and Moshe, and His people –
where is He, who brought them up from the sea[157]
with the shepherds of His flock?

---

155 | Cf. 59:16.

156 | Translation follows the *keri*. The *ketiv*: "Whenever they suffered, He did not cause them to suffer greatly."

157 | The name *Moshe* literally means "one who draws out"; see Exodus 2:10.

Where is He who placed among them
His holy spirit,
12 leading, at Moshe's right hand,
and with His arm of glory?
He split the waters before them
to make Him a name everlasting,
13 leading them through the deep
like a horse riding the desert,
never to fall;
14 as cattle descend the valley,
the LORD's spirit would guide them.
Thus You led Your people
to make You a name for glory.
15 Look down from the heavens and see –
from Your Sanctuary in its holiness and glory –
where, now, is all Your passion and might?
All Your great fervor and care
are held back now from me.
16 You are our Father
though Avraham would not know us,[158]
Yisrael would not recognize us.
You, LORD, are our Father,
named our redeemer since time began.
17 Why, LORD, have you led us astray from Your path
and hardened our hearts from fearing You?
Come back for Your servants' sake,
to the tribes of Your possession.
18 For such a short time Your holy people held it,
then enemies trampled down
Your Sanctuary.
19 We have become as ones You never ruled,
as ones never given Your name.
Would You but tear through the skies
and come down,
the hills would melt before You[159]
64 1 as fire burns to liquefy,
as water boils amid fire –
to make Your name known to Your foes –
and nations would quake before You.
2 Then, when You performed wonders
we never could have hoped for,
when You came down,
the hills melted before You,

158 | Neither Avraham nor Yaakov rescued us, but God.
159 | Cf. Judges 5:5.

3 and never has anyone heard,
anyone heeded,
has any eye borne witness
to any god but You
with all that You perform
for those who wait for You.
4 You struck down even those
who rejoice in doing justice,
who recall You, following Your ways –
for You raged; we sinned –
it was through them, always,
that we were spared.
5 All of us are defiled now,
the best of our actions a bleeding cloth
and all of us withered like leaves
until, like the wind, our sin bore us away,
6 and none call on Your name
or rouse themselves to grasp You,
for You have hidden Your face from us
and let our iniquities melt us away.
7 Now, Lord, You are our Father;
we are the clay, You our potter,
and all of us are Your hands' work.
8 Do not rage against us, Lord, with such a fury,
or remember forever our sin.
Please – look on and see – all of us, Your people.
9 Your holy cities have turned to wilderness;
Zion has turned to wilderness,
Jerusalem to wasteland;
10 our holy House, our glory,
where our ancestors sang Your praise
become a great conflagration;
and all we hold dear –
ruin.
11 Lord, from all this, will You yet hold back,
keep silence, torment us
so?

65 1 Though no one looked for Me, still I was found.
For those who did not seek Me, I was there.
I am here – I said – am here –
to a nation that never called My name;
2 I spread My hands out all the day
to a people that turned away –
walking the path to no good
after their wandering thoughts.

3 The people anger Me,
always there before Me
sacrificing in gardens,
burning incense on the slabs,
4 sitting among the graves
and passing the nights in caverns,
eating the meat of pigs and
filling their bowls with a broth of foulness,
5 saying, "Stand with your own kind;
do not come near me; I am holier than you" –
these people are smoke in My nostrils
from fire burning all the day.
6 Behold: it is written before Me:
I shall not be silent until I have repaid,
thrust everything back into their arms,
7 your iniquities with those of your parents,
so says the LORD.
Your parents who burned incense on the hills and
blasphemed Me from the mountaintops –
I have measured their payment out from the first
into their arms.

8 So says the LORD:
Just as there is yet wine in the bunch,
so that one will say, "Do not destroy this one,
for there is blessing in it yet,"
so will I intervene for My servants
not to destroy them all;
9 I will deprive Yaakov of progeny,
Yehuda of an heir to My mountains,
and My chosen ones will take possession;
My servants will live there;
10 the Sharon will be pasture to flocks,
the Valley of the Scourge[160] a resting place for cattle
for those of My people who sought Me out.
11 While you who forsake the LORD,
forgetting My holy mountain
while laying a table for Gad,
pouring lavish libations to Meni[161] –
12 I have marked you out for the sword;
you will all bow to the slaughter,
for I have called out to you, and you did not answer –
I spoke, but you were not listening;

160 | See Joshua 7:24–26.

161 | Gad was a god of fortune worshipped throughout the Near East, and Meni was a god worshipped by the Nabateans.

you did what was evil in My sight
and chose what I never desired.

13 And so, thus says the LORD GOD:
My servants will eat, but you will hunger;
My servants will drink, but you will thirst.
My servants will rejoice,
but you will be shamed;
14 My servants will sing out contentment,
but you will cry out in heartache,
will wail with a broken spirit.
15 You will leave behind your name
for My chosen few to swear by,
for the LORD GOD will annihilate you
and call His servants by a different name,
16 for those who bless themselves in the land
will bless themselves invoking the ever-faithful God,
and those who swear their oaths in the land
will swear by ever-faithful God,
for the early trials will be forgotten,
hidden away from My sight;
17 for I am creating new heavens,
a new earth,
and the first ones will not be remembered,
will not be taken to heart.
18 Rejoice, exult forever
in that which I create,
for I am creating Jerusalem as happiness,
her people as joy,
19 and I shall exult in Jerusalem,
rejoice in My people,
and no more will you hear in her
the sounds of weeping, of crying out.
20 There will not be any
youth or old person
who does not live out his days;
a man will die young one hundred years old,
and a sinner a hundred years old die accursed.[162]
21 They will build their houses and live,
plant vineyards, eat the fruit;
22 they will not build houses for others to dwell in
or plant and have others consume.
My people's lifetime is like that of a tree,
and those I have chosen will wear out

162 | Death at the age of one hundred will be assumed to be the fulfillment of a curse on a sinner, as most people will live much longer.

the works of their hands.[163]
23 They will not toil for nothing, will not
bear children to know horror,[164]
for they are the children the LORD has blessed,
their descendants with them,
24 and before they call out to Me, I shall answer –
while they are yet speaking, I shall respond.
25 Wolf and lamb will pasture as one,
and lion, like ox, will feed upon straw,
and dust will be the serpent's bread.[165]
There will be no wrong or violence
on all My holy mountain,
says the LORD.

66 1 Thus speaks the LORD:
The heavens are My throne;
the world, My footstool.
What house, then, would You build for Me, where
could I rest?
2 All this – My own hands made,
all these are Mine,
so says the LORD.
And these are the ones I look toward:
the poor, of humbled spirit,
who tremble at My words.
3 While he, killing his ox
is like a murderer of men,
the one who offers up a lamb
might so well behead a dog;
the offering brought
may just as well be pigs' blood;
and his remembrance incense
is a blessing of iniquity.
These men, they choose their paths,
their souls desire their disgusting things,
4 and so I too will choose – will choose their torments,
and bring to them what they most fear.
I called out – no one answered;
I spoke, but none was listening.
They did what was evil in My sight,
and chose what I never desired.[166]

---

163 | The tools and vessels they fashion will wear out long before the person who made them dies.

164 | Children will not die in their parents' lifetime.

165 | Cf. 11:6–9.

166 | Cf. 65:12.

5 You who tremble to hear His word –
listen to the LORD's word:
Your brothers said, the ones
who hated you,
who cast you out,
"Because of my name,
the LORD is honored."
We will see your joy –
and they will be shamefaced.[167]
6 A voice roaring out from the city –
a voice, out of the Sanctuary –
a voice – it is the LORD's –
as He repays His enemies.
7 Before she had writhed in labor
she gave birth;
before the agonies took her
she was delivered of a boy.
8 Who ever heard
of anything like this?
Who ever saw such
happenings as these?
Can the land give birth in a day?
Can a nation be born at a single step?
Yet Zion has labored, and
has birthed her children.
9 Would I bring on the labor
and not deliver?
So the LORD speaks:
Would I who fathered
close the womb?
So your God speaks.

10 Bring Jerusalem joy,
exult in her, all of you who love her;
celebrate her joy with her,
all of you who mourned her.
11 That you may suck your fill
from the bosom of her comforting;
may suckle, take delight
in the brilliance of her glory.

12 For thus says the LORD:
See Me make peace flow to her like a river,
and the substance of nations – like a rushing brook –

167 | These are the prophet's words of reassurance to those mocked by the hateful brothers, apparently a reference to Jews who rejected other Jews.

and you shall suckle.
You will be borne upon hips,
playing upon loving laps –
13 as a man is consoled by his mother,
just so shall I comfort you,
and in Jerusalem, you shall be consoled.
14 You shall look on, your heart rejoicing,
while your bones grow vigorous, like grass,
and the hand of the Lord becomes known to His servants,
and His rage known to all His foes.
15 For see: the Lord is coming in fire,
His chariots a storm wind,
to slake His fury in rage,
His rebuke in flames of fire.
16 For in fire, the Lord comes to judgment,
and by the sword, to all flesh,
and many are those
the Lord will execute.
17 Those in the gardens, sanctifying and
cleansing themselves,
one after the other in the midst of it,[168]
while eating the flesh of pigs and pests and mice,
they will all be gathered in together:
so the Lord has spoken.
18 For I – I know their works, their thoughts;
and time will come, to gather all nations and tongues,
and they will come, and look upon My glory.
19 I shall place a sign among them,
send out survivors from them
to all nations,
to Tarshish, Pul, and Lud,
to the great archers, Tuval, Yavan,[169]
to the distant coastlands
where none ever heard tell of Me
or saw My glory,
and they will tell of My glory to the nations.
20 And they will bring back all your brothers
from among all other nations,
an offering to the Lord,
on horseback and on chariot,
on camels, mules, dromedaries,
to My holy mount, Jerusalem –
so says the Lord –

168 | Cf. 65:3.
169 | Lands on the coasts of Asia Minor.

just as the children of Israel
would bring up their offerings
in pure vessels, to the LORD's House,
21 and from among them also I shall take
priests and Levites –
so says the LORD.
22 For just as the new heavens, the new earth
that I am now forming, will stand forever before Me,
so says the LORD,
so will stand
your children, your name.
23 And it will be – every New Moon,
every Sabbath –
all flesh will come
to worship Me,
so says the LORD.
24 Going out, they will see
bodies of those people who sinned against Me,
for the worms will not die
nor the fire be quenched –
and they will be repugnant to all flesh.

And it will be – every New Moon,
every Sabbath –
all flesh will come
to worship Me,
so says the LORD.

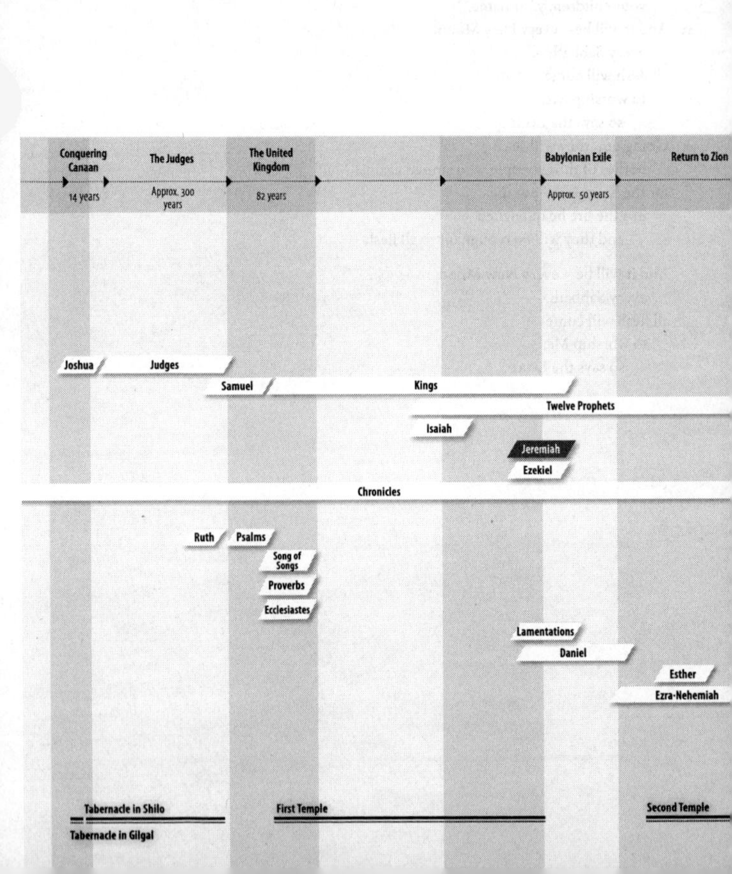
Conquering Canaan
14 years
The Judges
Approx. 300 years
The United Kingdom
82 years
Babylonian Exile
Approx. 50 years
Return to Zion
Joshua
Judges
Samuel
Kings
Twelve Prophets
Isaiah
Jeremiah
Ezekiel
Chronicles
Ruth
Psalms
Song of Songs
Proverbs
Ecclesiastes
Lamentations
Daniel
Esther
Ezra-Nehemiah
Tabernacle in Shilo
Tabernacle in Gilgal
First Temple
Second Temple

JEREMIAH/YIRMEYA

Jeremiah

JEREMIAH	The prophetic mission to establish an improved reality	Causes of the destruction and Yirmeya's attempts to prevent it	Yirmeya in conflict with the kings and false prophets	Prophecies of consolation and redemption	The period immediately before the destruction and its aftermath	Prophecies about the nations	Depiction of the destruction of Jerusalem and the Temple, and hints of hope
	Chs. 1–6	7–24	25–29	30–33	34–45	46–51	52
	Approx. 42 years						

1 1 The words of Yirmeyahu, son of Ḥilkiyahu, one of the priests who were
2 in Anatot in the land of Binyamin, to whom the word of the LORD came
in the days of Yoshiyahu son of Amon, king of Yehuda, in the thirteenth
3 year of his reign, and continued during the days of Yehoyakim son of
Yoshiyahu, king of Yehuda, until the end of the eleventh year of Tzidkiyahu
son of Yoshiyahu, king of Yehuda – until the exile of Jerusalem in the fifth
month:

4 The word of the LORD came to me:
5 "Before I formed you in the womb
I knew you.
Before you were born
I consecrated you.
I placed you as a prophet to the nations."

6 I said, "Please, Lord GOD, I am not capable of speaking,
for I am still only a boy."

7 The LORD replied to me, "Do not say, 'I am a boy,'
for you shall go to all to whom I send you,
and you shall speak as I instruct you.
8 Do not fear them,
for I am with you to rescue you,"
declares the LORD.

9 The LORD extended His hand and touched my mouth
and the LORD said to me,
"Look, I have placed My words in your mouth.
10 I have appointed you this day
against the kingdoms and against the nations
to uproot and tear down,
to destroy and demolish,
to build and to plant."

11 The word of the LORD came to me:
"What do you see, Yirmeyahu?"
I replied, "I see the branch of an almond tree."
12 And the LORD said to me:
"You have seen well,
for I am watchful about keeping My word."[1]
13 The word of the LORD came to me a second time:
"What do you see?"
I answered, "I see a boiling cauldron
facing the north."
14 And the LORD said to me:
"From the north disaster shall burst forth

1 | The Hebrew *shoked* (watchful) resonates with *shaked* (almond tree).

upon all the inhabitants of the land,
15 for I am about to summon all the tribes
of the kingdoms of the north,"
declares the LORD.
"They shall come;
each shall set up a throne
at the entrance of the gates of Jerusalem
against her ramparts roundabout
and against all the cities of Yehuda.
16 Thus will I pronounce My judgment upon them on account of their
wickedness:
they abandoned Me,
sacrificed to other gods,
and worshipped the works of their own hands.
17 As for you, be courageous;
stand up and speak to them as I will instruct you.
Do not break down because of them
lest I break you down before them.
18 I have made you today a fortress city,
an iron column,
and walls of bronze
against the entire land –
against the kings of Yehuda, its princes, its priests,
and the people of the land.
19 They will wage battle against you,
but they will not prevail,
for I am with you,"
declares the LORD,
"to rescue you."

2 1 The word of the LORD came to me:
2 "Go and proclaim to the people of Jerusalem:
This is what the LORD has said:
I recall on your behalf the devotion of your youth,
your bridal love,
when you followed Me into the wilderness,
a land unseeded.
3 Israel is a treasure to the LORD,
His choice harvest.
All who eat of it will be held to account.
Evil will befall them,"
declares the LORD.

4 Listen to the word of the LORD, House of Yaakov
and all the tribes of the House of Israel.
5 This is what the LORD said:

What fault did your forefathers find with Me
that they distanced themselves from Me?
They followed nothingness and became nothing.
6 They did not say,
"Where is the LORD
who lifted us up from the land of Egypt,
who guided us in the wilderness,
a land of deserts and pits,
an arid land, deathly dark,
a land never traversed by man,
where no one ever dwelt?"
7 I brought you to a fertile land, to eat its fruits and bounty,
but you came and defiled My land,
and made My heritage an abomination.
8 The priests did not say, "Where is the LORD?"
The teachers of the Torah did not know Me.
The shepherds[2] betrayed Me.
The prophets prophesied in the name of Baal.
They pursued that which was useless.
9 Therefore, I will continue to contend with them,
declares the LORD.
I will contend with their children's children.
10 Cross over to the islands of the Kittites[3] and observe.
Send emissaries to Kedar[4] and ponder well.
See if anything like this ever happened before.
11 Has a people ever exchanged its gods,
and they are non-gods?
Yet my nation exchanged its glory
for something useless.
12 Heavens, be astounded by this.
Storm and become utterly desolate,
declares the LORD.
13 For My nation has performed two wrongs:
they have forsaken Me,
the source of living waters,
to dig wells, broken wells
that cannot hold water.
14 Is Israel a slave?
Is he born to a maidservant?
Why has he become an object of plunder?
15 Young lions roar at him.
They voiced their cries.

---

2 | A metaphor for the rulers.

3 | Islands to the west.

4 | A desert tribe to the east.

They laid waste to his land.
His cities have been set afire,
with no inhabitants.
16 Even the men of Nof and Taḥpanḥes[5]
crush your skull.
17 This has been done to you
because you deserted the LORD your God
during the time He guided you upon the journey.
18 Now of what use is it to you to approach Egypt
to drink the waters of Shiḥor?
Of what use is it to you to approach Assyria
to drink the waters of the river?[6]
19 Your own evil will discipline you;
your own waywardness will rebuke you.
Know and see that your abandonment of the LORD your God
has been bad and bitter.
There is no fear of Me in you,
says the Almighty, LORD of Hosts.
20 I broke your yoke long ago.
I tore your restraints asunder.
You said, "I will never again transgress!"
Yet on every high hilltop
and under every leafy tree
you recline like a harlot.
21 I planted you as a choice grape:
perfect and genuine seed.
How did you change on Me into a weed?
Rotten grapes of a strange vine!
22 Although you scrub yourself with natron[7]
and heap soap on yourselves,
your guilt is stained before Me,
declares the Lord GOD.
23 How can you say that you were never defiled?
That you never followed the Be'alim?
Look back upon your path in the valley.
Recognize what you did,
like a young she-camel
clinging to her wild ways.
24 Like a wild ass
accustomed to the wilderness;
inhaling wind as she pleases,
her wailing cannot be silenced.

5 | Cities in Lower Egypt to whom the Israelites looked as allies against Nevukhadnetzar.

6 | *Shiḥor* is usually understood as the Nile, and "the River" is the Euphrates.

7 | A mineral used in ancient times as a cleanser. Cf. Proverbs 25:20.

Yet those who seek her need not be weary.
In her month they will find her.
25 Spare your foot from becoming bare
and your throat from suffering thirst!
But you said, "Never mind.
No. I have loved strangers;
it is them whom I will follow."
26 Like the shame of a thief when he is found out,
so will the House of Israel be shamed:
They, their kings, their noblemen,
their priests, and their prophets.
27 They say to the tree, "You are my father!"
And to the stone, "You gave birth to me!"
They have turned their backs to Me,
not their faces
but in their time of trouble they say,
"Arise and save us!"
28 Where are the gods that you have crafted for yourself?
Let them rise if they can save you in your time of trouble.
For your gods, Yehuda,
are as numerous as your cities.

29 Why do you contend with Me?
You have all rebelled against Me, declares the Lord.
30 I have punished your sons for naught,
for they did not learn their lesson.
Your sword has devoured your prophets
like a vicious lion.
31 I call upon this generation to acknowledge the word of the Lord!
Have I been a wilderness for Israel,
or a land of great darkness?
Why has My nation said,
"We have strayed;
we will never again approach You"?
32 Does a maiden forget her ornaments?
A bride her braided ribbons?
Yet My nation has forgotten Me
for days without number.
33 You have perfected the ways in which you search for love so well
that you have even taught those ways to sinful women.
34 The blood of the innocent poor
can be found on your skirts,
yet you did not find them tunneling into your home.
Despite all of this
35 you dare declare: "I am innocent;
surely He has turned His anger away from me!"

Be aware: I will judge you for saying,
"I did not sin."
36 How you have degraded yourself by perverting your ways.
You will yet be shamed by Egypt too,
just as you were shamed by Assyria.
37 From this[8] too you will depart
with your hands on your head.
The LORD despises those in whom you trust;
You will not succeed with them.

3 1 That is to say: [9] If a man sent away his wife,
and she walked away from him
and married another man,
would he return to her again?
Such a land would be utterly defiled.
You have strayed after many lovers,
and yet you dare return to Me?
demands the LORD.
2 Raise your eyes to the heights and observe:
Where have you not been debauched?
By the roadsides you sat in wait for them
like a nomad in the desert.
You defiled the land
with your promiscuity and your wickedness.
3 The rains were withheld,
and the spring rain did not come,
yet yours was the forehead[10] of a promiscuous woman;
you refused to be shamed.
4 By now, you should have called Me: "Father!
You were my childhood companion!"
5 Did you think He would bear a grudge forever
or preserve it for eternity?
Instead you spoke, did evil,
and you had your way.

6 The LORD spoke to me in the days of King Yoshiyahu:[11]
"Have you seen what wayward Israel has done?
She walks along every high mountain
and under every leafy tree;
she plays the harlot there.
7 I hoped that, having done all this, she would return to Me;
but she did not return,

8 | That is, from your alliance with Egypt.

9 | The voice in verses 1–5 is now the prophet's.

10 | Meaning willfulness.

11 | By which time the Ten Tribes of Israel had already been exiled (see II Kings, ch. 17, 18:1–9).

and her sister, treacherous Yehuda, took note.
8 I saw. For all the adulteries committed by wayward Israel
I sent her away and delivered a bill of divorce to her.
But treacherous Yehuda, her sister, still showed no fear.
Instead, she too went off and played the harlot.
9 With her casual promiscuity she defiled the land;
she debauched both stone and tree.
10 In spite of all this, her treacherous sister Yehuda
did not return to Me with all her heart,
but with deception,
declares the LORD."

11 The LORD said to me:
"Wayward Israel was more justified
than treacherous Yehuda.
12 Go, proclaim these words to the north, and say:
Return, wayward Israel –
declares the LORD.
I will not frown upon you,
for I am compassionate,
declares the LORD;
I will not bear a grudge forever.
13 Acknowledge your sin,
for you have betrayed the LORD your God.
You scattered your paths, following strangers
under every leafy tree.
You did not heed My voice,
declares the LORD.
14 Return, wayward children,
declares the LORD,
for I am your Master.
I will take you,
one from a city,
two from a family,
and I will bring you back to Zion.
15 I will provide you with shepherds true to My heart
who will shepherd you with wisdom and skill.
16 It will come to pass that you will multiply
and be fruitful in the land.
Then, declares the LORD,
there will no longer be a call for the Ark of the LORD's Covenant.
It will neither enter anyone's mind
nor be remembered
nor be missed;
nor will it be replaced by another.
17 At that time, they will call Jerusalem 'the LORD's throne';

all nations will assemble in the LORD's name in Jerusalem
and will no longer follow
the stubbornness of their evil hearts.

18 "In those days the House of Yehuda will join the House of Israel. They
will come together from the north to the land that I bequeathed to your
ancestors.
19 I had resolved that I would award you a special place among My children
and that I would grant you a precious land,
a glorious heritage for all nations.
I said: 'Call Me "my Father"
and never turn away from Me.'
20 But – as a woman betrays her lover –
so have you, the House of Israel, betrayed Me,
declares the LORD.
21 A clamor is heard from the hilltops,
the tearful supplications of the children of Israel,
for they have perverted their ways,
and they have forgotten the LORD their God.
22 Return, wayward children!
I will heal your waywardness."

Here we are. We come to You,
for You are the LORD our God.
23 In truth, false were the hopes offered by the hills
and the tumult upon the mountains.[12]
In truth, only in the LORD our God
is Israel's salvation.
24 The Shame[13] devoured the efforts of our ancestors
from the time of our youth:
their sheep, their cattle,
their sons, and their daughters.
25 We wallow in our shame;
our disgrace envelops us;
we sinned against the LORD our God,
we and our ancestors.
From the time of our youth until this very day
we did not heed the voice of the LORD our God.

4 1 If you, Israel, return to Me, declares the LORD, I will welcome your return.
If you remove your abominations from My presence, you shall not suffer
2 exile. You will utter oaths – exclaiming "as the LORD lives" truthfully, justly,
and righteously – so that other nations will bless themselves by Him and
come to take pride in Him.

12 | Places where idols were worshipped.

13 | The word "Shame" (*boshet*) is a derogatory substitute for "Baal."

3 For this is what the LORD said to the people of Yehuda and to Jerusalem:
Plow your untilled field well,
and do not sow among thorns.
4 Men of Yehuda and inhabitants of Jerusalem:
Circumcise yourselves before the LORD,
and remove the hardness of your hearts[14]
lest your evil deeds
cause My wrath to spread
like a fire burning out of control.
5 Tell it in Yehuda;
let it be heard in Jerusalem.
Say: "Sound the ram's horn in the land."
Call out loudly and tell one another,
"Let us gather and enter the fortified cities."
6 Raise a flag over Zion.
Take flight;
do not stand still.
I am about to deliver evil from the north –
a terrible destruction.
7 The Lion has come up from his lair.
The Destroyer of Nations has set forth.
He has departed from his place
in order to lay waste to your land.
Your cities will become desolate,
with no inhabitant.
8 For this reason, don sackcloth, lament, and wail,
for the LORD's wrath has not left us.

9 On that day –
declares the LORD –
the king will lose heart; so will the princes;
the priests will be stunned, the prophets stupefied.

10 I said: "Oh, Lord GOD,
in fact You deceived this people and Jerusalem
by telling them that there would be peace for them,
but the sword has reached the throat."

11 At that time it will be told to this people and to Jerusalem
that a desiccating wind will come from hill and desert
on the way to my people.
It will come neither to winnow nor to cleanse.
12 A wind so forceful will come upon us
that now,[15] I too will rebuke them harshly:
13 Behold, He rises like the clouds,

14 | Cf. Deuteronomy 10:16.

15 | That is, even before the wind has come.

His chariots like the whirlwind;
His steeds are swifter than eagles.
Woe to us, for we have been despoiled.
14 Jerusalem: Cleanse your heart from evil
so that you will be saved.
How long will your schemes of corruption
abide in you?
15 For a voice proclaims from Dan;
it announces misfortune from the Efrayim hills:
16 Let the nations be informed;
let it be announced about Jerusalem:
Besiegers are approaching from a distant land.
They have sounded their voices throughout the cities of Yehuda.
17 Like watchmen around the fields,
so have they encircled her
because she has rebelled against Me,
declares the Lord.
18 Your path and your deeds have done this to you.
This is your punishment so bitter.
It has touched your very heart.

19 My innards, my innards quake,
as do the chambers of my heart.
My heart pounds;
I cannot silence it,
for my soul has heard the call of the ram's horn,
the signal of war.
20 Destruction upon destruction has transpired.
The entire land has been despoiled.
Suddenly, my tents have been despoiled;
and so, in an instant, have my tent curtains.
21 How much longer will I see the flag[16]
and hear the call of the ram's horn?

22 For My nation is a fool;
they do not know Me.
They are stupid children;
they are not intelligent.
They are clever at doing evil,
but to do good?
That they do not know.
23 I gazed at the land –
it was void and desolate;[17]
and at the heavens,

16 | The flag of war.
17 | Cf. Genesis 1:2.

but gone was their light.
24 I gazed at the mountains –
they were shaking;
all the hills were aquiver.
25 I gazed, and behold:
mankind was gone.
All the birds of the skies had flown away.
26 I gazed, and behold:
the Carmel was the wilderness;
all its cities were torn down before the LORD,
before His fiery wrath.

27 This is what the LORD has said:
The entire land will be desolate,
but I will not completely eradicate it.
28 For this shall the land be ruined
and the heavens above darkened,
for I have declared My intentions;
I have not come to regret them,
nor will I retract them.
29 The entire city flees
from the sound of the horseman and the archer.
They have gone to the thick forests;
they climbed the cliffs.
The entire city is abandoned;
no man dwells there.
30 And you, despoiled one, what will you do?
Will you wear scarlet
and bedeck yourself with golden ornaments?
Will you line your eyes with kohl?
You will beautify yourself in vain.
Your lovers have rejected you.
They seek your death.
31 For I hear a voice like that of a sick person,
anguish like a woman delivering her firstborn.
It is the sound of Zion's daughter,
gasping and spreading her palms:
"Woe is me;
my soul is exhausted by these murderers."

5 1 Roam the streets of Jerusalem;
look about and determine;
search in her squares.
If you find a man,
if there is anyone who upholds justice,
who seeks faithfulness,

then I will forgive her.
2 Even those who exclaim, "As the LORD lives,"
do so in order to swear falsely.
3 LORD, Your eyes seek faithfulness.[18]
You struck them, but they were not pained.
You consumed them, yet they failed to take instruction.
They stiffened their faces harder than rock.
They refused to return.
4 I said to myself,
"These are but lowly folk.
They are foolish.
They know not the way of the LORD,
the Law of their God.
5 Instead, let me go to great men
and speak to them.
They surely know the way of the LORD,
the Law of their God."
But they too broke the yoke
and ripped apart what bound them.
6 Therefore the lion from the forest has mauled them;
the wolf of the plains will despoil them;
the leopard lies in wait over their cities.
Whoever escapes will be torn apart.
For their sins have been numerous,
and mighty have been their wayward acts.
7 How then can I forgive you?
Your children have abandoned Me.
They swear by non-gods.
I fed them well,
but they turned adulterous.
They trooped together to the harlot's house.
8 Like well-fed horses they awaken;
each has reveled with his neighbor's wife.
9 Should I not hold such people to account?
declares the LORD.
From a nation such as this
should I not exact retribution?

10 Climb the rows of her vineyards and do damage,
but do not totally destroy them.
Remove their spreading vines,
for they are no longer the LORD's.
11 For the House of Israel and the House of Yehuda
have utterly betrayed Me,

18 | Meaning honest people who will accept rebuke.

declares the Lord.

12 They have denied the Lord and said,
"He is nothing.
No harm will befall us;
we shall see neither sword nor famine.
13 The prophets shall be but wind;
the Word is not in them.
May what they prophesy be done to them."

14 Therefore, so says the Lord, God of Hosts:
Because you have said such words,
I will convert My words into fire in your mouth.
This people will be as kindling wood,
and it will consume them.
15 I will bring upon them, the House of Israel,
a nation from afar,
declares the Lord,
a powerful nation, an ancient nation,
a nation whose language you will not know[19]
and whose speech you will not understand.
16 His quiver is like an open grave.
They are all warriors.
17 He will devour your harvest and your bread;
they will devour your sons and daughters.
He will devour your flocks and your herds,
your vine and your fig tree.
He will devastate your fortress cities –
those in which you place such confidence –
by the sword.
18 Yet even in those days,
declares the Lord,
I will not make a full end of you.
19 And if you will ask, "For what reason
did the Lord our God do all this to us?"
Then you shall say to them
that just as you have abandoned Me
and worshipped alien gods in your land,
so shall you worship strangers
in a land which is not yours.

20 Proclaim this in the House of Yaakov,
and let it be heard in Yehuda:
21 Listen well to this,
stupid people without heart,

19 | Cf. Deuteronomy 28:49.

who have eyes but do not see
and ears but do not hear.
22 Me you will not fear?
declares the Lord.
Will you not tremble before Me,
who set the sand as a boundary to the sea,
an eternal boundary that it cannot pass?
The waters may rage,
but they are impotent;
the waves may roar,
but they cannot pass over it.
23 This people had a wayward and rebellious heart;
they turned aside and went their way,
24 and they did not say in their hearts,
"Let us revere the Lord our God
who has given us rain,
early and late, in the proper time,
who protects for us the weeks reserved for harvest."
25 Your sins have ended these things;
your transgressions have withheld the good from you.
26 For among My people wicked men are to be found.
They watch for the trap to come down;
they set up an ambush in order to catch men.
27 Like a cage full of fowl,
so are their homes full of deceit.
That is how they have grown great and become wealthy.
28 They have become fat and sleek.
They have surpassed the deeds of the wicked.
They have not judged justly,
even on behalf of the orphan,
and yet they prosper.
They did not judge the case of the poor.
29 Should I not hold such people to account?
declares the Lord.
Against a nation such as this
should I not avenge Myself?

30 An astonishing and ugly thing
has happened in the land.
31 The prophets prophesy falsehood;
the priests govern at their direction.
My people love it that way.
What will you do when it all ends?
6 1 Take refuge, Benjaminites,
out of the midst of Jerusalem;

in Tekoa, blow the ram's horn;[20]
above Beit HaKerem, raise a signal,
for evil looms from the north,
a great disaster.
2 I once likened you to a beautiful
and delicate woman, daughter Zion.
3 But now shepherds and their flocks approach her.
Against her they pitch their tents roundabout.
They graze, each in his place.
4 "Prepare for war against her.
Rise and let us go up at noon."
But woe to us – the day is departing.
The shadows of evening are growing long.
5 "Rise and let us go up at night.
Let us destroy her palaces."

6 For this is what the Lord of Hosts said:
Cut down trees,
cast up a siege ramp against Jerusalem,
for she is a city called to account,
ridden with oppression.
7 As a well flows with its water,
so does her wickedness flow.
Violence and plunder are heard within her.
Before Me constantly are sickness and suffering.
8 Correct yourself, Jerusalem,
lest My favor be withdrawn from you,
lest I render you desolate,
a land never inhabited.

9 This is what the Lord of Hosts said:
"Let the remnant of Israel be gleaned
like grapes off the vine.
Bring back your hand again
like a grape picker over his baskets."[21]
10 Whom can I address?
Whom can I forewarn
and expect that they will take heed?
Their ears are closed;
they cannot listen.
The word of the Lord has become a mockery to them.
They want none of it.
11 I am filled with the Lord's wrath
and am too weak to contain it.

---

20 | The city name Tekoa resonates with the Hebrew *tiku* (blow).

21 | The grape harvesters return to the vine to pluck every last grape.

Pour it upon a young child in the outdoors,
upon a group of young men joined together.
Husband and wife will be captured,
as will be the old man and the one full of days.
12 Their houses will be passed on to others,
fields and wives together,
for I will stretch out My hand
against the inhabitants of the land,
declares the Lord.
13 From their smallest to their greatest,
all are greedy for gain.
From prophet to priest,
all commit fraud.
14 They heal My people's brokenness dismissively,
saying, "Peace, peace,"
when there is no peace.
15 Were they ashamed
when they performed abominations?
They showed no shame
and knew no embarrassment;
therefore they will fall along with all who will fall.
When I hold them to account they will falter,
said the Lord.

16 This is what the Lord said:
Stand upon the roads and reflect.
Inquire about the ancient paths.
What is the good way?
Walk in it. You will find tranquility for your souls.
But you said, "We will not walk."
17 I set up watchmen over you:
"Listen to the call of the ram's horn."
But you said, "We will not listen."
18 Therefore, hear, O nations,
and know, O community,
what awaits them.
19 Hear, earth.
I am about to bring evil upon this people,
the fruit of their schemes.
For they did not listen to My words,
and as for My Law,
they rejected it.
20 For what purpose do I need frankincense brought from Sheba
or choice cane from some distant land?
Your burnt offerings are not desirable,

nor do I find pleasure in your sacrifices.
21 Therefore, this is what the LORD said:
I am about to place obstacles before this people
so that fathers and sons will stumble together.
The neighbor and his friend will perish.

22 This is what the LORD said:
A nation is about to come from the land of the north,
a powerful nation,
awakened from the ends of the earth.
23 They will grip both bow and spear.
They are cruel and will have no pity.
Their sound will rage like the sea.
They will ride upon horses,
each equipped to wage war
against you, daughter Zion.
24 We heard word of him,
and our hands weakened.
Distress gripped us:
a writhing, as of a woman giving birth.
25 Do not go out to the field.
Do not wander on the road,
for the enemy has a sword,
and terror is all around.
26 My dear nation,
gird yourself in sackcloth
and roll in the ash.
Mourn as if for an only child,
a bitter lament,
for the despoiler will come upon us suddenly.
27 I have made you a tower of strength for My people,
a fortress.[22]
You will know how to assess their ways.
28 They are all masters of rebellion, talebearers.
They are bronze and iron.
They are all corrupt.[23]
29 The bellows is charred;
the lead has dissolved in fire.
The refiner has refined in vain.
The dross has not been removed.
30 They are called rejected silver,
for the LORD has rejected them.

7 1 The word that came to Yirmeyahu from the LORD:

---

22 | Cf. 1:18.

23 | As metal contains impurities.

2 "Stand at the gate of the House of the LORD
and announce this message there.
Say: Hear the word of the LORD,
all you people of Yehuda who enter these gates
in order to worship the LORD."

3 This is what the LORD of Hosts, the God of Israel, has said:
Rectify your ways and your deeds,
and I shall allow you to dwell in this place.
4 Do not rely upon words of false assurance that say:
This is the Temple of the LORD,
the Temple of the LORD, the Temple of the LORD.[24]
5 For, if you indeed rectify your ways
and your deeds,
if you indeed perform justice
between a man and his fellow,
6 if you do not oppress the stranger, the orphan, and the widow,
if you do not spill innocent blood in this place,
and if you do not pursue alien gods to your detriment,
7 then I shall allow you to dwell in this place,
in the land that I gave to your forefathers
for ever and ever.
8 But here you are, relying upon words of false assurance
that are useless.
9 Will you steal, murder, fornicate,
swear falsely, offer sacrifices to Baal,
and pursue other gods that you have not known,
10 then come and stand before Me in this House,
which is called by My name,
and say, "We are saved,"
so that you might continue to commit all of these abominations?
11 Has this House that is called by My name
become a den of robbers in your eyes?
I myself have observed this,
declares the LORD.
12 But go now to My place which was in Shilo,
where I first made a dwelling for My name.
Observe what I did to it
on account of the wickedness of My people Israel.[25]
13 Now, because you have done all these deeds,
declares the LORD,
after I spoke to you repeatedly
and you did not listen,
after I called to you

24 | Meaning that God would never allow His Temple to be destroyed.

25 | See 1 Samuel, chapter 4.

and you did not respond,
14 I will do to this House that is called by My name,
and in which you place your trust,
and to the place that I gave to you and to your forefathers,
just as I did to Shilo.
15 I will cast you from My presence
just as I cast away all of your brothers,
all the seed of Efrayim.[26]

16 As for you, do not pray for this people,
do not raise a cry or a plea on their behalf,
and do not beseech Me,
for I will not listen to you.
17 Do you not see what they are doing in the cities of Yehuda
and in the streets of Jerusalem?
18 The children gather kindling wood,
the fathers ignite the fire,
and the women knead the dough
to bake cakes to the queen of the heavens.[27]
They pour libations to alien gods
in order to anger Me.
19 Is it Me that they anger?
demands the Lord.
Is it not themselves whom they harm,
bringing shame upon themselves?

20 Therefore, so said the Lord God:
My wrath and My fury are about to be poured out
upon this place,
upon man and beast,
upon the trees of the field
and the fruit of the earth.
It shall burn and not be extinguished.

21 This is what the Lord of Hosts, the God of Israel, said:
Heap your burnt offerings upon your other sacrifices
and eat the meat.
22 For when I brought your forefathers out of Egypt, I did not speak to them,
Nor did I command them
about matters of burnt offerings and sacrifices.
23 Rather, this is what I commanded them:
Heed my voice
so that I will be your God
and you will be My people.

26 | That is, the exiled Ten Tribes.

27 | A foreign deity (see also ch. 44).

Walk in all the ways as I will command you
so that it will be good for you.
24 But they did not listen,
nor even bend an ear.
They followed their own counsel,
their stubborn, wicked hearts.
They went backward, not forward.
25 From the day your forefathers left the land of Egypt
until this very day,
I sent to them all of My servants, the prophets –
early every day, and persistently.
26 But they did not listen to Me,
nor even bend an ear.
They stiffened their necks.
They did worse than their fathers.
27 You will speak all these words to them,
but they will not hear you.
You will call to them,
but they will not answer you.
28 You shall say to them:
"This is the nation that did not obey the voice of the LORD its God
and that did not accept correction.
Gone is faithfulness,
severed from their mouths."

29 Shear your hair and throw it away.
Raise a lament upon the high places,
for the LORD has despised
and has abandoned
the generation that enraged Him.

30 For the children of Yehuda have done evil in My eyes,
declares the LORD.
They have placed their vile objects in the House which is called by My name, thereby defiling it.
31 They have built the altars of Tofet, which are in the Valley of Ben Hinom,[28]
to burn their sons and daughters in fire,
something that I did not command
and that never entered My mind.

32 Therefore, days are fast approaching,
declares the LORD,
when men will no longer speak of "Tofet" and "Valley of Ben Hinom"
but rather of "Valley of Slaughter."
They will bury in Tofet

28 | The valley bounding Jerusalem to the west.

for lack of space elsewhere.
33 The carcasses of this people will become food
for the birds of the heavens
and the beasts of the earth,
and none will frighten them away.
34 I will silence from the cities of Yehuda
and the streets of Jerusalem
the sound of joy and the sound of happiness,
the voice of the groom and the voice of the bride,
for the land shall come to ruin.

8 1 At that time, declares the LORD,
they will remove the bones of the kings of Yehuda
and the bones of its princes,
the bones of the priests,
and the bones of the prophets,
and the bones of the inhabitants of Jerusalem
from their graves.
2 They will spread them beneath the sun, the moon,
and all the host of heaven that they loved,
and that they served,
after which they followed,
and which they sought,
and to which they bowed.
They will neither be collected nor reburied
but shall remain as dung upon the face of the earth.
3 Death will be preferable to life
for all the surviving remnant of this evil clan
in all the other places to which I have expelled them,
declares the LORD of Hosts.

4 Say to them: This is what the LORD said:
Did they ever fall
and not rise again?
Whenever they returned,
did He not return?
5 Why, then, do these people, Jerusalem,
rebel in an everlasting rebellion?
They hold fast to deceit.
They refuse to return.
6 I listened carefully, and I understood.
They do not speak properly.
No one regrets his misdeed
and says, "What have I done?"
They all persist in their course
like a horse plunging headlong into battle.
7 Even the stork in the sky knows its seasons;

the turtledove, the swallow, and the crane
know their time of arrival.
Yet my people do not know the judgment of the LORD.
8 How dare you assert, "We are wise;
with us is the LORD's teaching.
For naught was the pen fashioned,
and for naught is the scribes' rebuke"!
9 The wise men are put to shame,
broken and ensnared.
They have rejected the word of the LORD.
Theirs is an empty wisdom.
10 Therefore, I will give their wives over to others,
their fields to dispossessors.
From small to great,
all are greedy for gain.
From prophet to priest,
all commit fraud.[29]
11 They wish to heal my people's brokenness with ease,
saying, "Peace, peace,"
when there is no peace.
12 Were they ashamed when they performed abominations?
They showed no shame
and knew no embarrassment.
Therefore, they will fall
along with all who will fall.
When I hold them to account they will falter,
said the LORD.

13 I will eradicate them thoroughly,
declares the LORD.
No grapes on the vine.
No figs on the fig tree.
Even the leaf is withered.
That which I gave them will pass them by.
14 For what purpose do we sit still?
Assemble, and let us approach the fortress cities
and sit silently there.
The LORD our God has silenced us
and given us poisonous water to drink,
for we have sinned against the LORD.
15 We hope for peace,
but no good awaits us;
for a time of healing,
but instead – horror.

29 | Cf. 6:12–15.

16 From Dan[30] the snorting of his horses can be heard.
The entire land shudders from the neighing of his steeds.
They have come and have devoured the land and its bounty,
the city and its inhabitants.

17 I am about to let loose upon you snakes,
vipers against which there is no charm,
and they will bite you,
declares the Lord.

18 Though I struggle to contain my torment,
my heart is overwhelmed by woe.
19 Behold the sound of my people's cry from a distant land.
"Is the Lord no longer in Zion?
Is her King no longer there?"
"Why have they angered Me with their idols,
with their alien vanities?"
20 The harvest is over.
The summer is gone,
but we have not been saved.
21 Because of the collapse of my precious people,
I have collapsed.
I am despondent.
Desolation has possessed me.
22 Is there no balm in Gilad?[31]
Is there no healer there?
Why then has there not arisen a cure
for my precious people?

23 If only my head were water
and my eye a fountain of tears,
then I would weep day and night
for the slain of my precious people.
9 1 If only I were granted a wayfarer's lodging in the wilderness,
I would abandon my people and walk away from them,
for they are all adulterers,
a band of traitors.
2 They have drawn their tongue,
their bow is falsehood.
Not for faithfulness have they become powerful in the land.
From evil to evil they have advanced,
but Me they did not know,
declares the Lord.
3 Let each man be on guard against his fellow,
and let no one trust his own brother,

30 | In the north of Israel. The enemy would come from the north.

31 | Gilad was known for this substance (see, e.g., 46:11; Genesis 37:25).

for every brother acts deceitfully,
and every friend spreads slander.
4 Each man defrauds his fellow
and speaks untruth;
they have trained their tongues to speak lies.
They weary themselves with perversions.
5 You dwell in the midst of deceit.
In deceit they have refused to know Me –
declares the LORD.

6 Therefore, thus said the LORD of Hosts:
I am about to smelt them and test them,[32]
for what else can I do
on behalf of My precious people?
7 Their tongue is a sharpened arrow,
speaking deceit.
One speaks peaceably to another
but secretly plots an ambush.
8 Should I not hold them to account for these things?
demands the LORD.
For a nation such as this,
should I not exact retribution?

9 Over the mountains I will raise a cry and a wail,
and over pastures in the wilderness I will lament.
For they have been laid waste with not even a passerby.
The sound of cattle is no longer to be heard.
From the bird in the sky to the beast,
all have wandered, all are gone.
10 I will reduce Jerusalem to piles of rubble,
a dwelling place for jackals.
I will make the towns of Yehuda desolate,
with no inhabitant.

11 Every wise man knows this.
Let all to whom the LORD has spoken confirm it:
Why has the land been destroyed,
laid waste like a wilderness with no passerby?

12 The LORD said:
For they abandoned the teaching that I gave them.
They did not heed Me,
nor did they follow it.
13 Instead they followed the waywardness of their hearts
and the Be'alim, as their fathers taught them.
14 Therefore, thus said the LORD of Hosts,
the God of Israel:

32 | As metal is tested for quality after smelting.

"I am about to feed this people wormwood
and give them poisoned water to drink.
15 I will scatter them among nations
that neither they nor their ancestors ever knew.
I will send the sword after them
until I finish them off."
16 Thus said the Lord of Hosts:
Consider, then summon dirge singers
and let them come,
and send for skilled women[33]
and let them come.
17 Let them hurry and sound a wailing for us
so that our eyes shed tears
and our pupils drip water.
18 For the sound of wailing has been heard in Zion:
how we have been despoiled!
We are put to shame,
for we have left the land,
and they have cast down our dwellings.

19 Women, hear the word of the Lord,
and let your ears absorb the word of His mouth.
Teach your daughters wailing
and one another lamentation.
20 For death has climbed into our windows,
arrived in our palaces,
to cut down babes from the outdoors
and youth from the town squares.
21 "Speak!" Thus declares the Lord:
The carcasses of men will fall
like dung upon the open field,
like sheaves behind the reaper,
with no one to gather them.

22 Thus said the Lord:
Let not the wise man boast of his wisdom.
Let not the mighty man boast of his might.
Let not the wealthy boast of his wealth.
23 Someone may boast only
of his conscious devotion to Me,
for I the Lord act
with loving-kindness, justice, and righteousness in the world.
For it is these things that I desire,
declares the Lord.

24 Days are coming, declares the Lord, when I will call to account all

33 | Skilled in singing or composing dirges.

25 those who are circumcised only in foreskin:[34] Egypt, Yehuda, Edom, the
Amonites, Moav, and all whose hair is shaven at the temples, who dwell
in the wilderness. For all these nations are uncircumcised, but all of the
House of Israel is uncircumcised at heart.

10 1 Listen to the word that the LORD has spoken concerning you, House of
Israel.

2 This is what the LORD said:
Do not learn the ways of the nations;
do not fear heavenly portents,
even if the nations fear them,
3 for the laws of the nations are delusions.
It[35] is cut from a tree in the forest;
it is the handiwork of a craftsman with a chisel.
4 He embellishes it with silver and gold.
He fastens it with nails and hammers
so that it does not totter.
5 They are like a scarecrow in a cucumber patch;
they do not speak.
They must be carried,
for they cannot walk.
Do not fear them, for they can do no harm.
Neither is doing good in their capacity.

6 LORD, there is none like You –
You are great, and Your name is great in strength.
7 Who would not fear You, King of the nations?
For it befits You.
For among all the wise of the nations,
and among all their kingdoms,
there is none like You.
8 All together they are senseless and foolish.
Their code of conduct is a delusion
made of wood.
9 Beaten silver is brought from Tarshish,
and gold from Ufaz,
work of a craftsman and of a goldsmith's hands,
bedecked with blue and purple:
all the labor of skilled men.
10 But the LORD God is true.
He is the living God, the eternal King.
At His wrath the earth trembles.
Nations cannot endure His fury.

11 "This is what you must say to them:

34 | That is, whose hearts are not "circumcised" (cf. Deut. 10:16).

35 | Their god.

A god who did not create heaven and earth
shall perish from the earth
and from under these heavens."[36]

12 He makes the earth by His power,
establishes the world by His wisdom,
and stretches out the heavens by His understanding.
13 As He makes His voice heard,
there is rumbling water in the heavens,
and He raises clouds from the end of the earth.
He makes lightning bolts with the rain
and brings out wind from His storehouses.[37]
14 All humans are foolish,
without knowledge.
Every goldsmith is disappointed in his idol;
his molten image is a sham.
No breath animates them.
15 They are delusions,
works of mockery.
When they are called to account, they will perish.
16 Not like these is the portion of Yaakov,
for He formed all things.
Israel is the tribe He possesses.
Lord of Hosts is His name.

17 Gather your wares in from the land,
you who dwell under siege.

18 For thus said the Lord:
This time I will fling away those who dwell in the land
and confine them to close quarters
so that they can easily be found.

19 Woe unto me for my collapse.
My wound is severe.
I once thought:
This is my affliction; I can bear it.
20 My tent is despoiled;
all its cords are severed.
My children have left me;
they are gone.
There is no longer anyone to stretch out my tent,
no one to hang up my curtains.
21 For the shepherds became foolish.
They did not seek out the Lord;

36 | This verse is in Aramaic. It is perhaps a message from Yirmeyahu to the exiles in Babylon, whose spoken language was Aramaic.

37 | Cf. Psalms 135:7.

therefore, they did not succeed,
and all their flocks have scattered.

22 Hark! What we heard is now approaching,
a great commotion from a northern land
to render the cities of Yehuda desolate,
a dwelling place for jackals.

23 LORD,
I know that man does not determine his path.
No man who walks controls his footsteps.
24 LORD,
discipline me, but with justice,
not with Your wrath, lest You reduce me to nothing.
25 Pour out Your fury on the nations that do not know You
on those clans that do not invoke Your name,
for they have devoured Yaakov,
devoured him and finished him off
and laid his homeland waste.[1]

11 1 The word which came to Yirmeyahu from the LORD:

2 "Hear the terms of this covenant and speak to the men of Yehuda and to
3 those who dwell in Jerusalem. Say to them: This is what the LORD, God
of Israel, has said: Cursed is the man who shall not heed the words of this
4 covenant, which I commanded your fathers to keep at the time I delivered
them from the land of Egypt, the iron furnace, when I told them, 'Heed
My voice, and perform them exactly as I commanded you. Then you will
5 be My people, and I will be your God in order to uphold the oath which
I swore to your fathers, to give them a land flowing with milk and with
honey as at this day.'"

I responded and said: "Amen, LORD."

6 The LORD said to me, "Proclaim all these words in the cities of Yehuda and
in the streets of Jerusalem: Heed the terms of this covenant and perform
7 them. For I have forewarned your fathers from the day I raised them up
out of Egypt until this very day, consistently admonishing them: 'Heed
8 My voice!' But they did not listen, they did not even bend an ear. They
followed the stubbornness of their evil hearts, so I brought over them the
terms of this covenant, which I commanded them to follow, but they did
not follow."

9 The LORD said to me, "A conspiracy is to be found among the men of
10 Yehuda and the inhabitants of Jerusalem. They have returned to the sins
of their forefathers, who refused to heed My words. They followed other
gods and worshipped them. The House of Israel and the House of Yehuda
have broken My covenant that I made with their fathers."

1 | Cf. Psalms 79:6–7.

11 This is what the LORD therefore said: "I am about to bring upon them a disaster
from which they will not be able to extricate themselves. They will cry out to
12 Me, but I will pay them no heed. The cities of Yehuda and the inhabitants of
Jerusalem will then go and cry out to the gods to whom they offer sacrifices.
13 But they will certainly not save them in the time of their disaster. For your gods
have been equal to the number of your cities, Yehuda, and the altars you erected
to Shame[2] are as many as the streets of Jerusalem – altars upon which to offer
sacrifices to the Baal.

14 "As for you, do not pray on behalf of this people, and do not raise on their
behalf a song or a prayer, for I will not pay heed at the time they call out
to Me on account of their disaster."

15 For what purpose does My dear one come to My House?
Is it to perform her many sinful schemes?
Will sacral flesh absolve you?
For when you do evil, that is when you rejoice!
16 A verdant olive tree –
beautiful, with lovely fruit –
the LORD did call your name.
To the sound of a great roar
He has set fire to her
and crushed her branches.
17 The LORD of Hosts, who planted you, has spoken evil against you on
account of the evil that the House of Israel and the House of Yehuda have
done to themselves, angering Me by burning offerings to the Baal.

18 The LORD informed me, and so I knew.
Then You showed me their actions.
19 I was like a choice lamb led to slaughter.
I did not know that they plotted schemes against me:
"Let us poison his bread with a poisonous plant
and cut him off from the land of the living.
Let his name be mentioned no longer."
20 The LORD of Hosts is a righteous judge;
He discerns both mind and heart.
I will yet witness Your vengeance upon them,
for to You I have disclosed my disputes.

21 This is what the LORD therefore said concerning the men of Anatot who
seek your life, demanding, "You shall not prophesy in the name of the
22 LORD so that you will not die by our hand." This is what the LORD of Hosts
therefore said: I am about to hold them to account: the young men will die
23 by the sword; their sons and their daughters will die by famine. There will
be no remnant of them, for I will bring a disaster upon the men of Anatot
during the year of their retribution.

2 | See note on 3:24.

12 1 You are in the right, Lord, when I dispute with You.
Nevertheless, I will express my arguments with You:
Why does the way of the wicked prosper?
And why does every faithless traitor live securely?
2 You have planted them, and they have taken root.
They have even gone on to bear fruit.
You are near in their mouths
but distant from their inner thoughts.
3 You, Lord, know me. You see me;
You have discerned that my heart is with You.
Drive them out like sheep to the slaughter
and assign them to the day of slaying.

4 How long must the land mourn
and the grass of every field wither?
Must beasts and birds perish
because of the evil of those who dwell there,
who say, "He does not see our future"?

5 You ran with foot runners, and they exhausted you;
how do you presume to compete with horses?
In a peaceful land you were confident,
but how will you fare in the depths of the Jordan?
6 For even your brothers and your father's house,
even they have betrayed you.
Even they have summoned a mob against you.
Do not trust them when they speak well of you.

7 I have abandoned My House;
I have deserted My heritage.
I have given over My dear beloved
into the hands of her enemies.
8 My heritage has become for Me
like a lion in the forest.
She raised her cry toward Me;
therefore I despised her.
9 Has My heritage become like a bloodied bird of prey,
like a bird of prey with all circling around her?
Go and gather all the beasts of the field;
let them come and eat their fill.
10 Many shepherds have destroyed My vineyard,
trampled My portion,
turned My precious portion
into a desolate wasteland.
11 It has been rendered a desolation;
the desolate one pins her grief on Me.

The entire land has become desolate
yet no one takes it to heart.
12 The despoilers have come upon
every hilltop in the wilderness,
for the LORD's sword devours
from one end of the earth to the other.
There is no peace for anyone.
13 They have sown wheat,
and they have reaped thorns.
They suffered pain to no avail.
Be ashamed of your harvests
because of the burning wrath of the LORD.

14 This is what the LORD said: As for all My evil neighbors who have harmed
the heritage that I bequeathed to My people Israel, I am about to uproot
them from their land, and I will uproot the House of Yehuda from among
15 them. Then, after I have uprooted them, I will again show them compassion,
16 and I will return them, each to his heritage and each to his land. Then, if
they study well the ways of My people, to swear by My name, "As the
LORD lives," just as they taught My people to swear by Baal, then they
17 will flourish together with My people. But if they will not take heed, then
I will uproot that nation, uproot it and destroy it, declares the LORD.

13 1 This is what the LORD said: "Go and purchase a linen loincloth and place
it on your loins. Do not bring it into water."

2 I purchased the loincloth as the LORD instructed, and I placed it on my
loins.

3 4 The word of the LORD came to me a second time, saying, "Take the
loincloth that you purchased, that is on your loins, and get up and go to
Perat,[3] and hide it there in the crevice of a rock."

5 I went and hid it at Perat, just as the LORD commanded me.

6 After many days the LORD said to me, "Get up and go to Perat and remove
from there the loincloth that I commanded you to hide there."

7 I went to Perat and dug up the loincloth from the place where I had hidden
it, and behold, the loincloth was ruined, good for nothing.

8 The word of the LORD came to me.

9 This is what the LORD said: "Thus shall I bring ruin to the pride of Yehuda
10 and the great pride of Jerusalem. This evil people who refuse to heed
My words, who follow their own stubborn hearts, who have gone after
other gods and serve them and worship them, shall become like this
11 loincloth – good for nothing. For just as a loincloth clings to a man's loins,

3 | This likely refers to Wadi Kelt, located in the hills east of Jerusalem and Yirmeyahu's hometown of Anatot, rather than the Euphrates River.

so have I made all the House of Israel and all the House of Yehuda cling to
Me," declares the LORD, "to become My people for fame, praise, and glory.
But they would not take heed.

12 "Say to them this word: This is what the LORD, God of Israel, has said:
Every jug shall be filled with wine. When they respond, 'Do we not know
13 that every jug should be filled with wine?' say to them: This is what the
LORD has said: I am about to fill with drunkenness all who dwell in this
land, and the kings who sit upon David's throne, and the priests and the
14 prophets, and all who dwell in Jerusalem. I will smash them, each man
against his brother, fathers and sons together, declares the LORD; I will
neither pity nor show mercy nor spare them from ruin."

15 Take heed, listen, and be not haughty,
for the LORD has spoken.
16 Give honor to the LORD your God
before He brings darkness,
before your feet stumble upon the mountains of the night.
You will hope for light,
but He will make it deathly dark
and turn it into thick cloud.
17 If you will not take heed,
my soul will secretly weep
because of your pride;
my eyes will well up and drop tears,
for the LORD's flock is held captive.

18 Say to the king and to the queen mother:
Be humbled, be seated,
for your headpiece has come down,
the crown of your glory.
19 The cities of the south are enclosed;
there is no one to open them.
All of Yehuda has been exiled,
exiled completely.

20 Lift your eyes and see
those who approach from the north.
Where is the flock that you were given,
the sheep in which you took such pride?
21 What will you say when he holds you to account?
You taught them to rule over you like princes.
Will not pangs of pain grip you
like a woman in childbirth?
22 And when you say to yourselves,
"Why has all this happened to me?"
It is because of your many sins

that your skirts are exposed,
your heels laid bare.

23 Can the Kushite change his skin?
Or the leopard its spots?
Neither will you be able to do good,
so accustomed you are to doing evil.
24 I will scatter them like straw that tumbles
before the desert wind.
25 This is your lot,
your measure meted out by Me,
declares the LORD,
because you forgot Me
and trusted in falsehood.
26 I too will lift your skirts upon your face,
and your shame will be seen,
27 your adulteries and your loud orgies,
the lewdness of your harlotry;
on the hills in the fields
I saw your abominations.
Woe to you, Jerusalem.
If you will not become pure after all this,
when, then?

14 1 The word of the LORD came to Yirmeyahu
concerning the matter of the droughts:
2 Yehuda is aggrieved,
her gates weakened,
her inhabitants bent to the earth;
Jerusalem's screams rose.
3 The master shepherds sent their apprentices for water.
They came to the water holes but did not find water.
They returned with their vessels empty.
They were humiliated and ashamed,
and they covered their heads.[4]
4 Because the earth was parched,
for there had been no rain in the land,
the farmers were humiliated.
They covered their heads.
5 Indeed, even the hind in the field gives birth
but abandons its young because there is no grass.
6 The wild asses stand upon the heights
panting as jackals do.
Their eyes fail
because there is no vegetation.

4 | As was the custom of mourners.

7 If our sins testify against us –
then, LORD, act on behalf of Your name.
Our rebellious deeds are many.
We have sinned against You.
8 Hope of Israel,
its redeemer in times of trouble,
why be like a stranger in the land,
like a guest who stops by for a night?
9 Why be like a man taken by surprise,
like a warrior who cannot help?
You are in our midst, O LORD,
and we are called by Your name.
Do not desert us.

10 This is what the LORD said concerning this people: "Just as they love to
wander and never restrained their feet, so too does the LORD not accept
them. Now He will remember their transgressions and hold them to
account for their sins."

11 The LORD said to me:
"Do not pray for the benefit of this people.
12 When they fast,
I will not hear their cry;
if they offer a burnt offering or a grain offering
I will not accept them,
for I will finish them off
by the sword and by famine and by plague."

13 I protested, "Wait, Lord GOD! The prophets say to them: 'You shall not
see the sword, and no famine shall befall you, but I will grant you true
peace in this place.'"

14 The LORD said to me:
"These prophets prophesy falsehood in My name.
I did not send them, I did not command them,
and I did not speak to them.
A false vision, sorcery,
idolatry, and the fraudulence of their hearts –
that is what they prophesy to you."

15 This is what the LORD therefore said: "About the prophets who prophesy
in My name although I have not sent them, those who say, 'There will be
neither sword nor famine in this land,' those very prophets shall perish by
16 sword and famine. And the people to whom they prophesy will be thrown
about the streets of Jerusalem as a consequence of famine and the sword,
with no one to bury them: not them, nor their wives, nor their sons or
daughters. I will pour out their evil upon them.

17 "This is what you should say to them:
Let my eyes flow with tears
night and day and not cease,
for the maiden daughter, my people
has suffered a great collapse,
a most painful wound.
18 If I went out to the field,
those slain by the sword were there.
If I entered the city,
those struck ill by famine were there.
For even the priest and the prophet circle about a land
that they do not know."

19 Have You totally rejected Yehuda?
Have You become disgusted with Zion?
Why did You strike us
so that we have no cure?
We hope for peace,
but no good awaits us;
for a time of healing,
but instead – horror.
20 LORD, we acknowledge our wickedness
and the iniquity of our fathers,
for we have sinned against You.
21 Do not spurn us for Your name's sake.
Do not dishonor the throne of Your glory.
Remember, do not annul Your covenant with us.
22 Are there among the false gods of the nations any that give rain?
Do the heavens give showers by themselves?
It is You, the LORD our God,
so we place our hope in You,
for it is You who made all these things.

15 1 The LORD then said to me,

"Even if Moshe and Shmuel were to stand before Me, I would not show favor to this people. Send them away from My presence, and let them depart.

2 "Should they then say to you, 'Where shall we go?'
tell them that this is what the LORD said:
Those destined for death, to death;
for the sword, to the sword;
for hunger, to hunger;
and for captivity, to captivity.
3 I will appoint four families over them,
declares the LORD:

the sword to slay,
the dogs to drag away,
the birds of the sky
and the beasts of the earth
to devour and to destroy.
4 I shall make them an object of horror
for all the kingdoms of the earth
on account of Menashe the son of Ḥizkiyahu, king of Yehuda,
because of what he did in Jerusalem.[5]

5 "For who will have pity upon you, Jerusalem?
Who will console you?
Who will turn aside to inquire
about your well-being?
6 You abandoned Me," declares the LORD.
"You went backward.
I stretched out My hand against you and destroyed you.
I had become tired of relenting.
7 I will scatter them with a winnowing fork
to all the cities of the world.
I, bereaved, I destroyed My people.
They did not repent of their ways.
8 Their widows are more numerous to Me
than the sand of the seas.
I brought down upon mother and young lad
a marauder at noon.
I cast down upon them, suddenly,
anguish and horrors.
9 Diminished is she who gave birth to seven.
Her spirit is weakened.
Her sun set while it was yet day.
She is shamed and humiliated.
I will deliver their remnant to the sword,
to their enemies,"
declares the LORD.

10 Woe is me, my mother, that you gave birth to me –
a contentious man,
a quarrelsome man,
throughout the whole land.
I have no claims on anyone,
nor do they have claims on me.
Yet they all curse me.

11 The LORD responded:

5 | See II Kings 21:1–16.

"I swear that I will yet spare you for good,
and I swear that I will cause the enemy to appeal to you
in the time of evil and the time of distress.
12 Can iron shatter northern iron
reinforced with bronze?
13 I will turn your wealth and your treasure
into booty with no compensation
because of all your sins in all your territories.
14 I will bring you with your enemies
into a land you never knew,
for a fire is kindled in My nostrils,
blazing against you."

15 LORD, You know.
Remember me, take me into account.
Take revenge for me upon my pursuers.
Do not be overly patient in taking up my cause.
Know that I have borne humiliation
for Your sake.
16 Your words were found, and I devoured them.
Your word was for me a joy
and a source of happiness for my heart,
for I have been called by Your name,
O LORD, God of Hosts.
17 I never sat among a band of revelers
and made merry.
Because of Your hand,[6] I sat alone,
for You have filled me with a prophecy of wrath.
18 Why has my pain become endless
and my wound incurable,
refusing to heal?
You have become for me a deceptive stream,
waters that cannot be trusted.

19 Therefore, this is what the LORD said:
"If you return I will take you back,
and you will stand before Me.
If you will extract preciousness from rubbish,
you will have done as I decreed.
But let them return to you,
and do not allow yourselves to return to them.
20 Against these people I will make you
like a fortified bronze wall.
They will wage battle against you,
but they shall not prevail,

6 | Meaning God's prophecy, or perhaps God's wrath.

for I am with you to deliver you and rescue you,"
declares the LORD.[7]
21 "I will rescue you from the hands of the evil ones
and redeem you from the grasp of the violent."

16 1 The LORD's word came to me: "Do not take a wife, so that you will have
2 no sons or daughters in this place.

3 "For this is what the LORD said of sons and daughters born in this place
and of their mothers who bear them
and of their fathers who beget them in this land:
4 They will die of deadly diseases.
They will not be eulogized
and they will not be buried.
They will be like dung on the face of the earth.
They will be annihilated by the sword and by famine.
Their corpses will be food for the birds of the sky
and for the beasts of the earth.

5 "For this is what the LORD said:
Do not enter the house of funeral feasting,
do not go to eulogize,
and do not lament for them,
for I have withdrawn My peace
from this people,
declares the LORD,
My kindness and compassion.
6 Great and small alike will perish in this land
and not be buried.
There will be no eulogies for them,
no slashing,
no hair torn out for them.
7 No one will break bread for a mourner
to comfort them over the dead.
No one will offer to drink with them a cup of consolation
for father or for mother.
8 Do not enter the festival hall
to sit with them to eat and to drink.

9 "For this is what the LORD of Hosts, the God of Israel, said:
I am about to banish from this place,
before your eyes and in your days,
the sound of joy and the sound of happiness,
the voice of the groom and the voice of the bride.

10 "When you tell all these things to this people and they say to you, 'For
what reason did the LORD pronounce all this great evil over us? What

7 | Cf. 1:18–19.

is our transgression, and what sin have we sinned against the LORD our
11 God?' say to them: It is because your fathers abandoned Me, declares the
LORD. They followed other gods, served them, and worshipped them. They
12 abandoned Me and did not keep My teaching. And you did worse than
your fathers. Each of you pursues the stubbornness of his evil heart so as
13 not to obey Me. I will hurl you out of this land onto a land that neither
you nor your fathers ever knew. There you will serve other gods day and
night, for I will grant you no mercy."

14 Therefore, days are approaching, declares the LORD, when it will no longer
be said, "As the LORD lives who has brought the Israelites up from the land
15 of Egypt," but rather, "As the LORD lives who has brought the Israelites up
from the land of the north and from all the lands to which He had expelled
them"; I will return them to their own soil, which I gave to their fathers.

16 I am about to send for many fishermen,
declares the LORD,
and they will fish for them.
Afterward I will send for many hunters,
and they will hunt them down
from atop every mountain and from atop every hill
and from the crevices in the rocks.
17 For My eyes are upon all their ways;
they are not hidden from My presence,
and their sins are not concealed from before My eyes.
18 I will first exact retribution
for double their transgressions and sins –
for defiling My land
with the carcasses of their repulsive things and their abominations
with which they filled My inheritance.

19 The LORD is my strength and my might,
my refuge in a day of trouble.
To You the nations will come from the ends of the earth,
and they will say:
"Our ancestors inherited nothing but falsehood,
futility, and things of no use.
20 Can a human make gods for himself
when they are not gods?"
21 Therefore, I am about to make them know;
this time I will make them know of My power and My strength,
and they shall come to know that My name is the LORD.

17 1 Yehuda's sin is written with an iron pen
with a diamond point,
engraved upon the tablets of their hearts
and upon the corners of your altars.

2 As they yearn for their children,
so do they for their altars and their sacred trees[8]
beside verdant trees
upon the high hills.
3 Mountain dweller[9] –
because of the sin of your high places
in all your territories,
I will turn your wealth
and all your treasures
into booty upon the field.
4 You will forfeit, by your own fault,
the heritage which I have given you.
I will make you a slave to your enemies
in a land that you never knew,
for you kindled a fire in My nostrils
which shall blaze forever.

5 This is what the LORD said:
Cursed is he who trusts in man,
who makes flesh his strength
and who turns his heart away from the LORD.
6 He will be like a shrub in the desert,
never witnessing prosperity.
He will dwell scorched in the wilderness,
a salty, uninhabited land.

7 Blessed is the person who trusts in the LORD.
The LORD will be his protector.
8 He will be like a tree planted beside the water,
its roots spreading along the stream.
It need not be concerned when heat comes,
for its leaves will remain verdant.
It need not worry in a year of drought,
for it will never cease to produce fruit.
9 More devious is the heart than all else,
and it is hopelessly sick. Who can know it?
10 I, the LORD, search out the heart
and examine inner thoughts
so as to treat each person
according to his ways, according to the fruits of his actions.

11 Like the bird that hatches what she did not lay,
so is he who accumulated his wealth unjustly.
After half of his days, his fortune will leave him,
and in the end he will be proven a fool.

8 | Used in the worship of the goddess Ashera.
9 | Jerusalem is situated in the mountains of Yehuda.

12 Like the throne of glory,
elevated from the beginning,
so is the place of our Temple.
13 The hope of Israel is the LORD.
All who forsake You will be humiliated.
Those who stray from Me will be written in the earth,
for they have forsaken the source of living waters,
declares the LORD.

14 Heal me, LORD, so that I may be healed.
Save me so that I may be saved,
for it is You whom I praise.
15 "See," they say to me,
"where is the LORD's word?
Let it come now!"
16 I did not rush to serve as Your shepherd,
and I did not desire that fateful day.[10]
You know that!
The utterance of my lips was apparent to You.
17 Do not be a source of terror for me;
You are my protection in a day of evil.
18 Let my pursuers be humiliated,
but let me not be humiliated.
Let them be terrified,
but let me not be terrified.
Bring upon them the day of evil
and shatter them repeatedly.

19 This is what the LORD said to me: "Go and stand in the people's gate where
the kings of Yehuda enter and through which they leave, and in all the gates
20 of Jerusalem. Say to them: Listen to the LORD, you kings of Yehuda, and
all of Yehuda, and all the inhabitants of Jerusalem who enter through these
21 gates. This is what the LORD said: Be careful for your lives, and do not carry
any burden on the Sabbath day, nor bring them into the gates of Jerusalem.
22 Do not bring out a burden from your houses on the Sabbath day, perform
no work, and hallow the Sabbath day, as I commanded your fathers."

23 But they did not listen
nor even bend an ear.
They stiffened their necks so as not to listen
and so as not to take instruction.

24 If you obey Me, declares the LORD, so as not to bring any burden through
the gates of this city on the Sabbath day, and you hallow the Sabbath
25 day, so as not to perform any work on it, then through the gates of this
city shall come kings and princes, those sitting upon the throne of David,

10 | When I was called to prophecy.

riding chariots and horses, they and their princes, men of Yehuda and
26 dwellers in Jerusalem, and this city shall dwell forever. They shall come
from the towns of Yehuda and the environs of Jerusalem, from the land of
Binyamin, from the lowland and from the mountain and from the south,
bringing burnt offerings and sacrifices, grain offerings and frankincense,
27 and bearing thanksgiving offerings to the House of the Lord. But if you
do not obey Me to hallow the Sabbath day, so as not to carry in any burden
through the gates of Jerusalem on the Sabbath day, then I will send a fire
against her gates, and it will consume the fortresses of Jerusalem and not
be extinguished.

18 1 2 The word that came to Yirmeyahu from the Lord: "Rise and go down to
the house of the potter; there I will tell you My words."

3 So I went down to the potter's house and found him doing work upon his
4 wheel. Whenever the vessel that he was fashioning of clay would break in
the hands of the potter, he would remake it into a different vessel such as
it pleased the potter to fashion.

5 6 The Lord's word came to me: "Can I not do to you, House of Israel,"
declares the Lord, "what this potter does? Like clay in the hand of the
7 potter, so are you in My hand, House of Israel. At one moment I may
decree that a nation or a kingdom be uprooted, shattered, and destroyed.
8 But should that nation turn back because of the evil that I pronounced
upon it, I change My mind concerning the evil that I had planned to do
9 to it. And at one moment I may decree that a nation or a kingdom be built
10 and planted. But if it does what is evil in My eyes, not heeding My voice, I
change My mind about the good that I had thought to bestow upon it.

11 "Now, tell the men of Yehuda and those who dwell in Jerusalem that this
is what the Lord said: I am about to fashion[11] a disaster for you, and I am
devising a plan against you. Return now, each of you from his evil way, and
12 mend your ways and your actions. But they will say, 'It is futile. We will
follow our own plans, and each of us will do as his evil heart sees fit.'"

13 This is what the Lord therefore said:
"Inquire now among the nations:
Who has heard of such things?
She has committed a terrible scandal,
maiden Israel.
14 Would one forsake the snow from Lebanon
now flowing among the rocks in My field?
Would waters from afar, cold and flowing,
be abandoned?
15 For My people have forgotten Me.
They offer incense to vanity.

11 | Hebrew *yotzer*, which also means "potter" in the preceding verses.

They were made to stumble in their ways
and forsake the ancient paths,
to walk on byways,
on a way not cleared of stones,
16 to make their land a desolation,
a place of perpetual hissing.
Every passerby will gasp
and shake his head.
17 Like the east wind I will scatter them
before the enemy.
I will look upon their neck
and not upon their face
on their fateful day."

18 They said, "Let us devise plans against Yirmeyahu, for surely the Law will
not cease from the priest, nor counsel from the wise man, nor the word
from the prophet. Let us go and strike him with the tongue so that we need
no longer listen to all his words."

19 LORD, listen to me
and hear the voice of my adversaries.
20 Will good be repaid with evil?
They dug a pit to kill me.
Remember how I stood before You
to speak well of them,
to remove Your anger from them?
21 Therefore, give their children over to hunger.
Let their blood flow by the hand of the sword.
May their women become childless, bereaved, and widowed,
their men slain by pestilence,
and their young men struck down in battle by the sword.
22 May a scream be heard from their houses
when You bring troops upon them suddenly,
for they have dug a pit to trap me
and hidden snares for my feet.
23 You, LORD, know all their schemes to kill me.
Do not forgive their iniquity.
Do not erase their sin from Your presence,
and may they be made to stumble before You.
Act against them in Your moment of wrath.

19 1 This is what the LORD said: "Go along with some of the elders of the
2 people and some of the elders of the priests, and get a potter's jug. Then
go out to the Valley of Ben Hinom – it is by the entry to the Potsherd
Gate – and there proclaim the words which I will speak to you.

3 "Say: Hear the word of the LORD, kings of Yehuda and residents of
Jerusalem. This is what the LORD of Hosts, the God of Israel, has said: I
am about to bring such evil upon this place that the ears of all who hear
4 of it shall ring, because they have abandoned Me and made this into an
alien place. They sacrificed there to other gods whom neither they nor their
ancestors nor the kings of Yehuda ever knew. They filled this place with the
5 blood of innocents. They built altars for the Baal, to burn their children
in fire as burnt offerings to the Baal – something I never commanded or
spoke about and that never entered My mind.

6 "Therefore, days are soon coming, declares the LORD, when this place
will no longer be called the Tofet or the Valley of Ben Hinom, but rather
7 the Valley of Slaughter. I will spoil the scheme of Yehuda and Jerusalem
in this place. I will cause them to fall by the sword before their enemies,
into the hands of those who seek their lives. I will give their carcasses as
8 food to the birds of the heavens and the beasts of the earth. I will make
of this city a place of desolation and shrieking, for everyone who passes it
9 by will be horrified and will shriek over all its wounds. I will make them
eat the flesh of their sons and the flesh of their daughters. Everyone will
devour the flesh of his fellow during the siege and in the plight inflicted
upon them by their enemies, by those that seek their lives.

10 "Then smash the jug in front of those who accompanied you.

11 "Say to them: This is what the LORD of Hosts said: This is how I will smash
this people and this city, as one smashes a potter's vessel, so that it can
never again be repaired. They will be buried in the Tofet, there being no
place to bury them elsewhere.

12 "This is what I will do to this place," declares the LORD, "and to its residents.
13 This city will become a Tofet.[12] The houses of Jerusalem and the houses
of the kings of Yehuda will become impure like the place of the Tofet – all
those houses where they offered sacrifices on their rooftops to all the hosts
of heaven and poured libations to other gods."

14 Yirmeyahu returned from the Tofet, where the LORD had sent him to
prophesy, and he stood in the court of the House of the LORD and said
to all the people:

15 "This is what the LORD of Hosts, the God of Israel, said: I am about to
bring upon this city and upon all of her surrounding cities all the evil
which I have decreed against her. For they have stiffened their necks so as
not to heed My words."

20 1 Pashḥur son of Imer the priest, a high official in the House of the LORD,
2 heard Yirmeyahu prophesying these words. Pashḥur struck Yirmeyahu
the prophet and placed him in the stocks that were in the upper Binyamin

12 | See 7:31.

3 Gate, that was in the House of the LORD. The next day Pashḥur released
Yirmeyahu from the stocks, whereupon Yirmeyahu said to him, "The LORD
did not call your name Pashḥur, but rather Terror All Around.[13]

4 "For this is what the LORD said: I am about to make of you a source of
terror for yourself and for all your friends. They will fall before the sword
of their enemies as your eyes look on. I will deliver all of Yehuda into the
hand of the king of Babylon. Some he will exile to Babylon; others he will
5 slay by the sword. I will deliver all the wealth of this city – all the fruit of its
toil and all it holds dear and all the treasures of the kings of Yehuda – into
the hands of their enemies. They will plunder them and confiscate them
and bring them to Babylon.

6 "You, Pashḥur, and your entire household will go into captivity. You will
come to Babylon. There you will die, and there you will be buried, you
and all your friends for whom you prophesied falsely."

7 You persuaded me, LORD,
and I let myself be persuaded.
You overpowered me,
and You prevailed.
I have become a laughingstock all day long:
they all mock me.
8 For whenever I speak prophecy, I shout;
I call out, Injustice! Violence!
The LORD's word has brought upon me
derision and scorn all day long.
9 I said to myself: I will not make mention of it.
I will no longer speak in His name.
But it resides within me like a flaming fire,
locked into my bones.
I wearied of holding it back. I could not.
10 I have overheard the slanderous whispers,
a terror all around:
"Testify and let us testify."
All of my trusted friends
await my collapse. They say,
"Perhaps we can entrap him, overcome him,
and thereby take our revenge upon him."
11 But the LORD is with me like a mighty warrior.
Therefore my pursuers will stumble and not prevail.
They will suffer great shame and not succeed,
an eternal disgrace, never to be forgotten.
12 The LORD of Hosts discerns who is righteous.

13 | The name Pashḥur can have any of several positive meanings, e.g., *pash* meaning "great" and *ḥur* meaning "nobleman." Or it can be interpreted negatively: *pash* meaning "many (enemies)" and *seḥor* meaning "all around."

He sees into both heart and mind.
I will yet witness Your revenge upon them,
for to You I have disclosed my disputes.

13 Sing to the Lord,
praise the Lord,
for He has rescued the helpless
from the hands of evildoers.

14 Cursed be the day that I was born.
May the day that my mother gave birth to me not be blessed.
15 Cursed be the man who informed my father,
saying, "A son was born to you."
He caused him so much joy.
16 May that man be like the cities
that the Lord overturned without regret.[14]
May he hear shrieking each morning
and sobbing in the afternoon.
17 He should have killed me as I left the womb.
Then my mother would have been my grave
and her womb forever pregnant.
18 Why did I leave the womb
to see only misery and agony?
My days have ended in shame.

21 1 This is the word that came to Yirmeyahu from the Lord when King
Tzidkiyahu sent him Pashḥur son of Malkiya and Tzefanya son of Maaseya
2 the priest. They said, "Please inquire of the Lord on our behalf because
Nevukhadretzar, king of Babylon, is waging war against us. Perhaps the
Lord will act with us in accordance with all His wonders, so that our
enemy will withdraw from us."

3 4 Yirmeyahu said to them, "This is what you shall say to Tzidkiyahu: This is
what the Lord, God of Israel, said: I am about to turn back the weapons
that are in your hands with which you battle the king of Babylon and
the Chaldeans[15] who are besieging you from outside the wall, and I will
5 gather them in the midst of this city. I Myself will fight you with a hand
6 stretched forth and a with mighty arm, with anger and wrath and rage. I
will smite those who dwell in this city, man and beast – they shall die by
a great pestilence.

7 "After that, declares the Lord, I will deliver Tzidkiyahu, king of Yehuda, his
servants, the people, and all those in this city who survive the pestilence,
the sword, and the hunger into the hands of Nevukhadretzar, king of
Babylon, into the hands of their enemies, and into the hands of those who

14 | Referring to Sedom and Amora.
15 | An Aramean tribe prominent in Babylonia.

seek their lives. He will smite them by the sword and not have pity upon them, nor show mercy, nor show compassion.

8 "To this people you shall say: This is what the LORD said: Look, I am
9 placing before you the way of life and the way of death. Whoever remains
in this city will die by sword or famine or pestilence, but whoever leaves
and surrenders to the Chaldeans, who are now besieging you, will live, and
10 his life will be their prize of war. I will set My face against this city for evil,
not for good, declares the LORD. It shall be given into the hand of the king
of Babylon, and he will burn it with fire.

11 "And to the house of the king of Yehuda:
Listen to the word of the LORD.
12 House of David, this is what the LORD said:
Sit in judgment each morning
and save the victim of theft from the hand of his oppressor,
lest My wrath burst forth like a fire
and burn with none to quench it
because of your evil actions.
13 Look, I am against you, valley dwellers,
rock upon the plain, declares the LORD,
who say, 'Who can descend upon us?
Who can enter our homes?'
14 I will punish you as your deeds deserve,
declares the LORD.
I will kindle a fire in her forest
that will consume all her surroundings."

22 1 This is what the LORD said: "Go down to the palace of the king of Yehuda
2 and speak this word there. Say: King of Yehuda, who sits upon the throne
of David, heed the word of the LORD – you, your servants, and your
3 people who enter these gates. This is what the LORD said: Do justice and
righteousness; protect the victim of theft from the perpetrator; do not
deceive and do not cheat the stranger, the orphan, and the widow; and
4 spill no innocent blood in this place. If you will act in accordance with
this word, then kings who sit on David's throne will enter the gates of this
palace riding upon chariots and horses – he, his servants, and his people.
5 But if you do not heed these words, then by My own self I swear, declares
the LORD, that this palace will become a ruin.

6 "For this is what the LORD said
concerning the palace of the king of Yehuda:
Although you are like Gilad to Me,
like the peak of Mount Lebanon,
nevertheless I will make of you a wilderness,
cities uninhabited.
7 I will designate destroyers against you,

each man and his tools –
they will cut down your choicest cedars
and cast them onto the fire.

8 "Many nations will pass by this city, and one person will say to the other:
9 'For what reason did the LORD do this to this great city?' And they will
say, 'Because they abandoned the covenant of the LORD their God; they
bowed to other gods and worshipped them.'"

10 Weep not for the dead;
do not bemoan him.
Weep instead for him who departs,
never to return again
to see the land of his birth.

11 For this is what the LORD said concerning Shalum son of Yoshiyahu, king
of Yehuda, who reigned after his father Yoshiyahu: He who left this place
12 will never return again. For in that place where they will exile him, there
he shall die, and he will never see this land again:

13 Woe to him who builds his house without righteousness
and his lofts without justice;
who works his fellow for no pay
and never gives him his wages.
14 Who says, "I will build myself a house of grand dimensions,
with spacious lofts."
He makes himself windows
covered with cedarwood,
coated with precious paint.
15 Do you presume to reign
because you compete in cedarwood?
Indeed, your father ate and drank,
but he dispensed justice and righteousness;
therefore, things went well for him.
16 He took up the cause of the poor and the destitute
with good results.
That is the way to know Me, declares the LORD.
17 But your eyes and your heart
are concerned with nothing but your own gain,
with spilling the blood of the innocent,
with cheating and oppression.
18 Therefore, this is what the LORD said
concerning Yehoyakim the son of Yoshiyahu, king of Yehuda:
They will not eulogize him saying,
"Woe, my brother, my sister."
They will not eulogize him saying,
"Woe master, woe majesty."

19 Like the burial of a donkey will he be buried,
then dragged and flung
outside the gates of Jerusalem.

20 Climb upon Lebanon and shout;
raise your voice upon Bashan;
shout in all directions –
all your lovers have collapsed.
21 I spoke to you in your tranquil moments,
but you said, "I will not listen."
This has been your way since your youth:
you will not heed My voice.
22 Your shepherds will all be crushed by the wind;
your lovers will go into captivity.
Then you will be ashamed and humiliated
by all your evil.
23 Dweller in Lebanon,
nestled among cedars,
how much grace will you retain
when pains come upon you –
pangs as if to a woman in childbirth?

24 By My life, declares the Lord, even if Konyahu[16] son of Yehoyakim, king
of Yehuda, were a signet ring on My right hand, even from there I would
25 dislodge you. I will deliver you into the hands of those who seek your
life, into the hands of those of whom you are terrified, into the hand of
26 Nevukhadretzar, king of Babylon, and into the hands of the Chaldeans. I
will cast you and your mother who bore you into another land where you
27 were not born, and there you will both die. But to the land where they
greatly desire to return, there they will not return.

28 Is he a disgraced and broken idol,
this man Konyahu?
Is he an unwanted vessel?
Why have he and his seed been cast out
and flung into a land that they did not know?
29 Land, land, land –
heed the word of the Lord.
30 This is what the Lord said:
Write this man down as sterile,
a person who will not succeed in his lifetime,
for none of his descendants will rise
to sit upon the throne of David,
to reign ever again in Yehuda.

16 | Perhaps Yekhonya.

23 1 Woe to the shepherds who misguide and disperse the flock of My pasture,
2 declares the Lord.[17] Consequently, this is what the Lord, God of Israel,
said concerning the shepherds who now tend to my people: You have
dispersed My sheep; you drove them away. You did not guide them. I am
3 about to punish you for your evil deeds, declares the Lord. I will gather
the remnant of My flock from all the lands into which I have driven them,
and I will bring them to their home, where they will be fruitful and multiply.
4 And I will raise up shepherds who will tend to them so that they will no
longer fear, nor feel panic, and none shall be missing, declares the Lord.

5 Days are soon approaching, declares the Lord, when I will raise up a
righteous scion for David. He will reign as king and prosper and dispense
6 justice and righteousness in the land. In his days Yehuda will be saved, and
Israel will dwell in safety. And this is the name by which the Lord will call
him: Our Righteous One.

7 Therefore, days are approaching, declares the Lord, when they will no
longer say, "As the Lord lives, who has brought the Israelites up from
8 the land of Egypt," but rather, "As the Lord lives, who brought up and
delivered the descendants of the House of Israel from the northern land,
and from the lands to which I had expelled them," and they shall dwell
upon their own soil.

9 As for these prophets:
my heart breaks within me;
my bones all shudder;
I have become like a drunkard,
a man overcome by wine,
on behalf of the Lord and His holy words.
10 For adulterers fill the land;
the land is in ruins
because of false oaths;
pastures in the wilderness have withered.
Their pursuits are evil,
their heroism improper.
11 Even the prophet and even the priest act deceitfully.
Even in My House I discovered their evil,
declares the Lord.
12 Therefore their path shall become for them
like slippery ground in the darkness;
they shall be driven there,
and there they shall fall,
for I will bring evil upon them
in their year of retribution,
declares the Lord.

17 | Cf. Ezekiel 34:1–15.

13 Among the prophets of Shomron
I have witnessed inanity.
They have prophesied for the Baal
and have misled My people, Israel.
14 Among the prophets of Jerusalem
I have witnessed scandal,
adultery, walking in falsehood.
They support the hands of the wicked
so that no man repents his wickedness.
They have all become to Me like Sedom,
their inhabitants like Amora.

15 Consequently, this is what the LORD of Hosts said
concerning the prophets:[18]
I am about to feed them wormwood
and give them poison water to drink,
for from the prophets of Jerusalem
hypocrisy has gone forth to the entire land.

16 This is what the LORD of Hosts has said:
Do not heed the words of the prophets
who prophesy to you;
they are telling you nonsense.
They speak of the visions of their own hearts,
not from the mouth of the LORD.
17 Indeed, they say to those who despise Me,
"The LORD has spoken;
there will peace for you."
And to all who follow the desires of their own hearts they say,
"No evil shall befall you."
18 For who has stood in the counsel of the LORD,
and seen and heard His word?
Who has listened to His word and heeded it?

19 Behold, the tempest of the LORD
shall go forth with fury.
An earthshaking storm will come down
upon the heads of the wicked.
20 The LORD's wrath will not turn away
until it carries out and fulfills His heart's intentions.
In the days to come
you will understand this fully.
21 I did not send these prophets,
and yet they responded hastily;
I did not speak to them,

---

18 | That is, the false prophets.

and yet they prophesied.
22 Had they stood in My counsel,
they would have let My people hear My words
and brought them back from their wicked ways
and from their evil actions.

23 Am I a God only for those who are close,
declares the Lord,
but not a God for those who are distant?
24 If a person conceals himself in a hiding place,
will I not see him?
demands the Lord.
Do I not fill the heavens and the earth?
demands the Lord.

25 I have heard what the prophets who prophesy falsely in My name declare:
26 "I dreamed, I dreamed." How long will these prophets persist with these
false prophesies in their hearts, these prophets with fraudulent hearts?
27 They plan to make My people forget My name with the dreams that
they tell one another, just as their fathers forgot My name because of
the Baal.

28 The prophet who has a dream, let him relate the dream; but he who has
received My word, let him speak My true word. How can straw compare to
29 grain? demands the Lord. Behold, My word is like fire, declares the Lord,
30 and like a hammer that will shatter a rock. Therefore, I am against these
31 prophets, declares the Lord, who steal My words, one from the other. I
am against these prophets, declares the Lord, who use their own language
32 to speak as if I had spoken. I am against those who prophesy false dreams,
declares the Lord, those who relate them and mislead My people with
their falsehood and carelessness. I have neither sent them nor commanded
them, nor will they at all benefit My people, declares the Lord.

33 If this people, or a prophet or a priest, should ask of you, "What is the
burden of the Lord?"[19] you shall say to them, "What burden? I will
34 abandon you!" declares the Lord. The prophet or priest or the people
who shall say to you "burden of the Lord," I will punish that person and
his household.

35 This is what each person shall say to his neighbor and each person to his
36 kinsman: "What did the Lord answer? What did the Lord say?" But as
for "burden of the Lord," never mention that again, for "burden" is but a
word that people use. You have perverted the words of the living God, the
Lord of Hosts, our God.

37 This is how you should speak to the prophet: "What did the Lord answer
38 you? What did the Lord say?" If you continue to say "burden of the Lord,"

19 | The word "burden" (*masa*) also means "oracle," e.g., Isaiah 13:1.

then this is what the LORD said: Because you say this phrase, "burden of
the LORD," after I have sent word to you never to say "burden of the LORD,"
39 I am therefore about to eject you totally and remove from My presence
40 you and the city that I gave to you and your fathers. I will place upon you
eternal shame, eternal humiliation, that will not be forgotten.

24 1 The LORD showed me two baskets of figs placed before the Temple of
the LORD. This was after Nevukhadretzar, king of Babylon, had exiled
Yekhonyahu son of Yehoyakim, king of Yehuda, and the officers of Yehuda,
and the artisans and smiths,[20] from Jerusalem, and had brought them to
2 Babylon. In one basket were very fine figs, like well-ripened figs; in the
other basket were very bad figs, so bad that they could not be eaten.

3 The LORD said to me, "What do you see, Yirmeyahu?" And I replied, "Figs!
The fine ones are very fine, and the bad ones very bad, so bad that they
cannot be eaten."

4 5 The word of the LORD came to me: This is what the LORD, God of Israel,
said: "Like these fine figs, so will I show favor to the exiles of Yehuda
whom I have sent forth from this place to the land of the Chaldeans for
6 their benefit. I will watch over them benevolently and bring them back to
this land; I will build them up and not tear them down; I will plant them
7 and not uproot them. I will grant them the heart to know Me, for I am the
LORD. They will be My people, and I will be their God, for they will return
to Me with all their heart."

8 But of the bad figs, so bad that they cannot be eaten, the LORD said, "Like
those I will make Tzidkiyahu, king of Yehuda, his officers, and the remnant
of Jerusalem that has remained in this land, and those who dwell in the
9 land of Egypt.[21] I will make them a horror, an evil, for all the kingdoms of
the earth; a disgrace and an epithet, a sharp word and a curse, in all the
10 places to which I shall banish them. And I will send against them the sword
and famine and pestilence until they are finished off within the land which
I gave them and their fathers."

25 1 The word that came to Yirmeyahu concerning the entire people of Yehuda
in the fourth year of Yehoyakim son of Yoshiyahu, king of Yehuda, that
2 being the first year of Nevukhadretzar, king of Babylon. This is what
Yirmeyahu the prophet spoke to the entire people of Yehuda and to all
those dwelling in Jerusalem:

3 From the thirteenth year of Yoshiyahu son of Amon, king of Yehuda,
until this very day, it has been twenty-three years that the word of the
LORD has come to me. I have spoken to you diligently, but you have not
4 listened. The LORD sent you all of His servants, the prophets – early and
5 persistently – yet you did not listen, nor even bend your ear to hear. They

20 | See II Kings 24:14.

21 | Egypt was viewed as a place of refuge (see 41:16–17).

said, "Please turn back, each of you, from his wicked ways and evil deeds,
so that you may for ever and ever dwell upon the soil which the Lord gave
6 to you and to your fathers." Do not follow other gods, serving them and
worshipping them, so as not to anger Me with your actions and so that I
do not harm you.

7 But you did not listen to Me, declares the Lord, and thereby angered Me
by your actions, to your detriment.

8 Consequently, this is what the Lord of Hosts said: Because you have not
9 listened to My words, I am about to send for My servant Nevukhadnetzar,
king of Babylon, and I shall take all the tribes of the north, declares the
Lord, and bring them upon this land, upon its inhabitants, and upon all
these nations surrounding them. I will destroy them and make of them
10 a wasteland and a place of shrieking, an eternal ruin. I shall abolish from
them the sound of joy and the sound of happiness, the voice of the groom
and the voice of the bride, the sound of the mill and the light of the lamp.
11 The entire land shall become a ruin and a wasteland, and these nations
shall serve the king of Babylon for seventy years.

12 When these seventy years are completed, I will visit retribution upon the
king of Babylon and that nation, declares the Lord, for their sin, and as for
13 the land of the Chaldeans, I shall make it an eternal wasteland. I will bring
upon that land all that I have spoken against her, all that is written in this
14 book, which was prophesied by Yirmeyahu concerning all the nations. For
they too shall serve many nations and great kings, and I will repay them
according to their actions and handiwork.

15 For this is what the Lord, God of Israel, said to me: "Take this cup of the
wine of wrath from My hand, and give it to drink to all the nations to whom
16 I am sending you. They will drink and shiver and act foolishly because of
the sword that I am sending among them."

17 I took the cup from the hand of the Lord and I gave it to drink to all the
18 nations to whom the Lord had sent me. To Jerusalem and to the cities
of Yehuda, to her kings and to her officers, to lead them into destruction,
19 waste, and shrieking, and to a curse, just as on this very day. To Pharaoh,
20 king of Egypt, to his servants and officers, and to his entire nation. To the
conglomeration of peoples and to all the kings of the land of Utz; to all
the kings of the land of the Philistines – Ashkelon, Aza, Ekron, and the
21 22 remnant of Ashdod. To Edom and Moav and the Amonites. To all the
kings of Tyre, and to all the kings of Sidon; to the kings of the islands across
23 the sea. To Dedan and to Tema and to Buz, and to all in the distant reaches.
24 To all the kings of Arabia, and to all the kings of the conglomeration of
25 peoples that dwell in the desert. To all the kings of Zimri, and all the kings
26 of Elam, and all the kings of Media. To all the kings of the north, those
who are near and those who are far from each other, and to the kingdoms

of all the lands on the face of the earth, and the king of Sheshakh[22] will
drink after them.

27 "You shall say to them: This is what the LORD of Hosts, God of Israel,
has said: Drink, become drunk and vomit, fall and do not rise because of
28 the sword that I am sending into your midst. Should they refuse to take
the cup from your hand to drink, say to them: This is what the LORD of
29 Hosts said: You must drink! For I am about to bring evil upon the city
that is called by My name, and you expect to be absolved? You will not be
absolved, for I summon a sword to fall upon all the inhabitants of the land,
declares the LORD of Hosts.

30 "Now, you are to prophesy all these words to them
and say to them:
The LORD roars from on high;
from His holy dwelling place He raises His voice;
He roars and roars above His abode;
He shouts '*heidad*'[23] like the grape treaders
to all who dwell on earth.
31 A clamor has reached the end of the earth,
for the LORD has a dispute with the nations.
He enters into judgment with all flesh.
He has delivered them, the wicked, to the sword,"
declares the LORD.

32 This is what the LORD of Hosts said:
Evil is about to go forth
from nation to nation,
and a great storm
from the ends of the earth
will awaken them.
33 On that day, those slain by the LORD
will spread from one end of the earth to the other end of the earth –
they will not be eulogized;
they will not be gathered;
they will not be buried.
They will be like dung upon the face of the earth.
34 Wail, shepherds, and scream.
Roll in the dust, you masters of the flock,
for the days before your slaughter have expired.
I will smash you,
and you will fall like a precious vessel.
35 Flight shall be denied to the shepherds;

22 | Babylon (*Bavel*), written in the *atbash* cipher.

23 | An exclamation of effort or celebration, typically over the grape harvest, or a battle cry.

escape shall be denied to the masters of the flock.
36 Listen! Oh, the shouts of the shepherds
and the wails of the masters of the flock,
for the LORD has ruined their pasture.
37 The peaceful meadows will be demolished
by the burning anger of the LORD.
38 The young lion has left his lair,
for their land will soon be laid waste
by the wrath of the oppressor
and by His burning anger.

26 1 At the beginning of the reign of Yehoyakim son of Yoshiyahu, king of
2 Yehuda, this word came from the LORD. This is what the LORD said:
"Stand in the courtyard of the House of the LORD and speak to all who
dwell in the cities of Yehuda, who come to worship in the House of the
LORD, all the words which I commanded you to speak to them. Do not
omit a word.

3 "Perhaps they will listen and repent, each person from his evil way, so that I
will reconsider the evil that I plan to do to them because of the evil of their
4 deeds. Say to them: This is what the LORD said: If you do not listen to Me
5 to follow the teaching that I have placed before you, to obey the words of My
servants the prophets, whom I have sent to you early and repeatedly – though
6 you did not obey – I will make this House like Shilo, and this city I will turn
into a curse for all the nations of the earth."

7 The priests and the prophets and all the people heard Yirmeyahu speak these
8 words in the House of the LORD. When Yirmeyahu finished speaking all that
the LORD commanded him to speak to all the people, the priests and the
9 prophets and all the people seized him, saying, "You shall die! Why did you
prophesy in the name of the LORD, saying that this House will be like Shilo
and that this city will be destroyed, leaving no inhabitant?" All the people
10 crowded about Yirmeyahu in the House of the LORD. The officers of Yehuda
heard these words, and they went up from the king's house to the House of
the LORD and sat at the entrance of the new gate of the LORD.

11 The priests and the prophets said to the officers and to all the people, "This
man deserves the death penalty, for he prophesied against this city, as you
have heard with your own ears."

12 Yirmeyahu said to all the officers and to all the people, "The LORD sent me
to prophesy against this House and against this city all the words that you
13 heard. Now, rectify your ways and your deeds, and heed the voice of the
LORD your God. Then the LORD will reconsider the evil which He has spoken
against you.

14 "As for me, I am in your hands. Do to me whatever is good and proper in your
15 eyes. But know well that if you kill me, you will have brought the blood of

an innocent man upon yourselves and upon this city and its inhabitants. For, truthfully, the LORD did send me to you to speak all these words to you."

16 The officers and all the people said to the priests and the prophets, "This man does not deserve the death penalty, for he spoke to us in the name of the LORD our God."

17 Some men from among the elders of the land stood up and said to all the
18 assembled people, "Mikha the Morashtite would prophesy in the days of
Ḥizkiyahu, king of Yehuda. He addressed all the people of Yehuda, saying,
'This is what the LORD of Hosts said: Zion will be plowed over like a field,
Jerusalem will come to be a mound of ruins, and the Temple Mount an
19 overgrown hilltop shrine.'[24] Did Ḥizkiyahu, king of Yehuda, and all of Yehuda
put him to death? Did he not fear the LORD and beseech the LORD, so that
the LORD reconsidered the evil that He had spoken concerning them? We
would be bringing great evil upon ourselves.

20 "Another man would prophesy in the name of the LORD – Uriyahu son
of Shemayahu of Kiryat Ye'arim. He too prophesied against this city and
21 against this land as all of Yirmeyahu's words did. King Yehoyakim and all his
soldiers and all his officers heard his words, and the king sought to put him
to death, but Uriyahu heard and was afraid. He took flight and went to Egypt.
22 King Yehoyakim sent men to Egypt; he sent Elnatan son of Akhbor and his
23 companions to Egypt. They brought Uriyahu out of Egypt and delivered him
to Yehoyakim, who smote him by sword. He threw his carcass into the graves
of the common people."

24 But the power of Aḥikam son of Shafan stood by Yirmeyahu, refusing to surrender him to the hands of the people who would kill him.

27 1 At the beginning of the reign of Yehoyakim son of Yoshiyahu, king of Yehuda, this word came to Yirmeya from the LORD.

2 This is what the LORD said to me: "Make yourself the reins and bars of a
3 yoke,[25] and place them upon your neck, and send them to the king of Edom,
the king of Moav, the king of the Amonites, the king of Tyre, and the king of
Sidon, and by way of the emissaries who come to Jerusalem, to Tzidkiyahu,
4 king of Yehuda. And instruct them to tell their masters: This is what the
LORD of Hosts, God of Israel, has said, and this is what you should say to
your masters:

5 "It is I who made the earth – the humans and the animals upon the face of
the earth – with My great might and My arm stretched forth, and I gave
6 it to whom I saw fit. And now, I have delivered all these lands into the
hands of Nevukhadnetzar, king of Babylon, My servant. I have even given
7 him the beasts of the field to serve him. All the nations will serve him,

---

24 | Cf. Micah 3:12.

25 | See also 28:10.

his son, and his son's son, until his land's time will also come, and many
8 nations and great kings will subjugate him. The nation and kingdom
that will not serve him – Nevukhadnetzar, king of Babylon – and will
not submit its neck to the yoke of the king of Babylon, I will visit sword,
famine, and pestilence upon that nation, declares the LORD, until I finish
them off by his hands.

9 "As for you, do not listen to your prophets and diviners, your dreamers and
10 soothsayers and sorcerers, who tell you not to serve the king of Babylon. For
what they prophesy to you is false, with the result that it will remove you
11 from your land. I will drive you away, and you will be lost. But the nation
that will submit its neck to the yoke of the king of Babylon and serve him,
that nation I will leave upon its soil," declares the LORD. "They shall till it
and dwell on it."

12 I spoke similarly to King Tzidkiya of Yehuda, saying, "Submit your necks to
13 the yoke of the king of Babylon, serve him and his people, and survive. Why
should you and your people perish by the sword, by famine, and by pestilence,
as the LORD has spoken regarding that nation that will not serve the king of
14 Babylon? Do not listen to the words of those prophets who tell you not to
serve the king of Babylon, for falsehood is what they are prophesying to you.
15 For I did not send them, declares the LORD. They prophesy falsehood in My
name, with the result that I will drive you away and you will be lost – you and
the prophets who prophesy to you."

16 And to the priests, and to all these people, I said, "This is what the LORD said:
Do not listen to the words of your prophets, who prophesy to you saying that
the vessels of the LORD's House are about to be returned from Babylon – now,
17 quickly. For they prophesy falsehood to you. Do not listen to them. Serve the
18 king of Babylon and survive. Why should the city become a ruin? If they are
indeed prophets, and if the word of the LORD is indeed with them, let them
beg of the LORD of Hosts not to allow the vessels that remain in the House
of the LORD, and in the palace of the king of Yehuda, and in Jerusalem, to go
to Babylon.

19 "For this is what the LORD of Hosts has said about the pillars, and the Sea,
20 and the stands, and the other vessels that remain in this city,[26] those that
Nevukhadnetzar, king of Babylon, did not take when he exiled Yekhonya son
of Yehoyakim, king of Yehuda, from Jerusalem to Babylon, along with all the
nobles of Yehuda and Jerusalem.

21 "For this is what the LORD of Hosts, God of Israel, had said regarding the
vessels that remain in the LORD's House, and in the palace of the king of
22 Yehuda, and Jerusalem: To Babylon they shall be brought, and there they
shall remain until the day that I appoint for them, declares the LORD. Then I
will bring them up and return them to this place."

---

26 | See 1 Kings 7:13–50.

28 1 It was that year, at the beginning of the reign of Tzidkiya, king of Yehuda, in
the fifth month of the fourth year, that Ḥananya son of Azur the prophet,
who was from Givon, spoke to me in the House of the LORD, in full view of
2 the priests and all the people. He said, "This is what the LORD of Hosts, God
3 of Israel, said: I have broken the yoke of the king of Babylon. In two years
I will restore all the vessels of the LORD's House to this place, those that
4 Nevukhadnetzar king of Babylon took from here and brought to Babylon. I
will return Yekhonya son of Yehoyakim, king of Yehuda, and all of Yehuda's
exiles who have gone to Babylon, to this place – declares the LORD – for I
shall break the yoke of the king of Babylon."

5 Then Yirmeya the prophet spoke to Ḥananya the prophet in full view of the
priests and in full view of all the people who were standing in the LORD's
6 House. Yirmeya the prophet said, "Amen. May the LORD do that. May He
uphold the words that you prophesied regarding the return of the vessels
7 of the LORD's House and of all the exiles from Babylon to this place. But
please listen to the word that I am speaking in your ears, and in the ears
8 of all the people. The prophets who were before me and before you long
ago – they prophesied war, catastrophe, and pestilence to many lands and
9 to great kingdoms. The prophet who shall prophesy peace, when his words
come true, that prophet shall be acknowledged as one whom the LORD has
truly sent."

10 Then Ḥananya the prophet took the bar[27] from the neck of Yirmeya the
11 prophet and broke it. And Ḥananya spoke in full view of all the people
and said, "This is what the LORD said: Thus shall I break the yoke of
Nevukhadnetzar, king of Babylon, in two years, from the necks of all nations."
Yirmeya the prophet went on his way.

12 The word of the LORD came to Yirmeya after Ḥananya the prophet broke
13 the bar from the neck of Yirmeya the prophet, and He said, "Go and say to
Ḥananya: This is what the LORD said: You have broken bars of wood, but in
14 their stead you shall fashion bars of iron. For this is what the LORD of Hosts,
the God of Israel, had said: I have placed a yoke of iron upon the necks of
all these nations to serve Nevukhadnetzar, king of Babylon, and they shall
indeed serve him. I have even given him the beasts of the field."

15 Then Yirmeya the prophet said to Ḥananya the prophet, "Listen well,
Ḥananya. The LORD did not send you, and you have assured this people of
16 a lie. Therefore, this is what the LORD has said: I am about to send you away
from the earth. This year you shall die, for you preached insubordination
against the LORD."

17 And Ḥananya the prophet died that year in the seventh month.

29 1 These are the words of the letter that Yirmeya the prophet sent from
Jerusalem to the remaining elders of the exiles, and to the priests and

27 | The yoke mentioned in 27:2.

the prophets, and to all the people that Nevukhadnetzar had exiled from
2 Jerusalem to Babylon. This was after King Yekhonya and the queen
mother and the courtiers, the officers of Yehuda and Jerusalem, and the
3 craftsmen and artisans had departed from Jerusalem. This letter was sent
by the hand of Elasa son of Shafan and Gemarya son of Ḥilkiya, who were
sent to Babylon by King Tzidkiya of Yehuda to King Nevukhadnetzar of
Babylon. It said:

4 "This is what the Lord of Hosts, God of Israel, said to all the exiles that I
5 have exiled from Jerusalem to Babylon: Build houses and dwell in them;
6 plant gardens and eat their fruit. Take wives, and beget sons and daughters.
Take wives for your sons and give your daughters to husbands so that they
may give birth to sons and daughters. Multiply there; do not be diminished.
7 Seek the welfare of the city to which I have exiled you, and pray on its behalf
to the Lord, for in its peace there shall be peace for you.

8 "For this is what the Lord of Hosts, God of Israel, has said: Do not allow
the prophets among you and your diviners to mislead you. Do not heed your
9 dreams, those that you yourselves inspired. For they prophesy to you falsely
in My name. I did not send them, declares the Lord.

10 "But this is what the Lord has said: Only when Babylon's seventy years are
completed will I take note of you and will I fulfill for you My good word, to
11 bring you back to this place. For surely I know the plans that I have in store
for you – declares the Lord – plans for welfare and not for harm, to grant
12 you a hopeful future. Then, when you call upon Me and follow and pray to
13 Me, I will hear you. And when you search you will find Me, if you seek Me
14 with all your heart. I shall be accessible to you – declares the Lord – and I
shall bring back your captives and gather you from all the nations and from
all the places to which I have driven you, declares the Lord. I will bring you
15 back to the place from which I have exiled you. And yet you say, 'The Lord
has raised up prophets for us in Babylon.'

16 "But this is what the Lord said with regard to the king who sits upon David's
throne and with regard to all the people who dwell in this city, your brothers,
who did not go out into exile with you:

17 "This is what the Lord of Hosts said: I am about to send down upon you
sword, famine, and pestilence and treat you like putrid figs, so bad that they
18 cannot be eaten. I will chase after you with sword, famine, and pestilence. I
will make them into a source of trembling for all the kingdoms of the earth,
as a curse and an object of horror and shrieking and derision among all
19 the nations to which I will have driven you. Because they did not hear My
words – declares the Lord – when I sent them My servants, the prophets,
20 early and repeatedly, and yet you did not listen, declares the Lord. But you,
the entire exiled community, whom I sent off from Jerusalem to Babylon,
heed the Lord's word.

21 "This is what the LORD of Hosts, God of Israel, said concerning Aḥav son of
Kolaya and Tzidkiyahu son of Maaseya – who prophesy to you falsely in My
name. I am about to surrender them to the hand of King Nevukhadnetzar of
22 Babylon, and he will slay them before your eyes. From them a curse will be
taken up by all of Yehuda's exiles who are in Babylon. They will say, 'May the
LORD make you as Tzidkiyahu and Aḥav, whom the king of Babylon roasted
23 in fire.' Because they performed a vile deed in Israel, committing adultery
with the wives of others and speaking false words in My name, which I did
not command them. I know, and I am a witness, declares the LORD."

24 25 "And you[28] should say to Shemayahu the Nehelamite: This is what the LORD
of Hosts, God of Israel, said: Because you sent letters in your name to the
people in Jerusalem and to Tzefanya son of Maaseya the priest and to all the
26 priests, saying, 'The LORD has appointed you as priest in place of Yehoyada
the priest, to be overseers of the LORD's House over every madman who
pretends he is a prophet, whom you should consign to the stocks and to the
27 iron collar. Now, why have you not excoriated Yirmeyahu the Anatotite, who
28 pretends to be a prophet for you? For he did indeed send a message to us in
Babylon declaring: "The exile will be a long one, so build houses and dwell
in them, and plant gardens and eat their fruit."'"

29 And Tzefanya the priest read this letter to the ears of Yirmeyahu the
prophet.

30 31 Then the LORD's word came to Yirmeyahu, saying, "Send a message to all the
exiles, saying: This is what the LORD said regarding Shemaya the Nehelamite:
Because Shemaya has prophesied to you although I did not send him, and has
32 made you trust in a lie, therefore, this is what the LORD said: I am about to
punish Shemaya the Nehelamite and his descendants so that he will have no
one dwelling among this people; no one to see the good that I am going to
do for My people – declares the LORD – for he has preached insubordination
against the LORD."

30 1 The word that came to Yirmeyahu from the LORD:

2 This is what the LORD, God of Israel, said: "Write all the words that I speak
3 to you in a scroll. For look, days are coming," declares the LORD, "when I
will bring back from captivity My people Israel and Yehuda," said the LORD,
"and I will restore them to the land that I gave to their fathers, and they shall
possess it."

4 And these are the words that the LORD spoke concerning Israel and
Yehuda:

5 Thus said the LORD:
We heard the sound of trembling,
terror, and no peace.

---

28 | Yirmeyahu.

6 Ask now and observe.
Do males give birth?
Why then do I see every man
with his hands upon his loins
like a woman in labor
and every face turned green?
7 O! That day is great;
there is none like it!
It is a time of distress for Yaakov,
but he shall be delivered from it.

8 It will happen on that day, declares the LORD of Hosts, that I will break his[66]
yoke from upon your neck, and I will tear apart your bonds, and strangers
9 will no longer make you servants. Rather, they will serve the LORD their God,
and David their king, whom I shall raise up for them.

10 As for you, My servant Yaakov, do not fear,
declares the LORD,
and Israel, do not be terrified,
for I will deliver you from a distant land
and your descendants from their land of captivity.
For Yaakov it will again be
quiet and tranquil
with none to frighten him.
11 For I am with you,
declares the LORD,
to deliver you.
For I will make an end
of all the nations among whom I have scattered you,
but of you I will not make an end.
I will discipline you justly,
but I will surely not annihilate you.

12 For thus said the LORD:
Your bruise is incurable,
your wound severe.
13 There is none to plead your cause for healing.
You have no curative medicine.
14 All your supposed lovers have forgotten you;
they do not seek you out.
For I have struck you with an enemy's blow,
a cruel rebuke
for your many iniquities,
for your numerous sins.
15 Why do you cry out over your affliction?

66 | Nevukhadnetzar's.

Why is your pain incurable?
It is because of your many iniquities,
your numerous sins,
that I have done these things to you.
16 Therefore, all who devoured you
will be devoured,
and all of your oppressors, every one,
will fall into captivity.
Those who laid waste to you
will be laid waste,
and all who despoiled you,
I will make spoils of them.
17 I will surely raise up a cure for you,
and I will heal you of your wounds,
declares the LORD,
for they have called you an outcast, saying,
"This Zion, there is none to seek her out."

18 Thus said the LORD:
I am about to bring back the captives of Yaakov's tents
and will show compassion for his dwelling places.
The city will be rebuilt upon its mound,
and its citadel will be set upon its rightful place.
19 Out of them shall come thanksgiving
and the sound of merrymakers.
I will multiply them,
and they will not be diminished;
I will make them honored,
and they shall not be degraded.
20 Its children will be as before,
and its community will be established before Me.
I will punish all of its oppressors.
21 His leader shall be one of his own,
and his ruler shall come forth from his midst.
I will draw him near,
and he shall approach Me,
for who is it who will otherwise dare to approach Me?
declares the LORD.
22 And you shall become My people,
and I will be your God.

23 Behold, the tempest of the LORD
shall go forth with fury.
An earthshaking storm
will whirl down upon the heads of the wicked.
24 The LORD's burning wrath will not turn away

until it carries out and fulfills His heart's intentions.
In the days to come
you will understand this.[67]
25 At that time, declares the LORD,
I will be God to all the families of Israel,
and they will be My people.

31 1 This is what the LORD said:[68]
The people who escaped the sword
found favor in the wilderness –
Israel, on the way to its place of rest.
2 From afar the LORD appeared to me:
I have loved you with an everlasting love
and thereby drew you close with loving-kindness.
3 I will again rebuild you,
and you shall remain rebuilt,
maiden Israel.
You will again adorn yourself with timbrels
and go out to dance a dance of merrymakers.
4 You will again plant vineyards
on the hills of Shomron.
Planters will plant
and enjoy the fruit.
5 Indeed, there is a day when sentinels
shall call out over the Efrayim hills:
"Come, and let us go up to Zion,
to the LORD our God."

6 For this is what the LORD said:
Sing joyously for Yaakov
and shout publicly to the nations.
Give voice, give praise, and say,
"LORD, deliver Your people,
the remnant of Israel."
7 I am about to bring them from the northern land
and gather them from the ends of the earth.
The blind and the lame among them,
the pregnant woman together with one who has just given birth.
A great assembly will return here.
8 They will come weeping,
and with compassion I shall lead them.
I will guide them along streams of water
on a level path upon which they will not stumble,

67 | Cf. 23:19–20.

68 | Note that many English Bibles number the last verse of chapter 30 as the first verse of chapter 31, so that our verse 1 is their verse 2, and so on throughout the chapter.

for I have become a Father to Israel,
and Efrayim is My firstborn.

9 Nations, hear the word of the LORD,
and tell it to the distant isles.
Say, "He who has scattered Israel will gather him
and will watch over him as a shepherd does his flock."
10 For the LORD has released Yaakov
and has rescued him from the hands of one mightier than him.
11 They will come and sing on the heights of Zion
and will stream toward the LORD's goodness,
because of the grain and the new wine and olive oil,
and because of the young sheep and cattle.
Their lives will be like a well-watered garden;
they will no longer languish ever again.
12 Then maidens shall rejoice in dance,
young men and old together.
I shall turn their grief into joy;
I shall console them and gladden them in their grief.
13 I shall give the priests their fill of fatness,
and My people shall be satiated with My goodness,
declares the LORD.

14 This is what the LORD said:
A sound is heard in Rama:[69]
wailing, bitter weeping.
It is Raḥel, weeping for her children.
She refuses to be consoled
for her children,
for they are gone.

15 This is what the LORD said:
Restrain your voice from crying
and your eyes from tears,
for there is a reward for your labor,
declares the LORD,
and they will return from the land of the enemy.
16 There is hope for your future,
declares the LORD,
and your children will return to their own country.
17 I have indeed heard
Efrayim moaning for himself:
"You have disciplined me
and I accepted the discipline,
like an untamed calf.

---

69 | A town north of Jerusalem (see 40:1).

Bring me back and I shall return,
for You are the Lord, my God.
18 After I turned back, I was remorseful,
and after I became aware,
I struck myself upon my thigh.
I was ashamed and even humiliated,
for I carry the disgrace of my youth."
19 Is Efrayim not a precious son to me,
a delightful child?
Whenever I speak of him
I remember him all the more.
Therefore I long for him inwardly.
I will show him great compassion,
declares the Lord.

20 Set up road markers for yourself,
place high guideposts for yourself,
take note of the path by which you traveled.
Return, maiden Israel.
Return to these, your cities.
21 How long will you turn away,
wayward daughter?
For the Lord will create something new in the world:
A woman will go about in search of a man!

22 This is what the Lord of Hosts, God of Israel, said: They will again say these
words in the land of Yehuda and in its cities, when I bring them back from
their captivity:
"May the Lord bless you,
abode of righteousness,
holy mountain."
23 And they shall dwell there, in Yehuda and in all its cities, farmers and those
24 who move about with their flocks. I will refresh the weary and replenish every
languishing person.

25 At this I awoke and understood; I had slept pleasantly.

26 Days are soon coming, declares the Lord, when I will sow the House of
Israel and the House of Yehuda with the seed of people and the seed of cattle.
27 It will come to pass that just as I was watchful over them to uproot, to tear
down, to demolish, to destroy, and to harm, so will I be watchful over them
28 to build and to plant, declares the Lord. In those days they will no longer say,
29 "Fathers eat sour grapes, but the teeth of the children are set on edge." Instead,
everyone will perish for his own sins; anyone who eats sour grapes, only his
own teeth shall be set on edge.

30 Days are soon coming, declares the Lord, when I will make a new covenant
31 with the House of Israel and the House of Yehuda, not like the covenant that

I made with their fathers at the time that I held fast to their hands in order
to take them out of Egypt; they broke that covenant with Me although I was
32 master over them, declares the LORD. For this covenant, which I will make
with the House of Israel after these days, declares the LORD, I will deliver
My teaching into their midst and inscribe it upon their hearts, and I will be
33 their God, and they will be My people. No longer will each person teach a
neighbor and each person a brother, saying, "Know the LORD!" For they will
all know Me, from the least of them to their greatest, declares the LORD.
For I will forgive their iniquities
and no longer remember their transgressions.

34 This is what the LORD said:
He who assigns the sun to shine by day
and regulates the moon and stars to shine at night,
who first calms the sea and then makes its waves roar,
LORD of Hosts is His name.
35 If these statutes vanish from before Me,
declares the LORD,
then will the seed of Israel cease
to be a nation before Me for all time.

36 This is what the LORD said: If the heavens above be measured, and the
foundation of the earth below be explored, only then will I reject all the seed
of Israel for all that they have done, declares the LORD.

37 For days are soon coming, declares the LORD, when the city will be rebuilt for
38 the LORD from the Tower of Ḥananel to the Corner Gate. And a measuring
line shall go out again in front of it to the Hill of Garev and continue toward
39 Goa. And the entire valley of the corpses and ashes, and all the meadows up
to the Kidron Valley, up to the corner of the Horse Gate to the east, will be
holy to the LORD, never again to be uprooted or demolished.

32 1 The word that came to Yirmeyahu from the LORD during the tenth year of
Tzidkiyahu, king of Yehuda, that being the eighteenth year of Nevukhadnetzar.
2 The army of the king of Babylon was then besieging Jerusalem, and Yirmeyahu
the prophet was confined to the prison courtyard near the palace of the king
3 of Yehuda.[70] He had been confined by Tzidkiyahu, king of Yehuda, who had
said, "How dare you prophesy?"

This is what the LORD said: "I am about to give the city into the hand of the
4 king of Babylon, and he shall capture it. And Tzidkiyahu, king of Yehuda, shall
not escape the hand of the Chaldeans but shall certainly be delivered into the
hand of the king of Babylon, and will speak to him mouth to mouth and see
5 him eye to eye. He will lead Tzidkiyahu to Babylon, and there he will remain
until I call him to account," declares the LORD. "If you wage war against the
Chaldeans, you shall not be successful."

---

70 | See 37:21.

6
7 And Yirmeyahu said: The word of the LORD came to me: Ḥanamel, son of
your uncle Shalum, shall come to you and say, "Purchase for yourself my
field that is in Anatot, for yours is the right of redemption by purchase."[71]
8 Ḥanamel, my uncle's son, came to me – just as the LORD had said – to the
prison courtyard, and said to me, "Please purchase my field in Anatot, in
the territory of Binyamin, for yours is the right of inheritance, and it is your
right to redeem it. Purchase it for yourself." Then I knew that this was the
word of the LORD.

9 And so I purchased the field that was in Anatot from my uncle's son Ḥanamel.
10 I weighed out the silver to him: seven shekel and ten silver coins. I wrote it
upon a scroll and sealed it, and I had it witnessed; and I weighed out the
11 silver on a scale. I took the deed of purchase, sealed as prescribed by law and
12 custom, along with the unsealed document.[72] And I gave the deed of purchase
to Barukh son of Neriya son of Maḥseya in the presence of Ḥanamel my uncle,
in the presence of the witnesses who were listed in the deed of purchase,
and in the presence of all the men of Yehuda who were sitting in the prison
13
14 courtyard. In their presence I instructed Barukh, saying, "This is what the
LORD of Hosts, God of Israel, said: Take these scrolls, this deed of purchase,
the sealed section and the unsealed section, and place it in a clay vessel, so that
it might be preserved for many days."

15 For this is what the LORD of Hosts, God of Israel, has said: Houses, fields, and
vineyards shall once again be purchased in this land.

16 After I gave this deed of purchase to Barukh son of Neriya, I prayed to the
17 LORD, saying, "O Lord GOD! You made the heavens and the earth with Your
great strength and with Your arm stretched forth. Nothing is too wonderful for
18 You. You perform loving-kindness to thousands but repay the sins of fathers
unto the bosoms of their children after them. The great and mighty God, LORD
19 of Hosts is His name. Great in counsel, mighty in deed, Your eyes are open
to all of the ways of humans, to give each one according to his ways, to each
20 according to the fruits of his actions. You set signs and wonders in the land
of Egypt to this day[73] for Israel and for humankind, and You made a name
21 for Yourself as on this day. You brought out Your people Israel from the land
of Egypt with signs and wonders, a mighty hand and an arm stretched forth,
22 and with terrifying power. You gave them this land that You swore to their
23 fathers that You would give them, a land flowing with milk and with honey.
They came and possessed it, but they neither heeded Your voice nor followed
Your teaching. All that You had commanded them to do they did not do, and
24 so You caused all this disaster to come upon them. The siege ramps have
come near the city in order to capture it, and the city is about to be delivered,
because of the sword and the famine and the pestilence, into the hands of the

71 | See Leviticus 25:25.

72 | Common practice was to have both a sealed and an open copy of a deed.

73 | That are still spoken about today.

Chaldeans who are attacking it. That which you spoke about has happened,
25 and You see it for Yourself. And yet You say to me, Lord GOD, 'Purchase this
field for yourself for silver and have it witnessed, when the city is about to be
delivered into the hands of the Chaldeans'?"

26 27 And the word of the LORD came to Yirmeyahu: "Look, I am the LORD, God
28 of all flesh. Is anything beyond My power?" Therefore, this is what the LORD
said: "I am about to deliver this city into the hands of the Chaldeans and into
the hands of Nevukhadretzar, king of Babylon, and he will capture it. The
29 Chaldeans, who are attacking this city, will come and set fire to the city and
burn it down along with the houses that offered incense to the Baal on their
30 rooftops and poured libations to other gods, thereby arousing My anger. For
the Israelites and the people of Yehuda have been doing nothing but that
which is evil in My eyes from the time of their youth; for the Israelites are
only arousing My anger with their actions," declares the LORD.

31 "This city, from the time they built it until this very day, has aroused
My anger and My wrath so that it must be removed from My presence
32 on account of all the evil that the Israelites and the people of Yehuda
did to anger Me: them, their kings, their officials, their priests, and
their prophets, the prominent men of Yehuda, and the inhabitants
33 of Jerusalem. They turned their backs to Me, not their faces. I taught
them early and repeatedly; nevertheless, they neither listened nor took
34 instruction. They placed their vile objects in the very house which is
35 called by My name, to defile it. They built the altars for the Baal that
are in the Valley of Ben Hinom, to give over their sons and daughters
to Molekh – something that I did not command them and that never
entered My mind – to perform such a detestable thing, and so they
corrupted Yehuda.

36 "But now," so said the LORD, God of Israel, "about this city that you say is
delivered into the hands of the king of Babylon by the sword, by famine, and
37 by pestilence, I will gather them from all the lands to which I have driven
them in My anger and in My wrath and with great rage, and I will return them
38 to this place and settle them here in safety. They will be My people, and I will
39 be their God. I will give them one heart and one way to revere Me always in
40 order to benefit them and their children after them. I will make an eternal
covenant with them and never draw back from them, from benefiting them.
I will instill reverence for Me in their hearts so that they will never turn aside
41 from Me. I will rejoice over them to their benefit, and I will plant them in this
land faithfully, with all My heart and with all My soul."

42 For this is what the LORD said: "Just as I brought upon this people this great
disaster, so will I bring them all the good fortune that I have assured them.
43 Fields will be purchased in this land of which you say, 'It is desolate, devoid of
44 man and beast, delivered to the Chaldeans.' Fields will be purchased for silver,
written in a scroll, and sealed and witnessed in the land of Binyamin and in
the surroundings of Jerusalem, and in the cities of Yehuda and the cities in the

mountains, in the cities of the lowland and the cities of the south, for I will bring them back from their captivity," declares the LORD.

33 1 The word of the LORD came to Yirmeyahu a second time while he was still shut in the prison courtyard:
2 This is what the LORD, who is performing it, said –
the LORD is crafting it to make it last;
the LORD is His name –
3 Call to Me and I will answer you.
I will tell you great and unattainable things,
things that you never knew.

4 For this is what the LORD, God of Israel, said regarding the houses of this city
and the palaces that are being demolished on account of the siege ramps and
5 the sword: The kings of Yehuda are coming to do battle with the Chaldeans,
but they themselves fill the city with the corpses of the people whom I
struck in My anger and in My wrath, having hidden My face from this city on
6 account of all their wickedness. I shall offer her cure and healing, and I shall
7 heal them. I shall impart to them abundant and abiding peace. I will bring
them back from the captivity of Yehuda and the captivity of Israel and will
8 build them up as before. I will purify them from all their sins that they sinned
against Me. I shall forgive them for all the sins that they sinned against Me
9 and for their rebellion against Me. She shall become for Me a symbol of joy,
praise, and glory for all nations of the earth, who shall learn of the great good
that I have done for them and will fear and tremble over all the great good
and peace that I shall accomplish for her.

10 This is what the LORD said: Again will be heard in this place, that you say
is ruined and devoid of man and beast, the cities of Yehuda and the streets
11 of Jerusalem that are deserted, devoid of man and inhabitant and beast, the
sound of joy and the sound of happiness, the voice of the groom and the voice
of the bride, the voice of those who proclaim,
"Give thanks to the LORD of Hosts,
for the LORD is good
and His loving-kindness is forever,"
and the voice of those who bring offerings of thanksgiving to the House of the
LORD, for I will return the captives to the land as before, says the LORD.

12 This is what the LORD of Hosts said: There will again be in this place – now
a ruin with neither man nor beast in all of its cities – an abode for shepherds
13 resting their sheep. In the towns of the hills, in the cities of the lowlands, and
in the cities of the south, and in the territory of Binyamin, and in the environs
of Jerusalem, and in the cities of Yehuda, sheep will again pass under the
hands of the one numbering them, says the LORD.

14 Days are approaching, declares the LORD, when I will fulfill the good promise
15 that I made to the House of Israel and the House of Yehuda. In those days
and in that time, I will make a righteous scion blossom forth from David, and

16 he will dispense justice and righteousness in the land. In those days Yehuda
will be saved, and Jerusalem will dwell in safety, and this is what He will call
her: "The LORD is our righteous one."

17 For this is what the LORD said: There will never cease to be someone of
18 David's line to sit upon the throne of the House of Israel. And for the Levitical
priests there will never cease to be someone to offer burnt offerings, burn
grain offerings, and perform sacrifices before Me for all time.

19 The word of the LORD came to Yirmeyahu:

20 This is what the LORD said: If you are able to break My covenant with the day
and My covenant with the night, causing day and night not to occur in their
21 designated times, only then can My covenant with My servant David, that
his son will reign upon his throne, be broken, and similarly for the Levitical
22 priests, My ministrants. Just as the heavenly bodies cannot be counted, and
the sand of the sea cannot be measured, so will I increase the seed of my
servant David and of the Levites who minister to Me.

23 The word of the LORD came to Yirmeyahu:

24 Have you not observed what this people have said? "The LORD has rejected
these two families which He had once chosen."[74] They have scorned My
people, so that they will never again be a nation in their eyes.

25 This is what the LORD said: Only if I had no covenant with day and night,
26 and if I had not established the laws of heaven and earth, would I reject
the offspring of Yaakov and of David My servant, and not select any of his
offspring as rulers over the offspring of Avraham, Yisḥak,[75] and Yaakov – for
I will bring them back from their captivity and have compassion for them.

34 1 The word that came to Yirmeyahu from the LORD while Nevukhadretzar,
king of Babylon, his army, all the kingdoms under his dominion, and all the
2 peoples were attacking Jerusalem and its towns – this is what the LORD, God
of Israel, said: "Go and speak to Tzidkiyahu, king of Yehuda, and say to him:
This is what the LORD said: I am about to deliver this city into the hands of
3 the king of Babylon, and he will burn it down by fire. You will not escape him.
You will be seized and delivered into his hands. Your eyes will see the eyes
of the king of Babylon, and you will speak directly to each other. You will
4 be brought to Babylon. But hear the word of the LORD, Tzidkiyahu, king of
Yehuda. This is what the LORD said regarding you: You will not perish by the
5 sword. Rather, you will die peacefully. Just as incense was burned for your
ancestors, the kings of old who came before you, so will they burn spices for
you. They will eulogize you, saying, 'Alas, master!' For this is the word that I
asserted," declares the LORD.

---

74 | The dynasties of the priesthood and the kingship referred to in verse 21 above.

75 | A variant spelling of Yitzḥak. The verb "to laugh," on which the name is based, can itself appear in Biblical Hebrew both as *tzaḥak* and *saḥak*.

6 Yirmeyahu the prophet related all these words to Tzidkiyahu, king of Yehuda,
7 in Jerusalem while the army of the king of Babylon continued to attack
Jerusalem and all the remaining cities of Yehuda, Lakhish and Azeka, for they
alone were the fortified cities left of the cities of Yehuda.

8 The word that came to Yirmeyahu from the LORD after King Tzidkiyahu had
9 made a covenant with all the people of Jerusalem, proclaiming their freedom:
Everyone was to set free his Hebrew manservant and his Hebrew maidservant.
10 No one was to enslave his fellow man of Yehuda. All the officials and all the
people who had entered into the covenant obeyed in that each person set
free his manservant and his maidservant, Hebrew males and females, never
11 to enslave them again. They obeyed and set them free. After a time, they
regressed. They recovered the manservants and maidservants that they had
set free and forced them to be manservants and maidservants.

12 13 Then the word of the LORD came to Yirmeyahu from the LORD. This is what
the LORD, God of Israel, said: "I made a covenant with your ancestors at the
14 time I took them out of the land of Egypt, the house of bondage, saying, 'At
the beginning of the seventh year[76] each of you should set free your brother
Hebrew who had been sold to you and who served you for six years – send
him forth from you free.' But your ancestors did not heed Me and did not
even bend their ears.

15 "You repented today and did what was proper in My eyes, proclaiming
freedom, every person for his fellow, and you made a covenant in My presence
16 in the house which is called by My name. But you regressed and profaned My
name. Each of you recovered his manservant and his maidservant, whom you
had set free to do as they desire, and you forced them to remain manservants
and maidservants for yourselves."

17 Therefore, this is what the LORD said: "Because you did not heed Me to
proclaim freedom, everyone for his brother and everyone for his fellow, so
will I set free against you," declares the LORD, "the sword, the pestilence, and
the famine, and render you an object of shuddering for all the kingdoms of the
18 earth. And I will deliver to all the people who violated My covenant and did
not uphold the words of the covenant that they made in My presence, the calf
19 that they cut in two,[77] the sections of which they passed between – the officials
of Yehuda and the officials of Jerusalem, the courtiers and the priests, and all
20 the folk of the land who passed between the sections of the calf – I will deliver
them into the hands of their enemies, the hands of those that seek their lives,
and their corpses shall become fodder for the birds of the skies and the beasts
21 of the earth. I will deliver Tzidkiyahu, king of Yehuda, and his officials into
the hands of their enemies and into the hands of those who seek their lives
22 and into the army of the king of Babylon, which is withdrawing from you.[78] I

76 | See Exodus 21:2–3.

77 | An important covenantal ritual (see, e.g., Gen., ch. 15).

78 | Referring to when the Chaldeans were temporarily diverted from the siege (see ch. 37).

shall now utter a command," declares the LORD, "and I shall bring them back
to this city. They will attack it, capture it, and burn it down by fire. The cities
of Yehuda I shall render desolate, without an inhabitant."

35 1 The word that came to Yirmeyahu from the LORD in the days of Yehoyakim,
2 son of Yoshiyahu, king of Yehuda: "Go to the house of the descendants of
Rekhav[79] and speak to them. Bring them to the House of the LORD, to one
of the chambers, and give them wine to drink."

3 I took Yaazanya son of Yirmeyahu son of Ḥavatzinya, his brothers and all his
4 children and the entire house of the descendants of Rekhav, and I brought
them to the House of the LORD, to the chamber of the sons of Ḥanan son of
Yigdalyahu, the man of God, that was adjacent to the chamber of the officials
5 and above the chamber of Maaseyahu son of Shalum, the gatekeeper. I placed
goblets full of wine and cups before the sons of the house of Rekhav and said
to them, "Drink wine."

6 They said, "We will not drink wine because Yonadav son of Rekhav, our
ancestor, commanded us: 'Do not drink wine, neither you nor your children,
7 forever! You are not to build houses, nor sow seed, nor plant vineyards, nor
even possess them for yourselves. Instead, you are to live in tents all your lives
so that you will thrive for many days upon the land where you will reside.'
8 We heeded the voice of Yehonadav son of Rekhav our forefather in all that
he commanded us, never to drink wine, neither ourselves nor our wives, nor
9 our sons and daughters, and not to build houses in which to live, and not to
10 have vineyard, field, or seed. Rather, we live in tents. We heeded Yonadav
11 our ancestor, and we have done all that he commanded us. However, when
Nevukhadretzar, king of Babylon, rose up against the land, we said, 'Come
and let us go up to Jerusalem because of the army of the Chaldeans and
because of the army of Aram.' And so we live in Jerusalem."

12 13 Then the word of the LORD came to Yirmeyahu. This is what the LORD of
Hosts, God of Israel, said: "Go and say to the men of Yehuda and to those that
dwell in Jerusalem: It would befit you to take instruction to heed my words,
14 declares the LORD. Fulfilled are the words of Yehonadav son of Rekhav, who
commanded his descendants not to drink wine. They have not drunk wine
to this very day, for they heeded the command of their ancestor. But I spoke
15 to you persistently, and yet you did not heed Me. I sent to you My servants,
the prophets, again and again, to tell every one of you to turn away from his
evil path, to correct his actions, and not to follow other gods to worship them.
Then you would live upon the land which I gave you and your ancestors. But
16 you did not bend your ears. You did not listen to Me. For the children of
Yehonadav son of Rekhav obeyed their ancestor's command just as he had
commanded them, but this people have not obeyed Me.

17 "Therefore, this is what the LORD, God of Hosts, God of Israel, said: Now I

79 | See II Kings 10:15; I Chronicles 2:55.

will bring upon Yehuda, and upon all who dwell in Jerusalem, every disaster
which I have decreed upon them, for I spoke to them and they did not listen;
I called to them and they did not respond."

18 Yirmeyahu said to the house of the Rekhabites, "This is what the LORD
of Hosts, God of Israel, said: Because you listened to the command of
Yehonadav your ancestor, and kept all his precepts, and did exactly as he
19 commanded you, this is what the LORD of Hosts, God of Israel, therefore
said: There will never cease to be a descendant of Yonadav son of Rekhav
who will stand before Me, for all time."

36 1 In the fourth year of Yehoyakim son of Yoshiyahu, king of Yehuda, this word
2 came to Yirmeyahu from the LORD: "Take for yourself a scroll and write upon
it all the words that I have spoken to you concerning Israel, Yehuda, and all
the nations from the time I spoke to you in the days of Yoshiyahu until today.
3 Perhaps the House of Yehuda will hear of all the disasters that I plan to bring
upon them, and each of them will turn back from his evil way. I would then
forgive their sins and transgressions."

4 So Yirmeyahu summoned Barukh son of Neriya. From the mouth of
Yirmeyahu, Barukh wrote upon a scroll all of the LORD's words that He had
5 spoken to him. Yirmeyahu instructed Barukh, "I am constrained; I cannot go
6 to the House of the LORD. You go and read the scroll upon which you wrote
from my mouth the words of the LORD – in the hearing of the people in the
House of the LORD on a fast day. In doing so, you will be reading it in the
7 hearing of the people of Yehuda who come there from their towns. Perhaps
their pleas will be accepted by the LORD and each of them will turn back
from his evil ways, for great is the anger and wrath with which the LORD has
spoken against this people."

8 Barukh son of Neriya did just as Yirmeyahu the prophet instructed him,
reading from the scroll the words of the LORD in the House of the LORD.

9 In the fifth year of Yehoyakim son of Yoshiyahu, king of Yehuda, in the ninth
month, all the people of Jerusalem and all the people who came from the
10 towns of Yehuda to Jerusalem proclaimed a fast before the LORD. Barukh
read the words of Yirmeyahu from the scroll in the House of the LORD in
the chamber of Gemaryahu son of Shafan the scribe, in the upper courtyard
by the entrance of the New Gate of the House of the LORD, in the hearing
of all the people.

11 Mikhayehu son of Gemaryahu son of Shafan heard all the words of the LORD
12 from the scroll. He went down to the king's palace to the scribe's chamber
where all the officials had gathered: Elishama the scribe, Delayahu son of
Shemayahu, Elnatan son of Akhbor, Gemaryahu son of Shafan, Tzidkiyahu
13 son of Ḥananyahu, and all the officials. Mikhayehu told them all that he had
heard when Barukh read the scroll in the hearing of the people.

14 All the officials sent Yehudi son of Netanyahu son of Shelemyahu son of

Kushi to Barukh to say, "Come, and bring the scroll that you read in the
hearing of the people with you." Barukh son of Neriyahu took the scroll with
15 him and came to them. They said to him, "Be seated, please, and read it in
16 our presence." So Barukh read it in their presence. As they heard everything,
they looked at each other fearfully and said to Barukh, "We must certainly
tell the king about all this."

17 They asked Barukh, "Please, tell us how you were able to write all this from
his mouth."

18 Barukh replied, "He dictated all these words to me from his mouth, and I
wrote onto the scroll in ink."

19 The officials said to Barukh, "Go hide, you and Yirmeyahu. Let no one know
where you are."

20 They approached the king in the courtyard, having deposited the scroll in the
21 chamber of Elishama the scribe. They told the king everything. The king sent
Yehudi to retrieve the scroll, and he retrieved it from the chamber of Elishama
the scribe. Yehudi read it in the presence of the king and in the presence of
all the officials who were in attendance on the king.

22 The king was sitting in the winter quarters, it being the ninth month.[80] The
23 hearth was ablaze before him. As soon as Yehudi had read three or four columns,
he would cut them off with a scribe's knife and cast them into the fire in the
24 hearth until the entire scroll was consumed in the fire of the hearth. The king
and all his servants, having heard all of it, showed no fear and did not rend their
25 garments. Although Elnatan, Delayahu, and Gemaryahu had begged the king
26 not to burn the scroll, he did not listen to them. The king ordered Yeraḥme'el
the king's son, Serayahu son of Azriel, and Shelemyahu son of Avde'el to seize
Barukh the scribe and Yirmeyahu the prophet. But the LORD hid them.

27 After the king had burned the scroll and the words that Barukh had written
from the mouth of Yirmeyahu, the word of the LORD came to Yirmeyahu,
28 saying: "Do it again; take another scroll for yourself and write upon it all the
earlier words that were upon the first scroll that Yehoyakim, king of Yehuda,
29 burned. Concerning Yehoyakim, king of Yehuda, you shall say: Thus said the
LORD: You burned this scroll, asking how did you dare write upon it that the
king of Babylon would come and lay waste to this land and eradicate from it
humans and animals?

30 "Therefore, this is what the LORD said concerning Yehoyakim, king of
Yehuda: He will have no heir to sit upon the throne of David, and his corpse
31 will be exposed to the heat of day and the frost of night. I will hold him and
his offspring and his servants accountable for their sins. I shall bring upon
them and upon those who dwell in Jerusalem and upon every man of Yehuda
every disaster of which I have spoken to them, but they did not listen."

80 | The month of Kislev, which generally coincides with December.

32 Yirmeyahu took another scroll and gave it to Barukh son of Neriyahu the
scribe, who wrote upon it from the mouth of Yirmeyahu all the words of the
message that Yehoyakim, king of Yehuda, burned in the fire, with many more
words similar to them added.

37 1 Tzidkiyahu son of Yoshiyahu reigned as king instead of Konyahu[81] son of
Yehoyakim, for Nevukhadretzar, king of Babylon, made him king of the land
2 of Yehuda. Neither he nor his servants nor the people of the land heeded the
3 words of the LORD as spoken through Yirmeyahu the prophet. Nevertheless,
King Tzidkiyahu sent Yehukhal son of Shelemyahu and Tzefanyahu son of
Maaseya the priest to Yirmeyahu the prophet, saying, "Please pray on our
behalf to the LORD our God."

4 At that time Yirmeyahu walked about freely among the people, for they had
5 not placed him in prison. Now Pharaoh's army set out from Egypt, and when
the Chaldeans who were besieging Jerusalem heard of this, they withdrew
from Jerusalem.

6 7 The word of the LORD came to Yirmeyahu. This is what the LORD, God of
Israel, said: "This is what you are to say to the king of Yehuda, who sent you
to Me to inquire of Me: Pharaoh's army, which set out to help you, is about
8 to return to his land, to Egypt. The Chaldeans will return and attack this city.
They will capture it and burn it down with fire.

9 "This is what the LORD said: Do not deceive yourselves by assuming that the
10 Chaldeans will depart from us, for they will not depart. For even if you were
to smite the entire Chaldean army that is attacking you, leaving behind only
the gravely wounded, each of them would rise up from his tent and burn
down this city with fire."

11 When the Chaldean army had withdrawn from Jerusalem because of
Pharaoh's army,

12 Yirmeyahu went out from the city to go toward the land of Binyamin, to flee
13 from there into the midst of the people. He was at the Binyamin Gate. An
appointed guard was there whose name was Yiriya son of Shelemya son of
Ḥananya. He seized Yirmeyahu the prophet, saying, "You are surrendering
to the Chaldeans."

14 Yirmeyahu said, "That is a lie! I am not surrendering to the Chaldeans." But
Yiriya paid him no heed and held onto Yirmeyahu and brought him to the
15 officials. The officials were furious at Yirmeyahu and beat him. They put him
in a prison house, the house of Yehonatan the scribe, for they had made it
16 into a jail. Thus did Yirmeyahu come to the cistern house, to the prison cells.
He remained there for many days.

17 King Tzidkiyahu sent for him and brought him and questioned him secretly
in his palace: "Is there any word from the LORD?"

---

81 | Yekhonya, who reigned for only three months (see 24:1; II Kings 24:8–17).

Yirmeyahu replied, "There is," and continued, "you shall be delivered into the
18 hands of the king of Babylon." Yirmeyahu further said to King Tzidkiyahu,
"What crime did I commit against you, your servants, or this people that you
19 have put me into prison? Where are your prophets who prophesied to you
saying that the king of Babylon will not come upon you and upon this land?
20 And now, my master the king, please listen. May my plea be acceptable to you.
Do not send me back to the house of Yehonatan the scribe, lest I die there."

21 King Tzidkiyahu gave commands, and Yirmeyahu was confined in the
prisoners' courtyard. He was given a loaf of bread each day from the bakers'
street; until all the bread in the city was gone, Yirmeyahu remained in the
prisoners' courtyard.

38 1 Shefatya son of Matan, Gedalyahu son of Pashḥur, Yukhal son of Shelemyahu,
and Pashḥur son of Malkiya heard the words that Yirmeyahu was speaking to
2 all the people: "This is what the Lord said: Whoever remains in this city will
die by sword or famine or pestilence, but whoever goes out to the Chaldeans
will live. His life will be his prize in war, and he will live.

3 "This is what the Lord said: This city shall surely be delivered into the hands
of the army of the king of Babylon, and he shall capture it."

4 The officials said to the king, "Let this man be put to death, for he demoralizes
the men of war who remain in this city as well as all the people, speaking
such words to them. This man does not seek the welfare of this people, but
only disaster."

5 King Tzidkiyahu said, "He is in your hands, for the king can do nothing
against your will."

6 So they took Yirmeyahu and cast him into the pit of Malkiyahu the king's
son, which was in the prison courtyard. They lowered Yirmeyahu with ropes.
There was no water in the pit, only mud. Yirmeyahu sank into the mud.

7 Eved Melekh the Kushite, a eunuch, who was in the king's palace, heard that
8 Yirmeyahu was put into the pit. The king was then at the Binyamin Gate. Eved
9 Melekh left the king's palace and spoke to the king, saying, "My lord the king,
these men have done wrong by treating Yirmeyahu the prophet this way, by
casting him into the pit. He will surely die of hunger right where he is, for
there is no longer any bread in the city."

10 The king ordered Eved Melekh the Kushite as follows: "Take thirty men from
here under your authority and have them raise Yirmeyahu the prophet from
the pit before he dies."

11 Eved Melekh took the men under his authority and went to the king's palace
to a room beneath the treasury. From there they took ragged and worn-
12 out clothes and lowered them with ropes to Yirmeyahu in the pit. Eved
Melekh the Kushite said to Yirmeyahu, "Now place the ragged and worn-out

clothes under your armpits, under the ropes," and Yirmeyahu did just that.
13 They pulled Yirmeyahu out with the ropes and lifted him up from the pit.
Yirmeyahu stayed in the prison courtyard.

14 King Tzidkiyahu sent for Yirmeyahu, and they took the prophet to him near
the third entrance of the House of the LORD. The king said to Yirmeyahu, "I
ask you about the word of the Lord. Hold nothing back."

15 Yirmeyahu replied to Tzidkiyahu, "If I tell you, you will surely kill me; if I
advise you, you will not listen to me."

16 King Tzidkiyahu swore to Yirmeyahu in secret, saying, "As the LORD lives,
who made this life for us, I will not kill you, and I will not deliver you into
the hands of these men who seek your life."

17 Yirmeyahu said to Tzidkiyahu, "This is what the LORD, God of Hosts, God
of Israel, said: If you will go out to the officers of the king of Babylon, your
life will be spared, and this city will not be burned with fire. You and your
18 household will live. But if you do not go out to the officers of the king of
Babylon, then this city shall be delivered into the hands of the Chaldeans;
they shall burn it with fire, and you shall not escape from their hands."

19 King Tzidkiyahu said to Yirmeyahu, "I worry about the people of Yehuda
who have deserted to the Chaldeans lest they hand me over to them and
they torture me."

20 Yirmeyahu said, "They will not hand you over. Heed now the voice of the
21 LORD in what I say to you. It will benefit you, and your life will be spared. But
22 if you refuse to go out, this is what the LORD has shown me – look, all the
women remaining in the palace of the king of Yehuda are being led out to the
officers of the king of Babylon. And look, this is what they say:

'Your allies have seduced you,
and they have prevailed.
Now that your feet have sunk into the mire,
they have retreated backward.'

23 All your wives and sons are being taken to the Chaldeans, and even you shall
not escape their hands, for you shall be caught by the hand of the king of
Babylon, and you shall cause this city to be burned down by fire."

24 Tzidkiyahu said to Yirmeyahu, "Let no one else know of this conversation,
25 and you shall not die. Should the officials hear that I spoke to you, and should
they come to you and say, 'Tell us now what you said to the king – hold
26 nothing back and we will not kill you – and what the king said to you,' tell
them, 'I was presenting my plea before the king that he not send me back to
the house of Yonatan to die there.'"

27 All the officials did come to Yirmeyahu, and they interrogated him. He told
them precisely everything that the king had instructed him to tell. They ceased
speaking with him, for none of the conversation had been overheard.

28 Yirmeyahu stayed in the prison courtyard until the day that Jerusalem was captured.

It transpired when Jerusalem was captured...

39 1 In the ninth year of Tzidkiyahu, king of Yehuda, in the tenth month,
Nevukhadretzar, king of Babylon, and all his forces came to Jerusalem and
2 laid siege to it. In the eleventh year of Tzidkiyahu, on the ninth day of the
3 fourth month, the city was breached. All the officers of the king of Babylon
came and sat at the middle gate – Nergal Saretzer, Samgar Nevo, Sarsekhim
the Rav-Saris, Nergal Saretzer the Rav-Mag, and all the other officers of the
king of Babylon.

4 When Tzidkiyahu, king of Yehuda, and all the men of war saw them, they fled.
They left the city by dark of night by way of the royal garden through the gate
5 between the double walls. They went in the direction of the Arava.[82] But the
Chaldean force pursued them and caught up with Tzidkiyahu on the plains
of Yeriḥo. They took him and hauled him up before Nevukhadretzar, king
6 of Babylon, at Rivla in the land of Ḥamat, and he spoke harshly to him. The
king of Babylon slaughtered the sons of Tzidkiyahu before his eyes in Rivla.
7 The king of Babylon also slaughtered all the nobles of Yehuda. He blinded
8 Tzidkiyahu and chained him in bronze fetters to bring him to Babylon. The
Chaldeans burned down the royal palace and the people's houses with fire,
and they tore down the walls of Jerusalem.

9 As for the rest of the people who remained in the city and those that had
defected to him and the rest of the people who survived – Nevuzaradan, chief
10 of the guard, exiled them to Babylon. But Nevuzaradan, chief of the guard,
retained some of the poor people, who had nothing, in the land of Yehuda
and gave them vineyards and fields at that time.

11 As for Yirmeyahu, Nevukhadretzar, king of Babylon, ordered Nevuzara-
12 dan, chief of the guard, as follows: "Release him[83] and treat him with care.
Do nothing harmful to him; rather, do for him whatever he asks of you."
13 Nevuzaradan, chief of the guard, sent word along with Nevushazban the
Rav-Saris, Nergal Saretzer the Rav-Mag, and all the commanders of the king
14 of Babylon. They sent word and had Yirmeyahu released from the prison
courtyard. They entrusted him to Gedalyahu son of Aḥikam[84] son of Shafan
so that he would be taken to his house. He stayed among the people.

15 The word of the Lord had come to Yirmeyahu while he was still confined to
16 the prison courtyard: "Go and tell Eved Melekh the Kushite that this is what
the Lord of Hosts, God of Israel, said: I will bring My words to pass upon
17 this city, for disaster and not for good, and you will witness it at that time. I
will save you at that time, declares the Lord. You will not be turned over to

82 | Eastward, toward the Jordan River.

83 | From the prison courtyard.

84 | See 26:24.

18 the hands of the men whom you dread. I will surely rescue you so that you
will not fall by the sword. Your own life will be your prize in war because you
trusted in Me, declares the Lord."

40 1 The word came to Yirmeyahu from the Lord after Nevuzaradan, chief of
the guard, set him free from Rama, when he had taken him bound in chains
in the midst of all those of Jerusalem and Yehuda who were being exiled to
2 Babylon. The chief of the guard took Yirmeyahu and said to him, "The Lord,
3 your God, ordered disaster for this place. The Lord brought it about as He
had promised, for you all sinned against the Lord and did not heed His
4 voice, and this is what has happened to you. But now I have freed you from
the chains that were upon your hands. If it pleases you to come with me to
Babylon, I will take good care of you. If it displeases you to come with me
to Babylon, then do not. See this: the entire land is before you. Go wherever
pleases you and wherever seems proper to you to go."

5 And before Yirmeyahu turned to go, Nevuzaradan continued, "Go back
to Gedalya son of Aḥikam son of Shafan, whom the king of Babylon has
appointed over the towns of Yehuda, and stay together with him among the
people, or go wherever it seems proper for you to go." The chief of the guard
6 gave him food, provisions, and a gift and sent him off. Yirmeyahu came to
Gedalya son of Aḥikam at Mitzpa and stayed with him among the people
who were left in the land.

7 When all the army officers who were scattered in the countryside, they and
their men, heard that the king of Babylon had appointed Gedalyahu son of
Aḥikam over the land and that he had entrusted him with the men, women,
and children who were among the poor of the land who were not exiled
8 to Babylon, they came to Gedalya at Mitzpa – Yishmael son of Netanyahu,
Yoḥanan and Yonatan sons of Kare'aḥ, Seraya son of Tanḥumet, the sons of
Ofai the Netofatite, and Yezanyahu son of the Maakhatite, they and their
men.

9 "Do not be afraid to serve the Chaldeans," Gedalyahu son of Aḥikam son of
Shafan promised them and their men. "Stay in the land and serve the king of
10 Babylon, and all will be well for you. I intend to remain in Mitzpa to represent
you before the Chaldeans when they come to us. As for you, gather wine and
summer fruit and oil and store them in your vessels, and settle in the towns
that you have occupied."

11 Likewise, when all the people of Yehuda who were in Moav and among
the Amonites and in Edom and in all other lands heard that the king of
Babylon had granted a remnant in Yehuda and had appointed Gedalyahu
12 son of Aḥikam son of Shafan over them, all the people of Yehuda returned
from all the places where they had been dispersed and came to the land of
Yehuda, to Gedalyahu in Mitzpa. They gathered a great deal of wine and
summer fruit.

13 Yoḥanan son of Kare'aḥ and all the army officers who were in the countryside
14 came to Gedalyahu at Mitzpa. They said to him, "Are you aware that Baalis,
king of the Amonites, has sent Yishmael son of Netanya to take your life?" But
Gedalyahu son of Aḥikam did not believe them.

15 Yoḥanan son of Kare'aḥ secretly said to Gedalyahu in Mitzpa, "Let me go now
and slay Yishmael son of Netanya, and no one will know. Why should he take
your life? Then all of Yehuda who have gathered to you will scatter, and the
remnant of Yehuda will be lost!"

16 Gedalyahu son of Aḥikam said to Yoḥanan son of Kare'aḥ, "Do not do such
a thing. You are telling a lie about Yishmael."

41 1 In the seventh month, Yishmael son of Netanya son of Elishama, of royal
descent and among the king's chief officers, came with ten men to Mitzpa to
2 Gedalyahu son of Aḥikam. They ate a meal together there in Mitzpa. Yishmael
son of Netanya stood up, along with the ten men with him, and they struck
Gedalyahu son of Aḥikam son of Shafan with swords and killed him because
3 the king of Babylon had put him in charge of the land, and all the men of
Yehuda who were with Gedalyahu in Mitzpa and the Chaldeans who were
stationed there, the men of war, Yishmael killed.

4 5 It was the second day after Gedalyahu was killed, yet no one knew. Eighty
men came from Shekhem, Shilo, and Shomron with shaven beards and torn
clothing, having gashed themselves. They had grain offerings and incense
6 with them to bring to the House of the Lord. Yishmael son of Netanya went
out to greet them from Mitzpa, weeping as he went. When he met them, he
7 said to them, "Come to Gedalyahu son of Aḥikam." When they came into
the town, Yishmael son of Netanya – he and his ten men – killed them and
8 threw their bodies into the pit. There were ten men among them who said to
Yishmael, "Do not kill us, for we have hidden treasures in the field – wheat,
barley, oil, and honey." He desisted and did not kill them along with their
comrades.

9 The pit into which Yishmael cast the corpses of all the men whom he
murdered because of Gedalyahu was the very pit that King Asa had made to
defend himself against Baasha, king of Israel.[66] Yishmael son of Netanyahu
10 filled it with dead bodies. Yishmael made captives of the rest of the people who
were in Mitzpa – the daughters of the king and all the people remaining in
Mitzpa whom Nevuzaradan, chief of the guard, had entrusted to Gedalyahu
son of Aḥikam. Yishmael son of Netanya took them captive and set out to
cross over to the Amonites.

11 Yoḥanan son of Kare'aḥ, along with all his army officers, heard of all the evil
12 that Yishmael son of Netanya had done. They took all their men and set out
to do battle with Yishmael son of Netanya, and found him by the great pool

66 | See 1 Kings 15:16–22.

13 near Givon. When the people who were held by Yishmael saw Yoḥanan
14 son of Kare'aḥ and all his army officers, they rejoiced. All the people whom
Yishmael had taken captive from Mitzpa turned and went over to Yoḥanan
15 son of Kare'aḥ. Yishmael son of Netanya along with eight of his men escaped
from Yoḥanan and set out toward the Amonites.

16 Yoḥanan son of Kare'aḥ, along with all his army officers, took from Mitzpa
all the rest of the people whom he had recovered from Yishmael son of
Netanya after he had murdered Gedalya son of Aḥikam: men, soldiers,
women, children, and courtiers whom he, Yoḥanan, had recovered from
17 Givon. They left and stayed in the dwelling place of Kimham, near Beit Leḥem,
18 on their way to go to Egypt because of the Chaldeans, for they feared them,
for Yishmael son of Netanya had murdered Gedalyahu son of Aḥikam, whom
the king had put in charge of the land.

42 1 All the army officers, Yoḥanan son of Kare'aḥ, Yezanya son of Hoshaya, and
2 all the people, from the least to the greatest, stepped forward. They said to
Yirmeyahu the prophet, "Please accept our plea and pray to the Lord your
God on our behalf – on behalf of this entire remnant, for we remain but a few
3 of many, as your eyes can see. May the Lord your God tell us what path we
are to follow and what we are to do."

4 Yirmeyahu the prophet said to them, "I hear you. I will pray to the Lord
your God as you have requested. I will tell you every word that the Lord will
declare to you. I will hold nothing back."

5 They said to Yirmeyahu, "May the Lord be a true and trusted witness against
us if we do not do everything that the Lord your God will send you to tell
6 us. Whether good or bad in our eyes, we shall heed the voice of the Lord
our God to whom we have sent you so that it will go well with us, for we shall
obey the voice of the Lord our God."

7 8 At the end of ten days the word of the Lord came to Yirmeyahu. He
summoned Yoḥanan son of Kare'aḥ, all the army officers who were with him,
9 and all the people from the least to the greatest. He told them, "This is what
10 the Lord, God of Israel, to whom you sent me to present your plea, said: If
you will indeed dwell in this land, I will rebuild you and not tear you down.
I will plant you and not uproot you, for I have come to regret the disaster
11 that I inflicted upon you. No longer fear the king of Babylon as you fear him
now. Do not fear him, declares the Lord, for I am with you to save you and
12 to rescue you from his hands. I will grant you mercy, and he will show mercy
toward you and return you to your land.

13 "But if you say that you shall not dwell in this land, and that you shall not
14 heed the voice of the Lord your God – if you will say, 'No! We will go to
Egypt, where we will not see war, nor hear the sound of trumpets, and not
15 hunger for bread. There we shall dwell!' – in that case, listen to the word of
the Lord, remnant of Yehuda. This is what the Lord of Hosts, God of Israel,

said: If you indeed direct your course toward Egypt and come to settle there,
16 the sword that you fear will overtake you in the land of Egypt, and the famine
that you worry over shall pursue you there in Egypt, and there you shall die.
17 All those who directed their course toward Egypt to settle there shall die by
sword, famine, and pestilence. There shall be neither remnant nor survivor
18 from the disaster that I shall bring upon them. For this is what the LORD of
Hosts, God of Israel, said: Just as My anger and My wrath poured out upon
the inhabitants of Jerusalem, so will My wrath pour out upon you when you
arrive in Egypt. You will become an object of swearing and horror, of curses
19 and vilification. You shall never see this place again. The LORD has told you,
remnant of Yehuda: Do not go to Egypt.

20 "Know this well, for I warn you today. For you have misled me deliberately.
You sent me to the LORD your God, saying, 'Pray to the LORD our God on our
21 behalf. Tell us all that the LORD our God says, and we will do it.' Today I told
you. But you did not heed the voice of the LORD your God, hearing all that
22 I was sent to say to you. Now know this well: You will die by sword, famine,
and pestilence in the very place where you so desired to go and settle."

43 1 It was after Yirmeyahu had finished telling all the people all the words of the
LORD their God that the LORD their God had sent him to tell them, all those
2 words, that Azarya son of Hoshaya and Yoḥanan son of Kare'aḥ and all the
insolent men said to Yirmeyahu, "You tell a lie! The LORD our God did not
3 send you to say, 'Do not come to settle in Egypt.' Rather, Barukh son of Neriya
incited you against us in order to give us over to the hands of the Chaldeans
to kill us or to exile us to Babylon."

4 Yoḥanan son of Kare'aḥ and all the army officers and all the people did not
heed the voice of the LORD telling them to dwell in the land of Yehuda.
5 Yoḥanan son of Kare'aḥ and all the army officers led the entire remnant of
Yehuda who had returned from all the nations where they had been driven
6 to settle in the land of Yehuda – along with the men, women, and children;
the daughters of the king; every person whom Nevuzaradan, chief of the
guard, had left with Gedalyahu son of Aḥikam son of Shafan; Yirmeyahu the
7 prophet; and Barukh son of Neriyahu – and they went to the land of Egypt,
for they did not heed the voice of the LORD, and they arrived at Taḥpanḥes.

8 9 The word of the LORD came to Yirmeyahu in Taḥpanḥes: "In the presence
of the men of Yehuda, take some large stones in your hands and conceal
them in the mortar in the square that is at the entrance to Pharaoh's palace
10 in Taḥpanḥes. Say to them: This is what the LORD of Hosts, God of Israel,
said: I will soon send forth and lead Nevukhadnetzar, king of Babylon, My
servant, here. I will set his throne above these stones that I have concealed,
11 and he will raise his scepter over them. He will come and smite the land of
Egypt. Those destined for death will die, those destined for captivity will be
12 taken captive, and those destined for the sword will fall victim to the sword.
I will set fire to the temples of the gods of Egypt, and Nevukhadnetzar will

burn them and take the gods captive. He will wrap himself up in the land
of Egypt as a shepherd wraps himself up in his garment, and he will depart
13 from there in peace. He will smash the monuments at the house of the sun,[67]
which is in the land of Egypt, and he will burn the buildings of the gods of
Egypt by fire."

44 1 This was the word that came to Yirmeyahu for all the people of Yehuda
living in the land of Egypt, who lived in Migdol, Taḥpanḥes, and Nof, and in
2 the land of Patros; this is what the Lord of Hosts, God of Israel, said: You
yourselves have witnessed the entire disaster that I brought upon Jerusalem
and upon all the cities of Yehuda. Today they are a ruin with no one living in
3 them because of their evil that they perpetrated in order to anger Me, burning
incense to serve other gods whom they never knew – neither they nor you
4 nor your ancestors. I sent to them all My servants, the prophets, persistently,
5 imploring them not to commit this abomination that I despise. But they took
no heed, never even inclining their ears to turn away from their evil and not
6 burn incense to other gods. My anger and My wrath poured out and blazed
in the towns of Yehuda and in the streets of Jerusalem. They became a ruin
and desolation, as they are today.

7 Now this is what the Lord, God of Hosts, God of Israel, said: Why do
you do this terrible harm to yourselves, cutting off man and woman, child
and suckling babe, from the midst of Yehuda, not leaving yourselves any
8 remnant? For you anger Me with your actions by burning incense to other
gods in the land of Egypt where you have come to settle, causing yourselves
to be cut off and to become a curse and a disgrace among all the nations of
9 the earth. Have you forgotten the evils of your ancestors, the evils of the
kings of Yehuda and the evils of their wives, your own evils and the evils of
your wives that you committed in the land of Yehuda and in the streets of
10 Jerusalem? To this very day you have not been humbled; you do not fear;
you do not follow My teaching and My statutes that I placed before you and
before your ancestors.

11 This is what the Lord of Hosts, God of Israel, therefore said: I am about to
12 direct My face toward you for harm and to cut off all of Yehuda. I will seize
the remnant of Yehuda that directed their course to go to the land of Egypt
to settle there. They shall all be finished off in the land of Egypt; they shall fall
by sword and famine; they shall be finished off from the least to the greatest.
By sword and by famine they shall die; they shall become objects of swearing
13 and horror, of curses and vilification. I will punish those who dwell in the
land of Egypt just as I punished Jerusalem – with the sword, with famine, and
14 with pestilence. There will be neither refugee nor survivor from the remnant
of Yehuda who have come to settle in the land of Egypt. As for returning to
the land of Yehuda, where they so strongly desire to return to dwell, none
but refugees shall return.

67 | Temples to the sun god.

15 All the men who knew that their wives had burned incense to other gods
along with the great throng of women who were standing there and all the
16 people living in the land of Egypt, in Patros, responded to Yirmeyahu, "We
will not listen to you regarding the matter that you have told us in the name of
17 the LORD. We will continue to do all that we said we would, to burn incense
to the queen of the heavens and to pour libations to her exactly as we, our
ancestors, our kings, and our officials did in the towns of Yehuda and in the
streets of Jerusalem. There we had plenty of food, and we were successful and
18 suffered no harm. But when we ceased to burn incense to the queen of the
heavens and to pour libations to her, only then did we lack everything and
19 were finished off by the sword and by famine. When we burn incense to the
queen of the heavens and pour libations to her, is it without our husbands'
consent that we make wafers in order to sadden[68] her and pour libations to
her?"

20 Yirmeyahu spoke to all the people including the men and women and to
21 all the people who had responded to him with those words: "With regard
to your actions burning incense in the towns of Yehuda and in the streets of
Jerusalem – you, your ancestors, your kings, your officials, and the people of
the land – the LORD remembered those actions, and they remain upon His
22 heart. When the LORD could no longer forbear because of the wickedness
of your actions and because of the abominations that you performed, then
your land became a ruin, a desolation, and a curse with no one living there,
23 as it is today. Because you burned incense and sinned against the LORD, did
not heed the LORD's voice, and did not follow His teaching, statutes, and
testimonies, disaster therefore afflicted you, as it does today."

24 Yirmeyahu said to all the people and to all the women: "Heed the word of
25 the LORD, all of Yehuda that is in the land of Egypt. This is what the LORD
of Hosts, God of Israel, said: You and your wives have spoken with your
mouth and have acted with your hands, saying, 'We shall comply with our
vows, having vowed to burn incense to the queen of the heavens and to pour
libations to her.' So fulfill your vows; comply with your vows.

26 "Therefore, listen to the word of the LORD, all people of Yehuda living in the
land of Egypt: I have sworn by My great name, said the LORD, that My name
will no longer be invoked by any man of Yehuda anywhere in Egypt saying, 'As
27 the LORD God lives.' I will be watchful over them for harm and not for good.
Every man of Yehuda that is in the land of Egypt will be finished off by the
28 sword and by famine until they are gone. Those who escape the sword shall
return from the land of Egypt to the land of Yehuda few in number, and the
entire remnant of Yehuda that came to settle in the land of Egypt shall know
29 whose word shall stand, Mine or theirs. This will be the sign for you – declares
the LORD – that I will punish you in this place so that you shall know that My
promise to inflict harm upon you shall stand.

68 | Expecting that the saddening of the deity would cause her to rescue them.

30 "This is what the Lord said: I shall deliver Pharaoh Ḥofra, king of Egypt,
into the hands of his enemies and those who seek his life, just as I delivered
Tzidkiyahu, king of Yehuda, into the hands of Nevukhadretzar, king of
Babylon, his enemy, who sought his life."

45 1 The word that Yirmeyahu the prophet spoke to Barukh son of Neriya when
he was writing these words from Yirmeyahu's mouth on a scroll in the
fourth year of the reign of Yehoyakim, son of Yoshiyahu, king of Yehuda:
2 "This is what the Lord, God of Israel, said about you, Barukh: You said,
3 'Woe to me now, for the Lord has added agony to my pain. I am exhausted
4 by my sighing and have found no rest.' This is also what you shall say to
Him. But this is what the Lord said: That which I have built I will tear
down, and that which I have planted I will uproot. This applies to the entire
5 land. Yet you seek greatness for yourself? Do not seek it, for I am about
to inflict disaster upon all flesh – declares the Lord – but I will grant you
your life as a prize of war everywhere that you may go."

46 1 This came to Yirmeyahu the prophet as the word of the Lord concerning
2 the nations: Of Egypt, concerning the army of Pharaoh Nekho, king
of Egypt, located at the Euphrates River near Karkemish and which
Nevukhadretzar, king of Babylon, attacked during the fourth year of
Yehoyakim son of Yoshiyahu, king of Yehuda:

3 Prepare shield and buckler,
    and approach the battle.
4 Harness the horses;
    let the riders mount them.
Polish the spears;
    put on armor;
        stand erect with helmets on.
5 Why have I seen them thus: frightened,
    retreating, moving backward,
their mighty ones crushed,
    desperately fleeing and not looking back,
    terror all around?
        so says the Lord.
6 Let the swift not flee,
    and let the mighty not escape.
Up north, beside the Euphrates River,
    they stumble; they fall.
7 Who is this that rises like the Nile,
    whose waters pour forth like rivers?
8 It is Egypt that rises like the Nile,
    whose water pours forth like rivers,
and who says, "I will rise and cover the earth;
    I will destroy cities and their inhabitants."
9 Let the horses advance
    and the chariots charge madly,

and let the mighty go forth;
Kush and Put, who grasp the shield,
and the Lydians, who grasp and draw the bow.

10 That day will be a day of vengeance for the Lord GOD of Hosts, to take
revenge upon His enemies. The sword will devour, be sated, and overflow
with their blood; a sacrifice for the Lord GOD of Hosts, in the northern land,
by the Euphrates River.

11 Go up to Gilad and take balm, virgin daughter Egypt.
For naught will you apply many remedies;
there is no cure for you.
12 The nations have heard of your disgrace,
and your screams have filled the earth.
One mighty man has stumbled over the other mighty man;
together both have fallen.

13 The word that the LORD spoke to Yirmeyahu the prophet –
how Nevukhadretzar, king of Babylon,
would come to attack the land of Egypt:
14 Tell it in Egypt, let it be heard in Migdol,
and let it be heard in Nof and in Taḥpanḥes!
Say, "Stand firm and prepare yourself,
for the sword has devoured your surroundings."
15 Why have your warriors been swept away?
They did not stand
because the LORD pushed them down.
16 He made many falter.
Each man fell upon his comrade
and said, "Get up and let us return to our people
and to the land of our birth,
away from the sword of the oppressor."
17 There they will taunt:
"Pharaoh, king of Egypt, king over a multitude,
allowed the appointed time to go by."
18 As I live – declares the King,
LORD of Hosts is His name –
just as Tabor is among the mountains,
and Carmel is by the sea,
so will he come.
19 Make for yourselves baggage for exile,
you who dwell securely, daughter Egypt,
for Nof will become a desolation,
laid waste, with no inhabitant.

20 A very beautiful calf was Egypt,
but a murderous enemy attacks her from the north.

21 Even her hired soldiers within her army are like fattened calves.
They too shall turn away, flee together, and not stand firm.
Their day of doom has arrived,
when they will meet their fate.
22 Her voice will go forth like a snake's,
for they will attack her with force
and come upon her with axes like woodcutters.
23 They shall cut down her forest, declares the LORD,
although it cannot be fathomed.
There are more of them than locusts;
they are innumerable.
24 Shamed is daughter Egypt,
given over into the hands of the northern people.
25 Said the LORD of Hosts,
the God of Israel,
I will inflict punishment upon Amon of No,[69]
and upon Pharaoh, and upon Egypt,
upon her gods and upon her kings,
upon Pharaoh and all who trust in him.
26 I will give them over into the hands of those who seek their lives
and into the hands of Nevukhadretzar, king of Babylon,
and into the hands of his servants.
Afterward, she shall be inhabited as in days of old,
declares the LORD.

27 As for you, My servant Yaakov, do not fear,
and Israel, do not be terrified,
for I will deliver you from a distant land
and your descendants from their land of captivity.
For Yaakov it will again be
quiet and tranquil,
with none to frighten him.
28 And you, My servant Yaakov,
do not fear, declares the LORD,
for I am with you.
For I will make an end
of all the nations among whom I have scattered you,
but of you I will not make an end.
I will discipline you justly,
but I will surely not annihilate you.[70]

47 1 The word of the LORD that came to Yirmeyahu the prophet
concerning the Philistines
before Pharaoh attacked Aza:[71]

69 | A prominent Egyptian god.
70 | Cf. 30:10–11.
71 | A chief Philistine city.

2 Thus said the Lord:
Waters are about to rise from the north[72]
that will become like an overflowing river.
They shall flood the land and those who fill it,
the town and its inhabitants.
People will cry out;
all the land's inhabitants shall wail.
3 At the sound of the pounding hooves of his stallions,
the roar of his chariots,
and the rumbling of his wheels,
fathers will not turn around to save their children
because of their enfeebled hands,
4 because of the day that is coming
to devastate all the Philistines,
to cut off from Tyre and Sidon
every last ally.
For the Lord is devastating the Philistines,
the remnant of the island of Kaftor.
5 Aza has been shorn;
Ashkelon has been severed.
O remnant of her valley,
how long will you gash yourselves?[73]
6 O sword of the Lord,
how long will you be unquiet?
Withdraw into your scabbard;
rest and be silent.
7 How can she be quiet
when the Lord has ordered her
against Ashkelon
and has selected the seacoast
as her target?

48 1 Concerning Moav,
this is what the Lord of Hosts, God of Israel, said:
Woe to Nevo, for she has been devastated;
shamed, captured is Kiryatayim;
the fortress is shamed and shattered.
2 There shall no longer be glory for Moav.
In Ḥeshbon they have plotted disaster against her:
"Come and let us cut her off from being a nation."
You too, Madmen,[74] shall be silenced;
the sword shall pursue you.

72 | Whence the invaders would come.

73 | In mourning.

74 | A city in the region of Moav.

3 The sound of a scream from Ḥoronayim,
devastation, and a great collapse –
4 Moav is broken;
her young people have let loose a great scream.
5 On the ascent to Luḥit
weeping shall follow weeping;
on the descent from Ḥoronayim
enemies heard sounds of collapse.
6 Flee, save your lives,
and let them be like shrubs in the wilderness.
7 Because you have trusted
in your achievements and in your storehouses,
you shall also be taken captive,
and Kemosh[75] shall go into exile
together with his priests and his officials.
8 The marauder shall come to every town –
no town will be spared;
the valley ruined,
the plain destroyed,
as the LORD has said.
9 Give wings to Moav
so that she can take flight,
and her towns become a desolation
with no inhabitant in them.
10 Cursed is the one who performs the LORD's work deceitfully,
and cursed is the one who restrains his sword from shedding blood.
11 Moav has been tranquil from his youth
and has rested quietly upon his lees.
He has not been emptied from vessel to vessel
and has never gone into exile
so that his flavor has remained fresh,
and his fragrance has never altered.

12 Therefore, days are approaching,
declares the LORD,
when I will send forth spoilers
who will despoil him.
They will empty his vessels,
and they will smash his jugs.
13 And Moav will be shamed
because of Kemosh,
just as the House of Israel was shamed
because of Beit El,[76]
in whom they trusted.

---

75 | The god of Moav.

76 | A reference to the idolatrous calf situated there.

14 How dare you say: "We are mighty men,
soldiers adept at war"?
15 Moav is devastated;
his towns are gone.
His finest youths
have gone down to the slaughter,
declares the King –
LORD of Hosts is his name.
16 Moav's doom comes near;
his disaster hastens swiftly.
17 Grieve, all who dwell around him
and all who know his fame.
Say: "How has this mighty scepter,
this splendid staff,
been broken?"
18 Descend from glory
and sit in thirst,
she who dwells in daughter Dibon.
He who has devastated Moav
has come upon you.
He has destroyed your fortresses.
19 Stand by the road and stare,
dweller in Aroer.
Ask of him who flees
and of her who escapes:
say, "What has happened?"
20 Shamed is Moav,
for she is broken;
wail and shriek.
Tell it at the Arnon:
Moav is devastated.
21 Judgment has reached the tableland
upon Ḥolon, Yahatz, and Meifaat;
22 and upon Divon, Nevo, and Beit Divlatayim;
23 and upon Kiryatayim, Beit Gamul, and Beit Meon;
24 and upon Keriyot and Botzra –
and upon all the towns of the land of Moav,
far and near.
25 The horn of Moav has been cut off,
its arm broken,
declares the LORD.
26 Make him drunk,
for he has puffed himself up against the LORD.
Let him roll about in his vomit
so that he too becomes a laughingstock.

27 Was not Israel a laughingstock to you?
Was he found among thieves?
For whenever you spoke about him,
you shook with scorn.
28 Abandon towns
and dwell among rocks,
inhabitants of Moav.
Become like a dove that nests
in the sides of the entrance of a crevice.
29 We have heard of Moav's arrogance –
excessive arrogance –
his loftiness, his hubris,
his pride, and his haughty heart.[77]
30 I know, declares the Lord,
that his wrath has no basis,
and that his illusions have come to naught.
31 Therefore I will wail for Moav;
I will shriek on behalf of all of Moav;
for the people of Kir Ḥeres I will whimper.
32 Even more than weeping for Yazer
I weep for you, vineyards of Sivma,
whose branches once extended over the waters
and reached the Yazer Sea.
The devastator has fallen upon
your summer fruits and vintage.
33 Joy and gaiety
are dispelled from the fruitful field
and from the land of Moav.
I have made an end to the wine in the winepresses.
No one treads them with shouts of "*heidad*" –
the "*heidad*" is no longer the same "*heidad*."
34 The screams reached from Ḥeshbon to Elaleh.
They raised their voices as far as Yahatz,
from Tzoar up to Ḥoronayim
and up to Eglat Shlishiya.
Even the waters of Nimrim
shall become a desolation.
35 I will make an end in Moav,
declares the Lord,
of the one who gives an offering upon a high place
or burns incense to his god.
36 Therefore my heart moans for Moav like flutes;
my heart moans for Kir Ḥeres like flutes;

77 | Cf. Isaiah, chapters 15–16.

all the wealth it accumulated
is lost.
37 For every head is shaved,
every beard shorn.
On all hands there are gashes,
and on the loins sackcloth.
38 On all the rooftops of Moav
and in her squares there is only lament,
for I have broken Moav
like an unwanted vessel,
declares the LORD.
39 "How shattered!" they wailed.
How Moav has turned his back in shame
and become a laughingstock
and a source of horror
for all around him.

40 For this is what the LORD said:
He will soar like an eagle
and spread his wings toward Moav.
41 The towns are captured
and the fortresses seized.
On that day the heart of the mighty of Moav will become
like the heart of a woman in labor.
42 Moav is denied peoplehood,
for he has puffed himself up against the LORD.
43 Panic, pit, and a snare upon you,
inhabitant of Moav,
declares the LORD.
44 Whoever flees from the panic
shall fall into the pit,
and whoever climbs out of the pit
shall be caught in the snare,
for I shall bring upon her, upon Moav,
the year of its retribution,
declares the LORD.
45 Those who fled from the power
stood in the shadow of Ḥeshbon,
but a fire came forth from Ḥeshbon,
a flame from the midst of Siḥon.
It consumed the brow of Moav
and the foreheads of Shaon.[78]
46 Woe for you, Moav;
Kemosh's people are destroyed,

78| Cf. Numbers 21:27–30.

for they have taken your sons captive
and your daughters into captivity.
47 I will return the captives of Moav
in the days to come,
declares the Lord.
Thus far this is the judgment on Moav.

49 1 Concerning the Amonites,
this is what the Lord said:
Does Israel have no children?
Does he have no heir?
Why then did their king possess Gad
and their people settle in its towns?
2 Therefore, days are approaching,
declares the Lord,
when I shall let the trumpet blasts of war
be heard over Raba of the Amonites,
and she shall become a desolate mound,
her villages set on fire,
and Israel shall dispossess those who possessed him,
says the Lord.
3 Wail, Ḥeshbon,
for Ai has been devastated.
Shout, daughters of Raba;
gird sackcloth, lament,
rush about inside the fences,
for their king shall go into exile
together with his priests and princes.
4 Why do you boast about the valleys?
Your valley flows away,
wayward daughter,
she who trusts in her treasures,
saying, "Who dares come upon me?"
5 I am about to bring terror upon you,
declares the Lord God of Hosts,
from every direction.
Everyone will be driven forward
with none to gather the one who wanders off.
6 Afterward, I will return the captives of the Amonites,
declares the Lord.

7 Concerning Edom, this is what the Lord of Hosts said:
Is there no longer wisdom in Teiman?
Has good counsel been lost to those with understanding?
Has their wisdom decayed?
8 Inhabitants of Dedan,

flee, clear out, dwell in the depths,
for I have brought Esav's fate upon you
at the time I punished him.
9 If grape gatherers come upon you,
do they not leave gleanings?
Do not thieves of the night
consume only their fill?[79]
10 For I have exposed Esav;
I have revealed his secret places
so that he cannot hide.
His seed has been ravaged,
his brothers, his neighbors –
he is gone.
11 Leave your orphans to Me,
and I shall keep them alive,
and your widows shall come to rely on Me.

12 For this is what the LORD said:
Even those who are not sentenced
to drink the cup of wrath
must drink it,
and yet you expect to be absolved?
You will certainly not be absolved.
You shall certainly drink it.
13 For by My own self have I sworn,
declares the LORD,
Botzra[80] will become a desolation,
a disgrace, a wasteland, and a curse,
and all her towns shall be ruins forever.
14 I heard tidings from the LORD,
and an envoy is sent out among the nations:
"Assemble and come upon her;
rise up for battle."[81]
15 Look, I have made you small among nations,
scorned by humanity.
16 Your dreadfulness
and your haughty heart deceived you,
you who dwell in the cliff's niches,
who hold on to the height of the hill.
Should you raise your nest as high as the eagle's,
I shall bring you down from there,
declares the LORD.
17 Edom shall become a source of astonishment.

79 | Cf. Obadiah 1:5–6.
80 | An important city in Edom.
81 | Cf. Obadiah 1:1–2.

Whoever passes her by shall be astonished
and shall shriek over all her wounds.
18 As in the overturning
of Sedom and Amora and their neighbors,
says the Lord,
no one shall live there,
and no human shall stay there.
19 Look, like a lion coming up
from a thicket of the Jordan
against the secure pasture,
in a moment I will drive him[82] away from it.
I will appoint over her whomever I choose,
for who is like Me,
and who can summon Me?
Who is the shepherd who can stand up against Me?[83]
20 Therefore, hear the counsel
that the Lord has taken against Edom
and His plans regarding the inhabitants of Teiman:
Surely the weakest of sheep shall drag him away;
surely he will render their pastures desolate.
21 The earth trembles
at the sound of their collapse,
a shout,
the sound of which will be heard at the Sea of Reeds.
22 Look, he will fly up and soar like an eagle
and spread his wings over Botzra.
On that day the heart of the mighty of Edom will become
like the heart of a woman in labor.

23 Concerning Damascus:
Ḥamat and Arpad are put to shame,
for they heard bad tidings
and quivered,
fearful as if at sea,
unable to be calm.
24 Damascus has become feeble.
She has turned around to flee.
A shudder has possessed her;
anguish and pangs have seized her
like a woman giving birth.
25 "Why was the city of glory not fortified,
the town of my delight?"
26 Therefore, her young men will fall in her squares,

82 | Referring to Edom.
83 | Cf. 50:44–46.

and all men of war will be cut down on that day,
declares the Lord of Hosts.
27 I will set fire to the wall of Damascus,
and it shall devour the citadels of Ben Hadad.

28 Concerning Kedar[84] and the kingdoms of Ḥatzor
that Nevukhadretzar king of Babylon attacked,
this is what the Lord said:
Rise! Go up against Kedar
and plunder the peoples of the East.
29 They will take away their tents and their sheep;
their curtains, all their utensils,
and their camels they shall carry off for themselves,
and they will cry out at them,
"Terror all around."
30 Flee, wander far,
dwell in the depths, inhabitants of Ḥatzor,
declares the Lord,
for Nevukhadretzar, king of Babylon,
has taken counsel against you.
He has devised a scheme against you.
31 Rise and go up against the tranquil nation
that dwells securely,
declares the Lord,
that has neither gates nor bars,
that dwells alone.
32 Their camels shall be booty,
and their many cattle shall be spoils.
I shall scatter them in every direction,
to the end of every corner.
From every side I shall deliver their doom,
declares the Lord.
33 Ḥatzor shall become a jackals' haunt,
an eternal desolation.
No one shall live there,
and no human shall reside there.

34 The word of the Lord that came to Yirmeyahu the prophet concerning Eilam
35 at the beginning of the reign of Tzidkiya, king of Yehuda – this is what the
Lord of Hosts said:

I am about to break the bow of Eilam,
the mainstay of their might.
36 I shall bring upon Eilam four winds
from the four corners of the heavens,

---

84 | Kedar was a kingdom in the eastern desert; Ḥatzor was probably in the same area.

and I shall scatter them to all those winds
so that there shall be no nation
to which those driven from Eilam shall not come.
37 I shall shatter Eilam before their foes
and before those who seek their lives,
and I shall bring upon them disaster, My wrath,
declares the Lord.
I shall send the sword after them
until I finish them off.
38 I shall place My throne in Eilam,
and I shall remove from there kings and princes,
declares the Lord.
39 In the days to come
I shall return the captives of Eilam,
declares the Lord.

50 1 The word that the Lord spoke concerning Babylon, the land of the Chaldeans,
through Yirmeyahu the prophet:
2 Tell it among the nations, and let it be heard.
Raise a banner. Let it be heard,
and hold nothing back.
Say, "Babylon is captured,
Bel is shamed,
Merodakh[85] broken;
her statues shamed,
her idols broken."
3 For a nation from the north
has come upon her.
He shall render her land desolate,
and there shall be no inhabitant within her.
Humans and animals alike
shall wander off and be gone.
4 In those days, and at that time,
declares the Lord,
the people of Israel shall come,
they and the people of Yehuda together.
They shall go, weeping all the while,
and shall seek the Lord their God.
5 They shall ask for the way to Zion
with their faces turned toward it.
Come and let us join ourselves to the Lord
in an eternal covenant,

85 | Two names for the chief Babylonian god.

never to be forgotten.

6 My people were lost sheep.
Their shepherds misled them
and set them loose in the mountains.
They wandered from mountain to hilltop
and forgot their own resting place.
7 All who encountered them devoured them.
Her tormentors said, "We are not to blame
because they sinned against the Lord,
Righteous Pasture;
the Lord, the hope of their ancestors."

8 Wander away from the midst of Babylon,
depart from the land of the Chaldeans,
and be like male goats at the head of the flock.
9 For I am about to arouse and bring up against Babylon
an assembly of great nations from the land of the north.
They will array themselves in battle formation about her
and capture her there.
Their arrows are those of a murderous warrior
who does not miss his mark.
10 The Chaldeans shall become spoils,
and all those that spoil her will be sated,
declares the Lord.
11 For you have rejoiced,
you have celebrated,
you who pillage My possession.
You stomped like a threshing calf
and neighed like stallions.
12 Your mother is greatly shamed;
the one who gave birth to you is disgraced.
Look, the end of the nations will be
wilderness, parched land, and desert.
13 Because of the Lord's anger, she will not be inhabited
and shall become entirely desolate.
All who pass by Babylon
shall be stunned and shall shriek over her wounds.
14 Array yourselves in battle formation surrounding Babylon,
all you that bend the bow.
Shoot at her and spare no arrow,
for she has sinned against the Lord.
15 Shout against her from all sides;
she has raised her hand in surrender.
Her foundations have fallen;

her walls are destroyed.
It is the Lord's revenge,
so take revenge on her.
What she did, do to her.
16 Cut off the sower from Babylon
and he who wields the scythe at the time of the harvest.
Because of the sword of the oppressor,
everyone will turn back to his people
and everyone will flee to his land.

17 A scattered sheep is Israel; lions have driven it away. The king of Assyria was
the first to devour it, and now this last one, Nevukhadretzar, king of Babylon,
18 has gnawed its bones. Therefore, this is what the Lord of Hosts, God of Israel,
said: I shall now bring retribution upon the king of Babylon and upon his
19 land just as I did to the king of Assyria. I shall return Israel to his pasture; he
shall graze on the Carmel and the Bashan and will satisfy himself upon the
Efrayim hills and Gilad.

20 In those days and at that time,
declares the Lord,
the sin of Israel will be sought
but will be gone;
and the sins of Yehuda too,
but they will not be found,
for I will forgive those whom I will spare.

21 Go up against her, the land of Meratayim,
and against the inhabitants of Pekod;[86]
attack them by the sword and destroy them wherever they flee,
declares the Lord.
Do exactly as I command you.
22 There is the sound of war in the land
and of a great collapse.
23 How the hammer of the entire earth
has been cut down and broken!
How Babylon has become
an astonishment among nations!
24 I set a trap for you,
and you were ensnared, Babylon!
You were caught by surprise.
You were discovered, and you were seized,
for you strove against the Lord.
25 The Lord has opened His armory
and extracted the weapons of His wrath,
for this is a mission

86 | The location of Meratayim is unknown. Pekod is a region of southern Babylonia.

that the Lord GOD of Hosts is pursuing
in the land of the Chaldeans.
26 Come upon her from the farthest border;
open her granaries,
tread upon her as upon bundles of grain,
and destroy her completely.
Let there be no remnant of her.
27 Slay all her young bulls.
Let them go down to the slaughter.
Woe to them,
for their day has come,
the moment of their retribution.
28 The sound of those who flee,
refugees from the land of Babylon,
to tell in Zion
of the vengeance of the LORD our God,
vengeance for His Temple.
29 Summon archers against Babylon;
let everyone who bends the bow encamp around her;
let none escape.
Repay her according to her actions;
do to her all that she did,
for she has acted arrogantly toward the LORD,
toward the Holy One of Israel.

30 Therefore her young lads shall lie fallen in her squares,
and all who fought in her war
shall be still on that day, declares the LORD.

31 I am against you, arrogant one,
declares the Lord GOD of Hosts,
for your day has come,
the moment when I will hold you to account.
32 The arrogant one will stumble and fall
and will have no one to lift him.
I shall set fire to his cities,
and it will consume all its surroundings.

33 This is what the LORD of Hosts said:
The people of Israel are oppressed,
and the people of Yehuda along with them.
Their captors have all held them fast
and have refused to set them free.
34 Their redeemer is strong;
the LORD of Hosts is His name.
He will take up their cause:
He will calm the land

and disquiet the inhabitants of Babylon.
35 A sword upon the Chaldeans,
declares the LORD,
and upon the inhabitants of Babylon,
its officials, and its wise men.
36 A sword upon the diviners;
they shall be made fools.
A sword upon her mighty men;
they shall be broken.
37 A sword upon his horses and chariots
and upon the foreign troops in her midst;
they shall become as weak as women.
A sword upon her treasuries;
they shall be looted.
38 A drought upon her waters;
they shall dry up.
For it is a land of graven images
and acts as if mad before its dreadful deities.
39 Therefore, weasels shall dwell there with wildcats,
and owls shall dwell there,
but it will never again be inhabited by humans
and never be settled, in any generation.
40 As God overthrew Sedom
and Amora and their neighbors,
declares the LORD,
so shall no one dwell there,
and no human stay within her.
41 A people is coming down from the north;
a great nation with many kings
awakens from the remote parts of the earth.
42 They shall grasp bow and spear;
they are cruel and have no mercy.
The sound of them roars like the sea,
and they ride upon horses
arrayed like men of war
against you, daughter Babylon.
43 The king of Babylon heard a report of them,
and his hands became feeble.
Anguish gripped him;
he shook like a woman in childbirth.
44 Look, like a lion rising up
from the thicket of the Jordan
against the secure pasture,
in a moment I will drive him away from it.
I will visit upon him whomever I choose,

for who is like Me,
and who can summon Me?
Who is the shepherd who can stand up against Me?
45 Therefore, hear the counsel
that the LORD has taken against Babylon
and His thoughts regarding the land of the Chaldeans:
Surely the weakest of the sheep shall drive him away;
surely he will render their pasture desolate.
46 The land trembles
at the sound of Babylon's capture,
and a cry is heard among the nations.

51 1 This is what the LORD said: I am about to stir up against Babylon, and against
2 the hearts of those who dwell there and oppose Me,[87] a destructive spirit. I
shall incite foreigners against Babylon who shall scatter her and empty out
her land as they encircle her on the day of disaster.

3 To him who bends his bow
and to him who takes pride in his armor:
do not pity her young men;
completely destroy her army.
4 Let them fall as corpses in the land of the Chaldeans
and as wounded in her streets.
5 For Israel has not been forsaken,
nor Yehuda by his God,
by the LORD of Hosts,
although their land is full of sin
against the Holy One of Israel.
6 Flee from the midst of Babylon;
let each one save his own life
lest he be cut down along with her[88] sin,
for this is a moment of vengeance for the LORD;
He is paying her that which she deserves.
7 Babylon is like a golden cup in the hand of the LORD,
intoxicating the entire land.
The nations drank of her wine;
therefore the nations have gone mad.
8 Suddenly Babylon fell and has been broken.
Wail for her;
apply balm to her pain –
perhaps she will be healed.
9 We have tended to Babylon,
but she has not been healed.
Abandon her, and let each one of us return to his land,

87 | Hebrew *lev kamai*, i.e., the Chaldeans (*Kasdim*), written in the *atbash* cipher.
88 | Babylon's.

for her judgment has reached heavenward
and has been lifted into the skies.
10 The LORD has brought forth our vindication.
Come! Let us relate in Zion
the deeds of the LORD our God.

11 Polish the arrows;
gather the shields.
The LORD has stirred up the spirit of the kings of Media,[89]
for He has designs upon Babylon to destroy her.
This is the LORD's vengeance,
vengeance for His Temple.
12 Raise a banner upon the walls of Babylon.
Strengthen the watch,
set up watchmen,
and prepare ambushes,
for the LORD planned and has carried out
what He had spoken
against the inhabitants of Babylon.
13 You who dwelled upon mighty waters,
rich in treasures –
your end has come,
retribution for your crime.
14 The LORD of Hosts has sworn by Himself
that He will fill you with men as numerous as locusts,
and they will shout over you, "*Heidad*!"[90]

15 He makes the earth by His power,
establishes the world by His wisdom,
and stretches out the heavens by His understanding.[91]
16 As He makes His voice heard,
there is rumbling water in the heavens,
and clouds rise from the ends of the earth.
He makes lightning bolts with the rain
and brings out winds from His storehouses.
17 All humans are foolish, without knowledge.
Every goldsmith is disappointed in his idol:
his molten image is a sham;
no breath animates them.
18 They are delusions,
works of mockery.
When they are called to account, they will perish.

89 | Media was located east of Babylon. Babylon would later be conquered by Cyrus, the king of Media.

90 | See note on 25:30.

91 | Cf. 10:12–16.

19 Not like these is the portion of Yaakov,
for He formed all things,
and Israel is the tribe He possesses;
LORD of Hosts is His name.

20 You are a sledgehammer for Me,
a weapon of war.
With you I will shatter nations;
with you I will destroy kingdoms.
21 With you I will shatter horse and rider;
with you I will shatter chariot and driver.
22 With you I will shatter man and woman;
with you I will shatter old and young;
with you I will shatter lad and lass.
23 With you I will shatter the shepherd and his flock;
with you I will shatter the farmer and his team;
with you I will shatter governors and deputies.
24 I will repay Babylon and all the inhabitants of Chaldea
for all the evil they did to Zion
before your eyes, declares the LORD.

25 Look, I am against you, destructive mountain,
declares the LORD,
that destroys all the earth.
I shall stretch out My hand against you
and roll you down from the cliffs.
I shall make of you a burned-out mountain.
26 They shall not take from you
even a cornerstone
or a foundation stone,
for you shall remain a wasteland forever,
declares the LORD.
27 Raise a banner in the land,
sound a ram's horn among the nations,
prepare nations against her,
assemble upon her the kingdoms of Ararat, Mini, and Ashkenaz,[92]
appoint a chieftain over her,
and bring up horses like a swarm of bristling locusts.
28 Prepare nations for war against her:
the kings of Media,
her governors and all her deputies,
and all the lands under their rule.
29 The land will shake and tremble,
for the LORD's designs against Babylon shall stand:
to make of the land of Babylon a desolation

92 | Three kingdoms located north of Mesopotamia, allies or subjects of the Medes.

with no inhabitant.
30 The mighty of Babylon have ceased waging war.
They remain in fortresses.
Their strength is gone.
They have become like women:
her dwellings were set on fire;
her bolts are broken.
31 Runner runs to meet runner
and herald to meet herald,
to tell the king of Babylon
that his city has been taken from end to end.
32 The river crossings are seized,
the marshes burned in fire;
the men of war feel panic.

33 For this is what the Lord of Hosts, God of Israel, said:
Daughter Babylon is like a threshing floor
at the time we tread upon it.
In but an instant her reaping season will arrive.
34 "Nevukhadretzar, the king of Babylon, has devoured me,
crushed me,
set me up as an empty vessel,
swallowed me as a crocodile does,
filled his belly with my delicacies,
cast me away.
35 My stolen possessions and my flesh are upon Babylon,"
says she who dwells in Zion.
"My blood is upon the inhabitants of Chaldea,"
says Jerusalem.

36 Therefore, this is what the Lord said:
I will take up your cause
and take vengeance on your behalf.
I will dry up her sea
and cause her fountain to evaporate.
37 Babylon will become heaps of stones,
a haunt of jackals,
a desolation and a place of shrieking,
with no inhabitant.
38 They will roar in unison like young lions
and bray like lion cubs.
39 When they are warm,
I shall set out their drink.
I shall intoxicate them so that they will revel.
They shall sleep an everlasting sleep
and never awaken, declares the Lord.

40 I shall lead them down
like sheep to be slaughtered,
like rams together with male goats.
41 How Sheshakh[93] has been taken captive;
the praise of all the earth been seized!
How Babylon has become
a desolation among nations!
42 The sea has overcome Babylon;
she is enveloped by its raging waves.
43 Her towns have become desolate,
parched land and desert.
No one dwells in them,
and no person passes through them.
44 I shall bring retribution upon Bel in Babylon;
I shall make what he swallowed come up from his mouth.
No longer shall nations stream toward him.
Even the wall of Babylon has fallen.
45 Depart from its midst, My people;
let each one save himself from the LORD's wrath.
46 Do not be faint of heart and fearful
at the rumor that is heard in the land,
and later that year the rumor,
and in the next year the rumor
and violence in the land,
ruler against ruler.
47 Therefore, days are coming
when I shall take retribution
upon the graven images of Babylon;
its entire land shall be shamed,
and all her slain shall fall within her.
48 Heaven and earth
and all that is in them
shall rejoice over Babylon,
for marauders shall come against her from the north,
declares the LORD.
49 Because of Babylon
the slain of Israel lie fallen.
Because of Babylon
the slain of the entire land lie fallen.
50 Survivors of the sword, go!
Do not stand there.
Remember the LORD from afar,
and call Jerusalem to mind.
51 We are ashamed because we have heard of our disgrace.

93 | Babylon; cf. 25:26.

Embarrassment has covered our faces,
for strangers attacked
the holy places of the LORD's House.

52 Therefore, days are coming,
declares the LORD,
when I shall take retribution upon her graven images,
and all over her land,
the slain shall gasp their last gasp.
53 Even should Babylon ascend to the heavens
and fortify the heights of her strength,
marauders shall descend upon her from Me,
declares the LORD.

54 The sound of a cry from Babylon
and of a great collapse from the land of the Chaldeans,
55 for the LORD is marauding Babylon.
Gone from her is her great sound,
their waves that would rage like great waters,
giving forth their loud sound,
56 for a marauder is coming upon Babylon.
Her mighty men will be taken captive,
their bows broken,
for a God of recompense is the LORD;
He will indeed repay them.
57 I will intoxicate
her officials and her wise men,
her governors and her deputies,
and her mighty men.
They shall sleep an everlasting sleep
and never awaken,
declares the King;
LORD of Hosts is His name.

58 This is what the LORD of Hosts said:
The broad wall of Babylon
shall be demolished,
and her high gates shall be set afire.
Peoples shall toil for naught,
nations shall earn fiery destruction,
and they shall become exhausted.

59 The word that Yirmeyahu the prophet commanded to Seraya son of Neriya
son of Maḥseya when he went with Tzidkiyahu to Babylon in the fourth
60 year of his reign, and Seraya was his confidant: Yirmeyahu wrote down all
the disasters that would befall Babylon in one scroll; all these words were
61 written concerning Babylon. Yirmeyahu said to Seraya, "When you arrive in

62 Babylon, see that you read out all these words. Say, 'LORD, You declared that
this place shall be cut off, so that there shall be no inhabitant, neither human
63 nor beast, for it shall be an eternal wasteland.' When you finish reading this
64 scroll, tie a stone to it, cast it into the Euphrates, and say, 'So shall Babylon
sink and never rise from the disaster that I shall bring upon her, and they shall
become exhausted.'"

The words of Yirmeyahu extend to here.

52 1 Tzidkiyahu was twenty-one years old when he became king, and for eleven
years he reigned in Jerusalem.[94] His mother's name was Ḥamutal, daughter
2 of Yirmeyahu of Livna. He did what was evil in the eyes of the LORD, just as
3 Yehoyakim had done. And because of the LORD's fury against Jerusalem and
Yehuda, He cast them away from His presence.

Now Tzidkiyahu rebelled against the king of Babylon.

4 In the ninth year of his reign, on the tenth day of the tenth month,
Nevukhadretzar, king of Babylon, and all his forces attacked Jerusalem. They
5 encamped against it and built a siege wall all around, and the city remained
6 under siege until the eleventh year of King Tzidkiyahu. By the ninth day
of the fourth month, famine raged so fiercely in the city that there was no
7 food for the people of the land. The city was breached, and all the military
men fled and left the city by the dark of night through the gate between the
double walls by the royal garden, as the Chaldeans surrounded the city, and
8 made toward the Arava. But the Chaldean force pursued the king and caught
up with Tzidkiyahu on the plains of Yeriḥo, and all his forces scattered and
9 deserted him. They seized the king and hauled him up before the king of
10 Babylon at Rivla in the land of Ḥamat, where he spoke harshly to him. The
king of Babylon slaughtered Tzidkiyahu's sons before his eyes. He also slaugh-
11 tered all the officials of Yehuda in Rivla. He blinded Tzikdiyahu and chained
him in bronze fetters, and the king of Babylon brought him to Babylon and
put him in prison until the day of his death.

12 On the tenth day of the fifth month, in the nineteenth year of the reign of
Nevukhadretzar, king of Babylon, Nevuzaradan, chief of the guard, who
13 served the king of Babylon, entered Jerusalem. He burned down the House
of the LORD and the royal palace and all the houses in Jerusalem; he set fire
14 to every important building in Jerusalem. As for all the walls surrounding
Jerusalem, all the Chaldean forces with the chief of the guard tore them down.
15 As for some of the poor people, the rest of the people who remained in the
city, those who defected to the king of Babylon, and the rest of the artisans,
16 Nevuzaradan, chief of the guard, exiled them. But Nevuzaradan, chief of the
guard, retained some of the poorest of the land as vine dressers and field
workers.

17 The Chaldeans broke down the bronze pillars of the House of the LORD, the

94 | Cf. 39:1–7; II Kings 24:18–25:7.

stands, and the Bronze Sea that was in the House of the Lord, and carried
18 all the bronze off to Babylon. They took the pots, shovels, shears, basins, and
19 spoons and all the bronze vessels that had been used in service, while the chief
of the guard took the bowls, firepan, basins, pots, candelabra, spoons, and
20 jars – whatever was of gold and whatever was of silver. The two pillars, the
Molten Sea, the twelve bronze oxen that were underneath, and the stands that
King Shlomo had made for the House of the Lord – the weight in bronze of
21 all these vessels was incalculable. As for the pillars, each pillar was eighteen
cubits high and twelve cubits in circumference. It was four fingers thick and
22 hollow. Its capital was of bronze. The height of each capital was five cubits.
Meshwork and pomegranates surrounded the capital, all of bronze; and the
23 same for the second pillar and the pomegranates. There were ninety-six
pomegranates facing all directions, with room for one hundred pomegranates
around the meshwork.

24 The chief of the guard seized Seraya, the head priest, and Tzefanya, the deputy
25 priest, and the three guardians of the threshold. And from the city, he took
one official who was in charge of the military men, and seven men among
the king's personal attendants who were left in the city, the scribe of the army
commander whose duty was to rally the people of the land, and sixty of the
26 people of the land who were left inside the city. Nevuzaradan, the chief of the
27 guard, took them and led them to the king of Babylon in Rivla, and the king
of Babylon struck them down and put them to death in Rivla, in the land of
Ḥamat. Thus Yehuda was exiled from its own soil.

28 These are the people whom Nevukhadretzar exiled in the seventh year: 3,023
29 people of Yehuda. In the eighteenth year of Nevukhadretzar: 832 persons
30 from Jerusalem. In the twenty-third year of Nevukhadretzar, Nevuzaradan,
chief of the guard, exiled 745 people of Yehuda. All the people totaled 4,600.

31 In the thirty-seventh year following the exile of Yehoyakhin, king of Yehuda,
on the twenty-fifth of the twelfth month, Evvil Merodakh, king of Babylon, in
the year he became king, granted Yehoyakhin, king of Yehuda, pardon from
32 prison. He spoke kindly to him and set his throne above the thrones of the
33 kings who were with him in Babylon. He removed his prison garb, and he
34 dined in his presence for the rest of his life, and he was granted a permanent
allowance from the king of Babylon – a daily allowance for the rest of his life
until the day of his death.

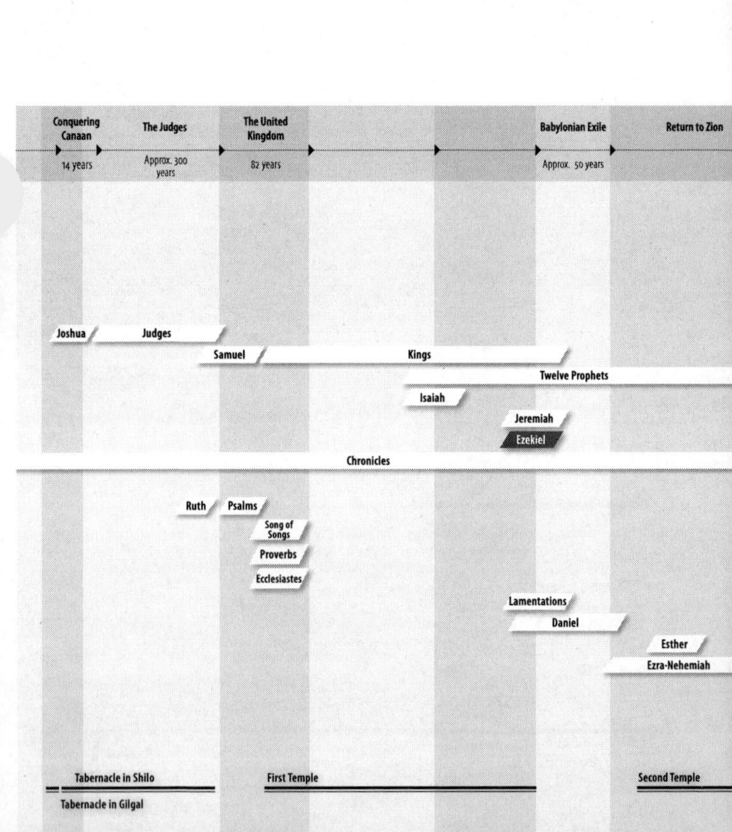

Conquering Canaan
14 years
The Judges
Approx. 300 years
The United Kingdom
82 years
Babylonian Exile
Approx. 50 years
Return to Zion
Joshua
Judges
Samuel
Kings
Twelve Prophets
Isaiah
Jeremiah
Ezekiel
Chronicles
Ruth
Psalms
Song of Songs
Proverbs
Ecclesiastes
Lamentations
Daniel
Esther
Ezra-Nehemiah
Tabernacle in Shilo
Tabernacle in Gilgal
First Temple
Second Temple

EZEKIEL/YEḤEZKEL

EZEKIEL	Initiation into prophecy, and the first message	Prophecies predicting the imminent destruction	Prophetic journey to Jerusalem – the destruction and its environment	Conflict with the people and the false prophets who denied the imminent destruction	Dramatizing the destruction and its environment through parables and descriptions	Prophecies concerning the nations	From destruction to consolation and redemption
	Chs. 1–3	4–7	8–11	12–15	16–24	25–32	36–48
	Approx. 22 years						

1 1 It was in the thirtieth year in the fourth month on the fifth day of the
month. I was in the exile, by the Kevar River; the heavens opened up, and I
2 saw Godly visions. On the fifth day of the month, the fifth year of the exile
3 of King Yoyakhin,[1] so it was: the word of the LORD came to Yeḥezkel son
of Buzi the priest, in the land of the Chaldeans by the Kevar River; there
the hand of the LORD was upon him.

4 And I looked:
Behold, a storm wind came from the north,
a great cloud and a flaring fire with a radiance around it,
and inside it, within the fire, the look of something luminous,
5 and within that was the form of four living beings.
This was their appearance:
they had the form of a man;
6 each one had four faces,
and each one of them had four wings;
7 their legs were straight-standing, and their feet were like a calf's hoof,
gleaming with a look of burnished bronze;
8 they had man's hands beneath their wings on their four sides,
and the four of them had faces and wings.

9 Their wings were joined to each other;
they did not turn when they moved
but moved in the direction of one of the faces.
10 Their faces were in the form of the face of a man
with the face of a lion on the right of the four,
the face of an ox on the left of the four,
and the face of an eagle[2]
on all four of them.
11 Their faces and their wings were separated above:
each one had two joining it to the others and two covering its body;
12 each moved in the direction of one of the faces –
wherever the spirit would move, they moved –
they did not turn when they moved.
13 The form of the living beings, their appearance, was like coals
burning,
like the appearance of torch flames;
it passed among the living beings;
the fire had a radiance, lightning flashed out from the fire,
14 and the living beings ran forward and back with the appearance of
darting flames.

---

1 | The year 592 BCE; see II Kings 24:11–17. "The thirtieth year" (v. 1) may be in reference to the Jubilee.

2 | Literally "vulture."

15 I looked at the living beings –
and there, a wheel was on the ground beside each of the living beings
with the four
faces.
16 The appearance of the wheels and their design had the look of an
aquamarine gem,
all four of them with the same form;
their appearance and their design were as though one wheel were
inside the other.
17 When they moved, they moved on any of their four sides;
they did not turn as they moved.
18 Their rims, towering, inspired fear;
and the rims of all four of them were covered, all around, with eyes.
19 When the living beings moved, the wheels moved beside them,
and when the living beings rose above the ground, the wheels also rose;
20 wherever the spirit would move, they moved;
there where the spirit moved, the wheels rose with them,
for the spirit of the living being was also in the wheels:
21 when they moved, they too moved,
and when they stood still, they too stood still,
and when they rose from the ground, the wheels too rose with them
because the spirit of the living being was in the wheels.

22 Above the head of the living being was the form of an expanse
with a look of ice, its overawing glare,
suspended over their heads from above,
23 and beneath the expanse, their wings reached out toward each other.
Each had a pair covering them –
each had a pair covering their bodies.
24 I heard the sound of their wings when they moved;
it was like the sound of great rushing waters,
like the voice of Shaddai,
a clamor like the noise of a gathered army.
Standing still, they lowered their wings;
25 a voice came from upon the expanse which was over their heads –
standing still, they lowered their wings.

26 Above the film which was over their heads,
with the appearance of a sapphire,
was the form of a throne;
and upon the form of the throne –
upon it, above –
was a form with the appearance of a man.

27 And I saw:
something that looked luminous,
the appearance of fire encasing it

from what appeared to be his waist and above;
and from what appeared to be his waist and below,
I saw an appearance like fire with a radiance around it –
28 it was like the appearance of a rainbow in the clouds on a rainy day;
the radiance around it had that appearance.
This was the appearance of the form of the glory of the LORD –
I saw it and I fell upon my face, and I heard a voice speak.

2 1 2 He said to me: "Man, stand on your feet, and I will speak to you." As He
spoke to me, a spirit came into me and set me on my feet, and I heard him
speaking to me.

3 He said to me: "Man, I am sending you to the sons of Israel, a nation
of rebels who have rebelled against me; they – and their fathers – have
4 transgressed against me until this very day. The sons are hard faced, tough
hearted – I am sending you to them, and you will say to them: 'So says the
5 Lord GOD.' Whether they listen or refuse, they are a defiant house, and
they will know that a prophet was among them.

6 "You, Man, do not fear them
and their words – do not fear;
thorns and thistles surround you
and you sit among scorpions;
their words do not fear,
before them do not quail –
for they are a defiant house;
7 speak My words to them
whether they listen or refuse,
for they are defiant.

8 "You, Man, listen to what I say to you – do not be defiant like this defiant
house; open your mouth and eat what I give you."

9 I looked – there was a hand reaching toward me, and there, within it, was
10 a written scroll. He spread it out in front of me and it had writing on the
front and on the back, and on it were written laments, keening, and woe.

3 1 And He said to me: "Man, what you find here, eat – eat this scroll and then
go, speak to the House of Israel."

2 3 I opened my mouth, and He fed it to me, this scroll, and said to me: "Man,
feed your stomach; fill your insides with this scroll that I am giving you." I
ate it, and in my mouth it had the sweetness of honey.[3]

4 And He said to me: "Man, go now! Come to the House of Israel and speak
5 My words to them. You are not being sent to a people of unfathomable
6 speech, of heavy tongue, but to the House of Israel; not to the many
peoples of unfathomable speech and heavy tongue whose words you

3 | Perhaps indicating an eventual positive outcome to the destruction.

cannot understand – if I were to send you to them, they would listen to
7 you. The House of Israel will not agree to listen to you, for they are not
prepared to listen to Me – the whole of the House of Israel are tough
browed and hard-hearted.

8 "Behold – I have made your face tough
before their faces
and your brow tough
before their brows;
9 like adamant, harder than flint
I have made your brow.
Do not fear them;
do not quail before them –
they are a defiant house."

10 And He said to me: "Man, everything that I say to you, take it into
11 your heart; let your ears hear it. Go now – come to the exiles, to the
sons of your people, and speak to them; say to them, 'So says the Lord
12 God' – whether they listen or refuse." A spirit then lifted me up, and I heard
a great, thunderous noise behind me: "Blessed is the Lord's glory from
13 its place!" – the sound of the wings of the living beings brushing against
each other and the sound of the wheels beside them, a great, thunderous
14 noise. A spirit lifted me up and took me away, and I went away bitter, my
15 spirit raging, with the hand of the Lord firm upon me, and I came to the
exiles in Tel Aviv[4] who were living on the Kevar River, and there, where
they sit, I sat there among them for seven days, desolate.

16 At the end of seven days –

17 The word of the Lord came to me, saying: "Man, I have made you
watchman for the House of Israel; when you hear a word from My mouth,
give them warning from Me.

18 "If I say to the wicked one, 'You will surely die,' and you do not warn him,
if you do not speak out to warn the wicked one off his wicked course so
that he should live, and he remains wicked, he will die for his iniquity – but
I will seek redress for his blood from your hands.

19 "But if you warn the wicked one and he still does not turn from his
wickedness, from his wicked course, he will die for his iniquity – but you
will have saved your own life.

20 "If the righteous one turns from his righteousness and does wrong, I
will put obstacles before him, and he will die; if you do not warn him, he
will die for his sin, and the righteousness that he has done will not be
remembered – and you, his blood will be on your hands.

---

4 | Literally "hill of new grain," this was an ancient Mesopotamian city whose precise location is unknown.

21 "But if you warn the righteous one so that he does not sin, if he remains
righteous and does not sin because he has been warned, then he will surely
live – and you will save your own soul."[5]

22 And the hand of the LORD came upon me there, and He said to me: "Get
23 up, go out to the valley, and I will speak to you there." I got up and went
out to the valley, and there was the glory of the LORD standing there – like
24 the glory that I saw on the Kevar River[6] – and I fell upon my face. A spirit
came into me and set me on my feet, and He spoke to me and said: "Come,
25 shut yourself in your house. You, Man, they have put ropes on you, they
26 have bound you with them, and you will not get out of them. I will stick
your tongue to the roof of your mouth, you will be struck silent, and you
27 will not be a man of rebuke to them – they are a defiant house. But when
I speak to you, I will open your mouth, and you will say to them, 'So says
the Lord GOD.' The one who listens will listen, and the one who refuses
will refuse, for they are a defiant house.

4 1 "Now you, Man, take a clay block, place it before you, and carve on it a
2 city: Jerusalem. Lay siege to her: build a siege wall against her, throw up
earthworks against her, set up encampments against her, and position
3 battering rams around her. Take an iron griddle and place it as an iron wall
between you and the city, and turn your face upon her – she will be under
siege, and you will besiege her. This is a sign for the House of Israel.

4 "And you, lie on your left side and let it bear the weight of the sins of the
House of Israel: you will bear their sin for the number of days that you lie
5 upon it. I set you as many days as the years of their sin: for 390 days you
6 will bear the sin of the House of Israel, and when you have completed
these, lie for a second time – on your right side – and bear the sin of the
House of Yehuda for forty days: a day for a year, I have set this for you, a
7 day for each year. Turn your face upon the siege of Jerusalem; bare your
8 arm and prophesy about her. Behold, I have bound you with ropes – you
shall not turn over from one side to the other until your days of siege are
complete.

9 "And you – take wheat, barley, beans, lentils, millet, and emmer wheat, put
them all into one utensil, and make bread for yourself from them. All the
days that you will be lying on your side – 390 days – you shall eat this.

10 "You will eat this, your food, at a weight of twenty shekel a day;
you will eat this from one day to the next,
11 and you will drink a small measure of water:
you will drink a sixth of a hin from one day to the next.
12 You will eat it as though it were a barley cake,
and you will bake it over dung – human excrement –
before their eyes."

5 | The prophecy of the "watchman" here in verses 16–21 is expanded in 33:1–20.

6 | See chapter 1.

13 And the LORD said: "This is how the children of Israel will eat their bread,
14 impure, among the nations that I will banish them to." And I said, "Ah, my
Lord GOD! Never before has my throat been defiled; I have never eaten
flesh from a carcass or mauled animal even as a youth, never until now,
15 and fouled meat has never entered my mouth." And He said to me: "I will
allow you cattle dung in place of human excrement; you shall make your
bread over that."

16 And He said to me: "See, I am going to break the staff of bread they lean
on in Jerusalem;
they will eat
bread weighed out, anxious;
water measured out, desolate,
they will drink;
17 and so, they will lack bread and water;
each man and his brother desolate,
they will waste away in their sin.

5 1 "And you, Man, take a sharp blade – a barber's razor – pass it over your
2 head and beard; take scales for weighing and divide up the hair. One-third
set aflame inside your city once the days of siege are over, one-third take
and strike with a sword on all sides, and one-third scatter to the winds and I
3 shall draw the sword after them. From this take a small measure, bind it up
4 in the hem of your garment, and again take from this and fling it into the
fire, burn it in the fire; fire will spread to all the House of Israel from this.

5 "So says the Lord GOD:
This is Jerusalem.
Amidst the nations I have placed her,
all around her the lands.
6 She has rebelled against My laws
with a wickedness greater than the other nations'
and against My statutes
even more than the lands all around her –
for they rejected My laws
and did not follow My statutes.

7 "So the Lord GOD says this:
Because you have surpassed
even those nations around you –
you did not follow My statutes,
you did not perform My laws –
and you did not even perform the laws of the nations around you.

8 "So the Lord GOD says this:
See, I am upon you – I, too,
I will execute My judgments among you
before the eyes of the nations;

9 I will do to you what I have not ever done,
the like of which I will never do again,
because of your abominations.
10 Parents will eat children among you,
children will eat their parents;
I will execute judgments upon you,
and I will scatter all that remains of you to the winds.

11 "And so, declares the Lord GOD, surely as I live, because you defiled My
Sanctuary with all your detestable things, all your abominations, I, I too,
will draw Myself back, and My eye will not pity; I will not show mercy:

12 "One-third of you will die of the plague
and destroyed by the famine among you,
one-third will fall to the sword on all sides,
and one-third I will scatter to the winds
and draw the sword behind them.
13 My anger will be exhausted,
I will let My fury at them die down,
and I will find relief;
they will know that I am the LORD;
I have spoken – in the passion of My anger,
in exhausting My anger upon them.
14 And I will give you over to ruin and reproach
among the nations around you
in the sight of every passerby;
15 it will be a reproach and a disgrace,
a warning and a horror
to the nations who are around you
when I execute judgments upon you in anger,
in fury, in furious rebuke.
I am the LORD; I have spoken.
16 When I set loose the terrible arrows of famine
among them to destroy them,
I will set them loose to destroy you,
and I will pile more famine upon you
and break the staff of bread you lean on.
17 I will set loose upon you famine and savage animals,
and they will bereave you;
plague and blood will pass through you;
I will bring the sword down upon you.
I am the LORD; I have spoken."

6 1 2 And the word of the LORD came to me, saying: "Man, set your face to the
3 mountains of Israel and prophesy to them; say: Mountains of Israel, listen
to the word of the Lord GOD. So says the Lord GOD to the mountains and
hills, to the ravines and valleys:

Behold, it is I – I will bring the sword down on you,
I will completely destroy your high places.
4 Your altars will be devastated,
your sun shrines will be smashed.
I will cut them down, your slain,
in front of your idols,
5 I will leave the corpses of the children of Israel
before their idols,
and I will scatter your bones
around your altars.
6 Everywhere you live
your cities will be laid waste,
and the high places will be devastated
so that your altars will be laid waste, desolate,
your idols smashed to pieces,
your sun shrines crushed,
and what you have crafted wiped out entirely;
7 the slain will fall there among you,
and you will know that I am the LORD.

8 "I will leave a remnant,
some survivors of the sword among the nations,
when you are scattered across the lands;
9 your survivors will remember Me
among the nations they are taken to as captives –
that I was grieved by their whoring heart that turned away from Me,
their eyes whoring after their idols,
and they will hate themselves for the evils they did,
for all their abominations.
10 They will know that I am the LORD;
not for nothing have I said
that I would inflict this great evil upon them.

11 "So says the Lord GOD: Beat with your hands, stamp with your feet, and
cry out at all the evil abominations of the House of Israel for which they
will fall to sword, famine, and plague.
12 Those far away will die from plague,
those close by will fall by the sword,
and those who remain, under siege, will die of famine;
I will exhaust My fury upon them,
13 and you will know that I am the LORD –
when their slain are among their idols, surrounding their altars,
on every high hill, every mountain peak,
beneath every green tree, beneath every lush oak,
that place where they burnt a sweet fragrance
to all their idols.

14 I will stretch out My hand over them;
I will turn the land over to waste and desolation
from the desert up to Divla,[7] everywhere they live.
And they will know that I am the LORD."

7 1 And the word of the LORD came to me, saying: "And you, Man – so says
2 the Lord GOD to the land of Israel:

"End, the end is come
to the four edges of the land;
3 now the end is upon you.
I will set loose My anger against you
and judge you according to your ways–
bring down on you all your abominations.
4 My eye will not pity you; I will not show mercy,
but I will bring your ways down upon you;
your abominations will be there in your midst,
and you will know that I am the LORD.

5 "So says the Lord GOD:
Evil, a unique evil,
see, it is come;
6 an end is come; it comes, the end,
awakened against you;
see, it is come.
7 The sun has set for you who live in the land;
the time is come,
it is near –
the day of panicked and not joyous cries on the hills.
8 It is close now.
I will pour My fury over you;
I will exhaust My anger upon you;
I will judge you according to your ways
and bring down upon you all your abominations.
9 My eye will not pity; I will not show mercy;
in accordance with your ways will I bring it down upon you;
your abominations will be there in your midst,
and you will know that I, the LORD, strike.
10 See – the day, here, it has come:
the dawn breaks,
the rod blossoms,
and insolence has budded,
11 violence grown into a rod of evil.
Nothing of them, none of their masses,
nothing of theirs, and none wailing for them.

7 | Referring to Rivla, a city in Syria that served as a Babylonian army center.

12 The time is come, the day is here:
the buyer is not to rejoice,
nor need the seller mourn,[8]
for wrath is upon her masses.
13 For the seller will not return to his sale
again while they both live,
for the prophecy to her masses will not be withdrawn,
and each man caught in his sin
will not hold fast to his life.
14 They blast the horns
and make everything ready,
but none go to war,
for My wrath is upon her masses.
15 The sword out there,
plague and famine within;
whoever is in the field,
by the sword he will die;
whoever is in the city,
famine and plague will destroy;
16 their fugitives will escape
to the mountains
like doves of the valley,
crying, all of them,
each man caught in his sin.
17 All hands will go limp,
all thighs wet with fear;
18 they will put on sackcloth,
they will be stifled with horror,
on every face shame,
all heads shaved.
19 Their silver they will fling into the streets;
their gold will be a thing defiled.
Their silver and gold will not save them
on the day of the LORD's rage;
their souls will not be satisfied,
their bellies not filled –
for this was the stumbling block of their sin.
20 He bestowed upon them majesty, the splendor from His adornment,
but they used it for their abominable, detestable things,
and so I will make it a thing defiled for them;
21 I will give it over into the hands of strangers to pillage,
to the wicked ones of the earth as spoil,
and they will desecrate it.

---

8 | The seller should not mourn the sale of his property, nor should the buyer rejoice about acquiring it, because neither will derive benefit from it in the impending exile.

22 I will turn My face away from them,
and they will desecrate My treasured place;
hooligans will come into her and desecrate her.

23 Forge the chains,
for the land is filled with blood crimes,
the city with violence;
24 I will bring the evil of the nations
and they will take possession of their houses;
I will put an end to the majesty of the powerful;
their sanctified places will be desecrated.
25 Terror is coming;
they will search for peace,
but – nothing.
26 Disaster upon disaster will come,
there will be report after report;
they will search for a vision from the prophet;
teaching will be lost from the priests
and counsel from the elders.
27 The king will mourn, the prince wear ruin,
and the hands of landed folk will quake;
according to their own ways will I deal with them,
with their own judgments will I judge them,
and they will know that I am the LORD."

8 1 It was in the sixth year in the sixth month on the fifth day of the month: I
was sitting in my house with the elders of Yehuda sitting before me when
the hand of the Lord GOD fell upon me there.

2 And I looked:

There was a form with the appearance of fire:
from what appeared to be his waist and below fire,
and from his waist and above the appearance of brilliance,
the look of something luminous.[9]

3 He stretched out the figure of a hand, which took hold of me by the locks
of my head, and a spirit lifted me up between the land and the heavens
and brought me to Jerusalem in a Godly vision, to the entrance of the
inner gate facing north where the statue of jealousy – that incites jealous
anger – stands.

4 And there was the glory of the God of Israel as in the vision that I saw in
5 the valley,[10] and He said to me, "Man, lift your eyes up toward the north."
I lifted my eyes up toward the north, and there, to the north of the gate of
6 the altar, was this statue of jealousy at the entry. He said to me, "Man, do

9 | Cf. the vision in 1:26–27; see also 43:3–4.

10 | Referring to 3:22–23, which refers in turn to chapter 1.

you see what they are doing – that the House of Israel is committing great
abominations here to drive Me away from My Sanctuary? You will see yet
greater abominations."

7 He brought me to the entrance to the court, and I saw there a single hole in
8 the wall, and He said to me, "Man, dig through the wall." I dug through the
9 wall, and there was a single entrance. He said to me, "Come through; look
10 at the evil abominations that they are carrying out here." I came through,
and there I saw every form of creeping thing and detestable animal and all
the idols of the House of Israel, all carved out on the surrounding walls.
11 Seventy men from the elders of the House of Israel were standing before
them, with Yaazanyahu son of Shafan[11] standing among them; each man
had his censer in his hand, and a dense cloud of incense was ascending.
12 And He said to me, "Do you see what the elders of the House of Israel are
doing in the dark, each in his room of graven images? For they say: 'The
13 LORD does not see us; the LORD has gone from the land.'" And He said
to me, "You will soon see greater abominations that they are committing."
14 He brought me to the entrance of the northern gate of the House of the
LORD, and there women were sitting, wailing over Tamuz."[12]

15 And He said to me: "Do you see, Man? You will yet see even greater
16 abominations than these." And He brought me to the inner court of the
House of the LORD, and there, at the entrance to the Sanctuary of the
LORD, between its hallway and the altar, were about twenty-five men with
their backs to the Sanctuary of the LORD and their faces to the east, and
17 they were bowing down eastward – bowing to the sun. And He said to
me, "Man, do you see? Is it so light a thing to the House of Yehuda – the
practice of these abominations here – that they have filled the land with
violence and anger Me further and even raise the branch to their noses?![13]
18 I, too, will act – with fury. My eye will not pity, I will not show mercy;
though loudly they call out to Me, I will not hear them."

9 1 And He called out loudly in my hearing, "Come out, officers of forces in
the city, each with his weapon of destruction in his hand!"

2 And six men came forward through the upper gate that faces north, each
with his bludgeon in his hand; among them was a man dressed in linen
with a scribe's instruments at his waist. They came forward and stood
3 beside the bronze altar. Now the glory of the God of Israel had moved
off the cherub it had rested upon the threshold of the House.[14] He called
to the man dressed in linen with the scribe's instruments at his waist.

4 The LORD said to him, "Pass through the city, through Jerusalem, and

11 | Possibly a descendant of Shafan the scribe, mentioned in II Kings, chapter 22.

12 | In Mesopotamian mythology, a god who dies every year when vegetation wilts; mourning aims to restore the vegetation.

13 | Possibly an idolatrous ritual or an offensive gesture.

14 | Beginning its gradual movement out of the city. See also 10:4, 18–19, and 11:22–23.

put a mark on the foreheads of the people sighing and crying over all the
abominations that are being done in her very midst."

5 And to the others He said in my hearing, "Pass through the city after him
6 and strike – do not let your eye pity, do not show mercy. The elderly, young
men, young girls, small children, women – kill, destroy, but do not go near
any person who has the mark upon them; begin with My Temple." And
7 they began with the elders who were before the House. He said to them,
"Defile the House; fill the courts with slain; go out!" And they went out;
8 they struck the city. And as they were striking it down, I alone was left; I
fell on my face, and I cried, "But my Lord God! Will you destroy all that
9 remains of Israel, pouring Your fury out over Jerusalem?" And He said to
me: "The iniquity of the House of Israel and Yehuda is extremely great;
the land is filled with blood, and the city is full of corruption, for they have
10 said, 'The Lord has gone from the land; the Lord does not see.' And so
I will not let My eye pity, I will not show mercy; their ways I will bring
down on their heads."

11 Then the man dressed in linen with the scribe's instruments at his waist
returned and reported, "I have done that which you commanded me."

10 1 I looked –

there, upon the expanse
that was above the heads of the cherubim,
something like a sapphire,
like the appearance of the form of a throne,
could be seen above them.[15]

2 He spoke to the man dressed in linen; He said, "Go into the space between
the wheelworks, beneath the cherub; fill your hands with burning coals
from between the cherubim and scatter them over the city." And he went
3 in before my eyes. The cherubim were standing to the right of the House;
4 the man went in, and the cloud filled the inner court. The glory of the
Lord rose from the cherub upon the threshold of the House; the House
was filled with the cloud, and the radiance of the glory of the Lord filled
5 the court; the sound from the wings of the cherubim could be heard all
the way to the outer court – like the voice of El Shaddai when He speaks.
6 When He commanded the man dressed in linen, saying, "Take fire from
between the wheelworks, from between the cherubim," the man came
7 and stood by the wheel. One of the cherubim reached his hand between
the cherubim and into the fire between the cherubim; he picked it up and
put it into the hands of the man dressed in linen, who took it and then
came out.

8 The cherubim appeared to have the figure of a man's hand
under their wings.

15 | Cf. 1:26.

9 And I looked:
There were four wheels alongside the cherubim,
one wheel by this cherub and one wheel by that cherub,[16]
and the appearance of the wheels was bright like a topaz gem.
10 In their appearance, all four had the same form of a wheel within a wheel;
11 when they moved, they moved in the direction of any of their four sides;
they did not turn when they moved,
for they moved toward whichever place their head turned toward;
they did not turn when they moved.
12 All of their bodies, their backs, their hands, their wings, and the wheels
were filled, all over, with eyes –
the wheels of the four of them.
13 It is these wheels that were called wheelworks in my hearing.
14 Each one had four faces:
the first face was the face of a cherub,
the second was the face of a man,
the third was the face of a lion,
and the fourth was the face of an eagle.
15 And the cherubim rose up –
these were the living beings that I saw by the Kevar River[17] –
16 and when the cherubim moved, the wheels moved with them;
and when the cherubim lifted up their wings
so that they could rise up above the land,
the wheels that were with them did not turn:
17 when they stood, they too stood,
and when they rose up, they too rose up,
for the spirit of the living beings was in them.
18 And the glory of the Lord left the threshold of the House
to stand upon the cherubim;
19 the cherubim lifted their wings, and they rose up from the ground
to leave – before my very eyes – with the wheels beside them;
they stood at the entrance of the eastern gate of the House of the Lord,
and the glory of the God of Israel was resting upon them from above.
20 These are the living beings that I saw beneath the God of Israel by the Kevar River,
and I knew that they were cherubim –
21 four, each one had four faces,
and each one had four wings,
and the form of a man's hand was beneath their wings;

16 | Cf. 1:15–21.

17 | See chapter 1.

22 the forms of their faces were those of the faces that I saw by the Kevar
River both in their appearance and in themselves; each moved in the
direction of one of the faces.

11 1 And a spirit lifted me up and brought me to the eastern gate of the House
of the LORD, which faces east, and there at the entrance to the gate were
twenty-five men. And I saw among them Yaazanya the son of Azur and
Pelatyahu son of Benayahu, officials of the people.

2 And He said to me: "Man, these are the men plotting sin and giving evil
3 advice in this city. They say, 'There is no need now for building houses;
4 the city, she is the pot – we are the meat!'[18] And so, prophesy against them;
prophesy, Man."

5 And so the spirit of the LORD fell upon me, and He said to me, "Say this:
So says the LORD:
This is what you said, House of Israel;
I know what comes up in your minds.
6 You have made your slain ever more numerous in this city;
you have filled her streets with slain.

7 "So the Lord GOD says this:
The slain you have put in her midst,
they are the meat, and she is the pot –
and you, I will remove from her midst.[19]
8 You feared the sword;
I will bring the sword down upon you,
declares the Lord GOD.
9 I will take you out from her midst;
I will give you over into the hands of strangers,
and I will execute judgments upon you.
10 You will fall by the sword,
upon the border of Israel I will judge you,
and you will know that I am the LORD.
11 She will not be a pot for you,
but you will be the meat in her;
I will judge you in the borders of Israel
12 and you will know that I am the LORD.
You did not follow My statutes,
you did not practice My laws,
but you acted according to the laws of the nations around you."

13 As I was prophesying, Pelatyahu son of Benaya fell dead, and I fell on my
face and cried a great cry: "Ah, my Lord GOD, You are destroying all that
remains of Israel!"

---

18 | That is, the city walls will protect us from destruction like the pot protects the meat.

19 | That is, I will remove you from the city like cooked meat is removed from a pot.

14 And the word of the Lord came to me, saying: "Man, your brothers,
15 your brothers, your very kinsmen, all of the House of Israel, entirely, the
inhabitants of Jerusalem say to them: 'They are far from the Lord; this
land has been given to us as a possession!'[20]

16 "And so, say: So says the Lord God:
Though I have placed them far away among the nations,
though I have scattered them over the lands
and am but a small sanctuary for them
in whichever lands they come to –

17 "So say: So says the Lord God:
I will gather you in from these other nations;
I will bring you in from the countries where you have been scattered,
and I will give you the land of Israel.
18 And they will come there,
and they will remove all the detestable things,
all the abominations, from her.
19 I will give them one heart –
I will put a new spirit into you –
I will remove the heart of stone from their flesh
and give them a heart of flesh,
20 so that they will follow My decrees
and keep My laws and fulfill them;
they will be My people,
and I will be their God.
21 And those whose hearts are drawn
to the heart of their detestable things and abominations,
I will bring their ways down on their heads,
declares the Lord God."

22 The cherubim lifted up their wings with the wheels beside them, and
23 above, upon them, the glory of the God of Israel. The glory of the Lord
rose from within the city and stood upon the mountain east of the city.

24 And a spirit lifted me up and brought back me to the Chaldeans, to the
exile, in a vision by the spirit of God, and the vision I had seen rose off me.
25 And to the exiles I related all the things that the Lord had shown me.

12 1 And the word of the Lord came to me, saying:
2 "Man, you are living in the midst of this defiant house;
they have eyes to see with, but they do not see;
they have ears to hear with, but they do not hear,[21]
for they are a defiant house.

20 | The current inhabitants of Jerusalem claim exclusive ownership of the city, since those exiled are far away.

21 | Cf. Psalms 115:5–6; Isaiah 6:9–10.

3 "You, Man, make an exile's bundle for yourself,
and go into exile by day before their eyes;
you will go into exile from your home to another place
before their eyes; perhaps they will see it –
for they are a defiant house.
4 Bring out your belongings as an exile's bundle
by day before their eyes –
by night you will go out before their eyes
like one going into exile.
5 Before their eyes
burrow through the wall
and take your bundle out through it,
6 before their eyes
carry it on your shoulder;
bring it out in the dark.
Cover your face so that you cannot see the land –
for I am making you a sign for the House of Israel."

7 I did as I had been commanded: I brought my belongings out as an exile's
bundle by day, and by night I burrowed through the wall with my hand;
in the dark I took it out and carried it on my shoulder before their eyes.

8 9 And the word of the Lord came to me in the morning, saying: "Man,
has not the House of Israel, that defiant house, asked you, 'What are you
10 doing?' Say to them: So says the Lord God: The prince is this burden
in Jerusalem,[22] and the whole of the House of Israel who are in its midst.
11 Say:
I am your sign;
just as I have done,
this is what will be done to them:
they will go into exile in captivity.
12 The prince who is in their midst
will carry the bundle on his shoulder in darkness and go out;
they will burrow through the wall to take him out through it;
his face will be covered
so that he will not see the land with his eyes.
13 I will spread My net over him;
he will be caught in My trap.
I will take him to Babylon,
the land of the Chaldeans,
but he will not see it,
and there he will die.
14 All who are around him, his attendants, all his forces,
I will scatter to the winds;

22 | The prince is Tzidkiya, who would be exiled (II Kings 24:18–25:21). *Masa* (burden) resonates with *nasi* (prince) and derives from the same Hebrew root.

I will draw the sword after them.
15 They will know that I am the LORD
when I strew them among the nations
and scatter them over the lands.
16 I will leave a small number of them
after sword, famine, and plague
to tell of all their abominations
among the nations that they go to,
and they will know that I am the LORD."

17 And the word of the LORD came to me, saying:
18 "Man, eat your bread trembling;
drink your water quaking and anxious.

19 "Say to the people of the land: So says the Lord GOD to the inhabitants of
Jerusalem in the land of Israel:
They will eat their bread anxious;
they will drink their water aghast.
And so, the land will be devastated of all that fills her
because of the lawlessness of all who inhabit her;
20 the populated cities will be laid waste,
and the land will be desolate;
and you will know that I am the LORD."

21 22 And the word of the LORD came to me, saying: "Man, to you on the soil
of Israel, what does this saying mean: 'Time passes; every vision comes
23 to nothing'? And so, say to them: So says the Lord GOD: I will bring an
end to this saying; they will no longer use it in Israel; instead, say to them:
'The days are near, each word of every vision.'

24 "Never again will there be any false visions
or fawning divinations among the House of Israel.
25 For I, the LORD, will speak;
every word that I speak will be fulfilled;
it will no longer be held off;
in your days, defiant house,
I will speak a word and fulfill it,
declares the Lord GOD."

26 27 And the word of the LORD came to me, saying: "Man, the House of Israel
says, 'The vision he sees is for many days in the future; he prophesies for
28 a far-off time.' So say to them: So says the Lord GOD: All My words will
no longer be held off; every word I speak will be fulfilled, declares the
Lord GOD."

13 1 2 And the word of the LORD came to me, saying: "Man, prophesy against
those prophets of Israel who prophesy; say to those who prophesy their
own hearts:

Hear the word of the Lord.
3 So says the Lord God:
Woe to those depraved prophets
who go after their own spirit,
who have seen nothing.
4 Like foxes among ruins
your prophets have become, Israel.
5 You have not gone up into the breaches
or built a fence for the House of Israel
so that they can stand strong in battle
on the day of the Lord.
6 They profess false visions, lying divinations,
saying, 'So declares the Lord,'
when the Lord had not sent them –
and expecting their words to be fulfilled.
7 Have you not professed false visions,
uttered lying divinations,
and said, 'So declares the Lord,'
when I have not spoken?

8 "So the Lord God says this:
Because you speak falsehood
and profess lies,
behold, I am upon you,
declares the Lord God.
9 My hand will be against the prophets
who assert false visions, those who divine lies;
they will not be part of the company of My people;
they will not be written in the annals of the House of Israel;
they will not come back to the soil of Israel;
you will know that I am the Lord God.
10 For the very reason that they have misled my people,
saying, 'All is well,' when all is not well,
the people build a thin wall,
and they daub it with whitewash.
11 Say to those daubing on the whitewash: It will fall;
there will be torrential rain;
you, hailstones, will fall;
storm winds will burst forth –
12 and when the wall falls,
will they not ask of you,
'Where is the whitewash that you daubed?'

13 "So the Lord God says this:
I will make storm winds burst forth in My fury;
there will be torrential rain in My anger;

and hailstones in fury, for destruction.
14 I will tear down the wall you daubed with whitewash;
I will raze it to the ground, bare its foundation;
it will fall, and you will be destroyed in her midst –
and you will know that I am the LORD.
15 I will exhaust My fury upon the wall,
upon those who daubed her with whitewash;
I will say to you: Gone is the wall,
gone are those who daubed it –
16 prophets of Israel who prophesy to Jerusalem,
asserting visions to her that all is well
when all is not well,
declares the Lord GOD.

17 "And you, Man, turn your face to the daughters of your people who prophesy
18 their own hearts; prophesy to them and say: So says the Lord GOD:
Woe to those women
who sew ribbon-amulets onto the joints of every arm,
who make veils for the heads of people of every stature –
in order to hunt others' lives;
you hunt the lives of My people,
but your own lives you preserve?
19 You have profaned Me to my people
for handfuls of barley and crumbs of bread,
proclaiming death to those who should not die
and life to those who should not live –
in your lies to My people, who listen to lies.

20 "So the Lord GOD says this:
Behold, I am against your ribbon-amulets
that you use to hunt people like birds;
I will rip them off your arms;
I will set free the people
whose lives you hunt like birds;
21 I will tear off your veils
and save My people from your grasp;
they will never again be prey in your grasp,
and you will know that I am the LORD –
22 for with lies you depress the hearts of the righteous
whom I would not cause pain
and strengthen the actions of the wicked
so that he does not turn from his evil course and live.
23 And so, you will never profess false visions
or divine divinations again;
I will save My people from your grasp,
and you will know that I am the LORD."

14 1 2 Men from the elders of Israel came to me, and they sat before me. And
3 the word of the LORD came to me, saying: "Man, these men have brought
their idols close to their hearts; they have placed the obstacle that is their
sin right before their faces; should they now be allowed to consult Me?
4 So, speak to them, say to them: So says the Lord GOD: Any man from the
House of Israel who brings his idols close to his heart and who places the
obstacle that is his sin before his own face and who then comes to the
prophet – I am the LORD – I will answer him when he comes with his
5 many idols in order to regain the hearts of the House of Israel, who have
all become estranged from Me with all their idols.

6 "So say to the House of Israel: So says the Lord GOD: Return, turn from
7 your idols; from all of your abominations turn your faces! For any man
from the House of Israel or the stranger who dwells in Israel who becomes
estranged from Me, brings his idols close to his heart, places the obstacle
that is his sin before his own face, and comes to the prophet to consult Me
8 through him, I am the LORD; it is I who will answer him. I will set My face
against that man; I will make him a sign, a cautionary tale; I will cut him
off from amongst My people, and you will know that I am the LORD.

9 "And if a prophet is tempted and speaks a word, I am the LORD; I have
tempted that prophet, and I will stretch My hand out over him and destroy
10 him from among My people Israel. They will bear their sin; the punishment
11 of the inquirer will also be that of the prophet, and so the House of Israel
will no longer stray from Me and no longer defile themselves with all their
transgressions. They will be My people, and I will be their God, declares
the Lord GOD."

12 13 And the word of the LORD came to me, saying: "Man, if a land sins against
Me by her faithlessness, and I stretch My hand out over her and break the
staff of bread she leans on, send her famine, and cut man and beast off from
14 her; if these three men were in her midst – Noaḥ, Daniel, and Iyov – their
righteousness would save them, declares the Lord GOD.

15 "And if I make wild animals pass through the land and bereave her, a
16 devastation none can pass through because of these beasts, if these three
men were there within her, surely as I live, declares the Lord GOD, even
if they would save sons and daughters – only they themselves would be
saved, and the land would be devastated.

17 "Or if I bring the sword down on that land and say, 'The sword will pass
18 through the land and cut man and beast off from her,' and these three men
were there within her, surely as I live, declares the Lord GOD, they would
not save sons or daughters; they alone would be saved.

19 "Or if I send a plague to that land and pour My fury out upon her in blood,
20 to cut man and beast off from her, and Noaḥ, Daniel, and Iyov were there
within her, surely as I live, declares the Lord GOD, they would save neither
son nor daughter – their righteousness would save their own souls.

21 "So says the Lord GOD: How much more so when I unleash on Jerusalem
My four terrible judgments: sword, famine, wild animals, and plague, to
22 cut off man and beast from her. And yet, a remnant will be left in her, will
be brought out, sons and daughters; they will come out to you, and you
will see their ways and their deeds, and you will be comforted over the
23 evil that I have brought upon Jerusalem, all that I have brought down on
her. They will comfort you – for when you see their ways and their deeds,
you will know that not for nothing have I done all that I have done to her,
declares the Lord GOD."

15 1 And the word of the LORD came to me, saying:

2 "Man, of all trees what is the grapevine,
the vine branch, among the trees of the forest?
3 Can wood be taken from it to be put to use?
Can you take a peg from it to hang utensils on?
4 See: given as fuel to fire,
both ends the fire consumes; its insides are charred.
Is it then fit for use?
5 See: when whole it cannot be put to use,
even less so when consumed by fire and charred –
how could it be put to further use?

6 "So the Lord GOD says this: Like the grapevine among the trees of the
forest, which I have given as fuel to fire, so have I given over the inhabitants
7 of Jerusalem. I will fix My face against them; they have escaped from fire,
but fire will consume them; you will know that I am the LORD when I set
8 My face against them. I will turn the land over to desolation because of
their faithlessness, declares the Lord GOD."

16 1 2 The word of the LORD came to me, saying: "Man, make known to Jerusalem
3 her abominations and say: So says the Lord GOD to Jerusalem:

"Your ancestry and your birth were in the land of the Canaanites. Your
4 father was Amorite, your mother Hittite; and as for your birth, on the
day you were born your cord was not cut, you were not washed clean
5 with water, you were not rubbed with salt, and you were not swaddled. No
eye took enough pity on you to do any of these things out of compassion
for you. You were thrown out into the open field, loathed, on the day you
6 were born. And when I passed by you, I saw you floundering in your own
blood, and I said to you, 'In your blood, live'; I said to you, 'In your blood,
live!'

7 "I made you flourish like the shoots of the field. You grew up, matured,
were beautifully adorned – your breasts were firm, your hair grew long –
8 but you were naked and bare. Then I passed by you and saw that you had
reached the age of love, so I spread my mantle out over you[23] and covered

23 | A metaphor for marriage (cf. Ruth 3:9).

your nakedness. I made My vow to you, entered into a covenant with you,
declares the Lord God, and you became Mine.

9 "I washed you with water, I rinsed your blood off you, and I anointed
10 you with oil. I clothed you in embroidered cloth, I placed on you leather
11 shoes, I wound about your head fine linen, and I covered you with silk. I
adorned you with jewelry; I put bracelets upon your arms and a necklace
12 around your neck. I put a nose ring in your nose, earrings in your ears, and
13 a glorious crown upon your head. You were adorned with gold and silver;
your clothing was fine linen, silk, and embroidered cloth; you ate fine flour,
honey, and oil; and you were exceptionally beautiful, fit to be a queen.

14 "You became known among the nations for your beauty, for with the
15 splendor I placed upon you it was perfect, declares the Lord God. But
you trusted in your beauty, and you used your fame to play the whore;
16 you showered your whoring upon every passerby – his for the taking!
You used your clothes to make yourself multicolored platforms that you
whored upon – such things will not come about, will not happen again.

17 "You took your glorious jewelry, made from the gold and silver I had given
18 you. You made yourself male images, and you whored with them. You took
your embroidered clothing to cover them. My oil and My incense you set
19 before them. The food I had given you – the fine flour, oil, and honey I
fed you – you set before them as a sweet fragrance; it was so, declares the
Lord God.

20 "You took the sons and the daughters you bore Me and sacrificed them
21 to them to devour – were your whorings not enough? You slaughtered
22 My children; you offered them up by passing them over to them. With all
your abominations, all your whoring, you did not remember the days of
your youth when you were naked and bare, when you were floundering
in your own blood.

23 "After all this, your wickedness – oh, what woe will come to you! declares
24 the Lord God – you then built yourself a platform, made yourself a raised
25 place in every square. At every crossroad you built raised places and made
your beauty disgusting, opening your legs to every passerby; you escalated
26 your whoring. You whored with the sons of Egypt, your large-membered
neighbors; you escalated your whoring to anger Me.

27 "So I stretched out My hand against you, reduced your portion and gave
you over to the will of your enemies, the daughters of the Philistines who
28 are themselves embarrassed at your depraved ways. Unsated, you whored
with the Assyrians; you whored with them, but you were still not satisfied.
29 You broadened your whoring to the land of merchants, Chaldea, but even
with this you were not satisfied.

30 "How languid is your heart, declares the Lord God, to have done all
31 these things, the acts of a brazen prostitute! Building platforms at every

crossroad, constructing raised places in every square. But you were not
32 like a regular whore; you scorned payment, the adulterous wife who takes
33 strangers instead of her husband. All prostitutes are given gifts, but you in
your whoring gave gifts to all your lovers, bribing them on every side to
34 come to you. You have been the opposite of other women – by whoring
unsolicited, by paying and not being paid a prostitute's fee, you were the
opposite.

35 "So, whore, hear the word of the Lord. So says the Lord God: Because
36 your lust was poured out and your nakedness bared in your whoring with
your lovers, and for all the idols of your abominations, and as you gave
37 them your children's blood, behold: I will gather together all the lovers
you pleased, all those you loved along with all those you hated; I will
gather them against you from all around, and I will bare your nakedness to
38 them – they will see you in all your nakedness. I will condemn you to the
punishment of the adulterous woman and the murderess, give you over to
39 bloody fury and passionate anger. I will give you over into their hands, and
they will tear down your platforms, pull down your raised places; they will
strip you of your clothes; they will take your glorious jewelry and leave you
40 naked and bare. They will bring against you a horde; they will stone you
41 and cut you down with their swords. They will burn down your houses;
they will execute judgments on you before the eyes of many women. Thus
will I put an end to your whoring; you will no longer pay a prostitute's fee.
42 I will let My fury at you die down; My passionate anger will turn away
43 from you; I will be silent, no longer will I be angry. Because you did not
recall the days of your youth but enraged Me with all of this – here, I will
bring your ways down upon your head, declares the Lord God, for have
you not acted with depravity on top of all your other abominations?

44 "Behold, all who use sayings will say of you, 'Like mother, like daughter.'
45 You are the daughter of the mother who despised her husband and children;
you are the sister of sisters who despised their husbands and children. Your
46 mother was a Hittite, your father an Amorite. Your older sister Shomron
and her daughters live to the north; your younger sister lives to the south,
47 Sedom and her daughters. Did you not follow their ways and act out their
abominations? Within a short time, you became more corrupt than they
48 were in all your ways. As I live, declares the Lord God, your sister Sedom
49 and her daughters did not act as you and your daughters have acted. The
sin of your sister Sedom was this: pride. She and her daughters had enough
bread and an easy tranquility and yet did not aid the hands of the poor and
50 needy. They were haughty and committed abominations before Me, and
so, when I beheld them, I did away with them.

51 "As for Shomron, she has not committed half of the sins you have. You
committed more abominations than they did; with all the abominations
52 you committed you made your sisters appear righteous! And so, bear your
disgrace: you have advocated for your sisters – because your sins were

more abominable than theirs, they appeared more righteous than you! So,
you, be ashamed; bear the disgrace of making your sisters appear righteous.
53 I will restore their fortunes, the fortune of Sedom and her daughters and
the fortune of Shomron and her daughters – and your fortune among
54 them – so that you will bear your disgrace and be disgraced by what you
55 have done in providing this comfort to them. Your sister Sedom and her
daughters will return to their former state; Shomron and her daughters
will return to their former state; and you and your daughters will return
56 to your former state. Was not Sedom, your sister, a byword in your mouth
57 during your proud days, before your own wickedness was revealed? Now
you are reproached by the daughters of Aram and all those around her,
the daughters of the Philistines, who treat you with contempt from all
58 sides. Your depravity, your abominations – you will bear them, declares
the LORD.

59 "So says the Lord GOD: I will do to you as you, who flouted the oath
60 and violated the covenant, have done, but I will remember My covenant
with you from the days of your youth, and I shall establish an everlasting
61 covenant with you. You will remember your ways; you will feel disgraced
when you receive your older sisters with your younger ones – I will give
them to you as daughters though they are not included in your covenant.
62 I will establish My covenant with you; you will know that I am the LORD.
63 And so you will remember and be ashamed; your voice will be silenced
in the face of your disgrace when I forgive you for all that you have done,
declares the Lord GOD."

17 1 2 And the word of the LORD came to me: "Man, pose a riddle; tell a parable
3 to the House of Israel; say: So says the Lord GOD:

"A great eagle
with great wings, long pinions,
his dense plumage a rich tapestry,
came to Lebanon
and took the crown of the cedar.
4 He plucked the topmost stalk
and carried it to the land of merchants,
placed it in a city of traders.
5 He took a seed from that land
and placed it in a field ready for seeding,
planted it on great flowing waters,
positioned it like a willow.
6 And it grew; it became a vine,
sprawling, low-growing,
bending its arms toward him,
its roots spreading below;
it became a vine,
it grew shoots,

and stretched out boughs.
7 And another great eagle
with great wings and full plumage –
behold, this vine reached its roots out toward him
to be watered, stretched its arms out to him
from its planting bed –
8 planted in a rich field by great flowing waters
to grow branches, bear fruit,
become a majestic vine.

9 "Say: So says the Lord God:
Will it thrive?
Surely he will tear up its roots,
he will rip off its fruit,
and it will wither.
All fresh leaves will wither;
it will take neither a strong arm
nor a great army
to tear it from its roots.
10 Even planted as it is,
will it thrive?
Surely when the east wind strikes
it will wither away;
upon the bed where it has grown
it will wither."

11 And the word of the Lord came to me: "Say this now to the defiant
12 house: Do you not know what these things mean? Say: Behold, the king of
Babylon came to Jerusalem and took her king and officials, and he brought
13 them to Babylon. He took one of the royal seed and made a covenant with
him; he brought him under oath and took away the leaders of the land so
14 that it would be a lowly kingdom that could not rise up, that would keep
15 his covenant to preserve itself. But he rebelled against him, sending his
messengers to Egypt for horses and a great army.[24] Will he thrive? Will he
who does these things escape? Will he violate a covenant and escape?

16 "As I live, declares the Lord God, in the domain of that king who made
him king, whose oath he flouted, whose covenant he broke with him – in
17 Babylon he will die. And in war Pharaoh will assist him with neither
numerous troops nor great hordes, nor when earthworks are thrown up
or a siege wall built against them for the destruction of numerous people.
18 He flouted the oath by breaking the covenant; he gave his word and yet
still did all these things; he will not escape.

19 "So the Lord God says this: As I live, My oath that he has flouted, My
20 covenant that he has broken I will bring back down upon his head. I will

24 | See II Kings 24:20.

spread My net over him; he will be caught in My trap; I will take him to
Babylon and enter into judgment with him there for his betrayal, through
21 which he betrayed Me. All his fugitives from all his forces will fall by the
sword, and those who remain will be scattered to the winds, and you will
know that I, the LORD, have spoken.

22 "So says the Lord GOD:
I will take from the soaring crown of the cedar and place it,
I will pluck from the topmost, tender stalks,
and I will plant it
upon a high and lofty mountain;
23 in the mountainous height of Israel I will plant it.
It will bear branches, grow fruit;
it will become a majestic cedar,
and every bird of every type
will settle beneath it;
in the shade of its arms they will dwell.
24 And all the trees of the field will know that I, the LORD,
have brought down the high tree
and raised the lowly tree;
I have withered the green tree
and made the withered tree bloom;
I, the LORD, have spoken and will do it."

18 1 2 And the word of the LORD came to me, saying: "What are you doing, using
this proverb on the soil of Israel: 'Fathers eat sour grapes, but the teeth of
3 the children are set on edge'? As I live, declares the Lord GOD, you will
no longer use this proverb in Israel.

4 "Behold: all lives are Mine; the life of father and son alike are Mine; that
5 person who sins will die. The person who is righteous, who acts in a way
6 that is just and right – he does not eat on the mountains or look up to the
idols of the House of Israel, he does not defile another's wife or approach a
7 menstruating woman,[25] he mistreats no one, he returns his debtor's pledge
to him, he commits no robbery, he gives his bread to the hungry, he covers
8 the naked with clothes, he does not lend with advanced interest or take
accrued interest,[26] he resists doing wrong, he judges between man and
9 man with true justice, he follows My statutes, keeps My laws, acts with
truth – he is righteous; he will live, declares the Lord GOD.

10 "If he bears a violent son, bloodshedder, who commits any one of
11 these – although he himself committed none of these – who eats on the
12 mountains, who defile another's wife, who mistreats the poor and needy,
commits robbery, does not return his debtor's pledge, who looks up to the
13 idols, who commits abominable things, who lends with advanced interest

25 | Leviticus 18:19.

26 | Leviticus 25:36.

and takes accrued interest, will he live? He will not live; he has committed
all these abominable acts; he will die – his blood is on his own head.

14 "And if he bears a son, who sees all the sins that his father has committed,
15 who considers them but does not act similarly – he does not eat on the
mountains, he does not look up to the idols of the House of Israel, he
16 does not defile another's wife, he mistreats no one, he does not retain his
debtor's pledge, he does not commit robbery, he gives his bread to the
17 hungry, he covers the naked with clothes, he refrains from harming the poor,
he takes neither advanced nor accrued interest, he keeps My laws, follows
My statutes – he will not die for the iniquity of his father; he will live.

18 "Because his father practiced extortion, robbed his own brother, acted in a
way that was no good among his people, behold: he will die in his iniquity.
19 And you say: Why does the son not bear the iniquity of the father? The
son has acted in a way that is just and right, has kept all My statutes, has
20 performed them – he will live. That person who sins will die; the son
will not bear the iniquity of the father, and the father will not bear the
iniquity of the son; the righteous one's righteousness will be on him, and
the wicked one's wickedness will be on him.

21 "The wicked one who turns back from all the sins he committed and keeps
all My statutes and acts in a way that is just and right – he will live; he
22 will not die. All the transgressions he committed will not be remembered
23 against him; through the righteousness he has performed he will live. Do I
desire the death of the wicked, declares the Lord God, not that he should
turn from his ways and live?

24 "And the righteous one who turns from his righteousness and does wrong
similar to all the abominable acts the wicked one committed, shall he
live? None of the righteous deeds he has done will be remembered; his
25 betrayal and the sins that he has sinned – because of these he will die. You
say, 'The way of the Lord is not fair.' Listen, House of Israel: Is My way not
26 fair? Surely, your ways are not fair. When the righteous one turns from
his righteousness and does wrong and dies for it, he dies for that which
27 he has done wrong. And when the wicked one turns from the wickedness
that he has done and acts in a way that is just and right, he preserves his
28 life. When he considers them and turns from all the transgressions he has
29 committed, he will live; he will not die. And the House of Israel says, 'The
way of the Lord is not fair.' Are My ways not fair, House of Israel? It is your
ways that are not fair.

30 "So I will judge you, House of Israel, each man according to his ways,
declares the Lord God; return – turn back from all your transgressions
31 so that they will not be the obstacle that is sin for you. Throw off all the
transgressions you have committed; make yourselves a new heart, a new
32 spirit. Why should you die, House of Israel? For I do not desire the death
of those who die, declares the Lord God; turn back and live!

19 1 "And you, raise a lament about the leaders of Israel; say:
2 What a lioness was your mother;
among lions she lay; among young lions she reared her cubs.
3 She raised one of her cubs as a young lion,
and he learned to tear apart prey and devour men.
4 But the nations heard about him,
and he was captured in their pit;
with hooks they brought him in
to the land of Egypt.[27]
5 She saw that in vain she waited, that hope was lost,
so she took another of her cubs;
she made him the young lion.
6 And he prowled among the lions as a young lion;
he learned to tear apart prey; he devoured men.
7 He seduced their widows, destroyed their cities;
the land and all within it were devastated at the sound of his roar.
8 But the nations set upon him from surrounding provinces;
they spread their net over him; he was captured in their pit.
9 With hooks they locked him in a cage
and brought him to the king of Babylon;
they brought him trapped in nets
so that his voice would no longer be heard
on the mountains of Israel.[28]

10 "Your mother was like a vine, like you,
planted by the water,
full of fruit and with full branches
from the great flowing waters.
11 She had strong branches
for the scepters of rulers;
her heights towered among the clouds;
in her height and abundant arms, she was striking.
12 But she was uprooted in fury
and hurled down to the ground;
the east wind withered her fruit;
they broke off, they withered,
the branches of her strength;
fire devoured her.
13 Now, planted in the desert
in a land of drought and thirst,
14 fire burst out
from the branch holding her shoots
and consumed her fruit;
no strong branch remained on her,

27 | Referring to Yehoaḥaz (see II Kings 23:33).
28 | Referring to Yehoyakhin (see II Kings 24:8–16).

no scepter to rule with.
This is a lament
and has become a lament."

20 1 And it was in the seventh year in the fifth month on the tenth day of the
month that men from the elders of Israel came and sat before me to consult
the LORD.

2 3 And the word of the LORD came to me: "Man, speak to the elders of Israel;
say to them: So says the Lord GOD: Have you come to seek Me? As I
4 live, I will not be sought by you, declares the Lord GOD. Will you accuse
them, Man, will you accuse them? Make known to them their fathers'
abominations.

5 "Say to them: So says the Lord GOD: On the day that I chose Israel, raising
My hand in promise to the descendants of the House of Yaakov and making
Myself known to them in the land of Egypt, I raised My hand in promise
6 to them, saying: 'I the LORD am your God.' On that day, I raised My hand
in promise to them to take them from the land of Egypt to the land that
flows with milk and honey, the most beautiful of all lands, that I had sought
7 out for them. I said to them: 'Throw off, each of you, the detestable things
before your eyes; do not defile yourselves with Egyptian idols: I the LORD
am your God.'

8 "But they defied Me; they were not prepared to listen to Me; none threw
off the detestable things before their eyes; they did not relinquish their
Egyptian idols. And I thought of pouring out My fury, exhausting My anger
9 upon them in the midst of the land of Egypt. But I acted for the sake of My
name so that it would not be desecrated in the eyes of the nations among
whom they were – and before whose eyes I had made Myself known in
10 taking them out from the land of Egypt. I took them out from the land of
Egypt and brought them into the wilderness.

11 "I gave them My statutes, made My laws known to them, by which a
12 person shall live. I even gave them My Sabbaths as a sign between Myself
and them so that they should know that I, the LORD, make them holy.
13 But the House of Israel defied me in the wilderness. They did not follow
My statutes; they rejected My laws, by which each person was to live;
they wholly desecrated My Sabbaths. I thought of pouring out My fury
14 upon them in the wilderness and destroying them, but I acted for the
sake of My name so that it would not be desecrated in the eyes of the
15 nations before whose eyes I had taken them out. I even raised My hand in
promise to them in the desert not to bring them to the land that flows with
milk and honey, the most beautiful of all lands, which I had given them,
16 because they rejected My laws, did not follow My statutes, desecrated My
17 Sabbaths – for their hearts followed after their idols. But My eye pitied
them, and I could not destroy them; I did not bring them to their end in
the wilderness.

18 "I said to their children in the wilderness: 'Do not follow the statutes
19 of your fathers, do not keep their laws; do not be defiled by their idols.
20 I the LORD am your God: follow My statutes, keep My laws, perform
them, make My Sabbaths holy – it will be a sign between Me and you to
21 know that I the LORD am your God.' But the children defied me: they did
not follow My statutes, the did not take care to keep My laws, by which
a person shall live, they desecrated My Sabbaths, and I thought to pour
22 out My fury upon them, exhausting My anger upon them there in the
wilderness. But I drew back My hand; I acted for the sake of My name so
that it would not be desecrated in the eyes of the nations before whose
eyes I had taken them out.

23 "Nevertheless, I raised My hand in promise to them in the wilderness – to
24 scatter them among the nations and strew them through the lands because
they did not perform My laws, they rejected My statutes, and they
desecrated My Sabbaths, their eyes bent toward the idols of their fathers.
25 So I further gave them statutes that were no good and laws they could not
26 live through; I defiled them through their gifts of giving over all the first to
emerge from the womb so that I might devastate them, so that they might
know that I am the LORD.

27 "And so, speak to the House of Israel, Man, and say to them: So says the
Lord GOD: In this, too, your fathers acted toward Me with contempt in
28 their betrayal of Me. I brought them to the land which I raised My hand
in promise to give to them; they saw each high hill, every lush tree, and
there offered up their offerings, there gave their enraging sacrifices with
29 the sweet fragrances they made, and there poured their libations. I said
to them: What is the high place that you hurry to? To this day it is called
Bama.[29]

30 "So say to the House of Israel: So says the Lord GOD: Do you defile
yourselves in the way that your fathers did; do you whore after their
31 detestable things? You defile yourselves when you offer your children
through fire as presents to all your idols – to this very day; shall I allow
you to seek Me, House of Israel? As I live, declares the Lord GOD, I will
32 not allow you to seek Me. And that which is in your thoughts will never be.
You say: We will be like the nations, like the families of the lands, serving
33 wood and stone. As I live, declares the Lord GOD, with a strong hand, with
34 an outstretched arm, and with an outpouring of fury, I will rule over you. I
will take you out from the nations; I will gather you in from the countries
where you have been scattered; with a strong hand, with an otstretched
35 arm, and with an outpouring of fury I will bring you into the wilderness
of the nations, and I will enter into judgment with you there, face-to-face.
36 Just as I entered into judgment with your fathers in the wilderness of the
land of Egypt, so will I enter into judgment with you, declares the Lord

29 | The name Bama (high place) can be read as a compound of *ba* (hurry) and *ma* (what).

37 God. I will make you pass beneath the rod;[30] I will bring you into the
38 bond of the covenant. I will purge you of the rebellious and of those who
transgress against Me; I will take them out of the land in which they are
living, but they will not come onto the soil of Israel. So you will know that
I am the Lord.

39 "And you, House of Israel – so says the Lord God: Go each of you to
worship his idols, now and beyond, if you will not listen to Me; you will
40 no longer desecrate My holy name with your gifts and your idols, because
on My holy mountain – on Israel's high mountain, declares the Lord
God – there, all of the House of Israel in its entirety will serve Me in the
land; there I will receive them; there I will seek your contributions and
41 your most choice offerings, with all your holy things. As with a sweet
fragrance I will accept you when I take you out from among the nations
and gather you in from the lands that you were scattered among; I will be
sanctified through you in the eyes of the nations.

42 "And you will know that I am the Lord when I bring you to the soil of
Israel, to the land that I raised My hand in promise to give to your fathers.
43 There you will remember your ways, all your deeds through which you
were defiled, and you will loathe yourselves for all the evil things that you
44 have done. And you will know that I am the Lord when I act toward you
for the sake of My name, not for your evil ways and your corrupt deeds,
House of Israel, declares the Lord God."

21 1 2 And the word of the Lord came to me: "Man, set your face toward Teiman,
3 proclaim to Darom, prophesy to the forestland of the Negev.[31] Say to the
forest of the Negev: Listen to the word of the Lord. So says the Lord
God:

See, I will kindle in you a fire;
it will devour in you every new tree
and every withered tree;
it will not go out, this raging blaze.
They, every face, will be scorched by it,
from the Negev up to the north.
4 All flesh will see
that I, the Lord, set it alight;
it will not be extinguished."

5 And I said: "Ah, but my Lord God! They say of me, 'He is just a teller of
parables.'"

6 7 And the word of the Lord came to me: "Man, set your face toward
Jerusalem and proclaim to the sanctuaries; prophesy against the soil of
8 Israel. Say to the soil of Israel: So says the Lord:

30 | As a shepherd counts his flock (cf. Lev. 27:32).

31 | Teiman, Darom, and Negev are terms for south, denoting the land of Israel from Yeḥezkel's vantage point.

Behold, I am coming down upon you;
I will draw My sword from its sheath;
I will cut off from you both righteous and wicked.
9 Since I will cut off from you righteous and wicked,
My sword will come out of its sheath
against all flesh, from south to north.
10 All flesh will know that I am the LORD;
I have drawn My sword from its sheath;
it will not be returned.

11 "And you, Man: Groan with a body shattered; in bitterness groan before
12 their eyes. And when they say, 'Why are you groaning?' say: Because of a
report that is coming:
Every heart will melt;
all hands will go limp;
every spirit will faint,
all thighs run wet with fear;
behold: it is coming; it will be,
declares the Lord GOD."

13 14 And the word of the LORD came to me: "Man, prophesy and say: So says
the Lord: Say:
A sword, a sword has been sharpened, polished,
15 to commit slaughter; sharpened,
and so that it will flash, polished.
Will we rejoice, rod of My son
that despises every tree?
16 It was given to be polished, to be wielded,
the sword was sharpened, polished,
to be given into the hand of a killer.
17 Cry out, wail, Man,
for it is against My people,
it is against all the leaders of Israel –
they are thrown to the sword with My people,
so slap your thigh in grief;
18 it is assured. What is?
That even the rod that despises will not be spared,
declares the Lord GOD.

19 "And you, Man, prophesy; clap your hands:
The sword will come again
and a third time,
the sword of slaying,
the sword of a great massacre
enclosing them;
20 so that hearts will crumble,
and many will fall

at each of their gates.
I have allowed sword slaughter;
O, shined so that it will flash,
honed for slaughter.
21 Sharp, to the right!
To the left!
Where is your blade aimed?
22 I, too, will clap My hands,
then let My fury die down.
I, the LORD, have spoken."

23 And the word of the LORD came to me: "And you, Man, mark out two
24 roads for the sword of the king of Babylon to advance upon, both exiting
from the same land, and clear space for a sign at the beginning of the road
25 leading to each city; clear space. Mark out a road for the sword to advance
upon – to Raba of the Amonites[32] and to Yehuda in fortified Jerusalem.
26 For the king of Babylon stands at the fork in the road, at the beginning
of the two roads, to perform a divination: shaking arrows, inquiring of
27 household gods, scrutinizing the liver. In his right hand is the omen that
signals Jerusalem: to post battering rams, to demand slaughter, to shout
out war cries; to post battering rams at the gates, to throw up earthworks,
28 to build a siege wall. It will be seen as a false divination in their eyes – for
they have had reassuring oaths sworn to them which recall the sin for
which they will be seized.

29 "So the Lord GOD says this: since you have recalled your sin by uncovering
your transgressions to reveal the iniquities in all your deeds – because your
sin has been recalled, by hand you will be seized.

30 "To you, disgraced, wicked leader of Israel whose day, the time of final
31 punishment, has come, so says the Lord GOD:
Remove the royal turban; lift off the crown!
This will no longer be thus;
exalt the lowly, and lower the exalted.
32 Ruin, ruined, wrecked
I will make it.
This, too, will not be
until he with just claim comes,
and I hand it to him.

33 "And you, Man, prophesy – say: So says the Lord GOD concerning the
Amonites and their taunts:
Sword, sword, unsheathed,
for slaughter polished
to its utmost so that it flashes,

32 | Raba, modern Aman, was the Amonite capital.

34 professing false visions
and lying predictions about you, sword,
have brought you down instead
onto the necks of the disgraced wicked,
whose day has come,
the time of final punishment.
35 Return it to its sheath!
In the place you were created,
in the land of your origin,
I will judge you.
36 I will pour out My rage upon you,
I will blast through you the fire of My wrath,
I will give you over into the hands of brutish men,
skilled at destruction.
37 You will be fuel for the fire,
your blood will be shed there in the land;
you will not be remembered –
for I, the LORD, have spoken."

22 1 2 The word of the LORD came to me, saying, "And you, Man, will you
accuse – will you accuse the bloody city? Make all her abominations
3 known to her. Say: So says the Lord GOD:
City that spills blood in her own midst, hastening her time
and making idols in her to defile her,
4 in spilling your own blood, you have become guilty;
in making your own idols, you have been defiled.
You have brought your days near;
you have come to the end of your years,
so I give you over as a reproach to the nations,
a mockery to all the lands.
5 Those near and far will mock you,
you of impure name, filled with panic.
6 Here are the leaders of Israel:
each used his power to spill blood among you;
7 they have dishonored mother and father within you;
they have oppressed the foreigner in your midst;
they have mistreated orphan and widow within you.
8 You despised My holy things;
you desecrated My Sabbaths.
9 Slanderers have been among you so as to spill blood;
on the mountains they have eaten among you;
depravities they have performed in your midst.
10 Their father's nakedness they have uncovered within you;
the impure, menstrual woman they have forced within you.
11 One man committed abominations with another's wife;
another has defiled his daughter-in-law with depravity;

another in you has forced his sister, the daughter of his
father – within you!
12 They have taken bribes within you so as to spill blood;
you have taken both advanced and accrued interest;
you have taken advantage of your friend with extortion;
and Me you have forgotten, declares the Lord God.
13 See: I clap My hands
over the dishonest gain you have taken,
and over the bloodshed, that were in your midst.
14 Will your heart stand firm,
will your hands stay strong
for the days when I deal with you?
I am the Lord; I have spoken and will do it.
15 I will strew you among the nations,
scatter you over the lands:
I will purge your impurity from you.
16 You will be debased in yourself
before the eyes of nations,
and you will know that I am the Lord."

17 18 And the word of the Lord came to me, saying, "Man, to Me the House of
Israel are dross; they are bronze, tin, iron, and lead in a crucible; they are
19 the dross of silver. So the Lord God says this:
Because you have all become dross,
I am gathering you in to Jerusalem.
20 Like silver and bronze, iron, lead, and tin
gathered into a crucible
to blast with fire to melt it –
so will I gather you in My anger and My fury
and put you in and melt you.
21 I will collect you together
and blast the fire of My wrath upon you;
you will be melted down within her.
22 Like the smelting of silver in a crucible,
this is how you will be smelted within her;
you will know that I am the Lord
and that I have poured My fury out upon you."

23 24 And the word of the Lord came to me, saying: "Man, say to her:
You are a land not cleansed,
not swept with rain on the day of rage.
25 Her prophets are a conspiracy in her midst:
like a roaring lion that tears apart its prey,
they have devoured people;
they have taken treasures and precious things;
they have made numerous widows in her midst.

26 Her priests have abused My teaching,
desecrated My holy things;
they have not distinguished between sacred and profane;
they have not taught the difference between impure and pure;
they have hidden their eyes from My Sabbaths,
and I have been profaned in their midst.
27 The leaders in her midst have been like wolves tearing their prey,
spilling blood, destroying people for malicious gain.
28 For them, her prophets have daubed with whitewash,
asserted false visions, and predicted lies,
saying, 'So says the Lord God,'
when the Lord has not spoken.
29 The people of the land practiced extortion and committed robbery,
mistreated the poor and needy,
and oppressed the foreigner without redress.
30 I searched for a man among them to build a fence,
to stand in the breach before Me
on behalf of the land so that I would not have to ruin her,
but I found no one.
31 I have poured My rage out upon them,
destroyed them in the fire of My wrath;
I have brought their ways down on their heads,
declares the Lord God."

23 1 2 And the word of the Lord came to me, saying: "Man, there were two
3 women, daughters of one mother, and they whored in Egypt. In their
youth they whored; there were their breasts caressed; there they fondled
4 their virgin's nipples. Their names: the older one was Ohola, and Oholiva
was her sister. And they became Mine and bore sons and daughters. Their
names: Shomron is Ohola, and Jerusalem is Oholiva.[33]

5 "Even while still Mine, Ohola whored and lusted after her lovers, the
6 Assyrians. They were warriors attired in blue, governors and officials,
7 young desirable men all of them, cavalrymen on horseback. She lavished
her whoring upon them, the finest of all the Assyrians, and defiled herself
8 with all the idols of each of those she lusted after. Still she did not abandon
her whoring with Egypt – for they had lain with her in her youth; they had
9 fondled her virgin's nipples and poured all their lusting onto her. So I gave
her over into the hands of her lovers, into the hands of the Assyrians after
10 whom she lusted. They exposed her nakedness; they took her sons and
daughters, and by sword they killed her. The punishments they inflicted
on her made her infamous among women.

11 "Her sister Oholiva saw this – yet she still made her lusting and her
12 whoring even more perverted than her sister's. She lusted after the

33 | Ohola literally means "tent"; Oholiva, "my tent is therein."

Assyrians, governors and officials, warriors impeccably attired, cavalrymen
13 on horseback – all of them dashing men. I saw that she defiled herself –
14 both of them took the same course. Then she added to her whoring: she
saw carved figures of men on the walls, images of Chaldeans imprinted
15 in bright red, girded at their waists with cloth belts, trailing turbans on
their heads, all with the appearance of officers, forms of Babylonians
16 born in Chaldea. As soon as she saw them she lusted after them and
17 sent messengers to them in Chaldea. And the Babylonians came to her
for lovemaking, and they defiled her with their lusting – she defiled
18 herself with them, then she recoiled from them. She flaunted her whoring,
flaunted her nakedness, and I recoiled from her – as I had recoiled from
19 her sister. She escalated her whoring – remembering the days of her youth,
20 whoring in the land of Egypt. And she lusted after their lovers whose
21 members were like a donkey's, whose emissions were like a horse's. You
sought out the depravity of your youth when the men of Egypt fondled
your nipples because of your young breasts.

22 "So, Oholiva, so says the Lord God: See that I will stir your lovers up
against you, those from whom you recoiled. I will bring them against you
23 from all around: Babylonians and all of the Chaldeans, Pekod, Shoa, and
Koa,[34] and all of the Assyrians along with them – dashing men, all of them
governors and officials, officers and dignitaries, all of them on horseback.
24 They will come down upon you – weapon, chariot, and wheel – with a
horde of armies; they will accost you all around with shield, buckler, and
helmet. I will give punishment over to them, and they will judge you with
25 their laws. I will bring down My passionate anger upon you: They will deal
with you with fury; your nose and your ears they will cut away, and what
remains of you will fall by the sword; they will take your sons and your
26 daughters, and what remains of you will be consumed by fire. They will
27 strip you of your clothes; they will take your glorious jewelry. I will put an
end to your depravity and your whoring with the land of Egypt; you will
not set your eyes upon them, and you will remember Egypt no more.

28 "For so says the Lord God: See that I am handing you over into the hands
29 of those you hate, into the hands of those from whom you recoil. They
will deal with you with hatred; they will take all you have worked for; they
will leave you naked and bare with the nakedness of your whoring, your
30 depravity and your licentiousness exposed. For whoring after nations
31 this will be done to you because you defiled yourself with their idols. You
followed in the ways of your sister, so I will put her cup into your hand.

32 "So says the Lord God:
You will drink from the deep, wide cup of your sister,
the cup of derision and contempt spilling over.
33 With drunkenness and grief you will be filled,

34 | Groups of Babylonian allies.

the cup of ruin and desolation,
the cup of your sister Shomron;
34 you will drink it, you will drain it,
you will gnaw at its shards,
and you will tear at your breasts;
for I have spoken, declares the Lord God.

35 "So the Lord God says this: Because you forgot Me and cast Me behind
your back, you must now bear the consequences of your depravity and
whoring."

36 And the Lord said to me: "Man, will you accuse Ohola and Oholiva?
37 Tell them of their abominations, for they have committed adultery, and
blood is on their hands; they committed adultery with their idols, and the
children that they bore Me they also passed over to their idols to devour.
38 What is more, this they have done to Me: on that same day they defiled
39 My Sanctuary, and they desecrated My Sabbaths; when they slaughtered
their children for their idols, on that same day they would then come to
My Sanctuary and desecrate it! See, this is what they did in My House. And
40 even more: they sent for men from afar to come; a messenger was sent to
them – and they came! For them you bathed, painted your eyes, adorned
41 yourself with jewelry. You sat on a lavish bed with a table set before it, and
42 you put My incense and My oil upon it. And the murmur of a careless
crowd was there; to the men among the mass of people they brought wines
from the desert; they placed bracelets on their arms and glorious crowns
43 on their heads. I thought the desire for whoring would leave her, haggard
44 from adultery, but she is unchanged. They came to her as though coming
to a prostitute; this is how they came to Ohola and Oholiva, depraved
45 women. Righteous people will sentence them to the punishment of the
adulteress and the punishment of the murderess – for they are adulteresses,
and they have blood on their hands.

46 "So says the Lord God: Bring a horde against them! Give them over to
47 terror, pillage! The horde will stone them with rocks, cut them down with
their swords, kill their sons and daughters; they will burn their houses
48 down with fire. I will put an end to depravity in the land; all women
49 will be warned not to imitate your depravity. They will inflict upon you
the outcome of your depravity, you will bear the consequences of your
idolatrous sin, and you will know that I am the Lord God."

24 1 And the word of the Lord came to me in the ninth year in the tenth
2 month on the tenth of the month:[35] "Man, write down the name of the
day, of this very day; the king of Babylon laid siege to Jerusalem on this
3 very day. Recount a parable to the defiant house; say to them: So says the
Lord God:

Put the pot onto the fire; put it on,

35 | The tenth of Tevet.

then pour water into it;
4 gather its carcass pieces into it,
every choice piece, thigh and shoulder;
fill it with the best bones.
5 Take the best of the flock,
then pile the bones up under it
and bring it to boil,
then cook the bones in it.

6 "So the Lord God says this:
Woe, bloody city,
pot with its insides rusted,
whose rust will not come off it;
empty it piece by piece;
the lot has not fallen to her,
7 for her blood is within her;
she placed it upon the bare rock
and did not spill it onto the ground
to cover it with earth.
8 To stir up fury, to take vengeance,
I put her blood upon the bare rock,
not to be covered up.

9 "So the Lord God says this:
Woe, bloody city;
I, in turn, will build up the pile.
10 Heap on more wood, light the fire,
cook the flesh well, mix the compound;
the bones will be charred.
11 Stand it upon the coals, empty,
so that the bronze heats up, scorches,
and her impurity melts down within her
so that her filth is gone completely.
12 Worn with useless toil,
its pervasive filth will not come off it
even through fire, such filth.
13 In your depraved impurity –
because I cleansed you, but you did not become pure –
you will never be purified of your impurity
until My fury against you dies down.
14 I am the Lord; I have spoken;
it is coming; I will do it;
I will not refrain, I will not pity, I will not relent;
according to your ways, your deeds, will you be judged,
declares the Lord God."

15 16 And the word of the LORD came to me: "Man, behold: I am taking from
you your eyes' delight with a sudden blow; you will not lament, you will
17 not cry, your tears will not fall. Moan silently for the dead but do not
mourn: bind on your turban, put your shoes on your feet; do not cover
your mouth, do not eat others' bread."

18 And I spoke to the people in the morning; my wife died in the evening; in
the morning I did as I was commanded.

19 And the people said to me, "Tell us, what do these things mean for us
20 that you are doing?" And I said to them: "The word of the LORD came
21 to me: 'Say to the House of Israel: So says the Lord GOD: I am going to
desecrate My Sanctuary – your power's majesty, your eyes' delight, your
soul's tenderness – and your sons and your daughters whom you have
22 left behind will fall to the sword. You will do as I have done: Your mouth
23 you will not cover; the bread of others you will not eat; your turbans will
remain on your heads, your shoes on your feet. You will not lament, you
24 will not cry; you will waste away in your sins and groan to each other. And
Yeḥezkel will be a sign to you: everything that he has done, so will you do
when it comes, and you will know that I am the Lord GOD.

25 "'And you, Man, on the day that I take way from them their stronghold,
their glory's joy, their eyes' delight, their soul's yearning, their sons and
26 daughters, on that day, a fugitive will come to you, for you to hear it with
27 your own ears. On that day your mouth will be opened with the fugitive,
and you will speak; you will no longer be struck silent; you will be a sign
to them, and they will know that I am the LORD.'"[36]

25 1 2 And the word of the LORD came to me: "Man, set your face to the
3 Amonites; prophesy against them; say to the Amonites: Listen to the
word of the Lord GOD: So says the Lord GOD:

Because you said, 'Ha!'
about My Sanctuary when it was desecrated,
about the soil of Israel when it was devastated,
about the House of Yehuda when they went into exile,
4 so I will give you over to the people of the East[37]
as a possession;
in you they will set up their camps,
in you put up their dwellings;
they will eat your fruits;
they will drink your milk.
5 I will turn Raba into a grazing place for camels,
Amon into a resting place for sheep,
and you will know that I am the LORD.

36 | This ends the period of Yeḥezkel's muteness described in 3:24–27.

37 | Nomads from the Arabian Desert.

6 "For so says the Lord GOD: Because you clapped your hands, stamped yor
feet, grew joyous with such absolute contempt about the soil of Israel,[38]
7 for this I am stretching My arm out over you – giving you over as spoil to
the nations; I will cut you off from among the peoples, I will make you
perish from among the lands, I will decimate you, and you will know that
I am the LORD.

8 "So says the Lord GOD: Because Moav and Se'ir have said, 'See, the House
9 of Yehuda is just like all the other nations,' for this I am exposing Moav's
flank, its cities, the cities at its edges, the glory of the land, Beit HaYeshimot,
10 Baal Meon, Kiryatayim. To the people of the East, together with the
Amonites, I will give it as a possession so that the Amonites will not be
11 remembered among the nations, and over Moav I will execute judgments;
they will know that I am the LORD.

12 "So says the Lord GOD: Because of how Edom acted, taking their vengeance
against the House of Yehuda and incurring great guilt for their vengeance
13 upon them, for this, so says the Lord GOD: I will stretch My arm out
against Edom and cut every man and beast off from her. I will give her over
to destruction; from Teiman to Dedan they will fall by the sword.[39] My
14 vengeance against Edom will be carried out by My people Israel; they will
act with My anger, My fury, against Edom; they will know My vengeance,
declares the Lord GOD.

15 "So says the Lord GOD: Because the Philistines acted in vengeance, took
their vengeance with absolute contempt, and wrought destruction with
16 an abiding hatred, for this, so says the Lord GOD: I am stretching My
hand out against the Philistines; I will cut off the Keretites;[40] I will cause
17 the remaining coastland to perish. I will carry out great acts of vengeance
against them with furious rebukes, and they will know that I am the LORD
when I take My vengeance against them."

26 1 And it was in the eleventh year on the first of the month, the word of the
2 LORD came to me: "Man, because Tyre said of Jerusalem: 'Aha! She has
been broken, the doorway of the peoples; it has passed round to me; I
3 will be filled now that she is laid waste,' for this, so says the Lord GOD:

Behold: I am upon you, Tyre;
I will heave many nations upon you
as the sea heaves up its waves.
4 They will destroy the walls;
they will demolish her towers;
I will strip her rubble off her,
turn her into a bare rock;

---

38 | Moav and Amon were enemies of Israel at this time (see II Kings 24:2).

39 | Teiman and Dedan were settlements in the desert of Edom.

40 | The Philistines are also called the Keretites and the dwellers of the coastland (e.g., Zeph. 2:5).

5 a place for spreading nets to dry, she will be
in the midst of the sea,
for I have spoken, declares the Lord God.
She will become spoil for the nations,
6 her daughters in the fields
will be killed by the sword,
and they will know that I am the Lord.

7 "For so says the Lord God:
Against Tyre I will bring Nevukhadretzar,
king of Babylon, from the north, a kings of kings,
with horse, chariot, cavalrymen,
with a horde and a great army.
8 By sword he will kill your daughters in the field;
he will construct a siege wall against you;
he will throw up earthworks against you,
set shields up against you.
9 He will pound his battering ram against your walls;
he will tear down your towers with his weapons.
10 From his legion of horses the dust will cover you;
from the sound of cavalrymen, wheel, and chariot
your walls will tremble
when he enters through your gates
like men charging a breached city.
11 With the hooves of his horses he will trample all of your streets;
he will kill your people by sword;
your strong pillars will fall to the groud.
12 They will plunder your riches,
pillage your merchandise,
tear down your walls,
pull down your delightful houses,
and your stones, your wood, your rubble
they will throw into the water.
13 I will put an end to the noise of your songs;
the sound of your lyres will be heard no more.
14 I will make you a bald, glaring rock;
you will be a place for spreading nets to dry;
you will never be rebuilt,
for I the Lord have spoken,
declares the Lord God.

15 "So says the Lord God to Tyre:
Surely,
from the sound of your downfall,
at the groaning of the slain,
when killing is raging in your midst,
the coastlands will tremble.

16 They will descend from their thrones,
all the princes of the sea;
they will take off their robes,
pull off their embroidered clothes,
dress themselves in quaking;
they will sit on the ground,
they will quake unceasingly,
they will be aghast at you.
17 They will raise a lament over you; they will say to you:
'How you have perished,
you praised city, who were settled from the seas,
who was so mighty on the seas – she was, along with her habitants –
who inspired terror over all its habitants.'
18 Now the coastlands quake on the day of your downfall;
the coastlands by the sea are terrified
at your demise.

19 "For so says the Lord God:
When I turn you into a destroyed city
like cities that lie unsettled,
when I heave the deep upon you
and the great rushing waters cover you over,
20 I will take you down
with those descending to the Pit,
to the ancient dead;
I will settle you there
in the netherworld of the dead,
like ancient ruins,
with those who descend to the Pit,
so that you will no longer be settled,
and I will make the land of the living glorious.
21 I will make you a horror; you will cease to be;
you will be searched for but will be not be found
ever again,
declares the Lord God."

27 1 2 And the word of the Lord came to me: "Man, raise a lament about Tyre.
3 Say to Tyre, who inhabits the gateway to the sea, who is trader of the
peoples to many coastlands: So says the Lord God:
Tyre, you have said,
'I am perfect in beauty';
4 in the heart of the sea were your borders;
builders perfected your beauty;
5 cypresses from Senir they used
to build your planks;
cedars from Lebanon
they used for your mast;

6 out of oaks from Bashan
they made your oars,
your deck of ivory-inlaid boxwood
from the islands of the Kittites;
7 embroidered linen from Egypt
was your sail, set as your flag,
blue and purple from the islands of Elisha[41]
your awnings.
8 The inhabitants of Sidon and Arvad
were your oarsmen;
the wise men in you, Tyre,
were your sailors,
9 the elders of Geval,[42] her wise men among you,
repaired your breaches;
all the seafaring ships and her sailors were among you
to bring you imports.
10 Persia, Lydia, and Put[43] peopled your army,
served as your men of combat;
they hung shield and helmet upon you,
making you splendid;
11 the sons of Arvad and Ḥeilekh were on the perimeter of your walls;
there were Gamadim in your towers;
they hung their quivers upon the perimeter of your walls,
and it made your beauty perfect.
12 Tarshish was your trader – due to your great wealth,
silver, iron, tin, and lead they gave for your wares.
13 Ionia, Tuval, and Meshekh[44] were your merchants –
living men and bronze vessels they gave you as imports.
14 From Beit Togarma,[45] horses, steeds, and mules
they gave for your wares.
15 The sons of Dedan were your merchants;
numerous islands traded under your aegis;
ivory tusks and ebony they brought as tributes.
16 Aram was your trader due to your abundant goods;
emerald, purple and embroidered cloths, fine linen, corals, and rubies
they gave for your wares.
17 Yehuda and the land of Israel were your merchants;
wheat of Minit,[46] millet, honey, oil, and balm they gave you as imports.

41 | Cyprus.
42 | Byblos, on the Lebanese coast.
43 | Put refers to Libya.
44 | Tuval and Meshekh are in Anatolia.
45 | Modern-day Gürün in central Turkey.
46 | In Amon (see Judges 11:33).

18 Damascus was your trader, because of your abundant goods and great wealth,
in wine of Ḥelbon and wool of Sahar.
19 Vedan and Ionia, from Uzal,
for your wares gave polished iron, cassia, and calamus as imports.
20 Dedan was your merchant
of saddlecloths for riding.
21 Arabia and all the chiefs of Kedar[47] were traders under your aegis;
in lambs, rams, and goats they traded with you.
22 The merchants of Sheba[48] and Rama were your merchants in all perfumes,
all precious stones, and gold that they gave for your wares.
23 Ḥaran, Kaneh, and Eden,
merchants of Sheba, Assyria, and Kilmad were your merchants;
24 they were your merchants
for exquisite clothing, blue and embroidered cloaks,
many-colored carpets bound with cords, preserved with cedar –
in your marketplace.
25 The ships of Tarshish transported your imports;
you were filled, heavily laden,
in the heart of the sea.
26 They rowed you,[49]
brought you to great rushing waters;
the east wind smashed you apart
in the heart of the sea.
27 Your wealth, your wares, and your imports,
your sailors and your pilots,
those who repair your breaches and who bring your imports,
and all your men of combat among you,
all the crew who are within you
will plummet into the heart of the sea
on the day of your downfall.
28 At the sound of your pilot's shouts
the billows will churn,
29 and all your oarsmen and sailors, all your pilots
will debark from their ships,
will stand on dry land.
30 They will make their voices heard over you,
and they will cry out bitterly;
they will put dirt on their heads,
dust themselves with ashes.
31 They will make themselves bald over you,

---

47 | A nomadic kingdom in the Arabian Desert.

48 | A kingdom in the southern Arabian Peninsula (see I Kings 10:1).

49 | Tyre is represented here as a ship.

gird themselves with sackcloth;
they will cry over you, their spirits bitter,
a bitter lament.
32 And in their wailing, they will raise a lament over you;
they will lament over you:
'Who was like Tyre,
silenced in the midst of the sea?'
33 When your wares were sent out on the seas,
you brought abundance to numerous peoples;
with your great wealth and imports
you made the kings of the earth rich.
34 Now, broken by the seas,
there in the depths of the water,
your imports and all of the crew within you
have plummeted down.
35 All the inhabitants of the coastlands
are aghast at your fate,
their kings appalled,
their faces thunderous.
36 Merchants among the other peoples
hiss at you;
a horror you have become;
you are gone, forever."

28 1 2 And the word of the Lord came to me: "Man, say to the ruler of Tyre: So
says the Lord God:
Because your heart grew arrogant,
you said, 'I am a god;
I sit upon the seat of a god
in the heart of the sea' –
but you are a man
and not a god;
you consider your heart
to be the heart of a god,
3 but are you wiser than Daniel?
Is no obscure matter hidden from you?
4 With your wisdom and understanding
you made yourself powerful;
you amassed silver and gold
in your treasuries;
5 with your great wisdom in commerce
you increased your riches,
and your heart grew arrogant
with your riches.

6 "So the Lord God says this:
Because you consider your heart

to be the heart of a god,
7 so will I bring strangers upon you,
the most terrifying of nations;
they will draw their swords upon the beauty of your wisdom;
they will defile your radiance.
8 They will take you down to the Pit;
you will die the death of the slain
in the heart of the sea.
9 Will you still say 'I am a god' before your slayer?
You are a man, not a god, in the hands of your killers.
10 You will die the death of the uncircumcised
at the hands of strangers;
thus have I spoken,
declares the Lord God."

11 And the word of the Lord came to me: "Man, raise a lament over the king
12 of Tyre; say to him: So says the Lord God:
You were the model of flawlessness,
full of wisdom, perfect in beauty.
13 You were there in Eden, the garden of God,
every precious stone as your wrapping,
carnelian, olivine, and green quartz,
aquamarine, rock crystal, and jasper,
sapphire, emerald, and garnet,[50]
gold the handiwork of your settings and grooves
that were set on the day you were created.
14 You were a sublime, shielding cherub;
I placed you there;
you were on the holy mountain of God;
you walked among the stones of fire.
15 You were faultless in your ways
from the day you were created
until wrongdoing was found in you;
16 because of your vast commerce
your midst was filled with corruption,
and you sinned.
I struck you from the mountain of God;
I have banished you, shielding cherub,
from among the stones of fire.
17 Your heart grew arrogant because of your beauty;
you perverted your wisdom along with your radiance;
I flung you to the ground,
brought you before kings to look on you.
18 Because of your many sins, your dishonesty in commerce,

50 | Cf. Exodus 28:17–20.

you desecrated your sanctuaries.
I brought fire from within your midst –
it consumed you;
I turned you into ashes on the ground
before the eyes of all who looked on you.
19 All your acquaintances among the peoples are aghast at your fate;
a horror you have become;
you are gone, forever."

20 21 And the word of the LORD came to me: "Man, set your face toward Sidon,
22 prophesy against her and say: So says the Lord GOD:
I am upon you, Sidon;
I will gain glory in your midst.
They will know that I am the LORD
when I execute judgments upon her,
when I am sanctified through her.
23 I will set plague and blood loose
against her in her streets,
the slain will fall within her
when the sword is bearing down on her from all around,
and they will know that I am the LORD.
24 The House of Israel will no longer suffer
stabbing briers, scratching thorns,
from those in their surroundings who scorn them,
and they will know that I am the Lord GOD.

25 "So says the Lord GOD: When I gather the House of Israel in from the
peoples where they have been scattered and I am sanctified through them
in the eyes of the nations, when they live on their land that I gave to My
26 servant Yaakov – they will live on it in safety; they will build houses, plant
vineyards, live safely; when I execute judgments over all those from their
surroundings who scorn them, they will know that I am the LORD, their
God."

29 1 In the tenth year in the tenth month on the twelfth of the month, the word
2 of the LORD came to me: "Man, set your face against Pharaoh, king of
3 Egypt; prophesy against him and against all of Egypt. Speak and say: So
says the Lord GOD: Behold, I am upon you, Pharaoh, king of Egypt, great
crocodile crouching in his Nile streams who says, 'It is mine, this Nile; I
made it for myself.'
4 I will fix hooks into your jaw;
I will make the fish from your streams stick to your scales;
I will drag you up out of your streams,
and all the fish from your streams will stick to your scales;
5 I will abandon you in the desert,
you and all the fish of your streams.
You will fall in the open field

and be neither collected nor gathered up;
to the animals of the land and the birds of the skies
I will give you over as food.
6 All the inhabitants of Egypt will know that I am the LORD –
for they were a reed staff to the House of Israel:
7 when they grasped hold of you, you crumbled,
tearing their shoulders;
when they leaned upon you, you broke,
buckling their loins.

8 "So the Lord GOD says this: I will bring the sword down upon you, cut off
9 man and beast from you. The land of Egypt will be desolate, ruined, and
they will know that I am the LORD. Because he said, 'The Nile is mine; I
10 made it,' for this, I am coming down upon you and your Nile streams. I will
turn the land of Egypt into a waste of desolate ruins from Migdol to Sevene
11 and to the border with Kush.[51] The foot of no man will pass through her;
the foot of no animal will pass through her; she will not be inhabited for
12 forty years. For forty years I will make the land of Egypt desolate among
desolate lands, and her cities will lie desolate among ruined cities. I will
strew Egypt among the nations, scatter them over the lands.

13 "Yet, so says the Lord GOD, at the end of forty years I will gather Egypt
14 in from the people among whom they were scattered. I will restore the
fortunes of Egypt; I will restore them to the land of Patros, the land of their
15 origin, and there they will be a lowly kingdom. She will be the lowest of
the kingdoms and will never again elevate herself above the nations; I will
reduce them to a state where they cannot dominate among the nations.
16 They will no longer be a source of trust for the House of Israel but merely
a reminder of Israel's sin in turning to them, and they will know that I am
the Lord GOD."

17 It was in the twenty-seventh year in the first month on the first day of the
18 month that the word of the LORD came to me: "Man: Nevukhadretzar,
king of Babylon, exerted his army to labor hard against Tyre. Every head
was rubbed raw, every shoulder worn down bare, but from Tyre neither
he nor his army received pay for the hard work with which they toiled
against her.

19 "So the Lord GOD says this: See that to Nevukhadretzar, king of Babylon, I
will give the land of Egypt. He will carry off her wealth, ransack her spoils,
20 and seize her loot; she will be the pay for his army. I shall give him the land
of Egypt as his payment, for which he has labored, which he has done for
Me, declares the Lord GOD.

21 "On that day I will make a horn of strength grow for the House of Israel,

51 | Migdol is in northern Egypt (see Ex. 14:2). Sevene is Aswan, in southern Egypt, near the border with Kush.

and you – I will let your voice be heard among them, and they will know
that I am the LORD."

30 1 2 And the word of the LORD came to me: "Man, prophesy; say: So says the
Lord GOD.
Howl it: 'Alas, the day!'
3 For a day is near;
the day of the LORD is near;
a day of cloud,
a time of nations it will be.
4 The sword will come to Egypt;
there will be anguish in Kush;
when the slain in Egypt fall,
they will take her wealth,
and her foundations will be torn up.
5 Kush and Put and Lydia,
all the mixed peoples and Kub,[52]
and people of allied lands with them
will fall by the sword.

6 "So says the LORD:
Those defending Egypt will fall;
the majesty of her power will collapse
from Migdol to Sevene;
there they will fall by the sword,
declares the Lord GOD.
7 They will be desolate among desolate lands,
her cities among the cities laid waste;
8 they will know that I am the LORD when I set Egypt afire
and all those who assist her are broken.
9 On that day messengers from Me will go forth in ships
to make secure Kush quake;
anguish will be among them on Egypt's day,
for see, it is coming.

10 "So says the Lord GOD:
I will put an end to the crowds of Egypt
by the hand of Nevukhadretzar, king of Babylon.
11 He along with his troops,
the most terrifying of nations,
will be brought to destroy the land;
they will draw their swords upon Egypt
and fill the land with the slain.
12 I will turn the streams to dry ground;
I will sell the land into the hands of evil people;

52 | Kush is in the south of Egypt, Put (Libya) is in its west, "the mixed peoples" (*kol ha'erev*) refers to Arabia to the east, and Lydia is in the north. Kub is otherwise unknown.

at the hands of strangers
I will devastate the land and everything in it;
I, the Lord, have spoken.

13 "So says the Lord God:
I will destoy idols
and end the false gods of Nof;[53]
there will no longer be a prince in the land of Egypt;
I will put fear into the land of Egypt.
14 I will devastate Patros;
I will set Tzoan afire
and execute judgments in No.
15 I will pour out My fury upon Sin, stronghold of Egypt;
I will cut off the masses of No.
16 I will set Egypt afire,
Sin will quiver in terror,
No will be broken open,
and Nof will face enemies daily.
17 The young men of Aven and Pi Beset will fall by the sword;
they will go into captivity.
18 In Taḥpanḥes day will darken
when I break Egypt's bars there
and the majesty of her power is put to an end;
cloud will cover her up,
and her daughters will go into captivity.
19 I will execute judgments in Egypt,
and they will know: I am the Lord."

20 And it was in the eleventh year in the first month on the seventh of the
21 month that the word of the Lord came to me: "Man, I have broken the
arm of Pharaoh, king of Egypt; see, it has not been bound up to heal nor
bound with a bandage to strengthen it enough to wield a sword.

22 "So the Lord God says this:
Behold, I am against Pharaoh, king of Egypt;
I will break his arms,
the strong one along with the broken one;
I will make the sword fall from his hand.
23 I will strew Egypt among the nations,
scatter them over the lands.
24 I will make the arms of the king of Babylon strong;
I will place My sword into his hands,
and I will break Pharaoh's arms;
he will groan with the moans of the mortally wounded
before him.
25 I will support the arms of the king of Babylon,

53 | This and the following are all major cities and regions in Egypt.

and the arms of Pharaoh will fall slack,
and they will know that I am the LORD
when I put My sword into the hand of the king of Babylon
and stretch it forth against the land of Egypt.
26 I will strew Egypt across the nations,
scatter them among the lands,
and they will know: I am the LORD."

31 1 It was in the eleventh year in the third month on the first of the month that
2 the word of the LORD came to me: "Man, say to Pharaoh, king of Egypt,
and to his crowds:
Who are you comparable to in your greatness?
3 Here is Assyria, a cedar in Lebanon with beautiful branches,
a wood giving shade with towering heights,
his crown among the clouds;
4 water made him grow; the deep waters made him soar;
her rivers ran around his plantings;
she sent her waterways out to all trees of the field.
5 And so, his height towered above all other trees of the field;
his branches became many, his boughs grew long
from the abundant water in his channel.
6 Upon his limbs nested every bird of the sky,
beneath his boughs birthed every animal of the field,
and in his shade lived each of the many nations.
7 He was beautiful in his greatness,
in the length of his branches,
for his roots reached down to abundant waters.
8 In the garden of God, the cedars could not overshadow him,
the cypress trees could not compare to his limbs,
and the plane trees could not equal his boughs;
none of the trees in the garden of God could compare to him in beauty.
9 I made him beautiful with his abundant branches,
and all the trees of Eden that were in the garden of God
envied him.

10 "So the Lord GOD says this:
11 Because he became towering in height
and placed his crown up among the clouds,
he grew arrogant because of his height.
I gave him over into the hands of the leader of the nations,
who dealt with him;
I drove him out due to his wickedness.
12 Strangers, the most terrifying of nations, have cut him down
and abandoned him;
his branches fell on the mountains, in all the valleys;
his boughs broke in all the land's ravines;

all the peoples of the land stepped out from under his shade;
they abandoned him.
13 Every bird of the sky will settle on his fallen trunk,
every animal of the field will nestle upon his boughs;
14 so that no watered trees
will become towering in their height
or place their own crowns up among the clouds,
and of all drinkers of water,
none of their mighty trees will stand at their full height,
for all of them will give in to death, to the netherworld,
among men who descend to the Pit.

15 "So says the Lord God:
On the day of his descent into Sheol,
I closed the deep waters upon him, covered him;
I held back her rivers, and abundant waters were restrained.
For him I cast Lebanon into darkness;
for him all the trees of the field languished.
16 With the sound of his fall I made the nations tremble
when I took him down to Sheol
with those gone down into the Pit;
in the netherworld all the trees of Eden –
the best, most choice of Lebanon,
all richly watered –
were comforted.
17 They too descended to Sheol with him,
to those slain by the sword
and his allies who sat in his shade among the nations.
18 To whom were you comparable like this
in glory and in greatness among the trees of Eden?
You will be brought down, too,
with the trees of Eden, to the netherworld;
you will lie among the uncircumcised
with those slain by the sword,
Pharaoh and all his crowds,
declares the Lord God."

32 1 It was in the twelfth year in the twelfth month on the first of the month
2 that the word of the Lord came to me: "Man, say a lament over Pharaoh,
king of Egypt; say to him:
You think yourself a young lion among the nations,
but you are like a crocodile in the seas,
pouncing in your rivers,
churning the waters with your feet,
turning up the mud of their rivers.

3 "So says the Lord God:
I will spread My net over you
with a horde of many people;
they will bring you up in My fishing net.
4 I will dash you to the ground,
I will hurl you onto the open field,
I will make every bird of the sky settle on you,
I will make all the animals of the land gorge upon you,
5 I will disperse your limbs over the mountains,
I will fill the valleys with your carcasses,
6 I will drench your floodlands with your blood up to the mountains,
and the ravines will be filled with you.
7 When you are extinguished, I will cover over the heavens,
I will darken their stars,
I will cover the sun over with clouds,
and the moon will not shine its light.
8 I will darken all the lights that shine in the sky, for you,
I will place your land in darkness,
declares the Lord God.
9 I will cause alarm in the hearts of many peoples
when I bring news of your collapse among the nations,
among lands you have never known.
10 I will make many peoples appalled at you;
their kings will bristle in horror
when I brandish My sword before them;
every man will quake in constant fear of his life
on the day of your downfall.

11 "So the Lord God says this:
The sword of the king of Babylon will come upon you;
12 I will bring down your hordes with the swords of warriors,
all the most terrifying of the nations;
they will devastate the majesty of Egypt;
all her hordes will be decimated.
13 I will cause all her livestock to perish from beside abundant waters;
the feet of men will no longer churn them,
nor will the hooves of livestock churn them.
14 Then will I settle their waters
and make their rivers flow like oil,
declares the Lord God.
15 When I render the land of Egypt desolate,
the land will be devastated of everything in it;
when I strike all her inhabitants,
then they will know that I am the Lord.
16 This is a lament – they will keen it;
the women of the nations will keen it;

over Egypt and all her hordes they will keen it,
declares the Lord God."

17 It was in the twelfth year on the fifteenth of the month that the word
18 of the Lord came to me: "Man, lament over the hordes of Egypt; take
them – take her, Egypt, and the daughters of majestic nations, down to the
19 netherworld with those gone down into the Pit. Are you more pleasant
than anyone else? Go down; be laid to rest with the uncircumcised!

20 They will fall among those slain by the sword;
she has been given over to the sword;
pull her and her hordes down.
21 From within Sheol, leaders of warriors
will say of him and those who help him,
'They have gone down and lie
with the uncircumcised, slain by the sword.'
22 There is Assyria and all her crowds;
all around him are his graves;
all of them the slain, fallen by the sword,
23 whose graves lie at the far edge of the Pit;
her crowds are around her grave,
all of them the slain, fallen by the sword,
those who struck terror in the land of the living.
24 There is Eilam, all her hordes around her grave,
all of the the slain, fallen by the sword,
who went down uncircumcised to the netherworld,
who spread their terror in the land of the living
and now bear their disgrace with those gone down into the Pit.
25 Among the slain they have made a bed for her with all her hordes;
her graves are all around him,
all of them uncircumcised, slain by the sword,
for though their terror spread through the land of the living,
they now bear their disgrace, placed among the slain
with those gone down into the Pit.
26 There is Meshekh and Tuval and all her horde;
her graves are all around him,
all of them uncircumcised, pierced by the sword,
though they spread their terror in the land of the living.
27 They do not lie with warriors felled by the uncircumcised,
who went down to Sheol with their weapons of war,
their swords placed beneath their heads;
their sins are upon their bones,
for terror of the mighty was in the land of the living.
28 But you: among the uncircumcised you will be broken,
and you will lie with those slain by the sword.
29 There is Edom, her kings and all her princes,

who, for all their might, are placed with those slain by the sword;
they will lie with the uncircumcised and those gone down into the Pit.

30 There are all the princes of the north and all the Sidonians,
who went down with the slain,
shamed despite the terror caused by their might,
lying uncircumcised with those slain by the sword,
bearing their disgrace with those gone down into the Pit.
31 Pharaoh will see them and be comforted for all his hordes,
Pharaoh and all his army, slain by the sword,
declares the Lord God.
32 For I have spread terror of Me through the land of the living:
he will be laid among the uncircumcised with those slain by the sword –
Pharaoh and all his hordes,
declares the Lord God."

33 1 2 The word of the Lord came to me:[54] "Man, speak to your people; say to
them: When I bring the sword upon a land, and the people of that land
choose a man from among them and appoint him as watchman for them,
3 and he sees the sword bearing down on the land, and he sounds the horn
4 and warns the people, if someone hears the sound of this horn and does
not heed the warning, and the sword comes and claims him – his blood
5 is on his own head. He heard the sound of the horn and did not heed the
warning; he is to blame for his blood: had he taken heed of the warning,
his life would have been saved.

6 "The watchman who sees the sword coming but does not sound the horn,
so that the people are not warned – if the sword comes and claims one of
them, that person's life has been claimed for his own iniquity, but I will
seek redress for his blood from the hand of the watchman.

7 "Man, I have made you the watchman of the House of Israel; when you
8 hear word from My mouth, give them warning from Me. If I say to the
wicked, 'Wicked man, you will surely die,' but you do not speak out to warn
the wicked one from his course – that wicked man will die for his iniquity,
9 but I will seek redress for his blood from your hands. But if you warn the
wicked man to turn from his course and he still does not turn from it – he
will die for his iniquity, but you will have saved your own life.

10 "You, Man, say to the House of Israel: You have all been saying, 'Our sins
and iniquities are upon us; we are wasting away in them; how can we
11 live?' Say to them: Surely as I live, declares the Lord God, I do not desire
the death of the wicked one but that he should turn from his course and

54 | Verses 1–20 here are a longer version of the prophecy of the watchman, which appears in 3:17–21.

live – turn, return from your evil ways! Why should you die, House of Israel?

12 "You, Man, say to your people: The righteous person's righteousness will not save him on the day he transgresses; the wicked person's wickedness – he will not stumble over it on the day he turns away from his wickedness; the righteous person will not be able to live by his righteousness on the day he sins.

13 "If I say to the righteous person, 'You will surely live,' but he relies on his
righteousness and does wrong, then of all his righteousness, none of it
14 will be remembered, and through the iniquity he has done he will die. If
I say to the wicked person, 'You will surely die,' and he turns from his sin
15 and does what is right and just – the wicked person restores a pledge, pays
back what he has stolen, and follows the laws of life, doing no wrong – he
16 will surely live; he will not die. All his sins that he committed will not be
remembered of him if he does what is just and right: he will surely live.

17 "Your people say, 'The way of the Lord is not just,' but it is their ways
18 that are not just! When the righteous man turns from his righteousness
19 and does wrong, he will die for it; when the wicked man turns from his
wickedness and does that which is just and right, by virtue of these deeds
20 will he live. You have all said, 'The way of the Lord is not just,' but I will
judge you, each man according to his ways, House of Israel."

21 It was in the twelfth year of our exile in the tenth month on the fifth of the
month that a fugitive came to me from Jerusalem and said, "The city has
22 been taken." The hand of the Lord had been upon me the evening before
the fugitive arrived and had opened my mouth by the time he came to
me in the morning; my mouth was opened; I was no longer struck silent.[55]
23
24 The word of the Lord came to me: "Man, the inhabitants of these ruins
on the soil of Israel say, 'Avraham was one person, and he inherited the
land; we are many, and to us the land has been given as a possession.'[56]

25 "So say to them: So says the Lord God: You eat with the blood, you lift
your eyes up to your idols, you shed blood – and you would inherit the
26 land? You stood by your sword, you practiced abominations, each of you
defiled others' wives – and you would inherit the land?

27 "So you will say to them: So says the Lord God: As I live, those who are in
the ruins will fall by the sword; those who are in the open field I will give
over to animals as food; those who are in strongholds and caves will die
28 by plague. I will hand the land over to waste and desolation, the majesty of
her power will cease to be, the mountains of Israel will be desolate, none
29 will pass through, and they will know that I am the Lord when I hand

55 | See 3:22–27 and 24:27.

56 | This statement is attributed to those who remained in the land after the exile.

the land over to waste and desolation because of all the abominations
they practiced.

30 "As for you, Man, your people who speak of you by the walls and in the
entrances of houses, who speak with one another, with each other, saying,
31 'Come and hear what word has come from the LORD,' they come to you as
a gathering of people, and they sit before you – My people – and hear your
words, but they do not perform them; they turn them into lustful talk in
32 their mouths while their hearts pursue their own gains. To them you are
like a singer of lustful songs with a lovely voice, playing music with skill;
33 they hear your words but perform none of them. When it comes – see, it
is coming – they will know that a prophet was in their midst."

34 1 The word of the LORD came to me: "Man, prophesy against the shepherds
2 of Israel;[57] prophesy and say to them, to the shepherds: So says the Lord
GOD:

Woe, shepherds of Israel who have been tending themselves
when surely it is the sheep the shepherds should tend.
3 You ate the fat,
you wore the wool,
and you slaughtered the fattest,
but you did not tend the sheep:
4 you did not strengthen the weak,
you did not nurse the sick,
you did not bind the broken,
you did not recover the stray,
and you did not search for the lost –
you ruled over them with force and with harshness.
5 They scattered, for they had no shepherd;
they became food for every animal of the field
and scattered.
6 My sheep are wandering
upon all the mountains, all the high hills;
My sheep have scattered over the face of the earth –
no one searches for them; no one seeks them out.

7 "So, shepherds, listen to the word of the LORD: Surely as I live, declares
8 the Lord GOD, because My sheep were spoils, My sheep became the
food of every animal of the field for want of a shepherd, and because My
shepherds did not search for My sheep but tended themselves and did
9 not tend My sheep, so, shepherds, listen to the word of the LORD: So says
10 the Lord GOD:

Behold, I am coming down upon the shepherds;
I will seek redress for My sheep from their hands
and put an end to their shepherding;

57 | Verses 1–16 are directed against the pre-exilic kings of Israel, referred to metaphorically as shepherds.

no more will the shepherds tend themselves;
I will save My sheep from their mouths;
it will not be their food.
11 For so says the Lord God:
Behold, it is I;
I will search for My sheep and care for them;
12 just as a shepherd cares for his flock
when he is among his sheep who have dispersed,
so will I care for My sheep –
I will save them
from all the places they have been scattered
on a day of heavy cloud, thick fog.
13 I will take them out from the nations;
I will gather them in from the lands
and bring them to their soil.
I will tend them
on the mountains of Israel, in the ravines,
in all the settled parts of the land.
14 I will tend them on good grazing-land;
the high hills of Israel will be their pasture;
there will they lie down on lush pasture;
they will graze on rich grazing-land in the hills of Israel.
15 I Myself will tend My sheep:
I will lay them down,
declares the Lord God;
16 I will seek the lost,
I will recover the stray,
I will bind the broken,
I will strengthen the sick,
but the robust, the strong, I will destroy;
I will tend them with justice.
17 As for you, My sheep, so says the Lord God:
Behold that I will judge
between one sheep and another, rams and he-goats.
18 Is it not enough for you to graze on good grazing-land;
must your feet trample the rest of your grazing-land?
And when you drink clear waters,
must you muddy the rest with your feet?
19 My sheep graze on what has been trampled by your feet
and drink from what has been muddied by your feet.

20 "So the Lord God says this to them:
Behold, it is I –
I will judge between the fat sheep and the thin sheep.
21 Because you pushed with flank and shoulder
and rammed all the weak with your horns

until you scattered them,
22 I will save My sheep;
they will no longer be spoils;
I will judge between one sheep and another.
23 I will establish over them one single shepherd
who will tend them;
My servant, David, he will tend them;
he will be a shepherd to them;
24 I, the LORD, will be their God,
and My servant David will be prince among them;
I, the LORD, have spoken.
25 I will make a covenant of peace with them,
I will rid the land of wild animals,
and even in the wilderness they will live securely
and sleep in the forests.
26 I will make them and all around My hill a blessing;
I will make rain fall at its right time –
they will be blessed rains;
27 the trees of the field will bear their fruit,
and the land will yield its produce.
They will be secure upon their soil,
and they will know that I am the LORD
when I break the bars of their yoke
and save them from those who enslave them.
28 They will no longer be spoils for the nations;
the animals of the land will not eat them –
they will live securely and without fear.
29 I will establish for them a planting of renown;
they will no longer be claimed by famine in the land;
they will no longer bear the insults of the nations,
30 and they will know
that I, the LORD their God, I am with them,
and that they, the House of Israel, are My people,
declares the Lord GOD.
31 You, My sheep,
sheep of My tending,
are people, and I am your God,
declares the Lord GOD."

35 1 2 The word of the LORD came to me: "Man, set your face against Mount Se'ir
3 and prohesy against it; say to it: So says the Lord GOD:
Behold, I am coming down upon you, Mount Se'ir;
I will stretch My hand out over you
and turn you into waste, desolation.
4 I will make your cities ruins,
you will be desolate;

you will know that I am the LORD.
5 Because you have displayed an endless enmity
and delivered the Israelites up to the sword
at the time of their ruin,[58]
at the time of final punishment,
6 so, as I live,
declares the Lord GOD:
I will turn you to blood
and blood will pursue you;
as you did not hate bloodshed,
blood will pursue you.
7 I will turn Mount Se'ir over to complete desolation
and cut off from it those who come and go.
8 I will fill its mountains with its slain;
your hills, your valleys, all your ravines –
those slain by the sword will fall into them.
9 I will turn you over to perpetual desolation;
your cities will not be reinhabited,
and you will know: I am the LORD.

10 "Because you said, 'The two nations and the two lands will be mine; we
11 will possess it,' and the LORD was there, so, as I live, declares the Lord
GOD, I will act according to the anger and the jealousy with which you
acted because of your hatred of them; I will make Myself known among
12 them when I judge you. You will know that I am the LORD. I have heard
all your abuse that you uttered against the mountains of Israel, saying,
13 'They are desolate; they have been given to us to consume.' You opened
your mouths wide against Me; you multiplied your words against Me – I
have heard it.

14 "So says the Lord GOD: As the entire earth rejoices, I will make you
15 desolate. Just as you rejoiced when the heritage of the House of Israel was
made desolate, so will I do to you: you will be desolate, Mount Se'ir and
the whole of Edom. They will know: I am the LORD.

36 1 "And you, Man, prophesy to the mountains of Israel and say: Mountains
2 of Israel, hear the word of the LORD: So says the Lord GOD: Because
the enemy said about you, 'Ha! The ancient high places have become
3 our possession,' so, prophesy; say: So says the Lord GOD: For this very
reason, they desolated and hounded you from all around so that you
would become a possession to the other nations and a topic of slander and
4 common gossip. So, mountains of Israel, listen to the word of the Lord
GOD: So says the Lord GOD to the mountains and hills, to the ravines and
valleys, to the desolate ruins and abandoned cities that were objects of
pillaging and derision to the other nations all around.

58 | See Obadiah and Psalms 137:7.

5 "So the Lord GOD says this: Surely in the fiery passion of My anger have
I spoken against the other nations and against all of Edom – who, with
wholehearted joy and absolute contempt, gave My land to them as a
possession so that her pastureland would be spoils.

6 "So, prophesy about the soil of Israel; say to the mountains and hills, to the
ravines and valleys: So says the Lord GOD: See that I have spoken, in the
passion of My anger and My fury, because you have borne disgrace from
7 the nations. So the Lord GOD says this: I raise My hand in promise that
the nations who are all around you will surely bear their own disgrace.

8 "And you, mountains of Israel,
you will extend your branches;
you will bear your fruit
for My people Israel,
for they are almost come.
9 For I am with you;
I will turn toward you,
and you will be tilled and sown.
10 I will make you densely populated,
the whole of the House of Israel;
the cities will be reinhabited,
the ruins will be rebuilt.
11 I will make you densely populated with people and animals;
they will multiply and be fertile,
and I will make you inhabited just as you were formerly
and make you thrive more than before,
and you will know: I am the LORD.
12 I will make people, My people Israel, walk on you;
they will possess you, and you will be their heritage,
and you will no longer bereave them.

13 "So says the Lord GOD: Because they said of you, 'You consume people;
14 you bereave your nations,' so:
you will no longer consume people;
you will not bereave your nations again,
declares the Lord GOD.
15 I will no longer allow the insults of the nations to be heard against
you,
you will no longer bear the reproaches of peoples,
and you will not cause your own nations to stumble again,
declares the Lord GOD."

16 17 The word of the LORD came to me: "Man, the House of Israel dwelled upon
their soil and defiled it with their ways and their deeds – their ways were like
18 the impurity of the menstrual woman before Me. I poured out My fury upon
them for the blood they spilled upon the land and the idols they defiled
19 her with. I scattered them among the nations – they were strewn across the

countries – and I punished them according to their ways and their deeds.
20 There, in whichever nations they came to, they desecrated My holy name
because it was said of them, 'These are the LORD's people, and they have
21 left His land.'[59] And I am concerned for My holy name, which the House of
Israel has desecrated among the nations to which they have come.

22 "So, say to the House of Israel: So says the Lord GOD: It is not for your sake
that I do this, House of Israel, but for My holy name that you desecrated
23 among the nations to which you came. I will sanctify My great name that
has been desecrated among the nations – that you desecrated among them.
The nations will know that I am the LORD, declares the Lord GOD, when
I am sanctified through you before their eyes.

24 I will take you from the nations;
I will gather you from all the countries
and bring you to your land.
25 I will sprinkle over you purifying waters,
and you will be cleansed;
I will cleanse you
of all your impurities and all your idols.
26 I will give you a new heart
and put a new spirit into you;
I will remove the heart of stone from your flesh
and give you a heart of flesh;
27 I will put My spirit into you;
make sure that you follow My decrees
and that you keep My laws and fulfill them.
28 You will live in the land that I gave to your fathers;
you will be My people, and I will be your God.

29 "I will deliver you from all your impurities; I will summon the grain,
30 make it plentiful; I will not bring famine upon you. I will make the fruit
of the trees and the produce of the fields plentiful so that you will no
31 longer have to endure the reproach of famine among the nations. You
will remember your evil ways and your actions that were no good; you
32 will loathe yourselves for your iniquities and your abominations. Not for
your sake do I act, declares the Lord GOD; let that be known to you; be
ashamed, disgraced by your own ways, House of Israel.

33 "So says the Lord GOD: On the day when I cleanse you of all your iniquities,
34 I will reinhabit the cities; the ruins will be rebuilt. The desolate land will
35 be tilled there, where she was desolate in the sight of every passerby. They
will say, 'This land that was desolate has become like the garden of Eden;
its towns that were ruined, devastated, and destroyed have been fortified
36 and inhabited.' And the nations that remain around you will know that I,

59 | The implication being that God could not defend His people in their land, and that God was somehow "defeated" by the Babylonians.

the Lord, have rebuilt what was destroyed, have sown what was desolated;
I the Lord have spoken and will do it.

37 "So says the Lord God: This, too – I will respond to the House of Israel's
request to do this for them: I will multiply their people like a flock of sheep,
38 like the flocks for sacred offerings, like the flocks of Jerusalem during her
holy times; this is how the ruined cities will be, filled with flocks of people,
and they will know that I am the Lord."

37 1 And the hand of the Lord came upon me. He brought me out by the spirit
2 of the Lord and set me down in the valley. It was full of bones. He led me
around through them all; there were so very many of them out upon the
3 valley, and they were utterly dry. And He said to me, "Man, can they come
to life, these bones?" And I said, "My Lord God, You know."

4 He said to me: "Prophesy to these bones; say to them: Dry bones – hear
5 the word of the Lord! So says the Lord God to these bones: See – I will
6 bring breath into you, and you will come to life. I will give you sinews, I
will make flesh grow on you, I will spread skin over you, I will put breath
into you, you will come to life, and you will know that I am the Lord."

7 I prophesied as I had been commanded. There was a noise as I was
prophesying, and then a rattling, and the bones moved together, each
8 bone to its bone. And I saw there on them sinews, flesh forming, and skin
spreading a cover over them – but there was no breath in them.

9 And He said to me: "Prophesy to the breath; Man, prophesy and say to
the breath: So says the Lord God: From the four winds, come; breath,
10 breathe into these slain so that they come to life." I prophesied as He had
commanded me, and the breath entered them, and they came to life; they
stood upon their feet, a vast army.

11 And He said to me: "Man, these bones are the whole House of Israel. See,
they say, 'Our bones are dried out, our hope is lost, and we are completely
12 cut off.' So, prophesy; say to them: So says the Lord God: See, I am
opening up your graves; I will lift you out of your graves, My people, and
I will bring you to the soil of Israel.

13 "You will know that I am the Lord when I open up your graves, when I
14 lift you out of your graves, My people. I will put My breath into you, and
you will come to life; I will set you upon your soil, and you will know that
I am the Lord; I have spoken, and I will do it, declares the Lord."

15 16 The word of the Lord came to me, saying: "And you, Man, take a branch
and write on it, 'For Yehuda and the children of Israel associated with
him.' Then take one branch and write on it, 'For Yosef – the branch of
17 Efrayim – and all of the House of Israel associated with him.' Bring them
18 together to make one branch, so that they are one in your hand. When
19 your people say to you, 'Tell us, what do these mean to you?' say to them:

So says the Lord God: See, I am going to take the branch of Yosef, which
is in the hand of Efrayim, and the tribes of Israel who are associated with
him, and join them with him, with the branch of Yehuda; I will make them
into one branch, and they will be one in My hand.

20 "Let these branches that you write upon be in your hand before their eyes.
21 Speak to them: So says the Lord God: See that I am taking the children of
Israel from among the nations that they went to; I will gather them from
22 all around, and I will bring them to their land. I will make them into one
nation in the land, in the mountains of Israel; one king will be king for all
of them, and they will no longer be two nations; they will no longer be
23 split into two kingdoms. They will no longer be defiled by their idols or
by their detestable things and all their transgressions; I will deliver them
from all the dwelling places where they have sinned; I will purify them,
24 and they will be My people, and I will be their God. My servant David will
be king over them; there shall be one shepherd for all, and they will follow
25 My laws, and they will keep My statutes and perform them. They will live
on the land that I gave to My servant Yaakov, where your ancestors lived.
They will live upon it, they and their children and their children's children,
for eternity, and David My servant will be their prince for eternity.

26 "I will make a covenant of peace with them; it will be an everlasting
covenant with them. I will place them securely there, I will make them
ever more numerous; I will place My Sanctuary among them for eternity.
27 My presence will be upon them; I will be their God, and they will be My
28 people. And the nations will know that I the Lord make Israel holy when
My Sanctuary is among them for all eternity."

38 1 2 The word of the Lord came to me: "Man, set your face toward Gog of the
land of Magog, the chief prince of Meshekh and Tuval.[60] Prophesy against
3 him; say: So says the Lord God: Behold – I am against you, Gog, chief
4 prince of Meshekh and Tuval. I will turn you around, fix hooks into your
jaw, and bring you out with all your troops, horses, and cavalry in complete
5 regalia, a great horde with shields and bucklers, all wielding swords. And
6 with them Persia, Kush, and Put, all with shields and helmets; Gomer and
all her forces; Beit Togarma from the far edges of the north and all her
7 forces – many peoples with you. Prepare, ready yourself, you and all of
the hordes assembled around you; you are their guarding commander.

8 "After many days you will be summoned; at the end of years, you will
come against the land which has been restored after the sword, which has
been gathered back from many nations upon the mountains of Israel that
long lay in ruins – she who will have been brought out from the nations,
9 a people who all now live securely. You will advance, you will come like

60 | Gog and Magog cannot be identified as real people or places. Meshekh, Tuval, and the other kingdoms mentioned here are located throughout the lands surrounding the Mediterranean (many are mentioned in chapter 27 above).

a devastating storm, and you will be like a cloud covering the land – you,
all your forces, and the many peoples with you.

10 "So says the Lord GOD: On that day, certain thoughts will occur to you;
11 you will devise an evil scheme. You will say, 'I will advance against the
land of open villages; I will come upon those who are tranquil, living
12 securely, all of whom live in unwalled towns and without bars or gates,' to
ransack spoils and seize loot, to turn your hand against reinhabited ruins
and a people gathered in from the nations who have built up livestock
13 and possessions, who live at the center of the land. Sheba, Dedan, and the
merchants of Tarshish and all her young warriors will say to you, 'Have
you come to ransack spoils? Have you assembled your hordes to seize
loot – to carry off silver and gold to take livestock and possessions, to
ransack great spoils?'

14 "So, prophesy, Man; say to Gog: So says the Lord GOD: Surely, on the day
15 that My people Israel lives securely, you will know it, and you will come
from your place, from the far edges of the north, you and many peoples
with you, all of them on horseback, with a great horde and a mighty army.
16 You will advance against My people Israel like a cloud covering the land.
This is what will be in the end of days, and I will bring you to My land so
that the nations will know Me when I am sanctified through you before
their eyes, Gog.

17 "So says the Lord GOD: It is you whom I spoke of in former days through
My servants the prophets of Israel, who in those days, for years, prophesied
that I would bring you against them.

18 "And it shall be, on that day, on the day that Gog comes onto the soil of
19 Israel, says the Lord GOD: My fury will blaze; in My passionate anger, in
the fire of My rage I have spoken: Surely on that day there will be a great
20 quaking upon the soil of Israel; they will quake before Me: the fish of the
seas and the birds of the sky, the animals of the field, every creeping thing
that crawls upon the earth, and every man on the face of the earth; the
mountains will be demolished, the terraces will collapse, and every wall
21 shall fall to the ground. I will call the sword down against him across My
mountains, says the Lord GOD; each man's sword will be turned against
22 his brother. I will execute judgment on him with pestilence and blood; I
will pour down torrential rain and crystal hailstone, fire and sulfur over
23 him and his troops, and over the many peoples who are with him. I will be
magnified, I will be sanctified, and I will make Myself known in the eyes
of many nations – and they will know that I am the LORD.

39 1 "And you, Man, prophesy against Gog and say: So says the Lord GOD:
Behold – I am against you, Gog,
chief prince of Meshekh and Tuval.
2 I will turn you around; I will drive you forward;
I will make you advance from the far edges of the north

and bring you to the mountains of Israel.
3 I will strike your bow from your left hand;
I will make the arrows fall from your right;
4 upon the mountains of Israel you will fall –
you, all your troops, and the peoples who are with you.
I will give you up to birds of prey of every kind
and to the animals of the field as food;
5 upon the open field you will fall,
for I have spoken, says the Lord God.
6 I will set loose fire on Magog
and on those living securely in the coastlands,
and they will know that I am the Lord.
7 I will make My holy name known among My people Israel;
I will no longer allow My holy name to be desecrated,
and the nations will know that I am the Lord, holy in Israel.
8 Behold: it is coming, it will be, says the Lord God:
This is the day I have spoken of.

9 "The inhabitants of the cities of Israel will come out, and they will kindle
and burn the weapons, the shields and bucklers, the bows and arrows,
and the clubs and spears; they will burn them as fuel for fire for seven
10 years. They will not take wood from the fields or chop down trees from
the forests, for they will fuel their fires with weapons. They will ransack
those who despoiled them and loot those who looted them, says the Lord
God.

11 "And it will happen on that day: I will grant Gog a burial place there in
Israel, the Valley of the Travelers, east of the sea, and it will block the
travelers. Here they will bury Gog and his horde; they will call it the Valley
of the Horde of Gog.

12 "For seven months the House of Israel will bury them to purify the land.
13 All the people in the land shall bury them, and it will make them renowned
14 on the day of My glory, says the Lord God. They shall select men to
cross the land constantly, burying the invaders' remains that lie upon
the ground – to purify it. They will search for a period of seven months.
15 Whenever these men assigned to cross the land see a human bone, they
shall place a sign next to it until the buriers have buried it in the Valley of
16 the Horde of Gog. There will also be a city named Horde. Thus they shall
purify the land.

17 "And you, Man, so says the Lord God, say to every type of bird and
every animal of the field: Assemble, come, gather from all around, for the
sacrificial feast that I am preparing for you, a great sacrificial feast upon
18 the mountains of Israel; you will eat flesh; you will drink blood. You will
eat the flesh of warriors; you will drink the blood of the princes of the
19 earth, rams, lambs, he-goats, and bulls – all fatlings of Bashan. You will
eat fat until you are full, you will drink blood until you are drunk from the

20 sacrificial feast I will prepare for you. At My table you will fill yourselves
on horses and chariots, warriors and all men of war, declares the Lord God.
21 I will manifest My glory among the nations; all the nations will see the
judgment that I have executed and the hand that I have placed upon them.
22 The House of Israel will know that I the Lord am their God – from that
23 day on. And the nations will know that it was for their iniquity that the
House of Israel was exiled. Because they betrayed me, I hid My face from
them and gave them over into the hand of their enemies, and they fell by
24 the sword, all of them. I have dealt with them according to their impurity
and transgressions; I have hidden My face from them.

25 "So the Lord God says this: Now I will restore the fortunes of Yaakov; I
will have compassion for the whole of the House of Israel and passionate
26 anger for the sake of My holy name. They will forget their disgrace and
all the betrayals by which they betrayed me – when they live in the land
27 securely and without fear, when I bring them back from among the nations,
when I gather them in from the lands of their enemies, and when I am
28 sanctified through them in the eyes of the many nations. They will know
that I the Lord am their God because I exiled them among the nations
and then collected them back to their land, leaving none of them behind.
29 I will not hide My face from them again, for I have poured out My spirit
upon the House of Israel, declares the Lord God."

40 1 It was in the twenty-fifth year of our exile, at the beginning of the year, on
the tenth of the month, in the fourteenth year after the city was destroyed;
on that very day the hand of the Lord was upon me, and He brought me
2 there. In visions of God He brought me to the land of Israel and set me
down near a very high mountain upon which, to the south, was something
3 like the structure of a city. He brought me over there and – behold! – there
was a man who looked as if made of bronze, and in his hand was a string
4 of flax and a measuring reed, and he was standing at the gate. The man
spoke to me: "Man, see with your eyes and listen with your ears, and pay
close attention to everything that I am showing you, for you have been
brought here in order that they be shown to you; tell the House of Israel
about everything you see."

5 And behold – there was a wall outside the house roundabout, and the
man had in his hand a measuring reed, six cubits long plus one more
handbreadth, and he measured the width of the structure, one reed
6 wide; and the height, one reed.[61] He came to the gate that faced eastward,
climbing its steps. He measured the doorpost of the gate, one reed deep,
7 and the other doorpost, one reed deep. And each of its side chambers was

61 | Many points in Yeḥezkel's vision are unclear, leading to a variety of interpretations of the Temple layout, but the scale of the Temple is clearly much larger than Shlomo's Temple; cf. 1 Kings, chapter 6. Note that the terms "width" and "length" refer to the shorter and longer measure of an object or area regardless of its orientation. For a diagram of the Temple in Yeḥezkel's vision, see the appendices.

one reed long and one reed wide, and between the side chambers were
five cubits. And the doorpost of the gate, between the entrance hall and
8 the inside one, was one reed. He measured the entrance hall of the inner
9 gate, one reed. He measured the entrance hall of the gate, eight cubits;
and its doorway columns, two cubits, this being the entrance hall of the
10 gate of the inner gate. And the side chambers of the eastern gate were
three on this side and three on the other. Each cluster of three measured
the same, and there was one measure for each of their doorway columns,
one on each side.

11 He measured the width of the opening in the gate, ten cubits; the length
12 of the gate was thirteen cubits. And there was a border of one cubit in
front of the side chambers and a border of one cubit on the other side, and
13 each side chamber was six cubits by six cubits. He measured the gate from
the roof of one side chamber to the roof of the opposite side chamber, a
width of twenty-five cubits; each doorway was directly across from another
14 doorway. Then he did the doorway columns, sixty cubits high, as well as
15 the columns of the courtyard all around the gate. The distance from the
front of the entry gate to the front of the entrance hall of the inner gate was
16 fifty cubits. And there were windows narrowing into the side chambers
and into their doorway columns within the gate roundabout, and into the
halls as well; and there were windows roundabout within, and on each
doorway column were decorations in the form of palm trees.

17 Then he brought me to the outer courtyard and behold – there were
chambers and a tiled pavement for the courtyard roundabout: there
18 were thirty chambers upon the tiled pavement. And the tiled pavement
continued to the sides of the gates along the length of the gates: this was
19 the lower tiled pavement. He measured the width from in front of the
lower gate to the outside of the inner courtyard, one hundred cubits both
eastward and northward.

20 He measured the length and width of the gate facing northward toward
21 the outer courtyard. Its side chambers were three on one side and three
on the other, and its doorway columns and its entrance hall had the same
measurements as the first gate: fifty cubits in length, and twenty-five cubits
22 wide. And its windows and its entrance hall and its decorations of palm
trees were the same as those of the gate facing eastward; people would
23 rise to it on seven steps, and its entrance hall would be before them. And
a gate to the inner courtyard was across from the gate facing north as from
the one facing east; he measured one hundred cubits from gate to gate.

24 He led me southward, and behold, there was a gate leading south, and he
measured its doorway columns and its entrance hall to be the same as the
25 measurements of the others. And it had windows roundabout, as did its
entrance hall, like those other windows. Its length was fifty cubits and its
26 width twenty-five cubits. People would ascend to it on seven steps, and its

entrance hall would be before them; and it had palm tree decorations upon
27 its doorpost columns, one on this side and one on the other. There was a
gate leading to the inner courtyard by way of the south and he measured
from gate to gate toward the south: one hundred cubits.

28 He brought me to the inner courtyard through the southern gate. He
measured the southern gate to be of the same measurements as the others.
29 And its side chambers and its doorway columns and its entrance hall
shared the measurements of the others; and it and its entrance hall had
windows roundabout. It was fifty cubits in length, and its width was twenty-
30 five cubits. And there were halls all around, with a length of twenty-five
31 cubits and a width of five cubits. Its entrance hall faced the outer courtyard
and had palm tree decorations on its doorway columns on both sides, and
people would ascend to it on eight steps.

32 Then he brought me to the inner courtyard by way of the east, and he
33 measured the gate to be the same as the others. And its side chambers
and its doorway columns and its entrance hall shared the measurements
of the others, and it had windows roundabout, a height of fifty cubits and a
34 width of twenty-five cubits. And its entrance hall faced the outer courtyard
and had palm tree decorations on its doorway columns on both sides, and
people would ascend to it on eight steps.

35 He brought me to the northern gate and measured it to be the same as the
36 others – its chambers, its doorway columns, and its entrance hall and it
had windows roundabout, a length of fifty cubits and a width of twenty-
37 five cubits. And its doorway columns led to the outer courtyard, and there
were palm tree decorations on its doorway columns on both sides, and
people would ascend to it on eight steps.

38 There was a chamber that had its entrance at the doorway columns of
39 the gate where the animals for burnt offerings were washed. And the
entrance hall of the gate had two tables on each side on which to slaughter
the animals brought to be burnt offerings, purification offerings, or guilt
40 offerings. And there were two tables outside on the slope rising toward
the northward gate, and there were two tables on the other side, at the
41 entrance hall of the gate. Four tables on this side and four tables on the
other side, alongside the gate; in all, eight tables upon which they would
42 slaughter. And there were four tables made of cut stone for the burnt
offering: they were one and a half cubits in length, one and a half cubits
wide, and one cubit high. On these they would also lay out the instruments
43 with which they slaughtered the burnt offering or the sacrifice. The rack of
double hooks of one handbreadth, to aid in the flaying of the animal, were
installed on the inside wall all around; the flesh of the animal would then
44 be brought to the tables. And outside the inner gate were the chambers for
the singers in the inner courtyard to the side of the northern gate, and they
faced toward the south; one chamber was to the side of the eastern gate,

45 facing north. And he spoke to me: "This chamber which faces southward is
46 for the priests who are guardians in charge of the house. And the chamber
which faces northward is for the priests who are guardians in charge of the
altar. These are the sons of Tzadok, of the sons of Levi, who approach the
LORD to serve Him."[62]

47 He measured the court to be a square one hundred cubits in length and
48 one hundred cubits in width; the altar was in front of the house. He took
me to the entrance hall of the house, he measured each doorway column
of the hall to be five cubits on this side and five cubits on that, and the
width of the gate was three cubits on this side and three cubits on that.
49 The length of the entrance hall was twenty cubits and its width was eleven
cubits, and there were steps by which people would ascend to it, and there
were pillars at each of the doorways, one on this side and one on that.

41 1 He then brought me to the Sanctuary. He measured the doorway columns
to be six cubits wide on this side and six cubits wide on the other; these
2 narrowed the width of the opening. And the width of the entranceway was
ten cubits, and the sides of the entranceway were five cubits long on this
side and five cubits on the other. He measured the Sanctuary's length to
be forty cubits and its width to be twenty cubits.

3 And he came to the inner sanctum and measured the doorway column of
the door, two cubits, and the entranceway, six cubits high; and the width of
4 the entranceway was seven cubits. He measured the inner sanctum's length,
twenty cubits, and width, twenty cubits, along the width of the Sanctuary.
5 He said to me: "This is the Holy of Holies." He measured the wall of the
House, six cubits, and the width of each side chamber, four cubits: so it
6 was roundabout the House on every side. And the side chambers adjoined
each other, thirty-three, and there were recesses in the wall of the House
roundabout for the side chamber ceilings to attach to, so they would
7 not be attached to the wall of the House. The side chambers became
progressively wider as they went up because the House was surrounded
by an inner system of stairs, which added width to the House as it rose. A
person would thus ascend from the lowermost level to the topmost level
by way of the middle level.

8 And so, I saw, the House had a raised platform roundabout: the foundations
9 of the side chambers were a full reed of six extended cubits. The width of
the side chamber wall on the outside was five cubits, as was the measure
of the open space between the outside wall of the side chamber structure
10 and the House. And separating all this from the chamber building were
11 twenty cubits, surrounding the House on all sides. The side chambers'
doors, which opened onto the open space, were one door to the north
and another door to the south, and the width of the open space was five

62 | Tzadok was one of the priests in the period of David, and was loyal to Shlomo (1 Kings 1:44).

12 cubits all around. Now the structure, facing the main enclosure along its
western edge, was seventy cubits wide, and the wall of the structure was
13 five cubits wide roundabout, and its length was ninety cubits. And he
measured the length of the House to be one hundred cubits; including the
main enclosure and the structure with its walls, it was one hundred cubits
14 in length. The width of the front of the House and the main enclosure
15 facing east was also one hundred cubits. He then measured the length of
the structure in front of the main enclosure, as he came back, along with
its supporting walls on both sides, to be one hundred cubits.

Now the Sanctuary, the inner sanctum, and the entrance hall of the
16 courtyard – all three of them had thresholds, and narrowing windows,
and supporting walls all around. Across the thresholds there was wooden
paneling all around and this overlay extended from the ground up to
17 the windows, as well as between the windows; similarly, the space over
the door all the way to the inner House and outside, and all the wall
roundabout, on the inside and on the outside, were paneled to measure.
18 And they were decorated with cherubim and palm trees, with a palm tree
19 in between one cherub and the next. And each cherub had two faces, such
that a human face faced the palm tree on this side and a lion's face faced
the palm tree on the other side. Thus was the whole House decorated
20 roundabout. Cherubim and palm trees were carved from the ground
21 and up over the door as well as along the wall of the Sanctuary. The
Sanctuary had square doorposts, as did the front of the inner sanctum:
the appearance of one pair was like that of the other.

22 The altar was of wood three cubits high, and its length was two cubits,
and its legs were of a piece with it. And its length and its sides were wood.
23 The man spoke to me: "This is the table placed before the LORD." The
24 Sanctuary and the inner sanctum each had double doors and each door
had two panels, two folding panels: two panels for one door and two panels
25 for the other. The doors of the Sanctuary were carved with cherubim and
palm tree carvings just like the decoration on the walls, and there was
thick wood paneling on the front of the entrance hall from the outside.
26 And there were narrowing windows with palm tree decorations on this
side and on that on the sides of the entrance hall, on the side chambers of
the House, and on the thick wood paneling.

42 1 He took me out to the outer courtyard; the path led to the north. He
brought me to the chamber building that ran alongside the main enclosure
2 and parallel to the structure, to the north. We faced a length of one hundred
cubits and entered by a door leading north; the width of the building was
3 fifty cubits. It ran alongside the space, twenty cubits across, belonging
to the inner courtyard, and paralleled the tiled pavement of the outer
4 courtyard. Its supporting walls faced one another in thirds. In front of
the chamber building was a walkway ten cubits wide leading to the inner
courtyard, a path of one cubit.

5 The chamber doors faced north. And the walls of the upper chambers
were narrower than those of the lower and central floors of the building
6 because the inner supporting walls consumed space. For these were three
stories high and did not have pillars like the courtyard pillars. Therefore,
7 the lower and middle floors lost floor space. There was a fence parallel
to the chamber building, extending by way of the outer courtyard to the
8 front of the chamber building. Its length was fifty cubits. For the length
of the chamber building belonging to the outer courtyard was fifty cubits,
and behold, the one across from the Sanctuary was one hundred cubits.
9 Below these chambers there was an entrance on the east side for a person
approaching from the outer courtyard.

10 And there were chambers set into the thickness of the eastward courtyard
11 wall, facing the sacred enclosure and facing the building. There was a
passageway in front of them, and they looked just like the chambers on the
northern passageway; their lengths were the same, as well as their widths,
12 as were their exits with their rules, and their entranceways. And as with
the entranceways to the chamber building on the southward passageway,
there was an entranceway at the main approach. This faced the platform
for singers, closest to those entering from the east.

13 Then he said to me: "The northern chambers and the southern chambers
which face the main enclosure are holy chambers where the priests who
approach the Lord may eat the holiest of sacrifices. There shall they place
the holiest of sacrifices, the grain offering and the purification offering and
14 the guilt offering, for the place is holy. Once the priests enter, they may
not leave the holy area to go to the outer courtyard; first they shall leave
the garments in which they minister there, for they are holy. They are to
put on other clothes and after that may approach the area designated for
the nation."

15 He finished the measurements of the inner House and took me out
through the gate looking out eastward and measured the whole perimeter.
16 He measured the eastern side with his measuring reed – five hundred
17 cubits with the measuring reed all around. He measured the northern
18 side – five hundred cubits with the measuring reed all around. He mea-
19 sured the southern side – five hundred reeds with the measuring reed. He
turned to the western side and measured five hundred reeds with the mea-
20 suring reed. He measured it in four directions; it had a wall roundabout
running a length of five hundred and a width of five hundred, to separate
the holy from the ordinary.

43 1/2 He led me to the gate, the gate facing out eastward. And behold! The glory
of the God of Israel was approaching by the eastern path with a sound
3 like the roar of vast waters, and the earth was lit up with His glory! It
looked like the vision that I had seen, like the vision I saw when I came to

prophesy the city's destruction,[63] visions like the vision I had seen at the
Kevar River,[64] and I fell upon my face.

4 Then the glory of the Lord entered the House by way of the gate facing
5 eastward. And a wind lifted me up and brought me to the inner courtyard,
and behold – the glory of the Lord filled the House.

6 I heard Him speaking to me from the House, then there was a man
7 standing next to me. He said to me: "Man, this is the site of My throne
and the place of My footstool, where I will dwell among the children of
Israel forever. And the House of Israel will no longer defile My holy name,
they and their kings with their whoring, and with the graves of their kings'
8 corpses decorated with altars. When they placed their thresholds near
My threshold and their doorposts near My doorposts, with only a wall
between Me and them, they polluted My holy name by the disgusting
9 things they did, so I destroyed them in My anger. This time they must keep
their whoring and the corpses of their kings far away from Me, so that I
may dwell among them forever.[65]

10 "You, Man, describe this House to the House of Israel so that they feel
11 ashamed of their sins, and let them take measure of the plan. And if they
do feel shame about all they have done, then make known to them the
design of the House and its architectural plan: its exits and entrances, all
of its structures and all of its rules, all its decorative shapes and all the
instructions about it. And write it down in front of them so that they can
preserve everything about its design and its rules so that they can carry
12 them out. This is the teaching of the House: the top of the mountain, all
its boundary roundabout, is holy of holies. Behold – this is the teaching
of the House:

13 "These are the dimensions of the altar[66] in cubits, each cubit being a five-
handbreadth cubit plus a handbreadth. But the base is a smaller cubit, as
is the cubit of its width, and the border at its edge all around is one half-
14 cubit, the same as for the top level of the altar. Now from the base on the
ground up to the lower ledge there are two cubits, and its excess width is
one cubit, and from the smaller ledge up to the top of the large ledge there
are four cubits, with an excess width of one cubit.

15 "Now the Harel hearth is four cubits, and from this Ariel upward, there
16 rise four horns. And the Ariel is twelve cubits long by twelve cubits wide,
17 square on its four sides. And the ledge is fourteen in length by fourteen in

63 | Literally "to destroy the city"; see the visions in chapters 8–11, which depict God's glory leaving Jerusalem as it is destroyed.

64 | See chapter 1.

65 | Cf. Exodus 25:8.

66 | See diagram of the Temple in Yeḥezkel's vision in the appendices.

width on its four sides, and the border surrounding it is half a small cubit.
A cubit of its base extends all around, and its ramp is off-center, shifted
eastward."

18 Then He said to me: "Man, thus says the Lord GOD: These are the statutes
pertaining to the altar on the day that it is fashioned, to enable you to bring
19 burnt offerings upon it and to sprinkle blood upon it. You will pass on to
the priests, the Levites who are of the seed of Tzadok who approach Me
to serve Me, the word of the Lord GOD: a young bull from the cattle herd
20 shall be a purification offering. Take from its blood and put some on the
four altar horns and four corners of the ledge and upon the border all
21 around: you shall purify it so that it can provide atonement. Then take
the bull of the purification offering and burn it in its designated place in
22 the bounds of the House, outside the Sanctuary. And from the second day
onward, you shall sacrifice a flawless male goat for a purification offering.
They shall purify the altar as they purified it before, by sacrificing the bull.
23 When you have finished the purification process, sacrifice a flawless young
24 bull from among the cattle and a flawless ram from among the sheep. You
shall bring them near the LORD, and the priests shall throw salt upon them
and offer them up as a burnt offering to the LORD.

25 "For seven days you shall bring the goat of a purification offering daily, as
well as a young bull from the cattle and a ram from the sheep; they are all
26 to be flawless. For seven days they shall cleanse the altar and purify it and
27 consecrate it. When these days are over, from the eighth day onward, the
priests may prepare your burnt offerings and your peace offerings on the
altar, and I shall respond favorably to you." So spoke the Lord GOD.[67]

44 1 He brought me back by way of the outer gate of the Sanctuary that faces
2 eastward, and it was closed. The LORD said to me: "This gate will stay shut;
it shall not be opened, and no man may enter through it; because the LORD,
3 God of Israel, entered through it, it shall remain closed. Regarding the
prince: as prince, he will sit within it to eat bread before the LORD, arriving
by way of the entrance hall of that gate and leaving the same way."

4 He brought me toward the northern gate to the front of the House. I
looked, and behold – the LORD's glory filled the House of the LORD, and
5 I fell on my face. The LORD said to me: "Man, pay attention, and see with
your eyes and hear with your ears all that I am saying to you about the
laws of the House of the LORD and all its teachings; and pay attention to
6 the rules about entering the House, about exiting the Sanctuary. And you
shall say to the rebels, to the House of Israel: Thus says the Lord GOD:
7 Enough with your disgusting activities, House of Israel, with your bringing
of strangers, uncircumcised of heart and uncircumcised of flesh, into My
Sanctuary to desecrate My House, offering up My bread, fat, and blood;

67 | Compare to the dedication of the altar in the Tabernacle in Leviticus 8:11–21; there, too, the ceremony lasts seven days (Lev. 9:34).

8 with your breaking of My covenant with all your disgusting deeds! You did
not dutifully protect My holy things. As guardians of My precious things
in My Sanctuary, you turned them into your own property!

9 "Thus says the Lord GOD: No stranger uncircumcised of heart or
uncircumcised of flesh shall enter My Sanctuary; this applies to any
10 estranged person among the children of Israel. But the Levites who
became distanced from Me when Israel went astray, who strayed from
11 Me to follow their idols, they shall bear their sin. They may be ministers
in My Sanctuary, in charge of the gates of the House and attending to the
House; they shall slaughter burnt offerings and sacrifices for the people,
12 and they shall stand before them to minister to them. But because they
ministered to them in front of their idols and became a stumbling block
of sin to the House of Israel, I have raised My hand against them; this is
13 the word of the Lord GOD, and they shall bear their sin.[68] Thus they shall
not come near Me to serve Me as a priest, nor approach any of My holy
offerings or the holy of holy offerings; let them bear their shame for the
14 disgusting things they did. I appoint them custodians of the duties of the
House, in charge of all its services and everything that is done within it.

15 "But the priests who are Levites descended from Tzadok, who protected
the preciousness of My Sanctuary when the children of Israel strayed
from Me, they are the ones who may draw near Me in order to serve Me,
and they shall stand before Me to offer Me fat and blood: this is the word
16 of the Lord GOD. They are the ones who will enter My Sanctuary, and
they shall approach My table to serve Me; they shall dutifully protect My
precious things.

17 "This is how it shall be when they approach the gates of the inner courtyard:
they will wear linen garments, and no wool shall be upon them when they
18 serve at the gates of the inner courtyard and within. There will be linen
turbans on their heads and linen trousers on their loins; they shall not
19 gird themselves in a way that causes perspiration. And when they leave
to go to the outer courtyard – to the outer courtyard to the people – they
shall remove the garments in which they serve, leaving them in the holy
chambers, and put on other clothing, in order not to give the impression,
by mingling with them wearing their holy garments, that the people are
equal to them in sanctity.

20 "They shall not shave their heads nor grow their hair long in disarray; they
21 shall keep their heads carefully trimmed. Nor shall any priest drink wine
22 when they enter the inner courtyard. And they shall not take as a wife a
widow or a divorcée.[69] Rather, they shall take as wives only virgins of the
23 seed of the House of Israel, or a widow who is the widow of a priest. And

68 | This idea does not appear in the Torah (Five Books of Moses), but see, e.g., Judges, chapter 17.

69 | Cf. Leviticus 21:7, which does not include the restriction on widows.

they shall teach My people the difference between the sacred and the
profane and make known to them the difference between impure and pure.
24 When there is controversy, they shall stand in judgment, adjudicating it
according to My laws. And they shall keep My teachings and My statutes at
25 all the times I have appointed, and sanctify My Sabbaths. The priest shall
not approach a human corpse and become impure because of it, though
for a father or a mother, for a son or a daughter, for a brother or for a sister
who is unmarried, they may become impure.[70]

26 "After a priest's purification process begins, seven days are counted for him.
27 And on the day he comes to the Sanctuary, into the inner courtyard, to
minister in the Sanctuary, he is to bring his purification offering – this is
28 the word of the Lord God. And this shall be the priests' inheritance: I am
their inheritance. Give them no territory to possess in the land of Israel; I
29 am their possession.[71] They shall eat the grain offering and the purification
offering and the guilt offering, and everything consecrated by vow in Israel
30 shall be theirs.[72] The choicest of all first fruits of every kind and every gift
offering out of all your various donations belongs to the priests. And your
first kneading you shall give to the priest so that a blessing settles upon
31 your home.[73] Whether it be bird or beast, the priests may not eat any
creature that died on its own or was torn to pieces as prey.

45 1 "When you allot the land as inheritance, you shall raise up a portion
of it as a gift to the Lord, a holy portion of the land measuring twenty-
five thousand reeds in length and ten thousand reeds in width. This is
2 consecrated ground within all of its boundary roundabout. Out of this,
there shall be dedicated a square plot for the Sanctuary, five hundred by
five hundred roundabout, with an open space of fifty cubits surrounding
3 it. And by this same measure you shall measure out a length of twenty-
five thousand and a width of ten thousand, and in it will be the Sanctuary,
4 the Holy of Holies.[74] This consecrated portion of the land belongs to the
priests who minister in the Sanctuary, those who approach to serve the
Lord. It shall give them a place for their houses as well as holy ground for
5 the Sanctuary. Another area twenty-five thousand long by ten thousand
wide shall be the heritable possession of the Levites who minister in the
6 House, to be divided into twenty sections. For the property of the city, set
an area of five thousand wide by twenty-five thousand long alongside the
7 consecrated portion: this shall belong to the entire House of Israel. And
the prince's portion shall be on both sides of the consecrated area and
the city's landholding, facing the consecrated area and facing the city's
landholding; on the west side extending westward, and on the east side,
eastward. And its length will parallel one of the tribes' portions, from the

70 | Cf. Leviticus 21:1–4.

71 | Cf. Deuteronomy 10:9.

72 | For this and the next verse, cf. Numbers 18:8–14.

73 | Cf. Numbers 15:20–21.

74 | That is, the Temple, which includes the Holy of Holies.

8 western boundary to the eastern boundary. This is the prince's territorial
possession in Israel so that My princes will no longer maltreat My nation;
instead, the rest of the land will be given to the House of Israel, according
to their tribes.

9 "Thus says the Lord God: You have gone far enough, O princes of Israel!
Stop your violence and robbery, do what is just and right! Remove from
My people your exacting taxes that evict them from their land, says the
10 Lord God. You shall have honest scales and honest measures of the ephah
11 and the *bat*.[75] The ephah and the *bat* contain the same amount, so the
bat contains one-tenth of a homer, and one-tenth of a homer is also an
12 ephah: their measure is relative to the homer. Now the shekel is twenty
gerah. Twenty shekel, twenty-five shekel, fifteen shekel together shall be
your maneh.[76]

13 "This is the contribution that you shall offer up: one-sixth of an ephah per
14 homer of wheat and one-sixth of an ephah per homer of barley. The rule
regarding oil: the *bat* is the measure of oil; you shall offer one-tenth of a
bat out of the *kor*, which is a homer of ten *bat*, for ten *bat* make up a homer.
15 And you shall offer one lamb out of two hundred from your flock in the
well-watered pastureland of Israel. These shall serve as the grain offering
and as the burnt offering and as the peace offering to atone for them, says
the Lord God.

16 "All the people of the land shall give this contribution to the prince of Israel.
17 And it shall be the prince's duty to provide burnt offerings and grain
offerings and libations on festivals, New Moons, and Sabbaths; at all the
times appointed for the House of Israel, he shall prepare the purification
offering and the grain offering and the burnt offering and the peace offering
to provide atonement for the House of Israel.

18 "Thus says the Lord God: In the first month, on the first day of the month,
19 you shall take a young bull with no blemish to purify the Sanctuary. And
the priest shall take from the blood of this purification offering and put it
on the doorposts of the House, on the four corners of the ledge of the altar,
20 and on the doorpost of the gate of the inner courtyard.[77] And so shall you
do on the seventh day of the month for anyone who has sinned by mistake
21 or due to ignorance: thus you shall provide atonement for the House. In
the first month, on the fourteenth day of the month, you shall bring the
Passover sacrifice, for a festival of seven days, unleavened bread shall be
22 eaten. On that day the prince shall prepare a bull as a purification offering
23 for himself and for all the people of the land. And on every one of the seven
days of the festival he shall prepare a burnt offering to the Lord: seven

75 | The ephah is a dry measure and the *bat* a liquid measure; each contained approximately 22 liters (cf. Lev. 19:35).

76 | The maneh and the shekel were measurements of weight. The shekel of pre-exilic Yehuda weighed 11.3 grams.

77 | Cf. Exodus 12:7, 22.

bulls and seven rams with no blemish every day for seven days, and a daily
24 purification offering consisting of one male goat. And he shall prepare a
grain offering consisting of one ephah for each bull and one ephah for
25 each ram and a hin of oil for each ephah.[78] In the seventh month, on the
fifteenth day of the month, during the festival, he shall prepare offerings
just like those on the seven days: a similar purification offering, a similar
burnt offering, and a similar grain offering, and a like amount of oil.

46 1 "Thus says the Lord God: The gate of the inner courtyard that faces
eastward shall be closed during the six days of labor, but on the Sabbath it
2 shall be opened, and on the day of the New Moon it shall be opened. The
prince shall enter from outside by way of the entrance hall of the gate and
shall stand by the doorpost of the gate. The priests shall prepare his burnt
offering and his peace offering, and he shall bow down at the threshold of
the gate and then leave, but the gate shall not be closed until the evening
3 so that the ordinary people can also bow down before the Lord at the
threshold of that gate on Sabbaths and New Moons.

4 "The burnt offering that the prince shall offer to the Lord on every
Sabbath day consists of six lambs with no blemish and a ram with no
5 blemish. And his accompanying grain offering shall be one ephah for the
ram; as for the lambs, his grain offering shall be whatever he chooses to
6 give as well as a hin of oil for each ephah of grain. And on the day of the
New Moon his offering shall consist of a young bull with no blemish as
7 well as six lambs and a ram, all without blemish. He shall prepare a grain
offering of one ephah for the bull and one ephah for the ram; as for the
lambs, his grain offering shall be whatever he chooses to give as well as a
8 hin of oil for each ephah of grain. And when the prince comes, he shall
enter by way of the entrance hall of the gate – and by way of it shall he exit.
9 But when the people come before the Lord on festivals, a person who
enters by way of the northern gate in order to bow down shall exit by the
southern gate, and a person who enters by way of the southern gate shall
exit by way of the northern gate. He shall not return by way of the gate
through which he entered but shall exit through the one across from it.
10 And the prince shall be among the people on those days: when they enter,
11 he enters, and when they leave, they leave together. And on the festivals
and at the appointed times the grain offering shall be an ephah for the bull,
an ephah for the ram, and as for the lambs, whatever he chooses to give as
well as a hin of oil for each ephah of grain.

12 "Now, should the prince make a voluntary offering, a burnt offering or
peace offering, voluntarily offered to the Lord on a weekday, the gate
facing eastward shall be open for him, and he shall prepare his burnt
offering or peace offering just as he would do on the Sabbath, but when
he leaves, the gate will be closed after his exit.

---

78 | A hin is one-sixth of a *bat*.

13 "And you shall prepare a daily burnt offering to the LORD consisting of a
lamb in its first year without blemish; you shall prepare it every morning.
14 And you shall prepare a grain offering for it every morning: one-sixth of
an ephah and one-third of a hin of oil to moisten the finely ground flour as
15 a grain offering to the LORD: a perpetual, everlasting decree.[79] Thus shall
they prepare the lamb and the grain offering with the oil every morning
as a regular burnt offering.

16 "Thus says the Lord GOD: Should the prince give a gift to one of his sons, it
is his estate that will belong to his sons; it is their possession by inheritance.
17 But should he give a gift from his estate to one of his servants, the servant
owns it until the year of freedom,[80] when it returns to the prince, for his
18 heritors are his sons: it belongs to them. This is so that the prince does not
take anything from the people's inheritance, throwing them wrongfully out
of their landholding. He shall pass his own landholding onto his sons so
that My people will not be scattered, each ousted from his landholding."

19 Then he led me through the entry passage at the side of the gate to the
holy chambers of the priests, which faced northward, and behold – there
20 was a space over there at the western end. He said to me: "This is the place
where the priests will cook the guilt offerings and the purification offerings,
where they will bake the grain offerings, so that they do not need to carry
them out to the outer courtyard to mingle with the people as if they were
holy, too."

21 He took me outside to the outer courtyard and had me pass by the four
corners of the courtyard, and behold, at every corner of the courtyard
22 there was another courtyard. In the four corners of the courtyard there
were roofless courtyards that were forty cubits long and thirty wide. All
23 four corner courtyards had the same measurements. And there was a
stonework platform roundabout inside them, roundabout each of the
four, and underneath the stonework platform there were cooking hearths
24 all around. He said to me: "This is the cooks' house, where those who
47 1 serve in the House cook the sacrifices of the people." Then he brought me
back to the entrance of the House, and behold, there was water coming
out from under the threshold of the House eastward, for the House faced
east, and the water flowed downward beneath the right-hand wall of the
2 House, south of the altar. He took me out through the northern gate and
led me around the outside path to the outer gate in an eastward direction,
and behold – water was trickling from the right-hand wall.

3 As the man went out eastward with the measuring line in his hand, he
measured off one thousand cubits. Then he led me through the water
4 there, ankle-deep water. He measured off one thousand cubits and led me
through the water there, knee-deep water. He measured off a thousand and

79 | Cf. Numbers 28:1–8.

80 | See Leviticus 25:9–24.

5 led me through water up to my loins. Then he measured off a thousand,
and there was a stream I could not cross – for the waters had risen to
6 become swimming waters, a stream that could not be walked through. He
said to me: "Have you seen this, Man?"

7 He led me and brought me back to the edge of the stream. When I got
back there – behold! there was a vast profusion of trees on both banks
8 of the stream. He said to me: "These waters flow out toward the eastern
region, descending to the Arava. Then they enter the sea;[81] it is to this sea
that these waters are sent forth, and the sea's waters will be healed thereby
9 from their saltiness. It shall come to pass that every living creature that
swarms shall survive wherever these streams flow, and there will be a great
abundance of fish because these waters will have arrived, and they will be
10 healed. Everything will live wherever this stream reaches. It shall come to
pass that fishermen will stand over the stream from Ein Gedi all the way to
Ein Eglayim. There will be an area to spread nets. The fish they catch will
11 be as varied as the fish of the Great Sea, and so abundant! But its swamps
12 and its marshes will not be healed; they are set aside for salt. Beside the
stream, rising on both banks, every kind of food tree shall grow, whose
leaves will never wither and whose fruit will never fail; it will bring forth
new fruit every month because its waters emanate from the Sanctuary. Its
fruit shall yield food, and its leaves, medicine.

13 "Thus says the Lord God: This shall be the border according to which you
shall give the land as inheritance to the twelve tribes of Israel. Yosef shall
14 receive two portions. You shall inherit it equally, one person like another;
as I swore to give it to your forefathers, so shall this land become your
possession.

15 "Now, this is the boundary of the land:

"On the northern side: from the Great Sea by way of Ḥetlon, Levo, Tzedad.
16 Ḥamat, Berota; Sivrayim, located between the border of Damascus and the
border of Ḥamat; Ḥatzer HaTikhon, which lies near the border of Ḥavran.
17 The border shall continue from the Sea up to Ḥatzar Einon at the border
of Damascus and everything northward, including the border of Ḥamat.
That is the northern side.

18 "As for the eastern side: between Ḥavran and Damascus, between the
Gilad and the land of Israel, the Jordan. You shall measure from the border
at the eastern sea. That is the eastern side.

19 "And the southern side: southward from Tamar up to the waters of Merivot
Kadesh, a wadi leading to the Great Sea. That is the south side, toward the
Negev.

---

81 | Referring to the Dead Sea.

20 "The west side shall be the Great Sea, from the border until opposite Levo
Ḥamat. That is the western side.

21 "You shall divide this land for yourselves according to the tribes of Israel.
22 You shall allot it as an inheritance for yourselves and for the strangers
who live amongst you, who bear children in your midst. These shall be
considered by you as citizens among the children of Israel. They shall
23 be allotted an inheritance among the tribes of Israel. It shall be that in
whatever tribe's territory the stranger lives, there shall you give him his
inheritance," says the Lord God.

48 1 "Now, these are the names of the tribes:

"From the northern edge, near the Ḥetlon Road toward Levo Ḥamat,
Ḥatzar Einan, the border of Damascus northward near Ḥamat, this shall
be his from the eastern edge to the sea: one portion for Dan.
2 And bordering Dan, from the eastern edge to the western edge, one
portion for Asher.
3 And bordering Asher, from the eastern edge to the western edge, one
portion for Naftali.
4 And bordering Naftali, from the eastern edge to the western edge, one
portion for Menashe.
5 And bordering Menashe, from the eastern edge to the western edge, one
portion for Efrayim.
6 And bordering Efrayim, from the eastern edge to the western edge, one
portion for Reuven.
7 And bordering Reuven, from the eastern edge to the western edge, one
portion for Yehuda.
8 And bordering Yehuda, from the eastern edge to the western edge, shall be
the gift portion that you shall designate, twenty-five thousand wide and as
long as any of the other portions – from the eastern edge to the western
edge – and the Sanctuary shall be within it.

9 "The gift portion that you shall designate for the Lord shall be twenty-five
10 thousand in length and ten thousand wide. And to these shall the holy
gift portion belong. To the priests – to the north a length of twenty-five
thousand, to the west a width of ten thousand, and to the east a width of
ten thousand, and to the south a length of twenty-five thousand; and the
11 Sanctuary of the Lord shall be within it. This sacred place shall belong to
the priests descended from Tzadok, who were guardians of My precious
things and who did not stray when the children of Israel went astray as the
12 other Levites did. And it shall be for them God's gift from the gift portion
of the land, holy of holies and bordering the Levites.

13 "The Levites, alongside the border with the priests shall have an area
twenty-five thousand in length with a width of ten thousand; the entire
14 length of twenty-five thousand and width of ten thousand. And they shall

not sell any part of it or exchange or transfer this choicest piece of the land,
for it is consecrated to the LORD.

15 "The five thousand that remain of the width, along the twenty-five thousand,
are for ordinary use for the city – for dwelling and for open space – and the
16 city shall be within this. And these are the city's dimensions: the northern
side, four thousand five hundred; the southern side, four thousand five
hundred; the eastern side, four thousand five hundred; the western
17 side, four thousand five hundred. The city shall have an open space – to
the north, two hundred and fifty; to the south, two hundred and fifty;
18 eastward, two hundred and fifty; northward, two hundred and fifty. And
the remainder in length parallel to the holy gift portion shall measure
ten thousand to the east and ten thousand to the west. This shall extend
alongside the holy gift portion, and its produce shall be food for people
19 who work in the city. The people who work in the city shall come from all
the tribes of Israel to cultivate it.

20 "The entire gift portion is twenty-five thousand by twenty-five thousand,
a square; and this shall you designate as the holy gift portion, with the
city property in it.

21 "What remains on both sides of the holy gift portion and the property of
the city belongs to the prince. Along the twenty-five thousand of the gift
portion up to the eastern border, and to the west along the twenty-five
thousand up to the western border, parallel to the tribes' portions, shall
be the prince's; the holy gift portion with the Sanctuary of the House are
22 within it. Thus the property of the Levites and the property of the city are
in the middle of that which belongs to the prince. The portion of the prince
shall be between the border of Yehuda and the border of Binyamin.

23 "And for the rest of the tribes, from the eastern side to the western side,
one portion for Binyamin.
24 And bordering Binyamin, from the eastern side to the western side, one
portion for Shimon.
25 And bordering Shimon, from the eastern side to the western side, one
portion for Yissakhar.
26 And bordering Yissakhar, from the eastern side to the western side, one
portion for Zevulun.
27 And bordering Zevulun, from the eastern side to the western side, one
portion for Gad.
28 And bordering Gad, at the Negev side southward, the border shall run
from Tamar by the waters of Merivat Kadesh to the wadi leading to the
Great Sea.
29 This is the land which you shall allot as inheritance to the tribes of Israel,
and these are their portions, says the Lord GOD.

30 "And these are the exits from the city:

31 From the northern side, which measures four thousand five hundred – the
gates of the city shall be named after the tribes of Israel – three gates
northward: one the Reuven Gate, one the Yehuda Gate, one the Levi
Gate.
32 And toward the eastern side, which measures four thousand five hundred,
three gates: one the Yosef Gate, one the Binyamin Gate, one the Dan
Gate.
33 And the southern side, which measures four thousand five hundred, three
gates: one the Shimon Gate, one the Yissakhar Gate, one the Zevulun
Gate.
34 Finally, the western side, four thousand five hundred, will have three gates:
one the Gad Gate, one the Asher Gate, one the Naftali Gate.
35 All around the city shall measure eighteen thousand, and its name from
that day on shall be:
The LORD Is There."

HAGGAI	Encouraging those who returned to Zion to rebuild the Temple Chs. 1–2		
ZECHARIAH	Zekharya's visions Chs. 1–6	Fasting over the destruction in an era of redemption 7–8	Regarding the kingdoms of Israel and the nations of the world 9–14
MALACHI	The poor spiritual state of those who returned to Zion Chs. 1–3		

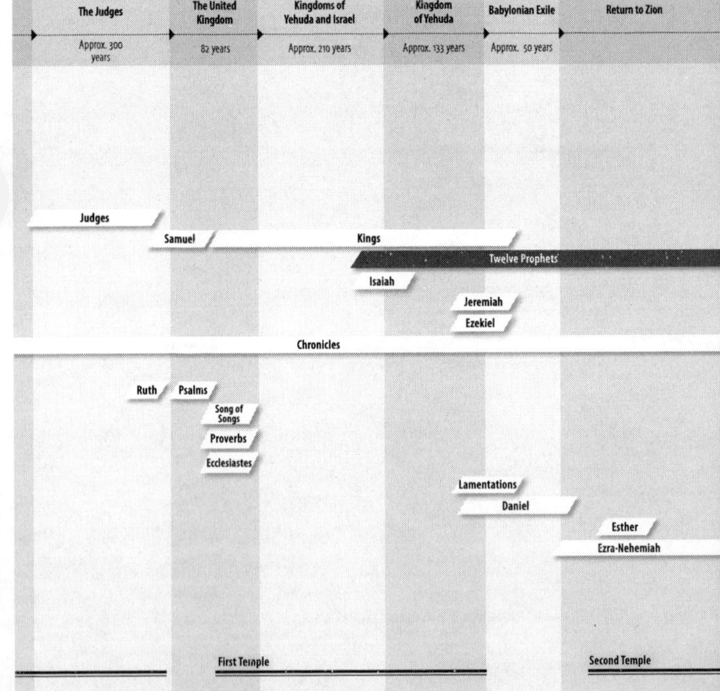

TWELVE PROPHETS/ SHENEIM ASAR

HOSEA	Relations between husband and wife as an allegory for relations between God and Israel Chs. 1–3	Rebuke and calls to repentance 4–14	
JOEL	The plague of locusts and its results Chs. 1–2	Promise of salvation for Israel and justice for the nations 3–4	
AMOS	Prophecies concerning the nations Chs. 1–2	Rebuke to a corrupt affluent society 3–6	From calamities to consolation 7–9
OBADIAH	Esav's relationship with Yaakov, and his judgment		
JONAH	Yona in the presence of God – flight and return Chs. 1–2	Yona in Nineveh – the argument over the fate of the city 3–4	
MICAH	Rebuke of a corrupt affluent society Chs. 1–3	Prophecies of redemption and ethics 4–7	
NAHUM	Punishment and destruction of Assyria – redemption for those enslaved by it Chs. 1–3		
HABAKKUK	The prophet's protest against the success of the wicked Ch. 1	God's response 2	The prophet's prayer 3
ZEPHANIAH	God judges the world – rebuke, punishment, and redemption Chs. 1–3		

HOSEA/
HOSHEA

1 1 This is the word of the Lord which came to Hoshea son of Be'eri in the
days of Uziya, Yotam, Aḥaz, and Yeḥizkiya, kings of Yehuda, and in the
days of Yorovam son of Yoash, king of Israel.
2 When the Lord first spoke to Hoshea,
the Lord said to Hoshea,
"Go, take for yourself a whoring woman and have children of a whore,
for the land is whoring itself away from the Lord."
3 So he went and married Gomer, daughter of Divlayim,
and she conceived and bore him a son.
4 And the Lord said to him, "Call him by the name of Yizre'el,
for soon I will punish the house of Yehu for the blood of Yizre'el,[1]
and I will put an end to the kingdom of the House of Israel.
5 And it will be on that day
that I will break the bow of Israel in the Yizre'el Valley."
6 Again she conceived and gave birth to a daughter,
and He said, "Call her by the name of Unloved,
for no longer will I have compassion on the House of Israel,
no more will I bear the burden of their sins;
7 but I will have compassion on the House of Yehuda,
and they will be saved by the Lord their God.
I will not save them by bow, nor by sword or battle,
not by horses nor by horsemen."
8 She weaned Unloved;
then she conceived and gave birth to a son.
9 And He said, "Call him Not My People,
for you are not My people,
and I will not be for you."

2 1 Yet the children of Israel will number like the sands of the sea,
not measurable or countable,
and rather than being told,
"You are Not My People,"
they will be told, "You are the sons of the living God."
2 Then the children of Yehuda and the children of Israel will gather
together;
they will designate one leader and escape from the land,
for the day of Yizre'el will be a great one.
3 Say then to your brothers "People,"
and to your sisters "Loved."
4 Berate your mother,
for she is not my wife,
nor I her husband.
Let her remove her prostitute's rouge from her face,
her adulterous acts from between her breasts,

1 | The site of Yehu's bloody revolt; see II Kings 9–10.

5 lest I strip her naked
as the day she was born
and make her as a desert wilderness.
I will make her into parched wasteland
and let her die from thirst.
6 As for her sons, I will have no mercy,
for they are the sons of a harlot,
7 for their mother has whored;
she has conceived them in shame.
She said, "I will follow after my lovers;
it is they who give me bread and water,
keep me in wools and linens,
lotions and wines,"
8 so I will obstruct her path with prickly shrubs;
I will fence her in with walls;
her way will be lost to her.
9 She will pursue her lovers
but not catch them;
she will search them out
but never find them.
Then she will say, "I will go and return to my first husband,
for I fared better then than now."
10 But she did not care to know
that it was I who furnished her with grain, wine, and oil,
I who lavished silver upon her
and gold which they used for Baal.
11 Hence I will take back My grain as it ripens in its season,
My wine as it ages;
I will seize My wools and My linens
meant to cover her nakedness.
12 And now I will expose her indecency for her lovers to see,
and there will be no one to rescue her from My hand.
13 I will put an end to all her joyous occasions –
her holidays, her New Moons, her Sabbaths,
and all her festive seasons.
14 I will ravage her vines and fig trees,
of which she once said, "These are my harlot's favors,
given to me by my lovers."
I will make them into abandoned woodlands,
and wild animals will feed on them.
15 I will revisit upon her the days of the Baalim,[2]
for whom she burned incense
and adorned herself with earrings and jewels,
how she followed after her lovers

2 | Canaanite gods mentioned frequently as objects of idolatrous worship by Israel.

and forgot Me.
So declares the LORD.

16 Behold, now I will coax her,
I will lead her back to the open desert,
and I will speak to her heart.
17 Then and there I will give her vineyards to her,
and the Valley of the Scourge[3] will be a doorway to hope;
she will return to Me in song as in the first days of her youth,
as on the day when she came up out of the land of Egypt.

18 It will be on that day, says the LORD:
you will call Me "my Husband";[4]
no longer will you call Me "my Master."[5]
19 I will eradicate the names of the Baalim from her mouth;
no more will they be mentioned by name.
20 On that day
I will make a covenant with them:
with the beasts of the fields,
and the birds of heaven,
and the crawling creatures of the ground.
I will break the bow
and the sword;
I will crush conflict out from the land,
and you will rest in safety.
21 I will betroth you to Me forever;
I will betroth you to Me in righteousness and justice,
in kindness and compassion.
22 I will betroth you to Me in faithfulness,
and you will know the LORD.

23 And it will be on that day:
I will answer, declares the LORD;
I will answer the heavens,
the heavens will answer the earth,
24 and the earth will answer the grain and the wine and the oil,
and they will answer to Yizre'el.
25 And I will sow her as My own in the land,
and I will have compassion on Unloved,
and I will say to Lo Ami,[6] "You are My people,"
and he will then say, "You are my God."

---

3 | See Joshua 7:24–26.

4 | Hebrew *ishi.*

5 | Hebrew *baali.* Both *baali* and *ishi* mean "my husband," but *baali* carries a connotation of dominance and evokes the Canaanite deity.

6 | "Not My people"; cf. 1:9.

3 1 The LORD said to me,
"Furthermore, go and love a woman loved by another,
and she an adulteress,"
as the LORD loves Israel
even as they turn to other gods
and adore their own drunken indulgence.
2 So then I paid her dowry of fifteen silver pieces
and a homer[7] and a half of barley,
3 and I said to her,
"Sit alone and wait for me for many days;
do not make a whore of yourself or be with any man;
neither will I come to you."
4 So too the children of Israel will wait alone for many days
with neither king nor leader,
without sacrifice or altars,
with no priestly garments or household shrines.
5 In time, the children of Israel will return;
they will seek the LORD their God
and David their king;
they will come trembling in awe back to the LORD
and His goodness
in the end of days.

4 1 Hear the word of the LORD, children of Israel,
for the LORD has a dispute with the people of this land –
for there is no truthfulness or kindness
and no awareness of God in the land.
2 False swearing and lying,
murder, thievery, and prostitution
are rampant, raging,
and bloodshed spills over into bloodshed.
3 For this the land will be laid waste,
all who dwell there wiped out:
beasts of the field
and birds of heaven,
even the fish in the seas will be swept away.
4 Still no man disputes another
nor admonishes his fellow man;
indeed, yours is like a nation at strife with their priests.
5 For this you will fall over in daylight,
and the false prophet with you at nightfall,
and I will cut off your nation.
6 My people are cut off for being unaware,
for as you spurned this awareness,

7 | A dry measure equaling approximately 220 liters.

I too will spurn you as My priest;
as you have forgotten the Law of your God,
I too will forget your children.
7 The greater they became, the greater their sins against Me;
I will turn their dignity into disgrace.
8 The priests feed on the purification offerings of My people
and yearn for their iniquity.
9 As the people
so too the priests;
I will punish each according to their ways,
and each will get what they deserve.
10 They will eat but not be satisfied;
they will whore but no offspring will come forth,
for they left the LORD and did not heed His laws.
11 Their heart leads them to harlotry and drunkenness.
12 My people look to their wooden figures for counsel,
to their sticks of magic to guide them,
for the prostituting spirit has steered them wrong,
and they whore themselves away from their God.
13 They sacrifice on the mountaintops,
offer incense on the hills
beneath the oak, the poplar, and the terebinth,
for their shade is bountiful.
And so your daughters will whore,
and your daughters-in-law will be adulterous.
14 But no, I will not punish your daughters for their whoring,
nor your daughters-in-law for their adultery,
for their men go with the whores
and sacrifice with the harlots;
surely a nation with no awareness will fall to its ruin.
15 Though you, Israel, whore yourself,
do not let Yehuda become guilty.
Do not come to Gilgal,
or make a pilgrimage to Beit Aven,[8]
or swear:[9] "As the LORD lives."
16 For Israel is as rebellious as an obstinate cow;
the LORD will graze them as a lone sheep in a wide pasture.
17 Efrayim[10] is entwined with idols;
leave him be.
18 When their drunkenness is done,
they whore with the harlots;

---

8 | A derogatory name for Beit El. Beit El and Gilgal were places of worship, sometimes idolatrous; see Amos 5:5.

9 | That is, swear falsely.

10 | A recurring metonym for the Kingdom of Israel.

her leaders love nothing more
than disgrace.
19 The wind will bind her in its billowing wings,
and they will come to be ashamed of their sacrifices.

5 1 Hear this, priests;
heed, House of Israel;
listen now, house of the king,
for judgment was entrusted to you,
but you set traps at Mitzpa
and spread nets out on Tavor.[11]
2 Those who strayed from Me are deep in the slaughter;
I will bring suffering on them all.
3 For I know all about Efrayim,
and Israel is not concealed from Me;
now you, Efrayim, have pursued prostitution,
and Israel has become defiled.
4 Their evil actions
do not allow them to return to their God,
for a whoring spirit has taken them over,
and they do not know the Lord.
5 The pride of Israel will bear witness against them.
The sins of Israel and Efrayim will make them falter,
and Yehuda too will falter with them.
6 They will go with their flocks and herds to seek[12] the Lord
but will not find Him,
for He has turned away from them.
7 They betrayed the Lord,
for they begot foreign children,
so soon there will come a month,[13]
and your fields will be consumed.

8 Blast the ram's horn in Giva,[14]
the trumpet in Rama;
sound the battle cry in Beit Aven;
they are closing in on you, Binyamin.
9 Efrayim will become desolate
on the day of punishment;
to the tribes of Israel I have declared
the truth of what will be.
10 The princes of Yehuda have become
like those who move back the boundary stones;

11 | Mitzpa and Har Tavor were respectively the southern and northern reaches of the Kingdom of Israel at the time.

12 | That is, by offering sacrifices.

13 | Meaning a month of destruction.

14 | These were three cities in the tribal territory of Binyamin.

upon them I will pour out My wrath like water.
11 Efrayim is oppressed,
crushed by decrees,
for he readily chose
to follow the commands of others.
12 And so I will be like a moth and eat away at Efrayim
and cause the House of Yehuda to rot from within.
13 Then Efrayim saw his sickness,
and Yehuda his oozing wound;
Efrayim hailed Assyria
and dispatched messengers to the great king,[15]
but he cannot heal you,
nor can he cure your wound.
14 For I will be like a lion to Efrayim
and like a young lion to the House of Yehuda.
For I – yes, I – will tear them to pieces and leave;
I will carry them off, and none will rescue them.
15 I will go and return to My place
until they realize their guilt and seek Me out,
for only in their distress
will they long for Me.

6 1 Come, let us return to the LORD,
for though He has ripped us apart, He will heal us,
for though He battered us, He will bandage us up.
2 After two days He will revive us;
on the third He will raise us up,
and we will live before Him.
3 Let us know, let us strive and eagerly seek knowledge of the LORD,
for as dawn breaks, He is surely there.
He will come to us as the rain,
as the final winter rains that replenish the earth.
4 What can I do for you, Efrayim;
what can I do for you, Yehuda?
Your goodness dissolves like morning mist;
like dew at daybreak it swiftly fades.
5 For this I have hewed at them by way of the prophets;
I have killed them with the strength of My words,
and your judgment will emerge like the morning light.
6 For it is goodness I yearn for, not sacrifice;
awareness of God rather than burnt offerings.
7 But they breached the covenant, as men do;
there they betrayed Me.
8 Gilad, a city full of sinners,

15 | This was the title of the Assyrian king.

is stained with tracks of blood.
9 As gangs of thieves stalk men,
bands of priests murder on the path to Shekhem,[16]
so purposeful is their evil.
10 In the House of Israel I have seen an appalling sight,
in Efrayim – prostitution,
Israel – defiled.
11 You too, Yehuda, reaped your harvest[17]
when I was ready to restore My people from captivity.[18]
7 1 When I would have wanted to heal Israel,
the iniquity of Efrayim
and the sinfulness of Shomron was exposed,
for they acted deceitfully;
so the thief barges in,
and gangs raid the open streets.
2 They do not think to themselves
that I remember all their wicked actions;
now they are besieged by their very misdeeds,
and they stand clearly before Me.
3 The king rejoices in their evil deeds,
the officials in their lies.
4 Adulterers, all of them:
their passions burn like an oven stoked by the baker,
barely pausing from the time the dough is kneaded
until rising.
5 On the day of our king,
officials make themselves ill from drinking skins of wine;
he too joins his hand with scoffers.
6 Their heart, like an oven, burns as they lie in wait;
all night their baker sleeps;
come morning, it burns like a raging blaze.
7 All of them heat up like an oven
and feed upon their judges;
their kings all fall;
not one cries out to Me.
8 Efrayim mixes with the nations;
unturned on a griddle, Efrayim has become like a burnt cake.
9 Foreign nations ate away his strength,
and he was unaware.
Old and frail, strewn with gray –
and he was unaware.

---

16 | Shekhem and Gilad were prominent Israelite cities.

17 | Received the punishment you deserved.

18 | This verse is unclear and subject to a wide variety of interpretations. The translation follows Radak and Metzudat David.

10 The pride of Israel will bear witness against them,
yet they do not return to the LORD their God
nor even seek Him out.
11 And so Efrayim has become like
an easily wooed, witless dove.
They appeal to Egypt,
and to Assyria they run.
12 Wherever they go,
I will snag them with My net;
I will bring them down like birds in the skies;
I will afflict them as was heard by the whole assembly.

13 Woe to them who have strayed from Me;
ruin unto them, for they have sinned against Me.
And I, how can I save them
when they speak lies against Me?
14 They do not cry out to Me in sincerity
but wail from their beds;
they gather over grain and wine
and rebel against Me.
15 I honed and strengthened their arms,
but they devise evil against Me.
16 They return, though not toward heaven,
and are misdirected like a faulty bow;
their leaders will fall by the sword
for the fire of their tongues;
for this they will be mocked
in the land of Egypt.[19]

8 1 Set the ram's horn to your lips:[20]
he will swoop like a vulture onto the House of the LORD,
for they have violated My covenant,
revolted against My Law.
2 To Me they will cry,
"O, our God, it is You; Israel knows You."
3 But Israel rejected the good;
so will be hounded by the enemy.
4 They have crowned kings without My sanction,
appointed princes without My say;
with their wealth and gold they made themselves idols,
bringing about their own demise.
5 Your calf has forsaken you, Shomron!
My anger burns against them;
how long until they become clean from this sin?

19 | To whom they appeal for aid.

20 | In other words, warn of an impending attack.

6 For this has been done by Israel –
the work of a craftsman;
it is not God;
so too, the calf of Shomron
will be reduced to shards.
7 For wind they will sow,
gales they will reap;
wheat stalks will not stand,
grains will not yield flour,
and were they to yield,
strangers would consume it.
8 Israel has been consumed
and now has become to the nations like an object of no value.
9 As they went up to Assyria
like an unruly donkey roaming aloof,
so Efrayim sold himself for lovers' favors.
10 Even as they sell themselves to the nations,
I will gather the nations against them,
and they will shudder
under the burden of the king and ministers.
11 For Efrayim has increased altars for sinning;
indeed, these altars have spawned his sins.
12 And though for him I wrote down My laws in their greatness,
they are considered as foreign by him.
13 As for the burnt sacrifices they offer Me,
that burning flesh – let them eat it;
the Lord does not accept them.
Now He will remember their transgressions
and hold them to account for their sins;
to Egypt they will return.[21]
14 For Israel has forgotten his Maker;
he has built palaces,
and Yehuda has increased fortified cities.
I will send a fire to his cities
to consume his castles.

9 1 Israel, do not celebrate;
you will know no joy like other peoples,
for you have whored; away from your God,
you have loved the harlot's payments
found on every thresher's floor.
2 The threshing floor and winepress will yield them no fodder,
and the new wine will fall short.
3 No more will they dwell in the Lord's land;

---

21 | See Deuteronomy 28:68.

Efrayim will go again to Egypt
and into Assyria, where they will eat impure food.
4 They will not pour wine in offering to the LORD,
nor will their sacrifices find favor with Him;
like the bread of grievers it will be;
all who eat of it will be defiled,
for their bread is merely to feed their hunger
and will not be brought to the House of the LORD.
5 What then will you offer on festival days,
on days of sacrifice to the LORD?
6 Though they have run from ruin,
Egypt will collect them,
Mof bury them;
their treasure-filled houses will be overrun by thistles,
and thorns will be in their tents.
7 Know, Israel:
the days of reckoning have come;
the days of requital are here.
You said, "This prophet is a fool;
the man with God's spirit is a madman";
as the enormity of your sins,
so the magnitude of the hatred.[22]
8 Efrayim's watchman[23] stands with his god;
he, a prophet, sets snares for all who follow his paths,
bringing hatred into the house of his god.
9 They have delved deeply into corruption
as in the days of the Giva.[24]
He will remember their iniquity;
He will punish their sins.

10 When I found Israel,
they were as grapes in the desert;
your fathers were to Me
like the first, ripe figs of the new season,
but when they arrived at Baal Peor,
they devoted themselves to shame[25]
and became detested – just as they had been loved.
11 As for Efrayim, their glory will take flight like a bird,
leaving nothing: no birth, none with child, not even conception.
12 Even were they to raise their children,
they would mourn every last one,
for woe to them

22 | Referring to divine hatred and rejection.
23 | Perhaps a reference to false prophets.
24 | See Judges 19:14–30.
25 | Hebrew *boshet*, a common epithet for the foreign god Baal.

when I turn from them.
13 Efrayim seemed to Me like Tyre nested in a lush haven,[26]
but no, Efrayim will send his sons
to the slaughter.
14 Give them, O Lord –
what can I ask you to give them?
Give them a grieving womb
and shriveled breasts gone dry.
15 Their wickedness, all of it was rooted in Gilgal;[27]
it is there that I hated them
on account of the evil of their ways.
I will banish them from My House;
no longer can I love them;
their leaders are all rebellious.
16 Efrayim has been struck down;
their roots have withered;
no longer can they bear fruit –
and even were they to give birth,
I would slay the treasured fruit of their womb.
17 He, my God, will reject them,
for they did not heed Him,
and they will be wanderers among the nations.

10 1 Israel is a withered, barren vine;
will he ever bear fruit again?
As he yielded fruit in plenty,
so he built altars profuse;
as his land filled with favor,
so pagan shrines flourished.
2 Their heart severed from Me,
now they will be held guilty.
He[28] will break down their altars,
bring ruin upon their pagan shrines.
3 For now they will say, "We have no king,
for we feared not the Lord.
And the king?
What could he do for us?"
4 They spoke deceptive words,
made covenants
with hollow oaths;
their false justice crops up like poison weeds
in the ruts of the field.

---

26 | Tyre was seen as a paragon of peace and security; cf. Ezekiel 28:2.

27 | Where Israelite sovereignty and monarchy originated; see Joshua, chapter 5; 1 Samuel 11:14–12:25.

28 | That is, the enemy.

5 The residents of Shomron are afraid
for the golden calf of Beit Aven;[29]
the people will mourn for it,
as will the priests who once rejoiced in its honor,
for it will be banished from them.
6 It too will be brought to Assyria
as tribute to the great king.
Efrayim will be seized with shame,
and Israel will be shamed by the counsel they gave.
7 Shomron's king will cease to be,
like froth on the water's surface.
8 The hilltop shrines of Aven will be ravaged,
that place of Israel's sin.
Thorns and thistles
will sprout up over their altars;
to the mountains they will say, "Conceal us,"
to the hills, "Descend upon us."

9 You have sinned, Israel,
ever since the days of Giva;[30]
unchanged they remain,
still believing
that they will not be overtaken at Giva
in war against the wicked ones.
10 At My will I will lash out at them,
and the nations will rally against them
when they are bound like two plowing cows.
11 Efrayim is a well-trained young cow
who loves to thresh;
I will stroke his fattened, strong neck;
I will harness Efrayim
and make Yehuda plow;
Yaakov will break up the dirt clods in the field.
12 Sow within yourselves honesty;
reap by the rule of goodness;
till the unbroken ground;
for now it is time to seek the Lord
until He comes to shower you with justice.
13 But instead, you have cultivated wickedness,
reaped wrongdoing,
eaten the fruit of your lies,
for your faith was in your own path,
in the might of your warriors.
14 And so the roar of battle will rise against your people,

29 | See note on 4:15.
30 | See above, 9:9.

and all your fortresses will be ravaged
as in the ravaging of Shalman[31] at Beit Arbel
on that day of war
when mothers were crushed to pieces
with their children.
15 So this, then, is what Beit El has made of you
as a result of your great evildoing;
at dawn the king of Israel
will be no more.
11 1 When Israel was a child, I already loved him;
from Egypt I called him to Me to be My son.
2 They[32] called to them,
but they only turned further away
to sacrifice to the Baalim,
to burn incense to the idols.
3 It was I who guided Efrayim's first steps,
carrying them in My arms,
but they never grasped that I was the one who tended them.
4 I led them with reins of human compassion,
with ties of love;
I was to them like him who lifts the harness from their mouths,
and I gently bent down to feed them.
5 I vowed that they would never return to Egypt,
but now Assyria is their king,
and to Me they refuse to return.
6 The sword will linger in their cities;
it will consume all their villages and devour them
because of their evil designs.
7 My people waver – whether to turn back to Me,
although Israel is summoned upward,
they will not praise Him together.
8 How can I relinquish you, Efrayim;
hand you over, Israel?
How can I make you like Adma[33]
and treat you like Tzevoyim?
My heart has turned upon Me;
My compassion has been kindled.
9 No, I will not unleash My burning wrath,
I will not turn again to destroy Efrayim –
for I am God, I am not a man;
within you, My holiness dwells;

---

31 | Perhaps Shalmaneser III of Assyria.

32 | That is, My prophets.

33 | Adma and Tzevoyim were destroyed along with Sedom and Amora; see Deuteronomy 29:22.

I will not enter the city with hatred.
10 They will follow after the LORD;
He will roar like a lion.
When He roars,
His children will rush forth from the west.
11 They will be like a frightened bird coming out of Egypt,
like a dove leaving the land of Assyria.
I will bring them to settle safely in their homes.
So declares the LORD.

12 1 Efrayim besieges Me with lies,
the House of Israel with deception,
but Yehuda still walks with God
and remains faithful to the Holy One.
2 Efrayim shepherds the wind;[34]
he chases the east winds.
Day and night
he increases lies and ruin;
he makes pacts with Assyria
and to Egypt bears oil.[35]
3 But also with Yehuda the LORD has a dispute:
He will visit upon Yaakov as he deserves,
as befits his deeds –
He will repay him.
4 In the womb he grasped his brother by the heel,[36]
and with all his strength he struggled with God.[37]
5 He struggled with an angel and prevailed;
he cried and pleaded with him;
in Beit El He found him,[38]
and there He spoke to us.
6 But the LORD, God of Hosts,
the LORD is His name.
7 Now you, too, return to your God,
uphold compassion and justice,
and long for your God forever more.
8 Still the merchant possesses false scales;
he loves to exploit.
9 Efrayim exclaims, "I have become wealthy;
I have found fortune from my own labors;
in all the fruits of my toil
they will find neither sin nor iniquity."

---

34 | A reference to useless activity; cf., e.g., Ecclesiastes 1:14.

35 | As a tribute.

36 | See Genesis 25:26.

37 | See Genesis 32:25–31.

38 | See Genesis 28:10–22; 35:1–8.

10 I am the LORD your God from the time you were in the land of Egypt;
once more I will settle you safely in tents as in days of old.
11 I have spoken by way of the prophets;
I endowed them with many visions,
and through images I communicated with the prophets.
12 As Gilad is rampant with iniquity, so too they are empty and vain;
in Gilgal they sacrifice oxen,
and their altars too
will become like rocks piled high in furrows of the fields.
13 Yaakov fled to the lands of Aram,
and Yisrael labored to acquire a bride;
for a bride he kept sheep.[39]
14 With a prophet the LORD brought Israel up out of Egypt,
and with a prophet He kept watch over us.
15 Efrayim has provoked bitter anger;
the guilt from the blood he shed will remain,
and the LORD will turn his scorn back upon him.
13 1 So it was: when Efrayim spoke, they trembled in fear;
he was esteemed in Israel,
but when found guilty of worshipping Baal, he was as dead.
2 Now their sinning goes on and on;
they cast graven images from their silver,
mold idols as they understood,
each entirely the craft of men;
of them they say,
"Men who offer sacrifices must kiss calves."[40]
3 So they will dissolve like morning mist,
like dew at daybreak that swiftly fades.
They will scatter like chaff from the threshing floor,
like smoke from the window.
4 I am the LORD your God
from the land of Egypt;
you know no God other than Me;
no one can save you except for Me.
5 I knew you, cared for you in the desert,
in the parched, bereft land.
6 But when they grazed, they became sated and satisfied;
their hearts became haughty –
then they forgot Me.
7 Therefore I will be as a lion to them;
as a leopard I will watch, lurking on the path.
8 I will fall upon them like a bear who mourns her whelps
and tear apart their sealed hearts;

39 | See Genesis, chapter 29.

40 | The idolatrous priests compel the worshippers to kiss golden calves as a sign of devotion.

there I will consume them like a lion;
wild beasts will shred them to pieces.
9 You have brought ruin upon yourself, Israel,
for your help is to be found in Me.
10 I am your King, then
who will save you in all your cities,
and what of your judges of whom you said,
"Appoint me a king and officers"?

11 In My rage I gave you a king,
and in My wrath I will take him away.
12 The sinfulness of Efrayim is tied together;
his sins are stored away.
13 Pangs of birth will overcome him,
but he is not a wise son,
for when the moment of birth comes,
he will break and not survive.
14 I will rescue them from Sheol;[41]
I will redeem them from the clutches of death.
I shall be your plague, O Death;
I will be your destruction, O Sheol;
any qualms will be concealed from My eyes.
15 For though he will flourish wildly among the reeds,
an east wind will come;
a gust from the LORD will rise from the wilderness.
His fountain will dry up;
his spring will parch;
his enemy will plunder
all of his treasures.
14 1 Shomron will be held guilty,
for she has rebelled against her God;
she will fall by the sword,
her young smashed to pieces,
her women with child ripped apart.

2 O Israel, return, go back to the LORD your God,
for you have stumbled in your own sinfulness.
3 Take words of remorse with you
and return to the LORD;
say to Him, "Forgive all of our sins; accept our goodness –
instead of calves we offer You our words of prayer.
4 Assyria will not save us;
no more will we ride upon horses;[42]
never again will we say, 'You are our god'

41 | Meaning the grave or the underworld.

42 | Symbolizing Egypt; cf., e.g., II Kings 18:24.

to the work of our hands,
for only in You will the orphan find mercy."
5 I will mend their rebellion
with gracious love,
for I have turned My anger away from them.
6 I will be as dew to Israel;
he will bloom like a lily
and set down roots as deep as the trees of Lebanon.
7 His branches will spread wide;
his splendor will be as the olive tree,
and his fragrance as the trees of Lebanon.
8 They who return will dwell beneath his shade;
they will revive once again as grain
and flower like vines;
their acclaim will linger as the scent
of the wine of Lebanon.
9 Efrayim will say, "What need do I have of these idols?"
And I will answer him; I will look after him.
I will be as a cypress tree, lush and leafy;
you will find in Me your source of fruit.
10 He who is wise will fathom these words;
the insightful will grasp them,
for the ways of the LORD are just,
and the righteous will walk in them,
but sinners will stumble over them.

JOEL/YOEL

1 1 This is the word of the LORD that came to Yoel the son of Petuel:
2 Listen, O elders;
take heed, all those who live on the land.
Has there been anything like this in your lifetimes
or in the lifetimes of your parents?
3 You will tell your children of this,
and your children will tell their children of this,
and their children will tell a different generation of this:
4 "What remains after the chewer-locusts
will be eaten by the locusts;
what remains after the locusts
will be eaten by the springing-locusts;
what remains after the springing-locusts
will be eaten by the finisher-locusts."
5 Wake, drunkards, and weep;
wail, drinkers of wine,

over the sweet wine you are denied drinking.
6 For a nation has risen up against My land –
innumerable, mighty,
with lion's teeth –
its fangs the fangs of a lioness.
7 It has laid My vines to waste
and splintered My fig trees.
It has stripped them bare
and cast them down, their cuttings bleached.
8 Wail like a young woman donning sackcloth
for her husband in her youth.
9 Grain offerings and libations have been cut off
from the House of the LORD.
The priests, attendants of the LORD,
are in mourning.
10 The field has been devastated;
the earth is in mourning.
The grain is devastated,
the young wine has dried up,
and the oil languishes.
11 Farmers, be ashamed;
vintners, bewail
the wheat, the barley,
the harvest of the field – destroyed.
12 The vine has withered,
and the fig tree languishes;
the pomegranate;
also the date.
The apple
and all the orchard trees wither.
Truly man is parched of joy.
13 Don sackcloth – mourn, O priests.
Wail, attendants of the altar.
Come sleep in sackcloth, attendants of my God,
for grain offerings and libations have been cut off
from the House of your God.
14 Sanctify a fast day,
convene an assembly,
gather the elders
and all those who live on the land
to the House of the LORD, your God,
and cry out to the LORD.
15 O, for the day,
the day of the LORD is nigh;
like havoc from Shaddai it will come.

16 Is not food cut off
in front of our very eyes;
happiness and joy
from the House of our God?
17 The seeds have shriveled
under the clods.
The storehouses
are desolate.
The granaries
have been destroyed;
the grain has dried up.
18 O, the animals, how they moan.
Herds of cattle are in confusion,
for they are without pasturage;
even the flocks of sheep suffer.
19 To You, my Lord, I cry out.
Fire has consumed the desert pasture,
and flame has been ignited in all the orchard trees.
20 Even the animals of the fields
long for You –
for the riverbeds are dry,
and fire has consumed the desert pasture.

2 1 Blow a ram's horn in Zion;
sound a horn on My holy mountain.
Let all those who live on the land
tremble,
for the day of the Lord is coming;
it is nigh.
2 It is a day of darkness and blinding black,
a day of clouds and mist
like dawn spread over the mountains.
There will be a great and mighty nation,
the likes of which has never been before
nor will ever be again
until the end of time.
3 Before it, the consuming fire;
after it, a burning flame.
The land, like Eden, before it;
after it, a barren desert.
It leaves not one survivor.
4 Its resemblance is to horses –
like war-horses, so they run.
5 Theirs is the pounding of chariots
dancing over the mountain peaks;
theirs is the crackle of a flame

as it consumes straw;
theirs is the shout
of a vast nation ready for battle.
6 Nations tremble before them;
they are all ashen faced.
7 They race like warriors;
like soldiers they ascend the wall:
Every soldier moving forward in position,
not one strays from the route.
8 They advance untouching,
every warrior moving forward
in position along the track.
They fall on the sword
but are not wounded.
9 They rush into the city,
race over the wall,
ascend into the houses
like thieves through the windows.

10 The earth trembles before Him,
the skies thunder,
the sun and the moon go dark,
and the stars draw in their light.
11 Then the LORD raises His voice before His troops –
for His camp is vast,
and mighty are the ones who carry out His words.
For great and terrifying is the day of the LORD –
who could withstand it?
12 Even now,
so says the LORD,
return to Me wholeheartedly,
with fasting, weeping, and grief.
13 Rend your hearts,
not your clothing,
and come back to the LORD your God.
For He is gracious and compassionate,
slow to anger and abounding in kindness;
He may well relent and forswear the evil.
14 Who knows? Maybe He will reconsider and relent[1]
and leave behind blessings;
offer grain offerings and libations
to the LORD, your God.
15 Blow a ram's horn in Zion,
sanctify a fast day,

1 | Cf. Jonah 3:9.

convene an assembly,
16 gather the people,
sanctify the masses,
convene the old, and
gather the children and infants.
Let the groom come from his room
and the bride from her wedding chamber.
17 Let the priests, attendants of the LORD, weep
between the hallway and the altar.
Let them say:
"Have compassion, O LORD, upon Your people,
and do not allow Your possession to become a reproach –
ruled by nations."
Why should it be said among the peoples,
"Where is their God?"
18 Then the LORD will be fiercely zealous toward His land,
and He will have mercy upon His nation.
19 He will reply and say to His nation:
So I will send to you grain,
and sweet wine, and young oil.
You will be sated with it.
I will no longer allow you to become
a reproach among the nations.
20 I will drive the northerner[2] away from you –
I will banish them to a dry and desolate land;
their vanguard to the east sea,
their rearguard to the west sea.[3]
Their foul smell will ascend,
their stench will rise,
for they have done terrible things.
21 Fear not, earth.
Rejoice! Be glad!
For the LORD has done great things.
22 Fear not, animals of My fields,
for the desert pasture is green with grass;
the tree has borne fruit:
the fig and vine have blossomed.
23 Rejoice and be glad
in the LORD, your God, children of Zion.
For He has given you the first rain out of generosity.
He will rain down for you the first and last rain
as it was in the beginning.

2 | Meaning the invading horde.

3 | The Dead Sea is located in the east of the land of Israel, and the Mediterranean to the west.

24 The granaries will fill with grain,
and the press will overflow
with sweet wine and young oil.
25 I will repay you for all the seasons
consumed by the locusts, the springing-locusts,
the finisher-locusts, and the chewer-locusts –
My great army, which I sent among you.
26 You will eat, eat and be sated,
and you will praise the name of the Lord, your God,
who has done wonders for you,
for My nation will never be ashamed.
27 You will know that I am among Israel,
and I am the Lord, your God;
there is no other.

My nation will never be ashamed.

3 1 Afterward, this is what will be:
I will pour My spirit out over humankind:
your sons and your daughters
will speak prophecy,
your elders
will dream dreams,
your young men
will see visions.
2 In those days,
even over the slaves and bondswomen
I will pour My spirit out.

3 I will turn the skies and land into omens:
blood and fire and plumes of smoke.
4 The sun will go dark,
the moon bloody,
before the coming great and terrifying day of the Lord.
5 And all those who call on the name of the Lord will escape,
for there will be a remnant on Mount Zion and in Jerusalem
as the Lord has said;
even among the survivors called by the Lord
there will be a remnant.[4]

4 1 For it will be in those days and at that time
that I will restore those held captive
from Yehuda and Jerusalem.
2 I will gather all the nations
and bring them down to the Valley of Yehoshafat.
There I will carry out judgment against them

4 | Cf. Obadiah 1:17; Isaiah 37:32; II Kings 19:31.

for the sake of My people –
My possession Israel,
whom they scattered among the nations –
and for the sake of My land,
which they divided among themselves.
3 They cast lots for My nation,[5]
and handed over young boys for the hire of a harlot,
and sold young girls for wine,
and they drank.

4 But what are you to Me, Tyre and Sidon, all the Philistine regions? Do you
deign to retaliate against Me? And if you retaliate, how quickly and easily
5 I will repay your deeds upon your head. You took My silver and gold and
6 carried My precious things away to your temples. You sold the Judahites
7 and Jerusalemites to the Ionians to cast them far from their borders. But
I will rouse them from the place to which you sold them, and I will repay
8 your deeds upon your head. I will sell your sons and daughters into the
hands of the Judahites, who will sell them to the people of Sheba – a far-off
nation. For the Lord has spoken.

9 Call this out to the nations:
Declare a war[6] and
let the warriors stir.
Let all the men of war
approach, ascend.
10 Beat your plowshares into swords
and your pruning hooks into spears.[7]
Let the weak say, "I am mighty."
11 Come swiftly, all you surrounding nations,
and gather together there.

O Lord, let Your warriors descend.

12 Let the nations stir and go up
to the Valley of Yehoshafat,
for it is there that I will sit and judge
all the surrounding nations.[8]

13 Hoist the sickle;
the harvest is ripe.
Come, trample;
the winepress is full.
The vats of wine overflow,
so great is the evil they have done.

5 | In order to divide up Israel's land.
6 | That is, commence a war; cf. Micah 3:5; Jeremiah 6:4.
7 | Cf. Isaiah 2:4; Micah 4:3.
8 | *Yehoshafat* literally means "the Lord judges."

14 Masses upon masses
in the Valley of Decision,
for the day of the Lord is nigh
in the Valley of Decision.
15 The sun and moon go dark,
and the stars draw in their light.
16 The Lord roars from Zion;[9]
from Jerusalem He raises His voice.
The heavens and the earth tremble.
But the Lord will be a shelter
for His people,
a stronghold
for the children of Israel.
17 So you will know that I am the Lord, your God –
the One who resides in Zion, My holy mountain.
Jerusalem will be sacred;
strangers will pass through her no longer.
18 On that day,
the mountains will drip with sweet wine,[10]
the hills will flow with milk,
and all of Yehuda's rivers will flow, full of water.
A spring will surge forth from the House of the Lord
and irrigate the Valley of Acacias.
19 Egypt will be desolate,
Edom a barren desert,
because of the violence they have perpetrated against Yehuda –
because of the innocent blood they spilled in their land.
20 But Yehuda will be forever settled,
Jerusalem to the end of time.
21 Even though I pardon,
I will not pardon the spilling of their blood,
for the Lord resides in Zion.

1 These are the words of Amos of the herdsmen of Tekoa, who prophesied AMOS
regarding Israel during the days of Uziya, king of Yehuda, and Yorovam the
1 son of Yoash, king of Israel, two years before the earthquake.[1] He said:
The Lord roars from Zion;
from Jerusalem He raises His voice:
2 The shepherds' pastures are in mourning,
and the peak of the Carmel withers.

9 | Cf. Amos 1:2; Jeremiah 25:30.

10 | Cf. Amos 9:13.

1 | See Zechariah 14:5.

3 So says the Lord:
On account of Damascus's three crimes and on account of the fourth, I will
not forgive them:[2] they threshed through Gilad with threshing sledges
of iron,[3]
4 so I will send a fire against the house of Ḥazael.
It will consume the fortresses of Ben Ḥadad.[4]
5 I will shatter the barred gates of Damascus.[5]
I will cut off any ruler from the Aven Valley
and any staff-bearer from Beit Eden.
The nation of Aram will be exiled to Kir,[6] says the Lord.

6 So says the Lord:
On account of Aza's three crimes and on account of the fourth, I will not
forgive them: they exiled an entire group of exiles, handing them over to
Edom,
7 so I will send a fire against Aza's wall.
It will consume her fortresses.
8 I will cut off any ruler from Ashdod
and any staff-bearer from Ashkelon.
I will set My hand against Ekron,
and the remnant of Philistines will be lost,
says the Lord God.

9 So says the Lord:
On account of Tyre's three crimes and on account of the fourth, I will not
forgive them: they handed over an entire group of exiles to Edom and did
not remember the brotherly covenant.[7]
10 So I will send a fire against Tyre's wall.
It will consume her fortresses.

11 So says the Lord:
On account of Edom's three crimes and on account of the fourth, I will
not forgive them: They have pursued their brother[8] in war and suppressed
their own mercy. They have allowed their anger to rage forever and nursed
their wrath unending,

---

2 | This is a common rhetorical device in Tanakh; cf., e.g., Proverbs 30:15. The last (or in these cases, only) item of the list mentioned is generally different or more extreme, roughly equivalent to "the final straw" in English.

3 | They used these machines to torture Gilad's inhabitants.

4 | Ḥazael and Ben Ḥadad were powerful kings of Damascus. See, e.g., I Kings 20; II Kings 8:7–15.

5 | This and the following were major Aramean cities. The following prophecies as well foretell doom for the major cities of the peoples in question.

6 | The place of their origins; see 9:7.

7 | Perhaps a reference to the covenant between David and Shlomo and the rulers of Tyre; see I Kings 5:21–25.

8 | Referring to Yisrael (Yaakov), who was the brother of Edom (Esav); see Genesis, chapter 23.

12 so I will send a fire against Yemen.
It will consume the fortresses of Botzra.

13 So says the LORD:
On account of the children of Amon's three crimes and on account of the
fourth, I will not forgive them: to expand their borders, they sliced open
the pregnant women of the Gilad,
14 so I will send a fire against the walls of Raba.
It will consume her fortresses
with a shout on a day of war,
a gale on a day of a storm.
15 Their king shall be taken into exile,
he and his princes together,
says the LORD.

2 1 So says the LORD:
On account of Moav's three crimes and on account of the fourth, I will
not forgive them: they immolated the corpse of the king of Edom down
to lime,
2 so I will send a fire against Moav.
It will consume the fortresses of the cities.
Moav will die in an uproar
with shouting, the sound of a ram's horn.
3 I will cut off any chieftain from within her,
and I will kill all her princes along with him,
says the LORD.

4 So says the LORD:
On account of Yehuda's three crimes and on account of the fourth, I
will not forgive them: they despised the LORD's Torah and did not keep
His statutes. Their own lies – the ones their fathers followed – led them
astray,
5 so I will send a fire against Yehuda.
It will consume the fortresses of Jerusalem.

6 So says the LORD:
On account of Israel's three crimes and on account of the fourth, I will
not forgive them. They sold the righteous for silver and the poor for the
price of shoes.
7 They are those who trample the dust of the earth atop the heads of the
poor; they turn the humble away from the path.
A man and his father visit the same girl to desecrate My holy name.
8 They spread confiscated clothing beside every altar and drink wine bought
with fines in the house of their gods.

9 But I had destroyed before them the Amorite, whose height was as tall as
cedars and whose strength was like that of oaks. Yet I obliterated their fruit
10 above and their roots below. I brought you up from the land of Egypt and

11 led you in the desert for forty years to inherit Amorite lands. I raised up
into prophets some of your sons and into nazirites some of your young
12 men. Is this not so, children of Israel? said the LORD. But you made the
nazirites drink wine and ordered the prophets not to prophesy.[9]

13 Behold, I will hold you back in your place, as a wagon loaded with sheaves
is held back.

14 The swift will lose the ability to flee; the strong will not gather their
15 strength; the warrior will not escape with his life. The bowman will not
stand; the fleet of foot will not escape; the horse rider will not escape with
16 his life. He who considers himself strongest among warriors will flee naked
on that day, says the LORD.

3 1 Hear this word, which the LORD has spoken about you, children of Israel:
2 About the whole family I brought up from the land of Egypt, it is only you
that I have known from among all the families on earth, so I will visit all
your sins upon you.

3 Would two walk together
if they had not met?
4 Would a lion roar in the forest
if it had not caught prey?
Would a young lion raise its voice from its den
if it had not seized prey?
5 Would a bird plunge into a trap on the ground
if it were not baited?
Would the trap spring up from the earth
if it had not trapped quarry?
6 Would a warning horn blow in the city
and the people not be afraid?
Would disaster come upon the city
were it not an act of the LORD?
7 The LORD GOD does not do anything without revealing His secret to His
servants, the prophets.
8 A lion roars;
who would not fear?
The LORD GOD speaks;
who would not prophesy?

9 Cause this to be heard in the fortresses of Ashdod
and the fortresses of Egypt.
Gather against the hills of Shomron and witness
much tumult within her and the oppressed in her midst.
10 They do not know how to act honestly, says the LORD, those who hoard
11 violence and theft in their palaces. Therefore, says the LORD GOD, an

9 | The nazirite is forbidden to drink wine (Num. 6:1–21).

enemy will surround the land and remove from you your defenses, and
your fortresses will be plundered.

12 So says the Lord:
Just as a shepherd salvages two thighs or a scrap of an ear from a lion, so
will the children of Israel, those who reside in Shomron, be saved with the
edge of the bed, with the cradle of Damascus.[10]

13 Proclaim; bear witness
against the House of Yaakov,
says the Lord God, God of Hosts:

14 For on the day on which I visit Israel's crimes upon them, I will visit them
upon the altars of Beit El. The altar horns will be hewn; they will fall to
15 the ground. I will strike the winter palace along with the summer palace:
the palaces of ivory will be lost. Many are the palaces that will be swept
away.

4 1 Hear this, O cows of the Bashan who are on Mount Shomron,
who oppress the poor,
who break the poverty stricken,
who say to their masters,
"Bring wine[11] and let us drink."
2 The Lord God swears by His holiness:
Days are coming upon you;
you will be carried away impaled on hooks,
and in fishing pots your children will be dragged away.
3 Women will flee through the breaches
and be cast into the palaces,[12]
says the Lord.
4 Come to Beit El and sin,
to the Gilgal and sin greatly.
Bring your sacrifices in the morning
and your tithes on the third day.
5 Burn your thanksgiving offering of leaven;
call for donations; let it be heard,
for this is what you love doing, children of Israel,
says the Lord God.
6 Yet I gave you clean teeth in all your cities,
a lack of bread in your places,
but you did not return to Me, says the Lord.
7 And I held back the rain from you three months before the harvest,

---

10 | The end of this verse is difficult. The word *eres* literally means bed. It may be a reference to Nergal Eresh, the Assyrian magnate in Damascus in the early eighth century who was a leader of the campaign (narrated in II Kings 13:5, without reference to Assyria) that ended the oppression of Israel by the Aramean Ḥazael and his successor Ben Ḥadad.

11 | "Wine" missing from the Hebrew, but implied.

12 | Of the enemy.

caused rain to fall on one city and not another;
one plot will be rained upon,
and one in which there will be no rain will wither away.
8 The residents of two or three cities
will wander to one city for water to drink,
but their thirst is not slaked,
yet you did not return to Me,
says the LORD.
9 I struck you with blight and mildew,
your many gardens and vineyards,
your fig and olive trees
devoured by the chewer-locusts,
but you did not return to Me,
says the LORD.

10 I sent a plague upon you like that which I sent against Egypt;
I slew your young men by the sword during the capture of your horses.
The stench of your slain camp rises in your noses,
but you did not return to Me,
says the LORD.
11 I overturned you as God overturned Sedom and Amora.
You became like a firebrand saved from the fire,
but you did not return to Me,
says the LORD.

12 Therefore, this is what I will do to you, Israel –
because of the above, this is what I will do:
prepare yourselves to meet your God, O Israel,
13 for it is He,
Mountain-shaper,
Wind-creator,
the One who tells man his thoughts.
He turns the dawn to dark
and treads over mountain heights;
the LORD, God of Hosts, is His name.

5 1 Hear these words that I raise
as a lament over you, House of Israel:
2 She has fallen, maiden of Israel;
she will not rise again.
She has been abandoned in her land;
there is no one to raise her up,
3 for so says the LORD GOD.
A city one thousand strong
will remain only one hundred strong,

and a city one hundred strong
will remain only ten strong
for the House of Israel,
4 for so says the LORD to the House of Israel.

Seek Me and live.

5 Do not go to Beit El seeking,
do not come to the Gilgal,
and pass not through Be'er Sheva.[13]
For the Gilgal will surely be exiled,
and Beit El will be as nothing.
6 Seek the LORD and live
lest the House of Yosef be split like fire
and Beit El be devoured with no one to extinguish it.
7 O, those who turn justice bitter
and cast righteousness to the ground.
8 O, He who formed Pleiades and Orion,
who turns morning to dread dark;
day to night He darkens;
He who calls to the ocean waters
and pours them out over the face of the earth,
the LORD is His name:

9 He who rains ruin upon the stronghold
so that ruin upon the fortress will come,
10 for they have hated the reprimander at their gates
and loathed the honest speaker.
11 Therefore, because you trample the poor
and confiscate their allotment of grain,
you have built houses of hewn stone
but will not live in them;
you have planted choice vineyards
but will not drink the wine,
12 for I know that your crimes are many
and your sins vast –
you, enemies of the innocent,
bribe takers;
they turn aside the poor at the gates.
13 Therefore, the wise are silent at this time,
for it is an evil time.
14 Seek good and not evil
so that you may live.
And if you do so, the LORD, God of Hosts,
will be with you as you said.

---

13 | All these cities contained shrines and sites of illicit worship.

15 Hate evil,
love good;
present justice at your gates.
Maybe the LORD, God of Hosts, will have pity
upon the remnant of Yosef.

16 Therefore – so says the LORD, God of Hosts, the LORD –
mourning in all the squares,
groaning in all the streets: oh, oh.
They will call the farmer to lament,
and the skilled mourners to mourn.
17 Mourning in all the vineyards,
for I will pass among you, says the LORD.

18 Hie, all those who long for the day of the LORD.
What is the day of the LORD to you, and why do you want it?
The day of the LORD is darkness and not light.
19 Like a man who runs from a lion,
then encounters a bear,
then comes home, lays a hand on the wall,
and a snake bites him,
20 is not the day of the LORD darkness and not light?
It has dimness and no shine.
21 I have hated, I have loathed
your holiday sacrifices,
and I will not take in the scent
of your festival offerings.
22 For even if you proffer Me burnt offerings
and your grain offerings,
I will not desire them,
and I will not look
at your peace offerings of fat cows.
23 Take away your clamoring songs;
I will not hear your harp tunes.
24 But let justice roll on like water
and righteousness like a roaring river.
25 Did you offer Me sacrifices and grain offerings
all those forty years in the desert, House of Israel?
26 Yet you bore Sikut, your king,
and Kiyun, your idol,
the star of your god
which you made for yourselves.[14]
27 So I will send you into exile
beyond Damascus,

14 | The identity of these foreign deities is unclear. Some have suggested that these are two Akkadian names for Saturn, vocalized as the Hebrew *shikkutz*, "abomination."

says the Lord.
God of Hosts is His name.

6 1 Woe, you who are settled secure in Zion,
who rest assured on Mount Shomron,
who are called "chief among nations";
the House of Israel flocks to them.
2 Yet go to Kalneh and look,
and from there to Ḥamat Raba;
go down to the Philistine Gat.[15]
Are you better than these kingdoms?
Is their territory greater than yours?
3 You who dismiss the day of evil
but embrace violent rule,
4 who lie on beds of ivory,
lounge upon your couches,
feasting on the choicest of sheep
and calves taken from their feeding stalls,
5 who play the harp –
with instruments they think themselves like David –
6 who guzzle wine from bowls,
anoint yourselves with the finest of oils,
but are not heartsick over Yosef's ruin;
7 therefore, you will now be the first of exiles,
a coterie of loungers removed,
8 the Lord God swears by Himself;
the Lord, God of Hosts, has spoken.
I despise the pride of Yaakov,
hate his palaces,
so I will hand over a city in its fullness.

9 This is what will be: If ten people initially survive by hiding in a house,
10 even so, they will die. Then the dead man's relative and loved one, stirring
themselves, will go and remove the corpses from the house. One of them
will call to the other, searching at the back of the house, "Is anyone alive
there?"

"Not one," he will say.

"Hush! Do not utter the name of the Lord,"[16] he will say.
11 For indeed, the Lord commands
and will shatter the great house to pieces

15 | Ḥamat and Gat had been centers of powerful city-states before being vanquished and destroyed.

16 | This cryptic phrase is explained by Radak and others as follows: The speaker is implying that this catastrophe has befallen us because we failed to mention the name of the Lord in our prayers and instead referred to idols. Therefore, let us now simply hush and suffer in silence.

and the small house to slabs.
12 Can horses gallop over rock?
Can anyone plow there with oxen?
Yet you have turned justice to poison
and the fruits of righteousness bitter.
13 Those who rejoice over Lo Davar,
who say that by our own strength we took Karnayim.[17]
14 Indeed I will raise a nation against you, House of Israel.
The LORD, God of Hosts, has spoken.
They will drive you from Levo Ḥamat
down to Arava Ravine.

7 1 The LORD GOD showed me this: He was forming a horde of locusts just
as the late wheat started to grow, the late wheat that sprouts after the
2 king's mowers have mowed. And as they consumed the land's greenery
completely, I said, "My LORD GOD, please forgive. How could Yaakov
3 survive this – he, who is so small?" And the LORD relented: "This shall
not be," said the LORD.

4 The LORD GOD showed me this: He was calling to fight with fire. It
5 consumed the mighty deep; it consumed the allotted land. I said, "My LORD
6 GOD, please stop. How could Yaakov survive this – he, who is so small?" And
the LORD relented: "This, too, shall not be," said the LORD GOD.

7 He showed me this: The LORD was standing high upon a leveled wall,[18]
8 holding a plumb line in His hand. The LORD said to me, "What do you
see, Amos?" and I said, "A plumb line." Then the LORD said, "I will place a
9 plumb line among My people, Israel. I will spare them no longer. Yisḥak's[19]
altars will be desolate, and Israel's temples will be destroyed. I will rise up
against the house of Yorovam with a sword."

10 Then Amatzya, priest of Beit El, sent the following message to Yorovam,
king of Israel: "Amos has conspired against you within the House of Israel.
11 The land cannot bear all he says. For this is what Amos says: 'Yorovam
will surely die by the sword, and Israel will be exiled from their land.'"

12 And to Amos, Amatzya said: "Seer, flee to the land of Yehuda. It is there
that you should eat your bread, and it is there that you should prophesy.
13 Prophesy no longer in Beit El, for it is a royal temple and a king's shrine."

14 Amos replied and said to Amatzya, "I am not a prophet nor of prophets
15 but a herdsman and a splicer of sycamore figs. It was the LORD who took

---

17 | Cities in Transjordan.

18 | The "plumb line" is a tool by which one makes an exact and precise determination of the angle of a wall. Thus, "plumb line" here is a metaphor for justice that is exact and precise, i.e., strict.

19 | A variant spelling of Yitzḥak. The verb "to laugh," on which the name is based, can itself appear in Biblical Hebrew both as *tzaḥak* and *saḥak*.

me from behind the flock of sheep and told me, 'Go, prophesy to My
people Israel.'

16 "And now, heed the word of the LORD: You say, 'Do not prophesy to
17 Israel; do not speak regarding the House of Yisḥak.' Therefore, says the
LORD, your wife will sell herself in the city, your sons and daughters will
be slaughtered by the sword, and your land will be divided. And as for
you, you will die in an impure land, and Israel will surely be exiled from
their land."

8 1 2 This is what the LORD GOD showed me: a basket of summer fruit. He said,
"What do you see, Amos?" and I said, "A basket of summer fruit." Then the
LORD said to me, "The end[20] is coming for My people, Israel. I will spare
them no longer.

3 "On that day" – the LORD GOD has spoken –
"Temple songs will become wails.
Many corpses everywhere,
and those who dispose of them
calling out, 'Silence.'"

4 Hear this, those who trample the poor,
who would decimate the destitute of the land,
5 those who say,
"When will the New Moon pass
so we can sell grain,
and the Sabbath
so we can open the storehouses,[21]
so we can diminish the weight of an ephah
but enlarge the shekel,[22]
skew false scales,
6 sell the needy for silver
and the poor for the price of shoes?
Let us sell chaff as grain."
7 The LORD swears by the pride of Yaakov:
I will forever remember what they have done.
8 Would the earth not shudder for this
and all its inhabitants mourn?
The earth will rise like the Nile,
churn and sink like the Nile of Egypt.
9 This is what will be on that day –
the LORD GOD has spoken –
I will cause the sun to set at noon
and the earth to go dark on a sunny day.
10 I will turn your holidays into mourning days

20 | Hebrew *ketz*, echoing "summer fruit" (*kayitz*).

21 | The verse reflects a practice to avoid work on the Sabbath and New Moon.

22 | Dishonestly skewing weights and measures; cf., e.g., Deuteronomy 25:13–16.

and all your songs to dirges.
I will cause sackcloth to be girded around every waist
and every forehead to be shorn bare.
I will make the grief of this day like the grief of the loss of an only child,
with a day of bitterness at its end.
11 Yes, days are coming –
the LORD GOD has spoken –
I will cast hunger over the land:
not hunger for bread
nor thirst for water,
but hunger to hear the words of the LORD.
12 They will wander from sea to sea
and from the north to the east
to seek the word of the LORD,
but they will not find it.
13 On that day, beautiful young women and young men
will faint of thirst.

14 O, those who swear by Shomron's sin
and say, "By the life of your god, Dan;
by the life of the way to Be'er Sheva,"[23]
They will fall and never stand again.

9 1 I saw my LORD standing beside the altar.
He said: "Strike the lintel,
and let the doorposts quake.
Their riches first,
then, by the sword, their children.
None who flee will escape;
no refugee will find safety.
2 Even if they burrow down to Sheol,[24]
there My hand will seize them;
even if they ascend to heaven,
from there I will pull them down;
3 even if they hide on the Carmel's peak,
there I will seek and seize them;
even if they secret themselves away from My eyes on the sea-floor,
there I will command the snake to bite them;
4 even if they are taken captive, marched before their enemies,
there I will command the sword to kill them;
I will set My eyes upon them
for evil, not good."
5 And my LORD, GOD of Hosts –
it is He – who but touches the earth, and it dissolves;

23 | See note on 5:5.
24 | The netherworld.

all inhabitants in mourning;
He makes all the earth rise like the Nile
and sink like the river of Egypt.
6 He who built His heavenly dome
and established His myriad forces upon the earth,
He calls to the sea
and spills it out over the land –
the LORD is His name.
7 Are you not to Me like the children of Kush, O children of Israel?
Did I not bring up Israel from the land of Egypt
as I brought the Philistines up from Kaftor
and Aram from Kir?[25]
8 Yes, the eyes of the LORD GOD are upon the sinning kingdom;
I will wipe it off the face of the earth,
but the House of Yaakov I will never destroy,[26]
says the LORD.
9 For I will but command,
and I will shake the House of Israel among all the nations
as one shakes a sieve;[27]
not one pebble will fall to the earth.
10 All the sinners of My nation
will be killed by the sword –
those who say,
"Disaster will not reach,
will not advance upon us."

11 On that day,
I will lift up David's fallen tabernacle,
repair its breaches,
and lift up its ruins,
rebuild it as it was in days of yore.
12 And so they will possess
the remnants of Edom and all the nations
who are called in My name,
says the LORD who does this.
13 Behold, days are coming.
The LORD has spoken.
The plow man will meet the reaper,
and the grape crusher the seed sower;[28]
the mountains will drip with sweet wine,
and all the hills will dissolve.

---

25 | All these migrations occurred around the same time.

26 | The sinners will be destroyed, and the remnant of Israel will be restored.

27 | Separating the worthy from the unworthy.

28 | Due to the great bounty, the summer reaping will last until the time of plowing in the late fall. Likewise for late-summer grape crushing and winter sowing.

14 I will bring back the exiled of My nation, Israel.
They will build ruined cities
and settle.
They will plant vineyards
and drink their wine.
They will grow gardens
and eat their fruit.
15 I will plant them on their land,
and never again will they be uprooted
from the land which I gave to them,
says the Lord, your God.

OBADIAH/ OVADYA

1 1 This is Ovadya's vision:

So says the Lord God to Edom –
we have heard tidings from the Lord:
and an envoy has been sent among the nations,
"Come, let us rise up in battle against her."
2 Look, I have made you small among nations;
you are utterly scorned.
3 The arrogance of your heart deceived you,
you who dwell in the cliff's niches,
your lofty abode,
saying in your heart,
"Who could bring me down to earth?"
4 But even if you rise as high as an eagle,
if you make your nest among the stars,
I shall bring you down from there,
declares the Lord.
5 If thieves come upon you,
bandits in the night,
do they not take only their fill?
If grape gatherers[1] come upon you,
do they not leave gleanings?
6 Yet how has Esav been ransacked,
his hidden treasures laid bare.
7 Your allies all
have forced you to the borders;
those with whom you had made peace
all deceived you, defeated you.
Those with whom you broke your bread laid a snare for you,
bereft of awareness.

1 | Hebrew *botzerim*, evoking the Edomite city of Botzra (see, e.g., Gen. 36:33; Is. 34:6, 63:1).

8 Behold, on that day,
says the LORD,
I will purge Edom of wise men,
the mountains of Esav of awareness.
9 Your warriors will be frightened, Teiman,
for the mountains of Esav will be unmanned by slaughter.
10 For the violence you wrought against your brother Yaakov
shame will cover you,
and you will be cut off forever.
11 The day you stood aside,
the day strangers took captive his forces,
and foreigners entered his gates,
casting lots for Jerusalem –
you too were like one of them.
12 Do not gloat over the day of your brother's destruction,
the day he becomes a stranger.
Do not rejoice over the children of Yehuda
on the day of their destruction.
Do not open your mouth
on the day of trouble.
13 Do not enter My people's gate
on the day of their ruin.
Do not gloat over its misfortune
on the day of its ruin.
Do not extend your hands to take its wealth
on the day of his ruin.
14 Do not stand at the crossroads
to cut down his refugees.
Do not surrender his survivors
on the day of trouble.
15 For the day of the LORD draws near
for all the nations.
What you have done shall be done to you;
what you have wrought will return upon your head.
16 What you drank on My holy mountain,
all the nations will always drink.
They will drink and they will swallow,
and they will be as if they never were.
17 There will be a remnant on Mount Zion,
and it will be holy,
and the House of Yaakov will possess their inheritance.
18 The House of Yaakov will be fire,
the House of Yosef, flame;
the House of Esav, straw.
They will blaze among them and consume them,

and there will be no survivors of the House of Esav,
for the LORD has spoken.

19 They will take possession of the Negev, along with the mountains of Esav,
and the Shefela, from the Philistines.
And they will take possession of the land of Efrayim
and the land of Shomron; and Binyamin, along with the Gilad –
20 they, the exiled force of the children of Israel
who are among the Canaanites as far as Tzarfat[2]
and the exiled of Jerusalem who are in Sepharad[3]
will take possession of the cities of the Negev.
21 And saviors shall go up to Mount Zion
to judge the mountains of Esav,
and dominion shall be the LORD's.

JONAH/YONA 1 1 The word of the LORD came to Yona son of Amitai: "Rise up – go to the
2 great city of Nineveh and cry out against it, for its cruel evil has come into
3 My sight." But Yona rose instead to flee to Tarshish, away from the LORD's
presence. He went down to Yafo, found a ship bound for Tarshish, paid
the fare, and went down inside the ship to sail away with them to Tarshish,
4 away from the LORD's presence. But the LORD hurled a great wind across
the sea; a great storm overcame the sea, and the ship threatened to break
apart.

5 The sailors were afraid and cried out, each to his god,[1] and they cast the
ship's cargo out into the sea to lighten the load, but Yona went down to
the bottom of the boat, lay down, and fell asleep.

6 The captain came up to him: "How can you sleep?" he said. "Rise up! Cry
out to your god! Perhaps your god will think kindly of us, and we will not
be lost."

7 The sailors said to one another, "Let us cast lots so that we may know on
whose account this cruel evil has come upon us." And they cast their lot,
8 and the lot fell upon Yona. "Tell us," they said to him, "you from whom
this cruel thing has come – what is your trade, and where are you coming
9 from? Which country is yours, and which is your people?" And he said
to them, "I am a Hebrew, and it is the LORD God of the heavens that I
fear – He who made both sea and dry land."

10 The men were filled with great fear and said, "What have you done?" for

---

2 | A town on the Phoenician coast (see I Kings 17:9).

3 | Possibly a reference to Sardis, in Asia Minor.

1 | The crew was multi-ethnic. A person's origin was identified by the god he worshipped.

11 they knew that he was fleeing the LORD's presence; he had told them. They
said, "What must we do to you to calm the sea for us?" – and the sea was
12 storming ever more fiercely. "Lift me up," he said, "cast me out into the
sea, and the sea will be still for you, for I know it is on my account that this
great storm has come upon you."

13 The men oared toward dry land but could not reach it, for the sea was
14 storming ever more fiercely around them. And they cried out to the LORD
and said, "Please, LORD, please – do not let us be lost on account of this
man's life, and do not stain our hands with innocent blood, for You are the
15 LORD, and whatever You desire, You perform." Then they lifted Yona up
and cast him out into the sea, and the sea ceased raging and grew still.

16 And the men were filled with a great fear of the LORD, and they offered up
a sacrifice to the LORD, and made vows.

2 1 The LORD sent a great fish to swallow up Yona; and Yona was inside the
2 belly of the fish for three days and three nights. And Yona prayed to the
LORD his God from the belly of the fish:

3 "From a narrow place[5] I cry out to the LORD,[6]
and He will answer.
From the belly of Sheol[7] I beg –
You hear my words.
4 You have cast me down into deep waters,
the heart of the sea –
the current engulfs me –
all Your torrents and storm waves
crash over me.
5 I said to myself,
I am flung away out of Your presence –
but I will yet see
Your holy Sanctuary again.[8]
6 The waters rush around me to my very life's edge,
deeps surround me,
weeds crown me.
7 I have sunk down to the roots of the hills;
the earth is forever barred before me.[9]
Yet You raise my life up
from the abyss,

5 | Meaning from a position of distress.

6 | The prayer is here translated in the present tense, rather than the past tense of the Hebrew. This makes it a prayer for rescue, which is immediately forthcoming. Alternatively, rendering in the past tense suggests that the great fish had rescued Yona from drowning in the sea and this is a prayer of thanksgiving.

7 | Sheol is the realm of death, the netherworld, the lowest place on earth.

8 | The Temple is where one is in God's presence. It is the antipode of Sheol.

9 | That is, the gates of Sheol are locked behind me and I cannot return to the living.

O Lord my God.
8 As my life closes over me
the Lord comes to my mind –
then my prayer comes to You,
comes to Your holy Sanctuary.
9 Those who cleave to empty folly
will yet forsake their faithfulness.[10]
10 But I, voicing thanks, shall bring You offerings.
I shall fulfill what I have vowed.
Rescue belongs to the Lord."
11 And the Lord spoke to the fish, and it vomited Yona out onto dry land.

3 1 2 So the word of the Lord came to Yona for a second time: "Rise up – go
to the great city of Nineveh and cry out to it the call that I convey to you."
3 And Yona rose and went to Nineveh as the Lord had said. Nineveh was
4 an immensely great city, three days' walk across. Yona began his journey,
a day's walk into Nineveh, and cried out, "Forty more days, and Nineveh
5 will be overturned!" And the people of Nineveh believed in God, and
declared a fast, and dressed themselves in sackcloth, from the greatest of
them to the least.

6 When word reached the king of Nineveh, he rose from his throne, took
off his mantle, covered himself with sackcloth, and sat down upon ashes.
7 And he had this proclaimed in Nineveh in the name of the king and his
nobles: "No person or animal – cattle or flock – may taste any morsel;
8 they may not pasture; they may drink no water. All must be covered in
sackcloth, man and beast, and must cry out to God with all their strength.
Let every man turn back from his cruel practices, from the violence that
9 stains his hands. Who knows? Perhaps God, too, will turn back and relent,
10 will turn back from His burning rage before we are all lost." And God saw
their actions – that they had turned away from their cruel practices – and
God relented from the evil He had spoken of bringing upon them, and
brought it not.

4 1 2 To Yona, this was a cruel evil, and he raged against it. And he prayed to
the Lord: "Please, Lord, is this not just what I said while I was still in my
own land? This is why I first fled toward Tarshish – because I knew that
You are a gracious and compassionate God, slow to anger, abounding in
3 kindness, and relenting from evil. Now, Lord, please take my soul away
from me, for death would be better than my life."

4 "Are you so enraged?" said the Lord.

5 Yona left the city and sat down to its east. He made himself a shelter and
sat in the shade beneath it, waiting to see what would become of the city.

---

10 | They will renounce their belief in other gods, or their expectation of receiving favor from those gods.

6 The Lord God sent a gourd plant, which grew up above Yona to shade
his head, to shield him from the cruel heat, and Yona rejoiced over this
7 gourd plant with great joy. But God sent a worm as dawn broke the next
8 day, and it attacked the gourd plant until it dried up entirely. As the sun
rose, God sent a scorching east wind, and the sun beat down on Yona's
head. He grew faint and longed in his soul to die. "Death," he said, "would
be better than my life."

9 God said to Yona, "Are you so enraged about the gourd plant?" Said Yona,
"I am enraged enough to die."

10 And the Lord said, "You cared about that gourd plant, which you did not
toil for and did not grow, which was born overnight and was lost overnight.
11 Am I not to care for the great city of Nineveh, which has in it more than
one hundred and twenty thousand people who do not know their right
hands from their left, and so many animals?"

MICAH/MIKHA

1 1 This is the word of the Lord that came to Mikha the Morashtite in the days
of Yotam, Aḥaz, and Yeḥizkiya, kings of Yehuda, in a vision concerning
Shomron and Jerusalem.

2 Listen, all peoples;
give heed, O earth and all its fullness.
May the Lord God be a witness against you,
the Lord from His holy Temple.
3 For behold the Lord – He is coming out of His place;
He will go down and tread upon the highest places
of the earth.
4 The mountains dissolve beneath Him,
and the valleys split open
like wax melting before fire,
like waters surging down a steep slope.
5 All this owing to Yaakov's sins,
to the wrongdoings of the House of Israel.
What then is the sin of Yaakov if not Shomron?
Who is behind the hilltop shrines in Yehuda
if not Jerusalem?
6 I will turn Shomron into a mass of stones in the fields,
a place for planting vineyards,
and will hurl her ruins into the valley
and bare her foundations.
7 All her statues
will be shattered;
all her tainted payment

will go up in flames;
all her idols
I will lay waste,
for she amassed it all from harlot's payment,
and to harlot's payment it will return.
8 Over this I will wail and lament;
I will walk barefoot, stripped bare,
my grief the cry of jackals,
my mourning like ostriches.[1]
9 For her blows are mortal;
they come all the way to Yehuda,
reaching the gates of my people,
even to Jerusalem.
10 Do not tell of this
in Gat,[2]
nor break out
in tears.
But within Beit Le'afra
immerse yourself in mourner's ashes.
11 Go then, residents of Shafir,
naked and shamed;
the dwellers of Tzaanan
could not escape;
so too the mourning in Beit HaEtzel will be great,
and your seat of safety will be snatched from you,
12 for though the residents of Marot
hoped for good,
disaster came down from the Lord
just to the gates of Jerusalem.
13 Hitch the chariot to the horses,
lady of Lakhish –
inciter of sin
for daughter Zion –
the rebellious acts of Israel
were first embraced in your midst.
14 So, then, give your gifts[3]
to Moreshet Gat;
the houses of Akhziv deceive, disappoint[4]
the kings of Israel.
15 I will yet bring a conqueror upon you,
O residents of Maresha;

1 | These animals lived in the wasteland and were considered despicable.
2 | The following are localities in the Kingdom of Yehuda.
3 | That is, parting tokens.
4 | Hebrew *le'akhzav*, resonating with *Akhziv*.

the esteemed men of Israel will flee
even to Adulam.
16 Shave your head; pull out your hair in mourning
over the children of your delight.
Make yourself bald like the vulture,
for they are gone from you into exile.

2 1 Woe to those who plot wicked deeds,
who plan evildoing from their beds;
come morning light they carry it out
merely because they have the power.
2 They lust for others' fields and seize them,
eye others' homes and assume them as theirs;
they exploit men and their households,
both man and his estate.

3 So says the Lord:
I too plot evil
against this tribe of people,
for you will not be able to move
your necks from there,
nor will you walk with your heads held high,
for the time of disaster has come.
4 On that day
you will be made an object of ridicule;
a woeful wail will arise,
and it will be said, "We are raided and ruined,
our people's portion seized.
How then does he take what is mine
and divide up our fields?"[5]
5 So then you will have no one
to cast the lots for dividing the land
among the community of the Lord.
6 "Do not preach,"
they preach,
for they will not be reproved
nor shrink back in shame.
7 Will it then be said in the House of Yaakov,
"Is the Lord's spirit wanting?
Can these truly be His deeds?"
Will My words not grant goodness
to those who walk righteously?
8 But instead, My people arise as their own enemy;
they strip fine outer garments from passersby;
those who felt safe become like hopeless men

5 | As booty.

returning from war.
9 You drive out the wives of My people
from their secure and joyful homes,
from their young children;
you forever remove the honor I gave them.
10 So get up and go;
this is not your place to rest,
for the defilement you brought will destroy;
it will bring down a harsh line of destruction.
11 For if there were a man with a spirit
of falsehood and lies
who would preach toward drink and drunkenness,
he would be welcomed as preacher of this people.

12 Gather – I will gather all of you, Yaakov;
collect – indeed I will collect the remnant of Israel.
I will place them together;
sheltered as sheep in a paddock
and as a flock in their pasture,
they will clamor, a commotion of men.
13 He, the breaker of the gate, will rise up before them;
they will burst through and cross over,
and their king will lead them
with the Lord at their head.

3 1 And I say:
Hear me, heads of Yaakov,
rulers of the House of Israel:
Is it not for you
to know what is just?
2 Haters of good,
lovers of evil,
you rip off their skin,
the flesh from their very bones,
3 you who feast on the flesh
of my people,
who strip off their skins
and crack their bones,
carving them like pieces into a pot
like meat in a caldron.
4 Then they[6] will call out to the Lord,
but He will not answer.
He will hide His face from them at that time,
for they have ingrained evil in their ways.

6 | The rulers.

5 So says the LORD:
As to those prophets
who mislead My people,
who call for peace
while sinking in their teeth[7]
but declare war
on those who do not feed them their fill,
6 thus night will come to end your vision;
darkness will fall upon your divination;
the sun will set on the prophets,
and their day will darken upon them.
7 The seers will be ashamed,
the diviners disgraced;
they will veil their mouths,[8] every one –
God does not answer.
8 But I, I am filled with the strength of the LORD's spirit
of justice and courage
to declare to Yaakov his transgressions,
to Israel his sins.

9 And I say: Hear me now, heads of Yaakov,
leaders of the House of Israel
who abhor justice
and all that is straight turn twisted,
10 who build Zion with bloodshed,
Jerusalem with iniquity.
11 Her leaders arbitrate for bribes,
her priests will teach for a price,
and her prophets for dividends will divine,
yet they rely upon the LORD, saying,
"Surely the LORD is in our midst;
no calamity can befall us."
12 And so because of you
Zion will be plowed over like a field;
Jerusalem will come to be a mound of ruins
and the Temple Mount
an overgrown hilltop shrine.

4 1 This will be in days to come:[9]
The mountain of the LORD's House will be
rooted firm, the highest of mountains,
raised high above all hills,
and all the peoples will stream to it.

7 | When satiated.
8 | In mourning.
9 | Cf. Isaiah 2:2–4.

2 Many nations will come, saying:
"Come, let us go up to the mount of the LORD,
to the House of Yaakov's God;
He will teach us of His ways;
we will walk in His pathways" –
for teaching will come forth from Zion,
from Jerusalem the LORD's word.
3 He will judge among peoples
and arbitrate for mighty nations, far away;
they shall beat their swords into plowshares,
their spears into pruning hooks.
Nation shall not raise sword against nation;
no more will they learn to make war.
4 Every man will sit beneath his grapevine,
under his fig tree with none to trouble him,
for the LORD of Hosts has spoken.
5 For all peoples
follow, each the call of his god;
we will follow the LORD our God, His call,
for ever and ever.

6 On that day, so says the LORD:
I will gather the lame,
draw close those driven away
and any I have afflicted.
7 I will set the lame as the remnant
and her who was far removed as a great nation,
and the LORD will reign over them
in Mount Zion
from then and forever.

8 And now you, Migdal Eder,[10]
the tower of daughter Zion to you will come;
the ruling power will return as first it was,
and the crown to daughter Jerusalem.
9 Now then,
why do you cry out loud?
Have you no king among you?
Is your advisor lost to you
that your agony overcomes you
like a woman in labor?
10 Suffer and strain
as a laboring woman, daughter Zion,
for now you will leave the city
and dwell in the open field.

10 | A town in the region of Beit Leḥem; see Genesis 35:21.

You will go as far as Babylon;
there you will be rescued;
it is there the LORD will redeem you
from the hand of your enemies.
11 Though now many nations
rally against you,
saying: "Let her be violated;
we will watch and gawk at Zion."[11]
12 But they know nothing of the LORD's thoughts;
they do not realize His design,
for He has gathered them
like sheaves on the threshing floor.
13 Rise and trample them, daughter Zion,
for I will make your horns iron,
your hoofs bronze.
You will crush multitudes of peoples.
You will dedicate their spoils to the LORD,
their riches to the Master of all the earth.
14 Now then, muster the warriors, O warrior daughter –
they have laid siege against us;
with their staff they lash the face
of the Judge of Israel.

5 1 You, Beit Leḥem Efrata,
minor among the clans of Yehuda –
from you, one will emerge
to rule Israel for Me,
one whose descent is from
an earlier time, from ancient days.
2 So, then, He will give them over
until that time when the laboring woman delivers.
Only then will the remaining brothers
return to the children of Israel.
3 And he will rise up and lead his flock with the strength of the LORD,
with the majesty of the name of the LORD his God,
and they will reside in safety,
for His greatness will be known to the ends of the earth.
4 This, then, will be peace
when Assyria comes to invade our land,
to trample our fortresses;
we will set against him seven shepherds
and eight commanders of men.
5 They will ravage the land of Assyria by sword
and the land of Nimrod[12] with the drawn blade,

11 | That is, at Zion's downfall.

12 | Assyria or Babylon (see Gen. 10:8–12).

and he will deliver us from Assyria when they invade our land
and trample our borders.

6 And the remnant of Yaakov
will be found amid countless peoples
as dew brought down from the Lord,
as ample rains shower upon grass;
they will not look to any man,
nor place their hopes in humankind.
7 The remnant of Yaakov will be among nations,
amid countless peoples,
like a lion among wild beasts of the forest,
like a young lion among flocks of sheep
whom, as they pass, he tramples and rips to pieces;
there is no one to save them.
8 Your hand shall be raised over your foes;
your enemies will be cut down.

9 On that day, so says the Lord:
I will cut out the horses from among you,
I will destroy your chariots,
10 and I will cut down the fortified cities of your land
and demolish all your fortresses.
11 I will cut out all practice of witchcraft,
and there will be no more fortune-tellers among you.

12 I will cut down your idols, the worship pillars from your midst;
no longer will you bow down to the craft of your hands.
13 I will rip out the Ashera[13] from your midst,
and I will destroy your cities.
14 I will lash out with My anger and wrath
in vengeance against nations
who did not heed My words.

6 1 Hear now what the Lord says:
Arise; argue your case before the mountains;
let the hills hear your plea.
2 Hear, O mountains, the Lord's dispute –
you, earth's everlasting foundations.
For the Lord has a dispute with His people;
He will contend with Israel:
3 My people!
How have I wronged you?
How have I worn you down?
Bear witness against Me,
4 for I brought you up from the land of Egypt;

---

13 | A prominent Canaanite goddess and the tree used in her worship.

I redeemed you from the house of slavery;
I sent Moshe, Aharon, and Miriam
to lead you.
5 My people, remember now
how Balak, king of Moav, schemed,
and how Bilam son of Beor responded;[14]
remember from Shitim to Gilgal[15]
so that you may come to realize
the righteous ways of the LORD.
6 What then can I offer the LORD
when I bow low to the God Most High?
Should I come before Him
with burnt offerings, with year-old calves?
7 Would the LORD want a thousand rams,
untold rivulets of oil?
Should I offer my firstborn as payment for my crimes,
the fruit of my womb for the sins of my being?
8 Man, God has told you what is good
and what the LORD seeks from you:
only to do justice, love goodness,
and walk modestly with your God.

9 The LORD's voice cries out to the city;
wise men will perceive Your name.
Heed the staff[16]
and Him who sanctioned it.
10 Are storerooms of evil still found
in the homes of the wicked?
And the scant measure
so detested by God?
11 Shall I be found innocent while using false scales
and a bag full of deceptive weights?
12 Her wealthy are filled with corruption;
her residents speak lies
with tongues of deceit in their mouths.
13 And so I will strike you with sickness,
ruin you for your sins.
14 You will eat and never be sated;
sickness will settle in your innards.
You will conceive
but bear no young,
and what you do bring forth
I will give over to the sword.

---

14 | See Numbers, chapters 22–25.

15 | Meaning the crossing of the Jordan in Joshua, chapters 2–5.

16 | The rod of punishment.

15 You will plant
but not reap,
you will tread olives
but have no oil to anoint,
and you will crush grapes
but drink no wine.
16 For the laws of Omri are upheld,
the conventions of Aḥav's house kept;[17]
you follow their counsel.
So then I will lay waste to you,
turn the people of this land into objects of disdain;
you will bear the shame of My people.

7 1 Woe is me!
I am like the last of summer fruit,
the gleanings of harvest.
No cluster of grapes is left to eat,
no first, ripe fig that I long for.
2 The righteous man is gone from the land;
no upright men remain;
all lie in wait for blood,
each snaring his brother in a net.
3 They extend their hands to enhance evil;
the official makes his request,
the judge names his price,
and the powerful man
states his heart's evil wish;
together they weave it.
4 The best of them are only prickly shrubs,
the most righteous worse than a thorn hedge.
The day you awaited will be the day of your reckoning;
now is your time of confusion.
5 Do not put your faith in a friend
nor place trust in a confidant;
guard your words
from her who lies in your arms.
6 For a son denigrates his father;
daughter rises up against mother;
women stand against their husbands' mothers;
a man's own household are his enemies.
7 Yet I, I will look toward the Lord;
I will await my God who will save me,
my God who will heed me.
8 My enemies, do not revel over me;

17 | For these kings' abuses, see 1 Kings, chapters 16–22.

though I fall I will rise;
though I sit in darkness,
the LORD is my light.

9 I will bear the rage of the LORD's anger,
for I have sinned against Him,
until He upholds my case
and favors my justice.
He will bring me out into the light;
I will behold His righteousness.
10 When my enemy sees this,
she will be covered with shame,
she who once said to me,
"Where is the LORD your God?"
My eyes will behold her defeat,
how she is now trampled
like mud in the streets.
11 The day for mending your walls,
that day is far away.
12 There will be a day
when they will come to you
from Assyria
and the cities of Egypt,
and from Egypt
to the river,
from sea to sea
and from mountain to mountain.
13 And their lands will be devastated
along with their people;
this is the fruit of their actions.

14 Shepherd Your people with Your staff,
the flock of Your legacy;
they will dwell safely in lush forest lands,
pasture in Bashan and Gilad[18]
as in ancient days.
15 As in the days when you came out of Egypt,
I will show My wonders.
16 Nations will see and be shamed
by the might they wielded;
they will place their hands over their mouths;
their ears will be deafened.
17 Like snakes they will lick the dust,
like slithering creatures of earth;
they will come quivering

18 | Rich pastureland east of the Jordan River; see Numbers 32:1–4.

out from their holes
in terror; they will come before the LORD our God,
and they will fear You.
18 Is there any God like You
who forgives iniquities,
who looks beyond the sins
of the remnant of His own people,
who does not hold onto His wrath forever
because He desires kindness?
19 He will again have compassion for us;
He will subdue our iniquities
and hurl all of our sins
into the deepest of seas.
20 You will show truth to Yaakov,
kindness to Avraham,
as You swore to our fathers
in the earliest days.

NAHUM/ NAḤUM

1 1 The oracle of Nineveh, a visionary book by Naḥum the Elkoshite.
2 The LORD is envious, an avenging God;
revengeful is the LORD, filled with burning fury;
the LORD takes vengeance on His foes;
He restrains His scorching wrath and awaits
His enemies.
3 The LORD is slow to anger,
immense in power.
Never will He let the guilty go unpunished.
The way of the LORD will be a raging whirlwind,
clouds as dust beneath His feet.
4 God berates the sea, parching it dry.
Each and every river He depletes.
Bashan and Carmel lie despondent,
the flowers of Lebanon
despondent, dying.
5 Mountains convulse before Him
and hills crumble;
the earth staggers from God's presence,
the world with all who live in it.
6 Who could possibly stand up to His rage?
Who could endure the fierceness of His fury?
His wrath rages like fire;
rocks shatter before Him.
7 Goodness is the LORD;

He, a refuge in days of distress,
knows who seeks His shelter.
8 With a ravaging flood
He will bring an utter end to this place.
As for His enemies,
He will pursue them into darkness.
9 What then do you contrive against the LORD?
He wreaks utter destruction
so that trouble will not strike a second time.
10 For they are ensnared as if by thorns,
soaked and soused with drink,
to be consumed entirely
like the driest of straw.
11 It is from you[1] that the architect of evil came,
he who plotted against the LORD,
who counseled to evil.

12 So says the LORD:
Though they are numerous and mighty,
still they shall be mowed down and disappear,
and as surely as I afflicted you,[2]
I will afflict you no more.
13 And now I will break off his yoke from you;
the straps of your shackles I will slash.
14 The LORD has ruled against you,[3]
that no seed will come from your name.
I will wipe out all idols and images
from the temple of your gods;
there I will prepare your grave,
for you are as nothing.

2 1 Behold: a messenger –
his feet tread upon the mountain; he bears tidings of peace.
O Yehuda, go ahead, celebrate your feasts;
once again you may fulfill your vows.
Never again will the wicked pass through you;
they will be utterly destroyed.
2 The hammer of war is rising against you;
fortify your defenses, guard your roads, ready yourself for battle,
summon all your strength.
3 For the LORD will restore the pride of Yaakov
like the pride of Israel.
For the plunderers have drained them bare;

1 | The prophet begins to address Nineveh, the capital of Assyria.
2 | The prophet now addresses Israel.
3 | The prophet returns to addressing Assyria.

they have trampled their vineyards.
4 The shields of his brave warriors are colored red;
his heroic troops are clad in crimson.
On this day as he prepares for battle,
the steel of the chariots glitters;
the cypress spears are poisoned and ready.
5 The chariots rush frenzied on the roadways,
clanging and ramming in the streets;
they appear like torches flashing,
strikes of lightning racing about.
6 He summons his warriors;
they stumble in their advance;
hastening to defend the walls,
they find the shielding barrier already in place.
7 The dams of the channels have been opened;
the palace washed away.
8 The queen, exposed in her disgrace, is taken away,
and like mournful doves, her handmaids wail
and beat their breasts in mourning.
9 Though Nineveh was a brimming pool from ancient times,[4]
now all flee from her.
"Stay, stay!"
but no one even looks back.
10 Plunder the silver,
plunder the gold.
Indeed, there is no limit to the storehouse of riches,
the endless articles of wealth.
11 She is devoid; she is devastated and drained;
their[5] hearts turn faint, knees buckle in fear; their loins are seized with trembling;
all gather, their faces blackened with ashes.
12 What then has become of the lion's den,
the pasture for grazing cubs
where the lion and lioness roamed freely with their whelp
and feared no one?
13 What then has become of the lion who ripped apart his prey, plentiful for his cubs,
who strangled victims for his lionesses,
who filled his caves with game,
his lair with spoils?
14 Behold, I will oppose you, says the Lord of Hosts.
I will burn your chariots up into smoke;
your young lions will be devoured by My sword,

4 | Meaning abundant in water and life.

5 | The remaining people of Nineveh.

I will sever your prey from the land,
the calls of your emissaries never again to be heard.

3 1 Woe to the bloodstained city,
the utterly treacherous place, suffused with plundering,
never lacking prey.
2 Hear the cracking whips,
the rattling wheels;
hear the pounding of stampeding horses,
the clatter of lurching chariots.
3 Mounted soldiers charge –
flame of the swords, flash of the spears;
masses lay slain, corpses upon corpses;
so endless are the carcasses
that they are stumbled over.
4 All this because of the many whorings of the prostitute –
this beautifully charming mistress of witchcraft,
who sells nations through her whoring,
and clans in her witchcraft.
5 Behold, I will oppose you, says the Lord of Hosts;
I will lift your skirts over your faces in disgrace;
I will reveal your nakedness to the nations,
to the kingdoms your shame.
6 I will hurl abhorrent filth upon you
and disgrace you;
I will make you into a repulsive, detestable public display.
7 So it will be that all who look upon you will flee
and say: Nineveh has been sacked,
but who will mourn for her?
Where could I ever find someone to comfort you?
8 Are you any better than Thebes,
situated amidst rivers, surrounded by water,
whose protective walls were the waters
and whose ramparts came from the depths of the sea?
9 The kingdom of Kush served as her strength;
the power of Egypt knew no limits.
She counted Put and Libyans
among her allies.
10 Yet even she was taken into exile, carried into captivity;
her babies were smashed to pieces at every street corner;
onlookers drew lots for her prominent people;
her powerful men were chained in shackles.
11 You too will be in a drunken stupor,
shriveled in hiding;
you too will beg for refuge
from the enemy.

12 All your fortresses will be
like the ripened first fruits of the fig tree:
lightly shaken, they drop easily
into the enemy's mouth.
13 Behold: your troops sit submissively like women; in your midst
the gates to your land fall gaping, open to your enemies;
fire consumes the bars of your gates.
14 Draw yourself water for the siege;
secure your strongholds;
prepare the clay and trample the mortar;
cast the bricks for the fortress.
15 But no matter what, there in your fortresses, fire will consume you;
the enemy sword will cut you down,
consume you like swarms of young locusts.
O, go ahead and multiply like young locusts;
make yourself many like banding locusts.
16 As you thrived,
your traders were more than the stars in the sky;
as locusts they stormed
and flew on.
17 Your rulers are like locusts, your generals like plagues of grasshoppers
who camp in hedges on cold days,
but as soon as the sun rises they swiftly flee,
who knows to where?
18 O king of Assyria, your shepherds sleep on duty;
your leaders are lounging;
your nation is scattered upon the mountains
with no one to gather them.
19 There is no healing your pain;
your blow is mortal.
All who hear what has become of you
will applaud your fall –
for are there any who have not suffered
your unrelenting evil?

HABAKKUK/ 1 1 The burden Ḥavakuk the prophet saw in a vision:
ḤAVAKUK
2 How much longer must I implore You, O Lord,
though You do not listen.
I scream out to You "violence!"
yet You bring no salvation.
3 Why then do You show me this evil?
You who see the oppression,

why are ruin and corruption before me
so that strife endures
and contention rises?
4 This then is why law will cease to exist
and justice will never prevail,
for the wicked besiege the righteous,
and justice becomes twisted.
5 Look around at the nations and witness:
feel stunned, bewildered, for I
will perform a deed in these very days
that you would not believe if you were told.
6 For behold, I am raising up the Chaldeans,
that harsh and impetuous nation
that sweeps the span of the earth
seizing homes not theirs –
7 they the dreaded and terrifying
who alone dictate law and power.
8 Their horses run faster even than leopards,
fiercer than wolves of the night;
their horsemen advance all over.
They come from far; horsemen come flying
like a vulture swooping swiftly to devour its prey.
9 They come intent on violence,
their faces relentless as the east wind,
and amass captives
countless as sand.
10 They ridicule kings
and scorn rulers;
every fortress is a mockery to them;
they pile dirt for siege ramps, and the city falls.
11 But then they will pass through as the wind blows
and be held guilty,
they who made their power their god.
12 But surely You are eternal,
O Lord my God, my Holy One,
You who will never die.
You, Lord, have assigned them to judge;
You, my Rock, have appointed them to rebuke.
13 You, with eyes too pure for seeing evil,
who cannot witness oppression,
how then can You look upon the wicked
and remain silent?
How can You allow the evil man to devour
a person more righteous than he?
14 How could You make man like fish in the sea,

like creeping creatures with none watching over them?
15 For they will all be caught by the fishhook,
entangled in their net
and gathered up into their trawl;
this will bring them happiness,
make them rejoice.
16 And so they worship their net,
make offerings to their trawl;
because of them their portions are plump,
their food plentiful.
17 And so they empty their nets
and with no mercy return to slaughtering nations.

2 1 I stand watch at my post;
I will not move from my lookout;
I wait to see what God will say to me
and how I will respond to the rebuke.
2 And the Lord answered me saying:
Write the vison
clearly onto the tablets
so that all may read it readily.
3 For there will be yet another vision in due time;
it will be a witness to the end
and not deceive.
Though it lingers, wait for it,
for when the time is right it will come;
it will not delay.
4 For behold – the arrogant man
his life will not be upright
but the righteous man lives on by his faith.
5 And just as wine betrays its drinker,
so too the haughty man is betrayed by his pride and knows no peace.
His greedy mouth gapes wide like Sheol;[1]
like death he swallows and is never sated.
Yet he conquers all nations around him
and amasses all peoples to himself.
6 Surely all these people tell tales of him,
sneer and mock him, saying:
Woe unto him who greedily takes what is not his;
for how long will he weigh himself down,
heavily in debt?
7 Suddenly your moneylenders will rise against you;
they will wake you and shake you,
and you will be their spoils.

---

1 | The netherworld.

8 And as you plundered countless nations,
so too all remaining nations will plunder you
for men's blood you spilt, for your assault upon lands,
the city, and all its inhabitants.

9 Woe to him who garners evil gains,
who brings ruin upon his home,
who places his nest up high
to keep himself out of harm's way.
10 You brought shame upon your household;
you destroyed many nations;
you are a sinner in your essence.
11 Even the stone set in the wall cries out,
and the wooden rafters answer.

12 Woe to him who builds a city with bloodshed,
who founds a town upon iniquity.
13 Is this not then from the LORD of Hosts
when peoples toil for the flames
and nations weary themselves for naught?
14 For then, the earth will be filled
with knowledge of the LORD's splendor
as waters cover the ocean floor.[2]

15 Woe to him who offers his companions drink,
spiking it with wrath;
he draws them into a drunken stupor
to see their nakedness.
16 You, sated by scandal rather than filled with glory,
now you too drink from the poisoned cup and become exposed;
the cup of the LORD's right hand will turn upon you,
and shame will replace your glory.
17 Your destruction of Lebanon will cover you with disgrace,
and the beasts you reduced to ruin will make you afraid
for men's blood you spilt, for your assault upon lands,
the city, and all its inhabitants.

18 Of what value is an idol created by a craftsman,
an image by a master of falsehood?
For the craftsman puts faith in his handiwork
but instead crafts mute idols.

19 Woe unto him that says to the wood, "Awake!"
To the lifeless stone, "Arise!"
Can it teach us?
Behold, it is wrapped with gold and with silver,

2 | Cf. Isaiah 11:9.

but no spirit breathes within it.
20 But the Lord is in His heavenly dwelling.
All the earth, be silent before Him.

3 1 A prayer Ḥavakuk the prophet sung with *shiggayon*:[3]

2 Lord, I have heard accounts of You and am afraid.
O Lord, in the coming years renew Your deeds;
in the coming years, make Yourself known;
in wrath, remember mercy.
3 God appears from Teiman,
the Holy One from Mount Paran.[4] Selah[5]
His splendor covers the heavens;
the earth is filled with His glory.
4 His radiance illuminates like light;
rays emanate from His every side;
therein lies His hidden strength.
5 Before Him will come plague,
fiery blight at His feet.
6 He stands and the earth shakes;
He looks and nations tremble;
age-old mountains shatter;
everlasting hills bow low;
all the world's ways are His.
7 I saw Kushan's tents afflicted
for sinning,
the curtains[6] in the land of Midyan
quiver.

8 Is the Lord angry at the rivers;
is it against the rivers that You rage?
Is Your fury against the ocean
so that You ride upon Your horses of war,
Your chariots of deliverance?
9 Your bow is unsheathed;
You keep Your word, Your oath to the tribes, Selah,
and split the earth open with rivers.
10 When the mountains see You they shiver;
streams of water flow through;
the deep sounds with thunder,
lifting its hands up high.
11 The sun, the moon stand still in their spheres;
by the light of Your bolts the world will march,

3 | Perhaps a tune or musical instrument; cf. Psalms 7:1.
4 | Localities in the southern desert.
5 | A liturgical or musical term of unknown meaning.
6 | That is, tent canvases.

by the glow of Your flashing spear.
12 In rage, You tread the earth;
in wrath, You trample nations.
13 You emerge to liberate Your people,
to liberate Your king.
You crush the head of the house of evil,
stripping it from the core up to its neck, Selah.

14 You pierce heads of cities with their own spears,
they who come in a storm to shatter me,
rejoicing as though
secretly devouring the needy.
15 You trample the ocean floor with Your steeds,
stirring mighty seas.
16 I hear this, and my gut churns;
my lips tremble at the sound.
Rot eats at my bones;
I shudder in my place.
Could I rest on the day of terror,
the day God rises up for His nation?
17 Though the fig tree will not flower,
nor will fruit fill the vines,
olives will grow gaunt
and grain fields yield no produce,
sheep will be removed from their pens,
and cattle will not be found in the sheds,
18 yet I will delight in the LORD;
I will rejoice in the God who will save me.
19 GOD, my LORD, my strength,
He makes my legs like a deer's
and guides me to stride to the heights.

This song is for the conductor;
to Him I offer my melodies.

ZEPHANIAH/TZEFANYA

1 1 This is the word of the LORD that came to Tzefanya son of Kushi son of
Gedalya son of Amarya son of Ḥizkiya in the days of Yoshiyahu son of
Amon, king of Yehuda:

2 I will erase everything
utterly from the face of the earth,
declares the LORD.
3 I will erase man
and animal,
birds of the sky
and fish of the sea;

misfortune will find
the evil men.
I will sever man
from the face of the earth,
so the LORD declares.
4 My hand will strike Yehuda
and all who dwell in Jerusalem.
I will sever every trace of Baal from this place,
every mention of pagan priests among priests;
5 those who bow before the hosts of the heavens on rooftops
and those who serve and swear loyalty
to the LORD and to Malkam[1] side by side;
6 those who have renounced the LORD
and those who never sought out the LORD
nor entreated Him.
7 Fall silent before the LORD GOD,
for the day of the LORD is near;
the LORD has readied a sacrificial feast;
His guests have been selected.

8 On the day of the LORD's feast
I will punish ministers, and kings' sons,
and all who dress in foreign clothes.
9 On that day I will punish
all who leap over the threshold in the manner of idolaters,[2]
and all who fill their master's palace
with violence and vice.

10 On this day, the LORD declares,
a cry will be heard from the Fish Gate,[3]
wailing from the second quarter,
and a shattering heartbreak from the hills.
11 Wail, you residents of the Makhtesh:
the merchants have been destroyed;
those weighed down by silver have been cut down.

12 And it shall come to pass:
I shall search Jerusalem with lamps;
I will punish men
who have settled like sediment,
saying in their hearts
that the LORD can do neither good nor harm.
13 Their wealth will be pillaged,

1 | God of the Amonites; see II Kings 23:13.
2 | See, e.g., I Samuel 5:5 for this practice.
3 | This and the following were localities in Jerusalem.

their homes laid waste;
they will build houses
but not dwell in them,
plant vineyards
but not drink of their wine.[4]
14 The terrible day of the LORD is near;
swiftly it draws near.
The LORD's day will resound
with bitter cries of brave men.
15 That day will be a day of wrath,
a day of trouble and torment,
a day of destruction and desolation,
a day of darkness and dread,
a day of concealment and clouds,
16 a day of blasting horns and trumpets of battle
against the fortified cities and fortressed towers.
17 I will besiege men with troubles;
they shall walk as if blind,
for they have sinned against the LORD,
and their blood shall spill like dust,
their flesh scattered like dung.
18 Neither their silver nor their gold
will save them.
On the day of the LORD's wrath,
in the fire of His fury,
all the land will be consumed;
for He will bring an end, a shocking end
to all who dwell in the land.

2 1 Gather yourselves together, collect yourselves,
O you unwanted nation,
2 before the ruling bears down upon you,
and the moment blows away like chaff,
before the LORD's wrath
befalls you,
before the day of the LORD's rage
comes upon you.
3 Seek out the LORD, all you humble folk
who have followed His Law.
Pursue righteousness, pursue decency;
possibly you might find refuge
on the day of the LORD's wrath.
4 For Aza shall be deserted
and Ashkelon desolate;

4 | Cf. Deuteronomy 20:5–7 and 28:30. Contrast with Deuteronomy 6:10–11.

Ashdod will be purged of its people in broad daylight
and Ekron ripped from its roots.[5]

5 Woe, coastland dwellers, people of Keretim;
the word of the Lord is averse to you;
O Canaan, land of the Philistines,
I shall destroy you
until no man remains.
6 And the coastland
will serve as pastures for shepherds,
pens and sheepfolds for flocks.
7 Those left of the House of Yehuda will be allotted this land;
here their flocks will feed.
Come evening their animals will lie down to rest
in the houses of Ashkelon,
when the Lord their God will remember them
and will restore them to their richness.
8 I have heard the slanderous smears of Moav
and the children of Amon's taunting
as they ridiculed My people
and gloated over their borders.
9 So says the Lord of Hosts, the God of Israel:
As surely as I live,
Moav shall become as Sedom
and the children of Amon as Amora –
a land of rustling thorny thistles
and stark salt pits,
a desolation everlasting.
My returning nation shall savor their spoils;
the survivors of My people shall stake their claim.
10 This, then, is what they will receive for their arrogance,
their slandering, their gloating
over the nation of the Lord of Hosts.
11 The Lord will inflict His terror upon them,
causing every earthly god to wither
and nations widespread to kneel down to Him,
each person from where he stands.
12 Even you Kushites, you too
will become victims of My sword.
13 He will reach His hand out to the North
and destroy Assyria;
He will reduce Nineveh to a desolate wasteland,
to parched desert dryness.
14 Herds from every land

5 | These curses are alliterative in Hebrew (e.g., *Azza azuva*).

will lie down in her midst;
both the pelican and the short-eared owl
will nest in the crevices of her columns,
their caws heard from the windows,
destruction seen from her doorways,
for the cedar rooftops have crumbled to ruins.
15 This, then, was the joyous city,
living without a care,
saying in her heart,
"I am superior; there is none beside me."
Alas, she has become
a desolate lair for beasts,
with every passerby
hissing and scornfully waving her off
with his hand.

3 1 Woe to her who is sullied and stained,
this city of deceit.
2 She who did not heed the voice,
she refused reproach.
In the LORD she has not placed her trust;
to her God she has not drawn herself close.
3 Sitting amidst her,
her rulers roar like lions over their prey;
her judges, wolves of the night,
do not leave even a bone for morning.
4 Her prophets are brazen
men of treachery;
her priests have profaned the holy,
pillaged the Law.
5 The LORD, righteous within her midst,
does no wrong;
morning after morning,
unfailingly,
His judgment comes to light –
but still the culprit knows no shame.
6 I have severed nations;
their fortresses lie abandoned.
I have turned their bustling boulevards into ruins
empty of passersby;
their cities, destroyed, have become desolate –
no man remains.
7 I said to Myself: Surely this will bring you to fear Me,
to heed My reproaches;
then her home will not be wiped out,
and all that I have designed against her will not befall –

but alas, eagerly they arose
and remained unrelenting in their corrupt ways.
8 So says the LORD: Only wait for Me,
wait for the day when I stand up in judgment
once and for all.
For it is My decree to gather the nations,
to amass the kingdoms;
I will pour out My wrath upon them,
all My burning anger,
and all the earth shall be consumed
by the fire of My rage.
9 Then I will transform the people's language
and turn their words into clear, clean speech
so that they may call upon the name of the LORD
and serve Him shoulder to shoulder.
10 From beyond the rivers of Kush,
even the peoples of Atarai and the daughter of Putzai[6]
will pay Me tribute.
11 On that day
you will no longer know shame for all the corrupt ways
in which you have sinned against Me,
for I will remove from your midst
those elated with pride,
and you shall no longer stand haughtily
on My sacred mountain.
12 I will leave the humble and destitute among you,
and they will find refuge in the LORD's name.
13 They who remain of Israel shall do no wrong;
they will speak no lies,
and words of deceit will not be found
upon their lips.
Like sheep they will graze and lie down,
and none shall cause them alarm.

14 Sing out, daughter Zion;
shout for joy, Israel;
be jubilant and rejoice wholeheartedly,
daughter Jerusalem.
15 The LORD has withdrawn His judgment;
He has banished your foes.
The LORD, King of Israel, is within you;
you will no longer fear evil.
16 Jerusalem on that day will be told:

6 | The identities of these peoples are unclear. Others understand *atarai* to mean "my supplicants" and *bat putzai* as "my scattered people."

Zion, do not be afraid;
do not throw your hands up in despair.
17 The LORD your God is among you;
He who is strong will bring salvation.
He rejoices, takes pleasure in you.
His love leads Him to be silent,
then He joyfully sings you songs of praise.
18 I will gather the mournful –
those who grieved for your lost celebrations
and all those burdened with shame.
19 Behold, I will confront all who then caused you to suffer.
I will rescue the lame
and draw close those driven away.

I will replace their shame with glory
and make them acclaimed throughout the lands.
20 At that time I will gather you together
and bring you home;
indeed, I will make you legendary and praised
among all the people of the earth.
Thus I will restore you and your people to your place
before your very eyes.
So says the LORD.

HAGGAI/ ḤAGAI

1 1 In the second year of King Daryavesh's reign, in the sixth month, on
the first day of the month, the word of the LORD came through Ḥagai
the prophet to Zerubavel son of She'altiel, governor of Yehuda, and to
Yehoshua son of Yehotzadak, the High Priest.

2 "So says the LORD of Hosts: This people says, 'The time has not come – the
3 time for the LORD's House to be built.'" Then the word of the LORD came
4 through the hand of Ḥagai the prophet: "Is it the time for you yourselves
to sit under roofs in your homes while this House lies desolate?

5 6 "Now says the LORD of Hosts: Take your ways to heart. You sow much but
bring in little, eat but are not satisfied, drink but remain sober. You clothe
yourselves but are not warmed, and anyone who earns wages receives them
into a pouch full of holes.

7 8 "So says the LORD of Hosts: Pay heed to your ways. Go up onto the
mountain, bring wood, and build My House. I will desire it and be glorified
9 by it, says the LORD. You expect much but receive little. You bring it home;
I cause it to wither. Why? Because of My House which remains desolate
while each of you keeps running back to his own house, says the LORD of
10 Hosts. Therefore, the skies lock up the dew above you;[1] the land locks
up its produce.

1 | Cf. Deuteronomy 11:17.

11 "I will call forth a drought over the land and the mountains; over the grains,
the young wine, and the fresh oil; over everything the land produces. I
will declare a drought over man and animal, even over the labor of their
hands."

12 Zerubavel son of She'altiel, Yehoshua son of Yehotzadak, the High Priest,
and all the remnant of the people listened to the voice of the Lord their
God and to the words of Ḥagai the prophet, for he was sent by the Lord
13 their God. The people feared the Lord. Then Ḥagai, messenger of the
Lord, sent by the Lord to the people, spoke: "So says the Lord: I am
with you."

14 Then the Lord roused the spirit of Zerubavel son of She'altiel, governor
of Yehuda, the spirit of Yehoshua son of Yehotzadak, the High Priest, and
the spirits of all the remnant of the people. They came and they carried
out the work on the House of the Lord of Hosts, their God.

15 This happened on the twenty-fourth day of the sixth month in the second
year of King Daryavesh's reign.

2 1 In the seventh month, on the twenty-first day of the month, the word of
2 the Lord came through Ḥagai the prophet: "Say now to Zerubavel son
of She'altiel, governor of Yehuda, and to Yehoshua son of Yehotzadak, the
3 High Priest, and to the remnant of the people: Who is there still among
you who saw this House in its first glory? As you see it now, it must seem
4 like nothing to you.[2] Now be strong, Zerubavel; the Lord has spoken.
Be strong, Yehoshua son of Yehotzadak, the High Priest; be strong, people
of the land; the Lord has spoken. Act, for I am with you; the Lord of
5 Hosts has spoken. That which I made into a covenant with you when you
left Egypt, that and My Spirit, stand here among you. Do not fear.

6 "For so says the Lord of Hosts: One more thing, but a small thing,[3] and I
7 will shake the heavens and the earth, the sea and the dry land. I will shake
all the nations, they will come with the riches of all the nations, and I will
8 fill this House with glory, says the Lord of Hosts. For Mine is the silver
9 and Mine the gold; the Lord of Hosts has spoken. The glory of this latter
House will be greater than the glory of the first, says the Lord of Hosts,
and I will bestow peace upon this place. The Lord of Hosts has spoken."

10 On the twenty-fourth day of the ninth month,[4] in the second year of
11 Daryavesh's reign, the word of the Lord came to Ḥagai the prophet: "So
12 says the Lord of Hosts: Now ask the priests for a ruling of Law: 'If a man
carries consecrated meat in the fold of his garment and with that fold
touches bread, or a cooked dish, or wine, or oil, or any other food, does
13 it become sanctified?'" The priests answered and said, "No." Ḥagai said,

2 | See Ezra 3:12.

3 | A small impediment; alternatively, "very soon."

4 | On the day the foundations for the Temple were laid; see verse 18.

"And if someone who has become impure through contact with the dead
touches any one of these things, does it become impure?" The priests
14 answered and said, "It becomes impure." Then Ḥagai spoke and said, "The
LORD has spoken: So too is this people, this nation before Me, and so is all
the labor of their hands. Everything they might offer there is impure.

15 "And now, pay heed from this day forward: Before stone was placed upon
16 stone in the Temple of the LORD, when you would come for a grain pile
of twenty, it was ten; and when you came to the vineyard to draw fifty
17 measures from a winepress, it would be twenty. I struck you with blight
and mildew; I struck you with hail. I struck all the labor of your hands. And
still you are not with Me – the LORD has spoken.

18 "Pay heed: From this day forward, from the twenty-fourth day of the ninth
month, from the day of the foundation of the Temple of the LORD, pay
19 heed. Is the seed still in the storehouse? Even the vine, fig, pomegranate,
and olive tree have not borne fruit. But from this day on, I will bless you."

20 Then on the twenty-fourth day of the month, the word of the LORD came
21 to Ḥagai a second time: "Tell Zerubavel, governor of Yehuda: I am going
22 to shake the heavens and earth, I will overturn the thrones of kingdoms,
and I will destroy the mighty dominion of nations; I will overturn the
chariot and its riders. The horses and their riders will fall, every man cut
23 down by the sword of his brother. On that day – the LORD of Hosts has
spoken – I will take you, Zerubavel son of She'altiel, My servant – the
LORD has spoken – and wear you close like a signet ring, for it is you whom
I have chosen. The LORD of Hosts has spoken."

ZECHARIAH/ZEKHARYA

1 1 In the eighth month of the second year of Daryavesh's reign, the word of
the LORD came to Zekharya son of Berekhya son of Ido the prophet:

2 "The LORD overflowed with fury against your forefathers.
3 Say to them:
So says the LORD of Hosts:
Come back to Me –
the LORD of Hosts has said –
and I will come back to you,
so says the LORD of Hosts.

4 "O, do not be like your forefathers, to whom the earlier prophets called,
saying:
So says the LORD of Hosts:
Return, please,
from your evil ways and your evil deeds.
They did not hear; they did not listen to Me –
the LORD has spoken.

5 Where are your forefathers?
Even the prophets – do they live forever?
6 Yet My words
and the rulings with which I charged My servants, the prophets,
did they not overtake your forefathers?

"They returned. They said: 'That which the LORD of Hosts devised to do to
us, befitting our ways and our deeds, indeed, He did with us.'"

7 On the twenty-fourth day of the eleventh month – which is the month of
Shevat – in the second year of Daryavesh's reign, the word of the LORD
came to Zekharya son of Berekhya son of Ido the prophet:

8 I saw in the darkness: a man mounted on a blood bay horse stood among
the myrtles in the deep, with blood bay, sorrel, and white horses behind
9 him. I said, "What are these, my lord?"

The angel with whom I spoke said to me, "I will show you what these are."

10 Then the man standing among the myrtles spoke. He said, "These are the
ones that the LORD sent to rove the land."

11 They spoke to the angel of the LORD, standing among the myrtles. "We
have roved the land. The whole land sits settled and quiet," they said.

12 The angel of the LORD spoke and said, "LORD of Hosts, how long will You
have no mercy on Jerusalem and the cities of Yehuda against whom You
have been filled with wrath these seventy years?"

13 Then the LORD answered the angel with whom I spoke with good words,
words of comfort.

14 So the angel with whom I spoke said to me, "Call out:
So says the LORD of Hosts:
I have been greatly zealous
on behalf of Jerusalem and Zion,
15 and I have been greatly furious
at those complacent nations.
I was only somewhat furious,
but they aided evil.
16 Therefore, so says the LORD:
I have returned to Jerusalem in mercy.
My House will be built in it –
the LORD of Hosts has spoken –
and a measuring cord will be drawn over Jerusalem.

17 "Call out again:
So says the LORD of Hosts:
Once again
My city will brim over with good,

and the Lord will again comfort Zion;
again He will choose Jerusalem."

2 1 2 I lifted my eyes and saw: There were four horns. I said to the angel with
whom I spoke: "What are these?" He said, "These are the horns that
scattered Yehuda, Israel, and Jerusalem."[1]

3 4 The Lord showed me four craftsmen. I said, "What are these coming to
do?" He said, "These are the horns that scattered Yehuda so that no man
could lift his head. And those, they are coming to terrify them, to cast
down the horns of the nations who lifted their horns against the land of
Yehuda, scattering her."[2]

5 I raised my eyes and saw: there was a man with a measuring cord in his
6 hand. "Where are you going?" I said. He said, "To measure Jerusalem. To
see how wide and how long she is."

7 Suddenly the angel with whom I spoke emerged, and another angel came
8 out to meet him. He told him, "Run, tell that attendant that Jerusalem shall
be settled beyond her walls from the abundance of people and animals
within her."

9 I will be for her –
the Lord has spoken –
an encircling wall of fire.
I will be the Glory within her.

10 Hie, hie, and flee from the northland –
the Lord has spoken –
for like the four winds I have spread you far –
the Lord has spoken.
11 Hie, Zion, escape,
O dweller with daughter Babylon,

12 for so says the Lord of Hosts:
In the wake of Glory
He sent me to the nations that have plundered you,
for he who harms you
harms that which is reflected in His eyes.
13 I will brandish My hand over them,
and they will be plundered by their slaves.
You will know that the Lord of Hosts sent me.

14 Shout out and be joyful, daughter Zion,
for I am coming,
and I will dwell in your midst –

1 | The Hebrew word *keranot* (horns) can also mean "corners." This could refer to the kings of Mesopotamia, who claimed to rule the four corners of the earth.

2 | The craftsmen might symbolize the rebuilding of the Temple, which took place at this time.

the Lord has spoken.
15 Many nations
will join themselves to the Lord on that day,
and they will be My people.
I will dwell in your midst,
and you will know
that the Lord of Hosts sent me to you.
16 The Lord will take possession of Yehuda
as His portion of holy ground,
and He will choose Jerusalem once again.

17 Hush, all flesh, before the Lord,
for He has stirred
from His holy abode.

3 1 Then He showed me Yehoshua the High Priest standing before an angel
2 of the Lord with the Adversary on his right to oppose him.[3] The Lord
said to the Adversary:

"The Lord drives you away, Adversary.
The Lord, who has chosen Jerusalem,
drives you away.
Yes, this is a firebrand saved from the fire."

3 And Yehoshua, wearing filthy clothing, was standing before the angel, who
4 spoke and said to those standing before him, "Take those filthy clothes off
him." Then the angel said to him, "See, I have removed your guilt from you
and dressed you in finery."

5 I said, "Place a pure turban on his head," and they placed a pure turban on
his head. They dressed him in clothing.[4]

The angel of the Lord remained standing.

6 Then that angel of the Lord testified regarding Yehoshua:

7 "So says the Lord of Hosts:
If you walk in My ways,
if you keep My watch,
if you judge My House,
and guard My courtyards,
then I will give you walkers
among these who are standing.[5]

8 "Listen, Yehoshua the High Priest, you and your friends who sit before you,
for they are men of wonders: Behold, I am bringing My servant Tzemaḥ.[6]

---

3 | Cf. Psalms 109:6.
4 | The priestly garments, symbolizing investiture (see Lev., ch. 8).
5 | That is, Yehoshua will be able to stand among the angels.
6 | *Tzemaḥ* means "plant" or "shoot," referring to a royal heir (cf. Is. 11:1).

9 Upon the stone that I set before Yehoshua, one stone with seven eyes,[7] I
will engrave its inscription, and I will wipe away the guilt of this land in
10 one day. On that day – the LORD of Hosts has spoken – you will call one
to another: Come under the shade of the vine; come under the shade of
the fig."

4 1 Then the angel with whom I had spoken returned and roused me like a man
2 stirring from his sleep. He said to me, "What do you see?" I said, "I see a
candelabrum of pure gold, its bowl at the top. It has seven lamps – seven – and
3 seven indentations for the lamps, which are at the top.[8] Next to it are two
4 olive trees, one to the right of the bowl and one to its left." I spoke and
5 said to the angel with whom I spoke, "What are these, my lord?" And the
angel with whom I spoke replied and said, "You know what these are." I
said, "No, my lord."

6 Then he spoke and said to me, "This is the word of the LORD to Zerubavel:

Not with valor
  and not with strength,
but with My spirit,
  says the LORD of Hosts.

7 "Who are you, great mountain before Zerubavel? Surely it will become a
level plain. He will remove the re-foundation stone[9] with clamor: Favor,
favor to her!"

8 9 Then the word of the LORD came to me: "Zerubavel's hands founded this
House, and his hands will complete it. You will know that the LORD of
10 Hosts sent me to you, for whosoever scorned the day of small things[10] will
rejoice seeing the measuring stone in Zerubavel's hand.

"These seven, they are the eyes of the LORD, roaming throughout the
land."

11 Then I spoke and said to him, "What are those two olive trees to the right
12 and to the left of the candelabrum?" And again I spoke. I said, "What are
these two olive branches next to the golden pipes that stream golden oil
13 from above?" He said to me, "You know what these are." I said, "No, my
14 lord." He said, "These are the two sons of the anointed ones[11] who stand
beside the LORD of all the land."

5 1 2 Once again I raised my eyes and saw a flying scroll. He said to me, "What
do you see?" I said, "I see a flying scroll twenty cubits long and ten cubits

---

7 | The eyes may symbolize God's providence and protection.

8 | Cf. Exodus 25:31–37.

9 | Referring to a stone from the old, ruined palace or temple that served as a symbolic foundation for the new.

10 | Meaning the day on which construction for the Second Temple was undertaken (see Hag. 2:3).

11 | Zerubavel and Yehoshua, anointed king and priest, respectively.

3 wide." And He said to me, "This is the curse emerging all over the land;
every thief has been spared what is written here. Every person who swears
4 has been spared what is written here. But I have brought it out – the LORD
of Hosts has spoken – and it will come into the house of the thief and the
house of the one who swears falsely in My name. It will lodge in his house
and destroy it, wood and stones and all."

5 Then the angel with whom I spoke approached and said to me, "Raise
6 your eyes and see. What is that approaching?" I said, "What is it?" He
said, "This is the ephah[12] emerging." He said, "This is their seeing eye all
over the land."

7 8 A lead weight is lifted. There is a lone woman sitting in the ephah. He said,
"She is the evil." He cast her into the ephah, then dropped the lead stone
onto its opening.

9 I raised my eyes and saw: there were two women approaching, wind in
their wings, and their wings were like the wings of a stork. They lifted
10 the ephah up between the earth and the heavens. I said to the angel with
11 whom I spoke, "Where are they taking the ephah?" He said to me, "To
build it a house in the land of Shinar,[13] established and placed there on
its foundation."

6 1 Once again I lifted my eyes and saw: four chariots emerging from between
2 two mountains. The mountains were of bronze. The first chariot was
hitched to blood bay horses; the second chariot was hitched to black
3 horses; the third chariot was hitched to white horses; and the fourth one
4 was hitched to brindle horses, mighty ones. Then I spoke and said to the
5 angel with whom I spoke, "What are these, my lord?" The angel spoke and
said, "They are the four winds of the skies, stationing themselves before the
6 LORD of all the earth. The chariot with the black horses is going out to the
northland, the white ones behind them. The brindle horses are going out
7 to the southland." Then these mighty ones went out and sought to go, to
rove the earth. So He said, "Go, rove the earth." And the chariots went and
8 roved the earth. He spurred me on and spoke to me, saying: "See, those
going out to the northland, they set My spirit upon the northland."[14]

9 10 Then the word of the LORD came to me: "Take from the exiles – from
Ḥeldai, from Tuvya, from Yedaya who came from Babylon – and come,
you yourself, on that day; come to the house of Yoshiya son of Tzefanya.
11 Take silver and gold; make crowns and set one on the head of Yehoshua
12 son of Yehotzadak the High Priest. Tell him, so says the LORD of Hosts:

There is a man;
  Tzemaḥ is his name.

---

12 | A dry measure, equivalent to approximately 25 liters.

13 | Another name for Bavel (see, e.g., Gen. 10:10).

14 | Conquerors such as the Babylonians generally invaded from the north (cf. Jer. 1:13–14).

He will come to flower
from where he is
and build
the Sanctuary of the Lord.
13 Lo, he will build
the Sanctuary of the Lord.

He will wear majesty;
he will sit and
rule on his throne.

"The priest, also, will sit on his own throne, and between them there will
be peaceful counsel.

14 "Let these crowns be a monument for Ḥelem, Tuvya, Yedaya, and Ḥen
15 son of Tzefanya in the Sanctuary of the Lord. Then those from afar will
come and build the Sanctuary of the Lord, and you will know that the
Lord of Hosts sent me to you.

"This is what will be if you indeed heed the voice of the Lord your God."

7 1 In the fourth year of King Daryavesh's reign, on the fourth of the ninth
month, Kislev, the word of the Lord came to Zekharya:

2 Beit-El, Saretzer, and Regem Melekh[15] and his men sent to entreat the
3 Lord, to ask the priests at the House of the Lord of Hosts and the
prophets, too: Should I weep in the fifth month,[16] deny myself as I have
done these many years?

4 5 Then the word of the Lord came to me: "Tell all the people of the land
and the priests as well: When you fasted and mourned during the fifth
and seventh[17] months these seventy years, was it for Me? Was it for Me
6 that you fasted? When you eat and when you drink, are you not the ones
eating and drinking?"

7 Were these not the words called by the Lord through the earlier prophets
when Jerusalem was settled and serene, her cities around her, too; when
the Negev and the lowlands were settled?

8 9 Then the word of the Lord came to Zekharya: "So says the Lord of Hosts:
10 Judge truthful justice; show kindness and compassion to one another. Do
not oppress the widow or orphan, stranger or poor person, and do not
11 think evil of your brother in your hearts. But they refused to listen. They
turned a stubborn shoulder and closed their ears so that they could not
12 hear; they set their hearts like adamant so as not to hear the Torah and
the words sent through the earlier prophets by the spirit of the Lord of

15 | Presumably Jewish leaders in the Babylonian exile.

16 | The fast of the Ninth of Av, commemorating the destruction of the Temple (II Kings 25:8).

17 | The fast of Gedalya, commemorating his assassination (Jer., ch. 41).

13 Hosts. Then a terrible fury arose from the LORD of Hosts: Because when
He called they did not hear Him, so they call and I do not hear, says the
LORD of Hosts.

14 "So in a storm I blew them away to all the nations who do not know
them.

"They left behind them a land barren of wayfarers. They laid this desired
land waste."

8 1 Then the word of the LORD of Hosts came:

2 So says the LORD of Hosts:
I was fiercely zealous
on Zion's behalf;
on behalf of her
I was zealous with a great wrath.

3 So says the LORD:
I have returned to Zion
and dwelled within Jerusalem.
Jerusalem will be called
City of Truth,
the Mountain
of the LORD of Hosts,
the Holy Mountain.

4 So says the LORD of Hosts:
Once again
old men
and old women
will sit in the squares of Jerusalem.
In old age
a man will lean
on the staff in his hand,
5 and the city squares
will be full and alive
with young boys and girls
playing in her open squares.

6 So says the LORD of Hosts:
Though it was wondrous in the eyes of this nation in those days,
would it be wondrous to My eyes?
The LORD of Hosts has spoken.

7 So says the LORD of Hosts: Behold, I will deliver My nation from the east
8 land and the land of the setting sun. I will bring them back, and they will
dwell within Jerusalem. They will be My nation, and I will be their God
in truth and beneficence.

9 So says the LORD of Hosts: Be strong! Be like those who heard these
words in those days from the prophets who were present on the day
the foundations were laid for the House of the LORD of Hosts, for His
10 Sanctuary to be built.[18] Previously, in those days, there were neither wages
for man nor recompense for animals; there was no peace from the enemy
for those who came and went. I set all of humanity against one another.

11 But now I will not be as in those first days for the remnant of this
12 people – the LORD of Hosts has spoken. These are the seeds of peace: the
vine will give its fruit, the land its produce, and the skies their dew. I will
13 give all of this to the remnant of this people to possess. Just as you were
a curse among the nations, House of Yehuda and House of Israel, to that
degree I will deliver you, and you will be a blessing.
Do not fear.
Be strong.

14 For so says the LORD of Hosts: Insofar as I planned to cause you trouble
when your forefathers angered Me, says the LORD of Hosts, and did not
15 relent, to that degree I have again planned in these days to do good with
Jerusalem and the House of Yehuda.
Do not fear.
16 This is what you should do:
Speak truthfully, one to another. In your gates render judgments of truth
17 and peace. Think not evil of one another in your hearts.
Do not love the false oath.
I hate all of these –
the LORD has spoken.

18 The word of the LORD of Hosts came to me:

19 So says the LORD of Hosts: The fasts of the fourth month and of the
fifth and the seventh and the tenth – all of these will be for the House of
Yehuda joy and happiness, and times set aside for good. Therefore, love
truth and peace.[19]

20 So says the LORD of Hosts: Once again nations, dwellers of many cities,
21 will come, and the dwellers of one city will go, saying one to another, one
by one, "Let us go entreat the face of the LORD, beseech the LORD of Hosts.
22 I too will go." Then many nations will come – great peoples – to beseech the
LORD of Hosts in Jerusalem, to entreat the face of the LORD.

23 So says the LORD of Hosts: It will be in those days that ten men of many
languages will cling, they will cling to the hem of a Jewish man and say,
"Let us go with you, for we have heard that God is with you."

---

18 | See Haggai 2:2–4 and Ezra, chapter 3.

19 | See notes on 7:3–5. The fast of the fourth month is the Seventeenth of Tammuz, commemorating the breach of Jerusalem's walls (see Jer. 39:2). That of the tenth month is the Tenth of Tevet, commemorating the beginning of the siege (see II Kings 25:1 and Ezek. 24:2).

9 1 An oracle:
The word of the Lord is in Ḥadrakh;[20]
Damascus is its resting place.
For the eyes of man
turn to the Lord
and to the tribes of Israel.
2 Even Ḥamat
will be bordered by it,
Tyre and Sidon,
for in great wisdom
3 Tyre built herself a tower;
she hoarded silver like dust
and gold like street mud,
4 but the Lord will dispossess her,
strike her forces at sea,
while she herself will be consumed by flame.
5 Ashkelon will look on in fear;
Aza will shudder and shake;
Ekron too,
for the one she looks to will be debased:
A king will be lost in Aza,
Ashkelon will be unpeopled,
6 a bastard will sit in Ashdod,
and I will cut off the majesty of the Philistines.
7 But I will wash away the blood in his mouth,
the detestable things between his teeth,
and he, he too will remain for our God
and be like a chieftain in Yehuda,
while Ekron will be like a Jebusite.
8 I will be an encampment around My House
against armies,
against those who come and go.
No more shall any oppressor overrun them,
for now I have seen with My eyes.

9 Rejoice mightily,
daughter Zion;
call out joyfully,
daughter Jerusalem.
Yes, your king is coming to you.
He is righteous and has prevailed –
humble, riding a donkey,
a yearling, purebred.
10 There will be no more chariots in Efrayim,

20 | A town in the region of Damascus.

nor horses in Jerusalem.
No longer will there be bows of war.
For he will speak words of peace with the nations,
and his rule will span
from sea to sea,
from the river to the ends of the earth.
11 You too:
for the sake of the blood of your covenant,
I released your prisoners
from a waterless pit.
12 Return to the stronghold,
O prisoners of hope.
Even today I will answer you,
messenger after messenger.
13 I aimed Yehuda like a bow;
Efrayim I filled like a quiver.
I roused your children, Zion,
against your children, Ionia,[21]
and wielded you like a warrior's sword.
14 The Lord God will appear above them;
His arrow flies like a strike of lightning.
The Lord God will sound a ram's horn
and rush in on southern storms.
15 The Lord of Hosts will protect them.
They will consume; they will conquer
slingstones.
They will drink, clamor as if with wine
brimming over like a bowl,
like the corners of the altar.
16 On that day
the Lord their God will save them
like sheep, His people,
for they are crown jewels
displayed above His land.
17 For how good is His good,
how lovely His beauty:
Young men like wheat;
young women blossoming with wine.

10 1 Ask the Lord for rain
in the time of spring showers,
and the Lord will strike lightning;

21 | Ionia was a region in Asia Minor inhabited by Hellenic (Greek-speaking) peoples; the name Yavan eventually came to refer in Hebrew to the Greek lands and peoples in general.

He will bring down torrents of rain;
He will give grass in the field
to man.
2 For the household idols spoke deceit,
and the seers falsely saw.
They tell of empty dreams;
their comfort means nothing.
Therefore they wandered like sheep;
they were defeated,
for they were without a shepherd.

3 My wrath is upon those shepherds,
and I will visit punishment upon those goat sires,
for the LORD of Hosts has redeemed His flock;
He has redeemed the House of Yehuda
and made them like His magnificent horse
charging in battle.
4 From Him the cornerstone;
from Him the tent peg;
from Him the bow of war;
from Him every ruler emerges
together.
5 They will be like heroes
treading through field mud in battle.
They will fight,
for the LORD is with them,
and they will put riders of horses to shame.
6 I will strengthen the House of Yehuda
and deliver the House of Yosef.
I will bring them back to roost
with My mercy upon them,
and they will be
as if I never abandoned them.
For I am the LORD, their God,
who will answer them.
7 Efrayim will be like a hero.
Their hearts will be glad like wine.
Their children will see and be glad.
Their hearts will rejoice in the LORD.
8 I will surely whistle for them, gather them in,
for I will redeem them,
and they will multiply
as once they multiplied.
9 I will scatter them like seeds among the nations;
in far-off places they will remember Me.
They will live

along with their children
and return.
10 I will bring them back from the land of Egypt;
from Ashur, I will gather them in
and bring them to the land of
Gilad and Lebanon,
and still, it will not be enough for them.
11 He will trawl trouble through the sea,
strike the ocean waves,
and dry will be the depths of the Nile.
Ashur's majesty will be cast down,
and rule shall pass away from Egypt.
12 I will strengthen them in the LORD,
and they will walk with His name –
the LORD has spoken.

11 1 Lebanon, open your doors,
and fire will consume your cedar trees.
2 Wail, O juniper tree, for the cedar,
devastated by august ones,
has fallen.
Wail, O oaks of the Bashan,
for the fortified forest
has been felled.
3 O, the sound, the wail
of the shepherds
for their devastated glory.
O, the sound, the roar
of young lions
for the devastated lush thicket along the Jordan.

4 So says the LORD, my God: "Herd the sheep marked for slaughter, those
5 whom buyers will kill and feel no guilt, whose sellers will say, 'Blessed be
the LORD, I will be rich'; whose shepherds have no mercy upon them.

6 "For I will no longer spare
the people of the land –
the LORD has spoken –
but indeed, I will
hand over every person into
the hands of their fellows,
into the hand of their king.
They will harrow the earth.
I will deliver no one
from their hands."

7 So I herded the sheep marked for slaughter, for they were ailing sheep. I

took two staffs – one I called Pleasant; the other I called Harmful. I herded
8 the sheep with them. I removed three shepherds in the space of one month,
for I had lost my patience with them, and they too were disgusted with
9 me. I said, "I will not herd for you; the dying will die, the lost will remain
10 lost, and as for those ewes that remain, they will eat one another's flesh." I
took my staff, I took Pleasant, and snapped it so as to annul my covenant,
the one I made with all the nations.

11 Yes, on that day it will be annulled, and those ailing sheep whom I guarded
12 will indeed know that this is the word of the LORD. I said to them, "If you
wish, pay me, but if not, do not." So they measured out my salary of thirty
13 shekel. Then the LORD said to me, "Throw it away to the treasury in that
eminent place where I granted them eminence." So I took the thirty shekel
14 and threw them into the Temple treasury. Then I snapped my second staff,
Harmful, so as to annul the brotherhood between Yehuda and Israel.

15 Then the LORD said to me, "Once again, take up the instrument of a foolish
16 shepherd, for I am going to establish a shepherd in this land:
He will not render an account of the lost,
nor seek out the young one.
He will not heal the broken,
nor provide for the lame.
But he will consume
the healthy fleshed
and break their hooves.

17 "Hie, worthless shepherd,
abandoner of sheep.
A sword be upon his arm,
and his right eye!
His arm will surely wither,
his right eye surely darken."

12 1 An oracle, which is the word of the LORD regarding Israel:
The LORD who spread out heaven,
laid the foundations of earth,
and created the spirit of man within him,
has spoken:

2 So it will be: that I will make Jerusalem as a cup of reeling for all those
nations surrounding her, even for Yehuda it will be so by a siege upon
Jerusalem.

3 On that day when the nations of the land gather against her, I will make
Jerusalem a boulder to all the nations; all those who dare lift it will surely
be deeply wounded.

4 On that day – the LORD has spoken –

I will strike every horse with terror
and their riders with insanity.
I will keep an open eye
on the House of Yehuda
but strike all the nations' horses with blindness.
5 Then the chieftains of Yehuda will say in their hearts: "I take strength from
the strength that the residents of Jerusalem find in the LORD of Hosts,
their God."

6 On that day, I will make the chieftains of Yehuda
like a fire basin alight among the trees,
like a flaming torch among the sheaves,
and they will consume everything
to the right and to the left of them:
all the surrounding nations.
7 Then Jerusalem will still remain in its place, in Jerusalem, and the LORD
will save the tents of Yehuda first so that the glory of the House of David
and the glory of the residents of Jerusalem does not become greater than
that of Yehuda.

8 On that day the LORD will protect the residents of Jerusalem.

On that day the most stumbling of them will be like David, and the House of David will be like a god, an angel of the LORD, before them.

9 On that day I will seek to destroy all the nations coming against Jerusalem.
10 Then I will pour out a spirit of favor and supplication over the House of
David and the residents of Jerusalem, and they will look to Me regarding
the one whom they stabbed. They will mourn for him as a person mourns
for an only child, and their bitterness will be the bitterness of the loss of
a firstborn.

11 On that day the mourning in Jerusalem will be greater than the mourning
12 of Hadad-Rimon[22] in the Valley of Megidon. The whole land will mourn,
every family on its own: the family of the House of David on its own, the
women on their own, the family of the house of Natan on its own, the
13 women on their own, the family of the House of Levi on its own, the
women on their own, the Shimi family on its own, the women on their
14 own, all the remaining families, every family, on its own, all the women
on their own.

13 1 On that day a spring will flow for the House of David and the residents of
2 Jerusalem, providing for water of lustration[23] and purification offering. On
that day – the LORD of Hosts has spoken – I will eradicate the names of

22 | Hadad and Rimon were names of Aramean gods; the verse may refer to an idolatrous rite.

23 | See Numbers 19:9.

the idols from the land. They will never be spoken of again. I will remove
the prophets and the spirit of impurity from the land.

3 And should a person prophesy still, then his father and mother, those who
bore him, will say, "You shall not live, for you have spoken falsely in the
name of the LORD." Then his father and mother, those who bore him, will
stab him in the act of his prophecy.

4 On that day the prophets will be ashamed of their vision, each one of
them, when they prophesy. They will no longer wear a mantle of hair to
5 deceive. He will say, "I am not a prophet; I am a worker of the land, made a
6 herdsman in my youth." And if someone should ask him, "What are those
bruises between your shoulders?" he will reply, "Those are the bruises I
received in the house of those who love me."

7 Awake, O sword,
against My shepherd,
against the man beside Me –
the LORD of Hosts has spoken.
Strike the shepherd
and let the sheep be scattered,
while I,
I will set My Hand
against the little ones.

8 This is what will be all over the land – the LORD has spoken – two-thirds
of the population will be cut down; they will die. One-third will remain.
9 I will pass that third through fire and refine them as one refines silver,
and test them as one tests gold.

He will call in My name,
and I will answer him.
I will say, "He is My nation,"
and he will say,
"The LORD is my God."[24]

14 1 Behold, a day of the LORD is coming; your spoil will be divided up in your
2 midst. I will gather all the nations to Jerusalem in war: the city will be
taken, the houses will be plundered, and the women will be raped; half
of the city will go into exile, but the remainder of the people will not be
3 cut off from the city. The LORD will go out, and He will fight against these
4 nations as He has fought on days of battle. On that day His feet will stand
upon the Mount of Olives which faces Jerusalem on the east, and the
Mount of Olives will split through its middle – into a great valley – from
east to west. Half the mountain will shift northward and half southward.
5 And you will flee from this Valley of the Mountains, for the Valley of the
Mountains will reach as far as Atzal; you will flee as you fled from the

24 | Cf. Hosea 2:25.

earthquake in the days of Uziya, the king of Yehuda, and the Lord will
6 come – my God, and all the holy ones with You. This is what will be: on
7 that day there will be neither bright light nor thick darkness. This is what
will be: there will be a day known to the Lord; it will be neither day nor
8 night, but at evening time there will be light. This is what will be: on that
day living waters will flow out from Jerusalem, half to the eastern sea and
9 half to the western sea; in summer and winter it will be so. Then the Lord
shall be King over all the earth; on that day the Lord shall be One and
10 His name One. Then the land will be smoothed out like a plain from Geva[25]
to Rimon, until the area south of Jerusalem, and Jerusalem will be lifted
up in her place. From the Gate of Binyamin to the site of the First Gate
and to the Corner Gate, from the Tower of Ḥananel to the king's winery,
11 they will inhabit her. There will be no more devastation, and Jerusalem
will live in safety.

12 This will be the plague that the Lord will bring upon all the peoples who
fought against Jerusalem: their flesh will rot away as they stand on their
feet, their eyes will rot in their sockets, and their tongues will rot in their
13 mouths. This is what will be: on that day the turmoil the Lord brings on
them will be great, and each man will seize another by the arm and raise
14 his fist against his neighbor's fist. And Yehuda too will fight in Jerusalem,
and the wealth of all the surrounding nations, great quantities of gold,
15 silver, and clothing, will be gathered in. There will be a plague just like
this plague on the horses, the mules, the camels, and the donkeys, and on
every animal in those camps.

16 This is what will be: all those remaining from all the nations who came
up against Jerusalem will go up year after year to bow down to the King,
17 Lord of Hosts, and to celebrate the Festival of Tabernacles. This is what
will be: the families of the land who do not go up to Jerusalem and bow
18 down to the King, Lord of Hosts, rain shall not fall for them. If the family
of Egypt does not go up, does not come, it shall not be upon them. This
will be the plague that the Lord will bring upon the nations who do not
19 go up to celebrate the Festival of Tabernacles. Such will be the punishment
of Egypt and the punishment of all the nations who do not come up to
celebrate the Festival of Tabernacles.

20 On that day even the bells of the horses will be inscribed "sacred to the
Lord," and the pots in the House of the Lord will be like basins before
21 the Altar. This is what will be: every pot in Jerusalem and in Yehuda will
be sacred to the Lord of Hosts, and all those who come to sacrifice will
take them and will cook in them. On that day, there will be no more need
for traders in the House of the Lord of Hosts.

---

25 | North of Jerusalem.

MALACHI/ MALAKHI

1 1 An oracle:
the word of the LORD to Israel through Malakhi.[1]

2 The LORD says, "I have loved you."
But you say, "How have You loved us?"
Is Esav not a brother to Yaakov?
So says the LORD: Yet I loved Yaakov
3 and hated Esav,
so I made his mountains desolate
and gave his inheritance over to desert jackals.

4 Even should Edom say,
"We have been destroyed,
but we will return and rebuild the ruins,"
says the LORD of Hosts,
they will build;
I will destroy,
and they will be called
the territory of evil
and the nation that suffers
the LORD's wrath forever.

5 Your eyes will see this, and you will say,
"The LORD is great beyond the territory of Israel."

6 A son honors his father,
and a slave his master;
if I am a Father,
where is My honor,
and if I am the Master,
where is My reverence?
So says the LORD of Hosts to you,
the priests who scorn My name.

Yet you say, "How have we scorned Your name?"
7 You offer defiled bread on My altar.

Yet you say, "How have we defiled You?"
In saying the LORD's table is repugnant.

8 When you offer a blind animal to be sacrificed,
is this no evil?[2]
And when you offer the lame and the sick,
is this no evil?

Offer it if you will to your governor.
Would he then accept you –

---

1 | Either the prophet's name or a title: "My servant."

2 | See the prohibition in Deuteronomy 17:1.

let you lift your face to him?
So says the Lord of Hosts.

9 Now, please, beseech God,
and let Him be gracious to us.
This was in your hands –
would He turn His face for any one of you?

So says the Lord of Hosts:
10 O, who is there among you
who would close the doors
so that you might not light
My altar for naught?

I have no desire for you,
says the Lord of Hosts.
I will accept no
offering from your hands.

11 For from one end of the earth to the other,
My name is great among the nations.
Incense is offered in My name,
a pure offering everywhere,
for My name is great among the nations,
says the Lord of Hosts.

12 Yet you desecrate it
by saying that the Lord's table is defiled
and its fruit too repugnant to be consumed.
13 You say,
"O, how wearisome,"
and you snort at it,
says the Lord of Hosts.
You bring what is stolen,
the Lord says,
what is lame,
what is ill;
you bring this offering.
Am I to accept it from your hands?

14 Cursed is the knave
who has a ram in his flock
but pledges and sacrifices
a damaged animal to the Lord.

For I am a great King, says the Lord of Hosts,
and My name is revered among the nations.

2 1 Now, this is your command, priests:

2 If you do not listen,
if you do not take it to heart
to honor My name,
says the LORD of Hosts,
then I will set a curse on you,
and I will curse your blessings –
indeed, I have cursed your blessing,
for you do not take it to heart.

3 I will drive away the crops because of you,
and I will scatter filth in your face,
the filth of your holiday sacrifices,
and you will be carried away after it.

4 And you will know that I sent you this command
so that My covenant may endure with Levi,
says the LORD of Hosts.

5 My covenant endures in him – life and peace.
I gave them to him so as to be revered.
He revered Me
and was in awe of My name.

6 True teaching was in his mouth,
no sin from his lips;
he walked with Me in peace and uprightness
and returned many from iniquity.

7 For a priest's lips
should safeguard knowledge,
and the people should seek teaching
from his mouth,
for he is a messenger
of the LORD of Hosts.

8 But you have strayed from the path
and caused many to stumble by your teaching.
You have destroyed the covenant of Levi,
says the LORD of Hosts.

9 So indeed I will make you
scorned and degraded before the whole nation
because you do not safeguard My ways,
and you distort the face of the Torah.

10 Do we not all have one Father?
Were we not all created by one God?

Why should a man
be faithless to his brother,

desecrating the covenant
of our fathers?

11 For Yehuda has been faithless,
and an abomination has been perpetrated
in Israel and Jerusalem.
For Yehuda, whom He loves,
has desecrated that which is holy to the LORD
and married the daughter of a foreign god.

12 Let the man who does this
be cut off by the LORD –
kith and kin[3] –
from the tents of Yaakov –
even one who brings offerings to
the LORD of Hosts.

13 And this you also do:
flood the LORD's altar with tears –
weeping and sighing
because He no longer turns toward the offerings
nor accepts favor from your hands.

14 And you say, "Why?"

For the LORD is witness
between you and the wife of your youth,
to whom you have been faithless,
though she is your companion
and your covenantal wife.

15 Did He not make them one being?
All remaining spirit accords with that.
And what does the One seek?
Children of God.

So take care of your spirits,
and let none of you be faithless
to the wife of your youth.

16 If anyone hates and sends her away,
says the LORD, God of Israel,
corruption covers his wedding clothes,
says the LORD of Hosts,
and so, take care with your spirit
and be not faithless.

---

3 | Hebrew *er ve'ona*, possibly echoing the children of Yehuda, Er and Onan (see Gen., ch. 38).

17 You have wearied the LORD with your talk.
But you say, "How have we wearied Him?"
By saying every evildoer is
good in the eyes of the LORD
and it is them whom He desires;
or, "Where is the God of justice?"

3 1 Behold: I am sending My messenger,
and he will clear a path before Me.[4]
Suddenly, the LORD whom you seek
will arrive at His Temple.
The angel of the covenant
whom you desire –
behold, he is coming,
says the LORD of Hosts.

2 Who can survive
the day of His coming,
and who can remain standing
when He appears?
For He is like the smelter's fire
and the washers' lye.

3 And He will sit smelting and purifying silver,
and He will purify the sons of Levi
and refine them like gold and silver,
and they will be the LORD's –
bringing offerings in righteousness.

4 Then the offering of Yehuda and Jerusalem will be pleasing to the LORD
as in days of old and years past.

5 I will draw close to you in judgment,
and I will be a swift witness
against the sorcerers and adulterers
and those who falsely swear;
against those who withhold payment
from the worker or the widow or the orphan;
against those who turn away the stranger.
They do not fear Me,[5]
says the LORD of Hosts.

6 For I am the LORD.
I have not changed.
And you, children of Yaakov,
you have not perished.

---

4 | Cf. Exodus 23:20.

5 | Cf. the prohibitions in Leviticus, chapter 19, especially verses 12–14.

7 Ever since the days of your forefathers
you have strayed from My statutes,
and you did not keep them.
Come back to Me,
and I will come back to you,
says the LORD of Hosts.
But you say, "How shall we come back?"

8 Can a person steal[6] from God?
Yet you steal from Me.
But you say, "What have we stolen from You?"
The tithes and donations.

9 You are being cursed with the curse
because you steal from Me – the whole nation.
10 Bring the entire tithe
to the treasury,
and it will be food for My House,
and put Me to the test, please, in this,
says the LORD of Hosts.

See if I do not open up the floodgates of heaven for you
and pour out blessings upon you endlessly.

11 I will drive away for you
that which devours.

Your produce will not be destroyed,
and your vines in the field will not be barren,
says the LORD of Hosts.

12 All the nations will
call you happy,
for you, yours will be
a desired land,
says the LORD of Hosts.

13 The LORD says, "You have spoken harshly against Me."
Yet you say, "What have we said of You?"

14 You say, "It is useless to serve God,
and what do we gain
in keeping His watch,
or by walking in dark sorrow
before the LORD of Hosts?

15 Now we call the arrogant happy;
evildoers have built themselves up;
they have tested God and escaped."

6 | The Hebrew *yikba* echoes the name Yaakov (v. 6).

16 Then those who fear the Lord spoke one to another,
and the Lord listened and He heard,
and it was written – a book of remembrance before Him
for those who fear the Lord and keep His name in mind.

17 And they shall be Mine,
says the Lord of Hosts,
on the day on which I
choose My cherished possession,
and I will take pity on them
as a man takes pity on his son
who serves him.

18 And you will once again distinguish
between the righteous and the wicked,
between one who serves God
and one who does not serve Him.

19 For behold, the day is coming,
burning like an oven;
the arrogant and the evildoers
will be straw,
and the coming day will consume them,
says the Lord of Hosts,
so that neither root nor branch will remain of them.

20 But for you, fearers of My name,
a sun of righteousness will shine
with healing under its wings,
and you will go out and
frolic like stall-fatted calves.

21 You will trample evildoers –
for they will be ashes under
the soles of your feet
on the day on which I act,
says the Lord of Hosts.

22 Remember the Teaching of Moshe My servant,
which I commanded to him at Ḥorev,
statutes and laws
for all of Israel.

23 Behold, I will send you Eliya the prophet
before the great and terrible
day of the Lord.

24 And he will return the hearts
of parents back to their children

and the hearts of children back
to their parents,
lest I come and lay the earth waste.

Behold, I will send you Eliya the prophet
before the great and terrible
day of the LORD.

WRITINGS/KETUVIM

PSALMS / TEHILLIM

PROVERBS / MISHLE

JOB / IYOV

SONG OF SONGS / SHIR HASHIRIM

RUTH / RUT

LAMENTATIONS / EIKHA

ECCLESIASTES / KOHELET

ESTHER / ESTER

DANIEL

EZRA • NEHEMIAH / NEḤEMYA

CHRONICLES / DIVREI HAYAMIM

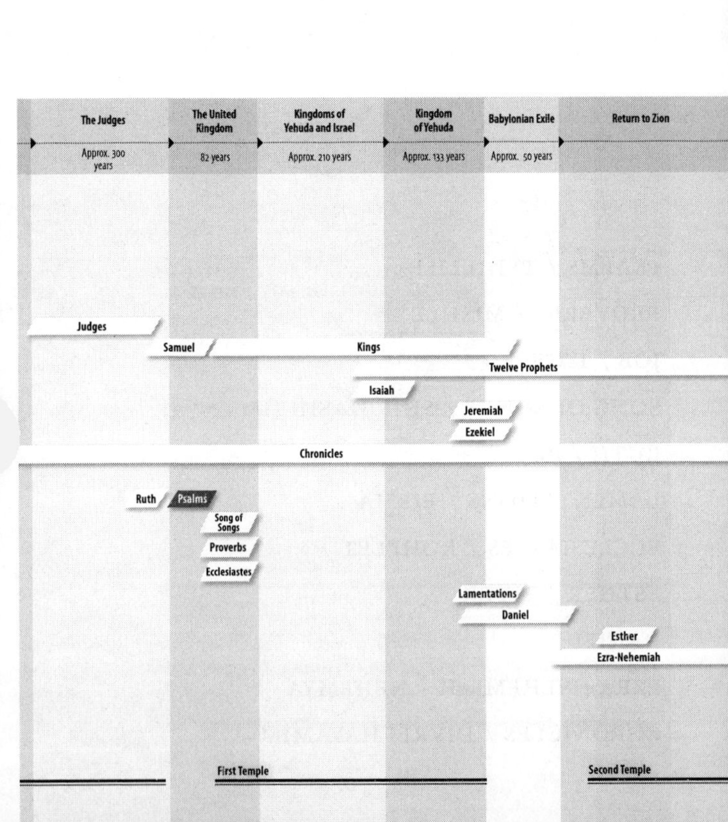
The Judges
The United Kingdom
Kingdoms of Yehuda and Israel
Kingdom of Yehuda
Babylonian Exile
Return to Zion
Approx. 300 years
82 years
Approx. 210 years
Approx. 133 years
Approx. 50 years
Judges
Samuel
Kings
Twelve Prophets
Isaiah
Jeremiah
Ezekiel
Chronicles
Ruth
Psalms
Song of Songs
Proverbs
Ecclesiastes
Lamentations
Daniel
Esther
Ezra-Nehemiah
First Temple
Second Temple

PSALMS/TEHILLIM

PSALMS	Book One	Book Two	Book Three	Book Four	Book Five
	Chs. 1–41	42–72	73–89	90–106	107–150

BOOK ONE

1 1 Happy is the one who does not walk in the counsel of the wicked,
who does not stand on the path of sinners,
who does not sit among the jeering cynics –
2 instead, the LORD's teaching is all his desire,
and he contemplates that teaching day and night.
3 He is like a tree planted on streams of water
yielding fruit in its season, its leaves never withering –
all it produces thrives.
4 Not so the wicked –
they are like chaff blown away by the wind.
5 Therefore, the wicked will not endure judgment,
nor the sinners among the righteous crowd.
6 For the LORD cares for the way of the righteous,
while the way of the wicked will be lost forever.

2 1 Why do the nations clamor;
why do the peoples plot futilities?
2 Kings of the earth stand ready;
leaders have bonded together
against the LORD and His anointed –
3 "Let us sever their bonds
and cast away their cords."
4 The One who dwells in heaven shall laugh;
the LORD will mock them,
5 then He will speak to them in His fury;
He will fill them with terror in His rage:
6 "I have set My king
over Zion My holy mountain."
7 I tell now of the LORD's decree:
He told me, "You are My child;
this very day I fathered you.
8 Just ask of Me –
I shall give you nations for your inheritance,
estate to the ends of the earth.
9 You will crush them with an iron rod;
You will shatter them like pottery."
10 And now, kings, be wise;
be warned, judges of the earth:
11 Serve the LORD with reverence
and tremble as you exalt.
12 Pay homage sincerely
lest He grow angry and you lose your way,
for His fury flares up in a moment.
Happy are all who seek refuge in Him.

3 1 A psalm *of David, when he fled from his son Avshalom.*[1]

2 Lord, my foes are so many –
so many rise up against me;
3 so many say of me,
"He has no salvation in God" – Selah[2] –
4 but You, Lord,
are the shield that protects me,
my honor; the One who raises my head.
5 My voice cries out to the Lord;
He answers me from His holy mountain – Selah.
6 I lie down to sleep;
I wake again, for the Lord sustains me.
7 I do not fear the myriads of men,
those encamped all around me.
8 Rise up, Lord;
save me, my God!
You have smashed all my foes across the jaw;
You have broken the teeth of the wicked.
9 Salvation is the Lord's –
Your blessing rests on Your people – Selah.

4 1 *To the lead singer,*[3] *accompanied by music*[4] *– a psalm of David.*

2 When I call out, answer me,
O God of my vindication;
in my distress You set me free –
show me grace and hear my prayer.
3 All you people –
how long will my honor be disgraced;
how long will you love emptiness;
how long will you seek illusions? – Selah.
4 Know that the Lord singles out those who are faithful to Him;
when I cry out to the Lord, He will hear.
5 Tremble and do not sin;
contemplate as you lie awake;
stay silent – Selah.
6 Offer sincere offerings,
and place Your trust in the Lord.
7 So many say, "Who will show us goodness?"
Direct the light of Your face upon us, Lord.

---

1 | See II Samuel, chapters 15–19.

2 | A term of uncertain meaning. It is most likely an instruction related to musical performance.

3 | The precise meaning of the Hebrew term *menatze'aḥ* remains unknown. It is often understood to refer to the leader of a group of musical performers.

4 | Hebrew *binginot*, another term of uncertain meaning referring to musical performance.

8 You have filled my heart with more joy
than others feel in their abundance of grain and wine.
9 In peace I shall lie down and sleep soundly,
for You alone, LORD, keep me safe.

5 1 *To the lead singer, on the* neḥilot[5] – *a psalm of David.*

2 Give ear to my words, LORD;
understand my reflections;
3 listen to the sound of my plea, my King and God,
for to You I pray.
4 LORD, hear my voice in the morning;
in the morning I plead before You in expectation,
5 for You are not a God who desires wickedness;
evil cannot abide with You.
6 The brazen will not stand before Your eyes;
You hate all evildoers.
7 You destroy those who speak lies;
men of blood and deceit the LORD despises.
8 But I, with Your great loving-kindness, will come to Your House;
I will worship at Your holy Sanctuary in reverence of You.
9 LORD, lead me in Your righteousness
because of my oppressors.
Make Your path straight before me,
10 for there is not a true word on their lips;
their insides churn with malice;
their slippery tongues lead
to the open grave of their throats.
11 Condemn them, God;
let them fall by their own counsel.
Drive them away for their many crimes,
for they have rebelled against You.
12 Let all those who take refuge in You rejoice;
let them ever sing for joy as You shelter them;
let those who love Your name exult in You,
13 for You bless the righteous, O LORD,
sheathing them with favor like a shield.

6 1 *To the lead singer, accompanied by music on the* sheminit[6] – *a psalm of David.*

2 LORD,
do not reproach me in Your anger;
do not punish me in Your fury.
3 Be gracious to me, LORD, for I am wretched;
heal me, LORD, for my bones shake with agony.

5 | A term of uncertain meaning, which many commentators relate to musical performance.

6 | A term of unknown meaning, perhaps a musical instrument with eight strings.

4 My soul is in grave agony –
and You, O Lord – oh, how long?
5 Come back, Lord – rescue my soul;
save me for the sake of Your love,
6 for there is no mention of You in death;
who can praise You from the grave?
7 I am weary with sighing –
each night I flood my bed with weeping;
I drench my couch in tears.
8 My eye grows dim from grief,
worn out from all my foes.
9 Leave me, all you evildoers,
for the Lord has heard the sound of my weeping;
10 The Lord has heard my pleas;
the Lord will accept my prayer.
11 Shame and agony will seize all my foes;
they will turn back in sudden shame.

7 1 *A* shiggayon[7] *of David, which he sang to the Lord concerning Kush,*[8] *a Benjaminite.*

2 O Lord my God,
in You I take refuge.
Save me and deliver me from all my foes
3 lest they ravage me like a lion,
tearing me apart, with no one to save me.
4 O Lord, my God,
if I have done this,
if there is guilt on my hands,
5 if I have repaid my allies with harm
or plundered my rivals without cause,
6 then let my enemies pursue and overtake me;
let them trample me into the ground
and lay my body in the dust – Selah.
7 Arise, O Lord, in Your anger;
rear up in wrath against my enemies
and rouse, for my sake,
the judgment You decreed.
8 The assembly of peoples will surround You;
take Your seat over them on high.
9 The Lord will judge nations;
vindicate me, O Lord,
according to my righteousness and integrity.

---

7 | A term of uncertain meaning that may pertain to musical performance. Cf. Habakkuk 3:1.

8 | Perhaps a reference to Sha'ul, son of Kish, who had persecuted David; see I Samuel, chapter 18 and onward.

10 Let the evil of the wicked come to an end,
and let the righteous stand firm –
You who search hearts and minds,[9]
O Righteous God.
11 My shield is God,[10]
who saves the upright of heart.
12 God vindicates the righteous,
growing livid every day.
13 If someone fails to repent
and sharpens his sword
and draws his bow and aims,
14 then he has prepared the instruments of his own death;
he has poisoned his arrows for himself,
15 for he has spawned evil,
he is pregnant with treachery,
and he breeds falsehood.[11]
16 He has dug a pit and hollowed it out,
and he himself will fall into that hole.
17 His treachery will come back on his own head;
his violence will crash down on his own skull.
18 I will praise the Lord for His righteousness;
I will sing to the name of the Lord Most High.

8 1 *To the lead singer, on the* gittit[12] *– a psalm of David.*

2 O Lord our Master,
how mighty is Your name throughout the earth;
Your majesty extends across the heavens!
3 From the coos of little ones and babies
You founded power against Your foes,
silencing enemies and avengers.
4 When I behold Your heavens,
the work of Your fingertips,
the moon and stars that You designed,
5 what are mortals, that You should be mindful of them;
human beings, that You should take note of them?
6 Yet You have set them just below God[13]
and crowned them with glory and splendor.
7 You made them rulers over Your handiwork;
You set it all beneath their feet –
8 all flocks and herds,
beasts of the field,

---

9 | Literally "kidneys."

10 | Literally "my shield is upon God."

11 | Cf. Isaiah 59:4; Job 15:35.

12 | An unknown musical term.

13 | Or "the angels."

9 birds of the skies, and fish of the sea –
whatever travels the paths of the seas.
10 O LORD our Master,
how mighty is Your name throughout the earth!

9 1 *To the lead singer,* Al Mot Labben[14] – *a psalm of David.*
2 I thank You, LORD, with all my heart;
let me tell of all Your wonders.
3 I rejoice and exult in You;
let me sing praise to Your name, Most High.
4 My enemies retreat;
they stumble and perish before You,
5 for You have upheld my case and my cause;
You have sat enthroned as righteous judge;
6 You have blasted nations and destroyed the wicked,
blotting out their names for ever and all time.
7 The enemies are finished, ruined forever;
You have overthrown their cities –
every trace of them is lost.
8 But the LORD abides forever;
He has established His throne for judgment.
9 He will judge the world with justice
and try the cause of peoples fairly.
10 The LORD is a stronghold for the downtrodden,
a stronghold in times of trouble.
11 Those who know Your name trust in You,
for You never forsake those who seek You, LORD.
12 Sing praise to the LORD who dwells in Zion;
tell of His deeds among the peoples.
13 For the avenger of blood remembers;
He does not forget the cry of the suffering.
14 Show me grace, LORD –
see how my enemies make me suffer,
You who lift me up from the gates of death,
15 so that I may sing all Your praises
at the gates of daughter Zion
and rejoice in Your deliverance.
16 The nations have fallen into their own pit;
their feet are tangled in their own hidden net.
17 The LORD is famed for His justice
while the wicked are ensnared by the work of their own hands –
higgayon[15] – Selah.

---

14 | The meaning of this phrase remains uncertain; perhaps it is related to the death (*mot*) of a son (*ben*) or someone called Labben.

15 | A term of uncertain meaning, probably a musical notation.

18 The wicked return to Sheol,[16]
all nations that forget God,
19 but the needy will not be forgotten for long;
the hope of the suffering will never be lost.
20 Arise, LORD; do not let mortals prevail –
let the nations be judged before You.
21 Strike them with fear, LORD;
let the nations know they are but mortal – Selah.

10 1 Why, LORD, do You stand far off,
hiding Yourself in times of trouble?
2 The proud wicked persecute the poor –
let them be trapped by their own devious schemes! –
3 for the wicked boast of their lust;
the avaricious curse and revile the LORD.
4 In their sheer arrogance, the wicked say,
"He will never call us to account";
in all their scheming, they say,
"There is no God."
5 Their ways always prosper –
Your justice is far above them.
As for their foes, they snort at them.
6 They say to themselves,
"I will not be shaken;
I will never encounter trouble."
7 Curses fill their mouths,
deceit and malice; treachery and cruelty lie beneath their tongues.
8 They lurk in backwater places,
murdering innocents where no one sees;
their eyes stalk the helpless.
9 They lurk, hidden like a lion in its lair,
lurk to snatch away the poor;
they snatch away the poor
and drag them off in their net.
10 They stoop, they crouch,
and the helpless fall prey to their clutches.
11 They say to themselves,
"God has forgotten –
He has hidden His face
and averted His gaze forever."
12 Rise up, LORD;
God, raise Your hand –
do not forget the poor!

16 | The underworld, the abode of the dead.

13 Why do the wicked revile God,
thinking, "You will never call us to account"?
14 You do see!
You do note treachery and torment
and take them into Your hands;
the helpless commit themselves to You;
You have always helped the orphan.
15 Break the arms of the wicked;
call the evil to account for their wickedness
until it is gone.
16 The LORD is King for ever and ever;
the nations shall perish from His land.
17 You have heard what the lowly desire, LORD;
strengthen their hearts and lend Your ear
18 to bring justice to the orphan and the downtrodden
so that mere earthly mortals
will never spread terror again.

11 1 *To the lead singer, of David.*

In the LORD I take shelter –
how can you say to me,
"Flee your mountain like a bird –
2 for look, the wicked,
they draw their bows taut,
set their arrows on the string
to shoot from the shadows at the upright –
3 for the foundations will soon be destroyed."
What are the righteous to do?
4 The LORD is in His holy Sanctuary;
the LORD is on His heavenly throne;
His eyes gaze down;
He examines humanity;
5 the LORD examines righteous and wicked.
He despises the lover of violence;
6 He will rain down soot and fire and sulfur on the wicked;
scorching winds are their portion.
7 For the LORD is righteous; He loves what is right.
The upright will gaze upon His face.

12 1 *To the lead singer, on the* sheminit[17] *– a psalm of David.*

2 Help, LORD, for the godly are no more,
for the faithful have faded from humanity.
3 People tell each other lies;
they are smooth talking and two faced.

---

17 | See note on 6:1.

4 May the LORD cut off all these smooth lips,
these arrogant wagging tongues
5 that declare,
"Our tongues shall prevail;
our lips are our own –
who is our master?"
6 "Because of the oppression of the poor,
the groans of the needy,
I will now rise up,"
declares the LORD.
"I will grant them the safety they sigh for."
7 The LORD's words are pure words,
like silver refined in an earthen furnace,
purified seven times over.
8 You, LORD, will watch over them
and protect them from this generation forever –
9 as the wicked strut around,
and obscenity is prized among humanity.

13 1 *To the lead singer – a psalm of David.*

2 For how long, LORD, will You forget me? Forever?
For how long will You hide Your face from me?
3 For how long will I have worries in my mind
and sorrow in my heart each day?
For how long will my enemy triumph over me?
4 Look at me; answer me,
O LORD my God.
Light up my eyes
lest I fall into a death sleep,
5 lest my enemy declare, "I have bested him!" –
lest my foes delight at my collapse.
6 But I have placed my trust in Your loyalty;
my heart will delight in Your salvation.
I will sing to the LORD,
for He has been good to me.

14 1 *To the lead singer, of David.*[18]

The brute says in his heart,
"There is no God."
They are corrupt; they wreak vile schemes;
there is no one who does good.
2 The LORD looks down from heaven at humanity
to see if someone has the sense to seek out God,

18 | Cf. Psalm 53, a slightly different version of this psalm.

3 but all have turned away,
altogether tainted;
there is no one who does good,
not even one.
4 Have they no knowledge, all those evildoers,
who devour My people as if devouring bread,
who do not call out to the LORD?
5 There they will be struck with terror,
for God is among the abodes of the righteous.
6 You would rebuff the counsel of the poor,
but the LORD is their shelter.
7 Oh, that Israel's salvation might come from Zion!
When the LORD restores His people's fortune,
Yaakov will rejoice;
Israel will be glad.

15 1 *A psalm of David.*

LORD, who may dwell in Your tent?
Who may live on Your holy mountain?
2 The one whose ways are blameless,
who does what is right,
who speaks truth from the heart;
3 the one who has no malice on his tongue,
who does no wrong to his fellow,
who does not cast a slur against his neighbor;
4 the one who scorns those who are vile,
who honors those who fear the LORD,
who keeps an oath even when it hurts;
5 the one who does not loan money for interest,
who does not take a bribe against the innocent –
anyone who acts thus will never be shaken.

16 1 *A* mikhtam[19] *of David.*

Protect me, God,
for in You I take refuge.
2 I said to the LORD,
"You are my LORD;
My favor comes from none but You."
3 As for the holy ones in the land,
the mighty who were all my delight,
4 may those who court other gods suffer many sorrows –
I will not pour out their libations of blood;
I will not bear their names on my lips.
5 The LORD is my chosen portion and my cup.

19 | Meaning is uncertain.

You direct my fate.
6 A sweet heritage has fallen to my lot;
my share is delightful to me.
7 I will bless the LORD who has guided me;
even at night, my conscience stirs me.
8 I have set the LORD before me always;
He is at my right hand; I shall not be shaken.
9 Therefore my heart is glad,
my spirit rejoices,
and my body rests secure,
10 for You will not abandon me to Sheol
nor let Your devoted one see the Pit.
11 You will teach me the path of life.
In Your presence is fullness of joy;
at Your right hand, bliss for evermore.

17 1 *A prayer of David.*

Hear, LORD, what is just;
listen to my plea;
give ear to my prayer, mouthed without deceit.
2 May I be vindicated before You –
Your eyes will behold what is right.
3 You have searched my heart,
visited me by night,
tried me, and found nothing amiss.
I shut my mouth tight against offense.
4 As for what others do,
by the words of Your lips
I myself keep away from the paths of the violent.
5 My steps have adhered to Your pathways;
my feet have never faltered.
6 I call on You
for You will answer me, God;
lend Your ear to me;
listen to my words.
7 Show Your wondrous loyalty,
You who save with Your right hand
those who seek refuge from adversaries.
8 Guard me like the apple of Your eye;
hide me in the shade of Your wings
9 from the wicked who assault me,
my deadly enemies who encircle me.
10 Their hearts are callous;
their mouths flaunt and gloat.
11 Now they close in around our steps,
combing the ground with their gaze

12 like a lion hungering for prey,
like a young lion crouching in ambush.
13 Rise up, LORD;
confront them; bring them down.
Rescue me from the wicked
with Your sword,
14 from people, O LORD, by Your hand,
from people whose share in life is fleeting.
As for those You treasure,
fill their bellies;
their children, too, will be sated
and leave what remains for their own little ones.
15 As for me, in justice I will gaze upon Your face;
wide awake, I am sated with Your image.

18 1 *To the lead singer – of the LORD's servant, of David*[20]
who uttered these words of song to the LORD;
on the day that the LORD saved him
from the hands of all his enemies and from the hands of Sha'ul,
2 *he said,*

I love You, O LORD, my strength.
3 The LORD is my Rock, my fortress, my rescuer;
my God is the Rock of my refuge,
my shield, the horn of my salvation, my haven.
4 Praise! When I call on the LORD,
I am saved from my enemies.
5 The cords of death assailed me;
deadly torrents engulfed me;
6 the cords of Sheol entangled me;
snares of death confronted me.
7 In my distress I called on the LORD;
I cried out to my God;
He heard my voice from His Temple,
and my cry rang in His ears.
8 Then the earth shook and shuddered;
the very mountain beds trembled;
they shuddered from His wrath.
9 Smoke issued from His nostrils;
devouring flames flared from His mouth;
from Him gleaming coals blazed forth.
10 He bent the heavens and descended,
dense cloud beneath His feet;
11 He mounted a cherub and flew,
soaring on wings of wind.

---

20 | Cf. II Samuel, chapter 22.

12 He enveloped Himself in darkness,
a shelter all around Him
of heavy storm clouds dark with rain.
13 The brilliant glow of His presence
pierced His clouds
with hail and fiery coals.
14 The LORD thundered from the heavens;
the Most High raised His voice
with hail and fiery coals.
15 He shot His arrows and scattered them;
He hurled lightning bolts and routed them.
16 The ocean bed was exposed,
the foundations of the world laid bare
by Your onslaught, LORD,
from the blast of Your breath.
17 From on high He reached down and took me;
He drew me out of the mighty waters.
18 He saved me from my fierce enemy,
from foes too strong for me.
19 They confronted me on my direst day,
but the LORD was my support.
20 He brought me out to freedom;
He rescued me because He delighted in me.
21 The LORD rewarded me as I deserved;
as my hands were clean, He repaid me,
22 for I kept the ways of the LORD
and did not betray my God,
23 for all His laws are before me;
I will not cast aside His statutes.
24 I am blameless to Him
and keep myself from sin,
25 so the LORD repaid me as I deserved,
as my hands were clean in His sight.
26 You deal loyally with those who are loyal;
to the blameless You show Yourself blameless;
27 You are pure with those who are pure,
but with the crooked, You twist and turn,
28 for it is You who brings salvation to a humble people
but humiliate haughty eyes,
29 for it is You who lights my lamp.
The LORD my God lights up my darkness;
30 with You I can rush a ridge;
with my God I can leap over a wall.
31 God's ways are blameless,
the LORD's words are pure;
He is a shield to all who take refuge in Him.

32 For who is a god besides the Lord;
who is a Rock besides our God?
33 God is the one who girds me with power;
He makes my way sound.
34 He makes my legs like a deer's
and stands me on the heights;
35 He trains my hands for battle
so that my arms can bend a bow of bronze.
36 You gave me the shield of Your victory;
Your right hand sustained me;
Your gentleness made me great.
37 You made my steps broad and firm;
my feet never faltered.
38 I pursued my enemies and overtook them,
never turning back until they perished.
39 I crushed them until they could rise no more;
they fell beneath my feet.
40 You girded me with power for battle
and sunk my adversaries far beneath me;
41 You made my enemies turn tail before me;
my foes, too, I destroyed.
42 They cried out, but there was no savior –
out to the Lord, but He did not answer them –
43 while I ground them up like dust in the wind;
I poured them out like street mud.
44 You rescued me from civil strife;
You have set me as the head of nations;
peoples I never knew of serve me.
45 They merely hear of me and obey;
foreign peoples come cringing before me.
46 Foreign peoples lose heart
and come trembling out of their forts.
47 The Lord lives!
Blessed is my Rock;
exalted is the God of my rescue! –
48 the God who grants vengeance to me,
who subjugates people under me.
49 My rescuer from my enemies,
You raise me above those who rise against me;
You save me from violent men,
50 so I praise You among the nations, Lord,
and sing to Your name.
51 He grants great victories to His king
and shows loyalty to His anointed,
to David and his seed forever.

19 1 *To the lead singer – a psalm of David.*

2 The heavens tell of God's glory;
the skies proclaim His handiwork.
3 Day to day pours forth speech;
night to night expresses knowledge.
4 There is no speech;
there are no words;
their voice is not heard,
5 yet their music carries across the land,
their words to the end of the earth.
In them[21] He has set a tent for the sun,
6 which emerges like a groom from his marriage chamber,
glowing like a champion about to run his course.
7 It rises at one end of the heaven and circuits to the other;
nothing can hide from its heat.
8 The LORD's teaching is perfect,
reviving the spirit;
the LORD's decree is steadfast,
making the simple wise.
9 The LORD's precepts are just, cheering the heart;
the LORD's commandment is radiant, lighting up the eyes.
10 Fear of the LORD is pure, enduring forever;
the LORD's judgments are true and righteous without exception –
11 more precious than gold, than boundless fine gold,
sweeter than honey, than nectar from the honeycomb.
12 Your servant, too, is careful of them;
in keeping them there is great reward.
13 Yet who can discern his errors?
Cleanse me of hidden faults.
14 Spare Your servant from the insolent;
let them rule me not.
Then shall I be blameless,
cleansed of grave sin.
15 May the words of my mouth
and my heart's reflections
please You, LORD,
my Rock and redeemer.

20 1 *To the lead singer – a psalm of David.*

2 May the LORD answer you in times of trouble;
may the name of Yaakov's God protect you.
3 May He send you help from the Sanctuary
and support you from Zion.

21 | Meaning in the heavens.

4 May He recall all your grain offerings
and accept your burnt offerings – Selah.
5 May He give you your heart's desire
and ensure that all your plans succeed.
6 We will shout for joy at Your salvation
and raise a banner in our God's name.
May the LORD grant all your requests.
7 Now I know that the LORD saves His anointed,
that He answers him from His holy heaven
with the saving power of His right hand.
8 Some trust in chariots,
others in horses,
but we call on the name of the LORD our God.
9 They crumple and fall,
but we rise up and stand firm.
10 LORD, grant victory!
May the King answer us when we call.

21 1 *To the lead singer – a psalm of David.*

2 LORD,
the king rejoices in Your might;
how he delights in Your victory!
3 You have granted him his heart's desire
and not denied the requests of his lips – Selah.
4 You have welcomed him with rich blessing
and set a golden crown upon his head.
5 He asked You for life, and You have granted it –
long life for evermore.
6 His glory is great through Your victory;
You lavish majesty and splendor upon him,
7 bestowing upon him eternal blessing,
cheering him with the joy of Your presence,
8 for the king trusts in the LORD;
with the loyalty of the Most High
he will never be shaken.
9 Your hand reaches all Your enemies;
Your right hand reaches those who hate You.
10 You set them ablaze like a furnace when You appear;
in His wrath, the LORD will engulf them,
and fire will consume them.
11 You wipe their offspring from the earth,
their seed from among men,
12 for they plotted evil toward You;
they devised schemes but could not succeed.
13 You will put them to flight,
aiming Your bow at their faces.

14 Rise up, Lord, in Your might;
we will sing and praise Your power.

22 1 *To the lead singer, a dawn song[22] – a psalm of David.*

2 O God, my God – why have You forsaken me?
So far from my salvation
are the words that I roar.
3 My God, I cry out to You by day,
but You do not answer,
and by night – without relief.
4 But You are the Holy One,
enthroned on Israel's praises.
5 In You our ancestors placed their trust;
they trusted,
and You delivered them.
6 To You they cried out
and were saved;
in You they trusted
and were not let down.
7 But I am a worm, not human –
scorned by men, disgraced among people.
8 Whoever sees me mocks me;
they curl their lips and shake their heads
9 "Look to the Lord – let Him deliver;
let Him save him, if He delights in him,"
10 for it is You who drew me out from the womb,
You who kept me safe at my mother's breast.
11 I have been in Your care since birth;
from my mother's womb, You have been my God.
12 Do not stray far from me,
for trouble is near,
with no one to help.
13 Many bulls surround me;
fierce beasts of the Bashan[23] close in on me.
14 Their jaws open wide against me
like ravenous roaring lions.
15 I dissolve like water,
all my limbs falling to pieces,
my heart melting like wax within me.
16 My strength is dried up like clay shards;
my tongue sticks to my palate;
You lay me down in the dust of death,
17 for hounds are all around me;

22 | The meaning of the Hebrew *ayelet hashaḥar* is uncertain. It is possibly a musical term.

23 | A territory notable for its pasture; see Numbers, chapter 32.

a vicious pack encircles me,
at my hands and feet like a lion.
18 I count all my bones
as they look on and gloat.
19 They divide up my garments among themselves
and cast lots for my clothing.
20 But You, LORD – do not be distant,
O my help; rush to my aid;
21 save my life from the sword,
my precious soul from those hounds;
22 rescue me from the lions' jaws;
deliver me from the horns of wild bulls.
23 I will tell of Your name to my kin;
I will praise You in the midst of the assembly.
24 You who fear the LORD, praise Him;
honor Him, all you seed of Yaakov;
revere Him, all you seed of Israel,
25 for He has not spurned or scorned
the suffering of the lowly;
He has not hidden His face from them;
when they cried out to Him, He listened.
26 You inspire my praise before the great assembly;
I will pay my vows before those who revere Him.
27 The lowly will eat and be satisfied;
those who seek the LORD will praise Him –
may your hearts rejoice forever!

28 Let all the ends of the earth remember
and turn to the LORD;
let all families of the nations
bow before You,
29 for the kingship is the LORD's;
He rules over the nations.
30 All those who thrive on the land will feast and worship;
all those who descend to the dust shall kneel before Him –
those who cannot endure.
31 Posterity will serve Him;
future generations will be told about the LORD,
32 and they, in turn, will tell of His righteousness,
of His deeds, to the people yet unborn.

23 1 *A psalm of David.*

The LORD is my Shepherd;
I lack nothing.
2 He lets me lie down in green pastures;
He leads me beside still waters.

3 He refreshes my soul,
guiding me along the right paths
for the sake of His name.
4 Though I walk through the valley of the shadow of death,
I fear no evil, for You are with me;
Your rod and Your staff encourage me.
5 You set a table before me in the face of my foes;
You anoint my head with oil;
my cup brims over.
6 May only goodness and kindness follow me
all the days of my life;
let me live in the LORD's House
for evermore.

24 1 *Of David – a psalm.*

The LORD owns the earth and all it contains,
the world and all who live in it,
2 for He founded it on the seas,
set it on the streams.
3 Who may ascend the LORD's mountain?
Who may stand in His holy place?
4 Those who have clean hands and pure hearts,
who do not take false oaths by My life,
who have not sworn deceitfully,
5 they shall receive blessing from the LORD,
due reward from the God of their salvation.
6 Such is the generation who seek Him –
Yaakov who seek Your presence, Selah.
7 Lift up your heads, O gates;
rise up, eternal doors,
so that the King of glory may enter.
8 Who is the King of glory?
It is the LORD, strong and mighty,
the LORD mighty in battle.
9 Lift up your heads, O gates;
lift them up, eternal doors,
so that the King of glory may enter.
10 Who is this King of glory?
The LORD of Hosts – He is the King of glory – Selah.

25 1 *Of David.*[24]

To You, O LORD, I lift up my soul;
2 in You, my God, I place my trust.
Do not let me be put to shame;

---

24 | This psalm takes the form of an alphabetical acrostic, with a few letters omitted.

do not let my enemies gloat over me.
3 Let none who hope for You be put to shame,
but let traitors, empty-handed, be ashamed.
4 Show me Your ways, Lord;
teach me Your paths.
5 Guide me in Your truth; teach me,
for You are the God of my salvation;
I constantly look to You in hope.
6 Remember Your compassion, Lord,
Your loyalty,
for they have always been.
7 Do not remember the sins of my youth or my offenses,
but remember me in keeping with Your loyalty,
in keeping with Your goodness, Lord.
8 Good and upright is the Lord;
therefore He shows sinners the way;
9 He guides the lowly along the right path
and teaches the lowly His way.
10 All the ways of the Lord are loyal and true
to those who keep His covenant, His rules.
11 For the sake of Your name, Lord,
forgive my sin though it is great.
12 Who, then, is one who fears the Lord?
He will show them which path to choose.
13 They will live good lives,
and their children will inherit the earth.
14 The Lord confides in those who fear Him;
to them He reveals His covenant.
15 My eyes are ever on the Lord,
for only He can free my feet from the net.
16 Turn to me and show me favor,
for I am lonely and suffering;
17 my heart swells with grief;
relieve me from my agony;
18 see my suffering and my pain,
and forgive all my sins.
19 See how many enemies I have
and their violent hatred toward me.
20 Protect me and save me;
let me not be put to shame,
for in You I take refuge.
21 Let integrity and decency keep me,
for I look to You in hope.
22 May God free Israel
from all its grief.

26 1 *Of David.*

Judge me, LORD,
for I have walked blamelessly;
I place my trust in the LORD;
I do not waver.
2 Test me, LORD; try me;
probe my heart and mind,[25]
3 for Your loyalty is before my eyes,
and I walk in Your truth.
4 I do not sit with corrupt people
or associate with hypocrites;
5 I despise the company of evildoers
and will not tolerate the wicked.
6 I wash my hands in innocence
and walk around Your altar, LORD,
7 raising my voice in thanksgiving
and telling of all Your wonders.
8 O LORD, I love the abode of Your House,
the dwelling place of Your glory!
9 Do not sweep me away with sinners,
my life with the men of blood
10 in whose hands are evil schemes,
their right hands full of bribes,
11 for I will walk on blamelessly;
redeem me and show me grace.
12 My feet stand on even ground;
among the crowd, I bless the LORD.

27 1 *Of David.*

The LORD is my light and my salvation –
whom need I fear?
The LORD is the stronghold of my life –
whom need I dread?
2 When evildoers close in on me to devour my flesh,
it is they,
my enemies and foes,
who stumble and fall.
3 Should an army besiege me,
my heart would not fear.
Should war break out against me,
I would still be confident.
4 One thing I ask of the LORD;
this alone I seek:

25 | Literally "my kidneys and heart."

to live in the LORD's House
all the days of my life,
to gaze on the beauty of the LORD,
and to worship in His Temple,
5 for He will keep me safe in His shelter in times of terror;
He will hide me under the cover of His tent;
He will set me high upon a rock.
6 Now my head is high above the enemies around me –
I will sacrifice in His tent with shouts of joy;
I will sing and chant praises to the LORD.
7 Hear my voice, LORD, when I call;
show me grace and answer me.
8 Of You my heart whispers, "Seek My presence" –
Your presence, LORD, I will seek.
9 Do not hide Your face from me;
do not turn Your servant away in anger.
You have been my help –
do not reject or forsake me, God, my savior.
10 Were my father and my mother to forsake me,
the LORD would take me in.
11 Teach me Your way, LORD;
lead me on a level path
because of my oppressors.
12 Do not abandon me to the will of my foes,
for false witnesses have risen against me,
breathing violence.
13 Were it not for my faith that I will see the LORD's goodness in the land of
the living....

14 Hope in the LORD;
be strong and brave of heart,
and hope in the LORD.

28 1 *Of David.*

To You, O LORD, I call;
O my Rock, be not deaf to my cry,
for if You remain silent,
I shall be like those who plummet to the Pit.
2 Hear the sound of my plea
when I cry out to You,
when I lift my hands
toward Your holiest Sanctuary.
3 Do not pull me away with the wicked,
with evildoers
who feign peace with one another
but harbor malice in their hearts.

4 Pay them back for their actions,
for their malicious acts;
pay them back for their deeds –
treat them as they deserve,
5 for they do not recognize the LORD's acts
or His handiwork.
May He break them down,
not build them up.
6 Blessed is the LORD,
who has heard the sound of my plea;
7 the LORD is my might and my protector;
my heart trusted Him, and I received help.
My heart exults,
and I praise Him with my song.
8 The LORD is their strength,
the saving stronghold of His anointed.
9 Save Your people;
bless Your heritage;
tend them and sustain them forever.

29 1 *A psalm of David.*

Render to the LORD, you angelic beings –
render to the LORD glory and might.
2 Render to the LORD the glory due His name;
bow to the LORD in the splendor of holiness.
3 The LORD's voice echoes over the waters;
the God of glory thunders;
the LORD thunders over the mighty waters.
4 The LORD's voice rings with power;
the LORD's voice rings with splendor!
5 The LORD's voice breaks cedars;
the LORD shatters the cedars of Lebanon –
6 He makes them skip like a calf,
Lebanon and Siryon[26] like a young wild ox.
7 The LORD's voice sparks fiery flames!
8 The LORD's voice shakes the desert;
the LORD shakes the desert of Kadesh.
9 The LORD's voice terrifies the deer
and strips the forests bare,
and in His Temple all say, "Glory!"
10 The LORD sat enthroned at the flood;
the LORD sits enthroned as King forever.
11 May the LORD give might to His people;
may the LORD bless His people with peace.

26 | Mountainous areas.

30 1 *A psalm of David – a song for the dedication of the House.*[27]

2 I will exalt You, LORD, for You have lifted me up;
3 You have not let my enemies gloat over me.
LORD, my God,
I cried out to You, and You healed me;
4 LORD, You lifted me from Sheol;
You saved me from plummeting to the Pit.
5 Sing to the LORD, you His devoted;
give thanks to His holy name,
6 for His wrath lasts but a moment,
but His favor a lifetime;
at night there may be weeping,
but the morning brings joy.
7 In my serenity
I said, "I shall never be shaken."
8 In Your favor, LORD,
You made me stand firm as a mountain,
but when You hid Your face,
I was terrified.
9 To You, LORD, I called;
to my LORD I pleaded,
10 "What gain would there be in my death[28]
if I went down to the grave?
Can dust praise You?
Can it declare Your truth?
11 Hear, LORD, and show me grace;
LORD, be my help."
12 You have turned my mourning into dancing;
You have untied my sackcloth and clothed me with joy
13 so that my soul[29] may sing to You and not be silent.
LORD my God, I will praise You forever.

31 1 *To the lead singer – a psalm of David.*

2 In You, LORD, I take refuge;
may I never be put to shame;
rescue me in Your righteousness.
3 Lend Your ear to me;
swiftly save me;
be my Rock of refuge,
a stronghold of salvation,
4 for You are my Rock and my fortress.
Lead me and guide me for the sake of Your name.

---

27 | Likely the Temple of Jerusalem.

28 | Literally "in my blood."

29 | Literally "glory."

5 Free me from this net they laid for me,
for You are my stronghold.
6 I place my spirit in Your hand –
You set me free, LORD, God of truth.
7 I despise those who rely on futilities –
as for me, I trust in the LORD.
8 I will delight and rejoice in Your loyalty:
You saw my suffering;
You knew of my grave danger;
9 You did not disclose me to enemy hands;
You let me go free.[30]
10 Show me grace, LORD,
for I am in danger;
torment wastes my eyes,
my being, my insides.
11 My life is spent with sorrow;
my years seep away in sighs;
my strength fades because of my sin;
my bones waste away.
12 I am the scorn of all my foes,
even more so to my neighbors;
I am a horror to my friends;
whoever sees me on the streets
shrinks away from me.
13 I have been forgotten like the dead,
like a long-discarded vessel,
14 for I have heard the whispers of many –
terror on every side![31] –
as they all conspire against me,
scheming to take my life.
15 But I place my trust in You, O LORD;
I say, "You are my God."
16 My fate is in Your hands;
save me from the hands
of my enemies and pursuers.
17 Shine Your face on Your servant;
save me in Your loyalty.
18 Let me not be put to shame, LORD,
for I call upon You;
let the wicked be shamed
and silenced to Sheol.
19 Let deceitful lips be stilled
that speak brashly against the righteous
with arrogance and contempt.

30 | Literally "You set my feet in a broad place."

31 | Cf. Jeremiah 20:10.

20 How great is the goodness
You keep in store for those who fear You;
You act for those who take refuge in You
in the full view of all.
21 Shelter them in Your safe presence
from human guile;
shield them within Your cover
from scathing tongues.
22 Blessed is the Lord
who has shown me His wondrous loyalty
in a city under siege.
23 Even when I said rashly,
"I am cut off from Your sight,"
You still heard the sound of my plea
when I cried out to You.
24 Love the Lord, all you His devoted ones;
the Lord protects the faithful
and amply punishes
those who act in arrogance.
25 Be strong and of determined hearts,
all you who wait for the Lord.

32 1 *Of David – a* maskil.[32]

Happy is the one whose offense has been forgiven,
whose sin has been covered over.
2 Happy is the one whom the Lord does not hold guilty,
whose spirit is devoid of deceit.
3 When I remained silent,
my body wasted away
from my howling all day long,
4 for day and night, Your hand weighed down upon me;
my vitality dried up as if scorched by summer heat – Selah.
5 I admitted my sin to You and did not cover up my guilt;
I said, "I confess my offenses to the Lord,"
and You forgave the guilt of my sin – Selah.
6 Thus let all those pray to You
at the moment of discovery[33]
so that the rush of mighty waters
will not reach them.
7 You are my shelter;
You keep me from danger;
You surround me with glad shouts of rescue – Selah.

---

32 | A musical term of uncertain meaning, perhaps related to instruction. Compare the use of this verb in verse 8.

33 | Meaning discovery of their sins.

8 I will instruct you and guide you
along the path you should follow;
I will counsel you and keep My eye on you.
9 Do not be senseless like a horse or mule
that must be curbed by bit and bridle –
far be it from you!
10 Many are the torments of the wicked,
while those who trust in the Lord
are surrounded by loving-kindness.
11 Rejoice in the Lord;
delight, righteous ones;
sing out loud, all you upright of heart!

33 1 Sing joyfully to the Lord, you righteous ones;
praise from the upright is beautiful.
2 Give thanks to the Lord with the harp;
sing praise to Him with the ten-stringed lute.
3 Sing Him a new song;
play your best with joyous shout,
4 for the Lord's word is right,
and all His deeds are faithful.
5 He loves righteousness and justice;
the earth is full of the Lord's loving-kindness.
6 By the Lord's word the heavens were made,
by His breath all their starry host.
7 He gathers the sea waters as if in a heap
and stores the depths in treasuries.
8 Let all the earth fear the Lord;
let all inhabitants of the world revere Him,
9 for He spoke and it came to be
at His command; it stood firm.
10 The Lord foils the plans of nations;
He thwarts the intentions of peoples.
11 The Lord's plans endure forever,
His heart's intents for all generations.
12 Happy is the nation whose God is the Lord,
the people He has chosen as His own.
13 The Lord looks down from heaven
and sees all of humanity;
14 from His dwelling place He watches
over all inhabitants of the earth.
15 He forms the hearts of all
and discerns all their deeds.
16 A king is not saved by a vast force;
a warrior is not delivered by great strength.
17 A horse is a vain hope for victory;

despite its great strength, it cannot bring salvation.
18 Yes, the eye of the Lord is on those who fear Him,
on those who place their hopes in His kindness,
19 rescuing them from death,
keeping them alive in famine.
20 We await the Lord;
He is our help and shield.
21 In Him our hearts rejoice,
for we trust in His holy name.
22 May Your loving-kindness be upon us, Lord,
for we place our hope in You.

34 1 *Of David, when he feigned insanity before Avimelekh,*[34] *who drove him away, and he left.*[35]

2 I will bless the Lord at all times;
His praise will be always on my lips.
3 My soul will glory in the Lord;
let the lowly hear this and rejoice.
4 Glorify the Lord with me;
let us exalt His name together.
5 I sought the Lord, and He answered me;
He saved me from all my fears.
6 Those who look to Him are radiant;
let their faces not be downcast.
7 This poor person called, and the Lord heard;
He saved him from all his troubles.
8 The Lord's angel encamps around those who fear Him
and comes to their rescue.
9 Taste for yourselves; see that the Lord is good;
happy are those who take refuge in Him.
10 Fear the Lord, you His holy ones,
for those who fear Him lack nothing.
11 Lions may grow weak and hungry,
but those who seek the Lord will never lack any good.
12 Come, my children, listen to me;
I will teach you the fear of the Lord.
13 Who among you desires life;
who longs to see many good years?
14 Then keep your tongue from evil,
your lips from speaking deceit.
15 Turn away from evil and do good;
strive for peace and pursue it.

---

34 | See 1 Samuel 21:11–16, which refers to the person here called Avimelekh as Akhish, king of Gat.

35 | This psalm takes the form of an alphabetical acrostic.

16 The eyes of the LORD are on the righteous;
His ears are attuned to their cry.
17 The LORD's face is set against those who do evil,
to erase their memory from the earth.
18 The LORD hears when they[36] cry out;
He delivers them from all their troubles.
19 The LORD is close to the brokenhearted;
He saves those who are crushed in spirit.
20 Many troubles may befall the righteous,
but the LORD delivers him from all of them;
21 He protects every one of his bones
so that none of them will be broken.
22 Evil will slay the wicked;
the enemies of the righteous will be condemned.
23 The LORD redeems the lives of His servants;
none who take refuge in Him will be condemned.

35 1 *Of David.*

Contend with those who contend with me, LORD;
fight those who fight me;
2 take up shield and armor
and rise up to help me;
3 unsheathe spear and javelin
against my pursuers.
Tell me, "I am your salvation."
4 Let those who seek my life
be shamed and humiliated;
let those who plot my ruin
retreat in disgrace.
5 Let them be like chaff in the wind,
driven by the LORD's angel;
6 let their way be dark and slippery,
with the LORD's angel in pursuit,
7 for they laid a trap for me without cause;
without cause they dug a pit for me;
8 let ruin ravage them suddenly;
let them be caught in their own trap
and fall into it to their utter ruin,
9 but my soul will delight in the LORD,
rejoicing in His salvation.
10 Every inch of my being declares,
"O LORD, who is like You?
You save the poor from those too strong for them,
the poor and needy from those who exploit them."

---

36 | This pronoun refers back to the righteous mentioned in verse 16.

11 False witnesses suddenly come forward,
interrogating me about things I know not;
12 they repay good with evil –
I am left bereaved,
13 for when they were ill I donned sackcloth,
made myself suffer with fasting,
prayer surging in my chest;
14 I went about as if it were my own friend, my own brother,
bowed in gloom as if mourning for my mother,
15 but when I stumbled, they swarmed in glee;
wretches suddenly swarmed about me,
tearing at me without cease.
16 With a vile, mocking leer
they gnash their teeth at me.
17 How long, Lord, will You look on?
Save me from their onslaught,
my precious life from lions.
18 I will thank You before a great assembly;
I will praise You before a mighty throng.
19 Do not let my treacherous enemies gloat over me
or those who hate me without cause narrow their eyes,
20 for they do not speak words of peace;
they devise treacherous schemes
against the harmless of the land.
21 Their mouths open wide against me,
calling "Aha! Aha! Our eyes have seen it!"
22 You have seen it, Lord;
do not remain silent;
O Lord, do not be far from me.
23 Awake and rise to my defense;
contend for me, my God, my Lord.
24 Vindicate me in Your justice, Lord my God;
do not let them gloat over me;
25 do not let them tell themselves,
"Aha! As we wished!"
Do not let them say,
"We have swallowed him up!"
26 Let those who gloat at my misfortune
be altogether shamed and disgraced;
let those who boast over me
don shame and humiliation.
27 May those who delight in my vindication
sing and rejoice;
may they always say,
"Great be the Lord
who delights in His servants' success."

28 Then will my tongue express Your justice,
Your praises all day long.

36 1 *To the lead singer – of the Lord's servant, of David.*

2 Well do I know
what vice whispers to the wicked;
there is no fear of God
before their eyes.
3 They flatter themselves in their own eyes
that their sin will not be discovered and hated.
4 The words they mouth are treacherous and deceitful;
they cannot contemplate doing good;
5 in bed they plot treachery;
they are set on a path of no good,
never spurning evil.
6 O Lord,
Your loyalty reaches the heavens,
Your faithfulness the skies;
7 Your justice is like the mighty mountains,
Your judgment like the great deep;
O Lord,
You save both human and beast.
8 How precious is Your loyalty, God;
people find refuge in the shade of Your wings;
9 they feast on the rich plenty of Your House;
You quench their thirst with Your river of delights,
10 for the fountain of life is with You;
by Your light we see light.
11 Extend Your loyalty to those who know You,
Your justice to the upright of heart.
12 Let no arrogant foot trample me;
let no wicked hand drive me away –
13 there evildoers lie fallen,
forced down, unable to rise.

37 1 *Of David.*[37]

Do not be incensed at the wicked
or let your envy be kindled by evildoers,
2 for they will soon wither like grass
and fade away like greenery.
3 Trust in the Lord and do good –
you will be settled in the land,
secure in your pasture.
4 Delight in the Lord,

37 | The first letters of every second verse of this psalm form an alphabetical acrostic.

and He will grant you your heart's desire.
5 Commit your way to the LORD;
trust in Him, and He will act:
6 He will bring out your vindication to light,
the justice of your cause like the noonday sun.

7 Wait for the LORD
silently, patiently;
do not be incensed
at those who succeed
through devious plots.
8 Release your anger;
abandon your wrath;
do not be incensed –
it leads only to harm,
9 for the wicked will be cut off,
while those who hope for the LORD
shall inherit the earth.
10 Very soon, the wicked will be no more;
you will look at their place to find them gone,
11 but the lowly shall inherit the earth;
they will delight in the wealth of peace.
12 The wicked scheme against the righteous,
gnashing their teeth at them,
13 but the LORD laughs at them;
He knows their day will come.
14 The wicked unsheathe their swords
and draw their bows
to bring down the poor and the needy,
to slaughter those whose path is straight.
15 Their swords will pierce their own hearts;
their bows will be shattered.

16 The righteous person's precious little is better
than the vast wealth of the many wicked,
17 for the arms of the wicked will be broken,
while the LORD supports the righteous.
18 The LORD cares for the days of the blameless;
their heritage will last forever.
19 They will not suffer shame when times are hard;
in famine they will still be sated,
20 but the wicked will perish;
the LORD's enemies are like meadow grass:
they vanish away like vanishing smoke.
21 The wicked borrows and does not repay;
the righteous are generous; they give and give,
22 for His blessed ones shall inherit the earth,

while those cursed by Him will be cut off.

23 It is the Lord who makes people's footsteps firm
when He delights in their way;
24 when they stumble, they will not fall,
for the Lord holds their hand.
25 I was once young; now I am old,
yet I have never seen the righteous forsaken,
with their children begging for bread.
26 They are always generous, lending freely,
and their children become a blessing.
27 Turn away from evil and do good,
and you will always dwell secure,
28 for the Lord loves justice;
He will never abandon His devoted ones.
They will always be kept safe,
while the children of the wicked will be cut off.
29 The righteous will inherit the earth
and be settled upon it forever.

30 Righteous mouths speak words of wisdom;
their tongues express justice.
31 Their God's teaching is in their hearts;
their steps will never falter.
32 The wicked lie in wait for the righteous,
seeking their death;
33 the Lord will not abandon them to their hands
or condemn them when they are judged.
34 Place your hope in the Lord
and keep His way –
He will raise you up to inherit the earth
as you will see
when the wicked are cut off.

35 I have seen a tyrant in his prime,
well rooted like a verdant native tree,
36 yet suddenly he passes on and is no more;
I looked for him, but he was nowhere to be found.
37 Watch and see, you blameless and upright,
that a future awaits the peaceful person
38 while sinners will be utterly destroyed;
the future of the wicked will be cut off.
39 The righteous's deliverance is from the Lord;
He is their refuge in times of trouble.
40 The Lord will help them and rescue them –
rescue them from the wicked and deliver them,
for they seek refuge in Him.

38 1 *A psalm of David,* lehazkir.[38]

2 Lord,
do not reproach me in Your rage
or punish me in Your fury,
3 for Your arrows strike me;
Your hand strikes me!
4 My body is not sound because of Your wrath;
my bones are not well because of my sin.
5 My offenses have piled up above my head
like a heavy burden,
too heavy to bear.
6 My wounds reek and fester
because of my foolishness.
7 I am utterly stooped over, hunched up,
my gait gloomy all day long,
8 for my insides burn fiercely;
my body is not sound.
9 I have grown so weak, so broken;
I roar out from the uproar in my mind,
10 "Lord, all I ache for is known to You;
My groans are not hidden from You."
11 My heart is throbbing;
my strength has left me;
the light is long gone from my eyes.
12 My loved ones, my friends –
they shrink away at my suffering;
those I was close to
keep their distance
13 while those who seek my life lay their snares;
those who seek my harm scheme viciously,
plotting their treacherous plots all day,
14 but I am like a deaf person who cannot hear,
like a dumb person who cannot speak;
15 I am like one who cannot hear
and cannot answer back,
16 yet for You, Lord, I wait in hope;
You will answer me, Lord my God,
17 for I fear they will gloat over me
and, when my foot slips, swagger over me –
18 for I am on the verge of collapse
and constantly in pain.
19 I admit my guilt;
I regret my sin.

---

38 | A musical term of uncertain meaning, literally "to evoke."

20 My mortal enemies are fierce;
so many hate me without cause.
21 Those who repay good with evil
oppose me for pursuing good.
22 Do not abandon me, LORD;
My God, do not stray far from me.
23 Rush to my help,
O LORD, my salvation.

39 1 *For the lead singer, for Yedutun*[39] *– a psalm of David.*

2 I was determined to watch my ways
and not to sin with my tongue;
I would keep my mouth shut tight
so long as the wicked were in my presence.
3 I remained silent;
I kept perfectly still,
but my pain grew intense –
4 my heart burned within me,
my thoughts blazed,
and I spoke up:
5 "Tell me when it will end, LORD,
the number of my days –
that I may know how fleeting I am."
6 You have measured out my days in handbreadths,
and my life span is as nothing before You.
Alas, all humanity, however firm it stands,
is but a mere breath – Selah.
7 Alas, people are but walking shadows,
their restless bustle but mere breath;
they hoard without knowing who will gather in.
8 And now, what can I wait for, LORD?
My only hope is You.
9 Save me from all my sins;
do not let me be scorned by fools.
10 I will keep silent; I will not open my mouth,
for it is Your doing.
11 Remove Your scourge from me;
I waste away from the blows of Your hand.
12 Punishing offense, You bring suffering,
crumbling people's treasures like a moth.
Alas, all humanity is but fleeting breath – Selah.
13 Hear my prayer, LORD;
give ear to my cry;
do not remain silent at my tears,

39 | A famed Temple musician; cf. Psalms 62, 77; 1 Chronicles 16:42, 25:6.

for to You I am but a passerby,
a mere transient like all my ancestors.
14 Let me be, so I may smile again
before I pass away and am no more.

40 1 *To the lead singer – of David, a psalm.*

2 I put all my hope in the LORD;
He bent down to me;
He heard my cry.
3 He raised me out of the pit of despair,
from the oozing mud;
He set my feet on solid stone
and steadied my footsteps.
4 He placed a new song on my lips,
a song of praise for our God;
the crowds will see and be struck with awe
and place their trust in the LORD.
5 Happy are those who make the LORD their trust
instead of turning to the pompous,
to followers of falsehood,
6 for You have done great things,
O LORD my God;
You have devised such wonders for us;
none can compare to You –
were I to tell of them, to speak of them,
there would be far too many to count.
7 For sacrifice or gift
You have no desire – that You have made clear.[40]
You never asked
for burnt offering or purification offering,
8 so I decided,
"Here – I come with the scroll that was written for me."
9 To do Your will, God, is my desire;
Your teachings course through my insides.
10 I proclaimed Your righteousness before the great assembly;
see – I have not sealed my lips, LORD, as You know.
11 I have not kept Your justice secret in my heart;
I proclaim Your devotion and salvation;
I have not denied Your loyalty and truth
before the great assembly.
12 As for You, LORD,
do not withhold Your compassion from me;
let Your loyalty and truth keep me always,
13 for endless evil has beset me;

40 | Literally "You have hollowed out ears for me."

my offenses have caught up with me, blurring my vision;
they far outnumber the hairs on my head,
and my heart fails within me.
14 Show me favor, LORD, and save me;
rush to my help, LORD!
15 Let those who seek to snatch away my life
be shamed and disgraced;
let those who wish me harm
retreat in humiliation;
16 let those who leer at me – "Aha! Aha!" –
wallow in their shame.
17 May all those who seek You
rejoice and delight in You.
May those who long for Your salvation
always proclaim, "The LORD is great!"
18 As for me, I am poor and needy;
may the LORD call me to mind.
You are my help and my rescuer –
my God, do not delay.[41]

41 1 *To the lead singer – a psalm of David.*

2 Happy are those who give thought to the weak;
may the LORD spare them in times of misery
3 May the LORD keep them and give them life
so that they will be happy in the land,
rather than give them up
to the will of their enemies.
4 May the LORD sustain them on their sickbeds;
You completely turned back their suffering.
5 I prayed,
"O LORD, show me mercy;
heal me, for I sinned against You."
6 My enemies speak of me with spite:
"When will he die and his name perish?"
7 If they visit, they babble insincerely
while malice swells in their heart –
as soon as they leave, they speak out.
8 All those who hate me whisper about me,
imagining the worst for me:
9 "Something deadly courses through him;
he will never rise from his bed again."
10 Even my trusted friend
– who ate of my bread! –

41 | Cf. Psalm 70, which parallels (with variants) the text of verses 14–18.

has treated me with cruel deceit.[42]
11 But You, Lord, show me grace;
raise me up so that I may pay them back –
12 by this I shall know that You delight in me;
my enemies will not crow over me.
13 As for me, because I am blameless
You support me;
You let me stand firm before You forever.
14 Blessed is the Lord, God of Israel,
for ever and ever,
Amen and Amen.

BOOK TWO

42 1 *To the lead singer – of the sons of Koraḥ,*[43] *a* maskil.[44]

2 As a deer pines for flowing streams,
my soul pines for You, God;
3 my soul thirsts for God, the living God –
oh, when will I come and appear before God?
4 My tears have been my fare day and night
as people ever taunt me, "Where is your God?"
5 Oh, the things I remember
as I pour out my soul:
how I would join the crowd
and march along
to the House of God
with elated song and the hum of praise
from the reveling throngs.
6 Why are you miserable, my soul?
Why do you grieve so within me?
Hope for God –
that I will yet praise Him
in the salvation of His presence.
7 My God –
my soul is miserable within me;
therefore I think of You
in the land of Jordan,
in the Ḥermon range,
from the Humble Mountain,
8 where deep calls to deep
in the roar of Your waterfalls;
all Your torrents and storm waves

42 | Literally "has made his heel great against me."

43 | A group of Levitical Temple singers; see II Chronicles 20:19.

44 | See note on 32:1.

crashed over me.[45]
9 By day, the LORD commands His loyalty;
by night, His song is with me –
a prayer to the God of my life.
10 Let me say to God, my Rock,
"Why have You forgotten me?
Why must I walk bent in gloom,
oppressed by my enemies?"
11 My enemies' scorn pierces my bones
as they ever taunt me, "Where is your God?"
12 Why are you miserable, my soul?
Why do you grieve so within me?
Hope for God –
that I will yet praise Him,
my salvation and my God.

43 1 Vindicate me, God; [46]
contend on my behalf
against an ungodly nation;
from treacherous, corrupt people
rescue me,
2 for You are the God of my refuge.
Why do You forsake me?
Why must I walk about bent in gloom,
oppressed by my enemies?
3 Send forth Your light and Your truth –
they will guide me;
they will bring me to Your holy mountain,
to Your dwelling place,
4 and I will come to the altar of God –
to God, my joy, my delight.
I will praise You with the lyre,
God, O my God!
5 Why are you miserable, my soul?
Why do you grieve so within me?
Hope for God –
that I will yet praise Him,
my salvation and my God.

44 1 *To the lead singer – of the sons of Koraḥ, a* maskil.

2 God,
we heard with our own ears;
our ancestors told us

---

45 | Cf. Jonah 2:4.

46 | This psalm represents the continuation of Psalm 42; note the shared refrain in 42:6, 42:12, and 43:5.

of the deeds You did in their days,
in days of old.
3 By Your hand You planted them,
dispossessing nations;
You brought evil upon peoples
and drove them out.
4 Not by their swords did they win the land,
nor did their arms bring them victory.
It was Your right hand,
Your arm,
the light of Your face,
for You showed them favor.
5 You are my King, God –
command victory for Yaakov.
6 Through You we will gore our foes,
in Your name trample our adversaries,
7 for I do not place my trust in my bow;
it is not my sword that will bring me victory.
8 It is You who bring us victory over our foes,
who bring shame to those who hate us.
9 In God we glory all day long,
and we will ever praise Your name – Selah.
10 Yet You have forsaken us and disgraced us;
You no longer accompany our armies.
11 You make us retreat before foes
while those who hate us plunder away.
12 You have allowed us to be devoured like sheep
and scattered us among the nations,
13 selling Your people for next to nothing,
making no profit from their sale.
14 You have made us the scorn of our neighbors,
the laughingstock of those around us,
15 a cautionary tale among the nations –
the peoples shake their heads.
16 All day long my disgrace haunts me;
my face is draped in shame
17 from the shouts of those who taunt and revile,
from the enemy and avenger.
18 All this has befallen us,
but we have not forgotten You;
we have not betrayed Your covenant.
19 Our hearts have not turned back;
our steps have not strayed from Your path
20 although You have broken us where jackals prowl
and draped us in death-shadow.

21 Had we forgotten the name of our God
or spread out our hands toward an alien god,
22 would God fail to discover this?
For He knows the secrets of the heart.
23 For Your sake we constantly face death;
we are considered mere sheep for the slaughter.
24 Stir – why do You sleep, LORD?
Rouse Yourself!
Do not forsake us forever.
25 Why do You hide Your face;
why do You forget our suffering and misery?
26 We are dragged down to the dust,
our bodies pressed to the earth.
27 Arise to help us;
redeem us for the sake of Your loyalty.

45 1 *To the lead singer – of the sons of Koraḥ, set to* shoshanim[47] *– a* maskil, *a love song.*

2 My heart is astir with glad words;
I dedicate this work to the king;
my tongue runs like a skilled scribe's pen.
3 You are the fairest of mortals;
your lips brim with grace;
for this, God has blessed you forever.
4 Fasten your sword on your thigh, mighty one,
in your majesty and splendor.
5 In your splendor, ride on triumphant
for the sake of truth, humility, and justice,
and may your right hand lead you to wondrous deeds.
6 Your arrows are sharp
in the hearts of the king's enemies;
peoples fall at your feet.
7 Your divine throne is eternal;
your royal scepter is a scepter of equity.
8 You love justice and despise evil –
for this, God – your God –
has anointed you out of all your fellows
with oil of bliss.
9 Your robes are all fragrant
with myrrh and aloe and cinnamon.
Lutes echo from ivory chambers,
delighting you.
10 The daughters of kings are among your noble ladies;
on your right stands the queen in gold of Ofir.

47 | A musical term of uncertain meaning, perhaps related to the meaning "lilies."

11 Hear me, daughter; look around and listen;
forget your own people and your father's house,
12 and let the king crave your beauty.
He is your master now; bow to him.
13 Daughter of Tyre,
the richest of peoples will seek your favor with gifts.
14 In all her glory, the princess is inside,
adorned in golden filigree;
15 she is led to the king in embroidered finery,
maidens, her friends, in her train;
they are brought to you,
16 led in gladness and joy;
they enter the king's palace.
17 Your sons will succeed your fathers;
you will make them princes throughout the land.
18 I have perpetuated your name for all generations;
therefore peoples shall praise you for ever and for all time.

46 1 *To the lead singer – a song of the sons of Koraḥ, on* alamot.[48]

2 God is our refuge and might,
ever present to help in times of trouble,
3 so we need not fear
when the world shifts,
when mountains crumble
into the heart of the sea –
4 though its waters rage and foam,
though the mountains shudder at its surge – Selah.
5 There is a river whose streams bring joy to the city of God,
to the holy dwelling place of the Most High.
6 God is in its midst; it will never crumble;
God will come to its aid at the break of day.
7 Nations rage; kingdoms crumble;
He sounds His voice, and the earth dissolves.
8 The Lord of Hosts is with us;
the God of Yaakov is our refuge – Selah.
9 Come, gaze at the works of the Lord,
at the desolation He has wrought upon the earth.
10 He has ended war all over the earth,
breaking bow and snapping spear,
burning chariots with fire.
11 Desist and know that I am God,
exalted among nations,
exalted over the earth.
12 The Lord of Hosts is with us;

48 | A musical term of uncertain meaning; cf. 1 Chronicles 15:20.

the God of Yaakov is our refuge – Selah.

47 1 *To the lead singer – a psalm of the sons of Koraḥ.*

2 Clap your hands together, all peoples;
shout out joyfully to God,
3 for the LORD, Most High, is fearsome,
the great King over all the earth.
4 It is He who subjugates peoples under us,
nations beneath our feet.
5 He chooses our legacy for us:
the pride of Yaakov, whom He loves – Selah.
6 God ascends amid shouts of joy –
the LORD – to the blast of the ram's horn.
7 Sing out to God, sing!
Sing out to our King, sing!
8 For God is King over all the earth –
sing a psalm of praise![49]
9 God reigns over nations;
God is seated on His holy throne.
10 The rulers of peoples have gathered,
the people of Avraham's God,
for all the earth's protectors are God's;
He is raised high above.

48 1 *A song – a psalm of the sons of Koraḥ.*

2 Great is the LORD, of highest praise
in the city of our God, His holy mountain,
3 beautiful in its heights,
the delight of all the earth,
Mount Zion, the slopes of Tzafon,[50]
city of the great King.
4 God is known as the protector
of its palaces.
5 See how the kings joined forces,
advancing together.
6 Astounded at the sight,
they panicked and fled –
7 there fear seized them,
the agony of a woman in childbirth,
8 like ships of Tarshish wrecked
by eastern winds.[51]

49 | Hebrew *maskil*. See note on 32:1.

50 | Literally "the North." The peak of Mount Zion (Moriah) was situated at the northern end of the city of Jerusalem, which was built on its southern slopes.

51 | Cf. 1 Kings 22:49.

9 The tales are all true –
we have seen for ourselves –
in the city of the Lord of Hosts,
in the city of our God.
May God preserve it forever – Selah.
10 Within Your Temple, God,
we meditate on Your love.
11 Your name, God, like Your praise,
reaches the ends of the earth;
Your right hand is filled with righteousness.
12 Let Mount Zion rejoice;
let the towns of Yehuda be glad
because of Your judgments.
13 Walk around Zion and encircle it;
count its towers;
14 note its strong walls;
make your way through its citadels
so that you may tell future generations
15 that this is God, our God,
for ever and ever;
He will guide us for evermore.

49 1 *To the lead singer – a psalm of the sons of Koraḥ.*

2 Hear this, all you peoples;
listen, all dwellers of this world,
3 low and high,
rich and poor alike.
4 My mouth will speak words of wisdom;
my heart's utterance, understanding.
5 I listen with care to a parable;
I expound my theme to the music of the harp.
6 Why should I fear when evil days come,
when wicked deceivers surround me –
7 those who trust in their wealth,
who boast of their great riches?
8 No person can ever redeem another
or pay God the price of his release;
9 the ransom of a life is costly;
no payment will ever be enough
10 to let him live forever,
never seeing the grave.
11 For all can see that wise men die
and that the foolish and senseless all perish,
leaving their wealth to others.
12 They think their houses will last forever,
their dwellings for all generations –

they give their names to their estates,
13 but a person, despite his wealth, cannot linger;
he is like the beasts that perish.
14 Such is the fate of the foolish,
the end of those pleased with their own words – Selah.
15 They go down to Sheol like sheep;
death will be their shepherd.
The upright will rule over them in the morning.
Their forms will decay in Sheol,
far from their noble mansions.
16 But God will redeem my life from Sheol,
for He will take me – Selah.
17 Fear not when people grow rich,
when their houses rise in esteem,
18 for they will take nothing with them in death;
their esteem will not descend with them.
19 Though they counted themselves blessed in life,
for people praise you when you prosper,
20 they too will join the ranks of their ancestors,
who will never see the light again.
21 A person with wealth but without understanding
is like the beasts that perish.

50 1 *A psalm of Asaf.*[52]

God, the Lord God,
speaks and summons the earth
from where the sun rises to where it sets.
2 From Zion, pure beauty,
God shines forth.
3 Let our God come;
let Him not hold back –
a devouring fire flares before Him;
a wild storm rages around Him.
4 He calls on the earth and the heavens above
for the judgment of His people:
5 "Gather My devoted ones to Me,
those who forged a covenant with Me by sacrifice."
6 The heavens tell of His justice,
for God Himself is the judge – Selah.
7 Listen, My people, and I will speak;
Israel, I will testify against you:
I am God, your God.
8 I do not rebuke you for your sacrifices
or for your burnt offerings ever before Me.

---

52 | A prominent Levitical Temple singer; see 1 Chronicles 16:7, 25:1–9; Nehemiah 7:44.

9 I claim no bulls of your house,
no he-goats from your folds,
10 for all the forest beasts are Mine,
the cattle of a thousand hills;
11 I know every bird of the mountains;
the creatures of the fields belong to Me.
12 Were I to hunger, I would not tell you,
for Mine is the world
and all that fills it.
13 Do I eat the flesh of bulls?
Do I drink the blood of he-goats?
14 Offer to God a thanksgiving sacrifice;
pay your vows to the Most High.
15 When you call Me in times of trouble,
I will rescue you, and you will honor Me.
16 But to the wicked, God says,
"How dare you recite My laws
or bear My covenant on your lips –
17 you who despise discipline
and toss My words behind you?
18 When you see a thief, you are drawn to him;
you associate with adulterers;
19 you speak evil freely;
your tongue adheres to deceit;
20 you sit and slander your brother,
maligning the child of your own mother.
21 If all this you do and I hold back,
You might imagine I am like you,
so I will rebuke you and charge you outright.
22 Consider this, you who forget God,
lest I tear you apart, with no one to save you:
23 those who bring Me offerings of thanksgiving honor Me,
and as for those who are following My way,
I will show them God's salvation."

51 1 *To the lead singer – a psalm of David,*
2 *when the prophet Natan came to him*
after he came to Batsheva.[53]

3 Show me grace, God, in Your loyalty;
in Your great mercy, erase my offense;
4 wash me well of my guilt;
purify me of my sin,
5 for I am aware of my transgression,
and my sin is ever before me.

53 | See II Samuel, chapter 12.

6 I sinned against You alone;
I committed what is evil in Your eyes,
so Your sentence is just,
and Your judgment is fair.
7 Yes, with guilt I came to be;
in sin did my mother conceive me.
8 Yes, You desire truth to course deep within me –
to teach wisdom to my innermost self.
9 Purge me with hyssop, and I will be pure;
wash me, and I will be whiter than snow.
10 Let me hear gladness and joy;
let the bones You have crushed rejoice.
11 Hide Your face from my sins;
erase all my guilt.
12 Create a pure heart for me, God;
renew a firm spirit within me.
13 Do not cast me away from Your presence
or take Your holy spirit away from me.
14 Restore your glad salvation to me;
let a willing spirit sustain me.
15 I will teach offenders Your ways,
and sinners will come back to You.
16 Save me from bloodshed, God,
God of my salvation;
my tongue will sing of Your justice.
17 O Lord, open my lips,
and my mouth will declare Your praise.
18 You have no desire for me to bring sacrifice;
You do not want burnt offerings.
19 To God, a broken spirit is an offering;
a crushed and broken heart, God, You will not spurn.
20 Favor Zion with Your goodness;
rebuild the walls of Jerusalem.
21 Then You will delight in sincere sacrifices,
burnt offerings and whole offerings;
then bulls will be offered up on Your altar.

52 1 *To the lead singer – of David, a* maskil,
2 *when Doeg the Edomite came and informed Sha'ul, telling him,*
"David went to the house of Avimelekh."[54]

3 Why do you boast of evil, powerful one?
God's loyalty is everlasting.
4 Your tongue wreaks malice,
carving mischief like a sharpened razor;

54 | See I Samuel 22:9.

5 you love evil more than good,
lying more than speaking truth – Selah.
6 You love all words of carnage,
all treacherous speech,
7 but God will tear you down once and for all;
He will snatch you up
and uproot you from your home,
your roots from the land of the living – Selah.
8 Then the righteous will look on in awe,
and they will mock him:
9 "Here is someone who would not make God his refuge
but trusted in his great wealth
and grew powerful through malice."
10 But I am like a flourishing olive tree
in the House of God;
I will trust in God's loyalty
for ever and for all time.
11 I will praise You forever
for what You have done;
I will proclaim that Your name is good
in the presence of Your devoted ones.

53 1 *To the lead singer, on* maḥalat[55] *– of David, a* maskil.[56]

2 The brute says in his heart,
"There is no God."
They are corrupt; they wreak vile schemes;
there is no one who does good.
3 God looks down from heaven at humanity
to see if someone has the sense to seek out God,
4 but all are treacherous,
altogether tainted;
there is no one who does good,
not even one.
5 Have they no knowledge, those evildoers
who devour my people as if devouring bread,
who do not call out to God?
6 There they were struck with terror,
such terror as never before,
for God scattered the bones of your attackers;
You have put them to shame,
for God has rejected them.
7 Oh, that Israel's salvation might come from Zion;
when God restores His people's fortune,

55 | An unknown musical term. See also 88:1.
56 | Cf. Psalm 14, a slightly different version of this psalm.

Yaakov will rejoice;
Israel will be glad.

54 1 *To the lead singer, accompanied by music – of David, a* maskil,
2 *when the Zifites came and told Sha'ul, "David is hiding among us."*[57]

3 God, save me by Your name;
with Your might, vindicate me.
4 God, hear my prayer;
give ear to the words I mouth,
5 for strangers have risen up against me;
cruel men seek my life,
men who have no regard for God – Selah.
6 Look – God is my helper;
the LORD is the one who sustains my life.
7 He will repay my oppressors for their evil.
By Your truth, destroy them.
8 To You I will offer a freewill sacrifice;
I will praise Your name, LORD, for it is good,
9 for He has saved me from all danger;
my eyes have seen my enemies' downfall.

55 1 *To the lead singer, accompanied by music – of David, a* maskil.

2 Give ear, God, to my prayer;
do not ignore my plea;
3 hear me and answer me.
Restless, I wail and cry out –
4 at the clamor of the enemy,
at the cruelty of the wicked,
for they bring evil crashing down on me;
they pounce on me with fury.
5 My heart trembles within me;
I am gripped with death terror;
6 fear and shaking seize me;
I am stifled with horror.
7 And I cried,
"If only I had wings like a dove,
I would fly away and find rest;
8 O, I would roam far away
and alight in the wilderness – Selah.
9 I would soon find shelter
from the raging wind and storm."
10 Thwart them, LORD;
confound their speech,
for I see violence and strife in the city.

---

57 | See 1 Samuel 23:19.

11 Day and night they patrol its walls;
evil and suffering are in its midst.
12 In its midst is corruption;
treachery and deceit never cease to haunt its square,
13 but it is not an enemy who taunts me –
that I could bear –
it is not a foe who looms over me,
for then I could hide.
14 It is you, a person like me –
my companion, my friend.
15 We shared sweet closeness
as we walked among the crowd
at the House of God.
16 May He set death upon them;
may they go down to Sheol alive,
for evil has permeated their minds,
their very being.
17 I will call out to God;
the LORD will save me.
18 Evening, morning, noon
I wail and cry out,
and He hears my voice.
19 He redeems me unharmed
from the battle I wage
as if many are on my side.
20 God, enthroned as of old,
will hear and humble them – Selah –
for they will never change;
they will never fear God.
21 That man[58] lashed out at his own allies;
he violated his pact.
22 His speech was smooth as butter,
but war was in his heart;
his words seemed soft as oil,
but they were drawn swords.
23 Cast your burden upon the LORD,
and He will sustain you;
He will never let the righteous be shaken,
24 but You, God, will plunge them down the deepest pit –
men of blood, deceitful men
will not live out half their days,
while I will trust in You.

58 | Referring to the duplicitous companion of verse 14.

56 1 *To the lead singer, on* yonat elem reḥokim[59] – *a* mikhtam[60] *of David, when the Philistines seized him in Gat.*[61]

2 Show me grace, God, for mortals hound me;
all day long my foes oppress me;
3 all day long my oppressors trample me;
so many attack me, Exalted One!
4 When I fear,
I trust in You –
5 in God, whose word I praise,
in God I trust; I do not fear –
what can mere flesh do to me?
6 All day long they move me to grief;
all their plans against me are evil;
7 they lie in wait,
tracing my footsteps,
eager to take my life.
8 Uproot them for their evil;
cast down such people in Your wrath, God!
9 You count my wanderings;
You store my tears in Your vial;
are they not in Your records?
10 Then, on the day that I call,
my enemies will retreat;
this I know, for God is with me.
11 In God, whose word I praise,
in the Lord, whose word I praise,
12 in God I trust; I do not fear –
what can man do to me?
13 I must fulfill my vows to You, God;
I will give thank offerings to You,
14 for You have saved me from death,
my feet from stumbling,
that I may walk before God in the light of life.

57 1 *To the lead singer,* al tashḥet[62] – *a* mikhtam *of David in the cave, when he was fleeing from Sha'ul.*[63]

2 Show me grace, God; show me grace,
for in You I take refuge.
I will take refuge in the shade of Your wings
until disaster has passed.

59 | The meaning of this phrase is uncertain.
60 | See note on 16:1.
61 | Perhaps referring to 1 Samuel 21:11–16.
62 | Perhaps "do not destroy." The meaning of the phrase in this context is uncertain.
63 | See 1 Samuel, chapters 24, 26.

3 I will call on God, the Most High,
to the God who grants me fulfillment.
4 He will send from heaven and save me;
He will bring those who crush me to shame – Selah.
God will send His loyalty and truth.
5 I am bounded by lions,
forced to dwell among ravenous beasts,
men whose teeth are spears and arrows,
their tongues sharpened swords.
6 Rise up, God, over the heavens;
unleash Your glory over all the earth.
7 They rigged a net to trip me up,
to entrap me;
they dug a pit in my path
but fell into it themselves – Selah.
8 My heart is sound, God;
my heart is sound –
I will sing and chant praises.
9 Stir, my soul!
Stir, harp and lyre!
I will stir the dawn.
10 I will praise You among the peoples, LORD;
I will chant Your praise among the nations,
11 for Your loyalty is as high as the heavens;
Your truth reaches the skies.
12 Rise up, God, over the heavens;
unleash Your glory over all the earth.[64]

58 1 *To the lead singer,* al tashḥet – *a* mikhtam *of David.*

2 Do you truly decree justice, powerful ones?
Do you judge people with equity?
3 No, your hearts churn out injustice;
your hands mete out violence in the land.
4 The wicked have been wayward since birth –
those liars, astray from the womb.
5 Their venom is like snake venom;
they are as deaf as the cobra that stops its ears
6 to tune out the whispers of the charmer,
the most skilled of enchanters.
7 God, crush the teeth in their mouths;
smash the fangs of these young lions, LORD.
8 May they melt away like water and vanish;
when they aim their arrows, let them crumble
9 like a snail dissolving as it moves,

64 | Regarding verses 8–12, cf. 108:2–6.

like a stillborn that never sees the sun.
10 Before your thorns harden to bramble,
He will whirl them away in wild fury.
11 The righteous will rejoice at the sight of vengeance
and rinse their feet in the blood of the wicked.
12 People will say,
"The righteous do harvest fruit;
there is, after all, divine justice on earth."

59 1 *To the lead singer,* al tashḥet – *a* mikhtam *of David*
when Sha'ul sent guards to David's house to kill him.[65]

2 Save me from my enemies, God;
protect me from those who rise against me.
3 Save me from evildoers;
deliver me from men of blood,
4 for look – they lurk in ambush –
fierce men lie in wait for me
for no crime or offense of mine, Lord;
5 for no fault of mine
they rush at me, ready to attack.
Look – rouse Yourself for my sake.
6 You, Lord God of Hosts,
are the God of Israel;
stir and call all the nations to account;
show no mercy to evil traitors – Selah.
7 They come out at nightfall,
growling like dogs,
prowling about the city.
8 See how they rant,
their lips like swords,
thinking, "Who can hear us?"
9 But You, Lord, mock them;
You hold all the nations in contempt.
10 O Mighty One,[66] I watch for You,
for God is my stronghold.
11 My loyal God will go out before me;
God will show me my enemies' downfall.
12 Do not kill them
lest my people forget,
but send them staggering by Your force;
bring them down, Lord, our shield.
13 For the sins of their mouths,
for the words of their lips,

65 | See I Samuel 19:11.

66 | Literally "His strength"; cf. verse 18.

let them be trapped by their own arrogance,
by the curses and lies they utter.
14 Destroy them in Your fury;
destroy them until they are no more.
Then it will be known to the ends of the earth
that God rules over Yaakov – Selah.
15 They come out at nightfall,
growling like dogs,
prowling about the city.
16 They stagger about, scavenging,
whining when they are discontent,
17 but I will sing of Your might;
each morning I will laud Your loving-kindness,
for You have been my stronghold,
my haven in times of trouble.
18 My Mighty One, to You I will chant praise,
for God is my stronghold,
the God who shows me loyalty.

60 1 *To the lead singer, on* shushan edut,[67] *a* mikhtam *of David, for instruction,*
2 *when he fought against Aram Naharayim and Aram Tzova,*
while Yoav returned and defeated twelve thousand men of Edom in the Valley of Salt.[68]

3 God,
You have forsaken us,
shattered us,
shown Your anger.
Now restore us!
4 You have made the land shudder
and split it open;
mend its cracks,
for it is falling apart.
5 You have made Your people suffer;
You have poured us poisoned wine,
6 but You have given those who revere You
a waving banner beyond bowshot – Selah.
7 That Your dear ones may be rescued,
let Your right hand bring victory – answer me!
8 God promised in His Sanctuary
that I would triumph.
I will divide up Shekhem
and measure out the Valley of Sukkot;
9 Gilad and Menashe will be mine;

67 | A musical term of uncertain meaning.

68 | See II Samuel, chapter 8, and I Chronicles, chapter 18.

Efrayim will be my chief stronghold,
Yehuda my scepter.
10 Moav will be my washbasin;
at Edom I'll fling my shoe;
Philistia, applaud me!
11 But who will bring me to the besieged cities?
Who will lead me to Edom?
12 Have You not forsaken us, God?
God, You no longer march out with our forces.
13 Come to our aid against the enemy,
for human help is worthless.
14 With God, we will triumph valiantly,
and He will trample our enemies.[69]

61 1 *To the lead singer, accompanied by music – of David.*

2 Hear my plea, God;
listen to my prayer.
3 From the end of the earth I call to You
when my heart is faint;
lead me up to a rock far above me,
4 for You have been my refuge,
a tower of strength against the enemy.
5 Let me dwell in Your tent forever
and take refuge in the shelter of Your wings – Selah –
6 for You, God, hear my vows.
Grant me the legacy of those who revere Your name.
7 Add days to the days of the king;
may he live on for many generations!
8 May he ever be seated in God's presence;
appoint loyalty and truth to keep him,
9 so I will ever sing praises to Your name,
fulfilling my vows day after day.

62 1 *To the lead singer, for Yedutun[70] – a psalm of David.*

2 For God alone my soul waits silently;
from Him is my salvation.
3 He alone is my Rock and salvation,
my stronghold – I will never be shaken.
4 How long will you come crashing down on people,
all you murderous men,
like a crooked wall,
a tottering fence?
5 Scheming to topple the people from their height,

---

69 | Cf. 108:7–14.
70 | See note on 39:1.

they relish lies;
their mouths bless
while their insides curse – Selah.
6 Wait for God in silence, my soul,
for my hope is from Him.
7 He alone is my Rock and salvation,
my stronghold – I will not be shaken.
8 My deliverance and honor rest on God,
the Rock of my strength;
in God is my refuge.
9 Trust in Him at all times, O people;
pour out your hearts before Him;
God is our refuge – Selah.
10 But people are mere breath;
humans are but an illusion;
placed on a scale all together,
they are lighter than a breath.
11 Place not trust in extortion
or false hopes in robbery;
should force pay off, give it no heed.
12 God made one pronouncement,
I heard these two:
That power belongs to God;
13 and that loyalty, Lord, is Yours,
for You will reward each person
according to his deeds.

63 1 *A psalm of David, when he was in the Wilderness of Yehuda.*[71]

2 O God,
You are my God;
I seek You desperately.
My soul thirsts for You;
my flesh longs for You
in a parched and weary land
that has no water,
3 so I have visions of You in the Sanctuary
of Your might and glory.
4 Your loving-kindness is better than life,
so my lips praise You,
5 so I will bless You as long as I live,
as I lift up my hands in Your name.
6 My soul will be nourished as with a rich feast;
my mouth will sing praises with joyful lips.
7 I think of You upon my bed;

71 | See 1 Samuel 23:14.

I contemplate You in the vigil of night,
8 for You have been my help,
and I revel in the shade of Your wings.
9 My soul clings to You;
Your right hand supports me.
10 As for those who seek to destroy my life,
may they reach the lowest depths of the earth.
11 May the sword spill their blood;
may they be the prey of foxes,
12 but the king will rejoice in God;
all who swear by Him will glory,
while the mouths of liars will be stopped up.

64 1 *To the lead singer – a psalm of David.*

2 Hear my voice, God, in my lament;
keep my life from the terror of the enemy.
3 Hide me from the band of wicked men,
from the riotous mob of evildoers
4 who sharpen their tongues like swords,
who aim bitter words like arrows
5 and shoot from ambush at the blameless,
shooting suddenly, without fear.
6 They arm themselves with evil schemes;
they plot to lay secret snares,
thinking, "Who can see them?"
7 They seek out vile crimes,
exhausting every possible plan
in the depths of the human mind and heart,
8 but God will shoot them down;
with a sudden arrow they will be wounded;
9 their own tongues will trip them up,
and all who see them will shudder.
10 Then all people will be struck with fear;
they will tell of God's works
and contemplate His deeds.
11 The righteous will rejoice in the LORD
and take refuge in Him;
all the upright of heart will exult.

65 1 *To the lead singer, a psalm – a song of David.*

2 Praise awaits You in Zion, God;
to You vows are paid.
3 Hearer of prayer,
to You all flesh will come.
4 When acts of sin overwhelm me,
You forgive our transgressions.

5 Happy are those whom You choose,
those You bring close to dwell in Your courtyards.
May we be sated with the goodness of Your House,
Your holy Sanctuary.
6 Answer us with wondrous deeds
in Your righteousness,
O God, our savior –
hope of all the ends of the earth
and the distant seas,
7 who set down the mountains in His power,
so girded in strength is He;
8 who stills the roaring seas,
the roaring of the waves,
the clamor of the nations.
9 Those who live at the ends of the earth
are awed by Your signs.
The lands of sunrise and sunset
You move to joyful song.
10 You care for the land and water it
and make it very rich,
with God-given streams brimming with water;
You provide the people's grain –
thus You have arranged it all.
11 Water its furrows;
level its ridges;
soften it with showers;
bless its growth.
12 You have crowned the year with Your goodness;
Your pathways overflow with richness.
13 The wild pasturelands overflow;
the hills are girded with joy.
14 The meadows are clothed with sheep;
the valleys are decked with grain –
they shout for joy; they burst into song.

66 1 *To the lead singer, a song – a psalm.*

Shout for joy to God, all the earth;
2 sing the glory of His name;
laud Him with glorious praise.
3 Proclaim to God,
"How wondrous are Your deeds!
In Your sheer strength,
Your enemies come cringing before You."
4 All the earth bows down before You
and sings to You,
singing to Your name – Selah.

5 Come, see the works of God,
the acts that move humanity to awe.
6 He turned sea to dry land;
they crossed the river on foot –
there we rejoiced in Him.
7 He rules over the world in His might,
His eyes keeping watch over the nations
so that the rebellious will not rise up – Selah.
8 Bless our God, O you peoples;
let His praise resound.
9 He keeps us among the living,
never letting our feet slip.
10 For You, God, have tested us,
refining us as silver is refined:
11 You led us into a trap,
placing shackles around our waists;
12 You let people ride over us;
we have been through fire and water,
but You brought us out to freedom.
13 I will enter Your House with burnt offerings;
to You I will honor my vows –
14 those that crossed my lips,
that my mouth uttered
in my distress.
15 Fat burnt offerings I will offer up to You,
the rich aroma of roasting rams;
I will prepare bulls and he-goats – Selah.
16 Come, listen, all you who fear God;
I will tell of what He did for me.
17 My mouth called out to Him,
high praise upon my tongue;
18 had evil been in my heart,
the Lord would not have listened,
19 but God did listen –
He paid heed to my prayer.
20 Blessed is God,
who has not turned away my prayer,
nor His loyalty from me.

67 1 *To the lead singer, accompanied by stringed instruments – a psalm, a song.*

2 May God be gracious to us and bless us.
May He shine His face upon us[72] – Selah.
3 Then will Your way be known on earth,
Your salvation among all the nations.

72 | Cf. the priestly blessing in Numbers 6:24–26.

4 Let the peoples praise You, God;
let all peoples praise You.
5 Let nations rejoice and sing for joy,
for You judge the peoples justly
and guide the nations of the earth – Selah.
6 Let the peoples praise You, God;
let all peoples praise You.
7 The earth has yielded its harvest;
may God, our God, bless us.
8 God will bless us,
and all will revere Him to the ends of the earth.

68 1 *To the lead singer, of David – a psalm, a song.*

2 Let God arise and His enemies be scattered;
let His foes flee before Him.[73]
3 As smoke disperses, disperse them;
as wax melts before fire,
may the wicked perish before God,
4 while the righteous rejoice and exult
before God, delighted and joyful.
5 Sing to God;
sing praises to His name.
Laud Him who rides the clouds –
the Lord is His name –
and exult before Him.
6 Father of orphans, judge of widows,
God is in His holy abode.
7 God brings the lonely back home
and sets captives free, to their delight,
but the rebellious must dwell in a parched wasteland.

8 O God, when You went out before Your people,
when You strode through the wilderness – Selah –
9 the earth shook;
the heavens, too, poured down before God,
Sinai itself before God,
God of Israel![74]
10 You, God, unleashed a lavish rain,
reviving Your weary heritage.
11 Your own flock settled there;
in Your goodness, God,
You provided for the lowly.
12 The Lord made His decree;
a great host of women spread the news:

73 | Cf. Numbers 10:35.

74 | Cf. Judges 5:4–5.

13 "Kings with their armies are fleeing, fleeing,
while housewives share out the spoil."
14 Even for those of you who lie among the sheepfolds,
the wings of the dove are inlaid with silver,
her pinions with glittering gold.
15 When Shaddai scattered the kings there,
it was like snow falling on Tzalmon.[75]

16 O mighty mountain, Mount Bashan,[76]
O Mount Bashan of many peaks,
17 why do you glare so, O many-peaked mountains,
at the mountain God desires for His abode?
Yes, the LORD will dwell there forever.
18 God's chariots are many myriads,
thousands upon thousands;
the LORD is among them
as at Sinai in holiness.
19 You ascended the heights
and carried off captives;
You received tributes from people,
even from those rebellious
against the LORD God's dwelling there.
20 Blessed be the LORD,
who bears our burdens every day;
God is our salvation – Selah.
21 Our God is for us a saving God;
God, the LORD, provides an escape from death,
22 but God will crush the heads of His enemies,
the hairy scalps of those who walk about in guilt.
23 The LORD decreed,
"I will bring them back from Bashan;
I will bring them back from the depths of the sea,
24 so that your feet may wade through blood,
so that the tongues of your dogs may take their share of the enemy."
25 They saw Your processions, God,
the processions of my God,
of my King, into the Sanctuary.
26 First came the singers;
next came the musicians
amid the girls playing tambourines.
27 Bless God in chorus,
the LORD, you of Israel's fountain!
28 There young Binyamin leads them,
the princes of Yehuda in their throngs,

75 | Perhaps a mountain in the vicinity of Shekhem mentioned in Judges 9:48.

76 | Located in the northern Transjordan region.

princes of Zevulun, princes of Naftali.
29 Your God has commanded your might,
the might, God, that You have shown us!
30 For Your Temple over Jerusalem,
kings will come to You bearing gifts.

31 Tame the beast of the marsh,
the herd of fierce bulls,
of feisty young calves, the peoples;
until they come cringing with pieces of silver,
scatter the peoples who delight in battle.
32 Let the nobles of Egypt come;
let Kush swiftly reach out its hands to God.
33 Kingdoms of earth, sing to God;
sing praise to the Lord – Selah.
34 To Him who rides the highest heavens of old,
listen! His voice rings out with might.
35 Ascribe might to God,
whose majesty is over Israel,
whose might fills the skies.
36 Your awe, God, emanates from Your Sanctuaries.
It is Israel's God
who gives might and power to the people.
Blessed is God!

69 1 *To the lead singer, set to* shoshanim[77] *– of David.*

2 Save me, God,
for the waters have reached my neck;
3 I am drowning in the mire of the deep
with nowhere to stand;
I have reached the watery depths,
and the current has swept me away.
4 I am weary from calling out;
my throat is hoarse;
my eyes are dim
from searching for my God.
5 There are more who hate me without cause
than there are hairs on my head,
so many treacherous foes
who long to destroy me.
Must I return
what I have not stolen?

6 God,
You know my folly;

77 | See note on 45:1.

my guilt is not hidden from You.
7 Let not those who hope for You
be shamed through me,
Lord God of Hosts;
let not those who seek You
be disgraced through me,
God of Israel.
8 For Your sake I bear taunting;
my face is draped in disgrace.
9 I have become a stranger to my brothers,
an alien to my mother's children,
10 for fervor for Your House has destroyed me;
the taunts of Your taunters have fallen on me.
11 When I wept and fasted,
I was taunted for it;
12 when I clothed myself in sackcloth,
I became a cautionary tale for them.
13 Loiterers at the gate gossip about me;
drunkards sing about me,
14 but as for me,
may my prayer come to You, Lord,
in a moment of favor.
God, in Your great loyalty,
answer me with Your true salvation.
15 Save me from drowning in the mud;
let me be saved from my haters,
from the watery depths.
16 Do not let me be swept away in the current
or swallowed by the deep;
do not let the Pit close its mouth over me.

17 Answer me, Lord, in Your good loyalty;
turn to me in Your great compassion.
18 Do not hide Your face from Your servant,
for I am in danger – hurry, answer me!
19 Draw near to me; redeem me;
free me from my enemies.
20 You know of how I am taunted,
of my shame and disgrace –
all my foes are before You.
21 Taunts have broken my heart,
and I am deathly ill;
I hope for consolation, but there is none;
for comforters, but find none –
22 they gave me poison for my fare
and vinegar to quench my thirst.

23 Let their own table be a deathtrap to them,
a snare for their friends.
24 May their eyes grow too dark to see;
may their loins ever tremble.
25 Pour Your wrath upon them;
let Your blazing fury overcome them.
26 May their encampment be laid waste,
their tents stand empty,
27 for they persecuted those You struck down
and recounted the pain of Your victims.
28 Add that offense to their offenses;
never let them share in Your favor.
29 Let them be blotted out from the book of life,
not ever inscribed among the righteous,
30 but as for me,
I am lowly and in pain;
Your salvation, God, will lift me up.
31 I will praise God's name with song;
I will glorify Him in thanksgiving.
32 This will please the LORD more than any ox
or any horned and cloven-hooved bull.
33 The lowly will see and rejoice;
take heart, you who seek God –
34 for the LORD listens to the needy
and does not neglect His captives.

35 Let heaven and earth praise Him,
the seas and all that stir within them,
36 for God will save Zion
and rebuild the towns of Yehuda;
they will settle there and take possession.
37 The seed of His servants will inherit it,
and those who love His name will dwell there.

70 1 *To the lead singer – of David,* lehazkir.[78]

2 O God, save me;
O LORD, rush to my help –
3 let those who seek my life
be shamed and disgraced;
let those who wish me harm
retreat in humiliation;
4 let those who leer "Aha! Aha!"
turn away in shame.
5 May all who seek You
rejoice and delight in You;

78 | See note on 38:1. This psalm is paralleled with slight variants in Psalms 40:14–18.

may those who long for Your salvation
always proclaim, "God is great."
6 As for me, I am poor and needy –
God, rush to me;
You are my help and my rescuer;
LORD, do not delay.

71 1 In You, LORD, I take refuge;
may I never be put to shame.
2 Deliver me; rescue me in Your righteousness;
lend Your ear to me and save me.
3 Be a Rock of refuge where I may always come;
command my salvation,
for You are my Rock and my fortress.
4 My God,
rescue me from the hands of the wicked,
from the grip of the evil and the violent,
5 for You are my hope,
O LORD GOD,
my trust since my youth.
6 I have relied upon You since conception;
from my mother's womb You brought me out;
I will praise You always.
7 I have set an example for many
while You have been my mighty refuge;
8 may my mouth be filled with Your praise,
Your glory, all day long.
9 Do not cast me away in old age;
when my strength fails, do not abandon me,
10 for my enemies say of me,
those who stalk me and conspire together,
11 "God has abandoned him.
Chase him and catch him,
for no one will save him."
12 God, do not stray far from me;
my God, rush to my help.
13 Let my accusers be shamed and ruined;
let those who seek my harm
be cloaked in disgrace and humiliation.
14 As for me, I shall always hope
and praise You ever more and more.
15 My mouth will tell of Your righteousness,
Your salvation all day long,
though it is immeasurable.
16 I will come tell of Your powerful deeds,
O LORD GOD;

I will proclaim Your righteousness –
Yours alone.
17 God, You have taught me since my youth;
to this day I tell of Your wonders.
18 Now that I am old and gray, God,
do not abandon me
until I tell the next generation of Your power,
all those to come of Your power.
19 Your righteousness, God, reaches the highest heights,
for You have done great things.
O God, who is like You?
20 You who have shown me great and terrible troubles
will revive me once more;
from the depths of the earth
You will once more raise me up.
21 You will increase my greatness
and comfort me again;
22 then I will praise You with the lyre
for Your faithfulness, my God;
I will sing praises to You with the harp,
O Holy One of Israel.
23 My lips will delight in singing praise to You,
my very being, whom You redeemed.
24 My tongue, too,
will express Your righteousness all day long,
how those who sought my harm
were shamed and reviled.

72 1 *Of Shlomo.*[79]

God,
grant Your judgment to the king,
Your justice to the king's son,
2 so that he may judge Your people fairly,
Your lowly ones with justice.
3 May the mountains yield peace for the people,
the hills righteousness;
4 may he bring justice to the lowly people,
save the children of the needy,
and crush the oppressor.
5 May they revere You as long as the sun shines,
as long as the moon glows, for generations untold.
6 May he be like rain falling on mown grass,
like showers watering the earth.
7 In his time, may the righteous bloom;

79 | See also Psalm 127.

may peace abound
until the moon ceases to be.
8 May he rule from sea to sea,
from the river to the ends of the earth.[80]
9 Let the desert nomads kneel before him;
let his enemies lick the dust;
10 let kings of Tarshish and the isles pay him tribute,
kings of Sheba and Seba offer gifts;
11 let all kings bow down to him,
and let all nations serve him,
12 for he brings salvation to the needy who cry out,
to the lowly with none to help them.
13 He pities the poor and the needy
and saves the lives of the needy,
14 redeeming them from deceit and violence,
for their blood is precious in his sight.
15 Long may he live!
May he be granted the gold of Sheba;
may they always pray on his behalf,
blessing him all day long.
16 May there be a wealth of grain in the land,
even on the mountaintops; let its fruit rustle like Lebanon
and the people[81] thrive in the towns like field grass.
17 May his name be forever;
may his name endure as long as the sun;
let all nations be blessed through him
and praise his fortune.
18 Blessed be the LORD God, God of Israel,
who alone does wonders;
19 blessed be His glorious name forever.
May the whole world be filled with His glory!
Amen and Amen!

20 *Here end the prayers of David, son of Yishai.*

73 1 *A psalm of Asaf.*[82]

BOOK THREE

God is truly good to Israel,
to those pure of heart;
2 but as for me, my feet nearly strayed,
my steps had all but slipped,
3 for I was envious of the revelers;
I saw the well-being of the wicked,
4 how they were free of death's torments

80 | Cf. Exodus 23:31.

81 | The word "people" does not appear in Hebrew and is taken as implied.

82 | See note on 50:1. Psalms 73–83 all mention Asaf in their titles.

with their sound, healthy forms,
5 with no part in human misery,
not suffering like other people.
6 Therefore they wear arrogance like a necklace
and drape themselves in violence;
7 their eyes bulge out;
their hearts overflow with fancies.
8 They mock and speak with malice;
from on high they plan oppression.
9 Their lips are aimed against the heavens;
their tongues prowl over the earth.
10 Thus His people are drawn back to them,
and they lap up their words.
11 They say, "How could God know?
What knowledge has the Most High?"
12 Look at these wicked people –
always at ease, amassing wealth.
13 All in vain have I kept my heart pure
and washed my hands in innocence –
14 when all day long I suffer from pain,
tormented each morning anew.
15 Were I to speak out in this way,
I would betray the circle of Your children.
16 When I tried to understand this,
it made me miserable
17 until I came to God's Sanctuary
and realized what their end would be.
18 You set them on a slippery path
and plunge them into devastation;
19 how they suddenly come to ruin,
swept away by utter terror,
20 like a dream upon waking, O Lord.
Upon rising You despise their image.
21 When my heart was sour and my conscience pricked,[83]
22 I was stupid and ignorant –
like a brute beast before You.
23 Yet I am always with You;
You hold my right hand.
24 You guide me with Your counsel;
You take me toward glory.
25 Whom else do I have in heaven?
With You, I desire nothing else on earth.
26 Though my flesh and heart waste away,
God is the Rock of my heart

83 | Literally "I was pierced in my kidneys."

and my portion forever,
27 for look – those far from You are lost;
You destroy all those who stray from You,
28 but as for me,
God's closeness is good for me.
I have made the LORD GOD my refuge,
to tell of all Your works.

74 1 *A* maskil *of Asaf.*

Why, God, have You forsaken us forever?
Your wrath smolders against the flock You tend.
2 Remember the congregation You made Yours long ago,
the tribe You redeemed as Your share,
Mount Zion where You dwell.
3 Rush over[84] to the endless devastation,
all the evil the enemy has wrought in the Sanctuary.
4 Your foes roared out in Your meeting place,
displaying their own signs as signs.
5 They are renowned as wielders of axes
against the tangled branches of trees,
6 then they smashed all its carvings
with pick and hatchet;
7 they burned Your Sanctuary down to the ground;
they desecrated Your name's dwelling place.
8 They said in their hearts, "We will crush them completely,"
and burned all God's meeting places in the land.
9 No signs appear for us,
no prophets are left,
and none of us know
for how long.
10 For how long, God, will the foe blaspheme?
Will the enemy revile Your name forever?
11 Why do You hold back Your right hand?
Thrust it out from Your bosom!
12 Yet You, God, are my King of old,
bringing salvation throughout the land.
13 In Your might You tore the sea to shreds
and smashed the heads of sea monsters on the waters.
14 You shattered the head of Leviathan[85]
and fed him to the desert peoples.
15 You split open spring and stream;
You dried up surging rivers.

84 | Literally "lift up your feet."
85 | The mythological sea beast; cf., e.g., 104:26; Isaiah 27:1; Job 40:25.

16 Yours is the day; Yours, too, is the night;
You fashioned luminary and sun.
17 You set all the boundaries of the earth;
summer and winter – You made them.
18 Remember this, Lord, when the enemy taunts,
when a brutish people revile Your name.
19 Do not give up Your dove to the wild beasts
or forget Your lowly flock forever.
20 Look to the covenant –
for the land's dark crevasses are haunted with violence.
21 Do not let the downtrodden turn away in disgrace;
let the lowly and needy praise Your name.
22 Arise, O God! Defend Your cause;
remember how brutes taunt You all day long.
23 Do not forget the voice of Your foes,
the ever-rising din of those against You.

75 1 *To the lead singer,* al tashḥet[86] – *a psalm of Asaf, a song.*

2 We praise You, God; we praise You,
and Your name is near.
They tell of Your wonders.
3 "At the appointed time I set,
I will judge with equity.
4 When the earth and all its dwellers dissolve,
it is I who hold its pillars firm" – Selah.
5 I warn the brazen, "Do not be brazen,"
and the wicked, "Do not raise your horn –
6 do not raise your horn up high,
preening with a haughty neck,"
7 for neither from the east nor from the west
nor from the wilderness is anyone raised up.
8 God alone is the judge;
it is He who brings down or raises up,
9 for in the Lord's hand there is a cup
of foaming wine, laced and brimming;
from this He will pour,
and all the wicked of the earth will drink
and drain it to its very dregs.
10 As for me, I will declare it forever;
I will sing praises to the God of Yaakov.
11 "I will hack off all the horns of the wicked,
while the horns of the righteous will be raised up."

76 1 *To the lead singer, accompanied by music – a psalm of Asaf, a song.*

---

86 | See note on 57:1.

2 God is renowned in Yehuda;
in Israel His name is great;
3 His tent is set in Salem,[87]
His abode in Zion.
4 There He shattered the bow's fiery shafts,
the shield and sword and weapons of war – Selah.
5 Dazzling You were,
mightier than the mountains of prey.
6 The fiercest of heart were plundered,
lulled into a trance;
the most powerful of warriors
could not lift their hands.
7 At Your onslaught, God of Yaakov,
horse and chariot were stunned.
8 You – O You are fearsome.
Who can stand before You
once Your anger is roused?
9 From the heavens You sounded Your decree;
the earth was stilled with fright
10 when God arose for judgment
to save all the lowly of the earth – Selah.
11 Human fury serves only to praise You
when You gird the last of Your fury.
12 Make vows and fulfill them to the Lord your God;
all around Him will bring tribute to the Fearsome One.
13 He humbles the spirits of princes;
He strikes fear in the kings of the earth.

77 1 *To the lead singer, for Yedutun[88] – a psalm of Asaf.*

2 My voice cries out to God –
my voice to God that He might hear me.
3 On the day of my distress I seek the Lord;
at night my hand reaches out unceasingly;
my soul refuses to be comforted.
4 I call God to mind and sigh in longing;
I reflect, and my spirit grows faint – Selah.
5 You hold my eyelids open;
I am anguished and cannot speak.
6 I think about the olden days,
the years long gone.
7 I recall my contemplation by night –
I reflect within my heart;
I search within my soul.

87 | Another name for Jerusalem; cf. Genesis 14:18.

88 | See note on 39:1.

8 Will the Lord forsake us forever
and never again show favor?
9 Is His loyalty gone forever,
His promise ended for all generations?
10 Has God forgotten to show grace
and in His wrath, curbed His compassion? – Selah.
11 And I said, "I am grieved
that the Most High's right hand has changed."
12 I will call to mind the Lord's acts;
I will recall Your wonders of old.
13 I will contemplate all Your works
and reflect upon Your acts.
14 God, Your way is holy.
What god is as great as our God?
15 You are the God who performs wonders;
You show Your might to the nations.
16 You redeemed Your people with Your own arm,
the children of Yaakov and Yosef – Selah.
17 When the waters saw You, God,
when the waters saw You, they shivered;
the very depths shuddered.
18 The clouds streamed with water;
the skies sounded with thunder;
Your bolts, too, flashed;
19 The sound of Your thunder rattled like wheels;
lightning lit up the world;
the earth trembled and shook.
20 You made Your way through the sea,
Your path through the mighty waters,
and Your footsteps left no trace.
21 You led Your people like a flock
by the hands of Moshe and Aharon.

78 1 A maskil *of Asaf.*

Hear my teaching, O my people;
lend Your ear to what I say.
2 I will open my mouth with a metaphor,
I will disclose an ancient mystery –
3 what we have heard, what we know,
and what our ancestors have told us
4 we will not hide from their children;
to the next generation
we will sing the Lord's praises
and the mighty deeds and wonders
He has done.

5 He established a decree in Yaakov
and founded the teaching in Israel,
charging our ancestors
to teach it to their children
6 so that the next generation would know it,
the children yet unborn,
and tell it, in turn, to their own children
7 and place their trust in God
and not forget God's acts
but keep His commandments
8 instead of being like their ancestors,
a wayward, rebellious generation,
a generation not firm of heart,
its spirit unfaithful to God.

9 The men of Efrayim, armed wielders of bows,
turned and fled on the day of battle.
10 They did not keep God's covenant
and refused to follow His teaching;
11 they forgot His acts
and the wonders that He showed them;
12 before their ancestors He worked wonders,
in the land of Egypt, in the fields of Tzoan:
13 He split the sea and led them across
and stood the waters like a wall;
14 He guided them with cloud by day,
with firelight all through the night;
15 He split rocks open in the wilderness
and gave them drink as from the great deep;
16 He brought out streams from stone
and made water run down like rivers.
17 Yet they continued to sin against Him,
to defy the Most High in the desert.
18 They were determined to test God
by demanding food for themselves;
19 they spoke out against God, saying,
"Can God spread a table in the wilderness?
20 Yes, He struck a rock and water flowed
and streams gushed forth,
but can He give us bread as well?
Can He provide meat for His people?"
21 When the Lord heard this, He grew furious;
fire flared out against Yaakov;
wrath blazed against Israel,
22 for they did not believe in God
and did not trust in His salvation,

23 but He commanded the skies above
and opened the doors of heaven;
24 He rained down manna upon them for food
and gave them the grain of heaven.
25 Each one ate a mighty feast;
He sent down abundant fare for them;
26 He stirred up the east wind across the heavens
and drove the south wind with His might
27 and rained down meat on them like dust,
winged fowl like ocean sand;
28 He made them fall inside His camp,
all around His dwelling place,
29 so they ate and ate their fill;
He brought them what they craved,
30 but before they tired of their cravings,
while their food still filled their mouths,
31 God's wrath flared up against them.
He killed the strongest ones among them;
He brought down the young men of Israel.

32 Despite all this they went on sinning
and did not believe in His wonders,
33 so He wasted their days like breath
and their years in dismay.
34 When He killed them, they sought Him out;
they came back and desperately sought God.
35 They remembered that God was their Rock,
God Most High their redeemer,
36 but they betrayed Him with their lips,
and with their tongues they lied to Him;
37 their hearts were not firmly with Him;
they were not faithful to His covenant,
38 but He is merciful;
He forgives offense and does not destroy.
He suppresses His anger again and again
and never rouses His full fury.
39 He remembers that they are but flesh,
a passing breath that never returns.
40 How often they defied Him in the wilderness,
aggrieving Him in the wasteland;
41 they tested God again and again,
provoking the Holy One of Israel.
42 They did not recall His power
on the day He redeemed them from the foe,
43 when He set out His signs in Egypt
and His wonders in the fields of Tzoan.

44 He turned their rivers to blood,
their streams undrinkable;
45 He unleashed swarms to consume them
and frogs to destroy them;
46 He gave their crops to blight,
their produce to the locust;
47 He killed their vines with hail,
their sycamores with frost;
48 He abandoned their livestock to the hail,
their cattle to bolts of lightning;
49 He unleashed against them His blazing fury,
wrath, rage, and misery,
a legion of destroying angels.
50 He leveled a path for His fury;
He did not spare their souls from death
but abandoned their lives to the plague.
51 He struck down every firstborn in Egypt,
the first fruits of manhood in the tents of Ham,
52 then He led His people on like sheep,
guiding them like a flock through the wilderness.
53 He led them in safety; they did not fear,
while the sea covered their enemies.
54 He brought them to His holy realm,
to the mountain His right hand had won.
55 He dispossessed nations before them,
allotted them shares of inheritance,
and settled the tribes of Israel in their tents,
56 but they tested and defied God Most High
and did not keep His decrees.
57 They turned back and rebelled like their ancestors,
treacherous as a faulty bow;
58 they angered Him with their high shrines
and aroused His jealousy with their idols.

59 God heard and grew furious
and utterly rejected Israel.
60 He abandoned the Sanctuary of Shiloh,
the tent where He dwelled among humanity.
61 He let His might fall captive,
His beauty into enemy hands;[89]
62 He abandoned His people to the sword,
so furious with His share was He.
63 His young men were consumed by fire;
His maidens had no wedding songs.

89 | See 1 Samuel, chapter 4.

64 His priests fell by the sword;
their widows never lamented them,
65 then the LORD awoke as if from sleep,
like a warrior shaking off wine,
66 and beat back His foes,
subjecting them to lasting shame.

67 Yet He rejected the tent of Yosef
and did not choose the tribe of Efrayim;
68 He chose the tribe of Yehuda,
Mount Zion that He loves.
69 He built His Sanctuary like the high heavens,
like the earth that He founded forever,
70 and He chose David, His servant,
taking him from the sheepfolds.
71 From among the ewes He brought Him
to tend to Yaakov, His people,
and Israel, His share.
72 He tended them with a sound heart
and guided them with a skillful hand.

79 1 *A psalm of Asaf.*

God,
the nations have invaded Your heritage,
defiled Your holy Temple,
and turned Jerusalem into ruins.
2 They have left Your servants' corpses
as food for the fowl of the heavens,
the flesh of Your devoted ones
for the beasts of the earth.
3 They have spilled their blood like water
all around Jerusalem,
with none to bury them.
4 We have become the scorn of our neighbors,
the laughingstock of those around us.[90]
5 How long, LORD?
Will You show Your anger forever,
Your indignation blazing like fire?[91]
6 Pour out Your fury
on the nations that do not know You,
on the kingdoms that do not invoke Your name –
7 for they have devoured Yaakov
and laid his homeland waste.[92]

90 | Cf. 44:14.
91 | Cf. 89:47.
92 | Cf. Jeremiah 10:25.

8 Do not hold our ancestors' sins against us;
let Your mercy rush toward us,
for we have sunk so low.
9 Help us, God of our salvation,
for Your name's glory;
Deliver us and forgive our sins
for the sake of Your name.
10 Why should the nations say,
"Where is their God?"
Let the vengeance of Your servants' spilled blood
be known among the nations
before our own eyes.
11 Let the captives' groans come before You;
with Your arm's great strength,
preserve those on the brink of death.
12 Pay back our neighbors sevenfold
with the very scorn they showed You, LORD,
13 then we, Your people and the flock You tend,
will give thanks to You forever;
throughout the generations
we will sing Your praise.

80 1 *To the lead singer, set to* shoshanim edut,[93] *a psalm of Asaf.*

2 Shepherd of Israel, give ear;
You who lead Yosef like a flock,
You who are enthroned on the cherubim, shine forth.
3 Before Efrayim, Binyamin, and Menashe,
stir Your strength
and come to save us.
4 God, bring us back;
let Your presence shine, that we may be saved.
5 O LORD, God of Hosts,
how long will You fume at Your people's prayers?
6 You have fed them tear-soaked bread
and made them drink tears by the bowlful.
7 You have set us in strife with our neighbors,
and our enemies mock us.
8 God of Hosts, bring us back;
let Your presence shine so that we may be saved.
9 You carried a vine out of Egypt;
You drove out the nations and planted it.
10 You cleared the ground for it;
it took deep root and filled the land.
11 The hills were covered by its shade,

93 | See note on 60:1.

mighty cedars by its branches.
12 Its boughs reached as far as the sea,
its shoots as far as the river.
13 Why have You broken through its walls
so that any passerby can pluck its fruit?
14 The wild forest boars gnaw at it;
the field creatures graze at it.
15 God of Hosts,
come back;
Look down from heaven and see;
take note of this vine,
16 this seedling Your right hand planted,
this shoot[94] You nurtured as Your own –
17 now burnt by fire, chopped down,
destroyed by the blast of Your presence.
18 Let Your hand rest on the person at Your right hand,
the person You nurtured as Your own,
19 then we will not turn away from You.
Give us life, and we will invoke Your name.
20 LORD, God of Hosts, bring us back;
let Your presence shine so that we may be saved.

81 1 *To the lead singer, on the* gittit[95] *– of Asaf.*

2 Sing for joy to God, our might;
shout out to the God of Yaakov.
3 Raise a song, beat the drum,
and play the sweet harp and lyre.
4 Sound the ram's horn on the New Moon,
on our feast day when the moon is full,
5 for it is a statute for Israel,
an ordinance of the God of Yaakov.
6 He established it as a decree for Yosef
when He rose against the land of Egypt,
where I heard a language that I did not know.
7 I relieved his shoulders of the burden;
his hands were freed from the builder's basket.
8 In distress you called, and I rescued you;
I answered you from the secret place of thunder;
I tested you at the waters of Meriva – Selah.
9 Hear, My people, and I will warn you,
Israel, if you would only listen to Me!
10 Let there be no strange god among you;
do not bow to an alien god.

94 | Literally "son."
95 | See note on 8:1.

11 I am the Lord your God
who brought you out of the land of Egypt –
open your mouth wide, and I will fill it.
12 Yet My people would not heed My voice;
Israel would not submit to Me,
13 so I left them to their stubborn hearts,
letting them follow their own devices.
14 If only My people would listen to Me,
if Israel would walk in My ways,
15 I would soon subdue their enemies
and turn My hand against their foes.
16 Those who hate the Lord would come cringing before Him;
their doom would last forever.
17 He would feed Israel[96] with the finest wheat;
with honey from the rock I would satisfy you.

82 1 *A psalm of Asaf.*

God stands in the divine assembly;
among divine beings He delivers judgment.
2 How long will you judge unjustly,
showing favor to the wicked? Selah.
3 Do justice to the weak and the orphaned;
vindicate the poor and destitute;
4 rescue the weak and needy;
save them from the hand of the wicked.
5 They do not know, nor do they understand;
they walk about in darkness
while all the earth's foundations shudder.
6 I once thought, "You are divine beings;
all of you are children of the Most High,"
7 but you shall die like mere men;
you will fall like any prince.
8 Arise, O God; judge the earth,
for all the nations are Your possession.

83 1 *A song, a psalm of Asaf.*

2 God,
do not remain silent;
be not deaf to me;
be not still, O God,
3 for look – Your enemies bustle;
Your haters have raised their heads;
4 they devise sly schemes against Your people;
they conspire against Your sheltered ones.

96 | Literally "him."

5 They say,
"Let us go and obliterate them as a nation,
and Israel's name will be mentioned no more."
6 Yes, their hearts conspire as one;
they have formed a pact against You:
7 the tents of Edom and the Ishmaelites,
Moav and the Hagrites,
8 Geval, Amon, and Amalek,
Philistia, and the people of Tyre;
9 Assyria, too, has joined them,
giving aid to the sons of Lot – Selah.
10 Treat them as You did Midyan[97] –
and Sisera and Yavin at Kishon Stream,
11 who perished at Ein Dor,
who turned into dung for the soil.
12 Render their nobles like Orev and Ze'ev,
all their princes like Zevaḥ and Tzalmuna,
13 who said,
"We will seize possession of God's meadows."
14 My God,
make them like thistledown,
like straw before the wind.
15 As fire burns up forests,
as flame sets the hills ablaze,
16 so shall You chase them with Your storm
and terrify them with Your whirlwind.
17 Fill their faces with humiliation
until they seek Your name, LORD.
18 May they ever be shamed and terrified;
let them be reviled; let them perish.
19 Then they will know that Your name,
Yours alone, is the LORD,
Most High over all the earth.

84 1 *To the lead singer, on the* gittit[98] *– a psalm of the sons of Koraḥ.*[99]

2 How lovely is Your dwelling place,
O LORD of Hosts.
3 My soul longs and pines for the LORD's courtyards;
my heart and my body sing out to the living God.
4 Even the bird makes a home for herself,
the swallow a nest where she lays her young –
near Your altars, LORD of Hosts,
my King and my God.

97 | For all the following events, see Judges, chapters 4, 6–8.

98 | See note on 8:1.

99 | See note on 42:1.

5 Happy are those who dwell in Your house;
they will ever praise You – Selah.
6 Happy are those whose strength is in You,
the paths ahead are in their hearts,
7 those who pass through the Valley of the Baca
make it into a spring
as if the early rain cloaks it with blessing,
8 so they go from rampart to rampart
and appear before God in Zion.
9 O Lord, God of Hosts,
listen to my prayer;
Give ear, O God of Yaakov – Selah.
10 See our shield, God,
and look upon the face of Your anointed one,
11 for a single day in Your courtyards
is better than a thousand elsewhere;
I would rather remain
at the threshold of the House of my God
than dwell in tents of wickedness,
12 for the Lord God is sun and shield;
the Lord will grant grace and glory;
He will not withhold good
from those who walk blamelessly.
13 O Lord of Hosts,
happy are those who trust in You.

85 1 *To the lead singer – a psalm of the sons of Koraḥ.*

2 You showed favor to Your land, Lord;
You restored Yaakov's fortune.
3 You forgave Your people's offense
and covered over all their sins – Selah.
4 You gathered up all Your anger
and turned back from Your blazing fury.
5 Bring us back, God of our salvation;
retract Your wrath against us.
6 Will You show Your anger against us forever,
drawing out Your fury throughout the generations?
7 Will You not give us life once more
so that Your people may rejoice in You?
8 Show us Your loyalty, Lord;
grant us Your salvation.
9 I wish to hear what God, the Lord, will speak
when He speaks of peace for His people and devoted ones –
may they not turn back to foolishness,
10 for His salvation is close to those who fear Him –
so that His glory will dwell in our land.

11 Loyalty and truth will meet;
justice and peace will kiss.
12 Truth will sprout up from the earth,
and justice will gaze down from heaven.
13 Yes, the LORD will grant goodness,
and our land will yield its fruit.
14 Justice will walk before Him,
marking a path for His steps.

86 1 *A prayer of David.*

Lend Your ear to me, LORD, and answer me,
for I am poor and needy.
2 Preserve my life,
for I am devoted.
You are my God;
save Your servant who trusts in You.
3 Show me grace, LORD,
for to You I call all day long.
4 Bring joy to the soul of Your servant,
for to You, LORD, I lift up my soul,
5 for You, LORD, are good and forgiving,
abounding in loyalty to all who call to You.
6 Give ear, LORD, to my prayer;
listen to the sound of my plea.
7 On the day of my distress I call to You,
for You will answer me.
8 There are none like You, LORD, among the gods,
and no works like Yours.
9 All the nations You have made
will come and bow before You, LORD,
adding glory to Your name,
10 for You are great and work wonders;
You alone are God.
11 Teach me Your way, LORD;
I will walk in Your truth.
Make my heart whole
to revere Your name.
12 I will praise You, LORD my God, with all my heart,
and give glory to Your name forever,
13 for Your loyalty to me is great;
You have saved my soul from the depths of Sheol.
14 God,
the insolent have risen against me;
a cruel mob seeks my life –
they have no regard for You,[100]

100 | Cf. 54:5.

15 but You, LORD, are a compassionate and gracious God,
slow to anger and abounding in kindness and truth.[101]
16 Turn to me and show me grace;
grant Your might to Your servant;
save the child of Your handmaid.
17 Show me a sign of favor
so that my haters will see and be shamed
when You, LORD, give me help and comfort.

87 1 *Of the sons of Korah – a psalm, a song.*

His foundation on the holy mountains –
2 the LORD loves the gates of Zion
more than all of Yaakov's dwellings.
3 Glorious things are said of you,
O city of God – Selah.
4 Among those who know me I mention Rahav[102] and Babylon,
Philistia, Tyre, or Kush –
"This one was born there" –
5 but of Zion it is said,
"One and all were born there,"
and the Most High Himself has established her.
6 The LORD will keep count in the record of peoples:
"This one was born there" – Selah.
7 They will dance and sing,
"All my springs well from you!"

88 1 *A song, a psalm of the sons of Korah –*
to the lead singer, mahalat le'annot[103] –
a maskil *of Heiman the Ezrahite.*[104]

2 O LORD, God of my salvation,
I cried out by day
and before You by night.
3 Let my prayer come before You;
lend Your ear to my plea,
4 for my soul is glutted with misery;
my life hovers on the brink of Sheol;
5 I am counted among those down in the Pit.
I am like one drained of vitality,
6 abandoned[105] among the dead
like corpses lying in the grave
whom You no longer recall,
cut off from Your care.

---

101 | Cf. Exodus 34:6.

102 | A mythical beast, here a symbolic designation for Egypt; cf. Isaiah 30:7.

103 | An unknown musical phrase; cf. 53:1.

104 | A famed Temple musician. See 1 Chronicles 15:17, 19, 25:4–6.

105 | Literally "freed."

7 You have set me in the deepest pit,
in the darkness, in the depths;
8 Your wrath weighs down upon me
with all Your overwhelming waves.
9 You have distanced my friends from me;
You made me a horror to them;
I am trapped with no way out.
10 My eyes are sore from suffering;
I call out to You, LORD, each day;
I stretch my hands out to You.
11 Will You work wonders for the dead?
Will the shades rise up and praise You? – Selah.
12 Is Your loyalty mentioned in the grave,
Your faithfulness in the realm of destruction?
13 Are Your wonders known in the darkness,
Your righteousness in the land of oblivion?
14 As for me – to You, O LORD, I cry out;
my prayers greet You each morning.
15 Why, O LORD, have You forsaken me;
why do You hide Your face from me?
16 Since my youth I have been poor, wasting away,
bearing Your terrors wherever I turn.
17 Your fury has washed over me;
Your agonies devastate me.
18 They surround me like water all day long,
completely encircling me.
19 You have distanced me from loved one and friend;
those who know me are but darkness.

89 1 *A maskil of Eitan the Ezrahite.*[106]

2 Let me sing of the LORD's loyalty forever;
I will spread word of Your faithfulness for all generations,
3 for I thought,
Eternal loyalty has been built,
constant as the heavens You established with Your faithfulness –
4 "I have formed a covenant with My chosen one;
I have sworn to My servant David.
5 I will establish your seed forever;
I have built your throne for all generations" – Selah.

6 The heavens praise Your wonders, LORD,
Your faithfulness among the holy assembly,
7 for who in the skies can compare with the LORD?
Who is like the LORD among the heavenly beings,

106 | See 1 Chronicles 15:17, 19.

8 a God so dreaded in the holy council,
fearsome to all around Him?
9 O LORD, God of Hosts,
who is as powerful as You, LORD?
Your faithfulness surrounds You.
10 You rule over the surging sea –
when its waves mount high,
it is You who stills them.
11 It is You who crushed Rahav[107] to a corpse;
with Your mighty arm You scattered Your enemies.
12 Yours are the heavens;
Yours, too, is the earth –
You founded the world and all that fills it.
13 The north and the south were created by You;
Tavor and Ḥermon[108] sing for joy of Your name.
14 Yours is an arm endowed with strength;
Your hand is mighty; Your right hand is raised high.
15 Righteousness and justice form the base of Your throne;
loyalty and truth go before You.
16 Happy are the people who know the joyful shout, LORD;
they walk in the light of Your presence.
17 They rejoice in Your name all day long,
raised up through Your righteousness,
18 for You are their beauty and might,
and our horn is raised high by Your favor,
19 for our shield belongs to the LORD,
our king to the Holy One of Israel.

20 Once in a vision
You spoke to Your devoted ones, saying,
"I have granted help for a hero;
I have raised up a chosen one from the people.
21 I have found David, My servant,
and with My holy oil anointed him
22 so that My hand will be ready to help him,
My arm to give him strength.
23 No enemy shall harm him,
no wicked one oppress him;
24 I will cut down his foes before him
and strike down his haters.
25 My faithfulness and loyalty are with him;
his horn will be raised up in My name.
26 I will set his hand upon the sea,
his right hand over the rivers.

107 | See note on 87:4; cf. Isaiah 51:9; Job 26:12.
108 | Prominent mountains in the Galilee and Golan regions, respectively.

27 He will say to me,
'You are my father,
My God,
the Rock of my salvation,'
28 and I will make him my firstborn,
most high over kings of the earth.
29 I will ever keep My loyalty for him,
My covenant ever faithful to him;
30 I will appoint his seed forever,
his throne as lasting as the heavens.
31 But if his children forsake My teaching
and do not follow in My laws,
32 if they violate My statutes
and do not keep My commandments,
33 I will punish their transgressions with the rod,
their offenses with wounds,
34 but I will never withdraw from him My loyalty,
nor betray My faithfulness;
35 I will not violate My covenant,
nor alter what My lips have uttered.
36 I have sworn by My holiness once and for all –
I will never be false to David.
37 His seed will continue forever,
his throne before Me like the sun,
38 established forever like the moon,
that faithful witness in the sky" – Selah.

39 But You – You have forsaken, You have spurned,
You grew furious at Your anointed.
40 You renounced Your servant's covenant
and defiled his crown in the dust.
41 You broke down all his walls,
and turned his fortresses to ruins.
42 All who pass by plunder him,
and he has become his neighbors' scorn.
43 You raised the right hand of his foes
and delighted all his enemies.
44 You even turned back the blade of his sword,
and did not bolster him in battle.
45 You brought his glory to an end
and hurled his throne to the ground.
46 You cut short the days of his prime
and cloaked him with shame – Selah.

47 How long, Lord?
Will You hide Yourself forever,
Your wrath blazing like fire?

48 Remember how brief my life is –
did You create humanity for naught?
49 Who can live without seeing death
or save himself from Sheol's grasp? – Selah.

50 Where are Your loyalties of old, LORD,
when You faithfully swore to David?
51 Remember, LORD, the taunts Your servants bore,
what I bore from so many people,
52 the taunts of Your enemies, LORD,
who taunted Your anointed at every step.
53 Blessed is the LORD forever,
Amen and Amen.

BOOK FOUR

90 1 *A prayer of Moshe, the man of God.*

LORD,
You have been our shelter in every generation.
2 Before the mountains were born,
before You brought forth the earth and the world,
from eternity to eternity,
You are God.
3 You turn mortals back into dust,
saying,
"Return, you children of men,"
4 for a thousand years in Your sight
are like yesterday that has passed,
like a brief watch in the night.
5 You sweep them away like a fleeting dream;
in the morning they are like grass newly grown –
6 in the morning it sprouts and flourishes;
by evening it withers and dries up,
7 for we are consumed by Your anger,
terrified by Your fury.
8 You have set our iniquities before Yourself,
our secret sins in the light of Your presence.
9 All our days pass away in Your wrath;
we spend our years like a sigh.
10 The span of our life is seventy years –
perhaps eighty, if we are strong –
but the best of them are toil and sorrow,
for they are soon gone, and we fly away.
11 Who can know the force of Your anger?
Your wrath matches the reverence due to You.
12 Teach us to count our days rightly,
that our hearts may grow wise.
13 Relent, O LORD! How much longer?

Show compassion for Your servants.
14 Nourish us each morning with Your loving-kindness
so that we may sing and rejoice all our days.
15 Repay us with joy for the pain You inflicted upon us,
for all the years we saw suffering.
16 Let Your deeds be seen by Your servants
and Your glory by their children.
17 May the LORD our God's sweetness be upon us.
Grant us success through our efforts,
and may our efforts succeed!

91 1 He who lives in the shelter of the Most High
dwells in the shadow of Shaddai.
2 I say of the LORD,
"My refuge and stronghold,
my God in whom I trust,"
3 for He will save you from the fowler's snare,
from deadly plague.
4 With His pinions He will cover you;
beneath His wings you will find shelter;
His loyalty is an encircling shield.
5 You need not fear terror by night,
nor the arrow that flies by day,
6 nor the plague that stalks in darkness,
nor disease that ravages at noon.
7 A thousand may fall beside you,
ten thousand at your right hand,
but it will not come near you.
8 You will only look with your eyes
and see the punishment of the wicked.
9 For you – "the LORD is my Refuge" –
you have made the Most High your abode.
10 No harm will befall you;
no sickness will come near your home,
11 for He will command His angels about you
to guard you in all your ways.
12 They will lift you in their hands
lest your foot stumble on a stone.
13 You will tread over lions and vipers;
you will trample on young lions and snakes.
14 "Because he loves Me, I will rescue him;
I will protect him because he acknowledges My name.
15 When he calls on Me, I will answer him;
I will be with him in distress;
I will rescue him and bring him honor.
16 With long life I will satisfy him

and show him My salvation."

92 1 *A psalm, a song for the Sabbath day.*

2 It is good to thank the LORD,
to sing psalms to Your name, Most High,
3 to sing of Your loving-kindness in the morning
and Your devotion at night
4 to the music of the ten-stringed lyre,
to the melody of the harp.
5 For Your work delights me, O LORD;
I sing for joy at the deeds of Your hands.
6 How great are Your deeds, LORD;
how profound Your thoughts!
7 A boor cannot know this,
nor can a fool understand:
8 though the wicked may spring up like grass
and all evildoers seem to flourish,
they will be destroyed for all eternity,
9 but You, LORD, are exalted forever,
10 for Your enemies, O LORD –
why, Your enemies will perish;
all evildoers will be scattered.
11 You raise up my horn like the wild ox;
I am anointed with fresh oil.
12 My eyes will see my enemies' downfall;
my ears will hear my wicked attackers' doom.
13 The righteous will flourish like a palm tree;
they will grow tall like a cedar in Lebanon.
14 Planted in the LORD's House,
they will blossom in the courtyards of our God.
15 Even in old age, they will still bear fruit,
always lush and fresh,
16 proclaiming that the LORD is upright.
He is my Rock, in whom there is no wrong.

93 1 The LORD reigns,
robed in majesty;
the LORD is robed,
girded with strength –
the world stands firm;
it will never be shaken.
2 Your throne has always stood firm;
You are of eternity.
3 The rivers rise up, O LORD;
the river sounds surge;
the rivers surge and swell and crash.

4 More powerful than the sounds of many waters,
than the mighty waves of the sea,
is the Lord on high.
5 Your decrees are most faithful;
holiness adorns Your House, Lord,
for evermore.

94 1 O God of retribution, Lord –
O God of retribution, shine forth!
2 Rise up, judge of the earth;
treat the arrogant as they deserve.
3 For how long, Lord,
for how long shall the wicked triumph?
4 They pour out insolent words;
all the evildoers are full of boasting.
5 They crush Your people, Lord,
and oppress Your own heritage.
6 They kill the widow and the stranger;
they murder the orphaned,
7 saying,
"The Lord does not see;
the God of Yaakov pays no heed."
8 Take heed, you most brutish people;
you fools, when will you grow wise?
9 Will He who implants the ear fail to hear?
Will He who forms the eye fail to see?
10 Will He who disciplines nations,
He who teaches man knowledge,
fail to punish?
11 The Lord knows
that the thoughts of man
are but mere fleeting breath.
12 Happy is the person whom You discipline, Lord,
whom You instruct in Your teaching,
13 lending him peace in times of trouble
until a pit is dug for the wicked,
14 for the Lord will not forsake His people,
nor abandon His heritage.
15 Judgment shall again accord with justice,
and all the true-hearted will follow it.
16 Who will protect me against the wicked?
Who will stand up for me against evildoers?
17 Had the Lord not been my help,
I would soon have dwelt in death's silence.
18 When I felt my foot was slipping,
Your loving-kindness, Lord, gave me support.

19 When my dread rose within me,
Your consolations soothed my soul.
20 Can a corrupt throne be allied with You,
a throne that brings misery through its law?
21 They join forces against the life of the righteous
and condemn the innocent to death,
22 but the LORD is my stronghold;
my God is the Rock of my refuge.
23 He will return their own evil back upon them
and with their own corruption destroy them –
the LORD our God will destroy them.

95 1 Come, let us sing for joy to the LORD
and shout out to the Rock of our salvation.
2 Let us greet Him with thanksgiving
and shout out to Him with songs of praise,
3 for the LORD is the great God,
the great King, above all divine beings.
4 The depths of the earth are in His hand;
the mountain peaks are His;
5 the sea is His, for He made it;
the dry land too, for His hands formed it.
6 Come, let us bow in worship
and kneel before the LORD our Maker,
7 for He is our God,
and we are the people of His pasture,
the flock He tends –
today, if you would heed His voice.
8 Do not harden your hearts as you did at Meriva,
as you did then at Masa in the desert[109]
9 when your ancestors tested Me
and tried Me though they had seen My deeds.
10 For forty years I was riled by that generation.
I said, "They are a people whose hearts go astray,
and they will not acknowledge My ways,"
11 so I swore in My anger,
"They will not enter My place of rest."

96 1 Sing to the LORD a new song;[110]
sing to the LORD, all the earth;
2 sing to the LORD, bless His name;
proclaim His salvation day by day.
3 Declare His glory among the nations,
His wonders among all peoples,

---

109 | See Exodus 17:7; Deuteronomy 33:8.
110 | Cf. 1 Chronicles 16:23–33.

4 for the LORD is great, of highest praise,
to be held in awe above all divine beings,
5 for all the gods of the peoples are mere idols –
it was the LORD who made the heavens.
6 Majesty and splendor are before Him;
strength and beauty fill His Sanctuary.
7 Render to the LORD, O families of the peoples,
render to the LORD glory and might.
8 Render to the LORD the glory due His name;
bring an offering, and come into His courts.
9 Bow to the LORD in the splendor of holiness;[111]
tremble before Him, all the earth.
10 Say among the nations, "The LORD is King."
The world stands firm; it will never be shaken.
He will judge the peoples with equity.
11 Let the heavens rejoice and the earth exult;
let the sea roar, and all that fills it;
12 let the fields revel, and all they contain,
then all the trees of the forest will sing for joy
13 before the LORD, for He is coming;
He is coming to judge the earth.
He will judge the world with justice
and the peoples with His faithfulness.[112]

97 1 The LORD is King; let the earth exult;
let the many islands rejoice.
2 Clouds and deep mist surround Him;
righteousness and justice form the base of His throne.
3 Fire blazes before Him,
burning His enemies on every side.
4 His lightning lights up the world;
the earth sees and trembles.
5 Mountains melt like wax before the LORD,
before the Master of all the earth.
6 The heavens proclaim His righteousness,
and all the peoples see His glory.
7 All who worship images and boast of idols
are put to shame;
all divine beings bow down to Him.
8 Zion hears and rejoices;
let the towns of Yehuda be glad
because of Your judgments, LORD,
9 for You, LORD, are supreme over all the earth;
You are exalted far above all heavenly powers.

111 | Cf. 29:1–2.
112 | Cf. verse 9.

10 O lovers of the LORD, hate evil,
for He protects the lives of his devoted ones,
delivering them from the hand of the wicked.
11 Light is sown for the righteous,
and joy for the upright of heart.
12 Rejoice in the LORD, righteous ones;
give thanks to His holy name.

98 1 *A psalm.*

Sing a new song to the LORD,
for He has done wondrous things;
His right hand and His holy arm
have brought about victory.
2 The LORD has made His salvation known,
displaying His righteousness before the eyes of the nations.
3 He has remembered His loving-kindness and loyalty
to the House of Israel;
all the ends of the earth have seen
the victory of our God.
4 Shout for joy to the LORD, all the earth;
burst into song, sing with joy,
make music.
5 Make music to the LORD on the harp;
sing along with the harp
6 with trumpets and the sound of the ram's horn;
shout for joy before the LORD, the King!
7 Let the sea roar, and all that fills it,
the world and all who live in it.
8 Let the rivers clap their hands
and the mountains sing together for joy
9 before the LORD,
for He is coming to judge the earth.
He will judge the world with justice
and the peoples with equity.[113]

99 1 The LORD reigns –
let the peoples tremble;
He sits enthroned on the cherubim –
let the earth quake.
2 Great is the LORD in Zion;
He is exalted over all the peoples.
3 Let them praise Your great and awesome name.
He is holy!
4 O mighty King who loves justice,

113 | Cf. 96:13.

You have established equity;
justice and righteousness in Yaakov
is Your doing.
5 Exalt the LORD our God
and bow at His footstool.
He is holy!
6 Moshe and Aharon of His priests,
Shmuel of those who called on His name –
they called on the LORD,
and He answered them.
7 He spoke to them in a pillar of cloud;
they observed His decrees
and the statutes He gave them.
8 LORD our God,
You answered them.
You were for them a forgiving God
though You punished their misdeeds.
9 Exalt the LORD our God
and bow at His holy mountain,
for the LORD our God is holy.

100 1 *A psalm of thanksgiving.*

Shout out to the LORD, all the earth!
2 Serve the LORD with joy;
come before Him in glad song.
3 Know that the LORD is God;
He made us, and we are His;
we are His people,
the flock He tends.
4 Enter His gates with thanksgiving,
His courts with praise;
thank Him
and bless His name,
5 for the LORD is good;
His loving-kindness is forever,
His faithfulness for all generations.

101 1 *Of David – a psalm.*

I will sing of loyalty and justice;
to You, LORD, I will sing praise.
2 I contemplate the way of the blameless –
when shall I reach it?
I walk about with a blameless heart
within my own home.
3 I will not set any depravity before my eyes.

I despise shifty dealing –
such things will not cling to me.
4 Perverse hearts will keep away from me;
I will have nothing to do with evil.
5 Those who slander their fellows in secret
I will destroy;
those of haughty eyes and proud hearts
I cannot bear.
6 My eyes are on the faithful ones of the land
to have them dwell with me.
Those whose ways are blameless,
they will serve me.
7 There shall not dwell within my house
anyone who practices deceit.
No one who speaks lies
shall endure before my eyes.
8 Morning after morning
I destroy all the wicked of the land,
ridding the Lord's city
of all evildoers.

102 1 *A prayer for the lowly when they grow overwhelmed*
and pour out their lament before the Lord.

2 O Lord, listen to my prayer;
let my cry reach You.
3 Do not hide Your face from me
on the day of my distress;
lend Your ear to me on the day that I call –
hurry, answer me! –
4 for my days dissipate like smoke;
my bones are scorched as in a furnace;
5 my heart is trampled and withered like grass;
I neglect to eat my food.
6 From the noise of my groans,
my bones cleave to my flesh.
7 I have become like a desert owl,
like an owl among ruins;
8 I lie awake; I have become
like a lonely bird upon a rooftop.
9 All day long my enemies taunt me;
my revilers use my name as a curse,
10 for I eat ashes for bread
and mingle my drink with tears
11 because of Your fury and wrath,
because You raised me up and flung me down.

12 My days are like lengthening shadows,
and I wither away like grass,
13 but You, LORD, are enthroned forever;
Your name endures for all generations.[114]
14 Rise up and have mercy on Zion;
the time has come to grant her grace;
the hour has arrived,
15 for Your servants love her very stones;
they even cherish her dust.
16 Then the nations will fear the name of the LORD,
all the kings of the earth Your glory –
17 when the LORD rebuilds Zion
and appears in His glory.
18 He turns to the prayer of the destitute
and does not show contempt for their prayers.
19 May this be inscribed for a generation to come,
that people yet unborn will praise the LORD.
20 For the LORD gazes down from His holy heights;
He looks down from heaven to earth
21 to hear the groans of captives,
to free those doomed to death;
22 so that the LORD's name may be proclaimed in Zion
and in Jerusalem His praise
23 when peoples gather together,
as well as kingdoms, to serve the LORD.
24 He has sapped my strength in midcourse
and shortened my days.
25 I say, "O my God,
do not take me away
when only half my days are done –
You whose years span the generations."
26 You founded the earth long ago;
the heavens are Your handiwork.
27 When they are long gone,
You will still stand;
they will all wear out like a garment;
You change them like clothing, and they fade away,
28 but You are always the same –
Your years never end.
29 May Your servants' children dwell in peace
and their own seed be established in Your presence.

103 1 *Of David.*

Bless the LORD, my soul,

114 | Cf. Lamentations 5:19.

His holy name with all my being;
2 bless the LORD, my soul;
forget none of His benefits –
3 He forgives all your sins,
He heals all your ills,
4 He redeems your life from the Pit,
He crowns you with love and compassion,
5 and He sates you with good in your prime
so that your youth is renewed like the eagle's.
6 The LORD executes righteousness
and brings justice to all the oppressed.
7 He revealed His ways to Moshe,
His deeds to the people of Israel.
8 The LORD is compassionate and gracious,
slow to anger, abounding in kindness.[115]
9 He does not contend for long
or bear a grudge forever;
10 He has not treated us according to our sins
or repaid us according to our misdeeds,
11 for as high as the heavens reach above the earth
is the strength of His love for those who fear Him;
12 as far as the east is from the west
He has distanced our transgressions from us.
13 As a father has compassion on his children,
so the LORD has compassion on those who fear Him,
14 for He knows how we are formed;
He remembers that we are dust.
15 Like grass are the days of mortals,
who spring up like wildflowers;
16 with a mere gust of wind they are gone,
leaving no trace behind them,
17 but the LORD's loyalty endures forever
for those who fear Him,
His righteousness
for their children's children,
18 for those who keep His covenant
and remember to obey His laws.
19 The LORD has established His throne in heaven;
His kingdom rules over all.
20 Bless the LORD, you His angels,
those mighty in power who do His bidding,
who obey His word.
21 Bless the LORD, all you His host,
you ministers who do His will;

115 | Cf. Exodus 34:6.

22 bless the Lord and all His works
in every part of His dominion.
Bless the Lord, my soul.

104 1 Bless the Lord, my soul.

O Lord my God,
You are exceedingly great,
clothed in majesty and splendor;
2 cloaked in a robe of light,
You have spread out the heavens like a tent.
3 He roofs His upper chambers with water;
He harnesses the clouds as His chariot
and rides on wings of wind.
4 He makes the winds His messengers,
flames of fire His ministers.
5 He has fixed the earth on its foundations
so that it will never be shaken.
6 You covered it with the deep like a cloak;
the waters stood above the mountains.
7 At Your onslaught they fled;
at the sound of Your thunder they rushed away,
8 flowing over the hills,
streaming down into the valleys
to the place You determined for them.
9 You set a boundary they were not to pass
so that they would never cover the earth again.

10 He makes springs flow in the valleys;
they make their way between the hills,
11 watering all the beasts of the field;
the wild donkeys quench their thirst.
12 The birds of the sky roost above them,
singing among the foliage.
13 He waters the mountains from His upper chambers;
the earth is sated with the fruit of Your work.
14 He makes grass grow for the cattle
and plants for human use
to bring forth food from the earth,
15 wine to cheer people's hearts,
oil to make their faces shine,
bread to sustain people's hearts.
16 The trees of the Lord drink their fill,
the cedars of Lebanon that He planted.
17 There birds build their nests;
the stork makes its home in the cypresses.
18 High hills are for the wild goats;

rocky crags are shelter for the hyraxes.
19 He made the moon to mark the seasons;
the sun knows when to set.
20 You cast darkness, night falls,
and all the forest creatures stir.
21 The young lions roar for prey;
they seek their food from God.
22 When the sun rises, they slink away
and settle down in their lairs.
23 People go out to their work,
to their labor until evening.

24 How many are Your works, LORD;
You made them all in wisdom;
the earth is full of Your creations.
25 There is the vast, immeasurable sea
teeming with countless creatures,
living things great and small.
26 There ships sail;
You created that Leviathan[116] for Your own pleasure.
27 All of them look to You in hope,
to give them their food when it is due.
28 They gather up what You give them;
when You open Your hand,
they are sated with good.
29 When You hide Your face,
they grow terrified.
When You take away their breath,
they die and return to dust.
30 When You emit Your breath,
they are created,
bringing new life to the face of the earth.

31 May the glory of the LORD last forever;
may the LORD rejoice in His works.
32 When He looks at the earth, it trembles;
when He touches the mountains, they smoke.
33 I will sing to the LORD all my life;
I will sing to my God as long as I live.
34 May my reflections delight Him;
I will rejoice in the LORD.
35 May sinners vanish from the earth
and the wicked be no more.
Bless the LORD, my soul.
Halleluya![117]

116 | See note on 74:14.

117 | Literally "praise the LORD."

105 1 Give thanks to the LORD; call on His name;[118]
proclaim His acts among the peoples.
2 Sing to Him; make music to Him;
tell of all His wonders.
3 Glory in His holy name;
let the hearts of the LORD's seekers rejoice.
4 Long for the LORD and His might;
seek out His presence always.
5 Recall the wonders He has done,
the marvels and judgments He has pronounced,
6 O seed of Avraham His servant,
O children of Yaakov, His chosen ones.
7 He is the LORD, our God;
His judgments are throughout the land.
8 He remembers His covenant forever,
His word of command for a thousand generations –
9 which He formed with Avraham,
swore to Yisḥak,[119]
10 and established with Yaakov as a statute,
as an eternal covenant for Israel –
11 saying, "To you I will give the land of Canaan
as your share of inheritance" –
12 when you were few in number,
scarce, strangers there,
13 wandering from nation to nation,
from one kingdom to another people.
14 Yet He let no one oppress them
and rebuked kings for their sake, saying,
15 "Touch not My anointed ones,
and do My prophets no harm."
16 He summoned famine to the land
and cut off all supply of bread,
17 but He sent a man before them –
Yosef, sold into slavery.
18 They pressed his feet into fetters,
and an iron collar closed around his neck;
19 until his words came to pass,
the LORD's decree purged him.
20 The king sent and set him free;
the ruler of peoples released him.
21 He made him master of his house,
ruler over all he owned

118 | For verses 1–15 of this psalm, cf. 1 Chronicles 16:8–22.
119 | A variant spelling of Yitzḥak. The verb "to laugh," on which the name is based, can itself appear in Biblical Hebrew both as *tzaḥak* and *saḥak*.

22 with the power to imprison princes at will
so that he could teach his elders wisdom.

23 Then Israel came to Egypt,
and Yaakov settled in the land of Ḥam.
24 He made His people most fruitful,
more numerous than their enemies.
25 He changed their hearts to hate His people,
to conspire against His servants.
26 He sent His servant Moshe
and Aharon, whom He had chosen,
27 and they performed His signs among them,
wonders in the land of Ḥam.
28 He sent darkness; it grew dark,
yet they still rebelled against His word.
29 He turned their water into blood;
He killed their fish;
30 their land teemed with frogs,
even in their royal chambers.
31 He gave the word, and swarms came,
and lice throughout their borders.
32 He made their rain into hail,
with flames of fire throughout their land.
33 He struck down their vines and figs
and shattered the trees throughout their borders.
34 He gave the word, and the locusts came,
grasshoppers without number;
35 they devoured all the grass in their land
and devoured the fruits of their soil.
36 He struck down every firstborn in their land,
all the first fruits of their manhood,
37 then He brought them out with silver and gold,
and none among His tribes did falter.
38 Egypt rejoiced when they went out,
for their terror had fallen upon them.

39 He spread out a cloud as a screen
and fire to light up the night.
40 They asked, and He provided quail;
He sated them with heavenly bread.
41 He opened up a rock, and water flowed out,
running like a river in the parched land,
42 for He remembered His holy word
to Avraham, His servant.
43 He brought His people out in joy,
His chosen ones in glad song.

44 He gave them the lands of the nations;
they took possession of the wealth of peoples
45 so that they might keep His statutes
and observe His teachings.
Halleluya!

106 1 *Halleluya!*

Thank the LORD for He is good;
His loving-kindness is forever.[120]
2 Who can articulate the LORD's mighty acts;
who can express all His praise?
3 Happy are those who keep justice,
who do what is right at all times.
4 Remember me, LORD, when You show Your people favor;
keep me in mind for Your salvation,
5 that I may share in the good of Your chosen ones,
rejoice in the joy of Your own nation,
and glory in Your heritage.

6 We have sinned like our ancestors;
we have offended;
we have done evil.[121]
7 Our ancestors in Egypt
did not appreciate Your wonders,
did not recall Your great loyalty –
they were defiant at the sea, at the Sea of Reeds,
8 yet He saved them for the sake of His name,
to make known His mighty deeds.
9 He blasted the Sea of Reeds, and it dried up;
He led them through the deep as through wilderness.
10 He saved them from the hands of haters
and redeemed them from the hands of enemies.
11 The waters covered their foes;
not one of them remained.
12 They had faith in His words
and sang His praises,
13 but they soon forgot what He had done
and would not await His counsel.
14 They were seized with craving in the wilderness
and tested God in the wasteland.
15 He granted what they asked for
but made them waste away.
16 They grew envious of Moshe in the camp,
of Aharon, the LORD's holy one.

120 | This verse is common in Psalms; cf. 107:1, 118:1, 29, 136:1.

121 | All the following events are recounted in the books of Exodus and Numbers.

17 The earth opened up and swallowed Datan
and closed over Aviram's mob,
18 then fire burned up their mob;
flame set the wicked ones ablaze.
19 They made a calf at Ḥorev
and bowed to a molten image,
20 exchanging their Glory
for a figure of a grass-eating ox.
21 They forgot God their savior,
who had done great things in Egypt,
22 wonders in the land of Ham,
awesome deeds at the Sea of Reeds.
23 He would have wiped them out
were it not for Moshe, His chosen one,
who stood in the breach before Him
to hold back His wrath from destroying them.
24 They spurned the most desirable land
and did not have faith in His promise.
25 They grumbled in their tents
and would not heed the LORD's voice,
26 so He raised His hand against them
to cast them down in the wilderness,
27 cast their seed among the nations,
and scattered them throughout the lands.
28 They embraced Baal Peor
and ate sacrifices of the dead.
29 Their practices provoked Him,
and a plague broke out among them,
30 then Pinḥas took a stand and intervened,
and the plague ceased.
31 This was counted to his merit
for all generations forever.
32 They moved Him to fury at the waters of Meriva,
and Moshe suffered because of them
33 when they defied his spirit,
and he spoke rash words.
34 They did not destroy the peoples
that the LORD bade them to destroy;[122]
35 they mingled with the nations
and learned their ways.
36 They served their idols,
which became a snare for them;
37 they sacrificed their sons
and their daughters to demons.

122 | See Judges. 2:1–5.

38 They spilled innocent blood,
the blood of their sons and daughters;
they sacrificed to the idols of Canaan,
and the land grew polluted with blood.
39 They defiled with their deeds,
and strayed with their practices;
40 the LORD's fury blazed against His people,
and He abhorred His share,
41 so He handed them over to the nations,
and their haters ruled over them.
42 Their enemies oppressed them,
and they were brought low by their power.
43 Many times He saved them,
but they were defiant in their schemes
and sank low in their guilt,
44 yet He saw their torment
when He heard their cry.
45 He remembered His covenant for their sake,
and He relented in His great loyalty.
46 He stirred compassion for them
in the hearts of all their captors.

47 Save us, LORD our God,
and gather us from the nations
so that we may give thanks to Your holy name
and glory in Your praise.
48 Blessed is the LORD, God of Israel,
for ever and ever,
and let all the people say "Amen."
Halleluya![123]

BOOK FIVE

107 1 Thank the LORD for He is good;
His loving-kindness is forever;[124]
2 let the LORD's redeemed say this –
those He redeemed from the enemy's hand,
3 those He gathered from the lands,
from east and west, from north and south.
4 Some lost their way in desert wastelands,
finding no inhabited towns;
5 hungry and thirsty,
their will to live grew faint.
6 They cried out to the LORD in their torment;
He rescued them from their distress;

123 | Cf. 1 Chronicles 16:35–36.
124 | See note on 106:1.

7 He led them by a straight path
to a town where they could settle.

8 Let them thank the Lord for His loving-kindness,
for His wondrous deeds for humanity,
9 for He quenches thirsty souls
and fills up hungry souls with goodness.
10 Some sat in darkness and death-shadow,
bound in cruel iron chains,
11 for they had defied God's words
and reviled the counsel of the Most High.
12 He humbled their hearts with toil;
they stumbled, with none to help.
13 They cried out to the Lord in their torment;
He saved them from their distress.
14 He brought them out from darkness and death-shadow
and broke apart their bonds.

15 Let them thank the Lord for His loving-kindness,
for His wondrous deeds for humanity,
16 for He shattered gates of bronze
and cut their iron bars.
17 Some were fools of sinful ways,
suffering because of their iniquities.
18 They found all food repulsive
and came close to the gates of death.
19 They cried out to the Lord in their torment;
He saved them from their distress.
20 He sent His word and healed them
and rescued them from their destruction.

21 Let them thank the Lord for His loving-kindness,
for His wondrous deeds for humanity;
22 let them sacrifice thanksgiving offerings
and tell of His deeds with joy.
23 Those who go down to the sea in ships,
sailing across the mighty waters –
24 they have seen the works of the Lord,
His wondrous deeds in the deep.
25 He spoke and stirred up a tempest
that lifted up the waves;
26 they rose to the heavens and plunged down to the depths,
their souls melted in misery.
27 They reeled and staggered like drunkards;
all their skill was to no avail.
28 They cried out to the Lord in their torment;
He brought them out from their distress.

29 He stilled the storm to a whisper,
and the waves of the sea grew calm.
30 They rejoiced when all was quiet,
then He guided them to their desired harbor.

31 Let them thank the LORD for His loving-kindness,
for His wondrous deeds for humanity.
32 Let them exalt Him before the assembly
and praise Him in the council of the elders.
33 He turns rivers into desert land,
springs of water into parched ground,
34 fruitful land into salt-sown waste
because of the corruption of its people.
35 He turns desert land into pools of water,
wasteland into flowing springs;
36 He brings the hungry to live there,
to build a town in which to live.
37 They sow fields and plant vineyards
that yield a fruitful harvest;
38 He blesses them, and they flourish.
He does not let their herds decrease,
39 but they shrink and languish
under tyranny, cruelty, and sorrow.
40 He pours contempt on nobles
and leads them astray into pathless chaos.
41 He lifts the destitute from poverty
and increases their families like flocks.
42 The upright see and rejoice,
while all wicked mouths are silenced.

43 Let the wise keep all this in mind;
let them reflect on the LORD's loving-kindness.

108 1 *A song – a psalm of David.*

2 My heart is sound, God;
my heart is sound[125] –
I will sing and chant praises
from my very soul.
3 Stir, harp and lyre!
I will stir the dawn.
4 I will praise You among the peoples, LORD;
I will chant Your praise among the nations,
5 for Your loyalty is higher than the heavens;
Your truth reaches the skies.
6 Rise up, God, over the heavens;

125 | For verses 2–6 and 7–14, cf. 57:8–12 and 60:7–14, respectively.

unleash Your glory over all the earth
7 so that Your dear ones may be rescued;
let Your right hand bring victory – answer me!
8 God promised in His Sanctuary
that I would triumph:
I will divide up Shekhem
and measure out the Valley of Sukkot;
9 Gilad and Menashe will be mine;
Efrayim will be my chief stronghold,
Yehuda my scepter.
10 Moav will be my washbasin;
at Edom I'll fling my shoe;
I will crow over Philistia,
11 but who will bring me to the fortified cities?
Who will lead me to Edom?
12 Have You not forsaken us, God?
God, You no longer march out with our forces.
13 Come to our aid against the enemy,
for human help is worthless.
14 With God, we will triumph valiantly,
and He will trample our enemies.

109 1 *To the lead singer, of David – a psalm.*

God of my praise,
do not remain silent,
2 for wicked mouths, deceitful mouths
have opened against me.
They speak to me with lying tongues;
3 they surround me with words of hatred,
attacking me without cause.
4 In return for my love they accuse me,
yet I pray for them.[126]
5 They repay me with evil for good,
with hatred for my love.
6 "Station a wicked person over him;
let an adversary stand on his right.[127]
7 When he is tried, let him be found guilty;
may his prayer count as offense.
8 May his days be few;
may another seize his post.
9 May his children become orphans,
his wife a widow;

126 | Literally "I am prayer."

127 | Verses 6–19 are understood as either a curse pronounced by the speaker against his enemies or a quotation of his enemies' curse against him.

10 may his children wander and beg,
foraging far from their ruined homes.
11 May a usurer seize all he owns
and strangers plunder his wealth.
12 May no one show him any kindness
and no one pity his orphans.
13 May his posterity be cut off,
their name erased by the next generation.
14 May the LORD recall his fathers' offense,
and may his mother's sin never be erased;
15 may these ever be before the LORD
until He cuts off their name from the earth,
16 for he was never mindful of showing kindness
but drove the poor, the needy, the heartsore
to death.
17 He loved to curse –
may curses come upon him –
and showed no desire for blessing –
may it keep far away from him;
18 he donned cursing as his attire –
may it seep inside him like water,
like oil within his bones.
19 May it cloak him like a garment,
always clasped around him like a belt."

20 May this be the due of my accusers from the LORD,
of those who speak evil against me,
21 and may You, God my LORD,
deal with me in keeping with Your name;
save me in Your good loyalty,
22 for I am but poor and needy,
and my heart is pierced within me.
23 I fade away like a lengthening shadow;
I am shaken off like a locust.
24 My knees give way from fasting;
my flesh is gaunt and lean.
25 As for me, I have become their scorn;
when they see me, they shake their heads.

26 Help me, LORD my God;
save me in keeping with Your loyalty,
27 and they will know that this is Your hand,
that You, O LORD, have done this,
28 so let them curse,
but You will bless;
they will rise and be shamed
while Your servant will rejoice.

29 My accusers will don disgrace;
their shame will cloak them like a robe
30 while my mouth will declare great thanks to the LORD;
I will praise Him in the midst of the crowd,
31 for He stands at the right hand of the needy
to save their lives from their condemners.

110 1 *Of David – a psalm.*

The LORD has spoken to my lord:
"Sit at My right hand
until I make your enemies
a stool for your feet."
2 Your mighty scepter
the LORD has sent forth from Zion;
dominate your enemies.
3 Your people offer themselves willingly
on your day of battle.
In sacred splendor adored from birth,
yours is the dew bloom of youth.
4 The LORD has sworn and will never retract:
"You are a priest forever
by My decree, a rightful king."
5 The LORD is at your right hand,
He who crushes kings
on the day of His wrath.
6 He executes judgment upon the nations –
so many corpses! –
crushing heads
far and wide.
7 He will drink from wayside streams
and thus hold his head high.

111 1 *Halleluya!*[128]

I will praise the LORD with all my heart
in the gathered assembly of the upright.
2 Great are the LORD's works,
sought by all who delight in them.
3 Majestic and splendid are His deeds;
His righteousness stands forever.
4 He has won fame for His wonders;
the LORD is gracious and compassionate.
5 He provides food for those who fear Him
and forever remembers His covenant.

128 | This psalm and the next form alphabetical acrostics built on the first letters of every half or third of a verse.

6 He has revealed His powerful deeds to His people
by granting them their share of the nations.
7 Truth and justice are His handiwork;
all His decrees are faithful,
8 steady for all eternity,
formed in truth and right.
9 He sent freedom to His people,
ordaining His covenant forever;
holy and awesome is His name.
10 Wisdom begins with fear of the LORD;
good sense is gained by all who practice it;
His praise stands forever.

112 1 *Halleluya!*

Happy are those who fear the LORD,
who deeply delight in His commandments.
2 Their seed will be powerful in the land,
a blessed upright generation.
3 Wealth and riches fill their homes;
their righteousness stands forever.
4 Even in the darkness
light glows for the upright;
they are gracious, compassionate, and just.
5 All is well for those who lend graciously,
who conduct their affairs with justice,
6 for they will never be shaken;
the righteous are remembered forever.
7 They will fear no evil tidings;
their hearts are firm; they trust in the LORD.
8 Their hearts are steady; they shall not fear;
in the end they will witness the fall of their foes.
9 They give freely to the needy;
their righteousness stands forever;
their horn will be raised up in glory.
10 The wicked shall see and grow furious,
gnash their teeth, and shrink away;
the desire of the wicked shall perish.

113 1 *Halleluya!*

Sing praise, servants of the LORD;
praise the name of the LORD.
2 Blessed be the name of the LORD,
now and for evermore.
3 From sunrise to sunset
may the LORD's name be praised.
4 The LORD is exalted above all nations;

His glory soars above the heavens.
5 Who is like the LORD our God,
who sits enthroned so high
6 yet looks down so low
to see the heavens and the earth?
7 He lifts the poor from the dust,
raises the needy from the refuse heap,
8 and seats them beside nobility,
beside the nobles of His people.[129]
9 He settles the childless woman in her home
as a joyous mother of children.
Halleluya!

114 1 When Israel came out of Egypt,
the House of Yaakov from a people of foreign tongue,
2 Yehuda became His sanctuary,
Israel His dominion.
3 The sea saw and fled;
the Jordan turned back.
4 The mountains skipped like rams,
the hills like lambs.
5 What happened, sea, that you fled?
Jordan, why did you turn back?
6 Why, mountains, did you skip like rams,
you hills like lambs?
7 Tremble, O earth, in the LORD's presence,
in the presence of the God of Yaakov –
8 He turned the rock into a pool of water,
the flint into a flowing spring.

115 1 Not to us, LORD, not to us,
but to Your name give glory
for Your love,
for Your faithfulness.
2 Why should the nations say,
"Where, now, is their God?"
3 Our God is in heaven;
He does as He pleases.
4 Their idols are silver and gold,
made by human hands.[130]
5 They have mouths but cannot speak,
eyes but cannot see;
6 they have ears but cannot hear,
noses but cannot smell;

129 | Cf. 1 Samuel 2:8.
130 | For verses 4–11, cf. 135:15–20.

7 they have hands but cannot feel,
feet but cannot walk;
no sound comes from their throat.
8 Their makers will become like them;
so will all who trust in them.
9 Israel, trust in the LORD –
He is their help and their shield.
10 House of Aharon, trust in the LORD –
He is their help and their shield.
11 You who fear the LORD, trust in the LORD –
He is their help and their shield.
12 The LORD remembers us and will bless us –
He will bless the House of Israel;
He will bless the House of Aharon;
13 He will bless those who fear the LORD,
small and great alike.
14 May the LORD grant you increase,
you and your children.
15 May you be blessed by the LORD,
Maker of heaven and earth.
16 The heavens are the LORD's,
but He has granted the earth to mankind.
17 It is not the dead who praise the LORD,
nor any of those who descend into silence,
18 but we who will bless the LORD
now and forever.
Halleluya!

116 1 I love the LORD,
for He hears my voice, my pleas;
2 He turns His ear to me
whenever I call.
3 The bonds of death encompassed me;
the pangs of the grave came upon me;
I was overcome by trouble and sorrow,
4 then I called on the name of the LORD:
"LORD, I pray, save my life."
5 Gracious is the LORD, and righteous;
our God is full of compassion.
6 The LORD protects the simple-hearted;
when I was brought low, He saved me.
7 Be at peace once more, my soul,
for the LORD has been good to you,
8 for You have rescued me from death,
my eyes from weeping,
my feet from stumbling.

9 I shall walk in the LORD's presence
in the land of the living.
10 I had faith
even when I said,
"I suffer terribly,"
11 even when I said rashly,
"All people are liars."
12 How can I repay the LORD
for all His goodness to me?
13 I will raise the cup of salvation
and call on the name of the LORD;
14 I will fulfill my vows to the LORD
in the presence of all His people.
15 The LORD grieves at the death
of His devoted ones.
16 Please, O LORD, I am Your servant –
I am Your servant, the child of Your handmaid;
You set me free from my chains.
17 To You I will bring a thanksgiving offering
and call on the LORD by name.
18 I will fulfill my vows to the LORD
in the presence of all His people,
19 in the courts of the House of the LORD,
in your midst, Jerusalem.
Halleluya!

117 1 Praise the LORD, all nations,
laud Him, all you peoples,
2 for His loving-kindness overwhelms us,
and the LORD's truth is everlasting.
Halleluya!

118 1 Thank the LORD for He is good;
His loving-kindness is forever.[131]
2 Let Israel say,
"His loving-kindness is forever."
3 Let the house of Aharon say,
"His loving-kindness is forever."
4 Let those who fear the LORD say,
"His loving-kindness is forever."
5 In my distress I called on the LORD;
the LORD answered me and set me free.
6 The LORD is with me; I have no fear.
What can man do to me?
7 The LORD is with me; He is my helper –

131 | For the first and last verses in this psalm, see note on 106:1.

I will see the downfall of my enemies.
8 It is better to take refuge in the LORD
than to trust in man.
9 It is better to take refuge in the LORD
than to trust in nobles.
10 The nations all surrounded me,
but in the LORD's name I drove them off.
11 They surrounded me on every side,
but in the LORD's name I drove them off.
12 They surrounded me like bees,
but they burned like a fire of thorns –
in the LORD's name I drove them off.
13 You pressed me so hard I nearly fell,
but the LORD came to my aid.
14 The LORD is my strength and song[132] –
and now my salvation.
15 Sounds of song and salvation
resound in the tents of the righteous:
"The LORD's right hand has done mighty deeds;
16 the LORD's right hand is lifted high;
the LORD's right hand has done mighty deeds."
17 I will not die but live,
and I will tell of the LORD's deeds.
18 The LORD has chastened me severely,
but He has not given me over to death.
19 Open for me the gates of righteousness
that I may enter them and thank the LORD.
20 This is the gateway to the LORD;
through it, the righteous shall enter.
21 I will thank You, for You answered me
and became my salvation.
22 The stone the builders rejected
has become the main cornerstone.
23 This was from the LORD;
it is wondrous in our eyes.
24 This is the day the LORD has made;
let us rejoice and be glad in it.
25 LORD, please save us;
LORD, please grant us success.
26 Blessed is the one who comes in the name of the LORD;
we bless you from the House of the LORD.
27 The LORD is God;
He has given us light.
Bind the festival offering with thick cords

132 | Cf. Exodus 15:2.

to the horns of the altar!
28 You are my God, and I will thank You;
You are my God, and I will exalt You.
29 Thank the LORD for He is good;
His loving-kindness is forever.

119 1 Happy are those whose way is blameless,[133]
who walk in the LORD's teaching.
2 Happy are those who keep His decrees,
who seek Him with all their heart,
3 who have done no wrong
and walk in His ways.
4 You have commanded that Your decrees
be carefully upheld.
5 If only my ways were firm
in upholding Your statutes,
6 then I would not be ashamed
when I behold all Your commandments.
7 I thank You with a sincere heart
as I learn Your just laws.
8 I will uphold Your statutes;
do not utterly forsake me.

9 How can youths keep their paths pure? –
by upholding Your word.
10 I sought You out with all my heart;
let me not stray from Your commandments.
11 I keep Your promise hidden in my heart
so that I will not sin against You.
12 Blessed are You, LORD;
teach me Your statutes.
13 My own lips recount
all the laws of Your mouth.
14 I rejoice in following Your decrees
as if in great wealth.
15 I reflect on Your precepts
and behold Your paths.
16 I delight in Your statutes;
I will never forget Your word.

17 Be good to Your servant
so that I may live to uphold Your word.
18 Uncover my eyes so that I may behold
the wonders of Your teaching.

133 | This psalm forms an alphabetical acrostic with twenty-two sections of eight verses. In each section, all the verses begin with the same letter.

19 I am but a stranger on earth –
do not hide Your commandments from me.
20 My soul is shattered with longing
at all times for Your laws.
21 You blast the cursed, the insolent
who stray from Your commandments.
22 Divest me of scorn and contempt,
for I keep Your decrees.
23 Even when princes sit to scheme against me,
Your servant reflects upon Your statutes.
24 Yes, Your statutes are my delight;
they are my advisors.

25 My soul clings to the dust;
give me life by Your word.
26 I recounted my ways, and You answered me;
teach me Your statutes.
27 Grant me insight to follow Your precepts,
and I will reflect upon Your wonders.
28 My soul weeps with grief;
sustain me by Your word.
29 Remove from me ways of falsehood,
and grace me with Your teaching.
30 I have chosen ways of truth;
I have set Your laws before me.
31 I cling to Your decrees;
LORD, let me not be shamed.
32 I rush to follow Your commandments,
for You broaden my heart.

33 Teach me the ways of Your statutes, LORD,
and I will keep to them to the end.
34 Grant me insight to keep Your teaching,
and I will uphold it with all my heart.
35 Guide me along the path of Your commandments,
for that is my desire.
36 Turn my heart to Your decrees
and not to gain.
37 Divert my eyes from false visions;
give me life through Your ways.
38 Fulfill for Your servant Your promise,
which is for those who fear You.
39 Remove the taunts I dread,
for Your laws are good.
40 See how I long for Your precepts;
in Your righteousness give me life.

41 Let Your loyalty come to me, LORD,
Your salvation, as You promised.
42 I will have a retort for those who taunt me,
for I trust in Your word.
43 Do not utterly strip the truth from my mouth,
for in Your laws I place my hope.
44 I will always uphold Your teaching,
for ever and ever.
45 I will walk about freely,
for I seek out Your precepts.
46 I speak of Your decrees in the presence of kings
without shame.
47 I delight in Your commandments,
which I love.
48 I reach out my hands to Your commandments,
which I love,
and reflect upon Your statutes.

49 Recall to Your servant Your word,
by which You have given me hope;
50 it is my comfort in my suffering
that Your promise gives me life.
51 The insolent mock me bitterly,
but I do not turn away from Your teaching.
52 I call to mind Your eternal judgments, LORD,
and I am comforted.
53 Scorching rage at the wicked grips me,
at those who abandon Your teaching.
54 Your laws are music to me
wherever I dwell.
55 At night I recall Your name, LORD,
and I uphold Your teaching;
56 It is my very own,
for I keep Your precepts.

57 The LORD is my share;
I promised to uphold Your word.
58 I implore You with all my heart:
show me grace as You promised.
59 I have considered my ways,
and my feet have turned back to Your decrees.
60 I rush – and never delay –
to uphold Your commandments.
61 The ropes of the wicked ensnare me,
but I do not forget Your teaching.
62 At midnight I rise to give thanks to You

for Your just laws.
63 I am a friend to all who fear You,
to those who uphold Your precepts.
64 Your loyalty, Lord, fills the earth;
teach me Your statutes.

65 You have shown Your servant favor
according to Your word, Lord.
66 Teach me good sense and knowledge,
for I believe in Your commandments.
67 Before my suffering I went astray,
but now I uphold Your promise.
68 You are good and do good;
teach me Your statutes.
69 Though the insolent falsely accuse me,
I will keep Your precepts with all my heart.
70 Their hearts are thick like fat,
whereas I delight in Your teaching.
71 My suffering was good for me
so that I might learn Your statutes.
72 For me, the teaching of Your mouth is better
than thousands of pieces of gold and silver.

73 Your hands formed me and firmed me;
grant me insight, and I will learn Your commandments.
74 Let those who fear You see me and rejoice,
for in Your word I place my hope.
75 I know, Lord, that Your laws are just
and that You made me suffer in faithfulness.
76 Now may Your loyalty comfort me
as You promised Your servant.
77 Let Your mercy come to me that I may live,
for Your teaching is my delight.
78 Let the insolent be ashamed for wronging me without cause
as I reflect upon Your precepts.
79 May those who fear You come back to me,
those who know Your decrees.
80 May my heart be soundly committed to Your laws
so that I will never be ashamed.

81 My soul pines for Your salvation;
in Your word I place my hope.
82 My eyes pine for Your promise,
saying, "Oh, when will You comfort me?"
83 Though I am like a wineskin shriveled in smoke,
Your statutes I have not forgotten.
84 How many days does Your servant have left?

When will You execute judgment on my pursuers?
85 The insolent have dug pits for me
in defiance of Your teaching.
86 All Your commandments are faithful,
but men pursue me without cause – help me!
87 They almost swept me off the earth,
but I never abandoned Your precepts.
88 In keeping with Your loyalty, give me life,
and I will uphold Your mouth's decrees.

89 Forever, LORD,
Your word endures in the heavens;
90 Your faithfulness endures throughout the generations;
You made the earth firm, and it stands.
91 By Your laws they stand today,
for all are Your servants.
92 Were Your teaching not my delight,
I would have perished in suffering.
93 I will never forget Your precepts,
for through them You give me life.
94 I am Yours – save me,
for I seek out Your precepts.
95 The wicked hoped to destroy me,
but I contemplate Your decrees.
96 I have seen that everything, however perfect, has a limit,
but Your commandments are boundless.

97 How I love Your teaching!
All day long I reflect upon it.
98 Your commandments make me wiser than my enemies,
for they are mine forever.
99 I have gained understanding from all my teachers,
for I reflect upon Your decrees.
100 I have attained more insight than some elders,
for I keep Your precepts.
101 I hold my feet back from every evil path
so that I may uphold Your word.
102 I have not turned away from Your laws,
for You Yourself have taught me.
103 How sweet Your promise is to my palate,
sweeter than honey to my mouth.
104 I gain insight from Your precepts,
so I despise all paths of falsehood.

105 Your word is a lamp for my feet,
a light for my path.
106 I have sworn – and I will keep my word –

to uphold Your just laws.
107 I have suffered gravely;
LORD, give me life in keeping with Your word.
108 Accept, LORD, what my mouth offers,
and teach me Your laws.
109 My life is constantly in danger,
but I do not forget Your teaching.
110 The wicked have set a trap for me,
yet I do not stray from Your precepts.
111 Your decrees are my everlasting share,
for they are the joy of my heart.
112 I have set my heart on fulfilling Your statutes
forever, to the end.

113 Hypocrisy I despise,
and Your teaching I love.
114 You are my shelter and shield;
in Your word I place my hope.
115 Turn away from me, evil ones,
so that I may keep the commandments of my God.
116 Sustain me as You promised, and I will live;
do not crush my hopes.
117 Care for me, and I will be saved;
I will ever heed Your statutes.
118 You reject all who stray from Your statutes,
for their deception is only false.
119 You discard like dross all the wicked of the land,
so I love Your decrees.
120 My flesh creeps from dread of You,
and Your laws I fear.

121 I have done what is just and right;
do not abandon me to my oppressors.
122 Secure the good of Your servant;
let me not be oppressed by the insolent.
123 My eyes pine for Your salvation,
for Your righteous promise.
124 Deal loyally with Your servant,
and teach me Your statutes.
125 I am Your servant – grant me insight
so that I may know Your decrees.
126 It is time for the LORD to act[134] –
they have violated Your teaching!
127 Yes, I love Your commandments
more than gold, more than finest gold.

---

134 | Or, "It is time to act for the LORD."

128 Yes, I keep in line with all Your precepts,
and I despise all paths of falsehood.

129 Wondrous are Your decrees,
so I keep them.
130 Your words shine light as they unfold,
granting insight to the simple.
131 My lips part to draw deep breath,
for I crave Your commandments.
132 Turn to me and show me grace
as You always do for those who love Your name.
133 Firm up my footsteps with Your promise,
and let no evil rule over me.
134 Free me from human oppression,
and I will uphold Your precepts.
135 Shine Your face upon Your servant,
and teach me Your statutes.
136 Streams of water flow down from my eyes
because they do not uphold Your teaching.

137 You are righteous, LORD,
and Your laws are upright.
138 You impose Your decrees with justice,
in deep faithfulness.
139 My fervor consumes me,
for my foes have forgotten Your words.
140 Your promise is deeply pure,
and Your servant loves it.
141 I am trivial and scorned,
but I never forget Your precepts.
142 Your righteousness is ever just,
and Your teaching is truth.
143 Danger and despair have found me,
but Your commandments are my delight.
144 Your decrees are ever just;
grant me insight, and I will live.

145 I call with all my heart – answer me, O LORD,
so that I may keep Your statutes.
146 I call out to You to save me
so that I may uphold Your decrees.
147 I greet the dawn and cry out;
in Your word I place my hope.
148 My eyes greet every watch of the night,
reflecting upon Your promise.
149 Hear my voice through Your loyalty;
LORD, through Your laws You give me life.

150 Pursuers of filth draw near –
 far away from Your teaching.
151 You draw close, LORD,
 and all Your commandments are truth.
152 I have long known of Your decrees,
 for You established them forever.

153 See my suffering and rescue me,
 for I have never forgotten Your teaching.
154 Contend on my behalf and redeem me;
 give me life through Your promise.
155 Salvation is far from the wicked,
 for they do not seek out Your statutes.
156 Your mercy is abundant, LORD;
 give me life through Your laws.
157 Though my pursuers and foes are many,
 I have not strayed from Your decrees.
158 When I see traitors I am disgusted –
 those who do not uphold Your promise.
159 See how I love Your precepts, LORD;
 in keeping with Your loyalty give me life.
160 The essence of Your word is truth;
 all Your just laws last forever.

161 Princes pursue me without cause,
 but it is Your word that my heart dreads.
162 I rejoice over Your promise
 like one who finds great wealth.
163 I despise and abhor falsehood;
 Your teaching I love.
164 Seven times a day I praise You
 for Your just laws.
165 Lovers of Your teaching enjoy great peace;
 no obstacles hold them back.
166 I hope for Your salvation, LORD,
 and I fulfill Your commandments.
167 I uphold Your decrees
 and love them dearly.
168 I uphold Your precepts and decrees,
 for all my ways are before You.

169 Let my plea reach You, LORD;
 grant me insight in accordance with Your word.
170 Let my supplication come before You;
 deliver me as You promised.
171 My lips shall stream with praise,
 for You teach me Your statutes.

172 My tongue shall sing of Your promise,
for all Your commandments are just.
173 Let Your hand be my help,
for I have chosen Your precepts.
174 I crave Your salvation, LORD,
and in Your teaching I delight.
175 Let me live so that I can praise You,
and may Your laws help me.
176 I have strayed like a lost sheep –
come and seek Your servant,
for I have never forgotten Your commandments.

120 1 *A song of ascents.*[135]

I called to the LORD in my distress,
and He answered me.
2 "LORD, save me from lying lips,
from a deceitful tongue."
3 What will be done to you,
and what will you gain,
O deceitful tongue? –
4 only a warrior's sharp arrows
and hot broomwood coals.
5 Woe to me that I dwell in Meshekh,
that I live among the tents of Kedar.
6 I have lived too long
among those who hate peace.
7 I am for peace,
but whenever I speak of it,
they are for war.

121 1 *A song of ascents.*

I lift my eyes up to the hills;
where will my help come from?
2 My help comes from the LORD,
Maker of heaven and earth.
3 He will not let your foot slip;
He who guards you does not slumber.
4 Behold – the Guardian of Israel
neither slumbers nor sleeps.
5 The LORD is your guardian;
the LORD is your shade at your right hand.
6 The sun will not strike you by day,

135 | The next fifteen psalms carry the same superscription. "Ascents" perhaps denotes a musical instruction, a literary structure, or the physical ascents to the Temple or from exile.

nor the moon by night.
7 The LORD will guard you from all harm;
He will guard your life.
8 The LORD will guard your going and coming,
now and for evermore.

122 1 *A song of ascents – of David.*

I rejoiced when they said to me,
"Let us go to the House of the LORD."
2 Our feet stood within
your gates, Jerusalem:
3 Jerusalem, built
as a city joined together.
4 There the tribes went up,
the tribes of the LORD,
as a decree to Israel,
to give thanks to the LORD's name,
5 for there the thrones of justice were set,
the thrones of the House of David.
6 Pray for the peace of Jerusalem:
"May those who love you prosper.
7 May there be peace within your ramparts,
tranquility in your citadels."
8 For the sake of my brothers and my friends,
I shall say,
"Peace be within you."
9 For the sake of the House of the LORD our God,
I shall seek your good.

123 1 *A song of ascents.*

To You, enthroned in heaven,
I lift my eyes.
2 As the eyes of slaves turn to their master's hand,
as the eyes of a slave-girl to her mistress's hand,
so our eyes turn to the LORD our God,
awaiting His favor.
3 Show us favor, LORD, show us favor,
for we have suffered more than enough contempt.
4 Too long have we suffered the scorn of the complacent,
the contempt of the arrogant.

124 1 *A song of ascents – of David.*

Had the LORD not been on our side –
let Israel say it –
2 had the LORD not been on our side
when men rose up against us,

3 they would have swallowed us alive
when their anger raged against us.
4 The waters would have engulfed us;
the torrent would have swept over us;
5 over us would have swept
the raging waters.
6 Blessed be the Lord,
who did not leave us as prey for their teeth.
7 We escaped like a bird from the fowler's snare –
the snare broke, and we escaped.
8 Our help is in the name of the Lord,
Maker of heaven and earth.

125 1 *A song of ascents.*

Those who trust in the Lord
are like Mount Zion, which cannot be shaken,
which stands firm forever.
2 As hills surround Jerusalem,
so the Lord surrounds His people,
now and forever.
3 The scepter of the wicked shall not rest
on the land allotted to the righteous,
so the righteous shall not set
their hand to wrongdoing.
4 Do good, Lord, to those who are good,
to those who are upright in heart.
5 As for those who turn aside to crooked ways,
may the Lord make them wander the ways of evildoers.
Peace be on Israel!

126 1 *A song of ascents.*

When the Lord brought back the exiles of Zion,
we were like dreamers –
2 then were our mouths filled with laughter,
our tongues with songs of joy;
then was it said among the nations,
"The Lord has done great things for them."
3 The Lord has done great things for us,
and we rejoiced.
4 Bring back our exiles, Lord,
like streams in the Negev.
5 May those who sowed in tears
reap in joy;
6 may those who go out weeping, carrying a sack of seed,
come back in glad song, carrying their sheaves.

127 1 *A song of ascents – of Shlomo.*

Unless the Lord builds the house,
its builders labor in vain.
Unless the Lord guards the city,
the guard keeps watch in vain.
2 In vain do you rise early
and stay up late,
you who eat hard-earned bread –
He provides for His loved ones while they sleep.
3 Children are a gift from the Lord,
the fruit of the womb His reward.
4 Like arrows in a warrior's hand
are the children of one's youth.
5 Happy are those who fill their quivers with them;
they shall not be put to shame
when they contend with the enemy at the gate.

128 1 *A song of ascents.*

Happy are all who fear the Lord,
who walk in His ways.
2 You shall eat the fruit of your labor;
You shall be happy and thriving.
3 Your wife shall be like a fruitful vine within your home,
your children like olive saplings around your table;
4 thus shall one who fears the Lord be blessed.
5 May the Lord bless you from Zion;
may you see Jerusalem thrive
all the days of your life;
6 may you live to see your children's children.
Peace be on Israel!

129 1 *A song of ascents.*

I have suffered so much torment since my youth –
let Israel say it –
2 I have suffered so much torment since my youth,
but my tormentors have never overcome me.
3 Plowmen plowed across my back,
making long furrows,
4 but the Lord is just;
He has cut the bonds of the wicked.
5 Let all who hate Zion
be driven back in shame;
6 let them be like weeds on rooftops
that wither before they are pulled up,
7 that will never fill a reaper's hand

or yield an armful for the gatherer of sheaves.
8 No passersby will say to them:
"The LORD's blessing be upon you;
we bless you in the name of the LORD."

130 1 *A song of ascents.*

From the depths I have called out to You, O LORD.
2 LORD, hear my voice;
let Your ears be attuned to the sound of my plea.
3 If You, LORD, keep account of sins,
O LORD, who could stand?
4 But with You there is forgiveness;
therefore You may be revered.
5 I wait for the LORD –
my soul waits –
in His word I put my hope.
6 My soul waits for the LORD
more than watchmen for the morning,
more than watchmen for the morning.
7 Israel, put your hope in the LORD,
for loving-kindness is the LORD's,
and great is His power to redeem.
8 It is He who will redeem Israel
from all their sins.

131 1 *A song of ascents – of David.*

LORD –
my heart is not proud,
my eyes not raised too high.
I do not concern myself with great affairs
or things beyond me,
2 but I have made my soul calm and quiet
like a soothed child against his mother;
like a soothed child
is my soul within me.
3 Israel, put your hope in the LORD,
now and for evermore.

132 1 *A song of ascents.*

LORD, remember David
and all his suffering.
2 He swore an oath to the LORD
and made a vow to the Mighty One of Yaakov:
3 "I will not enter my house
or go to bed,

4 I will not let my eyes sleep
or let my eyelids close,
5 until I find a place for the LORD,
a dwelling for the Mighty One of Yaakov."[136]
6 We heard of it in Efrat;
we found it in the fields of Yaar.[137]
7 Let us enter His dwelling;
let us worship at His footstool.
8 Advance, LORD, to Your resting place,
You and Your mighty Ark.
9 Your priests are robed in righteousness;
Your devoted ones sing for joy.
10 For the sake of Your servant David,
do not reject Your anointed one.[138]
11 The LORD swore to David a firm oath
that He will not revoke:
"One of your own descendants
I will set upon your throne.
12 If your children keep My covenant
and My decrees that I teach them,
then their children, too, for evermore
shall sit upon your throne,"
13 for the LORD has chosen Zion;
He desired it for His home:
14 "This is My resting place for all time;
here I will dwell, for that is My desire.
15 I will amply bless its store of food;
its poor I will sate with bread.
16 I will clothe its priests with salvation;
its devoted ones shall sing for joy.
17 There I will make David's horn flourish;
I will prepare a lamp for My anointed one.
18 I will clothe his enemies with shame,
but on him will rest a shining crown."

133 1 *A song of ascents – of David.*

How good and pleasant it is
when brothers dwell together –
2 like fragrant oil on the head
flowing down onto the beard,
Aharon's beard
that flows down over the collar of his robes,

---

136 | See II Samuel, chapter 7.
137 | Kiryat Ye'arim, the previous home of the Ark; see I Chronicles 13:5.
138 | Cf. II Chronicles 6:41–42.

3 like the dew of Ḥermon
that flows down the mountains of Zion.
There the LORD bestows His blessing,
life for evermore.

134 1 *A song of ascents.*

Come bless the LORD,
all you servants of the LORD,
you who nightly stand in the House of the LORD.
2 Lift up your hands toward the Sanctuary
and bless the LORD.
3 May the LORD –
Maker of heaven and earth –
bless you from Zion!

135 1 *Halleluya!*

Praise the name of the LORD;
praise Him, you servants of the LORD
2 who stand in the LORD's House,
in the courtyards of the House of our God.
3 Praise the LORD,
for the LORD is good;
sing praises to His name,
for it is lovely,
4 for the LORD has chosen Yaakov as His own,
Israel as his treasure,
5 for I know that the LORD is great,
that our LORD is above all gods.
6 Whatever pleases the LORD, He does
in heaven and on earth,
in the seas and all the depths.
7 He raises clouds from the ends of the earth;
He makes lightning bolts with the rain;
He brings out the wind from His storehouses.
8 He struck down the firstborn of Egypt,
humans and animals alike.
9 He sent signs and wonders into your midst, Egypt –
against Pharaoh and all his servants.
10 He struck down many nations
and slew mighty kings:
11 Siḥon, king of the Amorites,
Og, king of Bashan,
and all the kingdoms of Canaan,
12 and He gave their land as a heritage,
a heritage for His people Israel.

13 Your name, LORD, endures forever;
Your renown, LORD, for all generations.
14 For the LORD will vindicate His people,
bring solace to His servants.
15 The idols of the nations are silver and gold,
made by human hands.[139]
16 They have mouths but cannot speak;
eyes but cannot see.
17 They have ears but cannot hear;
there is no breath in their mouths.
18 Their makers will become like them;
so will all who trust in them.
19 House of Israel – bless the LORD!
House of Aharon – bless the LORD!
20 House of Levi – bless the LORD!
You who fear the LORD – bless the LORD!
21 Blessed is the LORD from Zion,
He who dwells in Jerusalem.
Halleluya!

136 1 Thank the LORD for He is good –
His loving-kindness is forever.[140]
2 Thank the God of gods –
His loving-kindness is forever.
3 Thank the LORD of lords –
His loving-kindness is forever;
4 the One who alone works great wonders –
His loving-kindness is forever;
5 who made the heavens with wisdom –
His loving-kindness is forever;
6 who spread the earth upon the waters –
His loving-kindness is forever;
7 who made the great lights –
His loving-kindness is forever;
8 the sun to rule by day –
His loving-kindness is forever;
9 the moon and the stars to rule by night –
His loving-kindness is forever;
10 who struck Egypt through their firstborn –
His loving-kindness is forever;
11 and brought out Israel from their midst –
His loving-kindness is forever;
12 with a strong hand and outstretched arm –
His loving-kindness is forever;

139 | For verses 15–20, cf. 115:4–11.
140 | See note on 106:1.

13 who split apart the Sea of Reeds –
His loving-kindness is forever;
14 and made Israel pass through it –
His loving-kindness is forever;
15 and hurled Pharaoh and his army into the Sea of Reeds –
His loving-kindness is forever;
16 who led His people through the wilderness –
His loving-kindness is forever;
17 who struck down great kings –
His loving-kindness is forever;
18 and slew mighty kings –
His loving-kindness is forever;
19 Siḥon, king of the Amorites –
His loving-kindness is forever;
20 and Og, king of Bashan –
His loving-kindness is forever;[141]
21 and gave their land as a heritage –
His loving-kindness is forever;
22 a heritage for His servant Israel –
His loving-kindness is forever;
23 who remembered us in our lowly state –
His loving-kindness is forever;
24 and rescued us from our tormentors –
His loving-kindness is forever;
25 who gives food to all flesh –
His loving-kindness is forever.
26 Give thanks to the God of heaven –
His loving-kindness is forever.

137 1 By the rivers of Babylon,
there we sat and wept as we remembered Zion.
2 There on the willow trees
we hung up our harps,
3 for there our captors asked us for songs,
our tormentors for amusement:
"Sing us one of the songs of Zion!"
4 How can we sing the Lord's song
on foreign soil?
5 If I forget you, O Jerusalem,
may my right hand forget its skill.
6 May my tongue cling to the roof of my mouth
if I do not remember you,
if I do not set Jerusalem above my highest joy.
7 Remember, Lord,

141 | See Numbers 21:21–35.

what the Edomites did on the day Jerusalem fell.
They said, "Tear it down;
tear it down to its very foundations!"[142]
8 Daughter of Babylon,
doomed to destruction,
happy are those who pay you back
for what you have done to us;
9 happy are those who seize your infants
and dash them against the rocks.

138 1 *Of David.*

I thank You with all my heart;
before the divine beings I sing Your praise.
2 I bow down toward Your holy Sanctuary
and give thanks to Your name
for Your loyalty and truth,
for You have exalted Your name
and Your word above all.
3 On the day I called You answered me;
You made my soul swell with might.
4 All kings of the earth will thank You, Lord,
for they have heard the words of Your mouth,
5 and they will sing of the Lord's ways,
for great is the glory of the Lord.
6 For the Lord is high up, yet He sees the lowly;
aloft, He discerns them from afar.
7 Though I walk among foes,
You preserve my life;
You thrust out Your hand
against my enemies' wrath,
and Your right hand saves me.
8 The Lord will fulfill His purpose for me;
Your loyalty, Lord, is forever;
never forsake Your handiwork.

139 1 *To the lead singer, of David – a psalm.*

O Lord,
You have searched me, and You know –
2 You know when I sit and when I rise;
You understand my thoughts from afar.
3 You trace my going out and lying down;
You are familiar with all my ways.
4 Even before a word is on my tongue,
You, Lord, know it all.

142 | See Obadiah 1:11–14.

5 You keep close guard behind and before me;
You have laid Your hand upon me.
6 Knowledge so wonderful is beyond me,
so high that it is above my reach.
7 Where can I escape from Your spirit?
Where can I flee from Your presence?
8 If I climb to heaven, You are there;
if I make my bed in the underworld, there You are.
9 If I rise on the wings of the dawn,
if I settle on the far side of the sea,
10 even there Your hand will guide me;
Your right hand will hold me fast.
11 Were I to say,
"Surely the darkness will hide me
and light become night around me,"
12 to You the darkness would not be dark;
night is light as day;
to You dark and light are one,
13 for You created my innermost being;[143]
You knit me together in my mother's womb.
14 I praise You because I am awesomely, wondrously made;
wonderful are Your works;
I know that full well.
15 My frame was not hidden from You
when I was formed in a secret place,
woven in the depths of the earth.
16 Your eyes saw my unformed substance;
in Your book it was all inscribed
when each part would be formed
before any of them came to be.
17 How precious to me are Your thoughts, God;
how vast in number they are.
18 Were I to count them,
they would outnumber the grains of the sand,
and when I wake again, I am still with You!
19 God, if only You would slay the wicked –
away from me, you men of blood!
20 They speak of You with evil intent;
Your adversaries misuse Your name.
21 Do I not hate those who hate You, LORD,
and loathe those who rise up against You?
22 I have nothing but hatred for them;
I count them my enemies.
23 Search me, God, and know my heart;

143 | Literally "my kidneys."

test me and know my innermost thoughts.
24 See if there is any grievous way within me,
and lead me in the everlasting way.

140 1 *To the lead singer – a psalm of David.*

2 Rescue me, LORD, from evil people;
keep me from violent people
3 who plot evil in their hearts,
who incite war day after day.
4 Their tongues are sharpened like a serpent's;
spider venom is beneath their lips – Selah.
5 Watch over me, LORD;
keep me from the grasp of the wicked;
from violent people
who plot to trip me up.
6 The haughty have laid a trap for me;
they spread out a net of ropes by my path;
they have set snares for me – Selah.
7 I said to the LORD,
"You are my God;
give ear, LORD, to the sound of my plea."
8 O GOD, LORD, my saving might,
shield my head when weapons clash.
9 O LORD, do not grant the desires of the wicked;
do not let them fulfill their schemes
lest they exalt themselves – Selah.
10 May the heads of those surrounding me
be overwhelmed by their own treacherous lips.
11 May fiery coals rain down on them;
may He cast them into the fire,
into chasms, never to rise.
12 Let no slanderer stand firm in the land;
may evil hound the violent,
blow upon blow.
13 I know that the LORD will uphold justice for the lowly,
the cause of the needy.
14 Yes, the righteous will give thanks to Your name;
the upright will dwell in Your presence.

141 1 *A psalm of David.*

I call to You, LORD – rush to me;
give ear to my voice when I call You.
2 Accept my prayer like incense before You,
my lifted hands like the evening offering.
3 Set a guard, LORD, over my mouth,
a keeper at the door of my lips;

4 do not let my heart turn to anything evil
or deal in deeds of wickedness with evildoers –
let me not feast on their decadence.
5 Let the righteous strike me,
in loyalty reproach me.
Let not fine oil distract my head,
but set my prayers ever against their evil deeds.
6 May their judges be felled by a rock
so that they will listen to my words,
for they are sweet.
7 As a person plows and breaks up the earth,
so our bones are scattered at the mouth of Sheol,
8 for my eyes are on You, God my Lord;
in You I take refuge – do not let my life ebb away.
9 Guard me from the snare they laid for me,
from the traps of evildoers.
10 May the wicked fall into their own nets
while I alone move on.

142 1 A maskil *of David while he was in the cave*[144] *– a prayer.*

2 My voice cries to the Lord;
my voice pleads with the Lord.
3 I will pour out my lament before Him,
tell my troubles to Him
4 when my spirit grows faint within me.
You know my path –
along the way I walk
they have laid a trap for me.
5 Look to the right and witness –
I have not one friend;
I have nowhere to flee;
no one cares for me.
6 I cry out to You, Lord –
I say, "You are my refuge,
my share in the land of the living."
7 Listen to my plea,
for I have sunk so low;
save me from my pursuers,
for they are too strong for me.
8 Set me free from this confinement
so that I may give thanks to Your name;
the righteous will gather around me
when You are good to me.

144| See 1 Samuel 24:3–4.

143 1 *A psalm of David.*

LORD, hear my prayer;
give ear to my pleas;
in Your faithfulness answer me,
in Your righteousness.
2 Do not visit judgment on Your servant,
for no living thing can be justified before You,
3 for the enemy hunted me down,
trampled my life to the ground,
forced me to dwell in darkness like those long dead,
4 so my spirit is faint within me;
my heart is stunned inside me.
5 I recall days of old;
I contemplate all Your works;
I reflect upon Your handiwork.
6 I spread out my hands to You;
my soul thirsts for You like a weary land – Selah.
7 Swiftly answer me, LORD;
my spirit pines away.
Do not hide Your face from me,
or I shall be like those who plummet to the Pit.
8 Let me hear Your loyalty in the morning,
for in You I trust;
let me know the way to go,
for to You I lift up my life.
9 Deliver me from my enemies, LORD;
in You I take cover.
10 Teach me to do Your will,
for You are my God;
Your good spirit
will guide me along level ground.
11 For the sake of Your name, LORD, let me live;
in Your righteousness bring me out of danger,
12 and in Your loyalty
destroy my enemies;
make all my mortal foes perish,
for I am Your servant.

144 1 *Of David.*

Blessed is the LORD, my Rock,
who trains my hands for war,
my fingers for battle.
2 He is my benefactor, my fortress,
my stronghold, and my refuge,
my shield in whom I trust,

He who subdues nations under me.
3 LORD, what is humanity that You care for it;
what are mortals that You think of them?
4 Humanity is no more than a breath,
its days like a fleeting shadow.
5 LORD, bend Your heavens and come down;
touch the mountains so that they pour forth smoke;
6 flash forth lightning and scatter them;
shoot Your arrows and panic them.
7 Reach out Your hand from on high;
deliver me and rescue me
from the mighty waters,
from the hands of foreigners
8 whose every word is worthless,
whose right hands are raised in falsehood.
9 To You, God, I will sing a new song;
to You I will play music on a ten-stringed harp.
10 He who gives salvation to kings,
who saves His servant David from the cruel sword,
11 may He deliver me and rescue me from the hands of foreigners
whose every word is worthless,
whose right hands are raised in falsehood.
12 Then our sons will be like saplings,
well nurtured in their youth;
our daughters will be like sculpted pillars,
fit to adorn a palace;
13 our barns will be filled
with every kind of provision;
our sheep will increase by thousands,
even tens of thousands, in our fields;
14 our oxen will draw heavy loads.
There will be no breach in the walls,
no going into captivity,
no cries of distress in our streets.
15 Happy are the people for whom this is so;
happy are the people whose God is the LORD.

145 1 *A song of praise of David.*[145]

I will exalt You, my God, the King,
and bless Your name for ever and all time.
2 Every day I will bless You
and praise Your name for ever and all time.
3 Great is the LORD, of highest praise;
His greatness is unfathomable.

145 | This psalm takes the form of an alphabetical acrostic.

4 One generation will praise Your works to the next
and tell of Your mighty deeds.
5 On the glorious splendor of Your majesty
and on the acts of Your wonders, I will reflect.
6 They shall talk of the power of Your awesome deeds,
and I will tell of Your greatness.
7 They shall celebrate the fame of Your great goodness
and sing with joy of Your righteousness.
8 The Lord is gracious and compassionate,
slow to anger and great in kindness.
9 The Lord is good to all,
and His compassion extends to all His works.
10 All Your works shall thank You, Lord,
and Your devoted ones shall bless You.
11 They shall talk of the glory of Your kingship
and speak of Your might,
12 revealing to humanity His mighty deeds
and the glorious majesty of His kingship.
13 Your kingdom is an everlasting kingdom,
and Your reign is for all generations.
14 The Lord supports all who fall
and raises all who are bowed down.
15 All raise their eyes to You in hope,
and You give them their food in due time.
16 You open Your hand
and satisfy the needs of every living thing.
17 The Lord is righteous in all His ways
and devoted in all He does.
18 The Lord is close to all who call on Him,
to all who truly call on Him.
19 He fulfills the will of those who revere Him;
He hears their cry and saves them.
20 The Lord guards all who love Him,
but all the wicked He will destroy.
21 My mouth shall speak the praise of the Lord,
and all creatures shall bless His holy name
for ever and all time.

146 1 *Halleluya!*
Praise the Lord, my soul.
2 I will praise the Lord all my life;
I will sing to my God as long as I live.
3 Put not your trust in nobles,
in mortal man who cannot save.
4 His breath expires;
he returns to the earth;

on that day his plans come to an end.
5 Happy are those whose help is the God of Yaakov,
whose hope is in the Lord their God,
6 who made heaven and earth,
the seas and all they contain –
He who keeps faith forever.
7 He secures justice for the oppressed;
He gives food to the hungry;
the Lord sets captives free.
8 The Lord gives sight to the blind;
the Lord raises those bowed down;
the Lord loves the righteous.
9 The Lord protects the stranger;
He gives courage to the orphan and widow
and thwarts the way of the wicked.
10 The Lord shall reign forever –
He is your God, Zion, for all generations.
Halleluya!

147 1 *Halleluya!*

How good it is to make music to our God;
how sweet it is to sing glorious praise.
2 The Lord rebuilds Jerusalem,
He gathers the scattered exiles of Israel.
3 He heals the brokenhearted
and binds up their wounds.
4 He counts the number of the stars,
calling each by name.
5 Great is our Lord and mighty in power;
His understanding has no limit.
6 The Lord gives courage to the humble
but casts the wicked to the ground.
7 Sing to the Lord in thanks;
make music to our God on the harp.
8 He covers the sky with clouds;
He provides the earth with rain
and makes grass grow on the hills.
9 He gives food to the beasts,
to young ravens when they cry.
10 He does not take delight in the strength of horses
or pleasure in the fleetness[146] of man.
11 The Lord takes pleasure in those who fear Him,
who put their hope in His loyalty.
12 Praise the Lord, Jerusalem;

146 | Literally "thighs."

sing to your God, Zion! –
13 for He has strengthened the bars of your gates
and blessed your children in your midst.
14 He has brought peace to your borders
and satisfied you with the finest wheat.
15 He sends His commandment to earth;
swiftly runs His word.
16 He spreads snow like fleece,
sprinkles frost like ashes,
17 scatters hail like crumbs.
Who can withstand His cold?
18 He sends His word and melts them;
He stirs up His wind, and the waters flow.
19 He has declared His words to Yaakov,
His statutes and laws to Israel.
20 He has done this for no other nation;
such laws they do not know.
Halleluya!

148 1 *Halleluya!*

Praise the Lord from the heavens;
praise Him in the heights.
2 Praise Him, all His angels;
praise Him, all His hosts.
3 Praise Him, sun and moon;
praise Him, all shining stars.
4 Praise Him, highest heavens
and the waters above the heavens.
5 Let them praise the name of the Lord,
for He commanded, and they were created.
6 He established them for ever and all time,
issuing a decree that will never change.
7 Praise the Lord from the earth:
sea monsters and all the deep seas;
8 fire and hail, snow, and mist,
storm winds that obey His word;
9 mountains and all hills,
fruit trees and all cedars;
10 wild animals and all cattle,
creeping things and winged birds;
11 kings of the earth and all nations,
princes and all judges on earth;
12 youths and maidens alike,
old and young together.

13 Let them praise the name of the LORD,
for His name alone is sublime;
His majesty is above earth and heaven.
14 He has raised the horn of His people,
glory for all His devoted ones,
for the children of Israel,
the people close to Him.
Halleluya!

149 1 *Halleluya!*

Sing to the LORD a new song,
His praise in the assembly of the devoted.
2 Let Israel rejoice in its Maker;
let the children of Zion exult in their King.
3 Let them praise His name with dancing,
sing praises to Him with timbrel and harp,
4 for the LORD delights in His people;
He adorns the humble with salvation.
5 Let the devoted revel in glory;
let them sing for joy on their beds.
6 Let high praises of God be in their throats
and two-edged swords in their hands
7 to impose retribution on the nations,
punishment on the peoples,
8 binding their kings with chains,
their nobles with iron fetters,
9 carrying out the judgment written against them.
This is the glory of all His devoted ones.
Halleluya!

150 1 *Halleluya!*

Praise God in His Sanctuary;
praise Him in His powerful skies.
2 Praise Him for His mighty deeds;
praise Him for His surpassing greatness.
3 Praise Him with blasts of the ram's horn;
praise Him with the harp and lyre.
4 Praise Him with timbrel and dance;
praise Him with strings and flute.
5 Praise Him with clashing cymbals;
praise Him with resounding cymbals.
6 Let all that breathe praise the LORD.
Halleluya!

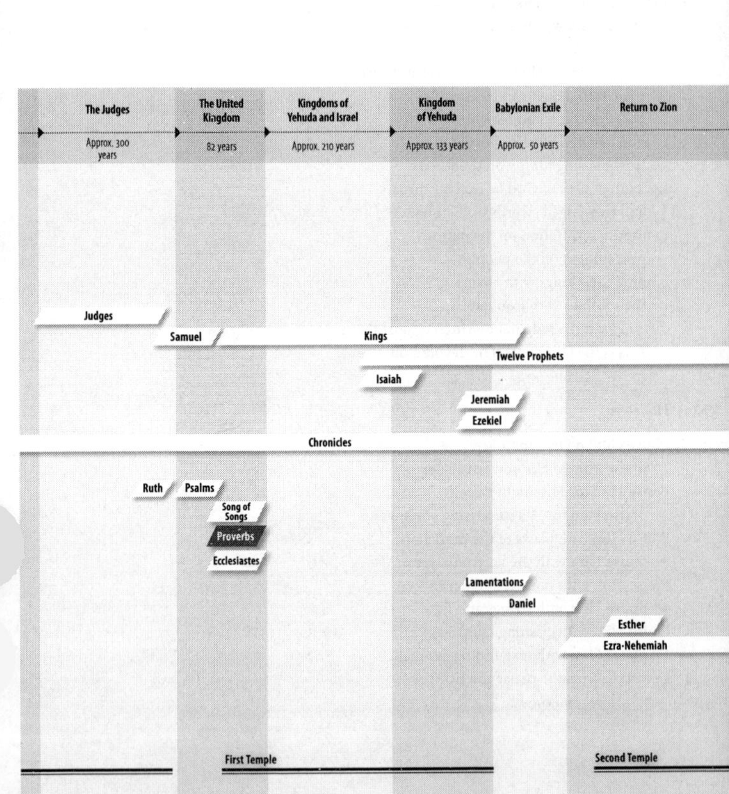
The Judges
The United Kingdom
Kingdoms of Yehuda and Israel
Kingdom of Yehuda
Babylonian Exile
Return to Zion
Approx. 300 years
82 years
Approx. 210 years
Approx. 133 years
Approx. 50 years
Judges
Samuel
Kings
Twelve Prophets
Isaiah
Jeremiah
Ezekiel
Chronicles
Ruth
Psalms
Song of Songs
Proverbs
Ecclesiastes
Lamentations
Daniel
Esther
Ezra-Nehemiah
First Temple
Second Temple

PROVERBS/MISHLEI

PROVERBS	The proverbs of Shlomo, king of Israel	Proverbs of Shlomo relating to the individual and the family	Words of wisdom	Proverbs of Shlomo that Ḥizkiya's people recorded	Statements of Agur, Aluka, and Lemuel
	Chs. 1–9	10:1–22:16	22:17–24:34	25–29	30–31

1 1 The proverbs of Shlomo son of David, king of Israel:
2 To become familiar with wisdom and instruction,
to comprehend intelligent sayings,
3 to gain sensible instruction –
righteousness, justice, and fairness,
4 to provide cleverness to the naive,
knowledge and counsel to the youth.
5 Let the wise hear and profit further
and the intelligent person acquire stratagems
6 by comprehending both proverb and adage,
the words of the wise and their riddles.[1]
7 Fear of the Lord is the beginning of knowledge;
fools scorn wisdom and instruction.

8 Heed, my son, your father's instruction,
and do not forsake your mother's teaching.
9 For they are like decorative ribbons for your head,
and like necklaces for your throat.
10 My son, if sinners tempt you
do not consent.
11 If they say, "Come along with us;
let us lie in hiding in order to shed blood;
let us ambush the innocent for no reason.
12 Let us swallow them alive like Sheol,[2]
the blameless like those who descend to the grave.
13 We will discover every sort of precious treasure
and fill our homes with loot.
14 Cast your lot among us;
there will be but one pocket for us all."
15 My son, do not go with them;
divert your foot from their path.
16 For their feet race toward evil,
and they rush to spill blood.[3]
17 For in the view of every winged creature,
the snare is spread for naught.[4]
18 Yet they lie in order to ambush their own blood
and hide in order to take their own lives.
19 So it is with everyone who lusts for gain,
which eventually takes the life of its possessor.

20 Wisdom will sing out in public
and give forth her voice in the squares.

---

1 | These are pedagogical devices for conveying wisdom.
2 | The netherworld.
3 | Cf. Isaiah 59:7.
4 | Birds, like criminals, do not think they will be caught.

21 From atop the crowded streets she will call;
at the entrance to the gates, in the city,
she will speak her message.
22 How long, you naive ones, will you cherish naivete,
you scoffers, the scoffing that you so desire?
Fools, how much longer will you despise knowledge?
23 Respond to my rebuke.
Look, I will express my sentiments to you.
I will inform you of my message.
24 Because I called and you refused,
I extended my hand,
but no one listened.
25 You abrogated my counsel,
and you refused my rebuke.
26 I too will laugh at your fate;
I will sneer when what you feared overtakes you.
27 When what you feared overtakes you like a disaster
and your fate arrives like a storm,
when trouble and woe come upon you,
28 then you will call for me, but I will not answer.
You will seek me, but you will not find me.
29 All this because they despised knowledge
and did not choose the fear of the Lord.
30 They did not consent to my counsel,
and they spurned all my rebukes.
31 So now they will eat the fruits of their ways,
and they will be sated with their own schemes.
32 For the nonchalance of the naive will kill them,
and the indifference of the foolish will do them in.
33 But he who heeds me shall dwell securely,
relieved of the fear of catastrophe.

2 1 My son, if you will accept my sayings
and keep my precepts close to you;
2 to listen attentively to wisdom
and bend your heart toward discernment,
3 indeed, if you will summon understanding
and give your voice over to discernment,
4 if you will seek it like silver
and search for it like buried treasure,
5 then you will understand the fear of the Lord
and achieve knowledge of God.
6 For the Lord grants wisdom;
from His mouth come knowledge and comprehension.
7 He preserves guidance for the upright
and shields those who walk in perfectness,

8 so as to protect the paths of justice
and guard the way of His righteous ones.
9 Then you will understand righteousness, justice, and rectitude –
every good pathway.
10 When wisdom and knowledge enter your heart,
your soul will be pleased.
11 Forethought will watch over you;
comprehension will protect you
12 to rescue you from an evil way,
from men who speak perversions,
13 who desert paths of rectitude
to follow roads of darkness;
14 who are happy to perform evil
and rejoice in wicked perversions –
15 their ways are crooked,
and they are misguided in their pathways –
16 to save you from the strange woman,[5]
from the exotic woman who polishes her words,
17 who abandons the companion of her youth
and forgets the covenant with her God –
18 she inclines toward death, her home;
her footsteps lead to ghostly spirits;
19 those who approach her shall not return
and will never regain the paths of life –
20 so that you will follow the way of good people
and keep to the paths of the righteous.
21 For the upright will dwell in the land,
and perfect ones will remain there,
22 but the wicked will be cut off from the land,
and the treacherous will be excised from it.

3 1 My son, do not forget my teaching,
and let your heart guard my precepts.
2 For they will add longevity, years of vitality,
and bring peace to you.
3 May loving-kindness and truth never leave you;
tie them around your neck;
inscribe them upon the tablet of your heart.
4 Find favor and approval
in the eyes of God and humans.
5 Trust in the LORD with all your heart;
do not rely upon your own understanding.
6 In all matters acknowledge Him,
and He will make your paths straight.

5 | Hebrew *zara*, a foreigner or outsider.

7 Do not be wise in your own eyes;
rather, fear the Lord and avoid evil.
8 That will be a cure for your flesh
and a healing potion for your bones.
9 Honor the Lord more than your wealth
and more than the best of all your produce.
10 Then your barns will be filled with plenty,
and your vats will burst with new wine.
11 My son, do not scorn the Lord's discipline,
and do not despise His rebuke.
12 For the Lord rebukes whom He loves,
as a father does a son he likes.

13 Fortunate is the person who has attained wisdom;
so is the person who has attained comprehension.
14 For its worth is better than the worth of silver,
and greater than gold is its value.
15 It is more precious than pearls,
and all your possessions cannot equal it.
16 Long life is in its right hand;
in its left hand is wealth and honor.
17 Its ways are the ways of pleasantness,
and all of its paths are peaceful.
18 It is a tree of life for those who grasp it;
those who hold fast to it are fortunate.

19 The Lord founded the earth with wisdom.
He established the heavens with discernment.
20 With His knowledge were the depths carved out,
and the sky dropped dew.
21 My son, do not allow them to elude your eyes.
Adhere to guidance and forethought.
22 They will be a source of life for your soul,
a charming decoration around your neck.
23 Then you will walk securely on your way,
and your foot will not stumble.
24 If you lie down, you will not fear;
when you lie down, your sleep will be sweet for you.
25 Fear neither sudden fright
nor the suffering of the wicked when it comes.
26 For the Lord will be your hope,
and He will protect your foot from the snare.

27 Do not withhold benefit from its owner
when it is in your power to act.
28 Do not say to your fellow, "Go, then come back, and tomorrow I will give
it to you,"

when you have it with you.
29 Do not plot evil against your fellow
when he dwells trustingly with you.
30 Do not quarrel with a person without cause
unless he has done you harm.
31 Do not envy the criminal,
and do not adopt any of his ways.
32 For the crooked are loathed by the LORD,
but with the upright He is intimate.
33 The LORD's curse is in the house of the wicked,
but He blesses the abode of the righteous.
34 At scoffers He scoffs,
but upon the humble He bestows grace.
35 The wise inherit honor,
whereas fools receive disgrace.

4 1 Hear, sons, a father's instruction.
Listen well and become familiar with understanding,
2 for I give you a valuable lesson.
Do not abandon my teachings.
3 I was a son to my father,
delicate and favored by my mother.
4 He taught me and said to me:
"Let your heart uphold my words;
guard my precepts and thrive.
5 Acquire wisdom, acquire understanding;
do not forget, and do not veer from the words of my mouth.
6 Do not abandon her, and she will watch over you.
Love her, and she will protect you.
7 The beginning of wisdom: acquire wisdom,
and, with all your acquisitions, acquire understanding.
8 Caress her and she will exalt you;
she will honor you when you embrace her.
9 She will place upon your head a charming ornament
and reward you with a crown of glory."

10 Hear, my son, and accept my words;
they will make many the years of life.
11 I taught you wisdom's way;
I guided you along pathways of rectitude.
12 When you walk, your footsteps will not be constrained,
and should you run, you will not stumble.
13 Hold fast to instruction; do not let go.
Guard her, for she is your life.
14 Do not enter the path of the wicked,
and do not tread in the way of evil ones.

15 Avoid it; do not traverse it;
swerve and pass by.
16 For they are unable to sleep if they have not done harm;
sleep is stolen from them if they have not misled others.
17 For they eat the bread of wickedness
and drink the wine of lawlessness.
18 The path of the righteous is like a shining light;
it increases its light until high noon,
19 whereas the way of the wicked is like darkness;
they know not over what they will stumble.

20 My son, listen well to my words;
bend your ear to my sayings.
21 Do not allow your eyes to be diverted from them;
guard them within your heart.
22 For they are a source of life for him who has discovered them,
healing for all his flesh.
23 More than all else that you guard, guard your heart,
for from it life grows.
24 Eliminate perverse speech,
and distance yourself from crooked lips.
25 Let your eyes gaze directly in front of you,
your eyelids straight ahead.
26 Align the pathways upon which you walk,
and let all your ways be righteous.
27 Do not veer to the right or to the left;
withdraw your foot from evil.

5 1 My son, listen well to my wisdom;
bend your ear to my understanding
2 in order to observe prudent thoughts
so that your lips will guard discretion.
3 For honey drips from the lips of the strange woman
whose palate is smoother than oil,
4 but her end is as bitter as wormwood,
as sharp as a double-edged sword.
5 Her feet descend to Death;
her footsteps hold open Sheol.
6 She does not aim toward a path of life;
her ways wander she knows not where.

7 Now, sons, hear me,
and do not veer from the sayings of my mouth.
8 Distance your way from her;
do not draw near to the door of her home
9 lest you give away your glory to others
and your years to a merciless man;

10 lest strangers derive satisfaction from your strength,
your efforts consumed in an alien's house.
11 In your final moments you will wail
as your flesh and frame decay.
12 You will say,
"How I did hate instruction, and my heart despised rebuke!
13 I did not hear the voice of my teachers,
and to my tutors I did not bend my ear.
14 I was very nearly completely evil,
exposed before congregation and community."

15 Drink water from your own cistern
and running water from your own well.[6]
16 Your wellsprings will burst outward,
streams of water flowing in the squares.
17 They will be yours, yours alone;
no strangers will share them with you.
18 Your fount will be blessed,
and you will rejoice with the wife of your youth.
19 An amorous doe, an alluring gazelle,
her breasts will sustain you at all times.
Indulge in her love always.
20 Why indulge, my son, with a strange woman?
Why embrace an exotic woman's bosom?

21 For a man's ways are before the Lord's eyes,
and He assesses all his footsteps.
22 His sins will ensnare the evil person!
He will be fettered by the bonds of his transgression.
23 He will die for not taking instruction,
and for indulging in his many follies.

6 1 My son, if you guaranteed a loan for your friend
or extended your hand[7] on behalf of a stranger,
2 you have been ensnared by the words of your own mouth;
you have been trapped by the words of your own mouth.
3 Do this, then, my son, and save yourself,
now that you have fallen into your friend's hand.
Quickly debase yourself and flatter your friend.
4 Do not allow your eyes to sleep,
nor your eyelids to slumber.
5 Save yourself as would a deer from the hunter's hand,
as would a bird from the hand of the trapper.

---

6 | Metaphors for the man's wife; see verse 18.

7 | That is, put up surety.

6 Take note of the ant, lazy one;
observe her ways and grow wise.
7 She has no captain,
no overseer, and no commander,
8 yet she prepares her bread in the summer
and stores up her food at harvest time.
9 How long, lazy one, will you lie idle?
When will you get up from your sleep?
10 A little sleep, a little dozing,
a little lying there with folded hands,
11 and poverty will arrive like a sudden intruder,
privation like a soldier bearing a shield.

12 The knave, the schemer,
he proceeds with a twisted mouth.
13 He winks his eyes,
stomps his feet,
signals with his fingers.
14 Perversions are in his heart.
He plots evil at every opportunity.
He incites strife.
15 Therefore he will suddenly meet his fate.
Unexpectedly he will collapse, beyond cure.

16 Six there are that the LORD despises,
and a seventh[8] which is anathema to Him:
17 haughty eyes, a false tongue,
and hands that shed innocent blood;
18 a heart that devises wicked schemes;
feet that hasten to race toward evil;
19 he who expresses deceptions, the false witness;
and he who incites strife among brothers.

20 Guard, my son, your father's precepts;
do not forsake your mother's teachings.
21 Bind them always within your heart;
wind them as an ornament around your neck.
22 When you walk about, she will guide you;
when you lie down, she will watch over you;
and when you awake, she will converse with you.
23 For the precept is like a lamp,
the teaching like light itself.
The admonishments of instruction are the road to life:
24 to keep you away from the evil woman,
from the smooth tongue of the foreign woman.

---

8 | The formulations "six ... and a seventh" and "three ... and a fourth" are familiar mnemonic devices; cf., e.g., 30:15; Amos, chapters 1–2.

25 Do not lust for her beauty in your heart,
and do not let her entice you with her eyelids.
26 Because, in exchange for a whore, a man will yield his last loaf of bread,
and a married woman will ensnare even an honorable person.
27 Can a man fetch fire in his lap
and not burn his clothing?
28 Can a man walk on coals
and not scorch his feet?
29 So it is with him who comes near his neighbor's wife;
none who touches her will remain unpunished.
30 They do not abhor the thief who steals
to satisfy his hunger when he is starving.
31 When discovered he might pay sevenfold
and even have to give away all his family's possessions.
32 But the adulterer is a mindless man;
only one who wishes to destroy himself will do this.
33 He will find only illness and shame;
his disgrace will never be erased.
34 Envy will stimulate the husband's wrath,
so that he will show no pity in the day of vengeance.
35 He will accept no ransom whatsoever
and will not consent to your most excessive bribe.

ז 1 My son, guard my words,
and keep my precepts close to you.
2 Guard my precepts and live –
my teachings as you would the pupil of your eyes.
3 Bind them upon your fingers;
inscribe them upon the tablet of your heart.
4 Say to Wisdom, "You are my sister!"
and call understanding a kinsman.
5 This will protect you from the strange woman,
the exotic woman who smooths her words.[9]

6 From the window of my home,
through the lattice I peered.
7 I saw among a group of innocents,
I discerned among the youngsters a mindless lad.
8 He was passing through the marketplace
near her corner,
marching along the road to her home –
9 in the dimness of dusk, in the darkness of nightfall,
pitch-black.
10 Suddenly a woman stands opposite him;
she poses as a harlot with seductive intent.

---

9 | A married woman seeking to seduce a young man.

11 She is wild and wanton;
her feet do not stay put in her own home.
12 One time outside the city, another time in the city squares,
she lurks near every corner.
13 She seizes him, kisses him,
and brazenly says to him:
14 "I owed a sacrificial peace offering;
today I fulfilled my vow.[10]
15 That is why I went out toward you,
to search for you,
and I found you!
16 I spread my couch with quilts
woven from Egyptian linen cords.
17 I have perfumed my bed
with myrrh, aloes, and cinnamon.
18 Come, let us gratify our lust until dawn;
let us make love playfully.
19 For the man of the house is not home;
he has gone far away on the road.
20 He took with him a purse filled with silver;
he will not return home until the full moon."
21 She has misled him with her countless persuasions;
with her smooth lips she has led him astray.
22 He follows her unwittingly;
he comes like an ox to the slaughter,
prancing into a halter
23 until an arrow pierces his liver.
He is like a bird rushing to the trap,
unaware that his life is at stake.
24 Now, sons, hear me;
listen well to the words of my mouth.
25 Let your heart not stray toward her ways;
do not wander into her paths,
26 for she has turned many into corpses,
and numerous are her victims.
27 Her home is on the way to Sheol,
descending to the chambers of death.

8 1 Does not wisdom call out;
does not understanding raise her voice?
2 Atop high places, at the roadside,
by the house at the crossroads she stands.
3 Beside the gates, at the city's entry,
at the entrance to the portals she sings out.

10 | Therefore she has meat for a meal to which she invites the lad.

4 To you, gentlemen, I call.
I raise my voice to all humanity.
5 Let the ignorant understand prudence;
let fools bring understanding to their hearts.
6 Hear me, for I speak noble words,
and my lips open with words of rectitude.
7 My palate pronounces truth;
wickedness is anathema to my lips.
8 In righteousness are spoken all the words of my mouth;
there is neither crookedness nor distortion in them.
9 They are all convincing to the contemplative person;
they are accurate for those who would find knowledge.
10 Accept my instruction, not silver;
accept knowledge rather than refined gold.
11 For wisdom is better than pearls;
all prized possessions do not compare to her.

12 I, Wisdom, reside with cleverness;
I have achieved the ability to think ahead.
13 Fear of the Lord is hatred of evil:
arrogance, pride, and the path of wrongdoing.
I despise a perverse mouth.
14 Counsel and guidance are mine.
I am the essence of understanding.
Courage is mine.
15 By me do kings reign,
and chieftains legislate righteousness.
16 By me do rulers rule,
and noblemen: all who judge righteously.
17 I will love those who love me.
Those who search for me will surely find me.
18 Wealth and honor are with me,
abundant riches rightfully obtained.
19 My fruit is better than the finest gold,
my produce better than refined silver.
20 On the path of righteousness will I walk
among the ways of justice.
21 To bequeath substance to those whom I love,
I will fill their storehouses.

22 The Lord created me at the beginning of His path
before His other deeds long ago.
23 From eternity I was formed,
from the start,
from the earliest times on earth.
24 When there were yet no depths, I was born,

when there were yet no wellsprings heavy with water.
25 Before the mountains were set down,
before the hills I was born:
26 when He had not yet made land and outdoors,
nor the beginning of the world's soil.
27 As He firmed up the heavens, there I was:
when He engraved the horizon on the surface of the deep,
28 when He fortified the clouds up above,
when strengthening the fountains of the deep,
29 when He set for the sea its limits
so that water would not transgress His command,
when He carved out the earth's foundations,
30 I was a disciple by His side.
I became a source of delight day by day,
bringing pleasure to Him all the time,
31 bringing pleasure to the world, His land,
and my delight to all humanity.

32 Now, children, hear me.
Fortunate are those who keep to my path.
33 Obey my instruction and become wise;
do not disregard it.
34 Fortunate is the person who heeds me,
persisting at my doors day by day,
staying at the doorposts of my doorways.
35 For he who finds me finds life
and gains favor from the LORD.
36 But he who turns away from me deprives himself;
all who hate me love death.

9 1 Wisdom built her house;
she sculpted its pillars, seven of them.
2 She prepared a feast of meat,
mixed her wine,
and even set her table.
3 She sent her maidservants to call out
from the ramparts upon the heights of the city:
4 "Whoever is ignorant, let him turn here."
And to the mindless one she said:
5 "Come, partake of my bread
and drink the wine that I have mixed.
6 Abandon ignorance and live well.
Walk down the road to understanding."

7 He who preaches to a scoffer gains shame for himself;
the same goes for someone who rebukes a wicked person for his fault.
8 Do not rebuke a scoffer lest he hate you;

rebuke a wise man, and he will love you.
9 Teach a wise man, and he will become yet wiser;
inform a righteous person, and he will add to his learning.
10 The prerequisite for wisdom is fear of the LORD;
knowledge of the Holy One leads to understanding.
11 For through me you will increase your days,
and years will be added to your life.
12 If you become wise, your wisdom will benefit you,
but if you scoff, you will suffer alone.

13 The foolish woman squawks nonsense;
she knows nothing.
14 She sits by the doorway of her house
or upon a seat on the city's heights
15 to call out to passersby
who walk along straight paths:
16 "Whoever is ignorant, let him turn aside here."
The mindless one, she says to him:
17 "Stolen waters are sweet,
and bread eaten secretly is pleasant."
18 He is unaware that the spirits of the dead are there;
those to whom she beckons are in Sheol's depths.

10 1 The proverbs of Shlomo:
A wise son brings joy to his father;
a foolish son is his mother's misery.
2 Treasures achieved by wickedness are of no benefit,
but righteousness rescues anyone from death.
3 The LORD will not allow the righteous to go hungry,
but He will deny the wicked what they crave.
4 A fraudulent scale causes poverty,
but the hand of the diligent grows rich.
5 The intelligent son stores away in the summer,
but the son who slumbers at harvest time brings shame.
6 Blessings envelop the head of the righteous,
but lawlessness covers the mouth of the wicked.
7 The mention of the righteous is a blessing,
but the name of the wicked will rot.
8 The wise of heart will seize precepts,
but the foolish of lips will become bewildered.
9 He who walks in perfectness will walk securely,
but whoever makes his ways crooked will be crushed.
10 He who winks his eye begets heartbreak,
and the foolish of lips will become bewildered.
11 The mouth of the righteous is a fount of life,
but lawlessness covers the mouth of the wicked.

12 Hatred awakens disputes,
but love covers over all wrongs.
13 Wisdom is found on the lips of the intelligent man,
but a rod is for the back of a mindless man.
14 The wise conserve their knowledge,
but the mouth of the fool is a disaster in the making.
15 The rich man considers his wealth his city of strength;
poverty is the poor man's disaster.
16 The righteous man's wages lead to life;
the produce of the wicked leads to want.
17 The path to life is for the one who heeds instruction;
he who shuns a rebuke misleads himself.
18 He who conceals enmity has lying lips;
he who spreads slander is a fool.
19 With too many words, no one can avoid wrongdoing.
He who restrains his lips is intelligent.
20 The righteous man's tongue is like refined silver;
the heart of the wicked is of little worth.
21 The lips of the righteous sustain a multitude,
but fools die because of their mindlessness.
22 It is the Lord's blessing that enriches;
it is not accompanied by disappointment.
23 For the fool, immorality is but play,
but wisdom is play for the man of intelligence.
24 That which the wicked man dreads will befall him,
but He will grant the righteous their desire.
25 As a sudden storm passes, so is the wicked man gone,
but the righteous man stands firm forever.
26 Like vinegar to the teeth and smoke to the eyes,
so is the lazy man to those who commission him.
27 Fear of the Lord increases a person's days,
but the years of the wicked are shortened.
28 The righteous can look forward to joy,
but the hope of the wicked is lost.
29 The Lord's way is a sanctuary of strength for the innocent,
but it is a disaster for those who wreak evil.
30 The righteous man will never ever falter,
but the wicked will not long dwell on earth.
31 The mouth of the righteous will utter wisdom,
but the perverse tongue will be severed.
32 The lips of the righteous know to win favor,
but the mouths of the wicked know only perversity.

11 1 False scales are anathema to the Lord;
an accurate weight is His desire.
2 When arrogance comes, then comes disgrace,

but with modest men comes wisdom.
3 The integrity of the upright guides them,
but the deviance of the treacherous ruins them.
4 Wealth will not help on the day of wrath,
but righteousness rescues anyone from death.
5 The righteousness of the blameless man will make straight his ways;
the wicked man will fall by his own wickedness.
6 The righteousness of upright men saves them,
but treacherous men are ensnared in their own mischief.
7 Hope is gone with the death of a wicked man;
the sinner's expectation comes to naught.
8 The righteous man is rescued from woe;
the wicked man suffers in his stead.
9 The liar destroys his fellow with his mouth,
but the righteous will be rescued through their knowledge.
10 When it goes well for the righteous, the city rejoices;
with the downfall of the wicked, there is song.
11 By the blessing of the upright the city is uplifted;
by the mouth of the wicked it is ruined.
12 A mindless man degrades his neighbor;
a man of discretion remains silent.
13 The talebearer reveals secrets;
the trustworthy spirit conceals the matter.
14 Without strategies a people falls;
salvation stems from abundant counsel.
15 Broken is the person who guaranteed a loan for a stranger,
while a person who detests pledges is secure.
16 A compassionate woman seizes honor;
ruthless men seize wealth.
17 A kind man does himself good,
but a cruel man tears his own flesh.
18 The wicked man earns false wages,
while he who sows righteousness earns a true reward.
19 Truly, righteousness assures life,
but he who pursues evil ensures his own death.
20 The crooked of heart are anathema to the LORD;
His pleasure is in those whose ways are blameless.

21 The wicked person will not be forgiven, even for a moment,
but even the descendants of the righteous will be spared.
22 Like a golden ring in a pig's snout
is a beautiful woman who lacks sense.
23 The righteous desire only good;
the wicked can hope only for wrath.
24 Some give freely and gain more thereby;
others refrain from generosity only to suffer loss.

25 He who is himself a blessing will prosper;
someone who sustains others, he too will be sustained.
26 The nation will curse the one who withholds grain,
but blessing will come upon the head of the one who provides.
27 He who searches for the good seeks favor;
he who pursues evil, evil will befall him.
28 He who trusts in his wealth will fall,
but the righteous will flourish like a leaf.
29 He who neglects his family inherits the wind;
the fool becomes a slave to the wise of heart.
30 The fruit of the righteous is a tree of life;
he who draws others to him is wise.
31 If the righteous person is repaid on earth,
certainly the wicked and the sinner will be.

12 1 The lover of instruction loves knowledge;
he who despises rebuke remains ignorant.
2 The good man obtains favor from the Lord;
the scheming man corrupts others.
3 A man cannot endure in wickedness,
but the righteous man's roots will not be shaken.
4 A meritorious woman is her husband's crown;
a vulgar woman is like rot in his bones.
5 The thoughts of the righteous are of justice;
the plans of the wicked are of deceit.
6 The words of the wicked are a deadly ambush,
but the mouth of the upright will save them.
7 Turn over the wicked, and they are gone,
but the house of the righteous will stand.
8 A man will be praised according to his intelligence,
but a twisted mind will be a mockery.
9 Better the modest person with a servant
than the pretentious one who lacks bread.
10 The righteous man knows his beast's needs;
the "compassion" of the wicked is but cruelty.
11 He who works his land will be sated with bread,
but he who trails idlers is mindless.
12 The wicked person covets the bastion of evil men,
but the root of the righteous will bear fruit.
13 In the treachery of lips lurks a terrible pitfall;
the righteous man avoids trouble.
14 From the fruits of a man's mouth he will be satisfied with good;
the recompense of a man's hands will come back to him.
15 The fool's way is correct in his own eyes,
but the wise man heeds counsel.
16 The fool's anger becomes known in a day,

but the clever man conceals his disgrace.
17 One who breathes faithfulness will testify truthfully,
but a testimony of untruths is deceitful.
18 Some utter words like the stabs of a sword,
but the tongue of the wise is healing.
19 Truthful speech endures forever,
but lying language lasts but a moment.
20 Deceit is in the heart of those who plot evil,
but for those who counsel peace there is joy.
21 No misfortune shall befall the righteous,
but the wicked are loaded with harm.
22 Lying lips are anathema to the LORD,
but those who act in faithfulness do His wish.
23 The clever man conceals his knowledge;
the heart of a fool proclaims nonsense.
24 The hand of the industrious will dominate;
the indolent will be subservient.
25 When worry enters a man's heart, he should suppress it
and gladden it with a good word.
26 The righteous man shows his fellow the way,
but the way of the wicked misleads them.
27 The cheat has no time to singe his quarry,
but the wealth of an honorable man is earned by diligence.
28 In the way of righteousness is life;
its path leads to immortality.

13 1 The wise son – the father's instruction.
The scoffer – he heard no rebuke.
2 A man enjoys good from the fruits of his mouth;
treacherous men enjoy lawlessness.
3 He who restrains his mouth protects himself;
he who spreads wide his lips prepares his downfall.
4 The indolent person craves but has nothing;
the industrious soul will have plenty.
5 The righteous man hates falsehood;
the wicked man defames and shames.
6 Righteousness guards the one whose way is blameless;
wickedness perverts the sinner.
7 Some pretend to be wealthy but have nothing;
others feign poverty but possess great treasure.
8 Wealth is a ransom for a man's life,
but only if the poor man hears no taunt.
9 The light of the righteous glows;
wicked men's candles sputter.
10 With arrogance comes strife;
wisdom abides with those who take counsel.

11 Wealth achieved through duplicity dwindles;
he who gathers little by little will increase.
12 Lengthy longing is a heartbreak;
fulfilled desire is a tree of life.
13 He who despises a commandment will meet with harm;
he who reveres a precept will be at peace.
14 The wise man's teaching is a fount of life;
it averts the snares of death.
15 Good sense wins favor;
the way of the treacherous is unyielding.
16 Every clever man acts thoughtfully;
a fool displays folly.
17 The wicked messenger falls into trouble;
the faithful envoy delivers healing.
18 Poverty and disgrace are for one who disregards instruction,
but whoever heeds rebuke will be honored.
19 A gratified desire is pleasant;
the anathema of fools is to turn away from evil.
20 He who walks with the wise will become wise,
but the companion of fools will fail.
21 Evil will pursue those steeped in sin;
as for the righteous, He will repay them with good.
22 The good man bequeaths to his sons' sons,
and the wealth of the sinner is hidden away for the righteous.
23 Abundant food may issue from poor men's plowing,
but many a field is barren because of improper care.
24 He who withholds the rod hates his child;
he who loves him will discipline him early.
25 The righteous man eats till he is satisfied;
the belly of the wicked will want food.

14 1 The wise among women builds her house;
the foolish woman tears it down with her own hands.
2 He who follows the correct path fears the Lord;
the errant in his ways derides Him.
3 In the mouth of the fool is the staff of pride;
the lips of the wise will protect them.
4 Without oxen the trough is bare;
abundant grain requires the ox's strength.
5 A trustworthy witness does not lie;
a false witness breathes lies.
6 The scoffer seeks wisdom but finds none,
but knowledge comes easily to the intelligent man.
7 Stay far away from the foolish man;
otherwise, you will never know wise speech.
8 The wisdom of the clever man is that he considers his course;

the folly of fools leads to delusion.
9 Fools discuss sinfulness;
upright men, goodwill.
10 The heart knows its own bitterness;
no outsider can share in its joy.[11]
11 The house of the wicked will be demolished;
the tent of the upright will blossom.
12 At times, the path before a man seems straight,
but it ends in paths of death.
13 At times, even laughter pains the heart,
and joy ends in misery.
14 The unrefined heart is satisfied with his conduct,
but the good man avoids him.
15 The simpleton believes everything;
the clever man considers his footsteps.
16 The wise man fears God and averts evil;
the fool assures himself and feels confident.
17 The short-tempered man will act foolishly;
the schemer will be despised.
18 Simpletons inherit foolishness;
the clever are crowned with knowledge.
19 Evil men will bow before good men;
so too will the wicked at the gates of the righteous.
20 Even his neighbor will despise the pauper,
but many are the friends of the rich.
21 He who derides his fellow is a sinner,
but he who shows favor to the lowly is fortunate.
22 Surely those who plot evil will go astray
while those who plan good will find kindness and faithfulness.
23 For every manner of toil there is gain,
but for mere talk there is only loss.
24 The wise wear their wealth as a crown,
but the folly of fools is idiocy.
25 A truthful witness saves lives;
he who breathes lies abets deceit.
26 In fear of the Lord there is a fortress of strength;
even a devout man's children will find a refuge.
27 Fear of the Lord is a fount of life;
it averts the snares of death.
28 A large population is a king's grandeur;
the lack of subjects is a disaster for the ruler.
29 Patience leads to great knowledge,
but impatience promotes folly.
30 A healing heart bring life to the flesh;

11 | In other words, no one really knows what another person is feeling.

envy is rot in the bones.
31 He who oppresses the poor blasphemes his Maker;
the one who shows pity to the pauper honors Him.
32 The wicked man is felled by his wickedness;
the righteous man finds refuge even in his death.
33 In the heart of the intelligent man wisdom rests quietly;
among fools it makes noise.
34 Righteousness exalts a nation,
and the kindness of peoples is a purification offering.
35 A king shows favor to a capable servant,
but he shows his wrath to one who causes shame.

15 1 A gentle response dispels wrath;
a worrisome word provokes anger.
2 The tongue of the wise enhances knowledge;
the mouths of fools spout folly.
3 The eyes of the Lord are everywhere,
watching both the evil and the good.
4 A healing tongue is a tree of life;
a distortion in it makes for a broken spirit.
5 The fool repels his father's instruction;
he who heeds rebuke grows clever.
6 In the house of the righteous there is great treasure;
in the wicked man's crop there is ruin.
7 The lips of the wise disseminate knowledge;
not so the hearts of fools.
8 Wicked men's offerings are anathema to the Lord;
the prayer of the upright is His desire.
9 The way of the wicked is anathema to the Lord;
He loves the pursuer of righteousness.
10 Instruction is harsh for anyone who forsakes the path;
he who hates rebuke shall perish.
11 Sheol and the netherworld are open before the Lord;
how much more so are the hearts of humans.
12 The scoffer dislikes receiving rebuke;
he will not call upon the wise.
13 A happy heart cheers the face;
with a sad heart comes a crushed spirit.
14 The heart of the intelligent man seeks knowledge;
the mouth of a fool keeps company with folly.
15 The poor man is miserable every day,
but the contented heart feasts always.
16 Better a little, with fear of the Lord,
than a great storehouse where there is turmoil.
17 Better a meal of greens with love present
than a fattened ox where hatred dwells.

18 The hot-tempered man incites strife;
the patient man calms a quarrel.
19 To the indolent, the way is a hedge of thorns;
to the upright, the path is paved.
20 A wise son brings joy to his father;
a foolish man shames his mother.
21 Folly is a joy to the mindless,
but the man of intelligence walks straight.
22 Without consultation, plans come to naught;
with many advisors, they succeed.
23 A man's response brings him joy;
how good is a timely word!
24 For the thinking man, the path of life is ever upward
so that he will avert Sheol below.
25 The Lord will extirpate the house of the haughty,
but He will secure the widow's boundary stone.[12]
26 Evil thoughts are anathema to the Lord,
but pure are words of pleasantness.
27 The man who pursues ill-gotten profit ruins his home,
but he who detests gifts will thrive.
28 The righteous man's heart reflects upon its response,
but the mouth of the wicked spouts evil.
29 The Lord is distant from the wicked,
but He hears the prayers of the righteous.
30 What brightens the eyes, gladdens the heart;
good tidings fatten the bones.
31 The ear that heeds a life-giving rebuke
resides among the wise.
32 He who disregards instruction despises himself;
he who heeds a rebuke acquires an understanding heart.
33 Fear of the Lord is wisdom's instruction;
before honor comes humility.

16 1 A person arranges the thoughts of his heart,
but the response comes from the Lord.[13]
2 A man's ways are all virtuous in his eyes,
but it is the Lord who assesses intentions.
3 Rely upon the Lord in all that you do,
and your plans will be secured.
4 The Lord made everything for His purpose,
even the wicked for his day of disaster.
5 Every haughty person is anathema to the Lord;
not for a moment will he be deemed innocent.
6 With kindness and truth, sin is forgiven;

12 | Protecting her property from encroachment.

13 | A person plans what he wants to say, but God determines what comes out of his mouth.

with fear of the Lord, evil is avoided.
7 When the Lord approves of a man's ways,
He will cause his enemies to make peace with him.
8 Better a little righteously attained
than great bounty gained unjustly.
9 If the heart of man scrutinizes his way,
the Lord will guide his footsteps.
10 There is magic upon the king's lips –
in judgment, his mouth will betray no one.
11 Just scales and balances are the Lord's;
all weights of the purse are His work.
12 Committing evil is anathema to kings,
for only with righteousness is a throne secured.
13 The wish of a king is for righteous lips;
he will love a person who speaks honestly.
14 A king's wrath is like death's messengers,
but the wise man can placate it.
15 A king's bright face signals life;
his approval is like a late winter rain cloud.
16 Acquiring wisdom is much better than refined gold;
acquiring understanding is superior to silver.
17 The path of the upright avoids evil;
he who would keep himself from harm will guard his way.
18 Before collapse comes pride!
Before failure, haughtiness of spirit!
19 Better a lowly spirit among the humble
than dividing spoils with the mighty.
20 He who thinks matters over will discover good;
he who trusts in the Lord is fortunate.
21 The wise of heart will be proclaimed intelligent;
sweet speech will increase learning.
22 A fount of life is intelligence to the one who has it;
the fools' instruction is folly.
23 The wise man's mind informs his mouth;
it adds instruction to his lips.
24 Pleasant words are like honeycomb:
sweet to the soul and healing to the bones.
25 At times, the path before a man seems straight,
but its end is in the paths of death.
26 The toiling person toils for himself,
for when his mouth makes its demands.
27 The villain mines for malice;
upon his lips is a scorching fire.
28 The perverse person incites strife;
the quarrelsome person alienates his companion.

29 The lawless man misleads his fellow;
he leads him along a base path.
30 He closes his eyes as he devises perversions;
he purses his lips as he executes evil.
31 Gray hair is a crown of glory;
it can be acquired through the way of righteousness.
32 Better a patient man than a mighty one;
better he who controls his mood than he who conquers a city.
33 Lots may be cast in a person's bosom,
but all decision is from the LORD.

17 1 Better dry bread with tranquility
than a house full of feasts with contention.
2 A competent servant will dominate a son who causes shame
and will share in the inheritance with the brothers.
3 A crucible is for silver and a furnace for gold;
it is the LORD who tests the heart.
4 The wicked man listens to sinful lips;
the liar gives ear to the tongue that speaks calamity.
5 He who mocks the pauper blasphemes his Maker;
he who rejoices over misfortune will not be deemed innocent.
6 Grandchildren are the crown of the aged;
the glory of children is their parents.
7 Exaggerated speech is unbecoming of a knave;
how much worse is false speech by a noble person.
8 A bribe is like a gemstone in the eyes of its possessor;
he will justify it to whomever he turns.
9 He who overlooks an offense seeks friendship;
he who repeats the matter alienates a companion.
10 One scolding will frighten a man of understanding
more than a hundred blows will a fool.
11 Surely the rebel courts disaster;
a cruel messenger will be sent against him.
12 Better that a man encounter a bereaved bear,
and not a fool in his folly.
13 A person who returns evil for good –
evil will never depart from his house.
14 He who initiates strife opens floodgates;
before the quarrel spreads, leave!
15 He who acquits the guilty, and he who condemns the innocent –
both are anathema to the LORD.
16 Of what use is money given to a fool
to acquire wisdom when he has no mind for it?
17 A good friend is always loving;
he is like a brother when trouble occurs.
18 A mindless man extends his hand;

he guarantees loans on behalf of another.
19 He who loves to offend loves dispute;
he who raises high his doorway invites collapse.
20 The crooked heart meets with no good;
he whose tongue is duplicitous will fall into evil.
21 He who begets a fool knows misery;
the father of the knave will never rejoice.
22 The happy heart enhances healing;
the crushed spirit dries up the marrow of the bone.
23 Bribes are taken from the lap of a wicked man
to pervert the paths of justice.
24 Wisdom is in front of the man of understanding;
in the eyes of the fool it is at the ends of the earth.
25 The foolish son causes his father pain,
and bitterness to her who bore him.
26 Surely, it is not good to punish the righteous
or flog noble men for their rectitude.
27 He who restrains his words appreciates knowledge;
he for whom speech is precious is a man of understanding.
28 Even a fool who keeps silent is deemed wise,
and he who shuts his lips, intelligent.

18 1 The loner follows his passions;
he rebuffs all guidance.
2 The fool does not desire understanding;
he wishes only to disclose his own thoughts.
3 When the wicked man comes, derision comes,
along with shame and disgrace.
4 The words of a person's mouth are deep waters;
a fount of wisdom is like a bubbling brook.
5 Tolerating the guilty is not good;
no more than subverting the innocent's judgment.
6 The lips of the fool cause disputes;
his mouth invites violence.
7 The mouth of the fool is its own pitfall;
his lips are his fatal snare.
8 The words of an argumentative person are like blows;
they pierce the belly's chambers.
9 The person who is careless in his work –
he, too, is brother to the destructive man.
10 The Lord's name is a tower of strength;
the righteous person runs there and is safe.
11 The rich man's wealth is his city of strength;
in his mind it is like a mighty wall.
12 Before collapse, a person's heart is haughty;
before honor comes humility.

13 He who responds before he has listened –
this is folly for him, and shame.
14 The brave person's spirit sustains him during his illness,
but a weak spirit, who can bear it?
15 An intelligent man's heart acquires knowledge;
the ear of the wise seeks knowledge.
16 A person's generosity widens his path;
it leads him into the presence of the great.
17 The first to present his case seems innocent
until his fellow comes and interrogates him.
18 Casting lots can quiet quarrels
and even separate powerful adversaries.
19 A brother wronged is like a fortified city;
such quarrels are like the bolts of a fortress.

20 A man fills his stomach by the fruits of his mouth;
he will be satisfied by the harvest of his lips.
21 Death and life are in the power of the tongue;
he who treats it lovingly will eat its fruit.
22 He who finds a wife finds what is good
and has derived favor from the LORD.
23 A poor person speaks beseechingly,
but the rich person responds with impudence.
24 A friendly man seeks many companions,
but one close friend is more loyal than a brother.

19 1 Better a pauper who walks in innocence
than a person with perverse lips who is a fool.
2 Ignorance, too, is of no benefit to a person;
he who hurries his footsteps sins.
3 A person's own folly distorts his path,
yet he takes out his anger on the LORD.
4 A person with wealth accumulates many friends,
but the pauper is separated from his friends.
5 He who testifies falsely will not be judged innocent;
he who spouts lies will not escape.
6 Many court the noble person;
all befriend the generous person.
7 The poor person's brothers all hate him;
his friends avoid him even more.
He pursues them with words, but they are futile.
8 He who acquires a mind loves himself;
he preserves understanding and will find success.
9 He who testifies falsely will not be judged innocent;
he who spouts lies will be doomed.
10 Luxury is unseemly for a fool;

it is yet worse for a slave to rule his masters.
11 A person's forbearance reflects his intelligence,
and it is to his glory that he overlooks offense.
12 Like a lion's roar is a king's rage;
his favor is like dew upon grass.
13 A foolish son is a father's heartbreak;
a wife's squabbles are like annoying drops of water.
14 Property and possessions are an ancestral inheritance;
an intelligent wife is from the LORD.
15 Laziness induces slumber;
an idle person will starve.
16 He who guards a precept guards himself;
he who abuses His ways will perish.
17 He who is kind to a pauper lends to the LORD;
He will repay him his kindness.
18 Discipline your son while there is yet hope;
do not be dissuaded by his weeping.
19 But excessive wrath pays a penalty;
spare him your wrath but continue your discipline.
20 Heed counsel and accept instruction;
you will then be wise in the end.
21 Many are the thoughts in the heart of man,
but it is the LORD's plan that will prevail.
22 What people seek from a person is his kindness;
better a poor man than one who lies.
23 Fear of the LORD leads a person to life:
he will endure in satisfaction and not be visited by misfortune.
24 The lazy man buries his hand in the bowl
but will not even return it to his mouth.
25 Strike the scoffer, and he will awaken from his ignorance;
rebuke an intelligent man, and he will advance his knowledge.
26 The son who embarrasses and disgraces
does violence to his father and drives his mother away.
27 My son, stop listening to instruction
that misinterprets words of knowledge.
28 A villainous witness scoffs at justice;
the mouth of the wicked conceals iniquity.
29 Punishments are readied for scoffers
and blows for the backs of fools.

20 1 Wine is a scoffer; beer is boisterous;
those who go astray with them will never be wise.
2 A king's terror is like a lion's roar;
he who provokes him endangers his life.
3 It is honorable for a man to refrain from dispute,
yet every fool gets entangled.

4 The lazy man does not plow in winter;[14]
he begs at harvest time, but there is nothing.
5 A plan in a man's mind is like deep water;
the thinking man will draw it out.
6 Many people are called faithful,
but the truly trustworthy person is rare.
7 The righteous man walks with perfectness;
fortunate are his children after him.

8 The king who sits firmly upon the throne of justice
disperses evil with his gaze.
9 Who can say "I have cleansed my heart;
I am pure of my sin"?
10 False weights, inaccurate measures:
both are anathema to the LORD.
11 A child may make himself strange while at play
but nevertheless be innocent and upright in his conduct.
12 An attentive ear and a discriminating eye –
the LORD made them both.
13 Do not cherish sleep lest you become impoverished;
keep your eyes open, and you will be sated with bread.
14 "Bad! Bad!" says the buyer,
but when he departs, he praises it.
15 There are many pearls and much gold,
but lips of knowledge are a rare vessel.
16 Take his garment, for he has put up security for a stranger;
if he did so on behalf of an alien woman – seize it!
17 The bread of betrayal tastes sweet to a man,
but afterward his mouth fills with gravel.
18 Plans will succeed if advice is taken;
therefore, wage war with great forethought.
19 He who reveals secrets is a talebearer;
do not mingle with a chatterer.
20 The lamp of him who curses his father and mother
will dim as darkness descends.
21 An inheritance initially obtained in haste
will not be blessed in the end.
22 Do not say, "I will repay evil."
Trust in the LORD; He will help you.
23 Fraudulent weights are anathema to the LORD;
false scales are wicked.
24 A person's footsteps derive from the LORD;
what can anyone know about where he is headed?
25 It is man's failing to blurt out sacred vows

14 | Winter is the rainy season, when the ground is prepared for planting.

and consider them only afterward.
26 The wise king disperses the wicked;
he rolls the wheel upon them.[15]
27 The LORD's lamp is a person's life;
it searches out all the belly's chambers.[16]
28 Kindness and truth will protect a king;
kindness will maintain his throne.
29 The splendor of youth is their strength;
the grandeur of the old is their gray hair.
30 Welts and bruises are cleansing salves for the wicked
as are blows to the belly's chambers.

21 1 The heart of a king is but a stream of water in the hand of the LORD:
to wherever He desires He directs it.
2 A man's ways are all correct in his eyes;
it is the LORD who holds him to account for his intentions.
3 Pursuing righteousness and justice
pleases the LORD more than sacrifice.
4 Lofty eyes and a haughty heart:
the schemes of the wicked are sinful.
5 The thoughts of the diligent lead only to gain;
all who are hasty only suffer loss.
6 Treasures achieved by a false tongue
are like a fleeting breath in search of death.
7 The violence of the wicked will drag them down,
for they refuse to do what is just.
8 Tortuous is the way of some men, and bizarre;
the pure person's actions are proper.
9 Better to sit on the corner of a roof[17]
than with a quarrelsome wife in the home of friends.
10 The wicked man craves evil;
even his comrade will not find favor in his eyes.
11 When a scoffer is punished, the simpleton grows wise;
when a wise man is taught, he[18] gains knowledge.[19]
12 The righteous man contemplates the wicked man's house
and consigns the wicked to evil.
13 He that stuffs his ear so as not to hear the cry of the poor,
he too will call out and not be answered.
14 Alms given in secret will subdue anger;

15 | A wheel rolled over wheat to separate the kernel from the chaff. Or, perhaps a chariot wheel rolled over the enemy.

16 | In other words, one's innermost thoughts.

17 | In isolation; see verse 19.

18 | Referring to the simpleton, when he sees the wise man being instructed. This follows *Mikra LeYisrael*.

19 | The simple person learns a lesson when he sees the scoffer punished and when he sees the wise person being taught.

a bribe in the bosom, fierce wrath.
15 Justice done is a joy for the righteous,
but it is the downfall of those who wreak evil.
16 A man who strays from the path of reason
will find rest in the company of ghosts.
17 He that loves luxury will become a needy man;
he that loves wine and oil does not get rich.
18 A wicked man ransoms the righteous;
the traitor redeems the upright.[20]
19 Better sit in a desert land
than with a quarrelsome wife and with anger.
20 Delightful treasure and oil are in the wise man's abode,
but the foolish man swallows it up.
21 He that pursues righteousness and kindness
finds life, virtue, and honor.
22 A wise man ascended to the fortress of the mighty
and brought down the strength of its fortress.
23 He that guards his mouth and his tongue
guards himself from troubles.
24 The arrogant villain – "scoffer" is his name –
commits villainy in a fit of rage.
25 A lazy man's craving will kill him,
for his hands refuse to work.
26 All day he craves and craves,
but the righteous man gives and does not withhold.
27 The sacrifice of the wicked is anathema,
all the more so if brought with nefarious intent.
28 The lying witness is doomed;
the man who listens speaks for eternity.
29 The wicked man's brazenness is upon his face;
the upright carefully considers his conduct.
30 There is neither wisdom nor understanding nor counsel
against the Lord.[21]
31 The horse may be prepared for the day of battle,
but deliverance is the Lord's.

22 1 A good name is preferable to great wealth;
good grace is better than silver and gold.
2 Rich man and poor man meet –
it is the Lord who made them both.
3 The clever man saw danger and hid;
the ignorant continued onward and suffered.
4 The result of humility is fear of the Lord –

20 | The wicked will serve as a ransom for the righteous and the traitor for the upright. Cf. 11:8.

21 | No amount of wisdom will avail if God does not wish it.

wealth, honor, and life itself.
5 There are thorns and snares upon the crooked path;
he who protects himself keeps far from them.
6 Train a youth in the way that befits him,
then even as he ages he will not turn away from it.
7 The rich man rules the destitute;
the borrower is slave to the lender.
8 He who sows injustice reaps naught,
and his rod of wrath will vanish.
9 The generous man will be blessed;
he gave of his own bread to the pauper.
10 Expel the scoffer, and strife departs;
gone are discord and disgrace.
11 The pure-hearted friend with gracious lips –
a king is his companion.
12 The eyes of the Lord watch over the man of knowledge
but disrupt the traitor's plans.
13 The lazy man says, "There is a lion out there!
If I venture into the streets I will be killed!"
14 The mouth of a promiscuous woman is like a deep pit;
he who is scorned by the Lord will fall into it.
15 Folly is bound up in the heart of a youth;
the rod of instruction will expel it far from him.
16 He who enriches the pauper will gain thereby;
he who bestows gifts upon the rich will only lose.
17 Bend your ear and listen to the words of the wise;
direct your heart to my knowledge.
18 It is pleasant that you preserve them in your belly
and that they stand firmly together on your lips.
19 That you put your trust in the Lord –
this I have demanded of you today – yes, you!
20 I have written these threefold
with great counsel and with forethought,
21 to inform you of the validity of these words of truth
so that you can respond with truthful words to those who sent you.
22 Do not steal from a pauper, thinking that he is helpless;
do not crush the poor man at the gate.
23 For the Lord will plead his cause
and confiscate the life of the one who confiscated his.
24 Do not befriend him who has a temper,
and do not even approach an irascible man,
25 lest you learn his ways
and set a trap for yourself.
26 Do not be among those who extend their hands
as guarantors for loans,

27 for if you are unable to pay,
why should he take your bed from under you?
28 Do not encroach upon the age-old boundary marker
that was set up by your ancestors.
29 If you see a man adept at his work,
he will one day serve kings;
he will not serve commoners.

23 1 When you sit down to break bread with a ruler,
consider well what is before you.
2 If you are a glutton,
put a knife to your throat.
3 Do not crave his delicacies;
they are the bread of lies.
4 Do not exhaust yourself in order to get rich;
follow your understanding – desist!
5 Blink your eyes at it; it is gone.
It has grown wings;
like an eagle it flies heavenward.
6 Do not eat a stingy man's bread;
do not crave his delicacies.
7 For he silently measures.
He will say to you, "Eat! Drink!"
But he does not mean it.
8 You will vomit the bread you ate,
and you will have wasted your pleasant words.
9 Do not address a fool;
he will ridicule the wisdom of your words.
10 Do not move the age-old boundary marker;
do not encroach upon the orphans' fields,
11 for their Redeemer is strong,
and He will take up their cause against you.
12 Apply your heart toward instruction
and your ears to knowledgeable sayings.
13 Do not withhold instruction from a youth;
if you strike him with the rod he will not die.
14 You will strike him with the rod
and thereby save him from Sheol.
15 My son, if your heart has grown wise,
my heart rejoices along with yours.
16 My mind[22]
takes delight
when your lips speak words of rectitude.
17 Do not envy sinners in your heart;

22 | Literally "my kidneys."

envy only those who fear the LORD constantly.
18 Indeed there is a future;
your hope will not be cut off.
19 You, my son, listen and grow wise;
let your heart march along the proper road.
20 Do not associate with those who guzzle wine,
who gorge themselves on meat.
21 For the drunkard and the glutton become impoverished;
drowsiness clothes them in tatters.
22 Listen to your father who begot you;
do not disdain your mother when she is old.
23 Buy truth; do not sell it.
Buy wisdom, instruction, and understanding.
24 The father of the righteous man will be glad,
and he who begets a wise man will rejoice.
25 Your father and your mother will rejoice,
and she who raised you will be glad.

26 My son, give your heart to me,
and let your eyes watch my ways.
27 For the harlot is like a deep pit,
and the alien woman is like a narrow well.
28 Like a beast of prey, she too lies in ambush;
she destroys the betrayers among men.
29 To whom is there woe, to whom wailing?
To whom quarrel, to whom delusion, to whom needless wounds?
To whom bloodshot eyes?
30 To those who linger late for wine
and come in search of mixed drinks.
31 Do not gaze at wine so red,
for he who keeps his eye upon the cup
thinks he is walking the straight and narrow.
32 But in the end, it is as if he is bitten by a snake
or stung by a viper.
33 Your eyes will see hallucinations;
your heart will speak distortions.
34 You will be like one who lies in the midst of the sea
or like one who lies upon the ship's prow.
35 "They struck me, but I felt no pain!
They pounded me, but I was unaware!
Whenever I wake up, I will pursue it all the more!"

24 1 Do not envy men of evil;
do not crave their company.
2 For their hearts contemplate violence,
and their lips speak harm.

3 With wisdom will a house be built;
with understanding it will hold firm.
4 With knowledge its chambers will be filled
with every sort of precious and pleasant treasure.
5 A wise man stands strong;
a man of reason conserves his resources.
6 For only with plans can you wage war;
victory is won with abundant counsel.
7 Wisdom is far removed from the fool;
at the gate of the wise he has nothing to say.
8 He who but considers doing evil –
him they will call "master of schemes."
9 Foolish thoughts are sinful;
men deem a scoffer anathema.
10 Because you weakened yourself on the day of another's distress,
your own strength will diminish.
11 If you failed to rescue those being taken to their death,
destined for slaughter –
12 you will object, "But, we didn't know of this!" –
He who assesses men's hearts discerns;
He who guards your life knows;
He will repay each man as he deserves.
13 My son, just as eating honey is as good
as sweet droplets upon your palate,
14 so too is striving to achieve wisdom for yourself.
If you succeed, there is a future;
your hope will not be cut off.

15 Wicked one! Do not ambush the righteous man's abode;
do not do violence to his place of rest.
16 Although the righteous man falls seven times, he rises,
but the wicked falter under duress.
17 Do not rejoice when your enemy falls;
let your heart not be glad when he falters,
18 lest the Lord take notice and be displeased
and remove His wrath from him.
19 Do not compete with evildoers;
do not envy the wicked.
20 For there is no future for evil;
the lamp of the wicked will be dimmed.
21 Fear the Lord, my son, and the king;
do not mingle with those who are disobedient.
22 For their day of retribution arrives suddenly,
and the decrees of both – who knows when?

23 These too are sayings of the wise:

Showing partiality in justice is not good.
24 He who says to the guilty, "You are innocent!"–
nations will curse him;
peoples will condemn him.
25 Those who offer rebuke will enjoy pleasantness;
the blessing of good fortune will come upon them.
26 He kisses with lips, does
the one who replies with forthright words.[23]
27 Prepare your outdoor work;
ready your field for yourself.
Afterward, build your house.

28 Do not offer unfounded testimony against your fellow;
you will crush him with your lips.
29 Do not say, "I will do to him as he did to me;
I will repay the man as he deserves."

30 I passed by the field of a lazy man,
by the vineyard of a mindless person;
31 it had become entirely overgrown with thorns,
its surface covered with weeds,
its stone fence demolished.
32 I observed and took it to heart;
I noted, and I took instruction.
33 A little sleep, a little dozing,
a little lying there with folded hands,
34 and poverty will come like a sudden intruder,
privation like a soldier bearing a shield.

25 1 These too are among the proverbs of Shlomo;
they were transcribed by the men of Ḥizkiya, king of Yehuda:
2 The glory of God is that He conceals things;
the glory of kings is that they search things out.
3 As high as the heavens, as deep as the earth,
the minds of kings are unknowable.
4 As dross is removed from silver
so that a vessel emerges for the silversmith,
5 so too must the wicked man be removed from the king's presence
so that his throne will be established in righteousness.
6 Do not flaunt yourself before a king;
do not stand in the place of great men.
7 For it is better that it be said to you, "Step up here,"
than to be humiliated before the nobleman –
this your own eyes have surely observed.
8 Do not enter into a dispute hastily,

23 | Forthright words (even if they are critical) are like giving a kiss.

for what will you do if your fellow puts you to shame in the end?
9 Dispute with him if you must,
but do not reveal another's secret,
10 lest a listener reproach you
and you be unable to retract your slander.
11 Like golden apples in silver settings,
so are words spoken in proper sequence.
12 Like a golden earring or an ornament of pure gold,
so does a wise man offer a rebuke to a listening ear.
13 Like the coolness of snow on a summer harvest day,
so is a messenger who is faithful to his senders.
He soothes his master's spirits.

14 Clouds and wind, but no rain!
So is the man who praises himself for gifts not given.
15 With patience even a tyrant can be won over;
a soft tongue can break a bone.
16 Have you found honey? Consume no more than you need,
lest you eat your fill and vomit it up.
17 So too, set foot in your friend's home but rarely,
lest he have his fill of you and come to hate you.
18 Like a club, a sword, and a sharpened arrow
is the man who bears false witness against his fellow.
19 Like a rotten tooth and a wobbly foot
is trust in a traitor in times of trouble.
20 A tattered garment on a cold day is like vinegar upon natron[24]
or like songs sung to a despondent heart.
21 If your foe is hungry, feed him bread;
if thirsty, give him water.
22 For you will be shoveling coals upon his head,
and the LORD will reward you.
23 The north wind produces rain;
a secretive tongue produces a scowling face.
24 Better to sit on the corner of a roof
than with a quarrelsome wife in the home of friends.
25 Like cool waters upon a thirsty throat
are glad tidings from a distant land.
26 Like a muddied spring and a ruined fountain
is the righteous man who bends before a wicked one.
27 Eating too much honey is not good,
and searching for honor is not honorable.
28 Like a breached city with no wall
is a man who has no control over his emotions.

---

24 | Natron is sodium bicarbonate (baking soda), used in biblical times as a cleanser. When mixed with vinegar, the solution froths and then quickly dissipates.

26 1 Like snow in the summer and rain at harvest time,
so is honor unseemly for a fool.
2 As a sparrow wanders and a swallow flies,
so will an undeserved curse come back to him who uttered it.
3 Like a whip for a horse and a bridle for a donkey,
so is a rod for the backs of fools.
4 Do not answer a fool according to his folly,
lest you become his equal.
5 Answer a fool according to his folly,
lest he consider himself wise.
6 It is like cutting off your feet or drinking down violence
to send messages in the hand of a fool.
7 Like removing the crutches[25] from a cripple,
so is a proverb in the mouth of a fool.
8 Like binding a pebble in a sling,
so is granting honor to a fool.
9 As a thorn comes into the hand of a drunkard,
so is a proverb in the mouth of a fool.
10 The quarrelsome man harms it all;
he hires both the fool and the disobedient.
11 As a dog returns to his vomit,
so does a fool repeat his folly.
12 You observed a man who is wise in his own eyes?
There is more hope for a fool than for him.
13 The lazy man says, "There is a young lion on the road;
a lion is in the midst of the streets."[26]
14 Just as a door twists on its hinges,
so does the lazy man on his bed.
15 The lazy man buries his hand in the bowl,
too tired to bring it to his mouth.
16 The lazy man is wiser in his own eyes
than seven sensible advisors.
17 Like someone who grasps a dog's ears
is he who angrily intercedes in a dispute not his.
18 Like someone acting as a madman,
shooting firebrands and deadly arrows,
19 so is the man who cheats his fellow and says,
"I was only joking."
20 Without wood, the fire will go out.
Without an argumentative man, strife is silenced.
21 As charcoal for embers and wood for a fire,
so does a quarrelsome person ignite dispute.
22 The words of an argumentative man are like blows;

25 | This admittedly unusual translation of a very obscure phrase is suggested by *Daat Mikra*.

26 | An excuse for not going out; cf. 22:13.

they pierce the belly's chambers.
23 Like cheap silver covering an earthen vessel,
so are enticing lips with evil intentions.
24 The foe disguises himself with his lips;
inside, he plots treachery.
25 His voice may sound gracious, but do not trust him:
he has seven abominations in his heart.
26 Hatred may be hidden in deep deception,
but its evil is exposed in public.
27 He who digs a ditch will fall into it;
he who rolls a stone will find it rolls back on him.
28 The false tongue hates those whom it oppresses;
the smooth tongue produces calamity.

27 1 Boast not about tomorrow,
for you do not know what might yet occur today.
2 Let another person praise you, not your own mouth;
a stranger, not your own lips.
3 Stone's weight, sand's burden –
the aggravation caused by a fool is heavier than both.
4 Wrath's cruelty, fury's torrent –
but who can withstand jealousy?
5 Better open rebuke
than concealed love.
6 A friend's bruises are well intended;
a foe's kisses are excessive.
7 A satisfied person tramples even honey;
to a hungry person everything bitter tastes sweet.
8 Like a sparrow that wanders from its nest,
so is a man who wanders from his home.
9 Oil and incense gladden the heart;
better a friend's sweetness than your own advice.
10 Forsake neither your friend nor your father's friend.
Enter not your brother's home at the time of your misfortune;
a close neighbor is better than a distant brother.
11 My son, become wise and gladden my heart;
I will then be able to respond to my critics.
12 The clever man saw danger and hid;
the ignorant continued onward and suffered.
13 Take his garment, for he has put up security for a stranger.
If he did so on behalf of a foreign woman – seize it!
14 He who blesses his fellow in a loud voice early in the morning –
it will be reckoned to him as a curse.
15 A quarrelsome wife is akin to
an annoying drip on a rainy day.
16 Confining her is like confining the wind;

he will have to call for the muscles of his right hand.
17 As iron sharpens iron,
so is a man gladdened by the presence of another.
18 He who tends to the fig tree shall eat its fruit;
he who takes care of his master shall be honored.
19 As water reflects the face shown to it,
so does one man's heart reciprocate another's.
20 Sheol and destruction are never satisfied;
human eyes, too, are never satisfied.
21 Silver is tested in a crucible and gold in a furnace;
so too can a man be tested by praise of him.
22 Even if you crush a fool with a mortar and pestle together with grain,
his folly will not depart from him.
23 Know well the appearance of your sheep;
pay attention to your flocks,
24 for wealth does not last forever,
nor is a crown always passed from generation to generation.
25 Grass is gone; fresh grass is revealed,
and the mountains' greenery accumulates.
26 Lamb's wool will be your clothing,
and your male goats will earn a field's price.
27 There will be enough goats' milk
to provide food for you and your household
and sustenance for your maidservants.

28 1 The wicked flee though there is no pursuer;
the righteous rest securely like a lion.
2 When the land is rebellious, its rulers are many;
with a man of understanding and knowledge, stability endures.
3 A pauper who oppresses the poor
is like a driving rain that leaves no food.
4 Those who forsake instruction praise the wicked;
those who observe instruction combat them.
5 Evildoers cannot understand justice;
those who seek the Lord understand it all.
6 Better a pauper who walks in innocence
than a man who is crooked in his ways but rich.
7 A wise son holds fast to instruction,
but a companion of gluttons shames his father.
8 He who amasses wealth by usury and interest
gathers it for the one who is kind to the poor.
9 He who turns his ear to avoid hearing instruction
renders even his prayers an anathema.
10 He who misleads the upright along an evil path
will fall into his own trap,
but the innocent will inherit goodness.

11 A rich man is wise in his own eyes,
but an insightful poor man will expose him.
12 When the righteous celebrate, there is great glory,
but when the wicked arise, people must hide.
13 He who would cover up his sins will not succeed,
but he who confesses and forsakes them will find compassion.
14 Fortunate is the person who is always cautious;
he who is obstinate will fall into disaster.
15 Like a roaring lion and a prowling bear
is a wicked tyrant over a helpless people;
16 so is the senseless prince who is oppressive.
He who hates sinful gain will prolong his days.
17 A person desperate because he has murdered another –
even if he flees to the pit, do not assist him.
18 He who walks in perfectness will be saved,
but he who is crooked in his ways will fall at once.
19 He who works his land will be sated with bread;
he who trails idlers will have plenty of poverty.
20 A trustworthy man has many blessings;
he who rushes to get rich will not escape the consequences.
21 Showing partiality is not right,
or that a man[27] should sin for a slice of bread.
22 Distracted by his wealth is the miser;
he is unaware that want will come upon him.
23 He who reproves a man
will eventually find more favor than someone who offers flattery.
24 He who robs his father and mother and insists that he has not sinned
is a vandal's accomplice.
25 The selfish man incites strife;
he who trusts in the Lord will be enriched.
26 He who trusts his own heart is a fool;
he who walks in wisdom will be safe.
27 He who gives to the poor will not lose thereby;
he who looks away will receive many curses.
28 When the wicked arise, a man had better hide;
with their destruction the righteous increase.

29 1 He who stiffens his neck when often rebuked
will collapse suddenly, beyond cure.
2 When the righteous ascend to greatness, the people rejoice;
when a wicked man reigns, the people lament.
3 A man who loves wisdom brings joy to his father;
he who keeps company with harlots squanders his fortune.
4 With justice, a king sustains the land;

27 | Meaning the judge.

the gift-seeking man lays it waste.
5 The man who flatters his fellow
spreads a net for his own feet.
6 The wicked man's sins are his own trap;
the righteous man sings and rejoices.
7 The righteous man knows the poor man's plight;
the wicked man does not understand such knowledge.
8 Scoffers inflame a city,
but the wise turn wrath away.
9 A wise man in a legal dispute with a fool –
he may show anger or he may smile,
but there is never satisfaction.
10 Murderers hate the innocent;
the upright seek to protect him.
11 The fool lets out all his anger;
the wise man calmly restrains it.
12 A ruler who listens to lies –
all of his servants become wicked.
13 The pauper and the scheming man meet;
the LORD illuminates the eyes of both.
14 A king who judges the poor truthfully –
his throne will be firm forever.
15 Rod and rebuke will yield wisdom;
a youth uncontrolled will disgrace his mother.
16 When the wicked ascend to greatness, sin increases,
but the righteous will witness their downfall.
17 Discipline your child; he will bring you comfort
and give you delight.
18 Without a vision the people become mutinous;
anyone who observes instruction is fortunate.
19 A slave cannot be controlled by words alone;
although he understands, he gives no response.[28]
20 Have you seen a man who hurries his speech?
There is more hope for a fool than for him!
21 He who pampers his slave from an early age
in the end will make him the master.
22 An angry man provokes conflict;
with a hot-tempered man there is much sin.
23 A man's pride will bring him down;
he who is lowly in spirit will grasp honor.
24 He who shares with a thief hates himself;
he will hear the oath but not testify.
25 A man's panic becomes a trap,

28 | The implication is that a slave can be controlled only by beating him. See also Exodus 21:20–21, 26–27.

but he who trusts in the LORD shall be lifted up.
26 Many seek an audience with the ruler,
but a man's judgment is from the LORD.
27 An unjust man is an abomination to the righteous;
he who walks a straight path is an abomination to the wicked.

30 1 The words of Agur[29] son of Yakeh, the Masaite;
the oration spoken by this man[30] to Itiel –
to Itiel and to Ukhal:[31]
2 I am more ignorant than any other man;
I lack human understanding.
3 I never studied wisdom,
nor do I have knowledge of holy beings.
4 Who rose to the heavens and descended?
Who gathered the wind in the hollow of his hands?
Who wrapped water in a cloak?
Who erected the ends of the earth?
What is his name or his son's name, if you know?
5 Every word of God is pure;
He is a shield to those who take refuge in him.
6 Do not add to His words,
lest He rebuke you, and you be exposed as a liar.
7 Two things I request of You;
do not deny them to me before I die.
8 Keep emptiness and falsehood far from me;
give me neither poverty nor wealth;
nourish me with my fixed portion of bread,
9 lest I become sated and deny
and say, "Who is the LORD?"
And lest I become impoverished and steal
and thereby defile the name of my God.

10 Do not malign a slave to his master
lest he curse you and you be found guilty.
11 There is a generation that curses its father
and does not bless its mother.
12 A generation pure in its own eyes
but not cleansed of its filth.
13 A generation – how haughty are its eyes,
its eyelids raised ever upward![32]
14 A generation whose teeth are swords
and whose jaws are knives

29 | Agur is an otherwise unknown foreign sage.
30 | Cf. Numbers 24:3.
31 | Perhaps Agur's sons.
32 | Raised eyes are a sign of arrogance.

ready to devour the poor from the earth –
the neediest of mankind.
15 The leech has two daughters:
"Give" and "Give."
There are three[33] that are never satisfied
and four that never say, "Enough!"
16 Sheol; the barren womb;
the earth is never satisfied with water;
and fire never says, "Enough!"
17 The eye that mocks its father
and belittles its mother's guidance –
ravens of the creek shall peck it out,
and eagles shall devour it.
18 Three things are too wondrous for me;
four I cannot know:
19 the way of the eagle in the heavens,
the way of the serpent upon the rock,
the way of a ship in the midst of the sea,
the way of a man with a young woman.
20 So too, the way of an adulterous woman:
she eats,[34] wipes her mouth,
and says, "I have done no wrong!"
21 The earth shudders because of three things,
and because of four it cannot carry on:
22 because of a slave who reigns,
because of a knave who is sated with bread,
23 because of a hated wife who gains authority,
and because of a slave girl who displaces her mistress.
24 There are four that are the smallest on earth,
yet they are exceedingly wise:
25 Ants are not a strong species,
yet they prepare their food in summer.
26 Hyraxes are not a mighty species,
yet they make their home in the rock.
27 The locust has no king,
yet he marches forth as a troop.
28 You can catch the lizard with your hands,
yet it resides in the palaces of kings.
29 There are three who are adept at marching
and four at walking:
30 The lion is the mightiest of beasts,
before nothing will he retreat;
31 the hunter's swift hound; the he-goat;

33 | See note on 6:16.

34 | A euphemism for sexual relations.

the king whom none will challenge.
32 If you are insulted, maintain your dignity;
if you consider otherwise, put your hand to your mouth.
33 Churning milk produces butter;
a churning nose produces blood;
churning anger produces strife.

31 1 The words to Lemuel, king;[35]
the oration with which his mother admonished him:
2 What? My son!
What? Child of my womb!
What? Child of my vows!
3 Do not waste your strength on women;
do not pursue the paths of kingly pleasures.
4 This is not for kings, Lemuel.
It is not for kings to drink wine,
nor for noblemen to ask, "Where is aged wine?"
5 Lest he drink and forget what is inscribed
and subvert the cause of all the downtrodden.
6 Leave aged wine for the bereaved
and wine for embittered souls.
7 Let him drink and forget his poverty
and never again remember his plight.
8 Speak up for the mute
and for the rights of all mortals.
9 Speak up; judge righteously;
advocate the cause of the poor and needy.

10 An exemplary woman who can find?
She is more valuable than pearls.
11 Her husband's heart trusts in her;
he will lack no benefit.
12 She will repay his favors, not his insults,
in all of her life's circumstances.
13 She searches for wool and flax,[36]
and her hands work adroitly.
14 She becomes like the merchant ships;
she brings her bread from afar.[37]
15 She rises while it is yet night;
she gives sustenance to her household
and portions to her maidservants.
16 When she sets her mind upon a field she buys it;
with the fruits of her labor she plants a vineyard.

35 | Identified by some commentators as Shlomo.
36 | Wool for winter wear and linen for summer.
37 | She resourcefully acquires imported food and other goods.

17 She girds herself with strength
and vigorously exerts her limbs.[38]
18 When she discerns that her wares are good,
her lamp is not extinguished by night.
19 She sets her hands to the distaff,
and her palms grasp the spinning rod.
20 She stretches out her palm to the poor
and extends her hands to the needy.
21 She need not fear for her household because of snow,
for her entire household is clothed in scarlet.[39]
22 She makes bedcoverings for herself;
linen and purple is her garment.
23 Her husband is well known in the city gates[40]
as he sits among the elders of the land.
24 She makes clothing and sells it
and offers belts to the merchant.
25 Strength and beauty are her garment;
she smiles as she faces the future.
26 She opens her mouth with wisdom,
and the teaching of kindness is upon her tongue.
27 She watches over the conduct of her household,
and she does not eat the bread of indolence.
28 Her children rise up and extol her;
so does her husband praise her:
29 "Many women have excelled,
but you have surpassed them all."
30 Charm is false and beauty – empty breath;
a woman who fears the Lord, she is praiseworthy.
31 Commend her for the fruit of her hands,
and let her deeds praise her in the city gates.

38 | In hard work.

39 | The finest clothing will protect her family from the cold. Scarlet and especially purple (v. 22) were expensive dyes.

40 | The legal and commercial gathering place of the city.

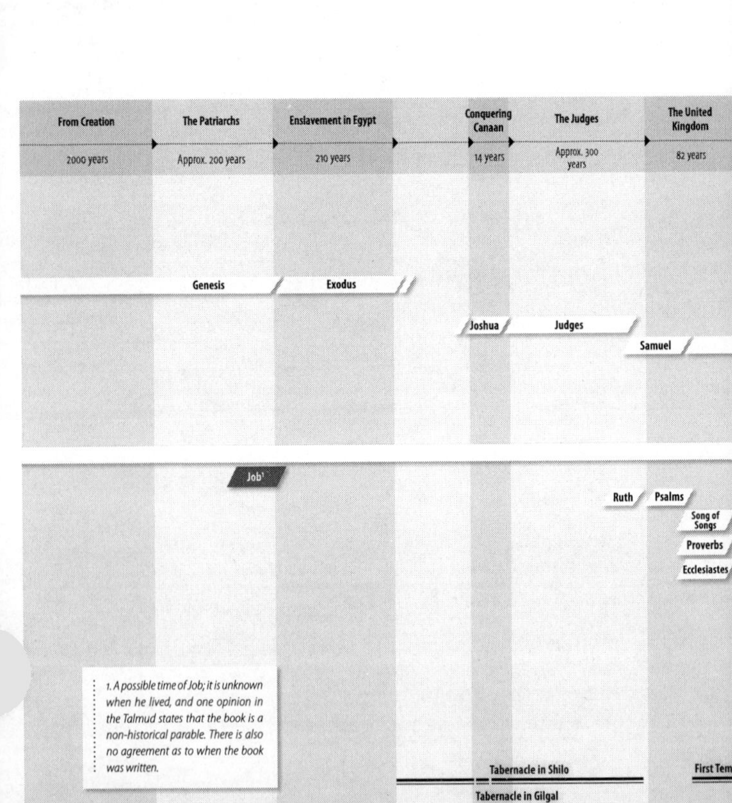

1. A possible time of Job; it is unknown when he lived, and one opinion in the Talmud states that the book is a non-historical parable. There is also no agreement as to when the book was written.

JOB/IYOV

JOB	Iyov's tragedies and his response to them	Discussion between Iyov and his friends regarding the reasons for the tragedies	Elihu's response to the discussion	God's response to Iyov	Iyov's response to God, and the end of the story
	Chs. 1–2	3–31	32–37	38–41	42

1 1 Once there was a man in the land of Utz,[1] and his name was Iyov. He was
2 innocent, honest, God-fearing, and always turned away from evil. He had
3 seven sons and three daughters. His livestock numbered seven thousand
sheep, three thousand camels, five hundred pairs of oxen, and five hundred
donkeys, and he had many workers. He was the greatest of the people of
4 the East. Now, his sons would hold a feast, each one at his house on his
set day; they would send for their sisters to come eat and drink with them.
5 And when the cycle of feast days had come full circle, Iyov would send a
messenger to his children and warn them to purify themselves. He would
get up early in the morning and offer as many sacrifices as he had children.
For Iyov said, "Maybe my children have sinned and cursed God in their
hearts." This is what Iyov did all of those days.

6 And the day came: The heavenly entourage came to stand in position
7 before the LORD, and the Adversary,[2] too, was among them. Then the
LORD said to the Adversary, "Where are you coming from?"

And the Adversary answered the LORD, "I was wandering the world, walking to and fro upon it."

8 The LORD said to the Adversary, "Have you noticed My servant, Iyov? For
there is no one like him in the whole world – an innocent, honest, God-
fearing man, who always turns away from evil."

9 "Is Iyov God-fearing for nothing?" the Adversary replied to the LORD.
10 "Have You not sheltered him and his house and everything that is his,
everything surrounding him? You have blessed the labor of his hands,
11 and his cattle bursts forth upon the land. But if You would cast forth
Your hand and lay it upon all that he has, I swear he would curse You to
Your face."

12 The LORD said to the Adversary, "I give everything that is his into your
hands, only do not lay a hand on him."

So the Adversary departed from before the LORD.

13 And the day came: His sons and daughters were eating and drinking wine
14 in the house of their oldest brother, when a messenger came to Iyov. He
15 said, "The cattle were plowing, and the donkeys were grazing nearby, when
a band from Sheba fell upon them and stole them. They slaughtered the
young men. I alone have escaped to tell you."

16 He was still speaking when another arrived and said, "A fire from God fell
from the heavens and engulfed the sheep and the young men. It consumed
them. I alone have escaped to tell you."

---

1 | In Transjordan (see Jer. 25:20; Lam. 4:21).

2 | A member of the heavenly court (see Zech. 3:1).

17 He was still speaking when another arrived and said, "The Chaldeans[3] split into three groups and raided the camels. They stole them and slaughtered the young men. I alone have escaped to tell you."

18 He was still speaking when another arrived and said, "Your sons and
daughters were eating and drinking wine in the house of their oldest
19 brother. Suddenly a great wind blew from beyond the desert. It slammed
into all four sides of the house, and the house collapsed upon the young
people and they died. I alone have escaped to tell you."

20 Iyov got up and tore his coat, he pulled out the hair on his head and fell
21 to the ground and bowed down.[4] He said, "I emerged naked from my
mother's womb, and naked I will return there.[5] The LORD has given, the
LORD has taken. May the LORD's name be blessed."

22 Despite all this, Iyov did not sin, nor accuse God of wrongdoing.

2 1 And the day came. The heavenly entourage came to stand in position
before the LORD, and the Adversary, too, was among them standing in
2 position before the LORD. Then the LORD said to the Adversary, "Where
are you coming from?"

And the Adversary answered the LORD, "I was wandering the world, walking to and fro upon it."

3 The LORD said to the Adversary, "Have you noticed My servant, Iyov? For there is no one like him in the whole world – an innocent, honest, God-fearing man, who always turns away from evil. He still holds on to his innocence, though you incited Me against him so that I would destroy him for nothing."

4 The Adversary replied to the LORD and said, "As flesh against flesh, a man
5 will give everything he has to save his own soul. But if You would cast Your
hand and lay it upon him and his flesh, I swear he would curse You to Your
face."

6 The LORD said to the Adversary, "He is in your hands, only do not kill him."

7 Then the Adversary departed from before the LORD, and he struck Iyov
8 with terrible boils from his heel to his head. He took a shard of pottery to
scratch himself with, and sat down in the dust.

9 His wife said to him, "Are you still holding on to your innocence? Curse God and die."

10 He replied to her, "You are speaking like a fool. Will we accept the good from God and not the bad?"

3 | A tribe from Babylonia.

4 | Acts of mourning.

5 | That is, I will be buried naked of possessions.

And in spite of everything, Iyov did not sin in his speech.

11 Now, three friends of Iyov – Elifaz the Temanite, Bildad the Shuhite, and
Tzofar the Naamatite – heard of the evil that had befallen him, and they
came, each from his home, and met together to nod in sorrow with him
12 and comfort him. They raised their eyes from afar and did not recognize
him, and they raised their voices and cried. They each tore their coat and
13 threw dust into the sky, letting it fall on their heads. They sat with him on
the ground for seven days and seven nights. And no one spoke a word to
him, for they saw how great was his pain.

3 1 After this, Iyov opened his mouth
and cursed the day he was born.
2 Iyov spoke up and said:

3 "Blot out the day of my birth
and the night that proclaimed:
A male has been conceived!
4 Darken that day!
May God want nothing of it;
may no glimmer of it ever appear.
5 May death-dark defile it,
cloud cover abide above it
in bleak and bitter terror;
6 may black oblivion take that night
and no day of the year,
no month ever claim it.
7 Make that night barren;
may no joy arise in its midst.
8 Let them damn that night, those sorcerers
who know how to wake Leviathan.[6]
9 Snuff out its first stars!
Let it hope for light and find none
and never behold the eyelids of dawn,
10 for it refused to lock that womb[7]
and hide agony from my eyes.
11 Why couldn't I have died
straight out of the belly?
12 Why did knees come to meet me;
of what use the breasts that nursed me?
13 For now I would be lying in quiet repose,
asleep and at rest,
14 with kings and advisors
who build up ruins for themselves,

6 | Leviathan is a crocodile or a mythical water creature.

7 | Iyov wishes he had been stillborn.

15 among nobles endowed with gold,
their houses heaped with silver –
16 or alongside a buried stillbirth,
an infant who never glimpsed the light.
17 There the fearful cease to tremble;
there the weary rest.
18 Captives are at ease
and ignore the oppressor's voice.
19 Meek and mighty are equals;
the slave is freed from his master.
20 Why does He waste light on the sufferer
or life on the embittered,
21 who wait for death in vain,
who seek it like a treasure,
22 who gleefully rejoice,
glad to reach the grave;
23 on a man whose path is hidden
because God has blocked his view?
24 My groaning is my bread;
my wails are rushing water.
25 What I feared has come to be;
what I dreaded has overwhelmed me.
26 I had no peace nor quiet nor rest;
and anguish has come."

4 1 Then Elifaz the Temanite spoke up and said:

2 "If someone ventures a word with you,
could you bear it?
But who can hold back?
3 See, you have taught many
and have strengthened weak hands;
4 your words could lift the stumbling
and brace buckling knees.
5 But now that it's your turn, you falter;
calamity strikes and you quail.
6 Isn't your piety your strength,
your integrity your confidence?
7 What guiltless man has ever fallen to ruin?
Since when are the virtuous destroyed?
8 From what I have seen, men who plow sin,
sow sorrow – reap them.
9 At the breath of God, they are gone;
one gust from His nostrils and they die.
10 The lion may roar, and he may howl,
but his teeth will break.

11 He will succumb for lack of prey,
and his cubs, abandoned, will waste away.
12 A word came to me in secret –
my ear caught only a trace
13 amid night-thoughts and visions
as slumber began to descend:
14 terror came, and a shudder –
my bones trembled,
15 a wind rushed past my face –
each hair on my flesh stood on end.
16 There it was – I could hardly make him out –
a figure before my eyes.
Silence, then a voice:
17 'Will God acquit a mere mortal?
What man is pure before his Maker?
18 If He cannot count on His own servants
and finds error even in His angels,
19 what then of people whose homes are clay,
whose origins are dust,
who are crushed like moths?
20 By evening they are shattered,
gone forever, and no one will know.
21 Their tent cords severed,
they die, having never grown wise.'

5 1 "Go ahead, cry out! But who will answer?
To which angel will you turn?
2 After all, rage kills the fool,
and passion destroys the feeble.
3 I remember seeing a fool taking root,
and at once I cursed his home.
4 His children now are defenseless,
helpless, rejected at the gate.
5 The hungry feast on his harvest,
making off with it in baskets,
and the thirsty lap up his riches.
6 Remember, affliction doesn't grow from the ground,
and sin doesn't spring up from the earth.
7 For man is born to suffer
as surely as arrows, flashing, whiz upward.
8 As for me, I would look to God;
it is to God I'd state my case –
9 who does great, unfathomable things,
wondrous deeds without number;
10 who lavishes rain upon the earth,
sends water across pastures;

11 who lifts up the lowly
and brings the bereaved to safety.
12 He thwarts the plans of the cunning,
sets victory out of their reach,
13 traps the wily in their designs,
for rash advice fails fast.
14 The day is dark wherever they turn;
by noon, they grope as if it were night!
15 But He saves the defenseless from the sword
and the poor from the powerful,
16 so there is hope for the wretched,
and injustice will shut its mouth.
17 See, happy is the man whom God reproves!
Do not scorn Shaddai's rebuke.
18 He injures but binds up the wound.
He strikes, but His hands heal.
19 From six disasters He will save you,
and even from the seventh you'll be spared.
20 He will deliver you from famine,
and in war will save you from the sword.
21 You will be sheltered from treacherous tongues
and have no fear of plunder;
22 you will laugh off scourge and pestilence,
stand fearless before wild animals,
23 and in a pact with the stones of the field,
be at peace with all creatures.
24 You will have tranquility in your tent,
look around your dwelling and find you lack nothing.
25 Rest assured – you will have bountiful seed,
offspring like grass across the earth,
26 and will be buried at a ripe old age
like grain in the season's fullness.
27 We have probed this and know it to be true.
Now take it to heart, and you will know it, too."

6 1 Then Iyov spoke up and said:

2 "If somehow my agony could be weighed,
if my calamity were placed on a scale,
3 it would be heavier than all the sand of the sea.
That is why I have not held back.
4 For Shaddai's arrows are all about me;
my spirit drinks their poison;
God has set His terrors against me.
5 Does a wild ass bray over grass
and an ox bellow over his fodder?

6 Who can stomach unsalted food?
Why drink flavorless juice?
7 I refuse to touch
such nauseating fare!
8 If only my plea were answered,
if God would grant my wish,
9 agree to crush me,
lift His hand and pierce me –
10 still I would be consoled,
even while writhing in relentless agony:
I have never hidden the Holy One's words.
11 What strength do I have left to hope?
And when is my end? How long do I have?
12 Am I solid as stone?
Is my flesh made of bronze?
13 Is there no help from within?
Has all counsel been driven from me?
14 Shame on him who fails his friend
and forsakes the fear of God!
15 My brothers have betrayed me like a wadi,
a channel where streams once coursed;
16 the streams are dark with ice,
hidden by a covering of snow.
17 As soon as it's dry, they vanish;
heat strikes, and at once they are gone.
18 Their paths wind about,
come upon wasteland, and vanish.
19 Tema's caravans[8] seek them out;
bands of Shebans look to them –
20 but their hopes are thwarted;
they arrive and are dismayed.
21 You are nothing to me!
You see my terror and stand aghast.
22 When ever have I said: 'Give me!
Pay a bribe on my behalf!
23 Save me from my enemy;
pay some tyrant my ransom'?
24 Teach me, and I will be quiet.
Just show me where I am wrong!
25 Indeed, honest words are provocative,
but what good is your reproach?
26 Who are you to come out with rebuke
while brushing off a despairing man's words?

8 | Desert nomads.

27 You would bargain for an orphan;
you would barter off your friend!
28 Now, if you will be so kind as to turn toward me,
I swear I will not lie to you.
29 Please, turn back; there is no wrong in me.
Come back – I remain in the right.
30 Is there error on my tongue?
Am I unable to discern lies?

7 1 "Isn't a man's life a term of hard service,
his days the days of a hired hand?
2 He is like a slave longing for shade,
a worker waiting for his wage.
3 I have inherited empty months;
nights of toil are now my lot.
4 When I lie down, I ask,
'When can I rise?' Night drags on,
and sleeplessness sates me till dawn.
5 My flesh is covered in maggots and earth,
my skin is blistered and oozing.
6 My days pass more quickly than a weaver's shuttle
carrying through the last thread of hope.[9]
7 Remember, my life is just a breath;
my eye will never again see goodness.
8 The eye that sees me will see me no more;
you will look, but I will no longer be here.
9 As a cloud fades and vanishes,
he who descends into Sheol[10] will not return;
10 he will never go home again;
the place will know him no more.
11 I will not hold back, either!
I will speak from the agony of my spirit,
bemoan the bitterness of my soul:
12 Am I Yam or the sea monster?[11]
Why do You place me under guard?
13 I tell myself, my couch will comfort me,
my bed will share my burden,
14 while You terrorize me with nightmares,
horrify me with visions,
15 until I would choose strangulation,
death, over these bones!
16 I am utterly spent. I will not live forever!

---

9 | A play on words: *tikva* means "hope" and also "thread" (cf. Josh. 2:18).

10 | The netherworld.

11 | Yam was the Canaanite sea-god. According to an ancient myth, God restrained the primeval sea monsters, the waters of chaos (cf. Is. 51:9–10).

Let me be. My days are vapor.[12]
17 What is man that You make so much of him,
that You pay him so much attention,
18 scrutinizing him every morning,
testing him every second?
19 When will You turn away from me
long enough for me to swallow my spit?
20 If I have sinned, what have I done to You,
warden of man?
Why have You made me Your target,
a burden to myself?
21 Why will You not pardon my crime
and forgive my error?
Soon enough, I will be lying in the dust;
You will look for me – but I will be gone."

8 1 And Bildad the Shuhite answered and said:

2 "How long will you prattle on like this?
The words of your mouth are one big wind!
3 Does God distort judgment,
and Shaddai – would He pervert justice?
4 When your sons sinned against Him,
He rightly did away with them.
5 But if you seek God
and implore Shaddai,
6 if you are pure and steadfast,
He will come to your protection
and restore your righteous home.
7 How humble your beginnings will seem
when in the end you are flourishing!
8 Just ask those who came before you
and heed our ancestors' inquiries,
9 for we were born yesterday and know nothing;
our lives are but shadows on this earth.
10 Surely they would teach you,
surely they would tell you
and bring these words from their hearts:
11 'Can papyrus grow without a marsh?
Will reeds flourish without water?'
12 Even while in flower, not yet plucked,
they'll wither faster than the brush.
13 That is the fate of one who forgets God:
the hope of the brazen comes to nothing.
14 His trust hangs on a thread;

12 | Fleeting and without substance (cf. Eccl. 1:2).

he relies on a spider's web.
15 Lean on his house – it will not stand!
Hold onto it – it will not last!
16 As for the righteous: moist in the sun,
shoots crop up in the garden,
17 winding around a heap of roots
and piercing through a bed of rocks.
18 Even if it's swallowed up then and there –
the place denying it: 'I have never seen you!' –
19 it will continue on its way
and spring up from other soil.
20 Remember, God does not abandon the blameless
and will not avail evil hands.
21 In time, He will fill your mouth with laughter
and your lips with cries of joy.
22 Your enemies will be clothed in shame,
and the tent of the wicked will cease to exist."

9 1 And Iyov answered and said:

2 "Of course, I know it is so:
man is no match for God.
3 Challenge Him? The chance
of getting an answer is one in a thousand.
4 A person may be shrewd, he may be strong –
but who has taken Him on and come out whole?
5 He moves mountains without their knowing,
upturns them in His wrath;
6 He jolts the earth from its place –
its pillars, they quake.
7 At His command, the sun will not rise,
and the stars will seal themselves shut.
8 Alone, He spreads out the heavens
and strides across Yam's back.[13]
9 He makes the Bear, Orion, the Pleiades,
and the chambers of the South.
10 He does great, unfathomable things!
Wondrous deeds without number!
11 Sure, He passes me, but I don't see Him;
He goes by, but I am oblivious.
12 He takes away – who can stop Him?
Who can ask, 'What are You doing?'
13 God does not avert His anger.

13 | See note on 7:12.

Even Rahav's[14] cohorts surrender beneath Him.
14 Who am I, then, to speak up to Him,
to carefully choose my words,
15 when, even if I am right, I will get no response
as I stand pleading before my judge?
16 If I call and He answers,
I doubt He would listen to me:
17 He will strike me down in a storm
and go on wounding me for no reason.
18 He will not let me breathe;
He has filled me with poison.
19 If it's a matter of might – it is all His!
And if justice – who will set my hearing?
20 If I am in the right, my mouth will convict me;
if I am innocent, He will prove me wrong.
21 I am blameless! I do not care about myself;
I despise my life.
22 It is all the same, anyway, so I say:
He destroys the righteous along with the wicked.
23 If a sudden scourge strikes,
He will scoff while the guiltless suffer.
24 The earth has been given to the wicked –
He covers the judges' faces –
if not He, then who?
25 Now my days sprint by like runners;
they flee and see no joy.
26 They rush by like reed-boats,
like a vulture swooping toward his prey.
27 If I say, 'I will forget my claim,
be free of this sorrow once and for all,'
28 knowing You will not clear me,
I would fear all my pain.-
29 I will be found guilty.
Why toil, then, in vain?
30 Even if I bathed in liquid snow,
and were pure down to my hands,
31 You would plunge me into the Pit
until even my clothes detested me.
32 For He is not a man, like me, to whom I can say,
'Come, let's take it to court!'
33 If only someone would arbitrate,
place his hand on both of us,
34 take His rod off my back

14 | Another mythical sea monster.

so that His terror would not haunt me,
35 I could speak my mind without fear,
for I have been untrue here to myself.

10 1 "I loathe my life.
I will say it, then, loud and clear,
and speak from the bitterness of my soul.
2 I will say to God: 'Do not condemn me!
Just tell me what Your accusation is!
3 Do You take pleasure in oppressing man;
do You so despise the work of Your hands
that You favor the advice of the wicked?
4 Do You have the eyes of flesh and blood?
Do You see as humans see?
5 Are Your days the days of mere mortals,
Your years the years of a man,
6 in that You seek my iniquity
and search out my every sin?
7 You know I have done nothing wrong;
still there is no escape from You!
8 Your hands have shaped and made me,
yet You ravage every part of me.
9 Remember, You kneaded me like clay,[15]
and You will return me to dust.
10 It was You who poured me out like milk
and like cheese congealed me.[16]
11 You have clothed me in skin and flesh,
woven bone and sinew;
12 You have granted me life and kindness
and kept my spirit under Your charge.
13 Yet these things You have hidden in Your heart –
I know how You operate –
14 when I sin, You will be watching!
You will not acquit me.
15 I will take the blame if I have done wrong!
But even if cleared I will not lift my head.
Enough of my disgrace now! Look at my suffering.
16 Something to be proud of – hunting me like a lion,
then coming back to work on me Your wonders.
17 You stir up Your hostilities toward me,
Your rage and fury mounting,
army after army upon me.
18 Why did You take me out of the womb?
I could have died, no eye having seen me.

15 | Created me (cf. Gen. 2:7).

16 | As an embryo gestating in the womb.

19 If only I could never have been –
brought straight from belly to grave!
20 Are my days not numbered as it is?
Let me be, turn away, allow me some relief
21 before I go, never to return,
to a land of gloom and death-dark,
22 a land whose brightness is like murk,
a land of death-dark, disorder,
black light ablaze.'"

11 1 Then Tzofar the Naamatite answered and said:

2 "Will a rant like yours go unanswered?
Is a smooth talker always in the right?
3 Will you keep on silencing people,
prattling on as you do, unrefuted?
4 You have said, 'My teaching is pure;
in Your eyes, I am blameless!'
5 But if only God were to speak up
and open His lips for you to hear,
6 He would share with you wisdom's secrets,
for its mysteries are twofold,[17]
and you would know God has made you forget your sins.
7 Can you fathom the essence of God?
Can you plumb the reaches of Shaddai?
8 It is higher than the heavens! What can you do?
It is deeper than Sheol! What can you know?
9 It is longer than the earth
and wider than the seas.
10 If He takes a man or delivers him to his enemy,
if He hems him in – who can reverse it?
11 For He knows duplicity when He sees it;
He spots falsehood and deceit.
12 A hollow man will have a brain
when a wild ass gives birth to a human!
13 But if you direct your heart
and spread out your hands toward Him –
14 if there is sin on those hands, cast it away,
and let no evil lodge in your tents –
15 then you will lift your unblemished face,
enduring and unafraid,
16 and you will forget all your suffering
as if it were water flowing through.
17 Your future will be brighter than noon,
and you will be radiant like daybreak;

---

17 | There is wisdom known to humans and wisdom known only to God.

18 sure that there is hope,
you will burrow in and rest secure.[18]
19 You will lie down fearing nothing,
and multitudes will seek your favor
20 while the wicked pine away
with nowhere in sight to run,
their hopes undone by despair."

12 1 And Iyov answered and said:

2 "You are the last of the wise, all right –
and with you, wisdom dies.
3 See, I too have a mind
and am no less than you.
Who has not grasped these things?
4 My friends have made a fool out of me,
a righteous man – now a laughingstock.
When they call to God, He answers them!
5 What pleasure the smug take in calamity,
too steady to stumble!
6 Their tents are calm when bandits come;
they are secure among the brazen –
all this by the very hand of God!
7 Ask the Behemoth,[19] and it will instruct you,
or a bird in the sky – it will tell you.
8 Just speak to the earth, and it will teach you;
the fish of the sea, they'll explain!
9 Who doesn't know these things:
'The LORD's hand has made all this,[20]
10 in whose hand is the soul of every living being
and the breath of all humankind;
11 can't the ear discern words
the way the palate tastes food?
12 Wisdom belongs to the old,
and acumen comes with longevity.
13 He has wisdom and might!
He has counsel and insight!
14 Indeed, what He destroys will not be rebuilt;
whoever He imprisons will not be freed.
15 When He stops the waters, there is drought;
when He sets them loose, they overturn the earth.
16 Strength and wisdom are His;

18 | The terms "burrow in" and "lie down" (v. 19) typically describe animals at rest.
19 | A mythical land animal, sometimes translated as "hippopotamus" (see 40:15).
20 | This section, in single quotation marks, is Iyov's parody of his friends' parroting of the Wisdom tradition.

deceived and deceiver under His sway.
17 He leads wise men away naked[21]
and turns judges into fools;
18 He undoes the belts of kings
and removes the sash around their loins;
19 priests He leads away naked,
ousting the devoted;
20 He strips orators of their words,
rids elders of all sense;
21 He pours contempt on nobles
and undoes the belts of conquerors;
22 He draws mysteries out of darkness
and brings death-dark to light.
23 He exalts nations, then obliterates them;
expands nations – then exiles them.
24 He confounds the leaders of the land,
sending them to wander a pathless wilderness
25 where they grope in the dark with no light
and stagger like drunkards.'

13 1 "All this I have seen with my own eyes;
my ears have heard and understood.
2 What you know, I know, too.
I am no less than any of you.
3 As for myself, I would rather speak to Shaddai –
I prefer to take it up with God –
4 but you are spreaders of lies
and worthless healers, all of you.
5 If only you would just be quiet –
then you would be wise!
6 Now, please hear me out
and listen to my charges.
7 Will you lie to God's face?
Do you deceive on His behalf?
8 Will you be taking His side?
Do you plan to speak for Him?
9 Would it go well if He examined you?
Or would you delude Him, too?
10 You can be sure He will set you straight
if you secretly play favorites.
11 Would His splendor not terrify you
and fear of Him not seize you?
12 Your aphorisms would turn to ash,
your answers to lumps of clay.

21 | A sign of madness.

13 Quiet now! Let me speak,
come what may.
14 Come what may,
I will take my flesh in my teeth
and put my life in my own hands!
15 Let Him kill me! I will wait for Him.[22]
I will argue my case before Him.
16 This, too, will be my salvation:
that blasphemers dare not come near Him.
17 Heed carefully my words;
let my declaration reach your ears.
18 I hereby present my case;
I know I am in the right.
19 Who dares contend with me?
I will hold my peace and die!
20 Just spare me these two things,
and I will not hide from You:
21 take Your hand off me,
and that Your terror would not haunt me.
22 Then call, and I will answer,
or I will speak and You will reply.
23 Just how many are my sins and offenses?
Show them to me!
24 Why do You hide Your face
as if I am Your enemy?
25 Would You chase a driven leaf
and hunt down dry straw?
26 You sentence me to poison
and hold against me my boyhood sins;
27 You have set my feet in lime[23]
so You can follow my every step,
tracking me all the time:
28 he will rot away like a wine skin,
like a moth-eaten shirt.

14 1 "Man, who is born of woman,
he is glutted with anguish; his days are few.
2 Like a flower, he blossoms, then withers;
like a shadow, he flees and cannot stay.
3 Why do You hound such a creature,
calling him to account?
4 Who can purify the defiled?
No one!

22 | This reading is based on the vocalized version, the *keri*. *Ketiv* (the written version) is "though I have no hope."

23 | Lime stuck to the bottom of one's feet makes footprints that can be tracked.

5 His days are determined:
You have set the number of his months
and drawn the line he may not cross.
6 Turn away from him and let him be!
Let him, like a hired hand, finish his day's work.
7 See, even a tree has hope:
if chopped down, it will sprout again –
its shoots will not relent –
8 and if its roots grow old in the earth,
if its stump succumbs to the dust,
9 a whiff of water and it will flower,
bursting forth like a new sapling.
10 But a man dies and wastes away;
he perishes, and where is he then?
11 Like water drained from the sea,
like a river scorched, run dry,
12 a man lies down, never again to rise;
until the skies fall he will not wake;
he will not be roused.
13 If only You would hide me in Sheol,
keep me there until Your wrath has passed,
set a time, then call me to mind.
14 If a man has already died, can he live again?
I will wait my entire term
until my relief [24] comes:
15 You will call, and I will answer You.
You will long for the work of Your hands.
16 When You follow my every step,
You won't search out my sin;
17 You will bundle and seal my wrongdoing
and plaster over my iniquity.
18 Yet, as a mountain falls and crumbles
and a rock is dislodged from its place,
19 as water wears away stones,
its torrents scouring the soil,
You ravage a man's hope:
20 You crush him forever, and he vanishes;
You mangle his face and banish him.
21 If his sons are revered, he will never know;
if they come to ruin, he will not notice.
22 Only his own flesh will feel the pain;
only his own spirit will grieve."

15 1 Then Elifaz the Temanite spoke up and said:

24 | To take my place in Sheol.

2 "Quite the wise man, spouting empty opinions,
belly bursting with hot air from the east,[25]
3 uttering worthless reproofs
and words that benefit no one.
4 What is worse, you do away with all piety
and sabotage any prayer to God.
5 Your mouth is schooled in sin,
so you make shrewd formulations.
6 It's your mouth that gives you away, not me –
your lips testify against you.
7 Are you the first ever to have been born?
Were you created before the hills?
8 Do you eavesdrop on God's council,
hoarding all His wisdom for yourself?
9 What do you know that we do not?
What understanding do you have that we lack?
10 There is a gray-haired man in our midst,
a man even older than your father!
11 Are these consolations insufficient?
Are the words too softly spoken?
12 Where are your thoughts taking you,
and what is that look in your eye
13 that you unleash your rage against God
and let such words escape your mouth?
14 Since when do mortals deserve to be acquitted?
Born of woman, how can they be right?
15 If God cannot even trust His angels,
and even the heavens are impure in His eyes,
16 how much more loathsome and corrupt,
then, is a man who drinks iniquity like water?
17 I will tell you! Listen to me:
I will relay exactly what I have seen,
18 what wise men have not withheld
but passed down from our fathers,
19 to whom alone the land was given;
no stranger ever passed among them.
20 All his days, the wicked man trembles,
the oppressor – in the years he has left.
21 The sound of terror is in his ears;
when it's quiet, robbers come near.
22 He cannot hope to escape the darkness;
he is fated for the sword.
23 He is cast out, food for vultures,
knowing his day of darkness is near.

---

25 | The east wind is hot and dry.

24 Distress and anguish terrorize him,
like a king before battle,
25 for he has stretched out his arm against God
and presumes to spar with Shaddai,
26 charging toward Him, neck raised
behind his thick, embossed shields,
27 for he has padded his face with fat[26]
and covered his loins with blubber.
28 He will live in plundered towns,
in houses long abandoned,
fated to become heaps of rubble.
29 He will have no riches, no enduring fortune,
no wealth extending across the land.
30 He will never escape the darkness.
Flame will shrivel his stalk,
and the wind of His mouth will sweep him away.
31 May no man be led astray by falsehood,
for falsehood will be his reward.
32 Withering before his time,
his branches never to be green again,
33 he is like a vine shedding unripe fruit,
like an olive tree casting off buds.
34 Remember, the brazen end up barren;
homes built on bribes burn down.
35 Pregnant with treachery, they breed sin,[27]
and their bellies conceive deceit."

16 1 Then Iyov spoke up and said:

2 "I have heard such talk before,
tormenting comforters that you are!
3 'Is there an end to words of wind?
What pains you so, that you go on and on?'[28]
4 I, too, could talk like you
were you in my shoes,
composing fine phrases against you,
shaking my head at your plight.
5 With my mouth, I would urge you on
and spare you my consolations!
6 Speaking up would spare me no pain,
and holding back, what would I lose?
7 But now, He has worn me out.
You have laid waste to all I know.

---

26 | A metaphor for rebelliousness (cf. Deut. 32:15).

27 | Cf. Psalms 7:15; Isaiah 59:4.

28 | Paraphrasing Elifaz in 15:2.

8 You have shriveled me up –
quite the sight to behold –
my emaciation testifying against me!
9 His rage has ravaged me, made me His prey.
How He bares His teeth!
My persecutor's gaze shoots through me.
10 Men gape at me open-mouthed,
strike my cheek in scorn,
band together against me.
11 God hands me over to evil men,
hurls me into the grip of the wicked.
12 I was at ease before He crushed me,
took hold of my neck, shattered me
and made me into His target.
13 His bowmen surrounded me;
He coldly sliced through my kidneys,
poured my juices out onto the ground;
14 He broke through me, gash by gash,
charging at me like a warrior.
15 I have sewn sackcloth onto my skin
and dug my horns into the dust.[29]
16 My face is red from weeping,
and death-dark covers my eyes,
17 though there is no wrongdoing on my hands,
and my prayer is pure:
18 'Earth! Do not cover up my blood!
Let my cry find no resting place!'
19 Even now, my witness is in heaven;
my defender is on high.
20 My intermediaries, my deriders –
it is to God my eyes shed tears.
21 A man may as well argue with God
as he would with his companions,
22 for in only a few years
I will go down that path of no return.

17 1 "My spirit is crushed,
my days have been snuffed out,
the graveyard awaits.
2 All about are people who jeer;
my eyes cannot bear it.
3 Be now my guarantor!
Who else will pledge on my behalf?
4 You cannot be exalted

29 | A sign of defeat. Raised horns signify victory (cf., e.g., 1 Sam. 2:1, 10).

for You have hidden reason from their hearts.
5 Who invites friends to a feast
while his children look on, starving?[30]
6 An exemplum, an epithet for all to behold,
that's what He has made me – a thing to spit at!
7 My eyes have grown dim from grief,
and all my limbs are like a shadow.
8 Decent people are outraged by this,
and the pure rise up against the godless.
9 The righteous man will hold fast to his path,
and those with clean hands will be strengthened.
10 But all of you, please come back!
Not a single one of you is wise!
11 My days are over; my plans,
my heart's desires, are severed.
12 They pretend that night is day,
that light is closer than the dark.
13 If I have set up my home in Sheol,
if I have laid out my bed in darkness,
14 called to the Pit: 'Father!'
and to the worm: 'My mother, my sister!'
15 where, then, will be my hope?
My hope – who can see it?
16 As it descends into Sheol,
together we will go down into the dust."

18 1 And Bildad the Shuhite answered and said:

2 "'How long will you all go on? Enough with words!
Think first. Then we can talk.'[31]
3 Why make us into beasts?
Do we strike you as that stupid?
4 How he ravages his soul in rage!
Will the earth be abandoned,
mountains moved, just for you?
5 The light of the wicked dissipates,
and the flame of his fire dies down;
6 in his tent, light turns to darkness,
and his lamp goes out on him.
7 His proud stride is diminished;
his own advice does him in;
8 his foot gets caught in a net,
and he heads straight into snares.
9 A trap grips him by the heel;

30 | Iyov's friends offer much advice but do not take it themselves.

31 | Bildad here is paraphrasing Iyov's earlier statements back to him (see 13:13, 16:3).

it tightens in knots around him;
10 a rope hides on the ground,
and his pitfall waits along the way.
11 On every side horrors terrify him,
and his feet falter.
12 His children are sure to starve,
calamity steadfast at his side;
13 disease ravages his skin,
and Death's firstborn devours his limbs.
14 Ripped from the safety of his tent,
he is brought before the King of Terrors;[32]
15 he lives in a home not his own,
brimstone scattered across his estate.
16 Underneath, his roots wither;
up above, his branches rot.
17 His memory vanishes from across the land,
and his good name vanishes.[33]
18 Thrust from light to darkness,
he is cast out of the world.
19 He leaves no child, no offspring,
not a single survivor where he sojourned;
20 in the West they are appalled by his fate;
in the East they are seized with terror.
21 That is the abode of the wicked,
the place for him who does not know God."

19 1 Then Iyov spoke up and said:

2 "How long will you go on afflicting me,
crushing me with words?
3 Ten times you have taunted me
shamelessly, full of disdain.
4 If I have erred,
that is my concern!
5 But if you have the gall to speak out,
holding my disgrace against me,
6 then know, at least, that God has done me wrong,
trapping me inside His net.
7 I cry foul but am never answered;
I call out but there is no justice.
8 He has blocked my way –
I cannot get through –
He throws darkness on my path.
9 He has stripped me of my honor

32 | Perhaps King of the Netherworld.

33 | Literally "he has no name"; his good reputation has disappeared.

and knocked the crown off my head.
10 From all sides He beats me down,
uproots my hope as He would a tree.
11 He has set His wrath ablaze,
considers me an enemy;
12 His troops move forward as one,
building their siege ramp against me,
and set up camp around my tent.
13 He has pushed my brothers away,
alienating all who knew me.
14 My family never comes;
my friends are gone.
15 I am a stranger, now, alien
to my maidservants, my household.
16 I call to my manservant, but he does not answer.
With my own mouth I implore him.
17 My wife is nauseated by my breath;
my own brothers can't stomach my stench.
18 Even hoodlums despise me,
defaming me behind my back.
19 Close friends are repulsed by me;
my loved ones have turned against me.
20 My bones cling to my skin and flesh;
my teeth are cemented shut.
21 Pity me, pity me, my friends!
Look how God's hand has struck me down!
22 Why do you go after me like God,
tearing me to shreds?[34]
23 If only my words were written,
then engraved in bronze
24 with a stylus of iron and lead,
carved in stone for eternity!
25 As for myself, I know my Redeemer lives,
and He will rise from the dust at last.[35]
26 And though they flay my skin,
from within this flesh I will see God.
27 I will see Him for myself
with my own eyes and no one else's.
My very kidneys will pine.[36]
28 If you say, 'How will we pursue him?
How will we uproot him?'[37] –

---

34 | Literally "never satiated with my flesh." "Devouring the flesh" of a victim is an idiom for slander; cf. 31:31; Psalms 27:2; Daniel 3:8.

35 | God will ultimately stand up to vindicate Iyov during his lifetime.

36 | The kidneys are the seat of the emotions.

37 | Literally "me." This translation accords with the manuscript variant "him."

29 you would be wise to fear the sword,
for wrath is sure to be avenged.
Beware, then, of justice."

20 1 Then Tzofar the Naamatite spoke up and said:

2 "Thanks to my inner sense of things,
my thoughts bid me to reply.
3 When I hear a biting reproach,
I am inclined from within to respond.
4 Don't you know that from the beginning,
ever since people were placed on earth,
5 the revelry of the wicked lasts but a moment,
and the joy of the defiant is gone in a flash?
6 A person may tower up into the skies,
and his head might graze the clouds,
7 but he vanishes forever like dung.
Onlookers wonder, 'Where did he go?'
8 He will fly away like a dream,
never to be found,
chased off like a night vision.
9 The eyes that glimpsed him never will again!
His home beholds him no more.
10 Poverty will crush his sons
when his own hands return his wealth.[38]
11 His bones – full of vigor, robust –
will lie down with him in the dust.
12 Though he hides evil, sweet there
under his tongue,
13 and, craving it, holds onto it,
loath to let it go,
14 the food in his bowels turns
to asp venom within.
15 He swallows his wealth then spews it out;
God hurls it from his belly.
16 It is poison of asps he sucks,
the viper's tongue that will kill him!
17 He will never see streams,
gleaming rivers of honey and curd.
18 His profits? He will not keep them,
and any earnings he will not enjoy,
19 for he has crushed what belongs to the poor,
robbed them of their homes and not rebuilt them.
20 Because his belly knows no quiet,
he will not escape with his pleasures.

---

38 | In other words, when the wicked person is forced to give up his ill-gotten wealth.

21 No one will be left to enjoy his bounty;
nothing good of his will last!
22 Just when he is satisfied,
calamity will strike:
the oppressed will overtake him.
23 The moment he is about to fill his belly,
the fire of God's fury will let loose,
warfare raining down on him.
24 He flees from a weapon made of iron?
A bronze bow will pierce him.
25 A blade is drawn? It comes out his back,
shooting through his bile.
Terror descends!
26 Thick darkness awaits his treasured ones.
Unfanned flames eat them alive,
devouring the last survivor in his tent.
27 The heavens lay bare his guilt,
and the earth rises up against him.
28 Waves surge into his house,
floods on the day of wrath.
29 And that is what has been prepared for the wicked,
their God-given portion."

21 1 Then Iyov spoke up and said:

2 "Hear now what I have to say,
and let that be your consolation!
3 Bear with me as I speak;
afterward, deride me.
4 Is my grievance against a mere mortal?
Why shouldn't my patience wear thin?
5 Turn toward me and be still;
put your hands on your mouths.
6 The thought of it horrifies me;
my flesh is seized with trembling.
7 Why do the wicked survive,
grow old and prosper,
8 their children right by their side,
their children's children ever before their eyes?
9 Their homes are untroubled, at peace,
and they are spared God's rod.
10 Their bulls breed without fail;
their cows give birth and do not miscarry;
11 they send their young to frolic like sheep;
their children hop and skip,
12 singing with the drum and lyre,

rejoicing to the sounds of the pipe.
13 They happily live out their days
and go down peacefully to Sheol.
14 They say to God, 'Turn away from us!
We have no use for Your ways!
15 Who is Shaddai that we should serve Him?
What would we gain by praying to Him?'
16 But their joy is not of their making.[39]
It is beyond me, the wicked man's thinking!
17 How often does the lamp of the wicked go out
and disaster overtake them?!
When does God, in His wrath, bring calamity?
18 How often are they like straw in the wind,
like chaff swept up in a storm?!
19 When does God store up punishment for his sons,
pay retribution so he will know,
20 so he will witness his ruin with his own eyes,
drink down the venom of Shaddai?
21 What will he care about the fate of his family
when the months allotted him are running out?
22 Who presumes to impart divine mysteries
to God, who judges on high?
23 One man dies in perfect health,
at ease and tranquil;
24 his pails are full of milk,
the marrow of his bones moist.
25 Another dies a bitter soul,
never having tasted prosperity.
26 Both lie down in the dust
under a blanket of worms.
27 Oh, I know your thoughts
and the schemes you plot against me.
28 You say, 'Where, then, is the noble man's house,
and where the tent of the wicked?'[40]
29 But haven't you asked those passing through?
You cannot deny their testimony:
30 on doomsday the wicked man is spared;
on the day of wrath he is delivered!
31 Who will confront him to his face?
Who will make him pay for what he has done,
32 tell him he will be carried to the grave,
that a watch will be kept at the mound,
33 that clods of earth from the wadi will be his comfort,

---

39 | The undeserved happiness of the wicked is given freely by God.
40 | You claim that all receive their just deserts.

that others will come after him,
that innumerable are those who precede him?
34 What are they for, these hollow consolations?
All that's left of your answers is betrayal."

22 1 And Elifaz the Temanite spoke up and said:

2 "Who is to say a man is of any use to God,
that the wise could be of help to Him?
3 What does Shaddai gain from your righteousness?
Does He profit from your blameless ways?
4 Would He litigate because He fears you?
Is that why He has brought you to judgment?
5 Clearly, your wickedness is immense,
your transgressions boundless!
6 You demand pledges from others without cause
and strip the naked of their clothes.
7 You withhold water from the thirsty
and deny the famished their bread.
8 The land belongs to the strong,
and those He favors settle it.[41]
9 You have sent widows away empty-handed
and shoved away the arms of orphans.
10 That is why traps surround you
and why you are suddenly struck by fear!
11 You cannot even see the darkness;
many waters blanket you.
12 Is God not in the highest heavens?
Can He not glimpse the topmost stars?
13 You said, 'What does God know?
How could He judge through the fog?
14 Clouds hide Him, and He does not see,
circling the rim of heaven.'
15 Haven't you noticed the ways of the world
that sinners have long trod –
16 who are cut off before their time,
their foundations washed away in a river?
17 They tell God, 'Turn away from us!
What can Shaddai do, after all?'
18 But He filled their houses with joy.
It is beyond me, the wicked man's thinking![42]
19 The righteous will see and delight,
and the pure are sure to scoff:
20 'You see! They were obliterated;

41 | This parodies Iyov's statement in 9:24.

42 | Echoing 21:13–16.

fire has devoured their wealth!'
21 Make amends with Him and be at one again.
Then – good things will find you.
22 Accept the teachings of His mouth,
and place His words in your heart.
23 If you return to Shaddai, you will be restored.
If you banish iniquity from your tent,
24 if gold is like dust to you
and Ofir[43] like stones in a stream;
25 if Shaddai will be your gold,
your shining silver,
26 if you entreat Shaddai
and lift your face to God,
27 when you implore Him – He will hear you,
and you will pay your vows in full.[44]
28 When you make a decree, it will come to pass.
Light will shine on your paths,
29 for God humbles the boastful
but delivers the lowly.
30 He rescues the innocent,
so you too will be delivered
by the purity of your hands."

23 1 And Iyov spoke up and said:

2 "Even now my complaint is bitter;
His hand weighs down on my moans.
3 If only I knew where to find Him,
if only I could approach His throne,
4 I would lay out my case before Him
and fill my mouth with my charges.
5 I would know how He would answer me
and understand what He tells me.
6 Would He come at me with force?
No! He would put forward His case.
7 There the righteous would be heard,
and I would escape my Judge forever.
8 But I go east, and He isn't there,
then west, but I cannot discern Him;
9 He hides in the north, but I cannot catch Him;
He cloaks Himself in the south, but I do not see Him.
10 He knows my ways; if He tested me,
I would emerge as pure as gold.
11 My feet have followed in His tracks;

---

43 | The gold of Ofir was especially fine.

44 | You will fulfill the vows made when entreating God once He has responded favorably.

I have held to His path and have not strayed.
12 Never diverging from the commandments of His lips,
I have held His words in my breast.
13 But He is of one mind. Who can turn Him back?
He does as He wishes.
14 When He carries out His decree,
He comes up with more of the same.
15 That is why I would shudder at His presence;
I would behold and dread Him.
16 God has weakened my heart;
Shaddai makes me shudder,
17 yet I am not annihilated by the darkness;
gloom does not shroud my face.

24 1 "Why has Shaddai not set times for judgment?
Why can't those who know Him foresee His days?[45]
2 Some take boundary stones,[46]
steal flocks, lead them off to graze.
3 They'll drive away an orphan's donkey;
they'll pawn a widow's ox as a pledge.
4 They shove the needy off the road,
force the wretched of the earth into hiding.
5 They go about their work like wild donkeys
in a wasteland, foraging for meat;
the wilderness sustains their young.
6 They harvest from fields not their own
and gather from the vineyards of the wicked.
7 They lie down naked, unclothed,
with nothing to cover them in the cold.
8 They are soaked from mountain rains,
cling to a stone for lack of shelter;
9 the wicked snatch orphans from breasts,
pawn the babies of the poor as pledges!
10 They have no clothes, go naked;
though famished, they must carry sheaves.[47]
11 As the olives drop they make oil;
while thirsty, they must tread grapes.
12 In town, people wail;
the throats of the dying cry out,
but God pays no heed.
13 They rebel against the light!
They do not know His ways;
they have not held to His paths.

45 | Days of wrath and judgment (see 20:28).

46 | That is, steal land.

47 | They must work for others while starving themselves.

14 The murderer rises in the evening;
he slays the needy and impoverished
like a robber in the night.
15 The eye of the adulterer, too, waits till dusk,
thinking, 'No eye will glimpse me.'
He hides his face.
16 In the dark, they break into homes.
By day, they seal themselves up;
they are not fond of light.
17 For them, daybreak is death-dark;
they will know the terror of death-dark!
18 May they float across the face of the waters;
may their plot of earth be cursed,
and may they never find refuge in vineyards.[48]
19 As heat and drought carry away snow-waters,
let Sheol take those sinners.
20 May the womb forget such a man,
a delicacy for maggots;
may he be forever forgotten
and corruption break like wood.
21 May his wife be barren, never to give birth,
his widow deprived of anything good.
22 Though he may draw in the mighty by force
and stand firm – may he have no trust in life.
23 Still, God keeps them safe; they rely on that,
and His eyes watch over their paths.
24 If only He looked up, they would cease to exist!
If He looked down, they would be gone;
they would wither like the tops of the stalks.
25 If this isn't the truth, prove me wrong!
Who can refute what I have said?"

25 1 Then Bildad the Shuhite spoke up and said:

2 "Dominion and dread are His;
He makes peace in His heights.
3 Could His armies be counted?
On whom does His light not shine?
4 How can mere mortals do right by God?
Born of woman, how can they be cleared?
5 If even the moon has no luster
and the stars are impure in His eyes,
6 what then of a mortal, a worm,
a human being, a maggot?"

48 | For vineyards as a hiding place, see Judges 21:20–21.

26 1 Then Iyov spoke up and said:

2 "What a help you are to the powerless,
your feeble arm coming to the rescue!
3 What use is advice devoid of wisdom,
clever insights freely bestowed?
4 Who put these words in your mouth?
Whose breath just came out of you?
5 The shades tremble
under the waters and their denizens!
6 Sheol lies naked before Him;
Avaddon's abyss is unveiled.[49]
7 It is He who hangs the earth over nothingness,
who stretches Tzafon[50] across the chaos,
8 who bundles water into clouds,
yet no billow bursts its seams;
9 He who covers the face of the full moon,
spreading His cloud over it,
10 He who delineates the waters' surface
at the edge between dark and light.
11 The pillars of heaven quake
from the shock of His roar.
12 With His might He strikes Yam;
by His guile He crushes Rahav.[51]
13 By His breath the heavens are bright;
His hand pierces through the fleeing serpent.
14 These are but hints of His ways,
mere whispers; who can hear them?
Who can fathom His mighty thunder?"

27 1 Iyov took up his theme again and said:

2 "By God, who has stripped me of justice,
and Shaddai, who has embittered my spirit,
3 so long as my life is in me
and God's breath is in my nostrils,
4 my lips will speak no wrong,
nor will my tongue utter deceit.
5 Heaven forbid I say you are right!
I will stand up for my integrity till the day I die.
6 I have held fast to my righteousness;
I will not let go;
my heart has never blasphemed:
7 'May my enemy end up like the wicked,

---

49 | Sheol and Abaddon are names for the netherworld.

50 | A mountain near the north Syrian coast.

51 | See notes on 9:8, 13.

my assailant like evildoers.'[52]
8 What hope will the brazen man have
when he petitions God?
9 Will God hear his cry
when calamity strikes?
10 Will he be able to entreat Shaddai,
to call out to God at any time?
11 I will teach you what is in God's hand
and will not hide what belongs to Shaddai:
12 you all have seen it,
so why do you prattle on:
13 'This is the God-given portion of the wicked,
the tyrant's heritage, straight from Shaddai.
14 Say he has many sons: they are marked for the sword;
his descendants will never have enough bread;
15 those who survive will be buried by a plague;
their widows will not mourn.
16 If he accumulates silver like dust
and amasses clothing like clay,
17 the righteous will wear what he's kept,
and his silver will go to the pure.
18 His house is like a moth's,
or like the booth a watchman makes.
19 He may lie down a wealthy man, but not for long:
when he wakes, that man will be gone.
20 Horror overtakes him like a torrent;
a storm makes off with him by night.
21 The east wind carries him off and away;
it hurls him from his place.
22 Unrelentingly He shoots at him;
he flees, how he flees from His hand!
23 Hands clap all about him;
he hears hissing from afar.'

28 1 "Now, silver has its source,
and gold – a place where it is refined.
2 Iron is pulled from the earth,
and copper drawn from stone.
3 He[53] cordons off the darkness,
probes the farthest reaches –
rock, gloom, death-dark.
4 He forges streams in far-off places
forgotten by wayfarers,
where few have stepped foot,

52 | Iyov has never cursed his enemies, even in his thoughts.
53 | God.

5 where the earth teems with sustenance
though it convulses like fire from below,
6 where stones are sapphire
and gold dust abounds.
7 No vulture knows the way there;
the buzzard's eye has not glimpsed it.
8 Not a single beast has reached it,
nor has the lion passed through.
9 He reaches down into flint,
upturning mountains at their roots.
10 He carves channels through rocks;
His eye sees every precious thing;
11 He binds up the rivers' flow
and brings that which they hide to light.
12 But where will wisdom be found,
and where is the place of understanding?
13 Mortals cannot surmise where it lies;
it will not be found in the land of the living.
14 The deep says: It is not in me!
The sea says: Nor is it with me!
15 It cannot be bartered for gold,
nor can it be weighed in silver;
16 it can't be exchanged for the gold of Ofir,
precious rock crystal, or sapphire.
17 It will not be measured in gold and glass
nor traded for fine golden vessels.
18 It cannot be mentioned
with coral or crystal;
wisdom's worth is beyond pearls.
19 It will not be measured in Kush's topaz
nor weighed against the purest gold.
20 But from where will wisdom come,
and where is the place of understanding?
21 For it is concealed from the eyes of every living being
and hidden from the birds of the sky.
22 Abaddon[54] and Death say,
'Our ears have heard rumor of it!'
23 God knows the way to it,
knows where it lies,
24 for He looks to the ends of the earth;
He sees beneath all the skies.
25 When He gave the winds their weight
and the water its measure,
26 when He meted out the rain

54 | See note on 26:6.

and set a path for the thundercloud,
27 He saw and appraised it,
measured and examined it.
28 He said to man,
'Now see that fear of the LORD is wisdom,
and turning from evil is understanding.'"

29 1 Iyov took up his theme again and said:

2 "If only I were as in months gone by,
the days God watched over me,
3 when He shone His lamp over my head,
when I walked by its light through darkness,
4 when I was young, in my prime,
and my tent knew God's protection,
5 when Shaddai was still with me,
when my servants surrounded me,
6 when He bathed my feet in cream
and the Rock poured streams of oil over me,
7 when I would go out to the city gates
and take my seat in the square.
8 On seeing me, young men would step back;
elders got up to stand.
9 Princes held back from speaking
and placed their hands on their mouths.
10 Nobles' voices turned to a hush,
tongues cleaving to palates.
11 When an ear heard and extolled me –
the eye that saw bore witness –
12 when I rescued the poor who cried out
and the helpless orphan,
13 when I received a beggar's blessing
and brought joy to the widow's heart,
14 when I wore righteousness and it clothed me –
justice was my robe and diadem –
15 when I was the blind man's eyes,
the lame man's legs,
16 when I was father to the destitute
and took up a stranger's cause,
17 I shattered the fangs of the wicked
and plucked the prey from his teeth!
18 I said to myself, I will die surrounded by family
and my days will be numerous as the sand;
19 my roots will be open to the waters,
and dew will lie along my branches.
20 My wealth will be restored

and the bow refreshed in my hand.
21 They listened to me eagerly,
kept silent at my counsel.
22 After I spoke, they said nothing;
my words poured down on them.
23 How they waited for my rainfall,
mouths open wide to receive it!
24 They would look my way when I smiled;
they never failed me when I showed them favor.
25 I set them on their path and took charge,
dwelt among them like a king over his troops,
like one who comforts mourners.

30 1 "But now they mock me,
men half my age whose
fathers I wouldn't deign to place
with the dogs tending my flock!
2 Of what use were their robust hands?
Thanks to them, the harvest was lost.
3 Wasted by want and famine,
they flee to the wilderness –
to gloom, ruin, and desolation;
4 left to pick from mallow bushes,[55]
broom roots are their bread.
5 Banished from society,
howled at like thieves,
6 settling in the gullies of riverbeds,
in crannies of earth and rock,
7 braying in bushes,
huddling under nettles,
8 rogues, nameless,
they are cut off from the land.
9 Now I'm the butt of their taunt-songs,
a ridiculous jingle –
10 they abhor me, avoid me,
and do not hesitate to spit in my face.
11 Because He has undone those belts and afflicted me,
they have loosened the bit from my face.
12 To my right the young mob rises,
sending me reeling,
building their siege ramp against me.
13 They break up my path,
increase my calamity;
no one holds them back.

55 | Whose flowers are inedible.

14 In a torrent they burst through,
coursing across the barren land.
15 Terrors turned loose on me
chase off my nobility like the wind;
my dignity vanishes like a cloud.
16 Now my spirit is emptied out;
days of affliction have taken hold.
17 Night gnaws at my limbs;
my sinews know no rest.
18 Changing my clothes takes all my strength;
they bind me, tight as a collar!
19 I am thrown into the mire;
I have become dust and ashes.
20 I call out to You, but You do not answer.
I wait – but You reflect.
21 You have turned cruel to me;
with all Your might You block my way.
22 You sweep me up, cast me to the wind,
and cunningly diffuse me.
23 I know You will send me off to death,
the meeting house of all the living.
24 If a poor man reached out his hand to me,
if in his misfortune he entreated me…
25 I swear I wept for the downtrodden!
I despaired over the needy!
26 I hoped for good, but evil came;
I longed for light, but darkness arrived.
27 My bowels seethe, refuse to be still.
Days of suffering come to meet me.
28 I walk, blackened, bereft of sun;
I rise up in the crowd and cry out;
29 I have been a brother to jackals,
a companion to ostriches;[56]
30 my skin is blackened, singed off,
my bones charred by the searing heat.
31 My lyre is given over to mourning
and my pipe to the sounds of weeping.[57]

31 1 "I had forged a covenant with my eyes
never to gaze upon a young woman,[58]
2 yet what was my God-given portion from above,
my inheritance from Shaddai on high?
3 Isn't calamity reserved for the wicked,

---

56 | These animals lived in the wasteland and were considered despicable.

57 | Such instruments were normally used on joyful occasions.

58 | God punished Iyov despite his chastity.

disaster for those who do evil?
4 Isn't it true He watches my ways
and counts my every step?
5 I swear I never walked with falsehood;
my feet have never rushed to deceive.
6 Let Him weigh me on honest scales;
God will know I am innocent,
7 and if my feet have strayed off course,
if my heart has chased after my eyes,
if any blemish has clung to my hands,
8 then may I sow while another eats
and my crops be uprooted!
9 If my heart has been seduced by another woman,
if I ever lurked around my neighbor's door,
10 then may my wife grind at the millstone
for someone else, and may others bend over her![59]
11 For this is an abomination,
a heinous crime,
12 a fire blazing all the way to Abaddon,
ravaging all my grain!
13 Have I ever scorned my servants,
man or woman, in their disputes with me?
14 What then will I do when God judges me?
When He calls me to account, what will I say?
15 Didn't He who formed me in the womb form them as well?
Were we not fashioned in the selfsame womb?
16 If I have withheld from the poor their desires,
let a widow's eyes pine away,
17 eaten my bread alone
and let no orphan partake of it –
18 from the time I was young, I raised him as if I were his father;
from my mother's womb I counseled her![60] –
19 if ever I glimpsed a wretched man unclothed
or a beggar lying uncovered,
20 if his loins did not bless me
as he warmed himself with my sheep's fleece,
21 if I ever lifted my hand against an orphan
when I saw my allies at the gate,
22 then may my shoulder fall out of its socket
and my elbow break off at its joint,
23 for I am haunted by God's terror.
I cannot bear His majesty!
24 If I have placed my faith in gold,

59 | Meaning, have sexual relations with her.

60 | The word "him" refers to the orphan and "her" to the widow.

if I pronounced, 'In you I trust,'
25 if I rejoiced in my opulence,
for my hand has found abundance,
26 if I ever gazed at the shimmering light,
the moon, magisterial in its course,
27 if my heart ever strayed in secret,
if I kissed my own hand,[61]
28 this too would be criminal,
for it would mean I had denied God on high.
29 I swear I never rejoiced in my enemy's downfall,
or exulted when evil found him,
30 or let my mouth sin,
wishing his death with a curse.
31 I swear no one in my vicinity ever exclaimed,
'Oh, how I'd love to tear him to shreds!'[62]
32 No stranger ever slept outside;
I opened my doors to the wayfarer.
33 I swear I never hid my sins like Adam
or concealed iniquity in my breast
34 because I feared a teeming mob,
felt terrified by slanderous clans,
or stood petrified at my doorstep.
35 If only I had a hearing –
take my signature! May Shaddai answer –
or let my rival write the indictment!
36 I would wear it on my shoulder,
tie it around me like a wreath.
37 I would tell Him of my every step,
approach Him as a prince.
38 If the land has ever cried out against me
or its furrows joined together to weep,
39 if I have eaten of its fruits without paying
or driven its rightful owners to despair,
40 then may nettles sprout up in place of wheat,
stinkweed instead of barley!
Iyov's words have reached their end."

32 1 Then the three men stopped answering Iyov, for he thought himself
2 righteous. But Elihu son of Barakhel the Buzite, of the Ram family, became
3 incensed.[63] He was angry at Iyov for justifying himself before God. He was
also angry at Iyov's three friends for not being able to find an answer and
4 for condemning Iyov. But Elihu waited for Iyov to finish speaking, for the

61 | A gesture of worship (see, e.g., 1 Kings 19:18).

62 | That is, defame him; see 19:22 and note there.

63 | A fourth friend, not mentioned before, enters the conversation.

5 men were older than he. Yet when he saw that the three men had no reply,
he grew angry.

6 So Elihu the son of Barakhel the Buzite replied and said:

"Me, I am young;
you, you are elders.
That is why I have been perturbed, afraid
of expressing my argument among you.
7 I said, let the wise speak;
let the many-yeared herald wisdom.
8 But wisdom is a spirit within mortals,
and it is the breath of Shaddai that teaches them insight.[64]
9 Not many become wise,
nor do many elders understand justice.
10 So I say, hear me out;
let me, too, express my argument.
11 Yes, I have been waiting for your words,
I have listened for your insights;
as you examined the remarks,
12 I have studied you.
No one has refuted Iyov.
None of you can reply to his claims.
13 Perhaps you say, we have found a strategy:
It is God who assails him, not a man.
14 But it is not against me that he contended with words;
I will not reply to him by repeating what you have said.
15 They were dismayed and did not respond.
Words fled from them.
16 I have waited for them to be quiet,
not to speak, not to respond.
17 Now, I too will say my part;
I too will express my argument,
18 for I am full of words;
my stomach clenches with them.
19 It is like unopened wine
rupturing new wineskins.
20 So let me speak and find relief;
let me open my mouth to reply,
21 but may I never turn my face toward any man
nor favor any title.[65]
22 May my Maker take me from this world
if I show favor.

33 1 "And yet, listen to my words now, Iyov;

64 | Every person, not only the wise elders, has the capacity to understand.

65 | Speak deferentially or show partiality.

hearken to all I say.
2 Now I have opened my mouth;
my tongue speaks from within my palate.
3 My words are the honesty of my heart,
and my lips have conveyed my argument in earnest.
4 The spirit of God made me,
and Shaddai's breath gave me life,
5 so if you can, reply to me.
Set your contentions before me.
6 I am like you before God;
I too was cut from clay.[66]
7 My dread will not terrorize you,
and my hand upon you will not weigh you down,
8 but what you said rings in my ears,
and I hear the sound of your words:
9 'I am pure, without transgression,
I am innocent, without iniquity,
10 yet He comes up with pretexts against me;
He thinks me an enemy.
11 He has set my feet in lime
so that He can follow my every step.'[67]
12 My reply to you: in this you are not right,
for God is greater than humanity.
13 Why do you seek a suit against Him, saying,
'He does not reply to all mankind's charges'?
14 For God speaks one way,
and two for those who cannot perceive it:
15 in a dream, a night vision,
when slumber falls upon men,
as they sleep in their beds,
16 He opens their ears to understanding,
and issues His directives
17 to turn them away from their misdeeds,
to conceal man's arrogance,
18 to save his soul from the grave
and his life from the sword.
19 He is chastened with pain, bedridden,
his every limb shivering mightily.
20 His palate will be revolted by bread
and his throat by delectable foods.
21 His flesh will putrefy out of sight,
his skeleton laid bare.
22 He will approach the grave,

66 | See Genesis 2:7.
67 | Cf. 13:27.

his life the place of the dead.
23 If for him there is a championing angel,
one out of a thousand
who can testify to his uprightness
24 and have mercy upon him, saying,
'Save him from descending into the grave;
I have found his ransom,'
25 then his flesh will be healthy as it was in his childhood,
restored, as in the days of his youth.
26 He will then beseech his God, God will long for him,
and he will see His face and shout with joy.
He will return to him what he deserves.
27 He will look upon people, and he will say,
'I have sinned; I have accused the Upright One of a crime,
and it was of no benefit to me.
28 God redeemed me from the grave,
and my life takes in the light.'
29 Yes, this is how God intervenes
two or three times with a man –
30 to bring him back from the grave
to be lit with the light of life.
31 Hearken, Iyov. Hear me.
Be silent and I will speak.
32 If you have words, respond to me;
speak, for I desire your acquittal.
33 But if not, you will listen to me.
Be silent, and I will teach you wisdom."

34 1 Then Elihu continued and said:

2 "Wise ones, listen to my words;
those who understand, lend an ear.
3 Just as the ear discerns words,
and the palate the taste of food,
4 let us examine this case
so that between us, we will know what is sweet.
5 For Iyov has said, 'I am innocent,
but God has stripped me of justice.
6 I am betrayed by those charges;
the arrows are fatal though I have not sinned.'
7 Oh, who is a man like Iyov,
who drinks mockery like water,
8 whose path is with those who do evil
and who consorts with wicked folk?
9 For he has said, 'What use is it to man
to do the will of God?'

10 So, men of wisdom, listen to me:
far be it from God to do evil,
from Shaddai to carry out injustice.
11 He repays a man according to his actions,
and according to his conduct He will provide for him.
12 This is the truth: God does no evil,
and Shaddai does not distort justice.
13 Who entrusted the earth to Him?
Who placed the world in His charge?
14 If He turns his attention to him,
He will take back his spirit and soul;
15 then all flesh will perish together,
and humanity will return to dust.
16 If you want to understand, hear this;
listen to the meaning of my words:
17 Would the hater of justice bind wounds?
Will you vilify the Perfectly Righteous?
18 Would He say of the king that he is base;
would He call nobles evil,
19 He who does not favor princes
nor acknowledge the ruler over the poor,
for they are all the works of His hands?
20 They die in a moment;
in the middle of the night they pass away.
The people are shaken,
because the mighty have been deposed,
but not at the hand of man.
21 His eyes are upon the ways of man,
and He sees all his steps.
22 There is no darkness, no death-dark,
that could hide evildoers.
23 After all, it is not for man to make a case,
to come before God in judgment.
24 He destroys the endlessly strong
and appoints others in their places.
25 Because He knows their actions,
they are crushed when the night is over.
26 He strikes them among evil men,
before everyone's eyes,
27 because they turned away from Him
and did not learn all His ways,
28 bringing upon Him the screams of the poor,
for He hears the howls of the destitute.
29 He makes silence; who can breach it?
He hides His face; who can see Him?

He sees nation and man as one
30 to hinder the rule of the evil,
of those who would snare the nation.
31 For to God, a person should say, 'I will bear it;
I will not remove the yoke.
32 What I cannot see, show me,
and if I have done evil, I will do it no longer.'
33 Did you think He should repay you as you see fit,
despite your rejection?
Did you think it was up to you and not Him?
Speak what you know.
34 Men of wisdom will tell me,
and wise men will hear me.
35 Iyov does not speak with knowledge,
and his words are not wise.
36 May Iyov be tested forever,
dealt with as evil men are,
37 for he continually increases his sin,
his iniquity among us is abundant,
and he speaks too much against God."

35 1 Then Elihu continued and said:

2 "Is this what you thought in your suit,
saying, 'I am more righteous than God'?
3 For you have asked what benefit you receive:
'What use is there in my not sinning?'
4 I will reply to you with words,
you and your friends as well.
5 Look up at the sky and observe;
peer into the heavens – they are higher than you.
6 If you sin, do you affect Him at all?
Even as your iniquities multiply, do you do anything to Him?
7 If you are in the right, what do you give Him;
what does He accept from you?
8 Your sin affects men like you,
and your goodness, humanity.
9 They scream out of conflict and oppression,
cry out under the fists of many persecutors,
10 but do not say, 'Where is God, my Maker,
the One who gives strength in the night?'[68]
11 But He has taught us more than the animals of the earth,
and He, more than the birds of heaven, has made us wise.[69]
12 When they shout, they will not be answered

68 | The oppressed fail to call upon God for help.
69 | Cf. 12:7.

because of their arrogance.
13 God will not listen to lies,
and Shaddai will not see them,
14 and though you say that He will not see it,
the case is before Him; wait for Him.
15 Now that there is deceit, He has grown angry
and knows no rest.
16 Iyov opens his mouth with false arguments
and without knowledge talks too much."

36 1 Then Elihu spoke again and said:

2 "Wait for me a bit, and I will teach you,
for God still has words:
3 'I will raise My argument from afar,
and I will give justice to My creatures.'
4 In truth, my words are not false;
my arguments with you are earnest.
5 Yes, God is mighty – and He does not despise
the mighty, strong of heart.
6 He does not let evildoers live
but gives the poor their due.
7 He does not take His eyes off the righteous.
He places kings on the throne
and ensconces them there. He raises them up.
8 But should He bind them in fetters,
seize them in torturous ropes,
9 then He will tell them of their actions
and their sins, which have multiplied.
10 He reveals rebuke to their ears
and says, 'If they return from wrongdoing,
11 if they listen and serve,
they will end their days well,
their years peacefully.
12 But if they do not listen,
the sword will overtake them;
they will die for lack of knowledge.'
13 The evildoers turn up their noses;
they do not call out even after He has bound them.
14 They die in their youth
among the male prostitutes.[70]
15 He will save the poor from their poverty,
and through distress opens their ears.
16 He has even distanced you from agony,
from the bottomless chasm.

70 | The depraved (see Deut. 23:18; 1 Kings 14:24).

Your table is laden with rich food.
17 Though you are beset by the evildoer's case,
law and judgment will support you.
18 Beware: do not let affluence seduce you,
nor a high ransom sway you.
19 Can you achieve salvation painlessly,
without great effort?
20 Hope neither through the night
nor for nations to rise from where they are.
21 Take care; do not turn toward evil
as you have in times of trouble.
22 Yes, God is exalted in His strength;
who is the Master like Him?
23 Who appointed His rule,
and who can tell Him, 'You have done wrong'?
24 Remember to declare that His deeds are great,
those that are recognized by man.
25 All of mankind has seen them;
humanity has gazed on them from afar.
26 Yes, God is unknowably great;
His days are innumerable.
27 He rains down drops of water
that pour down in a stream;
28 they flow down from the heights,
showering a multitude of people.
29 Can anyone understand the spreading of the clouds,
the thunder of His foggy veil?
30 He spreads His lightning over it,
covering the very roots of the sea.
31 With these He judges nations,
gives an abundance of food.
32 Lightning covers over the clouds;
at His command it meets its mark.
33 Its thunder proclaims Him,
as an angry blast rising upward.

37 1 "At this my heart quakes and falters in its place.

2 "Hear His thunder with trembling,
the rumble coming from His mouth.
3 Under all of heaven He flashes
his lightning to the ends of the earth.
4 After this He roars with His thunder,
rumbles in His loud voice.
He does not hold back; He makes His thunder heard.
5 God thunders in His voice wondrously.

He does great things, unfathomable to us.
6 He tells the snow, 'Fall upon the earth,'
the rain and the storm,
His mighty torrential rains.
7 He seals man in
so that all men know His work.
8 Even the animals retreat to their shelters
and curl up in their dens.
9 From the chamber comes the storm,[71]
and from the constellations, the biting cold.
10 With the breath of God, He brings ice;
many waters He turns solid;
11 He weighs down the fog with moisture,
and the clouds scatter His lightning.
12 It whirls and tumbles
in accordance with His directives,
whatever they are commanded to do
over all the settled lands.
13 He provides for His land,
whether for punishment or favor.
14 Hear this, Iyov;
be silent, and carefully contemplate God's wonders.
15 Do you know when God commands them
and lightning shines in His cloud?
16 Do you know the formation of fog,
the wonders of Him whose knowledge is perfect?
17 Why do your clothes grow warm
as the land is stilled by the south wind?
18 Have you beaten flat[72] the heavens with Him,
making them strong as a molten mirror?
19 Tell us what to say to Him;
wrapped in darkness we cannot argue in our ignorance.
20 When I speak, is He told of it?
Could a man so mired in confusion say anything?
21 And yet, even if the sun is unseen,
obscured high up in the heavens,
a wind passes and sweeps the clouds away;
22 golden rays from the north
cover God in His awesome glory.
23 Shaddai cannot be reached;
great in strength, great in justice,
mighty in righteousness, He does not afflict.

71 | The storms are kept in a chamber or vault until God lets them loose (cf. 38:22; Ps. 135:7).

72 | Hebrew *tarkia*, mirroring the description of the heavens as a metal sheet (*rakia*) in Genesis 1:6.

24 Therefore He is revered by men;
even the wise of heart cannot see Him."

38 1 Then the LORD answered Iyov from the whirlwind and said:

2 "Who dares darken wisdom with words
that know nothing?
3 Now, gird your loins like a man;
I will ask and you will tell Me.
4 Where were you when I laid the earth's foundations?
Speak if you have any understanding!
5 Who fixed its dimensions? Do you know?
Who stretched a measuring line across it?
6 On what ground were its pillars set;
who laid the cornerstone?
7 When the morning stars sang as one
and all the divine beings cried out for joy,
8 who barred Yam with double doors[73]
as it gushed forth from the womb,
9 as I clothed it in cloud,
swaddled it in fog,
10 and held to My boundary,
bolting up its double doors,
11 saying, 'Just this far and no more!
Here your proud torrents will stop.'
12 Have you ever commanded the daybreak,
marked the spot where dawn would rise
13 so that it could hold the edges of the earth
and shake the wicked out of it?[74]
14 Like clay whose mold has been lifted,[75]
the wicked catch the eye like a garment –
15 their light is lost,
their upraised arm broken at last.
16 Have you traveled as far as the sea's depths,
walked through them, plumbing the abyss?
17 Were the Gates of Death revealed to you?
The gates of death-dark, have you seen them?
18 Have you gazed hard at the earth's expanse?
Say so, if you know all!
19 Where is that path where light dwells?
And darkness, where is its place?
20 Can you take it to its limits?
Do you know the way there?

73 | See 7:12.

74 | The wicked are exposed in the daylight.

75 | The features of the earth can be seen, like an impression of a clay seal.

21 Of course you know – you were alive then!
You have lived so long![76]
22 Have you reached the stores of snow,
the treasuries of hail,
23 which I have kept for times of trouble,
for days of war, for battle?
24 Where is that path where lightning strikes,
scattering the east wind across the earth?
25 Who cleft a channel for the cascading waters,
a path for the thundercloud
26 bringing rain to uninhabited lands,
to wilderness no one enters,
27 to saturate a desolate wasteland
and make grass sprout from the ground?
28 Who fathered the rain?
Who gave birth to the beads of dew?
29 From whose belly did the ice emerge?
The frosts of the heavens,
who birthed them?
30 The waters fuse into stone:
the surface of the deep is frozen solid.
31 Can you bind the chains of the Pleiades
or let loose the reins of Orion?
32 Can you bring Canis Major and Minor in their season,
the Bear with her cubs – will you guide them?
33 Do you know the laws of heaven?
Will you establish its earthly dominion?
34 Can you lift your voice to the clouds
and make a gush of water rush over you?
35 Can you send off lightning bolts
so that they call to you: 'Here we are!'
36 Who has hidden wisdom deep inside,
endowed the heart with understanding?
37 Who colors the skies blue with wisdom,
tilts the pitchers of heaven?
38 Do you know how dust solidifies,
how clods of earth amass?
39 Do you hunt the lioness's prey,
and can you satisfy a lion's craving
40 as he crouches in his den,
poised to ambush from the thicket?
41 Who gives the raven its prey
when its young cry out to God
and wander about with nothing to eat?

76 | This is said sarcastically.

39 1 "Do you know the season the mountain goats give birth?
Do you watch as gazelles calve?
2 Can you count the months they fill;
do you know the time of their birth?
3 They crouch down, bring forth their young,
and cast away their offspring.
4 Their progeny thrive, grow in the wild;
once they leave, they never come back.
5 Who set the wild ass free?
Who cut the reins of the onager,
6 whose home I made in the wilderness,
whose dwellings lie in salt lands?
7 He scoffs at the clamoring city
and does not hear the taskmaster's shouts.
8 He roams the mountain pastures
in search of anything green.
9 Would the wild ox agree to serve you?
Would he lodge by your feeding trough?
10 Can you fetter him to the furrow?
Would he plow the valleys behind you?
11 Can you trust him to bring you a great yield?
Would you leave your hard labor to him?
12 Could you count on him to come back,
to gather your seed and harvest?
13 As for the ostrich – does her wing joyously beat?
Does she fly like the stork and falcon?
14 She leaves her eggs on the ground,
warming them in the dust,
15 forgetting a foot may crush them,
a wild beast could trample them.
16 She is harsh with her children as if they weren't her own.
She doesn't care that her efforts are in vain,[77]
17 for God has deprived her of wisdom;
He has not endowed her with understanding.
18 Otherwise she would soar on high,
scoffing at the horse and its rider.
19 Did you endow the horse with his valor?
Did you clothe his neck with a mane?
20 Do you make him rumble like locusts,
neigh in majestic terror?
21 He strikes the earth, reveling in his power
when he charges toward battle.
22 He laughs off fear and never recoils;
he does not flinch at the sword.

77 | Ostriches were thought to be uncaring (cf. Lam. 4:3).

23 A quiverful of arrows whizzes past him,
the spear's blade and the lance.
24 Raging and trembling he gallops;
he does not swerve as the horn sounds:
25 at its blast he cries 'Aha!'
From afar he catches a whiff of war,
the thundering of captains, battle cries.
26 Is it by your wisdom the hawk flies,
spreading his wings to head south?
27 Does the vulture soar at your bidding?
Is that why he builds his nest on high?
28 He makes his home in the rock,
on steep crags, a fortress.
29 From there he seeks out his food;
his eyes gaze out from afar.
30 His young gulp down blood;
where the dead are, he will be found."

40 1 Then the LORD spoke up to Iyov and said,

2 "Should he who argues make claims against Shaddai?
Should God reply to one who accuses Him?"

3 Iyov answered the LORD and said,

4 "I have been held worthless. What can I answer?
I will hold my hand to my mouth;[78]
5 I've spoken once and will say no more;
now twice. That is enough."

6 Then the LORD answered Iyov
out of the whirlwind and said:

7 "Now gird your loins like a man;
I will ask and you will tell Me.
8 Do you dare eschew My justice?
Would you dare indict Me
so that you can be in the right?
9 Do you have an arm like God's?
Can your voice thunder like His?
10 Then deck yourself in majesty, magnificence;
robe yourself in grandeur and glory!
11 Scatter your rage far and wide;
behold all the prideful – bring them low.
12 Behold the prideful and humble them;
trample the wicked wherever they are!
13 Bury them all in the dust;
shroud their faces in oblivion.

78 | I will be silent.

14 Then even I would praise you
for the deliverance won by your right hand.
15 Consider Behemoth;[79] I made him as I made you.
He devours grass as cattle do.
16 Behold – how strong his loins,
how mighty the muscles of his belly!
17 His tail stands erect like a cedar;
the tendons of his thighs are woven together.
18 His limbs are bronze conduits,
his bones like iron bars.
19 He is the first of God's works;
only his Maker can draw a sword against him.
20 The mountains bring him their harvest;
all beasts of the field frolic there.
21 He lies down under the lotuses,
under the cover of the marsh's reeds.
22 A thicket of lotus covers him;
the stream's willows surround him.
23 If a river rushes over him, he will have no fear,
steady while the Jordan gushes into his mouth.
24 Under his watchful eyes, who can take him
or run a grapnel through his nose?
25 Can you pull out Leviathan[80] with a hook,
tie up his tongue with a rope?
26 Can you wrap a bulrush around his nose,
pierce through his jaw with a prong?
27 Would he profusely plead with you?
Would he speak soft words to you?
28 Would he forge a pact with you
to forever be your slave?
29 Would you be able to play with him
like a bird, tie him down for your maids?
30 Will merchants bargain over him?
Will traders divvy him up?
31 Could you fill his skin with barbs,
his head with harpoons?
32 Lay a hand on him,
and you will forget what war is!

41 1 "You see, in his midst any hope will be crushed;
all fall to their knees at the sight of him;
2 no one is fierce enough to confront him;
who then can stand up to Me?
3 Whoever comes forward to take him on – I will reward him!

79 | See note on 12:7.

80 | See note on 3:8.

Everything under heaven is Mine.
4 I refuse to keep quiet about him,
his bravery, his indomitable prowess!
5 Who can strip away his outer trappings?
The folds of his jowls – who can delve inside?
6 Who can wrest open the gates of his face?
Sheer terror – the curve of his teeth!
7 His back is made of layers of shields[81]
locked shut and sealed.
8 Each is flush with the next;
not a breath can penetrate them,
9 each cleaving to the other,
interlocked and conjoined.
10 His sneezes are flashes of light;
his eyes are like the gleaming dawn.
11 Out of his mouth come flaming torches!
Burning sparks escape.
12 From his nostrils, smoke surges
as if from a steaming, boiling pot.
13 His breath ignites coals;
flames shoot from his mouth.
14 Strength abides in his neck;
his power rushes before him.
15 His cascading flesh clings together,
hard and immutable.
16 His heart is hard as rock,
hard as the lower millstone.[82]
17 Divine beings recoil before his majesty;
waves turn white at the devastation he brings.
18 He who approaches with a sword is doomed to fail –
so too with a spear, dart, or lance.
19 To him iron is straw;
bronze – rotted wood.
20 No arrow can drive him away;
slingstones look like stubble.
21 For him clubs are straw;
he scoffs at the rushing dart.
22 His underbelly is sharp as shards,
a threshing sledge across the mud.
23 He makes the depths boil like a pot;
he turns the sea into a seething cauldron.
24 He leaves behind him a gleaming wake;
the waters of the deep turn white.

81 | Hard scales.

82 | The heavy base of the mill on which the upper millstone turns to grind the grain.

25 No one on earth can overcome him;
no one was made so fearless.
26 He looks down at towering creatures;
he is king over every wild beast."

42 1 Iyov answered and said to the LORD:

2 "I know that You can do anything,
that no plan is beyond You.
3 'Who dares obscure wisdom when he himself knows nothing?'
Indeed, I have spoken but did not understand.
There are wonders beyond me I did not know.
4 'Hear now, and I will speak;
I will ask, and You will tell me...'[83]
5 I have heard You with my ears,
but now I see You with my eyes:
6 and so, I am utterly spent. I take pity
on dust and ashes."

7 After the LORD spoke these words to Iyov, the LORD said to Elifaz the
Temanite, "I am angry at you and your two friends, for you have not spoken
8 truthfully about Me, unlike My servant Iyov. Now take seven bulls and
seven rams, and go to My servant Iyov. Sacrifice them as a burnt offering
on your behalf, and Iyov My servant will pray for you. For I will accept his
prayer and will not commit any outrage against you, though you have not
spoken truthfully of Me, unlike My servant Iyov."

9 Then Elifaz the Temanite and Bildad the Shuhite and Tzofar the Naamatite
went and did as the LORD had told them. And the LORD lifted Iyov's face.
10 Then the LORD restored what Iyov had lost, for he prayed on behalf of his
friends. And the LORD doubled all that Iyov had.

11 And all his brothers and sisters and all those who knew him previously
came to break bread with him at his house; they grieved with him and
comforted him for all the suffering that the LORD had brought upon him.
Each person gave him one *kesita*[84] and one ring of gold.

12 The LORD blessed Iyov's later days more than his early days. He came to
have fourteen thousand sheep, six thousand camels, one thousand pairs
13 of oxen, and one thousand she-donkeys. He came to have seven sons and
14 three daughters: one was called Yemima, the second was called Ketzia, and
the third, Keren Hapukh.

15 Women more beautiful than Iyov's daughters could not be found in the whole
16 land. Their father gave them inheritances just as he did their brothers. After
all this, Iyov lived for one hundred and forty years. He saw his children and
17 grandchildren – four generations. Iyov died in old age, old and full in days.

83 | Echoing God's statement in 38:3.

84 | Apparently a unit of silver.

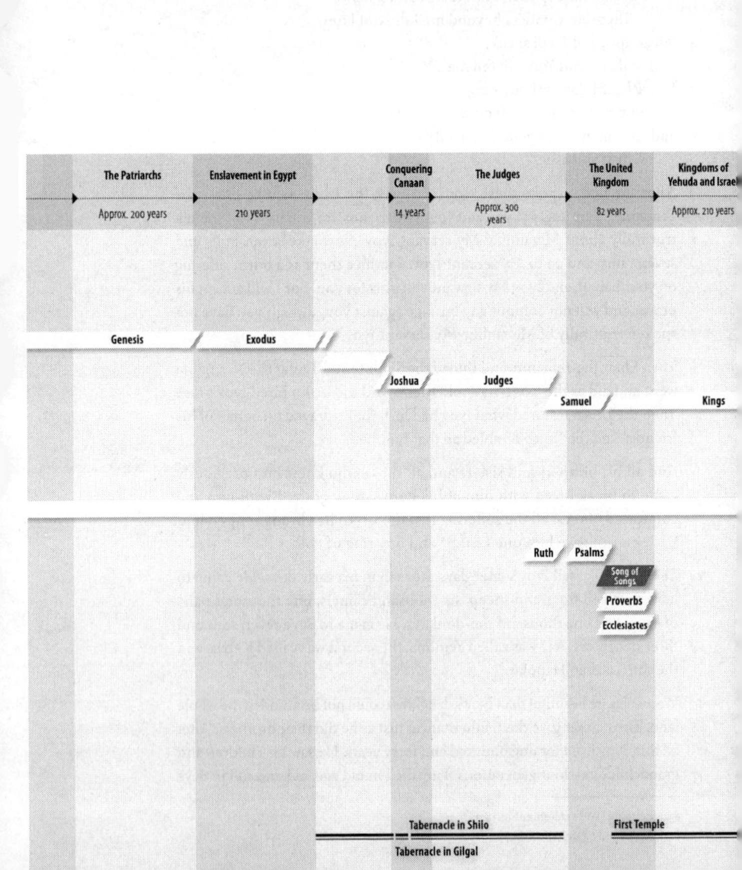

The Patriarchs
Approx. 200 years
Enslavement in Egypt
210 years
Conquering Canaan
14 years
The Judges
Approx. 300 years
The United Kingdom
82 years
Kingdoms of Yehuda and Israel
Approx. 210 years
Genesis
Exodus
Joshua
Judges
Samuel
Kings
Ruth
Psalms
Song of Songs
Proverbs
Ecclesiastes
Tabernacle in Shilo
Tabernacle in Gilgal
First Temple

SONG OF SONGS/ SHIR HASHIRIM

SONG OF SONGS	Song of yearning	Song of the wedding	Song of the missed opportunity and the desperate search	Song of the reunification
	Chs. 1–2	3:1–5:1	5:2–6:12	7–8

1 1 *Shlomo's Song of Songs,*

2 [*She*] Would that he would kiss me with that mouth.
Better than any wine is your love,
3 the fragrance of your oils finer;
your very name flows forth like fragrant oil;[1]
what wonder that all the maidens love you?
4 Come, draw me after you; come, let us run –
the king has brought me into his chambers.
In you our joy, our happiness:
your love possesses us more than any wine;
flowing freely falls this love.

5 [*She*] I am dark yet fair,
daughters of Jerusalem,
like the tents of Kedar,[2]
like the curtains of Shlomo.
6 Do not look at me: I am scorched black;
the sun has stared at me.
My mother's sons were furious:
they made me a keeper of the vineyards;
my own vineyard I did not keep.

7 Tell me, you whom I have loved,
where will you pasture,
where will you rest your flock at noon?
Do not make me swathe my face and wander
among all the herds of your friends.
8 [*He*] If you do not know,
most beautiful of women,
go out in the tracks of the flock;
bring your own young goats to pasture
beside the shepherds' huts.

9 [*He*] A mare among Pharaoh's chariots,
that is what you are to me, my love,
10 your cheeks fair in their strands of beads,
your neck bejeweled;
11 I would make you strands of gold –
with silver flecks.

12 [*She*] As long as my king[3] reclined to drink,
my musk root gave its scent,
13 my beloved a bundle of myrrh to me,
resting between my breasts;

1 | "Oil" (*shemen*) echoes "name" (*shem*); cf. Ecclesiastes 7:1.
2 | The tents of the tribes of Kedar were made from black goat hair.
3 | The beloved.

14 my beloved a cluster of henna to me
in the vineyards of Ein Gedi

15 [*He*] How beautiful you are, my love,
how beautiful, your eyes like doves.
16 [*She*] How beautiful you are, beloved, and how good.
Our bed is green, luscious;
17 our house is roofed with cedars;
its rafters are juniper trees.

2 1 I am a dune flower of the coast, I am
a lily of the valleys.
2 [*He*] A lily among thorn weeds
is my love among the maidens.
3 [*She*] An apple tree in the forest
is my beloved among young men.
I yearn for his shade; there I rest,
and his fruit fills my mouth with sweetness.

4 [*She*] He has brought me to the wine house,
and his ensign flying over me is love.
5 Sustain me with raisin cakes;
spread a bed for me among apples –
for I am sick with love.
6 My head rests in his left arm;
his right embraces me.
7 Swear to me, daughters of Jerusalem,
by the she-gazelles, by the does of the field,
swear that you will not waken, will not rouse,
this love before its time.

8 The voice of my beloved – I hear him coming,
springing over the hills,
leaping the slopes;
9 he is like a gazelle, my beloved;
he is like a young deer –
here he stands behind our wall,
gazing through the windows, catching
glimpses through every gap.

10 My beloved spoke; he said to me,
"Come, rise,
my love, my beautiful one,
let us leave.
11 Winter is over;
the rains have passed and left us.

12 On the land, buds have appeared.
The songbirds' time has come,
and the turtle dove's call sounds over our land.
13 The fig has put out her buds,
and the flowering vines give scent –
so come, rise,
my love, my beautiful one,
let us leave."

14 [*He*] My dove in the rock's cleft,
in the cliff's shadow –
show me your face;
let me hear your voice,
for lovely is your voice;
your face so fair.

15 [*She*] Catch the foxes,
the little foxes
ravaging the vineyards
just as our vineyard is in flower.
16 My beloved is mine, and I am his
who pastures among lilies.
17 Until the day has breathed its last
and the shadows have flown,
turn like a gazelle, my beloved,
turn like a young deer
to the riven hills.

3 1 Upon my bed at night[4]
I sought the one I love;
I sought him, I did not find him.
2 I shall rise, I shall go all around the town –
through the streets, across the squares –
searching for the one I love.
I searched for him but did not find him.
3 The guards found me, those who go around the town:
"The one whom I love – have you seen him?"
4 I had scarcely moved away from them
when I found the one I love.
I caught hold of him; I will not let him go
until I have brought him to my mother's house,
to the chamber where I was conceived.
5 Swear to me, daughters of Jerusalem,
by the she-gazelles, by the does of the field,
swear that you will not waken, will not rouse,
this love before its time.

4 | Meaning in a dream.

6 [*Friends*] Who is this rising from the wilderness
like plumes of smoke,
perfumed with myrrh and frankincense
more fragrant than all the merchants' powders?
7 Here is Shlomo's bed,
sixty soldiers all around it,
heroes of Israel,
8 each bearing his sword,
each schooled in war,
each with his sword at his thigh
for fear at night

9 King Shlomo built a palanquin
of Lebanon wood;
10 he ordered its pillars of silver,
its seat of gold;
its cushions are purple,
its space is lined with love
by the daughters of Jerusalem.
11 Go out now and see,
daughters of Zion;
look at Shlomo the king,
at the crown his mother gave him
on this his wedding day,
on the day his heart rejoiced.

4 1 [*He*] How beautiful you are, my love,
how beautiful, your eyes like doves
seen through your tresses;
your hair like a flock of goats
flowing down Mount Gilad.
2 Your teeth are like a perfect flock
rising up from washing:
each mother ewe bore twins,
not one among them lost.[5]
3 Your lips are a scarlet ribbon,
and your speech is fair;
your forehead like a pomegranate
glows through your tresses.
4 Your neck is like the Tower of David,
built in splendor,
a thousand shields adorning it,
the shields of all the heroes.

---

5 | That is, your teeth are white and none is missing.

5 Your two breasts are like young
twins of a she-gazelle,
pasturing in lilies.
6 Until the day has breathed its last,
and the shadows have flown,
I am going to the hill of myrrh,
to the slopes of frankincense.
7 And all of you is beauty, my love,
is flawless, wholly.

8 Come with me from Lebanon, bride;
come down with me from Lebanon;
from the peak of Amana come,
from the peaks of Senir and Ḥermon,[6]
from the lions' haunts,
the leopards' hills.
9 You have taken my heart, my sister,[7] my bride;
one glance of your eyes could take my heart,
any strand of the necklace you wear.
10 How beautiful your love is, my sister, my bride;
how much better than wine your love,
and finer than all perfumes the scent of your oils.
11 Your lips drip nectar, my bride;
honey and milk lie under your tongue,
and on your dress lingers
Lebanon's scent.

12 A locked garden is my sister, my bride,
a locked well, a spring sealed up –
13 yet your dry ground is a pomegranate grove
of sweetest fruits,
henna plants, musk root;
14 musk root and saffron,
calamus, cinnamon,
fragrant trees of every kind,
with myrrh plants and aloe,
with all the finest spices,
15 with a spring to water gardens,
a well of living waters,
waters flowing down from Lebanon.
16 [*She*] Wake now, north wind; south wind, come;
breathe life into my garden; let its perfumes flow.

---

6 | In the Anti-Lebanon mountain range.

7 | A term of endearment.

Let my beloved come to his garden
and eat his sweetest fruits.

5 1 [*He*] I have come into my garden, my sister, my bride;
I have gathered my myrrh and my balsam;
I have eaten my honeycomb with honey;
I have drunk my wine with milk.
[*Friends*] Eat, loved ones, eat;
drink, drink deep of love.

2 [*She*] I am asleep;
my heart is awake –
my beloved's voice, he is knocking –
"Open for me,
my sister, my love,
my dove, my perfection,
for my head is covered with dew,
my locks with drops of the night."
3 "I have taken off my dress;
how can I put it on again?
I have already washed my feet;
how can I dirty them?"
4 My beloved withdrew his hand from the door,
and my being longed for him.
5 I rose to open the door for my beloved;
my hands were dripping with myrrh,
my fingers streaming myrrh oil
over the handles of the latch.
6 I opened for my beloved –
he had slipped away, gone.
I fainted for him as he spoke –
I searched for him but could not find him;
I called out but he did not answer.
7 The guards found me, those who go around the town;
they beat me, they wounded me,
they pulled my shawl from me,
those guardians of the walls.
8 Swear to me, daughters of Jerusalem:
if you find my beloved,
swear that you will tell him –
tell him I am sick with love.

9 [*Friends*] What makes your lover more than other lovers,
most beautiful of women?
What makes your lover more than other men,
that this is what you have us swear?
10 [*She*] He is bright, my beloved; he is glowing;
you would know him among ten thousand.

11 His head shines like gold, fine gold,
his hair cascading curls,
raven black;
12 his eyes are like doves
at springs of water,
washed in milk,
at rest by the stream.
13 His cheeks are like beds of balsam,
like towers of perfume herbs.
His lips smell like lilies
flowing with myrrh oil.
14 His arms are like golden bars
set with stones of aquamarine,
his stomach like solid ivory
inlaid with lapis lazuli.
15 His legs stand firm as marble pillars
fixed on gold foundations.
To see him is like looking upon Lebanon,
and he is as choice as its cedars.
16 His mouth is filled with sweetness;
for all of him my longing.
This is my beloved, this is my love,
daughters of Jerusalem.

6 1 [*Friends*] Where has your beloved gone,
most beautiful of women?
Where has your beloved turned?
We shall search for him with you.

2 [*She*] My beloved has gone to his garden,
down to the beds of balsam
to pasture in the gardens,
to gather in lilies.
3 I am my beloved's – my beloved is mine –
who pastures among lilies.

4 [*He*] My love, you are as beautiful as Tirtza,[8]
as lovely as Jerusalem,
as terrifying as the ensigned armies.
5 Turn your eyes from me
for they have overwhelmed me.
Your hair is like a flock of goats
streaming down from Gilad.
6 Your teeth are like a flock of ewes
rising up from washing;

8 | Capital of the Northern Kingdom before Shomron.

each mother ewe bore twins,
not one among them lost.
7 Your forehead like a pomegranate
glows through your tresses.
8 Queens there are sixty,
eighty concubines,
and maidens there are without number.
9 But my dove, my perfection, is one –
one, unique to her mother –
the shining one she bore.
All the girls gaze at her – declare that she is blessed –
the queens and concubines – and speak her praise.

10 Who is this, like dawn to gaze upon,
beautiful as the moon,
shining like the sun,
as terrifying as the ensigned armies?

11 [*She*] I went down to the nut garden
to see the spring growth by the stream,
to see whether the vines were in flower,
whether the pomegranate buds had burst.
12 I did not know myself – I found myself
amid the chariots of my princely people.

7 1 [*He*] Turn, turn back, Shulamite;[9]
turn back, turn; let us see you.
Why do you gaze at the Shulamite
as if she were a Maḥanayim[10] dancer?

2 How lovely are your steps
in sandals, prince's daughter;
the turn of your thighs like jewelry,
work of the artist's hands;
3 your navel a circular bowl –
may it never want for wine;
your belly curved like baled wheat,
bounded round with lilies.
4 Your two breasts are like young
twins of a she-gazelle,

---

9 | Possibly a woman from the town of Shunem, or, alternatively, a feminine version of the name Shlomo.

10 | Literally "two camps," Maḥanayim may be the name of a place or a dance.

5 your neck an ivory tower,
your eyes like pools in Ḥeshbon,[11]
like pools by the Bat Rabim Gate,[12]
your nose like the Tower of Lebanon
gazing out to Damascus,
6 your head rising from you like the Carmel;
its curls shine like purple –
a king is tangled up among its tresses.
7 How beautiful you are, how good;
love with all its joys.

8 Your bearing is like a date palm,
your breasts its clustered fruits,
9 but I said, "I shall climb the date palm;
I shall take hold of its branches,"
and your breasts will be like clustered grapes,
your breath the scent of apples.
10 And your mouth is like good wine, inside –
[*She*] It is for my beloved, flowing freely,
bringing words to sleeping lips.
11 I am my beloved's,
and his longing is for me.

12 Come, my beloved, let us go to the fields;
let us lodge in the villages;
13 we will get up early and go to the vineyards
and see if the vine has flowered,
if its blossoms have opened out, and if
the pomegranate buds have burst;
there I shall give you my love.
14 The mandrakes impart their scent,
and on our own doorstep the sweetest
of fruits, new and old;
my beloved, I have hoarded them for you.
8 1 If only you could have been my brother,
could have suckled at my mother's breast.
I would find you outside,
I would kiss you,
yet none would shame me.[13]

---

11 | East of Jerusalem, a place of fertile fields and vineyards (Is. 16:8–10) and the capital of the kingdom of the Amorite king Siḥon.

12 | An unknown location, perhaps in Ḥeshbon.

13 | The lover wishes for a natural closeness to her beloved that would not be considered indecent.

2 I would lead you; I would bring you
to my mother's house;
you would teach me.
I would give you to drink
spiced wine, juice of my pomegranate tree.

3 My head rests on his left arm,
his right embraces me.
4 Swear to me, daughters of Jerusalem; tell me,
why do you seek to waken, why to rouse,
this love before its time?

5 [*Friends*] Who is this rising from the wilderness,
entwined with her beloved?

[*She*] Beneath the apple tree I roused you
where your mother bore you,
where in suffering she gave you birth.
6 Set me like a seal upon your heart,
like the seal upon your arm –
for love is as powerful as death itself,
and jealousy unyielding as Sheol;[14]
it burns with sparks of fire,
with the LORD's own flame.
7 Great waters cannot quench love,
nor torrents sweep it by.
If a man offered all his wealth for love –
they would laugh him to shame.

8 [*Brothers*] We have a little sister;
her breasts are not yet grown.
What shall we do for our sister
when a suitor comes for her?
9 If she is a wall,
we will build a silver watchtower;
if a door,
we will bar her up with cedar.

10 [*She*] But I am a wall;
my breasts are like towers.
It was then that I found
peace
in his eyes.

11 [*He*] Once, Shlomo had a vineyard at Baal Hamon.[15]
He gave the vineyard over to the keepers;

---

14 | The netherworld.

15 | An unidentified place meaning "master of wealth," perhaps hinting at Shlomo's riches.

each keeper brought him in
a thousand in silver from the fruits.
12 My vineyard stands before me, my own:
Shlomo, keep your thousand; pay
two hundred to the keepers of the fruits.

13 "You who still sit in the gardens,
friends listen for your voice.
Have me hear."

14 [*She*] Away with you, my beloved,
like a gazelle
or a young deer
over perfumed hills.

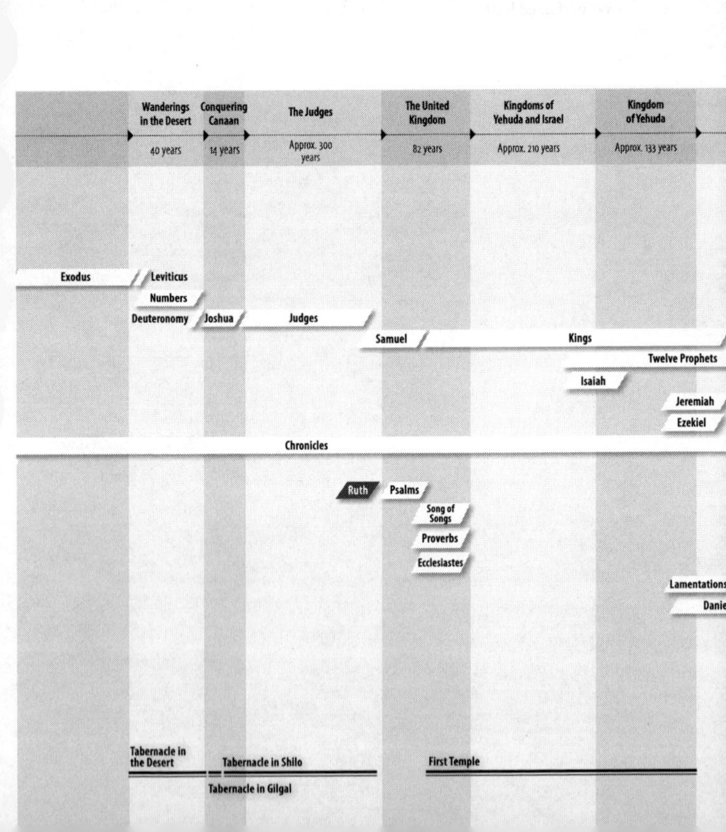
Wanderings in the Desert
Conquering Canaan
The Judges
The United Kingdom
Kingdoms of Yehuda and Israel
Kingdom of Yehuda
40 years
14 years
Approx. 300 years
82 years
Approx. 210 years
Approx. 133 years
Exodus
Leviticus
Numbers
Deuteronomy
Joshua
Judges
Samuel
Kings
Twelve Prophets
Isaiah
Jeremiah
Ezekiel
Chronicles
Ruth
Psalms
Song of Songs
Proverbs
Ecclesiastes
Lamentations
Tabernacle in the Desert
Tabernacle in Shilo
Tabernacle in Gilgal
First Temple

RUTH/RUT

RUTH	Naomi's family: Death, crisis, and alienation	Boaz and Ruth: Promises of sustenance and marriage	Naomi's family: Acceptance, marriage, and birth
	Ch. 1	2–3	4
	Approx. 10 years		

1 1 Once, in the days when the judges ruled,[1] there was a famine in the land.
One man set out from Beit Leḥem of Yehuda and journeyed to live for a
2 while in the land of Moav, and his wife and two sons came with him. This
man's name was Elimelekh, his wife's was Naomi, and his two sons' names
were Maḥlon and Kilyon, all Efratites[2] from Beit Leḥem of Yehuda. They
duly arrived in the fields of Moav, and there they stayed.

3 But then Elimelekh, Naomi's husband, died, and she was left there with
4 her two sons. Both of them married Moabite women – the first was called
5 Orpa, the second Ruth – and they lived there for some ten years. After
that, the two of them – Maḥlon and Kilyon – died as well, and the woman
6 was left bereaved of both her children and of her husband. She got up, her
daughters-in-law with her, to return from the land of Moav, for word had
reached her in the land of Moav that the Lord had brought His people to
mind and granted them bread.

7 So she left the place where she had been, both of her daughters-in-law with
8 her, and set off along the way back to the land of Yehuda. But to her two
daughters-in-law she said,
"Go on now, turn back,
each to your mother's home,
and may the Lord show you that kindness
that you have shown the dead and me.
9 The Lord grant that you find a place of rest,
each in your husband's home."
As she kissed them, they wept aloud
10 and said, "No. We shall return with you to your people."

11 Said Naomi,
"Turn back, daughters;
why would you come with me?
Have I still sons in my womb
who could be husbands to you?
12 Turn back, my daughters – go;
I am too old to be with a man.
Even were I to say, 'There is hope for me still,'
were I even this night to be married,
even if I could bear sons again,
13 are you to wait for them as they grow?
Would you be chained to them, never
to be with another man?
No, daughters, for your presence
is most bitter to me now,
for the hand of the Lord has beaten me."

---

1 | Before the establishment of the monarchy.

2 | Efrat is another name for Beit Leḥem.

14 Aloud they wept still more, then Orpa kissed her mother-in-law – but
Ruth clung to her.

15 And Naomi said,
"Your sister-in-law has turned back
to her people, to her gods.
Turn back after your sister-in-law."

16 But Ruth replied,
"Do not entreat me to leave you,
to turn back, not to walk after you.
For wherever you walk, I shall walk,
and wherever you stay, there I stay.
Your people is my people;
your God is my God.
17 Wherever you die, there I die,
and there shall I be buried.
So may the LORD do to me – and more –
for death alone will separate me from you."

18 Naomi saw that Ruth was determined to come with her, and she spoke to
19 her no more. The two of them walked on until they came to Beit Leḥem,
and when they arrived at Beit Leḥem, the whole town crowded around as
the women asked, "Can this be Naomi?"

20 She said to the women,
"Call me not Naomi. Call me Mara,[3]
for Shaddai has made my life bitter beyond words.
21 I was full when I left this place,
and empty has the LORD returned me.
Why call me, 'Naomi'?
the LORD has spoken up against me;
Shaddai has ruined me."

22 This is how Naomi, returning from the land of Moav with her daughter-
in-law, Ruth the Moabite, returned. They arrived at Beit Leḥem just as the
barley harvest began.

2 1 Naomi had a relative from her husband Elimelekh's family, a man of
2 substance and great strength: his name was Boaz. Ruth the Moabite said
to Naomi, "I shall go to the field and gather the fallen grains,[4] and follow
after anyone who should show me favor." Naomi said, "Go, then, my
3 daughter," and so she went. She came and started to gather in the field
after the harvestmen, and it chanced to be the field plot of Boaz that she
came to – that man of Elimelekh's family.

3 | Naomi means "pleasantness"; Mara means "bitterness."

4 | These grains were always left for the poor; see Leviticus 19:9–10.

4 And there came Boaz himself, arriving from Beit Leḥem and saying to the
harvestmen,
"The Lord be with you."
"The Lord bless you," they replied.

5 "Whose is that young woman over there?" asked Boaz of his servant in
6 charge of the harvestmen. "That is some Moabite girl," replied the servant
in charge of the harvestmen, "the one who came back with Naomi from
7 the land of Moav. She said, 'Let me come gleaning, gathering among the
sheaves where the harvestmen have been,' and so she came. She has been
standing out here from early morning until now and hardly sat at all in
the shelter."

8 Boaz went to Ruth and said,
"Daughter, take heed.
Do not go gleaning in any other field,
and do not leave this one;
cling close by my young women.
9 Keep your eyes on the field they are harvesting from
and follow after them.
I have instructed the young men by no means
to touch you.
When you are thirsty, go to the jugs
and drink of the water the young men have drawn."

10 Ruth fell upon her face, bowing low, and she asked him,
"Why is it that I have found favor in your eyes,
that you give me recognition such as this
when I am a stranger?"

11 Boaz said,
"I have heard of all you have done for your mother-in-law
ever since your husband died,
of how you left your father, your mother,
the land of your birth,
and came to a people you knew not the day before.
12 May the Lord repay your labors;
may your reward be full
at the hand of the Lord, God of Israel,
under whose mantle you come to take shelter."

13 "Sir," she said,
"I hope to find favor in your eyes,
for you give me solace,
for you have spoken to your servant's heart
though I am not fit to be your servant."

14 When the time came for eating, Boaz said to her, "Come here; eat of
this food and dip your bread in the vinegar." She sat down beside the

harvestmen, and he served her roasted grains, and she ate and had her fill
15 with more left over. And when she stood up to begin gleaning again, Boaz
instructed his workers,

"Let her glean among the sheaves as well;
do not disgrace her.
16 Drop some ears from the bundles as well;
leave them, let her glean them,
and do not reproach her."

17 Ruth carried on gleaning in the field until evening, then threshed what she
18 had gleaned; it was almost an ephah of barley.[5] She lifted it up and came
into the town. Her mother-in-law saw what she had gleaned; she produced
all that was left after she had eaten her fill and gave it to her.

19 "Where did you gather today," she asked, "and where did you work? Bless
whoever recognized you so." So Ruth told her mother-in-law under whose
patronage she had worked: "The man's name is Boaz, with whom I worked
20 today." Said Naomi to her daughter-in-law,
"The Lord bless him,
for he has not abandoned his kindness
to the living or the dead,"
and Naomi told her, "The man is our relative, one of our redeemers."

21 "He said to me as well," said Ruth the Moabite, "'Cling by my young men
22 until they finish all my harvest,'" and Naomi told her daughter-in-law Ruth,
"That is well, my daughter. Go out with his young women; do not go and
come to harm in other fields."

23 So it was that she clung by Boaz's young women to glean until the barley
harvest was over, and then the wheat, and after that she sat at home with
her mother-in-law.

3 1 "Daughter," said her mother-in-law Naomi to her, "do I not wish I could
2 find you a resting place that would be good for you? Now there is Boaz,
our relative, whose young women you were with, and he will be doing his
3 winnowing at the threshing floor tonight. You are going to wash yourself
and anoint yourself and put on your dress and go down to that threshing
floor. Do not let the man know that you are there until he has finished
4 eating and drinking. And when he lies down, take note of the place where
he lies, and afterward go there, uncover his feet, and lie down also – he
will tell you what to do next."

5 "I shall do," said Ruth, "all that you tell me to do."

---

5 | An ephah is about 21 quarts (19.87 liters), a very large measure for one person to glean and carry home.

6 She went down to the threshing floor and did exactly as her mother-in-law
7 had instructed her. Boaz ate and drank and was happy, and he went and lay
down beside the heap of grain. Then she came to him silently, uncovered
his feet, and lay herself down.

8 At midnight the man started and turned over – there was a woman lying at
9 his feet! "Who are you?" he said, and she answered, "I am your maidservant
Ruth – spread your mantle over your maidservant, for you are a redeemer."
10 And he replied, "The Lord bless you, daughter,
for this last kindness is yet greater than your first,
for you have not gone after the young men,
poor or rich.
11 Now, daughter, do not be afraid.
I shall do all that you ask,
for all within my people's gate know well
that you are a woman of great strength,
12 and I am indeed a redeemer to you,
but there is a redeemer still closer than me.
13 Stay on here tonight, and in the morning,
if he wishes to redeem you,
good: let him redeem.
And if he cares not to redeem you,
I shall redeem you myself, as the Lord lives –
stay until morning."

14 So she lay at his feet until morning and left before one person could
recognize another. "Let not a soul know there was a woman at the threshing
15 floor," said he. And then, "Give me the wrap that you are wearing; hold it
out." She did, and he measured six measures of barley into it; he placed it
upon her and went out into the city.

16 She came to her mother-in-law, "Who are you, my daughter?"[6] she said.
17 And Ruth told her all that the man had done for her. "He gave me these
six measures of barley," she said. "He said to me, 'Do not go back to your
18 mother-in-law empty-handed.'" Said Naomi,
"Sit down now, daughter,
until you find out how the matter will fall,
for that man will not rest unless the matter is settled today."

4 1 Boaz went up to the city gate and sat down, and the very redeemer of
whom he had spoken passed by. "Peloni Almoni," said Boaz, "come here
2 and be seated," and he turned aside and sat down. Then Boaz took ten men
from among the elders of the city, "Be seated here," he said, and they too
3 sat. Then he said to the redeemer,

6 | Meaning "how are you?" or "what transpired?"

"Naomi, who came back from the land of Moav,
must sell the field plot of our kinsman Elimelekh.
4 I said I would let you know of it, inviting you
to buy it in the presence of those sitting here,
in the presence of the elders of my people.
If you wish to redeem this, redeem;
and if you will not redeem it, tell me: let me know,
for there is none before you to redeem,
and I am next in line to you."

"I shall redeem," he said.

5 "On the day you buy that field from Naomi," said Boaz,
"and from Ruth the Moabite,
you will have bought the wife of a dead man with it,
to restore the dead man's name on his estate."

6 Said the redeemer,
"Such a redemption I could not perform;
it could be the ruin of my estate.[7]
You redeem in my place;
I cannot redeem."

7 In those long-ago days in Israel, a redemption or exchange – anything to
be officially enacted – was completed as follows. One man would take off
his shoe and would hand it to the other: that was the bond then recognized
8 among Israel. Now this redeemer said to Boaz, "Take possession," and he
took off his shoe.

9 "You are my witnesses this day," said Boaz
to the elders and to all the people present,
"that I take possession of all that was Elimelekh's
and all that was Kilyon's and Maḥlon's,
from Naomi's hand.
10 And with it I take Ruth the Moabite,
Maḥlon's wife, to be mine,
to rebuild the name of the dead on his estate.
And the dead man's name will not be cut off
from among his brothers, from the gate of his own city –
you are my witnesses this day."

11 And all the people at the gate and the elders said,
"We bear witness.
May the Lord make the woman who is joining your house
like Raḥel and like Leah,
who together built the House of Israel;

7 | Since a son born to Ruth and the redeemer would be considered Maḥlon's son, the field the redeemer stood to purchase would pass out of his estate.

may you go from strength to strength in Efrata
and your name be ever spoken in Beit Leḥem.
12 May your house be as the house of Peretz,
whom Tamar bore to Yehuda,
growing from the seed that the Lord will give you
from this young woman."

13 And so it was that Boaz took Ruth, and she became his wife, and he came
14 to her; the Lord granted her conception, and she bore a son. And the
women said to Naomi,
"Blessed be the Lord,
who has not withheld your redeemer on this day –
may the child's name be spoken in all Israel.
15 May he restore your spirit
and sustain your old age,
for your daughter-in-law, who loves you, she has borne him,
she who is better to you
than seven sons could be."

16 Naomi took the child and placed him in her bosom and became his nurse.
17 And her neighbors named him, saying, "A son is born for Naomi!" They
called him Oved. And that was Oved the father of Yishai the father of
David.

18 This is the line of Peretz:
Peretz was the father of Ḥetzron.
19 Ḥetzron was the father of Ram;
Ram was the father of Aminadav.
20 Aminadav was the father of Naḥshon;
Naḥshon was the father of Salma.
21 Salma was the father of Boaz;
Boaz was the father of Oved.
22 Oved was the father of Yishai –
and Yishai was the father of David.

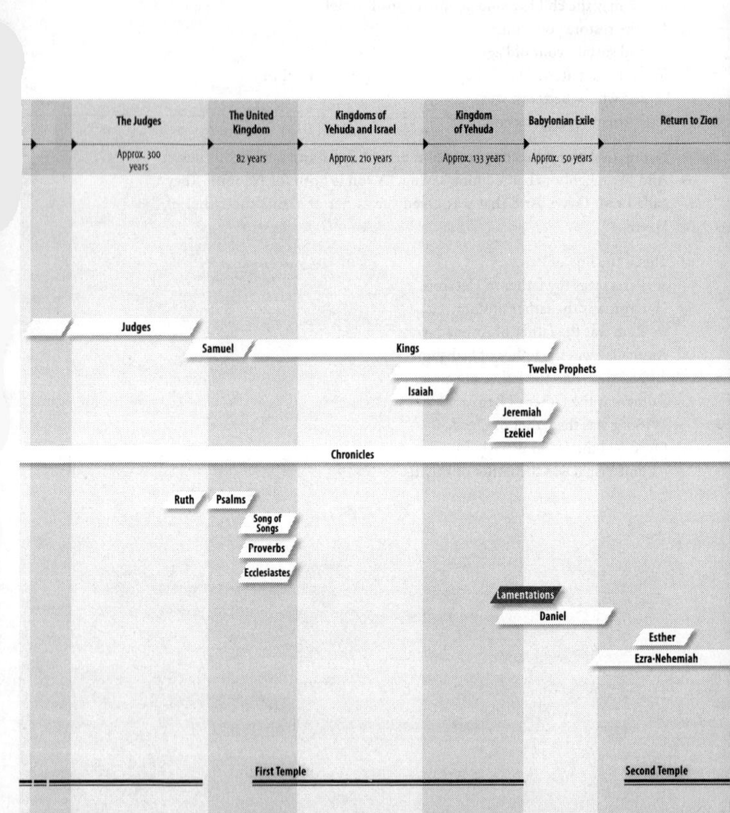

The Judges
The United Kingdom
Kingdoms of Yehuda and Israel
Kingdom of Yehuda
Babylonian Exile
Return to Zion
Approx. 300 years
82 years
Approx. 210 years
Approx. 133 years
Approx. 50 years
Judges
Samuel
Kings
Twelve Prophets
Isaiah
Jeremiah
Ezekiel
Chronicles
Ruth
Psalms
Song of Songs
Proverbs
Ecclesiastes
Lamentations
Daniel
Esther
Ezra-Nehemiah
First Temple
Second Temple

LAMENTATIONS/ EIKHA

LAMENTATIONS	Zion alone	Destruction and anger	Lamentation of "the man"	Horrors of the destruction	Petition and lament
	Ch. 1	2	3	4	5

1 1 How the city that overflowed with people
sits alone,[1]
become like a widow;
she who was great among nations,
princess of states,
now a forced laborer.
2 She weeps, weeps through the nights;
on her cheeks, tears.
Of all her lovers none console her;
all her friends have betrayed her,
become enemies to her.
3 Oppression has exiled Yehuda,
oppression and the harshness of her labor.
Confined among nations,
she finds no resting place;
all her pursuers caught up with her
in the narrow spaces.
4 The streets of Zion are grieving –
no one coming for the festival.
All her gates are desolate;
her priests are groaning;
her innocent girls are sorrowful,
and she – her life is bitter.
5 Her foes form the head of this beast now,
her enemies serene;
for the Lord has brought her suffering
for all her crimes.
Her little children walked away, captives,
before foes.
6 It is gone from daughter Zion –
all her splendor gone.
Her princes have become like
stags that find no pasture,
fleeing without strength
before pursuers.
7 She remembers, Jerusalem,
in her days of oppression and wandering,
all that she treasured
that was hers long ago,
how her people fell at the foe's hands
with none to help her;
they see her now, these enemies,
and laugh at her downfall.

1 | All chapters of Lamentations save the last are alphabetical acrostics.

8 She has sinned – Jerusalem sinned
and so has become an outcast.
All who once respected her abase her:
they have seen her naked.
Now she too is groaning,
sits apart.
9 Her impurity stains her skirts;
she forgot what her end would be.
Her fall was startling;
none console her.
"LORD, witness my oppression;
the enemy grew strong."
10 A foe has spread his hand
over all that she treasured.
The nations saw her;
they came to her Temple.
Those that You commanded
must never enter Your assembly.
11 All her nation groans:
they are seeking bread.
They gave up their treasures for food,
grasping at life.
"See this, LORD; look on –
I am abased.
12 May this never come to you, all you who cross my path.
Look on now and see –
is there any pain like mine?
Like that which was done to me,
like the suffering the LORD sent me
on the day His rage burned?
13 From above He sent down fire through my bones
and broke them all.
He spread a net for my feet,
sent me backward.
He rendered me desolate
all the day, ailing.
14 The yoke of my crimes, bound together,
the ropes twisted in His hand,
were raised to my neck
and brought my strength down.
My LORD has given me over
to those I cannot rise from.
15 He cast all my heroes aside –
the LORD in my midst.
He summoned forces forth
to break my young men.

The Lord trod red the winepress
of the virgin daughter Yehuda.
16 For these things I weep;
my eyes, my eyes stream water,
for the one who could console me is far away from me,
the one who would restore my life to me.
My children became desolate
when the enemy mastered."
17 Zion spreads her hands –
there is none to console her.
The Lord commanded enemies
against Yaakov all around,
Jerusalem an outcast among them, bleeding.
18 She says, "The Lord is just:
I had refused His word.
Listen, please, all peoples; witness this pain.
My young girls and youths have gone off in captivity.
19 I called out to my suitors; they have deceived me.
My priests and my elders have starved in the city;
they sought bread for themselves
to restore their lives.
20 See, Lord, I am anguished.
My stomach churns.
My heart turns within me,
for I have refused You.
Outside the sword bereaves me;
at home it is like death.
21 Hear me – I am groaning;
there is none to console me.
My enemies heard of my suffering – they rejoice:
You have done this.
When You bring the day You called for,
then they will be like me.
22 Let all their evil come before You,
and do to them everything
that You have done to me for all my crimes.
My groans compound;
my heart is ailing."

2 1 How in His rage the Lord darkens
the skies of daughter Zion;
He has flung from heaven down to earth
all of Israel's splendor.
He had no thought for His footstool[2]
on the day of His rage.

2 | The Temple, where the Divine Presence rested.

2 The LORD devoured, showed no mercy
for the sheepfolds of Yaakov,
devoured in His great rage
daughter Yehuda's fortresses –
down they came to earth
and brought low kingdoms, princes;
3 with burning rage He hacked off
the horn of Israel's pride,
held back His right hand
to let the enemy come.
He burnt like flames of fire in Yaakov,
consuming on all sides.
4 He trod[3] His bow like the enemy;
like a foe He raised His right hand
and killed all those the eye treasured.
In the tent of daughter Zion
He poured out rage like fire.
5 It was as if He were the enemy.
The LORD devoured Israel,
devoured all her palaces,
razed her fortresses;
in daughter Yehuda He caused much
moaning, mourning.
6 He uprooted His Shelter like a garden,
destroyed His Tent of Meeting.
The LORD erased the memory in Zion
of festival and Sabbath.
He debased, in His flaming rage,
king and priest.
7 The LORD shunned His altar,
renounced His own Temple,
gave over the walls of her palaces
into the enemy's hands.
They called aloud in the LORD's House
as if it were a festival.
8 The LORD planned demolition
for daughter Zion's walls.
He stretched out the plumb line,
devoured, did not hold back.
Now boundary and wall
are grieving, pitiful.
9 Her gates are sunk into the earth,
their bars broken and gone.

---

3 | God, pictured as the enemy, bends His bow and positions His arrows to shoot at Israel. See also 3:12.

Her king and ministers gone away among the nations,
there is no teaching.
Even her prophets
find no vision of the LORD.
10 The elders in daughter Zion
sit on the ground and are silent.
They lift up dust upon their heads,
wrap themselves in sacking;
the young girls of Jerusalem
lower their heads to the ground.
11 I have wept my eyes away;
my stomach churns;
my marrow is poured onto the earth
over my maiden nation's breaking,
as little ones, infants, faint
away in the town squares –
12 they say to their mothers,
"Where are grain and wine?"
as they faint away like the fallen
in the city squares,
as their lives are poured away
into their mothers' laps.
13 How can I bear witness, to what can I liken you,
daughter Jerusalem?
What can I compare you to and comfort you,
O virgin daughter Zion?
Your breaking as vast as the ocean,
who will heal you?
14 Your prophets brought you visions –
empty, meaningless –
but did not uncover your sins
to restore your fortunes.
They envisioned worthless
delusions for you; they misled you.
15 All who cross your path
slap their hands now in dismay.
They whistle and shake their heads
over daughter Jerusalem.
"Can this really be that city
that was called 'Perfect Beauty,'
'Delight of all the world'?"
16 All your enemies
gape their snarling mouths at you.
They whistle and grate their teeth;
they say, "We have devoured them:

this is the very day we hoped for –
we have done it, seen it."[4]
17 The Lord has completed
what He planned to do.
He has carried out His word,
His command of long ago.
He destroyed and showed no mercy,
brought the enemy joy over you;
He raised your foes' proud horn.
18 The heart cries out toward the Lord.
O wall of daughter Zion,
draw down, like a stream, your tears;
day and night
do not allow yourself rest;
let your eyes never be silenced.
19 Get up, give voice in the night
as every watch begins;
pour out your heart like water
in the presence of the Lord.
Lift up your palms to Him
over the lives of your little ones,
fainting away from hunger
at the end of every street.
20 See this, Lord, look on –
to whom have You done this?
Can women eat their own children,
the little ones they nurtured?
Can priest and prophet be murdered
in the Temple of the Lord?
21 On the ground, lying down in the streets –
youths, old men.
My own young girls and youths
have fallen to the sword.
You have killed on the day of Your rage,
have slaughtered, shown no compassion.
22 You call those living around me to come
as if it were a festival.
But there is no refugee or remnant
on the day of the Lord's rage.
All those I nurtured and raised,
my enemy disposed of.

4 | In the acrostics of chapters 2–4, the *peh* and *ayin* are reversed.

3 1 I am the man who has seen oppression[5]
through the staff of His rage.
2 It is I that He led, that He guided
into the darkness, not light.
3 It is to me alone that He returns,
turns His hand again against me all the day.
4 He has made my flesh and skin decay;
He has broken my bones.
5 He built a siege wall round me
of wormwood and of hardship.
6 He sat me down in darkness
like those forever dead.
7 He fenced me around – no escape;
made heavy the bronze that holds me.
8 Even as I cry out to be saved,
He has blocked my prayer.
9 He fenced off my way with hewn stone
and twisted my paths.
10 He is a bear lying in wait for me,
a lion in hiding.
11 He turns me from my path, gashes me,
renders me desolate.
12 He has trod His bow[6] and made me stand
the target to His arrow.
13 Into my very heart He shot
His quiver's load.
14 I am the laughingstock of all my people,
their mocking song all the day.
15 He has glutted me with bitterness
and quenched me with wormwood.
16 He crushed my teeth in grit,
trod me into the ashes.
17 Peace has deserted me:
I have forgotten what goodness is.
18 I said, "My endurance is lost,
and my hope of the Lord."
19 Keep in mind my affliction and wandering,
wormwood, venom.
20 Keep, keep in mind
my life, bowed low.
21 I make this reply to my heart,
and so I wait on.

---

5 | This chapter is a triple alphabetic acrostic, with twenty-two sets of three verses beginning with the same Hebrew letter.

6 | See 2:4.

22 The LORD's kindness – it is not finished;
His compassion is not spent.
23 New with each new morning,
how great is His faithfulness.
24 I said to myself, the LORD is what I have
and so I shall yet wait for Him.
25 The LORD is good to those who hope for Him,
to those who search for Him.
26 To hope is good in silence
for the LORD to come, to rescue.
27 It is good for a man
to bear the yoke in his youth.
28 He should sit alone and be silent:
this was inflicted on him.
29 Let him sink his teeth into the dust –
perhaps there is hope.
30 Let him offer his cheek to the one who beats him.
Let him be glutted with insult.
31 For the LORD will not shun him
through all eternity.
32 For if He brings sorrow,
He must, in His great kindness, have compassion.
33 He does not oppress from the heart
to bring men sorrow,
34 to trample underfoot
all the captives of this earth,
35 to twist a man's claim
before the Most High,
36 to let one's case be twisted –
and yet my LORD not see.
37 Who ever *spoke and it was so*
if the LORD did not command it?
38 Do not all evils and good emerge
from the mouth of the Most High?
39 How can a living man protest;
why should he protest his own sins?
40 Let us seek out our ways, understand them,
and come back to the LORD.
41 Let us raise our hearts with the palms of our hands
to God in heaven.
42 *We rebelled and refused You –*
but You did not forgive.
43 You covered us in rage and pursued us.
You killed; You showed no compassion.
44 You covered Yourself in a cloud
beyond the reach of prayers.

45 You have made us filth and loathing
among nations.
46 They gaped snarling mouths at us,
all our enemies.
47 Terror and snare were with us;
devastation, breaking.
48 Rivers of water ran from my eyes
at my maiden nation's breaking.
49 My eyes pour out and will not stop,
no respite
50 until the LORD shall look down
and see us from the heavens.
51 My eyes torment me
over all the daughters of my city.
52 He hunted me down like a bird,
my enemy, for no cause.
53 They closed off my life in a pit;
they laid the stone over me.
54 The waters came up over my head;
I said, "I am condemned."
55 LORD, I called Your name
from the very lowest of pits.
56 You have heard my voice;
do not close Your ears
to my need, to my pleading.
57 You once were close when I called You,
would tell me, "Do not fear."
58 You would fight my fight, my LORD,
redeem my life.
59 See, LORD, this twisted justice;
judge my case.
60 Witness all their vengefulness,
all that they plan to do to me.
61 Hear their insults, LORD,
and all their plans for me,
62 my attackers' mouthings, their mutterings
against me all the day.
63 Watch them as they sit or rise:
I am their mocking song.
64 LORD, return them payment
for all that they have done.
65 Bring them heartache,
Your curse on them.
66 Pursue them with rage and annihilate them
from under the skies of the LORD.

4 1 How dull gold has become;
how that finest gold has changed,
the sacred stones poured out
at the end of every street.
2 Precious children of Zion,
worth their very weight in gold –
how they are considered now like cheap clay jars,
work of the potter's hands.
3 Even jackals offer udders,
give their cubs to suck.
My maiden people is cruel
like desert ostriches.
4 The tongues of infants cling
to their mouths' roofs with thirst.
Little children beg for bread;
none break it for them.
5 Those who once ate the finest foods
sit desolate in the streets.
Those brought up in clothes of scarlet
now embrace the trash heaps.
6 My people's punishment is greater
even than that of Sedom,
which was overturned all in a moment;
no hand touched it.
7 Jerusalem's leaders were cleaner than snow
once, brighter than milk,
glowing redder than carnelians from within,
cut as finely as sapphires.
8 Now they are darker than pitch,
unrecognized on the streets,
skin shriveled against bones,
dry as wood.
9 Better to be killed by the sword
than killed by hunger.
The slain at least flow where they are stabbed,
do not starve for the yield of meadows.
10 The hands of loving women
have cooked their own children;
these have become their nourishment
in my maiden nation's breaking.
11 The Lord burned all His anger,
poured out all His flaming rage.
He set fire blazing in Zion;
it consumed all her foundations.

12 The kings of the world did not believe it –
  not anyone living on earth –
that a foe and enemy could come
  and enter Jerusalem's gates –
13 for the sins of her prophets,
  her priests' offenses,
who within her midst pour out
  the blood of righteous people.
14 They drift, blind, through the streets,
  disgusting with blood;
no one could possibly
  touch those clothes.
15 "Keep away, impure," they cry out;
  "away, away, do not touch,"
    floating, drifting away.
It is said among the nations,
  "They may stay no longer here.
16 It is the LORD's face that divides them.
  He will look on them no more."
They granted priests no honor
  and elders no favor.
17 And we: our eyes are worn out watching
  for our mirage of assistance,
waiting, ever waiting
  for a nation that knows no rescue.
18 They stalked our very steps,
  stopped us walking across our squares.
Our end comes close,
  our days are done,
    our end has come.
19 Our pursuers came swifter
  than the eagles of the sky.
They pursued us over mountains;
  in the steppes they lay in ambush.
20 Our life's breath,
  the LORD's anointed,
    was caught up in our slaughter,
the one whose shade we said
  we would live in among nations.
21 Rejoice, be merry, daughter Edom,
  sitting there in the land of Utz.
The cup will come to you in turn;
  you will get drunk and be laid bare.

22 Your offenses are done with, daughter Zion;
He will exile you no more.
Your offenses are noted, daughter Edom;
your sins have been exposed.

5 1 Remember, Lord, what has become of us.
See; witness our abjection:
2 our homeland turned over to strangers,
our homes to foreign men.
3 We are orphans now, fatherless,
our mothers are widows.
4 We pay to drink our water;
our wood comes at a price.
5 At our throats, they chase us;
we labor; they give us no respite.
6 We hold out a hand to Egypt,
to Assyria, for bread.
7 Our fathers sinned – they are gone now –
we bear their offenses.
8 Slaves now rule over us;
none will release us from their hands.
9 We risk our lives for bread
under the sword in desert lands.
10 Our skin burns like an oven
with the fevers of starvation.
11 They raped women in Zion,
virgin girls in the towns of Yehuda.
12 Princes were hung up by their hands;
no regard was shown to elders.
13 Young men bear the millstone;
boys stumble under loads of wood.
14 No more elders at the gates
or young men lost in song.
15 No more delight in our hearts;
our dance has turned to mourning.
16 The crown of our heads has fallen,
woe is to us: we have sinned.
17 For these things our hearts are ailing;
for this our eyes grow dark,
18 for Mount Zion, desolate –
foxes wander there.
19 But You, Lord, are enthroned forever;
Your rule endures for all generations.

20 Why would You forever forget us,
desert us, for days without end?
21 Bring us back to You, LORD, and we will come.
Renew our days to be as they once were;
22 even if You leave and loathe us now,
and rage against us with great passion.

Bring us back to You, LORD, and we will come.
Renew our days to be as they once were.

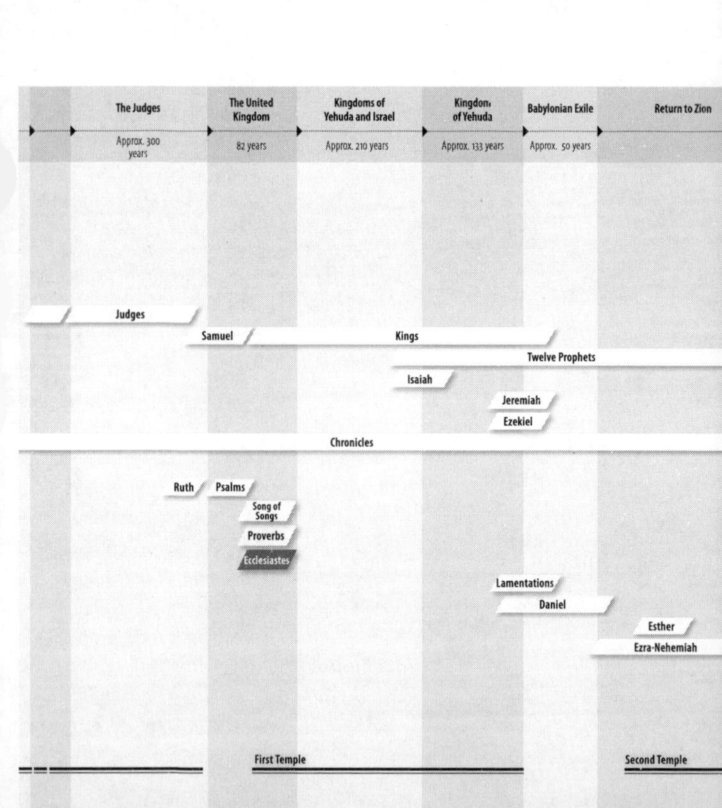

The Judges
Approx. 300 years
The United Kingdom
82 years
Kingdoms of Yehuda and Israel
Approx. 210 years
Kingdom of Yehuda
Approx. 133 years
Babylonian Exile
Approx. 50 years
Return to Zion
Judges
Samuel
Kings
Twelve Prophets
Isaiah
Jeremiah
Ezekiel
Chronicles
Ruth
Psalms
Song of Songs
Proverbs
Ecclesiastes
Lamentations
Daniel
Esther
Ezra-Nehemiah
First Temple
Second Temple

ECCLESIASTES/ KOHELET

ECCLESIASTES	Opening	Questioning and experimenting	Insights and counsel	Conclusion
	Chs. 1:1–11	1:12–6:12	7:1–12:7	12:8–14

1 1 The sayings of Kohelet son of David, king of Israel in Jerusalem.[1]

2 Fleeting breath, Kohelet said:
Fleeting breath – it is all mere breath.[2]
3 What profit remains for all the labor
one toils over beneath the sun?
4 One generation leaves, another comes;
the earth remains forever.
5 The sun rises, the sun sets;
it heaves toward its place and there it rises.
6 Blowing south, turning north,
turning, turning, blows the wind,
circling then turning, the wind returns.
7 All streams flow into the sea,
yet the sea is not full.
To the places where the streams first flowed
they return to flow again.
8 Everything is burdensome.
One can say nothing,
the eye can never see enough;
the ear is never filled with hearing.
9 What has been is what will be,
what was done will again be done,
and there is nothing new beneath the sun.
10 Some thing may make a person say,
"Look at this: it is new!" –
it already existed in all the
eons that came before us.
11 The people of old left no memory behind,
and those yet to come
will leave no more memorial
for those who will come after.

12 13 I, Kohelet, was king of Israel in Jerusalem. And I set my mind to studying
and exploring with wisdom all that is done beneath the sky – a wretched
occupation, that one, given by God to mortal man to oppress himself with.
14 I saw everything that is done beneath the sky. It is nothing but fleeting
15 breath, nothing but courting the wind. What is crooked can never be
straightened;
what is wanting can never be counted.
16 I said to my mind, I have gathered and built up more wisdom than anyone
who has ruled over Jerusalem before, and my mind has seen much of

1 | Presumably Shlomo, who is also associated with the books of Proverbs and Song of Songs.

2 | Transient and insubstantial, or incapable of being explained rationally. This language recurs throughout the book.

17 wisdom and insight. And I gave my mind over to understand wisdom, to
discern delirium and folly. I know that too is but courting the wind.
18 For in great wisdom lies great bitterness;
and one who gathers insight gathers pain.

2 1 I said to my mind, Come, let me quench myself with joy; let me sate myself
with good living. I found that, too, but fleeting breath.
2 "Delirium," I called laughter;
asked of joy, "What comes of this?"

3 And so I explored with my mind, steeping my body in wine, and grasping
folly, while my mind at the helm remained wise – that I might finally see
what path is good for mortal man to follow beneath the sky for as long
4 as he should live. I amassed a great estate. I built myself houses, planted
5 vineyards, acquired gardens and orchards for myself and planted them
6 with every kind of fruit tree. I ordered pools of water to be dug to irrigate
7 a forest burgeoning with trees. I bought slaves and maidservants, and
others were born in my house; I had livestock also, herds and flocks, more
8 than anyone else who came before me in Jerusalem. I collected silver and
gold and the treasures of kings and foreign lands; I brought in singers,
male and female, and all the delights of mankind; I took a woman, many
women.[3]

9 I grew great and gathered more than anyone who had come before me in
10 Jerusalem, while my wisdom still stood by me. I withheld from my eyes
nothing that they sought, nor did I withhold any joy from myself. For my
mind rejoiced in the fruits of my labor, and that was my reward for all my
11 toil. And then I turned to look at all my works, at the work of my hands, at
all that I had labored to achieve – and this is what I saw: all is but fleeting
breath, nothing but courting the wind, and there is no true profit beneath
12 the sun. And I turned to compare wisdom with delirium and folly, for who
is the man who will criticize the king after he has done what he has done?
13 And I saw that there is some advantage to wisdom over foolishness, like
the advantage of light over darkness. For
14 "the wise man has eyes in his head
while the fool walks in darkness";[4]
yet still I know, the same fate awaits them both.

15 I said to my mind, the fate of the fool awaits me also; why then should I
16 become wiser? And I told my mind that this too is empty breath. For the
wise man, like the fool, leaves no lasting memory. As soon as the coming
days arrive, all is forgotten. How can it be that the wise man dies like the
17 fool? I hated life; this that is done beneath the sun is evil to me. Nothing
but fleeting breath, nothing but courting the wind.

---

3 | Following Ibn Ezra. The word *shidda* occurs only here in Tanakh.

4 | Kohelet sometimes quotes known sayings, here indicated by quotation marks, and then refutes them.

18 And I hated all the toil of my labors beneath the sun; all to be left to some
19 person who will come after me. Who knows whether he will be wise or
foolish; either way, he will lord it over all that I toiled for wisely beneath
20 the sun; that too is empty breath. And I turned toward despair over all
21 the labor which I had toiled at beneath the sun. For so often a person
labors with wisdom and insight and skill – and then bequeaths his share
to someone who has not labored; this too is as empty as breath, and a
22 great evil. For what remains to a person of all the labor and of all the
23 thought that he has expended beneath the sky? All his days are pain, his
occupation bitterness, and even at night his mind does not rest – and this
too is empty breath.

24 There is nothing better for a person to do than to eat and drink and reap
25 some good from his labor; this I saw to be a gift from God. For who will
26 eat, who will hasten to satisfy my craving if not I? He gave wisdom and
insight and joy to those who are satisfied with what they have, but to the
misdirected He gave a preoccupation with gathering and collecting, only
to turn it all over to someone who pleases God. This too is empty breath;
it is courting the wind.

3 1 "Everything has its moment;
a time for every action
beneath the sky."

2 There is a time for birth — and a time for death;
a time to plant — and a time to uproot.
3 A time to kill, — a time to heal;
a time to tear down — and a time to build up.
4 A time to weep, — a time to laugh;
a time for eulogy — and a time for dance.
5 A time to cast away stones, — a time to gather them up;[5]
a time to embrace — and a time to hold back from embracing.
6 A time to seek, — a time to lose;
a time to keep — and a time to cast aside.
7 A time to tear, — a time to sew;
a time for silence — and a time for speech.
8 A time to love, — a time to hate;
a time for war — and a time for peace.

9 What profit then does he who toils gain from all his labor?

10 I have seen the occupation that God gave mortal man to torment himself
11 with. He made everything right in its proper time; He placed all the world
in their minds; yet no one ever fathoms what it is that God is forming from
beginning to end.

---

5 | This may refer to demolishing and constructing a building, or ruining a planting field by throwing stones into it.

12 And so I know that there is nothing better for them than to be happy and
13 to do what is good in their lifetimes. And if a man eats and drinks and reaps
14 some enjoyment from all his labor – that is a gift from God. And I know
that whatever God has made will exist forever.

There is no adding to it,
there is no taking away;
and God has made quite sure that He be feared.
15 That which has been is already here,
and that which will be has already been.
And God is seeking after the pursued.

16 Another thing that I saw beneath the sun:
in the place of justice – there is the evil;
where righteousness is – there evil is found.
17 I said to my mind: God will judge both the righteous and the wicked, for
18 the time will come for every deed, for all that is done; there. And I said to
my mind, as regards mankind: God set them apart only to find that they
19 are nothing but cattle. For the fate of man is the fate of cattle: the same
fate awaits them both, the death of one is like the death of the other, their
spirit is the same, and the preeminence of man over beast is nothing, for it
20 is all no more than empty breath. All end up in the same place; all emerge
21 from dust, and all go back to dust. Who can say that the spirit of man rises
22 on high while the spirit of a beast sinks into the ground? I saw that there
is nothing better for a man than to take pleasure in his work, for that is his
lot. For who will show him what will become of it all when he is gone?

4 1 I turned again and saw all those made victims beneath the sun. There they
were: the victims' tears and none to console them; power in the hands of
2 their oppressors and none to console them. And I praise the dead, who
3 have died already, more than the living who yet live. But better than either
are those who are yet to be, for they have seen none of the evil that is
wrought beneath the sun.

4 And I saw that all the striving and all the skill: it is all but one man's
jealousy of another. This too is empty breath and courting the wind.
5 "The fool crosses his hands
and eats his own flesh."
6 But better a handful gained peacefully,
than two hands full of labor and courting the wind.

7 8 I turned again and saw empty breath beneath the sun. It happens that a
man may be alone, with no fellow, no child even, no brother, yet there is
no end to all his labor. His eye, too, will never see enough of riches; yet he
never asks himself, "For whom, after all, am I laboring and denying myself
goodness?" This too is empty breath and a wretched business.
9 Two are better than one
for they have good return for all their labor.

10 For if one falls down, the other will raise him; but pity the one who falls
11 alone, for who will ever raise him? Two people lying down together are
12 warm, but how can one ever be warm alone? If one man should assault
another, two can stand against him, and a three-stranded thread is not
readily broken.

13 Better a poor but clever youth
than an old and foolish king,
14 who does not know how to take heed anymore. For he may come straight
15 out of debtor's prison to rule, though he was born poor in the old reign. Yes,
I saw all of life moving about beneath the sun, with the next child who will
16 stand in his place.[6] There is no end to this people, to all who came before
them, and those who come after them will likewise never rejoice in him.[7]
This too is empty breath, is courting the wind.

17 Watch your step when you go to the House of God. Better to take heed
than to bring a fool's offering, for they know not what doing wrong means.[8]
5 1 Do not hasten your lips, do not hurry your heart to make a vow in the
presence of God – for God is in heaven while you are here on earth; so let
2 your words be few. For as dreams come of too much preoccupation, so is
a fool's voice known by too many words.

3 If you make a vow to God, do not delay in fulfilling it, for there is no use
4 being a fool – whatever you vow, fulfill. Better not to vow than to vow and
5 not fulfill. Do not let your mouth lead your flesh to sin, and do not tell the
messenger that it was a mistake; why should you have God rage at your
6 words and destroy the work of your hands? For so many dreams and so
much empty breath, so many words – better only to fear God.

7 If you see oppression of a poor person or any perversion of law and justice
in the province, do not wonder at the fact, for every watchman has a
watchman over him, and there are higher ones yet above.[9]

8 Yet the earth below has the advantage over all; even a king is enslaved to
the field.[10]

9 One who loves money will never be satisfied with money, nor one who
10 loves abundance, with produce: that too is fleeting breath. As good things
multiply, so do those who would consume them; and what advantage
11 does it bring its master but longing eyes? The sleep of a worker is sweet

---

6 | The clever youth who will succeed the foolish king.

7 | The new king, even if he is wise and just, will not be acclaimed by the multitude of past or future generations.

8 | They do not understand that it is better to act well than to sin and atone with a meaningless sacrifice.

9 | Have faith that higher authorities will correct injustices.

10 | The meaning of this verse is unclear, perhaps referring to the need or value of cultivating fields.

whether he eats much or little, but the rich man's abundance will not let
him sleep in peace.

12 I have seen a sickly evil beneath the sun: wealth hoarded by its owner, only
13 to harm him. For the wealth is lost in some ill venture, and a child is born
14 to him when he has nothing to his name. Naked as he emerged from his
mother's womb, naked will he return.[11] And not the slightest thing from
all his labor will he retain to take with him.

15 This too is a sickly evil; just as a person comes, so shall he leave again.
16 And what profit does he gain for toiling in the wind? All his days he eats
in darkness with great bitterness, and sickness, and fury.

17 This is what I have seen that is good: to eat and to drink and gain satisfaction
from all the labor at which you toil beneath the sun all the days of the life
18 God has given you – for this is your share. For if God gives any man wealth
and belongings and grants him the power to eat of them, to take hold of
what is his, to take pleasure in the fruits of his labors – that is a gift from
19 God. For he will not much remember the hard days of his life; for God
has given him the joy of his heart to occupy him.

6 1 There is an evil I have seen beneath the sun, and the harm it does people
2 is great. There will be a man to whom God gives wealth and possessions
and honor so that he lacks nothing his heart desires. And then God will
not grant him the power to partake of it, and a stranger will consume it
all; this is empty breath and an evil sickness.

3 A man may have a hundred children and live for many years, and as many
as his years may be, if he is never satisfied with all that goodness – lacking
4 even a burial[12] – I say a stillborn child is better off than he. For he comes
with a breath and leaves in darkness, and in darkness is his name covered
5 over. That child will never see sunlight, will never know a thing, and yet
6 he has more peace than such a man. If a person lives a thousand years
twice over and sees no pleasure – well, do we not all go to the same place
in the end?

7 All of man's labor is only for his mouth; and still his throat is never sated.
8 What advantage does a wise man hold over a fool? And what does an
9 oppressed man profit from knowing how to walk through life? Is it better
for the eyes to see than for the spirit to enjoy? This too is empty breath
and courting the wind.

10 Whatever has been is already named – and it is known by now that this is
11 but a man, who cannot contend with one more powerful than he. There
are so many things, such bountiful production of empty breath, and what
12 profit do they bring to man? For who knows what is good for a man in his

---

11 | See Job 1:21.

12 | The placement of this phrase is problematic. It may refer to the man's burial or to the fact that the stillborn did not receive burials.

lifetime, during the numbered days of his breath that he lives as a shadow;
for who can tell what his fate will be beneath the sun?

7 1 "Better a good name than fine oil."
Better the day of death than of birth.
2 Better to frequent a house of mourning than a feast,
for that is the end of all men,
and the living do well to keep that in mind.
3 Better bitterness than laughter,
for while the face is troubled, the mind is bettering itself.
4 A wise man's heart is in the house of mourning,
and a fool's in the house of celebration.
5 Better to heed the rebuke of the wise
than to hear the song of fools.
6 For fools' cackling
is like the crackling of thorns under the pot.
That too is empty breath.
7 Lucre turns a wise man delirious,
and a gift makes him lose his wisdom.

8 The end of a thing is better than its beginning.
Patience is better than pride.
9 Do not be so quick to anger,
for anger lies in the lap of the fool.
10 Do not say, "What went wrong,
that times gone by were better than these?"
It is not wisdom that leads you to ask.

11 12 Wisdom is better with an estate, though it profits all who see the sun. For
then a man is in the shade of wisdom and the shade of money too. But
the profit of understanding is greater, for wisdom brings life to those who
master it.

13 Consider the acts of God – for nobody can straighten what He has made
14 crooked. On a good day, enjoy the good, and on a bad day consider: God
made both, one alongside the other; and no man can afterward find fault
with Him.

15 I have seen it all in the few days of my breath: righteous men who die in
their righteousness, and wicked ones who live long in their wickedness.
16 So do not be too righteous, and do not seek more wisdom, for why should
17 you become desolate? Do not be too wicked, and never be a fool, for why
18 should you die before your time? Better to hold the one, never loosening
your hand upon the other, for a God-fearing man will heed both warnings.
19 Wisdom gives the wise man more power than ten leaders wield in a city.

20 Yes, there is no one in this world so righteous that he only does good and
21 never sins. Do not take to heart all the words you hear said; do not hear

22 your slave when he insults you. For many times, as your heart well knows,
you yourself have insulted others.

23 I tried all this with my wisdom. I said, "I shall be wiser"; but it was far away
24 from me. All that has ever been is far away, deep beyond fathoming.

25 I turned my mind to understand and to explore, to seek wisdom and
reason; and to know the wickedness of foolishness, to know folly and
delirium.

26 And this is what I found: woman is more bitter than death, for she is all
traps, with nets laid in her heart; her arms are a prison; the man favored by
27 God escapes her while a sinner becomes entrapped. See what I found, said
28 Kohelet, searching one by one to find account. This too my soul sought and
did not find: one righteous man in a thousand I found, but among those
29 few even one such woman I did not. Yes, all that I found is this: that God
created man straightforward; but men go seeking endless accounts.[13]

8 1 Who is like a wise man
able to see meaning?
The wisdom a person has lights up his face,
and his countenance is changed.
2 Obey the king's word, I say,
and the word of your oath to God.
3 Do not take flight; walk clear away;
do not be present when evil is brewing,
for a king will do what it pleases him to do.
4 For a king's word rules,
and who can say to him, "What is it that you do?"
5 One who heeds commands will know no harm,
and a wise mind remembers the time of judgment.
6 For every thing has its time and its judgment –
and great is the evil man must suffer –
7 for man cannot know what will be,
for when it comes who will tell him?
8 Man has no power over the wind –
he cannot cage up the wind;
no one rules on the day of death,
no one will take your place in that battle,
and evil provides no escape for its masters.

9 All this have I seen, and I took it to heart: all that is done here beneath the
10 sun, wherever man wields power over man to harm him. As I looked around,
I saw wicked men coming from the holy place and buried honorably, while
those who acted with decency are forgotten by the town – here again:
11 empty breath. For it is not soon that judgment is passed after evil; and so a

13 | That is, reasons or schemes.

12 person's mind fills up with thoughts of doing evil. A sinner does a hundred
evil deeds and is granted long years for it. Yes, I know that good will come
13 to those who fear God – for fearing Him. And good will not come to an evil
man, and he will not live long – he passes like a shadow, for he does not fear
14 God. Yet see this thing of breath that happens on this earth: the righteous
who suffer the same fate as the wicked; and the wicked who enjoy the same
fate as the righteous – and I say: here again is empty breath.

15 And so I praise joy – for there is nothing as good for man beneath the sun
as to eat and drink and be happy. This is what he has to accompany him in
his labors throughout the life that God has given him beneath the sun.

16 When I set my mind to knowing wisdom, to seeing what it is that is done
17 upon this earth – and all day, all night, no sleep do our eyes see – I saw
all the work of God; I saw that no man can fathom the work that is done
beneath the sun. A person labors to seek it out and will never find it. If a
wise man says he knows – no! And never will he be able to discover it.

9 1 All this I took into my mind, trying to understand all this: that the righteous
and the wise and all their actions – all are in the hand of God. Their love,
2 their hate, none of it is known; it all just unfolds before them. All is as it
is for all. The same fate awaits the righteous and the wicked, the good and
the pure and the impure, the one who brings offerings and the one who
does not. For a good man just as for a sinner, for the one who swears falsely
3 along with the one who fears his oath. This is the evil in all that is done
beneath the sun: the same fate attends everyone. Therefore the hearts of
man contemplate evil; delirium clouds their minds all their lives – and
then they go to join the dead.

4 For anyone still bound to life has something to rely upon:
"Better to be a living dog
than a dead lion."
5 For the living know at least that they must die, while the dead know
nothing.
No longer rewarded for their actions,
their names are forgotten.
6 Their loves, their hates,
their passions – all are already lost.
No longer have they any share,
any part in what is done beneath the sun.

7 Go, eat your bread in joy,
drink your wine with a satisfied heart,
for God has accepted your deeds.
8 Let your clothes at all times be clean;
let your head never lack oil.
9 Enjoy life with the woman you love
all the days of fleeting breath

He has given you here beneath the sun,
for this is your share in life,
your due for all your toil,
all your labor beneath the sun.
10 Whatever you find it in your hands to do –
do that with all your strength.
For there is no action or thought,
no understanding or wisdom,
in Sheol,[14] where you are going.

11 Then I turned again and saw beneath the sun –
that the race is not won by the swift,
nor the war by the mighty;
bread is not promised to the wise,
nor to the intelligent, wealth,
nor to the knowing, favor,
for time and misfortune come to them all.
12 And man never knows when his time will come:
as fish are entrapped in the deadly net,
as birds are trapped in the snare,
so too are people caught at that time of harm
that falls upon them without warning.

13 This too I saw of wisdom beneath the sun – great beyond my understanding.
14 A small town. Few people in it. A great king came and surrounded it and
15 built great siege works all around. And one poor wise man was there to
be found, able to save the whole town by his wisdom. And not a soul
remembered that poor man.

16 And I said: Wisdom is better than might, but the wisdom of a poor man
is scorned, his words go unheeded.

17 The quiet words of the wise are heeded more
than the shout of a ruler among fools.
18 Better wisdom than weaponry –
yet one misjudgment can destroy much that is good.
10 1 Dead flies ferment and putrefy much perfume;
more costly than wisdom, than honor,
is one small dose of foolishness.
2 A wise man's mind is to his right
as the mind of a fool is to his left.
3 Even as he walks his chosen path his mind is lacking,
telling every passerby that he is a fool.

4 If a ruler's spirit turns against you, do not leave your place,
for appeasement can lay great sins to rest.[15]

14 | The netherworld.

15 | Calmness can pacify the ruler.

5 Here is an evil I have seen beneath the sun
like an error coming forth from the ruler's mouth:
6 fools are raised to the greatest heights
while rich men sit in the gutter.
7 I have seen slaves riding on horseback
and princes walking like slaves upon the ground.

8 He who digs the pit may fall into it,
and he who tears down walls – a snake may bite him.
9 He who quarries the stone will come to grief by it,
and he who chops the tree may by that tree be harmed.
10 If the ax grows blunt and is not polished,
then the one who wields it must add force;
for skill yields profit only through wisdom.
11 If the snake bites before he is charmed,
there is no profit to the charmer.

12 The words of the wise bring favor
while the mouth of a fool will swallow him up.
13 His speech begins with foolishness
and ends with evil delirium,
14 yet the fool speaks on and on.
Man does not know what will be;
yes, who may tell him what will come after?
15 The labor of fools exhausts them;
they do not even know the way to town.

16 I pity you, the land whose king is a lad,[16]
whose princes feast from the morning.
17 Happy the land whose king is a nobleman
and whose princes eat at the right time,
like the brave, without drunkenness.
18 "The roof caves in from much laziness,
and hands laid down spring leaks in the house."
19 Feasts are made for laughter, and wine fills life with joy –
and money will answer for everything.

20 Never curse a king, not even in your mind,
nor a rich man, even in your bedchamber,
for a bird of the sky will carry that voice;
a winged creature will repeat the word.
11 1 Cast your bread out onto the waters,
for in the long passage of days you will find it again.
2 Give of what is yours to seven, to eight,
for on this earth you cannot know what evil may yet come.

16 | A servant, not fit to rule.

3 If the clouds fill with rain,
they must empty it onto the earth.
If a tree falls to the south, to the north –
wherever that tree falls, there it will lie.
4 One who waits for the wind will never sow;
one who gazes at the clouds will never reap.[17]
5 And just as you know not the way of the wind,
nor what frame fills a pregnant woman's womb,
so you cannot know the work of God;
and everything is His work.
6 Sow your seeds in the morning,
and come evening do not lay your hands to rest –
for you do not know which will prove fit,
these seeds or those,
or whether the two are as good as one another.
7 There is a sweetness in the light;
it is good for the eyes to see the sun.
8 And should a man live many years,
he should rejoice in all of them,
remembering, too, the days of darkness,
for there will be many.
All that comes is but a breath.

9 Young man, rejoice now in your youth;
let your heart give you pleasure while you are young.
Follow your heart where it leads you,
your eyes where they allure you –
and know that God will bring you to judgment for all this.
10 So clear your heart of bitterness
and free your flesh of pain,
for youth and dark-haired days pass by like breath.
12 1 And remember your Creator
in these days of your youth
before the days of despair,
before years come when you shall say,
"There is nothing here that I desire."
2 Before the sun is darkened and the light,
the moon and stars
and clouds return again after the rain.[18]
3 The day when the guards of the house will shake
and the soldiers buckle,
when the grinders sit idle, grown few,
and the women at the windows sit in darkness.

---

17 | A farmer who waits for perfect weather will never plant or harvest.

18 | These verses may describe, metaphorically, the decline of the body in old age till death and burial.

4 When all the doors in the street are closed
  as the millstone falls silent,
and a man starts up at the sound of a bird,
  but the singing girls' voices drop low.
5 And a man lives in terror of the heights
  and all the pitfalls on the road.
The almond blossoms,
  the grasshopper bears its burden,
    the caper fruit breaks asunder,
but man is departing for his final home,
  and the mourners turn and turn about the streets.
6 Remember – before the silver cord snaps
  and the golden ball plunges downward,
the jug breaks on the edge of the spring,
  the basin is smashed against the well,
7 the dust returns to the earth where it began,
  and the spirit returns to God who gave it.
8 Fleeting breath, says Kohelet.
  It is all mere breath.

9 More – as Kohelet was wise, he also taught the people understanding;
10 and he weighed and explored and assembled many wise sayings. Kohelet
11 sought out choicest words and wrote honest words of truth. The words
of the wise are like goads; like pointed nails are the scholars' sayings. One
12 shepherd gave them all. And further than this, my son, take heed; there
is no end to the making of books, and much study wearies the flesh.

13 The final word: it has all been said. Hold God in awe, and heed His
14 commands, for that is all man has. And all that is done – God shall bring
it to judgment; all that is hidden, the good and the bad.

The final word:
  it has all been said.
Hold God in awe,
  and heed His commands,
    for that is all man has.

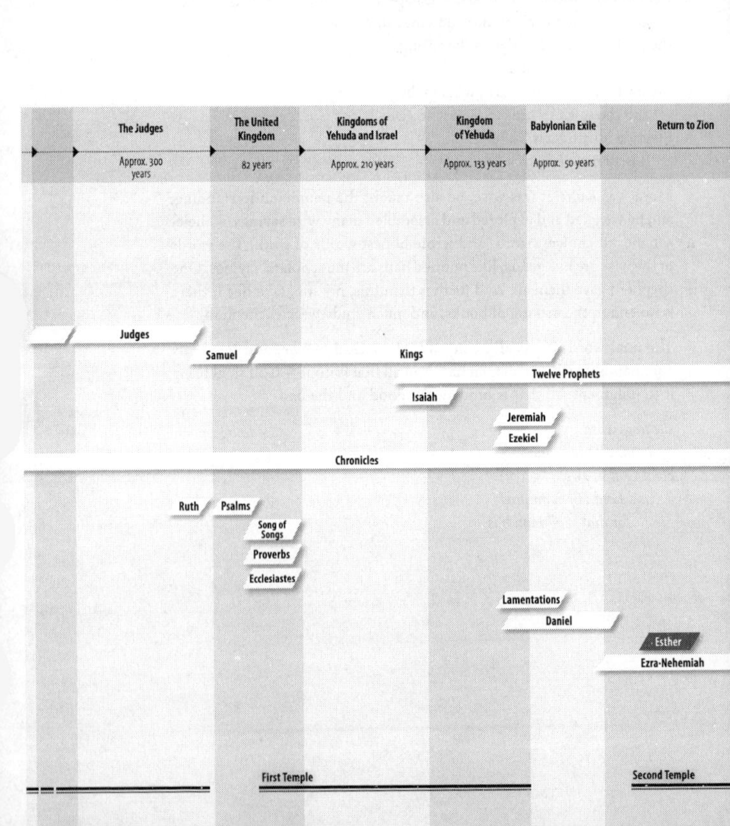
The Judges
Approx. 300 years
The United Kingdom
82 years
Kingdoms of Yehuda and Israel
Approx. 210 years
Kingdom of Yehuda
Approx. 133 years
Babylonian Exile
Approx. 50 years
Return to Zion
Judges
Samuel
Kings
Twelve Prophets
Isaiah
Jeremiah
Ezekiel
Chronicles
Ruth
Psalms
Song of Songs
Proverbs
Ecclesiastes
Lamentations
Daniel
Esther
Ezra-Nehemiah
First Temple
Second Temple

ESTHER/ESTER

ESTHER	Aḥashverosh's party	Choosing a queen to replace Vashti	Haman's decree	Salvation
	Ch. 1	2	3–5	6–10

1 1 It happened in the days of Aḥashverosh – Aḥashverosh who ruled 127
2 provinces from Hodu to Kush. At that time, when King Aḥashverosh sat
3 upon his royal throne in the imperial city of Shushan[1] in the third year of
his rule, he made a feast for his ministers and courtiers, the elite of Persia
4 and Media, all his noblemen and the ministers of his provinces. There, for
many days – 180 days in all – he displayed all the wealth of his noble reign
and the dazzling glory of his greatness.

5 When that time had passed, the king held a feast for all the people of
the imperial city of Shushan, from the greatest to the lowliest, in the
6 courtyard of the king's palace garden. There, swaths of fine fabric – of
precious white cotton and sky-blue wool – were caught up with cords of
the finest linen and purple and draped over silver bars and columns of
marble; and couches of gold and silver were arranged on a terrace paved
7 with alabaster and marble, with mother of pearl and black onyx. And the
guests were served drinks in vessels of gold, vessels unlike any other – royal
8 wine, abundant as the king's largesse. And the drinking followed a rule of
no duress, for the king had thus instructed all the overseers of his home:
honor the wishes of each and every man.

9 Meanwhile Vashti the queen made a feast of her own, a women's feast in
10 King Aḥashverosh's royal palace. And on the seventh day, when the king
had grown merry with wine, he instructed Mehuman, Bizta, Ḥarvona,
Bigta and Avagta, Zetar and Karkas – the seven eunuchs who attended
11 King Aḥashverosh – to bring Vashti the queen before the king in her royal
crown, to show the peoples and the ministers her charms, for she was
12 beautiful indeed. But Queen Vashti refused to come at the king's word,
conveyed through the eunuchs. So fury engulfed the king, and his rage
blazed inside him.

13 Now the king addressed the wise men, those well versed in procedure – for
it was the king's practice to consult with those who knew the law and
14 the statutes; and those closest to him were Karshena, Shetar, Admata,
Tarshish, Meres, Marsena, and Memukhan, the seven ministers of Persia
and Media who came freely into the king's presence and occupied the
15 highest positions in the realm. What, he asked, would the law have them
do with Queen Vashti for refusing to obey the word of King Aḥashverosh
as conveyed to her by the eunuchs?

16 And Memukhan replied before the king and the ministers: "It is not only
the king that Vashti the queen has wronged, but all the ministers and all
17 the peoples in all the provinces of King Aḥashverosh. For this tale of the
queen will go out to all the women, who will cast their husbands into their
contempt when they say, 'King Aḥashverosh commanded Vashti the queen
18 to be brought before him, but she did not come!' Yes, this very day, all the

---

1 | Shushan (Susa) was the main administrative capital of the Persian Empire. The imperial city (*bira*) of Shushan is the acropolis, and the "town of Shushan" (3:15) is the lower city.

ministers' wives of Persia and Media, who have heard what the queen did,
will tell all the king's ministers, and there will be no end to the contempt
and the fury.

19 "If, then, it so please the king, let a royal declaration be sent out from
him and be written among the laws of Persia and Media, never to be
contravened – that Vashti shall come no more before King Aḥashverosh
and that the king shall give her royal position to a woman who is better
20 than she. And the royal decree that the king will issue shall be heard in all
his empire, vast as it is: that all women must honor their husbands, from
the greatest of them to the least."

21 The proposal pleased the king and the ministers, and the king accepted
22 Memukhan's word. He sent scrolls to all the king's provinces – province
by province, each in its script, and people by people, each in its language –
ruling that every man must be master in his home, speaking the language
of his own people.

2 1 Some time later, when King Aḥashverosh's rage had subsided, he remembered
2 Vashti, and what she had done, and what had been decreed against her. The
king's attendants, those who served him closely, said, "Let beautiful young
3 virgins be sought for the king; let the king appoint officers in all the provinces
of his realm to gather every beautiful young virgin to the imperial city of
Shushan, to the harem, into the charge of Hegeh, the king's eunuch, the keeper
4 of the maidens, to be given their ointments there. Whichever young woman
the king likes best – let her become queen in Vashti's place!" The suggestion
pleased the king, and that is what he did.

5 Now there was a Jewish man in the imperial city of Shushan, and his name
was Mordekhai son of Yair son of Shimi son of Kish of the tribe of Binyamin.
6 He had been exiled from Jerusalem among the exiles expelled with Yekhonya,
7 king of Yehuda – exiled by Nevukhadnetzar, king of Babylon.[2] And Mordekhai was guardian to Hadasa – Esther – his uncle's daughter, for she had
no father or mother. The girl was lovely and beautiful, and when her father
8 and mother had died, Mordekhai had adopted her as his own child. When
the king's word and his law were heard, and vast numbers of young women
were gathered in the imperial city of Shushan into the charge of Hegai, Esther
too was taken to the king's palace into the charge of Hegai, the keeper of the
women.

9 The young woman pleased him, and she carried kindness with her, and
he hastened to give her all her ointments and meals and the seven young
maids from the king's palace to whom she was entitled; and he moved her
10 and her maids to the best of the royal maidens' quarters. And Esther made
no mention of her people or her birth, for Mordekhai had instructed her
11 strictly not to reveal them. But every single day Mordekhai would walk

2 | See II Kings 24:8–17.

around before the harem courtyard to find out whether Esther was well
and what was being done with her.

12 As each young woman would reach her turn to come before King
Aḥashverosh – after twelve months following her beauty regime, for that
was how many the days of their ointments were: six months in myrrh
13 oil and six months in perfumes and the women's ointments – the young
woman would come before the king. All that she asked for would be
given her to bring with her from the royal harem to the palace of the king.
14 She would enter in the evening, and in the morning she would return to
the royal harem, passing into the charge of Shaashgaz, the king's eunuch,
keeper of the concubines. Then she would come no more before the king
unless he desired her and she was called for by name.

15 When the time came for Esther daughter of Aviḥayil – Mordekhai's
uncle – whom Mordekhai had adopted as his own child, to come before
the king, she did not ask for anything except for what Hegai, the king's
eunuch, keeper of the women, told her to bring. Yet Esther carried grace
in the eyes of all who saw her.

16 Esther was taken to King Aḥashverosh, to his royal palace, in the tenth
17 month, the month of Tevet, in the seventh year of his reign. And the king
loved Esther more than all the other women, and she pleased him and
carried grace and kindness with her, more so than all the other virgins;
and he placed a royal crown upon her head and made her queen in Vashti's
18 place. And the king made a great feast for all his ministers and courtiers:
the feast of Esther. And he granted the provinces both a remission of their
dues and gifts as vast as the king's largesse.

19 As the virgins were gathered in for a second time, Mordekhai was sitting at
20 the King's Gate. Esther had not told of her birth or of her people, just as
Mordekhai had instructed her; for Esther still heeded Mordekhai's words,
just as she had when she had lived under his care.

21 As Mordekhai sat at the King's Gate at that time, fury engulfed Bigtan and
Teresh, two of the king's eunuchs, guards of the threshold, and they plotted
22 to lay their hands on King Aḥashverosh. But Mordekhai learned of the plot
and conveyed the knowledge to Queen Esther, and Esther told the king
23 in Mordekhai's name. The matter was investigated and found to be true,
and the two men were hung from a post;[3] and the story was written down
before the king in the scroll of the chronicles.

3 1 Some time after this, King Aḥashverosh promoted Haman son of Hamedata
the Agagite,[4] raising him to a seat above those of all his fellow ministers.
2 And all the king's courtiers serving at the King's Gate would kneel and bow

3 | The Persians "hung up" or impaled executed corpses for public display; cf. Deuteronomy 21:22–23.

4 | Descended from Amalek (see 1 Sam., ch. 15).

before Haman, for so had the king instructed, but Mordekhai would neither
3 kneel nor bow down. So the king's courtiers serving at the King's Gate
would ask Mordekhai, "Why do you not obey the king's command?"

4 When, day after day, they said this to him and he paid no attention, they
reported the matter to Haman, interested to see whether Mordekhai's word
5 would stand – for he had explained that he was a Jew. And Haman noticed
that Mordekhai, indeed, did not kneel or bow down before him, and it
6 filled Haman with rage. The thought of laying his hands only on Mordekhai
filled him with contempt, for they had told him who Mordekhai's people
were. No, Haman sought to destroy all of the Jews, all of Mordekhai's
people, all across the empire of Aḥashverosh.

7 And so in the first month, the month of Nisan, of the twelfth year of King
Aḥashverosh's reign, a *pur* – lots, in other words – was cast before Haman,
day for day and month for month, and it fell to the twelfth month, the
month of Adar.

8 Haman then spoke to King Aḥashverosh: "There is one people, scattered
and dispersed among the peoples across all the provinces of your realm,
whose laws are different from those of all the other peoples, and who do
not obey the king's own laws, and it really is not worth the king's while to
9 leave them so. If it so please the king, let it be decreed in writing to destroy
them, and I shall weigh out ten thousand talents of silver into the hands of
the administrators, to be delivered to the king's treasury."

10 The king removed the ring from his finger and gave it to Haman son of
11 Hamedata the Agagite, enemy of the Jews. And the king said to Haman,
"The silver is yours, and so is the people: do with them as you will."

12 The king's scribes were called on the thirteenth day of the first month, and
all that Haman commanded the king's viceroys, the administrators of every
single province and the ministers of every single people, was written to
province by province, each in its script, to people by people, each in its
language – written in the name of King Aḥashverosh and sealed with the
13 king's ring. Scrolls were sent out with the runners to all the provinces of
the king ruling that they kill, destroy, and annihilate all the Jews, young
and old, children and women alike, all in one day – the thirteenth day of
the twelfth month, which is the month of Adar – and seize the plunder.
14 The text of that letter was to be laid down as law in each and every province,
15 displayed for every people to see, to make them ready for that day. The
runners rushed out at the king's word, and the law was laid down in the
imperial city of Shushan. The king and Haman sat down to drink – and
the town of Shushan stood aghast.

4 1 Mordekhai understood all that had happened, and he tore his clothes
and dressed himself in sackcloth and ashes; and he walked out to the
2 middle of the town, crying out, a loud and bitter cry. He came as far
as the entrance to the King's Gate, for no one may enter the King's

3 Gate dressed in sackcloth. And in every single province, wherever the
king's word and law extended, deep mourning prevailed among the Jews,
fasting and weeping and grief; the multitudes lay down upon sackcloth
and ashes.

4 Esther's young maids and her eunuchs came and told her of this, and the
queen's whole body shook. She sent clothes for Mordekhai to put on, to
lay aside the sackcloth he was wearing, but he would not accept them.
5 So Esther called Hatakh, one of the king's eunuchs assigned to her, and
instructed him to go and speak to Mordekhai to find out what all this
6 was and why. Hatakh went out to Mordekhai, to the town square before
7 the King's Gate, and Mordekhai told him all that had happened to him,
and all about the silver that Haman had promised to have weighed out
8 to the king's treasury in return for the right to destroy the Jews. And
he gave him the text of the decree that had been issued in Shushan to
annihilate them, telling him to show it to Esther and to speak to her,
instructing her strictly to go to the king and plead with him, to implore
him to help her people.

9 10 Hatakh came and told Esther what Mordekhai had said. And Esther told
11 Hatakh, instructing him to repeat her words to Mordekhai: "All the king's
courtiers and all the people of his provinces know that there is only one
law for any man or woman who comes before the king, into the inner
courtyard, without being called: to be killed. Unless, that is, the king
extends the golden scepter toward him so that he may live on. As for me – I
12 have not been called to come before the king these thirty days past." And
they told Mordekhai what Esther had said.

13 Mordekhai sent back his reply to Esther: "Do not imagine that you can
14 escape to the king's palace from the fate of all the Jews. For if you keep
your silence at this time, relief and salvation will come forth for the Jews
from some other place, but you and your father's house will be lost forever.
And who can say; could it not be for just such a time as this that you came
into royalty?"

15 16 Esther sent back word to Mordekhai: "Go – gather all the Jews in Shushan
and fast for me: do not eat and do not drink for three whole days, day or
night; I and my maids will fast also. So shall I come before the king in
defiance of the law – and if I am lost, I am lost."

17 Mordekhai walked away; and he did all that Esther had instructed him
to do.

5 1 On the third day, Esther dressed herself in royalty and came to stand in
the inner courtyard of the king's palace, facing the king's palace, while
the king sat upon his royal throne in the great hall, facing the palace
2 entrance. When the king noticed Queen Esther standing in the courtyard,
she carried grace in his eyes, so the king extended the golden scepter in his

hand toward Esther, and Esther came forward and touched the scepter's
3 end. And the king said to her, "What brings you, Esther, my queen? And
what would you ask? Be it even half my kingdom, it shall be yours."

4 Esther said, "If it so please the king, may the king and Haman come today
to the feast that I have prepared for him."

5 And the king called out, "Make Haman hurry to carry out Esther's word!"
And the king and Haman came to the feast that Esther had prepared.

6 At that drinking feast, the king said to Esther, "What is your desire, then?
It shall be yours. What would you ask? Be it even half my kingdom, it shall
be done."

7 8 And Esther answered: "This is my desire and my request," she said. "If I
have the king's favor, and if it so please the king to grant what I desire, to
honor my request – let the king and Haman come again to the feast that I
shall prepare for them. And tomorrow I shall do as the king asks."

9 Haman went out on that day, happy and buoyant of heart. But when he
saw Mordekhai at the King's Gate, and when Mordekhai did not stand up
and did not tremble in his presence, Haman was filled with rage against
10 him. Yet Haman restrained himself until he reached his home, and then
11 he sent for all his friends and for his wife, Zeresh. And Haman told them
of his glorious wealth and the great number of his sons and all the ways
the king had elevated him and raised him above all the other ministers
12 and courtiers of the king. Finally Haman said, "And Esther brought no
one else but me with the king to the feast that she made, and tomorrow
13 too I am invited to her along with the king. Yet all this is worth nothing to
me whenever I see that Jew Mordekhai sitting there at the King's Gate."

14 Zeresh his wife replied, along with all his friends: "Let a post be erected full
fifty cubits high. In the morning, say the word to the king, and Mordekhai
shall be hung up from it. Then you will go happy to the feast with the king."
The idea pleased Haman, and he erected the post.

6 1 The king slept fitfully that night. He called for the scroll of the records, the
chronicles, to be brought to him, and they were read aloud before him.
2 There it was found written that Mordekhai had reported Bigtan and Teresh,
two of the king's eunuchs, guards of the threshold, who had planned to lay
3 hands upon King Aḥashverosh. The king said, "What honor or greatness
has been granted Mordekhai for doing this?" and the king's pages, those
who were attending him, said, "Nothing at all has been done for him."

4 "Who is in the courtyard?" asked the king. Haman had come to the
outer courtyard of the king's palace to speak to the king about hanging
5 Mordekhai on the post he had prepared for him. The king's pages said to
him, "Ah, there is Haman standing in the courtyard," and the king said,
"Show him in!"

6 In Haman came, and the king asked him, "What should be done for a man
the king wishes to honor?" Said Haman to himself, "Whom could the king
wish to honor more than me?"

7 8 So Haman told the king: "The man the king wishes to honor – let the
clothes of royalty be brought forth, clothes that the king himself has worn,
9 and a horse on which the king has ridden, on its head a royal crown; and
let these clothes and this horse be entrusted to one of the king's noble
ministers to dress the man the king wishes to honor. And let him lead
that man, riding on the horse, across the town square, crying out before
him as they go, 'This is what is done for the man whom the king wishes
to honor!'"

10 "Hurry!" said the king to Haman. "Take the clothes and the horse as you
have said, and do just that for Mordekhai the Jew, who sits at the King's
Gate – let no detail fall short of what you have described!"

11 So Haman took the clothes and the horse and dressed Mordekhai and led
him across the town square, crying out before him as they went, "This is
what is done for the man whom the king wishes to honor!"

12 Then Mordekhai returned to the King's Gate, and Haman rushed back
13 to his house grief stricken, covering his face. Haman told his wife Zeresh
and all his friends all that had happened to him, and his wise men with his
wife Zeresh said, "If this Mordekhai before whom you have begun to fall
is of Jewish blood, you will not overcome him; you will fall, you must fall
14 before him –" they were still speaking when the king's eunuchs arrived to
fetch Haman, with fearful haste, to the feast that Esther had prepared.

7 1 2 So the king and Haman arrived to drink with Queen Esther. On that
second day also, at the drinking feast, the king said to Esther, "What is
your desire, Esther, my queen? It shall be yours. What would you ask? Be
it even half my kingdom, it shall be done."

3 And Queen Esther answered: "If I have your favor, my king," she said, "and
if it so please the king – let me have my life as my desire, my people as my
4 request. For we have been sold, my people and I, to be killed, destroyed,
and annihilated. Had we but been sold as slaves and bondwomen, I would
have kept my silence, for that anguish is not worth any loss to the king."

5 King Aḥashverosh spoke; he said to Esther the queen: "Who is it – which
one – who put it into his heart to do such a thing?!"

6 "It is a foe, an enemy," said Esther, "this vicious man: Haman!" And Haman
7 was suddenly terrified before the king and the queen. The king rose up in
his rage and left the wine feast for the palace garden as Haman stood up
to entreat for his life with Esther the queen, for he saw that the king was
8 already set upon his downfall. By the time the king came back from the
palace garden to the feasting chamber, Haman had thrown himself onto

Esther's couch – "What!" said the king. "Would you take the queen too, and with me in the palace?!" The words came forth from the king's mouth, and Haman's face was covered over.

9 One of the eunuchs, Ḥarvona, said to the king, "You know, the post Haman prepared for Mordekhai, who spoke up so well for the king, is standing now in Haman's house, fifty cubits high." And the king said, "Hang him from it!"

10 Thus was Haman hung up from the very post he had prepared for Mordekhai – and the king's rage subsided.

8 1 On that day, King Aḥashverosh granted Queen Esther the entire estate
of Haman, enemy of the Jews, and Mordekhai came before the king, for
2 Esther had finally revealed what he was to her. The king took off the very
ring that he had once given to Haman and gave it instead to Mordekhai,
and Esther appointed Mordekhai to govern Haman's estate.

3 But then Esther spoke to the king again, falling down at his feet, weeping
and pleading with him to overturn the wickedness of Haman the Agagite
4 and the plot that he had thought up against the Jews. The king extended
his golden scepter to Esther, and Esther raised herself up and stood before
5 the king. She said, "If it so please the king, and if I have his favor, and if it
seems right to the king and I am pleasing in his eyes – let the decree be
written to revoke the scrolls that were the plot of Haman son of Hamedata
the Agagite, who wrote to destroy all the Jews in all the king's provinces.
6 For how can I live to see the evil that will come upon my people; how can
I live to see the loss of those I am born of?"

7 King Aḥashverosh said to Queen Esther and to Mordekhai the Jew, "Look,
I have given Esther Haman's estate, and he has been hung from the post
8 for laying hands upon the Jews. Now, write whatever you like about the
Jews in the king's name and seal it with the king's ring – but no writing
that has been written in the name of the king and sealed with the king's
ring can ever be revoked."

9 So at that time, the king's scribes were called – on the twenty-third day
of the third month, the month of Sivan – and they wrote down all that
Mordekhai dictated, to the Jews and to the viceroys, the administrators,
and the ministers of all the provinces from Hodu to Kush, 127 provinces,
to province by province, each in its script, to people by people, each in
10 its language, and to the Jews in their script and in their language. It was
written in the name of King Aḥashverosh and sealed with the king's ring,
and the scrolls were sent with the horseback runners, riding the swift
11 horses of the royal stable, the offspring of the royal mares, to convey
that the king had granted the Jews in every single town the right to come
together to stand up and defend their lives, to kill, destroy, and annihilate
all the armed hordes of the peoples and provinces who threatened them,

12 even the children and women, and to loot plunder, all on one day, the
thirteenth day of the twelfth month – the month of Adar – in all the
13 provinces of King Aḥashverosh. The text of that decree was to lay down
the law in every single province, displayed for every people to see, that
the Jews should make themselves ready for that day to wreak vengeance
14 on their enemies. The runners, riding the swift horses of the royal service,
galloped out at great speed, spurred on at the king's word, and the law was
laid down in the imperial city of Shushan.

15 So Mordekhai left the king's presence in royal clothes of sky-blue wool
and fine white fabric, wearing a great coronet of gold and a mantle of finest
linen and purple, and the town of Shushan was filled with jubilation and
16 happiness. And the Jews basked in light and happiness, joy and great honor.
17 And in each and every province, in each and every town, as far as the king's
word and law reached, happiness and joy touched the Jews, with feasting
and a holiday; and many of the local people joined the Jews, for awe of the
Jews had overwhelmed them.

9 1 On the thirteenth day of the twelfth month, the month of Adar, when the
king's word and his law were to come into effect, on the day when the Jews'
enemies had hoped to overcome them – it all was turned around, as the Jews
2 themselves overcame those who hated them. The Jews came together in their
cities throughout the provinces of King Aḥashverosh to lay hands upon those
who sought their harm, and no man could stand before them, for fear of them
3 had fallen upon all nations. And the ministers of the provinces, the viceroys
and the governors, and the administrators of the king's court, all promoted
4 the Jews, for fear of Mordekhai had fallen on them. For Mordekhai was great
now in the king's palace, and word of him was spreading to all the provinces:
this man, this Mordekhai, was becoming ever greater.

5 The Jews dealt all their enemies a terrible blow, of sword and slaughter and
6 destruction; they did whatever they pleased to those who hated them. In the
imperial city of Shushan the Jews killed and destroyed five hundred men, and
7 they killed Parshandata and
Dalfon and
Aspata and
8 Porata and
Adalya and
Aridata and
9 Parmashta and
Arisai and
Aridai and
10 Vayzata, the ten sons of Haman son of Hamedata, enemy of the Jews – but
they did not touch the plunder.

11 On that same day, the number of those killed in the imperial city of
12 Shushan was brought to the king, and the king said to Queen Esther, "The

Jews have killed five hundred men in the imperial city of Shushan alone,
as well as Haman's ten sons – what must they have done in the rest of the
king's provinces? And now, what is your desire? It shall be yours. What
13 would you ask further? It shall be done." Esther said, "If it so please the
king, may the Jews of Shushan be granted tomorrow also to do as they
14 did today, and let Haman's ten sons be hung from the post." Thus the
king commanded; the law was laid down in Shushan, and Haman's ten
15 sons were hung up. And the Jews of Shushan gathered on the fourteenth
day of Adar also and killed three hundred men in Shushan, never once
touching the plunder.

16 Meanwhile, the rest of the Jews in the king's provinces, having come
together and stood up to defend their lives, found rest from their enemies,
killing seventy-five thousand of those who hated them, though they did
17 not touch the plunder. That was on the thirteenth day of the month of
Adar. On the fourteenth day they rested, and they made it a day of feasting
and happiness.

18 The Jews who were in Shushan came together both on the thirteenth
and on the fourteenth, and rested on the fifteenth, and made that a day
19 of feasting and happiness. Thus it came about that provincial Jews living
in unwalled towns make the fourteenth day of the month of Adar a day
of happiness, of feasting and festivity, and of sending one another good
things to eat.

20 Mordekhai wrote all this down and sent scrolls to all the Jews in all the
21 provinces of King Aḥashverosh, near and far, to establish among them that
they should mark the fourteenth and fifteenth days of Adar every single
22 year: the days when the Jews rested from their enemies and the month
that was turned for them from sorrow to happiness, from mourning to
celebration – to make them days of feasting, happiness, sending one
23 another good things to eat, and giving gifts to the poor. And so the Jews
accepted upon themselves what they had already begun to perform and
all that Mordekhai had written to them.

24 For Haman son of Hamedata the Agagite, enemy of all the Jews, had
plotted against the Jews to destroy them, and had drawn the *pur* – lots – to
25 consume and to destroy them. When this came before the king, he declared
by the scroll that the evil plot Haman had hatched against the Jews must
come down upon his own head, and that he and his sons must be hung
from the post.

26 So these days were named Purim after the *pur*. So, following the words
27 of the letter and what they had seen and what had befallen them, they
established and accepted, for themselves and for their children, and for all
who would ever come to join their ranks, that they would keep these two
days, never to be neglected, as they are prescribed and at the right times,
28 every single year. Indeed, these days are remembered and marked in every

single generation, family by family, province upon province, town upon
town; and these days of Purim will never be neglected by the Jews, nor
will their memory ever cease to be among their children.

29 And Queen Esther daughter of Aviḥayil, together with Mordekhai the Jew,
30 wrote with all their authority to confirm this second letter of Purim. They
sent out scrolls to all the Jews across 127 provinces – all of Aḥashverosh's
31 realm – words of peace and truth. The scrolls were to confirm these days of
Purim in their times just as Mordekhai the Jew and Esther the queen had
fixed them, and indeed as they had all fixed their fast days and entreaties,
32 for themselves and for their children. Esther's words confirmed this
practice of Purim, and it was written down in the scroll.

10 1 As for King Aḥashverosh, he levied a tribute from the people of all the
2 land and of the islands of the sea. And the full account of his authority and
might, and all the greatness of Mordekhai, whom the king exalted – are
they not already written in the scroll of the chronicles of the kings of
3 Media and Persia? For Mordekhai the Jew was second in command to
King Aḥashverosh and revered too among the Jews – beloved of all
the multitudes of his brothers, working for the good of his people, and
speaking words of peace for all his children.

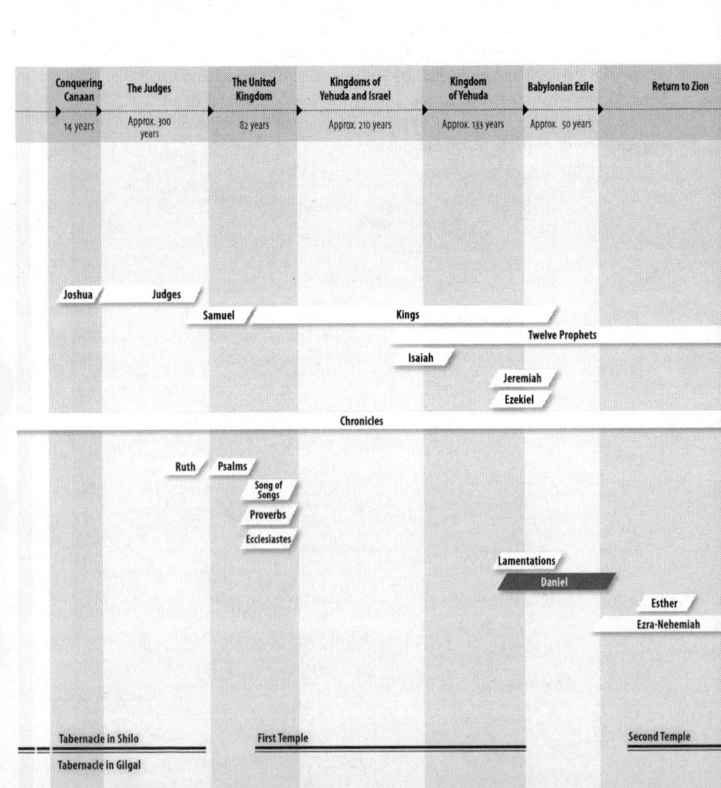

Conquering Canaan
14 years
The Judges
Approx. 300 years
The United Kingdom
82 years
Kingdoms of Yehuda and Israel
Approx. 210 years
Kingdom of Yehuda
Approx. 133 years
Babylonian Exile
Approx. 50 years
Return to Zion
Joshua
Judges
Samuel
Kings
Twelve Prophets
Isaiah
Jeremiah
Ezekiel
Chronicles
Ruth
Psalms
Song of Songs
Proverbs
Ecclesiastes
Lamentations
Daniel
Esther
Ezra-Nehemiah
Tabernacle in Shilo
Tabernacle in Gilgal
First Temple
Second Temple

DANIEL

DANIEL	Daniel, Ḥananya, Mishael, and Azarya in the Babylonian exile	Daniel and his friends entangled with the kings Nevukhadnetzar, Belshatzar, and Daryavesh	Daniel's visions and his prayer
	Ch. 1	2–7	8–12

1 1 In the third year of the reign of Yehoyakim, the king of Yehuda,
Nevukhadnetzar, the king of Babylon, came to Jerusalem and besieged
2 it. The LORD handed Yehoyakim, the king of Yehuda, over to him, along
with some of the vessels of the House of God, which he then carried off
to the land of Shinar,[1] to the temple of his god, and he brought the vessels
to the treasury of his god.

3 The king told Ashpenaz, his chief eunuch, to bring some Israelites, some of
4 royal lineage and some of the nobility – youths without blemish, attractive,
and adept in all wisdoms, who are lovers of knowledge and astute in
understanding, and disciplined enough to serve in the king's palace – and
5 to teach them the literature and language of the Chaldeans. The king
allotted them a daily portion of the king's food and of the wine that he
drank, and three years to train them, at the end of which some of them
6 would serve the king. Now among them were some Jews: Daniel, Ḥananya,
7 Mishael, and Azarya. The chief of the eunuchs renamed them: He called
Daniel Belteshatzar; Ḥananya, Shadrakh; Mishael, Meishakh; and Azarya
became Aved Nego.

8 Daniel resolved in his heart not to defile himself with the king's food or
with the wine that he drank. He requested permission from the chief
9 of the eunuchs that he not defile himself. Now God had given Daniel
10 the kindness and sympathy of the chief of the eunuchs. The chief of the
eunuchs said to Daniel, "I am afraid of my lord the king, who has allotted
your food and drink. If he should notice that you look more wretched in
comparison with the other youths your age, you would be endangering
11 my head with the king." Daniel said to the steward whom the chief of
the eunuchs had appointed over Daniel, Ḥananya, Mishael, and Azarya:
12 "Please, test your servants for ten days. Let them give us vegetables to eat
13 and water to drink. Then compare our appearance and the appearance
of the youths who eat from the king's food. In accordance with what you
14 observe, so shall you treat your servants." He acceded to their request and
15 tested them for ten days. And at the end of ten days they looked better and
healthier in appearance than all the youths who had been eating the king's
16 food. So the steward would take away the royal food and the wine they
17 were supposed to drink and would give them vegetables. As for all of these
four youths, God gave them knowledge and proficiency in all literature and
wisdom, and Daniel understood every kind of vision as well as dreams.

18 Now at the end of the time the king had allotted to bring them forth, the
19 chief of the eunuchs brought them before Nevukhadnetzar. The king
spoke with them, and out of all of them, not one was found to compare
with Daniel, Ḥananya, Mishael, and Azarya. They served in the king's
20 presence. And in every matter of wise understanding that the king sought
from them, he found them ten times better than all the magicians and

1 | Referring to Babylon; see Genesis 11:2.

21 exorcists throughout his kingdom. Daniel remained there until the first
year of King Koresh.

2 1 And in the second year of the reign of Nevukhadnetzar, Nevukhadnetzar
dreamed dreams; his spirit was troubled, and sleep was a struggle for him.
2 The king gave orders to summon the magicians and the exorcists and the
sorcerers and the Chaldeans to tell the king about his dreams. They arrived
and stood before the king.

3 The king said to them, "I dreamed a dream and my spirit was troubled to
4 understand the dream." The Chaldeans spoke to the king in Aramaic:[2] "O
king, live forever! Tell the dream to your servants and we will reveal its
5 interpretation." The king answered and said to the Chaldeans: "This matter
is decided as far as I am concerned: unless you make known to me the
dream and its interpretation, you shall be dismembered and your houses
6 turned into wreckage. But if you tell the dream and its interpretation, you
shall receive gifts and rewards and great honor from me, so tell me the
dream and its meaning."

7 They answered a second time and said, "Let the king tell the dream to his
8 servants and we will reveal its interpretation." The king answered and said,
"I know for sure that you are buying time, since you see that the matter
9 is already decided as far as I am concerned: unless you make the dream
known to me, there is one verdict for all of you, for you have conspired to
utter false and corrupt words before me until time passes. Therefore, tell
me the dream so that I can know that you can tell me its interpretation."

10 The Chaldeans answered the king and said: "There is no man on earth who
could address the king's concern, nor has any great or mighty king asked
11 such a thing of any magician, exorcist, or Chaldean. And the thing that the
king asks is difficult; there is no one else who could tell it before the king
12 except the gods, whose dwelling place is not with flesh." In response to
this, the king became enraged and very furious and he commanded that
all the wise men of Babylon be slain.

13 And the decree went forth and the wise men were about to be killed,
14 and Daniel and his companions were about to be killed.To this Daniel
responded with advice and reason to Aryokh, the chief executioner of
15 the king, who had gone forth to kill the wise men of Babylon. He spoke
and asked Aryokh, the king's officer, "Why this cruel decree from the
16 king?" Then Aryokh made the matter known to Daniel. So Daniel came
and requested of the king that he be given time to tell the interpretation
17 to the king.Then Daniel went to his house and made the matter known to
18 his companions Ḥananya, Mishael, and Azarya, so they might seek mercy
from the God of the heavens concerning this mystery, so that they would

---

2 | At this point the text switches from Hebrew to Aramaic until chapter 8.

not kill Daniel and his companions along with the rest of the wise men
of Babylon.

19 Then the secret was revealed to Daniel in a night vision, after which Daniel
20 blessed the God of the heavens. Daniel spoke and said: "May the name
of God be blessed from always to forevermore, for wisdom and power are
21 His. He changes the seasons and times, He deposes kings and enthrones
kings. He gives wisdom to the wise and knowledge to insightful knowers.
22 He reveals deep and hidden things. He knows what is in the darkness, and
23 light dwells with Him. To You, O God of my fathers, I give thanks and
praise, for now You have given me wisdom and power, for You have made
known to me that which we asked of You, for You have made known to us
the dream matter of the king."

24 Thereupon Daniel went to Aryokh, whom the king had appointed to kill
the wise men of Babylon; he went and said this to him: "Do not kill the
wise men of Babylon. Bring me before the king and I will tell him the
25 interpretation." So Aryokh, in great haste, brought Daniel before the king
and this is what he said to him: "I have found a man from the exiles of
Yehuda who can make known the interpretation to the king."

26 The king responded and said to Daniel, whose name was Belteshatzar, "Are
you able to make known to me the dream that I saw and its interpretation?"
27 Daniel answered the king and said: "The secret that the king demands is
28 one that no wise man, exorcist, magician, or diviner can tell the king, but
there is a God in heaven who reveals secrets, and He has made known to
the king Nevukhadnetzar what will come to pass at the end of days. Your
29 dream and the vision in your head while in bed is as follows: You, O king,
your thoughts arose when you were in bed, about what will come to pass
hereafter, and He who reveals secrets has made known to you that which
30 shall come to pass. But as for me, it is not because of any wisdom that I
have beyond other living things that this secret was revealed to me; rather
it was so that the interpretation be made known to the king, so that you
know the thoughts of your heart.

31 "You, O king, were looking, and – behold! – there was a huge figure. This
figure was great and its brightness was extraordinary. It was standing
32 facing you, and its appearance was terrifying. The head of this figure was
of fine gold, its breast and its arms were of silver, and its belly and thighs
33 were of bronze, its legs were of iron, its feet were partly of iron and partly
34 of clay. As you watched, a stone was carved out – not by hands – and it
smote the figure on its iron and clay feet, and smashed them into pieces.
35 Then, all at once, the iron, the clay, the brass, the silver, and the gold
shattered and became like the chaff of a summer's threshing floor; and
the wind carried them off, and no trace of them was found anywhere.
And the stone that smote the figure became a great mountain and filled
the whole earth.

36 37 "This is the dream; now we will relate its meaning before the king. You, O
king, king of kings, to whom the God of the heavens has given a kingdom
38 of strength, power, and prestige, and wherever dwell human beings, the
beasts of the field and the birds of the sky, He has put them in your hand
39 and made you ruler of them all: you are the head of gold. And after you
shall arise another kingdom, inferior to you, and another, third kingdom
40 of bronze, which will rule the whole earth. And the fourth kingdom will be
as strong as iron, in the way that iron smashes and pulverizes everything;
and just as iron shatters all other materials, so shall this kingdom shatter
41 and crush. And as for your having seen that the feet and toes were partly
of potter's clay and partly of iron: it shall be a divided kingdom, but some
resilience of iron shall be in it, just as you saw there was iron mixed into
42 the muddy clay. And just as the toes of the feet were part iron and part clay,
43 the kingdom will be partly strong and partly brittle. And as for your having
seen the iron mixed into muddy clay, the parts will mingle via procreation
but they will not hold fast together, just as iron does not mix into clay.
44 And during the days of these kings, the God of the heavens shall set up a
kingdom which shall never be destroyed, and this kingdom will never be
abandoned to the rule of any other nation; rather it will smash and put an
45 end to all these kingdoms, and it will last forever, in the way that you saw
a stone being carved out of the mountain without hands it smashed the
iron, the bronze, the clay, the silver, and the gold. A great God has made
known to the king what will happen hereafter. And the dream is certain
and its interpretation is precise."

46 Then the king Nevukhadnetzar fell upon his face and paid homage to
Daniel, and commanded that grain and wine offerings be proffered to
47 him. The king responded to Daniel and said, "Truly your God is the God
of gods and the ruler of kings and the revealer of secrets, for you have
48 been able to reveal this secret." Then the king exalted Daniel and gave him
many great gifts and made him ruler over the whole province of Babylon
49 and the chief officer of all the wise men of Babylon. Then Daniel made
a request of the king, so he appointed Shadrakh, Meishakh, and Aved
Nego over administration throughout Babylon, but Daniel remained at
the royal court.

3 1 Nevukhadnetzar the king made a figure of gold: its height was sixty cubits
and its width six cubits. He erected it in the Dura Valley in the province of
2 Babylon. Then Nevukhadnetzar the king sent messengers to assemble the
satraps, the prefects and the governors, the counselors, the treasurers, the
justices, the magistrates, and all the officials of the provinces to come to the
3 dedication of the figure which Nevukhadnetzar the king had erected. Then
the satraps, the prefects and the governors, the counselors, the treasurers,
the justices, the magistrates, and all the rulers of the provinces assembled
for the dedication of the figure which Nevukhadnetzar had erected, and
they stood facing the figure which Nevukhadnetzar had erected.

4 Then a herald proclaimed loudly: "You are commanded, O peoples,
5 nations, and speakers of various languages, when you hear the sound of
the horn, the pipe, the zither, the sambuca, the harp, the double flute, and
all kinds of music, you shall fall down and worship the golden figure that
6 Nevukhadnetzar the king has erected, and anyone who does not fall down
7 and worship will be thrown at once into the midst of the fiery furnace." As
a result, at the moment that all the people heard the sound of the horn,
the pipe, the zither, the sambuca, the harp, the double flute, and all kinds
of music, all the peoples, nations, and speakers of various languages fell
down and worshipped the golden figure that Nevukhadnetzar the king
had erected.

8 And then, at that very moment, some Chaldeans came forward and
9 slandered the Jews. They spoke and said to Nevukhadnetzar the king,
10 "O king, may you live forever! You, O king, have issued a decree that
every person who hears the sound of the horn, the pipe, the zither, the
sambuca, the harp, the double flute, and all kinds of music shall fall down
11 and worship the golden figure, and anyone who does not fall down and
12 worship shall be thrown into the midst of the fiery furnace. There are
some Jews whom you have appointed over the administration of Babylon:
Shadrakh, Meishakh, and Aved Nego. These men have not paid attention
to you, O king. They do not serve your god or worship the gold figure
you erected."

13 Thereupon Nevukhadnetzar, in fury and rage, gave an order to bring
Shadrakh, Meishakh, and Aved Nego. So these men were brought before
14 the king. Nevukhadnetzar spoke and said to them, "Is it true, Shadrakh,
Meishakh, and Aved Nego, that you do not serve my god and that you do
15 not worship the golden figure I have erected? Now if you are prepared to
fall down and worship the figure I have made when you hear the sound of
the horn, the pipe, the zither, the sambuca, the harp, the double flute, and
all kinds of music then all will be well with you, but if you do not worship,
at that very moment you shall be thrown into the midst of the fiery furnace,
and what god can rescue you from my hand?"

16 Shadrakh, Meishakh, and Aved Nego replied and said to the king, "O
Nevukhadnetzar, we do not need to answer you at all about this matter.
17 Behold, if He wishes, our God, whom we worship, is able to rescue us. He
can rescue us from the fiery furnace as well as from your hand, O king.
18 But even if He does not choose to save us, let it be known to you, O king,
that we will not serve your god and we will not worship the golden figure
you have erected."

19 Then Nevukhadnetzar became filled with fury, and the look on his face
changed toward Shadrakh, Meishakh, and Aved Nego. He spoke and
ordered to heat up the furnace seven times more than it was usually
20 heated. And he commanded the mightiest men in his army to tie up

Shadrakh, Meishakh, and Aved Nego and to throw them into the fiery
21 furnace. So those men were tied up still wearing their mantles, tunics,
hats, and clothes and were thrown into the midst of the fiery furnace.
22 Because the king's command was urgent and the furnace was heated
to excess, the flame of the fire killed those men who lifted Shadrakh,
23 Meishakh, and Aved Nego into it. And those three men, Shadrakh,
Meishakh, and Aved Nego, fell down tied up into the midst of the fiery
24 furnace. Then Nevukhadnetzar the king was amazed and rose in haste;
he turned and said to his advisors, "Didn't we just throw three men
tied up into the midst of the fire?" They answered and said to the king,
25 "That is true, O king." He replied and said, "But I see four men, unbound,
walking in the midst of the fire, and none of them are injured! And the
appearance of the fourth one is like an angel."

26 Then Nevukhadnetzar approached the opening of the fiery furnace and
spoke and said, "Shadrakh, Meishakh, and Aved Nego, servants of the Most
High God, come out and come here." Then Shadrakh, Meishakh, and Aved
27 Nego came out of the midst of the fire. And the satraps, the prefects, the
governors, and the king's advisors gathered round, looking at these men
over whose bodies the fire had no power: and the hair of their heads was
not singed, nor were their mantles damaged and not even a scent of fire
came from them.

28 Then Nevukhadnetzar spoke and said, "Blessed be the God of Shadrakh,
Meishakh, and Aved Nego, who has sent His angel and rescued His servants
who trusted in Him and defied the edict of the king, yielding their bodies
29 rather than serve or worship any god except their own God. I decree that
persons of any people, nation, or language who blaspheme against the
God of Shadrakh, Meishakh, and Aved Nego will be dismembered and
their houses reduced to refuse, because there is no other god who is able
30 to rescue like Him." Then the king promoted Shadrakh, Meishakh, and
Aved Nego in the province of Babylon.

31 Nevukhadnetzar the king, addressing all the peoples, nations, and speakers
of various languages who dwell in all the earth: "May your peace abound.
32 It is pleasing to me to tell of the signs and wonders that the Most High
33 God has performed with me. How great are His signs and how powerful
are His wonders! His kingdom is an eternal kingdom, and His rule is over
every generation.

4 1 2 "I, Nevukhadnetzar, was at peace in my house, relaxed in my palace. I saw
a dream that frightened me, and my thoughts in my bed and the visions
3 in my head upset me. Then I issued a command to bring all the wise men
of Babylon so they would make known to me the meaning of the dream.
4 When the magicians, the soothsayers, the Chaldeans, and the astrologers
arrived, I recited the dream before them but they could not make its
meaning known to me.

5 "And finally, Daniel, whose name is Belteshatzar like the name of my god,
and who has the spirit of the holy gods within him, came before me, and I
6 recited the dream before him: O Belteshatzar, chief magician, about whom
I know that the spirit of the holy gods is within you and that no mystery
can conquer you, tell the interpretation of the vision I saw in my dream.
7 There were visions in my head while I was lying in my bed: I was looking
and – behold! – there was a tree in the midst of the earth and its height
8 was colossal. The tree grew and became strong, and its height reached
9 the heavens and it was visible to the ends of all the earth. Its foliage was
beautiful and its fruit abundant, and it had food for all. Wild beasts were
taking shade under it, and in its branches were nesting the birds of the
heavens, and from it all flesh was being nourished.

10 "I was looking at the visions in my head as I lay in bed and – behold! – a
11 holy angel was coming down from the heavens. He called out forcefully
and thus did he speak: 'Cut down the tree and chop off its branches, bring
down its foliage and scatter its fruit. Let the beasts beneath it flee, as well
12 as the birds from its branches. However, leave the stump with its roots in
the earth, chained in a fetter of iron and bronze in the wild grass; let him
be drenched by the dew of the heavens; let his lot be with the beasts in the
13 grassland. Let his heart be changed from a human one, and let him be given
14 a beast's heart, and seven seasons will pass over him. This proclamation
is by decree of the angels and the matter is by order of the holy ones, in
order that everyone alive know that the Most High rules the kingdom of
man and He gives it to whomever He wishes, and He can appoint over it
15 the lowest of men.' This is the dream I saw, I, King Nevukhadnetzar; and
you, Belteshatzar, speak its interpretation, since all the wise men of my
kingdom are unable to make it known to me; but you are, for the spirit of
the holy gods is within you."

16 Then Daniel, whose name was Belteshatzar, was perplexed for a while,
his thoughts upsetting him. The king spoke up, saying, "Belteshatzar, do
not let the dream and its meaning upset you." Belteshatzar responded and
said, "My lord, may the dream be for your enemies, and its interpretation
17 for your foes. The tree that you saw, which grew and became strong until
its height reached the heavens and it became visible to the whole earth,
18 and its foliage was beautiful and its fruit abundant and it had food for
all; beneath it wild beasts dwelled and in its branches nested the birds
19 of heaven – it is you, O king, who has grown great and become strong,
and your greatness grew greater and reached the heavens, and your
20 dominion to the edge of the earth. And whereas the king saw a holy
angel descend from the heavens and say, 'Cut down the tree and destroy
it, but leave the stump with its roots in the earth, chained in a fetter of
iron and bronze in the wild grass, and let him be drenched by the dew
of the heavens and let his lot be with the beasts of the field until seven
seasons pass over him.'

21 "This is the interpretation, O king, and it is the decree of the Most High
22 which has come upon my lord the king. You will be driven out of human
society, and your dwelling place shall be with the wild beasts, and you will
be fed grass, like cattle, and be drenched by the dew of the heavens, and
seven seasons will pass over you, until you know that the Most High rules
23 the kingdom of man and He gives it to whomever He wishes. And whereas
they said to leave the stump with the roots of the tree, your kingdom awaits
24 you as soon as you come to know that the heavens rule. Therefore, O king,
may my advice please you: redeem your sins by giving charity and your
iniquities by acting mercifully toward the poor; perhaps your peacefulness
will be prolonged."

25 26 All this happened to Nevukhadnetzar the king. Twelve months later, he
27 was strolling on the roof of the royal palace in Babylon. The king spoke and
said, "Behold, this is the great Babylon, which I have built into the royal
28 seat by the force of my might and in honor of my splendor!" The word
was still in the king's mouth when a voice came down from the heavens:
"Regarding you it is decreed, Nevukhadnetzar the king: your kingdom has
29 been taken from you. And you shall be driven out of human society, and
your dwelling place will be with the beasts of the field; you will be fed
grass like cattle and seven seasons will pass over you, until you know that
the Most High rules the kingdom of man and He gives it to whomever
30 He wishes." At that very moment, the word about Nevukhadnetzar was
fulfilled, and he was chased out of human society and he ate grass, as cattle
do, and his body was drenched by the dew of the heavens until his hair
grew long like eagle feathers and his nails like bird claws.

31 "And when the designated time period ended, I, Nevukhadnetzar, raised
my eyes to the heavens, and my wits returned to me, and I blessed the
Most High, and I praised and glorified the One who lives forever, whose
reign is an eternal reign and whose sovereignty endures from generation to
32 generation. And all who inhabit earth count as nothing in comparison; and
He does as He wishes with the hosts of the heavens and the inhabitants
of earth and there is no one who can protest His power and say to Him,
'What are You doing?'

33 "At that very time my wits returned to me, and for the honor of my kingdom,
my splendor and my radiance returned to me. And I was sought by my
advisors and my noblemen, and I was reestablished over my kingdom,
34 and even more greatness was accorded to me. Now I, Nevukhadnetzar,
praise and exalt and give glory to the King of the heavens, whose every
deed is true, and whose ways are just, and who can humble those who act
arrogantly."

5 1 Beleshatzar the king made a great banquet for his one thousand nobles
2 and was drinking wine facing those thousand. Under the wine's influence,
Beleshatzar gave orders to bring the vessels of gold and silver which his

father, Nevukhadnetzar, had removed from the Temple in Jerusalem, so that the king and his nobles, his wives and his concubines might use them to drink.

3 So they brought the vessels of gold which they had removed from the
Temple, the House of God which is in Jerusalem, and the king and his
4 nobles, his wives and his concubines drank from them. They drank the
wine and toasted their gods of gold and silver, of bronze, iron, wood, and
stone.

5 Just then the fingers of a human hand emerged and were writing across
from the candelabra on the plastered wall of the king's palace, such that
6 the king could see the back of the hand that was writing. Then the king's
face blanched, and his thoughts frightened him, and the joints of his loins
loosened, and his knees knocked against each other.

7 The king cried out loudly to bring the soothsayers, the Chaldeans, and
the astrologers. The king sent word to the wise ones of Babylon and said,
"Whoever of you will read this writing and tell me its meaning shall wear
royal purple and have a golden chain on his neck and shall rule as the
8 third in power in the kingdom." Then all the wise ones of the king arrived,
but they were not able to read the writing or make its meaning known to
the king.

9 Then King Beleshatzar became very agitated and his face blanched and
10 his ministers were bewildered. The queen mother, in response to the
words of the king and his ministers, entered the banquet hall and spoke
up, saying, "O king, live forever! Do not let your thoughts upset you or
11 let your healthy look change. There is a man in your kingdom in whom
there is the spirit of the holy gods, and in your father's day he was found
to have insight and intelligence, and a wisdom like the wisdom of the gods.
And King Nevukhadnetzar, your father, appointed him to be the chief of
the magicians, soothsayers, Chaldeans, and astrologers – your father the
12 king! Since an extraordinary spirit and knowledge and intelligence – the
ability to interpret dreams and solve puzzles and resolve problems – were
found in this Daniel, whom the king named Belteshatzar, now let Daniel
be summoned and he will make the meaning known."

13 So Daniel was brought before the king. The king spoke and said to Daniel,
"You are Daniel, one of the exiles of Yehuda whom my father the king
14 brought here from Yehuda. And I have heard about you that the spirit of
the gods is within you, and that extraordinary insight and intelligence and
15 wisdom has been found within you. And just now there have been brought
before me the wise ones, the soothsayers, to read this writing so as to tell
16 me its meaning, but they could not tell me the meaning of the thing. And
I have heard about you, that you are able to interpret meaning and resolve
problems. Now if you can read the writing and make its meaning known

to me, you shall wear royal purple, a golden chain will be placed on your
neck, and you will rule as the third in power in the kingdom."

17 Then Daniel responded and spoke before the king, "Let your gifts remain
yours, and give your presents to another, but I shall read the writing for the
18 king and I shall make its meaning known to him. Regarding you, O king:
the Most High God gave sovereignty and greatness and honor and glory
19 to Nevukhadnetzar, your father. And because of the greatness that He gave
him, all nations, peoples, and speakers of all languages trembled in terror
before him. He would kill whomever he wished, and let live whomever he
wished. He would exalt whomever he wished, and debase whomever he
20 wished. And when he became haughty and his inclination to act wickedly
became powerful, he was deposed from his royal throne and his honor
21 was taken away. And he was driven from human society and his heart was
made like a beast's. His dwelling place was with the wild asses, and he was
fed grass, like cattle, and his body was drenched by the dew of the heavens,
until he recognized that the Most High God rules the kingdom of man and
that He appoints over it whomever He wishes.

22 "And you, Beleshatzar his son, have not humbled your own heart even
23 though you know all this. And you exalted yourself above the Lord of
the heavens, and you had the vessels of His House brought before you,
and you and your nobles, your wives and your concubines drank wine
from them, and you toasted your gods of silver and gold, of bronze, iron,
wood, and stone, who cannot see and cannot hear and cannot know. And
the God who holds your soul in His power and who owns all your paths
24 you did not honor. So there was sent from Him the back of a hand and
this writing was inscribed.

25 "And this is the writing which was inscribed: *Meneh, meneh tekel ufarsin.*
26 This is the interpretation of the message: *Meneh*; God has counted[3] your
27 kingdom and brought it to completion. *Tekel*; you have been weighed[4]
28 in the scales and been found wanting. *Peres*; your kingdom has been
29 divided[5] and given to Media and Persia." Then Beleshatzar gave an order,
and they robed Daniel in royal purple, and a chain of gold was placed on
his neck, and they publicly declared he would rule as third in power in
the kingdom.

30 That very night, Beleshatzar, the Chaldean king, was killed.

6 1 And Daryavesh the Mede received the kingdom when he was about
2 sixty-two years old. Daryavesh decided to appoint one hundred twenty
3 governors over his kingdom, to be located throughout his kingdom. And
above them were three ministers, of whom Daniel was one, to whom the

3 | Aramaic *mena.*

4 | Aramaic *tekilta.*

5 | Aramaic *perisat.*

governors would give an accounting, so that the royal treasury not be burdened.

4 Now the aforementioned Daniel surpassed the ministers and the governors
because of his extraordinary spirit, and the king intended to appoint him
5 over the whole kingdom. Then the ministers and governors sought to find
a fault against Daniel regarding affairs of state, but they could find no fault
or corruption because he was faithful, so no error or corruption was found
6 regarding him. Then those men said, "We will not find any fault against
this Daniel unless we find it in the law of his God."

7 Then these ministers and governors excitedly mobbed the king and said to
8 him, "O Daryavesh the king, live forever! All the ministers of the kingdom,
the supervisors and the governors, the counselors and the administrators
have resolved together that the king should enact a royal ordinance and
binding obligation that for thirty days, whosoever shall make any request
of any god or any man other than you, O king, shall be thrown into the
9 lions' den. Now, O king, enact the obligation and issue a written decree
that cannot be changed, as a law of Media and Persia that cannot be
10 annulled." Consenting to all this, King Daryavesh issued the obligation
in a written decree.

11 Now when Daniel learned that this law had been issued in a written
decree, he went to his house where he had open windows in his attic
facing Jerusalem, where three times a day he would kneel down and pray
and give thanks before his God, just as he had always done before this.
12 Then those men formed an excited mob and found Daniel petitioning and
supplicating his God.

13 Then they approached the king and said, concerning the king's edict, "Did
you not issue an obligation in a written decree that for thirty days, any
man who makes a request from any god or man other than you, O king,
would be thrown into the lions' den?" The king answered and said, "This
matter is valid as a law of Media and Persia, which cannot be annulled."
14 Thereupon they answered and said before the king, "Daniel, who is of
the exiles of Yehuda, has not paid attention to you, O king, nor to the
obligation that you issued as a written decree, and three times a day he
makes his petitions."

15 The moment the king heard about the matter he was very displeased, and
he made up his mind to rescue Daniel, and until sunset he made efforts
16 to save him. At that point those men excitedly mobbed the king and said
to the king, "Know, O king, that the law of Media and Persia is that no
obligation and ordinance which the king enacts can be changed."

17 Then the king issued a command, and they brought Daniel, and threw
him into the lions' den. The king spoke and said to Daniel, "May your
18 God, whom you serve constantly, rescue you." And a stone was brought

and placed on the opening of the den, which the king sealed with his own
ring and with the rings of his nobles so that nothing could be changed
19 with regard to Daniel. Then the king went to his palace and spent the
night fasting. They brought him no diversions, and sleep escaped him.

20 In the morning the king rose at the break of day and hurriedly went to the
21 lions' den. When he came near the den, he called out to Daniel in a pained
voice. The king spoke and said, "Daniel, servant of the living God, was your
22 God, whom you serve constantly, able to save you from the lions?" Then
23 Daniel spoke to the king, "O king, live forever! My God sent His angel,
who shut the mouth of the lions so they could not harm me, for I have been
found innocent before Him, and before you, O king, I have done no wrong."

24 Then the king was overjoyed, and commanded that Daniel be brought
out of the den. And Daniel was brought out of the den, and no injury was
25 found on him because he had faith in his God. And at the king's command
they brought those men who had slandered Daniel and threw them into
the lions' den, along with their children and their wives. Even before they
reached the bottom of the den, the lions overpowered them and shattered
all their bones.

26 Then Daryavesh the king wrote to all peoples, nations, and speakers of
27 all languages inhabiting the whole earth, "May your peace abound! I
have decreed that throughout the domain of my kingdom people should
fear and tremble before the God of Daniel, for He is the living God, and
He endures forever. His kingdom is indestructible and His dominion is
28 everlasting. He is rescuer and deliverer, and He makes signs and wonders
in the heavens and on earth; it is He who rescued Daniel from the lions."
29 And this Daniel prospered during the reign of Daryavesh and the reign of
Koresh the Persian.

7 1 In the first year of Beleshatzar, king of Babylon, Daniel saw a dream, and
visions in his head while in bed; then he wrote down the dream. He began
2 to speak. Thus Daniel spoke and said, "I was seeing my vision at nighttime
and – behold! – the four winds of the heavens were pounding the great sea.
3 And four powerful beasts arose from the sea, each different from the next.
4 The first one was like a lion that had the wings of an eagle. As I was watching,
its wings were plucked and it was lifted from the earth and raised onto two
legs like a man, and a human heart was given to it.

5 "And – behold! – there was another, second beast like a bear. It was raised
up on one side, and there were three ribs in its mouth between its teeth. And
6 this is what it was told: 'Arise! Devour much flesh.' After this, I kept watching
and – behold! – another, looking like a leopard. It had four wings of a bird
on its back, and the beast had four heads! And it was given dominion.

7 "After this, I kept watching the visions of the night and – behold! – a
fourth beast, terrible and terrifying and exceedingly powerful, and it had

enormous iron teeth! It devoured and crushed and then trampled what
remained with its feet. And it was different from all the beasts that preceded
8 it, and it had ten horns! I kept looking at the horns and – behold! – another,
small horn sprouted in their midst. And three of the earlier horns were
uprooted in front of it, and – behold! – this horn had eyes like human eyes
and a mouth speaking boastful things.

9 "I kept watching as thrones were set out and the Ancient of Days sat.
His clothes were white as snow and the hair of His head like clean wool.
10 His throne was sparks of fire, its wheels flaming fire. A river of fire was
streaming and flowing forth before Him. Thousands of thousands were
ministering to Him, and many tens of thousands stood before Him. The
court was sitting and the books were opened.

11 "I kept watching. Then, during the sound of the boastful words that the
horn was speaking, I kept watching as the beast was slain and its body
12 destroyed and given over to the burning fire. And the rest of the beasts
were stripped of their dominion, and an extension of life was given to them
until a time and a season.

13 "I was seeing visions of the night and – behold! – along with the clouds in
the heavens, one like a human being was coming and reached the Ancient
14 of Days and was presented before Him. And he was given dominion and
honor and kingship, and all the nations and peoples and speakers of all
languages will serve him. His dominion is everlasting dominion that will
not be removed, and his kingdom will not be destroyed.

15 "My spirit – I, Daniel – suffered within its vessel, my body, and the visions
16 in my head troubled me. I approached one of the attendants, seeking the
truth from him about all this, and he spoke to me and made the meaning
17 of the things known to me: 'These enormous beasts, of which there are
18 four: four kingdoms will arise from the earth. Holy ones of the Most High
will receive the kingdom and will inherit the kingdom for ever and ever.'

19 "Then I wished to be certain about the fourth beast, which was different
from all of them: exceedingly fearsome, with teeth of iron and claws of
bronze. It devoured and crushed and then trampled what remained with
20 its feet. And I wished to be certain about the ten horns that were on its
head and the other one that sprouted, with three falling before it, that
horn that had eyes in it and a mouth speaking boastful things, and whose
appearance was more powerful than the others.

21 "I kept looking, and that horn was waging war against holy ones and
22 prevailing over them until the Ancient of Days arrived and judgment was
passed in favor of the holy ones of the Most High. And the time arrived,
and holy ones took possession of the kingdom.

23 "This is what he said: 'The fourth beast means there will be a fourth
kingdom in the land that will be different from all the kingdoms. And it

24 will devour the whole earth and will crush it and trample it. And the ten
horns mean that from that kingdom, ten kings will arise. Then another
will rise after them, and he will be different from the first ones, and he will
25 bring about the downfall of three kings. He will speak words against the
Most High, and he will afflict the holy ones of the Most High and plan to
change the times and the Law. They will be handed over to him for a time
26 and times, and half a time. And the court will sit in judgment and do away
with his dominion, devastating and destroying it to finality.

27 "'And the kingship and the dominion and the grandeur of the kingdoms
underneath all the heavens will be given to the nation of the holy ones
of the Most High. Their kingdom is an eternal kingdom, and all rulers
28 will serve and obey it.'" Here the account concluded. I, Daniel, was very
alarmed by my thoughts, and my face blanched, but I kept the matter to
myself.

8 1 In the third year[6] of the reign of King Beleshatzar, a vision came to me – I,
2 Daniel – after the one that was first shown me. I was looking at the vision
and while I watched, it was me in Shushan the imperial city, which is in
the province of Eilam. And I saw in the vision that I was beside the river
3 Ulai. I raised my eyes and saw – behold! – there was a ram standing near
the river and it had two horns. Now the horns were tall, but one was taller
4 than the other; the taller one rose up last. I saw the ram goring westward
and northward and southward, and none of the animals could withstand
it and there was no rescue from its power; it did whatever it pleased and
grew bigger.

5 And as I was watching intently – behold! – a young he-goat came from the
west over the whole earth without touching the ground, and the goat had a
6 prominent horn between its eyes. The goat approached the ram with two
horns that I had seen standing near the river, and rushed toward it with
7 furious force. And I saw it reaching the ram and attacking with savage fury,
and it smote the ram and broke both of its horns. And the ram had no
power to withstand it; the he-goat threw it down to the ground, trampling
it. And there was no one to rescue the ram from its might.

8 And the he-goat grew to enormity, but, at the peak of its power, its great
horn was shattered, and there arose to prominence four in its place, facing
9 the four winds of the heavens. And from one of them there emerged one
small one; it grew exceedingly great toward the south and toward the east
10 and toward the beautiful land. It grew great, up to the host of the heavens,
knocking some of the host of stars down to earth and trampling upon
11 them. It even grew to challenge the prince of the host of heaven, who
was deprived of the daily sacrifice and whose Sanctuary foundation was
12 thrown down. And the army was set against the daily sacrifice because of
sin. It threw truth to the ground, acting and succeeding.

---

6 | At this point the text switches from Aramaic back to Hebrew.

13 I heard a holy one speaking, and another holy one said to whomever it was
who was speaking, "How long will this last, this vision of the removal of
the daily sacrifice and this sin-producing desolation and the giving over
14 of the Sanctuary and the multitudes for trampling?" He said to me, "For
two thousand three hundred evenings and mornings, then the Sanctuary
will be made right again."

15 While I, Daniel, was seeing that vision, seeking understanding – behold! –
16 standing across from me was a man-like figure. I heard a human voice from
between the banks of the Ulai calling out. It said, "Gavriel, explain the
17 vision to this one." He approached where I was standing and when he came
near I was overwhelmed and fell prostrate. He said to me, "Understand, O
18 mortal, that the vision refers to the end-time." And as he was speaking to
me, I fell asleep as I lay prostrate on the ground. He touched me and he
19 stood me up. He said, "Behold, I am informing you about that which will
come to be at the end of the time of wrath, for that period has an end.

20 "The two-horned ram that you saw represents the kings of Media and
21 Persia. The he-goat symbolizes the king of Ionia,[7] and the large horn
22 between its eyes is the first king. And that broken horn and the four that
rose in its place signify four kingdoms that will issue from that nation, but
23 not one of them with its strength. And at the end of their reign, when the
sinners have reached full measure, there will arise a fierce-faced king, one
24 who is skilled at intrigue. His power will grow strong, though not by his
own might; he will bring about amazing ruin and succeed in his activity.
25 He will devastate powerful peoples and the nation of holy ones. He will
succeed by his cunning, with deceit in his hand. He will boast in his heart
and destroy many by stealth. But when he stands against the prince of
26 princes he will be broken without a human hand being raised. The vision
of the evenings and the mornings that has been told is true. And as for you,
keep the vision undisclosed, for it is far in the future."

27 And I, Daniel, became weak and was ill for days. Then I arose and dealt with
the king's affairs, but I was in shock over the vision and not understanding
it.

9 1 It was the first year of Daryavesh son of Aḥashverosh, of Median stock,
2 who was made king over the kingdom of the Chaldeans. In year one of his
reign, I, Daniel, studied the books concerning the number of years that
the Lord told Yirmeya the prophet it would take to fulfill the desolation
of Jerusalem: seventy years.[8]

3 I turned my face unto the Lord God to petition Him with prayer and
4 entreaties, with fasting, sackcloth, and ashes. I prayed to the Lord my

7 | Ionia was a region in Asia Minor inhabited by Hellenic (Greek-speaking) peoples; the name Yavan eventually came to refer in Hebrew to the Greek lands and peoples in general.

8 | See Jeremiah 25:11–12, 29:10.

God and I confessed, saying, "O Lord, the great and awesome God,
who keeps the covenant and the love with those who love Him and keep
5 His commandments. We have sinned, offended, done evil, and rebelled,
6 straying from Your commandments and Your laws. We did not obey Your
servants, the prophets, who spoke in Your name to our kings, our princes,
and our fathers and to all the people of the land.

7 "Justice is Yours, O Lord, and ours is shamefacedness, even unto this
day, for the men of Yehuda, the inhabitants of Jerusalem and all of Israel,
near and far, in all the lands to which You have scattered them, because
8 of the treachery with which they betrayed You. Lord! Shamefacedness
is ours, belonging to our kings, our princes, and our fathers because we
have sinned against You.

9 "To the Lord our God belong mercy and pardon, even though we have
10 rebelled against Him and did not heed the voice of our Lord God to walk
according to His teachings which He set before us through His servants,
11 the prophets. And all of Israel transgressed against Your Law and turned
away, not heeding Your voice; the curse of breaking the oath that was
written in the teaching of Moshe, servant of God, was poured out upon
12 us because we sinned against Him. He fulfilled His word, that which He
had spoken regarding us and our judges who judged us, to bring upon us
a great evil the likes of which has never been done beneath all the heavens
as it was done in Jerusalem.

13 "Just as is written in the teaching of Moshe, all this evil came upon us, and
we did not seek to appease the Lord our God by turning back from our
14 sins and seeking to know Your truth. The Lord kept watch over the evil
and brought it upon us, for the Lord our God is just in all His deeds that
15 He has done, for we did not listen to His voice. And now, O Lord our
God, who took Your people out of the land of Egypt with mighty power
and have made a name for Yourself to this day – we have sinned; we have
behaved wickedly.

16 "Lord! In keeping with Your just acts, let Your anger and Your fury be
turned away from Your city Jerusalem, Your holy mountain. For due to
our sins and the transgressions of our fathers, Jerusalem and Your people
17 have become a disgrace to all around us. And now, let our God listen to the
prayer of Your servant and to his entreaties, and let Your face shine upon
18 Your desolate Temple, for the Lord's sake. Incline your ear, O my God,
and listen; open Your eyes to see our ruins and the city which is called by
Your name, for we are not relying on our righteousness in our entreaties
19 to You, but on Your great mercy. Lord, hear! Lord, forgive! Lord, pay
attention and act! Do not delay! For Your sake, O my God, because Your
city and Your people are called by Your name."

20 And I was still speaking and praying and confessing my sin and the sin of
my people Israel and pouring out my entreaty before the Lord my God

21 about my God's holy mountain. And I was still speaking my prayer when
the man Gavriel, whom I had seen at the start of the vision, approached
22 me, soaring in flight at the time of the evening offering. He gave me
understanding as he instructed me, saying, "Daniel, I have now come forth
23 to teach you understanding. At the very start of your entreaties, a word
came forth, and I have come to tell it because you are beloved. Understand
the word, and grasp the meaning of the vision.

24 "Seventy cycles of a week of years are decreed upon your people and on
your holy city to complete the transgressions, to finish the sins and to
atone for iniquity, and to bring everlasting justice, to validate the vision
25 and the prophet, and to anoint a holy of holies. You must know and be
aware of this: from the utterance of the word to restore and build Jerusalem
until there is an anointed leader will be seven cycles of seven years, and
during sixty-two cycles of seven years it will be rebuilt with a plaza and
26 a moat, albeit in times of distress. And after the sixty-two cycles of seven
years the anointed one will disappear; there will be none, and the army of
the next ruler will destroy the city and the Sanctuary. But his end will be
in a flood, and until the end of the decreed war there will be desolations.
27 He will make a strong alliance with the multitude for one seven-year cycle,
then for half of a seven-year cycle he will ban sacrifices and grain offerings;
and on the place they were brought will be desolating abominations until
the annihilation ordained is poured out upon the desolator."

10 1 In the third year of Koresh, king of Persia, a word was revealed to Daniel,
who had been named Belteshatzar. And the word was certain to come
true and involved a great army. He understood the word and gained
understanding from his vision.

2 3 In those days, I, Daniel, was mourning for three full weeks. I did not eat
baked delicacies, neither meat nor wine entered my mouth, and I did not
4 anoint myself with oil until the completion of three full weeks. And it was
the twenty-fourth day of the first month, and I was standing alongside the
5 great river, the Tigris. I raised my eyes and looked, and – behold! – there
6 was a man dressed in linen, and his waist was belted with fine gold. And
his torso was like aquamarine, and his face shone like lightning, and his
eyes were like fiery torches, and his arms and legs were like burnished
bronze, and the sound of his speech was like the sound of a multitude.

7 And only I, Daniel, saw this vision; and the people who were with me did
not see the vision, but a great terror fell over them, and they ran away to
8 hide; and I alone remained. And I looked at this great vision, and there was
no strength left in me; and my smile turned into ugliness, and I became
9 powerless. I heard the sound of his words, and while I listened to the
sound of his words, I was in a dream state, prostrate, my face to the ground.
10 And – behold! – a hand touched me and rocked me onto my knees and the
11 palms of my hands. He said to me, "Daniel, beloved man, understand the

words that I am speaking to you and stand up in place, for I have been sent
12 to you now." And when he said this to me I stood up trembling. He said
to me, "Do not be afraid, Daniel, for from the first day you set your heart
on understanding and humbling yourself before your God your words
13 have been heard, so I came in response to your words, but the prince of
the kingdom of Persia stood opposing me for twenty-one days, and then
Mikhael, one of the chief princes, came to help me after I had remained
there with the kings of Persia.

14 "And I have come to help you understand what will happen to your people
15 in the end of days, for there is another vision for those days." And as he
spoke the words to me, I turned my face to the ground and became dumb.
16 And – behold! – something like a human form was touching my lips, and
I opened my mouth and spoke, and I said to the one standing in front of
me, "My lord, during the vision I was seized by sudden pain, and I became
17 powerless. And how is this servant of my lord able to speak with you, my
lord? As for me, from now on I have no strength to sustain me, and no
breath is left in me."

18 19 The man-like one touched me again and strengthened me. He said, "Do
not be afraid, beloved man, you are safe; grow stronger and stronger." And
as he spoke to me I did become stronger, and I said, "Let my lord speak,
20 for you have strengthened me." He said, "Do you know why I came to you?
And now I must return to fight with the prince of Persia, and when I leave,
21 the prince of Ionia will arrive. Nonetheless, I shall tell you what is written
in the book of truth, and there is no one who supports me against these
except for Mikhael, your prince,

11 1 "and I, in the first year of Daryavesh the Mede, was serving as his strength-
2 ener and his refuge. And now I will tell you the truth: There are three more
kings in line to rule Persia, and the fourth will accumulate the most wealth
of all; and, empowered by his riches, he will stir up everyone against the
3 kingdom of Ionia. A mighty king will arise and rule a vast domain, accom-
4 plishing whatever he desires. But when he reaches full stature, his kingdom
will be shattered and scattered to the four winds of heaven. It will not
belong to his descendants, nor will it be comparable to his vast domain,
for his kingdom will be torn apart and belong to others, not to them.

5 "The king of the south will become strong, but one of his princes will be
6 stronger than he and govern a great domain. After a number of years they
will become allies, and the daughter of the king of the south will come to
the king of the north to manifest their peacemaking through marriage, but
she will not retain her military power, nor shall her father's power and army
suffice, but she shall be given over to death along with those who brought
7 her and him who begot her and strengthened her in those times. But from
a sprouting of her roots one will rise in his place. He will fight against the
army and will enter the fortress city of the king of the north and will act

8 against them and prevail. And he will also take captive their gods, with
their molten images and their precious vessels of silver and gold, bringing
them to Egypt. Then he will leave the king of the north alone for years.

9 "The king of the north will invade the kingdom of the king of the south
10 but then return to his own land. But his sons will become stirred up
and assemble a multitude of mighty forces. He will penetrate, invading,
sweeping through and passing beyond. Then he will turn around, stirred
11 up to attack again, until he reaches the fortress of the king of the south. The
king of the south will become bitterly angry and come forth to make war
with him, with the king of the north. The king of the south will assemble
a great multitude, and the multitude of the king of the north will be given
over to him.

12 "And as the multitude of captives are carried away, his heart will become
13 haughty. He will fell tens of thousands, but his triumph will not last. For
the king of the north shall again raise a multitude even greater than the first
and after a number of years will penetrate and invade with an enormous
14 army and plentiful supplies. And in those times, many will stand against the
king of the south. And renegade sons of your people will exalt themselves
to give substance to a vision and fail.

15 "And the king of the north shall invade and pour out mounds of earthen
siege works to capture a reinforced city. And the forces of the south will
not withstand the attack, not even his elite troops, for they will have no
16 strength to withstand it. And the one who invaded it will do as he wishes,
and no one will stand against him. He will rule the land of beauty by his
power of destruction.

17 "First he will be determined to invade with the force of his whole kingdom,
then he will act as if he is behaving peacefully, and he will give him the
daughter of one of his wives to destroy the kingdom. But this plot will not
18 succeed, and the kingdom of the south will not become his. Then he will
aim himself against the islands, and capture many of them, but a military
19 chief will put a stop to his insult, returning insult to him. He will then turn
back toward the fortresses of his own land, but he will stumble and fall
and never be found.

20 "And in his place there will arise a person who transfers there a collector
of tax for the splendor of the kingdom, but within a few days he will be
21 broken, and not in anger, nor in war. And there will arise in his place a
despicable person to whom royal splendor was not given. He will come
22 in peaceably but will seize the kingdom with deceitful trickery. Armed
forces will be swept away before him and broken, even the prince of
23 the covenant. And from the moment of forming an alliance he will act
24 deceitfully and will attack and overpower the ally with a small party. He
will peaceably enter even the prosperous places in the province and do that

which his fathers never did, nor his grandfathers: he will distribute spoils,
booty, and riches to them. And he will devise plots against strongholds
for another time.

25 "And he will summon his might and his courage against the king of the
south with a great army. And the king of the south will be roused to war
with a great and exceedingly powerful army, but he will not endure because
26 plots will be devised against him. Those who eat bread from his table will
destroy him, and his army will be swept away and many shall fall slain.
27 And both of these kings' hearts will be oriented toward evil; they will sit
at one table and exchange lies, but it will not succeed, because it is not yet
28 the appointed end-time. Then he will return to his land with great riches
and his heart set against the holy covenant. He will accomplish what he
wants, then return to his own land.

29 "At the appointed time, he will return and come to the south, but it will
30 not be the same at the latter time as it was in the former. When the ships
of Kitim come at him, he will lose heart and retreat and rage against the
holy covenant. And he will act: he will turn to and ally with those who have
31 forsaken the holy covenant. Armed forces will rise at his command; they
will desecrate the Sanctuary stronghold, and abolish the daily sacrifice, and
32 set up the desolating abomination. And those who act wickedly against
the covenant he will seduce by flatteries, but the people who know their
God will be strong and act.

33 "The nation's wise ones will instruct many, though for a time they will fall
34 by the sword, by flame, by captivity, by plunder. And when they fall, only
35 a few will help them, but many will join them with deceitful trickery. And
of the wise ones, some will fall, in order to refine, cleanse, and purify them
until the end-time, which is still appointed to come.

36 "And the king will do as he pleases, exalting himself and making himself
greater than any god. He will utter astonishing things against the God
of gods. He will prosper until the fury is complete, for that which is
37 determined must take place. He will have no regard for the gods of his
ancestors or for the one in whom women delight. He will have no regard
38 for any god because he will make himself greater than all. Instead, he will
honor the god of strongholds. A god whom his fathers did not know will
39 he honor with gold, silver, precious stones, and treasured things. And he
will build cities for defense of the strongholds, each with images of his god.
He will provide abundant honor to those who will acknowledge him; he
will appoint them as rulers over the many and distribute land for a price.

40 "And at the end-time, the king of the south will try to lock horns with
him, but the king of the north will storm over him with chariots and with
horsemen and with many ships. He will invade countries, despoil them,
41 and move on. He will also invade the land of beauty, and many cities
will fall, but these will escape his power: Edom and Moav, Yevus and

42 the choicest land of the sons of Amon. And he will attack and destroy
43 countries, and the land of Egypt will not escape. And he will have power
over the treasures of gold and silver, and over all the precious things of
Egypt, and the Libyans and Kushites will follow his entourage.

44 "But rumors from the east and the north will alarm him, so he will go forth
45 in a huge fury to destroy and to exterminate many peoples. And he will
set up splendid greeting pavilions between the seas and the beautiful holy
mountain. There he will arrive at his own end, and no one will help him.

12 1 "And at that time, Mikhael will arise, the great prince, guardian of the
children of your people. And there will be a time of great trouble, the
likes of which has not happened since nations came to be until that time.
And at that time, your people will escape, all of them found written in the
2 book.[9] And many of those sleeping in the dust of the earth will awaken,
some to everlasting life and some to humiliations and eternal degradation.
3 And those who are wise will shine like the radiance of the sky, and those
4 who lead the many to a righteous path will shine like stars forever. But you,
Daniel, keep the words secret and seal the book until the end-time. Many
will search here and there, and knowledge will increase."

5 Then I, Daniel, looked and – behold! – there stood two others, one on
6 this bank of the river and one on that bank of the river. One of them said
to the man dressed in linen, who was above the waters of the river, "Until
7 when shall this wondrous time last?" I could hear the man dressed in linen
who was above the waters of the river. He lifted his right hand and his left
toward the heavens. He swore by the Eternal One that it will be for a time,
times, and a half. And that when the shattering of the holy people's power
8 is complete, all these things will come to an end. Now I heard, but I did
not understand, so I said, "My lord, what will come after these things?"

9 He said, "Go on your way, Daniel, for the things are secret and sealed until
10 the end-time. Many people will become refined, cleansed, and purified,
but wicked people will do wicked things, and none of the wicked will
11 understand. But the wise will understand. And from the time that the
daily sacrifice will be taken away and the desolating abomination is set
12 up there will be 1,290 days. Happy is he who waits and reaches 1,335 days.
13 But you, go to your end and rest, and you will arise to your destiny at the
end of days."

9 | Meaning the book of life.

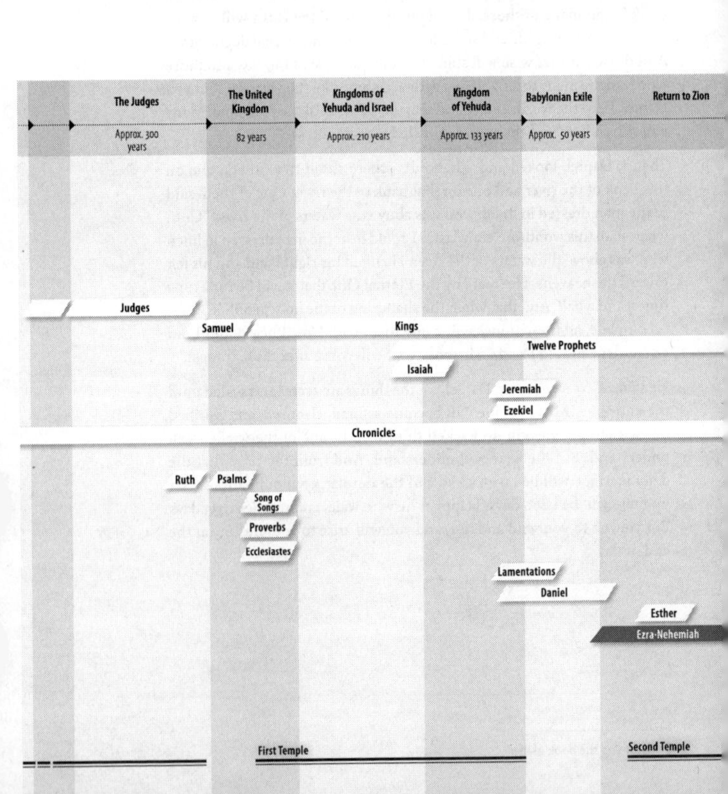

The Judges
Approx. 300 years
The United Kingdom
82 years
Kingdoms of Yehuda and Israel
Approx. 210 years
Kingdom of Yehuda
Approx. 133 years
Babylonian Exile
Approx. 50 years
Return to Zion
Judges
Samuel
Kings
Twelve Prophets
Isaiah
Jeremiah
Ezekiel
Chronicles
Ruth
Psalms
Song of Songs
Proverbs
Ecclesiastes
Lamentations
Daniel
Esther
Ezra-Nehemiah
First Temple
Second Temple

EZRA
NEHEMIAH/NEḤEMYA

EZRA · NEHEMIAH	Koresh's declaration, those who ascended the land as a result and their actions	Ezra's ascendance and his actions	Neḥemya's ascendance and his determined action	Neḥemya's second ascent: Attempts to repair the crisis
	Ezra, chs. 1–6	Ezra 7–10	Nehemiah 1–12	Nehemiah 13
			12 years	

1 1 In the first year of Koresh, king of Persia, when the LORD's word pronounced
by Yirmeyahu had come to pass,[1] the LORD stirred the spirit of Koresh,
king of Persia, and he issued a proclamation throughout his kingdom, by
word of mouth and written word as well:[2]

2 "Thus says Koresh, king of Persia: The LORD, God of the heavens, has
granted me all the kingdoms of the earth, and He has charged me to build
3 Him a House in Jerusalem, in Yehuda. Whoever is among you from all
His people, may his God be with him, and let him go up to Jerusalem, in
Yehuda, and build the House of the LORD, God of Israel, who is the God in
4 Jerusalem – and may his God be with him. As for anyone left behind in the
place where he lives, his townsmen shall aid him with silver, gold, supplies,
and beasts of burden, as well as gifts for the House of God in Jerusalem."

5 So all of the heads of the ancestral Houses of Yehuda and Binyamin and
the priests and the Levites, and all those whose spirit had been stirred by
God, prepared to go up and to build the House of the LORD, in Jerusalem.
6 And their neighbors supported them with vessels of silver, gold, supplies,
beasts of burden, and precious goods, aside from gifts which had been
7 donated. King Koresh took out the vessels of the House of the LORD that
Nevukhadnetzar had removed from Jerusalem and placed in the house of
8 his gods. Koresh, king of Persia, had them taken out by Mitredat, keeper
of the treasures, who counted them for Sheshbatzar, prince of Yehuda.
9 And this is an account of them: thirty golden dishes, one thousand silver
10 dishes, and twenty-nine knives; thirty golden bowls, four hundred ten
11 double silver bowls, and one thousand other vessels. All vessels of gold
and silver were five thousand four hundred in number; all were taken by
Sheshbatzar when the returning exiles were brought out from Babylonia
to Jerusalem.

2 1 And these are the people of the province, coming up from the captivity
of the exile, that Nevukhadnetzar, king of Babylon, had exiled to Babylon.
2 They returned to Jerusalem and Judea, each to his own town. Those who
came with Zerubavel, Yeshua, Neḥemya, Seraya, Re'elaya, Mordekhai,
Bilshan, Mispar, Bigvai, Reḥum, Baana – the people of the nation of
Israel – numbered as follows:

3 The sons of Parosh: 2,172.
4 The sons of Shefatya: 372.
5 The sons of Araḥ: 775.
6 The sons of Paḥat Moav – the sons of Yeshua and Yoav: 2,812.
7 The sons of Eilam: 1,254.
8 The sons of Zatu: 945.
9 The sons of Zakai: 760.
10 The sons of Bani: 642.

1 | See Jeremiah 25:11–12.

2 | Cf. II Chronicles 36:22–23.

11 The sons of Bevai: 623.
12 The sons of Azgad: 1,222.
13 The sons of Adonikam: 666.
14 The sons of Bigvai: 2,056.
15 The sons of Adin: 454.
16 The sons of Ater of Yeḥizkiya: 98.
17 The sons of Betzai: 323.
18 The sons of Yora: 112.
19 The sons of Ḥashum: 223.
20 The sons of Gibar: 95.
21 The sons of Beit Leḥem: 123.
22 The people of Netofa: 56.
23 The people of Anatot: 128.
24 The sons of Azmavet: 42.
25 The sons of Kiryat Arim, Kefira, and Be'erot: 743.
26 The sons of the Rama and of Gava: 621.
27 The people of Mikhmas: 122.
28 The people of Beit El and Ai: 223.
29 The sons of Nevo: 52.
30 The sons of Magbish: 156.
31 The sons of the other Eilam: 1,254.
32 The sons of Ḥarim: 320.
33 The sons of Lod, Ḥadid, and Ono: 725.
34 The sons of Yeriḥo: 345.
35 The sons of Senaa: 3,630.

36 The priests, sons of Yedaya, of the house of Yeshua: 973.
37 The sons of Imer: 1,052.
38 The sons of Pashḥur: 1,247.
39 The sons of Ḥarim: 1,017.

40 The Levites, sons of Yeshua and Kadmiel, of the sons of Hodavya: 74.
41 The singers, the sons of Asaf: 128.
42 The sons of the gatekeepers – the sons of Shalum, the sons of Ater, the
sons of Talmon, the sons of Akuv, the sons of Ḥatita, the sons of Shovai –
totaling 139.

43 The Netinim[3] – the sons of Tziḥa, the sons of Ḥasufa, the sons of Tabaot.
44 45 The sons of Keros, the sons of Siaha, the sons of Padon. The sons of
46 Levana, the sons of Ḥagava, the sons of Akuv. The sons of Ḥagav, the sons
47 of Shalmai, the sons of Ḥanan. The sons of Gidel, the sons of Gaḥar, the
48 sons of Re'aya. The sons of Retzin, the sons of Nekoda, the sons of Gazam.
49 50 The sons of Uza, the sons of Pase'aḥ, the sons of Besai. The sons of Asna,
51 the sons of Meunites, the sons of Nefusim. The sons of Bakbuk, the sons

3 | A group of Temple servants, whose origins and precise role in the Temple are not entirely clear (see Josh. 9:27; 1 Chr. 9:2).

52 of Ḥakufa, the sons of Ḥarḥur. The sons of Batzlut, the sons of Meḥida, the
53 sons of Ḥarsha. The sons of Barkos, the sons of Sisra, the sons of Tamaḥ.
54 The sons of Netziaḥ, the sons of Ḥatifa.

55 The sons of Shlomo's servants – the sons of Sotai, the sons of HaSoferet,[4]
56 the sons of Peruda. The sons of Yaela, the sons of Darkon, the sons of Gidel.
57 The sons of Shefatya, the sons of Ḥatil, the sons of Pokheret HaTzevayim,[5]
the sons of Ami.

58 The Netinim and Shlomo's servants totaled 392.

59 And these are those who came up from Tel Melaḥ, Tel Ḥarsha, Keruv, Adan,
Imer – but could not prove whether their ancestral house or descent were
60 of Israel: the sons of Delaya, the sons of Toviya, and the sons of Nekoda:
61 652. And of the sons of the priests: the sons of Ḥavaya, the sons of Hakotz,
the sons of Barzilai – he who married one of the daughters of Barzilai the
62 Gileadite and was called by their name. These sought the written record
of their genealogy, which could not be found, and they were therefore
63 repudiated from the priesthood. The governor instructed them that they
must not eat from the holiest offerings until the advent of a priest for the
Urim and the Tumim.[6]

64 65 The entire community altogether numbered 42,360. Aside from their male
and female slaves of whom there were 7,337, they also had 200 male and
66 67 female singers. Their horses – 736; their mules – 245 Their camels 435;
donkeys – 6,720.

68 Some of the clan leaders, when they arrived at the House of the Lord
in Jerusalem, willingly contributed to fix the House of God back on its
69 foundations. Each giving what they could, they donated to the project
treasury sixty-one thousand gold drachmas, five thousand silver mina, and
one hundred priestly robes.

70 And the priests, Levites, and others of the people, the singers, gatekeepers,
and the Netinim, settled in their towns, so that all Israel were in their
towns.

3 1 After the Israelites had settled in their towns, the seventh month arrived,
2 and the people assembled in Jerusalem as one. Then Yeshua son of
Yotzadak and his brothers the priests, and Zerubavel son of She'altiel and
his brothers, rose up and built an altar for the God of Israel, to present
3 burnt offerings as prescribed in the Torah of Moshe, man of God. They
established the altar upon its original foundations, for they were fearful of
the peoples of the land, and presented burnt offerings upon it to the Lord,
4 morning and evening. The people celebrated the Festival of Tabernacles

4 | Literally "the scribe," this name may have denoted the clan's profession.

5 | Literally "gazelle hunters," again perhaps the clan's vocation.

6 | An oracle worn by the High Priest (see Ex. 28:30; Lev. 8:8) which by this time was evidently no longer extant.

as prescribed, performing the designated number of daily offerings each
5 day in accordance with the law for each day.[7] Thereafter, they continued
to present the regular offerings, the offerings of the New Month and all
of the Lord's sacred assemblies, and the voluntary offerings brought for
6 the Lord. On the first day of the seventh month, the priests began to
present burnt offerings to the Lord, though the foundation of the Lord's
7 Sanctuary had not yet been laid. And the leaders paid the hewers and
stone masons in silver, and the Sidonians and Tyreans were given food
and drink and oil to bring cedar wood from Lebanon to the Sea of Jaffa,[8]
in accordance with the permission granted to them by Koresh, king of
Persia.

8 In the second year of their arrival in Jerusalem, for the House of God, in the
second month, Zerubavel son of She'altiel and Yeshua son of Yotzadak and
the rest of their brothers – the priests and the Levites, and all those who
had come from the exile to Jerusalem – began by appointing the Levites,
twenty years of age and above, to supervise the work of constructing the
9 Lord's House. Then Yeshua, his sons and brothers, and Kadmiel and his
sons, and the sons of Yehuda, rose up as one to supervise the builders of
the House of God, along with the sons of Ḥenadad, their sons, and their
brothers the Levites.

10 After the builders had laid the foundation for the Temple of the Lord, the
priests took up their positions in their vestments with trumpets, and the
Levites, the sons of Asaf, with cymbals, to praise the Lord as David, king
11 of Israel, had ordained. The Levites chanted hymns of praise thanking the
Lord, "For He is good; for His kindness to Israel is forever."[9] And all the
people raised a great shout in praise of the Lord, for the House of the
12 Lord had been established. But when many of the older priests, Levites,
and family heads who had seen the first House upon its foundations laid
their eyes on this House, they wept with loud voices,[10] while the crowds
13 raised their voices in a shout of joy. The people could not distinguish the
sound of the shout of joy from the voices of those who wept; for the people
raised a great shout, and the sound was heard from afar.

4 1 The adversaries of Yehuda and Binyamin heard that the returned exiles
2 were building a Sanctuary for the Lord, God of Israel. So they approached
Zerubavel and the family heads and said to them: "Let us join you in
building it, for we too worship your God and have been sacrificing to Him
ever since the days of Esar Ḥadon,[11] king of Assyria, who brought us here."

---

7 | See Numbers 29:12–38.

8 | Cf. the construction of Shlomo's Temple in I Kings 5:16–32.

9 | This phrase is common in Tanakh. Cf., e.g., Psalms 100:5, 106:1, 136:1; II Chronicles 5:13, 7:3.

10 | See Haggai 2:3.

11 | The successor of Sanḥeriv, who had exiled the ten tribes (see II Kings 19:37).

3 But Zerubavel and Yeshua and the rest of the family heads of Israel replied:
"You shall have no part with us building a House for our God; rather, it is
our people who, alone, shall build a House for the LORD, God of Israel, as
Koresh, king of Persia, has commanded us to do."

4 And so the people of the land undermined the people of Yehuda, and
5 made them afraid to build. They employed advisors to foil their plans
throughout the reign of Koresh, king of Persia, and through the reign of
Daryavesh, king of Persia.

6 During the reign of Aḥashverosh, at the outset of his reign, they wrote an accusation against the people of Yehuda and Jerusalem.

7 And in the days of Artaḥshasta, Bishlam, Mitredat, Tavel, and the rest of
his associates wrote to Artaḥshasta, king of Persia; the roll of letters was
8 written in Aramaic and translated into Aramaic.[12] Reḥum the chancellor
and Shimshai the secretary wrote a letter to King Artaḥshasta on the matter
9 of Jerusalem as follows: Reḥum the chancellor and Shimshai the secretary
and their associates: the men of Din-sharru, Afaresatekh, Tarpel, Persia,
10 Erekh, Babylon, Shushan, Dahav, and Elam,[13] and all the other nations
whom great, esteemed Asenapar[14] exiled and sent to settle in the city of
11 Shomron and in the rest of the province beyond the River:[15] And now,this
is the copy of the letter which they sent to him:

"To King Artaḥshasta, from your servants, the people of the province
12 beyond the River. And now, let it be known to the king that the Jews who
arose from your midst have come to us, to Jerusalem. They are rebuilding
the rebellious, evil city. They are close to completing the construction of
13 the walls and have laid the foundations. Now, let it be known to the king
that should this city be rebuilt and its walls completed – no tributes, head
taxes, or property taxes will be paid, and in the end, the interests of the
14 kingdom shall suffer. And now, since we consume the king's salt, and do
not wish to see anything unseemly occur to the king, we saw fit to send this
15 letter to inform the king, suggesting that you, O king, refer to the scrolls
of the records of your predecessors. In those scrolls you will discover and
learn that this city has a history of being rebellious and has inflicted harm
upon kings and provinces; from time immemorial, insurrections have
16 wreaked havoc within it – this is why this city was destroyed. We hereby
forewarn the king that if this city is built and its walls completed, you shall
cease to rule over the province beyond the River."

---

12 | As it presents these official letters, the text switches from Hebrew to Aramaic (until 6:18). Some of these letters may have been written in Old Persian and hence "translated into Aramaic."

13 | Verses 9–10 list the senders of the letter.

14 | Generally identified with Ashurbanipal (669–ca. 627 BCE), son of Esar Ḥadon.

15 | That is, east of the Euphrates River.

17 The king sent this edict: "To Reḥum the chancellor and Shimshai the
secretary and all their associates residing in Shomron and elsewhere in
18 the province beyond the River: Peace. And now: The letter you sent to
19 us has been read before me in translation. I commissioned a search, and
it has indeed been found that this city has, from time immemorial, risen
up against kings, and rebellions and insurrections have wreaked havoc
20 within it. Mighty kings have ruled over Jerusalem and the entire province
beyond the River, and these kings were paid their tributes, head taxes, and
21 property taxes. Now issue a decree commanding these people to remain
idle, so that this city is not rebuilt until another edict to that effect is issued
22 by me. Take care not to err in this matter so as not to aggravate the damage
to the king."

23 The moment King Artaḥshasta's letter was read before Reḥum and Shimshai
the secretary and their associates, they made haste and went to Jerusalem,
to oppose the Jews. They made them stop their work, using belligerent
24 force. Then[16] the work of building the House of God in Jerusalem ceased
and remained at a standstill until the second year of the reign of Daryavesh,
king of Persia.

5 1 And the prophets Ḥagai the prophet and Zekharya son of Ido prophesied
2 to the Jews in Yehuda and Jerusalem in the name of the God of Israel. So
Zerubavel son of She'altiel and Yeshua son of Yotzadak arose and began
to rebuild the House of God in Jerusalem with God's prophets supporting
them.

3 At that very time they were approached by Tattenai, governor of the
province beyond the River, and Shetar Bozenai and their associates, who
asked them: "Who authorized you to build this House and to perfect these
4 goods?" Then they[17] said to them: "What are the names of the men who
5 are involved in the construction?" But the providence of their God rested
upon the elders of Yehuda, so their adversaries did not stop them, waiting
until their report reached Daryavesh and a dispatch was received.

6 The following is the copy of the letter sent to King Daryavesh by Tattenai,
governor of the province beyond the River, and Shetar Bozenai and his
associates, the officials of the province beyond the River.

7 They sent him a report, which reads as follows: "To King Daryavesh,
8 all peace be with you. Let it be known to the king that we went to the
province of Yehuda, to the House of the great God. It is being built with
smoothed stones and wood is being embedded within its walls. This work
9 is progressing diligently and is enjoying great success. We demanded of
their elders: 'Who authorized you to rebuild this House and to perfect

16 | This verse returns to the original conflict in 4:1–3 regarding the construction of the Second Temple.

17 | Literally "we."

10 these goods?' We even asked for their names, so that we could write and
11 inform you of the names of the men who are their leaders. And this was
their reply to us: 'We are the servants of the God of the heavens and the
earth. We are rebuilding the House which was built many years ago; a great
12 king of Israel built it and completed it. But because our ancestors angered
the God of the heavens, He placed them in the power of Nevukhadnetzar,
the Chaldean, king of Babylon, who destroyed the House and exiled the
13 people to Babylon. However, in the first year of the reign of Koresh, king
of Babylon, King Koresh issued an edict that this Temple should be rebuilt.
14 Furthermore, regarding the silver and gold vessels of the House of God
that Nevukhadnetzar had taken away from the Sanctuary in Jerusalem
and brought to the sanctuary in Babylon – King Koresh released them
from the sanctuary in Babylon and handed them over to a man named
15 Sheshbatzar whom he appointed governor. And he said to him: "These are
the vessels. Take them, carry them with you, and place them in the Temple
in Jerusalem, and the House of God shall be rebuilt at its original site."
16 Then that Sheshbatzar came and laid the foundation of the House of God
in Jerusalem; and ever since, it has been under construction but has not
17 been completed.' Now, if it pleases the king, let a search be conducted there
in the royal archives in Babylon, to clarify whether an edict permitting
the building of the House of God in Jerusalem was indeed issued by King
Koresh. Let the king notify us what he wishes to do in this matter."

6 1 So King Daryavesh issued an edict, and they searched in the archive in
2 Babylon where the treasures were stored. But it was in the citadel of
Aḥmeta, in the province of Media, that one scroll was found, and this is
3 what was written therein: "A memorandum: In the first year of the reign of
King Koresh, King Koresh issued an edict regarding the House of God in
Jerusalem. He ordered that the House be rebuilt – a place where sacrifices
are offered – its foundations shall be fortified. Its height shall be sixty
4 cubits and its width sixty cubits. It shall have three courses of smoothed
stones and one course of wood, and the cost shall be paid out of the king's
5 coffers. Additionally, the gold and silver vessels of the House of God that
Nevukhadnetzar had taken from the Sanctuary in Jerusalem and brought
to Babylon shall be returned. Each one shall be replaced in the Temple in
Jerusalem; you shall deposit it in the House of God."

6 "Now, Tattenai, governor of the province beyond the River, and Shetar
Bozenai and associates, the surveyors of the province beyond the River:
7 keep your distance from there. Stop interfering with the work of this
House of God; let the governor of the Jews and their elders build this
8 House of God on its original site. I hereby issue a decree listing what you
must do to help these elders of these Jews rebuild this House of God; the
expense will be paid out of the king's coffers, from the taxes of the province
beyond the River. These funds shall be given to these men diligently so
9 that the work is not discontinued. And all that is needed: bulls, rams,

and sheep for offerings to the God of the heavens; wheat, salt, wine, and
oil – whatever is requested by the priests in Jerusalem – shall be provided
10 to them daily, without delay, so that they might offer fragrant sacrifices to
the God of the heavens and pray for the life of the king and his children.
11 I hereby decree that if anyone deviates from this edict, a beam shall be
removed from his house, and he will be impaled on it; his house shall be
12 made into a ruin for this. May the God who has established His name there
overthrow any king or nation who dares deviate thereupon by harming
this House of God in Jerusalem. I, Daryavesh, have issued this edict; let it
be implemented in full."

13 So Tattenai, governor of the province beyond the River, and Shetar Bozenai
14 and their associates followed Daryavesh's edict in full. And the elders of the
Jews went on with the building successfully encouraged by the prophecy
of Ḥagai the prophet and Zekharya son of Ido; they built the House and
completed it according to the command of the God of Israel and in keeping
with the edict of Koresh, Daryavesh, and King Artaḥshasta of Persia.
15 The construction of this House was completed by the thirteenth day of
16 the month of Adar, in the sixth year of the reign of King Daryavesh. The
Israelites, the priests and the Levites, and all the other returning exiles
17 celebrated the dedication of the House of God with joy. In honor of the
dedication of the House of God, they offered one hundred bulls, two
hundred rams, four hundred lambs as well as goats to atone for all of Israel.
18 There were twelve goats representing the twelve tribes of Israel. They
established the shifts of the priests and the divisions of the Levites for the
worship in the Temple in Jerusalem as prescribed in the book of Moshe.

19 The[18] returning exiles sacrificed the Passover offering on the fourteenth
20 day of the first month. For the priests and the Levites had all purified
themselves; every one of them was pure. They slaughtered the Passover
offering for all the returning exiles, and for their brothers the priests, and
21 for themselves. The Israelites who returned from the exile partook of it,
along with all those who separated themselves from the impurity of the
22 nations of the land and came to worship the Lord, God of Israel. They
celebrated the Festival of Unleavened Bread for seven days with joy, for the
Lord had brought them joy, by causing the king of Assyria[19] to change his
heart, supporting their construction of the House of the God of Israel.

7 1 Some time after this, during the reign of Artaḥshasta, king of Persia, came
2 Ezra, son of Seraya, son of Azarya, son of Ḥilkiya, son of Shalum, son of
3 4 Tzadok, son of Aḥituv, son of Amarya, son of Azarya, son of Merayot, son
5 of Zeraḥya, son of Uzi, son of Buki, son of Avishua, son of Pinḥas, son of
6 Elazar, son of Aharon the High Priest; this Ezra ascended from Babylon.
He was a scholar,[20] expert in the Torah of Moshe given by the Lord, God

18 | Starting with this verse, the text reverts from Aramaic to Hebrew.

19 | Daryavesh.

20 | Literally "scribe."

of Israel; the king granted him his every wish, for the hand of the LORD,
his God, was upon him.

7 In the seventh year of the reign of Artaḥshasta, some of the Israelites,
priests, Levites, singers, gatekeepers, and Netinim ascended to Jerusalem,
8 arriving in Jerusalem in the fifth month, during the seventh year of the
9 king's reign. It was on the first day of the first month that the pilgrims met
up to begin their journey from Babylon, arriving in Jerusalem on the first
10 day of the fifth month, for the good hand of his God was upon him. For
Ezra had set his heart on expounding the LORD's Torah and observing it;
he wished to teach Israel its laws and precepts.

11 This is the copy of the letter given by King Artaḥshasta to Ezra the priest,
the scholar: an authority of the LORD's commandments and His laws to
12 Israel.[21] "From Artaḥshasta, king of kings, to Ezra the priest, scholar of
13 the law of the God of the heavens, and so forth. And now, I hereby issue
an edict that any man in my kingdom who is of the nation of Israel or
its priests or Levites who is ready to go to Jerusalem, may go there with
14 you. Whereas, by the order of the king and his seven ministers, you are
hereby sent to supervise Yehuda and Jerusalem, in accordance with the
15 law of your God which you uphold. And to transport the silver and gold
donated by the king and his ministers to the God of Israel whose Temple
16 is in Jerusalem, along with any silver and gold you may acquire anywhere
in the province of Babylonia, as well as the donations of the people and
17 the priests to the House of their God in Jerusalem. Therefore, act diligently
and purchase offerings with this money: bulls, rams, lambs, and their
required grain offerings and wine libations, and offer them upon the altar
18 of the House of your God in Jerusalem. The rest of the silver and gold
may be put to use as you and your brothers see fit, according to the will of
19 your God. The vessels you are hereby entrusted with for the service of the
House of your God must be brought undamaged to the God of Jerusalem.
20 Whatever else is needed for the House of your God, that which you are
responsible to provide, may be charged to the king's coffers.

21 "I, King Artaḥshasta, have issued an edict to all Keepers of the Treasures
in the province beyond the River, ordering them to diligently grant every
22 request of Ezra, the priest, scribe of the law of the God of the heavens, up
to the sum of one hundred *kikar* of silver, one hundred *kor* of wheat, one
hundred *bat* of wine, one hundred *bat* of oil, and an unlimited amount
23 of salt. All that is required by the law of the God of the heavens shall be
provided assiduously for the House of the God of the Heavens, so that His
24 rage does not lash out upon the realm of the king and his sons. We also
inform you that no priest, Levite, singer, gatekeeper, Natin, or any other
person employed at the House of this God shall be subject to the payment
of tributes, head taxes, or property taxes.

---

21 | The entire text of this letter (7:12–26) is in Aramaic rather than Hebrew.

25 "And you, Ezra, use the wisdom of your God to appoint judges and
magistrates who will dispense judgment to all the people in the province
beyond the River, men with knowledge of the laws of your God; you shall
26 provide instruction to those who do not know them. Anyone who fails
to obey the laws of your God and the laws of the king shall be sentenced
promptly to death, corporal punishment, fine, or imprisonment."

27 Blessed is the LORD, God of our ancestors, for turning the king's heart
28 toward the cause of beautifying the House of the LORD in Jerusalem. And
for showing me kindness in the eyes of the king and his ministers and all his
valiant officers. So, by the grace of the LORD my God, I gathered courage
and assembled leaders from Israel to ascend to the land with me.

8 1 These are the heads of families – along with their family lines – who came
2 up with me from Babylon during the reign of King Artaḥshasta. From the
family of Pinḥas: Gershom; from the family of Itamar: Daniel; from the
3 family of David: Ḥatush, a descendant of Shekhanya. From the family of
Parosh: Zekharya; along with him were one hundred fifty men whose
4 lineage was recorded. From the family of Paḥat Moav: Elyeho'einai son
5 of Zeraḥya; along with him were two hundred men. From the family of
Shekhanya, the son of Yaḥaziel; along with him were three hundred men.
6 And from the family of Adin: Eved son of Yonatan, of the sons of Adin;
7 along with him were fifty men; from the family of Eilam: Yeshaya son of
8 Atalya; along with him were seventy men. And from the family of Shefatya:
9 Zevadya son of Mikhael; along with him were eighty men. From the family
of Yoav: Ovadya son of Yeḥiel; along with him were two hundred eighteen
10 men; from the family of Shlomit: Ben Yosifya; along with him were one
11 hundred sixty men; from the family of Bevai: Zekharya son of Bevai; along
12 with him were twenty-eight men; from the family of Azgad: Yoḥanan son
13 of Hakatan; along with him were one hundred ten men; and from the
family of Adonikam, the last ones,[22] and these were their names: Elifelet,
14 Ye'iel, and Shemaya; along with them were sixty men. And from the family
of Bigvai: Utai and Zakur; along with them were seventy men.

15 I assembled them at the river that flows to Ahava, and we encamped there
for three days; I noted the presence of Israelites and priests, but I did not
16 find any of the Levites there. So I called upon Eliezer, Ariel, Shemaya,
Elnatan, Yariv, Elnatan, Natan, Zekharya, and Meshulam, who were leaders,
17 as well as Yoyariv and Elnatan, who were teachers. I charged them with
the task of approaching Ido, the master of a place called Kasifya. I placed
words in their mouths to relay to Ido and his brother, Netinim[23] in Kasifya,
18 requesting that they send us men to serve in the House of our God. And
God's good hand was upon us; they sent us a wise man who was descended
from Maḥli son of Levi, the son of Yisrael, namely Shereveya and his sons
19 and brothers, eighteen men. And also Ḥashavya, along with Yeshaya who

22 | Likely the last members of the family to leave Babylon.

23 | See note on 2:43.

was from the family of Merari and his brothers and their sons, twenty men;
20 As well as two hundred twenty of the Netinim who had been dedicated to
the service of the Levites by David and his ministers, all listed by name.

21 I then proclaimed a fast there, upon the Ahava River, so that we might
abstain from sustenance before our God, asking Him for a smooth journey
22 for ourselves, for our small children, and for all of our possessions. For I
was ashamed to ask the king for a detachment of soldiers and cavalry to
protect us from enemies on the journey, since we had already said to the
king: "The hand of our God is upon those who seek Him in their favor,
23 but His fierce wrath is upon all those who forsake Him." So we fasted and
implored our God for this, and He granted our plea.

24 Then I set aside twelve of the leading priests in addition to Shereveya and
25 Ḥashavya and the ten kinsmen who were with them. I weighed the silver
and gold and vessels for them: all that the king and his ministers and
advisors and all the Israelites who had been present had donated to the
26 House of our God. These are the amounts I weighed for them: six hundred
fifty talents of silver and an additional one hundred silver vessels worth
27 one talent each; one hundred talents of gold; twenty golden bowls worth
one thousand gold darics,[24] and two vessels of brightly gleaming copper
28 as precious as gold. And I said to them: "You are holy to the Lord, and
the vessels are holy, and the silver and gold are a gift to the Lord, God of
29 your ancestors. Be vigilant and safeguard them until you weigh them in the
presence of the leaders of the priests and the Levites and the heads of the
fathers' households of Israel in Jerusalem, in the chambers of the House
30 of the Lord." So the priests and the Levites took it upon themselves to
transport the entire amount of silver, gold, and vessels to Jerusalem, to
the House of our God.

31 We journeyed from the Ahava River on the twelfth day of the first month,
heading for Jerusalem; the providence of our God was upon us, and He
saved us from falling into the hands of enemies and from ambushes on
32 33 the road. We arrived in Jerusalem and rested there for three days. On the
fourth day, the silver and gold and vessels were weighed in the House of
our God and entrusted to Meremot, son of Uriya the priest, along with
Elazar son of Pinḥas; also present were the Levites, Yozavad son of Yeshua
34 and Noadya son of Binui. Everything was counted out and weighed, and
the weight of the lot was recorded in writing on that occasion.

35 Those who returned from the captivity, the exiles, presented burnt offerings
to the God of Israel: twelve bulls representing all of Israel, ninety-six rams,
seventy-seven sheep, and twelve goats for atonement; all of these a burnt
36 offering to the Lord. And they delivered the king's orders to the king's
viceroys and to the governors of the province beyond the River, who held
the people and the House of God in great esteem.

24 | A Persian currency.

9 1 When all of this was over, the leaders approached me and said: "The people
Israel, and even the priests and Levites, have failed to separate themselves
from the people of the land. They engage in abominations in the manner
of the Canaanites, the Hittites, the Perizzites, the Jebusites, the Amonites,
2 the Moabites, the Egyptians, and the Amorites. For they have taken some
of their daughters as wives for themselves and for their sons, and the holy
seed has been mixed up with that of the people of the land; the leaders
3 and the officials have led the way in this unfaithfulness." When I heard
this, I rent my garment and my mantle, tore out hair from my head and
4 beard, and sat down, dumbfounded. And those who feared the word of
the God of Israel gathered around me because of the unfaithfulness of the
returned exiles. I myself sat there dumbfounded until it was time for the
afternoon offering.

5 At the time of the evening offering, I rose up from my fast, with my garment
and mantle torn. I knelt down on my knees and spread out my hands to
6 the Lord my God. And I said:

"My God! I am utterly mortified to face You, my God, for our sins have
increased so much that they have piled up above our heads, and our guilt
7 has mounted up to the heavens. Ever since the days of our ancestors, we
have been entrenched in great guilt, until this very day. Because of our sins,
we and our kings and priests have been handed over to foreign kings, to
the sword, to captivity, to pillage, and to shamefacedness, from which we
8 suffer to this very day. But now, for a short moment we have been granted
a pardon by the Lord our God, who has left us a remnant and has given
us a stake in His holy place. Our God has rekindled the light in our eyes,
9 allowing us to sustain ourselves a little in our bondage. For indeed, we are
slaves, but in our bondage, our God has not forsaken us. He has shown us
kindness through the kings of Persia, allowing us to sustain ourselves, to
exalt the House of our God and rebuild its ruins; He has built us a wall in
Yehuda and Jerusalem.

10 "And now, O our God, what can we say after this? Indeed, we have forsaken
11 Your commandments, which You gave through Your servants, the prophets,
who said:[25] The land that you are coming into to possess is an impure land,
polluted by the people of the land who, with their abominations, have filled
12 it with their impurity from end to end. And now, you shall not give your
daughters to their sons, and you shall not take their daughters for your sons,
and you shall not seek their peace or welfare, ever. Thus, you will be strong
and partake of the best of the land and bequeath it to your children forever.
13 After all that has befallen us due to our evil deeds and our great guilt, You,
our God, have punished us for less than the worth of our sins, having given
14 us this remnant. Shall we then disobey Your commandments yet again by

25 | See Leviticus, chapter 18.

intermarrying with these peoples who are replete with these abominations?
Would You not rage against us to the end, not leaving a remnant or a trace?
15 O LORD, God of Israel, You have dealt with us righteously, for we are a mere
remnant on this day; here we are before You with our guilt, though we are
unworthy of standing before You."

10 1 As Ezra prayed and confessed, weeping as he knelt down on his knees
before the House of God, a very large crowd of Israelites gathered around
him: men, women, and children, weeping a great deal.

2 Then Shekhanya son of Yeḥiel, of the sons of Eilam, spoke up, saying to
Ezra: "We have indeed been unfaithful to our God by marrying foreign
women of the peoples of the land; even so, there is still hope for Israel in
3 this matter. Now, let us make a covenant with our God to send away all
these women and their offspring, according to the counsel of the LORD
and of those who fear our God's commandments; everyone shall abide by
4 the law. Rise up, for it is your duty to take care of this matter; we will be
5 with you. Be strong and take action." So Ezra rose up and made the leaders
of the priests and the Levites and all of Israel take an oath that they would
act upon this, and they took the oath.

6 Then Ezra left his place before the House of God and went to the chamber
of Yoḥanan son of Elyashiv. He went there, all the while abstaining from
eating bread and drinking water, for he was still mourning the unfaithfulness of the returned exiles.

7 A proclamation was made throughout Yehuda and Jerusalem calling all
8 the returned exiles to assemble in Jerusalem, warning that anyone who
did not come within three days as prescribed by the leaders and elders
would have all his property confiscated and would be shunned from the
assembly of the exiles.

9 So all the people of Yehuda and Binyamin assembled in Jerusalem within
three days; it was the twentieth day of the ninth month. All of the people
sat in the plaza in front of the House of God, trembling because of the affair
10 and due to the heavy rains. Ezra the priest stood up and addressed them:
"You have been unfaithful by marrying foreign women, thus increasing the
11 guilt of Israel. But now, make your confession to the LORD, God of your
ancestors, and perform His will by separating yourselves from the peoples
12 of the land and from the foreign women." The whole assembly responded
13 loudly: "Indeed, we should do as you say. But there are many people, and
it is the rainy season so we cannot go on standing outdoors. In any event,
the task cannot be completed in a day or two, since we have sinned greatly
14 in this matter. Let our leaders stand in for the whole assembly: Every man
in any of our towns who has married a foreign woman shall come at his
designated time along with the elders and judges of that town until God's

15 rage over this affair has been turned away from us." Only Yonatan son of
Asael, and Yaḥzeya son of Tikva, objected to this, supported by Meshulam
and Shabtai the Levite.

16 So that is what the returned exiles did. Ezra the priest and men who were
heads of families sequestered themselves to represent their families, all
listed by name. They convened on the first day of the tenth month to
17 investigate the matter. They concluded the investigation regarding the
men who had married foreign women on the first day of the first month.

18 From the families of the priests they found that those who had married
foreign women were: From the family of Yeshua son of Yotzadak, and his
19 brothers: Maaseya, Eliezer, Yariv, and Gedalya. They pledged to send away
their wives; the guilty parties vowed to bring rams of the flock for their
20 21 guilt. From the family of Imer: Ḥanani and Zevadya. From the family of
22 Ḥarim: Maaseya, Eliya, Shemaya, Yeḥiel, and Uziya. And from the family
of Pashḥur: Elyo'einai, Maaseya, Yishmael, Netanel, Yozavad, and Elasa.
23 And of the Levites: Yozavad, Shimi, and Kelaya – that is, Kelita – Petaḥya,
24 Yehuda, and Eliezer. And of the singers: Elyashiv; of the gatekeepers,
Shalum, Telem, and Uri.

25 And of the Israelites: Of the sons of Parosh: Ramya, Yiziya, Malkiya,
26 Miyamin, Elazar, Malkiya, and Benaya. From the family of Eilam: Matanya,
27 Zekharya, Yeḥiel, Avdi, Yeremot, and Eliya. From the family of Zatu:
28 Elyo'einai, Elyashiv, Matanya, Yeremot, Zavad, and Aziza. From the family
29 of Bevai: Yehoḥanan, Ḥananya, Zabai, and Atlai. From the family of Bani:
30 Meshulam, Malukh, Adaya, Yashuv, She'al, and Ramot. From the family of
Paḥat Moav: Adna, Kelal, Benaya, Maaseya, Matanya, Betzalel, Binui, and
31 Menashe. From the family of Ḥarim: Eliezer, Yishiya, Malkiya, Shemaya,
32 33 Shimon; Binyamin, Malukh, and Shemarya. From the family of Ḥashum:
34 Matnai, Matata, Zavad, Elifelet, Yeremai, Menashe, and Shimi. From
35 the family of Bani: Maadai, Amram, and U'el; Benaya, Bedya, Keluhu;
36 37, 38 Vanya, Meremot, Elyashiv, Matanya, Matnai, and Yaasai; Bani, Binui,
39, 40 and Shimi; Shelemya, Natan, and Adaya; Makhnadvai, Shashai, Sharai;
41 42, 43 Azarel, Shelemyahu, Shemarya; Shalum, Amarya, Yosef. And from the
family of Nevo: Ye'iel, Matitya, Zavad, Zevina, Yadai, Yoel, and Benaya.
44 All these men had married foreign women, some of whom had produced
offspring.

NEHEMIAH/NEḤEMYA 1 1 The words of Neḥemya son of Ḥakhalya: In the month of Kislev in the
2 twentieth year,[1] I was in the citadel of Shushan.[2] There came Ḥanani, one
of my brothers, he and men from Yehuda whom I questioned about the
Jews, those survivors remaining from the captivity,[3] and about Jerusalem.

1 | The twentieth year of the reign of Artaḥshasta I, king of Persia, was 445 BCE, several decades after Koresh first issued his proclamation allowing the Jews to return to the land of Israel.

2 | A royal capital that was also the setting for most of the book of Esther.

3 | This phrase likely refers to the Jewish community of returnees from Babylonia.

3 And they told me, "Those remaining from the captivity in the province are
degraded and in dire distress while Jerusalem's wall has been everywhere
4 broken through, and her gates have been put to the torch." Upon hearing
these tidings, I sat down and wept, mourning for days while fasting and
praying before the God of the heavens.

5 I said,[4] "Please, LORD, God of the heavens, the great and awesome God,
who keeps His covenant of love with those who love Him and keep His
6 commandments, please, may Your ear heed and Your eyes be open to
hear Your servant's prayer that I am now praying before You day and
night on behalf of the Israelites Your servants, while confessing the sins
of the Israelites that we have sinned against You; I and my father's house
7 have also sinned. We have injured You grievously and have not kept the
commandments, statutes, and laws with which You charged Moshe, Your
servant.

8 "Remember, please, what You charged Moshe, Your servant, saying,[5] 'You
9 will break faith; I will disperse you among the nations – yet you will return
to Me; you will keep My commandments and observe them. If you should
be expelled to the farthest of horizons, even from there I will gather them,
10 bringing them to the place where I have chosen to house My name,' for
they are Your servants, Your people, whom You redeemed by Your great
11 power and Your strong hand. Please, O LORD – may Your ear heed Your
servant's prayer and the prayer of Your servants, eager to revere Your name.
Please let Your servant succeed today and grant him the mercy of this
man" – for I was official cupbearer to the king.

2 1 It was in the month of Nisan in the twentieth year of King Artaḥshasta,
while wine was before him, that I bore the wine and gave it to the king,
2 whom I did not displease. The king said to me, "Why is your face downcast?
Since you are not sick – it must be ill-heartedness." And I was filled with
trepidation.

3 Then I said to the king, "May the king live forever! Why should my face
not be downcast when the city that houses my ancestral tombs lies in
4 ruins with her gates consumed by fire?" The king said to me, "What is it
5 that you ask?" I prayed to the God of the heavens, and then I said to the
king, "If it pleases the king, and if your servant pleases you, send me to
6 Yehuda, to the city of my ancestral tombs, and I will rebuild her. And the
king said to me, as the queen consort[6] sat with him, "How long will you
be away, and when will you return?" It pleased the king to send me, and
we settled upon a time frame.

7 Then I said to the king, "If it pleases the king, let me be given missives to

4 | The language of this prayer parallels several other passages (cf. 9:32, and Deut. 7:9; I Kings 8:23–52; Dan. 9:4; and II Chr. 6:14–40).

5 | See, e.g., Deuteronomy 4:25–30, 12:11, 30:1–6.

6 | Cf. Psalms 45:10.

the governors beyond the River granting me passage so that I may come
8 to Yehuda. Likewise a missive to Asaf, the royal forester, so that he will
provide me with timber to roof the gates of the citadel of the House,[7] the
city wall, and the residence to which I will come." The king endowed me
9 in accordance with the good hand of my God upon me. So I came to the
governors beyond the River and presented to them the king's missives;
with me the king sent army captains and cavalry.

10 When Sanvalat the Horonite and Toviya the Amonite servant heard of
this, they took it exceedingly ill that someone had come seeking the good
of the Israelites.

11 12 I arrived in Jerusalem and was there for three days. Then I rose at night,
I and a few people with me, telling no one what my God was instilling
in my heart to accomplish for Jerusalem and taking no animals with me
13 except the one I rode. That night I exited through the Valley Gate facing
Ein HaTanin and the Dung Gate, all the while surveying the walls of
Jerusalem that are everywhere broken through and her gates consumed
14 by fire. I passed on to the Spring Gate and the King's pool, but there was
15 no room for the animal beneath me to pass. So instead that night I went
up the streambed, still surveying the wall, then turned back, reentered
through the Valley Gate, and so returned.

16 The officials did not know where I had gone or what I was doing, and I
had not yet told the Jews: the priests, the nobles and officials, and the
17 other participants in the project. Then I said to them, "You see our dismal
state with Jerusalem in ruins and her gates having been put to the torch.
Come – let us together rebuild Jerusalem's wall and no longer be degraded!"
18 I then revealed to them how my God's hand had favored me and the things
the king had said to me. They declared, "We will arise and rebuild," their
hands strengthened for the good.

19 Hearing of this, Sanvalat the Horonite, Toviya the Amonite servant, and
Geshem the Arab mocked and derided us, saying, "What do you think
20 you are doing? Are you rebelling against the king?" But I responded to
them, saying, "It is the God of heavens who will grant us success. We His
servants will arise and rebuild, while for you there is neither a share nor a
right nor any memory in Jerusalem."

3 1 Then Elyashiv the High Priest and his brother priests arose and built
the Sheep Gate, consecrating it and erecting its doors. They consecrated
2 from the Tower of the Hundred up to the Tower of Ḥananel. The people
3 of Yeriḥo built next, and Zakur son of Imri built next. The Fish Gate was
built by the sons of HaSenaa:[8] they roofed it and erected its doors, bolts,
4 and bars. Meremot son of Uriya son of HaKotz made repairs next to them,

---

7 | This likely refers to a fortified section of Jerusalem surrounding the Temple.

8 | Cf. the list of returnees in Ezra, chapter 2.

then Meshulam son of Berekhya son of Mesheizavel made repairs, then
5 Tzadok son of Baana. The Tekoites made repairs next to them, and their
chieftains did not bend their necks to the yoke of their lords.[9]

6 The Old Gate was repaired by Yehoyada son of Pase'aḥ and Meshulam son
7 of Besodeya, who roofed it and erected its doors, bolts, and bars. Melatya
the Gibeonite and Yadon the Meronite were repairing next to them along
with men of Givon and the Mitzpa, of the province beyond the River.
8 Uziel son of Ḥarhaya, of the smiths, made repairs next to them, as did
Ḥananya of the perfumers – and they plastered throughout Jerusalem up
9 to the Wide Wall. Refaya son of Ḥur, commissioner of a half district of
10 Jerusalem, made repairs next to them. And Yedaya son of Ḥarumaf made
repairs next to them as well as opposite his home while Ḥatush son of
11 Ḥashavneya made repairs next to him. Malkiya son of Ḥarim repaired a
second segment as did Ḥashuv, son of Paḥat Moav, including the Tower of
12 Furnaces. Next, Shalum son of HaLoḥesh, commissioner of a half district
of Jerusalem, made repairs, together with his daughters.

13 The Valley Gate was repaired by Ḥanun and the residents of Zanoaḥ. They
built it, erecting its doors, bars, and bolts as well as one thousand cubits
14 of the wall up to the Dung Gate. The Dung Gate was repaired by Malkiya
son of Rekhav, commissioner of the Beit HaKerem district. He alone
15 built it, erecting its doors, bolts, and bars. The Spring Gate was repaired
by Shalun son of Kol Ḥozeh, commissioner of the Mitzpa district, who
built it himself, constructing its ceiling and erecting its doors, bolts, and
bars in addition to the wall of the Shelaḥ pool in the king's garden up to
the stairs descending from Ir David.

16 Neḥemya son of Azbuk, half-district commissioner of Beit Tzur, followed,
repairing up to and opposite the tombs of David and up to the artificial
17 pool and the house of warriors. Following him, the Levites made repairs:
Reḥum son of Bani and next to him Ḥashavya, a half-district commissioner
18 of Ke'ila, made repairs along with his district. Their kinsmen followed in
making repairs: Bavai son of Ḥenadad, a half-district commissioner of
19 Ke'ila, and Ezer son of Yeshua, commissioner of the Mitzpa, who repaired
a second segment next to him opposite the elevated armory in the inner
corner.

20 Barukh son of Zakai followed, fervently repairing a second segment from
the inner corner up to the entrance to the house of the High Priest Elyashiv.
21 Meremot son of Uriya son of HaKotz followed, repairing a second segment
from the entrance of Elyashiv's house up to the edge of Elyashiv's house.
22 23 Following him, the priests, men of the vale,[10] made repairs. Binyamin

9 | This can be understood as a criticism of the chieftains for failing to participate in the reconstruction: They "did not bend their [*own*] necks to the yoke of their lords," i.e., the officials in charge of the construction.

10 | Perhaps the Jordan Valley.

and Ḥashuv followed, making repairs opposite their homes, followed by
Azarya son of Maaseya son of Ananeya, who made repairs near his own
home.

24 Binui son of Ḥenadad followed, repairing a second segment from the
25 house of Azarya to the inner corner all the way to the outer corner. Then
came Palal son of Uzai, opposite the inner corner and the Jutting Tower of
the upper royal residence of the Court of the Guard, followed by Pedaya
son of Parosh.

26 The Netinim residing in the Ofel[11] made repairs up to the Water Gate to
27 the east and the Jutting Tower. The Tekoites followed, repairing a second
segment opposite the Great Jutting Tower extending to the Ofel Wall.
28 Above the Horse Gate, the priests made repairs, each opposite his home.
29 Tzadok son of Imer followed, repairing opposite his home, followed
in repairing by Shemaya son of Shekhanya, guardian of the East Gate.
30 Ḥananya son of Shelemya and Ḥanun the sixth son of Tzalaf followed,
repairing a second segment, followed by Meshulam son of Berekhya,
31 who made repairs opposite his own chamber. Malkiya son of HaTzorfi
followed, making the repairs up to the house of the Netinim and the
32 Traders – opposite the Muster Gate and the Corner Ascent. The smiths
and the traders made repairs between the Corner Ascent and the Sheep
Gate.

33 When Sanvalat heard that we were rebuilding the wall, he was furious;
34 enraged, he jeered at the Jews. Speaking before his kinsmen and the
Samaritan forces, he said, "What are the miserable Jews doing? Will they
plaster, offer the consecration sacrifices, and reach the completion day?
Will they revive the stones from the rubble heaps after they have been
35 burned?" Toviya the Amonite, who was with him, said, "So what if they
are building? A climbing jackal could break through their stone wall!"

36 Hear, our God, how we are shamed! Heap their derision on their own
37 heads, rendering them spoils in a land of captivity. Do not cover their
crimes. Do not erase their sin from Your presence, for they have incited
anger against the builders.

38 So we built the wall and the entire wall was joined together up to its
halfway point, and the people acted with a willing heart.

4 1 But when Sanvalat and Toviya and the Arabs, Amonites, and Ashdodites
heard that the walls of Jerusalem were being rejuvenated as the breaks
2 began to be filled, they were incensed. They all then joined together to
3 wage war upon Jerusalem and cause confusion there. But we prayed to our
God and meanwhile set up a watch over the walls, day and night, against
4 them. Yehuda was saying, "The bearers' strength is sapped; the rubble has

11 | The Ofel was an elevated, fortified portion of Jerusalem, located to the south of the Temple Mount.

5 no end – we are simply unable to build the wall." Our enemies declared,
"They will neither know nor see until we come among them and slaughter
6 them – ending the entire endeavor." But when the Jews living among them
came, they told us ten times that at the places to which we always return,
they will come upon us.[12]

7 Therefore, in the lower places behind the wall, within the crags, I arrayed
the people, arranging them in families with their swords, lances, and bows.
8 I looked out, then got to my feet, saying to the nobles and officials and the
rest of the people, "Fear them not; remember the great and awe-inspiring
Lord, and fight for your kinsmen, for your sons and daughters, your wives,
9 and your homes." And when our enemies heard that we had been informed
and that God had thus foiled their plan, we all returned to the wall, each
of us to our tasks.

10 From that day on, half my men engaged in the work while half bore the
lances, shields, bows, and armor, with the officers following behind all the
11 House of Yehuda. They built the wall, and the bearers loaded – with one
12 hand doing the work and the other holding a weapon. The builders each
had their swords strapped at their hips as they built, and the horn blower
13 was by my side. For I had said to the nobles and officials and the rest of
the people, "The work is extensive and widely scattered as long as we are
14 spread along the wall, far away from each other. Wherever you hear the
sound of the horn, gather to us there – our God will fight for us."

15 So we engaged in the work, with half holding lances from the break of
16 dawn until the stars showed. At the same time I also said to the people,
"Each of you and your men must sleep in Jerusalem, serving as a watch by
17 night and a workforce by day." Neither I, nor my brothers nor my men
nor the watchmen following me ever undressed – each with his weapon
even at the water.[13]

5 1 There was a vehement outcry by the people and their wives against their
2 fellow Jews. Some said, "We have so many sons and daughters that we
3 need to buy grain in order to eat and so stay alive." Others said, "We
must mortgage our fields, our vineyards, and our homes to buy grain to
4 stave off starvation." And there were some who said, "We have had to
5 borrow money against our fields and vineyards to pay the king's levy. Is our
brothers' flesh not like ours? Their sons akin to our own? And yet we must
force our sons and daughters into servitude, and some of our daughters
have already been forced in that way while we stand helplessly by. Our
fields and vineyards have gone to others."

6 7 I was incensed when I heard of their cries and of these events. Taking
counsel from my heart, I upbraided the nobles and officials, saying to
them, "You are exacting exorbitant payments from your own brothers!"

12 | That is, they warned us of the impending attack.

13 | In other words, we were armed at all times, vigilant for potential threats.

8 Then I summoned them to a large assembly, and I said to them, "Insofar
as we could afford to, we have been buying back our brother Jews who
were sold to other nations,[14] but now you will sell your brothers to be
sold back to us?" And they were silenced and could find nothing to
say.

9 Then I said, "What you are doing is not right. You should walk in fear
10 of our God and of the derision of our enemies, the nations. And yes, I
too, my brothers, and my men have been demanding money and grain
11 in repayment of debt. Let us now end this exaction! Will you not return
to them this very day their fields, their vineyards, their olive groves, and
their homes and also forgo the money – be it even one hundred silver
coins – and the grain, wine, and olive oil that you are exacting from them?"
12 And they said, "We will restore it all and demand no more of them. We
will do just as you say." Whereupon I summoned the priests and had
13 them swear to act accordingly. I then shook out my pocket, declaring, "So
may God shake out of his home and possessions anyone who does not
act accordingly; just so may he be shaken out and left empty." The entire
congregation said "Amen" and praised the Lord – and the people acted
accordingly.

14 From the day he invested me as governor of the land of Yehuda – from
the twentieth to the thirty-second year of King Artaḥshasta – twelve
15 years – neither my kinsmen nor I partook of the governor's food tribute, for
the governors preceding me burdened the people heavily, taking bread and
wine from them as well as forty silver shekel while their men lorded over
16 the people. But I did not do so because of fear of God. I also supported
the work on the wall, and we did not acquire any fields;[15] rather, all my
men were gathered there for that enterprise.

17 At my table were one hundred fifty men from the Jews and the officials
18 as well as those joining us from the surrounding nations. One ox, six
choice sheep, and poultry were made for me each day – that was one day's
provision – and every ten days there was an abundant supply of wine. Yet
even so, I did not claim the governors' food tribute because the service
19 burdened this people too heavily. Remember me favorably, my God, for
everything I did on behalf of this people.

6 1 Now Sanvalat, Toviya, Geshem the Arab, and our other enemies heard
that I had rebuilt the wall and that not a single break remained, although
2 at that time I had not yet erected doors in the gates. Then Sanvalat and
Geshem sent to me, saying, "Come, let us convene together in Kefirim, in
3 Bikat Ono," all the while intending to do me harm. I sent them messengers
saying, "I am engaged in an epic enterprise and cannot come down lest the

---

14 | See Leviticus 25:47–49.

15 | I did not seize land from the poor as payment or collateral for financial support.

4 project cease while I withdraw to come down to you." They sent to me in
this manner four times, and I replied to them accordingly.

5 Then Sanvalat sent his man to me for the fifth time in this fashion, but
6 with an open missive in his hand. In it was written, "It is rumored among
the nations and confirmed by Gashmu[16] that you and the Jews plan to
rebel, and that is why you are building the wall, intending to be their king,
7 and additional such reports. Furthermore, you have set up prophets to
proclaim of you in Jerusalem, 'A king in Yehuda.' Now the king will hear
such reports! Come, let us deliberate together."

8 But I sent back to him, saying, "These reports you speak of never were, for
9 it is from your own heart that you are fabricating them." They are all trying
to intimidate us, saying, "They will withdraw their hands from the task,
leaving it undone." Now may my hands grow in strength!

10 Then I came to the house of Shemaya son of Delaya son of Meheitavel, who
was in seclusion, and he said, "Let us meet in the House of God, inside the
Sanctuary, while shutting the Sanctuary doors – for they are coming to kill
11 you. At night they are coming to kill you." But I said, "Should a man like
myself run away? And who am I to enter the Sanctuary and live? No! I will
12 not come in." Then I realized that it was not God who had sent him – his
13 prophecy about me was because Toviya and Sanvalat had hired him. He
was hired so that I would take fright and act in this way, sinning, so that
they could then defame and disgrace me.

14 My God, remember Toviya and Sanvalat for these actions of theirs, as well as
Noadya the prophetess and the other prophets who tried to intimidate me.
15 But the wall was completed on the twenty-fifth of Elul after fifty-two days.

16 When all our enemies heard, all the surrounding nations were afraid and
sank low in their own eyes, recognizing that this endeavor was brought
17 about by our God. Yet throughout this time the nobles of the Jews fre-
18 quently sent letters to Toviya while those from Toviya came to them. For
many in Yehuda were sworn to him as he was the son-in-law of Shekhanya
son of Araḥ, and his own son Yehoḥanan had married the daughter of
19 Meshulam son of Berekhya. Accordingly, they would mention his good
deeds to me while divulging my words to him, and all the while, Toviya
was sending out letters to intimidate me.

7 1 Once the wall had been built and I had erected the doors, the gatekeepers,
2 singers, and Levites were counted. Then I put my brother Ḥanani and
Ḥananya, commander of the citadel, in command of Jerusalem, for he was
widely known as a true and God-fearing man.

3 I gave orders to them: "Let the gates of Jerusalem not be opened until the
sun heats up, and while still stationed there, close the doors and bar them

16 | Gashmu is a variant of Geshem.

shut. Furthermore, let the inhabitants of Jerusalem be assigned to guard shifts, each to his watch or opposite his home."

4 Now while the city was large and extensive, her population was sparse,
5 and the rebuilt houses were few.[17] Then my God inspired me to gather the
nobles and officials and the people to register their genealogy, and I found
the genealogical record of those who first came up.[18]

6 In it I found written: These are the people of the province, coming up
from the captivity of the exile, that Nevukhadnetzar, king of Babylon, had
7 exiled. They returned to Jerusalem and Judea, each to his own town. Those
coming with Zerubavel, Yeshua, Neḥemya, Azarya, Raamya, Naḥamani,
Mordekhai, Bilshan, Misperet, Bigvai, Neḥum, Baana – the people of the
nation of Israel – numbered as follows:

8 The sons of Parosh: 2,172.
9 The sons of Shefatya: 372.
10 The sons of Araḥ: 652.
11 The sons of Paḥat Moav – the sons of Yeshua and Yoav – 2,818.
12 The sons of Eilam: 1,254.
13 The sons of Zatu: 845.
14 The sons of Zakai: 760.
15 The sons of Binui: 648.
16 The sons of Bevai: 628.
17 The sons of Azgad: 2,322.
18 The sons of Adonikam: 667.
19 The sons of Bigvai: 2,067.
20 The sons of Adin: 655.
21 The sons of Ater, with Ḥizkiya: 98.
22 The sons of Ḥashum: 328.
23 The sons of Betzai: 324.
24 The sons of Ḥarif: 112.
25 The sons of Givon: 95.
26 The people of Beit Leḥem and Netofa: 188.
27 The people of Anatot: 128.
28 The people of Beit Azmavet: 42.
29 The people of Kiryat Ye'arim, Kefira, and Be'erot: 743.
30 The people of the Rama and Gava: 621.
31 The people of Mikhmas: 122.
32 The people of Beit El and Ai: 123.
33 The people of the other Nevo: 52.
34 The sons of the other Eilam: 1,254.
35 The sons of Ḥarim: 320.

17 | Literally "no houses had been built," but the context implies that the housing was inadequate rather than nonexistent.

18 | This genealogical record also appears in Ezra, chapter 2, with minor variations.

36 The sons of Yeriḥo: 345.
37 The sons of Lod, Ḥadid, and Ono: 721.
38 The sons of Senaa: 3,930.

39 The priests – sons of Yedaya, of the house of Yeshua: 973.

40 The sons of Imer: 1,052.
41 The sons of Pashḥur: 1,247.
42 The sons of Ḥarim: 1,017.

43 The Levites – the sons of Yeshua and Kadmiel, of the sons of Hodva: 74.
44 The singers, the sons of Asaf: 148.
45 The gatekeepers – the sons of Shalum, the sons of Ater, the sons of Talmon, the sons of Akuv, the sons of Ḥatita, the sons of Shovai: 138.
46 The Netinim – the sons of Tziḥa, the sons of Ḥasufa, the sons of Tabaot,
47 48 the sons of Keros, the sons of Sia, the sons of Padon, the sons of Levana,
49 the sons of Ḥagava, the sons of Shalmai the sons of Ḥanan, the sons of
50 Gidel, the sons of Gaḥar, the sons of Re'aya, the sons of Retzin, the sons
51 52 of Nekoda, the sons of Gazam, the sons of Uza, the sons of Pase'aḥ, the
53 sons of Besai, the sons of Meunites, the sons of Nefishsim, the sons of
54 Bakbuk, the sons of Ḥakufa, the sons of Ḥarḥur, the sons of Batzlit, the
55 sons of Meḥida, the sons of Ḥarsha, the sons of Barkos, the sons of Sisera,
56 the sons of Tamaḥ, the sons of Netziaḥ, and the sons of Ḥatifa.

57 The sons of Shlomo's servants – the sons of Sotai, the sons of Soferet, the
58 sons of Perida, the sons of Yaala, the sons of Darkon, the sons of Gidel,
59 the sons of Shefatya, the sons of Ḥatil, the sons of Pokheret HaTzvayim, and the sons of Amon.

60 The Netinim and Shlomo's servants totaled 392.

61 And these are those who came up from Tel Melaḥ, Tel Ḥarsha, Keruv, Adon, and Imer but could not prove whether their ancestral houses or descent were of Israel:
62 the sons of Delaya, the sons of Toviya, and the sons of Nekoda: 642.
63 Of the priests: the sons of Ḥavaya, the sons of HaKotz, and the sons of Barzilai – he who married one of the daughters of Barzilai the Gileadite and was called by their name.
64 These sought the written record of their genealogy, which could not be found, and were therefore repudiated from the priesthood.
65 The governor instructed them that they must not eat from the holiest offerings until the advent of the priest for the Urim and Tumim.[19]

66 67 The entire community together numbered 42,360. Aside from their male and female slaves, of whom there were 7,337, they also had 245 male and female singers. (*In a few versions it is written:* Their horses – 736; their mules – 245.)
68 Camels: 435; donkeys: 6,720.

19 | An oracle worn by the High Priest (see Ex. 28:30; Lev. 8:8), which by this time was evidently no longer extant.

69 A few of the clan leaders donated toward the work. His Excellency the
governor donated gold to the treasury – one thousand drachmas and
70 fifty basins – as well as five hundred thirty priestly robes. Some of the
clan leaders also donated to the project treasury – twenty thousand gold
71 drachmas and two thousand two hundred silver mina – while the rest of
the people gave twenty thousand gold drachmas, two thousand silver mina,
and sixty-seven priestly robes.

72 And the priests, Levites, gatekeepers, singers, others of the people, and
the Netinim settled in their towns, so that all Israel were in their towns.

Now the seventh month arrived, and the Israelites were in their towns.[20]

8 1 All the people assembled together in the open plaza opposite the Water
Gate, calling upon Ezra the scholar[21] to bring out the scroll of the Torah
2 of Moshe: the Lord's command to Israel. So Ezra the priest brought
the Torah before the congregation – men and women and all who could
3 understand what they heard – on the first day of the seventh month. He
read it from the first light until midday in the plaza facing the Water Gate
before the men and the women and all who understood, and the ears of
all the people were attuned to the Torah scroll.

4 Ezra the scholar was standing upon a wooden platform erected for the
occasion. Next to him, on his right, stood Matitya, Shema, Anaya, Uriya,
Ḥilkiya, and Maaseya, and on his left were Pedaya, Mishael, Malkiya,
5 Ḥashum, Ḥashbadana, Zekharya, and Meshulam. Then Ezra, who was
elevated above all the people, opened the scroll before the entire people,
6 and as he did so, the people all stood up. Then Ezra blessed the Lord, the
almighty God, and the people answered, "Amen, Amen," while lifting up
their hands. They bowed and prostrated themselves before the Lord, faces
7 down to the ground, then Yeshua and Bani and Shereveya, Yamin, Akuv,
Shabtai, Hodiya, Maaseya, Kelita, Azarya, Yozavad, Ḥanan, Pelaya, and
the Levites explained the Torah to the people, who all the while remained
8 standing. They read from the scroll of God's Torah while explaining and
clarifying each detail to render the readings understandable.

9 Then Neḥemya, His Excellency the governor, along with Ezra the priest
and scholar and the Levites teaching the people, said to all the people,
"Today is sacred to the Lord, your God.[22] You should neither mourn nor
weep" – for the people were all weeping as they listened to the words of
10 the Torah. Then he told them, "Now go and feast on delicacies, drink sweet
things, and send servings of food to those who have none – for this day
is sacred to our Lord. Do not be sorrowful, for rejoicing in the Lord is
11 your strength and shelter." And the Levites quieted all the people, saying:
"Hush! This day is sacred – do not be sorrowful!"

20 | Cf. Ezra 3:1.

21 | See note on Ezra 7:6.

22 | See Leviticus 23:23–25.

12 So all the people went to dine and drink and to send servings of food to
one another and to make merry, for they understood what they had been
13 taught. And on the second day, all the clan leaders of the people gathered
with the priests and Levites around Ezra the scholar to ponder the words
14 of the Torah. And in the Torah they found written that the LORD had
commanded at the hands of Moshe that the Israelites should dwell in
15 booths during the festival of the seventh month and that they should
announce and have proclaimed throughout their towns and in Jerusalem,
"Go out to the hills and bring back leafy branches of olive, pine, myrtle,
and date, thickly leaved branches to construct booths as prescribed."[23]

16 So the people went out and brought branches and built booths for
themselves – on their rooftops or in their courtyards and in the courtyards
of God's House and in the plaza of the Water Gate and in the plaza of the
17 Efrayim Gate. The entire community who had returned from the captivity
constructed booths and dwelt in those booths, which the Israelites had not
done since the days of Yeshua bin Nun until that day. There was jubilant
18 rejoicing. And he read from the scroll of God's Torah every day from the
first day until the last. They held the festival for seven days and on the
eighth day, a sacred assembly, as ordained by law.

9 1 Then on the twenty-fourth of that month, the Israelites convened, fasting
2 and in sackcloth with earth on themselves. The seed of Israel separated
themselves from all those of foreign descent. Standing, they confessed
3 their sins and the wrongdoings of their ancestors. While still standing
in their places, they read from the scroll of the LORD their God's Torah
for a quarter of the day, and for another quarter-day they confessed and
prostrated themselves before the LORD, their God.

4 Standing on the Levites' platform Yeshua and Bani, Kadmiel, Shevanya,
Buni, Shereveya, Bani, and Kenani cried out in loud voices to the LORD,
5 their God. Then Yeshua and Kadmiel, Bani, Ḥashavneya, Shereveya,
Hodiya, Shevanya, and Petaḥya, the Levites, declared, "Rise and bless the
LORD your God from this world to eternity. May they bless Your glorious
name – exalted above any blessing or praise.

6 "You alone are the LORD – You created the heavens, the highest heavens
with all their hosts, the earth and all upon it, and the seas with all that
they contain. You give life to them all, and the hosts of heaven prostrate
7 themselves before You.[24] You are the LORD God who chose Avram, bring-
8 ing him out of Ur Kasdim and changing his name to Avraham. Finding
his heart faithful to You, You forged a covenant with him to give his seed
the land of the Canaanites, Hittites, Amorites, Perizzites, Jebusites, and
Girgashites, and You kept Your word because You are just.

23 | Leviticus 23:33–43.

24 | This passage contains allusions to many other biblical verses and episodes, especially in the Torah. Verse 6 parallels Psalms 148.

9 "You saw our ancestors suffering oppression in Egypt; You heard their cries
10 at the Sea of Reeds. You performed signs and wonders against Pharaoh, all
his servants, and all the people of his land because You knew with what
cruel wickedness they had treated them, thus making a name for Yourself
11 to this day. You split the sea for them so that they passed through it on
dry ground, but You hurled their pursuers into the depths like a stone into
raging waters.

12 "You guided them with a column of cloud by day and with a column of
13 fire at night to illuminate the way for them to walk. You descended on
Mount Sinai and spoke to them from heaven, giving them just laws and
14 true teachings, goodly statutes and commandments. You made Your holy
Sabbath known to them and charged them with commandments, statutes,
15 and teachings through the hand of Your servant Moshe. For their hunger
You gave them food from heaven and for their thirst extracted water for
them from the rock. You told them to enter and inherit the land that You
had raised Your hand in oath to give to them.

16 "But they and our fathers acted in willful wickedness, stiffening their
17 necks and disobeying Your commands. Refusing to listen, they did not
remember Your marvels which You performed for them. They stiffened
their necks and rebelliously turned their heads to return to their slavery.
But you are a God of forgiveness – compassionate and gracious, slow to
18 anger, abounding in kindness – and did not forsake them. Even though
they made themselves a molten calf, declaring, "This is your god who
19 brought you out of Egypt," and aroused great anger, You in Your infinite
compassion did not forsake them in the wilderness. The cloud column did
not cease guiding the way by day, nor did the nocturnal fire column cease
illuminating the way for them to walk.

20 "You conferred Your good spirit upon them for enlightenment, and You
did not withhold Your manna from their mouths while giving them
21 water to slake their thirst. For forty years You provided for them in the
desert – they lacked for nothing: their clothes did not wear out, nor did
their feet swell.

22 "You bestowed upon them kingdoms and peoples whom You then dispersed
to the far reaches. They inherited Siḥon's land, the realm of Ḥeshbon's king,
23 and the land of Og, king of the Bashan. You multiplied their descendants
like the celestial stars and brought them to the land that You had told their
24 ancestors to come to and possess. Then the sons came and took possession
of the land, for You subdued the Canaanite inhabitants before them,
delivering them into their hands – their rulers and the land's peoples – to
do with as they willed.

25 "They captured fortified cities and a rich fertile land, inheriting houses
full of all good things – hewn cisterns and vineyards, olive groves, and

plentiful fruit orchards. They ate and were satisfied, growing rich and fat,
luxuriating in Your great goodness.

26 “Yet they disobeyed and rebelled against You, casting Your Torah behind
their backs and slaughtering Your prophets who admonished them so as
27 to return them to You, thus arousing great anger. So You gave them into
the hands of their oppressors, who indeed oppressed them. Then, in the
time of their oppression, they cried out to You, and hearing from heaven,
You in Your infinite compassion sent them liberators, who delivered them
from the hands of their oppressors.

28 “But as soon as they were again at ease, they continued committing wrongs
against You – so You abandoned them to their enemies, who tyrannized
them. Then they returned, crying out to You, and You, hearing from heaven,
29 rescued them out of Your compassion time and again. You admonished
them so that they would turn back to Your teaching, but they acted wickedly, disobeying Your commands while transgressing Your laws – those
by which a person shall live. Instead, turning a stubborn shoulder, they
stiffened their necks and would not listen.

30 “You bore with them for many years, admonishing them at the hands
of Your prophets through Your spirit. They still would not listen, so You
31 delivered them into the hands of the peoples of the lands. But in Your
infinite mercy You did not annihilate them or forsake them, for You are a
compassionate and gracious God.

32 “Now, our God, the great, mighty, and awe-inspiring God, keeper of the
covenant and the love, do not deem as trivial all that hardship we have
encountered – our kings, princes, priests and prophets, our ancestors, and
33 all Your people – from the days of the Assyrian kings until today. You have
been just throughout all that has come upon us, for You have dealt in truth
34 while we have committed evil. Our kings and our princes, our priests, and
our ancestors did not act according to Your Torah; they heeded neither
Your commands nor the warnings through which You admonished them.
35 Despite their sovereign rule and the bountiful goodness You had bestowed
upon them in the expansive and rich land You had given them, they did
not serve You, nor did they repent or turn away from their evil deeds.

36 “Now here we are – subjugated – and it is in this land that You bestowed
upon our ancestors so that they could partake of her fruits and her bounty
37 that we are now subjugated. She yields abundant crops – for the kings
whom You have set over us for our sins. They reign as they will over our
bodies and our livestock.

“We are indeed in dire trouble and distress.

10 1 “Yet amid all this we commit to a faithful covenant and put it in writing
under the seal of our leaders, Levites, and priests.

2 "These are the signatories: His Excellency the governor, Neḥemya son
3, 4 of Ḥakhalya, and Tzidkiya, Seraya, Azarya, Yirmeya, Pashḥur, Amarya,
5, 6, 7 Malkiya, Ḥatush, Shevanya, Malukh, Ḥarim, Meremot, Ovadya, Daniel,
8, 9 Gineton, Barukh, Meshulam, Aviya, Miyamin, Maazya, Bilgai, and
Shemaya – these are the priests;
10 of the Levites: Yeshua son of Azanya, Binui, a descendant of Ḥenadad
11 and Kadmiel; their brothers: Shevanya, Hodiya, Kelita, Pelaya, Ḥanan,
12, 13, 14 Mikha, Reḥov, Ḥashavya, Zakur, Shereveya, Shevanya, Hodiya, Bani, and
Beninu;
15, 16 the leaders of the people: Parosh, Paḥat Moav, Eilam, Zatu, Bani, Buni,
17, 18, 19 Azgad, Bevai, Adoniya, Bigvai, Adin, Ater, Ḥizkiya, Azur, Hodiya, Ḥashum,
20, 21, 22 Betzai, Ḥarif, Anatot, Neivai, Magpiash, Meshulam, Ḥezir, Mesheizavel,
23, 24 Tzadok, Yadua, Pelatya, Ḥanan, Anaya, Hoshe'a, Ḥananya, Ḥashuv,
25, 26, 27 Haloḥesh, Pilḥa, Shovek, Reḥum, Ḥashavena, Maaseya, Aḥiya, Ḥanan,
28 Anan, Malukh, Ḥarim, and Baana;
29 and the rest of the people and the priests, Levites, gatekeepers, singers, and
Netinim, and all those who had separated themselves from the peoples
of the lands to be with God's Torah, with their wives, their sons, and
30 their daughters – all those able to understand – all these supported their
kinsmen, their lords, binding themselves by an oath, under the penalty of
a curse, to follow in the way of God's teaching as given into the hand of
God's servant Moshe and to keep and observe all the commandments of
the Lord our Master and His laws and precepts.

31 "So we will neither give our daughters to the peoples of the land nor take
32 their daughters for our sons.[25] And those peoples of the land who bring the
merchandise and assorted foods to sell on the Sabbath day – we will not
buy from them on the Sabbath or on any holy day. In the seventh year we
33 will forgo[26] the crops as well as each person's debt. We took certain charges
upon ourselves, imposing upon ourselves a third of a shekel yearly toward
34 the service of the House of our God: for the column bread,[27] for the regular
daily grain offering and the regular daily burnt offering, for the Sabbaths,
for the New Months, for the appointed times, for the designated sacred
offerings, for the purification offerings to atone for Israel, and for all the
labor of our God's House.

35 "We cast lots for the wood offering that the priests, the Levites, and the
people would bring to the House of our God at fixed times each and every
year, to be burned on the altar of the Lord our God, as is written in the

---

25 | See Deuteronomy 7:3. Ezra addressed this sin immediately upon his arrival in Jerusalem; see Ezra, chapters 9–10.

26 | Although this verse explicitly mentions only the obligation to forgive debt in the seventh year (Deut. 15:2), the Hebrew verb *natash* (literally "abandon") further alludes to Exodus 23:11, which employs the same verb to demand that farmers leave their land fallow during the seventh year.

27 | See Leviticus 24:5–9.

36 Torah.[28] Also to bring to the House of the LORD[29] the first fruits of our land
37 and all the first fruits of all trees each and every year; also the firstborn of
our sons and of our animals – as written in the Torah[30] – while the firstborn
of our cattle and sheep will be brought to the House of our God, to the
38 priests serving in our God's House.[31] The initial offering of our dough and
our donations of the fruit of all trees, and the wine and olive oil, we will
bring to the priests, to the chambers of the House of our God, and the
tenth from our lands to the Levites, those Levites receiving the tithes in
39 all our farming towns. The priest, descendant of Aharon, will be with the
Levites when the Levites tithe, and the Levites will bring the tithed tenths
40 up to the House of our God – to the chambers, to the treasury. For it is to
those chambers that the Israelites and the descendants of Levi will bring
the donations of the grain, wine, and olive oil, where the Temple vessels
are, as are the serving priests, gatekeepers, and singers – we will not forsake
the House of our God."

11 1 The ranking officers of the people settled in Jerusalem, and the rest of the
people cast lots: one in ten was to come settle in Jerusalem, the holy city,
2 while the other nine-tenths remained in the rural towns. And the people
blessed all those who volunteered to settle in Jerusalem.

3 These are the leaders of the province who settled in Jerusalem, while in
the towns of Yehuda, everyone settled on their own holdings, each in
their own towns[32] – Israel, the priests, the Levites, the Netinim, and the
4 descendants of Shlomo's servants. In Jerusalem resided some descendants
of Yehuda and some descendants of Binyamin. Among the descendants
of Yehuda were Ataya son of Uziya son of Zekharya son of Amarya son
5 of Shefatya son of Mahalalel, of the line of Peretz, and Masseya son of
Barukh son of Kol Ḥozeh son of Ḥazaya son of Adaya son of Yoyariv son
6 of Zekharya of the family of Shela. Altogether, the descendants of Peretz
living in Jerusalem numbered 468 skilled fighters.

7 These are the descendants of Binyamin: Salu son of Meshulam son of Yoed
son of Pedaya son of Kolaya son of Maaseya son of Itiel son of Yeshaya
8 9 followed by Gabai and Salai – 928, with Yoel son of Zikhri as their superior
officer and Yehuda son of Hasenua as second-in-command over the city.

10 11 Of the priests: Yedaya son of Yoyariv, Yakhin, Seraya son of Ḥilkiya son of
Meshulam son of Tzadok son of Merayot son of Aḥituv in charge of the
12 House of God, and their kinsmen acting in the service of the House – 822,
along with Adaya son of Yeroḥam son of Pelalya son of Amtzi son of
13 Zekharya son of Pashḥur son of Malkiya and his brothers, leaders of

28 | See Leviticus 6:5–6.

29 | See Exodus 23:19; Deuteronomy 26:1–11.

30 | See Exodus 13:13; Numbers 18:15.

31 | See, e.g., Deuteronomy 12:17.

32 | This list contains many parallels to 1 Chronicles, chapter 9.

clans – 242, along with Amashsai son of Azarel son of Aḥzai son of
14 Meshilemot son of Imer and their kinsmen, powerful men – 128, and their
superior officer was Zavdiel, of high lineage.

15 Of the Levites: Shemaya son of Ḥashuv son of Azrikam son of Ḥashavya
16 son of Buni. Shabetai and Yozavad of the Levite leaders oversaw the
17 external duties[33] of the House of God. Matanya son of Mikha son of Zavdi
son of Asaf was the first to open the prayers with thanks and gratitude,
seconded by Bakbukya from among his kinsmen and also by Avda son
18 of Shamua son of Galal son of Yedutun. All of the Levites in the holy city
numbered 284.

19 And the gatekeepers – Akuv, Talmon, and their kinsmen, who guard the
20 gates – 172. Now the rest of Israel, the priests, and the Levites were through-
21 out the towns of Yehuda – each one in his inherited property. The Netinim
resided in the Ofel, and Tziḥa and Gishpa oversaw the Netinim.

22 Uzi son of Bani son of Ḥashavya son of Matanya son of Mikha was the
superior officer of the Levites in Jerusalem. He was one of the descendants
of Asaf, those singers who accompanied the service of the House of God
23 in accordance with the king's command[34] and the singers' faithful com-
24 mitment.[35] Petaḥya son of Mesheizavel, of the descendants of Zeraḥ son
of Yehuda, was at the king's hand for all matters concerning the people.

25 As for the unwalled villages with their outlying fields, the descendants of
Yehuda resided in Kiryat Arba and its satellites, in Divon and its satellites,
26 27 in Yekavtze'el and its villages, in Yeshua, in Molada, in Beit Pelet, in Ḥatzar
28 Shual, in Be'er Sheva and its satellites, in Tziklag and Mekhona and its
29 30 satellites, in Ein Rimon, in Tzora, and in Yarmut, Zanoaḥ, and Adulam
and their villages, Lakhish and its fields, and Azeka and its satellites. Thus
they settled from Be'er Sheva to the Valley of Ben Hinom.

31 And the descendants of Binyamin – from Gava, Mikhmas, and Aya, and
32, 33 Beit El and its satellites, Anatot, Nov, Ananeya, Ḥatzor, Rama, Gitayim,
34 35, 36 Ḥadid, Tzevoyim, Nevalat, Lod and Ono and the Valley of the Smiths. The
Levite divisions were found throughout Yehuda and Binyamin.

12 1 These are the priests and the Levites who came up with Zerubavel son of
2 She'altiel and Yeshua: Seraya, Yirmeya, Ezra, Amarya, Malukh, Ḥatush,
3 4, 5 Shekhanya, Reḥum, Meremot, Ido, Ginetoi, Aviya, Miyamin, Maadya,
6, 7 Bilga, Shemaya and Yoyariv, Yedaya, Salu, Amok, Ḥilkiya, Yedaya – these
were the leaders of the priests and their kinsmen in the days of Yeshua.

---

33 | This service contrasts with the sacred rituals performed inside the Temple, perhaps including some combination of maintenance work, financial management, religious instruction, and bringing supplies to the Temple.

34 | This refers either to a command of the current Persian king or to rules originally established by King David for the First Temple.

35 | Perhaps a financial stipend that the king ordered be allotted to them or, more broadly, a "contract" regarding their responsibilities.

8 The Levites: Yeshua, Binui, Kadmiel, Shereveya, Yehuda, and Matanya
9 along with his kinsmen – in charge of the songs of thanksgiving – with
Bakbukya and Uni their kinsmen in shifts alongside them.

10 Now Yeshua[36] fathered Yoyakim, Yoyakim fathered Elyashiv, and Elyashiv –
11, 12 Yoyada. Yoyada fathered Yonatan, and Yonatan fathered Yadua. In the
days of Yoyakim, these priests were clan chiefs: for Seraya, Meraya; for
13, 14 Yirmeya, Ḥananya; for Ezra, Meshulam; for Amarya, Yehoḥanan; for
15 Melikhu, Yonatan; for Shevanya, Yosef; for Ḥarim, Adna; for Merayot,
16, 17 Ḥelki; for Ido, Zekharya; for Gineton, Meshulam; for Aviya, Zikhri; for
18 Minyamin and Moadya, Piltai; for Bilga, Shamua; for Shemaya, Yehonatan;
19, 20, 21 for Yoyariv, Matnai; for Yedaya, Uzi; for Salai, Kalai; for Amok, Ever; for
Ḥilkiya, Ḥashavya; and for Yedaya, Netanel.

22 In the days of Elyashiv, Yoyada and Yoḥanan, and Yadua, the Levites were
recorded according to their clan chiefs, as were the priests of the reign of
23 Daryavesh the Persian. For Levi's line, the patriarchal clans are written in
24 the book of Chronicles[37] up to the days of Yoḥanan son of Elyashiv. The
leaders of the Levites: Ḥashavya, Shereveya, and Yeshua son of Kadmiel
alongside their kinsmen to praise and give thanks as commanded by David,
25 the man of God – one shift opposite another. Matanya and Bakbukya,
Ovadya, Meshulam, Talmon, and Akuv – guards and gatekeepers in shifts,
26 stationed at the gate posterns. These were in the days of Yoyakim son of
Yeshua son of Yotzadak and in the days of Neḥemya the governor and Ezra
the priest and scholar.

27 At the dedication of Jerusalem's wall, they sought out the Levites in all of
their dwelling places to bring them to Jerusalem in order to celebrate the
dedication joyously with thanksgiving and music, with cymbals, harps, and
28 lyres. The clans of the singers assembled from the plain around Jerusalem
29 and from the villages of Netofa and from Beit HaGilgal and from the fields
of Geva and Azmavet – for the singers had built themselves villages around
30 Jerusalem. The priests and the Levites purified themselves, then purified
the people and the gates and the wall.

31 I then brought the leaders of the Jews to the top of the wall, having arranged
two sizable choirs of thanksgiving and a procession to the right atop the
32 wall toward the Dung Gate. Hoshaya followed them with half the ranking
33, 34 officers of Yehuda, and Azarya, Ezra, and Meshulam, Yehuda and Binyamin,
and Shemaya and Yirmeya.

35 Some of the descendants of the priests were accompanying on the trumpets;
Zekharya son of Yonatan son of Shemaya son of Matanya son of Mikhaya
36 son of Zakur son of Asaf and his kinsmen – Shemaya and Azarel, Milalai,

36 | This Yeshua is the first High Priest of the Second Temple (Ezra 3:2), not Yeshua the Levite mentioned two verses earlier.

37 | Based on the juxtaposition to the previous verse, this book was probably a chronicle from the days of King Daryavesh.

Gilalai, Maai, Netanel, Yehuda, Ḥanani – were accompanying on the
musical instruments assigned by David, the man of God. Ezra the scribe
37 preceded them. At the Spring Gate and opposite them, some climbed the
steps of the City of David, ascending the wall above David's palace up to
38 the Water Gate to the east. Meanwhile, the second thanksgiving choir
walked in the opposite direction, and I followed, with half the people,
on top of the wall, over the Tower of the Furnaces up to the Wide Wall
39 and over the Efrayim Gate and the Old Gate and the Fish Gate and the
Tower of Ḥananel and the Tower of the Hundred up to the Sheep Gate,
40 then stood at the Gate of the Guard. So the two processions came to a
standstill in the House of God – as did I and with me half of the officials.
41 The priests – Elyakim, Maaseya, Minyamin, Mikhaya, Elyo'einai, Zekharya,
42 Ḥananya – accompanied on the trumpets. Maaseya and Shemaya and
Elazar and Uzi and Yehoḥanan and Malkiya and Eilam and Azer – the
43 singers made music with Yizraḥya as their officer. On that day, they offered
many communal sacrifices and rejoiced, for God had filled them with
elation, and the women and children also rejoiced, and the jubilation of
Jerusalem was heard from afar.

44 On that day, men were appointed to supervise the chambers, to collect
within them the stores of the contributions, the firsts and the tithes from
the village fields – those portions allotted by the Torah to the priests and
Levites – for Yehuda rejoiced in the priests and Levites who stood and
45 served and who carried out the ritual duties of their God, the ritual duties
of purity and those of the singers and the gatekeepers, as charged by David
46 and his son Shlomo. For in the days of old, of David and Asaf, there were
already leaders of the singers and songs of praise and thanksgiving to God.
47 And during the days of Zerubavel and of Neḥemya, all Israel provided
the daily portions allotted for the singers and gatekeepers and dedicated
portions for the Levites, while the Levites in turn dedicated portions for
the descendants of Aharon.

13 1 On that day the book of Moshe was read aloud to the listening people,
and in it was found written that no Amonite or Moabite shall be admitted
2 to the congregation of God,[38] because they would not greet the Israelites
with food and water and hired Bilam to curse them – but our God turned
3 his curse into a blessing. And when they heard the Torah, they separated
all those of mixed lineage from Israel.

4 Previously, Elyashiv the priest had occupied a chamber of our God's House,
5 and he was connected to Toviya,[39] to whom he had assigned a substantial
chamber, one in which they had previously stored the grain offerings, the
incense, and the vessels as well as the tithes of grain, new wine, and olive

38 | This prohibition and its rationale appear in Deuteronomy 23:4–7; see also Ezra 9:1–2, 12.

39 | Perhaps by familial ties (cf. 6:17–18 above) or a friendship or alliance. Regardless, Toviya's Amonite lineage (see 2:10) was problematic.

oil, assigned by decree to the Levites, the singers, and the gatekeepers, as
well as the dedicated donations for the priests.

6 Throughout this period I was not in Jerusalem, for in the thirty-second
year of Artaḥshasta, king of Babylon, I came to the king; after some time
7 I requested leave from the king, then came to Jerusalem and recognized
the evil that Elyashiv had committed on behalf of Toviya, assigning him
8 a chamber in the courtyards of God's House. I was appalled and cast out
9 all the vessels of the house of Toviya from the chamber. I gave orders, and
they purified the chambers to which I then returned the vessels of God's
House and the grain offerings and the incense.

10 I also discovered that the portions allotted to the Levites had not been
provided and that the Levites and singers who performed the ritual
11 duties had fled, each to his field. I then upbraided the officials, demanding,
"Why has God's House been forsaken?!" I then reassembled them and
12 restationed them at their posts. And all Yehuda brought the tithes of
13 grain, wine, and olive oil to the storerooms. I then appointed treasurers
over these stores: Shelemya the priest, Tzadok the scribe, and Pedaya of
the Levites, along with Ḥanan son of Zakur son of Matanya, for they were
considered trustworthy, and they were the ones who were to distribute
the shares to their kinsmen.

14 My God, remember me for this and do not erase my loyal actions which
15 I have performed for the House of my God and its shifts of service. In
those very days in Yehuda I saw treading in winepresses on the Sabbath
and those bringing heaps of produce and loading the donkeys with wine,
grapes, figs, and all kinds of burdens, then bringing them to Jerusalem on
the Sabbath day – and I admonished them on that day when they were
16 selling the food.[40] And the Tyreans dwelling there would bring fish and
all manner of merchandise and sell it on the Sabbath to the Jews, and in
Jerusalem itself.

17 I upbraided the nobles of Yehuda, demanding of them, "What is this evil
18 thing you are doing, desecrating the Sabbath day? Your ancestors acted
just like this, so that our God brought all this evil upon us and upon this
city,[41] and now you are stoking anger against Israel by desecrating the
19 Sabbath." Then, when the shadows darkened the gates of Jerusalem before
the Sabbath, I ordered the doors shut, declaring that they should not be
opened until after the Sabbath. And I stationed some of my men at the
gates so that no loads could be brought in on the Sabbath.

20 Once or twice the traders and vendors of various goods camped overnight
21 outside Jerusalem. I warned them, saying: "Why are you camping outside
the wall? If you ever do this again, I will use violence against you!" From
22 then on they stopped coming on the Sabbath. Then I ordered the Levites

40 | See 10:32 above.

41 | This behavior is described in Jeremiah 17:19–27.

to come, once they had purified themselves, to guard the gates so as to
sanctify the Sabbath day. My God, remember this too on my behalf, and
be merciful to me in Your abundant kindness.

23 In those days I also saw those Jews who had brought home Ashdodite,
24 Amonite, and Moabite wives. As for their children, some spoke Ashdodite
and could not even speak Hebrew, and so it was for each people in their
25 native tongue. I upbraided them, cursed them, struck some of the men
and ripped out their hair, and made them swear an oath to God – that
you shall never give your daughters to their sons or marry their daughters
26 to your sons or to yourselves. Was it not with these that Shlomo, king of
Israel, sinned? Among all the many nations there was no king like him, he
was beloved by his God, and God made him king over all of Israel – yet
27 even he was led astray by the foreign women.[42] Shall we then listen to
you to commit all this great evil, breaking faith with our God by bringing
28 home foreign wives?! Even one of the sons of Yoyada son of Elyashiv the
High Priest was a son-in-law to Sanvalat the Horonite – and I made him
flee from me.

29 My God, remember this against them – the defilement of the priesthood
30 and the covenant of the priesthood and the Levites. But I purified them
of all foreign elements and established duty shifts for the priests and the
31 Levites – each for his official tasks – also for the first fruits and for the
wood offerings at fixed times.

Remember me favorably, O my God.

42 | See I Kings 11:1–11.

CHRONICLES

Geneological tables	End of Sha'ul's reign and David's reign in Jerusalem	End of David's reign and preparations for Shlomo's reign	Shlomo's reign	First kings of Yehuda: Reḥavam, Aviya, Asa, and Yehoshafat
I Chronicles chs. 1–9	I Chronicles 10–21	I Chronicles 22–29	II Chronicles 1–9	II Chronicles 10–20
	33 years		40 years	86 years

Family of the dynasty of Aḥav: Reigns of Yehoram, Aḥazya, and Atalya	The downfall of Aram and ascendance of Assyria: Reigns of Yoash, Amatzya, Uziya, Yotam, and Aḥaz	From the downfall of Assyria to the ascendance of Babylonia: Reigns of Ḥizkiya, Menashe, Amon, and Yoshiya	Final kings of Yehuda: Yehoaḥaz, Yehoyakim, Yehoyakhin, and Tzidkiya
II Chronicles 21–22	II Chronicles 23–28	II Chronicles 29–35	II Chronicles 36
15 years	153 years	117 years	22 years

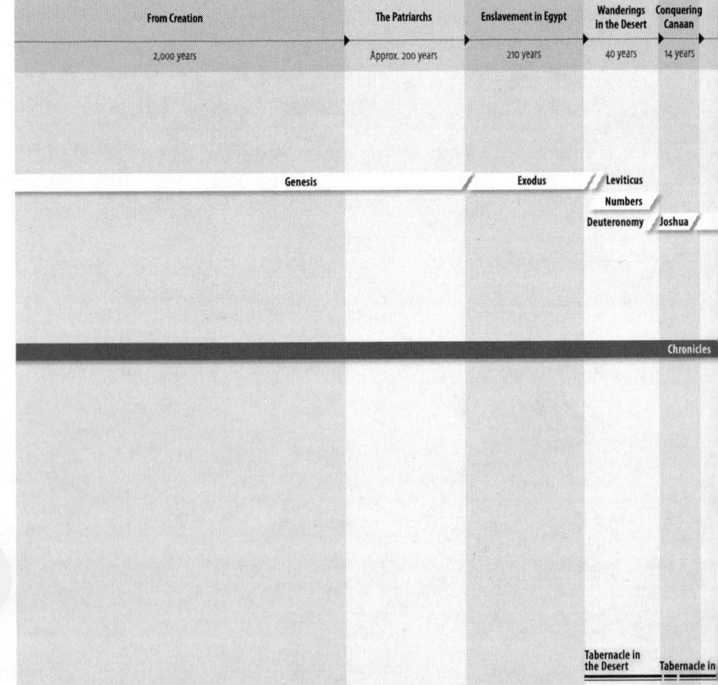

CHRONICLES/ DIVREI HAYAMIM

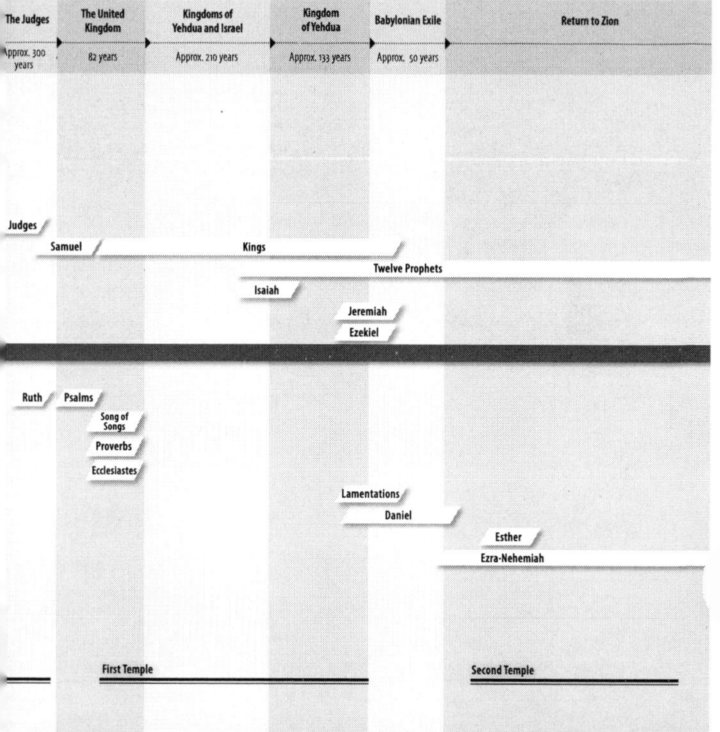

1 1, 2, 3 Adam, Shet, Enosh;[1] Keinan, Mahalalel, Yered; Ḥanokh, Metushelaḥ,
4 Lemekh; Noaḥ, Shem, Ḥam, and Yefet.

5 Yefet's sons were Gomer, Magog, Madai, Yavan, Tuval, Meshekh, and Tiras.
6 7 The sons of Gomer were Ashkenaz, Difat, and Togarma. The sons of Yavan
were Elisha, Tarshish, Kitim, and Rodanim.

8 9 The sons of Ḥam were Kush, Mitzrayim, Put, and Kenaan. The sons of
Kush were Seva, Ḥavila, Savta, Raama, and Savtekha. The sons of Raama
10 were Sheva and Dedan. Kush was the father of Nimrod, the first mighty
11 warrior on earth. Mitzrayim was the father of the Ludim, Anamim,
12 Lehavim, and Naftuḥim, Patrusim, Kasluḥim – from whom the Philistines
13 descended – and the Kaftorim. Kenaan was the father of Tzidon, his
14 15 firstborn, and Ḥet, and the Jebusites, Amorites, and Girgashites, the
16 Hivites, Arkites, and Sinites, the Arvadites, Zemarites, and Hamatites.

17 Shem's sons were Elam, Ashur, Arpakhshad, Lud, Aram, Utz, Ḥul, Geter,
18 and Meshekh. Arpakhshad was the father of Shelaḥ, and Shelaḥ was the
19 father of Ever. To Ever, two sons were born. One was named Peleg, for in
20 his time the earth was divided.[2] His brother was named Yoktan. Yoktan was
21 the father of Almodad, Shelef, Ḥatzarmavet, Yeraḥ, Hadoram, Uzal, Dikla,
22 23 Eival, Avimael, Sheva, Ofir, Ḥavila, and Yovav; all these were Yoktan's
sons.

24, 25 26, 27 Shem, Arpakhshad, Shelah; Ever, Peleg, Reu; Serug, Naḥor, Teraḥ; Avram,
that is, Avraham.

28 29 Avraham's sons were Yitzḥak and Yishmael. These are their descendants:
30 Yishmael's firstborn was Nevayot, then Kedar, Adbe'el, Mivsam, Mishma,
31 Duma, Masa, Ḥadad, Teima, Yetur, Nafish, and Kedma. These were
Yishmael's sons.

32 The sons of Ketura, Avraham's concubine: she bore Zimran, Yokshan,
Medan, Midyan, Yishbak, and Shuaḥ. The sons of Yokshan were Sheva and
33 Dedan. The sons of Midyan were Eifa, Efer, Ḥanokh, Avida, and Eldaa: all
these were descendants of Ketura.

34 35 Avraham had a son Yitzḥak. The sons of Yitzḥak were Esav and Yisrael. The
36 sons of Esav were Elifaz, Reuel, Yeush, Yalam, and Koraḥ. The sons of Elifaz
37 were Teiman, Omar, Tzefi, Gatam, Kenaz, Timna, and Amalek. The sons
of Reuel were Naḥat, Zeraḥ, Shama, and Miza.

38 The sons of Se'ir were Lotan, Shoval, Tzivon, Ana, Dishon, Etzer, and
39 Dishan. The sons of Lotan were Ḥori and Homam. Timna was Lotan's

1 | The narrative in Chronicles parallels that of the books of Genesis, Joshua, Samuel, and Kings, and some other books of the Prophets and Writings. Large portions of the text are similar or identical to the parallel accounts in these books.

2 | Peleg evokes the Hebrew *niflega* (divided). This is often understood to refer to the dispersion recounted in Genesis 11:1–9.

40 sister. The sons of Shoval were Alyan, Manaḥat, Eival, Shefi, and Onam.
41 Tzivon's sons were Aya and Ana. The son of Ana was Dishon. The sons of
42 Dishon were Ḥemran, Eshban, Yitran, and Keran. Etzer's sons were Bilhan,
Zaavan, and Yaakan. Dishon's sons were Utz and Aran.

43 These were the kings who reigned in Edom before any king reigned over
the Israelites:
Bela son of Beor. His city was named Dinhava.
44 When Bela died, Yovav son of Zeraḥ from Botzra succeeded him as king.
45 When Yovav died, Ḥusham from the land of the Temanites succeeded
him as king.
46 When Ḥusham died, Hadad son of Bedad, who defeated Midyan in the
country of Moav, succeeded him as king. His city was named Avit.
47 When Hadad died, Samla from Masreka succeeded him as king.
48 When Samla died, Sha'ul from Reḥovot HaNahar succeeded him as
king.
49 When Sha'ul died, Baal Ḥanan son of Akhbor succeeded him as king.
50 When Baal Ḥanan died, Hadad succeeded him as king. His city was named
Pa'i, and his wife's name was Meheitavel, daughter of Matred, daughter of
Mei Zahav.
51 And Hadad died.

52 53 The chiefs of Edom were Timna, Alva, Yetet, Oholivama, Ela, Pinon, Kenaz,
54 Teiman, Mivtzar, Magdiel, and Iram; these are the chiefs of Edom.

2 1 These are the sons of Yisrael: Reuven, Shimon, Levi, Yehuda, Yissakhar,
2 Zevulun, Dan, Yosef, Binyamin, Naftali, Gad, and Asher.

3 The sons of Yehuda were Er, Onan, and Shela; these three were born to him
from Shua's daughter, the Canaanite. Er, Yehuda's firstborn, was wicked in
4 the Lord's sight, and He took his life. Tamar, his daughter-in-law, bore him
Peretz and Zeraḥ. Yehuda's sons were five in all.

5 6 The sons of Peretz were Ḥetzron and Ḥamul. The sons of Zeraḥ were
7 Zimri, Eitan, Heiman, Kalkol, and Dara, five in all. Karmi's son was Akhar,
8 the scourge of Israel, who broke the ban,[3] and Eitan's son was Azarya.
9 The sons of Ḥetzron that were born to him were Yeraḥme'el, Ram, and
10 Keluvai. Ram was the father of Aminadav; Aminadav was the father of
11 Naḥshon, leader of the sons of Yehuda. Naḥshon was the father of Salma;
12 Salma was the father of Boaz. Boaz was the father of Oved; Oved was the
father of Yishai.

13 14, 15 Ishai was the father of his firstborn Eliav, Avinadav second, Shima third,
16 Netanel fourth, Radai fifth, Otzem sixth, David seventh;their sisters were
Tzeruya and Avigayil. The sons of Tzeruya: Avshai, Yoav, and Asael – three.
17 Avigayil bore Amasa, and the father of Amasa was Yeter the Ishmaelite.

---

3 | See Joshua 7:16–26.

18 Kalev son of Ḥetzron had children by his wife Azuva and by Yeriot; these
19 were her sons: Yesher, Shovav, and Ardon. When Azuva died, Kalev
20 married Efrat, who bore him Ḥur. Ḥur was the father of Uri, and Uri was
21 the father of Betzalel. Later, Ḥetzron came to the daughter of Makhir,
father of Gilad – he married her when he was sixty years old – and she
bore him Seguv.

22 Seguv was the father of Yair, who acquired twenty-three cities in the land of
23 Gilad. But Geshur and Aram seized the hamlets of Yair from them, Kenat
and its dependencies, sixty towns. All these were the sons of Makhir, father
24 of Gilad. After the death of Ḥetzron in Kalev Efrata, Aviya, Ḥetzron's wife,
bore Ashḥur, the father of Tekoa.

25 The sons of Yeraḥme'el, Ḥetzron's firstborn: Ram his firstborn, Buna, Oren,
26 Otzem, and Aḥiya. Yeraḥme'el had another wife, whose name was Atara;
27 she was the mother of Onam. The sons of Ram, Yeraḥme'el's firstborn:
28 Maatz, Yamin, and Eker. The sons of Onam: Shamai and Yada. The sons of
29 Shamai: Nadav and Avishur. The name of Avishur's wife was Avihayil, and
30 she bore him Aḥban and Molid. The sons of Nadav: Seled and Apayim;
31 Seled died childless. The sons of Apayim: Yishi. The sons of Yishi: Sheshan.
32 The sons of Sheshan: Aḥlai.The sons of Yada, Shamai's brother: Yeter and
33 Yonatan; Yeter died childless.The sons of Yonatan: Pelet and Zaza. These
were the sons of Yeraḥme'el.

34 Sheshan had no sons, only daughters. Sheshan had an Egyptian slave
35 whose name was Yarḥa. Sheshan gave his daughter in marriage to Yarḥa his
36 servant, and she bore him Atai. Atai was the father of Natan, Natan was the
37 father of Zavad, Zavad was the father of Eflal, Eflal was the father of Oved,
38 39 Oved was the father of Yehu, Yehu was the father of Azarya, Azarya was
40 the father of Ḥeletz, Ḥeletz was the father of Elasa, Elasa was the father
41 of Sisemai, Sisemai was the father of Shalum, Shalum was the father of
Yekamya, and Yekamya was the father of Elishama.

42 The sons of Kalev, brother of Yeraḥme'el: Meisha his firstborn was the
43 father of Zif and the people of Maresha, father of Ḥevron. The sons of
44 Ḥevron: Koraḥ, Tapuaḥ, Rekem, and Shema. Shema was the father of
Raḥam the father of Yorke'am, and Rekem was the father of Shamai.
45 46 The son of Shamai: Maon, and Maon was the father of Beit Tzur. Eifa,
Kalev's concubine, bore Ḥaran, Motza, and Gazez; Ḥaran was the father
of Gazez.

47 48 The sons of Yodai: Regem, Yotam, Geishan, Pelet, Eifa, and Shaaf. Kalev's
49 concubine, Maakha, bore Shever and Tirḥana, and she bore Shaaf father of
Madmana, Sheva father of Makhbena and father of Giva; Kalev's daughter
was Akhsa.

50 These were the sons of Kalev son of Ḥur, the firstborn of Efrata: Shoval
51 father of Kiryat Ye'arim, Salma father of Beit Leḥem, Ḥaref father of

52 Beit Gader. Shoval father of Kiryat Ye'arim had sons: Haroeh,[4] half of
53 the Menuḥot. The families of Kiryat Ye'arim: the Itrites, the Putites, the
Shumatites, and the Mishraites; from these came the Zoratites and the
54 Eshtaolites. The sons of Salma: Beit Leḥem, the Netofatites, Atrot Beit
55 Yoav, and half of the Manahatites, the Zorites. The scribal families that
dwelt at Yabetz: the Tiratites, the Shimeatites, and the Sucatites; these are
the Kinites who came from Ḥamat, father of Beit Rekhav.

3 1 These were the sons of David that were born to him at Ḥevron: the
firstborn Amnon to Aḥinoam the Jezreelite; the second, Daniel to Avigayil
2 the Carmelite; the third, Avshalom son of Maakha daughter of King Talmai
3 of Geshur; the fourth, Adoniya son of Ḥagit; the fifth, Shefatya, to Avital;
4 and the sixth, Yitre'am, to his wife Egla. Six were born to him in Ḥevron,
and he reigned there for seven years and six months, and for thirty-three
years he reigned in Jerusalem.

5 And these were born to him in Jerusalem: Shima, Shovav, Natan, and
6 Shlomo – four to Batshua daughter of Amiel; then Yivḥar, Elishama,
7 8 Elifelet, Noga, Nefeg, Yafia, Elishama, Elyada, and Elifelet – nine, all
9 David's sons beyond the sons of the concubines and Tamar, their sister.

10 The sons of Shlomo: Reḥavam, his son Aviya, his son Asa, his son
11 12 Yehoshafat, his son Yoram, his son Aḥazyahu, his son Yoash, his son
13 Amatzyahu, his son Azarya, his son Yotam, his son Aḥaz, his son Ḥizkiyahu,
14 his son Menashe, his son Amon, and his son Yoshiyahu.

15 The sons of Yoshiyahu: the firstborn Yoḥanan; the second, Yehoyakim;
16 the third, Tzidkiyahu; and the fourth, Shalum. The sons of Yehoyakim:
17 his son Yekhonya and his son Tzidkiya. The sons of Yekhonya, the captive:
18 his sons She'altiel, Malkiram, Pedaya, Shenatzar, Yekamya, Hoshama, and
19 Nedavya. The sons of Pedaya: Zerubavel and Shimi; the sons of Zerubavel:
Meshulam and Ḥananya and their sister Shlomit,

20 21 and Ḥashuva, Ohel, Berekhya, Ḥasdaya, and Yushav Ḥesed – five. The
sons of Ḥananya: Pelatya and Yeshaya, his son Refaya, his son Arnan, his
22 son Ovadya, and his son Shekhanya. The son of Shekhanya: Shemaya; the
23 sons of Shemaya: Ḥatush, Yigal, Bariaḥ, Ne'arya, and Shafat – six.[5] The
24 sons of Ne'arya: Elyo'einai, Ḥizkiya, and Azrikam – three. And the sons
of Elyo'einai: Hodavyahu, Elyashiv, Pelaya, Akuv, Yoḥanan, Delaya, and
Anani – seven.

4 1 2 The sons of Yehuda: Peretz, Ḥetzron, Karmi, Ḥur, and Shoval. Re'aya son
of Shoval was the father of Yaḥat, and Yaḥat was the father of Aḥumai and
Lahad; these were the families of the Zoratites.

---

4 | The descendants of Haroeh populated half of the city of Menuḥot, likely a variant name for Manaḥat; cf. verse 54.

5 | Some propose that one name has fallen out of the text; others explain that Shemaya is counted among the six immediate descendants of Shekhanya enumerated here.

3 These were of the father of Eitam: Yizre'el, Yishma, and Yidbash; their
4 sister's name was Hatzlelponi; Penuel was the father of Gedor, and Ezer
the father of Ḥusha. These were the sons of Ḥur, the firstborn of Efrata,
the father of Beit Leḥem.

5, 6 Ashḥur the father of Tekoa had two wives, Ḥela and Naara; Naara bore
him Aḥuzam, Ḥefer, Teimeni, and Aḥashtari; these were the sons of Naara.
7, 8 The sons of Ḥela: Tzeret, Tzoḥar, and Etnan. Kotz was the father of Anuv,
Tzoveva, and the families of Aḥarḥel son of Harum.

9 Yabetz was the most honorable of his brothers; his mother named him
Yabetz, "for I bore him in pain."[6]
10 Yabetz called out to the God of Israel, saying, "O, that You would bless me
and increase my borders, and that Your hand might be with me so that You
might keep me from harm to prevent my pain."
And God granted what he asked.

11 Keluv the brother of Shuḥa was the father of Meḥir, who was the father of
12 Eshton. Eshton was the father of Beit Rafa, Pase'aḥ, and Teḥina father of
13 Ir Naḥash; these were the people of Rekha. The sons of Kenaz: Otniel and
14 Seraya; and the sons of Otniel: Ḥatat and Meonotai, who was the father
of Ofra. Seraya was the father of Yoav father of Gei Ḥarashim, called thus
because they were craftsmen.[7]

15 The sons of Kalev son of Yefuneh: Iru, Ela, and Naam; and the sons of
16, 17 Ela: Kenaz. The sons of Yehalelel: Zif, Zifa, Tireya, and Asarel. The sons
of Ezra: Yeter, Mered, Efer, and Yalon. She conceived Miriam, Shamai, and
18 Yishbaḥ father of Eshtemoa, while his Judahite wife bore Yered father of
Gedor, Ḥever father of Sokho, and Yekutiel father of Zanoaḥ. These were
19 the sons of Bitya daughter of Pharaoh, whom Mered married. The sons of
the Judahite wife, sister of Naḥam, were the fathers of Ke'ila the Garmite
20 and Eshtemoa the Maakhatite. The sons of Shimon: Amnon, Rina, Ben
21 Ḥanan, and Tilon. The sons of Yishi: Zoḥet and Ben Zoḥet. The sons
of Shela son of Yehuda: Er father of Lekha, Lada father of Maresha, the
22 families of the house of the linen work at Beit Ashbe'a, Yokim, the men of
Kozeva, Yoash, Saraf who married into Moav, and Yashuvi Leḥem – the
23 records are ancient. These were the potters and residents of Neta'im and
Gedera; they lived there with the king in his service.

24, 25 The sons of Shimon: Nemuel, Yamin, Yariv, Zeraḥ, Sha'ul, his son Shalum,
26 his son Mibsam, and his son Mishma. The sons of Mishma: his son Ḥamuel,
27 his son Zakur, and his son Shimi. Shimi had sixteen sons and six daughters,
but his brothers did not have many children; none of their family grew as
28, 29 the Judahites did. They lived in Be'er Sheva, Molada, Ḥatzar Shual, Bilha,
30, 31 Etzem, Tolad, Betuel, Ḥorma, Tziklag, Beit Markabot, Ḥatzar Susim, Beit
32 Biri, and Shaarayim. These were their towns until David's reign, along

6 | The root letters *ayin-bet-tzadi* in the name Yabetz mirror those of *etzev*, "pain."

7 | *Ḥarashim* is Hebrew for "craftsmen."

with their villages: Eitam, Ayin, Rimon, Tokhen, and Ashan – five towns
33 along with all their settlements that surrounded these towns as far as Baal.
34 These were their abodes, and they kept genealogical records: Meshovav,
35 Yamlekh, Yosha son of Amatzya, and Yoel, and Yehu son of Yoshivya
36 son of Seraya son of Asiel. Elyo'einai, Yaakova, Yeshoḥaya, Asaya, Adiel,
37 Yesimiel, Benaya, and Ziza son of Shifri son of Alon son of Yedaya son of
38 Shimri son of Shemaya. These, listed by name, were the leaders of their
39 clans, and their ancestral houses spread far and wide. They journeyed to
the entrance of Gedor and up to the eastern side of the valley in search of
40 pastureland for their flock. They found good, rich pasture; the land was
41 vast, calm, and tranquil, for the previous dwellers were from Ḥam. Those
recorded by name arrived in King Yeḥizkiyahu's time. They attacked their
tents and the Meunites who were found there; they utterly destroyed
them – to this day – and settled in their place, for there was pastureland
for their flock there.

42 Some of them, of the Simeonites, journeyed to the mountains of Se'ir – five
hundred men with Pelatya, Ne'arya, Refaya, and Uziel, sons of Yishi, at
43 their head. They struck down the last remnant of Amalek and settled there
to this day.

5 1 The sons of Reuven, the firstborn of Yisrael – for he was Yisrael's firstborn,
but when he defiled his father's bed, his birthright was granted to the sons
of Yosef son of Yisrael, and he was no longer recorded as the firstborn.
2 Though Yehuda was the most powerful of his brothers, and a ruler came
3 from him, the birthright belonged to Yosef. The sons of Reuven the
4 firstborn of Yisrael: Ḥanokh, Palu, Ḥetzron, and Karmi. The sons of Yoel:
5 his son Shemaya, his son Gog, his son Shimi, his son Mikha, his son
6 Re'aya, and his son Baal; his son Be'era, who was exiled by King Tilegat
7 Pilne'eser of Assyria, was the leader of the Reubenites. And his kinsmen,
by their families, according to their genealogical records: Ye'iel the head,
8 Zekharyahu, and Bela son of Azaz son of Shema son of Yoel; he lived in
9 Aroer up to Nevo and Baal Meon. And on the eastern side, he lived up to
the outskirts of the wilderness on this side of the Euphrates, for their cattle
10 had increased in the land of Gilad. In Sha'ul's time, they waged war with
the Hagrites, who fell by their hand, and they pitched their tents all over
the region to the east of Gilad.

11 The sons of Gad lived across from them in the land of the Bashan up to
12 Salkha; Yoel was the head and Shafam the second-in-command, with Yanai
13 and Shafat in the Bashan. Their kinsmen by their ancestral houses: Mikhael,
14 Meshulam, Sheva, Yorai, Yakan, Zia, and Ever – seven. These were the sons
of Aviḥayil son of Ḥuri son of Yaroaḥ son of Gilad son of Mikhael son
15 of Yeshishai son of Yaḥdo son of Buz; Aḥi son of Avdiel son of Guni was
16 the head of their ancestral house. They lived in Gilad in the Bashan and
its dependencies and in all the pasturelands of the Sharon to their limits.

17 All these were recorded in genealogies during the time of King Yotam of
Yehuda and the time of King Yorovam of Israel.

18 The Reubenites, the Gadites, and half the tribe of Menashe were seasoned
warriors: bow drawers and bearers of shield and sword experienced in
19 warfare, 44,760 ready for war. They waged war with the Hagrites: Yetur,
20 Nafish, and Nodav. They overpowered them, and the Hagrites and all their
allies were delivered into their hands, for they cried out to God in battle;
21 He answered their pleas because they placed their trust in Him. They
captured their livestock: 50,000 camels, 250,000 sheep, 2,000 donkeys, and
22 100,000 human captives; many had fallen slain because the war was from
God, and they settled in their place until the exile.

23 The descendants of half the tribe of Menashe lived in the region; from
the Bashan up to Baal Ḥermon, Senir, and Mount Ḥermon, they were
24 numerous. These are the heads of their ancestral houses: Efer, Yishi, Eliel,
Azriel, Yirmeya, Hodavya, and Yaḥdiel, powerful men, men of renown,
25 the heads of their ancestral houses. But they broke faith with the God of
their ancestors and lusted after the gods of the people of the land whom
26 God had destroyed before them. And the God of Israel stirred the spirit of
King Pul of Assyria – the spirit of King Tilegat Pilneser of Assyria – and
he exiled the Reubenites, the Gadites, and half the tribe of Menashe and
led them away to Ḥelaḥ, Ḥavor, Hara, and the Gozan River to this day.

27 28 The sons of Levi: Gershon, Kehat, and Merari. The sons of Kehat: Amram,
29 Yitzhar, Ḥevron, and Uziel. The children of Amram: Aharon, Moshe, and
30 Miriam. The sons of Aharon: Nadav, Avihu, Elazar, and Itamar. Elazar was
31 the father of Pinḥas, Pinḥas was the father of Avishua, Avishua was the
32 father of Buki, Buki was the father of Uzi, Uzi was the father of Zeraḥya,
33 Zeraḥya was the father of Merayot, Merayot was the father of Amarya,
34 Amarya was the father of Aḥituv, Aḥituv was the father of Tzadok, Tzadok
35 was the father of Aḥimaatz, Aḥimaatz was the father of Azarya, Azarya
36 was the father of Yoḥanan, and Yoḥanan was the father of Azarya – he was
the one who served as priest in the House that Shlomo built in Jerusalem.
37 38 Azarya fathered Amarya, Amarya was the father of Aḥituv, Aḥituv was
39 the father of Tzadok, Tzadok was the father of Shalum, Shalum was the
40 father of Ḥilkiya, Ḥilkiya was the father of Azarya, Azarya was the father
41 of Seraya, and Seraya was the father of Yehotzadak. Yehotzadak went
into exile with the Lord's exile of Yehuda and Jerusalem at the hand of
Nevukhadnetzar.

6 1 2 The sons of Levi: Gershom, Kehat, and Merari. These are the names of the
3 sons of Gershom: Livni and Shimi. The sons of Kehat: Amram, Yitzhar,
4 Ḥevron, and Uziel. The sons of Merari: Maḥli and Mushi. These are the
5 families of the Levites according to their ancestors – of Gershom: his son
6 Livni, his son Yaḥat, his son Zima, his son Yoaḥ, his son Ido, his son Zeraḥ,

7 and his son Ye'aterai. The sons of Kehat: his son Aminadav, his son Koraḥ,
8 9 his son Asir, his son Elkana, his son Evyasaf, his son Asir, his son Taḥat, his
10 son Uriel, his son Uziya, and his son Sha'ul. The sons of Elkana: Amasai
11 12 and Aḥimot, his son Elkana, his son Tzofai, his son Naḥat, his son Eliav,
13 his son Yeroḥam, and his son Elkana. The sons of Shmuel: his firstborn
14 Vashni and Aviya. The son of Merari: Maḥli, his son Livni, his son Shimi,
15 his son Uza, his son Shima, his son Ḥagiya, and his son Asaya.

16 These are the ones whom David appointed over the singing in the House
17 of the LORD once the Ark came to rest. They served with song in the
Tabernacle of the Tent of Meeting until Shlomo built the House of the
18 LORD in Jerusalem; they performed their service as they were bid. These
are the men who performed along with their sons: the Kehatites, Heiman
19 the singer son of Yoel son of Shmuel son of Elkana son of Yeroḥam son of
20 Eliel son of Toaḥ son of Tzuf son of Elkana son of Maḥat son of Amasai
21 22 son of Elkana son of Yoel son of Azarya son of Tzefanya son of Taḥat son
23 of Asir son of Evyasaf son of Koraḥ son of Yitzhar son of Kehat son of Levi
24 son of Yisrael; his kinsman Asaf, who stood on his right, that is, Asaf son
25 of Berekhyahu son of Shima son of Mikhael son of Baaseya son of Malkiya
26 27 son of Etni son of Zeraḥ son of Adaya son of Eitan son of Zima son of Shimi
28 29 son of Yaḥat son of Gershom son of Levi; with their kinsmen, the sons of
30 Merari, on the left: Eitan son of Kishi son of Avdi son of Malukh son of
31 Ḥashavya, son of Amatzya son of Ḥilkiya son of Amtzi son of Bani son of
32 Shemer son of Maḥli son of Mushi son of Merari son of Levi.

33 Their kinsmen, the Levites, were on duty for all the service of the
34 Tabernacle of the House of God. Aharon and his sons made offerings on
the altar of burnt offerings and on the incense altar, performing all the
work of the Holy of Holies and atoning for Israel according to all that
35 Moshe, God's servant, had commanded. These are the sons of Aharon:
36 his son Elazar, his son Pinḥas, his son Avishua, his son Buki, his son Uzi,
37 38 his son Zeraḥya, his son Merayot, his son Amarya, his son Aḥituv, his son
39 Tzadok, and his son Aḥimaatz. These are their dwelling places throughout
their encampments within their borders: to the sons of Aharon of the
40 families of Kehatites, for the lot fell to them, they assigned Ḥevron in the
41 land of Yehuda and its surrounding pasturelands, but they assigned the
42 fields of the city and its villages to Kalev son of Yefuneh. To the sons of
Aharon they gave the cities of refuge: Ḥevron, Livna with its pasturelands,
43 Yatir, Eshtemoa with its pasturelands, Ḥilez with its pasturelands, Devir
44 with its pasturelands, Ashan with its pasturelands, and Beit Shemesh with
45 its pasturelands. From the tribe of Binyamin: Geva with its pasturelands,
Alemet with its pasturelands, and Anatot with its pasturelands; in all,
thirteen cities for their families.

46 To the remaining families of Kehatites of the tribe, ten cities were assigned
by lot to half the tribe of Menashe.

47 To the Gershomites according to their families from the tribe of Yissakhar,
the tribe of Asher, the tribe of Naftali, and the tribe of Menashe in the
Bashan – thirteen cities.

48 To the Merarites according to their families from the tribe of Reuven, the
tribe of Gad, and the tribe of Zevulun, twelve cities were assigned by lot.
49 50 The Israelites gave the Levites cities and their pasturelands. They assigned
by lot these cities, mentioned by name, to the tribe of the Judahites, the
tribe of the Simeonites, and the tribe of the Benjaminites.

51 Some of the Kehatite families had the cities of their territory from the
52 tribe of Efrayim. They gave them the cities of refuge: Shekhem with its
pasturelands in the hill country of Efrayim, Gezer with its pasturelands,
53 54 Yokme'am with its pasturelands, Beit Ḥoron with its pasturelands, Ayalon
55 with its pasturelands, and Gat Rimon with its pasturelands. For the
remaining families of Kehatites from half the tribe of Menashe: Aner with
its pasturelands and Bilam with its pasturelands.

56 To the Gershomites from half the tribe of Menashe: Golan in Bashan
57 with its pasturelands and Ashtarot with its pasturelands; from the tribe
of Yissakhar: Kedesh with its pasturelands, Dovrat with its pasturelands,
58 59 Ramot with its pasturelands, and Anem with its pasturelands; from the
tribe of Asher: Mashal with its pasturelands, Avdon with its pasturelands,
60 61 Hukok with its pasturelands, and Reḥov with its pasturelands; from the
tribe of Naftali: Kedesh in Galilee with its pasturelands, Ḥamon with its
pasturelands, and Kiryatayim with its pasturelands.

62 To the remaining Merarites from the tribe of Zevulun: Rimono with
63 its pasturelands and Tavor with its pasturelands. Beyond the Jordan at
Yeriḥo, on the east side of the Jordan, from the tribe of Reuven: Betzer
in the wilderness with its pasturelands, Yahtza with its pasturelands,
64 65 Kedemot with its pasturelands, and Meifaat with its pasturelands. From
the tribe of Gad: Ramot in Gilad with its pasturelands, Maḥanayim
66 with its pasturelands, Ḥeshbon with its pasturelands, and Yazeir with its
pasturelands.

7 1 2 The sons of Yissakhar: Tola, Puah, Yashuv, and Shimron – four. The sons
of Tola: Uzi, Refaya, Yeriel, Yaḥmai, Ivsam, and Shmuel; heads of their
ancestral houses of Tola, they were powerful men in their generation. In
3 David's time, they numbered 22,600. The son of Uzi: Yizraḥya. The sons
of Yizraḥya: Mikhael, Ovadya, Yoel, and Yishiya – five, all of them heads.
4 And with them by their generations, according to their ancestral houses,
5 were military battle units – 36,000, for they had many wives and sons. Their
kinsmen, belonging to all the families of Yissakhar, powerful warriors, were
87,000 in all according to their genealogical record.

6 7 Binyamin: Bela, Bekher, and Yediael – three. The sons of Bela: Etzbon,
Uzi, Uziel, Yerimot, and Iri – five, heads of ancestral houses, powerful

8 warriors; according to the genealogical records, they were 22,034. The
sons of Bekher: Zemira, Yoash, Eliezer, Elyo'einai, Omri, Yeremot, Aviya,
9 Anatot, and Alemet; all these were the sons of Bekher. According to their
genealogical record by their generations, heads of their ancestral houses,
10 powerful warriors, they were 20,200. The son of Yediael: Bilhan; the sons of
Bilhan: Yeush, Binyamin, Ehud, Kenaana, Zeitan, Tarshish, and Aḥishaḥar.
11 All these were the sons of Yediael, heads of the fathers, seasoned warriors,
12 a force of 17,200 ready for war. Shupim and Ḥupim were the sons of Ir;
Ḥushim the son of Aḥer.

13 The sons of Naftali: Yaḥatziel, Guni, Yetzer, and Shalum, the descendants
of Bilha.

14 The sons of Menashe: Asriel, whom his Aramean concubine bore; she
15 bore Makhir the father of Gilad. And Makhir took wives for Ḥupim and for
Shupim. The name of his sister was Maakha, and the name of the second
16 was Tzelofḥad; Tzelofḥad had daughters. Maakha the wife of Makhir bore
a son, and she named him Peresh. The name of his brother was Sheresh,
17 and his sons were Ulam and Rekem. The son of Ulam: Bedan. These were
18 the sons of Gilad son of Makhir son of Menashe. His sister Hamolekhet
19 bore Ish Hod, Aviezer, and Maḥla. The sons of Shemida were Aḥyan,
Shekhem, Likḥi, and Aniam.

20 The sons of Efrayim: Shutalaḥ, his son Bered, his son Taḥat, his son Elada,
21 his son Taḥat, his son Zavad, and his son Shutelaḥ as well as Ezer and
Elad; the men of Gat, who were born in the land, killed them because
22 they went down to raid their cattle. Their father Efrayim mourned for a
23 long time, and his brothers came to comfort him. He was intimate with
his wife, she conceived and bore a son, and he named him Beria because
24 evil had befallen his house.[8] His daughter was She'era, who built lower
25 and upper Beit Ḥoron and Uzen She'era. Also his son Refaḥ, his sons
26 Reshef and Telaḥ, his son Taḥan, his son Ladan, his son Amihud, his
27 son Elishama, his son Non, and his son Yehoshua. Their property and
28 settlements were Beit El and its dependencies, on the east Naaran, on the
west Gezer and its dependencies, and Shekhem and its dependencies up
29 to Aya and its dependencies. Next to the descendants of Menashe: Beit
She'an and its dependencies, Ta'nakh and its dependencies, Megiddo and
its dependencies, Dor and its dependencies; in these lived the sons of
Yosef son of Yisrael.

30 The sons of Asher: Imna, Yishva, Yishvi, and Beria, and Seraḥ their sister.
31 The sons of Beria: Ḥever and Malkiel, who was the father of Birzayit. Ḥever
32
33 was the father of Yaflet, Shomer, and Ḥotam and their sister Shua. The
sons of Yaflet: Pasakh, Bimhal, and Ashvat; these were the sons of Yaflet.
34 The sons of Shemer: Aḥi, Roga, Ḥuba, and Aram. The sons of Helem,
35
36 his brother: Tzofaḥ, Imna, Shelesh, and Amal. The sons of Tzofaḥ: Suaḥ,

8 | "Beria" evokes the Hebrew *beraa*, "in evil."

37 Ḥarnefer, Shual, Beri, Yimra, Betzer, Hod, Shama, Shilsha, Yitran, and
38 39 Be'era. The sons of Yeter: Yefuneh, Pispa, and Ara. The sons of Ula: Araḥ,
40 Ḥaniel, and Ritzya. All these sons of Asher were heads of the ancestral
house and elite, powerful warriors. According to their genealogical record,
the number of their fighting force was 26,000.

8 1 Binyamin was the father of Bela, his firstborn, Ashbel the second, Aḥraḥ
2, 3 the third, Noḥa the fourth, and Rafa the fifth. Bela had sons: Adar, Gera,
4, 5, 6 Avihud, Avishua, Naaman, Aḥoaḥ, Gera, Shefufan, and Ḥuram. These were
the sons of Eḥud; they were the ancestral heads of the inhabitants of Geva,
7 and they were exiled to Manaḥat: Naaman, Aḥiya, and Gera – he exiled
8 them and was the father of Uza and Aḥiḥud. Shaḥarayim was the father of
children in the country of Moav after he had sent away Ḥushim and Baara
9 his wives; he fathered sons by his wife Ḥodesh: Yovav, Tzivya, Mesha,
10 Malkam, Yeutz, Sakheya, and Mirma; these were his sons, ancestral heads.
11 12 Through Ḥushim, he also fathered Avituv and Elpaal. The sons of Elpaal:
Ever, Misham, Shemed – who built Ono and Lod with its dependencies
13 Beriya and Shema – they were the ancestral heads of the inhabitants of
14 Ayalon, who drove away the inhabitants of Gat – Aḥyo, Shashak, and
15, 16, 17 Yeremot. Zevadya, Arad, Eder, Mikhael, Yishpa, and Yoḥa were sons of
18 Beria. Zevadya, Meshulam, Ḥizki, Ḥever, Yishmerai, Yizlia, and Yovav
19, 20, 21 were the sons of Elpaal. Yakim, Zikhri, Zavdi, Elienai, Tziletai, Eliel, Adaya,
22, 23, 24 Beraya, and Shimrat were the sons of Shimi. Yishpan, Ever, Eliel, Avdon,
25, 26 Zikhri, Ḥanan, Ḥananya, Eilam, Antotiya, Yifdeya, and Penuel were the
27 sons of Shashak. Shamsherai, Sheḥarya, Atalya, Yaareshya, Eliya, and
28 Zikhri were the sons of Yeroḥam. These were the ancestral heads, heads
of their generations; these resided in Jerusalem.

29 The father of Givon lived in Givon, and the name of his wife was Maakha;
30 31 his firstborn son was Avdon, then Tzur, Kish, Baal, Nadav, Gedor, Aḥyo,
32 and Zekher. Miklot was the father of Shima, and they too lived in
33 Jerusalem alongside their kinsmen, together with their kinsmen.[9] Ner
was the father of Kish, Kish was the father of Sha'ul, and Sha'ul was the
34 father of Yehonatan, Malkishua, Avinadav, and Eshbaal. Yonatan's son was
35 Meriv Baal, and Meriv Baal was the father of Mikha. The sons of Mikha:
36 Piton, Melekh, Taare'a, and Aḥaz. Aḥaz was the father of Yehoada, Yehoada
37 was the father of Alemet, Azmavet, and Zimri, and Zimri was the father
38 of Motza. Motza was the father of Bina, his son Rafa, his son Elasa, and
his son Atzel. Atzel had six sons, and these are their names: Azrikam,
39 Bokheru, Yishmael, She'arya, Ovadya, and Ḥanan; all these were the sons
of Atzel. The sons of his brother Eshek: his firstborn Ulam, Yeush the
40 second, and Elifelet the third. The sons of Ulam were powerful warriors
of Ulam – bow drawers and men of substance who had many children and
grandchildren – 150; all these were descendants of Binyamin.

9 | Both the descendants of Miklot and the descendants of Yeroḥam mentioned in verses 26–28 shared Jerusalem with their kinsmen from other tribes; cf. 9:3.

9 1 All of Israel were registered by genealogy; they are recorded in the Book of
the Kings of Israel. And Yehuda was exiled to Babylon because they broke
2 faith. The first to settle on their own holdings, in their own towns, were
3 Israel, the priests, the Levites, and the Netinim.[10] In Jerusalem resided
4 some Judahites, Benjaminites, Efraimites, and Manassites: Utai son of
Amihud son of Omri son of Imri son of Bani, of the descendants of Peretz
5 6 son of Yehuda; of the Shilonites, the firstborn Asaya and his sons;and of the
7 descendants of Zeraḥ, Yeuel and their kinsmen – 690. Of the Benjaminites:
8 Salu son of Meshulam son of Hodavya son of Hasenua, Yivneya son of
Yeroḥam, Ela son of Uzi son of Mikhri, Meshulam son of Shefatya son of
9 Reuel son of Yivneya, and their kinsmen by their generations – 956. All
these men were heads of their ancestral houses.

10 11 Of the priests: Yedaya, Yehoyariv, Yakhin, Azarya son of Ḥilkiya son of
Meshulam son of Tzadok son of Merayot son of Aḥituv in charge of the
12 House of God; Adaya son of Yeroḥam son of Pashḥur son of Malkiya, and
Maasai son of Adiel son of Yaḥzera son of Meshulam son of Meshilemit son
13 of Imer, together with their kinsmen, heads of their ancestral houses – 1,760
powerful men for the work of the service of the House of God.

14 Of the Levites: Shemaya son of Ḥashuv son of Azrikam son of Ḥashavya;
15 of the descendants of Merari, Bakbakar, Ḥeresh, Galal, and Matanya son
16 of Mikha son of Zikhri son of Asaf, Ovadya son of Shemaya son of Galal
son of Yedutun, and Berekhya son of Asa son of Elkana, who lived in the
villages of the Netofatites.

17 And the gatekeepers: Shalum, Akub, Talmon, and Aḥiman, and their
18 kinsman Shalum was the head; they had previously been stationed at the
king's gate toward the east – these were the gatekeepers of the Levite camp.
19 Shalum son of Koreh son of Evyasaf son of Koraḥ and his kinsmen of the
Korahite ancestral house were in charge of the work of the service, keepers
of the Tent threshold. Their ancestors had been in charge of the Tent of the
20 Lord, keepers of the entrance. Pinḥas son of Elazar had been their ruler in
21 times past; the Lord was with him. Zekharya son of Meshelemya was the
22 gatekeeper of the entrance to the Tent of Meeting. In all, 212 were selected
to be gatekeepers of the threshold; they were listed by genealogy in their
villages. David and Shmuel the seer had established them in permanent
23 office, and they and their descendants guarded the gates of the House
24 of the Lord and of the House of the Tent; the gatekeepers stood at all
25 four sides: east, west, north, and south. Their kin from their villages were
26 to come in every seven days to be with them in turn, for the four chief
gatekeepers – who were Levites – were on permanent duty; they were
27 in charge of the chambers and the treasuries of the House of God. They
lodged near the House of God, for they were responsible for guard duty
28 and for unlocking it every morning. Some of them were in charge of the

10 | A group of servants in the Temple, apparently of non-Jewish extraction, whose origins are not fully known.

service vessels, of bringing in a certain number and bringing out a certain
29 number; some of them were in charge of the vessels, including all the
sacred vessels, and of the fine flour, the wine, the oil, the frankincense, and
30 31 the spices. Some of the priests prepared mixtures of the spices. Matitya of
the Levites, the firstborn of Shalum the Korahite, was in permanent charge
32 of the pan-bread preparation while some of their Kehatite kinsmen were
in charge of the showbread, making them every Sabbath.

33 Then there were the singers, the ancestral heads of the Levites; they lived
in the chambers exempt from other duties because they worked day and
34 night. These were the ancestral heads of the Levites according to their
generations; these resided in Jerusalem.

35 In Givon lived the father of Givon, Ye'iel, and the name of his wife was
36 Maakha. His firstborn son was Avdon, then Tzur, Kish, Baal, Ner, Nadav,
37 38 Gedor, Aḥyo, Zekharya, and Miklot; Miklot was the father of Shimam, and
they too, opposite their kinsmen, lived in Jerusalem with their kinsmen.
39 Ner was the father of Kish, Kish was the father of Sha'ul, and Sha'ul was
40 the father of Yehonatan, Malkishua, Avinadav, and Eshbaal. Yehonatan's
41 son was Meriv Baal, and Meriv Baal was the father of Mikha. The sons
42 of Mikha: Piton, Melekh, and Taḥare'a. Aḥaz was the father of Yara, Yara
was the father of Alemet, Azmavet, and Zimri, and Zimri was the father of
43 Motza. Motza was the father of Bina, his son Refaya, his son Elasa, and his
44 son Atzel. Atzel had six sons, and these are their names: Azrikam, Bokheru,
Yishmael, She'arya, Ovadya, and Ḥanan; these were the sons of Atzel.

10 1 The Philistines fought against Israel; the men of Israel fled before the
2 Philistines and fell slain on Mount Gilboa. And the Philistines closed in
on Sha'ul and his sons; the Philistines struck down Yonatan, Avinadav, and
3 Malkishua, the sons of Sha'ul. And the battle weighed heavily upon Sha'ul,
and when the archers found him, he shook, frightened by the archers.
4 "Draw your sword and stab me with it," Sha'ul said to his arms bearer, "lest
these heathens come and torture me." But his arms bearer was not willing
5 due to his great reverence, so Sha'ul took the sword and fell upon it. When
his arms bearer saw that Sha'ul was dead, he too fell on the sword and died.
6 7 Sha'ul, his three sons, and all his house died together on that day. When all
the men of Israel in the valley and on the other side of the Jordan realized
that Sha'ul and his sons had fled and died, they abandoned their cities and
fled. And Philistines came and settled in them.

8 The next day, when Philistines came to strip the corpses, they found Sha'ul
9 and his sons fallen on Mount Gilboa. They stripped him, carried off his
head and his armor, and sent word throughout the land of the Philistines,
10 bringing tidings to their idols and to the people. They deposited his armor
in the temple of their gods and fastened his skull in the temple of Dagon.

11 Now when all the people of Yavesh Gilad heard of everything that the
12 Philistines did to Sha'ul, all their boldest men set out, carried off Sha'ul's

corpse and the corpses of his sons, and brought them to Yavesh. They
buried their bones beneath the terebinth in Yavesh and fasted for seven
13 days. Thus Sha'ul died for breaking faith with the LORD, for failing to keep
14 the LORD's word, and for inquiring of a necromancer; he did not inquire of
the LORD, so He put him to death and turned the kingship over to David
son of Yishai.

11 1 Now all the tribes of Israel gathered to David at Ḥevron.
2 "Look, we are your own flesh and blood. All along, even when Sha'ul was
king, you were the one who led Israel out and brought them back. And
the LORD your God said to you, 'You shall shepherd My people Israel, and
3 you shall be ruler over Israel.'" All the elders of Israel came to the king at
Ḥevron; David formed a covenant with them at Ḥevron before the LORD,
and they anointed David as king over Israel, fulfilling the word of the LORD
through Shmuel.

4 David and all Israel went to Jerusalem, that is, Yevus, where the Jebusites
5 had settled the land. The people of Yevus said to David, "You shall not enter
here." But David captured the stronghold of Zion, that is, the City of David.
6 Then David said, "Whoever is the first to attack the Jebusites will be made
a leader and an officer." The first to go up was Yoav son of Tzeruya, and he
7 was made the leader. David settled in the stronghold, and for that reason it
8 was called the City of David. He built up the city all around in a complete
9 circuit from the Milo while Yoav repaired the rest of the city. And David
grew in greatness; the LORD of Hosts was with him.

10 These are the leaders among David's warriors who gave him great support
in his kingdom, together with all of Israel, to appoint him as king in
11 accordance with the LORD's word about Israel. This is an account of
David's warriors: Yoshovam son of Ḥakhmoni was the head of the Thirty;
he wielded his spear against three hundred victims at one time.

12 Next in rank was Elazar son of Dodo the Ahohite; he was among the
13 warriors of the Three. He was with David in Pas Damim where the
Philistines had gathered for war. There was a plot of land full of barley,
14 and the troops fled from the Philistines. But they took their stand in the
middle of the plot, defended it, and defeated the Philistines; the LORD
saved them with a great victory.

15 Once, the chief three of the Thirty went down to the rock to David in the
cave of Adulam, when an army of Philistines was encamped in the Refaim
16 Valley. At the time, David was in the stronghold while the Philistines were
17 then stationed at Beit Leḥem. David was seized with a craving and said,
"Oh – if only someone could give me water to drink from the well of Beit
18 Leḥem by the gate." So the three warriors infiltrated the Philistine camp,
drew water from the Beit Leḥem well by the gate, and carried it back. But
when they brought it to David, he would not drink it and poured it out in
a libation to the LORD.

19 “The Lord forbid that I do such a thing!” he said. “Shall I drink the
lifeblood of men who risked their very lives by going?” And he would not
20 drink it. These were the feats of the three warriors. Avshai, the brother
of Yoav, was the head of these three. He wielded his spear against three
21 hundred victims. He was famous among the three. Of the three in the
second rank he was the most honored and so became their leader, though
he never reached the rank of the Three.

22 Benaya son of Yehoyada, from Kavtze'el, was a powerful man who achieved
great feats. He defeated the two leonine warriors of Moav, and he climbed
23 down into a pit and overpowered a lion on a snowy day. He defeated an
Egyptian man of formidable proportions, five cubits tall. The Egyptian
held a spear like a weaver’s beam, but he charged down at him with a
pole, snatched the spear from the Egyptian’s hand, and killed him with
24 his own spear. These were the feats of Benayahu son of Yehoyada, and he
25 was famous among the three warriors. He was among the most honored
of the Thirty, though he never reached the rank of the Three, and David
appointed him over his bodyguard.

26 The most valiant of the warriors were:
Asael brother of Yoav, Elḥanan son of Dodo from Beit Leḥem,
27 Shamot the Harorite, Ḥeletz the Pelonite,
28 Ira son of Ikesh the Tekoite, Aviezer the Anatotite,
29 Sibekhai the Hushatite, Ilai the Ahohite,
30 Mahrai the Netofatite, Ḥeled son of Baana the Netofatite,
31 Itai son of Rivai from Giva of the Benjaminites, Benaya of Pirathon,
32 Ḥurai of Naḥalei Gaash, Aviel the Arbatite,
33 Azmavet the Bahrumite, Elyaḥba the Shaalbonite,
34 the sons of Hashem the Gizonite, Yonatan son of Shageh the Hararite,
35 Aḥiam son of Sakhar the Hararite, Elifal son of Ur,
36 Ḥefer the Mekheratite, Aḥiya the Pelonite,
37 Ḥetzro the Carmelite, Naarai son of Ezbai,
38 Yoel brother of Natan, Mivḥar son of Hagri,
39 Tzelek the Amonite, Naḥrai the Berotite, the arms bearer of Yoav son of
Tzeruya,
40 Ira the Itrite, Garev the Yitrite,
41 Uriya the Hittite, Zavad son of Aḥlai,
42 Adina son of Shiza the Reubenite, a leader of the Reubenites, and thirty
with him.
43 Ḥanan son of Maakha, Yoshafat the Mitnite,
44 Uziya the Ashteratite, Shama and Ye'iel, sons of Ḥotam the Aroerite,
45 Yediael son of Shimri and his brother Yoḥa the Tizite,
46 Eliel the Mahavite, Yeribai and Yoshavya, sons of Elnaam, Yitma the
Moabite,
47 Eliel, Oved, and Yaasiel the Mezobaite.

12 1 These people came to David in Tziklag while he was still held in check by

2 Sha'ul son of Kish; they joined his warriors, his allies in battle: archers who
could use both their right and left hands for slinging stones and shooting
3 arrows – they were of Sha'ul's kin from Binyamin. At the head were Aḥiezer
and Yoash, sons of Shema'a of Giva; Yeziel and Pelet, sons of Azmavet;
4 Berakha and Yehu of Anatot; Yishmaya of Givon, a warrior of the thirty in
5 charge of the Thirty; Yirmeya, Yaḥaziel, Yoḥanan, and Yozavad of Gedera;
6 7 Eluzai, Yerimot, Be'alya, Shemaryahu, and Shefatyahu the Ḥarufite; Elkana,
8 Yishyahu, Azarel, Yoezer, and Yoshovam the Korahites; and Yoela and
9 Zevadya sons of Yeroḥam of Gedor. Warriors of the Gadites defected to
David in his wilderness stronghold, experienced men of war who wielded
shield and spear – their faces were like the faces of lions, and they could
10 race over the hills like deer. At the head was Ezer, with Ovadya the second,
11 12 Eliav the third, Mishmana the fourth, Yirmeya the fifth, Atai the sixth,
13 14 Eliel the seventh, Yoḥanan the eighth, Elzabad the ninth, Yirmeyahu the
15 tenth, and Makhbanai the eleventh. These were heads of the army from
the Gadites; the least of them was worth a hundred, and the greatest a
16 thousand. These are the ones who crossed the Jordan in the first month
when all its banks were overflowing; they drove away all those in the
valleys to the east and to the west.

17 Some of the Benjaminites and Judahites came to David at his stronghold.
18 David went out to meet them in response.
"If you came to me in peace to help me," he said to them, "my heart will
be bound to yours; but if you came to betray me to my enemies though
my hands have done no wrong, may the God of our ancestors see and
condemn you!"

19 Suddenly the spirit seized Amasai, the head of the thirty:

"We are yours, David.
We are with you, son of Yishai –
peace!
Peace to you
and peace to all who help you,
for it is God who helps you."

So David accepted them and assigned them as heads of the force.

20 Some of Menashe defected to David when he came with the Philistines
to fight against Sha'ul, but he did not help the Philistines because their
chieftains took counsel and sent him away, saying, "At the cost of our
21 heads, he will defect to his master Sha'ul." As he went to Tziklag, some
of Menashe defected to him: Adnaḥ, Yozavad, Yediael, Mikhael, Yozavad,
22 Elihu, and Ziletai, heads of the clans of Menashe. They helped David
against the raiders, for they were all valiant warriors, and they became
23 officers of the army. Day by day, men kept coming to David to support
him until his forces were as great as the heavenly forces.

24 These are the numbers of the divisions of the armed troops who came over
to David in Ḥevron to transfer Sha'ul's kingship to him in accordance with
the word of the LORD.

25 The Judahites, bearing shield and spear, 6,800 armed troops;

26 of the Simeonites, warriors ready for battle, 7,100;

27 28 of the Levites, 4,600; Yehoyada, leader of the house of Aharon, and 3,700
29 with him; Tzadok, a valiant young warrior, and 22 officers from his father's
house;

30 of the Benjaminites, Sha'ul's own kin, 3,000 – even now, most of them kept
their allegiance to the house of Sha'ul.

31 Of the Efraimites, 20,800 warriors, famous throughout their ancestral
houses;

32 from half of the tribe of Menashe, 18,000 who were singled out by name
to come and make David king;

33 of the Issakharites, men who understood the times and knew what
Israel would do, 200 at their head, and all their brothers were at their
command;

34 of Zevulun, 50,000 seasoned warriors, ready for battle with all weapons of
war, giving support with undivided loyalty;

35 of Naftali, 1,000 officers along with 37,000 with shield and spear;

36 of the Danites, 28,600 ready for battle;

37 of Asher, 40,000 seasoned warriors ready for battle.

38 From across the Jordan, from the Reubenites, Gadites, and half the tribe
of Menashe – 120,000, with all weapons of war.

39 All these men of war, offering support with all their hearts, came to Ḥevron
to make David king over all of Israel, and all the rest of Israel as well were
40 of one heart: to make David king. They stayed with David for three days,
41 feasting and drinking, for their brothers had prepared for them. And those
who were nearby, as far as Yissakhar, Zevulun, and Naftali, brought food
on donkeys, camels, mules, and cattle: baked goods, cakes of figs and
raisins, wine, oil, and an abundance of cattle and sheep, for there was joy
in Israel.

13 1 David took counsel with the officers of thousands and hundreds, with
2 every leader. And David said to all the assembly of Israel: "If you approve,
and if it is the will of the LORD our God, let us send word far and wide to
our brothers who remain in all the lands of Israel, together with the priests
and Levites in the cities of their pasturelands, so they may gather to us.

3 Then we will bring the Ark of our God back to us, for we did not seek it
out in the days of Sha'ul."

4 And all of the assembly agreed to do so, for the idea seemed right in the
5 eyes of all the people. So David assembled all of Israel – from Shiḥor of
6 Egypt to Levo Ḥamat – to bring the Ark of God from Kiryat Ye'arim. David
went up with all of Israel to Baala of Kiryat Ye'arim of Yehuda, to bring up
from there the Ark of God, of the Lord Enthroned upon the Cherubim,
7 which is called by the Name. They mounted the Ark of God onto a new
8 cart from the house of Avinadav, with Uza and Aḥyo driving the cart and
David and all of Israel reveling before God with all their might, with song
and with lyre, with harp and with timbrel, with cymbal and with trumpet.
9 When they came to the threshing floor of Kidon, Uza reached out his hand
10 to grasp hold of the Ark, for the oxen had stumbled. And the Lord's rage
flared up against Uza; He struck him down for having reached out his hand
11 toward the Ark, and he died there before God. David was enraged that the
Lord had burst out against Uza, so that place has been called Peretz Uza[11]
12 to this day. David feared God on that day, and he said, "How will I bring
13 the Ark of the Lord to me?" David did not remove the Ark of the Lord
to him in the City of David; he had it redirected to the house of Oved
14 Edom the Gittite. The Ark of God remained at the house of Oved Edom
the Gittite for three months, and the Lord blessed the house of Oved
Edom and all that was his.

14 1 King Ḥiram of Tyre sent envoys to David, and cedar logs, stonemasons,
2 and carpenters to build him a house. And David knew that the Lord had
established him as king over Israel and that the kingship had been exalted
for the sake of His people Israel.

3 David took more wives in Jerusalem, and David fathered more sons and
4 daughters. These are the names of those born to him in Jerusalem: Shamua,
5 6 Shovav, Natan, and Shlomo; Yivḥar, Elishua, and Elpelet; Noga, Nefeg,
7 and Yafia; Elishama, Be'elyada, and Elifelet.

8 When the Philistines heard that David had been appointed as king over
Israel, all the Philistines marched in to hunt David down. When David
9 heard, he marched out to preempt them. The Philistines came and raided
the Refaim Valley.

10 David inquired of the Lord, "Shall I go up to the Philistines? Will You
deliver them into my hands?"

"Go up," the Lord replied to him, "for I will surely deliver the Philistines
into your hands."

11 They marched up to Baal Peratzim, and there David defeated them. And
David said, "God has blasted my enemies away by my hand like a blast of

---

11 | Literally "outburst of Uza."

12 water," so he named that place Baal Peratzim.[12] They abandoned their idols
there, and David gave orders to burn them with fire.

13 But the Philistines returned once more and went raiding in the valley.
14 David inquired of God once more, and God said, "Do not go up after them;
turn around to go behind them and advance upon them opposite the baca
15 trees. As soon as you hear the sound of marching echoing across the tops
of the baca trees, go out to attack, for then God will go out before you to
16 strike down the Philistine force." And David did as God commanded him,
and he defeated the Philistine force from Givon up to Gezer.

17 David's fame grew throughout the lands, and the LORD spread fear of him
throughout the nations.

15 1 David made himself houses in the City of David. He prepared a place for
2 the Ark of God and pitched a tent for it. Then David declared, "No one
should bear the Ark of God except for the Levites, for the LORD has chosen
them to bear the Ark of the LORD and to serve Him forever."

3 David assembled all of Israel to Jerusalem to bring up the Ark of the
4 LORD to the place he had prepared for it. Then David gathered all the
descendants of Aharon and the Levites:

5 Of the Kehatites, the leader Uriel and his kin, 120;

6 of the Merarites, the leader Asaya and his kin, 220;

7 of the Gershomites, the leader Yoel and his kin, 130;

8 of the sons of Elitzafan, the leader Shemaya and his kin, 200;

9 of the sons of Ḥevron, the leader Eliel and his kin, 80;

10 of the sons of Uziel, the leader Aminadav and his kin, 112.

11 David summoned the priests Tzadok and Evyatar and the Levites Uriel,
12 Asaya, Yoel, Shemaya, Eliel, and Aminadav and told them, "You are the
ancestral heads of the Levites; you and your kin must sanctify yourselves.
Then you will bring up the Ark of the LORD, God of Israel, to the place I
13 have prepared for it. Because it was not you the first time, the LORD our
God burst out against us, for we did not seek Him in the right way."

14 The priests and Levites sanctified themselves to bring up the Ark of the
15 LORD, God of Israel, and the Levites carried the Ark of God as Moshe had
commanded according to the word of the LORD: bearing poles upon their
16 shoulders. David ordered the Levite leaders to position their brothers the
singers with musical instruments – lyres, harps, and cymbals – to play out
loud, raising sounds of joy.

17 So the Levites appointed Heiman son of Yoel, and of his kinsmen Asaf

---

12 | From the Hebrew *peretz*, meaning "bursting out" or "blast"; cf. 13:11.

son of Berekhyahu, and of their Merarite kin Eitan son of Kushayahu,
18 along with their kinsmen within the second order: Zekharyahu, Ben,
Yaaziel, Shemiramot, Yeḥiel, Uni, Eliav, Benayahu, Maaseyahu, Matityahu,
19 Elifelehu, Mikneyahu, Oved Edom, and Ye'iel, the gatekeepers. The singers
20 Heiman, Asaf, and Eitan played on cymbals of bronze; Zekharya, Yaaziel,
Shemiramot, Yeḥiel, Uni, Eliav, Maaseyahu, and Benayahu played the
21 *alamot*[13] on harps while Matityahu, Elifelehu, Mikneyahu, Oved Edom,
22 Ye'iel, and Azazyahu led with the *sheminit* on lyres. Kenanyahu, the chief
23 musician of the Levites, conducted the music, for he was skilled. Berekhya
24 and Elkana were gatekeepers for the Ark while Shevanyahu, Yoshafat,
Netanel, Amasai, Zekharyahu, Benayahu, and Eliezer the priests sounded
the trumpets before the Ark of God, with Oved Edom and Yeḥiya as
25 gatekeepers for the Ark. Thus David, the elders of Israel, and the officers
of thousands went with joy to bring up the Ark of the Lord's Covenant
from the house of Oved Edom.

26 Because God supported the Levites who carried the Ark of the Lord's
27 Covenant, they sacrificed seven bulls and seven rams. David was clad
in a robe of fine linen, as were all the Levites who carried the Ark, the
musicians, and Kenanya, the chief musician of the singers; David also
28 wore a linen ephod.[14] And all of Israel brought up the Ark of the Lord's
Covenant with joyous shouting, with the sound of the ram's horn and
trumpets and cymbals, and the music of lyres and harps.

29 As the Ark of the Lord's Covenant reached the City of David, Mikhal,
Sha'ul's daughter, was watching through the window, and when she saw
David – the king! – dancing and reveling, she felt a rush of contempt for
him.

16 1 They brought the Ark of God, set it up within the tent that David had
pitched for it, and offered up burnt offerings and peace offerings before
2 God. When David had finished offering the burnt offering and the
3 peace offerings, he blessed the people in the name of the Lord. He then
distributed a loaf of bread, a share of meat, and a cake of raisins to all the
4 people of Israel, every single man and woman. He appointed some of the
Levites as attendants before the Ark of the Lord to invoke, thank, and
5 praise the Lord, God of Israel: Asaf was the head, Zekharya his second,
Ye'iel, Shemiramot, Yeḥiel, Matitya, Eliav, Benayahu, Oved Edom, and
6 Ye'iel with lyres and harps, Asaf sounding the cymbals, and the priests
Benayahu and Yaḥaziel with trumpets continually before the Ark of God's
7 Covenant. On that day, for the first time, David gave thanksgiving to the
Lord through Asaf and his kinsmen:

8 Give thanks to the Lord; call on His name;[15]

---

13 | *Alamot* and *sheminit* (v. 21) are musical terms of uncertain meaning; cf. Psalms 6:1, 46:1.
14 | An outer garment worn by the priests (see Ex., ch. 28).
15 | Cf. Psalms 105:1–15.

proclaim His acts among the peoples.
9 Sing to Him,
make music to Him,
tell of all His wonders.
10 Glory in His holy name;
let the hearts of the LORD's seekers rejoice.
11 Long for the LORD and His might;
seek out His presence always.
12 Recall the wonders He has done,
the marvels and judgments He has pronounced.
13 O seed of Yisrael His servant,
O children of Yaakov, His chosen ones.
14 He is the LORD, our God;
His judgments are throughout the land.
15 Remember His covenant forever,
His word of command for a thousand generations –
16 which He formed with Avraham,
swore to Yitzḥak,
17 and established with Yaakov as a statute,
as an eternal covenant for Israel,
18 saying, "To you I will give the land of Canaan
as your share of inheritance,"
19 when you were few in number,
scarce,
strangers there,
20 wandering from nation to nation,
from one kingdom to another people.
21 Yet He let no one oppress them
and rebuked kings for their sake, saying,
22 "Touch not My anointed ones,
and do My prophets no harm."
23 Sing to the LORD, all the earth;[16]
proclaim His salvation day by day;
24 declare His glory among the nations,
His wonders among all peoples,
25 for the LORD is great, of highest praise,
to be held in awe above all divine beings –
26 for all the gods of the peoples are mere idols;
it was the LORD who made the heavens.
27 Majesty and splendor are before Him,
might and joy in His place.
28 Render to the LORD, O families of the peoples –
render to the LORD glory and might –
29 render to the LORD the glory due His name.

16 | Cf. Psalms 96:1–13.

Bring an offering and come before Him;
bow down to the LORD in the splendor of holiness.
30 Tremble before Him, all the earth –
the world stands firm; it will never be shaken.
31 Let the heavens rejoice and the earth exult;
let them say among the nations, "The LORD is King."
32 Let the sea roar, and all that fills it;
let the fields revel, and all they contain;
33 then the trees of the forest will sing for joy
before the LORD, for He is coming to judge the earth.
34 Thank the LORD for He is good;
His loving-kindness is forever.
35 Say,
"Save us, God of our salvation;
gather us and rescue us from the nations,
so that we may give thanks to Your holy name
and glory in Your praise."
36 Blessed is the LORD, God of Israel,
for ever and ever.

37 And all the people said, "Amen," and "Praise the LORD!" He then left Asaf
and his kinsmen there before the Ark of the LORD's Covenant in constant
38 daily service before the Ark. Oved Edom and his kin numbered sixty-eight;
39 Oved Edom son of Yeditun and Ḥosa were to be gatekeepers. Tzadok the
priest and his kin, the priests, remained in the presence of the LORD's
40 Tabernacle at the high shrine at Givon to offer up burnt offerings regularly
to the LORD, morning and evening, on the altar of burnt offering in accordance with all that is written in the LORD's Law that He commanded
41 Israel to follow. With them were Heiman and Yedutun and the rest of the
chosen who were singled out by name to give thanks to the LORD, for His
42 loving-kindness lasts forever; Heiman and Yedutun accompanied them
with trumpets and cymbals and played instruments for the sacred song.
Yedutun's sons were posted at the gate.

43 Then all the people went back home, and David turned around to bless
his own house.

17 1 Once he had settled in his palace, David said to the prophet Natan, "Here I
am dwelling in a cedarwood palace while the Ark of the LORD's Covenant
is dwelling beneath tents."

2 "Do whatever you have in mind," Natan said to David, "for God is with
you."

3 But that same night, the word of God came to Natan:

4 "Go and say to My servant David: Thus says the LORD: You shall not
5 be the one to build a house for Me to dwell in. For I have not dwelt in a

house from the day I brought the Israelites out to this day; I have gone
6 from tent to tent, from Tabernacle to Tabernacle. But wherever I roamed
throughout Israel, have I ever spoken a word to any of the judges of Israel
whom I charged to shepherd My people, saying, 'Why have you not built
Me a cedarwood palace?'

7 "Now, you shall say so to My servant David: Thus says the LORD of Hosts:
I took you out of the pasture, from following the sheep, to be ruler over
8 My people Israel. I have been with you wherever you went, and I have cut
down all your enemies before you. I will make for you a name – one of the
9 greatest names on earth. I will set aside a place for My people Israel and
let them take root and settle down within it, and they will be disturbed no
10 longer; violent men will no longer wear them down as they once did in
the days when I appointed judges over My people Israel. I will subdue all
of your enemies; moreover, I declare that the LORD will establish a house
11 for you. For it will be when your days are done and you must go the way
of your ancestors, I will raise up your own seed after you – among your
12 own sons – and I will establish his kingship. He will build Me a house, and
13 I will firmly establish his throne forever. I will be a Father to him, and he
will be a son to Me; My loyalties will never stray from him, as I removed
14 them from him who was before you. I will set him in My house and in My
kingship forever, and his throne will be secure forever."

15 Natan related all these words and all this vision to David.

16 Now King David came and sat before the LORD.

"Who am I, O LORD God, and who is my house," he said,
"that You have brought me so far?
17 And yet even this is small in Your eyes, God,
as You also speak of Your servant's house in the distant future
and perceive me as a worthy man, O LORD God.
18 But what more could David add,
for the honor You have given Your servant?
You know Your servant.
19 It is for the sake of Your servant, O LORD, and Your own will,
that You brought about this greatness,
to make all this greatness known.
20 O LORD, there is no one like You and no god besides You,
as we have heard all along.
21 And who is like Your people Israel –
the only nation on earth God went to redeem as His own people,
making a name for Yourself of greatness and wondrous deeds
by driving out nations
before the people You redeemed for Yourself from Egypt.
22 You have made Your people Israel Your own people forever,
and You, O LORD, have become their God.

23 Now, O Lord,
let the promise You made regarding Your servant
and regarding his house endure forever;
do as You have promised.
24 May Your name endure and be exalted forever;
let them say,
'The Lord of Hosts, God of Israel, is the one God of Israel,'
and may the House of David be established before You.
25 As You, My God, have revealed to Your servant
that You will build him a house,
Your servant has been moved to pray before You.
26 And now, O Lord –
You are God,
and You have promised this grace to Your servant.
27 And now –
may it please You to bless Your servant's house to be before You forever,
for You, O Lord, have blessed it and are blessed forever."

18 1 Some time later, David defeated the Philistines, and subjugated them,
and seized Gat and its dependencies from the hand of the Philistines.
2 He defeated Moav, and Moav became tribute-bearing vassals to David.
3 David defeated King Hadadezer of Tzova near Ḥamat as he set out to
4 establish his rule by the River Euphrates; David captured 1,000 chariots,
7,000 riders, and 20,000 infantrymen from him and hamstrung all the
5 chariot horses, retaining 100 chariot horses. Aram of Damascus came to
King Hadadezer of Tzova's aid, but David struck down 22,000 of Aram's
6 men. David then took over Aram of Damascus, and the Arameans became
David's tribute-bearing vassals. And the Lord granted victory to David
wherever he went.

7 David took the golden quivers that were with Hadadezer's officials and
8 brought them to Jerusalem. And from Tivḥat and Kun, Hadadezer's cities,
David confiscated vast amounts of bronze, which Shlomo used to make
the bronze sea, the pillars, and the bronze vessels.

9 When To'u, king of Ḥamat, heard that David had defeated the entire force
10 of King Hadadezer of Tzova, he sent his son Hadoram to King David to
greet him and congratulate him for having conquered Hadadezer in battle,
for Hadadezer had been at war with To'u. With him was a vast array of gold
11 and silver and bronze vessels. King David devoted those, too, to the Lord,
in addition to all the silver and gold he had carried off from all the nations
of Edom, Moav, the Amonites, the Philistines, and Amalek.

12 Avshai son of Tzeruya struck down 18,000 of Edom in the Valley of Salt. He
13 stationed governors in Edom, and all Edom became David's vassals. And
the Lord granted victory to David wherever he went.

14 David reigned over all of Israel, upholding justice and righteousness for all

15 his people. Yoav son of Tzeruya was the commander of his army; Yehoshafat
16 son of Aḥilud was royal herald; Tzadok son of Aḥituv, and Avimelekh
17 son of Evyatar, were priests; Shavsha was royal scribe; Benayahu son of
Yehoyada commanded the Keretites and Peletites; and David's sons were chief ministers to the king.

19 1 Some time later, King Naḥash of the Amonites died, and his son reigned in his place.

2 "I will show loyalty to Ḥanun son of Naḥash," said David, "just as his father
showed loyalty to me." David sent messengers to offer condolences for
his father, and David's officials reached the land of the Amonites to offer
3 condolences to Ḥanun. But the ministers of the Amonites said to Ḥanun,
"Do you really think that David honors your father because he sent you condolences? No – his officials came to you to scout and spy out the city to overthrow it."

4 So Ḥanun had David's officials seized; he shaved them, cut off half of their uniforms – up to their hips – and sent them off.

5 When David was informed about the men, he sent word out to them, for the men were utterly humiliated.

"Remain in Yeriḥo until your beards grow," said the king, "and then return."

6 When the Amonites realized that they had become odious to David,
Ḥanun and the Amonites sent a thousand talents of silver to hire chariots
7 and riders from Aram Naharayim, Aram Maakha, and Tzova. They hired
32,000 chariots along with the king of Maakha and his men, who came and
set up camp before Meideva while the Amonites gathered from their towns
8 and arrived for battle. When David heard, he sent Yoav together with his
9 entire military force. The Amonites advanced and deployed for battle by
the city entrance, while the kings who had come were stationed separately,
10 in the open field. Yoav saw that he was faced with battle before him and
behind him, so he selected all of Israel's elite troops and deployed against
11 Aram. He handed command of the remaining troops to his brother Avshai
and deployed them against the Amonites.

12 "If Aram overpowers me, come to my aid," he said, "and if the Amonites
13 overpower you, I will come to your aid. Let us be strong and remain strong
for the sake of our people and for the sake of the cities of our God, and
14 may the LORD do as He sees fit." Then Yoav and all the troops with him
charged out to battle against Aram, who fled before them.

15 When the Amonites saw that Aram had fled, they too fled before Yoav's
16 brother Avshai and entered the city; thus Yoav came to Jerusalem. But
when Aram saw that they had been defeated by Israel, they sent messengers and summoned the Arameans who were across the Euphrates, with

17 Shofakh, Hadadezer's army commander, at their head. When this was
reported to David, he mustered all of Israel and crossed the Jordan to
reach them, and he drew up his forces against them. When David drew
18 up his forces against Aram in battle, they fought back against him, but
still Aram fled before Israel, and David killed 7,000 riders and 40,000
infantrymen from Aram. And as for Shofakh, their army commander, he
put him to death.

19 When all those who were subject to Hadadezer realized that they had
been routed before Israel, they surrendered to David and became subject
to him. And Aram was not willing to come to the Amonites' aid again.

20 1 The next spring – when kings launch campaigns – Yoav led the army forces
and ravaged the land of the Amonites; he came and laid siege to Raba
while David stayed in Jerusalem. Yoav defeated Raba and destroyed it.

2 David took their king's crown from upon his head and found that it
weighed a talent of gold and was set with jewels, and it was placed on
3 David's head. And he brought out great masses of spoil from the city. As
for its people, he brought them out and set them to work with saws and
iron picks and axes; David did the same thing for all the Amonite towns.
Then David and all the troops returned to Jerusalem.

4 Some time later, battle broke out with the Philistines at Gezer; this time,
Sibekhai the Hushatite defeated Sipai, a descendant of the Refaim,[17] and
they were subdued.

5 Yet another war broke out against the Philistines, and Elḥanan son of Yair
defeated Laḥmi, brother of Golyat the Gittite, whose spear shaft was like
a weaver's beam.

6 Yet another war broke out, in Gat. There was a man of gigantic proportions
who had six fingers and six toes on his hands and feet, twenty-four in all; he,
7 too, was descended from the Rafa. When he taunted Israel, Yehonatan son
8 of Shima, David's brother, struck him down. All these were descendants
of the Rafa in Gat, and they fell at the hand of David and his subjects.

21 1 An adversary[18] rose up against Israel and incited David to number Israel.
2 "Go and count Israel from Be'er Sheva to Dan," said David to Yoav and the
officers of the people, "then report back to me so that I will know their
number."

3 "May the Lord increase His people a hundred times over," said Yoav, "but
my lord the king, they are all my lord's subjects – why should my lord make
such a request? Why should he bring guilt to Israel?"

---

17 | A race of giants. See, e.g., Deuteronomy 2:11.

18 | A member of the celestial host. Cf. I Samuel 24:1, and see also Zechariah 3:1–2; Job, chapters 1–2.

4 But the king's word prevailed against Yoav, and Yoav set out, traveled all
5 around Israel, and came to Jerusalem. Yoav delivered the census figures of
the population to David: in all of Israel there were 1,100,000 sword-drawing
6 men, while in Yehuda there were 470,000 sword-drawing men – but he
did not count Levi and Binyamin among them, for the king's order was
7 abhorrent to Yoav. This affair was grave in the eyes of God, and He struck
against Israel.

8 "I have sinned grievously by doing this thing," David said to God. "Now
please excuse Your servant's offense, for I have been so foolish."

9 The Lord spoke to Gad, David's seer.

10 "Go and tell David – thus says the Lord – I am holding three things over
you; choose one of them, and I will bring it upon you."

11 Gad came to David and said to him, "Thus says the Lord: Make your
12 choice: either three years of famine, or three months of devastation by
your foe while your enemy's sword overwhelms you, or three days of the
Lord's sword – that is, sickness in the land, with the angel of the Lord
bringing destruction within every border of Israel. Now consider what
reply I should bring back to Him who sent me."

13 "I am in grave torment," David said to Gad. "Let me fall into the hand
of the Lord, for His mercy is exceedingly great; do not let me fall into
human hands."

14 The Lord sent a sickness against Israel, and 70,000 people in Israel fell.
15 God sent an angel to destroy Jerusalem, but as he was about to wreak
destruction, the Lord looked down and relented from the evil.

"Enough," He said to the destroying angel. "Now stay your hand." And the
angel of the Lord halted by the threshing floor of Ornan the Jebusite.

16 David looked up and saw the Lord's angel standing between earth and
heaven with his sword drawn in his hand, stretched forth against Jerusalem.
And David and the elders, covered in sackcloth, fell upon their faces.

17 "I am the one who said to number the people," David said to God. "I am
the one who sinned, and I have committed grave evil. But this flock – what
have they done? O Lord, my God, let Your hand move against me and my
father's house, but upon Your people, let there be no plague."

18 Then an angel of the Lord charged Gad to say to David, "Go up and
erect an altar to the Lord by the threshing floor of Ornan the Jebusite,"
19 and David went up at Gad's word, which he spoke in the Lord's name.
20 As Ornan turned back, he saw the angel, and his four sons with him
21 hid – Ornan had been threshing wheat. As David approached Ornan,
Ornan looked out and saw David, and he came out of the threshing floor
and bowed to David with his face to the ground.

22 "Give me the site of the threshing floor so that I may build an altar to the
LORD upon it," David said to Ornan. "Give it to me for the full price so
that the plague will cease among the people."

23 "Take it," Ornan said to David, "and let my lord the king do as he sees
fit. Look, I will provide you with the oxen for burnt offerings and
threshing boards for wood and wheat for a grain offering – I will provide
everything."

24 "No," said King David to Ornan, "for I must purchase it at the full price – I
will not bring what is yours to the LORD and offer a burnt offering at no
cost."

25 26 So David paid Ornan six hundred shekel of gold for the site, and David
built an altar there for the LORD and sacrificed burnt offerings and peace
offerings. He called out to the LORD, and He answered him with heavenly
fire upon the altar of burnt offerings.

27 Then the LORD commanded the angel, and he placed his sword back in
its sheath.

28 At that time, when David saw that the LORD had answered him at the
threshing floor of Ornan the Jebusite, he offered his sacrifices there
29 because the LORD's Tabernacle that Moshe had made in the wilderness
and the altar of burnt offerings were at the high shrine in Givon at the time.
30 David could not go before it to inquire of God because he was terrified of
the LORD's angel's sword.

22 1 "This is the House of the LORD God," said David, "and this is the altar for
Israel's burnt offerings."

2 Then David gave orders to assemble all the foreigners who lived in the land
of Israel, and he appointed masons to cut hewn stones for the construction
3 of God's House. David prepared vast amounts of iron for nails for the
gate doors and for clamps, as well as immeasurable amounts of bronze
4 and countless cedar logs, for the Sidonians and Tyrians had brought vast
amounts of cedarwood to David.

5 "My son Shlomo is young and inexperienced," said David, "and the House
to be built for the LORD must be incomparably magnificent, of fame and
glory throughout all lands – I will now make preparations for it." And so
6 David made many preparations before his death, and he summoned his
son Shlomo and commanded him to build a House for the LORD, God
of Israel.

7 "My son," David said to Shlomo, "I set my heart upon building a House
8 for the name of the LORD my God. But the word of the LORD came to me,
saying, 'You have shed much blood and waged mighty wars – you will
not build a House for My name, for you have shed too much blood upon
9 the earth before Me. Now a son has been born to you; he will be a man of

peace. I will give him rest from all his surrounding enemies, for Shlomo
will be his name,[19] and I will grant peace and calm to Israel in his time.
10 He will build a House in My name; he will be a son to Me, and I a Father
11 to him, and I will establish his royal throne over Israel forever.' Now, my
son, may the Lord be with you so that you may succeed in building the
12 House of the Lord your God, as He spoke of you. But may the Lord grant
you wisdom and understanding and appoint you over Israel in order to
13 keep the Torah of the Lord your God. You will prosper if you take care to
keep the laws and rulings that the Lord commanded Moshe for Israel. Be
14 strong and brave; do not quake or cower. Here I have struggled to prepare
for the House of the Lord: a hundred thousand talents of gold, a million
talents of silver, and immeasurably vast amounts of bronze and iron. I have
15 prepared wood and stone which you will supplement. With you are many
craftsmen: masons, cutters of stone and wood, and experts in every craft.
16 The gold, silver, bronze, and iron cannot be counted; arise and take action,
and may the Lord be with you."

17 David then commanded all the officials of Israel to assist his son Shlomo:
18 "The Lord your God is with you, and He has granted you rest on every
side, for He gave the people of the land into my hands, and the land lies
19 conquered before the Lord and His people. Now set your hearts and
souls to seeking out the Lord your God; arise and build the Temple of
the Lord God in order to bring the Ark of the Lord's Covenant and the
sacred vessels of God into the House to be built for the Lord's name."

23 1 When David was old and full of days, he made his son Shlomo king over
2 3 Israel. He assembled all of Israel's officials, priests, and Levites. The Levites
of thirty years old and up were counted, and they numbered 38,000 men.
4 "Of these, 24,000 shall oversee the work of the House of the Lord, 6,000
5 shall be officers and judges, 4,000 shall be gatekeepers, and 4,000 are to
6 praise the Lord with instruments that I have made for praise." David then
organized them into divisions according to the sons of Levi – Gershon,
Kehat, and Merari.

7 8 The Gershonites: Ladan and Shimi. The sons of Ladan: the head was
9 Yeḥiel, then Zetam and Yoel – three. The sons of Shimi: Shelomot, Ḥaziel,
10 and Haran – three. These were the ancestral heads of Ladan. The sons of
Shimi: Yaḥat, Zina, Yeush, and Beria; these were the sons of Shimi – four.
11 Yaḥat was the head, and Ziza was the second, but Yeush and Beria did not
have many children, so they were counted as a single ancestral house.

12 13 The sons of Kehat: Amram, Yitzhar, Ḥevron, and Uziel – four. The sons
of Amram were Aharon and Moshe. Aharon was set apart to be sanctified
for the holiest of holies, he and his sons forever – to sacrifice before the
14 Lord, to serve Him, and to bless in His name forever. As for Moshe, the
15 man of God, his sons were associated with the tribe of Levi. The sons of

19 | The name Shlomo evokes the Hebrew *shalom* (peace).

16 Moshe: Gershom and Eliezer. Of the sons of Gershom, Shevuel was the
17 head. As for the sons of Eliezer, Reḥavya was the head, and Eliezer had no
18 other sons, but the sons of Reḥavya were very many. Of the sons of Yitzhar,
19 Shlomit was the head. The sons of Ḥevron: Yeriyahu was the head, Amarya
20 the second, Yaḥaziel the third, and Yekamam the fourth. The sons of Uziel:
Mikha was the head and Yishiya the second.

21 The sons of Merari: Maḥli and Mushi. The sons of Maḥli: Elazar and Kish.
22 Elazar died with no sons, only daughters, and the sons of Kish, their kin,
23 married them. The sons of Mushi: Maḥli, Eder, and Yeremot – three.

24 These are the descendants of Levi according to their ancestral houses,
the ancestral heads as listed by name and by the number of sons who
performed the work for the service of the House of the Lord from twenty
25 years old and up. For David said, "The Lord, God of Israel, has granted
26 rest to His people, and He will dwell in Jerusalem forever, so the Levites
no longer need to carry the Tabernacle and all the vessels for its service."
27 Therefore, one of the final acts of David was to count the sons of Levi
28 twenty years old and up, for their station was beside the sons of Aharon
for the service of Lord's House – to oversee the courtyards, the chambers,
the purification of all that was sacred, and any work for the service of God's
29 House: the showbread, the fine flour for grain offerings, the unleavened
wafers, the pan offerings, the offerings mixed with oil, and all quantities
30 and measurements. They were also to stand each morning to give thanks
31 and sing praise to the Lord, as well as in the evening, and whenever burnt
offerings were offered up to the Lord on the Sabbath, New Moons, and
festivals in accordance with the required number – continually in the
32 Lord's presence. They were to keep watch over the Tent of Meeting, over
what was sacred, and to attend the sons of Aharon, their kin, for the service
of the House of the Lord.

24 1 As for the division of the sons of Aharon, the sons of Aharon were Nadav,
2 Avihu, Elazar, and Itamar. Nadav and Avihu died before their father, and
3 they had no children, so Elazar and Itamar served as priests. David, Tzadok
of the sons of Elazar, and Aḥimelekh of the sons of Itamar divided them up
4 into offices of their service. It was found that there were more male heads
of the sons of Elazar than of the sons of Itamar, and they divided them up
accordingly: the sons of Elazar with sixteen heads of ancestral houses and
5 the sons of Itamar with eight ancestral houses. They divided them by lot,
equally, for there were both officers of the Sanctuary and officers of God
among the sons of Elazar and the sons of Itamar.

6 Then Shemaya son of Netanel, the scribe from Levi, recorded them in
the presence of the king, the officers, the priest Tzadok, Aḥimelekh son
of Evyatar, and the ancestral heads of the priests and Levites: for every
ancestral house selected for Itamar, two ancestral houses were selected
for Elazar.

7, 8 The first lot fell to Yehoyariv, the second to Yedaya, the third to Ḥarim, the
9, 10 fourth to Seorim, the fifth to Malkiya, the sixth to Miyamin, the seventh to
11 Hakotz, the eighth to Aviya, the ninth to Yeshua, the tenth to Shekhanyahu,
12, 13 the eleventh to Elyashiv, the twelfth to Yakim, the thirteenth to Ḥupa,
14 the fourteenth to Yeshevav, the fifteenth to Bilga, the sixteenth to Imer,
15 16 the seventeenth to Ḥezir, the eighteenth to Hapitzetz, the nineteenth to
17 Petaḥya, the twentieth to Yeḥezkel, the twenty-first to Yakhin, the twenty-
18 second to Gamul, the twenty-third to Delayahu, and the twenty-fourth to
Maazyahu.

19 Their duties for their service were to come to the House of the Lord
according to the requirements of their ancestor Aharon as the Lord, God
of Israel, had commanded him.

20 The rest of the sons of Levi: the son of Amram, Shuvael; the sons of Shuvael,
21 Yeḥdeyahu and Reḥavyahu; and the son of Reḥavyahu, Yishiya, the head.
22 23 Of the Izharites: Shelomot and the son of Shelomot, Yaḥat. The sons
of:[20] Yeriyahu, Amaryahu the second, Yaḥaziel the third, and Yekamam
24 25 the fourth. The son of Uziel, Mikha and the son of Mikha, Shamir. The
26 brother of Mikha, Yishiya and the son of Yishiya, Zekharyahu. The sons
27 of Merari: Maḥli and Mushi. The sons of Yaaziyahu, his son – that is, the
28 sons of Merari through his son Yaaziyahu: Shoham, Zakur, and Ivri. Of
29 30 Maḥli: Elazar, who had no sons. Of Kish: the son of Kish, Yeraḥme'el. The
sons of Mushi: Maḥli, Eder, and Yerimot. These were the sons of Levi
31 according to their ancestral clans. Like their brothers, the sons of Aharon,
they too cast lots in the presence of King David, Tzadok, Aḥimelekh, and
the ancestral heads of the priests and Levites – each ancestral head and
his younger brother.

25 1 David and the army officers singled out the sons of Asaf, Heiman, and
Yedutun for service: they were to play in prophetic ecstasy on lyres, harps,
and cymbals. The list of skilled men who performed this service:

2 Of the sons of Asaf: Zakur, Yosef, Netanya, and Asarela – Asaf's sons
charged by Asaf, who prophesied by the king's orders.

3 Of Yedutun: the sons of Yedutun: Gedalyahu, Zeri, Yeshayahu, Ḥashavyahu,
and Matityahu – six[21] charged by their father Yedutun, who played on the
harp in prophetic ecstasy, giving thanks and praising the Lord.

4 Of Heiman: the sons of Heiman: Bukiyahu, Matanyahu, Uziel, Shevuel,
Yerimot, Ḥananya, Ḥanani, Eliata, Gidalti, Romamti Ezer, Yoshbekasha,
5 Maloti, Hotir, and Maḥaziot; all these were sons of Heiman, the king's
seer, in accordance with God's promise to exalt him – God gave Heiman
6 fourteen sons and three daughters. All these were charged by their father

20 | The sons of Ḥevron. "Ḥevron" is not explicit in the Hebrew, but cf. 23:19.

21 | Verse 17 indicates that the sixth son is Shimi.

with the music in the House of the Lord, with cymbals, harps, and lyres
for the service of the House of God. Directly charged by the king were Asaf,
7 Yedutun, and Heiman. Together with their brothers who were trained in
making music for the Lord, the total number of skilled players was 288.

8 They cast lots to determine shifts for small and great alike, for skilled player
together with student.

9 The first lot fell for Asaf – to Yosef;
the second to Gedalyahu, he and his brothers and sons – twelve;
10 the third to Zakur, his sons, and his brothers – twelve;
11 the fourth to Yitzri, his sons, and his brothers – twelve;
12 the fifth to Netanyahu, his sons, and his brothers – twelve;
13 the sixth to Bukiyahu, his sons, and his brothers – twelve;
14 15 the seventh to Yesarela, his sons, and his brothers – twelve; the eighth to
Yeshayahu, his sons, and his brothers – twelve;
16 the ninth to Matanyahu, his sons, and his brothers – twelve;
17 the tenth to Shimi, his sons, and his brothers – twelve;
18 the eleventh to Azarel, his sons, and his brothers – twelve;
19 the twelfth to Ḥashavya, his sons, and his brothers – twelve;
20 the thirteenth to Shuvael, his sons, and his brothers – twelve;
21 the fourteenth to Matityahu, his sons, and his brothers – twelve;
22 the fifteenth to Yeremot, his sons, and his brothers – twelve;
23 the sixteenth to Ḥananyahu, his sons, and his brothers – twelve;
24 the seventeenth to Yoshbekasha, his sons, and his brothers – twelve;
25 the eighteenth to Ḥanani, his sons, and his brothers – twelve;
26 the nineteenth to Maloti, his sons, and his brothers – twelve;
27 the twentieth to Eliyata, his sons, and his brothers – twelve;
28 the twenty-first to Hotir, his sons, and his brothers – twelve;
29 the twenty-second to Gidalti, his sons, and his brothers – twelve;
30 the twenty-third to Maḥaziot, his sons, and his brothers – twelve;
31 the twenty-fourth to Romamti Ezer, his sons, and his brothers – twelve.

26 1 As for the divisions of gatekeepers:

Of the Korahites: Meshelemyahu son of Koreh of the sons of Asaf.
2 Meshelemyahu's sons: Zekharyahu the firstborn, Yediael the second,
3 Zevadyahu the third, Yatniel the fourth, Eilam the fifth, Yehoḥanan
4 the sixth, and Eleiho'einai the seventh. Oved Edom's sons: Shemaya
the firstborn, Yehozavad the second, Yoaḥ the third, Sakhar the fourth,
5 Netanel the fifth, Amiel the sixth, Yissakhar the seventh, and Peuletai
6 the eighth – for God had blessed him. The sons born to Shemaya were
7 dominant in their father's house, for they were worthy men. The sons of
Shemaya: Otni, Refael, Oved, and Elzavad; his worthy brothers were Elihu
8 and Semakhyahu. All these sons of Oved Edom's – they and their sons and
brothers – were worthy men with a strong capacity for work; sixty-two
9 from Oved Edom. Meshelemyahu's sons and brothers were worthy, able

10 men – eighteen. Ḥosah of the Merarites' sons: Shimri the head was not
11 the firstborn, but his father designated him as chief; Ḥilkiyahu the second,
Tevalyahu the third, and Zekharyahu the fourth. The sons and brothers of
Ḥosa were thirteen in all.

12 These divisions of gatekeepers by their chief men had shifts just like their
13 kin who served in the House of the Lord. For each gate they cast lots for
small and great alike according to their ancestral houses.

14 The lot for the east fell to Shelemyahu, and when they cast lots for his son
15 Zekharyahu, a wise counselor, his lot came out for the north. For Oved
16 Edom the south, and for his sons the storehouse. For Shupim and Ḥosa the
west, with the Shalekhet Gate by the ascending road. Watch corresponded
17 to watch: on the east were six Levites; on the north, four each day; on
18 the south, four each day as well as two and two at the storehouse; for the
19 vestibule to the west, four for the road and two for the vestibule. These were
the divisions of gatekeepers among the Korahites and the Merarites.

20 Of the Levites, Aḥiya was in charge of the treasuries of the House of the
Lord and the treasuries of the dedicated items.

21 The sons of Ladan, the sons of the Gershonites belonging to Ladan, were
22 the ancestral heads of Ladan the Gershonite: Yeḥieli. The sons of Yeḥieli,
Zetam and his brother Yoel, who were in charge of the treasuries of the
23 House of the Lord. Of the Amramites, the Izharites, the Hebronites, and
24 the Uzielites: Shevuel son of Gershom son of Moshe was chief officer
25 of the treasuries. His kin, of Eliezer, were his son Reḥavyahu, his son
26 Yeshayahu, his son Yoram, his son Zikhri, and his son Shlomit; this Shlomit
and his brothers were in charge of all the treasuries of items that had been
dedicated by King David, the ancestral heads of the officers of thousands
27 and hundreds, and the army officers – they had dedicated part of the spoils
28 of war for the maintenance of the House of the Lord. All that Shmuel the
seer, Sha'ul son of Kish, Avner son of Ner, and Yoav son of Tzeruya had
dedicated – and all that anyone else had dedicated – was under the charge
of Shlomit and his brothers.

29 Of the Izharites, Kenanyahu and his sons were appointed for external
30 duties in Israel, as officials and judges. Of the Hebronites, Ḥashavyahu
and his kin – 1,700 worthy men – were in charge of Israel on the west bank
31 of the Jordan for all the work of the Lord and the king's service. Among
the Hebronites, Yeriya was the leader of the Hebronites according to the
genealogy of his father's house: in the fortieth year of David's reign, worthy
32 men were sought out and found in Yazeir of Gilad. King David appointed
him and his kin, 2,700 worthy men, over the Reubenites, the Gadites, and
half the tribe of Menashe, for anything concerning the word of God and
the king's orders.

27 1 This is the list of the Israelites, the ancestral heads, the officers of thousands

and hundreds, and their officials who served the king in all matters concerning the divisions that marched back and forth every month of the year. Each division had 24,000.

2 Yoshovam son of Zavdiel was in charge of the first division for the first
3 month, and there were 24,000 in his division. Descended from Peretz,
he was the leader of all the army commanders during the first month.

4 Dodai the Ahohite was in charge of the division for the second month; Miklot was chief officer of his division, and in his division were 24,000.

5 The third army commander for the third month was the leader Benayahu
6 son of Yehoyada the priest; in his division were 24,000. This same Benayahu
was a warrior of the Thirty who led the Thirty, and his son Amizavad was
in his division.

7 The fourth for the fourth month was Asael brother of Yoav and his son Zevadya after him; in his division were 24,000.

8 The fifth for the fifth month was the officer Shamhut the Izrahite; in his division were 24,000.

9 The sixth for the sixth month was Ira son of Ikesh the Tekoaite; in his division were 24,000.

10 The seventh for the seventh month was Ḥeletz the Pelonite, descended from Efrayim; in his division were 24,000.

11 The eighth for the eighth month was Sibekhai the Hushatite, of the Zerahites; in his division were 24,000.

12 The ninth for the ninth month was Aviezer the Anatotite, of Binyamin; in his division were 24,000.

13 The tenth for the tenth month was Mahrai the Netofatite, of Zeraḥ; in his division were 24,000.

14 The eleventh for the eleventh month was Benaya the Piratonite, of the Efraimites; in his division were 24,000.

15 The twelfth for the twelfth month was Ḥeldai the Netofatite, of Otniel; in his division were 24,000.

16 In charge of the tribes of Israel: over Reuven, the chief officer was Eliezer
17 son of Zikhri. Over Shimon, Shefatya son of Maakha. Over Levi, Ḥashavya
18 son of Kemuel. Over Aharon, Tzadok. Over Yehuda, Elihu, of the brothers
19 of David. Over Yissakhar, Omri son of Mikhael. Over Zevulun, Yishmayahu
20 son of Ovadyahu. Over Naftali, Yerimot son of Azriel. Over the Efraimites,
Hoshe'a son of Azazyahu. Over half the tribe of Menashe, Yoel son of
21 Pedayahu; over half of Menashe in Gilad, Ido son of Zekharyahu. Over
22 Binyamin, Yaasiel son of Avner. Over Dan, Azarel son of Yeroḥam. These
23 were the officers of the tribes of Israel. David did not take a census of

those under twenty years old because the LORD promised to increase
24 Israel like the stars of the heavens. Yoav son of Tzeruya began to number
them – although he did not finish; for this, wrath rose against Israel, and
the count was not entered into the account in King David's chronicles.

25 The royal treasuries were overseen by Azmavet son of Adiel, while over the
treasuries of the fields, cities, villages, and towers was Yehonatan son of
26 27 Uziyahu. Over the field preparation for agriculture, Ezri son of Keluv; over
the vineyards, Shimi the Ramatite, while over the vineyard produce for the
28 wine cellars, Zavdi the Shifmite. Over the olive groves and sycamore trees
29 in the plains, Baal Ḥanan the Gederite; over the oil stores, Yoash. Over the
cattle grazing in the Sharon, Shirtai the Sharonite; over the cattle in the
30 valleys, Shafat son of Adlai. Over the camels, Ovil the Ishmaelite; over the
31 donkeys, Yeḥdeyahu the Meronotite; over the flocks, Yaziz the Hagarite.
All these were the officials who managed the property that belonged to
King David.

32 Yehonatan, David's uncle, was a wise advisor and scribe; and Yeḥiel the
33 Hakhmonite was with the king's sons. Aḥitofel was the king's advisor, while
34 Ḥushai the Arkite was Friend of the King. After Aḥitofel was Yehoyada son
of Benayahu and Evyatar, and the king's army commander was Yoav.

28 1 David assembled in Jerusalem all the officers of Israel – the officers of
the tribes, the officers of the divisions that served the king, the officers of
thousands and the officers of hundreds, and the officers of all the property
that belonged to the king and his sons – along with the officials, the
2 warriors, and all the powerful men. King David rose to his feet and said:

"Hear me, my brothers and my people – I had my heart set on building a
resting place for the Ark of the LORD's Covenant and for the footstool of
3 our God, and I made preparations for building. But God said to me, 'You
will not build a House for My name, for you are a man of war, and you
4 have shed blood.' Yet the LORD, God of Israel, chose me out of all my
father's house to be king over Israel forever, for He chose Yehuda as ruler,
and within the House of Yehuda, my father's house; and out of my father's
5 sons, it was me He wished to make king over all Israel. And out of all my
sons – for the LORD has granted me many sons – He has chosen my son
6 Shlomo to sit on the throne of the LORD's royal dominion over Israel. And
He said to me, 'Your son Shlomo will be the one to build My House and
My courtyards, for I have chosen him as My son, and I will be his Father.
7 I will establish his kingdom forever so long as he adheres firmly to My
commandments and rulings as he does now.'

8 "And now, before the eyes of all Israel, the LORD's assembly, and in the
hearing of our God: keep and seek out all the commandments of the
LORD your God so that you will inherit the good land and leave it to your
children after you forever.

9 "As for you, my son Shlomo, know the God of your father and serve Him

with a full heart and a willing soul, for the LORD searches all hearts and
understands the design of all thoughts. If you search for Him, He will be
10 there for you, but if you forsake Him, He will abandon you forever. Look
now, for the LORD has chosen you to build a House for the Sanctuary – be
strong and take action."

11 Then David gave to his son Shlomo the design for the Hall, its buildings,
its upper chambers, its inner chambers, and the place for the Ark and its
12 covering; all his inspired designs for the courts of the House of the LORD,
for all its surrounding chambers, for the treasuries of the House of God,
13 and for the treasuries of the dedicated items; along with the divisions of
priests and Levites and all the work of the service of the House of the
14 LORD and all the vessels for the service of the House of the LORD; the
weight of gold for all golden vessels for each and every kind of service
and the weight of silver for all vessels for each and every kind of service;
15 the weight of the gold candelabra and their golden lamps, with the weight
needed for each candelabrum and its lamps and the weight of silver needed
for each candelabrum and its lamps in accordance with the use of each
16 candelabrum; the weight of gold needed for the tables for showbread for
17 each table, and silver for the silver tables; pure gold for the forks, basins,
and pitchers; the weight of gold needed for every bowl and the weight of
18 silver needed for every bowl; the weight of refined gold needed for the
incense altar; and gold for the design of the chariot – the cherubim that
spread their wings to shelter the Ark of the LORD's Covenant.

19 "All is written down, under the inspiration of the LORD given me to
20 understand – all the work of the building design," David said to his son
Shlomo. "Be strong and brave – do not quake or cower, for the LORD God,
my God, is with you. He will never let you go or leave you until all the
21 work for the service of the House of the LORD is complete. Look – here
are the divisions of priests and Levites for all the service of the House of
God; skilled, willing men will be with you for every job and task; and the
officers and all the people are at your every command."

29 1 King David said to the whole assembly, "Shlomo my son, whom God has
singled out, is young and inexperienced, but the task at hand is great – for
2 the palace is not for man but for the LORD God. With all my might I have
made preparations for the House of my God – the necessary gold, silver,
bronze, iron, and wood, as well as stones of rock crystal and stones for
setting, stones of antimony, colored stones, all kinds of precious stones,
3 and vast quantities of marble. What is more, out of my devotion to the
House of my God, I have given over my own private treasure of gold and
silver to the House of my God in addition to all that I prepared for the Holy
4 House: three thousand talents of gold – Ofir gold – and seven thousand
5 talents of refined silver to overlay the walls of the buildings, the necessary
gold and silver for all the work of the craftsmen. Who, then, is willing to
offer freely and devote himself today to the LORD?"

6 Then the leaders of the ancestral houses, the officers of the tribes, the
officers of thousands and hundreds, and the officers of the king's service
7 made willing donations: for the work of God's House they gave five
thousand talents and ten thousand darics of gold, ten thousand talents
of silver, eighteen thousand talents of bronze, and one hundred thousand
8 talents of iron. Whoever had precious stones with him gave them to the
treasury of the House of the LORD in the care of Yeḥiel the Gershonite.
9 The people rejoiced over the donations they made so willingly, for they
had offered freely to the LORD with whole hearts. King David, too, was
stirred with great joy.

10 David blessed the LORD in front of the entire assembly, and David said,

"Blessed are You, O LORD God of Israel, our Father
for ever and ever.
11 Yours, O LORD, is the greatness and the might,
the glory and the fame and the splendor.
Yes, all that is in heaven and earth is Yours;
Yours, O LORD, is the kingdom;
You are exalted as head above all.
12 Wealth and honor come from You,
and You rule over all;
in Your hand is power and might;
Your hand gives greatness and strength to all.
13 Now, our God,
we thank You
and praise Your glorious name,
14 for who am I, and who are my people,
that we should have the power to offer so freely?
For all is from You,
and we have given You only what is Yours.
15 For to You we are but passersby,
mere transients like all our ancestors;
our days are like shadows over the earth –
there is no hope.
16 O LORD our God,
all this abundance we have prepared,
to build You a house for Your holy name,
is from Your hand, and all is Yours.
17 I know, my God,
that You search hearts
and desire what is upright;
I, with an upright heart,
willingly offer all this.
And now I see Your people, who are present here,
offering freely and joyously to You.

18 O Lord, God of Avraham, Yitzḥak, and Yisrael our ancestors,
keep such desires and thoughts
in the hearts of Your people forever;
direct their hearts to You.
19 And grant that my son Shlomo
will keep Your commandments, decrees, and laws
with a whole heart
and do all these things
and build the palace for which I have prepared."

20 Then David declared to the whole assembly, "Now bless the Lord your
God!" And the whole assembly blessed the Lord, God of their ancestors,
and bowed down low and prostrated themselves before the Lord and
the king.

21 On the following day, they made sacrifices to the Lord and offered up burnt
offerings to the Lord: a thousand bulls, a thousand rams, and a thousand
sheep along with their libation offerings and sacrifices in abundance for all
22 of Israel. On that day they feasted and drank before the Lord with great
joy. They proclaimed Shlomo son of David as king once more, anointing
23 him before the Lord as prince and Tzadok as priest. And Shlomo ascended
the Lord's throne in his father David's place; he flourished, and all of Israel
24 obeyed him; all the officers and warriors as well as all of King David's
25 sons pledged their allegiance to King Shlomo. The Lord granted Shlomo
supreme greatness in the eyes of all Israel and endowed him with a royal
majesty beyond that of any king of Israel before him.

26 27 Thus David son of Yishai was king over all Israel. The length of time that
he reigned over Israel was forty years: he reigned in Ḥevron for seven years,
28 and he reigned in Jerusalem for thirty-three. He died at a ripe old age, full
29 of days, wealth, and honor, and his son Shlomo reigned in his place. The
earlier and later deeds of King David are recorded in the chronicles of the
seer Shmuel, the chronicles of the prophet Natan, and the chronicles of the
30 seer Gad, along with all the accounts of his rule, his might, and the events
that befell him and Israel and all the kingdoms of the land.

II CHRONICLES

1 1 Shlomo son of David gained power over his kingdom; the Lord his God
2 was with him, and He granted him supreme greatness. Shlomo gave orders
to all of Israel: to the officers of thousands and hundreds, to the judges, and
3 to all the leaders of all Israel, the ancestral heads. And Shlomo and all his
assembly went to the high shrine at Givon because the Tent of Meeting that
4 Moshe, the Lord's servant, had made in the wilderness was there – although
David had brought up the Ark of God from Kiryat Ye'arim to the place that
5 David had prepared for it, having pitched a tent for it in Jerusalem – and the
bronze altar that Betzalel son of Uri had made was there before the Sanctuary
6 of the Lord, and Shlomo and the assembly made inquiry at it. Shlomo went
up there to the bronze altar before the Lord at the Tent of Meeting, and he
offered up a thousand burnt offerings upon it.

7 That night God appeared to Shlomo and said to him, "Ask – what shall I
give you?"

8 And Shlomo said to God, "You treated David my father with great loyalty
9 and made me king in his place. Now, O LORD God, let Your promise to
my father David be fulfilled, for You have made me king over a people as
10 abundant as the dust of the earth. Now grant me wisdom and knowledge
so that I may lead this people out and bring them back, for who will judge
this great people of Yours?"
11 "Because this was your desire," God said to Shlomo, "and you did not ask
for wealth, possessions, honor, or the lives of your enemies, nor did you
ask for a long life, but you asked instead for the wisdom and knowledge
12 to judge My people over whom I made you king, wisdom and knowledge
are granted to you, and I will give you wealth, possessions, and honor as
well – such as kings before you have never had and kings after you never
will."

13 So Shlomo came down from the high shrine in Givon, from before the
Tent of Meeting, to Jerusalem, and he reigned over Israel.

14 Shlomo amassed chariots and horsemen; he had 1,400 chariots and 12,000
horsemen. He stationed them in the chariot towns and with the king in
15 Jerusalem. The king made silver as common in Jerusalem as stones, while
16 cedars were as common as sycamores in the lowlands. Shlomo's horses
were procured from Egypt and Keveh; the king's traders would import
17 them from Keveh at a set price. The cost of importing a chariot from
Egypt was 600 pieces of silver, while a horse was 150; these, in turn, were
18 exported to all the kings of the Hittites and all the kings of Aram. And
Shlomo gave orders to build a House for the LORD's name and a royal
house for himself.

2 1 Shlomo designated 70,000 men as carriers, 80,000 men as quarriers in the
mountains, and 3,600 to oversee them.

2 Shlomo then sent to King Ḥuram of Tyre, saying, "You once dealt with
3 my father David, sending him cedars to build a house to dwell in. I am
now building a House for the name of the LORD my God, devoting it to
Him to offer before Him fragrant incense, the daily showbread, and burnt
offerings each morning and evening, and on the Sabbaths and the New
Moons and the festivals of the LORD our God, as ordained for Israel forever.
4 The House I am building must be great, for the LORD our God is greater
than any other god.

5 "Yet who has the power to build Him a House when the heavens – even
the highest heavens – cannot contain Him? And who am I to build Him a
House except as a place to sacrifice before Him?

6 "Now send me a man skilled in working with gold, silver, bronze, and iron;
and with purple, crimson, and blue; one who is skilled in the art of engraving

to be with the skilled workers whom my father David provided for me in
7 Yehuda and Jerusalem. Send me cedar, cypress, and sandalwood from
Lebanon, for I know how skilled your servants are at cutting cedarwood –
8 now my own servants together with your servants will prepare vast
quantities of timber for me, for the House I am building will be massive
9 and magnificent. I will provide your servants, the woodcutters who cut the
timber, with twenty thousand *kor*[1] of beaten wheat, twenty thousand *kor*
of barley, twenty thousand *bat*[2] of wine, and twenty thousand *bat* of oil."

10 King Ḥuram of Tyre answered in writing and sent this to Shlomo: "Because
the Lord loves His people, He has made you king over them.

11 "Blessed is the Lord, God of Israel, who made the heaven and earth,"
Ḥuram continued, "for having granted King David a wise son, endowed
with intelligence and understanding, who will build a House for the Lord
12 and a house for his kingdom. Now I have sent a skilled man endowed with
13 understanding – Ḥuram Avi, the son of a Danite woman and a Tyrian
father. He is skilled at working with gold, silver, bronze, iron, stone, and
wood; with purple, blue, fine linen, and crimson; he can engrave anything
and work with any kind of medium he is given along with your own
craftsmen and the craftsmen of my lord, your father David.

14 "As for the wheat, barley, oil, and wine my lord has spoken of – let him
15 send it to his servants. We will cut down as many trees from Lebanon as
you need and bring them to you as rafts by sea to Jaffa, and you will convey
them up to Jerusalem."

16 Shlomo then counted all the foreigners in the land of Israel after the census
17 his father David had taken: 153,600 were found. He assigned 70,000 of
them as carriers, 80,000 as quarriers, and 3,600 as overseers to set the
people to work.

3 1 Shlomo began to build the House of the Lord in Jerusalem on Mount
Moria where He had appeared to his father David, on the site that David
2 had prepared on the threshold of Ornan the Jebusite. He began construction on the second day of the second month in the fourth year of
his reign.

3 These are the foundations that Shlomo laid for the construction of the
House of God: its length in cubits of the old standard was sixty cubits, and
4 its width was twenty cubits. The length of the Hall in front of the House
was equal to the width of the House, twenty cubits, and its height was one
5 hundred twenty cubits. He overlaid the interior with pure gold. He paneled
the main part of the House with cypress wood and overlaid that with fine
6 gold, embossing it with shapes of palm trees and chains, and he adorned
the House with precious stones for splendor – the gold was Parvayim gold.

1 | A dry measure equivalent to approximately 400 liters.

2 | A liquid measure equivalent to approximately 43 liters.

7 He paneled the House with gold – the beams, the thresholds, its doors, and
its walls – and engraved cherubim on the walls.

8 He made the place of the Holy of Holies; its length, along the width of the
House, was twenty cubits, and its width was twenty cubits, and he paneled
9 it with fine gold, using six hundred talents. The weight of the nails was fifty
shekel of gold, and he paneled the upper chambers with gold.

10 In the place of the Holy of Holies, he made two sculptured cherubim and
11 overlaid them with gold. The wings of the cherubim were twenty cubits
long: one wing, five cubits long, touched the wall of the House, while the
12 other wing, five cubits long, reached the other cherub's wing; the other
cherub's wing, five cubits long, reached the wall of the House, while the
other wing, five cubits long, was joined to the wing of the other cherub.
13 The wings of these cherubim spanned twenty cubits; they stood on their
feet with their faces toward the House.

14 He made the veil of blue, purple, and crimson thread and fine linen and
15 decorated it with cherubim. He made two pillars, each thirty-five cubits
high, at the front of the House, with a capital five cubits high atop them.
16 He made chains in the Inner Sanctuary and set them on top of the pillars;
he fashioned one hundred pomegranates and placed them on the chains.
17 He set up the pillars in front of the Hall, one to the right and one to the
left; he named the one on the right Yakhin and the one on the left Boaz.

4 1 He made an altar of bronze twenty cubits long, twenty cubits wide, and ten
2 cubits high. He made the Molten Sea,[3] ten cubits across from rim to rim and
perfectly round. It was five cubits high and thirty cubits in circumference.
3 Figures of oxen[4] were beneath it all around it, clustered around the Sea
4 ten to a cubit; two rows of oxen were cast together with it. It stood upon
twelve oxen, three facing north, three facing west, three facing south, and
three facing east; the Sea was on top of them, and all their haunches turned
5 inward. It was a handbreadth thick, and its rim was like the rim of a cup,
like the petals of a lily; its capacity was three thousand *bat*.

6 He made ten lavers, placing five on the right and five on the left; these
were for rinsing what was used for the burnt offering, while the Sea was
for the priests to wash in.

7 He made the ten golden candelabra as instructed and set them in the
8 Sanctuary, five on the right and five on the left. He made ten tables and
placed them in the Sanctuary, and he made a hundred basins of gold.

9 He made the priests' courtyard, the great court, and doors for the court;
10 he overlaid its doors with bronze. He placed the Sea on the right side, in
the southeast corner.

---

3 | A large tank made of cast metal.

4 | The parallel verse in I Kings 7:24 reads "bulb-shaped knobs" in place of "figures of oxen."

11 Ḥuram crafted the pots and the shovels and the basins. And so Ḥuram completed all the work for the House of God as commissioned by King Shlomo:

12 Two pillars and two globe-shaped capitals for the pillar tops;

two pieces of meshwork to cover the two globe-shaped capitals for the pillar tops;

13 and four hundred pomegranates for the two pieces of meshwork – two rows of pomegranates for each piece of meshwork that covered the two globe-shaped capitals on top of the pillars.

14 He made the stands and the lavers for the stands;

15 one Sea with twelve oxen beneath it;

16 pots, shovels, and forks, and all their equipment that Ḥuram Avi crafted
for King Shlomo, for the House of the Lord, were of burnished bronze.
17 The king had them cast in clay molds on the Jordan plain between Sukkot
18 and Tzeredata. Shlomo made such vast amounts of all of these vessels that
the weight of the bronze was not determined.

19 Shlomo made all the vessels for the House of God, the golden altar, and
20 the tables for displaying the showbread. The candelabra and their lamps,
which were to burn as instructed in front of the Inner Sanctuary, were of
21 solid gold; the flowers, the lamps, and the tongs were all of gold, of purest
22 gold. The shears, basins, spoons, and firepans were of solid gold; the doors
at the entrance to the innermost House, to the Holy of Holies, and the
doors of the Hall of the House, were of gold.

5 1 When all the work that Shlomo did for the House of the Lord was finished, Shlomo brought what David, his father, had dedicated – the silver, the gold, and all the vessels – and placed them in the treasury of the House of God.

2 Then Shlomo assembled the elders of Israel – all the heads of the tribes,
the patriarchal ancestral leaders of the Israelites – to Jerusalem, to bring up
3 the Ark of the Lord's Covenant from the City of David, which is Zion. All
the men of Israel assembled before the king in the seventh month during
4 the festival.[5] When all the elders of Israel had arrived, the Levites lifted
5 up the Ark and brought up the Ark, and the Tent of Meeting, and all the
6 sacred vessels in the Tent. While the Levite priests brought them up, King
Shlomo and the whole community of Israel, who had joined him before
the Ark, sacrificed sheep and oxen – far too many to number or count.

7 The priests brought the Ark of the Lord's Covenant to its place – to the
House's Inner Sanctuary, the Holy of Holies, to under the shade of the
8 cherubim's wings. The cherubim's wings were spread over the place of
the Ark so that the cherubim covered the Ark and its poles from above.

5 | That is, Sukkot, the Festival of Tabernacles.

9 The poles extended beyond the Ark so that the ends of the poles were
discernible from the Inner Sanctuary, but they could not be seen from the
10 outside, and they are there to this day. The Ark contained nothing but the
two tablets Moshe gave at Ḥorev when the Lord made a covenant with
the Israelites as they left Egypt.

11 And as the priests left the Holy Place – for all the priests present had
12 sanctified themselves, regardless of their divisions – all the Levite
musicians – Asaf, Heiman, and Yedutun, their sons, and their kin, dressed
in fine linen – stood at the east end of the altar with cymbals, harps, and
13 lyres, while a hundred twenty priests sounded the trumpets. The trumpet
players and the singers joined together as one, playing in unison, to praise
and give thanks to the Lord. As they lifted up their voices, with trumpets
and cymbals and musical instruments, praising the Lord – "For He is
good, for His loving-kindness is forever" – the House, the House of the
14 Lord, filled with cloud. The priests could not stand and serve because of
the cloud, for the glory of the Lord had filled the House of God.

6 1 Then Shlomo declared,

"The Lord promised that He would dwell in deep mist;
2 I have built You an exalted House,
a permanent place for Your abode."

3 The king turned his face and blessed the whole assembly of Israel as the
whole assembly of Israel stood.

4 "Blessed is the Lord, God of Israel," he said, "who made a promise to my
father David with His own mouth and has now fulfilled it with His own
hands, saying:
5 'From the day I brought My people out of the land of Egypt, I never chose
a city from among all the tribes of Israel to build a House where My name
6 would be, nor did I choose a man as ruler over My people Israel. Then I
chose Jerusalem as the place where My name will be, and I chose David
to be over My people Israel.'

7 "My father David had his heart set on building a House for the name of
8 the Lord, God of Israel. But the Lord said to my father David, 'Though
you have set your heart on building a House for My name, and though
9 you have set your heart well, you will not be the one to build the House.
But your son, the issue of your own loins – he will be the one to build a
House for My name.'

10 "The Lord has fulfilled the promise He made; I have risen in my father's
stead, and I sit upon Israel's throne as the Lord promised. I have built the
11 House for the name of the Lord, God of Israel. And there I have placed
the Ark, which contains the covenant that the Lord formed with the
Israelites."

12 And he stood before the Altar of the LORD, facing the whole assembly of
13 Israel, and he raised his hands. Shlomo had made a bronze laver that was
five cubits long, five cubits wide, and three cubits high and had placed it in
the courtyard; now he stepped onto it and knelt, facing the whole assembly
of Israel, and raised his palms heavenward.

14 "O LORD, God of Israel," he cried,
"there is no god like You in heaven or on earth.
O keeper of the covenant and the love for Your servants, who walk before
You with all their heart,
15 You kept what You promised to my father David; You made him a promise
with Your own mouth, and You have fulfilled it with Your own hand this
very day.
16 Now O LORD, God of Israel, keep the promise You made to Your servant
David, my father, saying, 'No one of your lineage shall be cut off from
sitting on the throne of Israel before Me, but only if your sons keep to the
path of My teaching, as you walked before Me.'
17 Now, O LORD, God of Israel, let the promise You made to Your servant
David be realized.
18 For will God truly dwell with humanity on earth? If the heavens – the
highest heavens – cannot contain You, how will this House that I have
built?
19 Yet, turn to the prayer of your servant, O LORD my God, and to his plea;
Listen to the cry and the prayer your servant offers before You.

20 "Let Your eyes be open to this House day and night,
to the place where You determined to put Your name.
Listen to the prayer Your servant offers at this place.
21 Listen to the pleas of Your servant and of Your people, Israel, who pray at
this place.
Listen from Your heavenly abode; listen and forgive.

22 "Should a person wrong another who then imposes an oath upon him, and
he thus becomes cursed, and he comes before Your altar in this House with
23 the curse – listen from the heavens, take action, and judge Your servant.
Avenge the wicked by bringing his own ways upon his own head, and
vindicate the righteous by rewarding him as befits his righteousness.

24 "Should Your people Israel be defeated by an enemy because they have
sinned against You, and they come back, acknowledging Your name in
25 prayer and pleading before You in this House – listen from the heavens,
forgive the sin of Your people Israel, and bring them back to the land You
gave to them and to their ancestors.

26 "When the heavens are stopped up and there is no rain because they have
sinned against You, and they pray at this place and acknowledge Your name,
27 repenting from their sins so that You will answer them – listen from the
heavens and forgive the sin of Your servants and Your people Israel, having

taught them the proper path to follow. Shower rain upon the land You gave
to Your people as their share.

28 "Should there be famine in the land, should there be sickness, should there
be blight, mildew, locust, or larvae, should enemies harass them in the land
29 within their own gates – oh, any suffering or any disease! – and anyone
from Your people, Israel, offers any prayer or any plea, moved by his own
30 suffering and pain, and raises his palms toward this House – listen from
Your heavenly abode and forgive. Treat each person according to his ways,
31 for You know his heart – for You alone know the hearts of humanity – so
that they will revere You and follow in Your ways for as long as they live
upon the soil that You gave to our ancestors.

32 "Should the foreigner, too, not of Your people Israel, come from a distant
land for the sake of Your great name and Your mighty hand and Your
33 outstretched arm; should he come and pray at this House – listen from
Your heavenly abode and fulfill all that the foreigner calls out to You. For
then all the peoples of the land will know Your name and revere You as
Your people Israel does, for then they will know that it is Your name that
is proclaimed over this House.

34 "Should Your people go out to war against their enemies, wherever You
might send them, and they pray toward this city You have chosen and the
35 House I built for Your name – listen from the heavens to their prayer and
plea, and uphold their cause.

36 "Should they sin against You – for there is no person who does not sin – and
You rage against them and deliver them over to their enemy, who drags
37 them off as captives to a land far or near, but they take it to heart in the land
where they are being held captive, and they repent and offer pleas to You
in the land of their captivity, declaring, 'We have sinned and offended and
38 done evil,' and they come back to You with all their heart and all their soul
in the land of their captivity, and they pray toward their own land which
You gave to their ancestors, to the city that You chose and the House that
39 I built for Your name – listen from Your heavenly abode to their prayer
and their pleas, uphold their cause, and forgive Your people who sinned
against You.

40 "Now, my God, let Your eyes be open
and Your ears be attuned
to the prayers of this place.
41 And now, O Lord God,
advance to Your resting place,
You and Your mighty Ark.
Your priests, O Lord God, are robed in victory;
Your devoted ones will rejoice in goodness.
42 O Lord God, do not reject Your anointed one.
Remember Your loyalty to Your servant David."

7 1 As Shlomo concluded his prayer, fire flared down from the heavens
and consumed the burnt offering and the sacrifices, and the LORD's
2 glory filled the House – the priests could not enter the LORD's House
3 because of the divine glory that filled the LORD's House. When all the
Israelites saw the fire and the LORD's glory descending to the House, they
kneeled down on the floor with their faces to the ground, bowed down,
and gave thanks to the LORD, "for He is good, for His loving-kindness
is forever."

4 5 And the king and all the people offered sacrifices before the LORD; King
Shlomo offered a sacrifice of 22,000 cattle and 120,000 sheep – thus the
6 king and all of Israel dedicated the House of God. The priests stood at
their posts as well as the Levites with their instruments for the LORD's
music, those that King David had made to give thanks to the LORD – for
His loving-kindness is forever! – whenever David offered praise through
them. The priests, facing them, sounded the trumpets, and all of Israel
stood by.

7 On that day, Shlomo consecrated the center of the courtyard in front of the
House of the LORD, for it was there that he prepared the burnt offerings
and the fats of the peace offerings. The bronze altar that he had made could
not contain all of the burnt offering, the grain offering, and the fats.

8 At that same time, Shlomo celebrated the festival for seven days together
with all of Israel; they were a massive assembly from Levo Ḥamat to the
9 Ravine of Egypt. On the eighth day they held an assembly, for they had
celebrated the dedication of the altar for seven days and the festival for
10 seven days. And on the twenty-third day of the seventh month he sent
the people back to their homes, joyful and glad at heart for the goodness
11 the LORD had shown to David and Shlomo and His people Israel. Shlomo
had finished building the House of the LORD and the king's own house.
He managed to fulfill all that he had in mind for the House of the LORD
and his own house.

12 Now the LORD appeared to Shlomo by night and said to him,
"I have heard your prayer,
and I have chosen this place as a place of sacrifice for Me.
13 Should I stop up the heavens and there is no rain,
or command the locust to devour the land,
or send forth disease among My people –
14 if My people, who are called by My name,
humble themselves and pray and seek My presence
and turn back from their evil ways –
then I will listen from heaven
and forgive their sins
and heal their land.
15 Now My eyes will be open and My ears attuned

to the prayers of this place.
16 Now I have chosen to consecrate this House
for My name to be there forever;
My eyes and My heart will be there for all time.
17 As for you –
if you walk before Me as your father David did,
fulfilling all I have commanded you,
keeping My laws and My rulings,
18 then I will establish your royal throne
in accordance with My covenant with your father David:
'No one of your lineage will be cut off from ruling over Israel.'

19 "But if you turn back from Me
and abandon the commandments and laws I set before you
and serve other gods and worship them,
20 then I will uproot them from the land that I gave them
and I will cast this House –
which I sanctified for My own name –
from My presence,
leaving it as a proverb and a byword among all the nations.
21 And whoever passes by this once-exalted House will reel
and say,
'Why did the LORD do this to this land and this House?'
22 And they will answer,
'Because they left the LORD, the God of their ancestors,
who brought them out of the land of Egypt,
and they embraced other gods and worshipped them and served them.
For this, He brought all this evil upon them.'"

8 1 At the end of the twenty years that Shlomo had spent building the House
2 of the LORD and the king's own house, Shlomo built up the cities that
Ḥuram had given to him, and he settled Israelites there.

3 4 Shlomo went to Ḥamat Tzova and seized it. He built Tadmor in the
5 wilderness, and in Ḥamat he built all the store towns. He built Upper
Beit Ḥoron and Lower Beit Ḥoron and fortified cities with walls, gates, and
6 bars, as well as Baalat and all of Shlomo's store towns, chariot towns, and
cavalry towns – all that Shlomo desired to build in Jerusalem, Lebanon,
7 and throughout the land of his dominion. As for all the people who
remained among the Hittites, the Amorites, the Perizzites, the Hivvites,
8 and the Jebusites, who were not of the Israelites – some of their remaining
descendants, whom the Israelites had not destroyed, Shlomo drafted them
9 for forced labor to this day. Shlomo never reduced the Israelites to slavery
for his work, for they were military men, his commanding officers, and the
10 officers of his chariots and cavalry. These were King Shlomo's ministers of
prefects: two hundred fifty supervised the people.

11 Shlomo brought Pharaoh's daughter up from the City of David to the
palace he had built for her, saying, "My wife will not live in the house of
King David of Israel, for wherever the Ark of the Lord has been is holy."

12 At that time, Shlomo offered up burnt offerings to the Lord on the Lord's
13 altar that he had built in front of the Hall, performing the constant daily
service as the laws of Moshe dictated: on Sabbaths, New Moons, and the
three annual festivals: the Festival of Unleavened Bread, the Festival of
14 Weeks, and the Festival of Tabernacles. He maintained his father David's
orders regarding the division of priestly duties, the Levites' shifts to sing
praise and serve before the priests according to the constant daily service,
and the division of gatekeepers for each gate, following the orders of David,
15 the man of God. They did not deviate from any of the king's orders to the
priests and the Levites regarding these matters, or regarding the treasuries.
16 Thus all Shlomo's work was accomplished from the day the foundations of
the Lord's House were laid until its completion; the House of the Lord
was completely finished.

17 Shlomo then went to Etzyon Gever and Eilot on the seacoast in the land
18 of Edom. Ḥuram sent him ships with his own servants, who were familiar
with the sea, and together with Shlomo's servants, they traveled to Ofir.
There they collected gold – 450 talents – and brought it to King Shlomo.

9 1 Now the Queen of Sheba had been hearing of Shlomo's fame, and she came
with a vast entourage to test him with riddles in Jerusalem, with camels
bearing spices, an immense wealth of gold, and precious stones. She came
2 to Shlomo and told him all that she had in mind. Shlomo addressed all of
her words; nothing remained hidden from Shlomo, and there was nothing
3 he failed to address. When the Queen of Sheba saw Shlomo's wisdom and
4 the House he had built, and the fare of his table and how his subjects were
seated, and his servants' attendance and attire and his cupbearers and their
attire, and the burnt offerings he offered up in the House of the Lord, she
was left breathless.
5 "What I heard in my land about your deeds and your wisdom is true," she
6 said to the king. "I never believed their words until I came and saw it with
my own eyes – and I was not told even half of your great wisdom; you have
7 surpassed the rumors I heard. How fortunate are your people, and how
fortunate are these attendants of yours who are always in your presence
8 and hear your wisdom. Blessed be the Lord your God, who delighted in
you and set you upon His throne as king for the Lord your God; because
your God loves Israel and wishes to establish them forever, He has made
you king over them to uphold justice and righteousness."

9 She gave the king one hundred twenty talents of gold and a great wealth of
spices and precious stones; never again has there been a wealth of spices
10 like the Queen of Sheba's gift to King Shlomo – the servants of Ḥuram
and Shlomo who conveyed gold from Ofir had also brought sandalwood
11 and precious stones, and the king had the sandalwood made into banisters

for the House of the Lord and the royal house, and harps and lyres for
the musicians, the likes of which had never been seen before in the land
12 of Yehuda – and he gave the Queen of Sheba all that she desired, far more
than she had brought to the king. Then, together with her servants, she
took her leave and journeyed back to her own land.

13 The weight of gold that Shlomo received in a single year was 666 talents
14 beside imports from traveling merchants and traders; all the Arabian kings
15 and the governors of the land would bring gold and silver to Shlomo. King
Shlomo made two hundred shields of beaten gold – six hundred pieces of
16 beaten gold went into each shield – and three hundred bucklers of beaten
gold – three hundred pieces of gold went into each buckler – and the king
placed them in the House of the Lebanon Forest.

17 The king made an enormous ivory throne and overlaid it with pure gold.
18 Six steps led up to the throne; a golden footstool was attached to the
throne, and there were armrests on both sides of the seat. Two lions were
19 positioned by the armrests, and twelve lions stood there on the six steps
on either side. Nothing like it was ever made in any other kingdom.

20 All the king's drinking vessels were of gold, and all the utensils of the
House of the Lebanon Forest were of solid gold. Silver counted for nothing
21 in the days of Shlomo, for the king's ships traveled to Tarshish with Ḥiram's
servants; every three years, the ships would come from Tarshish loaded
with gold and silver, ivory, monkeys, and peacocks.

22 King Shlomo surpassed all the kings of the earth in wealth and in wisdom;
23 all the kings of the earth sought an audience with Shlomo to hear the
24 wisdom that God had granted him. And each one brought his tribute:
vessels of silver and vessels of gold, garments, weapons, spices, horses, and
mules according to the yearly due.

25 Shlomo had four thousand horse stables and chariots and twelve thousand
horsemen. He stationed them in the chariot towns and with the king in
26 Jerusalem. He ruled over all the kings from the River[6] to the land of the
27 Philistines and up to the border of Egypt. The king made silver as common
in Jerusalem as stones, while cedars were as common as sycamores in the
28 lowlands. Shlomo's horses were imported from Egypt and from all over
the world.

29 The rest of Shlomo's history, earlier and later, is recorded in the chronicles
of the prophet Natan, the prophecy of Aḥiya the Shilonite, and the
30 oracles of the Seer Yedo[7] about Yorovam son of Nevat. Shlomo reigned
31 in Jerusalem over all of Israel for forty years. Then Shlomo slept with his
ancestors, and they buried him in the City of David, his father, and his son
Reḥavam reigned in his place.

---

6 | The Euphrates.

7 | Believed to be the same as the prophet Ido mentioned in 12:15 and 13:22.

10 1 Reḥavam went to Shekhem, for all of Israel had come to Shekhem for his
2 coronation. Yorovam son of Nevat heard this when he was in Egypt, for
he had escaped from King Shlomo. Now Yorovam returned from Egypt.
3 They sent for and summoned him, and Yorovam came with all of Israel,
who made the following speech to Reḥavam:

4 "Your father made our yoke heavy – now relieve the heavy workload and
the harsh yoke your father placed upon us, and we will serve you."

5 "Leave for three days," he said to them, "and then come back to me," and
the people left.

6 King Reḥavam consulted with the elders who had served his father Shlomo
during his lifetime.

"How would you advise to answer this people's request?" he said.

7 "If you treat this people kindly today," they told him, "and appease them
by speaking kind words, then they will become your servants forever."

8 But he rejected the advice that the elders gave him and consulted with
the youngsters who had grown up with him and who now served him.

9 "What do you advise?" he asked them. "How should we answer this
people's request? They told me, 'Relieve the yoke your father placed upon
us.'"

10 The youngsters who had grown up with him said, "This is what you should
say to the people who told you, 'Your father made our yoke heavy – you
should relieve us.' Tell them this: 'My little finger is thicker than my father's
11 loins. Now, my father burdened you with a heavy yoke, but I will increase
your yoke; my father flogged you with whips – I will use scorpions.'"

12 Yorovam and all the people came to Reḥavam on the third day, just as the
king had commanded them, saying, "Come back to me on the third day."
13 14 The king answered them harshly, rejecting the advice of the elders. He
answered them as the youngsters had advised, saying, "I will burden you
with a heavy yoke and make it even heavier; my father flogged you with
15 whips, but I will use scorpions!" The king would not listen to the people,
for it was part of God's plan in order to fulfill the promise that the Lord
had made to Yorovam son of Nevat through Aḥiyahu the Shilonite.

16 When all Israel saw that the king would not listen to them, the people
retorted to the king,

"We have no part in David
nor any share in the son of Yishai!
Every man to your tent, O Israel!
Now look to your own house, O David!"

17 And all Israel went back to their tents. But as for the Israelites who lived
in the towns of Yehuda, Reḥavam ruled over them.

18 King Reḥavam sent out Hadoram, who was in charge of the forced labor,
but Israelites pelted him with stones, and he died. At that, Reḥavam forced
19 his way onto his chariot, to flee to Jerusalem. And the Israelites have
rebelled against the House of David ever since.

11 1 When Reḥavam reached Jerusalem, he assembled the House of Yehuda
and Binyamin – 180,000 elite fighters – to fight against Israel, to restore the
2 kingship to Reḥavam. But the word of the LORD came to Shemayahu, man
3 of God: "Say to Reḥavam son of Shlomo, king of Yehuda, and to all of Israel
4 who live in Yehuda and Binyamin: 'Thus says the LORD: Do not advance,
and do not fight with your brothers. Let every man go back home, for it is
through Me that this has come about.'" And they heeded the LORD's word
and turned back from the campaign against Yorovam.

5, 6 Reḥavam settled in Jerusalem and built fortified cities in Yehuda. He built
7, 8 up Beit Leḥem, Eitam, Tekoa, Beit Tzur, Sokho, Adulam, Gat, Maresha,
9, 10 Zif, Adorayim, Lakhish, Azeka, Tzora, Ayalon, and Ḥevron, which are in
11 Yehuda and in Binyamin, as fortified towns. He reinforced the fortresses
and stationed commanders in them along with stores of food, oil, and wine,
12 and he supplied every city with shields and spears; by greatly increasing
their strength, he maintained control of Yehuda and Binyamin.

13 From all over Israel, the priests and the Levites left their own borders
14 and presented themselves to him; the Levites left their land and their
holdings and went to Yehuda and Jerusalem because Yorovam and his sons
15 prevented them from ministering to the LORD – he appointed his own
16 priests for the shrines and idols and for the calves that he had made – and
they were followed by all those of the tribes of Israel whose hearts were
devoted to seeking the LORD, God of Israel; they came to Jerusalem to
17 offer sacrifice to the LORD, the God of their ancestors. They strengthened
the Judahite kingship and supported Reḥavam son of Shlomo for three
years, because for three years they followed in David and Shlomo's path.

18 Reḥavam married Maḥalat, the daughter of Yerimot son of David, and
19 of Aviḥayil the daughter of Eliav son of Yishai. She bore him sons:
20 Yeush, Shemarya, and Zaham. After her, he married Maakha, daughter
21 of Avshalom, and she bore him Aviya, Atai, Ziza, and Shlomit. Out of all
his wives and concubines, Reḥavam loved Maakha, Avshalom's daughter,
the most – he married eighteen wives and sixty concubines and fathered
22 twenty-eight sons and sixty daughters – and Reḥavam designated Aviya
son of Maakha as head and prince over his brothers, for he intended to
23 make him king. He strategically positioned his sons in all the fortified
cities throughout the regions of Yehuda and Binyamin, provided them
with ample food, and secured many wives for them.

12 1 As Reḥavam's kingdom grew stronger and more established, he aban-
2 doned the teachings of the LORD, he and all Israel with him. In the fifth year
of Reḥavam's reign, because they broke faith with the LORD, King Shishak

3 of Egypt launched an attack on Jerusalem with 1,200 chariots, 60,000 riders,
and countless troops that came with him from Egypt – Libyans, Sukkites,
4 and Kushites. He captured Yehuda's fortified cities and invaded as far as
Jerusalem.

5 The prophet Shemaya came to Reḥavam and the officers of Yehuda, who
had assembled at Jerusalem because of Shishak, and said to them,

"Thus says the Lord: You abandoned Me, so I, too, have abandoned you to the hands of Shishak."

6 The officers of Israel and the king humbled themselves and declared, "The
7 Lord is right." When the Lord saw that they had humbled themselves, the
word of the Lord came to Shemaya: "They have humbled themselves; I
will not destroy them. I will grant them some measure of deliverance, and
8 My fury will not be poured out on Jerusalem through Shishak. But they
will become subjects to him so that they will know the difference between
service to Me and service to kingdoms of other lands."

9 King Shishak of Egypt attacked Jerusalem, and he seized the treasures of
the House of the Lord and the treasures of the royal palace; he seized
10 everything. He even seized the golden shields that Shlomo had made. King
Reḥavam had bronze shields made in their place and entrusted them to the
11 chief sentry who guarded the entrance of the palace. Whenever the king
went to the House of the Lord, the sentry would come and carry them
and then return them to the sentry armory.

12 Once he had humbled himself, the Lord's wrath subsided, and He did
not inflict complete destruction; some goodness was found in Yehuda.

13 King Reḥavam established a strong reign in Jerusalem. He was forty-one
years old when he became king, and for seventeen years he reigned in
Jerusalem – the city where the Lord had chosen to establish His name
out of all the tribes of Israel. His mother's name was Naama the Amonite.
14 And he did what was evil, for he did not set his heart on seeking out the
Lord.

15 The rest of Reḥavam's history, earlier and later, is recorded in the chronicles
of the prophet Shemaya and of the seer Ido, in charge of genealogy. There
16 was ongoing war between Reḥavam and Yorovam. And Reḥavam slept
with his ancestors, and he was buried in the City of David. And his son
Aviya reigned in his place.

13 1 In the eighteenth year of King Yorovam, Aviya became king over Yehuda.
2 For three years he reigned in Jerusalem, and his mother's name was
Mikhayahu, the daughter of Uriel of Giva.

3 War continued between Aviya and Yorovam. Aviya went out to battle with
a military force of 400,000 elite fighters while Yorovam drew up his battle
lines against him with a force of 800,000 elite warriors.

4 Then Aviya stood up on the top of Mount Tzemarayim, which is in the
hill country of Efrayim.
"Listen to me, Yorovam and all of Israel," he said.
5 "You certainly know that the LORD, God of Israel, gave kingship over Israel
to David forever, to him and his sons as a covenant of salt.

6 "Yet Yorovam son of Nevat, Shlomo's servant, rose up and rebelled against
7 his master. And worthless, depraved men gathered about him and defied
Reḥavam son of Shlomo; Reḥavam was young and soft-willed, and he
could not withstand them.

8 "And now, you believe you are able to withstand the kingdom of the LORD
in the charge of David's descendants because you are a vast multitude and
because you have golden calves that Yorovam made for you as gods?

9 "Have you not rejected the LORD's priests – the sons of Aharon and the
Levites?

"Like the peoples of other lands, you made your own priests – whoever shows up for ordination with a young bull or seven rams becomes a priest of non-gods.

10 "As for us – the LORD is our God, and we have not abandoned Him;
the priests ministering to the LORD are the sons of Aharon, and the Levites
are performing their service.
11 They offer sacrifices to the LORD – burnt offerings every morning and
evening and fragrant incense;
they set rows of bread on the pure table;
they light the golden candelabrum with its lamps every evening,
for we keep the charge of the LORD our God
while you have abandoned Him.
12 Here, now, at our head are God and His priests
with their battle trumpets to sound the battle cry against you!
Do not fight with the LORD, the God of your ancestors,
for you cannot succeed!"

13 Meanwhile, Yorovam had led the ambush around to attack them from
behind, so his men were in front of Yehuda, and his ambush was behind
14 them. When Yehuda turned around, battle suddenly raged before them
and behind them, and they cried out to the LORD as the priests blasted the
15 trumpets. The men of Yehuda raised the battle shout, and as they shouted
16 out, God defeated Yorovam and all of Israel before Aviya and Yehuda. The
Israelites fled before Yehuda, and God delivered them into their hands.
17 Aviya and his men dealt them a deadly blow, and 500,000 of Israel's elite
warriors fell slain.

18 Thus Israel was defeated at that time while the Judahites grew strong
19 because they relied on the LORD, God of their ancestors. Aviya pursued
Yorovam and seized towns from him: Beit El with its villages, Yeshana with

20 its villages, and Efrayin with its villages. Yorovam never regained his power
21 in Aviyahu's time; the LORD struck him down, and he died. But Aviyahu
grew in strength; he married fourteen wives and fathered twenty-two sons
and sixteen daughters.

22 The rest of Aviya's history, his ways and words, are recorded in the tales of
23 the prophet Ido. And Aviya slept with his ancestors and was buried in the
City of David, and his son Asa reigned in his place. In his time, the land
saw peace for ten years.

14 1 2 Asa did what was good and right in the eyes of the LORD his God. He
removed the foreign altars and the shrines; he razed the worship pillars
3 and cut down the sacred trees.[8] And he commanded Yehuda to seek the
LORD, God of their ancestors, and to keep the Torah and commandments.
4 He removed the shrines and the sun altars from all the towns of Yehuda,
and the kingdom saw peace under his rule.

5 He built fortified cities in Yehuda, for the land was peaceful; there were
6 no wars during these years, for the LORD had granted him rest. He said
to Yehuda, "Let us build these cities and surround them with walls and
towers, with gates and bars. The land still stretches out before us, for we
have sought the LORD our God; we sought Him, and He granted us rest
all around." So they built and they flourished.

7 Asa had an army of 300,000 from Yehuda, armed with buckler and spear,
and 280,000 from Binyamin, armed with shield and bow; all these were
8 powerful warriors. Zeraḥ the Kushite marched out against them with an
army of a million men and three hundred chariots, and they came as far
9 as Maresha. Asa marched out before him, and they drew up their battle
lines in the Valley of Tzefat at Maresha.

10 Then Asa called out to the LORD his God.
"O LORD," he said, "to You there is no difference between helping the
powerful and the powerless. Help us, O LORD our God, for upon You we
rely, and in Your name we confront this multitude. O LORD, You are our
God; let no mortal prevail against You."

11 And the LORD defeated the Kushites before Asa and Yehuda, and the
12 Kushites fled. Asa and his men pursued them as far as Gerar, and the
Kushites fell until none were left alive, for they had been broken before the
13 LORD and His army. The men of Yehuda carried off masses of spoil; they
ravaged all the towns around Gerar – which had been seized with terror of
the LORD – and they plundered all the towns, for they were full of goods.
14 They also ravaged livestock enclosures and captured flocks of sheep and
camels. Then they returned to Jerusalem.

---

8 | Hebrew "*asherim*": trees, wooden posts, or images representing the Canaanite fertility goddess Ashera.

15 1 2 The spirit of God came upon Azaryahu son of Oded. He approached Asa
and said to him,

"Listen to me, Asa, and all Yehuda and Binyamin:
The Lord is with you so long as you are with Him;
if you seek Him, He will be there for you,
but if you abandon Him, He will abandon you.
3 For a long time, Israel has been without a true God,
without guiding priests, without Torah,
4 but in their distress they came back to the Lord, God of Israel –
they sought Him, and He was there for them.
5 In those times, traveling back and forth was not safe,
for great turmoil stirred all the people of the lands.
6 Nation was crushed by nation, city by city,
for God frenzied them with a torrent of troubles.
7 Now take courage, and do not let your hands go limp –
for your work shall be rewarded."

8 When Asa heard these words, the prophecy of the prophet Oded, he took
courage. He purged the abominations from all the land of Yehuda and
Binyamin and the towns he had taken over in the hill country of Efrayim,
and he repaired the Altar of the Lord in front of the Hall of the Lord.
9 He gathered all of Yehuda and Binyamin and those that lived among
them from Efrayim, Menashe, and Shimon, for there had been a mass
immigration of Israelites when they saw that the Lord his God was with
10 him. They gathered in Jerusalem in the third month in the fifteenth year
11 of Asa's reign and offered sacrifices to the Lord on that day from the spoil
12 they had brought: seven hundred oxen and seven thousand sheep. And
they entered into a covenant to seek the Lord, the God of their ancestors,
13 with all their hearts and all their souls. Whoever would not seek the Lord,
God of Israel, would be put to death, whether young or old, man or woman.
14 They pronounced this oath to the Lord in a loud voice, with shouting out,
15 blasting the trumpets and rams' horns. And all of Yehuda rejoiced over
the oath, for they had sworn it with all their hearts and sought Him with
all their desire. And He was there for them, and the Lord granted them
rest on every side.

16 King Asa even deposed his mother Maakha from the position of queen
mother because she had made a monstrous image for Ashera;[9] Asa cut
down her monstrous image, crushed it, and burned it by the Kidron Valley.
17 Though the high shrines were not removed from Israel, Asa's heart was true
18 all the days of his life. He brought his father's sacred items and his own
19 sacred items into the House of God: silver, gold, and the vessels. And no
war took place until the thirty-fifth year of Asa's reign.

---

9 | See note on 14:2.

16 1 In the thirty-sixth year of Asa's reign, Basha, king of Israel, marched against
Yehuda and fortified Rama to prevent Asa, king of Yehuda, from marching
2 out into battle. So Asa took silver and gold from the treasuries of the House
of the Lord and the royal palace and sent it to Ben Hadad, king of Aram,
who resided in Damascus, with this message:

3 "There is an alliance between me and you and between my father and your
father. Look, I have sent you silver and gold; go and break your alliance
with Basha, king of Israel, so that he will withdraw from me."

4 Ben Hadad complied with King Asa and sent his military officers to the
towns of Israel; they attacked Iyon, Dan, and Avel Mayim and all the
5 store towns of Naftali. When Basha heard, he ceased construction in
6 Rama, halting his work. King Asa then summoned all of Yehuda to seize
the stones and wood that Basha had been using to fortify Rama, and with
them he in turn fortified Geva and Mitzpa.

7 Soon after, the seer Ḥanani came to King Asa of Yehuda and said to him,
"Because you relied on the king of Aram instead of relying on the Lord
8 your God, an army of the king of Aram has escaped you. The Kushites and
the Libyans were a mighty force indeed, with chariots and riders abundant,
but when you relied upon the Lord, He delivered them into your hands,
9 for the eyes of the Lord roam all over the land, giving strength to those
whose hearts are completely with Him.
This time you have been foolish, and from now on you will have war."

10 Asa was angry at the seer, and in his rage over this, he had him thrown
into prison; Asa also dealt harshly with certain people at the same time.

11 Asa's history, earlier and later, is recorded in the Book of the Kings of
12 Yehuda and Israel. In the thirty-ninth year of his reign, Asa suffered from
a foot disease, and his disease grew severe. Yet even in his illness he did
13 not seek help from the Lord but from healers. And Asa slept with his
14 ancestors; he died in the forty-first year of his reign. They buried him in the
tomb he had hewn for himself in the City of David. They laid him out on a
bier that had been covered with all kinds of spices and perfumes, artfully
prepared, and lit an enormous fire in his honor.

17 1 His son Yehoshafat reigned in his place, and he grew more powerful against
2 Israel. He stationed forces in all of Yehuda's fortified cities, and he stationed
garrisons in the land of Yehuda and in the towns of Efrayim that his father
3 Asa had taken over. The Lord was with Yehoshafat, for he followed in the
4 ways of David as his father did at first, and he did not seek the Baalim. He
sought his father's God and followed His commandments – unlike the
5 ways of Israel. And the Lord established the kingdom firmly in his grasp.
All Yehuda paid tribute to Yehoshafat, and he had great wealth and honor.
6 His heart soared with the Lord's ways; moreover, he removed the high
shrines and the sacred trees from Yehuda.

7 In the third year of his reign he sent his officials Ben Ḥayil, Ovadya,
Zekharya, Netanel, and Mikhayahu to teach in the towns of Yehuda
8 together with the Levites Shemayahu, Netanyahu, Zevadyahu, Asael,
Shemiramot, Yehonatan, Adoniyahu, Toviyahu, and Tov Adoniya, with
9 the priests Elishama and Yehoram accompanying the Levites. They taught
in Yehuda with the scroll of the LORD's Torah, making their way around
10 all the towns of Yehuda and teaching among the people. All the kingdoms
of the lands surrounding Yehuda were struck with fear of the LORD, and
11 none made war against Yehoshafat. Some of the Philistines offered gifts
to Yehoshafat and silver as tribute; the Arabians brought him 7,700 rams
and 7,700 he-goats.

12 Yehoshafat steadily rose in greatness. He built fortresses and store towns
13 in Yehuda; he led great industry in the towns of Yehuda and a powerful
14 military force in Jerusalem. They were enlisted this way according to their
ancestral houses: Yehuda's officer of thousands was the officer Adna in
15 charge of 300,000 warriors; next to him was the officer Yehoḥanan in
16 charge of 280,000; next to him was Amasya son of Zikhri, a volunteer
17 for the LORD's service, in charge of 200,000 warriors. From Binyamin
18 the warrior Elyada in charge of 200,000 armed with bow and shield, and
19 next to him Yehozavad in charge of 180,000 armed troops. These were in
the king's service in addition to those that the king had stationed in the
fortified cities throughout Yehuda.

18 1 Yehoshafat had great wealth and honor, and he made a marriage alliance
2 with Aḥav. After some years, he went down to Aḥav in Shomron. Aḥav had
many sheep and oxen slaughtered for him and for the people with him, and
3 he persuaded him to march up to Ramot Gilad. Aḥav, king of Israel, said
to Yehoshafat, king of Yehuda, "Will you go with me to Ramot Gilad?"
"I am ready, as you are," he said to him. "My troops are your own troops; we
4 will accompany you in battle." Then Yehoshafat said to the king of Israel,
"Please, inquire of the LORD today."

5 So the king of Israel gathered the prophets, four hundred men, and said
to them, "Shall we go to battle over Ramot Gilad, or should I refrain?"
"Advance!" they said, "and God will deliver them to the king's hand."
6 "Is there no other prophet of the LORD here?" said Yehoshafat. "Let us
inquire through him."
7 "There is another man through whom we could inquire of the LORD," the
king of Israel said to Yehoshafat, "but I despise him; he will not prophesy
good for me, only evil all the time – he is Mikhayehu son of Yimla."
"Do not say such a thing, O king," said Yehoshafat.
8 So the king of Israel summoned one of the eunuchs and said, "Bring
Mikhayehu son of Yimla at once."

9 The king of Israel and Yehoshafat, king of Yehuda, each sat upon their
thrones attired in robes; they sat by the threshing floor at the entrance of

the gate of Shomron, and all the prophets were prophesying before them.
10 Tzidkiyahu son of Kenaana had made himself horns of iron.
"Thus says the Lord," he said, "with these you shall gore Aram until their
11 demise." And all the prophets echoed his prophecy: "Advance to Ramot
Gilad, and be victorious," they were saying. "The Lord will deliver it to
the king's hand."

12 Then the messenger who had gone to summon Mikhayehu told him, "Look
here – the words of the prophets are unanimous; they favor the king. May
your words be like their words – speak favorably."
13 "As the Lord lives," said Mikhayehu, "I will speak only what my God says
to me."
14 He came up to the king, and the king said to him, "Mikha – shall we go to
battle over Ramot Gilad, or should I refrain?"
"Advance and be victorious," he said, "and they will be delivered into your
hands."
15 "How many times must I have you swear?" the king said to him. "You must
speak only the truth to me, by the name of the Lord."
16 "I saw all of Israel scattered over the hills," he said, "like sheep without a
shepherd. And the Lord said: These have no masters. Let each man return
home in peace."
17 "Did I not tell you?" the king of Israel said to Yehoshafat. "He never
prophesies good for me – only evil!"
18 "Therefore listen to the word of the Lord," he continued. "I saw the Lord
sitting on His throne, with all the heavenly hosts standing to His right and
19 to His left. And the Lord said, 'Who will lure Aḥav, king of Israel, so that
he will advance and fall at Ramot Gilad?' This one said this, and that one
20 said that. Then a spirit came forward and stood before the Lord and said,
'I will lure him.'
"'How?' said the Lord.
21 "'I will go out and become a false spirit in the mouths of all his prophets,'
it said. "'Lure him – you will succeed,' He said. 'Go out and do so.'

22 "And now look – the Lord has placed a false spirit in the mouths of these
prophets of yours, and the Lord has pronounced evil for you."

23 Tzidkiyahu son of Kenaana came forward and slapped Mikhayehu across
the cheek. "Which way did the spirit of the Lord pass from me to speak
to you?" he said.
24 "Oh, you will see on that day," Mikhayehu said, "when you enter the
innermost room to hide."
25 "Seize Mikhayehu!" said the king of Israel. "Hand him over to Amon, the
26 city governor, and to Yoash, the king's son, and say, 'Thus says the king:
Put this one in prison, and feed him only scant bread and scant water until
my safe return.'"

27 "If you indeed return safely, then the LORD did not speak through me," said
Mikhayehu, and added, "Listen, all peoples!"[10]

28 So the king of Israel and Yehoshafat, king of Yehuda, advanced to Ramot
29 Gilad. "I will disguise myself and go into battle,"[11] the king of Israel said
to Yehoshafat, "while you should wear your robes." And the king of Israel
30 disguised himself, and they went into battle. Now the king of Aram had
instructed his chariot commanders as follows: "Do not attack anyone, great
31 or small, except for the king of Israel." When the chariot commanders saw
Yehoshafat, they thought, "He must be the king of Israel." They charged
toward him to attack, but Yehoshafat cried out, and the LORD came to his
32 aid; God diverted them away from him. When the chariot commanders
realized that he was not the king of Israel, they turned back away from
him.

33 But one man drew his bow at random, and he struck the king of Israel in
between the joints of his armor. He called out to his chariot driver, "Steer
34 back around and get me out of the camp, for I am wounded." As the battle
raged that day, the king was propped up in his chariot facing Aram until
the evening; he died as the sun was setting.

19 1 2 Yehoshafat, king of Yehuda, returned home safely to Jerusalem. But the
seer Yehu son of Ḥanani went out to meet him.
"Should you help the wicked and love those who hate the LORD?" he said
to King Yehoshafat. "For this, the LORD's wrath is unleashed against you.
3 Yet there is still some goodness found within you, for you have purged the
sacred trees from the land, and you have set your heart on seeking God."

4 Yehoshafat dwelled in Jerusalem, and he went out again among the
people – from Be'er Sheva up to the hill country of Efrayim – to bring
5 them back to the LORD, God of their ancestors. He appointed judges in
6 the land in all the fortified cities of Yehuda, city by city. He said to the
judges, "Consider what you do, for you are judging not for the people's
7 sake but for the LORD's, and He is with you in judgment. Now, may fear of
the LORD be upon you; act with care, for there is no corruption with the
8 LORD our God, or favoritism, or accepting bribes." When they returned
to Jerusalem, there too, Yehoshafat appointed certain Levites, priests, and
some of Israel's ancestral heads to pass judgment for the LORD and to settle
9 disputes. He commanded them, saying, "Thus you shall act: with fear of
10 the LORD, faithfully, and with whole hearts. Whenever your brothers
bring a case before you from their hometowns – whether it concerns
bloodshed, law and commandment, statutes, or rules – you must instruct
them so that they do not incur guilt before the LORD, bringing wrath

---

10 | Cf. Micah 1:2.

11 | Literally "disguise yourself," but this must be understood as referring to the king of Israel himself.

11 upon you and your brothers; if you act thus, you will not incur guilt. The
head priest Amaryahu is over you in all matters concerning the Lord,
and Zevadyahu son of Yishmael, the leader of the house of Yehuda, in all
matters concerning the king; the Levites shall serve as your officers. Act
with courage, and may the Lord be with the good."

20 1 Some time later, the Moabites and Amonites, together with some
2 Amonites,[12] advanced against Yehoshafat for battle. They came and told
Yehoshafat, "A vast multitude is advancing against you from across the
sea, from Aram; they are now in Ḥatzetzon Tamar" – that is, Ein Gedi.

3 Yehoshafat was afraid, but he was determined to seek the Lord, and he
4 proclaimed a fast for all of Yehuda. Yehuda gathered together to appeal to
the Lord; they came from all the towns of Yehuda to appeal to the Lord.
5 Yehoshafat stood among the assembly of Yehuda and Jerusalem in the
House of the Lord before the new courtyard.

6 "O Lord, God of our ancestors," he said,
"You are God in heaven,
and You rule over all the kingdoms of the nations.
Power and might are in Your hand;
You cannot be overcome.
7 You, our God, dispossessed the people of this land
before Your people Israel;
You gave it to the seed of Avraham,
who loved You, forever.
8 There they settled,
and there they built a Sanctuary for Your name, saying,
9 'Should evil come upon us,
sword, judgment, disease, or famine,
we will stand before this House –
before You, for Your name is on this House –
and we will cry out to You in our distress;
You will hear, and You will save.'
10 And now, here are the people of Amon and Moav and Mount Se'ir;
You did not allow Israel to travel through them
when they came from the land of Egypt –
they circumvented them and did not destroy them –
11 but see how they repay us;
they come to drive us out from Your possession,
which You gave us as ours.
12 Our God, will You not pass judgment against them?
For we are powerless against this vast multitude
that advances toward us.
We know not what to do;

12 | Hebrew *Amonim*. Radak understands the latter group to be the Meunites, as the terms *Amonim* and *Meunim* are interchangeable elsewhere; cf. 26:7–8.

our eyes are upon You."

13 All of Yehuda stood before the LORD with their little ones and wives and
14 children. And in the midst of the crowd, the spirit of the LORD came upon
Yaḥaziel son of Zekaryahu son of Benaya son of Ye'iel son of Matanya, a
Levite of the sons of Asaf:

15 "Listen, all of Yehuda and the people of Jerusalem and King Yehoshafat,"
he said.

"Thus says the LORD to you:
Do not be frightened or dismayed
in the face of this vast horde,
for this battle is not yours,
but God's.
16 Tomorrow, charge down at them
as they ascend the Ascent of the Blossom;
you will encounter them at the end of the wadi
before the wilderness of Yeruel.
17 You will not need to fight this battle –
take your positions and stand still,
and you will see the LORD's victory among you,
Yehuda and Jerusalem.
Do not be frightened or dismayed,
tomorrow, go out before them,
and the LORD will be with you."

18 And Yehoshafat bowed with his face to the ground, and all of Yehuda
and the people of Jerusalem flung themselves down before the LORD
19 in worship of the LORD. Then the Levites – of the Kehatites and the
Korahites – stood up to sing praise to the LORD, God of Israel, in loud,
powerful voices.

20 They rose early in the morning and set out for the wilderness of Tekoa.
As they set out, Yehoshafat stood and said, "Listen to me, Yehuda and the
people of Jerusalem: have firm belief in the LORD your God, and you will
stand firm; have firm belief in His prophets, and you will succeed."

21 When he had given counsel to the people, he gave the cue to those who
were to sing and give praise to the LORD in the splendor of holiness as
they went out before the army, declaring, "Give praise to the LORD, for
His loving-kindness is forever."
22 And as they burst into joyful song and praise, the LORD set ambushes
against the people of Amon, Moav, and Mount Se'ir, who were advancing
23 against Yehuda, and they were routed. The Amonites and Moabites rose
against the people of Mount Se'ir to destroy and annihilate them, and
once they had finished off the people of Se'ir, they proceeded to destroy
one another.

24 When Yehuda reached the wilderness's vantage point, they looked out
toward the hordes and saw nothing but corpses sprawled all over the
25 ground; none had escaped. When Yehoshafat and his men advanced
to seize the spoil, they found vast quantities of goods and precious
objects among the corpses; they loaded themselves up until they could
carry no more. It took them three days to carry off the spoil, there was so
26 much. On the fourth day they gathered at Berakha Valley, for there they
blessed the Lord – for this reason, that place is called the Berakha Valley
to this day.

27 Then, with Yehoshafat at their head, all the men of Yehuda and Jerusalem
returned to Jerusalem with joy, for the Lord had granted them joy over
28 their enemies. They came to Jerusalem with harps and lyres and trumpets
29 to the House of the Lord. And fear of God was on all the kingdoms of
the lands, for they heard that the Lord had fought against the enemies
30 of Israel. So Yehoshafat's kingdom was at peace, for his God had granted
him rest on every side.

31 Thus Yehoshafat reigned over Yehuda. He was thirty-five years old when
he became king, and for twenty-five years he reigned in Jerusalem. His
32 mother's name was Azuva daughter of Shilḥi. He followed in the ways of
his father Asa and did not turn away from them, doing what was right in
33 the eyes of the Lord. Only the high shrines were not removed, and the
hearts of the people were not devoted to the God of their ancestors.

34 The rest of Yehoshafat's history, earlier and later, is recorded in the
chronicles of Yehu son of Ḥanani, which were copied into the Book of
the Kings of Israel.

35 Later Yehoshafat, king of Yehuda, formed an alliance with Aḥazya, king of
36 Israel, whose ways were wicked. They joined forces to build a fleet of ships
37 to travel to Tarshish, and they built a fleet at Etzyon Gever. But Eliezer son
of Dodavahu of Mareshah prophesied against him, saying, "When you
joined forces with Aḥazyahu, the Lord burst out against your work." And
the ships were wrecked and not fit to sail to Tarshish.

21 1 And Yehoshafat slept with his ancestors and was buried with his ancestors
2 in the City of David. And his son Yehoram reigned in his place. He had
brothers, the sons of Yehoshafat: Azarya, Yeḥiel, Zekharyahu, Azaryahu,
Mikhael, and Shefatyahu; all these were sons of King Yehoshafat of Israel.
3 Their father gave them many gifts, silver and gold and precious things,
along with fortified cities in Yehuda, but he gave the kingship to Yehoram
4 because he was the firstborn. Once Yehoram had ascended his father's
throne and gained power, he had all his brothers killed by the sword along
5 with some of Israel's officials. Yehoram was thirty-two years old when he
6 became king, and for eight years he reigned in Jerusalem. He followed in
the ways of the kings of Israel, as the house of Aḥav had done, for Aḥav's
daughter was his wife, and he did what was evil in the eyes of the Lord.

7 But the LORD was not willing to destroy the House of David for the sake
of the covenant He had made with David, because He had promised to
grant him and his descendants a lamp for all time.

8 In his time Edom rebelled against Yehuda and appointed their own king.
9 Yehoram crossed over with his officers and all his chariots; he advanced
at night to attack Edom, who had surrounded him and his chariot officers.
10 Edom has rebelled against Yehuda ever since; it was also then that Livna
rebelled against his rule because he abandoned the LORD, God of his
ancestors.

11 He even made high shrines in the hills of Yehuda, led the people of
Jerusalem astray, and corrupted Yehuda.

12 A letter came to him from the prophet Eliyahu saying,
"Thus says the LORD, God of your father David: Because you did not follow
in the ways of your father Yehoshafat and in the ways of Asa, king of Yehuda,
13 but followed in the ways of the kings of Israel and, like the house of Aḥav,
led Yehuda and the people of Jerusalem astray, and because you killed your
14 brothers from your father's house, who were better than you –
the LORD is about to unleash a devastating plague among your people,
15 your sons and wives, and all your possessions. And you yourself will suffer
from severe sickness, from a bowel disease – until your bowels slip out
from sheer sickness, day by day"

16 And the LORD stirred against Yehoram the spirit of the Philistines and
17 the Arabs who neighbored the Kushites. They marched up against Yehuda,
invaded them, and captured all the possessions that were found around
the royal palace, as well as his sons and wives. The only son that was left
to him was Yehoaḥaz, his youngest son.

18 After all this, the LORD struck him with an incurable bowel disease.
19 Gradually, his bowels slipped out from sheer sickness, and at the end of
the second year he died in gruesome agony. The people did not make a
great fire in his honor as they did for his ancestors.

20 He was thirty-two years old when he became king, and for eight years he
reigned in Jerusalem. No one was sorry when he died, and they buried
him in the City of David, but not in the royal tombs.

22 1 The people of Jerusalem made Aḥazyahu, his youngest son, king in his
place because all the older sons had been killed by the raiders who
infiltrated the camp with the Arabs. Thus Aḥazyahu, son of King Yehoram
of Yehuda, became king.

2 Aḥazyahu was forty-two years old when he became king, and he reigned
in Jerusalem for a single year; his mother's name was Atalyahu daughter
3 of Omri. He too followed in the ways of the house of Aḥav, for his mother
4 taught him wicked ways. Like the house of Aḥav he did what was evil in

the eyes of the LORD, for they had become his counselors after his father's
death, to his undoing.

5 It was their counsel that he followed in accompanying Yehoram son of
Aḥav, king of Israel, to war against Ḥazael, king of Aram, at Ramot Gilad
6 where the Arameans defeated Yoram. He went back to Yizre'el to recover
from the wounds he had sustained in Rama when fighting against Ḥazael,
king of Aram. Azaryahu son of Yehoram, king of Yehuda, went down
7 to visit Yehoram son of Aḥav in Yizre'el while he was injured. Through
Aḥazyahu's visit to Yoram, God brought about his downfall, for when he
arrived, he went out with Yehoram to meet Yehu son of Nimshi, whom the
8 LORD had anointed to destroy the house of Aḥav. As Yehu was executing
judgment on the house of Aḥav, he encountered the Judahite officers
and Aḥazyahu's nephews who attended Aḥazyahu, and he killed them.
9 He then sought out Aḥazyahu and had him captured as he was hiding in
Shomron, and he was brought to Yehu. He put him to death and buried
him, for they said, "He was the son of Yehoshafat, who sought the LORD
with all his heart." The house of Aḥazyahu was not powerful enough to
rule the kingdom.

10 When Atalyahu, the mother of Aḥazyahu, saw that her son was dead, she
11 swiftly assassinated all those of royal descent in the house of Yehuda. But
Yehoshavat, the daughter of the king, took Yoash, Aḥazyahu's son, stole
him away from where the princes were being put to death, and placed him
in the bed-chamber together with his nurse. Because Yehoshavat, King
Yehoram's daughter and the wife of the priest Yehoyada, was Aḥazyahu's
sister, she hid him from Atalyahu so that she would not put him to death.
12 He stayed with them in the House of God, hiding for six years, while Atalya
reigned over the land.

23 1 By the seventh year, Yehoyada had gained power, and he formed a pact
with the officers of hundreds – Azaryahu son of Yeroḥam, Yishmael son
of Yehoḥanan, Azaryahu son of Oved, Maaseyahu son of Adayahu, and
2 Elishafat son of Zikhri. They made their way around Yehuda and gathered
the Levites and ancestral heads from all the towns of Yehuda, then came
to Jerusalem.

3 Then all the assembly formed a covenant with the king in the House of
God. "Here is the king's son," he said to them. "He shall reign as the LORD
promised David's descendants would.
4 This is what you must do: out of the priests and Levites on weekly duty,
5 a third of you shall be gatekeepers, a third of you shall be stationed at
the royal palace, and a third at the Foundation Gate. All the people shall
6 be in the courtyards of the House of the LORD. No one must enter the
House of the LORD except for the priests and the Levites on duty; they
may enter because they are consecrated, but all the people must keep the
7 LORD's charge. The Levites must surround the king on all sides and make

sure every man's weapon is poised, and whoever enters the House must
be killed. And stay with the king when he goes or comes."

8 The Levites and all of Yehuda did all that the priest Yehoyada instructed
them, and each took their men – those on weekly duty and those off weekly
9 duty, for the priest Yehoyada had not dismissed the divisions. The priest
Yehoyada then gave the officers of hundreds David's own spears, shields,
10 and quivers, which were in the House of God. He then stationed all the
people – each man with his weapon poised – from the south end of the
House to the north end of the House, by the altar and the House, all
11 around the king. They brought out the king's son, set the crown and the
royal insignia upon him, and declared him king. Yehoyada and his sons
anointed him and shouted, "Long live the king!"

12 Atalyahu heard the sound of the people thronging and praising the king,
13 and she came to the people at the House of the Lord. When she looked up
to find the king standing on the platform by the entrance with officers with
trumpets beside the king, all the people of the land rejoicing and blowing
the trumpets, and singers with their instruments leading the celebration,
14 Atalyahu rent her clothes and shouted, "Treason! Treason!" But Yehoyada
brought out the officers of hundreds, the force commanders.
"Take her out through the ranks," he said to them, "and put anyone who
follows to the sword," for the priest thought, "They should not put her to
15 death in the House of the Lord." They cleared the way for her, and she
entered the royal palace through the Horse Gate, and there they put her
to death.

16 Then Yehoyada forged a covenant between him and all the people, and
17 with the king, to be the Lord's people. All the people came to the temple
of Baal and tore it down, shattered its altars and images, and killed Matan,
the priest of Baal, in front of the altars.

18 Yehoyada then assigned the duties of the House of the Lord to the charge
of the Levite priests that David had appointed over the House of the Lord
to offer the Lord's burnt offerings, as written in Moshe's teaching, in joy
19 and song as David set down. He appointed gatekeepers at the gates of
the House of the Lord to prevent the entry of anyone with any kind of
impurity.

20 Then he had the officers of the hundreds, the nobility, the leaders of the
people, and all the people of the land escort the king down from the House
of the Lord. They came in through the upper gate of the royal palace, and
21 they set the king upon the royal throne. All the people of the land rejoiced,
and calm settled over the city. As for Atalyahu, they had put her to death
by sword.

24 1 Yoash was seven years old when he became king, and for forty years he
2 reigned in Jerusalem. His mother's name was Tziya of Be'er Sheva. Yoash
did what was right in the eyes of the Lord all the days of Yehoyada the

3 priest. Yehoyada arranged two wives for him, and he fathered sons and
daughters.

4 After some time, Yoash decided to restore the House of the Lord. He
5 gathered the priests and the Levites and said to them, "Go out to the
towns of Yehuda and collect the money due annually from all of Israel to
repair the House of your God. Take care of it right away." But the Levites
did not act right away.

6 The king summoned Yehoyada, the head, and said to him, "Why have you
not required the Levites to bring the tax imposed by Moshe, the Lord's
servant, from Yehuda and Jerusalem and from the assembly of Israel for the
7 Tent of Testimony?" For the followers of the wicked Atalyahu had violently
broken into the House of God and even used all the sacred objects of the
House of the Lord for the Baalim.

8 At the king's command, they made a chest and placed it outside the gate
9 of the Lord's House. A proclamation was issued in Yehuda and Jerusalem:
to bring to the Lord the tax that Moshe, servant of God, imposed on
10 Israel in the wilderness. And all the officials and all the people brought it
11 gladly, and they dropped it into the chest until it was full. Whenever the
Levites saw that there was a considerable amount of money in the chest,
they would bring it to the king's officers, and the royal scribe, and the
chief priest's clerk would come and empty the chest, then put it back in its
12 place. They did this regularly and collected a large amount of money. The
king and Yehoyada gave it to those who oversaw the work on the House
of the Lord; they hired masons and carpenters to restore the House of
13 the Lord as well as smiths of iron and bronze to repair the House of the
Lord. The craftsmen did their work well, and they carried out the repair
work; they restored the House of God to its original condition and made
14 reinforcements. When they had finished, they brought the remaining
money to the king and Yehoyada, and it was made into vessels for the
House of the Lord: utensils for the service and the burnt offerings, spoons,
and vessels of gold and silver. Burnt offerings were offered up regularly in
the House of the Lord all the days of Yehoyada.

15 Yehoyada grew old and full of days, and he died; he was one hundred
16 thirty years old when he died. They buried him in the City of David among
the kings because of the good he had done in Israel and for God and His
House.

17 After the death of Yehoyada, the officials of Yehuda came and pandered
18 to the king, moving the king to obey them. They abandoned the House of
the Lord, the God of their ancestors, and they worshipped sacred trees
and idols; this offense stirred up divine fury against Yehuda and Jerusalem.
19 He sent prophets among them to bring them back to the Lord, and they
warned them, but they would not pay any heed.

20 Then the spirit of God seized Zekharya son of Yehoyada the priest, and
he stood above the people.

"Thus says God," he said to them. "Why do you transgress the LORD's
commandments when you cannot succeed? Because you have abandoned
21 the LORD, He has abandoned you." But they conspired against him, and
at the king's command, they pelted him with stones in the courtyard of
22 the House of the LORD. Yoash would not remember the loyalty his father
Yehoyada had shown him, and he killed his son. As he died he said, "May
the LORD see and avenge."

23 At the end of the year, the Aramean army marched up against him. They
invaded Yehuda and Jerusalem and killed all the leaders of the people from
24 among the people and sent all their spoil to the king of Damascus. Though
the Aramean army had come with but few men, the LORD delivered a vast
force into their hands, for they had abandoned the LORD, God of their
ancestors – and on Yoash, they executed judgment.

25 When they withdrew from him, leaving him gravely wounded, his servants
conspired against him for murdering the sons[13] of Yehoyada the priest.
They killed him in his bed, and he died. And they buried him in the City of
26 David, but they did not bury him in the royal tombs. These were the ones
who conspired against him: Zavad son of Shimat the Amonite woman and
Yehozavad son of Shimrit the Moabite woman.

27 The accounts of his sons, the many pronouncements against him, and the
restoration of the House of God are recorded in the annotations of the
Book of Kings. And his son Amatzyahu reigned in his place.

25 1 Amatzyahu was twenty-five years old when he became king, and for twenty-
nine years he reigned in Jerusalem. His mother's name was Yehoadan of
2 Jerusalem. He did what was right in the eyes of the LORD, though not with
3 a whole heart. Once he had the kingdom firmly in his grasp, he killed the
4 officials who had struck down the king, his father. But he did not execute
their sons, in accordance with what is written in the Torah, the book of
Moshe, as the LORD commanded, "Parents shall not die for their children,
nor children for their parents. A person shall die only for his own sin."[14]

5 Amatzyahu gathered the men of Yehuda and assigned all of Yehuda and
Binyamin, according to ancestral house, under officers of thousands and
officers of hundreds. He mustered those who were twenty years old and
up and found that there were 300,000 men fit for military service, able to
6 wield spear and shield. Then he hired 100,000 from Israel for one hundred
talents of silver.

7 But a man of God came to him and said, "O king, the army of Israel must
not accompany you, for the LORD is not with Israel – not with any of the

13 | Verses 20–21 above describe only the killing of Zekharya.

14 | Deuteronomy 24:16.

8 people of Efrayim. Unless you go by yourself and battle fiercely, God will
bring you down before the enemy, for God has the power to aid or to
overthrow."
9 "But what of the hundred talents I gave for the Israelite mercenaries?"
Amatzyahu said to the man of God.
"The LORD can give you much more than that," said the man of God.

10 So Amatzyahu discharged the mercenaries who had come to him from
Efrayim, sending them back home; they were furious with Yehuda, and
they went back home in a fierce rage.

11 Amatzyahu took courage and led his troops down to the Valley of Salt,
12 and he struck down ten thousand of the men of Se'ir. And the men of
Yehuda took another ten thousand captives alive; they brought them to
the clifftop and threw them down from the clifftop; they were all dashed to
13 pieces. But the mercenaries Amatzyahu had sent back without letting them
accompany him in battle attacked the towns of Yehuda from Shomron to
Beit Ḥoron, struck down three thousand people, and seized large amounts
of spoil.

14 When Amatzyahu came back from slaughtering the Edomites, he brought
the gods of the people of Se'ir. He set them up as his gods and bowed
15 and offered sacrifices before them. Then the LORD's fury raged against
Amatzyahu, and he sent a prophet to him.
"Why did you seek out that people's gods when they could not save their
own people from your hands?" he said to him.
16 "Who made you the king's counselor?" he said, cutting him off. "Leave off!
Why should you be struck down?"
So the prophet left off, but added, "I know that God has planned to destroy
you because you acted thus and would not listen to my counsel."

17 Then Amatzyahu, king of Yehuda, took counsel and sent to Yoash son
of Yehoaḥaz son of Yehu, king of Israel, saying, "Come, let us meet
face-to-face."
18 Yoash, king of Israel, sent a response to Amatzyahu, king of Yehuda:
"The thistle in Lebanon sent to the cedar in Lebanon, saying, 'Give your
daughter as a wife for my son.' But a wild beast in Lebanon passed by and
trampled the thistle.
19 You boast that you have defeated Edom, and your arrogant heart craves
more glory. Now stay at home; why should you provoke disaster and fall
down together with Yehuda?"

20 But Amatzyahu paid no heed, for God had determined to hand them
21 over because they had sought out the gods of Edom. Yoash, king of Israel,
marched up and met Amatzyahu, king of Yehuda, face-to-face in Beit
22 Shemesh of Yehuda. Yehuda was routed before Israel, and every man
23 fled back to his tent. As for Amatzyahu, king of Yehuda, the son of Yoash

son of Yehoaḥaz – Yoash, king of Israel, captured him in Beit Shemesh
and brought him to Jerusalem. He demolished four hundred cubits of
24 the Jerusalem wall from the Efrayim Gate to the Corner Gate. And with
all the gold and silver, all the vessels to be found in the House of God
under Oved Edom's care, the royal treasures, and hostages, he returned
to Shomron.

25 Amatzyahu son of Yoash, king of Yehuda, lived on for fifteen years after
26 the death of Yoash son of Yehoaḥaz, king of Israel. As for the rest of
Amatzyahu's history, earlier and later, it is recorded in the Book of Kings
27 of Yehuda and Israel. From the time that Amatzyahu turned away from
the Lord, a conspiracy was formed against him in Jerusalem, and he fled
to Lakhish, but they sent after him to Lakhish and assassinated him there.
28 They conveyed his body back by horse and buried him with his ancestors
in the city of Yehuda.

26 1 Then all the people of Yehuda took Uziyahu, who was sixteen years old,
2 and made him king in place of his father Amatzyahu. He was the one
who rebuilt Eilot and restored it to Yehuda once the king slept with his
3 ancestors. Uziyahu was sixteen years old when he became king, and for
fifty-two years he reigned in Jerusalem. His mother's name was Yekholya
4 of Jerusalem. He did what was right in the eyes of the Lord just as his
father Amatzyahu had done.

5 He was determined to seek God in the time of Zekharyahu, who understood God's visions. As long as he sought the Lord, God made him pros-
6 per. He went out to fight against the Philistines and breached the walls of
Gat, Yavneh, and Ashdod, and he built cities in Ashdod and among the
7 Philistines. God helped him against the Philistines, the Arabs who live
8 in Gur Baal, and the Meunites. The Amonites offered tribute to Uziyahu,
and his fame reached all the way to the border of Egypt, for he grew very
powerful.

9 Uziyahu built towers in Jerusalem on the Corner Gate and the Valley
10 Gate and at the Angle,[15] and he reinforced them. He built towers in the
wilderness and dug many cisterns because he had a wealth of livestock in
the lowlands and on the plain; he had farmers and vinedressers in the hills
and the fertile lands, for he had a deep love for the soil.

11 Uziyahu had a military force of soldiers ready for war, organized by
divisions commanded by Ye'iel the recruitment officer and Maaseyahu
the captain under the direction of Ḥananyahu, one of the royal officers.
12 13 The ancestral heads in charge of the fighting men numbered 2,600; they
commanded an army of 307,500 ready for war, a powerful force to support
14 the king against the enemy. Uziyahu provided shields and spears, helmets
and mail, and bows and slingstones for his entire army.

15 | A certain spot in the eastern wall.

15 In Jerusalem he invented ingenious devices that could shoot arrows and
large stones from the towers and corner defenses. And his fame spread far
and wide, for he had been miraculously helped until he grew powerful.

16 But as he grew powerful, his arrogant heart grew corrupt, and he broke
faith with the LORD his God: he entered the LORD's Sanctuary to offer
17 incense on the incense altar. Azaryahu the priest followed him with eighty
18 of the LORD's priests – powerful men – and confronted King Uziyahu.
"It is not for you, Uziyahu, to offer incense to the LORD," they said to
him. "That is for the priests, the descendants of Aharon, who have been
consecrated to offer incense. Leave the Sanctuary because you broke
faith – it will bring you no glory from the LORD God."
19 Uziyahu – with the incense burner in his hand, about to offer incense –
flew into a rage, but as he raged at the priests, skin-blight broke out on his
forehead before the priests in the House of the LORD by the incense altar.
20 Azaryahu the head priest and all the priests turned to him – and suddenly,
he had skin-blight on his forehead! They rushed him out of there, and he
too was in a hurry to leave, for the LORD had struck him.

21 King Uziyahu remained a blighted man until his dying day. He remained
in secluded quarters, blighted, banned from the House of the LORD, while
his son Yotam took charge of the palace and governed the people of the
land.

22 As for the rest of Uziyahu's history, earlier and later, it is recorded by the
23 prophet Yeshayahu son of Amotz. And Uziyahu slept with his ancestors,
and they buried him with his ancestors in the open field near the royal
burial grounds, for they said, "He is blighted." And his son Yotam reigned
in his place.

27 1 Yotam was twenty-five years old when he became king, and for sixteen
years he reigned in Jerusalem. His mother's name was Yerusha daughter
2 of Tzadok. He did what was right in the eyes of the LORD just as his father
Uziyahu had done, but he did not enter the LORD's Sanctuary. And the
people were still corrupt.

3 He built the upper gate of the House of the LORD and did extensive
4 construction on the Ofel Wall. He built towns in the hill country of Yehuda
and fortresses and towers in the woodland.

5 He fought against the king of the Amonites and overpowered them,
and that year, the Amonites paid him one hundred talents of silver, ten
thousand *kor* of wheat, and ten thousand *kor* of barley. The Amonites gave
him the same amount in the second and third years as well.

6 And Yotam grew powerful, for he was committed to the ways of the LORD
7 his God. The rest of Yotam's history, and all his wars and ways, are recorded
8 in the Book of Kings of Israel and Yehuda. He was twenty-five years old

9 when he became king, and for sixteen years, he reigned in Jerusalem. And
Yotam slept with his ancestors, and they buried him in the City of David.
And his son Aḥaz reigned in his place.

28 1 Aḥaz was twenty years old when he became king, and for sixteen years
he reigned in Jerusalem. But he did not do what was right in the eyes of
2 the Lord like his ancestor David. He followed in the ways of the kings of
3 Israel and even made images for the Baalim; he offered sacrifices in the
Valley of Ben Hinom and burned his sons to death in fire, imitating the
abominations of the nations whom the Lord had dispossessed before
4 the Israelites. He made sacrifices and offerings at the high shrines and on
hilltops and under every shady tree.

5 The Lord his God handed him over to the king of Aram. He defeated
him, took a great number of his people captive, and led them to Damascus.
He was also handed over to the king of Israel, who dealt him a crushing
6 blow. Pekaḥ son of Remalyahu killed 120,000 of Yehuda in a single day,
all powerful warriors, for they had abandoned the Lord, God of their
7 ancestors. Zikhri, a warrior of Efrayim, killed Maaseyahu the king's son,
and Azrikam the chief officer of the palace, and Elkana, second to the
8 king. And the Israelites took 200,000 of their brothers captive – women,
boys, and girls; they also seized vast amounts of spoil from them, and they
brought the spoil to Shomron.

9 But a prophet of the Lord by the name of Oded was there, and he went
out before the army arriving at Shomron.

"Behold!" he said to them. "In His wrath against Yehuda, the Lord, God of
your ancestors, has handed them over to you. But you have killed them in
10 such anger that it has reached the heavens. Do you now intend to subjugate
the people of Yehuda and Jerusalem as your own slaves and maidservants?
Are you not guilty of an offense against the Lord your God yourselves?
11 Now listen to me: send back those you took captive from among your
brothers, for the Lord's wrath rages against you."

12 Certain leaders of Efrayim – Azaryahu son of Yehoḥanan, Berekhyahu son
of Meshilemot, Yeḥizkiyahu son of Shalum, and Amasa son of Ḥadlai –
then rose before the incoming army.
13 "You must not bring the captives here," they said to them. "It will only cause
us to offend the Lord. Do you wish to exacerbate our offense and our sins?
For our offense is already grave, and His wrath rages against Israel."

14 So the soldiers released the captives and the spoil in the presence of the
15 officers and the whole crowd. Then the aforementioned men took the
captives, and from the spoil they clothed all those who were naked. They
provided them with clothes, shoes, food, drink, and balm, helped the weak
mount donkeys, and led them to their kinsmen in Yeriḥo, city of palms.
Then they went back to Shomron.

16 17 At that time, King Aḥaz sent to the kings of Assyria for aid. For the
Edomites had invaded once more, defeating Yehuda and taking captives,
while the Philistines had raided the towns in the lowlands and the Negev
18 of Yehuda. They captured Beit Shemesh, Ayalon, Gederot, Sokho with
its villages, Timna with its villages, and Gimzo with its villages, and they
19 settled there. For the Lord had humbled Yehuda because of King Aḥaz of
Israel, for he had let Yehuda run wild and had broken faith with the Lord.
20 King Tilegat Pilne'eser of Assyria indeed came to him, but to oppress
21 him, not to support him. For Aḥaz had ransacked the House of the Lord
and the palace of the king and the officials and paid tribute to the king of
Assyria – to no avail.

22 In his time of crisis, he still broke faith with the Lord, that King Aḥaz.
23 He sacrificed to the gods of those who had defeated them – Damascus –
thinking, "If the gods of the kings of Aram are helping them, I will sacrifice
to them, and they will help me." But they only led to his ruin and to the
ruin of all Israel.

24 Aḥaz gathered all the vessels of the House of God, broke them in pieces,
and shut up the doors of the House of the Lord. And he made himself
25 altars in every corner of Jerusalem. In every town in Yehuda, he built
high shrines for sacrifices to other gods, angering the Lord, God of his
ancestors.

26 The rest of his history and all his ways, earlier and later, are recorded in
27 the Book of Kings of Yehuda and Israel. And Aḥaz slept with his ancestors,
and they buried him in the city of Jerusalem, but they did not bring him to
the royal tombs of Israel. And his son Yeḥizkiyahu reigned in his place.

29 1 Yeḥizkiyahu became king at the age of twenty-five, and for twenty-nine
years he reigned in Jerusalem. His mother's name was Aviya daughter of
2 Zekharyahu. He did what was right in the eyes of the Lord just as his
ancestor David did.

3 In the first month of the first year of his reign, he opened the doors of the
4 House of the Lord and repaired them. He brought in the priests and the
Levites and gathered them in the eastern square.

5 "Listen to me, Levites," he said to them. "Now sanctify yourselves and
sanctify the House of the Lord, God of your ancestors – remove the
6 contamination from the Holy Place. For our fathers have broken faith and
done what is evil in the eyes of the Lord our God. They abandoned Him
and turned away from the Lord's dwelling place; they turned their backs.
7 They also shut the doors of the Hall and put out the lamps; they never
burned incense and never offered up burnt offerings in the Sanctuary to
8 the God of Israel. And the Lord grew furious with Yehuda and Jerusalem,
and He made them an object of shock, a place of desolation and shrieking,
9 as you see with your own eyes – our fathers fell by the sword, and our sons
and daughters and wives were taken captive because of this.

10 "Now – I have set my heart on forming a covenant with the LORD, God
11 of Israel, so that His fierce anger will leave us. Now – my sons, do not be
passive, for the LORD has chosen you to stand and serve before Him, to
be His ministers and make offerings to Him."

12 Then the Levites arose: Maḥat son of Amasai and Yoel son of Azaryahu,
of the sons of the Kehatites; of the sons of Merari, Kish son of Avdi and
Azaryahu son of Yehalelel; of the Gershonites, Yoaḥ son of Zima and Eden
13 son of Yoaḥ; of the sons of Elitzafan, Shimri and Yei'el; of the sons of Asaf,
14 Zekharyahu and Matanyahu;of the sons of Heiman, Yeḥiel and Shimi; and
15 of the sons of Yedutun, Shemaya and Uziel. They gathered their kinsmen
and sanctified themselves, and as the king had commanded by the word
of the LORD, they went in to purify the House of the LORD.

16 The priests went in to purify the inner section of the House of the LORD,
and they brought out all the impurity that they found in the LORD's
Sanctuary to the courtyard of the House of the LORD; the Levites then
took it and carried it out to Kidron Valley.

17 They began the sanctification on the first day of the first month, and by
the eighth day of the month they reached the Hall of the LORD; they
sanctified the House of the LORD in eight days, and by the sixteenth of
the first month, they had finished.

18 They went in to King Ḥizkiyahu and reported, "We have purified the entire
House of the LORD, the altar of burnt offerings and all its utensils, and
19 the table for the showbread and all its utensils. All the vessels that King
Aḥaz despised when he broke faith during his reign, we have restored and
sanctified – and here they are before the Altar of the LORD."

20 King Yeḥizkiyahu rose early, gathered the city officials, and went up to the
21 House of the LORD. They brought seven bulls, seven rams, seven lambs,
and seven buck goats for a purification offering on behalf of the kingdom,
the Sanctuary, and Yehuda, and he ordered the descendants of Aharon,
22 the priests, to offer it up on the Altar of the LORD. They slaughtered the
bulls, and the priests received the blood and dashed it against the altar;
they slaughtered the rams and dashed the blood against the altar; they
23 slaughtered the lambs and dashed the blood against the altar. Then they
led the goats for the purification offering before the king and the assembly,
24 and they rested their hands upon them. The priests slaughtered them and
offered their blood as a purification offering on the altar to atone for all of
Israel, for the king had designated the burnt offering and the purification
offering on behalf of all Israel.

25 He stationed the Levites at the House of the LORD with cymbals, harps,
and lyres, as ordered by David, the seer Gad, and the prophet Natan, for
26 the LORD's commandment was issued through His prophets. The Levites
27 stood with David's instruments, the priest with trumpets. Ḥizkiyahu then

gave the order for the burnt offering to be offered up on the altar, and as
the burnt offering began, the song to the Lord and the trumpets began as
28 well, accompanied by the instruments of David, king of Israel. The whole
crowd worshipped as the singers sang and the trumpets played on until
29 the burnt offering was finished. Once the offering was finished, the king
30 and everyone in his presence kneeled and worshipped. King Yeḥizkiyahu
and the officials ordered the Levites to sing praise to the Lord with the
words of David and the seer Asaf, and they praised them in sheer joy, knelt
down low, and bowed.

31 Then Yeḥizkiyahu spoke up and said, "You have now consecrated yourselves
to the Lord. Come forth and bring sacrifices and thanksgiving offerings
to the House of the Lord!" And the crowd came bearing sacrifices and
thanksgiving offerings, and all those with a generous heart brought burnt
32 offerings: the number of burnt offerings that the crowd brought was
seventy bulls, one hundred rams, and two hundred lambs – all these
33 were for burnt offerings to the Lord. There were six hundred bulls and
34 three thousand sheep for sacred offerings, but the priests were too few
to manage the flaying of all the burnt offerings, so their Levite kinsmen
assisted them until other priests had sanctified themselves, and the work
was done. The Levites were more conscientious than the priests about
sanctifying themselves.

35 Besides the great number of burnt offerings, there were also the fat from
the peace offerings and the libations for the burnt offerings. Thus the
36 service of the House of the Lord was reinstated. And Yeḥizkiyahu and
all the people rejoiced over what God had provided for the people, for it
had come about so suddenly.

30 1 Yeḥizkiyahu sent to all Israel and Yehuda – he even wrote letters to
Efrayim and Menashe – to come to the House of the Lord in Jerusalem
2 to celebrate Passover before the Lord, God of Israel. The king and his
officials, together with all the assembly in Jerusalem, decided to celebrate
3 Passover in the second month – they were not able to celebrate on the
usual date because not enough priests had sanctified themselves, and the
4 people had not yet gathered to Jerusalem – and the plan seemed right to
5 the king and all the assembly.[16] So they issued a proclamation to spread
the word throughout Israel from Be'er Sheva to Dan to come and celebrate
Passover before the Lord, God of Israel, in Jerusalem, for they had rarely
kept it as prescribed.

6 The couriers set out all over Israel and Yehuda with letters from the king
and his officials proclaiming the royal decree:

"Israelites, come back to the Lord, God of Avraham, Yitzḥak, and Yisrael,
and He will come back to the remnant of you who escaped from the hands

16 | Cf. Numbers 9:6–13.

7 of the kings of Assyria. Do not be like your fathers and brothers who
broke faith with the LORD, God of their ancestors – He gave them up to
desolation as you can see.

8 "Now – do not stiffen your necks like your fathers; yield to the LORD and
come to His Sanctuary, which He has sanctified forever. Serve the LORD
9 your God, and His fierce wrath will turn away from you. If you come back
to the LORD, your brothers' and children's captors will show them mercy,
and they will come back to this land, for the LORD your God is gracious
and merciful, and He will not turn His face away from you if you come
back to Him."

10 As the couriers passed from city to city in the land of Efrayim and Menashe
11 and up to Zevulun, they were ridiculed and mocked. Yet some people from
Asher, Menashe, and Zevulun humbled themselves and came to Jerusalem.
12 In Yehuda God's hand was upon them and made them one in heart to keep
the king's and the officials' order about the word of the LORD.

13 So a multitude of people gathered to Jerusalem to celebrate the Festival
14 of Unleavened Bread in the second month – a massive crowd. They set to
work and removed the altars that were around Jerusalem; they removed all
15 the incense altars and cast them into the Kidron Valley. They slaughtered
the Passover sacrifice on the fourteenth of the second month. Having
been ashamed, the priests and the Levites had sanctified themselves and
16 brought burnt offerings to the House of the LORD. Now they took up
their usual positions as dictated by the teaching of Moshe, man of God,
17 with the priests dashing the blood that the Levites handed to them. Many
among the crowd had not sanctified themselves, and the Levites were
in charge of slaughtering the Passover sacrifice for all those who were
18 impure so that it would be holy to the LORD. Most of the people – many
of them from Efrayim, Menashe, Yissakhar and Zevulun – ate the Passover
sacrifice without purifying themselves despite what was prescribed. But
Yeḥizkiyahu prayed on their behalf, saying, "May the God LORD atone for
19 all those who have set their heart on seeking God the LORD, God of their
20 ancestors, even if they are not purified for the Sanctuary." The LORD heard
Yeḥizkiyahu and forgave the people.

21 The Israelites who were in Jerusalem celebrated the Festival of Unleavened
Bread for seven days with great joy. Day by day, the Levites and the priests
sang praise to the LORD, playing to the LORD on powerful instruments.
22 Yeḥizkiyahu spoke encouragingly to all the Levites who showed great
promise in their service to the LORD.

They ate the food of the festival for seven days, sacrificing peace offerings
and giving thanks to the LORD, God of their ancestors.

23 Then all the assembly agreed together to celebrate for another seven days,
24 and they celebrated for seven days in joy, for Ḥizkiyahu king of Yehuda

provided the assembly with a thousand bulls and seven thousand sheep,
the officials provided the assembly with a thousand bulls and ten thousand
25 sheep, and the priests had sanctified themselves in great numbers. And
there was rejoicing among all the assembly of Yehuda, the priests, and
the Levites, all the assembly that had come from Israel, and the outsiders
26 who had come from the land of Israel to live in Yehuda – there was great
joy in Jerusalem, for nothing like this had happened in Jerusalem since the
27 days of Shlomo son of David, king of Israel. And the Levite priests rose
and blessed the people; their voices rang out, and their prayers reached
His Holy abode in heaven.

31 1 When all of this was over, all Israel who were present went out to the towns
of Yehuda and tore down the worship pillars, cut down the sacred trees,
and razed the high shrines and the altars throughout Yehuda, Binyamin,
Efrayim, and Menashe, to the very last one. Then all the Israelites went
back, each to his own property in his own town.

2 Yeḥizkiyahu appointed the divisions of priests and Levites, division by
division, each of the priests and Levites according to their service: for
burnt offerings and peace offerings, to minister, and to give thanks and sing
3 praise at the gates of the Lord's courts. The king's contribution from his
own possessions was for the burnt offerings: for the morning and evening
burnt offerings and for the burnt offerings for the Sabbaths, the New
4 Moons, and the festivals, as written in the Lord's Torah. And he ordered
the people, the inhabitants of Jerusalem, to give the portions due to the
priests and the Levites in order to encourage their devotion to the Lord's
5 Torah. As soon as word spread, the Israelites brought large amounts of
their first grain, wine, oil, honey, and all their produce – they brought
6 generous tithes of everything. The people of Israel and Yehuda living in the
towns of Yehuda also brought tithes of cattle and sheep and tithes of sacred
items that they had consecrated to the Lord their God, and they laid it
7 out in many heaps. By the third month, the heaps began to accumulate,
8 and they were finished by the seventh month. When Yeḥizkiyahu and the
officials came and saw the heaps, they blessed the Lord and His people
9 Israel. Yeḥizkiyahu questioned the priests and the Levites about the heaps,
10 and the priest Azaryahu, head of the house of Tzadok, answered him.
"Since they began to bring the contributions into the House of the Lord,"
he said, "we have eaten our fill and had plenty left over, for the Lord has
blessed His people, and this great amount still remains."

11 Yeḥizkiyahu then gave orders to arrange store chambers in the House of the
12 Lord, and they arranged them; they faithfully brought in the contributions,
the tithes, and the consecrated items. The chief officer in charge of them
13 was Kananyahu the Levite, with his brother Shimi as second, while Yeḥiel,
Azazyahu, Naḥat, Asael, Yerimot, Yozavad, Eliel, Yismakhyahu, Maḥat, and
Benayahu were overseers assisting Kananyahu and his brother Shimi by
appointment of King Yeḥizkiyahu and of Azaryahu, the chief officer of the

14 House of God. Koreh son of Yimna the Levite, keeper of the east gate, was
in charge of the freewill offerings to God, of distributing the contribution
15 reserved for the Lord, and of the most holy offerings. Eden, Minyamin,
Yeshua, Shemayahu, Amaryahu, and Shekhanyahu were his loyal assistants
in the priestly towns, distributing their kinsmen's portions by division to
16 great and small alike in addition to distributing the daily rations to all males
three years and up – registered by genealogy – who came to the House of
the Lord for service in shifts according to their divisions.

17 The priests were registered according to their ancestral houses while
Levites from twenty years and up were listed according to their offices
18 within their divisions. Both groups were registered by genealogy with
all their young children, their wives, their sons, and their daughters, for
19 in their duty they led lives of holiness. As for the priestly descendants of
Aharon in the fields of common land adjoining their cities, in every city
the aforementioned men distributed portions to every male priest and to
every Levite who was registered by genealogy.

20 Yeḥizkiyahu instituted this throughout Yehuda; he did what was good and
21 right and true before the Lord his God. Every task he undertook – for the
service of the House of God, the Torah, and the commandment of seeking
his God – he did with all his heart, and he was successful.

32 1 After these faithful deeds came Sanḥeriv, king of Assyria. He invaded
Yehuda and set up camp next to the fortified cities, intending to conquer
2 them for himself. When Yeḥizkiyahu saw that Sanḥeriv had come and
3 was intent on war over Jerusalem, he took counsel with his officials and
warriors about stopping the flow of springs that were outside the city, and
4 they supported him. A great crowd gathered, and they stopped up all the
springs and the wadi that flowed through the land, saying, "Why should
the kings of Assyria come and find water in abundance?"

5 Determined, he repaired all the breaches in the wall, raised up towers over
it, and built another wall outside it. He reinforced the Milo in the City
6 of David, and he commissioned weapons and shields in abundance. He
appointed battle officers over the people and gathered them to him by the
square at the city gate to encourage them with these words:

7 "Be strong and determined; do not fear or hesitate in the face of the
Assyrian king and all the horde that accompany him, for what is with us is
8 far greater than what is with him. With him is but an arm of flesh; with us
is the Lord our God to help us and fight our battles." And the people were
encouraged by the words of King Yeḥizkiyahu of Yehuda.

9 After this, King Sanḥeriv of Assyria – who was stationed at Lakhish
with all his forces – sent his servants with this message to Jerusalem to
King Yeḥizkiyahu of Yehuda and to all the people of Yehuda who lived in
Jerusalem:

10 "Thus says Sanḥeriv, king of Assyria: In what do you place your trust,
11 that you remain under siege in Jerusalem? Yeḥizkiyahu is misleading
you – condemning you to die in hunger and in thirst – by saying, 'The
12 Lord our God will save us from the king of Assyria's hand.' Is this not
the same Yeḥizkiyahu who removed his high shrines and altars and told
Yehuda and Jerusalem, 'Before a single altar you shall worship and offer
13 sacrifices'? Are you unaware of what my ancestors and I have done to all
the peoples of other lands? Have the gods of the nations of other lands
14 managed to save their lands from my hand? Who among all the gods of
these nations utterly destroyed by my ancestors managed to save their
people from my hand, that your God will manage to save you from my
hand?

15 "Now do not let Ḥizkiyahu deceive you or mislead you thus; do not believe
him, for no god from any nation or any kingdom has managed to save his
people from my hand or the hand of my ancestors. Your God will not
manage to save you from my hand either."

16 His servants continued to disparage the Lord God and His servant
17 Yeḥizkiyahu; he also wrote letters that ridiculed the Lord, God of Israel,
claiming about Him, "Just as the gods of the nations of other lands failed
to save their nations from my hand, the God of Yeḥizkiyahu will fail to
18 save His people from my hand." They shouted out in Hebrew at the people
of Jerusalem on the wall to frighten and intimidate them so as to capture
19 the city. They spoke about the God of Jerusalem as if they were speaking
about the gods of the peoples of other lands, made by human hands.

20 Then King Yeḥizkiyahu and the prophet Yishayahu son of Amotz prayed
21 about this and cried out to heaven. And the Lord sent an angel who
annihilated every warrior, commander, and officer in the camp of the
king of Assyria, who then slunk back to his land in utter disgrace. When
he reached the temple of his gods, some of his very own sons struck him
down by the sword.

22 Thus the Lord saved Yeḥizkiyahu and the people of Jerusalem from the
hands of King Sanḥeriv of Assyria and everyone else; He provided for
23 them in every way. Many came to Jerusalem to offer tribute to the Lord
and treasures to Yeḥizkiyahu, king of Yehuda, and he was exalted in the
eyes of all the nations ever after.

24 At that time, Yeḥizkiyahu became ill, on the verge of death. He prayed to
25 the Lord, and He answered him and gave him a sign. But Yeḥizkiyahu did
not respond as would befit the favor he had been granted, for he had grown
26 arrogant, and wrath came upon him and upon Yehuda and Jerusalem. Then
Yeḥizkiyahu humbled himself because of his arrogant heart – he and the
people of Jerusalem – and the wrath of the Lord did not come upon them
in Yeḥizkiyahu's time.

27 Yeḥizkiyahu had great riches and honor, and he made himself treasuries
for silver, gold, gems, spices, decorative shields, and all kinds of precious
28 objects, as well as storehouses for produce of grain, wine, and oil, stalls for
29 all kinds of animals, and stables for livestock. And he acquired cities and
vast flocks of sheep and cattle, for God had endowed him with a wealth
of possessions.

30 This was the same Yeḥizkiyahu who dammed the upper pool of the waters
of Giḥon and directed them down to the western side of the City of David.
Yeḥizkiyahu was successful in all that he did.

31 As for the delegation of Babylonian officials that sent to him to inquire
about the sign that was in the land – God left him to his own devices to
test him, to learn all that was in his heart.

32 The rest of Yeḥizkiyahu's history and his loyal deeds are recorded in the
vision of the prophet Yeshayahu son of Amotz in the Book of Kings of
33 Yehuda and Israel. And Yeḥizkiyahu slept with his ancestors, and they
buried him in the upper section of the tombs of David's descendants; all
of Yehuda and the people of Jerusalem honored him upon his death. And
his son Menashe reigned in his place.

33 1 Menashe was twelve years old when he became king, and for fifty-five
2 years he reigned in Jerusalem. He did what was evil in the eyes of the LORD,
imitating the horrors of the nations whom the LORD had dispossessed
3 before the Israelites. He rebuilt the high shrines that his father Yeḥizkiyahu
had torn down, and he erected altars for the Baalim, made sacred trees,
4 and bowed down to all the heavenly hosts and served them. He even built
altars in the House of the LORD, of which the LORD had said, "My name
5 will be in Jerusalem forever." He built altars for all the heavenly hosts in
6 both courtyards of the House of the LORD; he passed his sons through
the fire in the Valley of Hinom; he practiced augury, divination, and
soothsaying, and consulted ghosts and spirits – he did so much that was
evil in the eyes of the LORD, angering Him.

7 He placed a carved idol that he had made in the House of God, of which
God promised to David and his son Shlomo: "In this House, and in
Jerusalem, which I have chosen out of all the tribes of Israel, I will establish
8 My name forever. And never again will I turn Israel's feet away from the
land that I granted your ancestors – so long as they carefully observe all
that I commanded them, all the Torah, statutes, and laws given through
Moshe."

9 But Menashe led Yehuda and the people of Jerusalem astray to do even
worse evil than the nations that the LORD had destroyed before the
10 Israelites. The LORD spoke to Menashe and his people, but they would not
11 listen. So the LORD brought the army officers of the king of Assyria against
them; they captured Menashe with hooks, bound him with fetters, and

12 led him to Babylon. In his distress, he pleaded for the favor of the LORD
13 his God and humbled himself deeply before the God of his ancestors. He
prayed to Him; He responded to his prayer and heard his plea, and He
returned him to his kingdom in Jerusalem. Menashe recognized that the
LORD is God.

14 After that, he built an outer wall for the City of David to the west of
the Giḥon, in the wadi, reaching the Fish Gate and encircling the Ofel;
he raised it up high. And he appointed military commanders in all the
fortified cities in Yehuda.

15 He removed the foreign gods and the idol from the House of the LORD
along with all the altars he built on the hill of the House of the LORD and
16 in Jerusalem, and he cast them outside of the city. He restored the Altar of
the LORD and sacrificed peace offerings and thanksgiving offerings upon
17 it, and he ordered Yehuda to serve the LORD, God of Israel. The people
still offered sacrifices upon the high shrines, but only to the LORD their
God.

18 The rest of Menashe's history, his prayer to his God, and the words of the
seers who spoke to him in the name of the LORD, God of Israel, are in the
19 chronicles of the kings of Israel. His prayer and God's response to it, all
his sins and how he broke faith, and the places where he built high shrines
and set up sacred trees and idols before he humbled himself are recorded
20 in the chronicles of Ḥozai. And Menashe slept with his ancestors, and he
was buried by his palace. And his son Amon reigned in his place.

21 Amon was twenty-two years old when he became king, and for two years
22 he reigned in Jerusalem. He did what was evil in the eyes of the LORD, as
his father Menashe had done. He sacrificed to all the idols that his father
23 Menashe had made and worshipped them. But he did not humble himself
before the LORD as his father Menashe had humbled himself; instead,
24 Amon incurred more and more guilt. So his servants formed a conspiracy
25 against him and assassinated him in his palace. But the people of the land
struck down all those who had conspired against King Amon, and the
people of the land made his son Yoshiyahu king in his place.

34 1 Yoshiyahu was eight years old when he became king, and for thirty-one
2 years he reigned in Jerusalem. He did what was right in the eyes of the
LORD, following in the ways of his ancestor David; he strayed neither
right nor left.

3 In the eighth year of his reign, though he was still young, he began to seek
out the God of his ancestor David; and in the twelfth year, he began to
purge Yehuda and Jerusalem of the high shrines and sacred trees and idols
4 and images. Under his supervision they smashed the altars of the Baalim,
cut down the sun altars that were built above them, razed the sacred trees,
the idols, and the images, ground them to dust, and scattered them over

5 the graves of those who had sacrificed to them. He burned the bones of
the idolatrous priests on their own altars and thus purged Yehuda and
Jerusalem.

6 In the towns of Menashe, Efrayim, Shimon, and as far as Naftali – with
7 ruins all around – he smashed the altars, ground the sacred trees and the
idols to dust, and cut down all the sun altars all over the land of Israel. Then
he went back to Jerusalem.

8 In the eighteenth year of his reign, after purging the land and the House, he
sent Shafan son of Atzalyahu, Maaseyahu the city governor, and Yoaḥ son
9 of Yoaḥaz, the herald, to repair the House of the Lord his God. They came
to Ḥilkiyahu the High Priest and gave him the silver that had been brought
to the House of God – that which the Levite guardians of the threshold
had collected from Menashe, Efrayim, and all the remnant of Israel, and
10 from Yehuda, Binyamin, and the people of Jerusalem.[17] They gave it to the
foremen in charge of the House of the Lord, and they paid it out to the
workers in the House of the Lord who worked to keep the House in repair,
11 and they gave some to the carpenters and the builders to purchase quarry
stones and timber for binders and for roof beams for the buildings that
12 the kings of Yehuda had let fall into ruin. The people were honest workers,
and they were supervised by the Levites Yaḥat and Ovadyahu of the sons
of Merari, and Zekharya and Meshulam of the sons of Kehat, who were in
13 charge. Other Levites, all of them skilled with musical instruments, were
in charge of the porters, directing all those who worked at various tasks;
other Levites were scribes, officers, and gatekeepers.

14 As they took out the money that had been brought to the House of the
Lord, Ḥilkiyahu the priest found a scroll of the Lord's Torah given by
15 Moshe. Ḥilkiyahu remarked to the scribe Shafan, "I found a scroll of the
teaching in the House of the Lord," and Ḥilkiyahu gave the book to
Shafan.

16 Shafan brought the book to the king and further reported to the king:
17 "Your servants are fulfilling all that has been assigned to them. They have
melted down the silver found in the House of the Lord, and they have
18 paid it out to the foremen and to the workers." Then Shafan the scribe told
the king, "The priest Ḥilkiyahu gave me a scroll," and Shafan read from it
before the king.

19 20 When the king heard the words of the teaching, he rent his clothes. And
the king gave orders to Ḥilkiyahu, Aḥikam son of Shafan, Avdon son of
21 Mikha, Shafan the scribe, and Asaya, the king's servant: "Go, inquire of
the Lord on my behalf and on behalf of those who are left in Israel and
Yehuda, about the words of this scroll that has just been found. For great

17 | See note on 19:8.

was the fury the LORD poured out on us when our ancestors did not keep
the LORD's word and do all that was prescribed in this book."

22 The priest Ḥilkiyahu and those sent by the king went to Ḥulda the prophet,
wife of Shalum son of Tok'hat son of Ḥasra, keeper of the wardrobe – she
lived in Jerusalem in the Mishneh[18] – and they spoke to her about this.
23 She said to them, "Thus says the LORD, God of Israel: Say to the man who
24 sent you to me: Thus says the LORD: I am about to bring disaster upon
this place and its inhabitants – all the curses written in the scroll they read
25 out before the king of Yehuda. Because they left Me and made sacrifices to
other gods to anger Me with all their practices, My fury will be poured out
26 on this place, and it will not be extinguished. And to the king of Yehuda,
who sent you to inquire of the LORD, say this: Thus says the LORD, God of
27 Israel: Concerning the words that you heard, because you softened your
heart and you humbled yourself before God when you heard His promise
about this place and its people, and you humbled yourself before Me and
rent your clothes and wept before Me, I, too have heard. The LORD has
28 spoken. I will gather you to your ancestors, and you will be gathered to
your grave peacefully; your own eyes will not see all the disaster I will bring
upon this place and its inhabitants." And they reported back to the king.

29 30 The king sent and gathered all the elders of Yehuda and Jerusalem. And the
king went up to the House of the LORD along with all the men of Yehuda
and the inhabitants of Jerusalem, the priests and the Levites and all the
people, great and small. And in their hearing, he read out all the words
of the scroll of the covenant that had been found in the House of the
31 LORD. The king stood in his place and reinstated the covenant before the
LORD: to follow the LORD and to keep His commandments, decrees, and
laws with all his heart and all his soul, to fulfill the words of the covenant
32 as written in this book. He then pledged all those who were present in
Jerusalem and Binyamin, and the people of Jerusalem committed to the
covenant of God, the God of their ancestors.

33 Then Yoshiyahu removed all the abominations from all the territory that
belonged to the Israelites and obliged all who were in Israel to worship
the LORD, their God; all his life, they did not stray from the LORD, God
of their ancestors.

35 1 Yoshiyahu celebrated Passover for the LORD in Jerusalem; they slaughtered
2 the Passover sacrifice on the fourteenth of the first month. He reappointed
the priests to their shifts and encouraged them in the service of the House
3 of the LORD. And he instructed the Levites, who taught all Israel and who
were holy to the LORD, "Place the holy Ark in the House built by Shlomo
son of David, king of Israel; no longer shall you carry it on your shoulders.
4 Now serve the LORD your God and His people Israel; group yourselves
according to your ancestral houses in your divisions as instructed by

18 | A quarter in the city.

5 both David, king of Israel, and Shlomo his son. Take positions in the
Sanctuary grouped according to the ancestral houses of your kinsmen, the
6 common people, with the Levites divided by ancestral house. Slaughter
the Passover sacrifice once you have sanctified yourselves, and prepare
it for your kinsmen to fulfill the LORD's word given through Moshe."

7 Yoshiyahu donated flocks to the people for Passover sacrifices for all those
present, a total of 30,000 lambs and kid goats and 3,000 bulls; these were
8 of the king's own possessions. His officials also made a voluntary donation
to the people, the priests, and the Levites. Ḥilkiya, Zekharyahu, and Yeḥiel,
the chief officers of the House of God, gave 2,600 Passover sacrifices and
9 300 bulls to the priests. Kananyahu and his brothers Shemayahu and
Netanel, as well as Ḥashavyahu, Ye'iel, and Yozavad, the officers of the
Levites, donated 5,000 Passover sacrifices and 500 bulls to the Levites.

10 When the preparations for the service were complete, the priests stood
in position and the Levites in their divisions as the king had ordered.
11 They slaughtered the Passover sacrifice, and the priests dashed the blood
12 they received, while the Levites did the flaying. And they set aside the
parts of the burnt offering, arranging them according to the groups of the
common people's ancestral houses, to offer them to the LORD as written
13 in the book of Moshe, and they did the same for the bulls. They cooked
the Passover sacrifice with fire, as required, and they cooked the sacred
offerings in pots, kettles, and pans, then carried them quickly to all the
14 people. After that, they made preparations for themselves and for the
priests; the priestly descendants of Aharon were busy offering up the
burnt offerings and the fats late into the night, so the Levites made the
preparations for themselves and for the priestly descendants of Aharon.
15 The singers, the sons of Asaf, were at their posts as ordered by David, Asaf,
Heiman, and Yedutun, the king's seer, while the gatekeepers were stationed
at every gate; they were not to neglect their duties, for their fellow Levites
16 made the preparations for them. Thus all the necessary preparations for the
LORD's service were completed on that day, the Passover was celebrated,
and the burnt offerings were offered up on the Altar of the LORD as king
17 Yoshiyahu had commanded. The Israelites who were present celebrated
Passover at that time and the Festival of Unleavened Bread for seven days.
18 There had not been such a Passover celebration in Israel since the days of
the prophet Shmuel; none of the kings of Israel ever celebrated Passover
as Yoshiyahu did with the priests, the Levites, all of Yehuda, the Israelites
19 who were present, and the people of Jerusalem. It was in the eighteenth
year of Yoshiyahu's reign that this Passover was celebrated.

20 After all this, after Yoshiyahu had set the House in order, King Nekho of
Egypt marched up to fight in Karkemish on the Euphrates, and Yoshiyahu
21 went out to meet him. He sent messengers out to meet him, saying, "What
have I to do with you, king of Yehuda? It is not you that I am marching

against today, but against my rival house, and God has bid me to make
haste. Do not meddle with God, who is with me, and He will not destroy
you."

22 But Yoshiyahu would not turn away from him; instead, he donned his royal
armor in order to fight against him and did not heed the words that Nekho
23 quoted from God. And he joined the battle in the Valley of Megiddo. The
archers shot King Yoshiyahu, and the king said to his servants, "Take me
away, for I am gravely wounded."

24 His servants took him out of the chariot, transferred him to his deputy's
chariot, and conveyed him to Jerusalem, where he died. He was buried
in the tombs of his ancestors. And all of Yehuda and Jerusalem mourned
25 for Yoshiyahu. Yirmeyahu composed a lament for Yoshiyahu that all the
keening men and women sing in their laments for Yoshiyahu to this day;
it has become part of Israelite custom and was incorporated into the
laments.

26 The rest of Yoshiyahu's history and his loyal deeds are recorded in the
27 Lord's teaching. And his history, earlier and later, is recorded in the Book
of Kings of Israel and Yehuda.

36 1 The people of the land took Yehoaḥaz, Yoshiyahu's son, and made him
2 king in his father's place in Jerusalem. Yoaḥaz was twenty-three years old
3 when he became king, and for three months, he reigned in Jerusalem. But
the king of Egypt deposed him in Jerusalem and imposed a fine on the
4 land of one hundred talents of silver and one talent of gold. The king of
Egypt made his brother Elyakim king over Yehuda and Jerusalem, and he
changed his name to Yehoyakim. As for his brother Yoaḥaz, Nekho took
him and brought him to Egypt.

5 Yehoyakim was twenty-five years old when he became king, and for eleven
years he reigned in Jerusalem. He did what was evil in the eyes of the Lord
6 his God. Then Nevukhadnetzar, king of Babylon, marched up against him,
7 and he bound him in fetters to lead him to Babylon. Nevukhadnetzar
brought some of the vessels from the House of the Lord to Babylon, and
he kept them in his palace in Babylon.

8 As for the rest of Yehoyakim's history and the horrors he performed and
what was found against him, they are recorded in the Book of Kings of
Israel and Yehuda. And his son Yehoyakhin reigned in his place.

9 Yehoyakhin was eight years old when he became king, and for three
months and ten days he reigned in Jerusalem. He did what was evil in
10 the eyes of the Lord. In the spring, King Nevukhadnetzar sent and had
him brought to Babylon along with the precious objects in the House
of the Lord, and he made his brother Tzidkiyahu king over Yehuda and
11 Jerusalem. Tzidkiyahu was twenty-one years old when he became king,
12 and for eleven years he reigned in Jerusalem. He did what was evil in the
eyes of the Lord his God, and he would not humble himself before the

13 prophet Yirmeyahu, who spoke for the Lord. He also rebelled against
King Nevukhadnetzar, who had made him swear by God.[19] He stiffened
his neck and set his heart against returning to the Lord, God of Israel.

14 All the upper classes of the priests and the people broke faith time and
again, imitating all the abominations of the nations; they defiled the House
15 of the Lord that He had consecrated in Jerusalem. The Lord, God of
the ancestors, sent His messengers to them time after time, for He had
16 compassion on His people and His dwelling place, but they continued to
scorn God's messengers and mock His words and ridicule His prophets
until the Lord's wrath rose against His people to the point of no return.
17 He unleashed the king of the Chaldeans against them, and he slew their
young men by the sword in their Temple with no pity for any young man
18 or maiden, the old, or the frail – they were all handed over to him. And
every last vessel in the House of God, great and small, and the treasuries of
the House of the Lord and the treasuries of the king and his officials – he
brought everything to Babylon.

19 They burned down the House of God and tore down the wall of Jerusalem;
20 they burned all its palaces with fire and destroyed all its treasures. He
exiled the remnant who had survived the sword to Babylon, and they
became slaves for him and his sons until the Persian Empire rose to
21 power – fulfilling the word of the Lord as pronounced by Yirmeyahu:
until the land had paid back its Sabbatical years, it lay Sabbath-fallow all
the days of its desolation until seventy years were fulfilled.

22 In the first year of Koresh, king of Persia, when the Lord's word pronounced by Yirmeyahu had come to pass, the Lord stirred the spirit
of Koresh, king of Persia, and he issued a proclamation throughout his
kingdom by word of mouth and written word as well:

23 "Thus says Koresh, king of Persia: The Lord, God of the heavens, has
granted me all the kingdoms of the earth, and He has charged me to build
Him a House in Jerusalem in Yehuda. Whoever is among you from all His
people, may the Lord his God be with him, and let him go up!"

19 | An oath of fealty.

REFERENCE MATERIAL

TIMELINES AND GENEALOGIES

TIMELINE OF THE BOOKS OF TANAKH

1. *A possible time of Job; it is unknown when he lived, and one opinion in the Talmud states that the book is a non-historical parable. There is also no agreement as to when the book was written.*

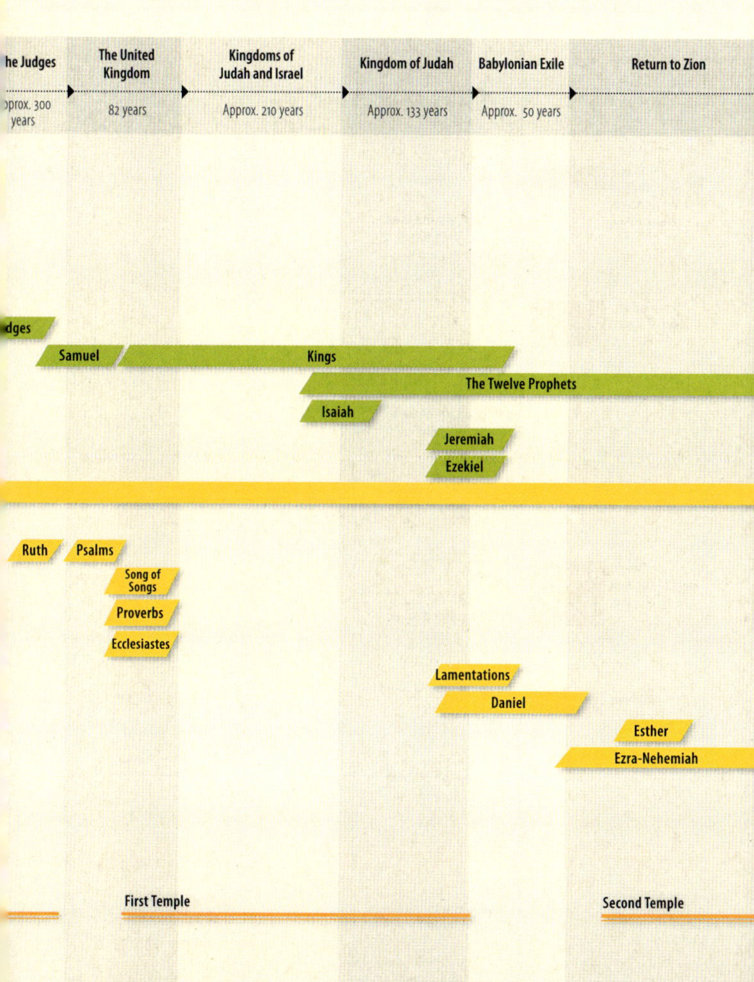

he Judges
pprox. 300 years
The United Kingdom
82 years
Kingdoms of Judah and Israel
Approx. 210 years
Kingdom of Judah
Approx. 133 years
Babylonian Exile
Approx. 50 years
Return to Zion
dges
Samuel
Kings
The Twelve Prophets
Isaiah
Jeremiah
Ezekiel
Ruth
Psalms
Song of Songs
Proverbs
Ecclesiastes
Lamentations
Daniel
Esther
Ezra-Nehemiah
First Temple
Second Temple

LEADERS OF ISRAEL
(FROM ENTERING THE LAND TO THE DIVISION OF THE KINGDOM)

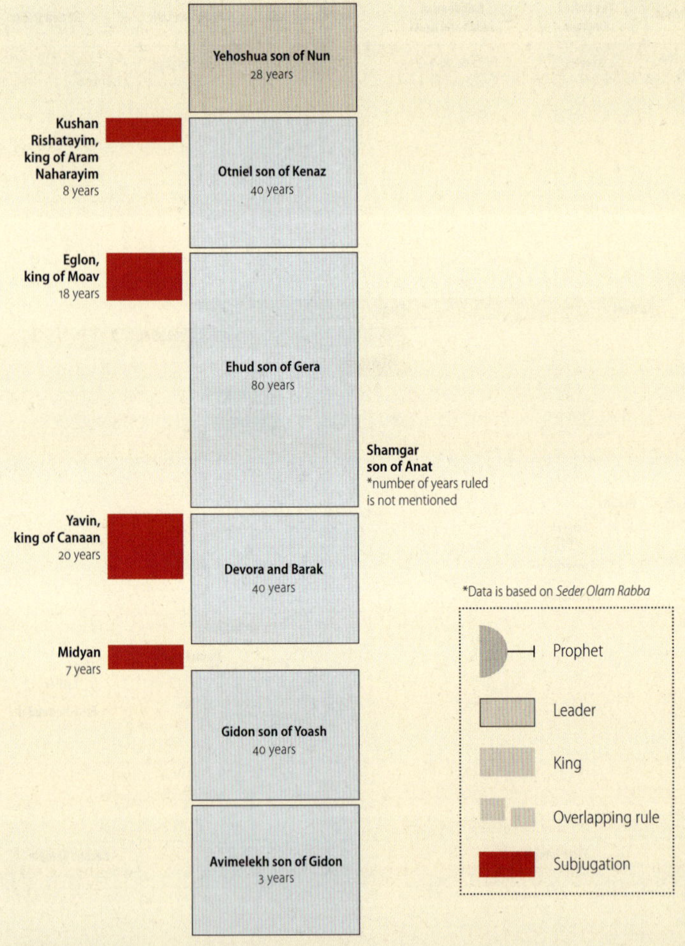

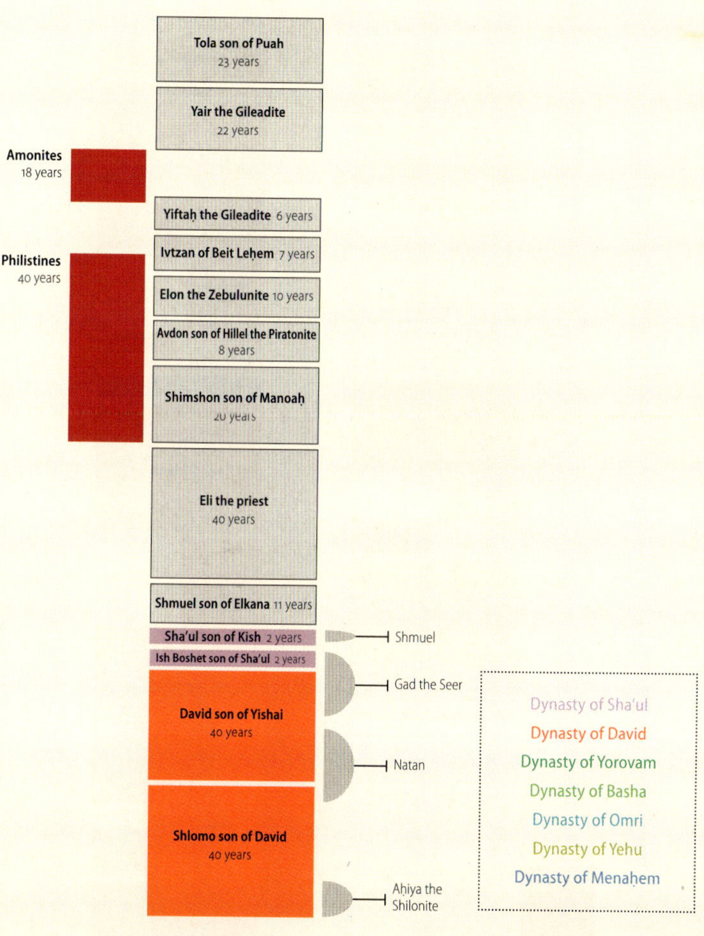
Tola son of Puah
23 years
Yair the Gileadite
22 years
Amonites
18 years
Yiftaḥ the Gileadite 6 years
Philistines
40 years
Ivtzan of Beit Leḥem 7 years
Elon the Zebulunite 10 years
Avdon son of Hillel the Piratonite
8 years
Shimshon son of Manoaḥ
20 years
Eli the priest
40 years
Shmuel son of Elkana 11 years
Sha'ul son of Kish 2 years
Shmuel
Ish Boshet son of Sha'ul 2 years
Gad the Seer
David son of Yishai
40 years
Natan
Shlomo son of David
40 years
Aḥiya the
Shilonite
Dynasty of Sha'ul
Dynasty of David
Dynasty of Yorovam
Dynasty of Basha
Dynasty of Omri
Dynasty of Yehu
Dynasty of Menaḥem

LEADERS OF ISRAEL
(FROM THE DIVISION OF THE KINGDOM TO THE RETURN TO ZION)

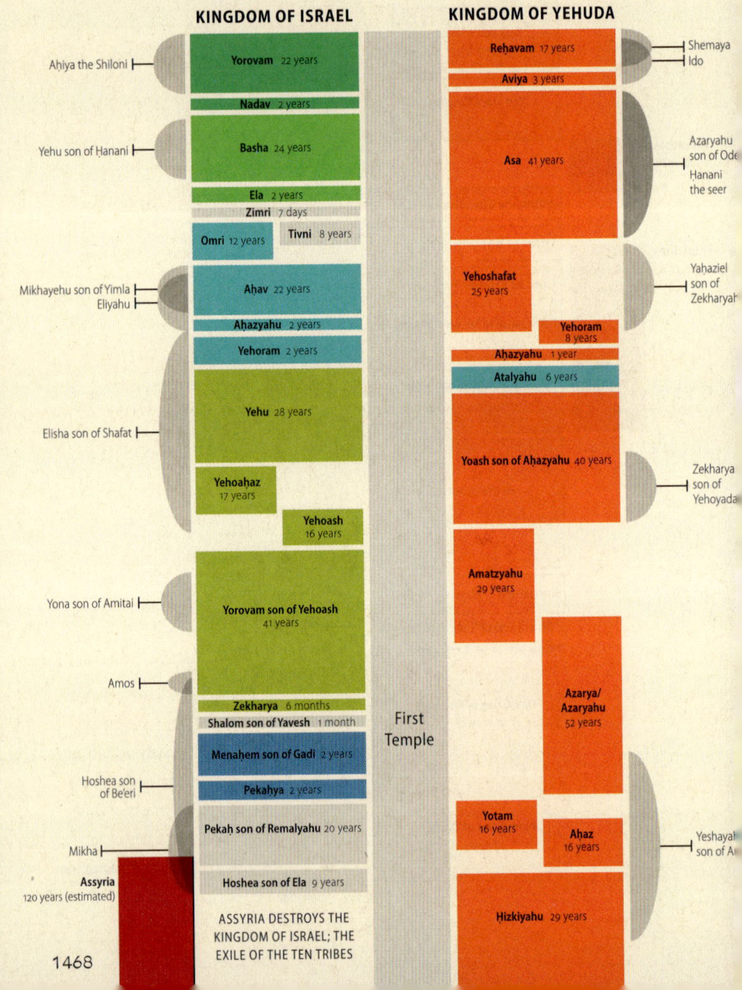

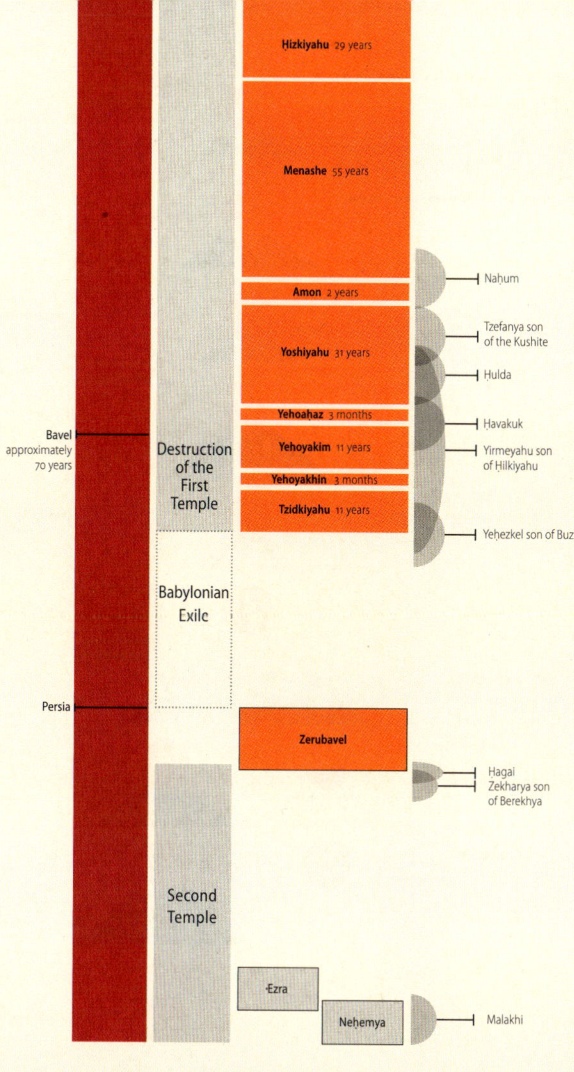

Ḥizkiyahu 29 years
Menashe 55 years
Amon 2 years
Yoshiyahu 31 years
Yehoaḥaz 3 months
Yehoyakim 11 years
Yehoyakhin 3 months
Tzidkiyahu 11 years
Naḥum
Tzefanya son of the Kushite
Ḥulda
Ḥavakuk
Yirmeyahu son of Ḥilkiyahu
Yeḥezkel son of Buzi
Bavel
approximately 70 years
Destruction of the First Temple
Babylonian Exile
Persia
Zerubavel
Ḥagai
Zekharya son of Berekhya
Second Temple
Ezra
Neḥemya
Malakhi

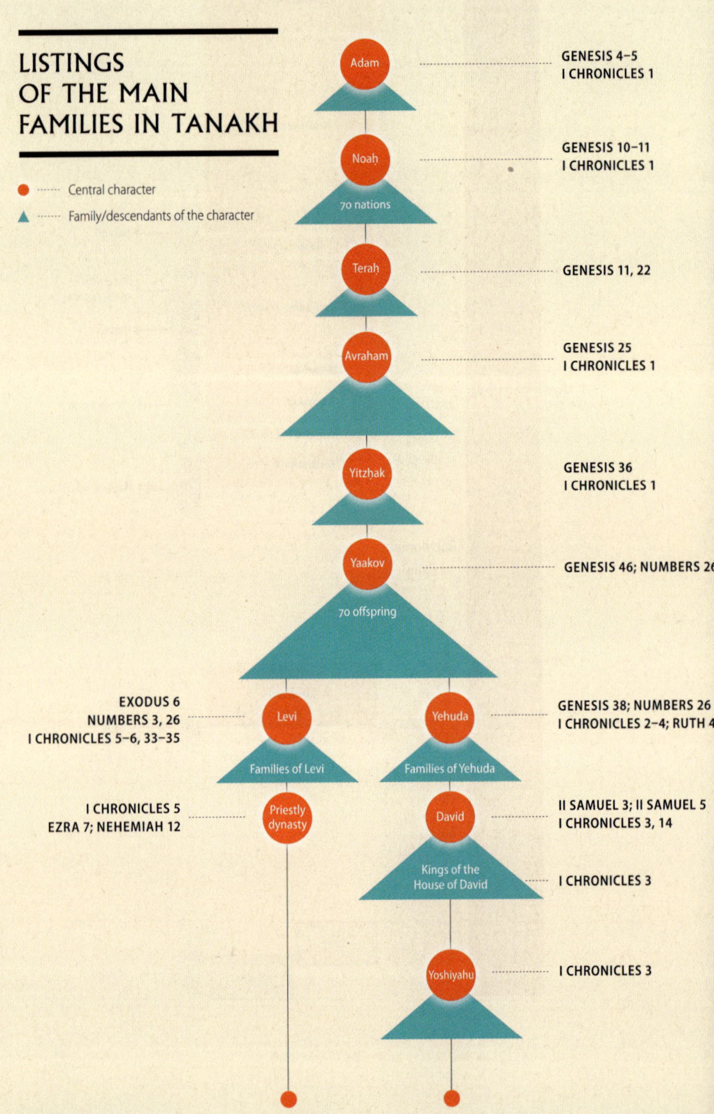
LISTINGS OF THE MAIN FAMILIES IN TANAKH
Central character
Family/descendants of the character
Adam
GENESIS 4–5
I CHRONICLES 1
Noaḥ
70 nations
GENESIS 10–11
I CHRONICLES 1
Teraḥ
GENESIS 11, 22
Avraham
GENESIS 25
I CHRONICLES 1
Yitzḥak
GENESIS 36
I CHRONICLES 1
Yaakov
70 offspring
GENESIS 46; NUMBERS 26
EXODUS 6
NUMBERS 3, 26
I CHRONICLES 5–6, 33–35
Levi
Families of Levi
Yehuda
Families of Yehuda
GENESIS 38; NUMBERS 26
I CHRONICLES 2–4; RUTH 4
I CHRONICLES 5
EZRA 7; NEHEMIAH 12
Priestly dynasty
David
II SAMUEL 3; II SAMUEL 5
I CHRONICLES 3, 14
Kings of the House of David
I CHRONICLES 3
Yoshiyahu
I CHRONICLES 3

FROM ADAM TO NOAḤ

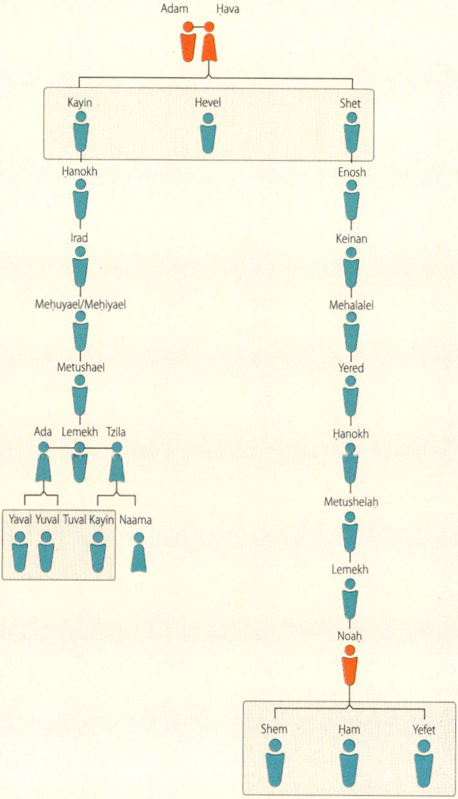

Adam
Ḥava
Kayin
Hevel
Shet
Ḥanokh
Irad
Meḥuyael/Meḥiyael
Metushael
Ada
Lemekh
Tzila
Yaval
Yuval
Tuval Kayin
Naama
Enosh
Keinan
Mehalalel
Yered
Ḥanokh
Metushelaḥ
Lemekh
Noaḥ
Shem
Ḥam
Yefet

Main character
Husband-wife
Relationship to concubine

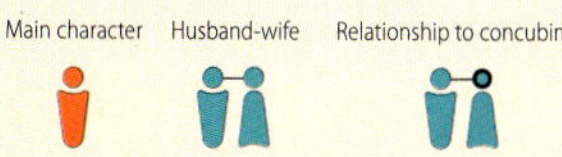

GENESIS 4–5; I CHRONICLES 1

NOAḤ'S DESCENDANTS

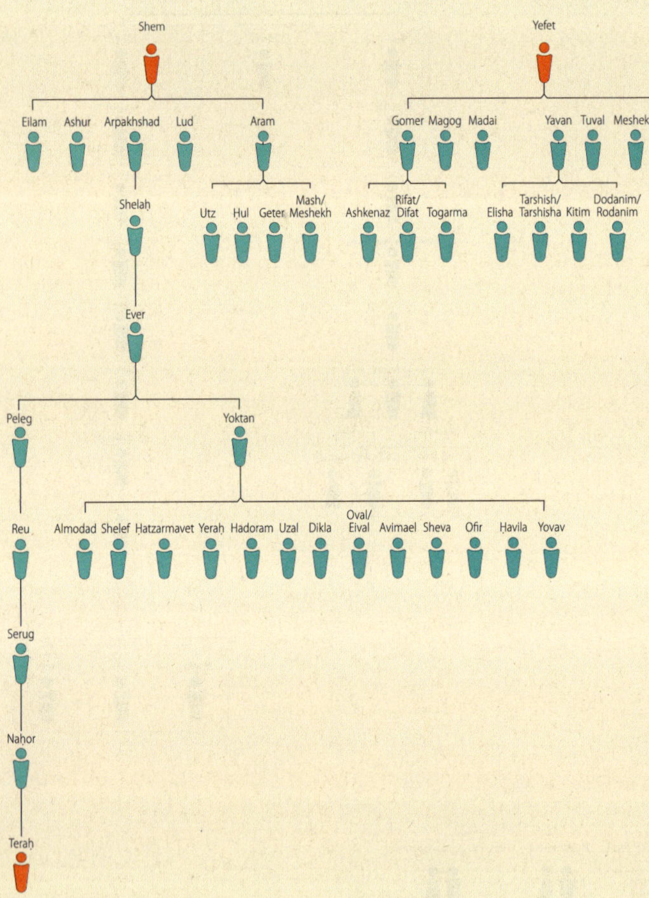

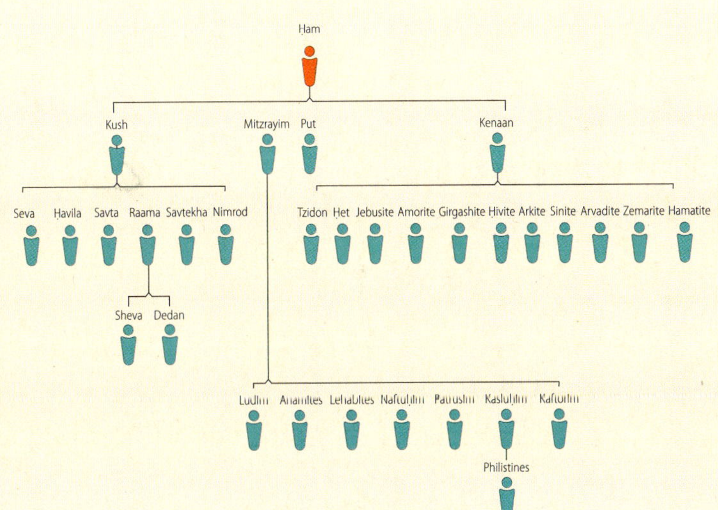
Ḥam
Kush
Mitzrayim
Put
Kenaan
Seva
Ḥavila
Savta
Raama
Savtekha
Nimrod
Sheva
Dedan
Tzidon
Ḥet
Jebusite
Amorite
Girgashite
Ḥivite
Arkite
Sinite
Arvadite
Zemarite
Hamatite
Ludim
Anamites
Lehabites
Naftuḥim
Patrusim
Kasluḥim
Kaftorim
Philistines

TERAḤ, AVRAHAM, AND YITZḤAK'S DESCENDANTS

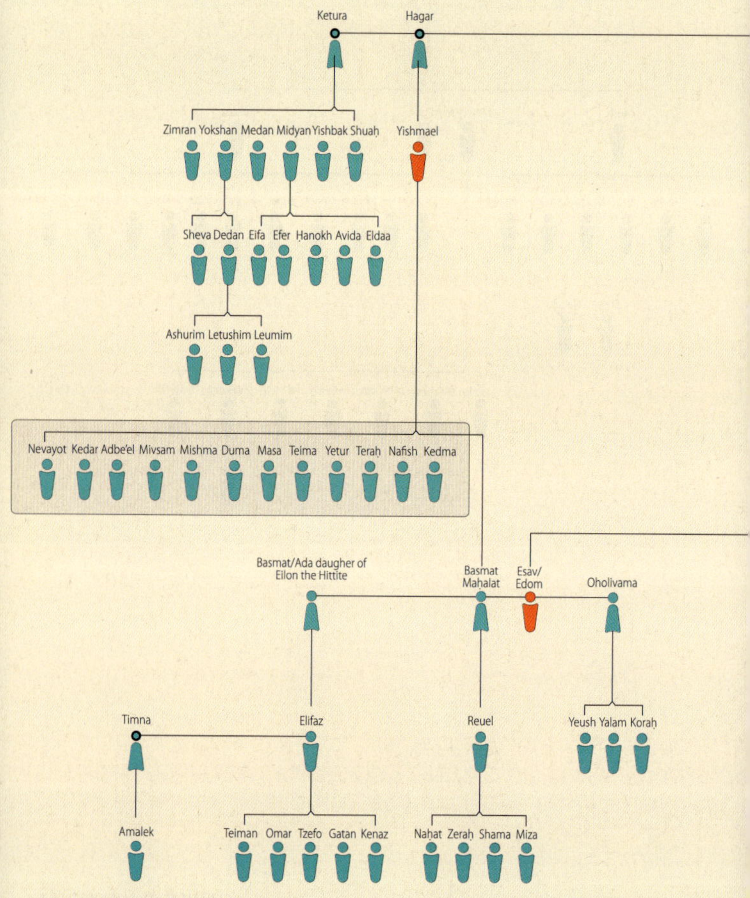

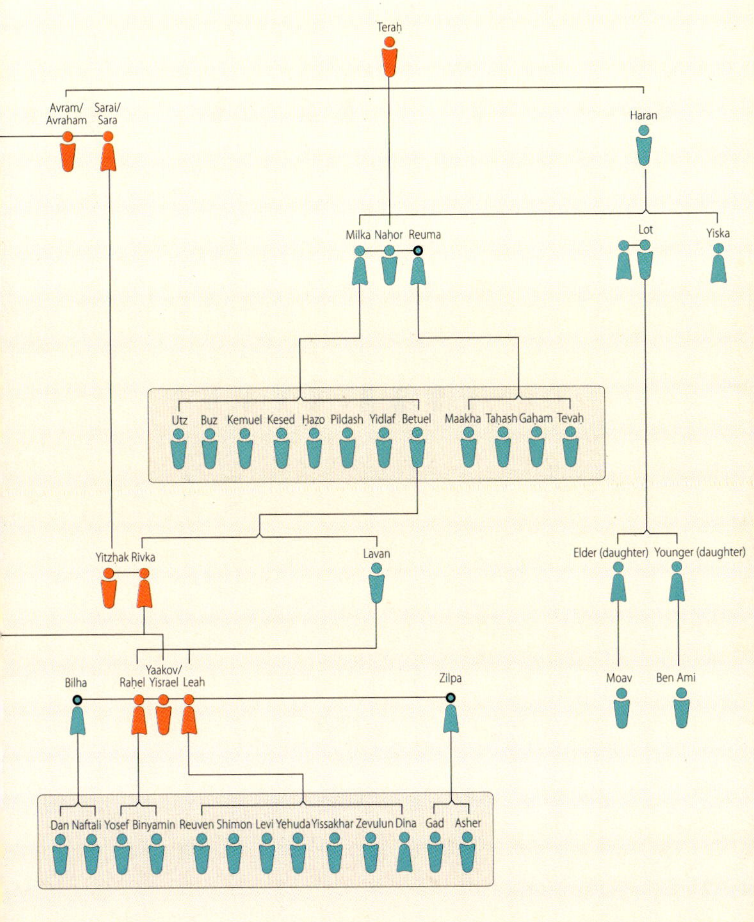

GENESIS 11, 22, 25, 36; I CHRONICLES 1

YISRAEL'S DESCENDANTS

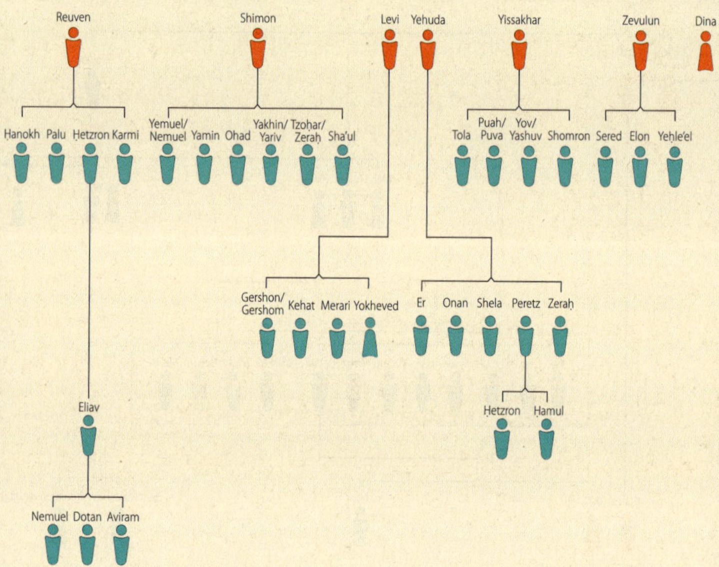

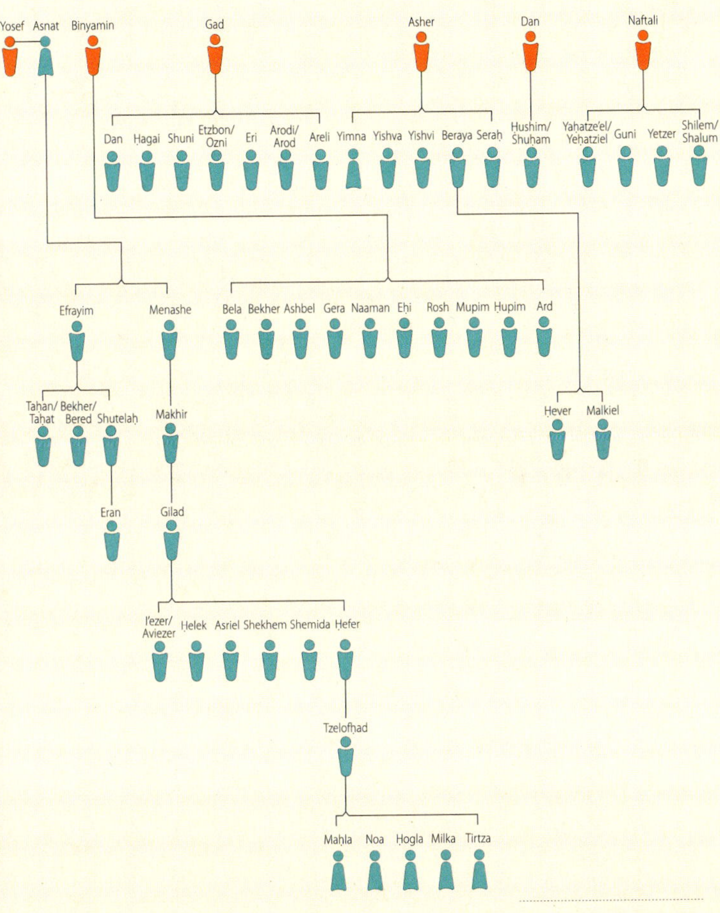

GENESIS 46; NUMBERS 26

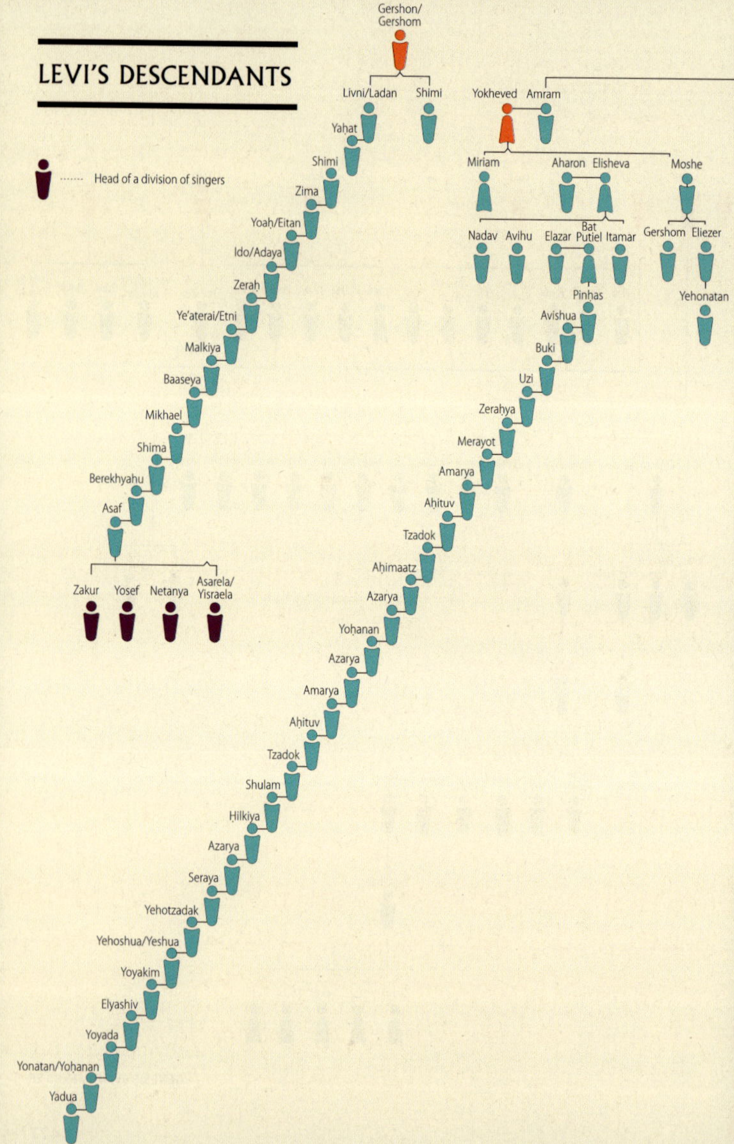

LEVI'S DESCENDANTS
Head of a division of singers
Gershon/
Gershom
Livni/Ladan
Shimi
Yaḥat
Shimi
Zima
Yoaḥ/Eitan
Ido/Adaya
Zeraḥ
Ye'aterai/Etni
Malkiya
Baaseya
Mikhael
Shima
Berekhyahu
Asaf
Zakur
Yosef
Netanya
Asarela/
Yisraela
Yokheved
Amram
Miriam
Aharon
Elisheva
Moshe
Nadav
Avihu
Elazar
Bat
Putiel
Itamar
Gershom
Eliezer
Yehonatan
Pinḥas
Avishua
Buki
Uzi
Zeraḥya
Merayot
Amarya
Aḥituv
Tzadok
Aḥimaatz
Azarya
Yoḥanan
Azarya
Amarya
Aḥituv
Tzadok
Shulam
Ḥilkiya
Azarya
Seraya
Yehotzadak
Yehoshua/Yeshua
Yoyakim
Elyashiv
Yoyada
Yonatan/Yoḥanan
Yadua

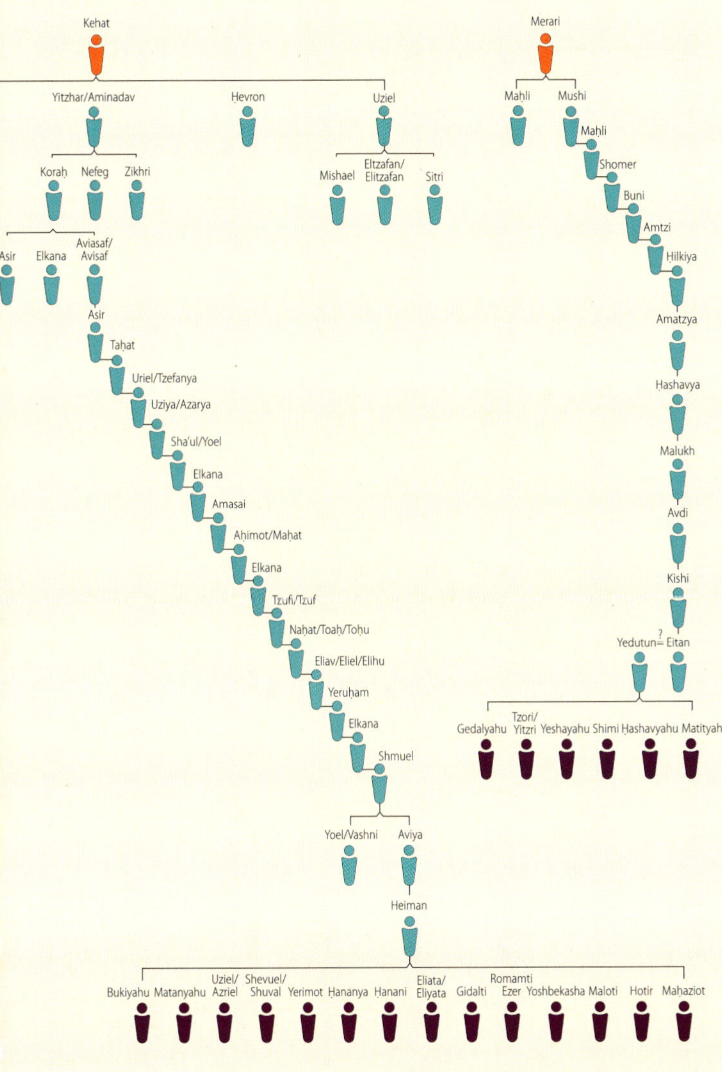

EXODUS 6; NUMBERS 3, 26; JUDGES 18; I CHRONICLES 5–6, 23–25; EZRA 7; NEHEMIAH 12

MAIN FAMILIES OF YEHUDA

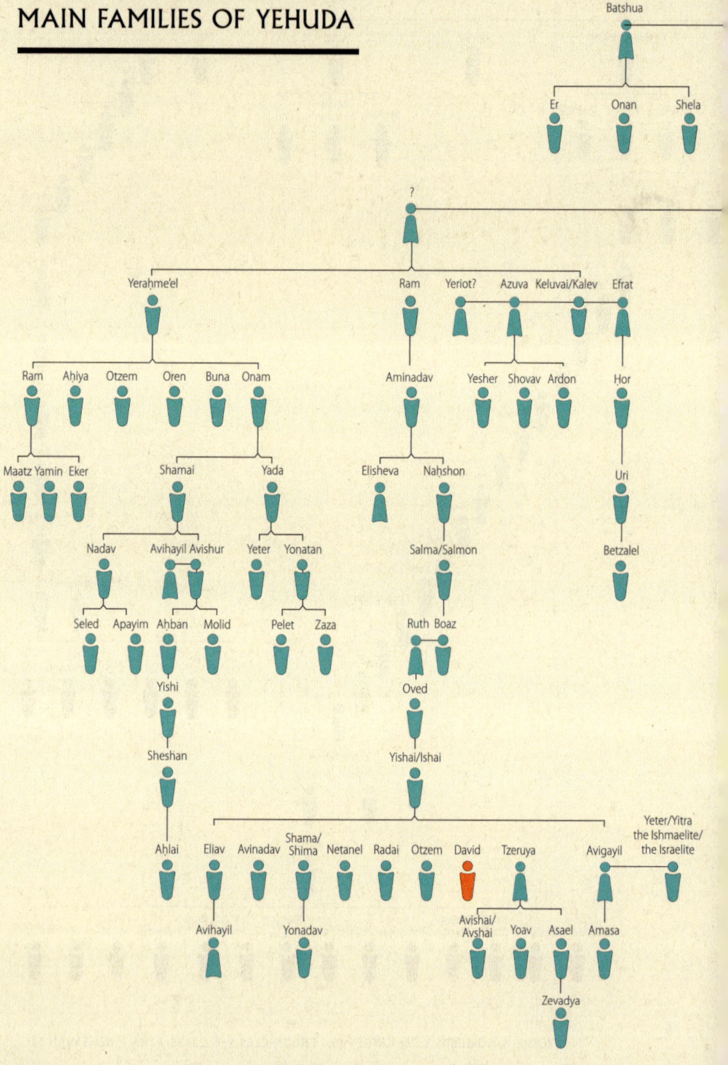

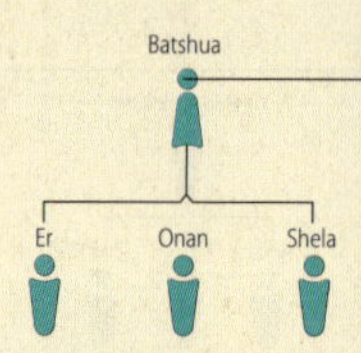

Batshua
Er
Onan
Shela
?
Yeraḥme'el
Ram
Yeriot?
Azuva
Keluvai/Kalev
Efrat
Ram
Aḥiya
Otzem
Oren
Buna
Onam
Aminadav
Yesher
Shovav
Ardon
Ḥor
Maatz
Yamin
Eker
Shamai
Yada
Elisheva
Naḥshon
Uri
Nadav
Avihayil
Avishur
Yeter
Yonatan
Salma/Salmon
Betzalel
Seled
Apayim
Aḥban
Molid
Pelet
Zaza
Ruth
Boaz
Yishi
Oved
Sheshan
Yishai/Ishai
Aḥlai
Eliav
Avinadav
Shama/Shima
Netanel
Radai
Otzem
David
Tzeruya
Avigayil
Yeter/Yitra the Ishmaelite/the Israelite
Avihayil
Yonadav
Avishai/Avshai
Yoav
Asael
Amasa
Zevadya

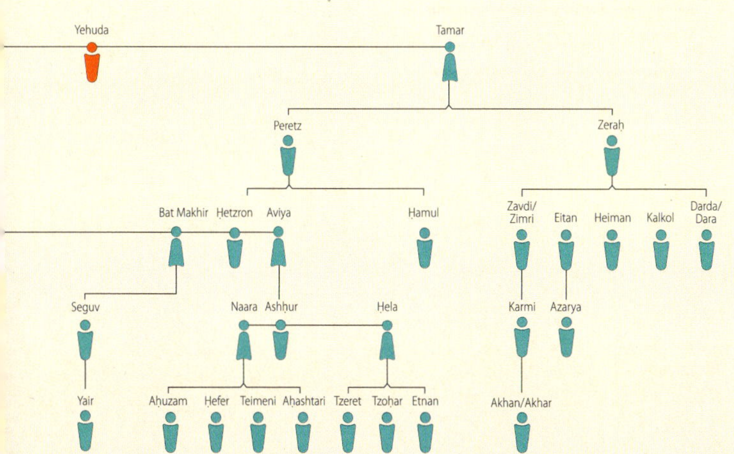

GENESIS 38, 46; NUMBERS 26; JOSHUA 7; I SAMUEL 16–17; II SAMUEL 2, 13, 17; I KINGS 5; RUTH 4; I CHRONICLES 2–4; II CHRONICLES 11

DAVID'S DESCENDANTS

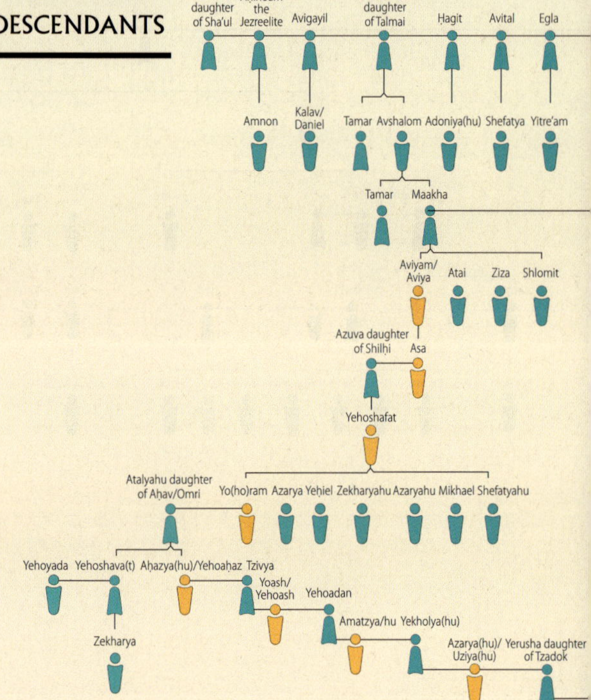

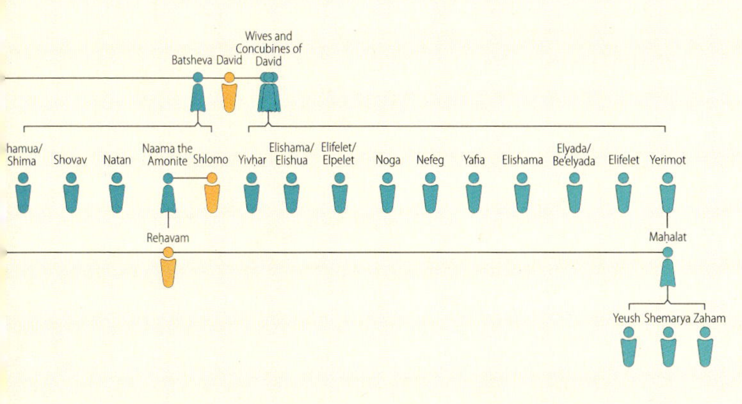

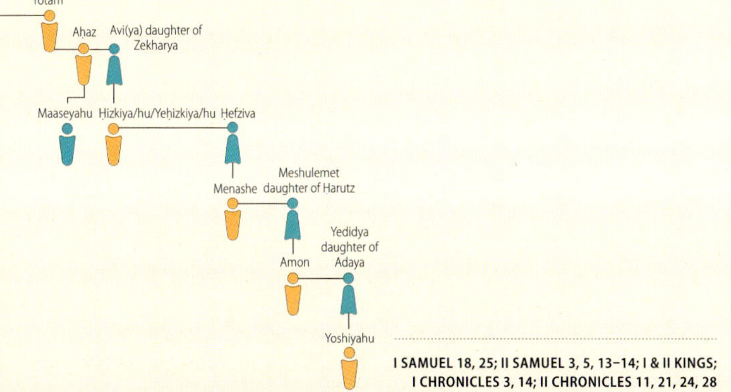

I SAMUEL 18, 25; II SAMUEL 3, 5, 13–14; I & II KINGS; I CHRONICLES 3, 14; II CHRONICLES 11, 21, 24, 28

YOSHIYAHU'S DESCENDANTS

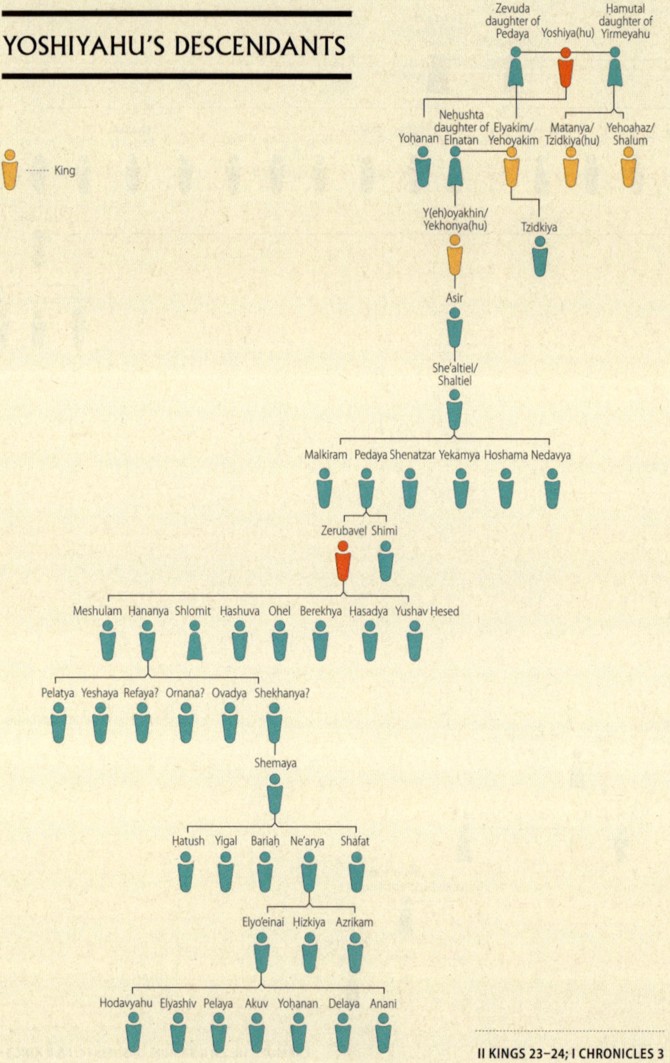

King

Zevuda daughter of Pedaya
Yoshiya(hu)
Ḥamutal daughter of Yirmeyahu

Yoḥanan
Neḥushta daughter of Elnatan
Elyakim/ Yehoyakim
Matanya/ Tzidkiya(hu)
Yehoaḥaz/ Shalum

Y(eh)oyakhin/ Yekhonya(hu)
Tzidkiya

Asir

She'altiel/ Shaltiel

Malkiram
Pedaya
Shenatzar
Yekamya
Hoshama
Nedavya

Zerubavel
Shimi

Meshulam
Ḥananya
Shlomit
Ḥashuva
Ohel
Berekhya
Ḥasadya
Yushav Ḥesed

Pelatya
Yeshaya
Refaya?
Ornana?
Ovadya
Shekhanya?

Shemaya

Ḥatush
Yigal
Bariaḥ
Ne'arya
Shafat

Elyo'einai
Ḥizkiya
Azrikam

Hodavyahu
Elyashiv
Pelaya
Akuv
Yoḥanan
Delaya
Anani

II KINGS 23–24; I CHRONICLES 3

MAPS

1. NOAH'S DESCENDANTS

2. AVRAHAM'S JOURNEY TO THE LAND

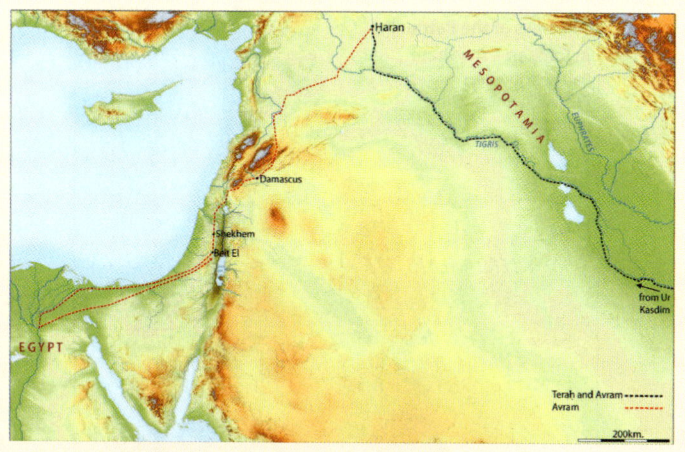

3. AVRAHAM'S TRAVELS

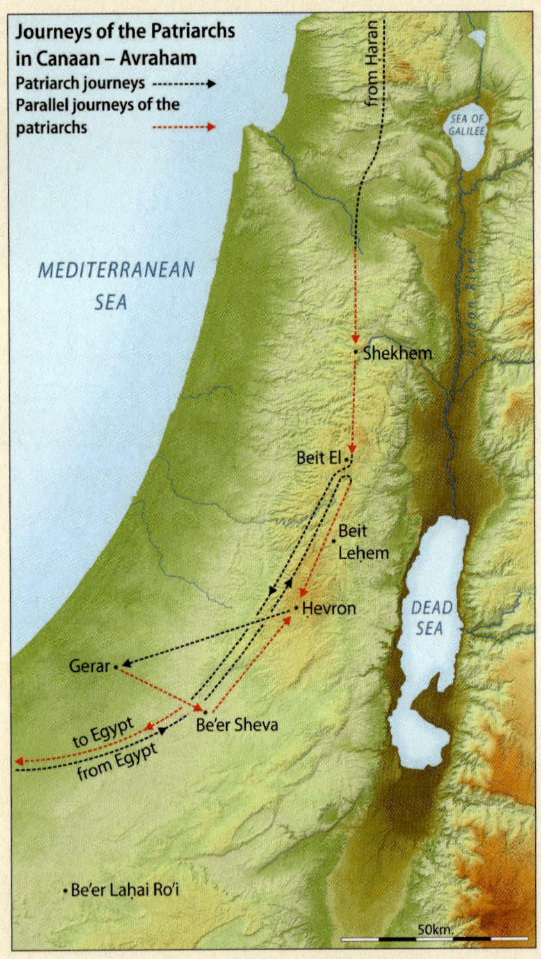

4. YITZḤAK'S TRAVELS

5. YAAKOV'S TRAVELS

6. PATH OF THE EXODUS FROM EGYPT

7. WANDERINGS OF THE CHILDREN OF ISRAEL

8. THE WARS OF YEHOSHUA (JOSH. 6–11)

9. TRIBAL DIVISION OF LAND

10. JUDGES

Tyre
DAN
Barak son of Avinoam
Kedesh Naftali
MEDITERRANEAN SEA
NAFTALI
ASHER
SEA OF GALILEE
Eilon the Zevulunite
ZEVULUN
Dor
Megiddo
Kamun
YISSAKHAR
Yair the Gileadite
LAND OF TOV
Tolah son of Puah
MENASHE
Jordan River
Mitzpeh Gilad
Yiftah the Gileadite
Ofra
Shekhem
Piraton
Gidon son of Yoash
Sukkot
Hillel son of Avdon
Eli
Yafo
Shilo
GAD
Devora
Shmuel
Ramatayim Tzofim
EFRAYIM
Raba of the Amonites
Beit El
Yazeir
Shamgar son of Anat
Rama
BINYAMIN
DAN
Yevus/Jerusalem
Ashdod
Tzora
Shimshon
Beit Lehem
Avtzan
REUVEN
YEHUDA
Hevron
DEAD SEA
Devir
Otniel son of Kenaz
Arad
Be'er Sheva
SHIMON
50km.

11. BORDERS OF THE LAND OF ISRAEL

A. BORDERS OF THE LAND IN PARASHAT MASEI (NUM. 34)

B. BORDERS OF THE LAND AT THE BEGINNING OF DAVID'S REIGN (II SAM. 5:1–5)

C. BORDERS OF THE LAND DURING SHLOMO'S REIGN (I KINGS 4–5)

D. BORDERS OF THE LAND DURING YOROVAM II'S REIGN (II KINGS 14)

12. PHILISTINE WARS AND THE WANDERINGS OF THE TRIBE OF DAN

13. TRAVELS OF THE TABERNACLE AND THE ARK

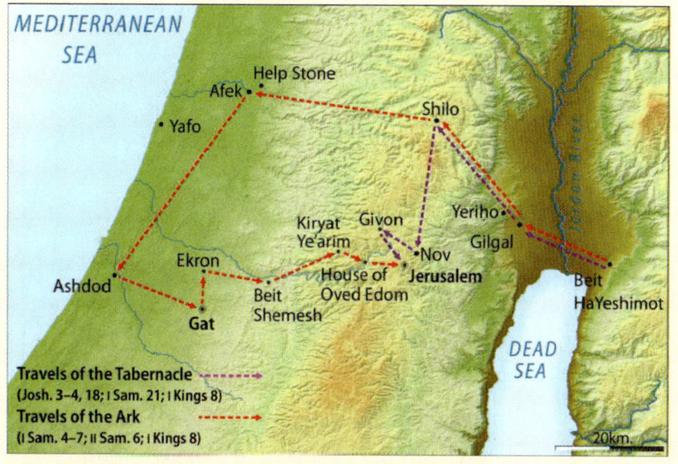

14. DAN TO BEER SHEVA

15. DAVID'S CAMPAIGNS

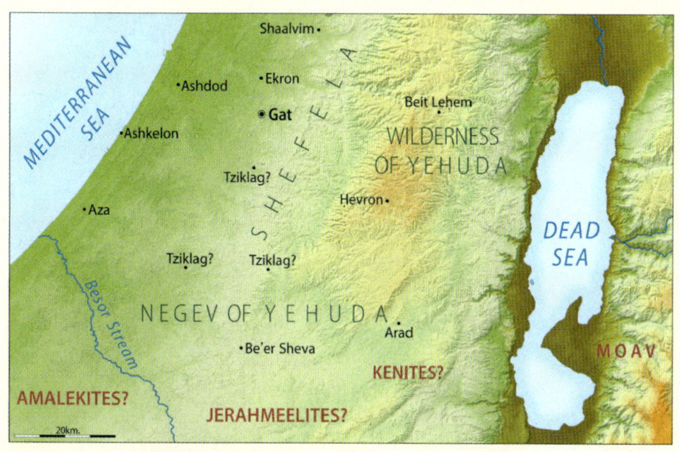

16. KEILA

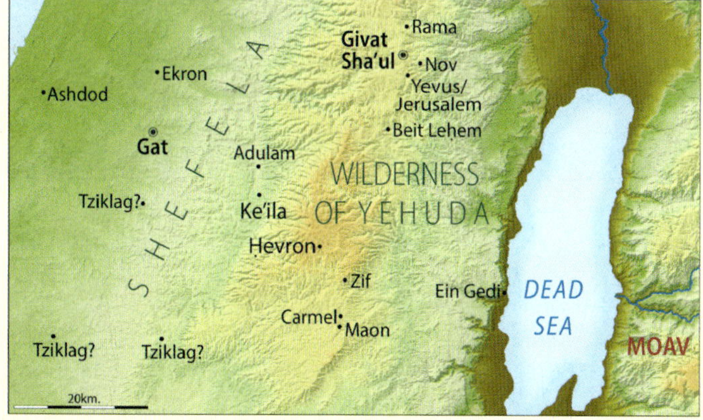

17. TOWNS IN YEHUDA

18. DAVID'S EMPIRE

19. WALLS OF JERUSALEM

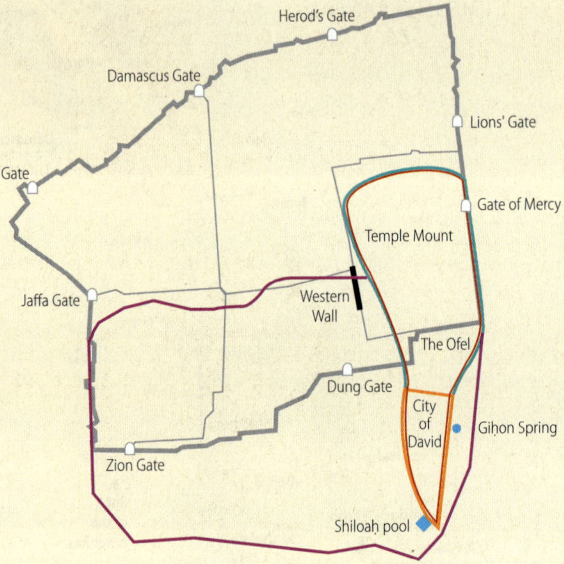

Herod's Gate
Damascus Gate
Lions' Gate
New Gate
Gate of Mercy
Temple Mount
Jaffa Gate
Western
Wall
The Ofel
Dung Gate
City
of
David
Giḥon Spring
Zion Gate
Shiloaḥ pool

Walls of Jerusalem during First Temple period:

- Canaanite wall, 18th century BCE
- Shlomo's wall, 10th century BCE
- Ḥizkiyahu's wall, 8th century BCE

- Original wall of Jerusalem in the Second Temple period – Neḥemya's wall, 5th century BCE
- Current walls of Jerusalem, built in 16th century CE

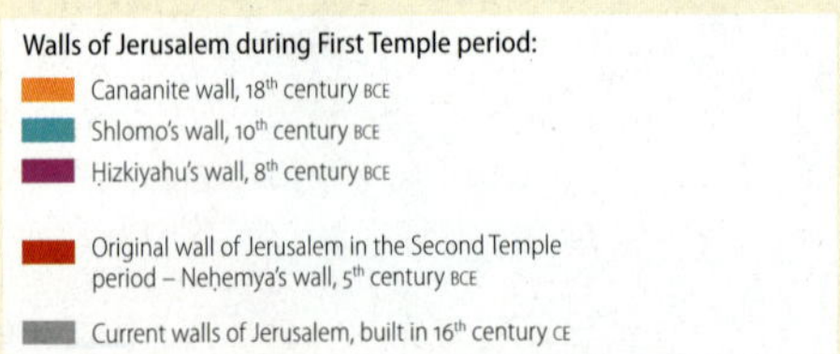

TRIBAL ENCAMPMENTS AND TEMPLES

ORDER OF TRIBAL ENCAMPMENTS

NUMBERS 2

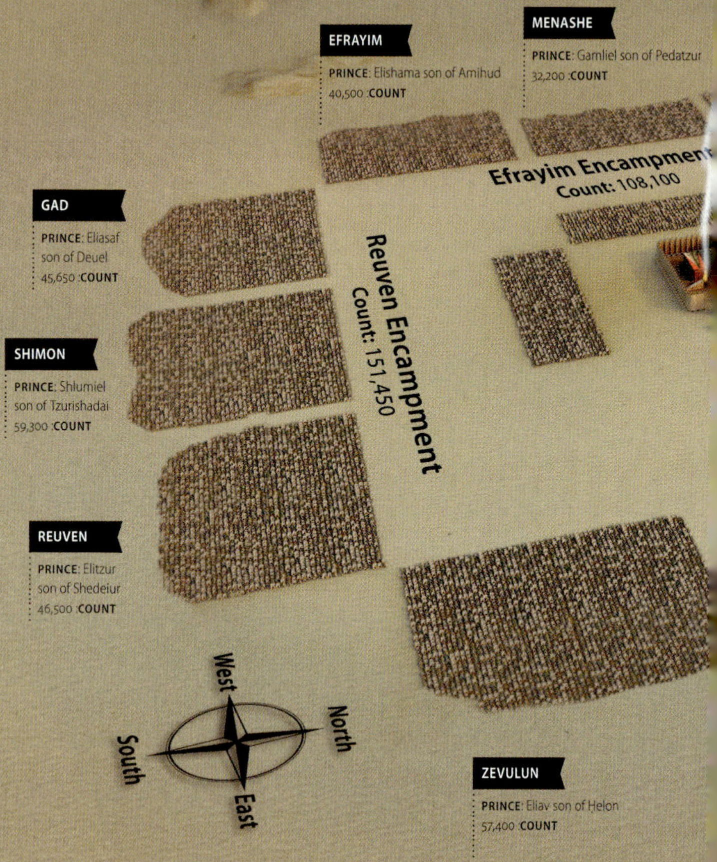

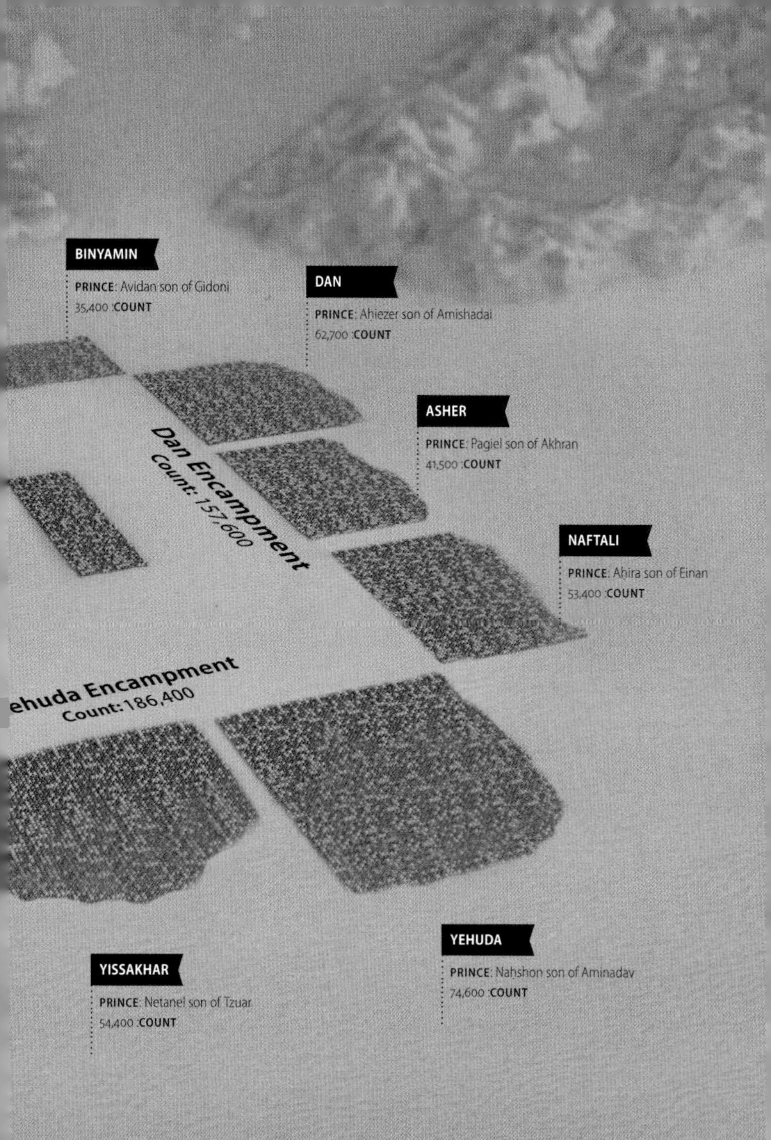

BINYAMIN

PRINCE: Avidan son of Gidoni

35,400 :COUNT

DAN

PRINCE: Ahiezer son of Amishadai

62,700 :COUNT

ASHER

PRINCE: Pagiel son of Akhran

41,500 :COUNT

Dan Encampment

Count: 157,600

NAFTALI

PRINCE: Ahira son of Einan

53,400 :COUNT

ehuda Encampment

Count: 186,400

YEHUDA

PRINCE: Nahshon son of Aminadav

74,600 :COUNT

YISSAKHAR

PRINCE: Netanel son of Tzuar

54,400 :COUNT

GERSHON

PRINCE: Eliasaf son of Lael

FAMILIES: Livni and Shimi

7,500 :**COUNT**

ROLE: Carrying the cover of the Tabernacle, the screen of the Tabernacle, and the sheets of the courtyard

KEHAT

PRINCE: Elazar son of Aharon

FAMILIES: Amram, Yitzhar, Hevron, and Uziel

8,500 :**COUNT**

ROLE: Carrying the vessels of the Tabernacle and the curtain

ENCAMPMENT OF THE LEVITES AND THEIR ROLES

NUMBERS 3

MERARI

PRINCE: Tzuriel son of Aviḥail

FAMILIES: Maḥli and Mushi

6,200 :**COUNT**

ROLE: Carrying the boards of the Tabernacle and the poles of the courtyard

MOSHE, AHARON, AND HIS SONS

PRINCE OF THE PRINCES OF THE LEVITES: Elazar, son of Aharon the priest. In addition to this role, he was also in charge of carrying the oil, the incense, and the daily grain offering

TABERNACLE IN THE DESERT

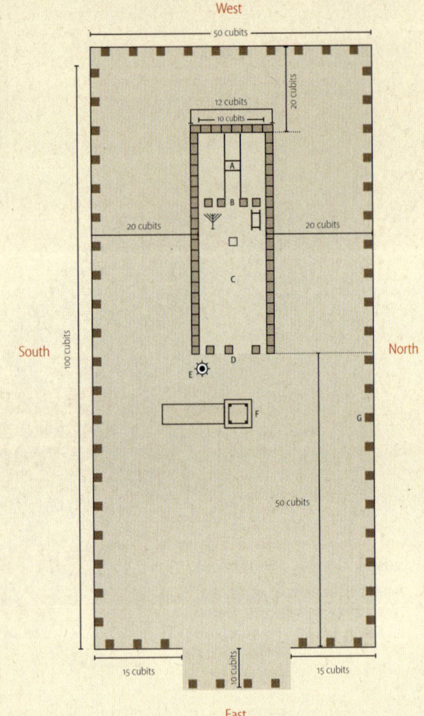

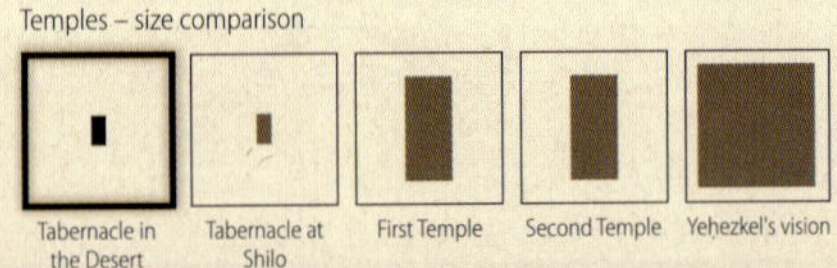

TABERNACLE AT SHILO

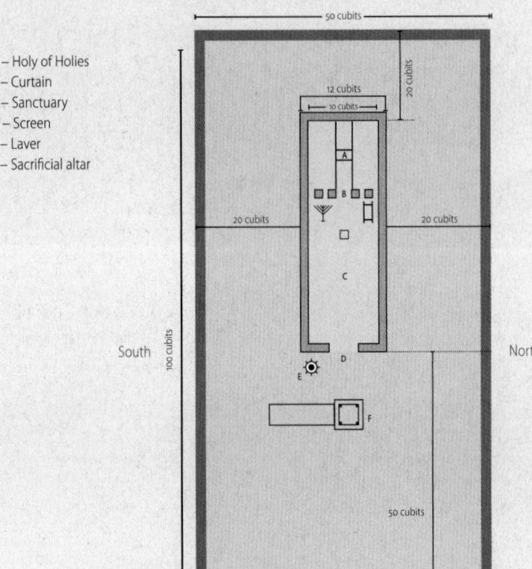

Temples – size comparison

Tabernacle in the Desert | Tabernacle at Shilo | First Temple | Second Temple | Yeḥezkel's vision

FIRST TEMPLE

A – Inner Sanctuary
B – Sanctuary
C – Hall
D – Laver
E – Sacrificial altar
F – Shlomo's Sea
G – Courtyard (estimated size)

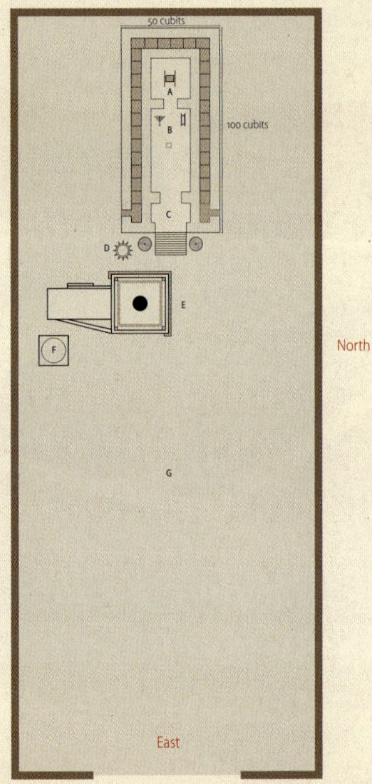

Temples – size comparison

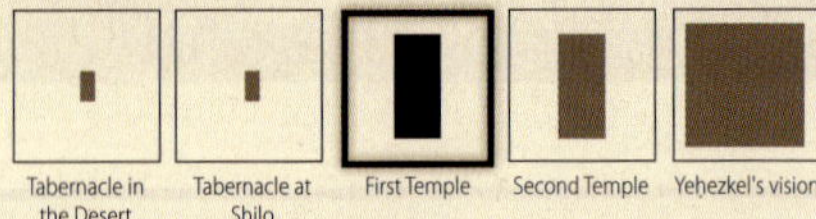

SECOND TEMPLE

A – Holy of Holies
B – Sanctuary
C – Hall
D – Rampart
E – Sacrificial altar
F – Priests' courtyard
G – Israelites' courtyard
H – Women's courtyard

We have no information about the Temple built by those who ascended from Babylon. Therefore, we present here a diagram of Herod's Temple, on the assumption that the dimensions remained as they had been from the foundation of the Second Temple.

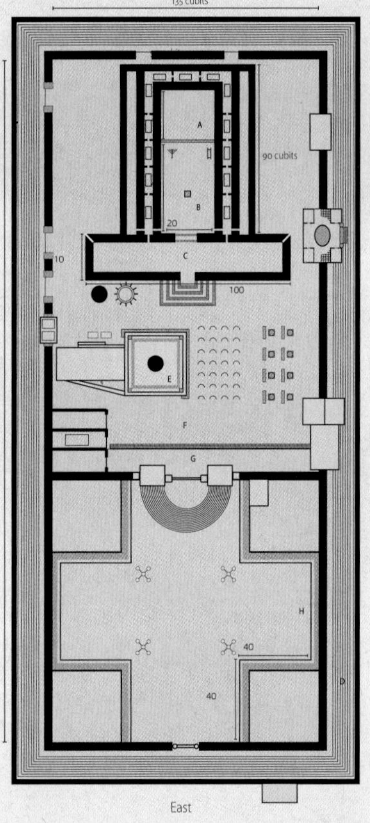

Temples – size comparison

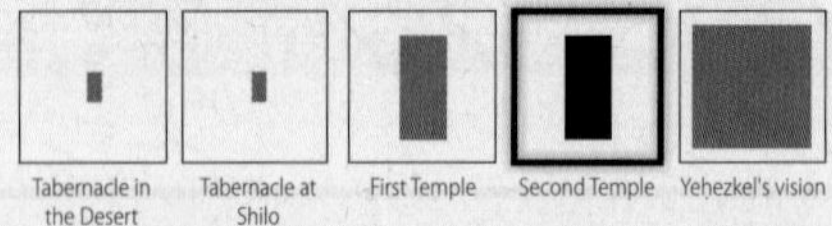

THE TEMPLE IN YEḤEZKEL'S VISION

A – Holy of Holies
B – Sanctuary
C – Sacrificial altar
D – Inner courtyard
E – Outer courtyard
F – Temple Mount

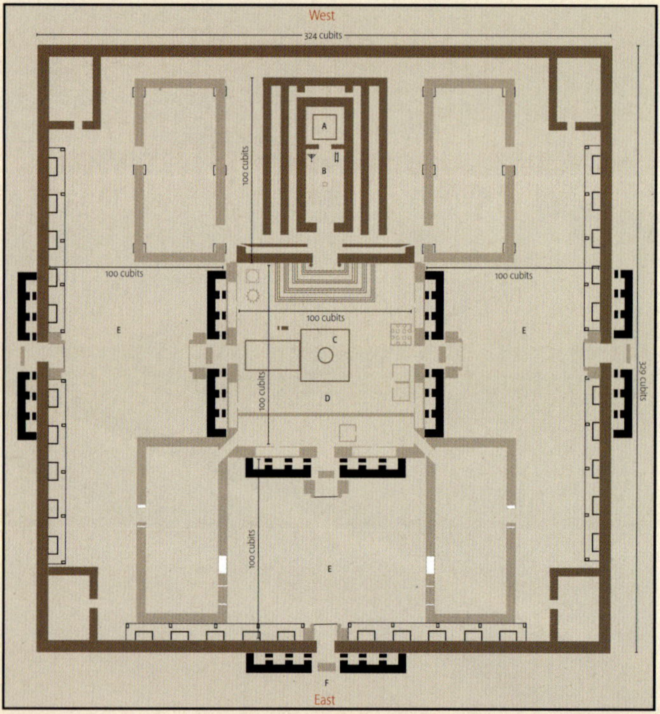

West
324 cubits
A
B
100 cubits
100 cubits
100 cubits
100 cubits
C
E
E
D
100 cubits
329 cubits
100 cubits
E
F
East

Temples – size comparison

Tabernacle in the Desert
Tabernacle at Shilo
First Temple
Second Temple
Yeḥezkel's vision

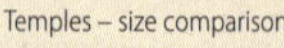

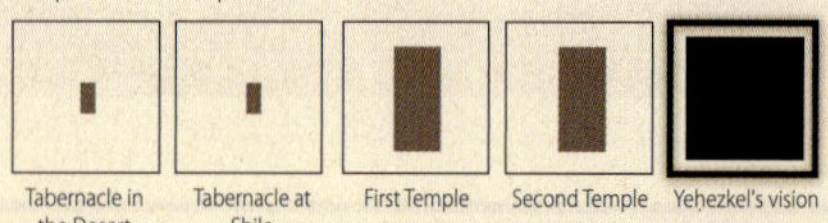

THE TABERNACLE AND ITS VESSELS

INTRODUCTION TO THE TABERNACLE

RABBI MENACHEM MAKOVER

The Torah dedicates five *parashot* to the Tabernacle, from *Parashat Teruma* through *Parashat Pekudei* (Ex. 25:1–40:38). This indicates the significance of the Tabernacle – the location of the revelation of the Divine Presence and the site where sacrifices are offered. In these *parashot*, the Torah describes the structure of the Tabernacle, its vessels, and the priestly vestments in great detail, with regard to both the command to make them and the implementation of the command, as well as their construction.

Notwithstanding this great level of detail, there are numerous opinions among the Sages and the later commentators about many of the specifics. The most significant tannaitic source on this topic is the compendium known as *Baraita deMelekhet HaMishkan*. There are also several extensive discussions in the Talmud. Among the early commentators, Rashi provided the most expansive interpretations of the structure, in his commentary to the Torah. Most of the other commentators based their explanations on Rashi's. Maimonides did not discuss the Tabernacle directly, but in his *Laws of the Chosen Temple* he issued rulings regarding the vessels that often differ from Rashi's interpretations.

In this appendix, we have generally followed Rashi, as he is the primary biblical exegete. In some places we have also mentioned other opinions. There are also several later commentators who expounded upon Rashi's explanations, most significantly the author of *Maaseh Ḥoshev*.

The command to construct the vessels and the Tabernacle itself appears in the Torah in a highly organized manner. *Parashat Teruma* (Ex. 25:1–27:19) begins by discussing the vessels: the Ark, the table, and the candelabrum. After this, it describes the structure of the Tent of Meeting that stood in the center of the Tabernacle courtyard, the sacrificial altar, and the structure of the courtyard. In *Parashat Tetzaveh* (Ex. 27:20–30:10) we learn about the priestly garments, the incense altar, and at its conclusion, about the bronze laver (basin). The commentaries have provided various explanations for this sequence, and in this appendix, we have generally tried to follow it. For the sake of clarity, though, we have deviated from the sequence regarding the incense altar and the bronze laver (basin).

With regard to the boards of the Tabernacle, the Torah uses the expression, "acacia wood, standing." The Sages interpret this homiletically: "Perhaps you will say that their hope is lost, and their chances are gone. For this reason, the verse states, 'Acacia wood, standing' – to teach that they are standing forever" (Yoma 72a). The Tabernacle includes an aspect of eternity, and therefore it is relevant and significant in all generations to study about its structure and vessels.

GENERAL TERMS

HANDBREADTH: This measurement is mentioned in the Torah in the verse describing the frame of the table (Ex. 25:25). According to Rashi and Maimonides, the handbreadth is a measurement equivalent to the width of four fingers held together.

Halakha – A handbreadth is equivalent to 7.6 centimeters according to Maimonides, 8 centimeters according to Rabbi Ḥaim Naeh, and 9.6 centimeters according to the Ḥazon Ish.

CUBIT: This measurement is defined as the length of the forearm, from the elbow to the end of the middle finger. The standard cubit generally referenced by the Sages is equivalent to six handbreadths, and this is the cubit referenced in the biblical passages relating to the Tabernacle. There is also a measurement known as a "minor cubit," which is equivalent to five handbreadths.

Halakha – According to Maimonides, a standard cubit is equivalent to 45.6 centimeters. According to Rabbi Ḥaim Naeh it is 48 centimeters, and according to the Ḥazon Ish it is 57.6 centimeters.

TALENT (*kikar*): The unit of weight called a talent is mentioned in the Torah as the weight of the golden candelabrum (Ex. 25:39) and of the silver sockets (Ex. 38:27). The sacred talent, used in the Tabernacle, was twice the weight of an ordinary talent. According to Maimonides, a desert talent (that was in use at the time of the Tabernacle) is 21.25 kilograms, and thus a sacred talent is equal to 42.5 kilograms.

CRAFTS FOR CONSTRUCTING THE TABERNACLE

SKILLED CRAFTSMANSHIP: According to Rashi's interpretation (Ex. 26:1), this term refers to a type of weaving that produces two different patterns on each of the two sides of the woven material (images of lions on one side and images of eagles on the other). This type of weaving was used for the curtain, the sheets of the Tabernacle, the ephod, and the breast piece.

RAW MATERIALS: In the construction of the Tabernacle, skilled craftsmanship was used only with threads spun of twenty-four strands: six white flax and eighteen dyed wool – six sky blue, six purple, and six scarlet. These were all twisted together into a single thread. In the ephod and the breast piece there were also four threads of gold intertwined with each group of dyed threads that were twisted together.

EMBROIDERED WORK: This term refers to embroidering a single pattern or image onto fabric in a manner that causes it to appear on both sides. This type of embroidery was used in the screen at the entrance to the Tabernacle, the screen at the entrance to the courtyard, and the priests' sashes.

RAW MATERIALS: See above, "Skilled Craftsmanship."

WOVEN WORK: This refers to weaving threads with a loom to produce fabric. This type of weaving was used for the High Priest's robe and the tunics.

PERFUMERS' BLEND: This refers to the craft of blending a mixture of ground plants and spices. This type of mixture was used in producing the anointing oil and the fragrant incense.

GEM CUTTER'S WORK: This is the craft of carving gemstones from their natural source. This was used in preparing the rock crystal stones for the ephod and the breast piece.

BRAIDED INTO CORDS: This refers to a method of braiding threads for chains. This method was used with the golden threads that attached the ephod to the breast piece.

PROCESSING RAW MATERIALS – WOOD, STONE, AND METAL

Flattened boards of acacia wood

Acacia wood before processing

Polished gemstones

Uncut gemstones

Gold ore

Purified gold

Silver ore

Purified silver

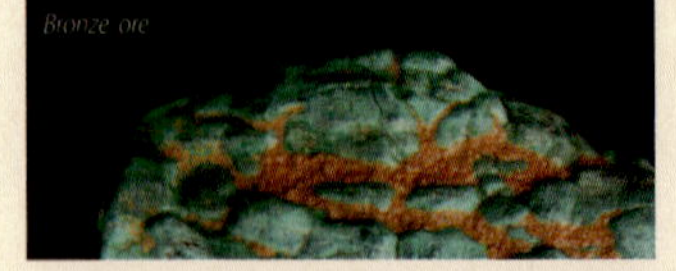
Bronze ore

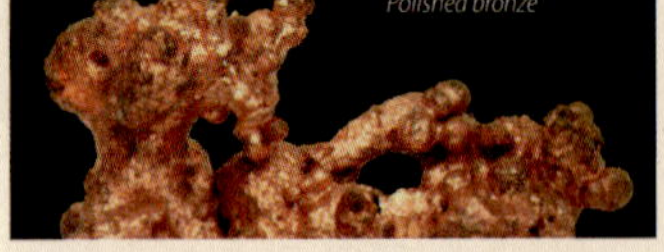
Polished bronze

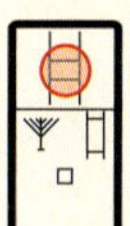

GOLD PLATING

CROWN

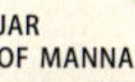

JAR OF MANNA

ARK OF THE COVENANT

Exodus 25:10–22
Exodus 37:1–9

LOCATION: The center of the Holy of Holies.

RAW MATERIALS: Acacia wood and pure gold.

DIMENSIONS: **WIDTH:** 1.5 cubits (approx. 72 cm).
LENGTH: 2.5 cubits (approx. 1.2 m).
HEIGHT (including cherubim)**:** 1.5 cubits (approx. 72 cm).

STRUCTURE: The Ark was made of three boxes – an inner box made of gold, a middle box made of wood, and an external box made of gold. Outside of the Ark there was a pottery jar containing manna (in the volume of an omer, which according to Maimonides is equivalent to approx. 2.16 l). Later, Aharon's staff that had miraculously blossomed was also placed there. The fragments of the first, broken, tablets of testimony, and the unbroken second tablets of testimony were placed inside the Ark. Later, the original Torah scroll written by Moshe was also inserted into the Ark.

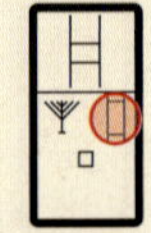

THE TABLE *Exodus 25:23–30, Exodus 37:10–16*

LOCATION: The northern part of the Sanctuary.

RAW MATERIALS: Acacia wood and pure gold.

DIMENSIONS: **WIDTH:** One cubit (approx. 48 cm).
LENGTH: Two cubits (approx. 96 cm).
HEIGHT (without the tubes)**:** 1.5 cubits (approx. 72 cm).

STRUCTURE: The table, and the frame that sat on it, were made of wood and plated with pure gold. At the sides of the frame were four tubes, with supports between them. The twelve loaves of showbread were placed on the supports.

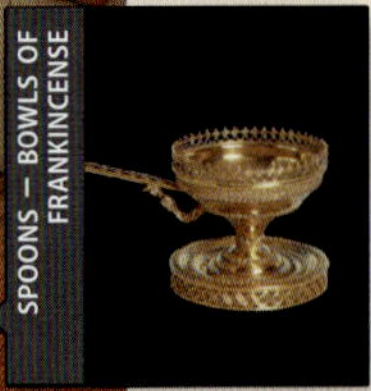

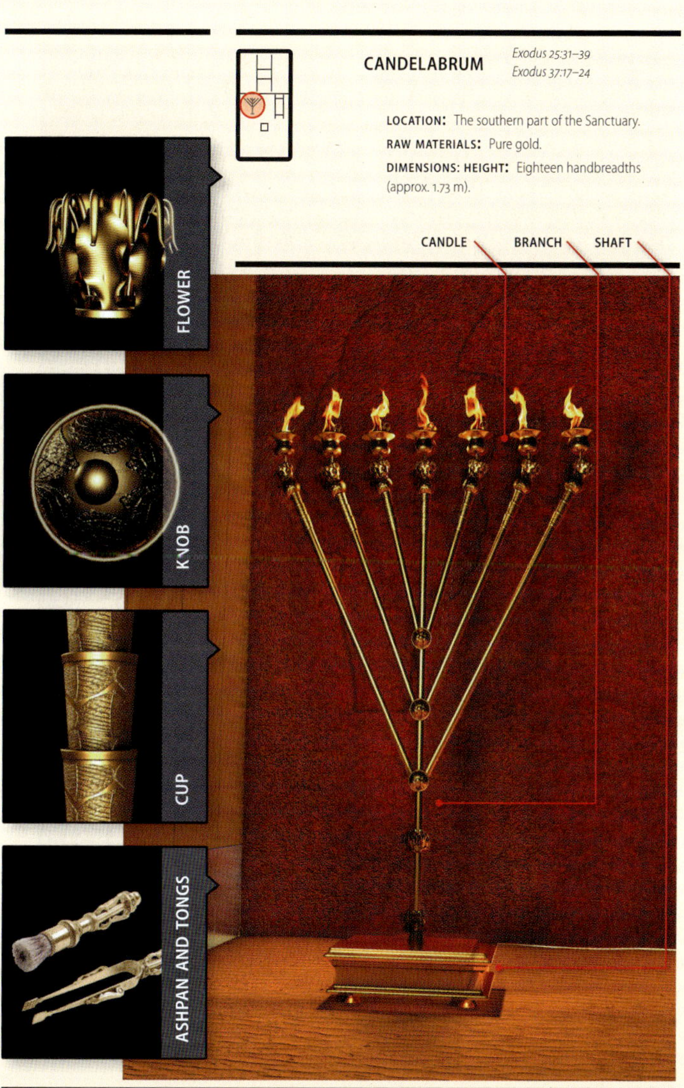

CANDELABRUM
Exodus 25:31–39
Exodus 37:17–24
LOCATION: The southern part of the Sanctuary.
RAW MATERIALS: Pure gold.
DIMENSIONS: HEIGHT: Eighteen handbreadths (approx. 1.73 m).
CANDLE
BRANCH
SHAFT
FLOWER
KNOB
CUP
ASHPAN AND TONGS

GOLD PLATING

The incense altar does not appear in the list of the other sacred vessels in Parashat Teruma *Ex. 25:1–27:19) but only in* Parashat Tetzaveh (Ex. 30:10-27:20) *after the list of the priestly vestments.*

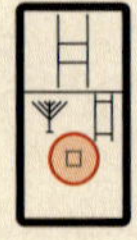

THE INCENSE ALTAR

Exodus 30:1–10
Exodus 37:25–28

LOCATION: The center of the Sanctuary.

RAW MATERIALS: Acacia wood and pure gold.

DIMENSIONS: **WIDTH:** One cubit (approx. 48 cm).
LENGTH: One cubit (approx. 48 cm).
HEIGHT (including horns): Two cubits (approx. 96 cm).

STRUCTURE OF THE TABERNACLE

STRUCTURE OF THE TABERNACLE *Exodus 26:1–14, Exodus 36:8–19*

FUNCTION: The three different sheets were designed to cover the Tent of Meeting.

DESCRIPTION: The bottom sheet, which was laid directly over the Tabernacle's boards, is called the Tabernacle. Above it was placed the goats'-hair sheet, which was longer and wider than the Tabernacle. A person who stood outside the Tent of Meeting was unable to see the Tabernacle, as the goats'-hair sheet concealed it. The goats'-hair sheets hung down an extra two cubits at the facade of the Tabernacle, above the entrance to the tent, and a single cubit extended in the back onto the ground ("the extra overhang"). The goats'-hair sheets were attached with ropes to bronze spikes that were inserted in the ground. Above the goats'-hair sheet was placed the cover of the Tent. This covered only the upper portion of the Tent of Meeting.

THE TABERNACLE

FUNCTION: To provide a covering for the Tent of Meeting.

RAW MATERIALS: Six strands of white linen, and eighteen strands of colored wool – six sky blue, six purple, and six scarlet red. All the strands were twisted together to form a single thread.

STRUCTURE: Ten sheets, each of which was twenty-eight cubits long and four cubits wide (approx. 13.4 m x 1.92 m).

ATTACHMENT OF THE SHEETS: The ten sheets were sewn together into two separate **couplings**, each of which was composed of five sheets. The two couplings were attached to each other with fifty golden clasps. These clasps were inserted through fifty sky-blue loops that were attached to the edges of the couplings.

The line of the attachments formed by the golden clasps was positioned directly over the curtain.

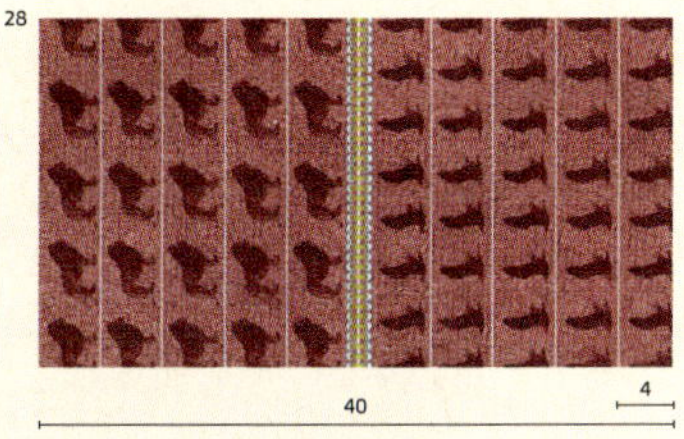

GOATS'-HAIR SHEETS

FUNCTION: To provide a tent covering above the sheets of the Tabernacle.

RAW MATERIALS: Goats'-hair.

STRUCTURE: Eleven sheets, each of which was thirty cubits long and four cubits wide (approx. 14.4 m x 1.92 m).

ATTACHMENT OF THE SHEETS: The eleven sheets were combined into two **couplings**, one made from six sheets and the other from five sheets. These two couplings were attached to each other with fifty bronze clasps. These clasps were inserted through fifty loops that were attached to the edges of the couplings.

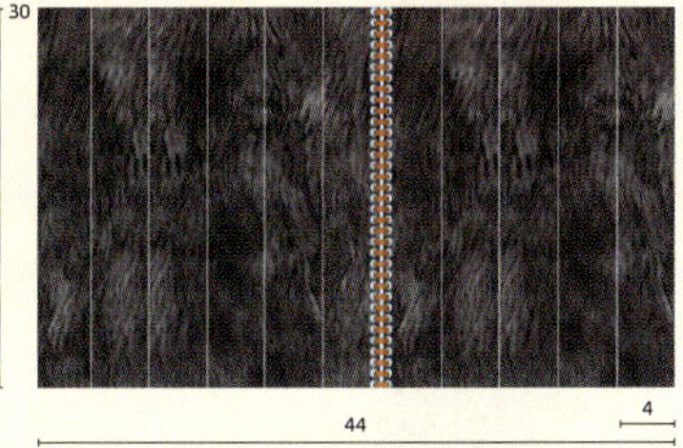

COVER OF THE TENT

FUNCTION: To provide a covering above the goats'-hair sheets.

RAW MATERIALS: Rams' hides dyed red, and *tahash* skin.

STRUCTURE: A single sheet, half of which was made from rams' hides dyed red, and half from *tahash* skin. It was thirty cubits long and ten cubits wide (approx. 14.4 m x 4.8 m).

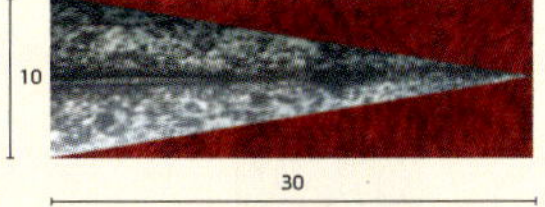

THE TABERNACLE BUILDING *Exodus 26:15–30, Exodus 36:20–34*

FUNCTION: To support the Tabernacle (the bottommost sheet that covers the holy vessels), and contain the holy vessels.

DESCRIPTION: The **boards** were placed within **silver sockets** to form a three-sided structure, with an opening on the fourth side. The boards were attached to one another at the top by **rings**, and the structure was strengthened by the use of **crossbars** on all sides.

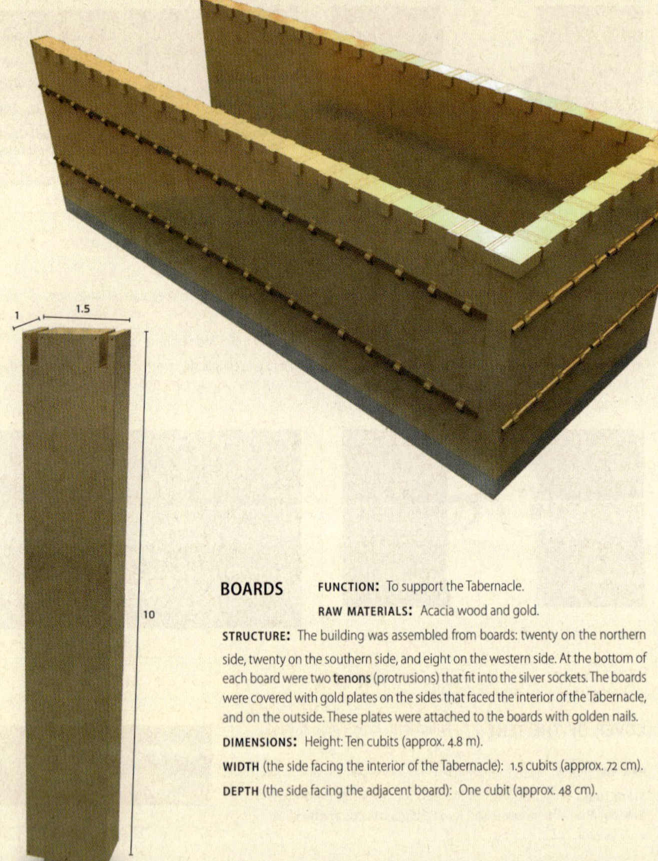

BOARDS

FUNCTION: To support the Tabernacle.

RAW MATERIALS: Acacia wood and gold.

STRUCTURE: The building was assembled from boards: twenty on the northern side, twenty on the southern side, and eight on the western side. At the bottom of each board were two **tenons** (protrusions) that fit into the silver sockets. The boards were covered with gold plates on the sides that faced the interior of the Tabernacle, and on the outside. These plates were attached to the boards with golden nails.

DIMENSIONS: Height: Ten cubits (approx. 4.8 m).

WIDTH (the side facing the interior of the Tabernacle): 1.5 cubits (approx. 72 cm).

DEPTH (the side facing the adjacent board): One cubit (approx. 48 cm).

RINGS

FUNCTION: To secure the tops of the boards.

RAW MATERIALS: Gold.

Each of the boards had a groove cut into the top, near the edge of the board. The rings were inserted into these grooves to hold the boards together. At the corners, where two sides of the building met, the ring was inserted on one of the boards, and was designed to fit its width.

DIMENSIONS: Apparently slightly more than one cubit by two fingerbreadths (approx. 50 cm x 4 cm).

SILVER SOCKETS

FUNCTION: To support the boards of the Tabernacle, and protect them.

RAW MATERIALS: Silver.

Each socket had a single impression into which one of the tenons of the board was inserted. In other words, underneath each board there were two sockets; a total of ninety-six sockets on the three sides of the structure.

DIMENSIONS: Height: One cubit (approx. 48 cm).

WIDTH (the side facing the interior of the Tabernacle): Seventy-five cubits (approx. 36 cm).

DEPTH (the side facing the adjacent socket): One cubit (approx. 48 cm).

The impression in each socket measured half a cubit by one-fourth of a cubit (approx. 24 cm x 12 cm).

CROSSBARS

FUNCTION: To hold the boards together and stabilize the walls of the structure.

RAW MATERIALS: Acacia wood and gold.

Each side of the Tabernacle was secured with five round crossbars – two upper crossbars that met in the middle of the wall on the outside, two lower crossbars that met in the middle of the wall on the outside, and a single central crossbar that was inserted into holes that cut through the boards (this crossbar was not visible from the outside). The four external crossbars were attached to the boards by rings. The crossbars and the **rings** were plated with gold.

DIMENSIONS: Thickness: At least one handbreadth (approx. 8 cm).

LENGTH OF THE FOUR EXTERNAL CROSSBARS: On the long walls, fifteen cubits (approx. 7.2 m), and on the short side, six cubits (approx. 2.9 m).

LENGTH OF THE CENTRAL CROSSBAR: On the long walls, thirty cubits (approx. 14.4 m), and on the short side, twelve cubits (approx. 5.8 m).

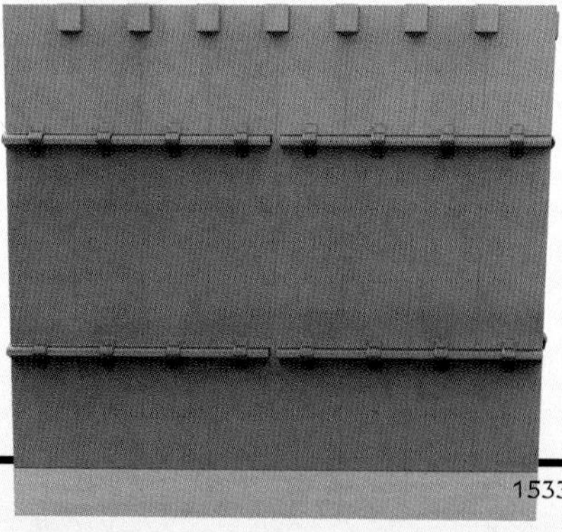

SCREENS *Exodus 26:31–37, Exodus 36:35–38*

RAW MATERIALS: Six threads of white flax and eighteen threads of colored wool – six sky blue, six purple, and six scarlet.

STRUCTURE: The curtain and the screen were supported by poles. These poles were supported by hooks that were attached to pillars made of acacia wood.

DIMENSIONS OF THE CURTAIN AND THE SCREEN:

HEIGHT: Ten cubits (approx. 4.8 m).

WIDTH: Ten cubits (approx. 4.8 m).

THE CURTAIN

FUNCTION: To separate between the Sanctuary and the Holy of Holies.

METHOD OF WEAVING: Artistic work with the form of cherubim.

LOCATION: Underneath the clasps of the sheets of the Tabernacle, twenty cubits (approx. 9.6 m) from the door of the Tabernacle.
The curtain was supported by four pillars made of gold-plated acacia wood. The pillars were ten cubits (approx. 4.8 m) high and one cubit by one cubit (approx. 48 cm x 48 cm) wide. Each pillar stood on a silver socket.

THE SCREEN AT THE OPENING OF THE TENT OF MEETING

FUNCTION: To serve as the door to the Tent of Meeting.

METHOD OF WEAVING: Woven work.

LOCATION: Entrance to the Sanctuary.
The screen was supported by five pillars made of gold-plated acacia wood, with gold tops and hoops. The pillars were ten cubits (approx. 4.8 m) high and one cubit by one cubit (approx. 48 cm x 48 cm) wide. Each pillar stood on a bronze socket.

THE LAVER AND ITS BASE

Exodus 30:18–21
Exodus 38:8

FUNCTION: To serve as a vessel for the priests for washing their hands and feet prior to the service.

RAW MATERIALS: Bronze from the **mirrors of the assembled women**.

DESCRIPTION: In the lower section of the laver, there were spouts for washing hands and feet. The base of the laver was like a large bronze bowl.

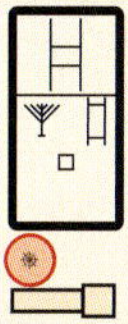

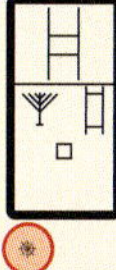

The laver and its base do not appear in Parashat Teruma *(Ex. 25:1–27:19) together with the altar of acacia wood, but only in* Parashat Ki Tisa *(Ex. 30:11–34:35), after the command* ***to collect half shekels.***

THE SACRIFICIAL ALTAR

Exodus 27:1–8
Exodus 38:1–7

LOCATION: The Tabernacle courtyard, opposite the entrance to the Tabernacle.

RAW MATERIALS: Acacia wood and bronze.

DIMENSIONS: **WIDTH:** Five cubits (approx. 2.4 m).
LENGTH: Five cubits (approx. 2.4 m).
HEIGHT (including horns)**:** Ten cubits (approx. 4.8 m).

STRUCTURE: The **foundation** of the altar protruded one cubit outward and was one cubit high. In the center of the altar was the **grate**, which was a bronze net to which were attached four rings for the carrying poles. Above this was the **ledge**, which was a protrusion one cubit wide. At the top of the altar there were **four horns** at the four corners. The altar was hollow, made from boards, meaning that four boards of acacia wood were attached to one another, creating a hollow space between them. Each time the Tabernacle was assembled, this hollow space was filled with dirt, which was visible at the top of the altar. The walls of the altar were plated with bronze, as were the carrying poles (made from acacia wood). It is clear from the text (Ex. 20:23) that there was a ramp leading to the top of the altar.

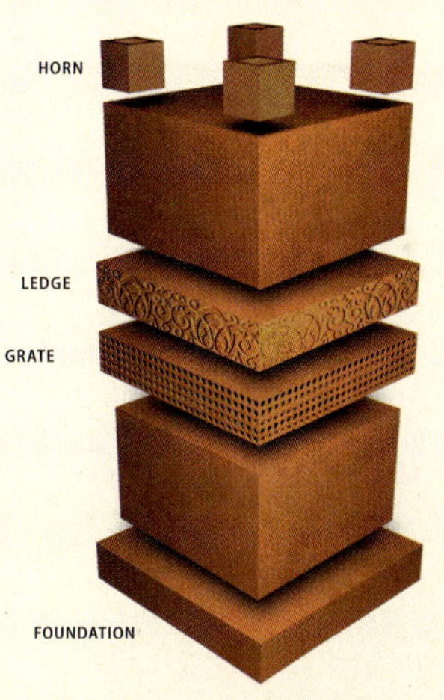

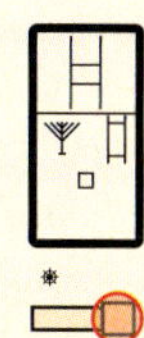

BRONZE VESSELS

FIVE BRONZE VESSELS WERE USED IN THE TABERNACLE SERVICE:

POTS: Bowls for collecting the ashes to remove them from the altar.

SHOVELS: Small rakes for sweeping the ashes into the pots.

BASINS: Cups for collecting the blood of sacrifices and sprinkling it on the altar.

FORKS: Used to turn the sacrificial meat on the altar.

FIRE PANS: Large pans for carrying coals from the bronze altar.

BASIN

FORK

FIRE PAN

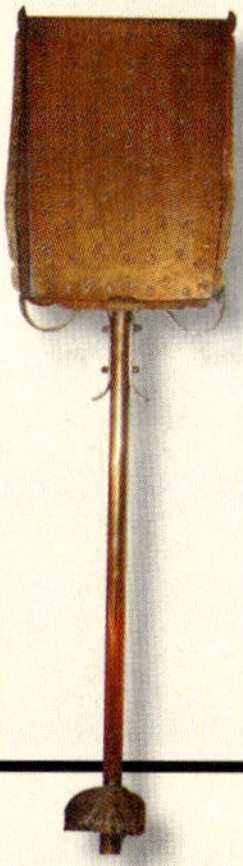

SHOVEL

POT

THE TABERNACLE COURTYARD *Exodus 27:9–19, Exodus 38:8–20*

DESCRIPTION: The Tent of Meeting was surrounded on all four sides by partitions called **hangings**. These hangings were supported by **pillars** mounted on **sockets** together with **hooks and loops**. These formed the Tabernacle courtyard. At its entrance was the **courtyard screen.**

DIMENSIONS: LENGTH: One hundred cubits (approx. 48 m).
WIDTH: Fifty cubits (approx. 24 m).
HEIGHT (of the pillars)**:** Fifteen cubits (approx. 7.2 m).

HANGINGS

FUNCTION: To enclose the Tabernacle courtyard.

RAW MATERIALS: Six threads of twisted flax.

TYPE OF WEAVING: Twisting.

DIMENSIONS: LENGTH of the edges at the sides of the Tabernacle: One hundred cubits (approx. 48 m).

LENGTH of the edge at the back of the Tabernacle: Fifty cubits (approx. 24 m).

LENGTH of each edge opposite the entrance to the Tabernacle, on each side of the screen: Fifteen cubits (approx. 7.2 m).

At the top, the hangings were attached to small boards. These boards were hung by clips from the tops of each of the pillars. At the bottom, the hangings were attached to cords that were tied to bronze stakes. These stakes pulled the hangings down.

PILLARS

FUNCTION: To support the courtyard hangings.

RAW MATERIALS: Acacia wood (apparently) and silver.

DIMENSIONS OF EACH PILLAR: HEIGHT: Fifteen cubits (approx. 7.2 m).

WIDTH: One cubit (approx. 48 cm).

DEPTH: One cubit (approx. 48 cm).

DESCRIPTION: Each pillar was supported by a bronze socket whose dimensions matched those of the pillar. Silver loops encircled the pillar, and its top was plated with silver. At the top of the pillar, the board that the hangings were hung from was attached. The pillars were attached to the bronze stakes with cords.

THE SCREEN OF THE GATE

FUNCTION: To serve as the entrance gate to the courtyard.

RAW MATERIALS: Six threads of white flax and eighteen threads of colored wool – six sky blue, six purple, and six scarlet.

TYPE OF WEAVING: Embroidery.

LOCATION: At the entrance to the courtyard between two hangings each fifteen cubits high, ten cubits from the courtyard.

DIMENSIONS: LENGTH: Twenty cubits (approx. 9.6 m).

HEIGHT: Fifteen cubits (approx. 7.2 m).

STRUCTURE: The screen of the gate was supported by four pillars (which were identical to the other pillars of the courtyard).

PROCESSING RAW MATERIALS – FLAX, WOOL, AND SKINS

Flax during processing

Processed flax

A strand of spun wool

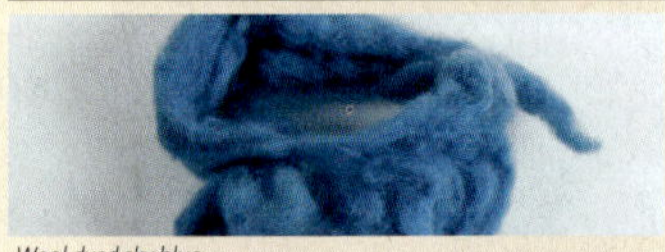
Wool dyed sky blue

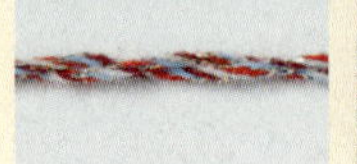
A thread spun from strands of dyed wool, a strand of flax, and a strand of gold

Flax threads

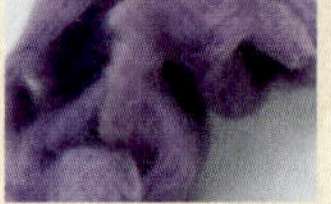
Wool dyed purple

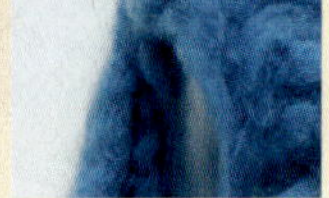
Wool dyed sky blue

An example of woven work

Wool dyed scarlet

Strands of beaten gold

Taḥash skin

Ram's hide dyed red

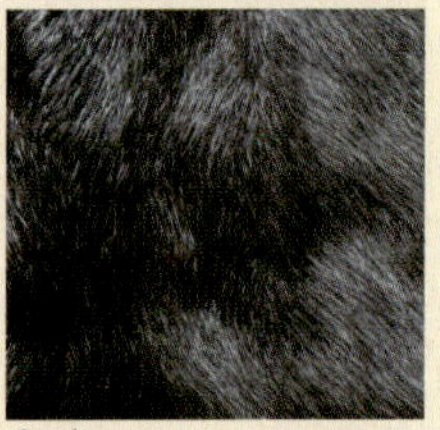
Goatskin

SACRED VESTMENTS

THE VESTMENTS OF AHARON THE PRIEST *Exodus 28:2–43, Exodus 39:2–31*

RAW MATERIALS: Gold, pure gold, threads of white flax, threads of wool dyed sky blue, purple, and scarlet, and precious stones.

DESCRIPTION (*according to the order of dressing detailed in Exodus 29:5*):

First, Aharon would put on the **linen trousers**. After that, he would put on the **tunic**, which covered his entire body. He then tied the **sash** around his waist, and above all of these, he wore the **robe**. Above the robe, he wore the **ephod**. At the upper edge of the ephod was a **decorated belt** to which rings were attached. A cord of sky blue was attached to these rings, used to attach the **breast piece** to the ephod. On his head, Aharon wore the **miter**, and above this the golden **headplate**.

BREAST PIECE

Exodus 28:15–30, Exodus 39:8–21

RAW MATERIALS: Four threads of gold, six threads of white flax, and eighteen threads of dyed wool – six sky blue, six purple, and six scarlet.

METHOD OF WEAVING: Skilled craftsmanship with a single golden thread on each of the four sets of threads.

DIMENSIONS: The breast piece was a folded rectangle that looked like a square when viewed from the front.

LENGTH: Before folding: One cubit (approx. 48 cm); after folding: Half a cubit (approx. 24 cm).

WIDTH: Half a cubit (approx. 24 cm).

DESCRIPTION: The breast piece was a square piece of woven fabric (a rectangle folded in half). Aharon wore the breast piece above his heart. On the breast piece, twelve stones were mounted in gold filigree settings. On these stones, the names of the twelve tribes of Israel were engraved "like a seal" (Ex. 28:21, 39:14). On the two upper edges of the breast piece, two golden rings were sewn. These rings were attached to pure gold chains to the gold filigree settings that were on the upper part of the shoulders of the ephod. Golden rings were also sewn to the two lower corners. These were attached with a sky blue cord to the golden rings that were on the lower part of the shoulders of the ephod. These connections held the lower edge of the breast piece adjacent to the upper edge of the decorated belt. The Urim and Tumim, which consisted of the ineffable name of God written on parchment, were inserted into the breast piece.

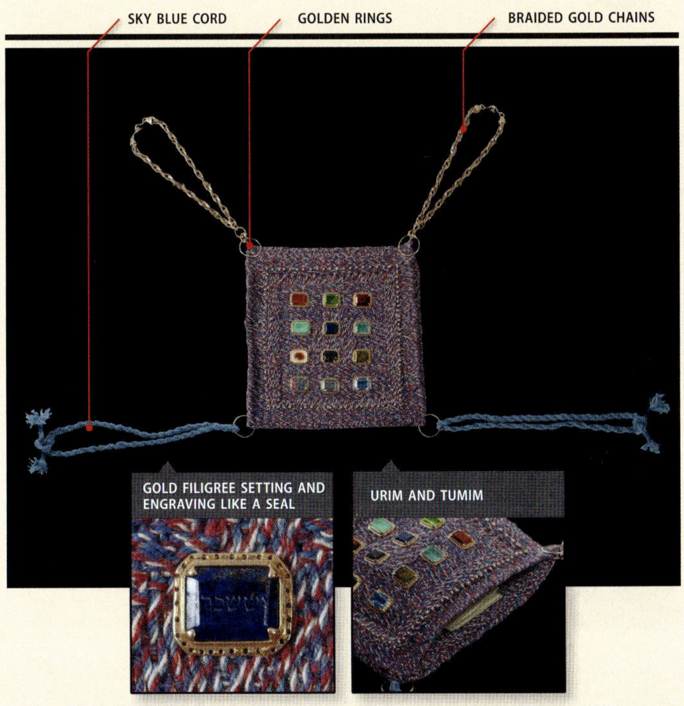

STONES OF THE BREAST PIECE

ZOHAR AMAR

In this appendix, we present an approach that applies a consistent system of identifying these stones. In our opinion, precedence should be given to the translation of Onkelos (although his explanations are not completely clear). This is because even if this translation underwent a later redaction, it was originally composed in the land of Israel a relatively short time after the destruction of the Second Temple. Hence, it may well preserve some of the memories of the actual Temple.

Carnelian: A quartz stone from the chalcedony mineral group, which contains a small amount of iron oxide, giving it a brown-orange-red hue. Its chemical formula is SiO_2. This stone is mentioned first, apparently due to its significance and unique popularity in the Biblical period. Indeed, it is the most common gemstone found in archaeological excavations from the Near East.

Olivine: This stone is also known as peridot, a silicate (meaning containing the element silicon, Si) compound also containing iron and magnesium. Its chemical formula is $(Mg,Fe)_2SiO_4$. It has been identified with the *τopázion* stone mentioned in Greek sources (and in fact, there is an etymological similarity between this term and the Hebrew *pitda*) which became popular in the Hellenistic period. This stone was imported from an island in the Red Sea that was within the borders of Ethiopia (Kush). This association leads to the expression *pitdat Kush* ("Kush's topaz") mentioned in Job 28:19.

Garnet: The Hebrew term *bareket* is related to the terms *barak* and *bazak* (lightning), and thus it seems that this is the "carbuncle" stone mentioned in ancient sources. This stone is red or purplish in color. Its chemical formula is $Fe_3Als(SiO_4)_3$.

Emerald: The emerald is mentioned in ancient Greek sources, sometimes as a general term for precious stones that are varieties of the mineral aquamarine. These stones are green in color because of the penetration of chromium and vanadium into the crystal. Its chemical formula is $Be_3Al_2(SiO_3)_6$. In nature, it generally appears in the form of hexagonal rods

Lapis lazuli: The term used by Onkelos in his translation [*shavziz*] is unclear. We suggest that the correct identification is lapis lazuli, a blue stone with a golden sheen caused by its pyrite inclusion. Its chemical formula is $(Na,Ca)_8Al_6Si_6O_{24}(S,SO)_4$. This identification is supported by Onkelos's translation of a parallel verse mentioning this blue stone called *sapir* (Ex. 24:10), as well as the Targum Yerushalmi translation, which references the blue stone with gold highlights mentioned in Greek sources called *sapperos*. The lapis lazuli was one of the most sought-after precious stones in ancient times. From the Roman period onward, the valuable blue corundum brought from India was also called by this name.

Green quartz: The meaning of the Hebrew word *yahalom* is unclear. According to Greek and Aramaic translations, it appears that it is an alternate name for the rubies mentioned in the prophets (Is. 54:12). However, the Greek translation *laspis* refers to a green stone, and thus it is reasonable to think that it is a type of green chalcedony such as plasma, or green jasper. Its chemical formula is SiO_2.

Amber: Onkelos's translation (*kankhiri*) may be equivalent to the Greek *lyncurion* mentioned in the Septuagint. The *inbar*, or amber, is actually fossilized sap of conifer trees with a yellow or orange hue. Another possibility is the sanburs plant mentioned in Greek sources.

Jet: The Aramaic translations identified the *shevo* as a stone coming from Thracia, or Thrace. This stone has been identified with the jet, which is fossilized charred wood. Ancient sources state that it is similar in appearance to the gagate stone, identified with the Greek translation *achates*. Other commentators, however, have identified the *shevo* as turquoise.

Sardonyx: This is a gemstone with a dark circle against a bright background in its center, resembling the eye of a cow, which is the meaning of the Aramaic term *ein egla* used by Onkelos. It is mentioned in ancient sources with the name *sardonyx*. This gemstone from the quartz family is characterized by bands of various colors: red, brown, white, or black. Its chemical formula is SiO_2. This identification is not compatible with the widespread identification of *aḥlama* as amethyst.

Aquamarine: The term "aquamarine" is etymologically similar to Onkelos's Aramaic translation *krom yama*, which incorporates the Greek *chrom* ("color" or "shade," used particularly in rabbinic sources with regard to varying shades) and the Aramaic *yam*, meaning "sea." As its name implies, the aquamarine is a type of beryl tinted in the bluish-green color of the sea. Its chemical formula is $Be_3Al_2(SiO_3)_6$.

Rock crystal: Onkelos translates this as *burla*, which is similar to the Greek gemstone name beryl. However, in Aramaic this term, or the alternate *bdolḥa*, was usually used for crystal. The particular stone in question here is related to the pure quartz family. It is a form of crystal resembling glass with various levels of translucency. It is one of the silicate minerals, which are composed of silicon and oxygen atoms. Its chemical formula is SiO_4.

Jasper or Opal: This is the gemstone known in Latin as *pantera* or *panther*. In Greek it is called *panchrus*, which means "all colors." It is characterized by reflections in a variety of colors: red, purple, green, and more. This description could fit the jasper, and even more so, the opal.

EPHOD

Exodus 28:1–12, Exodus 39:2–7

RAW MATERIALS: Four threads of gold, six threads of white flax, and eighteen threads of colored wool – six sky blue, six purple, and six scarlet.

METHOD OF WEAVING: Skilled craftsmanship, with one golden thread intertwined into each of the four groups of threads.

DESCRIPTION: The ephod covered Aharon from his back and on his sides from the lower back down to his heels. He tied the ephod with a type of belt known as the decorated waistband.

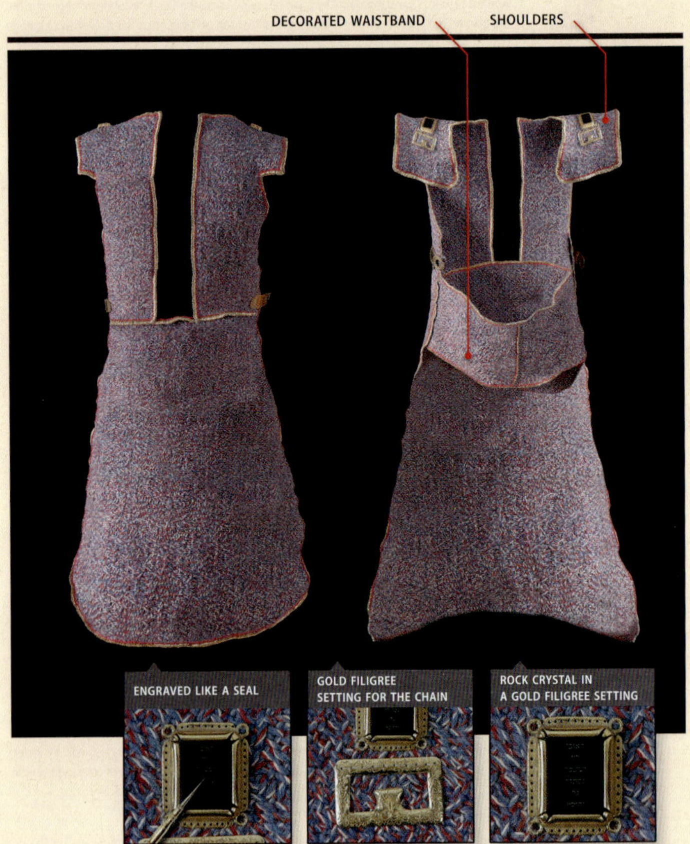

THE ROBE OF THE EPHOD *Exodus 28:31–35, Exodus 39:22–26*

RAW MATERIALS: Colored threads of flax – for the robe itself, twelve sky-blue threads, and for the pomegranates twenty-four threads – eight dyed sky blue, eight purple, eight scarlet – and also pure gold.

TYPE OF WEAVING: Woven work.

DESCRIPTION: The robe was a type of a gown that covered Aharon's entire body, with holes for his arms, head, and legs. The opening at the neck was woven doubly ("like the neck of a coat of mail"). The lower edge of the robe had thirty-six golden bells with clappers in front, and thirty-six at the back. Between every two bells, there was a pomegranate made from colored flax.

HEADPLATE

Exodus 28:36–38
Exodus 39:27

RAW MATERIALS: Pure gold, threads dyed sky blue.

DESCRIPTION: The headplate was tied onto Aharon's head with three double strands of sky blue – two from the two sides and the third in the center. The center one was pulled over the miter.

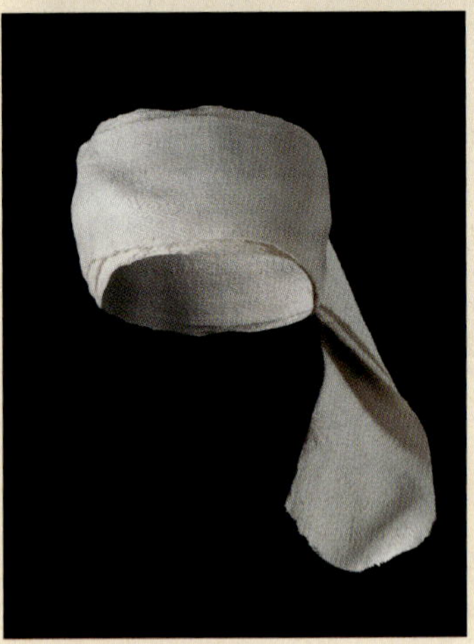

MITER

Exodus 28:39
Exodus 39:28

RAW MATERIALS: Six threads of flax.

DIMENSIONS: Width: Approximately three fingerbreadths (approx. 6 cm).

LENGTH: Sixteen cubits (approx. 7.7 m).

DESCRIPTION: Aharon's miter was a strip of linen fabric that was wrapped around his head.

TUNIC

Exodus 28:39
Exodus 39:27

RAW MATERIALS: Six threads of flax.

METHOD OF WEAVING: Woven work, quilted.

DESCRIPTION: The tunic was woven from a single piece of fabric long enough to reach the feet. The sleeves were attached to it by sewing.

SASH

Exodus 28:39
Exodus 39:29

RAW MATERIALS: Six threads of white flax and eighteen threads of colored wool – six sky blue, six purple, and six scarlet.

METHOD OF WEAVING: Embroidered work with flax embroidered with wool.

DIMENSIONS: Width: Approximately three fingerbreadths (approx. 6 cm).

LENGTH OF THE OPEN SASH: Thirty-two cubits (approx. 15.4 m).

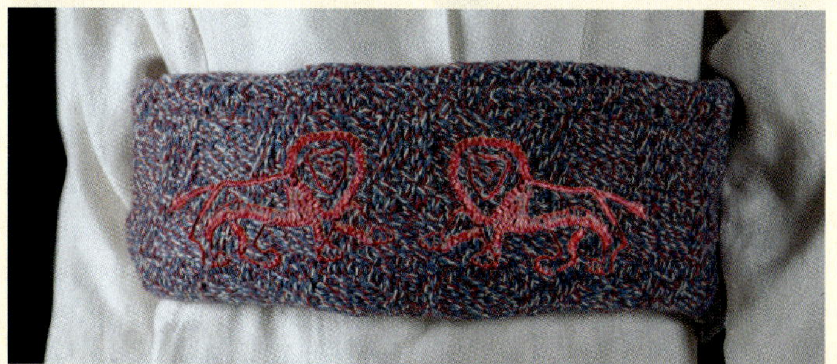

AHARON'S SONS' GARMENTS

Exodus 28:40, Exodus 39:27–29

DESCRIPTION: Aharon's sons wore four garments, three of which were made exclusively of linen: a tunic, a cap, and linen trousers. In addition, they wore a sash as a belt.

LINEN TROUSERS

Exodus 28:42
Exodus 39:28

RAW MATERIALS: Six threads of flax.

DESCRIPTION: Aharon and his sons wore the trousers under their tunics. They extended from above the navel down to the ankles. A cord was threaded through the upper edge of the garment to tighten the trousers.

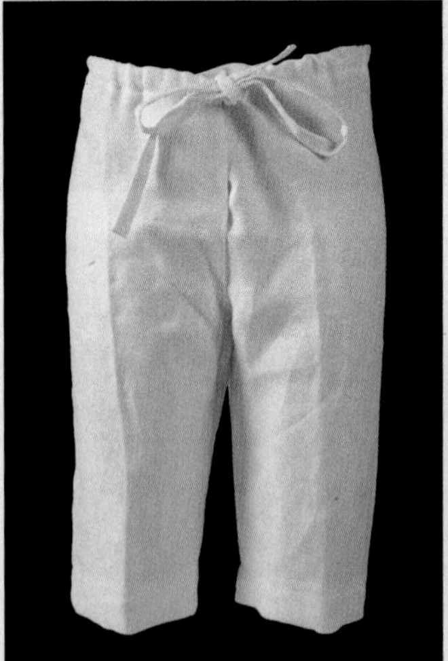

OFFERINGS

THE LAWS OF OFFERINGS – INTRODUCTION

RABBI MENACHEM MAKOVER

The book of Leviticus is devoted to the many details of the laws of offerings. Our Torah devotes the greater part of one entire book of the Torah to this topic. The service of the offerings is one of the three pillars upon which the world stands: Torah, divine service in the Temple, and acts of kindness (*Mishna Avot* 1:2).

According to the Sages (Avoda Zara 8a), the service of the offerings is as old as the world itself; the first one to offer an offering to God was Adam after he was banished from the Garden of Eden. The first offerings mentioned in the Torah in detail are the ones brought by Noaḥ after leaving the ark (Gen. 8:20): "Then Noaḥ built an altar to the Lord and, taking of each of the kinds of pure animals and pure birds, sacrificed burnt offerings on the altar." After that, our patriarchs, Avraham, Yitzḥak, and Yaakov, also built altars and brought offerings. It is thus clear that the service of offerings has very deep roots in the Torah.

In the book of Leviticus, the children of Israel were given very detailed commands and instructions regarding offerings, which apply for all generations. At the first stage, this service was carried out in the temporary Tabernacle, later on in the more permanent Tabernacle at Shiloh, and finally in the eternal Temple that stood on Mount Moriah in Jerusalem. In this appendix, we have chosen to explain the service of the offerings as it was carried out in the Temple, as most of the discussions in the literature of the Sages focus on this period and not on the Tabernacle in the desert. This is because even during the interim period before the Temple was constructed, the Temple was the goal for which people were striving, and it was only there that the service of the offerings could be completely fulfilled. The service of the offerings will be renewed in the future when the Temple is rebuilt, as Maimonides has written (*Laws of Kings* 11:1), "The king Messiah shall arise in the future, and will restore the dynasty of David as of old...and all the laws [of the Torah] will be observed in his days as were in the past; **we will bring offerings**...according to all of the Torah's commands."

There are several different categories of offerings. Here we shall list them and describe some of their essential characteristics:

- **OFFERINGS OF THE MOST SACRED ORDER:** These are offerings with the highest level of sanctity. They are brought primarily to achieve atonement. These include burnt offerings, purification offerings, guilt offerings, and communal peace offerings.
- **OFFERINGS OF LESSER SANCTITY:** These are brought primarily for the sake of coming closer to God, offering thanksgiving, and strengthening the covenant. Offerings of the most sacred order must be slaughtered to the north of the altar, and the parts that are eaten (from the purification offerings, guilt offerings, and communal peace offerings) must be consumed within the Temple courtyard. Conversely, offerings of lesser sanctity may be slaughtered anywhere within the courtyard, and the parts that are eaten may be consumed anywhere in Jerusalem.
- **ANIMAL OFFERINGS:** These come from cattle, sheep, or goats. These comprise the majority of the offerings.
- **BIRD OFFERINGS:** These consist of doves or pigeons; **GRAIN OFFERINGS:** These are offerings brought from plants, primarily wheat.
- **OBLIGATORY OFFERINGS:** These include the daily burnt offering and additional offerings; **VOLUNTARY OFFERINGS:** These are made up of voluntary burnt offerings, peace offerings.
- **COMMUNAL OFFERINGS:** These include the daily offering; **INDIVIDUAL OFFERINGS:** One example is the burnt offering of appearance, brought on the festivals.

The procedures for bringing the offerings include several obligatory acts of service: slaughtering the animal, receiving the blood, bringing the blood to the altar, and sprinkling the blood upon the altar. Additional acts of service, such as burning the limbs of the offering, are not essential acts (meaning that if they are not properly performed, the offering remains valid). The procedures for the offerings must be carried out correctly, regarding both the laws of the offering and the thoughts and intentions of the priests who carry out the service.

Hasidic writings explain (see *Beit Yaakov* by the Rebbe of Izhbitza, *Vayikra* 2) that the purpose of the service of the offerings is that the sanctity that is revealed in the Temple not remain in the purely elevated, spiritual realm. Rather, the revelation of sanctity must also elevate the physical, animalistic aspects of the world. The essence of the offering is thus a connection between diverse worlds, unifying the material and physical worlds. The animal that ascends on the altar is converted into "a pleasing aroma"; the Godly spark that exists in the animal is elevated to its source, and with this the animalistic essence is redeemed – thus also redeeming those who bring the offering.

May it be His will that we merit the rebuilding of the Temple, speedily in our days.

In this appendix, we have attempted to explain the procedures of the animal, bird, and grain offerings in a clear and understandable manner. First, we present the animals that are brought, and the raw materials used in the grain offerings. Each of these is accompanied by an icon. Next, we have given a brief explanation of each step in the procedures for each offering, and here as well there is an icon for each act. In the descriptions of the procedures for each individual offering, we have employed the same icons, with brief explanations for the sake of clarity. In addition, we have provided a small diagram of the Tabernacle indicating the precise location where the services for each offering take place.

ANIMALS

CATTLE (בקר)

"**Cattle**" is a general term that includes the **calf** and the **bull**.

A pink border indicates females; a blue border indicates males.

CALF (עגל/עגלה)

Cattle is called by this term during its first year of life, at which time it is valid as an offering.

BULL (פר)

Cattle is called by this term from the second year onward. It is valid as an offering until the end of its third year of life.

COW (פרה)

This term is used from the second year onward. It is valid as an offering until the end of its third year of life.

ANIMAL

FLOCKS (צאן)

"Flock" is a general term that includes **sheep** and **goats**.

A pink border indicates females; a blue border indicates males.

SHEEP

RAM (איל)

This term refers to a male sheep from the age of one year and thirty-one days onward. It is valid as an offering until the end of the second year of its life.

SHEEP (כבש)

The animal is called a sheep during the first year of its life.

GOATS

HE-GOAT (שעיר)

This term refers to a male goat from the age of one year onward. It is valid as an offering until the end of the third year of its life.

GOAT (עז)

The animal is called this during the first year of its life.

BIRDS (עופות)

PIGEON (יונה)

The pigeon is valid as an offering from its youth.

DOVE (תור)

The dove is valid as an offering when mature.

PARTS OF THE OFFERINGS

SACRIFICIAL PORTION (אימורים)

This term refers to the internal fats of the animal that are offered on the altar. They are found in the hind portion of the animal, in the vicinity of the kidneys, liver, and hip bone. When offering a sheep, the tail and the vertebrae connected to it are also burned.

HIDE (עור)

The hide of the animal is given to the priests (with the exception of purification offerings that are brought into the holy place). This constitutes one of the twenty-four gifts of the priesthood.

BLOOD (דם)

Immediately after the animal is slaughtered, the blood is collected from its neck into a vessel. The primary atonement brought about by the offering is connected to placing this blood on the altar, or to sprinkling it in the Sanctuary or the Holy of Holies.

MEAT (בשר)

This refers to the remaining limbs of the animal. In a burnt offering, these are also burned on the altar. For other types of offerings, they are eaten by the priests, and at times by the owner of the offering.

PLANT-BASED OFFERINGS

BARLEY (שעורה)

Barley was used in some of the grain offerings (the omer offering and the offering of the suspected adulteress).

WHEAT (חיטה)

The flour for the grain offerings was made from wheat.

OIL (שמן)

Oil was produced from choice olives and used in the preparation of grain offerings.

WINE (יין)

Wine was poured on the altar.

FRANKINCENSE (לבונה)

Most grain offerings had frankincense added.

SALT (מלח)

Everything offered on the altar was salted.

WEIGHTS AND MEASURES

Length			
Unit	Equivalent	Centimeters	Sample Biblical Reference
fingerbreadth		20 cm	Jeremiah 52:21
handbreadth	4 fingerbreadths	80 cm	Exodus 25:25
span (distance between thumb and little finger)	3 handbreadths	240 cm	Exodus 28:16
cubit	2 span	48 cm	Exodus 26:16 Judges 3:16

Weight			
Unit	Equivalent	Grams	Sample Biblical Reference
gerah		0.8	Exodus 30:13
shekel	20 gerah	19.2	Exodus 38:24
maneh	50 shekel	480	Ezekiel 45:12
talent	60 maneh	28,800	Exodus 25:39

Dry Measures			
Unit	Equivalent	Liters	Sample Biblical Reference
kab		1.38	II Kings 6:25
omer	1.8 kab	2.49	Exodus 16:16
(Rabbinic: tarkav)	1.66 omer	4.14	
se'a	2 tarkav	8.29	II Kings 7:1
ephah	3 se'a	24.88	Ezekiel 45:24
homer	10 ephah	248.9	Isaiah 5:10

Dry Measures			
Unit	Equivalent	Liters	Sample Biblical Reference
log		0.34	Leviticus 14:12
tenth of an ephah	7.2 log	2.49	Leviticus 14:12
hin	0.166 ephah	4.14	Exodus 30:24
(rabbinic: jug)	2 hin	8.29	
bat	3 jug	24.88	I Kings 7:26
kor	10 bat	248.9	Ezekiel 45:14

SERVICE OF THE OFFERINGS

THE STRUCTURE OF THE TABERNACLE AND THE STRUCTURE OF THE TEMPLE

The primary service of the offerings took place in the courtyard of the Tabernacle. The courtyard was an open area surrounded by the sheets, and in its center was the Tent of Meeting. The Tent was built from boards that were plated with gold, and over them, sheets. In the Temple, the courtyard was surrounded by a wall; in its center was the Sanctuary of the House of God. The sacrificial altar stood to the east of the entrance to the Tent of Meeting. In the Temple, the altar that stood opposite the Sanctuary was larger (see elaboration below).

In the Tabernacle, the area of the Holy of Holies was ten cubits by ten cubits. In the Temple, it was twenty cubits by twenty cubits.

The holy place in the Tabernacle was twenty cubits long and ten cubits wide. In the Temple, these measurements were doubled to forty cubits by twenty cubits. In the Tabernacle, the curtain divided between the holy place and the Holy of Holies. In the First Temple, there was a wall one cubit thick separating the two sections, whereas in the Second Temple there were two curtains separated by a cubit.

In the holy place, there were three vessels: the candelabrum, the table, and the incense altar. The candelabrum was in the south, and opposite it to the north was the table – both of these were closer to the Holy of Holies than the incense altar, which was in the center of the holy place. The Ark was in the Holy of Holies.

Offerings of the most sacred order were slaughtered in the northern part of the courtyard, as illustrated below:

NORTH

WEST

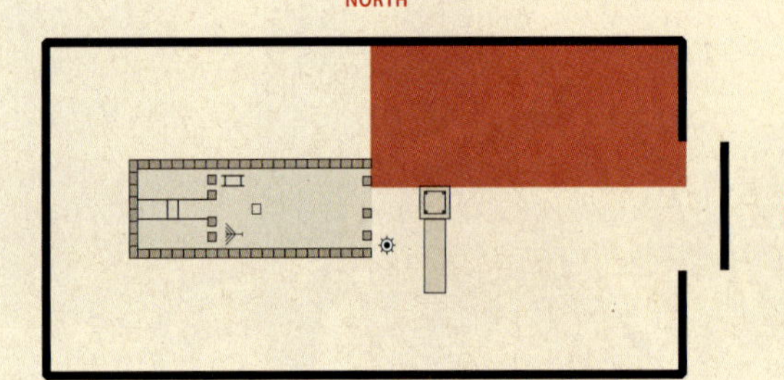

EAST

SOUTH

Offerings of lesser sanctity could be slaughtered anywhere in the courtyard, as illustrated below:

NORTH

WEST

EAST

SOUTH

STRUCTURE OF THE ALTAR

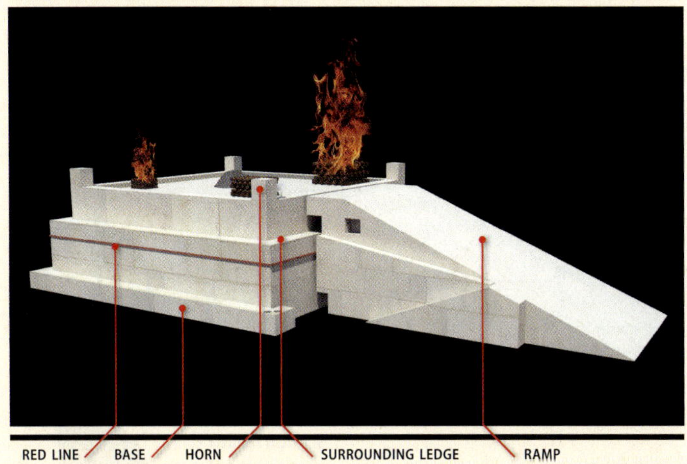

The altar of the Second Temple is described in tractate Middot (3:1).

The width of the altar at its bottom was thirty-two cubits, and it got progressively smaller at higher levels. At the bottom was the base of the altar. It was a single cubit wide, and it surrounded the altar on the north and on the west, with an additional cubit protruding to the south and an additional cubit protruding to the east.

There were certain services that were performed on the lower section of the wall of the altar. Therefore, at the halfway mark (five cubits from the ground), there was a red line that served as the boundary between the upper and lower parts of the altar.

Five cubits above the base was the surrounding ledge, a type of path that surrounded the altar, with a width of a single cubit. For certain services, the priests would stand on this ledge.

Three cubits above the surrounding ledge was the roof of the altar, and in its four corners there were four horns, each one cubit high. Hence, the total height of the altar, including the horns, was ten cubits.

To the south of the altar was the ramp that was used to ascend the altar.

On the roof of the altar there were three arrangements of wood. The first was called the large arrangement, and it was where the offerings were burned. It was located in the southeastern part of the altar. The second arrangement was called the incense arrangement, as coals were taken from it to burn the incense on the golden altar in the holy place. The third arrangement was used to fulfill the commandment "A daily fire shall be kept alight on the altar" (Lev. 6:5). This arrangement of wood had no other use.

THE WORK OF THE OFFERINGS

TRANSPORTING THE BLOOD

After receiving the blood from the slaughtered animal in a vessel, the priest walks with the blood toward the altar so that it can be placed there. For purification offerings in which the blood is sprinkled inside the holy place, the priest brings the blood into the holy place for sprinkling.

PRESENTING THE BLOOD

The priest presents the blood of the offering in one of five different ways:

1. **Two presentations which are four:** For burnt offerings, guilt offerings, and peace offerings, the priest sprinkles the blood on the lower part of the altar, on the point of two of the corners (the northeastern corner and the southwestern corner). The blood therefore spreads out onto all four sides of the altar.

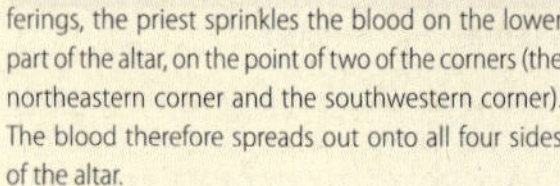

2. **Four presentations on the four horns:** For a purification offering in which the blood is sprinkled on or near the altar, the priest ascends to the surrounding ledge of the altar and places the blood on each one of the four horns of the altar. At each horn, the priest dips his right finger into the blood and smears it on the point of the horn.

3. **Pouring out over the base:** For a firstborn animal, an animal tithe, and the Passover offering, the priest pours all of the blood over the base of the altar (with the exclusion of the southeastern corner, where there was no base).
4. **Sprinkling:** The priest sprinkles the blood with his finger inside the Sanctuary or the Holy of Holies. After sprinkling it, he puts some of the blood on the horns of the golden altar.
5. **Extraction:** The priest presses the body of the bird against the wall of the altar, so that the blood will run down the wall and onto the base.

LAYING OF HANDS

The owner of the offering leans both of his hands, with all of his strength, on the animal's head.

CONFESSION

The owner of the offering makes a statement while laying his hands on the animal. For purification offerings, he confesses his sin; for offerings that are not brought to atone for a sin, he makes a statement of thanksgiving and praise of God.

SLAUGHTERING

The priest severs the two organs of the animal that must be severed – the trachea and the esophagus. This act can also be done by a non-priest.

PINCHING THE NECK

The priest slices through the neck of the bird with his thumbnail. As with ordinary slaughter, he must sever the correct organ (for a purification offering from a bird it is sufficient to sever a single organ).

RECEIVING THE BLOOD

The priest receives the blood from the slaughtered animal in a vessel.

TRANSPORTING THE SACRIFICIAL PARTS

The priest walks to the ramp with the parts of the animal that are to be burned. For a burnt offering, he brings all of the animal's limbs, and for other offerings, he brings only the sacrificial parts.

WAVING

The owner of the offering stands at the east of the courtyard holding the sacrificial parts of the animal, together with the breast and the thigh. The priest places his hand under the owner's hand, and together they wave the parts back and forth, and up and down.

SALTING

The priest salts all of the parts that will be placed on the altar before they are placed there. There was a single pile of salt on the ramp, and another pile on the altar itself.

BURNING

The priest throws all of the parts that are offered into the fire of the large arrangement of wood.

POURING THE REMAINING BLOOD

After presenting the blood, the priest pours the blood that remains in the vessel onto the base of the altar.

SKINNING

The priest strips the hide of the animal. This act may also be performed by a non-priest.

BUTCHERING

The priest cuts the animal into pieces. For a public burnt offering, the bull is divided into twenty-four parts, a ram is divided into eleven, and a sheep or goat is divided into eight. For an individual burnt offering it may be divided into any number of parts.

REMOVING THE SACRIFICIAL PARTS

The priest removes the inner fats and the organs that are to be burned on the altar: the fat that is on the entrails, the two kidneys and the fat that is on them, the fat on the loins, and the diaphragm of the liver (for a sheep, the tail is also burned).

EATING

For those offerings that are eaten, after the sacrificial parts are burned, the remainder of the animal must be eaten within the span of a single day and a single night (that is, the day that the offering is brought, and the night that follows), or two days and a single night (meaning the day the offering is brought, the night that follows, and the next day). For offerings of the most sacred order, male priests eat the meat of the offering in the Temple courtyard. Meal offerings are also eaten by male priests in the courtyard.

The priest eats the meal offering

The priest eats the offering

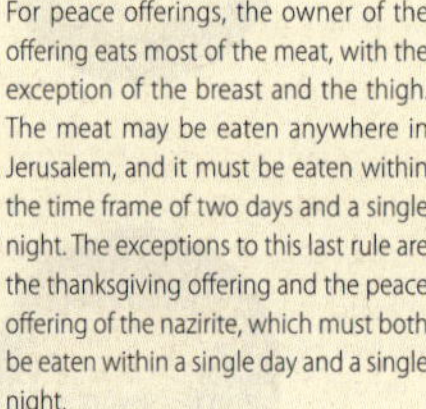

For peace offerings, the owner of the offering eats most of the meat, with the exception of the breast and the thigh. The meat may be eaten anywhere in Jerusalem, and it must be eaten within the time frame of two days and a single night. The exceptions to this last rule are the thanksgiving offering and the peace offering of the nazirite, which must both be eaten within a single day and a single night.

The owner eats the offering

For offerings of lesser sanctity, the portions given to the priests may be eaten by the priests and their families anywhere in Jerusalem. The time frame for eating this meat is the same as for the rest of the offerings: two days and a single night, except for the thanksgiving offering and the peace offering of the nazirite, which must both be eaten within a single day and a single night.

The priest and his family eat the offering

TYPES OF OFFERINGS

TYPES OF OFFERINGS

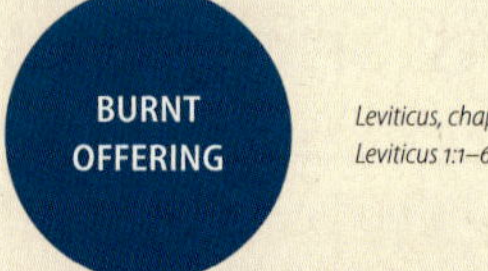

Leviticus, chapter 1
Leviticus 1:1–6

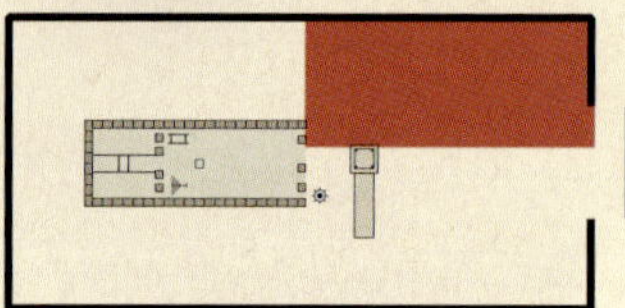

The burnt offering is one of the offerings of the most sacred order. It is an individual offering and is entirely burned on the altar (with the exception of the hide). The Torah explains that a person can bring a burnt offering voluntarily, as a vow offering or a gift offering. According to the Sages, a burnt offering can atone for the sin of failing to fulfill a positive commandment, for transgressing a prohibition that entails fulfillment of a positive commandment, or for sinful thoughts.

There are also obligatory burnt offerings, such as one of the two birds brought by a poor person obligated to bring a sliding-scale offering (that is, an offering that varies according to a person's financial means). Some communal offerings are also burnt offerings, such as the daily offering and some of the additional offerings. These are also considered obligatory.

BURNT OFFERINGS FROM ANIMALS

THE ANIMALS

BURNT OFFERINGS FROM BIRDS

THE PROCESS OF BRINGING THE OFFERING

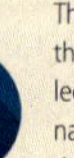

The priest ascends to the surrounding ledge of the altar and pinches the neck of the bird at the southwestern corner (above the red line), while severing the two organs and separating the head from the body. After this, the priest extracts the blood of the bird onto the wall of the altar, at the upper portion of the altar. The priest then ascends to the top of the altar, salts the head of the bird, and burns it. The priest then returns to the surrounding ledge, removes the crop and the skin with the feathers and innards, and throws them onto the place of the ashes located to the east of the altar's ramp. After this, the priest tears open the body of the bird from its back, but does not need to separate it completely. He ascends to the top of the altar, salts the bird's body, and burns it.

BURNT
OFFERING

Leviticus, chapter 2
Leviticus 1:1–6

The grain offerings are offerings brought from plants. They are brought as individual or communal offerings, sometimes obligatory and sometimes voluntary. The services of the grain offerings are parallel to those of the animal offerings: The removal of a handful is parallel to slaughtering, placing the handful in the service vessel is parallel to receiving the blood, bringing the handful to the altar is parallel to bringing the blood to the altar, and burning the grain is parallel to burning the sacrificial parts. Generally, the grain offerings come from fine wheat flour, with the exceptions of the omer offering, and the grain offering brought by the woman suspected by her husband of adultery – these two offerings consist of barley. Also, the grain offerings are generally brought as unleavened bread, with the exception of the two loaves brought on the Festival of Weeks, and some of the loaves brought with the thanksgiving offering.

GRAIN OFFERING FROM FINE FLOUR

EATEN BY

INGREDIENTS

METHOD OF PREPARING THE OFFERING: Oil is placed in a vessel. Then flour is added to the oil and additional oil added to the flour. The flour and oil are then mixed together, additional oil is poured on top, and a handful of frankincense is placed on the mixed flour.

The priest then walks with the flour offering to the altar, and presents it opposite the southwestern corner, until the vessel touches the wall of the altar. (Additionally, the omer offering and the grain offering brought by the woman suspected by her husband of adultery are also waved, and the two loaves brought on the Festival of Weeks are waved but are not presented at the altar.)

The priest moves the frankincense to the side and removes a handful of flour from a place where oil has accumulated. This handful must measure more than the volume of two olives. He places this handful in a service vessel. The priest then collects the frankincense from the top of the mixed flour and brings the handful and the frankincense up to the altar, salts them, and burns them on the large arrangement of wood.

The remaining flour is baked and eaten by male priests in the Temple courtyard.

GRAIN OFFERING BAKED IN AN OVEN (LOAVES AND WAFERS)

EATEN BY

INGREDIENTS

METHOD OF PREPARING THE OFFERING: The fine flour is placed in a vessel, oil is poured on top of it, and it is mixed with warm water. Each tenth of an ephah (about 2 kg) is divided into ten parts and moistened with water. These portions of dough are baked on the floor of the oven; if they are thick they are loaves, and if they are thin they are wafers.

For a grain offering of wafers, each wafer is smeared with oil after it is baked, with a *log* of oil for each tenth of an ephah.

After this, the priest crumbles the loaves and presents the crumbs at the southwestern corner of the altar. He takes a handful and places it in a service vessel, adds frankincense, and brings it up to the altar. There the priest salts the handful and the frankincense and burns them on the large arrangement of wood.

The remaining part of the flour offering is eaten by male priests in the Temple courtyard.

GRAIN OFFERINGS PREPARED IN A GRIDDLE OR PAN

EATEN BY

INGREDIENTS

METHOD OF PREPARING THE OFFERING: Oil is placed in a vessel. Fine flour is added to the oil, mixed together, and kneaded in warm water. Then each tenth of an ephah is split into ten parts. Each one of these parts is shaped into dough, moistened with water, and baked in a griddle or a pan inside an oven. After the baking, each piece of dough is broken into four parts. The owner of the offering then pours the remainder of the oil onto the pieces, places frankincense on top, and hands it to the priest.

After this, the priest brings the grain offering to the altar and presents it at the southwestern corner, until the vessel touches the wall of the altar. The priest then takes a handful of pieces, places it in a service vessel, and brings this handful and the frankincense up to the altar. There the priest salts and burns them.

The remaining part of the flour offering is eaten by male priests in the Temple courtyard.

THE OMER OFFERING

EATEN BY

INGREDIENTS

This grain offering, made of barley, is brought on the sixteenth day of the month of Nisan. The barley is harvested on the night after the first day of Passover, and after it is brought to the Temple it is roasted in fire. After that the grains are ground, and the flour is sifted in thirteen sieves in succession. A tenth of an ephah of the resulting flour is then mixed with a *log* of oil, and a handful of frankincense is added. The grain offering is waved (it is waved forward and backward, up and down) at the eastern side of the altar and presented at the corner of the southwestern corner of the altar. There the priest takes a handful, places it in a service vessel, and brings the handful and the frankincense up to the altar. On the altar, the priest salts the handful and the frankincense and burns them.

The remaining part of the flour offering is eaten by male priests in the Temple courtyard.

GRIDDLE-CAKE GRAIN OFFERING

INGREDIENTS

This grain offering is brought every day and is paid for by the High Priest. Half of it is brought in the morning and half in the afternoon. An ordinary priest also brings a similar offering on the day that he begins his service in the Temple; this offering is called the grain offering of initiation.

For the griddle-cake offering, the High Priest brings a complete tenth of an ephah of flour and places it in a service vessel. After this, he divides it into two parts, adds oil, mixes it, blanches it in boiling water, and kneads six loaves from each half of the tenth of the ephah (making a total of twelve loaves). After this, he places a quarter of a *log* of oil on each loaf (a total of three *log* of oil), bakes the loaves slightly, and then roasts them a bit in their oil. Half of the loaves are burned in the morning with half a handful of frankincense, and the other half are burned in the afternoon with half a handful of frankincense.

For the grain offering of initiation, the tenth of the ephah is not split into two parts; instead the entire quantity is burned together with a handful of frankincense.

GRAIN OFFERING OF A SINNER

EATEN BY

INGREDIENTS

In the context of a sliding-scale offering (see below), the sinner brings an offering commensurate with his financial status. The poorest people bring a grain offering.

The owner of the offering brings a tenth of an ephah of fine flour without oil, frankincense, or water (this is called a dry grain offering). The priest presents the offering at the southwestern corner of the altar, removes a handful and places it in a vessel, and brings the handful to the top of the altar. There the priest salts the handful and burns it.

The remainder is eaten by male priests in the Temple courtyard.

PEACE OFFERINGS

Leviticus, chapter 3
Leviticus 7:11–34

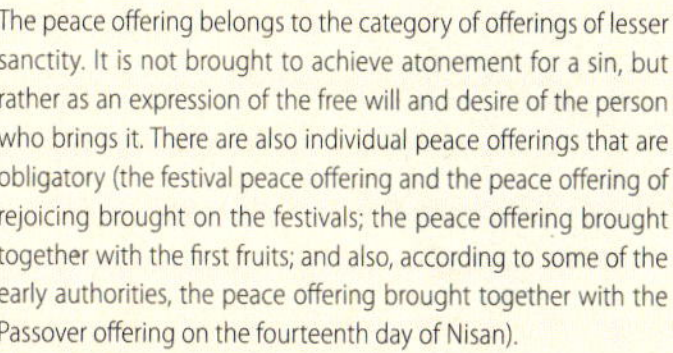

The peace offering belongs to the category of offerings of lesser sanctity. It is not brought to achieve atonement for a sin, but rather as an expression of the free will and desire of the person who brings it. There are also individual peace offerings that are obligatory (the festival peace offering and the peace offering of rejoicing brought on the festivals; the peace offering brought together with the first fruits; and also, according to some of the early authorities, the peace offering brought together with the Passover offering on the fourteenth day of Nisan).

There are also communal peace offerings that are obligatory: the communal peace offering of two sheep that accompanies the two loaves on the Festival of Weeks. These are offerings of the most sacred order.

The peace offering may be slaughtered in any part of the Temple courtyard. After the sacrificial portions are brought, the priests receive the breast and the thigh, and the rest of the meat belongs to the owner of the offering.

There are two special types of peace offerings that are brought with accompanying bread: the thanksgiving offering and the peace offering brought by a nazirite. These two offerings must be eaten within a time frame of a single day and a single night, as opposed to all other peace offerings, which have a longer time frame of two days and a single night.

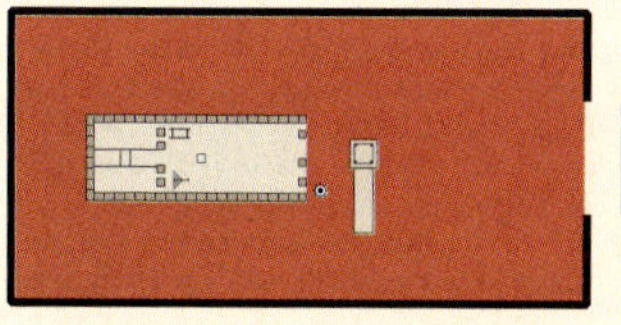

INDIVIDUAL PEACE OFFERINGS

PROCEDURE FOR BRINGING THE OFFERING

EATEN BY

TIME FRAME FOR EATING

THE ANIMALS

THANKSGIVING OFFERING

Together with the thanksgiving offering, the owner brings four types of bread. These breads are baked in different ways, according to the following division: Thirty of the loaves are unleavened bread (ten baked in an oven; ten baked as wafers; and ten soaked loaves, meaning that the fine flour is blanched in boiling water, baked, and then fried), and ten loaves of leavened bread. When the sacrificial portions are waved together with the breast and the right thigh, four loaves of bread (one of each type) are also waved. After bringing the sacrificial portions, the four loaves that were waved are given to the priests, and the remainder belong to the owner of the offering.

TYPES OF OFFERINGS

PURIFICATION OFFERINGS

Leviticus 4:1–5, 13
Leviticus 6:17–23

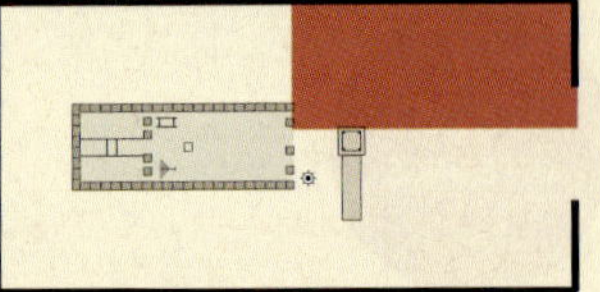

The purification offering belongs to the category of offerings of the most sacred order.

There are two types of purification offerings: **internal** and **external**.

The **internal purification offerings** are called this because the priest brings the blood of the offering into the Sanctuary and sprinkles it there. This type of purification offering is brought for sins committed by the entire nation, or by the High Priest. These include: the bull of the High Priest on the Day of Atonement, as well as the goat brought as a purification offering to God on this day; the bull brought for an unwitting communal sin, which is brought when the Sanhedrin issues an erroneous ruling regarding a matter which carries a punishment of *karet* (severance from the community); the goat brought for idolatry, offered when the Sanhedrin issues an erroneous ruling regarding the prohibition of idol worship; and an offering brought by the High Priest to atone for an erroneous halakhic ruling. After burning the sacrificial portions of the internal purification offering, the meat and the hide are taken outside of Jerusalem, and they are burned there in the place of the ashes.

An **external purification offering** is brought by a person who unintentionally transgressed a prohibition that carries a punishment of *karet* (in a case where a person transgresses intentionally). The blood of this offering is placed on the four horns of the external altar. There are also communal external purification offerings brought as part of the additional offerings on the Sabbath, festivals, and the New Moon (according to the Sages, these goats atone for the defiling of the Temple or its sacrificial foods).

INTERNAL PURIFICATION OFFERING

PROCEDURE FOR BRINGING THE OFFERING

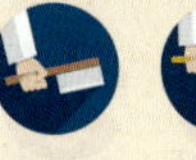

THE ANIMALS

EXTERNAL PURIFICATION OFFERING

PROCEDURE FOR BRINGING THE OFFERING

THE ANIMALS

For an individual: 

For the leader (king): 

TIME FRAME FOR EATING

EATEN BY

SLIDING-SCALE OFFERING

The **sliding-scale offering** is an additional type of external purification offering. This offering atones for an oath of testimony, an oath of utterance, and the defiling of the Temple or its sacrificial foods. The unique aspect of this purification offering is that the specific offering brought is determined by the economic status of the person bringing it: a wealthy individual brings an offering from the flock (a female goat or sheep), a poor person brings a bird, and the poorest person brings the grain offering of the sinner.

SHEEP

Equivalent to an **external purification offering**

BIRD

The poor person's offering is composed of two doves or two pigeons, one brought as a purification offering and one brought as a burnt offering.

PURIFICATION OFFERING OF A BIRD

PROCEDURE FOR BRINGING THE OFFERING

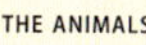

TIME FRAME FOR EATING

EATEN BY

For the purification offering of a bird, the neck is pinched at the southwestern corner of the altar (beneath the red line) without separating the bird's head from its body. The blood is sprinkled directly from the bird onto the wall of the altar, at the southwestern corner beneath the red line. Then the blood is extracted from the bird's head and body simultaneously on the base of the altar. The entire bird is then eaten by male priests in the Temple courtyard on the day it was brought or the night that follows (and according to a decree of the Sages, it must be eaten before midnight).

BURNT OFFERING OF A BIRD

PROCEDURE FOR BRINGING THE OFFERING

THE ANIMALS

The priest ascends to the surrounding ledge of the altar and pinches the neck of the bird at the southwestern corner (above the red line), while severing the two organs of the neck and separating the head from the body. After this, the priest extracts the blood of the bird onto the wall of the altar, at the upper portion of the altar. The priest then ascends to the top of the altar, salts the head of the bird, and burns it. The priest then returns to the surrounding ledge, removes the crop and the skin with the feathers and innards, and throws them onto the place of the ashes located to the east of the altar's ramp. After this, the priest tears open the body of the bird from its back but does not need to separate it completely. He ascends to the top of the altar, salts the bird's body, and burns it.

GRAIN OFFERING OF THE SINNER

Explained above; see the other grain offerings

Leviticus 5:14–26
Leviticus 7:1–7

The guilt offering belongs to the category of offerings of the most sacred order. This is an obligatory offering, brought in one of six different cases:

The provisional guilt offering: Brought by a person who is in doubt whether or not he unintentionally transgressed a prohibition that would obligate him to bring a purification offering.

The guilt offering for robbery: Brought by a person who denied under oath that he owed someone money, and then later admitted that he had lied.

The guilt offering for misuse of consecrated property: Brought by a person who unintentionally benefited from consecrated items.

The guilt offering of the espoused maidservant: Brought by someone who engaged in sexual relations with a woman who was half Canaanite maidservant and half free woman, and who was betrothed to a Hebrew servant.

The guilt offering of the nazirite who became defiled: Brought on the eighth day of impurity by a nazirite who became ritually impure, whether intentionally, unintentionally, or by accident.

The guilt offering of the leper: Brought by a purified leper on the eighth day of his purification.

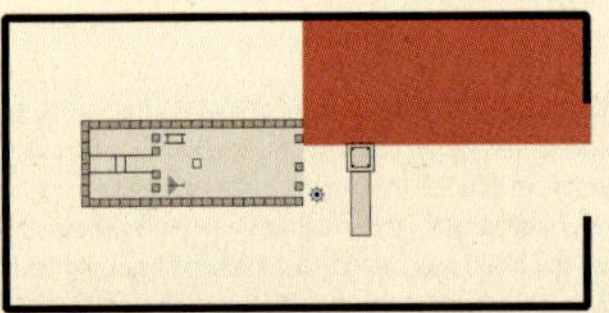

PROCEDURE FOR BRINGING THE OFFERING

THE ANIMALS

TIME FRAME FOR EATING

EATEN BY

NAZIRITE	*Numbers 6:1–21*	A person who has taken a vow to be a nazirite for a certain period of time is commanded during this period to let the hair on his head grow out, and he is also prohibited from becoming impure through contact with a dead person and from drinking wine or eating or drinking anything else made from grapes (including the fruit itself as well as inedible parts, like seeds).

A NAZIRITE WHO COMPLETES HIS PERIOD OF SEPARATION IN PURITY

The nazirite brings three offerings:

ANIMALS

The purification offering is brought according to the regular procedure.

ANIMALS

The burnt offering is brought according to the regular procedure.

ANIMALS

EATEN BY

TIME FRAME FOR EATING

The peace offerings of the nazirite are special peace offerings that share certain similarities with the thanksgiving offering. The nazirite brings, together with the ram, twenty loaves of unleavened bread baked in an oven: ten loaves of fine flour and ten unleavened wafers. The loaves are smeared with oil prior to baking them, whereas the wafers are smeared with oil after baking.

Following the slaughtering of the offering, the sprinkling of its blood, and the removal of the sacrificial portions, the priest removes the breast and thigh, and cooks the remainder of the ram in the Chamber of the Nazirites, which was located in the southeastern corner of the Women's Court of the Temple. The nazirite shaves his hair and throws it onto the fire that is underneath the pot in which the meat of the offering is being cooked. After this, the priest takes the cooked (right) arm of the ram and one-tenth of the loaves (two loaves, one of each type), and places them on the hands of the nazirite along with the breast and the thigh and the sacrificial portions. He then places his own hands under the nazirite's hands, and together they wave these portions. From this point forward, the nazirite is permitted to drink wine and to contract ritual impurity by contact with a dead person. After this, the priest salts the sacrificial portions and burns them on the altar. The breast and the thigh are eaten by priests, as is the case with all peace offerings. The cooked arm and the two loaves that were waved are also eaten by priests. The remainder of the meat and the loaves belong to the nazirite.

A NAZIRITE WHO BECAME IMPURE

A nazirite is enjoined from becoming impure. If he contracted ritual impurity, he must have water of purification (water that has ashes of the red heifer mixed into it) sprinkled upon him on the third and seventh days after he became impure. On the seventh day, the nazirite shaves all of his hair and immerses in a ritual bath. On the eighth day, the nazirite brings a burnt offering and a purification offering, both from birds (two doves or two pigeons), as well as a sheep as a guilt offering.
After bringing the purification offering, the nazirite restarts his period of separation, following all of the rules according to the full period that he vowed (the days that he had observed prior to becoming impure do not count toward the fulfillment of the vow).

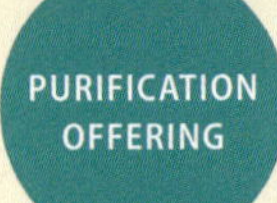

BIRDS

The purification offering of birds is brought according to the regular procedure.

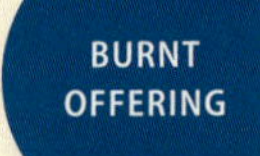

The burnt offering of birds is brought according to the regular procedure.

ANIMALS

The guilt offering is brought according to the regular procedure.

For your convenience, below is a reminder of the symbols used in these charts.

RAM	FEMALE SHEEP	DOVE OR PIGEON	DAY
SHEEP	THE PRIEST AND HIS FAMILY	OWNER	NIGHT

LIBATIONS

Numbers 15:1–16

When an animal is offered as a burnt offering or a peace offering, whether as an individual or communal offering, one also brings a grain offering of fine flour mixed with oil, as well as wine for a libation on the altar. The purification offering and guilt offerings of one afflicted with blight are also accompanied by libations.

The grain offering is brought up to the altar, and the wine of libation is poured into a bowl located on the southwestern corner of the altar.

The quantity of wine and oil varies according to the type of animal offered.

	GRAIN OFFERING		LIBATION
	FINE FLOUR	OIL	WINE
SHEEP OR GOAT	A tenth of an ephah	One-fourth of a hin	One-fourth of a hin
RAM	Two-tenths of an ephah	One-third of a hin	One-third of a hin
BULL OR CALF	Three-tenths of an ephah	One-half of a hin	One-half of a hin

Hin: 4,147 cubic centimeters   A tenth of an ephah: 2,488 cubic centimeters

ADDITIONAL OFFERINGS *Numbers 28:9–30:1*

	DATE / ANIMAL	SHABBAT	NEW MOON	PASSOVER	FESTIVAL ADDITIONAL OFFERING
BURNT OFFERING	BULL		2	2	2
BURNT OFFERING	RAM		1	1	1
BURNT OFFERING	SHEEP	2	7	7	7
PURIFICATION OFFERING	HE-GOAT		1	1	1
PEACE OFFERING	SHEEP				
SOURCE		Numbers 28:9–10	Numbers 28:11–15	Numbers 28:16–25	Numbers 28:26–31
COMMENTS				*These offerings were brought on each of the days of Passover. On the sixteenth of Nisan, an additional sheep was also brought in conjunction with the omer offering.*	

In *Parashat Pinḥas* (Num. 28:9) the Torah details the additional offerings to be brought on Shabbat and festivals, in addition to the fixed daily offering.

FESTIVAL OF WEEKS SHEEP BROUGHT ON FESTIVAL OF WEEKS	ROSH HASHANA (NEW YEAR)	DAY OF ATONEMENT	FESTIVAL OF TABERNACLES	THE EIGHTH DAY A SACRED ASSEMBLY
Leviticus 23:18–20	Numbers 29:1–6	Numbers 29:7–11	Numbers 29:12–34	Numbers 29:35–38
These offerings are brought in conjunction with the "Two Loaves."	*These offerings are brought in additional to the additional offerings for the New Moon.*	*In addition to these, a goat was brought as an internal purification offering (the second goat, parallel to the scapegoat).*	*On the first day of the Festival of Tabernacles, thirteen bulls are brought; on the second day, twelve. This daily reduction continues until the seventh day, when seven bulls are brought.*	

PURIFICATION OF THE PERSON WITH AN IMPURE BLIGHT

...the priest shall command two living ritually pure birds, and cedarwood, scarlet wool, and hyssop to be brought for the one who is to be purified. *Leviticus 14:4*

Bird: According to the Sages, the term "bird" is a general term for all pure birds (*Sifrei, Devarim, Re'eh* 98). The specific bird used in the purification of a person with an impure blight is known in Hebrew as *dror* (Nega'im 14:1). The *dror* is described as an undomesticated bird that lives in proximity to humans but cannot adjust to life in captivity: "it lives (*dara*) in the house like the field," and it "does not accept [human] authority" (Beitza 24a). It is virtually certain that this refers to the bird known today in Modern Hebrew as *dror*, the true sparrow (of the genus *Passer*). This bird is pure, and various Jewish communities have preserved a tradition permitting eating it, including the communities from Germany, Italy, Yemen, and the land of Israel.

SPARROW

Cedar: The cedar mentioned in the Bible refers primarily to the Lebanon cedar (*Cedrus libani*) – the finest construction wood used in the ancient world, from which temples and royal palaces were built. This was due to its long, straight trunk and fragrant xylem, which can be preserved for hundreds of years. The tree is found in the wild in the mountains of Lebanon and can grow to heights of dozens of meters, making it a symbol of great height (Ps. 92:13; Amos 2:9), as opposed to the hyssop and scarlet wool, which symbolize lowliness.

CEDAR OF LEBANON

Hyssop: The description of the *ezov* in the literature of the Sages does not leave any room for doubt – when used without additional clarification, the term *ezov* is the species known today as biblical hyssop (*Majorana syriaca*), in Arabic, *saatar*. This is a tall shrub with leaves covered in feltlike, greenish-gray hairs with white blossoms. The plant emits a strong and characteristic aroma, and is used as a spice.

HYSSOP

Scarlet wool: *Tolaat shani* is mentioned together with sky blue and purple as the colors used in several of the vessels in the Temple. For example, the priests' sash was embroidered with these colors (Ex. 39:29). In the ancient world, there were several insects from which the scarlet color could be extracted. In the land of Israel, a parasitic insect called kermes (*kermes echinatus*) can be found on oak trees. During the month of July, one can collect them together with their eggs and use these to dye wool a reddish-orange color.

SCARLET WOOL

RED COW *Numbers 19:1–22*

A person who has contracted ritual impurity because of direct contact with a corpse or by being in the same tent as a corpse can become purified via the red cow.

This cow must be completely red in color; if it has even two white or black hairs, it is invalid. It must be three or four years old and not have any blemishes, just like all animals sanctified for offerings. It also must never have been used for work and never even have had a yoke placed on its neck (which would invalidate it even if it did not actually pull a plow).

The cow is burned outside of the Temple Mount, on the Mount of Olives. Any priest – not only the High Priest – may burn the red cow.

According to the description appearing in the Mishna (Para, ch. 3), the cow is brought from the Temple Mount to the Mount of Olives across a special bridge, so that the people involved in its preparation do not risk becoming ritually impure due to impurity imparted by a grave in the depths below.

To emphasize the halakha that a *tevul yom* (one who was ritually impure who immersed that day and is waiting for nightfall for the purification process to be completed) is fit to be involved with the preparations of the cow – a ruling that was contested by the Sadducees – they would intentionally defile the priest tasked with burning the cow shortly before burning it. The priest would then immediately immerse in a ritual bath on the Mount of Olives before commencing the procedure.

The cow would be bound and laid on an arrangement of wood that had been prepared in advance. The priest would stand facing west, toward the Temple Mount, slaughter the cow with his right hand, and catch the blood with his left. He would then sprinkle some of the blood with his right finger seven times in the direction of the Holy of Holies and wipe the remaining blood onto the body of the cow. After this, the priest would descend from the arrangement of wood and light it. As the cow was burning, the priest would throw cedarwood, hyssop, and scarlet cloth into the fire.

After the burning was complete, the priests would beat the burnt cow and the wood with sticks and sift them with sieves, repeating this process multiple times until the entire pile was reduced to ashes. These ashes would then be divided into three parts: One part was kept in the rampart of the Temple Mount, a second part was stored on the Mount of Olives and was used to purify the people, and the third part was divided among the different priestly watches.

When a person comes to be purified using the ashes of the cow, a priest must bring spring water in a vessel and place some of the ashes into it, of sufficient quantity to be seen above the water. The person performing the purification then dips three bundles of hyssop into the water and sprinkles it on the person or vessel that requires purification. A single act of sprinkling can be used to purify several people or vessels; anything touched by the smallest quantity of the water is purified, provided that the person performing the procedure intended such.

This sprinkling is to be done on the third and seventh days of the purification process. On the seventh day, following the sprinkling, the purified person immerses in a ritual bath, and at nightfall his purification is complete.

RED COW

YOKE

RITUAL BATH
From the Second Temple Period

SEXUAL RELATIONS PROHIBITED BY THE TORAH

Leviticus 18:6–23
Leviticus 20:10–21

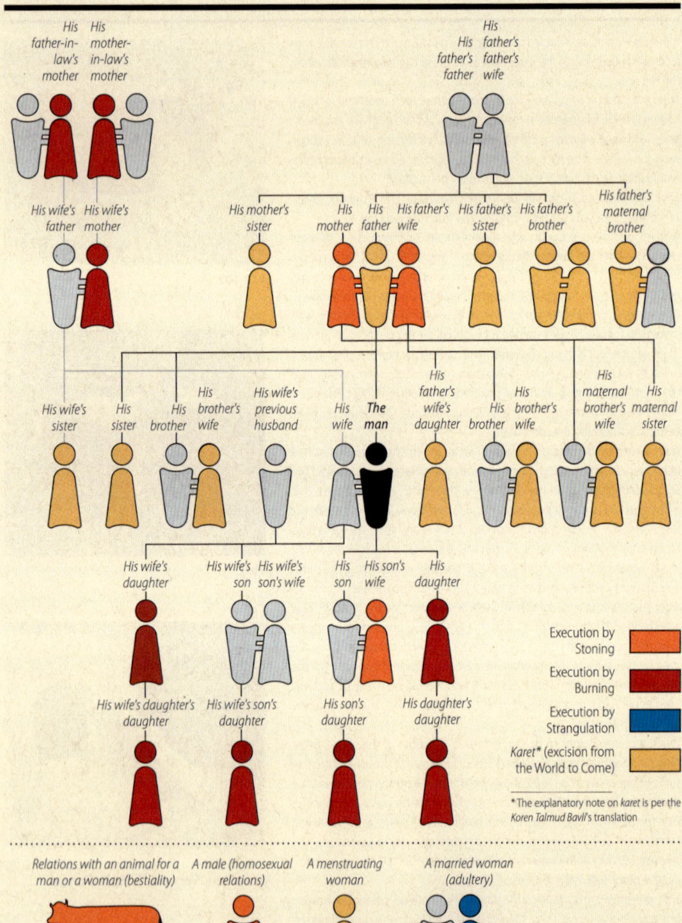

LIVING CREATURES

LIVING CREATURES IN THE BOOK OF LEVITICUS

ZOHAR AMAR

If the offering for the LORD is to be a burnt offering of fowl, one may offer doves or pigeons. *Leviticus 1:14*

Dove: The dove is a member of the Columbidae family and is generally identified as the European turtledove (*Streptopelia turtur*). The Hebrew name *tor* comes from the sound made by the bird, *tur-tur*. This is a migratory bird that summers in the land of Israel and whose presence is particularly prevalent during the migration seasons.

These migration seasons correspond to the times of the festivals, primarily Passover and the Festival of Tabernacles, at which time they were offered in the Temple. According to halakha, this bird can be brought as an offering only as an adult.

EUROPEAN TURTLEDOVE

Pigeon: The domestic pigeon (*Columba livia domestica*) was the most common domesticated bird used for food in biblical times. For offerings in the Temple, one must specifically bring a chick, not a mature bird (indicated by the Hebrew *ben yona*). The reason may be that the young chick, which has not yet grown feathers and begun to fly, may be close in size to its parents, but its meat is softer and finer, making it more suitable for offering on the altar.

PIGEON

IMPURE BIRDS

Among the birds, the following you shall regard as detestable – being detested they shall not be eaten: the griffon vulture, the bearded vulture, the lappet-faced vulture, the kite, any kind of buzzard, any kind of raven, the ostrich, the swift, the gull, any kind of sparrow hawk, the little owl, the fish owl, the short-eared owl, the barn owl, the pelican, the vulture, the stork, any kind of heron, the hoopoe, and the bat. *Leviticus 11:13-19; compare to similar passage in Deuteronomy 14:12-18*

Some of the names of the birds mentioned here are names of entire families, which is why the Torah uses the expression "any kind." According to ancient systems of taxonomy, species that are today considered distinct but are similar in appearance and behavior were categorized together. Regarding the kosher status of birds, the Torah uses a process of elimination: only the impure birds, which are prohibited, are listed. This is because the pure, permitted birds are more numerous than the impure ones (Ḥullin 63b). In principle, therefore, anyone who could identify all of the impure birds would be permitted to eat any other birds that exist anywhere in the world. However, over the course of many generations, the definitive identification of some of the impure birds has been forgotten. Therefore, the halakha relies on tradition as well as on inspection based on signs that the Sages have recorded (Ḥullin 59a, 63b). Possible identifications are found in the early translations (such as the Septuagint and the *Targumim*) as well as the literature of the Sages, but their meaning is not always clear. By the Middle Ages, we already see disputes among the authorities regarding the correct identification of most of the birds. Rav Se'adya Gaon, in his Arabic translation, is the only authority to systematically identify all of the birds. Conversely, Rashi identifies only some of them, and other European commentators also disagree with one another. Only with regard to the identity of a small number of birds is there a near-unanimous consensus: the kite, raven, little owl, ostrich, and hoopoe. Names of birds in Modern Hebrew (which are assigned by the Academy of the Hebrew Language) are generally based on one possible identification and thus should not be viewed as definitive. The reader should relate similarly to the photographs in this article. According to this opinion, only three of the Modern Hebrew names for birds reflect a definitive or probable identification. At the same time, an analysis of all of the potential available identifications indicates that there is agreement that none of the impure birds are pure herbivores, as all of them eat certain animals, such as small mammals, reptiles, or insects. There is also general agreement that the category of impure birds includes all predators (including scavengers and those that eat marine animals).

Griffon vulture: The *nesher* first appears here, in the list of impure birds, and is mentioned a total of twenty-eight times in the Bible – more than any other impure bird. This fact attests to its importance in the ancient world, where it was considered the king of the birds. Undoubtedly, in the context of the land of Israel, the name refers specifically to the griffon vulture (*Gyps fulvus*), known as *nesher* also in Modern Hebrew. Its size, wide wingspan, and significant gliding ability gave it its status as a symbol and a basis for parables (see, e.g., Deut. 8:49; Jer. 49:22; Prov. 30:19). The *nesher* nests on high rocks. It is a pure scavenger that eats carrion exclusively and is able to identify food sources from a great distance (see Job 39:27–30). Its head is bald, with no feathers (Mic. 1:16), which enables it to dig deeply into the carcass of its prey when eating it. The name *nesher* has been preserved in Semitic languages, as can be seen in Rav Se'adya Gaon's translation *nasar*. In Europe, however, this bird is uncommon, and therefore some commentators (see *Tosafot*, Ḥullin 63a) erroneously identified it as the predatory eagle (*Aquila sp.*). This identification was also aided by references in various sayings of the Sages and explanations by European commentators, who were influenced by the image of the eagle as the symbol of the Roman Empire and other nations.

GRIFFON VULTURE

Bearded vulture: The *peres* is a bird that is not commonly found among human populations (Ḥullin 62a), and its identification is not definitive. Rav Se'adya Gaon translates it into Arabic as *akab*, which is a type of eagle (*Aquila sp.*) with several different species that live in different habitats. Most contemporary researchers, though, identify it as the bearded vulture (*Gypaetus barbatus*), a rare bird that is either solitary or lives in pairs. This identification is aided by the etymological analysis of the name *peres*, which is connected to this bird's ability to carry its food (generally dead animals) to a great height, smash it against rocks, and split open its bones (see Mic. 3:3). Onkelos translates the name as *ar*, which is also the name of a city in the region of Moav and perhaps hints at the bird's habitat (see Num. 21:15). That city is translated by Onkelos as *Liḥayat*, which means "beard" in Arabic. The name reflects a characteristic of this bird, which has hard whiskers growing from its beak that look like a beard. This is also the source of its scientific name.

BEARDED VULTURE

Lappet-faced vulture: We cannot know for certain the correct identification of the *ozniya*. Already in the time of the Sages, this bird was not commonly found among human populations (Ḥullin 62a). The Hebrew name and its Aramaic version (*uzya*) both indicate a bird that is strong and bold (*az*) in its behavior. In the Hebrew of the Mishna, this bird is known as *oz*; at that time people would use the bones from its wings to prepare various utensils (Kelim 17:14). In his Arabic translation, Rav Se'adya Gaon translates the name of this bird as *anka*, a term used in Arabic literature for a giant mythological bird; Rabbi Avraham Ibn Ezra criticized him sharply for this translation. However, others explained that he was referring to an actual bird. Today, it is generally accepted to identify the *ozniya* as the lappet-faced vulture (*Torgos tracheliotus*) – the largest of the raptors that lived in the land of Israel in the past. Today, however, it has become extinct in the region, with the exception of an occasional one flying over the skies of the Negev Desert. It is a scavenger, with a wingspan of almost 3 meters and a strong beak that is capable of penetrating very thick hides, like those of an elephant or a camel.

LAPPET-FACED VULTURE

Kite: In the list of impure birds in the book of Deuteronomy, the name *daya* appears, as well as the name *raa*. Among the Sages, there is an opinion that all three of these names (*daa*, *daya*, and *raa*) refer to the same creature (Ḥullin 63b). In the Aramaic translations, the term used is *dayta*. In his Arabic translation, Rav Se'adya Gaon renders it *ḥada*, which refers to the *Milvus sp.*, a type of raptor known as the kite. In Modern Hebrew, this bird is also called *daya*.

BLACK KITE

Buzzard: The expression "any kind of buzzard" indicates that the term the Torah uses is a general one, as the Sages said: "There are one hundred different types of impure birds in the east, and they are all types of buzzards" (Ḥullin 63b). From a verse in Job (28:7) it seems that this is a sharp-eyed bird that is able to see great distances: "No vulture knows the way there; the falcon's eye has not glimpsed it." A rabbinic hyperbole even suggests that a buzzard in Babylonia could identify carrion in the land of Israel (Ḥullin 63b).

These qualities are characteristic of several different raptors, and beyond this there is no agreement among the early translations or later commentators. Hence, a specific identification is elusive.

In Modern Hebrew, the term is used specifically for the European honey buzzard (*Pernis apivorus*), which is the most common raptor among those that pass through the land of Israel in their migrations..

EUROPEAN HONEY BUZZARD

Raven: There is a general consensus that "any kind of raven" includes the genus crow (*Corvus sp.*) with all of its species (Ḥullin 63a), and similar birds from the Corvidae family. The name *orev* has been preserved in Semitic languages, such as Rav Se'adya Gaon's Arabic translation *gharab*. Among all the songbirds, the raven is the largest and the loudest. It is an omnivore, eating both plants and carrion, and it also is a predator that eats small chicks and eggs, among other things. The raven can be a hostile attacker, using its feet to secure its prey.

COMMON RAVEN

Ostrich: All of the early traditions agree that the *bat yaana* is the ostrich (*Struthio camelus*), called *yaen* in Modern Hebrew, *naamit* by the Sages, and *naama* in Rav Se'adya Gaon's Arabic translation. However, many contemporary researchers have rejected that identification, suggesting instead a nocturnal predator such as the Pharaoh eagle-owl. According to this theory, the *bat yaana* mentioned in the Bible is a flying bird that lives among ruins and is characterized by its wailing sound, whereas the ostrich does not fly and supposedly does not make a sound. However, in light of the strong consensus of traditional sources, this argument should be rejected. The Sages emphasized that although the ostrich is a strange and unusual creature (according to ancient folklore its origin was a union between a bird and a camel), it is to be treated as a bird in all matters (Jerusalem Talmud, Kilayim 8:5). Although the ostrich does not appear to have a mechanism for making sounds like other birds do, ostrich chicks are able to chirp, and the male is able to produce a strong, dull sound that can be heard from a distance.

OSTRICH

Swift: The *Targum Yerushalmi* translates this as *ḥatifta*, and apparently following this tradition, Rav Se'adya Gaon renders it *ghutaf* in Arabic. This is a generic name for birds of the swallow family – an unusual family among the songbirds that is distinguished by the speed of its members' flight and their navigational abilities. Their name is related to their food, which primarily consists of insects that they grab quickly in their mouths while in flight. This family includes many species from different genera: *Ḥirundo sp.*, *Riparia sp.*, and *Delichon sp.* In Modern Hebrew, the name *taḥmas* is applied to a different order of birds, the Caprimulgiformes (*Caprimulgus sp.*), which includes several birds that are rare in the land of Israel. These birds are active at dusk and at night, and also trap insects during flight like the swallows. It appears that the Torah did not designate a separate name for them. The source of the scientific name, which means "goat milkers," is in an ancient belief that this bird steals milk from goats.

SWALLOW

Gull: The identification of the biblical *shaḥaf* with the gull (*Larus sp.*), which is also given this name in Modern Hebrew, is based on the Septuagint and the Vulgate. The meaning of the Hebrew word, or its Aramaic equivalent, *shaḥfa*, is not clear, although some suggest that it refers to an ailment that was somehow connected to the bird or its thin flesh. Rav Se'adya Gaon translates it to Arabic as *saaf*, which is a type of raptor whose exact identity is also unclear. According to Rabbi Yona Ibn Janaḥ, the association is based on the similarity between the names *shaḥaf* and the Arabic *saḥaaf*, which means "tuberculosis."

GULL

Sparrow hawk: All ancient translations and commentators, including Rav Se'adya Gaon and Rashi, identified "any kind of *netz*" with the bird also called *netz* in Modern Hebrew, the hawk (*Accipiter sp.*). These birds are diurnal raptors with short wings and long tails, and they live in woodlands and forests. They primarily eat other birds, as the Mishna states, "Small fowl are mauled by the hawk" (Ḥullin 3:1). It is possible that the biblical term also includes all other small raptors, such as the falcon (*Falco sp.*).

EURASIAN SPARROW HAWK

Little owl: There is widespread agreement among the commentators that the *kos* is a nocturnal raptor. Onkelos uses the term *kadya*, and the Talmud explains that this refers to birds whose "eyes face in front of them, like humans" (Taanit 23a). It is quite certain that these sources refer to the bird known today as the little owl (*Athene noctua*). This fits Rav Se'adya Gaon's Arabic translation *bom*, and Rashi's French *chouettes*.

LITTLE OWL

Fish owl: According to most commentators, this is a bird that eats fish. The Septuagint identifies it as the cormorant (*Phalacrocorax sp.*), a bird that is excellent at fishing. The Vulgate translates it *mergulus*, referring to types of ducks that dive in the water to trap marine animals. In the Aramaic translations and the Talmud, the name that appears is *shalinuna min yama*, meaning "that draws fish from the sea" (Ḥullin 63a). Rashi there explains that the term refers to a "water raven" – a folk term for the cormorant. Based on the logic that the other birds listed in conjunction with the *shalakh* are nocturnal raptors (the little owl, short-eared owl, and barn owl), it would be possible to suggest the brown fish owl (*Bubo zeylonensis*) as a possibility, since this bird does trap fish, although nowadays it is very rare in the Middle East. Rav Se'adya Gaon translates it to Arabic as *zamag* – a raptor similar to the eagle. Today, the name *shalakh* is used in Modern Hebrew for the osprey (*Pandion haliaetus*).

LARGE CORMORANT

Owl: According to most opinions, the *yanshuf* is a nocturnal raptor. The Aramaic translations render it *kafufa*, referring to a bird similar to the little owl, with a face similar to that of a human or an ape (Nidda 23a). The name *yanshuf* also hints at its nocturnal character, as *neshef* means "night" (Rabbi Avraham Ibn Ezra). Rashi's translation seems to hint at the tawny owl (*Strix aluco*). Nowadays in Modern Hebrew the term *yanshuf* is used for any bird from the genus *Asio*.

OWL

Barn owl: The identification of the *tinshemet* is the subject of much dispute. Onkelos translates it as *buta* – apparently a nocturnal raptor that makes sounds. Rav Se'adya Gaon translates it into Arabic as *shahin*, which is the migratory peregrine falcon (*Falco peregrinus*), and according to Rashi it is a bat. In Modern Hebrew, the term *tinshemet* is applied to the western barn owl (*Tyto alba*), a common nocturnal raptor that makes blowing sounds.

BARN OWL

Pelican: The *kaat* is mentioned five times in the Bible, although it is possible that the bird mentioned in the Torah is not identical to the *kaat midbar* of Psalms (102:7). The Septuagint, the Vulgate, and Rav Se'adya Gaon all translated the term in the Torah as the water bird known today as a pelican (of the genus *Pelecanus*). This bird is also called *kuk* in Aramaic and Hebrew (Ḥullin 63a). It is possible that the name *kaat* comes from the manner in which this bird feeds its chicks from within its own throat, giving the appearance of vomiting (*kaa*) its food. Based on other biblical references, most of the researchers have suggested that this is a nocturnal raptor that vomits out small, round pellets of indigestible food.

PELICAN

Vulture: The most accepted identification for the *raḥam* is the bird that is also called by this name in Modern Hebrew: the Egyptian vulture (*Neophron percnopterus*). This is a raptor known for its black and white wings that are similar to those of a white stork (*ḥasida*), which may explain why the two are listed in succession in the same verse. Onkelos translates *ḥasida* as *ḥuraita*, meaning "white," and *raḥam* as *yerakrika*, meaning "yellowish," because of the color of its neck and head – unique features of this particular bird. The name *raḥam* has also been preserved in conjunction with this bird to this day in the Arabic name *ragham*, which is also the translation provided by Rav Se'adya Gaon. In the *Targum Yerushalmi* and the Talmud the name given is *sharakraka* (Ḥullin 63a). As a result, some contemporary researchers have suggested that it refers to the bird known today as the *sharakrak* – the bee-eater (*Merops sp.*) – or a different bird that is characterized by a whistling sound (*sherika*). However, it is also possible that this term has the same connotation as that used by Onkelos, as the root ש-ר-ק can also refer to a yellowish color, which would indicate the distinctive color of the Egyptian vulture's head and neck. According to the Sages, the Hebrew name *raḥam* (meaning "compassion") is given because this bird is a symbol of one who acts with compassion and concern to its family members (a tradition also preserved in the Arabic zoological literature).

VULTURE

Stork: The biblical *ḥasida* is a migratory bird that passes through the land of Israel, which is recognizable by its impressive wingspan (Jer. 8:7; Zech. 5:9). In the Aramaic translations and in the literature of the Sages, it is referred to as a white kite. According to Rashi, this bird is the *chigunia* (*Ciconia sp.*), an identification that is accepted by most researchers, and which is also called by the name *ḥasida* in Modern Hebrew. This identification seems to fit the descriptions in the Bible, and the explanation of the Sages: "Why is it called *ḥasida*? Because it engages in acts of kindness (*ḥesed*) with its companions" (Ḥullin 63a). The Romans referred to the white stork as *pia avis* – the generous or kind bird. It is possible that this reputation comes from the loyalty that the birds show to their monogamous mates, and to the widespread belief at the time that these birds also excel at honoring and aiding their parents. In spite of this, though, Rav Se'adya Gaon translates the biblical *ḥasida* as *sakar*, which is a saker falcon (*Falco cherrug*).

WHITE STORK

Heron: The phrase "any kind of heron" indicates that the term *anafa* is a name of an entire category that includes many species. The Septuagint and Vulgate translate it as *charadrius*, a word that is used today to indicate a genus of birds that lives in wet habitats. The *Targum Yerushalmi* translates the *anafa* as the black kite. According to Rav Se'adya Gaon, this bird is a member of the parrot family. Rashi translates it as "heron," and this is also the bird known as *anafa* (*Ardea sp.*) today. Support for this identification can be seen in its similarity to the stork, which is mentioned immediately before it. The Sages interpret the name as follows: "*Anafa* – this is a bird that becomes angry easily, and why is it called *anafa?* Because it commits adultery (*niuf*) with others" (Ḥullin 63a). This characteristic could be descriptive of different types of birds that live in flocks, which gather together noisily and appear to be fighting with one another. In truth, the name *anafa* can be understood as coming from the root *af*, which can mean "nose" (a reference to its long beak) and also "anger."

HERON

Hoopoe: The identification of the *dukhifat* as the hoopoe (*Upupa epops*), which is also identified this way in Modern Hebrew, is definitive. In Aramaic, it is called *nagar tura*, or "wild rooster" (Gittin 68b), because of the distinctive plume of feathers on its head that resembles a rooster's crest. This plume spreads out and closes intermittently, and this gives rise to a number of midrashic interpretations of the name *dukhifat*: "The one whose comb is bent (*hodo kafut*); this is the bird that brought the *shamir* [a unique worm] to the Temple" (Ḥullin 63a).

HOOPOE

Bat: The biblical *atalef* is identified with all of the species in the order of bats (Chiroptera), mammals with thin skin and membranes that attach its long arms together to form a type of wing. Unlike in modern taxonomy, the ancients categorized animals according to their external characteristics and behavior, and therefore all winged creatures (including winged insects that are called "swarming, flying creatures") were considered birds. This includes the bat. Because of its unusual hybrid status as a flying mammal, it is listed last.

BAT

SWARMING, FLYING CREATURES THAT CRAWL ON ALL FOURS

All swarming, flying creatures that crawl on fours are detestable to you, but you may eat those swarming, flying creatures that crawl on four legs, with legs jointed above their feet with which they hop on the ground. Of these you may eat the following: any kind of locust, bald locust, cricket, or grasshopper. *Leviticus 11:20-22*

Various species of flying insects are permitted to be eaten. These are the indications that the Torah specifies: it must have four legs used for walking, an additional pair of legs used for hopping, and wings. The Torah lists the names of only four such creatures. However, the Sages added additional indicators of kosher insects and through careful analysis of the verses arrived at a list of eight permitted insects (Mishna Ḥullin 3:7; Talmud Bavli there, 65a–b). There are also additional indicators, such as a U-shaped mark on the lower belly, and there is also a tradition identifying the specific species. At the time of the Sages, there was still a clear tradition identifying the various species of insects, but by the Middle Ages this tradition began to be forgotten. In our time, the only insect about which we have a firm tradition (preserved by the Yemenite and some North African communities) is the locust.

Below are suggested identifications for the insects mentioned in the Torah:

Any kind of locust: This is a generic name for different species of swarming grasshoppers, and especially for the desert locust (*Schistocerca gregaria*). The mature winged grasshopper migrates with the aid of the wind, and at times gathers into large swarms that can cause immense damage to agricultural crops. At times of drought and famine, these insects served as sources of food for humans, and in ancient times were even considered a delicacy. In Aramaic, these insects are known as *govai*, and in Arabic, *jarad*.

DESERT LOCUST

The *solaam* is translated into Aramaic as *rashun* or *rashuna*, which apparently means "head." In classical Arabic, the name of this creature is "long nosed." It seems that it should be identified with a group of grasshoppers from the subfamily Acridinae which are known by their sharp head and long antennae that resemble horns (apparently this is what is known as the *eil kamtza*). There are signs identifying these creatures as pure, and some remnants of a tradition permitting eating them have been preserved among some of the Jews of Yemen.

ACRIDINAE

Any kind of cricket: A definitive identification of the biblical *ḥargol* is elusive. The Talmud says it is a creature that "has a tail" (Ḥullin 65b), and on that basis, some have suggested identifying it with the katydid or bush cricket, known in Modern Hebrew by the name *ḥargol*. One of the distinguishing characteristics of this family of insects (Tettigonioidea) is a lengthy ovipositor (a tube used for laying eggs) that resembles a tail. It is possible that this is the insect referred to by the Torah.

Any kind of Grasshopper: In the Torah this term is used to refer to a specific species of grasshopper. It appears that this is similar to the locust in its general appearance and characteristics, but smaller and more limited in its ability to fly.

GRASSHOPPER

HYRAX AND HARE

Among those that chew the cud or have divided hoofs you must not eat the following: the camel, because though it chews the cud, it does not have divided hoofs, and so it is impure for you; the hyrax, though it chews the cud, does not have divided hoofs and so it is impure for you; the hare, though it chews the cud, does not have divided hoofs and so it is impure for you; the pig, though it has fully divided hoofs, does not chew the cud and so it is impure for you. *Leviticus 11:4–7*

It seems that the animals mentioned in these verses were chosen due to their common denominator of having one of the two signs of pure animals. However, even the one sign that they do have is not precise as it is in the case of the pure animals. For example, the definition of "chewing the cud" that was used in ancient taxonomy is not identical to the modern definition – it is broader: the ancient definition includes impure animals whose anatomical system or behavior appears externally similar to those of pure animals but is different in how it actually works. This fact, though, has no halakhic significance, since anyway these animals lack the other signs of purity.

Hyrax: The biblical *shafan* is generally identified, based on Rav Se'adya Gaon's Arabic translation *wabar*, as the rock hyrax (*Procavia capensis*). This identification fits the biblical description of a small animal that lives in groups and whose primary habitat is among the rocks (Ps. 104:18; Prov. 30:26). The rock hyrax does not chew its cud as do pure animals, who have a digestive system divided into four chambers. Its digestive system consists of a simple stomach, a very long small intestine, then a cecum resembling a pouch, then an intermediate intestine, followed by two additional ceca for food that was not digested. This complex structure, consisting of multiple microbiological digestive chambers that utilize various enzymes and bacteria, is capable of achieving a level of digestive efficiency comparable to that of pure ruminants. In certain circumstances, it also moves its jaws in a circular motion similar to that of ruminants chewing their cud.
There are, however, some commentators who believe that the true identity of the biblical *shafan* has been forgotten, or that the creature has become extinct. Another formerly popular theory, influenced by medieval Sephardic commentators, is the European rabbit (*Lepus cuniculus* = *Oryctolagus cuniculus*), which comes from the Iberian Peninsula and North Africa.

HYRAX

Hare: According to an ancient tradition preserved in the Aramaic translations, it is virtually certain that this term refers to the animal known today in Modern Hebrew as *arnevet*, the cape hare (*Lepus capensis*). The hare does not have a complex digestive system consisting of four chambers as the pure mammals do, but it does have a digestive system characteristic of herbivores: a stomach, a long small intestine, a large intestine, and an especially lengthy cecum. Furthermore, the hare's chewing motions are similar to those of pure ruminants – the lower jaw moves repeatedly in a wide circular motion. Additionally, because their food is rich in cellulose and takes a long time to digest, they engage in the process of coprophagy; that is, they eat the feces that are produced by the cecum, directly from the anus, so that they can be swallowed and digested a second time. This enables a fuller digestion and utilization of the nutrients in the food. This behavior can be viewed as a type of chewing the cud.

HARE

THE EIGHT CREEPING CREATURES

Among the creatures that creep along the ground, the following are impure for you: the marten, the mouse, every kind of spiny-tailed lizard, the legless lizard, the chameleon, the lizard, the skink, and the mole rat. *Leviticus 11:29-30*

A number of halakhot separate the group of eight creeping creatures from other impure animals, specifically with regard to their carcasses: they impart ritual impurity by contact but not by carrying, and the minimum measure for imparting impurity is a lentil-bulk, as opposed to an olive-bulk. This leads to various halakhic ramifications, for example, with regard to eating *teruma* and sacrificial foods. Also, there are specific halakhot relating to this group of animals with respect to trapping them and wounding them on Shabbat.

The eight creeping creatures have been identified using various methods. From most of the translations, it seems that the common denominator that defines them halakhically is that they are terrestrial vertebrates, that is, small mammals and reptiles with short limbs that move close to the ground. About half of the names have been definitively or almost definitively identified, and the others with various degrees of likelihood. Below, we will present their identities according to our research and will relate partially to other commentaries as well.

Marten: According to most of the ancient translations, the *ḥoled* is the ferret (*Mustela*), which is considered the smallest predator in nature. It is an animal with a very long and flexible body, enabling it to maneuver in narrow passageways. Zoological-archaeological finds have proven that in the past this animal lived in the land of Israel in proximity to human settlements. A different identification that is accepted by some contemporary researchers – based on Rav Se'adya Gaon's writings – is the animal known in Modern Hebrew as the *ḥoled*, the Middle East blind mole rat (*Aspalax ehrenbergi*), but this is more likely the *tinshemet* – meaning that either way, it is one of the eight creeping creatures.

FERRET

Mouse: There is no doubt about the identification of the *akhbar* as the common house mouse (*Mus musculus*). All the commentators agree that this is a generic term for the mouse and all similar rodents, which in ancient systems of taxonomy were considered a single species. This category therefore also includes the rat (of the genus *Rattus*) and various field mice, the most common of which is Günther's vole (*Microtus guentheri*), one of the most damaging pests for farmers.

COMMON HOUSE MOUSE

Spiny-tailed lizard: It is virtually certain that the *tzav* is a lizard from the dragon lizard family (Agamidae), most probably the spiny-tailed lizard (of the genus *Uromastix*), as explained by Rav Se'adya Gaon. The biblical name is preserved in the modern Arabic term *sab*. Etymologically, the name *tzav* means "round" or "wide," assumedly referring to the animal's wide belly. Rashi, however, identifies the *tzav* as a toad (of the genus *Bufo*). The mistaken idea that the biblical *tzav* should be identified with the tortoise (of the genus *Testudo*), called *tzav* in Modern Hebrew, is a late one. The Torah specifically indicates that the name *tzav* is a generic one that includes other animals, by use of the phrase "every kind of spiny-tailed lizard" (Lev. 11:29).

SPINY-TAILED LIZARD

Legless lizard: The identification of this creature is uncertain. According to the Septuagint and the Vulgate, it is the shrew (of the genus *Crocidura*); according to Rav Se'adya Gaon, it is the monitor lizard (of the genus *Varanus*); and according to Rashi, it is the hedgehog (of the *Erinaceus* genus). Our suggestion is the European legless lizard (*Ophisaurus apodus*), which is the only member of this family native to the land of Israel. This is a lizard with no legs, which can reach up to 1.2 meters in length. The creature is not poisonous, but its similarity in appearance to a snake alarms many people, who often kill it as a result. This fits the description of the *anaka* in the Midrash (*Tanḥuma, Balak* 9).

EUROPEAN LEGLESS LIZARD

Chameleon: The *koaḥ* has also not been definitively identified. The Septuagint and the Vulgate identify it as the chameleon (of the genus *Chamaeleo*). The Aramaic translations simply preserve the biblical name, so it is difficult to discern what they intended. However, it is somewhat likely that they also were referring to the chameleon, which is a distinctive type of lizard. In the area of the land of Israel there is only one native species of this lizard: the Mediterranean chameleon (*Chamaeleo chamaeleon*). The name *koaḥ* in Syrian refers to breathing, and in Arabic it refers to coughing. This terminology is appropriate for the chameleon – at times of danger, it breathes in air and then exhales it in a noisy fashion. Rav Se'adya Gaon identifies the *koaḥ* as the starred agama; however, most researchers follow a different etymological theory and understand *koaḥ* as a reference to strength and power, which would be appropriate for the desert monitor (*Varanus griseus*), a particularly large lizard that has therefore been given the name *koaḥ* in Modern Hebrew.

CHAMELEON

Lizard: According to all traditions, the name *litaa* refers to a group of reptiles from the Lacertidae or Gekkonidae families (or perhaps from both of them). This identification is aided by a statement in the Mishnah about the fact that these animals sometimes continue to move after they are dead: "If their heads have been removed, even though they continue to twitch, they are impure, such as the tail of a *litaa*, which continues to twitch [after it is dead]" (Ohalot 1:6).

LEBANON LIZARD

Skink: According to most of the ancient translations, the *ḥomet* is related to the *litaa*. This leads to the question of whether the Lacertidae and Gekkonidae families are considered one group or separate ones. If we assume that they are grouped together under the category *litaa*, then the *ḥomet* should be a different class of reptiles similar to those (as the Septuagint translates it) "resembling *litaa*." Onkelos translates it *ḥamta*, which may be related to the words for sand or dirt. It is therefore possible that the *ḥomet* is a member of the skink family (Scincidae), or more precisely, its subterranean species or those whose legs move them in varied steps similar to snakes, like the *Ophiomorus latastii* or the wedge-snouted skink (*Sphenops sepsoides*) species – both of which live in sand. Conversely, though, Rav Se'adya Gaon translated the *ḥomet* as a chameleon, and Rashi translated it as a type of snail.

WEDGE-SNOUTED SKINK

Mole rat: The Torah mentions two different species with this name: an impure bird (Lev. 11:18; Deut. 14:16), and a creeping creature. The Septuagint and Onkelos identify the creeping creature with the Middle East blind mole rat, a blind rodent that lives in underground tunnels in the land of Israel that is known in Modern Hebrew as *ḥoled* (*Aspalax ehrenbergi*). When caught from behind, this animal sometimes makes a blowing sound (*neshifa*), which may explain the biblical name. The Vulgate and Rashi identify it with the European mole (*Talpa europea*), which is not native to the land of Israel. (The *Aspalax ehrenbergi* is from the rodent family and the mole is an insect eater; nevertheless, in spite of the taxonomic distance and dietary distinctions between them, they are considered a single species because of the similarities in their appearance and habitat.) Rav Se'adya Gaon is the exception; he identifies the *tinshemet* as the gecko.

MIDDLE EAST BLIND MOLE RAT

All creatures that swarm on the earth are detested; they shall not be eaten. Of these swarming things you shall not eat any, those that move on their bellies or crawl on all fours or on many feet – for they are all detestable. *Leviticus 11:41-42*

Multipeds: This category is identified by *Targum Yonatan* with the centipede genus *Scolopendra*, a poisonous creature with many legs on both sides of its body. Rashi translates it into French as *cempiés* – which means "centipede." Although the literal meaning of "centipede" is "one hundred legs," this term includes arthropods from the subphylum Myriapoda.

CENTIPEDE

TERUMA AND TITHES
IN THE LAND OF ISRAEL

TERUMA AND TITHES IN THE LAND OF ISRAEL

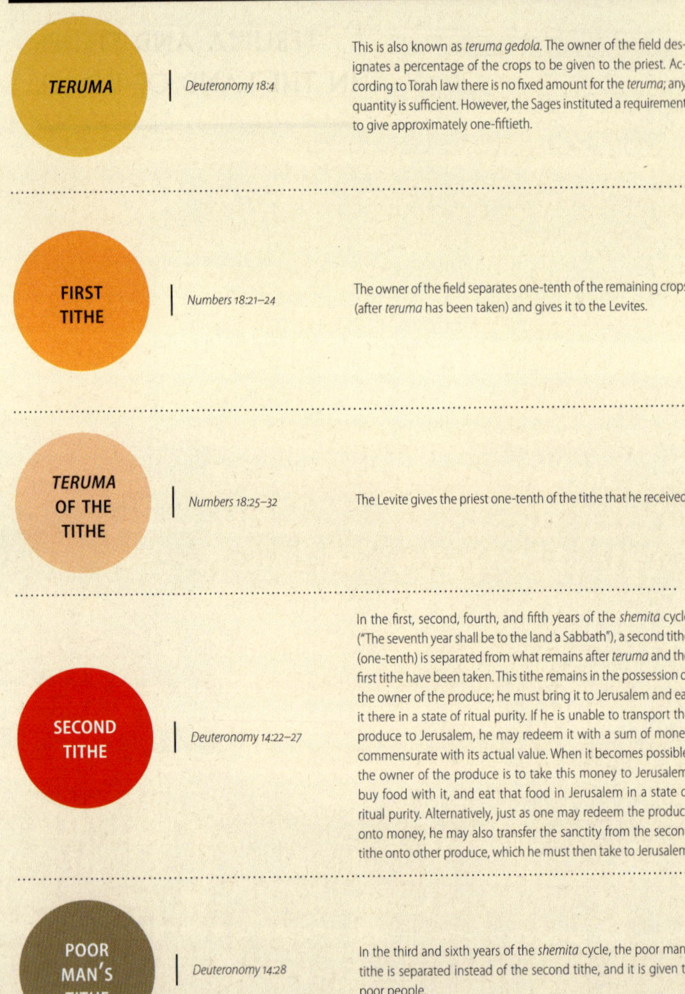

TERUMA	*Deuteronomy 18:4*	This is also known as *teruma gedola*. The owner of the field designates a percentage of the crops to be given to the priest. According to Torah law there is no fixed amount for the *teruma*; any quantity is sufficient. However, the Sages instituted a requirement to give approximately one-fiftieth.
FIRST TITHE	*Numbers 18:21–24*	The owner of the field separates one-tenth of the remaining crops (after *teruma* has been taken) and gives it to the Levites.
***TERUMA* OF THE TITHE**	*Numbers 18:25–32*	The Levite gives the priest one-tenth of the tithe that he received.
SECOND TITHE	*Deuteronomy 14:22–27*	In the first, second, fourth, and fifth years of the *shemita* cycle ("The seventh year shall be to the land a Sabbath"), a second tithe (one-tenth) is separated from what remains after *teruma* and the first tithe have been taken. This tithe remains in the possession of the owner of the produce; he must bring it to Jerusalem and eat it there in a state of ritual purity. If he is unable to transport the produce to Jerusalem, he may redeem it with a sum of money commensurate with its actual value. When it becomes possible, the owner of the produce is to take this money to Jerusalem, buy food with it, and eat that food in Jerusalem in a state of ritual purity. Alternatively, just as one may redeem the produce onto money, he may also transfer the sanctity from the second tithe onto other produce, which he must then take to Jerusalem.
POOR MAN'S TITHE	*Deuteronomy 14:28*	In the third and sixth years of the *shemita* cycle, the poor man's tithe is separated instead of the second tithe, and it is given to poor people.

ERADICATION OF TITHES

Deuteronomy 26:12

The owner of the produce must remove all tithes from his possession and give them to the appropriate recipients: *teruma* and *teruma* of the tithe to a priest, first tithe to a Levite, poor man's tithe to a poor person, and he must bring the second tithe to Jerusalem. This must be completed before the eve of Passover in the fourth year, and in the *shemita* year. If he is unable to bring the second tithe or the money on which it was redeemed to Jerusalem, he must destroy it. First fruits must also be destroyed if they remain in his possession at these times.

CONFESSION OF TITHES

Deuteronomy 26:13–15

After eradicating the tithes, the owner makes a declaration on the afternoon of the first day of Passover and in the *shemita* year. The text of this statement (known as confession) is listed explicitly in the Torah. It consists of a declaration that the owner of the produce has fulfilled all of the laws of tithes appropriately. Ideally, this commandment is meant to be fulfilled in the Temple, but if he made the declaration somewhere else, he has nonetheless fulfilled the commandment.

FIRST FRUITS

Exodus 23:19, 34:26
Deuteronomy 26:1–11

Every year, between the Festival of Weeks and the Festival of Tabernacles, the first fruits of the seven species are brought to the Temple (if one did not bring them by the Festival of Tabernacles, they may be brought until Ḥanukka). According to Torah law, there is no minimum amount that must be brought for the first fruits, but the Sages instituted a requirement to bring one-fiftieth of the crop. The owner of the produce brings the first fruits to the Temple in a vessel, waves it together with the priest, and recites the "Declaration of the First Fruits" (Deut. 26:5–10). After this, the owner of the first fruits places them next to the altar, bows, and exits. The priests on duty at the time eat the fruits in a state of ritual purity. The Sages also determined that the person bringing the first fruits must also bring a peace offering along with them.

SHEMITA

Exodus 23:11
Leviticus 25:1–7

After six years of working the land, the seventh year is a Sabbatical year for the land. There are four agricultural labors explicitly forbidden by the Torah during this year: sowing, pruning, reaping, and harvesting grapes. Additionally, the owner of the field must relinquish ownership of any produce that grows during this year.

RELEASE OF LOANS

Deuteronomy 15:1–2

At the end of the *shemita* year, the commandment of releasing loans takes effect. All creditors are commanded to forgive any loans owed to them and to make no further attempts to collect them.

ASSEMBLY (*HAKHEL*)

Deuteronomy 31:1–13

In the year following the *shemita* year, on the Festival of Tabernacles, there is a commandment to read passages from the Torah to pilgrims who have ascended to Jerusalem. The purpose of this is to "encourage them to fulfill the commandments and to strengthen the observance of the true religion" (Maimonides, *Hilkhot Ḥagiga* 3:1). The passages that are read all come from the book of Deuteronomy. The king conducts the public reading from a special wooden stage that is erected in the Women's Court of the Temple.

COMMANDMENTS IN THE SEVEN-YEAR CYCLE

An icon surrounded by a circle indicates a specific event

TERUMA
FIRST TITHE
TERUMA OF THE TITHE
SECOND TITHE
POOR MAN'S TITHE
ERADICATION OF THE TITHE
CONFESSION OF TITHES
FIRST FRUITS
RELEASE OF LOANS
ASSEMBLY (*HAKHEL*)

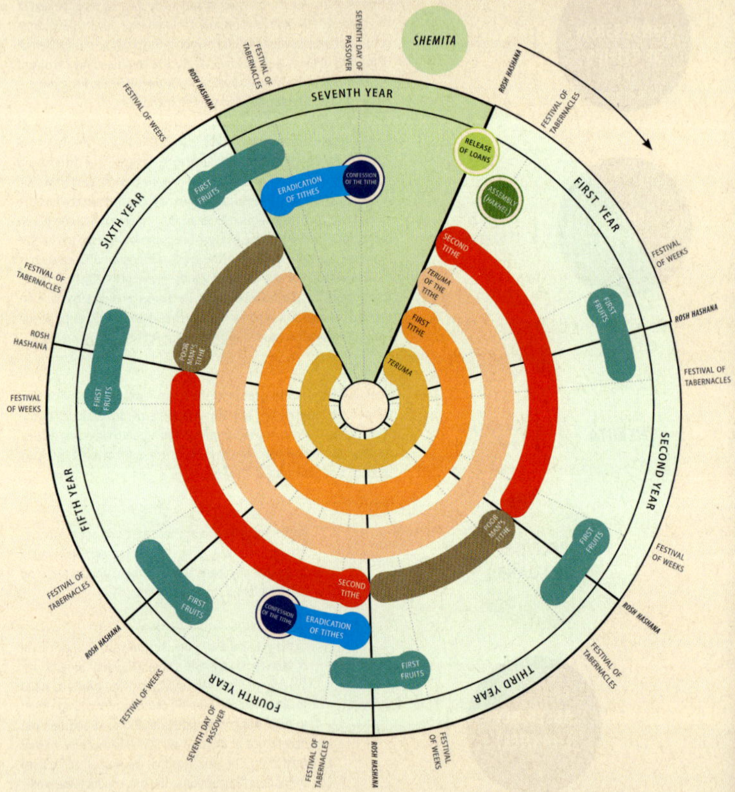

SEPARATING TERUMA AND TITHES I

First, approximately 2 percent of the crops are separated as *teruma*. Then, one-tenth of the remaining amount (9.8 percent of the total) is separated as the first tithe and given to the Levite. From this tithe, the Levite separates a tithe (0.98 percent of the total); this is the *teruma* of the tithe.

In addition to the first tithe, one must also separate an additional tithe (either the second tithe or the poor man's tithe) from the produce that remains after the first tithe has been taken (8.82 percent).

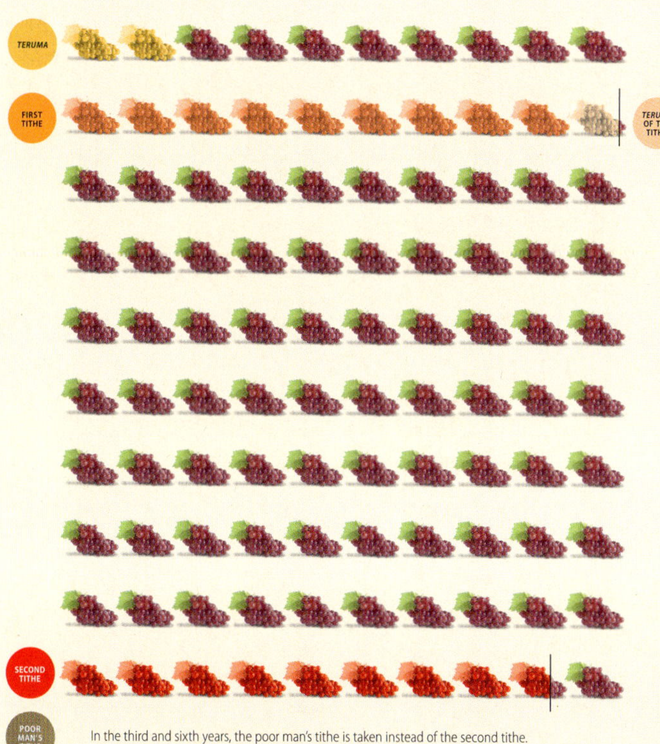

ARCHAEOLOGICAL ARTIFACTS

LETTER OF THE REAPER FROM ḤASHAVYAHU STRONGHOLD

The letter is a twenty-seven-hundred-year-old ostracon (inscription on a pottery shard), dated to the time of King Yoshiyahu. It was discovered in a fortress known as the Ḥashavyahu Stronghold, adjacent to Kibbutz Palmachim. It is written in Ancient Hebrew script, with no final letters and no punctuation. The ostracon records the complaint of a sharecropper against a tax collector who was sent to collect a debt and confiscated the sharecropper's only garment. The ostracon is on display in the Israel Museum, and a copy is on display at the Sea Museum (Bet Miriam) on Kibbutz Palmachim.

Source: Exodus 22:23–25

Background: Six ostraca were discovered in the guardhouse of the Ḥashavyahu Stronghold, all written in Ancient Hebrew script in pale ink. The most interesting is the "Letter of the Reaper," apparently intended for the commander of the stronghold. In the letter, a sharecropper complains about the tax collector, Hoshiyahu son of Shevi, who had accused him of the crime of tax evasion and therefore confiscated his only garment. The ostracon begins with the words "May my master the minister hear the words of of his servant" and continues to describe the work of the reaper. According to his claim, he had submitted the assessed amount of produce that he had been commanded to reap, but the tax collector did not believe him, and took his garment. To support his claim, the reaper is prepared to bring as witnesses his fellow reapers, claiming, "My brothers will attest to my credibility; I am free of guilt." The ostracon ends with the plea "and return your servant's garment." The description of events in the letter is consistent with the biblical prohibition against confiscating a debtor's only garment, lest he have nothing with which to cover himself at night. This demonstrates that this action was an accepted pressure tactic in ancient times, one that is denounced by the Torah.

SHILOAḤ TUNNEL

The Shiloaḥ Tunnel is accredited to King Ḥizkiyahu. It is a water channel that brings water from the Giḥon Spring, located outside of Jerusalem, to the city. The tunnel was first discovered at the end of the nineteenth century, together with the "Shiloaḥ Inscription" that describes how it was dug. This inscription – written in Ancient Hebrew script – is one of the few that have survived from the First Temple period. Visitors can view the tunnel in the City of David National Park. The inscription, however, is on display in the Istanbul Archaeology Museums.

Sources: II Kings 20:20
Isaiah 22:11
II Chronicles 32:2–4
II Chronicles 32:30

Background: After King Ḥizkiyahu declared a tax rebellion against Sanḥeriv, king of Assyria, the latter embarked on a campaign of conquest and destruction against the cities of Yehuda. Ḥizkiyahu prepared for a lengthy siege on his capital, Jerusalem. He fortified the city, forcing him to leave its primary water source – the Giḥon Spring – outside of the walls, due to its low topographical height, near the bottom of the slope leading to the Kidron Valley. So that he would not lose this important water source, and so that it would not be available to enemy soldiers, Ḥizkiyahu came up with a brilliant engineering solution: he stopped up the source of the Giḥon to the east of the city and diverted the water through an excavated tunnel 600 meters long that ran beneath the houses of the city to a pool inside the fortified city walls. This gave the city a powerful water source within its walls. Ultimately, the army of Sanḥeriv withdrew and the city was spared.

THE WIDE WALL

The Wide Wall is a section of a city wall, approximately 40 meters in length and built from uncut fieldstones, that was discovered in the Jewish Quarter in Jerusalem's Old City. The width of the wall reaches 7 meters, and its height when it was standing was approximately 10 meters. It was built by King Ḥizkiyahu as part of the preparations for the siege of Sanḥeriv, king of Assyria, approximately twenty-seven hundred years ago. The Wide Wall can be viewed in an open pit on Bonei Haḥoma Street near the Cardo. The parts of the wall that remain buried under the modern street are indicated with red-colored tiles along the street.

Sources: Isaiah 22:10
Nehemiah 3:8
Nehemiah 12:38
II Chronicles 72:5

Background: As part of his preparations for the impending siege, Ḥizkiyahu fortified the city with a wall that enclosed the City of David as well as today's Mount Zion and Jewish Quarter. An especially fortified wall was built along the northern side, which was particularly vulnerable due to the flat topography in that area. This wall was built along a shallow valley known as the Transversal Valley, which passes from east to west (along the route of today's David Street and Street of the Chain). To build it, several residential houses that were located along its path were destroyed; the remains of these houses can be seen in contemporary excavations. The discovery of the Wide Wall settled a long-raging archaeological argument by proving that First Temple–period Jerusalem extended beyond the City of David and the Temple Mount, and reached the "Western Hill" (today's Mount Zion and Armenian Quarter). It is possible that the "Wide Wall" mentioned twice in the book of Nehemiah (3:8, 12:38) as a Jerusalem-area landmark is in fact the wall of Ḥizkiyahu.

BULLA OF GEMARYAHU SON OF SHAFAN

The bulla of Gemaryahu son of Shafan is a small seal impression that was discovered in the City of David, as part of a collection of fifty-one bullae. It is made of silt pottery, and it contains the words "of Gemaryahu son of Shafan" in Ancient Hebrew script. This indicates that it belonged to Gemaryahu son of Shafan, a scribe and senior officer in the royal court of Yehoyakim, king of Yehuda. Bullae of this type were generally used to seal confidential documents. This artifact is on display at the Israel Museum.

Sources: Jeremiah 29:3
Jeremiah 32:11–14
Jeremiah 36:10–12, 25

Background: In ancient times, personal or legal documents would be rolled up and sealed for privacy with a block of silt, which would be stamped with a seal containing the name of the sender or a clerk who worked on his behalf. Legal documents such as bills of sale would be written in two copies – one which would be rolled up and sealed with a bulla so that it could not be altered, and a second copy that was open and could be read. In the City of David a royal archive was discovered that had stored documents such as these and that was burned during the destruction of the city at the end of the First Temple period. The documents themselves were destroyed, but the bullae that sealed them became hardened and were preserved. Gemaryahu son of Shafan, whose seal was discovered in the archive, was from a family of nobility, scribes of the king who lived in Jerusalem around twenty-six hundred years ago. His father, Shafan, was the scribe of King Yoshiyahu, and his nephew, Gedalya son of Aḥikam, was the last governor of Yehuda. His name was the only one from among the bullae in the archive that is known from Tanakh. However, at later dates several other bullae related to biblical figures, such as Yehukhal son of Shelmiyahu, Gedalyahu son of Pashkhur, Barukh son of Neriya, and even King Ḥizkiyahu, were discovered.

SANḤERIV'S PRISMS

Sanḥeriv's Prisms are large clay cylinders surrounded by six flat sides, inscribed with an Akkadian text depicting eight military campaigns conducted by Sanḥeriv. Three complete and virtually identical copies of the prisms have been found in the region of Mesopotamia; these can be seen in the British Museum, the University of Chicago, and the Israel Museum. In addition to these complete prisms, fragments of at least eight others have also been found; most of these fragments are stored in the British Museum. Among other things, the prisms provide a detailed description, taking up thirty-one lines, of Sanḥeriv's conquest of the land of Yehuda in the year 701 BCE. The description includes a list of cities that he conquered and the abundant spoils he took from King Ḥizkiyahu, and also references the siege of Jerusalem.

Sources: II Kings 18:13–36; 19
Isaiah 36–37
II Chronicles 32:1–23

Background: The kings of Assyria were accustomed to providing elaborate descriptions of their military accomplishments, in the form of dedicatory inscriptions written in Akkadian on stone or ceramic tablets, describing events, conquests, and battles. Sanḥeriv's Prisms declare that he conquered forty-six fortified Judahite cities, in addition to an unspecified number of unfortified villages. They detail the tribute paid to him by Ḥizkiyahu, which included 30 talents of gold and 800 of silver, precious gems, ivory and ebony artifacts...as well as his daughters, concubines, and other people, and musicians that he sent to Nineveh as tribute (a less detailed and similar, though not identical, account appears in II Kings 18:13–16). The prism states that Sanḥeriv placed a protracted siege on Jerusalem, and trapped King Ḥizkiyahu "like a bird in a cage." It does not, however, claim that he conquered Jerusalem; indeed, the Tanakh states that Sanḥeriv was forced to withdraw and Jerusalem was ultimately spared (II Kings 19:32–37; Is. 37:33–37; II Chr. 32:20–22). The great significance of the prism is the fact that it provides an anchor for dating the historical accounts in the Tanakh (Sanḥeriv's siege of Jerusalem was in 701 BCE) as well as in the comparison of the events recorded in the prism with the biblical account.

YEHOSHUA'S ALTAR ON MOUNT EIVAL

Sources: Exodus 20:22–23
Deuteronomy 27:1–10
Joshua 8:30–34
Ezekiel 43:15
(laws of constructing an altar)

The altar on Mount Eival is a rectangular platform made of uncut fieldstones. Its dimensions are 7.5 x 9 meters, and its height is approximately 3 meters. The platform is surrounded on three sides by a wide stone enclosure that is lower than the altar. Adjacent to it is a large courtyard surrounded by a fence. The courtyard is divided in half by a ramp that ascends from outside of the compound directly to the top of the altar. Its identification as an altar is based on its shape, and on the rich finds of ashes and animal bones at the site. The exceptionally well-preserved altar can be visited on Mount Eival.

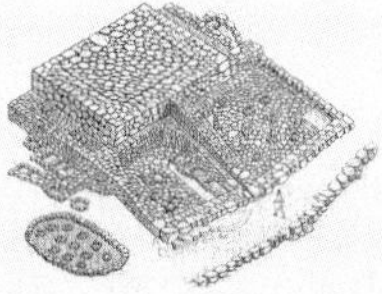

Background: The altar on Mount Eival corresponds in many ways to depictions of altars in the Tanakh and Mishna: Its stones are uncut, it is made of a frame of "whole stones" (see Deut. 27:6), filled and sealed; and the ascent to the altar is by a ramp, not by stairs (see Ex. 20:23). The altar is surrounded by a wide stone enclosure that is shorter than the altar, enabling priests to encircle it, which recalls the "surrounding ledge" described in the Mishna (e.g., Zevaḥim 5:3). Also, a large quantity of burnt animal bones was found at the site. These bones come only from kosher animals, and a large percentage are from one-year-old male sheep, goats, and bulls, all of which are fit for use as burnt offerings (see Lev. 1). Usage of the site has been dated to the late thirteenth and early twelfth centuries BCE, primarily based on pottery sherds found at the site. These findings, and others, led the excavator, Adam Zertal, to conclude that this is the historic altar built by Yehoshua.

At the same time, there are several puzzling features of this altar that deviate from what one might expect of Yehoshua's altar – it is rectangular, not square as are the others detailed in the Tanakh. In addition to the animal bones mentioned above, the finds include many burnt bones of fallow deer – a kosher animal, but one that is not mentioned in the laws of offerings in Leviticus. Also, the corners of this altar point almost exactly to the four points of the compass – as opposed to the altar in the Temple, whose sides, not corners, were aligned with these directions. Finally, the altars described in the Tanakh all have horns protruding from the four corners. By contrast, the altar on Mount Eival does not have horns (although since the upper layer of stones was not preserved, it is possible that it once did). For these reasons and others, many scholars reject associating this cultic site with Yehoshua.

MESHA STELE

The Mesha Stele is a basalt stele that was erected twenty-nine hundred years ago in the city of Dibon in the Transjordan by Mesha, king of Moav. It is 1 meter tall and 60 centimeters wide, and it features a Moabite inscription thirty-four lines long (the original inscription had thirty-six lines), written in Hebrew Phoenician script, describing the victories of Mesha over the Kingdom of Israel. The stele was first discovered in the nineteenth century and was the first extrabiblical historical source to confirm an account in the Tanakh. It is on display in the Louvre in Paris.

Sources: II Samuel 23:20
II Kings 3:4–27
(regarding the term "Ariel" in Moabite)

Background: It was common for ancient kings to commemorate their military successes and conquests with steles that were erected in their capital cities or in the conquered cities. They would generally also express gratitude to their gods for the victories. The Mesha Stele is an example of this phenomenon. It states that in his days, the Moabite god Chemosh punished his people and caused them to be enslaved by the kings of Israel, Omri and Aḥav. However, ultimately, in his mercy, Chemosh freed Mesha from the yoke of oppression and even enabled him to capture some cities from Israel. According to the stele, Mesha also seized Ariel Doda, which may be a reference to a warrior named David, perhaps someone from the Kingdom of Yehuda who went to help the Israelite army. The stele lists the names of cities and people that are known from Tanakh, which made it the first external contemporaneous source that does so. Due to the great interest in the stele, the Bedouin who first found it smashed it to pieces, hoping to sell each one for large sums. Because of this, the portions of the stele that exist today are broken and fragmentary. The text has been completed with the aid of a copy that was made from it before it was shattered.

PRIESTLY BLESSING PLATES

Two small silver plates, containing the priestly blessing and carefully rolled up, were found in a First Temple burial cave in Ketef Hinom near the old train station in Jerusalem. Each one features the blessing with a shortened text written in Ancient Hebrew script that is slightly different from the biblical one. The plates are dated to approximately 600 BCE, indicating the antiquity of the priestly blessing as well as its popularity in the First Temple period. The plates are displayed in the Israel Museum.

Source: Numbers 6:24–26

Background: A complex of elaborate burial caves dating to the time of King Yoshiyahu was discovered at Ketef Hinom. One of them included a hoard of jewelry and other objects that were intended to escort the dead on their journey to the next world. Included among these items were silver plates that apparently functioned as amulets. The opening of the plates was delayed for several years until a method was discovered that could be used to do so without damaging them. One of the plates contains the words, "May the Lord bless you and watch over you. May the Lord make His face shine upon you and be gracious to you." The other one says, "May the Lord bless you and watch over you. May the Lord make His face shine upon you and grant you peace" (see text to right of image). Together, the two contain an almost complete version of the Masoretic text of the blessing that appears in the Torah, and it therefore appears that they were based on this text. These plates are the oldest known copies of a biblical text, as well as the first known example of a text containing the Tetragrammaton. This fact is particularly interesting given that in the Hinom Valley directly below these burial caves, Jews carried out the idolatrous worship of Molekh during this exact time period.

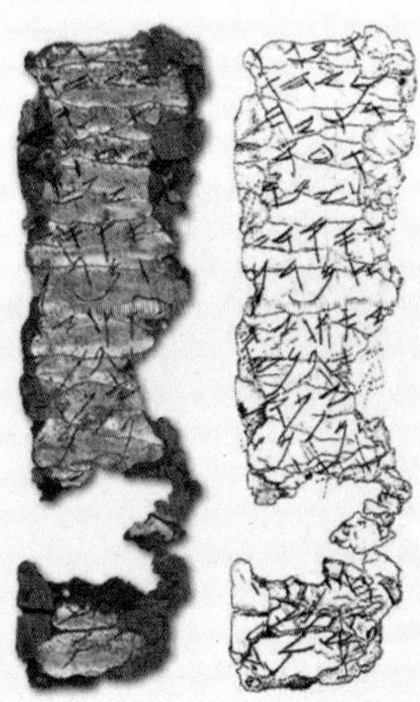

WISEMAN CHRONICLE ABOUT THE EXILE OF YEHOYAKHIN

The Wiseman Chronicle is a Babylonian list written in cuneiform script on pottery, covering the campaigns of Nevukhadnetzar II during the first eleven years of his reign (605–594 BCE). This chronicle describes wars fought by the Babylonians in Syria and the land of Israel, including a description of the conquest of Jerusalem during the days of Yehoyakhin. The chronicle lay dormant in the archives of the British Museum for decades until it was studied. It was first published in 1956 by the British Assyriologist Donald Wiseman.

Sources: II Kings 24:1–20 (especially v. 12)
Jeremiah 25:1–10
Jeremiah 52:28
Esther 2:5–6
II Chronicles 36:9–10

Background: According to the chronicle, the seventh year of Nevukhadnetzar's reign was devoted entirely to the siege and conquest of Jerusalem – a detail that indicates its importance. In the month of Kislev, "he camped against the city of Yehuda. On the second day of the month of Adar, he conquered the city and captured its king, appointing in his place a different king who was to his liking. He accepted its generous gifts and brought them to Babylon." The chronicle beautifully supplements the account in Kings describing the capture of Yehoyakhin, the appointment of Tzidkiyahu in his place, and the plundering of the royal and Temple treasuries. Due to this chronicle, we are able to pinpoint an exact date for the conquest of Jerusalem: 597 BCE. The king Yehoyakhin was taken to exile afterward, at the end of Nevukhadnetzar's seventh year (according to the book of Jeremiah) or at the beginning of his eighth year (according to the book of Kings). The exiles included the upper echelon of the nation, among them the family of Mordekhai the Jew.

MODEL TEMPLE FROM KHIRBET QEIYAFA

The model temple from Khirbet Qeiyafa is a 35-centimeter-high stone model in the shape of a temple that was discovered in the Ela Fortress near Beit Shemesh. The fortress is located on an Israelite archaeological mound that has been dated to the times of David and Shlomo. It is possible that it can be identified with the city Shaarayim that is mentioned in the story of David and Golyat.

On the model, one can see a doorway that recedes inward, surrounded by three frames, one inside the next. The upper lintel is decorated with seven rectangular protrusions, each of which is divided into three vertical strips. These strips apparently symbolize the edges of wooden beams supporting a roof, which were arranged in groups of three.

Sources: I Samuel 17:52 (regarding the city Shaarayim)
I Kings 6:4–5, 31, 33
I Kings 7:2–5
Ezekiel 41:5–6

Background: In the biblical description of the construction of the House of the Lebanon Forest in Shlomo's palace, several enigmatic expressions appear: "side chambers," "paned windows," and "window." The model of the Temple from Khirbet Qeiyafa demonstrates a type of elaborate architecture used in public buildings and may therefore enable us to understand those expressions. The side chambers are the beams supporting the roof – the roof of the House of the Lebanon Forest was supported by forty-five beams that were arranged in fifteen groups; the openings were rectangular with paned windows, which are the upper lintels arranged in three receding steps; and the window is the doorframe, which is also arranged in three receding steps. In the description of the Temple itself, it says that the entrance to the Sanctuary was "four-sided" (I Kings 6:33), and the entrance to the Inner Sanctuary was "five-sided" (v. 31). In light of the model Temple, we can suggest that these doors were made with four or five receding frames, similar to the three in the model. The model also enables us to understand the heavenly Temple envisioned by Yeḥezkel, if we explain the word *tzlaot* there as well to refer to roofing beams arranged in groups of three.

YOROVAM'S TEMPLE AT TEL DAN

Tel Dan is an archaeological site located in the Tel Dan Nature Reserve in the north of Israel. The city of Dan was settled already in the time of Avraham, and a cultic site was active there during the period of the Judges, until the destruction of Shilo. Many unique artifacts from various periods were discovered at the site, including an altar dated to the days of Yorovam son of Nevat in the tenth century BCE. The altar also remained in use during the reigns of Aḥav and Yorovam son of Yoash. The altar is 18 meters wide and is made of uncut fieldstones, in accordance with the Torah's laws for the construction of an altar. It also features holes for draining the blood of offerings.

Sources: Genesis 14:14
Joshua 19:47 (regarding the city of Dan)

Exodus 20:22–23
(laws of constructing an altar)

Judges 18:29–31; Amos 5:14
(Dan as a site of cultic worship)

I Kings 10:28–29
I Kings 12:28–33
I Kings 15:20
II Kings 10:29

Background: The golden calves and altars that Yorovam erected at Beit El and Dan were designed to serve the ten tribes that had broken away from the Kingdom of Yehuda, to serve as an alternative to the Temple in Jerusalem. Therefore, we may surmise that these altars were built in a manner similar to the one in Shlomo's Temple. The altar was destroyed when the Aramean king Ben Hadad attacked Dan, but Aḥav restored it, and added to it ashlar stones cut in a Phoenician style – perhaps under the influence of his wife Izevel, who was of Phoenician background. When the house of Omri was overthrown and replaced by the house of Yehu, the site fell into disuse. In the days of Yorovam son of Yoash, worship was renewed there and an elaborate staircase 8 meters wide was built next to the altar. A new altar, 3 meters high and with four horns, was built next to the platform. Many bones of kosher animals, as well as three firepans and copper bowls similar to those described in conjunction with the Temple in Jerusalem, were found at the site. The rich finds assist us in visualizing the Temple in Jerusalem.

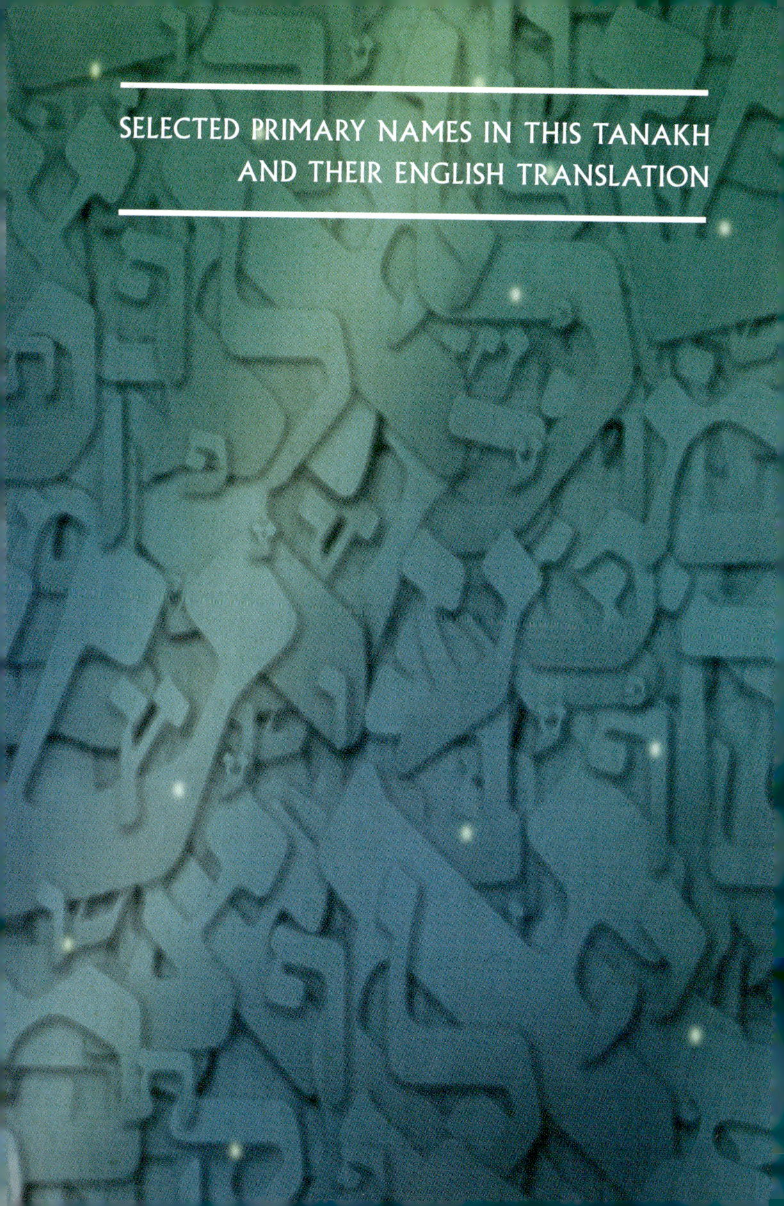

SELECTED PRIMARY NAMES IN THIS TANAKH AND THEIR ENGLISH TRANSLATION

SELECTED PRIMARY NAMES IN THIS TANAKH AND THEIR ENGLISH TRANSLATION

Transliteration • English
In Alphabetical Order

Adalya • Adalia
Admata • Admatha
Adoni Tzedek • Adoni Zedek
Adoniram • Adoram
Adoniya • Adonijah
Aharon • Aaron
Aḥashverosh • Ahasuerus
Aḥav • Ahab
Aḥaz • Ahaz
Aḥazya • Ahazia
Aḥazyahu • Ahazia
Aḥikam • Ahikam
Aḥimaatz • Ahimaaz
Aḥiman • Ahiman
Aḥimelekh • Ahimelech
Aḥinoam • Ahinoam
Aḥitofel • Ahitophel
Aḥyo • Ahio
Akhan • Achan
Akhish • Achish
Akhsa • Achsah
Amatzya • Amazia
Amatzyahu • Amaziah
Aminadav • Aminadab
Amrafel • Amraphel
Aram Beit Reḥov • The Syrians of Beth-Rehob
Aram Damesek • The Syrians of Damascus
Aram Maakha • Syria-Maachah
Aram Tzova • Syrians of Zoba
Arav • Arab
Arpakhshad • Arphaxad
Artaḥshasta • Artaxerxes
Artza • Arza
Arvana • Araunah
Asael • Asahel
Asnat • Asenath
Atalya • Athaliah
Aviezer • Abiezer
Avigayil • Abigail
Aviḥayil • Abihail
Avihu • Abihu
Avimelekh • Abimelech
Avinadav • Abinadab
Aviram • Abiram
Avishag (the Shunamite) • Abishag
Avishai • Abishai
Avital • Abital
Aviyam • Avijam
Avram • Abram
Avraham • Abraham
Avner • Abner
Azarya • Azariah
Baal Zevuv • Baal Zebub (Beelzebub?)
Barukh • Baruch
Basha • Baasha
Basmat • Basemath
Batsheva • Bath-Sheba
Beit Leḥem • Bethlehem
Ben Hadad • Ben-Hadad
Benaya • Benaiah
Betuel • Bethuel
Betzalel • Bezalel
Bikhri • Bichri
Bilam • Bileam
Bilha • Bilhah
Binyamin • Benjamin
Bitya • Bithiah
Daryavesh • Darius
Datan • Dathan
Delila • Delilah
Devir • Debir
Devora • Deborah
Dina • Dinah
Efrayim • Ephraim
Efron • Ephron
Eilon • Elon
Eitan • Ethan
Elazar • Eleazer
Elḥanan • Elchanan
Eliav • Eliab
Elisheva • Elisheba
Elitzafan • Elizaphan
Elitzur • Elizur
Eliyahu • Elijah
Eltzafan • Elzaphan
Elyakim • Eliakim
Elyasaf • Eliasaph
Elyashiv • Eliashib
Esav • Esau
Etam • Etham
Etzer • Ezer
Ever • Eber
Evi • Ebi
Evvil Merodakh • Evil-merodach
Evyatar • Abiathar
Gavriel • Gabriel
Gedalya • Gedaliah
Geḥazi • Gehazi
Gemarya • Gemariah
Geshuri • Geshurites
Gidon • Gideon
Giḥon • Gihon
Gilad • Gilead
Girgashi • Girgasite
Golyat • Goliath
Hadasa • Hadassah
Ḥagai • Haggai
Ḥagit • Haggith
Ḥam • Ham
Ḥamor • Hamor

Ḥana • Hannah
Ḥamutal • Hamutal
Ḥana • Hannah
Ḥanamel • Hanameel/Hanamel
Ḥananya • Hananiah
Ḥanokh • Enoch/Hanoch
Ḥanun • Hanun
Ḥaran • Haran
Ḥarvona • Harbona/Harbonah
Hatakh • Hatach
Ḥava • Eve
Ḥavakuk • Habakkuk
Ḥazael • Hazael
Ḥefziva • Hephzi-bah
Heiman • Heman
Ḥeshbon • Heshbon
Ḥet • Heth
Ḥetzron • Hezron
Hevel • Abel
Ḥever • Heber
Ḥiel • Hiel
Ḥilkiya • Hilkiah
Ḥilkiyahu • Hilkiah
Ḥiram • Hiram
Ḥizkiya • Hezekiah
Ḥizkiyahu • Hezekiah
Ḥofni • Hophni
Ḥogla • Hoglah
Ḥor • Hur
Hoshea • Hosea
Ḥovav • Hobab
Ḥulda • Huldah
Ḥur • Hur
Ḥushai • Hushai
Ikhavod • I-chabod
Itamar • Ithamar
Iyov • Job
Izevel • Jezebel
Jebusite • Jebusite
Kalev • Caleb
Kayin • Cain
Ke'ila • Keilah
Kedorlaomer • Chedorlaomer
Kehat • Kehath/Kohath
Kehatite • Kohathites
Keinan • Kenan
Keinite/s • Kenite/s
Kenaan – note this is the spelling for the person, not the place.
Place is Canaan • Canaan

Keren Hafukh • Keren-happuch
Keretite • Cheretites
Ketura • Keturah
Ketzia • Keziah
Kilav • Chileab
Kilyon • Chilion
Kohelet • Koheleth/Ecclesiastes
Koraḥ • Korah
Koresh • Cyrus
Kozbi • Cozbi
Kush • Ethiopia
Kushite • Ethiopian
Lavan • Laban
Lemekh • Lamech
Maakha • Maachah
Maakhatite • Maachathites
Madai • Medes
Maḥla • Mahla
Maḥlon • Mahlon
Makhir • Machir
Malakhi • Malachi
Malki Tzedek • Melchizedek
Manoaḥ • Manoah
Matanya • Mattaniah
Matityahu • Mattithiah
Mefivoshet • Mephibosheth
Meḥuyael • Mehujael
Meidad • Medad
Memukhan • Memucan
Menashe • Manasseh
Merav • Merab
Merodakh • Merodach
Metushael • Methusael
Metushelaḥ • Methuselah
Midyan • Midian
Mikha • Micah
Mikhael • Michael
Mikhal • Michal
Mikhayehu • Micaiah
Milka • Milcah
Moav • Moab
Molekh • Molech
Mordekhai • Mordecai
Moshe • Moses
Naama • Naamah
Nadav • Nadab
Naftali • Naphtali
Naḥash • Nahash
Naḥor • Nahor
Naḥshon • Nahshon

Naḥum • Nahum
Natan • Nathan
Naval • Nabal
Navot • Naboth
Neḥemya • Nehemiah
Neriya • Neriah
Nevayot • Nebaioth
Nevukhadnetzar • Nebuchadnezzar
Nevuzaradan • Nebuzaradan
Noaḥ • Noah
Novaḥ • Nobah
Oholiav • Aholiab
Oholivama • Aholibamah
Orev • Oreb
Orpa • Orpah
Otniel • Othniel
Ovadya • Obadiah
Ovadyahu • Obadiah
Oved • Obed
Oved Edom • Obed-edom
Pekaḥ • Pekah
Pekaḥya • Pekahiah
Penina • Peninnah
Peretz • Perez
Peretz Uza • Perez-uzzah
Pharaoh Nekho • Pharaoh Necho
Pikhol • Phichol
Pinḥas • Phinehas
Potifar • Potiphar
Potifera • Potipherah
Puah • Puah
Raḥav • Rahab
Raḥel • Rachel
Rav-Shakeh • Rabshakeh
Refael • Raphael
Refaim • Giants
Reḥavam • Rehoboam
Rekhav • Rechab
Retzin • Rezin
Reuven • Reuben
Reva • Reba
Ritzpa • Rizpah
Rivka • Rebecca
Sanḥeriv • Sennacherib
Sara • Sarah
Seraḥ • Serah
Seraya • Seraiah
Sha'ul • Saul/Shaul
Shafan • Shaphan
Shekhem • Shechem

Shemaya • Shemaiah
Shet • Seth
Sheva • Sheba
Shevna • Shebna
Shifra • Shiphrah
Shimi • Shimei
Shimon • Simeon
Shimshon • Samson
Shishak • Shishak
Shlomo • Solomon
Shmuel • Samuel
Siḥon • Sihon
Teraḥ • Terah/Terach
Tiglat Pileser • Tiglath-Pileser
Tirtza • Tirzah
Tivni • Tibni
Toviya • Tobijah
Toviyahu • Tobijah
Tuval Kayin • Tubal-cain
Tzadok • Zadok
Tzalmuna • Zalmunna
Tzefanya • Zephaniah
Tzelofḥad • Zelophehad
Tzeruya • Zeruiah
Tzidkiya • Zedekiah
Tzidkiyahu • Zedekiah
Tzila • Zillah
Tzipora • Zipporah
Tziva • Ziba
Tzofar • Zophar
Tzur • Zur
Uriya • Uriah
Uriyahu • Uriah
Utz • Uz
Uza • Uzzah
Uziel • Uzziel
Uziya • Uzziah
Uziyahu • Uzziah
Yaakov • Jacob
Yael • Jael
Yahotzadak • Jehozadak
Yair • Jair
Yakhin • Jachin
Yarden • Jordan
Yaval • Jabal
Yavan • Javan
Yavesh • Jabesh
Yavin • Jabin
Yedaya • Jedaiah
Yedutun • Jeduthun
Yefet • Japheth
Yegar Sahaduta • Yegar-Sahadutha
Yeḥezkel • Ezekiel
Yeḥizkiya • Hezekiah
Yeḥizkiyahu • Hezekiah
Yehoaḥaz • Jehoahaz
Yehoash • Jehoash
Yehonadav • Jonadab
Yehonatan • Jonathan
Yehoram • Jehoram
Yehoshafat • Jehoshaphat
Yehoshua • Joshua
Yehotzadak • Jehozadak
Yehoyada • Jehoiada
Yehoyakhin • Jehoiachin
Yehoyakim • Jehoiakim
Yehoyariv • Jehoiarib
Yehu • Jehu
Yehuda • Judah
Yehudit • Judith
Yekhonya • Jeconiah
Yemima • Jemima
Yered • Jared
Yerubaal • Jerubbaal
Yeshaya • Isaiah
Yeshayahu • Isaiah
Yeter • Jethro
Yevus • Jebus
Yiftaḥ • Jephthah
Yirmeya • Jeremiah
Yirmeyahu • Jeremiah
Yishai • Jesse
Yishmael • Ishmael
Yiska • Iscah
Yisrael • Israel
Yissakhar • Issachar
Yitro • Jethro
Yitzḥak • Isaac
Yitzhar • Izhar
Yoaḥaz • Jehoahaz
Yoash • Joash
Yoav • Joab
Yoel • Joel
Yoḥanan • Johanan
Yokheved • Jochebed
Yona • Jonah
Yonadav • Jonadab
Yonatan • Jonathan
Yoram • Joram
Yorovam • Jeroboam
Yosef • Joseph
Yoshafat • Joshaphat
Yoshiya • Josiah
Yoshiyahu • Josiah
Yotam • Jotham
Yotzadak • Jozadak
Yoyada • Joiada
Yoyakhin • Joiachin
Yoyakim • Joiakim
Yoyariv • Joiarib
Yuval • Jubal
Ze'ev • Zeeb
Zekharya • Zechariah
Zeraḥ • Zerah
Zerubavel • Zerubbabel
Zevaḥ • Zebah
Zevulun • Zebulun
Zilpa • Zilpah

IMAGE CREDITS

All images are copyright © Koren Publishers Jerusalem Ltd., except:

Page 1463, Timelines and Genealogies, © Todd Bolen/BiblePlaces.com

Page 1485, Maps, © ingram

page 1505, Tribal Encampments and Temples, © HaRav Menachem Makover, courtesy of *Harenu Bevinyano*; pages 1506–1507, order of tribal encampments, © HaRav Menachem Makover, courtesy of *Harenu Bevinyano*; pages 1508–1509, encampment of the Levites, © HaRav Menachem Makover, courtesy of *Harenu Bevinyano*; pages 1510–1519, the Temples, © HaRav Menachem Makover, courtesy of *Harenu Bevinyano*

Pages 1521, The Tabernacle and Its Vessels, © HaRav Menachem Makover, courtesy of *Harenu Bevinyano*; page 1523, embroidered fabric, gold chain and perfumers' blend, © **courtesy of the Temple Institute**; woven work, © **איתי צורף, רישיון־השימוש**; page 1524, accacia wood, © Forest & Kim Starr; flattened boards, © David Lipchik; uncut gemstones, © Cold River Mining; polished gemstones, © Rudra Jeevan; purified gold, purified silver, silver ore © Rob Lavinsky, iRocks.com; gold ore, © PHGCOM; polished copper, © Jonathan Zander (Digon3), page 1525–1528, vessels of the tabernacle and the covenant © HaRav Menachem Makover, courtesy of *Harenu Bevinyano*; pages 1529–1536, structure of the Tabernacle, © HaRav Menachem Makover, courtesy of *Harenu Bevinyano*; page 1537, top timages; © HaRav Menachem Makover, courtesy of *Harenu Bevinyano*; bottom images © **courtesy of the Temple Institute**; pages 1538–1539, tabernacle courtyard, © HaRav Menachem Makover, courtesy of *Harenu Bevinyano*; page 1540, processed flax, © Kate Poland, Cordwainers Garden; flax during processing, © Kristin Ledgett; flax threads, © Anne Shoring, Artisan Yarns; strands of beaten gold, © Needlepoint.fr; ram's hide dyed red, © Layne De Monbrun, Centralia Fur & Hide Inc; wool dyed scarlet blue, purple, scarlet, and woven work, © **courtesy of the Temple Institute**; goat skin, © Shutterstock

Pages 1541–1543, Sacred Vestments, © **courtesy of the Temple Institute** page 1544, Leshem, © Shutterstock / ntv; Shoham, © Didier Descouens; Tarshish, © Rob Lavinsky, iRocks.com; Bareket, © JJ Harrison / https://www.jjharrison.com.au; Yahalom, © Géry PARENT; page 1545, Ahlama, © Shutterstock / Albert Ross; Odem, © Quatrostein; Nofekh, © Shutterstock /photo - world; Sapir, © Hannes Grobe; Shevo, © Geni; Pitdah, © Aomai / Template:R.Weller/Cochise College; Jasper, © Aramgutang, page 1546–1550, Sacred Vestments, © **courtesy of the Temple Institute**

Pages 1551, Offerings, © antoniogravante; page 1553, calf, © **יאסר שואהנה**; bull, © Lehava Sakhnin via the PikiWiki - Israel free image collection project; cow, © Hohum; page 1554, sheep, © Joaquim Alves Gaspar; ram, © Martin Stoltze; goats, © Firo002/Flagstaffotos; he goat, © RomanLevashov; page 1555, pigeon, © Miguel González Novo; dove, © Jörg Hempel; page 1556, wheat, © Dominicus Johannes Bergsma; barley, © Alexander von Halem; wine, © iroo02/Flagstaffotos; olives, © Giancarlo Dessì; salt, © Dana Claudat; frankincense, © Prof. Zohar Amar

Pages 1559–1561, Service of the Offerings, © **courtesy of the Temple Institute**

Page 1565, Types of Offerings, © 4028mdk09 page 1566, 1569, 1570, 1572, structure of the altar, © HaRav Menachem Makover, courtesy of *Harenu Bevinyano* page 1578, bird, © David Friel; cedar, © Patche99z; hyssop, © **ידידיה מגדלבאום**; scarlet wool, © Prof. Zohar Amar page 1579, red cow, © iStock; yoke, © John Gevers; ritual bath, © **טל שוורץ**; page 1581, Living Creatures, © Moujib Aghrout page 1582, dove, © Miguel González Novo; pigeon, © J.M.Garg; page 1583, griffon vulture, © Matthias Kabel; page 1584, bearded vulture, © Norbert Potensky; lappet-faced vulture, © Matthias Zepper; black kite, © Tim Sträter; page 1585, buzzard, © Maky Orel; raven, © Ianaré Sévi; ostrich, © Math Knight; page 1586, swift, © Ken Billington; gull, © Dario Sanches; sparrow hawk, © Peter Trimming; page 1587, little owl, © Trebola; fish owl, © Ken Billington; owl, © Ron Knight; page 1588, barn owl, © Peter Trimming; pelican, © Mike, Michael L. Baird; vulture, © Artemy Voikhansky; page 1589, stork, © Carlos Delgado; heron, © Alain Carpentier; hoopoe, © Antony Grossy; page 1590, bat, © Anton Croos, locust, © Joachim Frische page 1591, acridinae, © Shutterstock/ Hayk_Shalunts; grasshopper, © Armin Kübelbeck; page 1592, hyrax, © Shirley Saramito; hare, © benjamint; page 1593, ferret, © Keven Law; mouse, © George Shuklin; page 1594, spiny-tailed lizard, © Arpingstone; legless lizard © TimVickers; chameleon © Benny Trapp; page 1595, lizard, © **דליק כלבלב**; skink, © Benjamint444, mole rat, © Jörg Hempel; page 1596, multiped, © **ערן פינקל**; page 1597, wheat field, © CastielSagan

Page 1603, Archaeological Artifacts, © Prof. Aren M. Maeir, Tell es-Safi/Gath Archaeological Project; page 1604, Letter of the reaper, © Hanay; page 1606, Shiloah Tunnel, © **תמר הירדני**; page 1607, Bulla of Gemaryahu, © Photography: **קלרה עמית, יורם להמן, יעל יולוביץ, מיקי קורן, מריאנה סלצברגר**, courtesy of the Israel Antiquities Authority; page 1608, Sanḥeriv's Prism, © Hanay; page 1609, Yehoshua's altar on Mount Eival, © courtesy of the estate of Adam Zertal; page 1610, Mesha Stele, © Mbzt 2012; page 1611, Priestly blessing, © **תמר הירדני**; page 1612, Wiseman Chronicle, © Todd Bolen/BiblePlaces.com; page 1613, Khirbet Qeiyafa, © Prof. Yosef Garfinkel; page 1614, Yorovam's Temple, © Mboesch

Page 1615, Selected Primary Names, © Eliyahu Misgav

KOREN PUBLISHERS JERUSALEM